This book is to be returned on or before
the last date stamped below.

New Testament Theology

By the same author

New Testament Introduction
The Pastoral Epistles (Tyndale New Testament Commentary)
Galatians (New Century Bible)
The Pastoral Epistles and the Mind of Paul
Epistles from Prison
Jesus the Messiah
A Shorter Life of Christ
The Apostles

NEW TESTAMENT THEOLOGY

Donald Guthrie, BD, MTh, PhD

*formerly Vice-Principal and Lecturer
in New Testament, London Bible College*

Inter-Varsity Press

Inter-Varsity Press
38 De Montfort Street, Leicester LE1 7GP, England
P.O. Box 1400, Downers Grove, Illinois 60515, U.S.A.

Inter-Varsity Press, England, is the publishing division of the Universities and Colleges Christian Fellowship (formerly the Inter-Varsity Fellowship), a student movement linking Christian Unions in universities and colleges throughout the British Isles, and a member movement of the International Fellowship of Evangelical Students. For information about local and national activities in Great Britain write to UCCF, 38 De Montfort Street, Leicester LE1 7GP.

InterVarsity Press, U.S.A., is the book-publishing division of InterVarsity Christian Fellowship, a student movement active on campus at hundreds of universities, colleges and schools of nursing. For information about local and regional activities, write Public Relations Dept., InterVarsity Christian Fellowship, 6400 Schroeder Rd., P.O. Box 7895, Madison, WI 53707-7895.

R02413

225.9
GUT

ISBNs: UK 0-85111-742-2
*   USA 0-87784-965-X*

Library of Congress Catalog Card Number: 81-47066

Printed in the United States of America

British Library Cataloguing in Publication Data

Guthrie, Donald
    New Testament theology.
    1. Bible. New Testament—Commentaries
    I. Title
    225.9   BS2341.2

ISBN 0-85111-742-2

19   18   17   16   15   14   13   12   11   10   9   8
99   98   97   96   95   94   93

Dedicated to my wife Mary
and to my children Eleanor, Alistair, Rosalyn,
Anthony, Adrian and Andrew

Contents

CONTENTS

CONTENTS

9

CONTENTS

CONTENTS

13

CONTENTS

14

CONTENTS

Preface

It may be wondered whether there is need for a book like this. Such a question must no doubt face anyone writing on any subject. The least an author can do is to state his own reason for producing his book. In view of the many existing books on NT theology some justification is needed for writing another. My main aim has been to produce a book which pays attention to the different sources of material within the NT, but which at the same time presents the teaching under its major themes. It may therefore serve the purpose of a handbook to Christian doctrine.

It is my hope that this book will be a useful tool in the hands of all serious students of the NT. It is further hoped that it will go some way towards demonstrating the considerable amount of unity within the NT and will help to offset the prevailing tendency to stress the diversity.

I am indebted particularly to two of my colleagues in the Tyndale Fellowship, Professor I. Howard Marshall of Aberdeen University and Dr Richard T. France of Tyndale House, Cambridge, who have both carefully read through the manuscript and made many valuable suggestions. There is no doubt that this book would have been the poorer without their help, but I alone am responsible for its final form. I wish to record my thanks to my publishers who have supplied encouragement to me from the inception of the idea some years ago. I am also grateful to several of my students or former students for their assistance. Sally Jiggins BA, Maria da Silva and Rhona Pipe BD, between them undertook the not inconsiderable task of turning my hand-written manuscript into typescript, and Brian Capper BA gave invaluable assistance in preparing the Bibliography and Index of Authors from my footnotes.

Donald Guthrie

Abbreviations

ABBREVIATIONS

MNT	*The Moffatt New Testament Commentary*
MS(s)	Manuscript(s)
NBD	*The New Bible Dictionary*
NCB	*New Century Bible*
NEB	New English Bible
NICNT	*The New International Commentary on the New Testament*
NIGTC	*The New International Greek Testament Commentary*
NIDNTT	New International Dictionary of New Testament Theology
NIV	New International Version of the Bible
NovT	*Novum Testamentum*
NT	New Testament
NTD	*Das Neue Testament Deutsch*
NTS	*New Testament Studies*
NTT	*New Testament Theology*
OT	Old Testament
Peake	*Peake's Commentary on the Bible*
RB	*Revue Biblique*
RHPR	*Revue d'Histoire et de Philosophie Religieuses*
RScR	*Revue des Sciences Religieuses*
RSV	Revised Standard Version of the Bible
RThPh	*Revue de Théologie et de Philosophie*
RV	Revised Version of the Bible
SJT	*Scottish Journal of Theology*
StEv	*Studia Evangelica*
Strack-Billerbeck	*Kommentar zum Neuen Testament aus Talmud und Midrash* von H. L. Strack und P. Billerbeck
StTh	*Studia Theologica*
TB	*Tyndale Bulletin*
TDNT	*Theological Dictionary of the New Testament* (Eng. trans. by G. W. Bromiley from German *Wörterbuch*, ed. G. Kittel and G. Friedrich)
ThB	*Theologische Blatter*
ThLZ	*Theologische Literaturzeitung*
ThZ	*Theologische Zeitschrift*
THNT	*Theologischer Handkommentar zum Neuen Testament*
TNT	*Theology of the New Testament*
TNTC	*Tyndale New Testament Commentaries*
TR	Textus Receptus
TSF Bulletin	*Theological Students Fellowship Bulletin*
VGT	*The Vocabulary of the Greek Testament illustrated from the Papyri and Other Non-literary Sources*, J. H. Moulton and G. Milligan
Vig Chr	*Vigiliae Christianae*
Vox Ev	*Vox Evangelica*
VT	*Vetus Testamentum*
WC	*Westminster Commentaries*
WMANT	*Wissenschaftliche Monographien zum Alten und Neuen Testament*
WTJ	*Westminster Theological Journal*
ZNW	*Zeitschrift für die Neutestamentliche Wissenschaft*
ZPEB	*Zondervan Pictorial Encyclopaedia of the Bible*
ZTK	*Zeitschrift für Theologie und Kirche*

Introduction

Anyone undertaking to write a NT theology is at once faced with the question whether he is attempting the impossible, for there are not wanting those who would deny that there is such a thing. Others would prefer to speak of religion rather than theology, while some would attempt a compromise and speak of 'thought' rather than theology, fearing that the latter word is too closely bound up with a system of doctrine. It will at once be seen that any writer attempting the task must make clear at the outset his definition of NT theology and its scope. He must also come to terms with the relationship between theology and history since his understanding of this will determine his method.

A brief survey of the development of the study of New Testament theology

Prior to the Reformation there was little or no interest in biblical theology. The focus was wholly upon dogmatics which in turn was dominated by the traditional teaching of the church. Church tradition was more important than the biblical evidence, although the latter was used to bolster up the traditional dogmas. Since no freedom of interpretation was allowed to the individual scholar, exegesis was non-existent and ecclesiastical teaching never challenged. This approach reached its official expression in the edicts of the Council of Trent. While paying tribute to the importance of the biblical texts, the Council conceded that the ecclesiastical traditions were of equal weight. But this was not the kind of milieu which would encourage the development of a genuine biblical theology. Modern Catholicism, at least in its more liberal schools of thought, has nevertheless given more serious attention to the examination of the biblical texts.

It is one of the most notable features of the thought of the Reformers that they were determined to break away from ecclesiastical tradition and it is therefore not surprising to discover among them a tremendous upsurge of interest in biblical theology. Indeed, because the reformers substituted the authority of the biblical text for the authority of the church, the attempt to construct an orderly account of biblical teaching was, in fact, indispensable. Moreover, the belief in the divine origin of the text of Scripture gave all doctrine based upon it the stamp of its own authority. Protestant scholarship at that time was not scientific in its approach to biblical evidence. Interpretations were often subjective, rather than based on historical research. Nevertheless the Reformers' view of theology undoubtedly laid the foundation for all subsequent interest in biblical theological studies. In place of the forced exegesis of much medieval scholasticism, the Reformers argued for the plain meaning of Scripture, which encouraged the quest for greater facility in the biblical languages and paved the way for an understanding of Scripture independent of the decisions of church councils or the ideas of the creeds. The systematizing of thought in Reformation theology was very different from the philosophical frameworks used by the previous dogmaticians. It should be noted, however, that as yet no distinction was made between OT and NT theology. All parts of Scripture were equally valid for the support of doctrine and no suggestion of a specifically NT theology appears at this time.

Indeed, throughout the post-Reformation period until the dawn of rationalism, Protestant theology made no provision for progressive revelation and this led to a view of Scripture as a mine of proof-texts to support doctrinal systems.[1] The idea of a NT theology would have been alien at this time since Christ could be seen in the OT as in the NT, and the unity of Scripture prevented the view that NT theology should be studied as a distinct entity. What was most serious during this period was the lack of any consideration of the historical background in which the Christian theology developed. The context of scriptural statements was less important than their content, but exegesis was inevitably dominated by dogmatic considerations.

It is the rise of the modern critical period, covering the last two centuries, which has caused the field of NT theology both to come into its own and yet at the same time to suffer many setbacks. The first real differentiation between dogmatic and biblical theology was made in 1787 by J. P. Gabler,[2] who criticized the former because it consisted of what men by the use of their reason philosophized, and urged attention to the latter because it

---

[1] Cf. W. G. Kümmel, *The New Testament: The History of the Investigation of its Problems* (Eng. trans. 1972), p.98.

[2] The title of J. P. Gabler's work is *Oratio de justo discrimine theologiae biblicae et dogmaticae regundisque recte utriusque finibus* (*Discourse on the proper distinction between biblical and dogmatic theology and the correct determination of their boundaries*) (1787). Kümmel gives an extensive quotation of this work, *op. cit.*, p. 98. A German translation of Gabler's essay has been included in *Das Problem der Theologie des Neuen Testaments* (ed. G. Strecker, 1975), pp. 32–44, a recognition of its importance in the development of the study of NT theology.

consisted of a historical discipline. Other rationalistic interpreters of NT theology followed Gabler's lead, although their work was mainly aimed to support from the biblical texts the principles of the age of reason.[3]

The earlier rationalistic attempts gave way to an approach to the NT which was affected by the Hegelian philosophy, which influenced the approach of scholars to history. Indeed, it led to so radical a reconstruction of early Christian history, that the theology of the early period was inevitably affected. F. C. Baur's criticism of the biblical texts was based on his prior acceptance of an early tension between the Petrine and Pauline factions, leading him to see the NT as an *eirenicon* between them. But theology could not be based on an interpretation which had been imposed on the NT text. Indeed the result of this kind of movement was an over-emphasis on historical considerations and a lack of interest in NT thought except as re-edited in line with Baur's reconstruction.[4] Although this thesis has long since been disbanded, Baur's influence over theological studies in the NT field was extensive.[5] It contributed to the quest for the historical Jesus which dominated the theological scene through the next half-century.

This historical movement found an able exponent in Holtzmann, whose work on NT theology may be regarded as the classic statement of 'liberal' thinking.[6] He definitely rejected any approach to NT theology based on a dogmatic framework and also rejected the idea of revelation. He nevertheless used theological topics for the classification of his material. Holtzmann's position is of interest because he based his approach to the literature on a historical-critical analysis which did not maintain the full authenticity of the texts. During this period there were still many scholars who built their theology on a more conservative basis, among the more notable of whom were Hofmann, Tholuck, Bernard Weiss, Zahn and Feine. These all inclined towards a more historical approach than the dogmaticians had adopted, although they still maintained that the text was the vehicle of revelation. The most outstanding work from a conservative theological standpoint was the *New Testament Theology* of A. Schlatter,[7] who, although recognizing the need for historical orientation, nevertheless

---

[3] *Cf.* G. E. Ladd, *TNT* (1974), pp.14f. for details.

[4] *Cf.* A. Schweitzer, *Paul and his Interpreters* (Eng. trans. 1912), pp. 12ff., for discussion of Baur's approach to Paul's theology. He shows that Baur speaks more as a pupil of Hegel than as a historian.

[5] R. Morgan, *The Nature of New Testament Theology* (1973), pp. 13f., points out that Baur's reconstruction failed because it did not do justice to the complexity of early Christian history. He also confused the chronology. But Morgan considers that Baur's conception of the relation between theology and history found its true successor in W. Wrede.

[6] For an appraisal of Holtzmann's work, *cf.* R. Morgan, *op. cit.*, 7ff. H. J. Holtzmann's *Theology* was published in 1897 under the title *Lehrbuch der neutestamentlichen Theologie* (2 vols.). *Cf.* also Schweitzer's review of Holtzmann's work, *op. cit.*, pp.100ff. W. Wrede comments on this on p.93 of the essay mentioned in the next note.

[7] A. Schlatter's *Neutestamentliche Theologie* ([2]1922–3) was in two parts: 'Die Geschichte des Christus' and 'Die Theologie der Apostel' (this included Paul's theology and Luke and Matthew).

retained a dogmatic interest. His views will be considered in the next section. In America a *New Testament Theology* was produced by G. B. Stevens[8] at the end of the nineteenth century. This kept clear of dogmatic structures and concentrated on a descriptive account of the various groups of literature.

A major event in the approach to NT theology was the appearance of Wrede's essay on *The Task and Methods of New Testament Theology* (1897).[9] This was a thorough-going attempt to argue for a historical approach in contrast to a dogmatic approach. Wrede insisted that the NT was concerned with religion rather than with theology, an issue which will be discussed in the next section. There is no doubt that Wrede over-reacted against dogmatic considerations in his approach to NT thought, with the result that for him NT theology resolved itself into a history of early Christian religion. Nevertheless Wrede's insistence that theology must be studied in its historical context has exerted a powerful influence on subsequent studies.

Wrede was a representative of the *Religionsgeschichte*[10] movement which was based on an historical approach. The interest in setting out an account of the Christian religion necessitated a comparative study of other religions to bring out ways in which the former had been influenced by the latter. The NT ceased to be an authoritative source of early Christian theology, but rather became a part of the total picture of first-century religion.[11] This undoubtedly led to an over-emphasis on Jewish apocalyptic.[12] Neither approach led to a true picture of NT theology, and certainly neither fulfilled Wrede's demands for a historical approach, for both presented reconstructions which were historically dubious. Much of Schweitzer's reaction was caused by his opposition to the 'Jesus of history' movement, based as it was on a wholly non-eschatological approach. A further result from these movements was the tendency to set the Hellenistic background of Paul against the Jewish apocalyptic background of Jesus. No unified theology of the NT was possible in these circumstances. Consequently any NT theology was bound to involve most emphasis on either the teaching of Jesus *or* the teaching of Paul and John. Since through the rise of form criticism a sceptical attitude has developed towards the historical Jesus, especially in Bultmann's presentation, the teaching of Jesus has been largely discounted

---

[8] G. B. Stevens, *TNT* (1899).

[9] This essay of Wrede is included under this title in R. Morgan's book, *op. cit.*, pp.68–116.

[10] A recent book giving a survey of this approach is C. Colpe's *Die religionsgeschichtliche Schule* (1961).

[11] *Cf.* W. Bousset, *Kyrios Christos* (1913, Eng. trans. 1970); R. Reitzenstein, *Die hellenistischen Mysterienreligionen nach Ihre Grundgedanken und Wirkungen* ([3]1927). Schlatter's wise words of warning against treating all religious data as a unitary thing went unheeded (*cf.* R. Morgan, *The Nature of New Testament Theology*, p.144): 'The necessary task of New Testament theology remains undone so long as it lurches up and down the wide front of the statistics and history of all religions in an attempt to establish how far back anticipations of and analogies to the ideas of the New Testament can be found.'

[12] A. Schweitzer, *The Quest of the Historical Jesus* (1906, Eng. trans. [3]1954). He gives his own views, in response to Wrede's *The Messianic Secret in the Gospels*, on pp.328ff.

and NT theology has concentrated on the Pauline epistles and the fourth gospel, both of which were considered to be strongly Hellenistic. Indeed Bultmann's *New Testament Theology* is a classic example of this tendency.

It would not, however, be true to say that Bultmann's *New Testament Theology*[13] was, or even aimed to be, a purely historical account. He introduced a dogmatic element which was very different from the older traditional dogmatic approach. Drawing his inspiration from existential philosophy, he maintained that the theological texts had a continuing relevance, but must constantly be reinterpreted. The NT texts on which he based his reassessment had themselves been interpreted through the mythological approach of their age and it was therefore essential to subject them to a process of demythologization before the timeless truths, which alone could challenge for decision, could be uncovered. No connection was seen between the historical Jesus and the Christ of faith, and this naturally coloured Bultmann's whole approach to theology.[14]

Not all Bultmann's followers have been as sceptical regarding the historical Jesus. Nevertheless, the production by Hans Conzelmann of *An Outline of the Theology of the New Testament*[15] is still far removed from the older approaches which gave full weight to the teaching of Jesus. In Conzelmann's presentation Jesus becomes only slightly more credible as a historical figure. The *Theology* is still dominated by the attempt to reinterpret the NT in terms of existential philosophy, and it must be seriously questioned to what extent such a reinterpretation can legitimately be called NT theology.

During this period of existential philosophical influence, a parallel movement was devoting increasing attention to biblical theology, which had itself suffered neglect during the 'Jesus of history' movement. Against the fragmented approach of various other movements, the biblical theology movement strove to discover some unity within the variety of the NT. Most notable among the exponents of this movement is Oscar Cullmann[16] whose main emphasis is on *Heilsgeschichte*, the view that God's acts as well as his words are fundamental to salvation, a view which challenges the premises of existentialism. History is seen, therefore, to be of great importance in the approach to NT theology. Cullmann's main theological

[13] R. Bultmann, *TNT*, 2 vols. (Eng. trans. 1956). He considered that 'New Testament Theology consists in the unfolding of those ideas by means of which Christian faith makes sure of its own object, basis and consequence' (1, p.3). He does not, however, enlarge on this. He begins with the kerygma. To him the message of Jesus was a presupposition for NT theology rather than a part of it.

[14] R. Morgan, *op. cit.*, p.37, sums up Bultmann's theology as rooted in man. He comments that according to this view man is the object of theology. This, of course, makes theology dependent on anthropology.

[15] H. Conzelmann, *An Outline of the Theology of the New Testament* (Eng. trans. 1969). Conzelmann includes only a very brief introduction to his method, which covers a brief historical survey (pp. 3ff.).

[16] O. Cullmann, *Christ and Time* (Eng. trans. 1951); *Salvation in History* (Eng. trans. 1967). Although Cullmann has not produced an NT theology, he has written a major work on Christology from a *Heilsgeschichte* point of view, *i.e.* his *Christology of the New Testament* (Eng. trans. ²1963).

work, however, has been in the field of Christology. The same may be said of Floyd Filson,[17] who takes a somewhat similar approach. Neither, however, has produced a complete theology of the NT.

Alan Richardson's book *An Introduction to the Theology of the New Testament*[18] was based on the assumption that NT thought forms a unity and this led him to adopt a thematic approach. Whereas he paid some attention to the historical background, his work has not escaped the charge that he played down too much that background. He has been criticized for failing to distinguish between the theologies of the different NT authors.[19] Nevertheless Richardson was certainly more aware of the common basis of the NT than his immediate predecessors had been. E. Stauffer's *New Testament Theology*[20] is structured on a different pattern and has a different aim. He is more concerned to set out a theology of history from the NT world of thought.

The first part of J. Jeremias' *New Testament Theology*,[21] which deals with the teaching of Jesus, attaches much more importance to that teaching than Bultmann, and is less influenced by dogmatic considerations. He devotes little attention in this work, however, to discussing the methodology of NT theology. Other German writers who have produced works in this field are W. G. Kümmel and L. Goppelt (two volumes), together with two Roman Catholics, M. Meinertz (two volumes) and K. H. Schelkle (four volumes). Kümmel[22] concentrates on Jesus, Paul and John and in so doing has exposed himself to the criticism that he has been too much influenced by the theory of dominating personalities.[23] Goppelt[24] divides his theology into two parts, the first dealing with the activities of Jesus (theologically considered), the second with the variety and unity of the apostolic witness

[17] F. V. Filson, *The New Testament against its Environment* (1950). Filson has also produced a work on Christology, *Jesus Christ, the Risen Lord* (1956).

[18] A. Richardson, *An Introduction to the Theology of the New Testament* (1958), has a brief preface explaining his method (pp. 9ff.). In considering whether it is right to assume that the apostolic church possessed a common theology, Richardson maintains that the only way of confirming this is to construct an hypothesis and test it out. He employs the principle of interpretation reflected in the historic Christian faith, which he finds leads to a more coherently and rationally satisfying 'history' than liberal-humanist or existential principles.

[19] R. Morgan, *op. cit.*, p. 58, considers that in some respects Richardson's work looks 'like a return to the pre-modern, unhistorical textbooks of biblical dogmatics'.

[20] E. Stauffer, *New Testament Theology* (Eng. trans. 1955), presented his material against the background of apocalyptic. His work in its German edition (1941) antedated Bultmann's *Theology of the New Testament* and was not influenced by existential philosophy.

[21] J. Jeremias, *New Testament Theology* I: *The Proclamation of Jesus* (Eng. trans. 1971).

[22] W. G. Kümmel, *The Theology of the New Testament: According to its Major Witnesses, Jesus – Paul – John* (Eng. trans. 1974).

[23] *Cf.* E. Käsemann, 'The Problem of a New Testament Theology', *NTS* 19, 1972–3, p. 238, who links this view with the idealist's view of history, which stresses the influence of strongly dominating personalities.

[24] L. Goppelt's *Theologie des Neuen Testaments* (1975–6) is arranged in two volumes *Jesus Wirken in seiner theologischen Bedeutung* and *Vielfalt und Einheit des apostolischen Christuszeugnisses*.

to Christ. Meinertz[25] presents his evidence under the literary divisions of the NT and selects his themes according to their suitability to the literature being considered, but Schelkle[26] has chosen a thematic approach. The French Roman Catholic J. Bonsirven[27] based his theology on four parts – Jesus Christ, primitive Christianity, St Paul, and mature Christianity, somewhat similar to Meinertz's arrangement.

In his *Theology of the New Testament*,[28] G. E. Ladd claims to have adopted a historical approach, because he believes that NT theology has a descriptive function. According to him, the task of the NT theologian is to bring out the rich variety of NT thought, although he sees in all the sources a testimony to God's redemptive act in Christ. He sees NT theology as laying the foundation for the systematic theologian.[29]

It will be seen from this brief survey that there is no common agreement on what a NT theology should aim to achieve.[30] Most have preferred an approach which presents the evidence as a collection of different theologies and the thematic approach has been mainly out of favour, for fear it would detract from the inner cohesion of the individual thinkers whose literary works make up the NT. More will be said in the following sections about the methodological questions which are raised. One could justly conclude that it is an impossible task to write an NT theology which would meet all the requirements of the various schools of thought. In the final analysis each interpreter can do no more than produce a work which gives priority to the aims he considers most important. He has an obligation, however, to outline his objectives and to give some indication of the reasons why he has chosen them.

The nature and method of New Testament theology

There have not been many carefully thought out discussions on the nature of NT theology: the wide variety of works on this subject testifies to the lack of any general agreement about its nature, and about the aim of anyone attempting to write a NT theology. Two important essays which appeared at the beginning of the twentieth century merit consideration today because

---

[25] M. Meinertz, *Die Heilige Schrift des Neuen Testaments*, Ergänzungsband 1: *Theologie des Neuen Testamentes* (2 vols., 1950).

[26] K. H. Schelkle, *Theologie des Neuen Testaments* (1968–76). English translations of this work have been published under the title *Theology of the New Testament*. The four volumes deal with the following subdivisions of New Testament theology: 1: Creation, world – time – man; 2: God was in Christ; 3: Morality; 4: Creation and redemption.

[27] J. Bonsirven, *Théologie du Nouveau Testament* (1951).

[28] G. E. Ladd, *TNT*.

[29] A. M. Hunter has not been included in the text because he has not written an NT theology as such, but he has nevertheless provided an excellent brief introduction to the study of the subject in his *Introducing New Testament Theology* (1957).

[30] For a survey of the problems involved in writing an NT theology and a summary of some major recent attempts, *cf.* I. H. Marshall's article 'New Testament Theology', *The Theological Educator*, Spring 1979.

they raise in concise form the problems and tensions which modern NT theologians are still facing. Wrede's article has already been referred to (see p. 24), but we need to give attention to the particular issues he raised. He may be regarded as the representative of the thorough-going historical school. We have also already mentioned Schlatter's *New Testament Theology*, but his essay on 'The Theology of the New Testament and Dogmatics' brings out the principles on which his theology was based. Schlatter's essay had less impact than Wrede's, but it still deserves consideration by anyone coming to the task of writing NT theology in the last quarter of the twentieth century.

In addition to comments below on these two essays, attention will be given to R. Morgan's essay on 'The Nature of New Testament Theology',[31] and the article by E. Käsemann on 'The Problem of a New Testament Theology', in which he briefly sets out what he calls theses for regulating the study of the subject.

The distinction between theology and religion

Wrede tried to deal with the NT purely as a historian. He was reacting against the older dogmatic approach in the same way as Gabler, who clearly influenced him. He was convinced that the link between biblical and dogmatic theology must be cut.[32] But to do this he was obliged to maintain that the biblical texts were concerned with the history of religion. This meant the virtual abandonment of NT theology. Indeed, in the original German edition of Wrede's essay, he used the word *sogennanten* (so-called) to show that he regarded the term 'NT theology' as a misnomer.

Wrede's quest, however, implied more than the challenging of the term 'theology'. By 'religion' he meant a description of early Christian experience from a historical point of view. In this approach doctrine is inapplicable.[33] Indeed, it is integral to Wrede's view of NT theology that all dogma is rejected, including any idea of the authoritative character of the text. With the rejection of an inspired text and the substitution of religion for theology, Wrede saw no reason to restrict himself to the NT canon. His new approach was two-fold: on the one hand he was selective with regard to the NT books, and on the other hand he appealed beyond the NT alto-

---

[31] Wrede's, Schlatter's and Morgan's essays are all published in R. Morgan, *The Nature of New Testament Theology*.

[32] *Cf.* Wrede, in Morgan, *op. cit.*, p. 69. He criticized the use of the word 'normative' in relation to NT theology, because he saw it as a dogmatic predicate which says nothing about the characteristics of the material as documents. But see the later discussion on the normative character of NT theology (below, pp. 32f.).

[33] Wrede, *op. cit.*, p. 75, goes so far as to regard the use of the name 'doctrinal concept' in relation to the NT as a crime. His idea is that the term 'doctrine' is applicable only 'when thoughts and ideas are developed for the sake of teaching'. He considers that this rarely happens in the NT, which shows the very narrow definition of the word in his use of it.

gether to the writings of the sub-apostolic fathers. His reason for doing this was that he could find no justification for drawing a distinction between the canonical and non-canonical writings, since he did not in fact admit 'canonicity' (see later discussion).[34]

There is no doubt that Wrede's attempt to make the distinction between theology and religion was salutary, for the NT must not be regarded as a lifeless repository out of which systems of doctrine may be dug. If the pulse of early Christian life is not felt in the theology, it will unquestionably lead to dead theologizing. But did Wrede go too far in insisting on religion instead of theology?

As generally understood the word 'theology' is narrower in its conception than 'religion', especially when used in a Christian context. While 'theology' is not necessarily restricted to doctrine, it tends to signify a system of beliefs. On the other hand the concept of 'religion' is broad enough to include not only doctrinal beliefs, but anything which bears on the religious life of the people. The question arises how far such a wide concept is useful, or indeed valid, when dealing with NT thought. It cannot fail to introduce an element of vagueness. A treatment of NT religion would present something of a hotch-potch of various disconnected ideas which had contributed in different ways to the religious life of the early church. It would not be concerned to trace any connection between the various themes, but would be a kaleidoscope of early Christian experiences and activities. Its wide variations would, therefore, be considered enriching. There are undoubtedly attractive features about such an approach. It absolves the investigator from coming to grips with many teasing problems. It is content simply to present a descriptive account of early Christian experiences and activities.

The religion-instead-of-theology approach is nevertheless open to objections. Such an approach lays no claim to provide a normative pattern. It may provide some impetus if studied with its exemplary value in mind, but there is no reason to suppose that it must be relevant to later Christian centuries. It has little more than an antiquarian interest in the material. It certainly cannot provide anything authoritative. It does not see NT thought as a revelation from God and therefore valid for all ages. It reduces to an account of men's quest for God in the first century, which may, of course, be repeated in some of its aspects in each succeeding century; but the exegete is left in fact to make his own choice.

Very different from this is the approach which sees the NT teaching as an abiding revelation from God, which therefore concentrates on what God has to say to man rather than on man's various religious experiences

[34] In commenting on Wrede's emphasis on the history of religions, R. Morgan, *op. cit.*, pp. 12f., writes, 'The theological motive for this shift of emphasis in New Testament studies was that the old authority of the biblical text as revelation had disintegrated in the light of historical research.'

in his search for God. If divine truth of an authoritative kind is conveyed in the NT, the interpreter is circumscribed in his task. He is not at liberty to pick and choose. He must take all or nothing. He must also see the teaching as a whole and not in unconnected snippets. He cannot concentrate on one aspect (*e.g.* Paul's theology) to the exclusion of the rest. Nor can he create his own ideas about the comparative importance of different emphases.[35] He is committed to discover the unifying factors because he knows that revelation cannot be contradictory.

It must be noted, of course, that not all who would reject the 'religion' approach would agree that theology is definitive or necessarily revelation. Many would consider it legitimate to concentrate on ideas or concepts, but would deny all thought of unity. If the NT consists of a variety of theologies rather than a unity presented from different aspects we need to consider whether its value as revelation is modified. It may be said that interpreters who consider that the NT consists only of 'theologies' place themselves midway between the two approaches discussed above. It is evident that the interpreter's view of the character of the NT as revelation has a profound effect on the methodology he uses. The problem of the unity of the NT will be discussed later (pp. 49 ff.).

The relation between New Testament theology and dogmatics

The reaction against dogmatics, of which Wrede's essay was the most articulate example, was not representative of all points of view. Adolf Schlatter addressed himself to the question of the relation between a historical approach to the NT and a dogmatic interest in the text.[36] It is as well to note first of all what Schlatter meant by dogmatics in relation to NT studies. He claims to use it with respect to 'that shared knowledge and faith which unites us into a church'.[37] This distinguishes it from individual opinions. On the strength of this definition he considered that dogmatics looks to the present (*i.e.* to ourselves), whereas historical work looks to the past (*i.e.* to the experience of others). But he denied that the two disciplines were mutually exclusive. 'Since Christianity is based upon the New Testament, the interpretation of the New Testament is an act which

---

[35] An existential interpreter like E. Fuchs would not agree on this. Indeed, he regards NT theology as an abbreviation for the enquiry about theology in the NT; *cf.* 'The Theology of the New Testament and the Historical Jesus', in his *Studies of the Historical Jesus* (Eng. trans. 1964), pp. 167–190. His approach is representative of many modern NT theologians who hold to a canon within the canon. Fuch's own emphasis is on faith as a language event.

[36] A. Schlatter's essay on NT theology was written after his *Neutestamentliche Theologie*, but it sets out the principles on which the earlier work was based. The original essay was published in 1909 in *Theologische Bücherei*, Bd 41), but has appeared in an English translation as, 'The Theology of the New Testament and Dogmatics', in R. Morgan's *The Nature of New Testament Theology*, pp. 117–166.

[37] Schlatter, *op. cit.*, p.119.

touches its foundations.'[38] Schlatter even went as far as to say that 'system' is as appropriate to historical work as to dogmatics, in the sense that our knowledge of history is not limited to 'scattered and contradictory observations'. He considered that 'the harmonious ordering of our thoughts is an indication that our work has been successful'. The force of Schlatter's plea has been largely lost because of a modern hardening against all thought of harmonization.[39] But his opinion merits rethinking.

If the NT historian is to make sense of what he finds, he cannot avoid a study of doctrine. Nor can he keep his own convictions out of the question, for, as Schlatter remarked, 'At no point in our lives do we have the task of self-annihilation.'[40] He maintained that the present interacts with the past to clarify the past.[41] This brings dogmatics and biblical theology into close proximity.

It will be seen at once that this involves a totally different approach to NT theology from Wrede's proposals. Schlatter gave much greater significance to revelation, pointing out that if the NT is made dependent on 'the tarnished products of human work, Pharisaism and Hellenism, rabbinate and gnosticism, instead of on God's activity alone',[42] it may be claimed that 'divine origin' and 'historical mediation' are mutually exclusive. But Schlatter did not accept this as a necessary antithesis, although he issued some perceptive warnings against appealing to other religious backgrounds as if these formed a unitary whole. Schlatter's retention of the idea of revelation as an essential factor for a genuine understanding of NT theology has not been given the weight that it deserves.

In considering Schlatter's contribution to the debate on NT theology, we must note that there has been modern recognition of his importance; Käsemann goes as far as to rank Schlatter as Bultmann's 'one and only peer'.[43] Moreover, Käsemann regards him as the real originator of the new quest for the historical Jesus. Morgan sees some similarity between Bultmann's existential emphasis and Schlatter's position.[44] The fact is, Schlatter's call for a theological approach rather than a purely historical approach has had wider influence in recent years. Morgan,[45] however, criticized him for maintaining traditional views of authorship and for plac-

---

[38] *Ibid.*, p. 120.

[39] It is all too often assumed without debate that 'harmonizing' is in itself intellectually taboo. But this does less than justice to the evidence, for it places a premium on diversity and assumes that no two early witnesses could be expected to agree. Undoubtedly some attempts at harmonization for purely dogmatic reasons are rightly to be rejected.

[40] *Op. cit.*, p. 125.

[41] *Ibid.*, p. 126.

[42] *Ibid.*, p. 151.

[43] E. Käsemann, 'The Problem of a New Testament Theology', *NTS* 19, 1972–3, p.239.

[44] *Op. cit.*, p. 28.

[45] *Ibid.*, p. 29.

ing too much weight on particular personalities, but he commends him for recognizing development within the NT.

If we are to continue to give due weight to the character of the NT as revelation, some consideration must be given to the significance of the doctrinal concepts within the NT. It is a corollary that the doctrinal teaching of the NT would not be expected to provide a hotch-potch of disparate ideas totally unconnected with the ongoing convictions of the Christian church. To recognize the need for some continuity between NT theology and Christian convictions does not mean, however, that the NT theologian is entitled to impose on the NT a dogmatic structure which is derived from the historic dogmatic formulations.[46] At most, NT theology can provide the basic materials for dogmatic theology which in any age must continually be checked against NT concepts. Yet there are major themes which arise out of a study of the NT, which are not imposed upon it by dogmatic considerations, although they may find parallels in later credal formulations. Schlatter maintained that the sovereignty of God, Christ, sin, justification, love and faith establish the content of NT theology.[47] These he claimed were derived from the NT itself.

The relationship between NT theology and a dogmatic interest becomes acute in a different form in the theology of Bultmann. His existential presuppositions virtually impose a structure on his NT theology, which goes beyond the purely historical approach. Further comment will be made on Bultmann's position in the section on theology and history, but for our present purpose it is worthy of note that there is some kinship between the conservative Schlatter and the existentialist Bultmann.

In considering the relationship between NT theology and dogmatics one important question which arises is whether there is any sense in which NT theology can be normative. If it is regarded as wholly descriptive, it might lead to the position in which the NT theologian is little more than a kind of museum keeper who displays his ancient exhibits to the best possible advantage, but can do nothing to demonstrate their modern relevance. But such a view of the theologian's task lacks all dynamic and does not match up to the continuing importance of the NT in the experience of Christians.

The real issue is how far NT theology can be considered normative. If it needs reinterpreting in every age, as Bultmann maintains, first-century thought patterns can certainly not be considered normative, not at least in an objective manner. But if the NT presents an authoritative revelation, is there no sense in which it can be considered normative for every age?

---

[46] E. Käsemann, *op. cit.*, p. 236, recognized the pressing need today for a connection between analytic and systematic thought. He thinks that otherwise we end up in total isolation from one another. He likens specialization to people digging their own pits from which they can see little of the sky or of the world around them.

[47] *Op. cit.*, p. 161.

Man's cultural background has certainly changed since first-century times. His understanding of his own environment is immeasurably enlarged. But does this make the NT less relevant for today? It would only do so if man's basic need had changed. But the fact is, with all his sophisticated scientific progress he is still faced with similar questions about his relationship to God. If salvation was by knowledge, it would be necessary to produce a NT theology in very different terms from the original first-century concepts. But the twentieth century has not yet demonstrated that man's knowledge can save him. The fact is, the basic problem with which the NT deals is how sinful man may approach a holy God and this is the same for all ages. It is our contention, therefore, that NT theology is authoritative and therefore normative in the essentially spiritual area with which it deals. No-one would suppose the NT to be normative in its scientific understanding.

Yet in calling NT theology normative, care must be taken to ensure that something more is intended than the repetition of early Christian beliefs, which must be presented to every age *in toto* for imitation. The normative character of NT theology rests in the changelessness of man's basic need for God, but each age must bring its own consciousness of need to the understanding of the NT. In other words, if it is to be truly normative, NT theology must awaken twentieth-century readers to an awareness that what it is saying has relevance to their present needs. If in this respect it appears to be encroaching on the preserves of dogmatic theology, it is only because there is no clear-cut dividing line between them (see previous discussion on pp. 30f.).

It is equally true, if not considerably more so, that the NT theologian must first himself face the relevance of what he writes. He cannot expect it to be relevant to others if it has not first become meaningful to himself. He must in fact approach his task in faith, even if he be charged with bringing to it a bias which renders his work historically unacceptable. For unless the theologian can respond to the basic message of the NT, he will become a mere antiquarian, observing remote past opinions about Jesus Christ. But such an observer would not be an acceptable historian. Even modern man fears the risk of dogmatic bias less than that of total isolation. The present author, therefore, offers no apology for approaching NT theology unashamedly from the standpoint of faith. The facets of doctrine discussed have been tested in Christian experience and bear comparison with the historic Christian declarations of faith.

Nevertheless, the NT must be allowed to speak for itself and not be encased in those historic declarations. In each age it is incumbent on historic Christianity to test again the validity of its present dogmatic formulations against the living doctrines which emerge from the NT. For the NT itself is the mainspring of the church's doctrines, however valid the systematic theologian's task of setting those doctrines against the background of wider historical and cultural considerations.

The limitations of a purely literary approach

Partly as a reaction against the older purely dogmatic approach to Scripture, which viewed it as supernatural revelation divorced from its historical background, the early critical scholars insisted on treating the NT on the same footing as any other literary work. There was no doubt some justification in this, but it led to an over-emphasis on literary analysis which in many cases has obscured the uniqueness of the NT. It is clearly important to discuss the extent to which the NT can be approached in the same way as other literature. No-one would deny that it is perfectly proper to consider the human agencies behind the NT, the men of flesh and blood who penned its words, and to attempt to discover the sources of their material. Hence some comparisons must be made with the methods used by other writers.

But care must be taken not to blur the obvious distinction in subject matter. The NT literature centres on a person who contributes an element of uniqueness to the literature about him. This is not to be interpreted as a plea to hedge the NT around with an impenetrable wall against all criticism, for that would be indefensible. But nevertheless anyone who approaches the literature without being conscious of its unique character is in no better position than those who approach a study of Christ predetermined to see him in purely humanist terms. Neither will arrive at a true picture.

There is, of course, a dilemma here, for the interpreter cannot approach his texts with an open mind if he accepts their uniqueness as a presupposition. But neither can he arrive at a true understanding of his texts unless he is prepared to admit that he is faced with a mystery which cannot be resolved in purely human terms. If he regards an approach to the texts which restricts him to human tools as the only authentic method,[48] he will have no alternative but to strip the texts of elements which do not fit into his understanding (as, for instance, in the case of the actual resurrection of Christ). Yet this methodology makes the texts bow to the presuppositions of the exegete, and places his own theories in a position of greater authority than the texts themselves.

If on the other hand the NT exegete recognizes that in the texts he is faced with a mystery which cannot be solved in purely human terms, he will set a limit on the extent to which he is entitled to depend on literary studies. He cannot avoid pursuing literary parallels; but he will be influenced not merely by parallel wording, but by a comparison of the entire context of

---

[48] Schlatter, in Morgan's *The Nature of New Testament Theology*, p. 155, points out that historical criticism is never based on historical fact alone, but always has roots in the critic's own dogma. In his opinion our convictions do not come from history alone, but from the effects of that history in our experience.

the parallel writing with that of the NT. Hence rabbinic parallels have validity only when they are seen against the wide differences between Judaism and Christianity in their over-all approaches.

This leads to a comment on what one scholar has called 'parallelomania',[49] a literary disease which pushes the quest for parallels to excess. Again this has arisen only in those schools of thought which have not paid enough attention to the particular character of the NT texts. If parallels are used as a means of determining unauthenticity, as, for instance, in Bultmann's approach to NT interpretation, they form an extremely important part of the principles of criticism and become a powerful tool for measuring truth.[50] But there is no justification for attaching such importance to mere parallels. Some further investigation is needed to establish whether there is any connection between the texts being compared. It is not sufficient, for instance, to assume that, because both Jesus and the early Christians were Jewish, it is legitimate to use any Jewish parallels as evidence of dependence and therefore of unauthenticity. The probability of the Jewish teaching in question having influenced the gospel writers must be demonstrated. In other words there must be both a chronological and a geographical probability to back up the parallel. Otherwise at best it can be regarded only as a hypothetical possibility. The NT theologian must bear in mind that a parallel must not be treated as a source and cannot be regarded as providing on its own a guide to exegesis. Too often theories have been constructed on no other grounds than supposed parallels, resulting in distortions.

An equally serious problem of much literary criticism of the NT texts is the tendency to over-emphasize the differences.[51] This has resulted in a multiplication of different strands. Hence not only is the Pauline theology set over against the other strands within the NT, because Paul has his own special characteristics; but also within the Pauline epistles differences are magnified into inconsistencies, and Pauline authorship for certain letters is denied. In many cases a totally different result would follow if similarities rather than differences were stressed.[52] But some types of literary criticism

[49] S. Sandmel, 'Parallelomania', *JBL* 81 (1962), pp. 2–11.

[50] *Cf.* M. D. Hooker, 'On using the wrong tool', *Theology* 75, 1972, pp. 570–581, for a powerful criticism of methodology of this kind. *Cf.* also D. G. A. Calvert's article, 'Distinguishing the Authentic Words of Jesus', *NTS* 18, 1971–72, pp. 209–218.

[51] W. Wrede in Morgan, *op. cit.*, p. 186 n. 26, warns against this tendency: 'The tendency to emphasize differences and contradictions, even where they are not important, is partly a reaction against harmonization in the interests of dogmatics. This is quite natural, but is none the less itself a kind of dogmatizing.'

[52] R. Morgan, *The Nature of New Testament Theology*, p. 20, agrees that someone who accepts Ephesians, Colossians and the pastorals 'will have a very different picture of Paul from someone who does not.' He admits that historical criticism does not result in widespread critical agreement. An example of radical fragmentation within a Pauline epistle is J. C. O'Neill's treatment of Romans, *Paul's Letter to the Romans*, (1975). But theological differences have played an important part in the challenge to the authenticity of many Pauline epistles.

blow up differences at the expense of similarities.[53] An important illustration of this is in the field of Christology where differences of emphasis have been construed into different 'Christologies'. Although some significance may certainly be attached to special themes, where these stand out in contradistinction to the general teaching (as for instance when Paul expounds his Adam theology), yet this does not justify a wholesale magnification of differences. Literary criticism exceeds its brief when it constructs a number of different theologies out of shifts of emphasis found in various NT books.[54] It is more reasonable for the NT theologian to expect some kind of basic unity rather than the reverse.

Why should it even be thought probable that different church leaders and church groups should develop along independent lines?[55] Is it not more plausible to suppose that a basic common understanding of the gospel existed, and that specific emphases were not deviations but merely different facets of a complex whole? More will be said on this when the basis of unity within the NT is discussed below. For the moment it is desired only to enter a caveat against the fragmentation of NT thought which then becomes a *sine qua non* in approaching NT theology.

The weakness of a wholly analytical approach

From the last point arises the whole problem of analytical methodology. Is it a right approach, for example, to make a fragmented study of the synoptic gospels, the fourth gospel, the Pauline epistles and various other streams of thought? To answer this question we must consider the nature of an analytic as compared with a synthetic approach. The analytical approach takes up one type of literature (*e.g.* the synoptic gospels) and treats the major themes of that source as the sum total of the writer's tenets. Under this kind of methodology it is inevitable that some themes will loom larger than they should. Is it right, for instance, to make synoptic theology wholly revolve around the kingdom theme? Or, to put it another way, should we approach the gospels as if the main theme of the early Christians was eschatology? Such an approach is bound to highlight dif-

---

[53] In his recent book *Unity and Diversity in the New Testament* (1977), J. D. G. Dunn has not avoided the fault of over-analysis although he does attempt to maintain a core of unity.

[54] Although Schlatter, in Morgan's *The Nature of New Testament Theology*, p. 140, claimed that NT theology must be divided up into as many theologies as there are NT authors, he nevertheless set this within the context of the community. He was therefore strongly against the view that these separate theologies were conflicting. Wrede, in Morgan, *op. cit.*, p. 74, conceded that some of the NT books are too brief to be treated separately. Since he was concerned to discover the characteristic religious emphasis in each, he found little scope for this in 1 and 2 Peter, Jude and James because of their brevity.

[55] H. Riesenfeld, 'Reflections on the Unity of the New Testament', *Religion* 3, 1973, pp. 35–51., makes some pertinent comments on this theme. He denies that there was conflict between different churches over the circulation of different parts of the NT. Further comments are made on this theme below, pp. 49ff.

ferences between the synoptics and John,[56] and between both and Paul. Analytical work of this kind has value if it avoids assuming that any work exhausts its author's theology. On the other hand the synthetic approach examines the individual aspects to see where they fit into the total picture. It should be noted, however, that the analytic and synthetic approaches are not mutually exclusive.

The place of personality in New Testament theology

Because God chose to make his revelation known through men, we cannot overlook the important part played by their personality in the presentation of their message. Did their own inclinations colour their thinking, and must allowance be made for this in assessing their theology? It would be best here to concentrate attention on the case of Paul.

The apostle's habit of producing letters which are for the most part far removed from theological treatises presents a problem. Clearly in some letters (*e.g.* Corinthians) his own personality not only shines through, but in fact dominates the subject matter. What can be gleaned from these letters about Paul's theology is purely incidental. The subject matter is mainly practical, rather than theological. Very different is Paul's letter to Rome, where he seems to have worked out an overall plan for the letter, which he adheres to in a much more orderly way than is discernible in the other letters. Personality and circumstances combine to provide the right setting for the most theological of all his letters.

But from the obvious fact that Paul's personality has a bearing on his theology some scholars have deduced that he has corrupted the pure gospel of Jesus by overlaying it with dogma. This was a particular theme of the nineteenth-century liberal school whose aim was to liberate NT theology from Paul's dogmatic influence. He was essentially the corrupter. Yet how psychologically probable is such a view? Could Paul have hammered out an independent line at variance with the primitive teaching? The shade of Baur, with his polarization of opposing movements under the dominant personalities of Peter and Paul, was not yet completely forgotten at the turn of the century. The inadequate experiment of the Tübingen school should provide a warning against too much concentration on personalities.

A modern movement like *Redaktionsgeschichte* also tends to concentrate on personalities (see further the comments on p. 48). It may be said that this is preferable to the earlier concentration on units of tradition which were assumed to have circulated anonymously. Instead of having a synoptic

---

[56] Not only is there need for caution over a methodology which drives too deep a wedge between the theology of John and the synoptics, but also between the separate synoptic evangelists. As Riesenfeld, *op. cit.*, pp. 42f., remarks, what the gospels have in common must be more significant and important than what is peculiar to each, since as far as we know they were not in competition with one another before the time of Marcion.

theology, we now have theologies of each separate gospel. Suddenly the authors have come into their own. But again a caution is needed, lest it be supposed that any of these personalities could or would have developed a theology of his own, unconnected with the views of the early communities as a whole. It would be better to speak of the special theological emphases rather than the theology of each evangelist. It is legitimate to examine the different emphases, but when these are treated as coherent 'theologies' confusion is bound to occur. Moreover, this question of personality in theology is profoundly affected by the important consideration of apostolicity (see further discussion on p. 971ff.). It is scarcely credible, for instance, that any nonentity could have worked out his own theological ideas and then got them accepted as authentic teaching. The great lengths to which Paul went, and clearly felt obliged to go, in order to prove his authority to take a different line from what was advocated by some who claimed the support of James, is evidence of his consciousness that his innovations might be challenged. It was not enough for anyone to take an independent line. It all depended on the identity and authority of the person. The schisms at Corinth, although deplored by Paul, are a notable testimony to the 'pull' of important personalities.

In view of this we need to examine to what extent the highly individualistic theology of Paul can in any sense be considered characteristic for his own time. Because of its striking features when compared with the other NT literature, it is tempting either to use the Pauline theology as basic and to attempt to fit other ideas into his framework, or else to regard Paul's system as a more intellectualized approach which obscured rather than clarified the 'simple' gospel. Neither view is satisfactory, for both give too much weight to the personality of Paul. He did not regard himself as an innovator, except perhaps in certain practical matters such as marriage, where he admits nevertheless that others may have other opinions. He seems, however, to be concerned to reflect the usage of the churches generally (as in 1 Cor. 14:33).

It may be questioned whether the practice of speaking of theology in terms of personality, as Pauline, Johannine, Petrine, Lucan, is strictly valid within NT theology, for it encourages individuality. It would be preferable to speak of the theology of the different writings. Nevertheless, it has become so much a part of contemporary procedure that it would be pedantic to suggest that it should be avoided. Provided a caution is exercised that the basic core of Pauline theology is not to be regarded necessarily as exclusive to Paul, no damage will be done to the right appreciation of NT theology as a whole. It may well be that Paul was expressing in a more precise way concepts which also formed an essential part of general Christian beliefs. When, for instance, he expounds his great theme of righteousness in his Roman letter, there is no need to suppose that all the concepts would come fresh to the readers, although Paul's expression of the doctrine is certainly unique. Indeed, the somewhat complicated character of the argument in this letter presupposes a considerable amount of theological background on the part of the readers. Much is assumed. The apostle takes it for granted, for example, that his readers will have a working acquaintance with the idea of righteousness.

Another factor which makes it unsatisfactory to place too much stress on personal theologies in the NT is the fragmentary character of the evidence. It is a misnomer, for instance, to speak of a Petrine theology when the literature is not only restricted in quantity, but also in purpose. It cannot be expected that brief letters written from a mainly practical point of view will provide an adequate guide to the total theology of any one writer.[57] As already pointed out, even with Paul's letters, the total material available is small. Where evidences of theological thought are fragmentary, it is wrong methodology to regard such thought as representing the writer's whole range of theology. For instance, if Paul concentrates in Ephesians on one aspect of the atonement – that of Jewish-Gentile reconciliation – it cannot be supposed that all other aspects are excluded. Such a deduction would imply that no-one could express a new aspect of truth without excluding, if not negating, all other aspects which he has previously expressed. Moreover, if a letter is written to Christians suffering persecution (as 1 Peter), it is not to be wondered that much is made of hope. Yet it would be wrong to suppose that a theology of hope was a dominant characteristic of Peter. It was simply what was needed at that particular time for those particular readers.

A further consideration is necessary in dealing with the place of personality in theology. What part is played by the different intellectual backgrounds of the writers? Should more weight be given to an obviously theological thinker like Paul, compared with an equally obviously non-theological thinker like James? A man's educational background may perhaps determine the degree of precision we would expect from his theological statements; but we must not lose sight of the fact that ideas more loosely expressed might be as theologically significant. In other words, it is imperative to take the total evidence into account. It is possible to be misled into thinking that theology is wholly a matter of intellectual concepts instead of embracing the whole life. Many-sided personalities will lead to a many-sided presentation of theological truth. There can be no doubt that God in his wisdom chose different personalities to bring richness and variety to his revelation.

In dealing with personality some comment must be made on the frequently alleged dichotomy between the creative theologian Paul and the

---

[57] As Wrede, *op. cit.*, p. 74, rightly pointed out.

'stereotyped' doctrine of the pastoral epistles.[58] The presentation of Paul as a 'creative' theologian in this alleged dichotomy blurs, if it does not pre-judge, the issue, for it presupposes that the most characteristic feature of Paul was his creativity, which leads to the conclusion that anything non-creative is not Pauline. The error lies in the assumption that a creative mind must always be creative and would find any codification of doctrine into 'the deposit' or 'the truth' totally unacceptable. But is not this particular conception of 'creativity' something imposed on Paul from without? It is asking too much to suppose that the apostle could not have conceived of the whole body of doctrine under a caption like 'the truth'. If he could not have conceived of 'truth' in this way, it would be necessary to suppose that he envisaged the possibility of further revelations of truth after his own death. But who would carry on his flights of creativity? Is it not more reasonable to restrict Paul's creativity to a greater clarification of truths already basic to all Christian thought? It is again the analytical approach which has been responsible for denying that such basic common doctrine existed and which has therefore over-emphasized the significance of Paul's creativity. The same tendency has been extended to the theology of the evangelists. This is not, of course, to deny the essentially living quality of Paul's theological thinking. He brings amazing insights to his expositions, but this is short of 'creativity' if that word is used in the sense of producing something entirely new as compared with previously existing material.

The place of the canon in New Testament theology

It might appear unnecessary to raise the issue of the relationship between the NT canon and NT theology were it not that this issue has already become a matter of debate on two different fronts. It has been noted that Wrede in his quest for religion not only refused to restrict himself to the NT docu-ments, but made no distinction between the canonical and non-canonical sources. Wrede argued that no NT writing was born with the predicate 'canonical' attached.[59] From this he deduced that anyone who accepted without question the NT canon placed himself under the bishops and theo-logians of the second- to fourth-century church. But this is a misrepresen-tation of the facts. The canon may have been recognized by the bishops and theologians, but it was not initiated by them. Wrede's view on this issue has been sufficiently criticized to allow us to conclude that his con-tention has not been self-evidently established.[60] We may in fact state that

[58] Cf. the discussion of this issue in my *The Pastoral Epistles* (*TNTC*, 1957), pp. 38ff.

[59] Cf. Wrede, *op. cit.*, pp. 70f.

[60] Morgan, *op. cit.*, p. 3, criticizes Wrede for maintaining that where the doctrine of inspiration is discarded, it is impossible to maintain the dogmatic conception of the canon. But he supports Wrede's view that the literature must be evaluated without regard for its ecclesiastical status. Morgan, however, denies any distinction between the apostolic and sub-apostolic ages. A view of this kind must devalue the canon.

the concept of NT theology demands the understanding of the collection of NT literature in a special way. As Schlatter rightly pointed out in distinguishing between the NT writings and the later literature, 'By canonizing these writings, the generations following the apostles expressed where they found that word through which the church emerged and receives for all time its connection with the Christ.'[61] It is right to conclude that NT theology is based upon an accepted canon of literature.

The second front on which comment must be made is the problem whether or not it is right to speak of a 'canon within the canon' and if so what effect this must have on the study of NT theology. In other words the issue is whether NT theology can legitimately be based on part only of the NT, or whether the interpreter is obliged to take the whole of the canonical literature into account. The idea of a canon within the canon has been brought into focus recently by E. Käsemann's strong advocacy of it. But the idea is not in itself new. Martin Luther began the trail by his attitude towards certain NT books being less valuable than others, although it has been questioned whether it is accurate to speak of a canon within the canon in relation to Luther's attitude.[62] Bultmann, in his *New Testament Theology*, virtually adopted a limited canon by concentrating on Paul (*i.e.* on some of the epistles attributed to him) and on John. Kümmel does the same in his work, although he conceded more importance to the teaching of Jesus. It will be seen at once that the limits of NT theology are set, not by the NT itself, but by the prior decisions of the interpreter. But is this a legitimate procedure?

If we accepted a purely descriptive function for NT theology it might not matter too much if some of the minor parts of the NT literature were omitted. But if there is any sense in which NT thought possesses a normative force, the interpreter is not at liberty to pick and choose what he considers to be of value and omit the rest. Such a procedure is in any event open to question even for those who adopt a descriptive interpretation.

It has been suggested that the usage of the different sections of the church has established not one but several canons within the canon.[63] But this is no basis for deciding the scope of NT theology. If certain groups stress one part of the canon more than another, it is part of the function of NT theology to supply a corrective. It is not a complete answer to maintain that the canon within the canon is the common faith in the exalted Jesus, for this confuses the meaning of the word 'canon'. What we are concerned to establish is what written material supplies the basis of our study and we

---

[61] *Cf.* Schlatter, *op. cit.*, p. 146.

[62] *Cf.* N. B. Stonehouse, 'Luther and the New Testament Canon', in his *Paul before the Areopagus, and Other New Testament Studies* (1957), pp. 186–197.

[63] *Cf.* the concept of a canon within the canon in the discussion of J. D. G. Dunn, *Unity and Diversity*, pp. 374ff.

cannot accept as adequate any view which depends on a selective approach to the NT.

Another question arises which has a direct bearing on our use of our sources. Are we concerned to distinguish between books which are regarded as unquestionably authentic and those which among many scholars are not? The Pauline epistles present the most pressing problems here. Since some dispute the Pauline authorship of Ephesians, Colossians, the Pastorals, how valid is it for the NT theologian to split the Pauline theology accordingly? Clearly different interpreters will give different answers according to their stance on these literary questions. It must be admitted by all serious scholars that there is no consensus of opinion which enables anyone to speak unhesitatingly of deutero-Pauline epistles in contradistinction from the general. No NT theology is on a solid foundation if it rests on the changing position of NT hypotheses. Nevertheless neither can it ignore serious research. The position adopted in this book maintains that all the Pauline epistles belong to the same category. This is not, however, to exclude the possibility of development within the Pauline epistles.

In a later section the problem of the unity of the NT will be discussed, but for the moment it needs to be noted that 'unity' is closely linked with 'canon'. An authoritative collection of books like the NT canon must be held together by some overriding concept. Whereas diversity is in line with the idea of a canon within the canon, unity is more difficult to square with that view. This is not to say that diversity is excluded if the whole canon is considered, for there is no doubt that such diversity exists. There may be some truth in saying that the canon 'canonizes the diversity of Christianity',[64] so long as this is understood to mean the diverse forms in which the essential unity has come to be expressed. Käsemann[65], on the other hand, regards the NT as fragmentary and any apparent unity as the result of early catholicizing. It is obvious that this fragmentary view of the sources must affect the structure of the theology constructed from them. All that can be done is for each interpreter to make clear the position adopted with regard to the canon.

The relation between history and theology

The problem of history and theology is crucial in the modern debate on NT theology. Since the early part of this century, academic theology has been obsessed with the debate over the Jesus of history. Mention has already

---

[64] Cf. ibid., p. 376.

[65] Cf. E. Käsemann, 'The Canon of the New Testament and the Unity of the Church', in his Essays on New Testament Themes (Eng. trans. 1964), pp. 95–107, originally published in German in EvT 11, 1951–2, pp. 13–21. Both in this article and in the NTS 19, 1972–3, article (especially p. 242), Käsemann stresses the fragmentary character of the NT. As a result he considers that the variableness of the primitive Christian kerygma must have been greater than the NT canon leads us to suppose (cf. Essays on New Testament Themes, p. 100).

been made of the need for the historical background of the evidences of NT theology to be taken into account, but the problem now confronting us is the more fundamental one of the validity of the history itself.

Nineteenth-century thought had raised the issue as a result of the emergence of rationalism – as with men like Reimarus, Baur and Strauss. But until the twentieth century no book on NT theology was orientated to a non-historical approach to Jesus. Indeed, works like Holtzmann's *Theology* were built up on the basic assumption that the history of Jesus could be known. There was point therefore in giving a place of importance to the teaching of Jesus. But twentieth-century interpretation of NT theology has to take into account the scepticism regarding the historical Jesus which has developed in the wake of Bultmann's position.[66] A theology based on this approach will have a very different starting point from a theology which gives greater validity to the historical records. Because of this it will be necessary to discuss in general how modern historiography affects theology.

MODERN VIEWS OF HISTORY

It has been regarded almost as axiomatic that the gospels could be relied on to supply the gist of the teaching of Jesus. But when modern historiography challenges the possibility of an objective approach to history, the biblical theologian must face the challenge to decide how valid it is. If it is right to suppose, with Collingwood,[67] that no historian can honourably accept history from another, but must make his own investigations until he himself becomes part of the history, the gospels would be called into question. The theologian of the gospels would then be required to approach them with historical scepticism. That would be part of his basic equipment. It would be his task to determine what was authentic or not. But this approach is open to challenge. History is more than what takes place in the mind of the historian. The historian's task is to examine his facts, not to create them. On the other hand, the theologian's reconstruction, for instance, of the Christology of the synoptic gospels will depend on how much he regards the teaching of Jesus to consist of the views of the Christian community or to be a true reflection of what Jesus taught. Although it need hardly be said that the evangelists were not unbiased historical observers because they were committed to faith in what they

[66] *Cf.* R. Bultmann, *History and Eschatology* (Eng. trans. 1957), pp. 3ff., for a concise discussion of his view of historiography. For a brief critique of Bultmann's position, *cf.* G. H. Clark, 'Bultmann's Historiography', in C. F. H. Henry (ed.), *Jesus of Nazareth: Saviour and Lord* (1966), pp. 213–223. *Cf.* also Bultmann's earlier discussion in *Jesus and the Word* (Eng. trans. 1935).

[67] *Cf.* R. G. Collingwood, *The Idea of History* (1946), p. 256. D. E. Nineham, 'Eye-witness Testimony and the Gospel Tradition', *JTS* 11 (1960), pp. 253ff., cites Collingwood's opinion approvingly. But F. F. Bruce, 'History and the Gospel', in *Jesus of Nazareth: Saviour and Lord*, p. 99 n.1, questions whether Collingwood's work can be considered as revolutionary as he himself thought.

wrote, nevertheless this does not mean that they could not produce dependable facts. It will be necessary to give some indication of theological movements which are based on this modern approach to history in order to explain why their perspective is not adopted in this work.

HISTORY AND EXISTENTIALISM

In the particular view of history mentioned above, the philosophy of existentialism found a congenial partner. If all that matters is a present encounter with Christ, the history becomes unimportant. In fact, if the objective element is removed from history, what is left is at least intelligible to existentialism, if not to those who see other grounds for a historical approach. If the modern historian comes to the text with the conviction that he must become a part of the history he is studying, this ties in well with the existentialist's demand for understanding when he is confronted with the text of Scripture. Since Bultmann is the leading exponent of this latter view, it will be valuable to outline his view of history and show how existentialism affects his approach to NT theology.

Bultmann maintains that a historian approaches his data in a different way from a scientist. He imagines that the latter is impersonal, but the former is not. This, however, may be strongly challenged, for no scientist can approach his data without presuppositions.[68] If these presuppositions are wrong his enquiries will lead nowhere and he will be forced to try other theories. But he does not and cannot approach with a blank mind.

In explaining his existential approach to history, Bultmann speaks of 'dialogue with history',[69] but what precisely he means by this is a matter of debate. The idea seems to be that as the theologian comes to the history books about Jesus he achieves 'being' by entering into an encounter with the text and therefore making the text part of himself. He seems to mean more than interpreting or evaluating the text. The text challenges the interpreter. Dialogue with history is only possible if a full understanding of the background can be achieved, but no modern historian has access to the psychological information needed to understand the first-century background. Indeed Bultmann maintains it to be impossible, which means that his dialogue with history must be almost entirely subjective. Moreover, what history there is, according to his theory, is almost wholly the history of early Christian thinking, not the history of the event. Not more than forty of the sayings of Jesus are, in his view, authentic.[70]

This at once raises the problem of the means by which certain material can be considered authentic and other material unauthentic. For Bultmann

---

[68] For a critique of this view, *cf.* G. H. Clark, *op. cit.*, pp. 216f.

[69] *Cf.* R. Bultmann, *Jesus and the Word*, p. 3.

[70] *Cf.* R. Bultmann, *The History of the Synoptic Tradition* (Eng. trans. 1963, ²1968) and his essay in *Form Criticism* (with K. Kundsin, Eng. trans. 1934, r.p. 1962).

the answer lies in the so-called 'laws of tradition'.[71] It is first assumed that such laws exist, that is, that whenever traditions are handed on they follow the same pattern. For Bultmann's theory this means that the most characteristic feature of tradition-growth is borrowing. It is this assumption that led him to formulate his law of dissimilarity, which postulated that any material paralleled in contemporary Jewish or Christian literature must have been borrowed from such sources. If this is a true law of tradition it means that much in the gospels does not come from specifically Christian sources, although it has to be taken into account in examining early Christian thinking. We have already noted that there is no reason to suppose that parallel ideas necessarily indicate borrowing. Moreover, if some ideas did not occur in common, communication would be impossible. It is more reasonable to suppose that the accounts are rooted in reliable history.

Another matter which affects Bultmann's approach to the sources of NT theology is his extensive use of the category of myth. His own definition is as follows: 'Mythology is the use of imagery to express the other worldly in terms of this world, and the divine in terms of human life, the other side in terms of this side.'[72] Many of the most characteristic features of the NT become suspect after being classed in this category – for instance, the descending dove and the heavenly voice at the baptism of Jesus. This is all bound up with Bultmann's notion of the first-century picture of the world (*Weltbild*) which is reflected in the writers of the NT and which is totally unacceptable to modern scientific man. The three-tier universe, which is claimed to be behind NT thought, is considered naive by modern sophisticated man. Bultmann, having classed much of the material as myth, then holds that 'mythology would lead not only to a *sacrificium intellectus*, but would make faith equivalent to works'.[73] But what Bultmann is in fact doing is to reject the NT *Weltbild* solely on the ground that it differs from his own. Yet there is nothing to show that his own view is correct, or that it necessarily exclusively represents current ideas. Those not committed to an existential approach do not find such a sharp cleavage between the NT view and modern scientific opinion about the world. No-one need suppose, for instance, that the heaven above, the underworld below and the earth

---

[71] For further comment on these laws of tradition, *cf.* M. D. Hooker, *Theology* 75, 1972, pp. 570–581. H. E. W. Turner, in his book *Historicity and the Gospel* (1953), has a chapter on 'The Quest for Criteria' (pp. 58–118) in which he discusses the more general search for historical criteria. For a brief summary of Bultmann's position, *cf.* my *New Testament Introduction* (³1970), pp. 195ff.

[72] R. Bultmann, 'New Testament and Mythology', *Kerygma and Myth* 1 (ed. H.-W. Bartsch, Eng. trans. 1953), p. 10 n.2. This definition of myth has been criticized for being too narrow. K. Barth, *Kerygma and Myth* 2 (ed. H.-W. Bartsch, Eng. trans., 1962, p. 109), called it a 'curiously formal definition of myth'. Bultmann himself seems to introduce modifications in his later essay, 'Bultmann replies to his critics' *Kerygma and Myth* 1, pp. 196f., in which he concedes the use of analogy. *Cf.* also his discussion, 'On the Problem of Demythologizing', in *New Testament Issues* (ed. R. Batey, 1970), p. 42.

[73] R. Bultmann, *Jesus Christ and Mythology*, (Eng. trans. 1960), p. 17.

as the centre of conflict in between is intended as an explanation of cosmology. The spiritual conflict is real enough in whatever terms it is expressed. And the conflict is still present. The spatial imagery may not be acceptable to Bultmann, but it vividly portrays the nature of the conflict.

It is Bultmann's desire to present the thought of the NT in terms of modern existential philosophy that forces him to follow a process of demythologization.[74] If the NT is couched in terms of first-century myths, it will be unacceptable to modern intellectuals until the mythical elements are stripped off and the kernel is reinterpreted. These myths expressed the tensions of first-century Christians in their endeavour to understand the meaning of existence. The modern theologian must therefore express the same tensions by clothing the ideas in the terms of twentieth-century existential philosophy. Of course, since each age is duty-bound to reinterpret in terms of its own age, there is no guarantee that the existential reinterpretation will not itself need reinterpreting in a succeeding age. This does not worry Bultmann, but it means that there can be no abiding authority in the interpretation. It will be seen that a NT theology built on such a structure will be vastly different from one which proceeds on the assumption of a dependable and authoritative text.

Bultmann's principles of interpretation will not be followed in this book for several reasons. His existential philosophy is not embraced because it does not provide a satisfactory approach to NT theology. Instead of clarifying the issue, it obscures theology by using terms in an almost nonintelligible way.[75] Since theology is meant to be understood, no attempt will be made to impose on NT thought what is germane to a modern world view at the expense of either clarity or truth. Further, the subjectivity of Bultmann's opinions at once raises suspicions about the validity of his method. There is no room for this approach within the framework of an authoritative view of the NT. The world of NT times and the modern world have in common that both contain people with the basic need to be relieved of fear, anxiety, guilt. The supposed difference in *Weltbild* is superficial compared with this common factor. In any case the only hope that Bultmann can offer such people in need is an existential encounter which will

---

[74] *Cf.* R. Bultmann, 'The Case for Demythologizing: A Reply', *Kerygma and Myth* 2, pp. 181–194. For a critique, *cf.* I. Henderson, *Myth in the New Testament* (1952); J. D. G. Dunn, 'Demythologizing – the Problem of Myth in the New Testament', in *New Testament Interpretation* (ed. I. H. Marshall, 1977), pp. 285–307. For other books which deal with mythology, *cf.* J. Macquarrie, *The Scope of Demythologizing*, (1960); G. Miegge, *Gospel and Myth in the Thought of Rudolph Bultmann* (Eng. trans. 1960); F. Gogarten, *Demythologizing and History* (Eng. trans. 1955); H. Schlier, 'The New Testament and Myth', in his *The Relevance of the New Testament* (1967), pp. 76–93. J. M. Robinson, 'The Pre-History of Demythologization', *Int* 20, 1966, p. 71, considers that Bultmann's demythologization essay in 1941 was influenced by H. Jonas' previously published work on Augustine.

[75] This is brought out by Karl Barth in his essay, 'Rudolf Bultmann – An Attempt to Understand Him', *Kerygma and Myth* 2, pp. 83–132.

give them a challenge to a new understanding of themselves.[76] But there is nothing to alleviate guilt. Although further reference will be made in the body of the book to Bultmann's views, enough has been said to explain why his methodology must be rejected.

ATTEMPTS TO GET AWAY FROM HISTORICAL SCEPTICISM

The unsatisfactory character of extreme historical scepticism displayed by Bultmann is seen in reactions which have taken place within his own school. The total discontinuity between the apostolic faith and the historical Jesus was seen to be unrealistic. The structure of theology which emerged from the resurrection onwards needed more explanation than the mere 'thatness' of the cross. This realization has led such men as Käsemann, Bornkamm, Fuchs and others [77] to seek for a broader historical link between the historic events and the apostolic *kerygma*. There has been no agreement between them on what was more authentic. Käsemann sees it in the preaching of Jesus, Bornkamm in his attitude to people, and Fuchs in his interest in social outcasts. What is significant is that this reaction has been in the direction of greater historicity, although the movement is far from laying a satisfactory historical basis for Christian theology. There is the same devotion to existentialism as the only intellectually respectable approach to life, although rather less divorce between the Jesus of history and the Christ of faith.

The approach of James M. Robinson[78] in America has been strongly influenced by this reaction, which he has chronicled and called the 'New Quest of the Historical Jesus'. His own contribution centres on what he calls the self-understanding of Jesus, by which he means Jesus' understanding of existence. This offers no more objective basis for NT theology than Bultmann's theories have done.

It is important to note that both Bultmann and the New Quest show marked similarities in their theology with the methods of early gnosticism which became the first major challenge to apostolic Christianity. Its view of the historical Jesus is akin to docetism, and Bultmann and his supporters have not adequately avoided the charge of adopting a similar error.[79] Like the gnostics, they have sought to combine Christian ideas with contemporary ideas. This approach cannot avoid the charge of syncretism. It is

---

[76] Barth, *op. cit.*, p. 116, is surely right in charging Bultmann with clamping the gospel in the vice of existentialism which recognizes only the existence of the human subject.

[77] *Cf.* E. Käsemann, *Essays on New Testament Themes*, which includes his well-known essay on 'The Problem of the Historical Jesus', first published in 1951, which can be regarded as the beginning of the New Quest; G. Bornkamm, *Jesus of Nazareth* (Eng. trans. 1960); E. Fuchs, *Studies of the Historical Jesus* (Eng. trans. 1964).

[78] J. M. Robinson, *A New Quest of the Historical Jesus* (1959).

[79] Barth, *op. cit.*, p. 111, says, 'I cannot deny that his (Bultmann's) demythologized New Testament looks suspiciously like docetism.'

ironical in this respect that Bultmann has maintained that some of the NT theological ideas which he rejects, such as the redemptive theme, and the pre-existence of Christ, are mainly due to gnostic influence.[80] Apart from the fact that he is using the term gnosticism in a way that is open to question (*i.e.* of first-century movements), his failure to see parallels between this procedure and his own methodology is striking.

ATTEMPTS TO REDISCOVER THE THEOLOGY OF THE GOSPELS

Because of the reduction of genuine material in the gospels, it is not surprising that the theology of the synoptic gospels plays an insignificant part in Bultmann's understanding of the documents. His own *New Testament Theology* devotes only a few pages to the teaching of Jesus in the synoptic gospels. A newer movement which began within the same school has sought to concentrate on the theology of the evangelists. This is *Redaktionsgeschichte*. Its main contention is that form criticism, by focusing on the anonymous units of traditions, overlooked the individual contribution of the evangelists. It has been some gain, for greater attention has been paid to the authors, who had previously been regarded as no more than compilers. But the result of *Redaktionsgeschichte* has been a multiplication of theologies. Whereas for long the fourth gospel has furnished its own 'Johannine theology', the synoptics had been linked together. The new movement, however, sees a distinctive theology in each of the synoptics. The basic method of approach is to suppose that each evangelist selected material from the traditions and sources to give a particular slant to his theological ideas. Conzelmann,[81] for instance, reckons that Luke had a special approach to time, in which he saw the time of Jesus as the middle of time, and the time before (Israel's history) and the time after (the church's history) as governed by this idea. The distinctiveness of Luke's understanding of the middle of time is the suspension of satanic activity. Luke's gospel does not obviously give this impression and one suspects that Conzelmann has imposed his own interpretation upon Luke. The main problem with this kind of radical *Redaktionsgeschichte*, apart from its dependence on existentialism, is that it heightens any distinctive emphases in the gospels into separate theologies. Indeed, it may be said that such a *Redaktionsgeschichte* approach has brought into prominence a tendency, which has been inherent in the more extreme form critical movements, to over-emphasize the variety of theologies within the NT at the expense of its unity. This raises an acute problem which will be dealt with in the next section.

One other aspect of radical *Redaktionsgeschichte* which is important to note is that it assumes that the evangelists could not be both historians and

---

[80] *Cf.* his essay in *Kerygma and Myth* 1, pp. 1–8.
[81] H. Conzelmann, *The Theology of St Luke* (Eng. trans. 1960).

theologians. Its advocates, having already discarded the gospels as historical accounts, find no tension here, but simply refer to the evangelists as theologians. On the other hand, those who see historical worth in the accounts do not for that reason reject the suggestion that each evangelist had a theological interest. It is more correct to speak of them as both historians and theologians rather than either one or the other.[82] The combination of both ensures that the theology is based on the history and has not created the history. It is also possible and desirable to recognize that each evangelist in expressing his own point of view is not independent of the basic apostolic doctrine expressed in other literature. But this point will be clarified in the next section.

Variety and unity within the New Testament

When the earlier dogmatic approach to NT theology is compared with modern approaches, what stands out is the contrast between the earlier unified theology and the modern diversity. The older concept of unity was undoubtedly based directly on the view of revelation and inspiration held. If all parts of the literature are equal in value, irrespective of the historical background, unity is assured. Particularly is this the case if the concept of progressive revelation is denied. The concept of theological unity in the NT is of great importance, but its basis must be carefully examined. It cannot be taken as assumed, especially in view of the strong modern rejection of the idea. Nevertheless anyone who sets out to write an NT theology must state in the clearest possible terms whether he is going to treat the NT literature as a collection of disconnected sections and aim to display their diversity as if that in itself was his main aim; or whether he is going to approach the texts as a means of revealing various aspects of a united whole. No-one can deny that a decision on this matter has a profound effect on the presentation of NT teaching. The matter may be discussed under several sub-sections.

THE NATURE OF THE VARIETY

First of all, the materials for NT teaching come from different types of literature. It is inevitable that the form in which the teaching is expressed will be influenced by the type of literature in which it occurs. In the NT the four types (gospels, acts, epistles and apocalypse) all have their distinctive characteristics and all lead to different literary 'shells' for preserving the teaching. In the gospels the teaching is found in various aspects – the sayings of Jesus, the doings of Jesus, the theological comments of the evangelists. Even within the sayings of Jesus there are various types – 'I' words, parables, epigrammatic statements, discourses. But does the rich

---

[82] As I. H. Marshall does in his *Luke: Historian and Theologian* (1970).

variety of forms support a corresponding variety of teaching? That is the crucial question, and the answer is not obviously in the affirmative. Moreover, the speeches of Acts are an essentially different kind of literary form from the epistles, and it would be unreasonable to suppose that the teaching will be presented in the same way in each. Much wrong exegesis and wrong approach to NT theology has resulted from an over-emphasis on the variety of teaching, without sufficient attention being paid to the significance of the literary forms. It is further obvious that no systematic theology is presented anywhere in the NT and this inevitably makes the task of the NT theologian more difficult. The theological statements and ideas are scattered about among practical letters, an incomplete history, gospels designed primarily to present a particular view of Christ, and an apocalypse which concentrates on one major area of interest. It is from this wholly disparate collection of material that the NT theologian is expected to present in a clear way the basic apostolic teaching.[83] Wrede's argument for a description of NT religion rather than of theology is not without some appeal in this connection. But since we have already seen reason to reject Wrede's plea, we are obliged to come to terms with the variety of truth in the NT.

Not only is there a problem about the vague theological nature of some of the material, but there is variety within similar kinds of material. The epistles, for example, contain many different emphases and some scholars see a genuine Pauline theology and a deutero-Pauline theology, a Petrine and pseudo-Petrine (or a double pseudo-Petrine) theology, a theology of Hebrews and another of James and yet another of John. What are we to make of this wide variety? What we make of it will undoubtedly be determined by our starting point. It is, for instance, possible to distinguish between Paul's conception of justification-faith and James' works-faith so as to make them mutually exclusive and therefore contradictory. But it is equally possible to resolve the supposed contradiction. For some scholars any resolution of difficulties is excluded as unacceptable, with the result that there is always a bias towards diversity rather than unity. This is especially true of the gospels, where the different emphases in each are often heightened into different theologies, with an emphasis on diversity.

The splintering of theology into a number of components which bear no necessary relation to each other makes the conception of a unified faith more remote. The parts are not regarded as being like the pieces of a jigsaw puzzle, which, however individually shaped each piece happens to be,

---

[83] Although the forms within the literature varied, there is no evidence from the early period that one type of literature (*e.g.* epistles) was ever invoked to prevent the circulation of another (*e.g.* gospels). *Cf.* Riesenfeld, 'Reflections on the Unity of the New Testament', *Religion* 3, 1973, p. 41, who asks why the collection of Christian writings functioned as an organic unity. He considers that no satisfactory solution can be given by those whose work has led to the disintegration of the NT.

nevertheless fit together into a united whole.[84] Many modern approaches are more like the situation where several jigsaws are mixed up together and the various pieces refuse to fit because they do not belong. The question whether or not there is a unifying pattern is clearly of crucial importance.[85]

Before discussing this problem there is another which affects the whole question, and that is whether or not it is right to speak of development of theology within the NT.[86] The idea of progressive revelation is familiar in OT interpretation and also in the area of the relation of the OT to the NT. The Christian revelation is obviously an advance on the OT revelation. With Christ the OT ritual system became obsolete, as the epistle to the Hebrews makes clear. But is there a development of doctrine within the NT? One obvious area where this is undeniable is the difference between the gospels and the rest of the NT. Before the death and resurrection of Christ the revelation given to the disciples was limited. In the nature of the case Jesus could not give a full explanation of his own death to his disciples until they had grasped the fact of it. But after the resurrection the apostolic preachers were guided into an understanding of it, although again not in any stereotyped way, but with a rich variety. The understanding of the person of Christ did not come in a cataclysmic way. It seems rather to have been revealed piecemeal. It is of great importance to bear this in mind, in order to avoid the error of looking for developed statements of doctrine, where the development had not yet occurred.

THE RELATION OF PAUL TO JESUS

Unquestionably the major problem within the variety of NT theology is the relationship between the theology of Paul and the teaching of Jesus.[87] There are three possible ways of approaching the matter. It has been argued that the pure Christian teaching is that of Jesus and that Paul has obscured, if not corrupted, this teaching by theologizing upon it. Or the opposite has been maintained, in which case Paul's theology provides the key for the understanding of Jesus. The *via media* regards Paul's teaching as a

[84] Morgan, *op. cit.*, p. 15, uses the jigsaw illustration to express caution about making forced connections. But he thinks the vast majority of the pieces are missing.

[85] H. Riesenfeld, *op. cit.*, p. 36, makes some acute observations on the task facing critical research. A multitude of theologies, Christologies and other themes 'have to be attributed to different milieux and currents in primitive Christianity. By something of a circular argument these settings and currents of thought are assumed to have existed, although at the same time we have no further knowledge about them than that which is given in those texts ascribed to them.'

[86] E. Käsemann, 'The Problem of a New Testament Theology', *NTS* 19, 1972–73, p. 238, considers that the old liberal idea of an organic development is now bankrupt. But he goes to the other extreme and asserts that we have only fragments, which effectively excludes any kind of development. At the same time he criticizes H. Braun's view that what we meet in the NT is no more than a series of disparate conceptions (p. 240).

[87] For an historical account of the Paul versus Jesus issue during the twentieth century, *cf.* H. Ridderbos, *Paul and Jesus* (1958), pp. 3–20; *cf.* also F. F. Bruce, *Paul and Jesus* (1974).

blossoming out of what was in embryo in the teaching of Jesus. In the first two cases there is a dichotomy in the theology and in the third a synthesis. There have been many variations within each group but the basic ideas are as set out above.

Much of the confusion which has arisen has been due to the assumption that whereas Jesus taught in a wholly Jewish environment, Paul was affected by Hellenistic or gnostic influences. A dichotomy is understandable if it is assumed that Paul has taken the simple gospel of Christ and expressed it in terms amenable to a non-Jewish cultural background. But there is no doubt that the Hellenizing and gnostic elements have been grossly exaggerated. The *Religionsgeschichte* school has been largely to blame. Bousset, for example, drew a sharp distinction between the confessional beliefs of the Jewish and Hellenistic sections of the early church and maintained that the NT presentation has been confused as a result. The strong appeal by Bultmann to the gnostic redeemer myth has maintained the rift, but in any case his rejection of the historical Jesus makes such a cleavage inevitable.

The tendency to make Jesus and Paul oppose each other is not peculiar to the twentieth century for it has strong roots in the nineteenth century. F. C. Baur blazed a trail with his view that Paul opposed the more primitive Petrine party and the clash was resolved only by the orthodox combination of both in the early second century in face of the threat of gnosticism.[88] In spite of the fact that Baur's Hegelian reconstruction has been abandoned, he left a legacy of antithesis between Paul and Jesus which has never been entirely eradicated from many critical approaches to the NT.

This is not the place to discuss the historical background to the controversy, but it is clearly necessary to give reasons why the mediating position has been adopted in the following work. Several considerations have a direct bearing on the matter and these will be outlined.

Paul's knowledge of the historical Jesus raises the *first* problem. Throughout his letters, it must be admitted, he shows little interest in the historical Jesus. He is absorbed with the heavenly Christ. At first sight it might be maintained that Paul was not concerned with the Jesus of history, but he obviously assumes more than he states.[89] The death and resurrection of Jesus are central and are treated as historical events. Apart from this Paul speaks of the poverty of Christ (2 Cor. 8:9), of his affection (Phil. 1:8), of his meekness and gentleness (2 Cor. 10:1) and of his commands (1 Cor. 7:10,25). Although slight, these allusions do not go back to a vacuum. It may be wondered why Paul does not sometimes cite an incident or saying

---

[88] For a detailed account of Baur and the Tübingen School, *cf.* Horton Harris, *The Tübingen School* (1975). Harris points out that Baur could not conceive of a harmonization between Paul and Peter and therefore concluded that such a harmonization could not have happened (p. 259).

[89] *Cf.* J. W. Fraser, *Jesus and Paul. Paul as Interpreter of Jesus from Harnack to Kümmel* (1972), especially pp. 90–102 on Paul's knowledge about Jesus.

of Jesus to support some discussion. But it cannot reasonably be argued from his omitting to do this that he was either ignorant of or indifferent to the historical life of Jesus.[90] His theology makes clear that his exalted Lord is also a perfect man, which implies of necessity a perfect human life (see pp. 224ff.).

The *second* consideration is the need to define what traditions Paul received about the historical Jesus. This is a wide area of study and can only be briefly outlined. That Paul did receive earlier traditions is clear from 1 Corinthians 15:1ff., which is a key passage for appreciating the connection between Paul and the kerygma (for further discussion see p. 57f. below). What is important to note here is that not only are the death and resurrection spoken of as historical facts – so also is the burial. Moreover some kind of theological interpretation is contained in the words 'died for our sins'. The specific list of resurrection witnesses shows further how acutely conscious Paul was of the historical basis of the Christian faith.

Another specific tradition was the Lord's Supper, details of which had similarly been transmitted to him. He relates this also as a historical fact, specifically referring to the night of the betrayal. Paul was conscious of carrying on what Jesus had inaugurated.

The *third* consideration is to explain why Paul introduces many concepts which do not occur in the teaching of Jesus. Some of his most characteristic ideas concern the person and work of Christ and their application to man. It is evident that no full explanation by Jesus of his mission and death was possible before his death occurred. But what evidences are found point the way for the Pauline expositions. It cannot be maintained that Paul foisted on to the simpler teaching of Jesus his own complicated dogmatic statements, although it can be held that the germ in Jesus' teaching blossoms into full flower in Paul's theology. What Jesus came to mean for the mind of Paul is not alien to Jesus' own self-testimony, nor to the general early Christian understanding of him. In this matter the more extreme form-critical approach has been confusing, not to say misleading, in attributing so much of the teaching of Jesus to the community; for had this really happened, it is incredible that echoes of the developed Pauline theology would not inadvertently have strayed into the gospels.

The position adopted in the following studies is that what is inherent in the gospels becomes emergent in Paul, often adapted to a wholly different audience. It cannot be too strongly stressed that Paul as much as Jesus thought in harmony with an OT background, and Paul's doctrine will certainly not be understood unless this is borne in mind. Whatever part Hellenistic influences played in the moulding of his thought, his basic

---

[90] H. Riesenfeld, *Religion* 3, p.45, asks whether any Christian missionary could have based his preaching exclusively on the Pauline epistles without mentioning any of the material which is in the gospels, and have produced an impressive result.

background was Jewish; and it must be assumed that, where he expresses concepts which found parallels in the OT, those concepts will be best understood in the light of this fact. This will explain why in the studies on Pauline theology, the Hellenistic influences will be played down. It is not now possible to maintain with such confidence as that displayed by some scholars that a cleavage existed between Hellenistic and Hebraic Christianity.[91] If the Dead Sea Scrolls have demonstrated the existence of Hellenistic strands in non-conformist Judaism, there is no reason to suppose that a similar mixture could not have existed in Christianity.

THE BASIS OF UNITY IN NEW TESTAMENT THEOLOGY

Anyone maintaining a unified theology in the NT must, in the prevailing climate of opinion, be prepared to state what he considers the unifying factor to be. Much of this will be clarified in the methodology used in this book, but it is right that a brief statement should here be made of the principles of unity employed. When faced with a number of different ideas, as every NT theologian is, the interpreter must be aware of the danger of pressing into a unity what may never have been intended to be taken as such. Yet with this caution in mind, the interpreter would be failing in his task if he did not seek out some unity of thought.

The key figure in NT theology is Jesus Christ. It requires little effort to demonstrate that he is the main binding force throughout the NT. But this in itself is not enough to establish the basic unity of the NT, for it has been maintained that differing Christologies appear. This contention of basically different Christologies will be shown later to be a misleading understanding of the evidence, in the section on Christology. It would be better to speak of various *aspects* of Christology. No part of the NT is intelligible apart from an understanding of Christ as portrayed in it. Every part makes some contribution, although some are slight on Christology (as, for instance, James). The variety of ideas about Jesus Christ presents an enriching picture, but all the ideas are concerned about the same person who lived, died and rose again. There are different portraits of the same Jesus. Some statements present his messianic office, some his kingly reign, some his lordship, some his humanity, some his creative activity, and many other aspects. NT theology is essentially theology about Christ. It is for this reason that Christology comes to be the primary doctrine to be considered.[92] This is not because of any dogmatic influence, but purely because

---

[91] *Cf.* I. H. Marshall's article, 'Palestinian and Hellenistic Christianity: Some Critical Comments', *NTS* 19, 1972–3, pp. 271–287.

[92] It is a noticeable weakness of Bultmann's NT theology that he merges Christology into soteriology. His main concern is undoubtedly anthropology.

it is most logical to look for the basic unity of the NT in him who became the centre of Christian belief.[93]

The importance of the work and mission of Christ. If the NT did nothing more than focus attention on the various aspects of Christ, setting him out in his rich and powerful variety, it would not be enough unless it told us something about his relevance to man. Hence the saving activity of Christ must be linked with his person. While this also finds many different expressions within the NT, there is a basic conviction that Christ's mission enables man to come to God in face of the sin which has wrought havoc in the relationship. All the rich aspects of the NT doctrines of grace and atonement are foundational to an understanding of the unity of the NT. Those who approach the numerous strands from an anthropological point of view will see no more than various different attempts on man's part to explain his understanding of his relationship to God. But a theocentric approach will see God in Christ reconciling the world to himself and making that activity known in a variety of different ways, but always from the standpoint of the divine initiative. This largely covers what has come to be called the *Heilsgeschichte* approach, which centres in the acts of God in history, but must also, of course, include the explanation of those acts in the utterances of God through and to men. Such an approach is specific enough to make the unity in the NT conceivable and general enough to allow for many variations within the unity. It implies within it the expression of God's activity in the believer in both its individual and corporate aspects, both present and future.

The fulfilment motive. One of the most powerful influences on the thought of early Christians was the conviction that what had been predicted by the Hebrew prophets had been fulfilled in Jesus Christ. Whereas there is variation in the amount of emphasis that is placed on this theme, it is present in most of the NT books and undoubtedly forms a strong link between the various sources of teaching. This concerns not only OT citations, but also the application of so many OT concepts to Jesus Christ. The fulfilment idea ensured a considerable measure of continuity, since the OT served as a check on wide variations of interpretation.

The community idea. Another widespread conviction was that all Christians (those in Christ) were bound together into a new community. This idea again runs through all the literature. The body of believers, the church of

---

[93] In his book on *Unity and Diversity in the New Testament*, J. D. G. Dunn narrows down the basis of unity to 'Jesus, the man, the exalted one' (P. 369). In this his aim is to maintain the unity between the historical Jesus and the exalted Christ. But he has exaggerated the diversity to such an extent, that his 'unifying strand' seems altogether too thin in comparison.

Christ, is seen both in its local and its universal dimensions. There is no suggestion that groups of Christians could each forge their own theological position. In fact the opposite is nearer the truth in view of warnings against certain errors or practices which would have caused dissensions had they been tolerated. There is a basic assumption in the NT books that believers should form a unity and this in itself presupposes that there was general agreement on the basic doctrines. The body of Christ is never presented as a loosely knit collection of church groups which lacked understanding of what they stood for.

The future hope. Without any dissentient voices, the NT testifies to the firm conviction that Jesus will return. Details are clearer in some books than others, but the thread of eschatological hope runs strongly through early Christian faith. This fact is more significant than the problems raised by the delay in the Lord's coming. Moreover, there is a firm belief that many of the promises would reach their fulfilment only in a future age. This view that the future holds the key to the present may be said to be a dominant feature of NT belief.

The Spirit. One of the most striking features of NT literature is the all-pervasive activity of the Holy Spirit. There was undoubtedly a strong dependence on the Holy Spirit from the incarnation of Jesus to the various stages of the development of the church; and although there are different emphases, there is a remarkable consistency about this factor. NT theology is bound together by the bond of the Spirit.

THE LIMITS OF HARMONIZATION IN THEOLOGY

The concept of harmonization in any form in the theological field is taboo among many NT theologians. It is assumed at once that anyone seeking to resolve difficulties or searching for agreements is suspect of imposing a preconceived unity on the evidence. This approach has contributed to the fragmentation of NT theology.[94] If Jesus' teaching about the kingdom is set alongside the comparative lack of kingdom teaching in the epistles, is it to be considered illegitimate to look for ways of linking that teaching with other concepts in the rest of the NT? It is often more credible to suppose that agreement exists than to suppose that it does not. Harmonization must be allowed its proper place in the interpreting of NT thought, although any unnatural straining to achieve agreement must be rejected. Undoubtedly the use of strained harmonization for dogmatic purposes has been responsible for the modern rejection of all types of harmonizing. But it is as

[94] H. Riesenfeld, *art. cit.*, p. 39, uses the illustration of the picking apart of the separate parts of a flower in order to study its components. And yet studied in isolation the various parts turn out to be poor and lifeless. No-one who sees only the separate parts will have a true conception of what the flower is like.

illogical to suppose that no attempt should be made to reconcile evidence, as it would be in a court of law to suppose that the only function in examining evidence was negative (to discover discrepancies) and never positive (to propose a valid reconstruction to account for apparently contrary evidence).

In view of what has already been said about the authority of the NT writings, it is a sound principle of exegesis that different parts of the same teaching may be expected to be non-self-contradictory.[95]

THE RELATION BETWEEN NEW TESTAMENT THEOLOGY
AND THE KERYGMA

So much is heard about the kerygma in modern discussions of NT theology that its significance must be understood in order to provide a right approach to the doctrine. It should first be noted that the term seems to be used in different ways by different scholars. When used by Dodd it denotes the content of the early Christian preaching,[96] whereas in Bultmann's use it involves the process of preaching itself.[97] In the latter case it is considered wrong to think of any body of doctrine which was being preached. Rather it is maintained that Christ came alive and challenged men in the act of being proclaimed. The sense in which we intend to discuss the kerygma here is the former, since we are concerned to establish the connection between what the early Christians proclaimed and what stand out as the basic data for NT theology.

Naturally, the proclamation of the first preachers would not be expected to present developed theology. But it is important to know whether their early ideas were in substantial agreement with the later presentations in the epistles. The work of Dodd[98] has established that there is a substantial basis of agreement between the early sermons and certain passages which he discovers in the Pauline epistles and which demonstrate particularly that behind the Pauline theology is a solid substratum of primitive teaching. Reference has already been made to 1 Corinthians 15:1ff. and this forms a key passage in Dodd's study. Among other passages are Romans 1:1–4 and Romans 10:8–9. A summary of Paul's kerygma might read as follows: (i) Prophecies had been fulfilled and the new age inaugurated; (ii) Jesus was born of the seed of David; (iii) he died, according to the Scriptures, to

---

[95] To quote Riesenfeld again (*art. cit.*, pp. 41f.) – 'The most remarkable feature in primitive Christianity is in fact not the diversity of congregations, writings and beliefs, but that homogeneity which made possible the acceptance and constant use of a diversity of writings which already at an early stage were considered authoritative.'

[96] C. H. Dodd sets out his views in his *Apostolic Preaching and its Developments* (1936).

[97] Bultmann is not consistent in his use of the term kerygma, for he can speak of demythologizing it, 'New Testament and Mythology', in *Kerygma and Myth* 1 (ed. H.-W. Bartsch, Eng. trans. 1953) pp. 1–44, which must involve its content.

[98] *Cf.* Dodd, *op. cit.*, pp. 7–35, on 'The Primitive Preaching'.

deliver man from this present age; (iv) he was buried; (v) he rose again on the third day according to the Scriptures; (vi) he has been exalted as Son of God and as Lord of the living and the dead; and (vii) he will return as judge and saviour.

With few exceptions these features echo the main features of the earliest proclamation in Acts. The importance of this is that it demonstrates a direct link between the theology of Paul and the earliest kerygma. The exercise could be extended to show close connections between the kerygma and other NT books. Indeed the kerygma can be said to be the link between the historical Jesus and the epistles. In no sense, however, can the teaching of the epistles be regarded as kerygma. The distinction between the kerygma and the didachē, first proposed by Dodd, is valid, provided the line of demarcation is not too finely drawn. By didachē Dodd meant instruction as distinct from proclamation. NT theology, while mainly concerned with the didachē, must take account of the kerygma. What is proclaimed still forms, as it did then, a vital part of what Christianity is all about.

We might raise the question whether in any sense Bultmann's use of the term kerygma has value for an approach to NT theology which does not share his presuppositions. His insistence that the proclamation must challenge constantly to a decision contains partial truth if understood in a certain way. In contrast with the theology of the nineteenth-century liberal school, Bultmann's demands a response. The same may be said of the traditional understanding of the NT, although the concept of faith in the two systems differs radically. This will become clear in the section dealing with faith (see pp. 573ff.). As already noted, NT theology arose from a living faith and cannot be appreciated as a collection of objective doctrines which men long ago once happened to believe. The objective character of the doctrines must be affirmed, but not to the extent of reducing them to dead orthodoxy.

THE EFFECT OF APOLOGETICS ON THEOLOGY

The importance of background studies in NT theology must be recognized because the Christian message had to relate to the contemporary world (see next section). The possibility of deliberate use of contemporary ideas in order to express the message more adequately must certainly be borne in mind. Some clear examples of this are found, for instance, in the wisdom (*sophia*) and fullness (*plērōma*) concepts of Paul. In these and many other cases, Paul takes current terms from contemporary Greek life and invests them with new spiritual meaning. John appears to do the same, as, for instance, with the word *Logos*. There are grounds for thinking that some use is made of terminology which was drawn directly from pre-gnosticism and used for apologetic purposes. This is entirely different from the view that non-Christian thought has been responsible for the shaping or even creating of NT ideas.

Undoubtedly the greatest apologetic element in the NT is that which explains the Christian approach to the OT. This is further commented on below under background studies and will be fully discussed in the later chapter on Scripture (see pp. 953ff.), but for our present purpose it should be noted that the desire of the early Christians to back up their teaching with scriptural proof contains a strong apologetic element. This accounts for the influence of OT thought on most of the NT and explains why the NT theologian must be prepared to dig deep into OT sources for much of his understanding of NT truths.

CONCLUSION

To sum up the unity and diversity of NT theology, we need to clarify certain features. The idea of unity relates to the conviction that there is only one gospel which the NT presents. There is simply no evidence to show that there were many gospels. In view of this our understanding of diversity must work within the limits of this gospel. Variations in the method of presentation there certainly are, but these may be classed as diversities only in the sense of variations in the expression of the same fundamental gospel. If diversity is used in the sense of contradiction, it is difficult to see how this can be maintained without calling in question the basic gospel. Undoubtedly, different writers will vary their expression according to the different purposes they have in mind. That is to be expected; but this is very different from the theory that there was no general agreement about the basic truths, no idea of orthodoxy to set over against heresy. The following study will bring out the rich variety of NT thought, but will also hope to demonstrate in a substantial way the unity of NT thought.

The relevance of background studies
for New Testament theology

It is impossible to study NT theology in isolation. It arose in a world of various religious influences and the theologian must take account of these influences if he is to arrive at a true understanding of NT doctrine. It is for this reason that background studies have played an important role in NT theological interpretation during the last hundred years. Nevertheless, a difficult problem arises over the degree of importance that should be assigned to them. Care must be taken to ensure that the background studies do not become more important than the biblical text, as happens when the text is bent towards the background, rather than seen as a unique contribution which frequently stands in contrast to the surrounding influences. It is going too far to suggest, for example, that because several points of contact can be found with Hellenistic thought in a gospel such as John's, the whole book must be regarded as a Hellenistic presentation. The Hellenistic parallels are valuable in throwing light on the meaning of individual statements, but cannot determine the theological milieu of the whole book.

Under background studies the three main areas are the OT, Palestinian Jewish literature, and Hellenistic literature. The relative importance of these will now be discussed.

THE OLD TESTAMENT BACKGROUND

It is clear in the most cursory survey of NT literature that a close connection exists between the OT and the NT. Attempts to dispense with the former can lead only to a distortion of the latter. The considerable number of quotations from the OT which appear in the NT bear impressive testimony to the importance attached to a continuity between the Christian era and the OT. The theme of promise and fulfilment links the two. The Scripture of the early church was the OT, and it was to be expected that the apostles would base much of their exegesis on OT predictions. Nevertheless, important as they are, the profusion of citations does not constitute the major contribution of OT studies to NT theology; it is rather the OT colouring in the concepts which were taken over and then invested with new meaning by Jesus and his apostles. Only an appreciation of OT usage can explain many NT concepts. Such a term as 'righteousness', for example, must be considered against the revelation of the OT on this matter, rather than based purely on a general philological study.

A variety of methods are used in the quotations from the OT in the NT, in many of which the idea of authority shines clearly through. There is no doubt that the NT writers shared the same approach as the Jewish teachers towards the inspiration of the OT text (see pp. 953ff.). Certainly Jesus had a high view of Scripture, and the epistles show this to have been shared by the apostles. The frequency with which the formula 'It is written' occurs demonstrates the powerful effect the OT was considered to have on the NT truths which it was claimed to support. This is particularly characteristic of the Pauline epistles. In some cases it does not even depend on the relevance of the original context. A notable example is the grouping of various texts on a common theme, as found in Romans 3. A similar witness to the authority invested in the OT texts is seen in Matthew's frequent use of the formula 'this was to fulfil what was spoken by. . .', or similar wording, to show a variety of ways in which the OT was fulfilled in the ministry of Jesus. No interpreter of NT theology can bypass the important contribution of the OT in the shaping of NT thought.

This fact, however, raises a difficulty, for it becomes essential to formulate some principles of interpretation of the OT in order to bring out the nuances in its use. Notice must be taken of the rabbinical methods, the

Qumran methods and the Hellenistic methods as well as the various approaches found in the NT itself, in order to compare and contrast the Christian approach with other approaches to the OT. Much of the significance of the epistle to the Hebrews lies in its grappling with the problem of OT interpretation. The contribution of this epistle to the theology of the NT is without doubt profoundly affected by its approach to this problem. The concept of the high priesthood of Christ, for instance, finds its basis in the OT cultus, even if it is seen to supersede the old order. In the course of our examination of NT thought it will frequently be necessary to set it against the background of its OT antecedents. Although in a sense the inadequacies of the OT cultus are often reflected in the NT, there is no suggestion that the OT can therefore be ignored. Significantly the earliest person to fall into this trap ended with a totally inadequate concept of Christian theology. Marcion's attempt to dispense with the OT met with determined resistance from orthodox Christian leaders who recognized the dangers in this approach.

The need for the theologian to define his understanding of the relationship between the OT and NT revelation [99] is more pressing than in the case of the relationships between NT theology and any other of the background studies, because of the authoritative character of the OT. It cannot be set on an equal footing with such studies as rabbinics, Qumran and Philonic studies, for example, since the NT nowhere affords to any of these a comparable authority. Indeed none of them is mentioned. The OT cannot be regarded as simply one source among many, for it is unique among all the background studies. It demands that the NT theologian make some attempt to explain the continuity as well as the differences between the OT and the NT, and this will be done in our present studies in the section devoted to Scripture (see pp. 953ff.). Suffice it here to say that some idea of progressive revelation which sees an advancement in NT theology over OT theology, at least in several important respects, seems unavoidable if the full glory of the revelation of God's truth in Christ is to be seen.

An important corroboration of this is the position of John the Baptist.[100] He appears in the role of an OT prophet, indeed the last and greatest of them. His task is to announce the dawn of the new age. In doing so he announces the decrease of his own importance and the increase in the importance of the Messiah. Although he testifies to his own unworthiness, the importance of his office lies in its link between the old order and the new. It is significant that Jesus rated John among the greatest to be born of women, a fitting reminder of Jesus' view of his prophetic office. More-

---

[99] For a detailed discussion of the relation between the OT and the NT, *cf.* D. L. Baker, *Two Testaments, One Bible* (1976).

[100] On John the Baptist, *cf.* C. H. Kraeling, *John the Baptist* (1951); C. Scobie, *John the Baptist* (1964); W. Wink, *John the Baptist in the Gospel Tradition* (1968).

over, in his initial preaching Jesus proclaimed the same theme as John the Baptist – repent for the kingdom is near. Due weight must be given to the ministry and witness of John the Baptist as a prelude to a right understanding of the ministry of Jesus.

THE PALESTINIAN JEWISH LITERATURE

What has been said above highlights the need for as much understanding as possible of the historical period between the OT and the NT. This period is the period of preparation for the coming of Christ. An understanding of the milieu of thought, which dominated the Jewish world in the century or so before the coming of Christ, contributes much to our grasp of the relevance as well as the uniqueness of his mission and message. The gospels describe the interaction between Jesus and his contemporaries. If the message was made relevant to those contemporaries it must have been clothed in concepts readily understood. The universal application of the message depends to some extent on a correct interpretation of it in its historical context – hence the value of intertestamental studies. But the NT theologian must approach such studies with caution. He must constantly remember as already pointed out (p. 35) that parallels do not in themselves furnish an infallible key for a right understanding of NT theology. Even if isolated Jewish parallels do exist, the need to interpret them in terms of their total context places a different complexion at once on the Jewish statements when they are compared with the NT parallels. A broad approach to intertestamental studies will reveal a marked difference between the character of NT theology and its immediate Jewish predecessors. It is the task of the theologian to show the major features of that difference. Indeed if there had been no vital difference, there would have been no explanation of the emergence of Christianity out of Judaism.

Apocalyptic. The literature which is grouped under the general name of apocalyptic serves as a link between the prophetic period and the NT era.[101] These works enjoyed widespread popularity, although it is difficult to determine the number of people to whom they appealed since apocalyptic was essentially literary. There is no reason to suppose, however, that the main ideas were not diffused among a much wider Jewish audience than those among whom the books circulated. The literature is important because it provides valuable insights for understanding certain features of NT theology, such as the Son of man concept and various facets of eschatology.

Apocalyptic literature is generally esoteric, symbolic and pseudonymous.

---

[101] For discussions on the significance of apocalyptic, cf. D. S. Russell, *The Method and Message of Jewish Apocalyptic* (1964); idem, *Apocalyptic: Ancient and Modern* (1978); M. Rist, 'Apocalypticism' in *IDB* 1, pp. 157ff. H. H. Rowley, *The Relevance of Apocalyptic* (³1963); P. D. Hanson, *The Dawn of Apocalyptic* (1975); idem, 'Apocalypticism', Supplementary Volume, *IDB* (1976), pp. 28ff.; L. Morris, *Apocalyptic* (1972).

In spite of its heterogeneous character it has a recognizable form in the same way as the prophetical writings. It differs from the latter in that it did not originate, as they did, in the spoken word. There is no doubt that a major factor in the development of apocalyptic was the cessation of prophecy and a greater concentration on the importance of the Torah. In view of the closure of the Canon, the apocalyptists had to seek other ways of communicating what they believed to be God's message. It was for this reason that most apocalypses were pseudonymous. By this means ancient men could still speak authoritative words to a much later generation. These largely pessimistic books nevertheless performed one important function in relation to the NT. They brought into sharp focus the hope of a messianic deliverer, but there was no clear picture of who the Messiah was to be. The deliverance hoped for was in any case largely political and nationalistic in contrast to the NT idea of salvation, although the notion of an idealized New Jerusalem was not entirely lacking. It was in the absence of uniformity or precision in the presentation of messianic hopes that apocalyptic showed most vividly the weakness of its position and thus prepared the way for the more adequate Christian message. It is significant that the period of the apocalyptists overlapped the beginning of the Christian era, but by AD 100 it was a spent force within Judaism. Apocalyptic continued to enjoy some popularity among the Christians, even to the extent of Christian production of apocalyptic-style literature or else Christian interpolations into older Jewish works (*Sybilline Oracles*), which is evidence that the Christian faith found certain features of the apocalypses congenial.

The Apocalypse of John comes closest in form to this kind of literature in the NT, but even here the differences are more significant than the similarities. For a proper approach to NT interpretation an understanding of apocalyptic is important, but the NT theologian must resist the temptation to allow too much weight to it. Apocalyptic can do no more than shed light on the environment in which the Christian faith grew. It cannot provide any explanation of the origin of that faith. Its role is essentially subsidiary.

Closely akin to the apocalyptic movement and itself a strong supporter of it is the community at Qumran.[102] The discovery of the extensive library of this community has illuminated one little-known sector of Judaism in the period from a century before Christ until the Jewish war, which culminated in the sack of Jerusalem (AD 70). There is little doubt that this nonconformist Jewish group were Essenes, a particularly ascetic sect. Essenes are nowhere mentioned in the NT, but this does not mean that Qumran studies have no relevance for the NT theologian. The discovery

---

[102] For a general survey of the Qumran Community, *cf.* F. F. Bruce, *Second Thoughts on the Dead Sea Scrolls* (1956); G. R. Driver, *The Judean Scrolls* (1965); A. R. C. Leaney, *The Rule of Qumran and its Meaning* (1966); G. Vermes, *Dead Sea Scrolls: Qumran in Perspective* (1977).

that Greek ideas infiltrated so rigid a Jewish group has caused a reappraisal of the relation between NT thought and Hellenism. Particularly has this affected the interpretation of John's gospel, for it can no longer be claimed that Judaism kept Hellenism at bay during the period of the emergence of the Christian church.[103] It is not impossible, in fact, to place John's gospel in an earlier Jewish milieu, instead of regarding it as a later Hellenistic production.

It cannot be claimed that Qumran studies have supplied much additional evidence for the use of the NT theologian. Yet by providing insights into a Jewish splinter group, Qumran has become an indispensable part of background studies, especially in relation to its exegesis of the OT[104]. The idea of an eschatological community may find some parallels with the Christian church, but the essentially inward character of the former contrasts vividly with the essentially out-going character of the latter. The rapid spreading of the Christian faith from Jerusalem to the centre of the known world (as Acts relates) is in striking contrast to the small exclusive group by the shores of the Dead Sea, which even discouraged contact with fellow Jews in Jerusalem. To turn from the law-centred writings of the devotees at Qumran to the grace-dominated writings of the NT is to enter a different world of spiritual liberty. At some points in the exposition of NT themes, the Qumran usage may throw light on the NT, and these features will be noted. The same caution that applied to apocalyptic must apply here, for undoubtedly Qumran has more divergences than parallels when compared with the NT. It should be noted, however, that there were some features of Qumran piety which paralleled the greater spirituality of the NT age (*e.g.* in the *Hodayot*). Yet for the most part, the legalistic approach was dominant.

The Apocrypha. Some reference must be made to the Apocrypha, for although non-canonical, this collection of books played an important part in the Jewish and Christian scene in the first century AD. They were apparently not placed on an equal footing with the OT by the Christians, for they are never cited in the NT, although there are echoes of some of them (such as Wisdom and Ecclesiasticus). The books found their way into the Greek Scriptures, but never received sanction among the Hebrew-speaking Jews. They cannot form a basis for NT interpretation for this reason. Nevertheless

---

[103] This was noted in J. A. T. Robinson's essay 'The New Look on the Fourth Gospel', originally in *StEv* 1 (ed. K. Aland, 1959), but reprinted in Robinson's *Twelve New Testament Studies* (1962), 94–106. This lead has been followed in most recent exegetical works on John's gospel.

[104] For some useful books dealing with Qumran exegesis of OT passages, *cf.* F. F. Bruce, *Biblical Exegesis in the Qumran Texts* (1959); R. N. Longenecker, *Biblical Exegesis in the Apostolic Period* (1975). *Cf.* also W. H. Brownlee, 'Biblical Interpretation among the Sectaries of the Dead Sea Scrolls', *Biblical Archaeologist* 14, 1951, pp. 54–76.; J. A. Fitzmyer, 'The Use of Explicit Old Testament Quotations in Qumran Literature and in the New Testament', *NTS* 7, 1961, pp. 297–333.

they reflect what some men were thinking in the intertestamental period and provide much useful background data. Yet what is of most positive value in the Apocrypha is but a continuation of OT ideas. There are, moreover, instances of the intrusion of extraneous material, as for instance, Persian ideas in the book of Tobit. Recognition of this fact draws attention to the remarkable absence of such influences in the NT, in spite of the claims of the *Religionsgeschichte* school. Indeed, a thorough examination of background studies leads to a firm conviction of the uniqueness of the revelation of God in Christ, and therefore the unique character of NT theology.

Rabbinic studies. Our next consideration is the value of rabbinic studies.[105] After the closure of the OT canon, oral tradition developed in a way which gave it equal authority with the written law, because it was believed to be a true exposition of the written law. Moreover, it was believed to go back to the authority of Moses himself (so *Pirke Aboth* 1:1). The 'tradition of the elders' played a definitive part in the pharisaic religious outlook in the time of our Lord, and some understanding of this background clearly facilitates a better understanding of the context in which his teaching was given.

The major problem in relating rabbinic teaching to the NT is the difficulty of dating much of this material. The weakness of some rabbinic studies in relation to NT thought is the lack of sufficient differentiation between early and later material.[106] It is doubtfully assumed that the later evidence reflects earlier practice. It must further be borne in mind that the fall of Jerusalem in AD 70 caused a major upheaval in Judaism and it cannot too readily be assumed that what was maintained in writings after that date must necessarily represent the position in the pre-fall era. It cannot be denied that the NT interpreter is bound to take account of the milieu of rabbinic thought, since one of the main backgrounds to the teaching of Jesus must have been current Jewish discussions. Indeed an understanding of first-century teaching and practice is indispensable to a right understanding of Jesus' criticism of the Pharisees. Nevertheless, caution must be exercised in the use of such evidence, because of the uncertainty of dating.

In the Pauline epistles there is much that can be illuminated by rabbinic Judaism. The great Christian apostle had been brought up in this milieu of thought and carried over into Christian discussion some of the thought forms of his former faith. He occasionally uses Jewish methods of approach – as, for instance, when he strings together a collection of OT quotations (as in Rom. 3), or when he argues on a grammatical point (as in Gal. 3). Rabbinic studies have unquestionably shed much light on Pauline theology,

---

[105] On rabbinic studies as a background to NT theology, *cf.* W. D. Davies, *Paul and Rabbinic Judaism* (1948); R. A. Stewart, *Rabbinic Theology* (1961); F. C. Grant, *Ancient Judaism and the New Testament* (1960); J. Bowker, *The Targums and Rabbinic Literature* (1969); E. P. Sanders, *Paul and Palestinian Judaism* (1977).
[106] *Cf.* G. F. Moore, *Judaism* (1927).

but the distinctive features of his theology stand out all the more strongly when set against such a background. It can often be seen that what the rabbis were searching after comes to clear fruition in Paul. It can equally be seen where rabbinic teaching was very definitely on the wrong track as, for instance, in its dependence on the efficacy of the law. The whole core of Paul's theological emphasis on justification by faith becomes intelligible against the current Jewish approach to man's justification.

It must be questioned whether Bultmann, in applying his law of dissimilarity for determining the genuineness of the sayings of Jesus, uses rabbinic material in a valid way. He assumes that parallels with Jewish material renders sayings unauthentic, which is based on the assumption that what is similar must have been derived from Jewish sources. But as already noted such an approach would make it impossible for Jesus to communicate with his own contemporaries in categories of thought that they would understand.

HELLENISTIC LITERATURE

There are two main categories which fall under the broad description of Hellenistic literature, *i.e.* Jewish and Greek. Under the former are the extensive works of Philo, while the latter covers such diverse literature as the Hermetica, gnostic works and mystery religious literature.

Philo. This Alexandrian Jew who lived *c.* 20 BC – AD 40 has exercised considerable influence in NT studies, although many of the earlier claims have been mellowed by studies in other fields, particularly Qumran.[107] Philo's aim was to demonstrate an OT origin even for Greek ideas and for this purpose he indulged in widespread and often fantastic allegorizing of the OT text. His works abound moreover in quotations from Greek writings and present the best example of the attempt to merge Jewish and Greek ideas. His influence was certainly powerful in Alexandria, but it is less certain to what extent his influence permeated to the writers of the NT.

For long it was confidently assumed that Philo's usage lay behind the prologue to John's gospel, and the *Logos* concept was accordingly interpreted in wholly Hellenistic terms. But many scholars now believe that it is possible to trace Jewish influence in the prologue (see pp. 321f.). This is not to say that these two sources are mutually exclusive, but the dominance of Philo over the interpreter has certainly lessened. Another area where Philo is believed to have exerted his influence is in the epistle to the Hebrews. This is largely due to Philo's acceptance of the Platonic theory of ideas in which the true world lies behind the apparent world. This spatial

[107] E. R. Goodenough, *An Introduction to Philo Judaeus* (1962); H. A. A. Kennedy, *Philo's Contribution to Religion* (1919); N. Bentwich, *Philo-Judaeus of Alexandria* (1910, r.p. 1948); R. Williamson, *Philo and the Epistle to the Hebrews* (1970).

dualism can certainly find some parallels in the theology of Hebrews, where the earthly things are seen to be shadows of the heavenly. But this epistle departs from Philo's stance on so many issues that the most that could be claimed for the author is that Philonic influence was minimal.

Admittedly in the Melchizedek section there is a slight tendency towards allegory and in the whole epistle a widespread appeal to and reverence for the LXX text as in Philo. Moreover, several other common features occur such as the antitheses between the created and uncreated, the past and the future, and the transitory and the eternal. Nevertheless, there is a fundamental difference of approach. Philo does not treat the OT as history, even in its historical sections. The writer to the Hebrews sees God working in history. Indeed in this respect, unlike Philo, he is thoroughly biblical. His aim is to bring out how perfectly Christ fulfils the true spiritual meaning of the OT. The cultus is seen to be obsolete, but the OT itself is still authoritative.

The Christian church had to face the challenge of Hellenism and Philo's form of it had sufficient influence for some adaptation to be made. But there is no section of NT theology which can be said to be indebted to Philo, except in a superficial way.

Hermetica. A considerable body of literature exists under the title of Hermetica. This consists of Egyptian philosophic tracts under the name of Hermes. Appeal to this literature as a guide to NT interpretation came into its own with the writings of C. H. Dodd,[108] and especially in his exposition of John's gospel. It must be borne in mind that unlike the other background material already mentioned, the Hermetica did not come from a Jewish milieu, but are the product of paganism. In spite of this Dodd finds some remarkable parallels between the Hermetica and the fourth gospel.[109] But it may be questioned to what extent the interpretation of John is dependent on the Hermetica. Indeed, extreme caution is needed because much of the Hermetica literature cannot be dated until very much later than the NT era. Dodd assumes that many of the ideas were current during the early part of the second century. If he is correct, it would not be possible to claim any more than a common milieu. In this case, the fourth gospel would be regarded as interpreting the Christian gospel in contemporary language.

Any suggestions of this kind must be balanced against the not inconsiderable evidence for placing the fourth gospel in a totally different environment, as, for instance, in a Jewish setting, which seems probable in the light of the Qumran evidence. It is more reasonable to suppose that a

---

[108] On the Hermetica, *cf.* C. H. Dodd, *The Bible and the Greeks* (1935); A. D. Nock and A. J. Festugière (eds.), *Corpus Hermeticum*, 4 vols. (1945–54). Some of the Nag Hammadi Texts in Codex VI are Hermetic works (*cf. The Nag Hammadi Library in English* (ed. J. M. Robinson, 1977), pp. 278f., 292f.).

[109] C. H. Dodd, *The Interpretation of the Fourth Gospel* (1954).

gospel like John's should be evaluated against a typically Jewish background, than against a pagan Egyptian background. Geographical considerations favour the former more than the latter. Moreover, the whole of Dodd's thesis depends on a particular view of the origin of John's gospel. If there is any truth in the Hermetica theory, it must mean that the teaching of Jesus recorded in the fourth gospel is a Johannine interpretation which bears little or no relation to what Jesus actually taught. But the evidence produced is not based on indisputably first-century texts, and it is therefore difficult for such a position to be satisfactorily maintained. Nevertheless, Hermetica studies undoubtedly show the wide relevance of the Johannine teaching to meet the challenge from pagan philosophical, as well as from Jewish, quarters.

Gnosticism. In the past, NT interpreters have too often been misleading when applying gnostic studies to the NT. The problem has arisen because no distinction was being made between gnosis and gnosticism.[110] The latter term properly refers to developed gnostic systems which did not come into existence until the second century AD. The former term refers to the general ideas of gnosticism in its pre-developed state, a kind of pre-gnosticism. This earlier trend must have existed in the first century, which would explain why the NT makes passing references to it. Since gnosis was syncretistic, and sought to combine several strands of religious thought into a whole, it early became a serious threat to Christianity. Its whole purpose would be alien to a faith which claimed to be sufficient in itself (as the gospel of Jesus Christ does). As soon as philosophical and oriental mystical features began to be mixed with the Christian faith, it could not fail to distort the latter. This accounts for the strong line which the NT takes against aberrations.

What then is the value of gnostic studies to the student of NT theology? The answer must be 'very little'. Its value is mainly negative. It provides another slant on contemporary opinion against which the Christian gospel must be set. Men were experimenting in various ways to discover the satisfaction for which they longed. The later widespread appeal of gnosticism shows that this particular movement was thought to provide an answer. It had the advantage of enabling people to retain some of their existing beliefs while being susceptible to other ideas.

One of the more thorough-going appeals to gnosticism to furnish an

---

[110] *Cf.* R. M. Wilson, *The Gnostic Problem* (1958); *Gnosis and the New Testament* (1968); E. M. Yamauchi, *Pre-Christian Gnosticism* (1973); E. Lohse, *The New Testament Environment* (Eng. trans. 1974), pp. 253–277. Of these writers, Wilson and Yamauchi are critical of the theory of pre-Christian gnosticism, but Lohse considers it is now generally recognized, although he admits that there are 'very few literary attestations'. Yamauchi, however, denies that there are any attestations at all. For evidence for the gnostic background to early Christianity, *cf.* J. M. Robinson, in the Introduction to *The Nag Hammadi Library in English*, pp. 1–25.

explanation of NT thought is Bultmann's use of the gnostic redeemer myth as the source of the redemptive idea in Pauline theology and the idea of the revealer in Johannine theology.[111] This is another case of the use of a wide range of material drawn mostly from literature much later than the NT age. There is certainly no gnostic literature which can confidently be assigned to the first century.

In view of this, gnosticism is another area whose usefulness for NT theology must be considered minimal. This is not, of course, to maintain that gnostic studies have no value, for they are essential for a true appreciation of the developing church. Moreover, the obscurity of thought which abounds in gnostic writings emphasizes by way of contrast the straightforwardness of NT thought. There are times when gnostic terms occur in the NT and these seem to be instances where the Christian thinkers took over ideas which were being bandied about in pagan circles and invested them with entirely new meanings (*e.g.* the *plērōma*).

Mystery religions. It was the 'history of religions' school which popularized comparisons between Christianity and the mystery religions with a view to finding in the latter a source for the ideas of the former.[112] Whatever justification the advocates of this school thought they had, their method was at fault in several particulars. They assumed as unchallengeable that Christianity was but one of a number of religions which had, in fact, influenced each other. With such a presupposition it did not seem incongruous to claim, for instance, that the Lord's Supper was somehow connected with the notorious bulls' blood-bath of the mystery religions. Once such a point of view was adopted it became imperative for the investigator to discover many features in NT theology which were based on the mysteries (including the word *mystērion* itself).

So alien are some of these interpretations to an unbiased understanding of NT thought that the 'history of religions' school did not gain widespread support. But some dependence on the mystery religions has remained in Bultmann's approach to NT theology, and for this reason it must be taken note of in NT studies. Yet it should be pointed out that the open 'mystery' of the gospel is diametrically contrasted with the secret initiation required by the mystery religions. Again, background studies bring into clear focus

---

[111] For Bultmann's views, *cf.* his commentary on *John* and his *TNT*. He depended heavily on the opinions of Reitzenstein, who, however, cited only later evidence for the redeemed Redeemer notion. For a refutation of Bultmann's position, *cf.* Yamauchi, *op. cit.*, pp. 163ff.; *cf.* also R. M. Wilson, 'Some Recent Studies in Gnosticism', *NTS* 6, 1959–60, p. 43, who questions whether the 'pure' form of the redeemer myth ever existed except as a scholar's reconstruction. Wilson was commenting on Schmithal's excursus on the subject in his *Gnosticism in Corinth* (1956, Eng. trans. 1971).

[112] On the mystery religions, *cf.* H. A. A. Kennedy, *St Paul and the Mystery Religions* (1913); R. Reitzenstein, *Die hellenistischen Mysterienreligionen* (³1927); H. Rahner, *Greek Myths and Christian Mysteries* (1963); B. M. Metzger, 'Considerations of Methodology in the Study of the Mystery Religions and Early Christianity', *HTR* 48, 1955, pp. 1–29.

the immeasurable superiority of the Christian gospel to its environment.

This brief survey of background studies has focused on the diverse background against which NT theology must be approached. Christian concepts must in some way be related with contemporary ideas, for they did not develop in complete isolation. Nevertheless, caution must be exercised to avoid over-emphasizing background elements, for this has caused many of the problems which have arisen in the course of the development of NT interpretation. It would clearly be wrong to suppose that Christian theology was an extensive borrower from a wide range of non-Christian sources. An over-enthusiasm to trace the sources of concepts has led to a drastic reduction of that uniqueness which characterizes the gospel as a whole. No-one would think of assessing the significance of a motor car by analysing its separate parts and searching for their origin. The uniqueness of any creation consists in more than the fresh material which is introduced when it is compared with previous creations. It consists of the effectiveness of the concepts as a whole. If this is true of human creations, how much more is it true of divine revelation?

A real understanding of this feature will protect the NT theologian from the pitfall of supposing that he must necessarily allow contemporary usage to determine the meaning of NT concepts. The problem surrounding the Son of man title is a case in point. By different uses of the contemporary parallels, various opinions have been reached as to what the title actually meant to Jesus, who, according to the gospels, was the only one to use it. It becomes a question then of deciding how far the context of the title in the gospel passages themselves is not more important than parallels elsewhere. The approach to be adopted in the following study of NT theology is to give greater weight to the text itself than to the parallels, although due attention will be given to the latter.

Questions of authenticity

Anyone writing a NT theology is bound to adopt a certain point of view with regard to the validity of the evidence at his disposal. He therefore has a responsibility not only to make clear what that point of view is, but also how it relates to other points of view. Because of the central place of Jesus within NT theology, the view taken about the authenticity of his teaching will clearly be a determining factor in the production of a theological framework. If the teaching as recorded in the gospels is a fair record of what Jesus thought and taught, considerable weight can be placed on his teaching as a major contribution towards an understanding of NT theology. But if the authenticity of the sayings of Jesus is constantly in dispute, the teaching of Jesus will no longer be a dominant consideration in a NT theology (as it is not, for instance, in Bultmann).

Difficulties arise over some theories of redaction criticism which, if adopted, make an integrated approach to NT theology more difficult. If, for instance, the theology of each evangelist is more important than the teaching of Jesus which each records, this would indicate a collection of different theologies rather than the notion of a unified NT theology. In the following studies the texts have been taken as reliable accounts of the teaching of Jesus. It is clear, therefore, that those who regard some of that teaching as non-authentic will not be disposed to put the same weight on it, but will incline to see it as the evangelist's own reflections. Those adopting this view will inevitably regard part of the evidence as less authoritative than if it were accepted as the genuine teaching of Jesus.

The difference in approach will be most evident in John's gospel. Those who regard the teaching attributed to Jesus as an interpretation by the evangelist of that teaching will probably want to modify the importance attached to some of the following discussions. To cite one example, the 'I am' sayings, which have been taken as evidence of the awareness by Jesus of his own uniqueness, would clearly have less point if their authenticity were questioned, as it is by many scholars. In that case the evidence becomes the evangelist's idea of what Jesus thought about himself, thus expressing his own Christological reflections. It has not been possible to discuss authenticity questions regarding all the sayings appealed to, although some indication of conflicting opinion has, in many cases, been given in the footnotes.

Another problem arises from the NT epistles, where discussions of authorship have led some scholars to dispute the authenticity of some of the letters (*e.g.* Ephesians, the pastoral epistles, 1 Peter). Where differences are made between the 'genuine' Pauline epistles and the 'deutero-Pauline' epistles on theological grounds, it plainly affects the weight given to the latter. It has clearly not been possible to defend the position taken up in this book on each issue. The general questions of introduction have been discussed elsewhere. All the Pauline epistles have been treated as valid sources for Paul's thoughts, although it is recognized that not all scholars would concur with this point of view. Nevertheless, many who would not accept Paul as author of some of the epistles attributed to him would nonetheless agree that there is at least some Pauline influence in those epistles.

The position adopted in this book is the result of a careful consideration of the evidence, and it is hoped that the survey of the evidence itself will prove valuable, not only to those who accept the same position, but also to those who would attach different and often lesser values to the sources of information.

The structure of New Testament theology

The interpreter's own understanding of the scope of his work will obviously determine his method in setting out the materials. There are only two basic methods open to him. Either he may split the NT into its different literary groups and present the theological opinions of each of these groups; or he may decide to select certain major themes and make these the main divisions of work. The former of the two methods presents the least number of difficulties for methodology, for once the theologian has class-ified his groups of sources his task consists of describing the special char-acteristics of each. This methodology is admirable if NT theology is regarded purely as a descriptive science. The purpose would then be to initiate the reader, for instance, into a survey of synoptic, Pauline or Johannine theology. Such a method provides a ready-made handbook for the analytical approach, but tends to lead to a splintering of theology, against which a warning has already been given.

Admittedly, the theologian who chooses the thematic method avoids one problem, but confronts many others. He has to face the relation of his work to the historical method. If he has rejected the view that he is at liberty to draw proofs from any part of the NT in support of a thematic idea without reference to the historical context, he must propose a satis-factory alternative. He could choose to include the context with his proof-texts, which would at least avoid the worst aspect of the proof-text method, but this would not make for clarity. The method chosen in this book is to group the teaching on each theme under the various sources to give them historical perspective and then to summarize the NT teaching as a whole on each main area of interest. Even this method may lead to lack of clarity at some points, but the interpreter is bound to come up against that, whatever his methodology. At times he has no alternative but to choose the lesser of two evils. The advantage of this scheme is that it presents what the NT says on each important theme, sets out the evidence in a historical form and gives a concise summary of all the major aspects, which will demon-strate both the variety and unity of NT thought.

For this purpose the following scheme for the classification of sources will be followed: the synoptic gospels, the Johannine literature, (gospel and epistles) Acts, the Pauline epistles, Hebrews and the other NT books. The book of Revelation has been treated separately from the gospel and epistles of John, but this is not intended to imply that it has no connection with them; rather, its particular form lends itself better to separate treatment. Some prior decisions have naturally to be made regarding the homogeneity of these groups and it is not possible to discuss here in full the reasons for the classification. Problems of introduction and decisions concerning them must affect the weight which is attached to any evidence. Discussions on these matters have been given elsewhere.[113] It has been decided against

---

[113] *Cf.* my *New Testament Introduction* (³1970).

splitting the synoptic theology into the separate theologies of the individual authors after the manner of redaction criticism, although any special emphasis of a separate writer will be pointed out. Similarly, in treating the Johannine theology as distinct from the synoptics, it is not intended to suggest that their differences should be heightened.

The major problem in the thematic approach is to decide on the themes and then to provide some rationale for the order in which they are studied. Here is where the individual preference of the interpreter is most apparent. Whatever choices he makes will be questioned by those who would have made different choices. Indeed a glance at the schemes proposed by a wide selection of recent theologies reveals how highly individualistic the choice is. Some concentrate on the idea of development. Others make little attempt to trace connections. It is more important to explain the reason underlying the scheme adopted and to leave the reader to decide for himself if this rationale is justified.

Two considerations have influenced the layout of this *Theology*. The first is that the subject matter is approached from the conviction that it is a revelation of God rather than an exploration of man. The other has been the needs of the user of the book. It has been borne in mind that those who want to know what the NT teaches will have questions to which answers are sought. They are questions which have been relevant to man in all ages and therefore will not be striking for their originality. Any parallels our divisions may have with those of historic dogmatic theology arise only because the major areas of spiritual enquiry are essentially timeless. Other than this the NT has been allowed to speak for itself within these areas.

The first doctrine must then be that of God, for this is basic to any God-centred theology. There will be no attempt to formulate the doctrine of his existence, for everywhere the NT assumes belief in God. In this section will be found an outline of his functions and attributes as portrayed in the NT. Special attention will be given to his creative activity to show his essential relation to man.

Attention will next be given to the subject of man and his world, in which the NT view of the constitution of man, his environment and his basic needs in relationship to God are discussed. It is the clear statement in the NT of man's sinful condition which makes relevant what it has to say about God's redemptive activity.

This brings us to the section on Christology, which seeks to deal with the nature of Jesus Christ. The section will be concerned with more than the Christological titles, although these will form the starting point. Since Christology is so central to NT theology, the problems which it raises will need to be considered in some detail.

Our next discussion will focus on the closely linked subject of the mission of Christ, under which general title will be considered the kingdom teaching, the intimations of the meaning of the death of Christ in the gospels, and the interpretation of that death in the Acts, epistles and apocalypse, but especially in the teaching of Paul and the epistle to the Hebrews. This section will inevitably touch on the NT view of salvation, which nevertheless comes into clearer focus later when the application of the work of Christ to Christian living is discussed.

Before dealing with this theme, however, another important theme will be considered. The person and activity of the Holy Spirit is a subject of vital importance, not only for understanding, but also for life. The variety of aspects of the Spirit's work will be examined.

Next follows the important section on the Christian life, which deals with such crucial matters as faith and forgiveness, grace, new life, sanctification and law. This involves a discussion of how the Christian deals with the ill effects of the old life.

So far the approach has been individual, but there is need to discuss the NT teaching on the church, not only with regard to its constitution, aims and destiny, but also with regard to its worship and practices. It is logical to follow this with a discussion on future destiny, to bring out the NT teaching on the future of mankind and the future of the world.

A section is included on NT ethics, because it is considered of great importance to link morality to doctrine and to show it to be, in fact, an essential part of NT theology. It is not intended in this section to give more than basic ethical principles as far as these are discernible in the NT. Of great importance will be the various ways in which Christian theology carries with it ethical obligations. Also included in this section will be a discussion of the NT teaching on social involvement.

This will be followed by a special section on Scripture, because of its importance for a right understanding of the NT. The discussion will deal mainly with the Christian approach to OT, but will also discuss such matters as inspiration and authority as far as the NT supplies data on these themes.

All of these major themes are subjects which in all ages have been of interest to Christians. On all of them the NT gives specific answers which are as relevant today as they were when first given. It is remarkable that although it does not pose the questions in any formal way, it nevertheless enables the enquiring mind to discover the answers. Those who approach the NT in dependence on the Holy Spirit will discover for themselves that NT theology is more than an amassing of dry facts. It is, in fact, a dynamic experience of God's revelation in Christ.

Chapter 1

God

SOME BASIC ASSUMPTIONS

The NT makes no attempt to prove the existence of God. The theistic proofs belong to the later period of apologetics and systematic theology. NT theology begins with some tremendous assumptions – that God exists, that he created man and continues to maintain interest in man. Indeed, the whole structure of early Christian thought takes this for granted. The NT makes no sense at all unless these basic assumptions are true. It provides only two options – either to accept the assumptions in faith or else to reject them and consequently reject the whole revelation based upon them. Whatever the value of attempting to prove philosophically the existence of God, the NT offers no guidance. It may be thought that this seriously limits the validity of an approach to theology via NT teaching, but this can be countered by the fact that Christian theology can be fully understood in the end only by those who exercise faith. It is perhaps a salutary reminder that neither the NT nor NT theology is dominated by a purely intellectual approach. At the same time it must be affirmed that the assumptions with which the NT begins are thoroughly valid. God's existence and his interest in his creation offer a reasonable explanation of man's own existence.

The writers of the NT all share the view of God which is seen in the OT. The creation story concentrates on God's creative initiative, and this view of God as originator of the created world is basic to OT thought. Moreover it is assumed that the creator is also sustainer of his creation. The heavens and earth are the work of his hands and he is seen to possess supreme power within the order of nature. In the intertestamental period the Jews firmly believed the same basic creative relationship between God and his world, adding to it the conviction that it was the Torah (Law) through which God created, a view which came close to personifying the Torah.[1]

---

[1] It should be noticed that the Torah was only one of the intermediaries which was conceived to link the transcendent God with the world of men (*cf.* Wisdom, Memra). The ascription to these intermediaries of

This was necessary because of the prevalent transcendental view of God during the intertestamental period.[2] The Most High was removed so far from his own creation that he needed some intermediary to maintain contact with the world. There is nothing of this remoteness in the NT approach.[3] The NT view of God is linked with the OT revelation, not with current Jewish speculations.

Nevertheless, the transcendence of God finds some support in the majesty and particularly the holiness of God, which is so characteristic of OT writings, especially of the Prophets. The statement in Isaiah 57:15 illustrates the essential difference between the OT view and much Jewish transcendental theology – 'For thus says the high and lofty One who inhabits eternity, whose name is Holy: "I dwell in the high and holy place, and also with him who is of a contrite and humble spirit." ' This combination of loftiness and tenderness is an essential feature of the NT, and makes the NT view of God intelligible. This high moral view was in strong contrast to the contemporary multifarious and often immoral deities worshipped by non-Jewish people at the time when the NT came into being. It is impossible to appreciate the NT revelation apart from maintaining its close connection with the OT view of God. Those movements, among which Marcionism was the earliest,[4] which have created a cleavage between OT and NT, begin their approach to NT thought with a serious disadvantage for they have no clue to the understanding of the basic NT view of God. It did not arise *ex nihilo*; it was the result of a long period of revelation of which the NT was the consummation.

---

a share in creation was a natural development. *Cf.* W. O. E. Oesterley, *The Jews and Judaism during the Greek Period* (1941), pp. 103f., for a discussion of transcendence during the intertestamental period. *Cf.* from a Jewish point of view E. G. Hirsch's article 'God' in the *Jewish Encyclopaedia* 6, pp. 2ff. For a Christian Jewish assessment of the Torah, *cf.* P. Borchsenius, *Two Ways to God* (1968), pp. 47–57, especially pp. 54, 55. God himself is said to have consulted the Torah before creating the world, *cf.* J. Neusner, *First Century Judaism in Crisis* (1932), p. 98.

[2] Not all Jewish scholars would admit that transcendentalism was the exclusive tendency of the intertestamental period. J. Abelson, *The Immanence of God* (1912), is at some pains to show that signs of a shift from transcendentalism to immanence were already present. He admits that there are both elements in the Hebrew Bible, although he thinks that the transcendent view is paramount (pp. 46–54.).

[3] E. P. Sanders, *Paul and Palestinian Judaism* (1977), p. 44, criticizes Bultmann for maintaining that the remoteness of God was the Jewish view. *Cf.* R. Bultmann's discussion on 'God, the Remote and the Near' in *Jesus and the Word* (Eng. trans. 1956), pp. 59f. Sanders is emphatic that the rabbis did not think of God as inaccessible (*op. cit.*, p. 215). He cites P. Kuhn, A. M. Goldberg and E. E. Urbach as recent Jewish writers on rabbinic theology who support this view. What is most important for our present purpose is that both in the OT and in first-century Judaism there was a sense of God's glory, which would have been shared by the early Christians.

[4] Marcionism was based on the idea of two gods, of which the OT creator God was rejected as incompatible with the NT. Nevertheless Marcion did not deny that there was an element of righteousness in the OT view of God. *Cf.* E. C. Blackman's discussion, *Marcion and his Influence* (1948), pp. 113f., in which he criticizes Harnack's view that for Marcion the supreme God alone was good, while the OT God was inferior, *cf.* A. von Harnack, *Marcion: Das Evangelium vom fremden Gott* (r.p. 1960), p. 109. He considers this to be overdrawn. Without a doubt, however, Marcion's exegesis of the NT was vitiated by his lack of appreciation of its connection with the OT revelation of God.

Linked with the high OT view of the holiness of God was the complementary view of his covenant love.[5] It is important to recognize in approaching the NT that the OT view of God's love is righteous love, a love
which at no time is viewed as sentimental. It is as much a demanding love
as a giving love. God's acts of love towards Israel showed what he expected
– a people prepared to respond to the covenant conditions. But they also
showed his longsuffering and patient love when Israel failed. This view of
God again differed strongly from the ideas of contemporary paganism,
where it was usual to regard the deity as an object to fear, and consequently
to be placated. The NT view that God is love is an extension of this OT
view and is deeply indebted to it. Nowhere in the NT is there any discussion
as to why God should love. It is the unchallenged assumption that he does.

There is no doubt that the OT conception of God also includes the idea
of judgment.[6] This in fact is an aspect of his righteousness. A wrong
emphasis upon it, however, has led to the view that there is a strong
distinction between the OT and NT ideas. There are passages in the OT where
God commands wholesale slaughter of peoples, and these passages are seen
to be alien to the NT God of love. This draws attention to the fact that
some concept of progressive revelation is indispensable, if the OT is to form
a true basis for an approach to the NT doctrine of God. The imprecatory
passages in the OT reveal a God of justice in the concepts of the time, but
although the justice of God is not absent from the NT, the mercy of God
comes into clearer focus in the revelation in Christ. In considering the NT
concept, it will be necessary to examine both those aspects which are
parallel with the OT and those which are more distinctive in the NT.

GOD AS CREATOR, FATHER AND KING

So basic to all parts of the NT is the doctrine of God that much of the

---

[5] N. Snaith, *The Distinctive Ideas of the Old Testament* (1944), pp. 94f., brings out clearly the covenant
connection in the OT idea of *hesed*, which he describes as covenant love. Not only in OT times, but also in
rabbinic Judaism, the covenant is central for an understanding not only of religion, but more particularly
of the view of God. It is dominated by God's personal relationship with men, not by metaphysical
speculation about him. For the importance of this in rabbinic Judaism, *cf.* Sanders, *op. cit.*, pp. 240ff. T.
C. Vriezen, *An Outline of Old Testament Theology* (Eng. trans. 1970), p. 316, admits that there is great
tension between God's love and his holy being, but denies that in the OT he is ever made an arbitrary
despotic ruler. E. Jacob, *Theology of the Old Testament* (Eng. trans. 1955), p. 110, rightly regards the love
of God in the OT as a manifestation of his sovereignty. He admits that love has a different tone in the OT
from the NT because in the former it was addressed in a general way to the people as a nation (p. 112).

[6] J. L. McKenzie, *A Theology of the Old Testament* (1974), p. 153, suggests that the oldest use of the word
'judgment' is probably synonymous with the word 'salvation'. See also L. Koehler, *Old Testament Theology*
(Eng. trans. 1957), pp. 218f. A forensic use of the term is certainly implied in parts of the OT. The Word
of the Lord becomes a criterion for judgment for instance in the prophecy of Jeremiah (*cf.* J. G. S. S.
Thompson, *The Old Testament View of Revelation*, 1960, pp. 72f.). The justice of God burns in the words
of God. In Judaism, the controlling factor in religion was the will of God, and this naturally raised the
question of justice when that will was disobeyed. The sovereignty of God is an essential part of the OT
view of the holiness of God (*cf.* T. C. Vriezen, *op. cit.*, pp. 297ff.).

evidence consists of assumptions rather than specific statements. Nevertheless there are many statements which are highly significant. We shall discuss the following aspects – God as Creator, the providence of God, God as Father, God as King and Judge, various other titles for God, and then in summary form the attributes of God.

God as Creator

There is no doubt that the Christians assumed without discussion that God is the originator of the universe.[7] They took this over from the OT and also from the teaching of Jesus. In the synoptic gospels the most explicit statement recorded of the teaching of Jesus on this theme is found in Mark 13:19 ('from the beginning of the creation which God created'). Jesus also cites with full acceptance the OT statement that God made man male and female (Mk. 10:6; Mt. 19:4). No other suggestion regarding the origin of creation is anywhere even hinted at in the gospel writings.

In his speech to the Athenians, Paul boldly announced the kind of God whom he worshipped as 'the God who made the world and everything in it, being Lord of heaven and earth' (Acts 17:24). His creative power is also seen in the statement that men are his offspring (Acts 17:29). In his speech at Lystra Paul makes a similar assertion about God's creative power (Acts 14:15).

In the epistles of Paul the relationship between Creator and creatures is assumed in Romans 1:25. Moreover, creation is said to reflect the work of the Creator (Rom. 1:20). Indeed, it shows something of the character of God (his eternal power and deity). It can do this only because it is the direct work of his hands. There are specific assertions that all things were made by God (Rom. 11:36; 1 Cor. 8:6; 11:12; Eph. 3:9). Paul criticizes those who prohibit what God created for man's good (1 Tim. 4:3). The same creation theme is found in Revelation 4:11, where adoration of God is centred on his creative work ('for thou didst create all things, and by thy will they existed and were created'). *Cf.* also Revelation 10:6.

The NT reflects the same conviction that the OT shows, that the creation is not co-eternal with the Creator. In several passages the phrase 'before the foundation of the world' is used of God. In John, Jesus speaks of the glory he shared with the Father before the world was made (17:5,24). Paul speaks in the same vein in mentioning the choice of God (Eph. 1:4). A similar idea concerning the predestined role of Christ appears in 1 Peter 1:20. There is no doubt that all three writers held that the Creator existed apart from the material existence of his creation.

---

[7] G. Wingren, *Creation and Law* (1961), pp. 3ff., maintains creation, as in the creeds, must be the starting point in approaching biblical theology. He criticizes those who, like Cullmann, begin with Christology. His contention is that creation focuses attention on God and avoids an anthropological approach to theology. Any system which is based exclusively on the NT is in danger of adopting such a view.

The NT writers do not discuss the method of creation. In the epistle to the Hebrews it is declared to have been brought about 'by the word of God' (11:3), an allusion to the sovereign commands of God at creation (*cf.* Gn. 1:3). More important than the method is the agent. Whereas in Genesis the agency of the Spirit is mentioned, in the NT on many occasions creation is said to have been effected through Christ.[8] This has great significance for our later discussion of the person of Christ (see pp. 342ff.). But for our present purpose it serves to put the NT view of creation in a somewhat different context from the OT view. The emphasis on the creative activity of Christ in no way lessens the creative activity of God. Indeed, the creative act is seen as a unity. In the prologue of John's gospel the matter is clearly presented. The Word, who was with God and was God, was the agent of creation – 'all things were made through him, and without him was not anything made that was made' (Jn. 1:3). The same theme comes in Colossians 1:16 – 'for in him (*i.e.* Christ) all things were created, in heaven and on earth . . . all things were created through him and for him.' Similarly the writer to the Hebrews declares in reference to the Son: 'Whom he (God) appointed the heir of all things, through whom also he created the world' (1:2). Moreover in the same passage, the Son is said to uphold the universe (*ta panta*) by the word of his power.

These passages clearly teach, not only that God created through (*dia*) Christ but also for (*eis*) him, which gives some indication of the divine purpose for the created order. The infinite wisdom of the Creator is seen in his making the creation Christocentric rather than anthropocentric. The NT does not support the view that the world belongs to man, except in the idealistic sense fulfilled only in Jesus Christ (Heb. 2:8). Creation itself is bound up with man's condition, as Paul clearly recognized in speaking of the groaning of creation for deliverance (Rom. 8:19ff.). Modern anxiety over man's misuse of creation has brought this into focus and has shown the extraordinary relevance of Paul's concept. The whole ecological problem of the wasting of resources and the pollution of what remains conflicts directly with the NT view of creation as made 'for' Christ. This leads naturally into our next discussion of the NT idea of providence.

The providence of God

It is as important to consider the NT teaching on God's providential dealing with his creation, as to note its basic assumptions about his creative work. The NT provides an answer to the problem of God's continued activity within the created order. No support is given for the view that, having created the world, God left it to its own devices. A very different picture

---

[8] G. Wingren, *ibid.*, pp. 31ff., discusses the meaning of creation in Christ. He considers that the real understanding is reached when the question is asked 'whether man is *destined for Christ* from his own inescapable existence and position as created man' (p. 33).

lies behind the NT approach. Providence is based on the character of God.

In the teaching of Jesus, there is a specific emphasis on God's special care for his creatures. To show the detailed nature of God's providential care, he states that not even a sparrow, which men rank as little, falls to the ground apart from the Father's will (Mt. 10:29). This is further substantiated by the view that the heavenly Father feeds the birds, without their having to sow, reap or store their food (Mt. 6:26ff.). There is no discussion of the problems raised when conditions occur which cause starvation to animals and birds. The intention of the passages cited is rather to portray a God who is concerned about his creation. Even more significant is his knowledge of the hairs of the head, which vividly demonstrates his interest in the minutest details of human life (Mt. 10:30). Moreover, sun and rain are under his control and operate irrespective of the worthiness of the recipients (Mt. 5:45).[9]

The very fact that Jesus uses the title 'Father' applied to God when mentioning his providential care shows how comprehensive is his view of fatherhood. More will be said on this in the next section, but no statement on providence is possible without including God's fatherly concern for his creation. This is brought out in such a petition as the prayer for bread in the Lord's Prayer (Mt. 6:11; Lk. 11:3), which is based on faith in God the Father's providential care. The same basic assumption is made by Paul in his Lystra address (Acts 14:17) in stressing God's control of the seasons, and in his Areopagus address (Acts 17:25) in affirming that God gives to all life and breath.

In the epistles God's providence is again assumed as passages like Romans 1:19f. and James 1:17 show. Although it is maintained that providence affects all men, some distinctions are made over God's special concern for those who believe in him, mainly in the realm of spiritual blessings.[10] According to Romans 8:28 God exercises control over all aspects of the lives of believers, which arises from his special concern as Father for his children (see next section).

God as Father

It is the idea of the fatherhood of God which is most characteristic of NT teaching and especially of the teaching of Jesus. Whereas the contemporary pagan world held its gods in fear, the Christian view of God's fatherhood

---

[9] Cf. R. A. Ward's discussion of Matthew's wording in 5:45 in *Royal Theology* (1964), pp. 26ff., in which he sees this as evidence that God is the sustainer of the universe according to the teaching of Jesus. This author also discusses whether here and elsewhere Jesus reflects an acceptance of a naïve world-view. Although the words of Jesus are cast in poetic form (*cf.* T. W. Manson, *The Sayings of Jesus* (1949), p. 112,) it cannot be supposed that for him there was no reality of an active creator behind the words.

[10] For a succinct statement on the providence of God in the NT, see A. W. Argyle, *God in the New Testament* (1965), pp. 71ff.

brings an unparalleled element of intimacy into man's relation with God.[11] Nevertheless, while there are unique aspects in Jesus' concept of God as Father, the idea is not absent from the OT or from Jewish usage.[12] God is conceived of as Father of his people. The king could be conceived of as an individual son of God. Israel could be called 'my son'. But this tended to be a nationalistic idea rather than an individual relationship. At the same time, bearing in mind the Hebrew concept of solidarity, it should be noted that this corporate fatherhood did not exclude the idea of individual relationship. Indeed it prepared the idea for its full development in the NT.

Some of the Psalms, which are expressions of individual piety, come close to the more intimate character of God as seen in the NT, but the father-son relationship is not specifically formulated. The idea of God as shepherd (as in Ps. 23; Is. 40; Ezk. 34), while introducing an amazingly tender view of God, falls short of the acceptance of God as Father. In Jewish thinking in the intertestamental period glimpses of God as Father in an individual sense are found, but in no sense is this a characteristic view of God during this period.[13] With the advent of Christ these adumbrations of fatherhood emerge into a view of God which shows that the most intimate form of human relationships (father-children) is but a reflection of the essential characteristic of God (see comment on Eph. 3:14,15 below).

In the NT the fatherhood of God is seen in three ways. He is Father of Jesus (see the discussion on Jesus as Son of God, pp. 301ff.), he is Father of the of the disciples of Jesus, and he is Father of all creation. It is important to note that the father-child relationship in reference to God is almost wholly reserved for those who are believers. The relationship is the result of the redemptive activity of God. The creative relationship has already been discussed under the providence of God. Our concern here will be over the special relationship with believers.

The most notable instance in which Jesus assumed the fatherhood of God for his disciples is the form of the prayer he taught them. The Lord's Prayer, with its direct address to God as Father, is appropriate to the

[11] For a general discussion of the theme of God's fatherhood in the NT, *cf.* J. Jeremias, 'Abba', *The Prayers of Jesus* (1967), pp. 11–65.; H. F. D. Sparks, 'The Doctrine of the Divine Fatherhood in the Gospels', *Studies in the Gospels* (ed. D. E. Nineham, 1955), pp. 241–262.; H. Montefiore, 'God as Father in the Synoptic Gospels', *NTS* 3, 1956, pp. 31–46.; A. W. Argyle, *op. cit.*, pp. 57–90.; J. S. Lidgett, *The Fatherhood of God* (1902), pp. 12–48.

[12] G. Vermes, *Jesus the Jew* (1973), pp. 206–210, and K. Berger, 'Zum traditionsgeschichtlichen Hintergrund christologischen Hoheitstitel', *NTS* 17, 1970–71, pp. 391–426ff. Both trace the Father-Son concept used by Jesus in Jewish thought. See next footnote.

[13] Although the basic Jewish view was that God was Father of the nation of Israel, the idea of the individual as a son is not entirely absent (*cf.* Ecclus. 4:10; Psalms of Solomon 17:30; Jubilees 1:24–25). Nevertheless there is a distinction between the Jewish approach and the teaching of Jesus. R. Bultmann, *Jesus and the Word*, p. 192, is probably correct in claiming that there is no question of Jesus introducing a new conception of God. But there is no denying that he brought to the conception a clarity and intimacy not previously known.

disciples only because it is basic to Jesus' own approach to God.[14] Not only is there a general concept of God's fatherhood but an individual emphasis, as the personal pronoun in 'Our Father' shows. This intimate concept is all the more striking in view of the following words which stress the hallowed character of God. The individualizing of relationships was never intended to lessen man's sense of awe in his approach to God. Care must be taken not to reduce the NT view of the fatherhood of God to the level of human experience. No father-son relationship among men is ever perfect, because no human father is perfect. But in God the perfect pattern of true father-hood is always seen. In view of this the prayer 'Our Father' was a remarkable advance on all previous views of God and provided an indication that Christian teaching was going to revolutionize man's concept of God.

Another remarkable aspect of God is seen in Jesus' teaching in the Sermon on the Mount, where the expression 'your heavenly Father knows' is applied to everyday needs (Mt. 6:32). The explanation of how the creator cares for his creatures (such as birds, Mt. 6:26) is given in terms of fatherhood rather than creatorship, thus introducing the concept of individual concern. This viewpoint is particularly emphasized in the rest of the NT where the title Father is frequently and quite naturally applied to God. In the opening salutation in all the epistles under Paul's name God is described as Father. It forms a basic assumption behind all that the apostle writes in these letters. Moreover, it is frequently reflected in the course of the discussions, whether doctrinal or practical. Indeed there is no one concept of God which dominates the theology of the NT more than this.

The title 'Father' is sometimes qualified to give added richness to the concept. God is many times described as the Father of Jesus Christ, but he is also Father of glory (Eph. 1:17), Father of spirits (Heb. 12:9), Father of lights (Jas. 1:17).[15] All human fatherhood is seen to derive from the fath-

[14] For a full discussion of the fatherhood of God reflected in the Lord's prayer, cf. E. Lohmeyer, *The Lord's Prayer* (Eng. trans. 1965), pp. 32–62. In comparing the synoptic usage with John's gospel, Lohmeyer points out the teaching of Jesus is that God is called 'your Father' because he is 'my Father' (p. 56). R. Bultmann, *TNT* 1 (Eng. trans. 1956), pp. 23f., draws attention to the marked difference between the simplicity of 'Father' as used by Jesus and the ornate, although often liturgically beautiful forms of address used in Jewish prayers. He cites the 'Prayer of Eighteen Petitions' as an example.

[15] In these expressions where a genitive is added there is some question about the sense in which the fatherhood should be understood. In Eph. 1:17 the genitive seems rightly to qualify the noun in an adjectival sense in which case the NEB rendering 'the all-glorious Father' is justified; cf. M. Barth, *Ephesians* (AB, 1974), p. 148, who nevertheless thinks the expression may denote God as the source of the splendour which produces light in man's hearts. C. L. Mitton, *Ephesians* (NCB, 1976), *ad loc.*, accepts the NEB rendering, while F. F. Bruce, *Ephesians* (1961), p. 39, considers the expression emphasizes the unique glory of God's fatherhood as the archetype of fatherhood. The expression 'Father of Spirits' is generally taken in the sense of Father of our Spirits (*i.e.* our spiritual Father) to distinguish God from those who are our natural forebears. Cf. F. F. Bruce, *Hebrews* (NICNT, 1964), pp. 359f. This contrasts two degrees of fatherhood, natural and spiritual, and it implies that if the former commands submission, the latter would certainly do so. The concept 'Father' here seems to involve the sense of creatorship. This is even more clear in the third phrase 'Father of lights' in Jas. 1:17. There is a Jewish parallel in the Damascus Document which describes God as 'Prince of Lights' (cf. M. Dibelius – H. Greeven, *James* (Eng. trans. *Hermeneia*,

erhood of God (Eph. 3:14,15), which shows that God is not called Father on the basis of a human analogy, as if human fatherhood was the nearest approximation to the relationship between God and man. Fatherhood is seen rather to be inherent in the nature of God.

But we need to enquire what 'fatherhood' means when applied to God. As far as believers are concerned it means that God is the source of their spiritual life and pours out his love upon them. He is concerned with their welfare (Rom. 8:28) and also with their discipline (Heb. 12:5ff.).

We may note in passing that it is in John's gospel that the fatherhood of God is seen most clearly in relation to Jesus. We shall discuss under Christology the absolute use of the title in the frequent statements of Jesus about God which shows how fundamental this concept was for him. The only close parallel in the synoptic gospels to this father-son relationship occurs in the celebrated passage in Matthew 11:25ff., where the forms 'Father', 'My Father' and 'the Father' all occur.[16] But the fact that such a statement occurs is evidence that this is not a Johannine invention, although it must be noted that the prominence of the idea in John's gospel is no doubt due to its interest for the mind of the author.[17] More will be said about these Johannine passages when the sonship of Jesus is discussed (see p. 312f.). But for our present purpose there is one significant statement on the subject of fatherhood which requires mention because it not only draws a distinction between God as Father of Jesus and God as Father of the disciples, but also shows the connection between them. The words of Jesus addressed to Mary which she was to report to the disciples (Jn. 20:17), 'I am ascending to my Father and your Father, to my God and your God,' are so expressed

---

1976, from *KEK*, 1964), p. 100). Although the primary reference may be to God as the creator of the heavenly bodies (C. L. Mitton, *James*, 1966, p. 53), there is undoubtedly an extended allusion to God as source of intellectual, spiritual and moral lights; *cf.* R. J. Knowling, *James* (*WC*, pp. 190f.), *ad loc.*, J. B. Mayor, *James* (³1913), *ad loc.*. All that can be said is that fatherhood in the more intimate sense is not supported by this reference.

[16] Mt. 11:25 was for long considered to be a product of Hellenistic Christianity, but there is less support for this view among many recent scholars. *Cf.* T. W. Manson, *The Sayings of Jesus* (1949), p. 79, who strongly maintains its Palestinian origin. *Cf.* also W. L. Knox. *Some Hellenistic Elements in Primitive Christianity* (1944), p. 7, who denies that the form and language are Hellenistic. On the other hand S. Schulz, *Q – Die Spruchquelle der Evangelisten* (1972), pp. 213–228, and R. Bultmann, *History of the Synoptic Tradition* (Eng. trans. 1963), pp. 159f., still regard it as Hellenistic. *Cf.* also A. M. Hunter, 'Crux Criticorum – Matt. xi. 25–30 – a Re-appraisal', *NTS* 8, 1961–2, pp. 241ff., who goes back to Hosea as a background, but who argues that no precise parallel can be expected in view of the uniqueness of Jesus. *Cf.* also the discussion of J. D. G. Dunn, *Jesus and the Spirit* (1975) and J. Jeremias, *The Prayers of Jesus*.

[17] H. Conzelmann, *An Outline of the Theology of the New Testament* (Eng. trans. 1969), pp. 99ff., in discussing the distinction between 'my' Father and 'your' Father, concludes that it is a matter of the Christological style of the community. He does not regard the distinction as original to Jesus. But his conclusions are based on critical methods which can be challenged. He disposes, for instance, of the 'My' Father form in Mt. 11:27 on the grounds that the word 'my' is absent from Luke's version. J. Jeremias, *The Central Message of the New Testament* (1965), pp. 23ff., argues that the article in 'the Father' in this statement is generic, not ontological. He takes it in the sense that only a father knows a son, so only a son knows a father. *Cf.* J. A. T. Robinson, *The Human Face of God* (1973), p. 186.

83

as to make this distinction clear.[18] It is in a unique sense that Jesus can be said to be the Son of God the Father. Nevertheless this special sense is not unconnected with the special father-son relationship which God maintains with those who are in Christ.

A further observation which is of great importance in any assessment of the NT view of God and which distinguishes the NT from the OT is the use of the form 'Abba' by Christians (Rom. 8:15; Gal. 4:6), undoubtedly based on Jesus' own use of the term in addressing God (Mk. 14:36). This Aramaic form of address to a father was originally a form used by young children, but it had acquired an extended meaning in familiar usage, roughly equivalent to 'dear father'.[19] It is a unique form, for it finds no parallels either in the OT or in Judaism as an address to God.[20] Its use by Jesus shows how completely his view of God as Father is divorced from any formal approach. The Abba form conveys a sense of intimacy and familiarity which introduced an entirely new factor into man's approach to God.

God as King and Judge

Throughout the NT are found traces of the idea of God as King. It comes into focus especially in the phrase kingdom of God or kingdom of heaven.[21] The full implications of this concept will be discussed later in the section on the mission of Christ (see p. 409ff.). But clearly the idea of kingdom implies a King who exercises his rule over his subjects. There are many OT passages in which God is seen as King, and this furnishes a solid basis for the NT usage. In the contemporary world of NT times, most kings were tyrants, but this idea is nowhere suggested in the NT as applicable to God. Kingship implies sovereignty, which in its proper function carries with it responsibility. This is not to say that the idea of sovereignty is necessarily the major idea of the kingdom. Indeed the kingdom stands also for the

[18] On this Johannine passage, cf. J. Jeremias, op. cit., p. 55, and G. Dalman, The Words of Jesus (Eng. trans. 1902), pp. 190, 281.

[19] W. G. Kümmel, TNT, p. 75, while recognizing the extraordinary nature of Jesus calling God 'my Father' (see p. 40), does not recognize the implication of this for Jesus' awareness of sonship. Jeremias, NTT 1, pp. 64ff., claims that God in Judaism was never addressed as Abba, as he was by Jesus. D. Flusser, Jesus (Eng. trans. 1969) cautions that the evidence for charismatic prayer in Jewish literature is sparse and may account for the lack of the Abba usage. G. Vermes, Jesus the Jew (1963), pp. 210f., claims that Hasidic piety addressed God as Father. But the only two examples he notes are not actual addresses to God as Father, cf. Schrenk, TDNT 5, pp. 979ff.

[20] Cf. O. Hofius, NIDNTT 1, p. 614.

[21] On God as King, cf. A. W. Argyle, op. cit., pp. 35–56; G. E. Ladd, TNT, pp. 81–90.; H. Conzelmann, TNT, p. 101, notes in passing the paucity of references to God as King (Basileus) in spite of the frequency of the expression 'Kingdom of God'. In his opinion the latter phrase was not derived from God's title as King. It is nearer the truth to say that both concepts are so intimately connected with each other that it is impossible to give intelligible meaning to 'Kingdom of God' without implying at the same time the notion of the sovereignty of God. In our later discussions of basileia we shall note that the dominant idea is 'rule' rather than 'realm', and this focuses attention on sovereignty. It is worth noting that in the earliest records in Palestinian Judaism where God is addressed as 'Father', the word occurs in the form 'Our Father our King' (cf. J. Jeremias, The Prayers of Jesus (Eng. trans. 1967), p. 27).

entire blessings of salvation. Yet the two ideas are closely linked, since for believers the sovereignty of God has no meaning apart from the salvation which he has effected. The subjects of the kingdom are those who have committed themselves wholly to carrying out the will of the King. The fact that Jesus himself said so much about the kingdom of God shows that he regarded the sovereignty of God as assumed. He did not, in fact, demonstrate why people should acknowledge the right of God to make sovereign demands on them. He took it for granted. Central to this idea is the assumption that the will of God was a norm for people.[22] This comes out clearly in the Lord's Prayer.

This idea of kingship springs from the creatorship of God. When the early Christians prayed they acknowledged this fact, addressing God as 'Sovereign Lord, who made the heaven and the earth and the sea and everything in them' (Acts 4:24). He who creates has a right to direct. Indeed the creature has no right to question the decisions of the Creator. Paul recognized this when he used the potter illustration in Romans 9:19ff. (drawn from Isaiah).[23] Sovereignty is therefore seen to be an inherent part of the creative activity of God.

In harmony with the idea of kingship is the use of the title Lord as applied to God. This is another title which is prevalent in the OT and assumed in the NT. The title 'Lord your God' is used in two of the citations made by Jesus at his temptation, when refuting the devil (Mt. 4:7,10; Lk. 4:8,12). Lordship and sovereignty demand such rigorous standards of allegiance that the mere announcement of these themes is sufficient rebuff for the tempter. God's sole right to worship and homage is not open to question. For man to act in any other way would result in his falling into temptation and consequently dishonouring God.

It is the throne imagery used of God in the NT which links the twin concepts of King and Judge. When speaking of oaths, Jesus forbade swearing by heaven 'for it is the throne of God' (Mt. 5:34; 23:22). There is no need to be literalistic in understanding the meaning of 'throne' in this

---

[22] The importance of the will of God for an understanding of NT theology cannot be over-emphasized. Bultmann, from an existential point of view, speaks of God as the 'Demand-er', although he recognizes in the teaching of Jesus that the 'Demand-er' is also a God of forgiveness (*TNT* 1, p. 24). It is because the demand of God is so central, that Bultmann assigns so important a place to obedience (*cf.* pp. 12f.). Kümmel, *TNT* p. 53, speaks of God's unconditional will. So it is essential to grasp the absolute character of God's demands on people if man's basic need is to be properly understood.

[23] It is important not to take the potter illustration out of its immediate context, as J. Murray, *Romans* (*NICNT*, 1967), *ad loc.*, rightly points out. He attempts to limit the potter's right over people to people as sinners, not simply as creatures. This distinction is over-fine, for it is because of people's rebellion against the will of God that they have become sinners. C. K. Barrett, *Romans* (1957), p. 188, faces the criticism that people are not pots with the remark that a detail of the analogy should not be stressed and the main point missed, *i.e.* the final responsibility of God for what he does in history. F. J. Leenhardt, *Romans* (Eng. trans. 1957), p. 256, reckons that Paul's illustration here concerns God in providence, not as creator.

context. The significance clearly depends on the royal status of God, of which 'throne' is an appropriate symbol. In the previously mentioned statement in Matthew 11:25ff., which parallels the Johannine Father-Son Christology, Jesus addresses God as 'Father, Lord of heaven and earth', another evidence for the sovereignty of God. The idea of a court of heaven is hinted at in the saying in Luke 12:8f., which predicts that the Son of man acknowledges men 'before the angels' (a reverent periphrasis for God). This throne idea occurs many times in other parts of the NT as will next be seen. It contributes not a little to the basic concept of God as king.

In the book of Acts and in the epistles the idea of the kingdom is less frequent and consequently the concept of God as King is not as prominent. Sometimes the early preachers preached about the kingdom (Acts 8:12; 28:31), but more often they are said to have preached Christ (Acts 5:42; 8:5; 9:20; 17:18; cf. also 1 Cor. 1:23; 15:12; 2 Cor. 1:19). For the early Christians Jesus was seen to be the embodiment of the kingdom. This led to less emphasis on the kingdom itself, but in no sense lessened the conviction that the reign of God had been inaugurated. His kingly function was everywhere assumed rather than expressed.

In Paul's epistles there are many indirect indications that the apostle thought of God in terms of sovereignty. God is more powerful than the rulers of this age (1 Cor. 2:6ff.). All the powers of evil (the principalities and powers) are incapable of interfering with God's purposes in Christ (Rom. 8:37–39). Indeed they have already been conquered (Col. 2:15). Paul sees the final act of history as God subduing his enemies 'under his feet' (1 Cor. 15:23ff.). In the apostle's thought there is little real distinction between the kingdom of God and the kingdom of Christ, although Christ will deliver the kingdom to God (1 Cor. 15:24). What is central to Paul's thinking in this context is the supreme sovereignty of God over everything. The pastoral epistles contain one statement which clearly brings this aspect to the fore when God is described as 'the blessed and only Sovereign, the King of Kings and Lord of Lords' (1 Tim. 6:15).[24]

The doctrine of God in the epistle to the Hebrews is central to the theme of the whole epistle. Since the content is concerned with the way of approach to God, it is of great importance to note the exalted concept of God which is found in this epistle. At the beginning the focus falls on the 'Majesty on high', with the Son seated at his right hand (1:3). This emphasis on the right hand of majesty[25] as the position of honour recurs at two other points in the epistle (8:1; 12:2), showing it to be a key concept which links

[24] Although the word translated 'sovereign' (*dynastēs*) was frequently used of a prince who possessed only delegated authority, in this context it carries with it a sovereignty which knows no superior, as the title King of kings shows. *Cf.* D. Guthrie, *The Pastoral Epistles* (1957), p. 116.

[25] The expression 'at the right hand of the majesty on high' is undoubtedly influenced by Ps. 110 which plays an important part in this epistle. The phrase 'majesty on high' expresses the dignity and exalted character of God. *Cf.* F. F. Bruce, *Hebrews, ad loc.*

the parts into a whole. The high priest not only pleads before the throne, but actually shares the throne. The royal nature of God is in this manner vividly demonstrated. The same idea is found in 1 Peter 3:22, where angels, authorities and powers are said to be subject to Jesus Christ 'at the right hand of God'.

In the book of Revelation, the enthronement idea in relation to God is so marked that in the vision in 4:2 God is simply denoted by the phrase 'the One seated on the throne', an expression which is repeated in 5:1 (*cf.* also 7:15). At the end of the book the vision concentrates on the great white throne in the scenes of judgment (20:11). Moreover it is 'he who sat upon the throne' who makes 'all things new' (21:5). His throne is central in the vision of the new Jerusalem (22:1f.). In addition, in Revelation 6:10 God is addressed by the martyrs as Sovereign Lord. A significant aspect of this motif of divine kingship in this Apocalypse is that God is frequently described as 'Almighty' (4:8; 11:17; 15:3; 16:7,14; 19:6,15), a title which strongly emphasizes the sovereign power of God.[26]

The king concept is closely allied to that of judge. The certainty of God's judgment was a major assumption behind the sternness of John the baptist's preaching (*cf.* Mt. 3:7ff; Lk. 3:7ff., although absent from Mark's account). No questions were raised over this judgment theme, for the idea of God as judge was everywhere assumed. Jesus makes the same assumption when he alludes to the future judging activity of God (*cf.* Mt. 7:1,2; 11:22–24; 12:36–37). There has been a tendency to play down this aspect of Jesus' view of God, but the importance of it cannot be assessed purely on the number of times the theme occurs.[27] True sovereignty would be unintelligible apart from some provision for the accountability of the subjects to the King. In one of his parables Jesus contrasted an unjust judge with the vindicating judgment of God (Lk. 18:7). Moreover, in John's gospel, he positively associated himself with the judging activity of God (Jn. 8:16).

For Paul the idea of God as Judge was an integral part of his gospel (*cf.* Rom. 2:16). Indeed, there was no doubt in his mind that God would judge the world (Rom. 3:6). He speaks positively about 'the judgment seat of God' (Rom. 14:10) and uses it as a basis for his condemnation of Christians who were judging their brethren. What is not regarded as an approbation for man is nevertheless of the essence of the divine nature. It is assumed as right and proper in the NT that the divine king should exercise his prerogative of judgment. There is admittedly a certain element of severity about

---

[26] The title *Pantokratōr* (Almighty) is the LXX equivalent of 'Lord of Hosts'. In the NT it is used only in the book of Revelation. The whole book shows not only that God is omnipotent by right, but in actual fact. The final consummation lies in the future but the reality of it is here and now, *cf.* G. B. Caird, *Revelation* (BC, 1966), p. 141.

[27] W. G. Kümmel, *TNT*, pp. 39f., while he admits that Jesus shared the contemporary Jewish convictions about God as Judge, nevertheless suggests that it was only to a slight extent characteristic of, and essential for, his conception of God.

this aspect of God (*cf.* Pet. 2:4ff.). Paul, who admits the severe side of God, is nevertheless careful to link it with the kindness of God (Rom. 11:22).[28] In the Apocalypse it is God who gives judgment against the symbolic Babylon. Indeed throughout the book it is the One on the throne who subdues all rebellious elements. The theme of judgment merits separate treatment and will be discussed in the section on the future (see pp. 848ff.).

Various other titles for God

SPIRIT

The NT presents the nature and character of God in a number of different titles which express various facets, not in a formal way, but nonetheless significantly. In John's gospel Jesus declares that God is Spirit (Jn. 4:24). The precise nature of God's spirituality is left unexpressed but there was no need for any further explanation.[29] John's readers would know that the statement could mean nothing less than that God cannot be defined in material categories – no doubt a necessary assertion at a time when gods of wood and stone were common. Moreover, it is the spiritual nature of God which makes the doctrine of the Holy Spirit intelligible.[30]

SAVIOUR

Although the title 'Saviour' is more generally applied to Jesus Christ in the NT, it is nevertheless also used of God and in this respect tallies with a dominant activity of God in the OT. The main occurrences of the title are in the Pastorals (1 Tim. 2:3; Tit. 2:10, 13; 3:4), but it also occurs with an OT flavour in Mary's song (Lk. 1:47), and in the doxology in Jude 25. Although the title is rare, the activity implicit in the title permeates the whole NT.[31] Indeed, Christian theology centres in the theme of God saving his people.

MOST HIGH

This is a title of supreme dignity which expresses the superiority of God over all other gods.[32] It is used by the soothsayer in Acts 16:17, by the

[28] The combination of goodness and severity is found in many OT passages (*cf.* Ps. 125:4, 5; Is. 42:25–43:1, 50:10–11). Paul would take this for granted. In Rom. 11:22 the possibility of being 'cut off' shows the nature of Paul's understanding of the severity of God.

[29] Involved in the spiritual nature of God is his life-giving activities. In John's gospel spirit and life are closely connected (*cf.* 6:63). See L. Morris' discussion, *John* (*NICNT*, 1971), pp. 271f.

[30] The particular aspect of spirituality which is brought out in 1 Pet. 4:6 seems to be its eternal quality. The believer's life in the Spirit becomes in 'God's likeness' (*kata Theon*) which contrasts with those under judgment. It marks the difference between death and life. *Cf.* E. G. Selwyn, *The First Epistle of Peter* (1946), pp. 215f.

[31] In view of the dominance of the idea of 'saving' and 'salvation', it is remarkable that the term occurs so rarely in the NT. One explanation is that *sōtēr* was used both in the Greek mysteries religions (of Asclepios, the god of healing) and in Caesar worship (of the Roman emperor). *Cf.* A. W. Argyle, *op. cit.*, pp. 115f., who cites W. Bousset, *Kyrios Christos* (1913), pp. 204ff. (see pp. 310–317 in Eng. trans., 1970).

[32] This title 'Ēl 'Elyôn, is generally considered to be among the most ancient names for God in the OT. It occurs frequently in the Psalms. *Cf.* G. Bertram, *TDNT* 1, pp. 619f., who considers that the Greek

demon possessing the man of Gerasa (Lk. 8:28/Mk. 5:7), by Jesus himself when exhorting people to love their enemies (Lk. 6:35) and by Zechariah in his song about John the Baptist (Lk. 1:76). It is also used in the description of Melchizedek's priesthood (Heb. 7:1).

GOD OF THE PATRIARCHS

Several times God is specifically mentioned as God of Abraham, Isaac and Jacob (Mt. 8:11, 22:32; Mk. 12:26f.; Lk. 20:37; Acts 3:13; 7:32). Similarly he is called God of our fathers (Acts 22:14). In a Jewish setting the linking of God with the patriarchs would be highly significant. It would convey much more than a nationalistic deity. It would show that the present nature of God was recognized as being identical to that seen when God dealt graciously with the fathers of the Jewish race.[33] It stresses the continuity between Christian revelation and the OT.

ALPHA AND OMEGA

Only in Revelation 1:8 and 21:6 does this description of God occur. Later in the book it is used of Christ (Rev. 22:13). It must be understood as figurative of All-inclusiveness, in the sense that both beginning and end and all between must be related to God.[34] It is especially meaningful in a book which deals so much with the end-time. It conceives of the whole span of history in terms of God's activity. There are no blank periods. This concept ties in closely with the concept of God as Creator.

THE ATTRIBUTES OF GOD

Anyone who seeks an answer to the question, 'What is the God of the NT like?', will find no formal statements, but a mass of incidental indications, which nevertheless are invaluable in throwing light on many facets of the

---

equivalent of this title (*hypsistos*) does not correspond to the NT revelation of God 'no matter whether it be understood as a solemn liturgico-hymnal expression of sublimity, a religious philosophico-theological term to denote transcendence, or a traditional proper name for God'. It is not clear why a name as little used as this in the NT must for that reason be considered to be contrary to the NT revelation. It is but part of a total picture of supreme dignity. Because Luke has a fondness for this expression, it is sometimes supposed that the only NT evidence for Jesus using it (Lk. 6:35) must be attributed to Luke's editorial adaptation of his material. G. Dalman, *Words of Jesus* (Eng. trans. 1902), p. 199, for instance, argued this on the basis that in the parallel saying in Mt. 5:45, the expression is not used. Matthew may have edited the words in accordance with his usual style. It cannot be said definitely that Jesus did not use the title.

[33] God is addressed in the Prayer of Eighteen Petitions as God of Abraham, God of Isaac and God of Jacob, as well as God Most High, among other titles (*cf.* Bultmann, *TNT*, p. 24).

[34] For a detailed examination of the Alpha-Omega theme, *cf.* G. R. Beasley-Murray, *The Book of Revelation* (NCB, 1974), pp. 59ff. He takes Rev. 1:8 to imply that God is the sovereign Lord of all times and ages. He shows that this use of the letters of the alphabet was common among the Jews. The expression had particular point for the readers of the book of Revelation who were clearly passing through a period of trial and needed reassuring that God was in control of all times and circumstances.

character of God. There is nothing to suggest that there were differences of opinion in the NT about what God is like. Whereas some parts bring certain facets into focus more than other parts, there is no doubt that a unified picture is presented. While it is impossible to arrange the evidence in systematic form, it will be helpful to group the main ideas under the following considerations – the glory of God, the wisdom of God, the holiness of God, the righteousness of God, the love and grace of God, the goodness of God, the uniqueness of God, and the unity of God.

The glory of God

There is a strong OT background to the frequent references to the glory of God. Whereas the Hebrew word for 'glory' (*kābôḏ*) was used of anything which possessed splendour, honour, conspicuousness, it soon came to have a special significance when applied to God.[35] It came in fact to stand for the revelation of God, as when the psalmist maintained that the heavens declare the glory of God (Ps. 19:1). OT history is seen as a record of God's revelation of his glory in his activities on behalf of his people. A more developed sense of the same idea is the use of 'glory' to denote the presence of God in a theophany, which was later to become known in Jewish theology as the Shekinah *(šᵉkînâ)*.[36] But it is the translation of the Hebrew *kābôḏ* into the Greek *doxa* which provides the key for understanding the NT idea of the glory of God.[37] We shall note that in the NT there are two senses in which *doxa* is used, as visible glory (in the sense of seeing the glory of God) and as uttered praise (in the sense of ascribing glory to God).

It is astonishing how frequently the NT writers mention the glory and majesty of God. Moreover, men are prompted to glorify God. To ascribe glory to God in face of the mysterious working of his power is often spontaneous. The shepherds did so at the birth of Jesus (Lk. 2:20); so did the people who observed the healing of the paralytic (Mk. 2:12; Lk. 5:25–26; Mt. 9:8) and the healing of numerous sick people (Mt. 15:31). At the raising of the dead man at Nain (Lk. 7:16) and the restoration of sight to the blind at Jericho (Lk. 18:43), Luke records the same reaction. It is moreover stated by Jesus that when he returns he will come in the glory

[35] *Cf.* the remarks of B. Ramm, *Them He Glorified* (1963), pp. 10f. Ramm maintains that the glory of God is not an attribute of God like wisdom, but an attribute of his total nature (p. 18). He also links glory with beauty in God (as Augustine and Barth also do), pp. 20, 21. J. Moltmann, *Theology and Joy* (Eng. trans. 1973), pp. 58f., discusses the 'beauty' of God, linking it with the OT and NT evidence for 'glory' applied to God.

[36] On the idea of *Shechinah, cf.* G. B. Gray, *HBD* 2, p. 183. For a Jewish exposition of this theme, *cf.* J. Abelson, *The Immanence of God*, especially pp. 77–149.

[37] *Cf.* L. H. Brockington, 'The Septuagintal Background to the New Testament use of *doxa*', *Studies in the Gospels* (ed. D. E. Nineham, 1957), pp. 1ff. *Cf.* G. von Rad, *TDNT* 2, pp. 238–242, for the OT usage of the corresponding Hebrew word *kābôḏ*. In the same volume G. Kittel explores the NT meaning, *ibid.*, pp. 247f.

of the Father (Lk. 9:26). The most vivid demonstration of the glory of God in the ministry of Jesus was the transfiguration, in which the splendour of God was fleetingly seen in a complete transformation of the appearance of Jesus (Mt. 17:1ff.; Mk. 9:2ff.; Lk. 9:28ff.).[38] This glory of Christ is inseparably linked with the glory of God. It is understandable that a later commentary on this event speaks of the Majestic Glory of God (2 Pet. 1:17).

John makes clear in his account that the glory which he and others had observed in the ministry of Jesus had a divine source (Jn. 5:41ff.). Indeed the glory of Jesus Christ is again inextricably bound up with the glory of God (Jn. 1:14; 11:4,40; 13:31). Whatever glorifies the Son of man is said to glorify God (13:31f.). The essential point to notice is that God is not only assumed to be glorious, but is the pattern for the measuring of glory in others, even in the case of his Son (*cf.* Jn. 17:5).[39] No glory can be greater than God's. In Acts Luke describes Stephen as seeing the 'glory of God' and the Son of man at the right hand of God (Acts 7:55). The Jerusalem church is said to ascribe glory to God when hearing the reports of Peter and Paul respectively (Acts 11:18; 21:20).

In Pauline theology the same theme is implicit. The pattern for measuring man's shortcomings is 'the glory of God' (Rom. 3:23), which implies that man's sin has made it impossible for him to be the reflector of God's glory as he should have been.[40] Nevertheless, through the process of justification Paul sees the possibility of men again sharing in God's glory (Rom. 5:2). When describing the glory of Christ, he equates it with the glory of God (2 Cor. 4:4ff.). He sees an interaction between the glory of God and glory shared by Christians (2 Cor. 3:18). On one occasion he describes God as the 'Father of glory' (Eph. 1:17). He includes several doxologies which ascribe glory to God (Rom. 16:27;[41] Phil. 4:20; 2 Tim. 4:18). All that man does must be done to God's glory (*cf.* Rom. 15:7; 2 Cor. 4:15; Phil. 1:11; 2:11). Moreover, eternal destruction is seen as exclusion from the presence of God and the glory of his might (2 Thes. 1:9), which shows that any

[38] *Cf.* A. M. Ramsey's study on *doxa*, *The Glory of God and the Transfiguration of Christ* (1949).

[39] For a discussion from a radical point of view of the glory of Christ in John's gospel, *cf.* E. Käsemann, *The Testament of Jesus* (Eng. trans. 1968), pp. 4–26. *Cf.* also W. Thüsing, *Die Erhöhung und Verherrlichung Jesu im Johannesevangelium* (²1970), pp. 206f., where he discusses the meaning of Jn. 17:5. The whole book concentrates on the theme of glorification and the tension created by the human life of Jesus.

[40] There is some difference of opinion over the interpretation of *doxa tou Theou* here. C. K. Barrett, *Romans, ad loc.*, sees it as the glory with which man was created, a glory nevertheless received from God. *Cf.* also C. E. B. Cranfield, *Romans (ICC,* 1975) 1, *ad loc.* K. Barth, *Romans* (Eng. trans. 1933), p. 101, however, follows Bengel in taking the glory of God to be his consciousness. C. H. Dodd, *Romans (MNT,* 1932) *ad loc.*, interprets it of the image of God, but M. Black, *Romans (NBC,* 1973), *ad loc.*, disputes this. What is undeniable is that the original glory was derived from God.

[41] The grammatical problems surrounding the construction of the Rom. 16:27 doxology make it uncertain whether Paul was ascribing *doxa* to God or to Christ. It is questionable whether the apostle would have drawn a fine distinction between the two concepts. C. K. Barrett, *op. cit., ad loc.*, considers that the defective construction would remind readers of both.

obscuring of God's glory is the worst possible happening in man's experience.[42]

In the rest of the NT this concept of God's glory is continued. Christ is said to reflect God's glory (Heb. 1:3), which seems to mean that Christ represents in his person the majesty and power of God, in a sense similar to the OT idea of the glorious presence of God.[43] Man's chief end is to glorify God (1 Pet. 2:12; cf. 4:11). Christians are said to be called 'to his own glory and excellence' (2 Pet. 1:3), an idea fully in accord with Pauline thought. In both 2 Peter 3:18 and Jude 25, there is the familiar ascription of glory to God. In the Apocalypse, the theme of God's glory occurs mainly in the interludes which focus on worship (cf. Rev. 4:11; 7:12; 19:2). In a picturesque description of the temple, John speaks of it being filled 'with smoke from the glory of God and from his power' (15:8), as if it possessed some all-pervasive quality which cannot be missed.[44] Perhaps the most striking and solemn focus on God's glory is at the hour of judgment when the flying angel bids men to fear God and give him glory (14:7). The vision of the New Jerusalem is in marked contrast, for it already possesses the glory of God (21:11).[45]

Another closely allied facet is the description of God as light (1 Jn. 1:5), no doubt arising from the connection in man's mind between light and glory (cf. also John's prologue).[46] Concentration on the glory of God floods all man's activities with light. This idea occurs also in the Apocalypse, which describes the New Jerusalem as having no need of other light since the glory of God is its light (Rev. 21:23).

Enough has been said to demonstrate the great importance in NT thought of the theme of God's glory as a basic assumption about the nature and

[42] The linking of God's presence with his glory is significant, because in Paul's mind God can never be separated from his glory. In the expression 'glory of his might', the genitive is one of origin, which shows that God's power proceeds from his glory (cf. E. Best, 1 and 2 Thessalonians (BC, 1972), ad loc.). Although 2 Thes. 1:9 need not be taken to imply exclusion, since apo could be understood in other ways, it fits the context better and is normally to be expected with this preposition.

[43] It makes little difference whether in Heb. 1:3 apaugasma is rendered 'radiance' or 'reflection', for the glory in both is directly derived from God. F. F. Bruce, Hebrews, ad loc., takes it in the former sense, and H. W. Montefiore, Hebrews (BC, 1964) takes it in the latter sense. But Montefiore admits that the two senses interpenetrate.

[44] There are OT precedents for the association of smoke and glory (cf. Is. 6:4; Ex. 40:35; 2 Ch. 7:1f. and Ezk. 44:4). The vivid imagery in Rev. 15:8 is intended to impress on the reader the overwhelming sense of awful holiness (cf. G. R. Beasley-Murray, Revelation, pp. 237f.).

[45] It is not surprising that 'the glory of God' dominates the book of Revelation with its forward vision, since the NT generally supposes that the revelation of God's glory will not be complete until the last day. It is in this sense that it would be right to describe it as eschatological.

[46] In his treatment of leading ideas in the fourth gospel, C. H. Dodd, The Interpretation of the Fourth Gospel (1953), pp. 201f., links Light with Glory and Judgment. Since in Judaism the Shekinah was conceived as light, it is not surprising that 'glory' and 'light' are associated in the NT. Cf. also the section in E. K. Lee's book, The Religious Thought of St John (1950), on God as light, pp. 32ff. Lee takes 1 Jn. 1:5 as meaning that God is light in the sense of the inherent quality of God, not simply in the sense of his intelligibility or self-revelation.

character of God. Now we must consider how it bears upon other aspects of God. It cannot fail to promote a reaction of awe. It provides a ready preparation for the view of God's power, which is everywhere assumed in the NT. So glorious a being could never be impotent (*cf.* Rom. 4:21; 11:23; 1 Cor. 2:5; 2 Cor. 9:8). Indeed the description 'the power of God' when used absolutely aptly indicates this dynamic aspect of God's character (*cf.* 2 Cor. 6:7; 13.4; 2 Tim. 1:8).

The 'power of God' is regarded as an object of knowledge (Mk. 12:24). It can be used as a title synonymous with God (as in Mk. 14:62; Lk. 22:69).[47] The all-inclusive ability of God is vividly brought out in the statement of Jesus that all things are possible with God (Mk. 10:27; Lk. 18:27; *cf.* the angel's word to Mary, Lk. 1:37). There is no discussion of any problems which this raises, like the moral impossibilities (*cf.* Heb. 6:18 where it is an axiom that God cannot lie). The NT sees the omnipotence of God only in the context of the total portrayal of his character. There is nothing arbitrary or capricious about God's use of his power, for he cannot act contrary to his own character.[48] That power is used for good ends, as when he uses it to guard his people (1 Pet. 1:5; Jn. 10:29). The only fitting approach of the creature is an attitude of humility under his mighty hand (1 Pet. 5:6). It is not surprising that among the attributes of God celebrated in the liturgical passages in the Apocalypse, might and power figure prominently (*cf.* Rev. 4:11; 5:12–13; 7:12; 19:1; *cf.* also the doxology in Jude 25).

With so exalted a view of the glory and power of God, it is not surprising that the NT writers at times allude to the mysteries of God. The apostle Paul speaks of 'the depths of God' (1 Cor. 2:10),[49] which are known only to the Spirit of God. There is a whole area of knowledge of God which is beyond man's grasp. God is in a sense incomprehensible, although the Spirit's revelations of him are sufficient for man's understanding of his redemptive purposes. There is no question of man being able to set his own limits on God's nature and attributes. What he knows is at most no

---

[47] 'The Power' was a rabbinic term for God, *cf.* G. Dalman, *Words of Jesus* (Eng. trans. 1902), pp. 200f. Along with other periphrases it was intended to avoid anthropomorphism. It stood essentially for a God who was powerfully active.

[48] There is a close connection between God's power and his providence. To maintain providence God must have the resources to do it. Neither the OT nor the NT questions his possession of that power. In the OT in addition to the manifestations of his power in maintaining the created order, there are special demonstrations of power in God's activities on Israel's behalf. The concept of the power of God in the NT concentrates on his acts of salvation (Rom. 1:16). The consummation comes when all the kingdoms of the world become the kingdoms of our Lord and his Christ (Rev. 11:15).

[49] Some have interpreted this reference to the 'depths' of God in a gnostic sense (so U. Wilckens, *Weisheit und Torheit* (1956), cited by, but not supported by, H. Conzelmann, *1 Corinthians* (Eng. trans. *Hermeneia*, 1975, from *KEK* 1969), p. 66. Wilckens supposes that 'depths' are to be identified with the revealer, but Conzelmann finds this explanation of Paul's words incomprehensible. *Cf.* also C. K. Barrett's comments, *1 Corinthians* (BC, [2]1971), *ad loc.* He contends that Paul is combating the view that men could plumb the depths of God's being. F. W. Grosheide, *1 Corinthians* (*NICNT*, 1953), p. 68, understands the phrase to mean 'God himself in his infinitude'.

more than a glimpse at the whole reality. A massive area of mystery must remain. Paul can speak of God's servants as 'stewards of the mysteries of God' (1 Cor. 4:1), which shows that an element of mystery [50] will always attend the proclamation of the gospel. This sense of awe is well brought out by the apostle at the conclusion of Romans 11, where he speaks of the unsearchable character of God's judgments and the inscrutable nature of his ways (verse 33). No-one has known the mind of God, as Isaiah 40:13–14, which Paul quotes, so patently implies. The mysterious character of God does not find such clear expression in other parts of the NT, but is assumed. There is no suggestion anywhere that God is limited to man's capacity to conceive him. A due sense of the mystery of God is indispensable to an understanding of the NT revelation of God's dealing with men. Many of the exegetical problems which have arisen have been caused by man assuming that God's mind is precisely analogous to his own. This will become clear when the wisdom of God is discussed in the next section.

Some comment must be made on the connection between the NT view of God's mysteriousness and that of contemporary Judaism. In the latter, transcendental ideas had generally so removed God from contact with man, except through intermediaries, that to many he had become remote.[51] The sense of mysteriousness was heightened by the avoidance of the sacred name and the substitution of an alternative title (*Adonai*). Undoubtedly these ideas were ennobling when compared with contemporary paganism, but they tended to suggest that God was wholly Other. It was the achievement of NT revelation to retain a sufficient air of mystery to remind man of his own limited understanding of God, but at the same time to unveil a means by which some aspects of the mysteriousness become knowable.[52]

The wisdom and knowledge of God

The Jewish wisdom writers often speak of wisdom, but not so much as an attribute of God[53] as an emanation from God (Wisdom 7:25). She is described as the brightness of his everlasting light (Wisdom 7:26). She is

[50] For the NT use of *mystērion* in relation to the things of God, *cf.* G. Bornkamm, *TDNT* 4, pp. 817–824. He denies any connection between the NT usage and the mystery cults. He points out that since the 'mystery of God' is disclosed in revelation, 'its concealment is always manifest with its proclamation' (p. 822). This is seen in three antitheses between (i) the then and the now, (ii) the rulers of the world and those who love God, and (iii) the now and the one day.

[51] It has already been pointed out in footnote 2 that the transcendental emphasis must not be regarded as the only emphasis in rabbinic Judaism, although it was the most dominant. See also the remarks on remoteness in footnote 3.

[52] It is a mistake to suppose that no sense of the mysteriousness of God pervades the NT revelation. An over-emphasis on the love of God has all too often led to a soft view of him which has removed the element of awe. *Cf.* R. Otto, *The Idea of the Holy* (Eng. trans. 1927), especially the section on 'The Numinous in the New Testament', pp. 98–109.

[53] For a discussion of God as Wisdom, *cf.* E. K. Lee, *op. cit.*, pp. 97ff. *Cf.* also W. F. Howard, *Christianity according to St John* (1943), pp. 48ff., for the influence of wisdom on John's Logos concept, with its strongly divine character.

created, but created before all things (Ecclus. 1:4,7ff.; 24:14;) and is in fact the principle of creation (Ecclus. 24:10ff.; 42:21; Wisdom 7:21; 9:2). This concept is more relevant to the NT concept of Christ (see discussion on pp. 324ff.); nevertheless, there is the strong implication that this personification of wisdom proceeds from God and therefore witnesses to an essential attribute of God.

In the NT the concept of the wisdom of God is not prominent except in Paul. The phrase occurs once in Luke 11:49 as a formula introducing an oracular utterance.[54] This is sometimes regarded as meaning 'God in his wisdom', but it could imply a quality in the being of God.[55] Since it introduces a citation, it supports the veracity of the words by the inscrutable wisdom of God. If God is wisdom, what he says must be true. In the rest of Luke's writings, wisdom is linked with the Spirit.

Paul contrasts the wisdom of God with man's wisdom (1 Cor. 1:20) and shows its superiority. Man's wisdom is in fact turned to foolishness in the light of God's wisdom. This implies that the latter is the standard by which all other wisdom is gauged. In the same letter Paul speaks of the secret and hidden wisdom of God (1 Cor. 2:7), which can nevertheless be imparted. It is clear that Paul identifies the wisdom which can be communicated with what the apostles proclaimed. Since in the same passage he identifies Christ as 'our wisdom' (1 Cor. 1:30), he is evidently thinking of the wise acts of God in the salvation of man. This is regarded in NT thought as the supreme manifestation of wisdom. Indeed, it is through the church that 'the manifold wisdom of God' is made known even to spiritual powers (Eph. 3:10). What is important for our present purpose is that God's work for man is seen to spring from his wisdom. It is no wonder that Paul marvels at the depth of the 'wisdom and knowledge of God' (Rom. 11:33).

Some distinction has to be drawn between wisdom and knowledge in relation to men, but this distinction is not so appropriate to God.[56] If wisdom is the right use of knowledge, perfect wisdom presuppose perfect knowledge. The NT writers never doubt the perfect knowledge of God. Matthew reports the saying of Jesus that 'your Father knows what you need before you ask him' (6:8), which shows the precise and detailed knowledge of God about the movements and needs of his creatures. He sees what men do in secret (Mt. 6:4,6). Jesus declared that nothing was

[54] Cf. J. M. Creed, *The Gospel According to St Luke* (1930), *ad loc.*
[55] See the discussion in E. E. Ellis, *The Gospel of Luke* (NCB, 1966), *ad loc.*
[56] While there is a clear connection between the wisdom and knowledge of God, a distinction between them could be maintained. F. J. Leenhardt on Romans 11:33 regards wisdom as relating to the execution of God's compassionate purposes, and knowledge to the initiative of God's love in salvation (he takes *gnōsis* in the sense of *proegnō* in Rom. 8:29), *Romans* (Eng. trans. 1961, from CNT, 1957), *ad loc.* Cf. R. Bultmann, *TDNT* 1, pp. 703ff., for a discussion of *gnōsis* in early Christian usage. H. Schlier, *Der Römerbrief* (1977), p. 345, thinks that Paul probably distinguished beween wisdom and knowledge, although he admits the possibility that they may express the same idea. It should be noted that both were current terms in contemporary thought.

hidden that would not be made known (Mt. 10:26).[57]

This perfect knowledge of God is extended in some NT statements to include foreknowledge. It is a logical development. Paul insists that in the perfect planning of God to provide a people conformed to the image of God, he knew beforehand those who were to share that image (Rom. 8:29). Paul's statement has provoked endless debate because it appears to limit man's free will and some discussion of this problem will be included later (see pp. 622ff.). But for the present it must be noted that Paul does not discuss the foreknowledge of God; he simply takes it for granted. He does not doubt that if God knows the present, he must also know the future. This seems to be an essential part of his total conception of God (cf. also Eph. 1:5).

A similar understanding is basic to the Johannine theology, where God's gift of his people to his Son is emphasized in the prayer of Jesus (Jn. 17). The same intimate knowledge of his Son which is possessed by the Father is a pattern for his own followers' knowlege of the Son (Jn. 10:14f.).[58] Indeed such knowledge is extended to include not only the present 'fold', but also the 'other sheep' (Jn. 10:16), another indication of perfect foreknowledge.

There are certain deductions from this conviction that God is all-wise and all-knowing. Such perfect understanding means that when God wills, his plans and purposes are perfect and can never be in error. Indeed, although there are few specific statements in support of this in the NT, it does not seem to be questioned. What God says must be true. He never lies (Tit. 1:2). It is impossible for him to prove false (Heb. 6:18). The absolute truth of God guarantees the consistency of his wisdom and knowledge. There is no suggestion that he ever modifies his plans in the light of his own progressive experience. This aspect of God, which will be expounded more fully in the discussion on the uniqueness of God (see p.110ff.), is essential if his acts in history are to have continuing validity.

The NT writers generally are conscious of the controlling character and obligatory nature of the will of God.[59] Jesus himself shows the deepest

[57] It was the task of the disciples to make things known (*i.e.* the kingdom), for it is clearly the purpose of Jesus that what had been regarded as a mystery should become unveiled. *Cf.* P. Bonnard, *Matthieu* (*CNT*, 1963), p. 151, on this verse.

[58] A difficulty would arise if the *kathōs* in Jn. 10:14 were taken to imply exact correspondence, for it could not be supposed that disciples know the Son in the same sense as the Son knows the Father. But the *kathos* need not be understood in this way. As L. Morris points out (*John, NICNT,* 1971, p. 511 n.42,), it is not so much the degree of knowledge as its reciprocal character which is in view.

[59] It is characteristic of rabbinic Judaism to show great regard for the will of God. Indeed it was insistence on the need for obedience to that will (as seen in the Torah) which led to concentration on regulations for daily life. As E. P. Sanders points out, these commandments were not intended as a burden (*Paul and Palestinian Judaism*, pp. 110ff.). The point that he is making is that the will of God was accepted as calling for implicit obedience. The sense of burden develops when consciousness of one's own liability to obey comes sharply into focus. The rabbis regarded disobedience to the will of God as sin. Bultmann, *TNT* 1, pp. 11f., discusses Jesus interpretation of what he calls 'The demand of God'.

awareness of this. The focus of the Gethsemane experience [60] falls on the words of Jesus, 'Not as I will, but as thou wilt' (Mt. 26:39; *cf.* also verse 42). What God willed must be best for the Son even if it involved an act of self-sacrifice from which the Son momentarily shrank. It is the will of God which dominates the darkest hour of Jesus. It is against this background that the petition 'Thy will be done' in the Lord's Prayer finds significance (Mt. 6:10). To do the Father's will is a sign of belonging to the family of God (Mt. 12:50).[61] This acceptance of the ruling character of God's will is also frequently found in the epistles. Paul begins several letters with the declaration of his apostleship 'by the will of God' (1 Cor. 1:1; 2 Cor. 1:1; Eph. 1:1; Col. 1:1; 2 Tim. 1:1). Moreover, his movements are controlled by God's will (Rom. 15:32). Indeed, even in his approach to those who challenged his policies, Paul asserts that God imposes limits upon him (2 Cor. 10:13). On the other hand God's will is also seen to be a mystery (Eph. 1:9).

Life for the Christian is life according to God's will (Heb. 10:36).[62] That will is never considered to be optional. Even the quest for maturity is subject to the permissive will of God (Heb. 6:3). It is a question of man's will in conjunction with God's. James can point out that all plans should be linked with the Lord's will because life itself is dependent on it (Jas. 4:15).[63] The same idea is expressed in 1 Peter 3:17; 4:2 (*cf.* also 1 Jn. 2:17). Those enduring suffering 'according to God's will' should entrust themselves to a faithful creator (1 Pet. 4:19). The ever present problems involved in God's willing suffering for his people are nowhere discussed. Does this mean that the NT writers were unaware of the problem? This cannot be maintained in view of the intensity of the Gethsemane experience of Jesus. It must be assumed, therefore, that the Christians were convinced about the all-inclusive character of God's wisdom and the perfection of his will. This is bound up with the conviction of God's providential care for his

---

[60] There is a close connection between the agony in Gethsemane and the temptation of Jesus, in that doing the Father's will is the ultimate triumph over all self-centred methods. *Cf.* P. Bonnard, *op. cit.*, 383. This acceptance of God's will as supreme stands out in vivid contrast to the violent aims of the Zealots in their pursuit of what they considered to be God's will.

[61] Naturally, to do the will of God can relate only to that aspect of the will of God that can be done. It is an essentially practical assessment. *Cf.* W. Hendriksen, *Matthew* (1973), p. 543, in a comment on Mt. 12:50. F. V. Filson, *Matthew* (*BC*, 1960), p. 154, comments that this reference reminds us that God was not considered to be morally indifferent. 'As Father he is to be obeyed, respected, loved'.

[62] In the context of Heb. 10:36, the 'will of God' 'suggests a contrast to man's will through the discipline of suffering'; B. F. Westcott, *op. cit.* (1892), *ad loc.* The epistle sets the pattern of Christ himself setting out to do the will of God (Heb. 10:5ff.).

[63] When James urges the use of such an expression as 'if the Lord wills', he is echoing the usage of conventional piety, but he means more than a form of words, *cf.* C. L. Mitton's useful discussion of this phrase, *James*, pp. 170f. The commitment to the will of God is well brought out in one of the *Aboth* sayings (ii.4) in the *Mishnah* (H. Danby's translation, 1933, p. 448) which shows a similar approach to that of James.

people (see previous section p. 79f.). If suffering comes, God must have a purpose in it.[64]

Much confusion arises from the fact that it is generally assumed that all suffering should be avoided. The notion that God could use suffering does not come naturally. But the NT approach to suffering constantly takes it into the sphere of God's purpose. Although it is true that suffering is nowhere explained, there is enough evidence to show what the Christian attitude towards it should be. There is no suggestion that God is less than wise or good because suffering exists. Since the supreme example of suffering lies at the heart of God's redemptive activity in Christ, it cannot be maintained that suffering is alien to the purpose of God. It will always remain a mystery why God chose to redeem mankind the way he did, but this very fact must be taken into account in considering the NT view of God.

Arising from the necessity for Christ to suffer comes the problem of suffering for Christians. It is not surprising that in a hostile world Christians will meet with opposition on account of their faith. This is the key to the advice given in 1 Peter, where to suffer for Christ's sake is seen to be highly probable and in no sense a matter of which to be ashamed. Indeed 1 Peter 4:14 affirms that a special blessing rests on those who are reproached for the name of Christ. This is the least problematic aspect of suffering. Paul, in recounting his experiences in 2 Corinthians 4:7–5:10, in no way criticizes God for the hardships he has endured. He sees these hardships as tools in the hand of God. The present momentary affliction is regarded as 'slight' (2 Cor. 4:17) compared with the weight of glory to follow. Later in the same epistle the apostle gives details of this 'slight' affliction (*cf.* 6:4ff; 11:23ff.), which consists of a harrowing list of calamities which have been seldom equalled or surpassed and yet he has arrived at a triumphant attitude towards them. There is no hint anywhere in this epistle that he resents or questions the wisdom of God in allowing suffering.

In Romans 5:3 Paul actually rejoices in suffering because it develops the quality of endurance. In this same context he speaks of God's love being poured out in our hearts. The two things are clearly not incompatible in his mind.

This positive approach to suffering is found in other parts of the NT. James advises his readers to count it a matter for rejoicing if they meet various trials (Jas. 1:2 ff.). The Apocalypse shows God's concern over the suffering of his people, especially for those who have been martyred for their faith (Rev. 6:9ff.).

---

[64] E. G. Selwyn, *1 Peter*, pp. 78ff., discusses providence and suffering in this epistle. He points out that the modern view that suffering is contrary to God's will finds no countenance in this epistle. The same could be said of the NT as a whole. What is more important than the transitory suffering is the conviction that God's will is right.

It cannot be said that the NT answers all the intellectual problems which arise from God's permitting human suffering, but it does enable Christians to face suffering without losing confidence in the perfection of God's wisdom.

The holiness of God

One of the most characteristic qualities of God in the OT is his holiness. Although people and things and places are described as holy, this is only in the sense of being set apart for God. Holiness is essentially an attribute of God. It marks him out as being utterly pure in thought and attitude. In the prophecy of Isaiah 'the holy One' is a characteristic name for God (*cf.* Is. 6). It is this quality of holiness which creates at once a barrier in man's approach to God, since man becomes conscious of his own lack of holiness in the presence of God. It is because Israel had a holy God that demands were made upon her people to become a holy people, which they certainly failed to fulfil.

Undoubtedly this conviction that God is holy forms an important element in the NT account of salvation. Jesus once addressed God as 'holy Father' (Jn. 17:11). When faced with the ordeal of his passion Jesus was most conscious of the absolute holiness of his Father who had sent him. This ascription of holiness to God is characteristic of the Johannine writings, for it occurs also in 1 John 2:20 and several times in the Apocalypse (Rev. 4:8; 15:4; 16:5). In the most moving of the liturgical passages, the theme of the living creatures centres in the thrice repeated 'Holy' ascribed to him who sits on the throne, which is clearly reminiscent of Isaiah 6:3 (Rev. 4:8). It is clear that the basic assumption of God's holiness is taken over from the OT where it is especially prominent, not only in the levitical ceremonial, but also in the prophetic declarations. It is not surprising that the holiness of God's name figures in the Magnificat with its strong OT flavour (Lk. 1:49). From the levitical source comes the citation in 1 Peter 1:16 (from Lv. 11:44–45) which regards the holiness of God as a pattern for man's holiness. There is no suggestion in the NT that God's character and actions are anything but holy. His purity of thought and deed is unassailable.

The righteousness and justice of God

So far the only moral characteristic of God which has been mentioned is his absolute truthfulness and his holiness. But more needs to be said about the righteousness of God, for this is basic to the whole plan of salvation. In the OT righteousness in God means more than that God always acts in a morally right way. It includes also the fact that God acts on behalf of his people when they are unjustly oppressed. In the NT the apostle Paul is the great exponent of this important characteristic of God. He does not question that God is righteous. He begins his exposition in the epistle to the Romans with the assertion that God's righteousness has been revealed (Rom. 1:17).[65] This is reiterated in Romans 3:21,22. Exegetes debate whether the righteousness of God in these contexts concentrates on what can be imparted rather than what is inherent to God; whatever their conclusion, the association of God and righteousness is clear enough.[66] True righteousness comes from God (cf. Rom. 10:3; Phil. 3:9). In 2 Corinthians 5:21 Paul even states that Christ was made sin 'so that in him we might become the righteousness of God'. Further discussion will later be given on the process of justification (see pp. 501ff.), but at this stage we must acknowledge that such statements as 2 Corinthians 5:21 make sense only if God himself is essentially righteous. Indeed Paul describes the Christian's new nature as 'created after the likeness of God in true righteousness and holiness' (Eph. 4:24), showing righteousness as an essential constituent in God's image.

It may seem surprising that the theme of God's righteousness is not more prominent in the teaching of Jesus, although it is certainly assumed. The demand for righteousness in men presupposes the righteousness of God (Mt. 5:20; 6:33).[67] The most significant statements are those in John's gospel in which Jesus incorporated the idea into his terms of address to God as 'righteous Father' (Jn. 17:25). Righteousness is of utmost import-

---

[65] There has been much debate over whether Paul's use of the expression 'the righteousness of God' (*dikaiosynē Theou*) is intended to refer to a quality in God or not. The genitive may be taken in three ways: (i) as an objective genitive, in which case the righteousness is that which God grants (so Luther); (ii) as a subjective genitive, in which case it refers to that which belongs to God; (iii) as a genitive of origin, in which case it is God's righteousness, but proceeds from God to men. Even under (i) and (iii) there have been many different interpretations of what is meant by righteousness. There is a reluctance among many recent writers to regard righteousness as an attribute of God. E. Käsemann, 'God's Righteousness in Paul', Eng. trans. of his article in *ZTK* 58, 1961, pp. 367–378, in *Journal for Theology and the Church* 1, 1965, pp. 100–110, and reprinted in *New Testament Questions for Today* (1969), pp. 168–182, takes God's righteousness in the sense of his power which creates salvation. By this means Käsemann seeks to retain the subjective sense, but wants to give it a dynamic force. A similar view was earlier proposed by A. Schlatter, *Gottes Gerechtigkeit; ein Kommentar zum Römerbrief* (⁴1965), 36ff., and A. Nygren, *Romans* (Eng. trans. 1952), pp. 146, 152. Käsemann's view was developed by his pupils, C. Müller, *Gottes Gerechtigkeit und Gottes Volk* (1964), who sees righteousness as God's victory, and P. Stuhlmacher, *Gottes Gerechtigkeit bei Paulus* (1963), who regards it as an exclusive redemptive act. J. A. Bollier is another advocate of the subjective interpretation ('The Righteousness of God', *Int* 8, 1954, 404ff.).

The Catholic writer, K. Kertelge, '*Rechtfertigung' bei Paulus* (1967), denies that righteousness is descriptive of God's essence, but maintains that it denotes God's activity. For a discussion of these various viewpoints, cf. J. A. Ziesler, *The Meaning of Righteousness in Paul* (1972), pp. 9ff., and cf. also M. T. Brauch's appendix, 'Perspectives on God's Righteousness in Recent German Discussion', in E. P. Sanders, *Paul and Palestinian Judaism*, 523–542. Ziesler himself gives a detailed linguistic study of the word righteousness and its cognates.

[66] H. Conzelmann, 'Die Rechtfertigungslehre des Paulus: Theologie oder Anthropologie?', *EvT* 28, 1968, pp. 389–404, and R. Bultmann, '*DIKAIOSYNĒ THEOU*', *JBL* 83, 1964, pp. 12ff., both rejected the view that relates righteousness to the character of God (the subjective interpretation). They understand the term anthropologically, in which case it has no contribution to make to an understanding of the righteousness of God.

[67] In Matthew's use of the term 'righteousness', there is the sense of conformity to the will of God (cf. G. Schrenk, '*dikaiosynē*', *TDNT* 2, pp. 198f.). If what is done in accordance with God's will is righteousness, that will itself must partake of the character of its own demands.

ance when God's judgments come into view. An absolutely righteous God must judge in an absolutely righteous way (*cf.* Rom. 2:5).

This latter concept involves the idea of God's impartiality. It was difficult for Jews to accept this idea, for they were convinced that Israel was a favoured nation, which made it superior to the Gentile peoples in the sight of God.[68] It was this strong bias which threatened to cause real problems when Jews and Gentiles had to mix in the early Christian communities. Peter needed a special vision to convince him that God was impartial (Acts 10:34), and until he was convinced of this he was unprepared to visit a Gentile home to preach the gospel. It became obvious to him through the vision that his former view of God was defective. That he had thoroughly grasped the impartiality of God is seen from his statement in 1 Peter 1:17. By then it had become axiomatic that God the Father 'judges each one impartially according to his deeds.' (*Cf.* Heb. 6:10; Rom. 3:5).

Another Jew who made a *volte-face* when he became a Christian was Saul of Tarsus. More than any other he wrestled with the problem of God's special concern for the Jewish people, but as a Christian he never doubted that God was impartial and that both Jew and Gentile must be included in the plan of salvation on an equal footing.[69] On two occasions he asserted as axiomatic that God shows no partiality (Rom. 2:11; Gal. 2:6),[70] the second of which deals with the apostolic office. The idea definitely excluded any notion of favouritism with God, which would not be in keeping with absolute justice.

An important side to the righteousness and justice of God is his wrath. There are sufficient instances of emphasis on God's wrath in the NT to make it important to define its meaning. The precise meaning has been subject to debate. Indeed of all the aspects of God in the NT this is perhaps the most questioned. Some reduce wrath (*orgē*) to the effect of human sin, thus getting rid of all notion of anger in God because this is considered to be irrational.[71] But this is an unsatisfactory way of dealing with the NT

---

[68] Although there were rabbis who were prepared to concede that Gentiles could be righteous (provided they kept the Torah), the general approach was that salvation did not stretch to those outside the covenant. A similar view is found in the Dead Sea Scrolls. *Cf.* E. P. Sanders' discussion on this, *op. cit.*, pp. 206ff., 240ff.

[69] Sanders, *op. cit.*, p. 499, brings out an important aspect in the change in Paul's thinking when he states that before his conversion the apostle would not have been able to think that Jews were sinners, whereas as a Jew he would have been convinced that Gentiles were. In that case Jews and Gentiles were definitely not on the same footing. Paul's conversion, with its conviction that Jews were equally sinners before God radically changed his approach to universalism.

[70] See the comment on 'partiality' in my commentary on *Galatians* (NCB, 1969), *ad loc.*

[71] *Cf.* C. H. Dodd, *Romans*, pp. 22ff., for an exposition of this view. He considers that Paul retains the concept of the 'wrath of God' to describe 'an inevitable process of cause and effect in a moral universe'. He concludes that 'we cannot think with full consistency of God in terms of the highest human ideals of personality and yet attribute to him the irrational passion of anger.' Irrational anger must certainly be ruled out, but the NT view of God's wrath is not based on such an interpretation. C. K. Barrrett, *Romans*, p. 33,

evidence. In Romans the expression 'the wrath of God' occurs in 1:18 (*cf.* 5:9; 12:19; 13:5; *cf.* also 9:22), and it is impossible in this case to empty the phrase of any relevance to the attributes of God. Paul speaks of a wrath of God which has been revealed (*apokalyptetai*) in precisely the same way as he has just previously stated that God's righteousness has been revealed.[72] It is inescapable that Paul intended a connection between the two concepts. It seems most reasonable to suppose that 'wrath' is the negative aspect of God's righteousness.[73] It does not express anger in the sense in which it is applied to man, *i.e.* of an uncontrolled outburst of passion (which would certainly be an irrational concept), but it must express the revulsion of absolute holiness towards all that is unholy. This is in harmony with the context where 'wrath' is explicitly said to be against (*epi*) ungodliness and wickedness.[74] The same may be said of Romans 5:9 where salvation is said to be from 'the wrath' which may well denote the wrath of God, as an expression of God's rejection of all that is sinful. Salvation of the sinner does not affect God's attitude towards sin.

It is not sufficient to define wrath as the principle of retribution in a moral universe without connecting the principle to its source, *i.e.* to the nature of God. Unless we find some place for the moral displeasure of God, we shall make light of his judgment, which finds no small place in NT thought.[75] When Paul says in Colossians 3:6 that the wrath of God is coming, he must mean more than that a principle of retribution is approaching.[76] The expression has more force if the condemnation of the

---

is nearer the point when he says, 'Wrath is God's personal (though never malicious or, in a bad sense, emotional) reaction against sin.' C. E. B. Cranfield, *Romans*, 1, p. 109, asks the pointed question whether even human goodness can exist without indignation against wickedness.

[72] The use of the same verb (*apokalyptetai*) in both Rom. 1:17 and 1:18, must mean that Paul intended the latter to be understood in terms of the former. This means that both righteousness and wrath are revealed in the proclamation of the gospel. *Cf.* Cranfield, *op. cit.*, pp. 109f.

[73] J. Murray, *Romans*, p. 35, is clear that the wrath of God cannot be emptied of its emotional and affective character, although he recognizes a vital distinction between man's anger and God's wrath. 'Wrath is the holy revulsion of God's being against that which is the contradiction of his holiness.' M. Black, *Romans*, p. 48, regards God's wrath as a manifestation of his righteousness. He does, however, concede an element of truth in Dodd's view.

[74] Murray, *op. cit.*, p. 36, rightly says, 'There is a positive outgoing of the divine displeasure'.

[75] Many scholars note that God's wrath is an eschatological term, although it clearly has a present significance. It is at the last judgment that God's wrath will be manifested, but there is a constant reaction of God's holiness against sin. See C. K. Barrett, *op. cit.*, p. 34, on its eschatological significance. Nevertheless C. E. B. Cranfield, *op. cit.*, p. 107, rightly criticizes Barrett for his view that wrath is a clear signal of the revealing of God's righteousness, on the grounds that the 'observable situation' of which Barrett speaks would have to be something entirely new.

[76] The eschatological aspect is again present in this context and is more explicit than in Rom. 1:18. R. P. Martin, *Colossians: The Church's Lord and the Christian's Liberty* (1972), p. 110, notes that Paul's eschatology is flexible enough to hold together both time-aspects (future and present). In commenting on Col. 3:6, E. Lohse, *Colossians and Philemon* (Eng. trans. *Hermeneia*, 1971, from *KEK*, 1968), p. 139, denies that wrath indicates an emotion of God, but God's judgment of wrath. Yet God's judgment cannot be wholly detached from his continual reaction against sin. 'Wrath' cannot, in short, be received as a term which describes only God's final act of judgment. *Cf.* G. Stählin, *TDNT* 5, 424f., for a recognition that an

evils mentioned in the previous verse is based on the active opposition of God against them (*cf.* also Eph. 5:6). It should be noted that when the apostle assures the Thessalonians that God has not destined us for wrath (1 Thes. 5:9), he is writing to Christians and his words cannot cancel out the statements about God's wrath elsewhere.

The gospels have only one direct statement on the subject of God's wrath. In John 3:36 Jesus asserts that the wrath of God abides on those who disobey the Son, in which case it is connected with God's love for the Son. Love and wrath are evidently not incompatible in the same person. Indeed intense love must have an element of jealous regard for the object of love and reaction against those who reject the object of love. Some concept of wrath is needed to safeguard the purity of divine love.[77] In the Apocalypse this theme of wrath is given a particular setting in scenes of final judgment. On the opening of the sixth seal, the inhabitants of the earth cry to the mountains and rocks to hide them from the 'face of him who is seated on the throne, and from the wrath of the Lamb' (Rev. 6:16), which vividly portrays some active 'wrath'. Moreover, the idea of judgment occurs in Revelation 14:10 as the wine of God's wrath poured into the 'cup of his anger', while the idea is further developed when the harvesting angel throws the vintage into 'the great wine press of the wrath of God' (14:19). The vision portrays a terrifying picture of God's wrath which is impossible to whittle away. Similarly the seven bowls are said to be 'full of the wrath of God' (15:7; *cf.* 15:1; 16:1). The closing vision of the warrior executing judgment has as its climax his treading of the 'wine press of the fury of the wrath of God the Almighty' (19:15), a vigorous expression of the positive wrath of God. Nevertheless, the distinctive feature of the book of Revelation is the description of wrath as the wrath of the Lamb, which unmistakably links it with the cross, and sets its manifestation in history.[78]

It is not surprising that the writer of the epistle to the Hebrews describes God as a 'consuming fire' (12:29) and also speaks of a 'fearful prospect of judgment, and a fury of fire which will consume the adversaries' (10:27).[79] Earlier in the same epistle, the statement that God swore in his wrath (cited

---

element of God's displeasure must be retained. A. T. Hanson in his study, *The Wrath of the Lamb* (1957), concludes that the wrath of God in the NT in not an attitude of God, but a condition of men. He, therefore, regards it as impersonal.

[77] G. Stählin, *op. cit.*, p. 425, sees wrath and love as mutually inclusive, and regards the wrath of God as arising from his love and mercy. 'Only he who knows the greatness of wrath will be mastered by the greatness of mercy'.

[78] The expression 'wrath of the lamb' is remarkable in this respect, for nowhere else in the NT are 'wrath' and 'sacrifice' so closely knit. This has led A. T. Hanson, *op. cit.*, p. 178, to the conclusion that wrath in the book of Revelation is more profoundly Christian than elsewhere in the NT. We would prefer to say that the basic exposition of wrath in the NT is linked with the total work of God in salvation, and that it finds its most explicit expression in this book.

[79] There is some debate over the meaning of *pyros zēlos* in Heb. 10:27. *Cf.* A. T. Hanson, *op. cit.*, appendix 5, pp. 213f.

from Ps. 95) is twice made in the course of the discussion of God's dealing with his disobedient people (3:11; 4:3). It is impossible to conclude that the NT writers had any view of the righteousness of God which did not include an element of wrath.

The love and grace of God

That God is a God of love is another assumption which is basic to all parts of the NT. It has a firm basis in the OT[80] and Jewish literature,[81] but takes on a sharper focus and a more dominant role in the NT. In the gospels the notion comes to the surface more clearly in John than in the synoptics. A statement like that made by Jesus in Luke 11:42, that the Pharisees were neglecting the justice and love of God (*i.e.* love towards God), is sufficient to show that there was no fundamental contradiction between righteousness and love in man; and there is no reason to suppose that there is in God. In the synoptic gospels, the love of God is assumed rather than stated.[82] In the Johannine account the Father's love for the Son is the main evidence that love is an essential characteristic of God (Jn. 3:35; 5:20; 10:17; 15:9; 16:27; 17:23f.). Jesus was deeply conscious of the Father's love for him as the foundation stone and pattern of God's love for people (17:23). It is integral to the teaching of Jesus that for man the most desirable thing is to be the object of God's love (Jn. 14:21, 23). The most significant feature in the statement that God so loved the world that he gave his Son (Jn. 3:16) is not that God loved, but that he loved so comprehensively.

The apostle Paul pursued the same line of thought. In the epistle which most emphasizes the righteousness of God, he can speak with equal certainty about the love of God. God's love has been poured into our hearts through the Spirit (Rom. 5:5), a vivid way of speaking of the communicating of God's love to man. That love is most seen in God's saving work for sinners (Rom. 5:8). The consequence for believers is that they will never be separated from that love (Rom. 8:39). Love makes them more than conquerors (Rom. 8:37). Indeed, the love of God is a familiar part of such benedictions as 2 Corinthians 13:14 (*cf.* also 2 Cor. 13:11) and Ephesians 6:23. It comes in Paul's prayers for the Thessalonians (2 Thes. 2:16;

[80] The love of God in the OT is concerned more with the nation than with individuals. There are in fact surprisingly few instances where particular persons are singled out as objects of God's love. A. W. Argyle remarks about the testimony of Hellenistic Judaism, that although God's love is extended to the whole creation, it is still specially set by an act of will and choice upon Israel (*God in the New Testament*, p. 76).

[81] In Judaism there were isolated statements which underlined the importance of God's love, but it cannot be said that this concept was foundational in Jewish theology. *Cf.* G. Quell and E. Stauffer, 'agapē', *TDNT* 1, pp. 38ff. 'The lofty sayings about love remain isolated. The underlying basis of Judaistic theology and ethics is still righteousness – in spite of everything'.

[82] For a thorough discussion of the synoptic evidence, see C. Spicq, *Agapē in the New Testament*, 1 (1963). *Cf.* also J. Moffatt, *Love in the New Testament* (1929), pp. 67–130. He comments that Jesus never speaks of God as love or as loving people, and yet he implies it (p. 67). His use of the title Father testifies to this. As Argyle (*op. cit.*, p. 77) rightly notes, Jesus revealed God's love less by words than by deeds of compassion and forgiveness.

3:5). In the latter prayer the love of God is regarded as the aim to which the Christians' minds should be directed ('may the Lord direct your hearts to the love of God'). A similar idea occurs in Jude 21.

The clearest expression of the loving character of God is found in 1 John, which contains the statement that God is love (1 Jn. 4:8, 16).[83] This focuses attention on the essential character of love in God to the extent that love can be regarded as summing up in itself God's approach to people. This love must be sharply distinguished from man's love. It is God who loves, who initiates love, not man (1 Jn. 4:10, 19). John is overwhelmed by the thought of God's love which has enabled people to become sons of God (1 Jn. 3:1). Moreover, if people are to love each other, God's love must be the source (1 Jn. 4:7). In fact those who do not show love to those in need are closing their own hearts to the abiding presence of God's love (1 Jn. 3:17). It is clear that John is not expounding a merely ontological characteristic of God, a quality locked up in the heart of God. Indeed, it may be questioned whether such an abstract form of love is conceivable, since love must have an object. The fact that so much is made in John's gospel of the Father's love for the Son is a strong indication that it is within the Godhead that God's love has an object. The NT is mainly concerned, however, with man as the object of God's love.

Closely allied to the same idea is the use of the title 'Beloved' of Jesus by the voice from heaven at his baptism (Mt. 3:17; Mk. 1:11; Lk. 3:22; *cf.* also 2 Pet. 1:17). This has most force as a title, but even if the word (*agapētos*) is used adjectivally, it still bears strong witness to the intensity of love between God the Father and the Son.[84] Moreover, the extraordinary nature of the pronouncement shows the importance for men generally to understand the motive behind the whole mission of Jesus. A similar form of address is found at the transfiguration (Mt. 17:5; Mk. 9:7; *cf.* Lk. 9:35).

There are two other aspects of God which are so closely linked to love that they may properly be considered in conjunction with it. First there is the understanding that God is a God of grace. The whole concept of grace will need to be explored when the doctrine of salvation is examined (see p. 602ff.), but for our present purpose it is necessary to note that 'the grace of God' denotes an essential feature of God's love. When applied to God, the word grace denotes the favour of God towards those who do not deserve his favour, and therefore came to be used particularly of God's saving work in Christ.[85] In the epistles it has become a basic assumption,

---

[83] J. Moffatt, *Grace in the New Testament* (1931), 253, remarks about 1 Jn. 4:16, 'This is not an abstract reflection upon the divine nature, much less an intuition of some inward light on an eternal unity, but a deduction from the revelation of God in the life and career of Jesus Christ'.

[84] This kind of love is what A. W. Argyle, *op. cit.*, p. 78, describes as 'the electing love', which called Jesus to suffer and die.

[85] For a discussion of the usage of the concept of 'grace' (*charis*) in the NT, *cf.* H. H. Esser, *NIDNTT* 2, pp. 118ff.

so much so that it frequently occurs in the opening salutations and in the concluding benedictions, especially in the Pauline letters. God is seen as one who bestows unmerited favours on the objects of his love. God's grace is more than his gracious acts, although it includes these.[86] It involves his nature. His love is of such a quality that it gives unstintingly. Grace is another name for the outgoing character of his love. Sometimes God's grace becomes almost objectified in the results that it achieves, as when Luke can say that men saw the grace of God in believers (Acts 11:23). An even more suggestive expression is that in Acts 13:43 where Paul and Barnabas are described as urging their hearers to 'continue in the grace of God', which means that they are to expose themselves to God's grace.

It is to be noted that the word 'grace' does not occur at all in the synoptic gospels. But this does not mean that the grace of God is not in view, for Jesus revealed in his own acts and teaching the initiative of God. The mission of Jesus was a supreme revelation of the God of grace. There is never any suggestion that man could do anything to win favour with God.

The apostle Paul was deeply convinced of his indebtedness to God's grace. He saw his own calling as an act of grace (Gal. 1:15). He had no doubt that Christians are saved by God's grace (Rom. 3:24; 5:15; Eph. 2:5; Tit. 2:11). He was overwhelmed by the superlative quality of that grace (2 Cor. 9:14; Eph. 2:7). He sees it as a subject for praise (Eph. 1:6). He never tires of speaking of it. He views it as a communicable gift (e.g. 1 Cor. 1:4; 3:10; 15:10; 2 Tim. 1:9). It is diametrically opposed to any method depending on human effort (Gal. 2:21; Rom. 11:6).[87] If there was one characteristic of God which captured the imagination of Paul more than another, it was the grace of God.[88]

Other NT writers are similarly impressed. In Hebrews the throne of God is described as the throne of grace (Heb. 4:16),[89] because it is characteristic

---

[86] This does not mean that grace is a static quality in God. It is rather the quality which prompts the acts of God. Argyle, op. cit., p. 82, defines the NT concept of the grace of God as 'his unmerited and prevenient love towards man which takes the initiative in freely giving and forgiving. . .' In grace is manifested the total plan of salvation.

[87] R. Bultmann sees a difference between the Jewish view of merit and the Christian view in this approach to grace (Jesus and the Word, p. 148). E. P. Sanders has been critical of Bultmann's appeal to the doctrine of merit (op. cit., 43ff.), but this criticism does not alter the fact that any emphasis on man's achievements must affect one's view of God's grace.

[88] It makes an interesting study to note the forms of salutation and conclusion in Paul's epistles. Every one of them mentions grace at the beginning and the end. J. Moffatt, op. cit., 135ff., shows how novel this is by comparison with contemporary letters. Paul's reference to grace is not formal, but expressive of deep conviction that the gospel was based on the unmerited favour of God. It is significant that the often repeated expression 'Grace . . . from God' emphasizes that the greeting was to be understood theologically.

[89] B. F. Westcott, Hebrews, p. 109, says that the 'throne of grace' is 'that revelation of God's presence in which His grace is shown in royal majesty'. It is possible, however, that the expression may be the anti-type to the OT mercy-seat (so F. F. Bruce, Hebrews, p. 86), in which case the grace is the favour of God seen in his atoning work. According to J. Héring, Hebrews, p. 36, the genitive is used in a very loose way as a genitive of quality (i.e. merciful-ness).

of his royal activity. James can speak of God's gift of grace to the humble (Jas. 4:6), a thought which is also found in 1 Peter 5:5. This latter epistle speaks of the manifold character of God's grace (4:10),[90] describes God as the God of all grace (5:10) and indeed states that the whole purpose of the writing was to declare 'the true grace of God' (5:12).

The second aspect of God closely allied to love is the mercy of God. The root meaning of 'mercy' is compassion, hence its close link with love. It is essentially outgoing. Mercy is also inseparably linked with grace,[91] but is more specifically connected with righteousness. It is when the righteous judgments of God are considered that his mercy becomes a vivid reality. If he must condemn what is unrighteous because he himself is righteous, he extends mercy to those who would otherwise be condemned because mercy is as much a part of his nature as righteousness. This idea of God's mercy is not unique to the NT. It finds its roots in the OT.[92] It is reflected in Mary's song (Lk. 1:54) and in Zechariah's (Lk. 1:72, 78). Luke records the exhortation of Jesus, 'Be merciful, even as your Father is merciful' (6:36), which sets the pattern for man's approach in accordance with the basic nature of God. The publican's prayer for mercy, also recorded by Luke, presupposes that God was disposed to a merciful approach to sinners (18:13).

Again the apostle Paul is deeply conscious of the mercy of God (Rom. 9:15–16,18) as part of God's prerogative. He several times speaks of obtaining mercy, which means receiving the results of God's merciful acts (Rom. 11:30–32; 1 Cor. 7:25; 2 Cor. 4:1; 1 Tim. 1:16). There is no suggestion that the quality of mercy is alien to God, nor that it conflicts with his essential righteousness. It is part of the apostle's understanding of the total nature of God. Indeed, Paul uses the striking expression 'Father of mercies' of God in 2 Corinthians 1:3, which draws attention to his compassionate nature. It echoes Ex.36:6; Psalm 86:15; 145:8 which speak of God as merciful and gracious. Peter is similarly convinced of the importance of mercy in the incorporation of Gentiles into the people of God (1 Pet. 2:10). James also, in appealing to the OT, regards as axiomatic that the Lord is compassionate and merciful (Jas. 5:11).

[90] In 1 Pet. 4:10, God's manifold grace describes the infinitely variegated forms of God's freely bestowed bounty (*cf.* J. N. D. Kelly, *Peter and Jude* (BC, 1969), *ad loc.*). E. Best thinks that this epistle lacks something of the wonder seen in Paul's use of grace, but he admits that grace stands for God's gracious activity towards men (*1 Peter*, NCB, 1971, p. 72). The distinction between gracious acts and gracious character is, however, very fine.

[91] R. C. Trench, *Synonyms of the New Testament*, [9]1880), pp. 166ff., maintains that grace is concerned over man's guilt, while mercy is concerned with his misery. For a discussion of the use of *eleos* (mercy) in the NT, *cf.* H. H. Esser, *NIDNTT* II, pp. 596ff.

[92] In Jewish thinking the mercy of God was generally mentioned in connection with obedience to the covenant. In the Dead Sea Scrolls the Jewish doctrine is that the reward of the good is by mercy, while punishment of the wicked is deserved (*cf.* E. P. Sanders, *op. cit.*, p. 293). The basis of this view is that man's works, through contributory to, can never be entirely sufficient for salvation. God's mercy must have a place.

The apostle Paul sometimes uses another word – kindness (*chrēstotēs*) – when describing the gracious attitude of God. He once links it with the quality of severity (Rom. 11:22). It may seem difficult to see how these two facets of God's character can exist in one person, but Paul is not worried by this difficulty. To him both kindness and severity are essential characteristics. He sees God's kindness as intended to lead people to repentance (Rom. 2:4), although he recognizes that his Jewish contemporaries have incurred the righteous judgment of God (Rom. 2:5). The close connection between God's grace and his kindness is clearly seen in Ephesians 2:7 where God's immeasurable riches of grace are equated with his kindness towards us in Christ. Kindness is therefore practically synonymous with grace. This may be seen in the statement in 1 Peter 2:3 that the Christians addressed have tasted the kindness of the Lord. Kindness is further linked with the goodness of God in Titus 3:4, where both are stated to have 'appeared' (*i.e.* in the provision of salvation for man).

The goodness and faithfulness of God

There are a few significant statements in the NT which focus on the goodness of God and which deserve separate consideration. The concept of goodness is difficult to define but is nevertheless generally recognized. It is closely linked with the moral holiness of God. It is significant that the word 'good' (*agathos*) is applied exclusively to God by Jesus when declining the rich young man's address to him as 'good teacher' (Mt. 19:17; Mk. 10:17; *cf.* Lk. 18:18–19).[93] The statement 'Only one is good, God', makes clear that the character of God is such that it is itself the standard that should determine all human notions of goodness.[94] Jesus was not on this occasion disclaiming that he was good, but was challenging the right of any man to be the arbitrator of goodness since this belongs to God alone. Whatever goodness anyone else possesses is derived from him.[95] This is supported by such an OT statement as Psalm 53:1ff., which is cited by Paul in Romans 3:12, and which affirms that no-one is good. Paul uses it to demonstrate man's need, but he does not bring out so specifically as Jesus had done the unique goodness of God.

---

[93] There is a difference between the forms in which Matthew and Mark record these words. In Mark's account Jesus says, 'Why do you call me good?', whereas Matthew has 'Why do you ask me about what is good?' Mark's account may suggest that Jesus himself is not good and it has therefore been suggested that Matthew has modified the words to avoid such a misunderstanding (*cf.* G. M. Styler, 'Stages in Christology in the Synoptic Gospels', *NTS* 10, 1963–4, pp. 404ff.). Yet both accounts point to God as the ultimate source of all goodness and this is undoubtedly where the emphasis falls.

[94] It is important to note the radical distinction between defining what is good in terms of God and defining the good apart from God. As J. I. Packer says, 'Man is good, and things are good, just so far as they conform to the will of God' (*NBD*, p. 482).

[95] It is well to remember that God's works are good even when man corrupts and distorts them (*cf.* G. Wingren, *op. cit.*, p. 47).

Although the faithfulness of God is a different kind of attribute from goodness, it may be linked with it in the sense that were God faithless to his word he could not be good. Paul was deeply impressed with the faithfulness of God. He is faithful in calling people into fellowship with his Son (1 Cor. 1:9) and in guarding them against excessive testing of their faith (1 Cor. 10:13) or from the attacks of the evil one (2 Thes. 3:3). The faithfulness of God is even cited by Paul as a guarantee of the dependability of his own word – whether yes or no (2 Cor. 2:18). Moreover, God remains faithful even when men are faithless (2 Tim. 2:13). There is a rock-like quality about the apostle's conviction about God's reliability.

In other NT writings the idea is not prominent, but does occur. In Hebrews 10:23, the unwavering faithfulness of God becomes the basis for the appeal to the readers to hold fast to the confession of their hope. In the list of heroes of faith Sarah is said to have considered him faithful who had promised (Heb. 11:11), showing the close connection between human faith and God's faithfulness. Peter refers to the faithfulness of the Creator as an inspiration to sufferers (1 Pet. 4:19), while John mentions God's faithfulness to forgive sins (1 Jn. 1:9). There is an implicit assumption that God can be relied on to fulfil his promises.

We may perhaps include in this section a note about the expression 'the God of peace' which is particularly familiar through the concluding salutation in Romans 15:33 and in 1 Thessalonians 5:23. The more widely used form of the idea 'peace from (*apo*) God' occurs in the opening greetings in all Paul's epistles and in 1 Peter 1:2. It appears that the quality which God can impart has become an ascription to him. The form 'God of peace' is suggestive because it points to the absence of conflict in God. Indeed 1 Corinthians 14:33 brings this out explicitly – 'God is not a God of confusion, but of peace.' Peace therefore describes an attitude of God as well as a quality which he imparts. Peace cannot be bestowed 'from God' unless it is an integral part of his nature. Man in his fallen state is in a perpetual state of tension until reconciled to God. But such a state of tension does not exist in God. There is no suggestion anywhere in NT teaching that God is ever uncertain as to his actions, nor frustrated in his plans. His mind is always in a state of equilibrium. It is no wonder that Paul in desiring to allay anxiety among Christians, not only exhorts them to commit themselves to God, but also assures them that the peace of God will garrison their hearts and minds (Phil. 4:7). In the same passage he assures his readers of the continued presence of the God of peace (Phil. 4:9).

This peace and serenity of God may perhaps be represented symbolically in the Apocalypse by the sea of glass before the throne of God (Rev. 4:6). It is characteristic of NT theology that at the heart of the universe and behind all the turbulent affairs of men is a God of peace.

The uniqueness of God

It has been the habit of systematic theologians to discuss the incommunicable attributes of God under a separate category from those that can be shared. These attributes are those that establish the uniqueness of God as compared with man. But the NT writers do not discuss such matters. With their strong OT background they assume the uniqueness of God and therefore do not hesitate to ascribe to him attributes which are totally inapplicable in a human context. Even so, such ascriptions are sparse, which suggests that they formed part of the basic assumptions of the NT writers and only incidentally came to expression. There is moreover a complete absence of any speculative element.

That God is unchangeable is part of the OT heritage and finds explicit acknowledgment in the quotation from Psalm 102:25–27 in Hebrews 1:10f. This characteristic evidently made a profound impression on the writer for he mentions it again in 6:17.[96] It is, on the other hand, implicit in the NT appeals to the fulfilment of OT predictions. It assumes that God, who has revealed himself in the past, is the same as the one who now reveals himself in Jesus Christ. The unchangeable nature of God is the rock on which the old and new covenants can stand together. It is important in this connection to draw a distinction between the nature of the revelation of God achieved at any point in history and the essential characteristics of the God so revealed. It cannot be maintained that no advancement has been made in man's understanding of God since the OT revelation, but NT theology is based on the assumption that God himself has not changed in the process. Indeed we may go further and state that there is no suggestion in the NT that it is possible for God to change. This aspect of changelessness is, in fact, essential if NT theology is to have any abiding validity.

Another consideration is the invisibility of God. The Johannine statement 'no-one has ever seen God' (Jn. 1:18) is fully in accord with the OT conceptions.[97] This invisibility is one of the foundations of the revelatory character of the mission of Jesus. Paul makes clear that God the Creator has made himself known in his works (Rom. 1:19),[98] but in saying this he implies that there are aspects of God which cannot be known. In 1 Timothy 1:17 is included in the somewhat formalized ascription to God, his invisi-

---

[96] Heb. 6:17 speaks of the unchangeable character of God's purpose. This must not be made to suggest that God's unchangeable purpose stands over against the nature of God as if he were bound by his own immutable purposes, for what God intends is an exact revelation of what he is. As H. W. Montefiore (*Hebrews*, p. 112) points out, God cannot deny his own moral nature.

[97] While there are some OT statements which might suggest that some had seen God (*e.g.* Ex. 24:9–11), yet the OT theophanies are at most only partial revelations of God. The statement in Jn. 1:18 is in line with Ex. 33:20. *Cf.* L. Morris, *John*, p. 113.

[98] C. E. B. Cranfield, *Romans* 1, p. 113, notes that the expressions 'what is knowable' (*to gnōston tou Theou*) should probably be understood in the sense of 'God, in so far as He is objectively knowable' (*i.e.* of 'being experienceable'). This would not imply that a complete knowledge is possible. Cranfield thinks that Paul was wanting to preserve the truth of 'the mysteriousness and hiddenness of God'.

bility,[99] which is specifically mentioned only here in the NT.[100]

Closely linked and occurring in the same statement in 1 Timothy 1:17 is the idea of the immortality of God, which occurs also in Romans 1:23. The concept may be indebted more to Hellenistic than to Jewish thought, but the abiding 'living' character of God is supported by the frequent NT use of the description 'the living God' (Heb. 3:12; 9:14; 10:31; 12:22; Acts 14:15; Mt. 16:16; 26:63). The possibility of the death of God could not be further removed from NT thought.[101] A God who is changeless must be a God who is immortal. Such a God can rightly be described as 'eternal' (Rom. 16:26).

The unity of God

Our purpose here will be to bring together the main NT evidence for the trinity and then to assess its significance. It must be remembered that although the intertestamental Jews were strongly monotheistic, there are not wanting indications in the OT that God was not regarded as rigidly one.[102] Such an expression as 'the Lord of hosts' at least implies that God is not alone (*cf.* 1 Ki. 22:19ff.; Ps. 89:5–8). The armies of heaven or the 'sons of God' (as in Jb. 1:6; 38:7; Ps. 29:1; 89:6) show that God has agents. Some have even seen the expression 'Lord of hosts' as equivalent to Yahweh *who is* hosts, but perhaps not too much should be made of this. Of greater significance is the frequently mentioned 'angel of Yahweh', who sometimes appears in human form, but is nevertheless recognized as God (*cf.* Gn. 16:7–14; 18:1ff.; Ex. 3:2–6;). Nevertheless at times the 'angel' is distin-

---

[99] J. N. D. Kelly, *The Pastoral Epistles* (BC, 1963), p. 56, observes that 'invisible' was a commonplace in Jewish thought about the Godhead.

[100] Note also the expression in 1 Tim. 6:16 denoting that God dwells in light unapproachable. The metaphor of the brilliance of light is closely linked with the idea of invisibility. *Cf.* W. Hendriksen, *Commentary on 1 and 2 Timothy and Titus* (1957), p. 208, on this passage.

[101] The 'death of God' theologians certainly do not base their view on the NT, but begin with a total secular view of the world. Their attempt to approach 'Christian' theology through the eyes of modern non-theistic secular society unavoidably results in a complete distortion of the NT evidence. But this does not disturb the 'death of God' advocates, for they begin with the assumption that the NT category of God is now outgrown. For an exposition of their views and an assessment of the influences which produced such a totally non-exegetical approach to Christian thought, *cf.* K. Hamilton, *God is Dead: the Anatomy of a Slogan* (1966). *Cf.* also T. J. J. Altizer, *The Gospel of Christian Atheism* (1966); P. M. van Buren, *The Secular Meaning of the Gospel* (1963). These latter two works are a significant example of the radical type of 'theology' which results when an inadequate (or rather in this case, a non-existent) God supplies the key to the system. The NT theologian is concerned with the religious ideas of his sources irrespective of whether these ideas are culturally acceptable. It is the task of the systematic theologian to present the basic facts of the NT in the setting of contemporary society, but he cannot begin with a viewpoint which is totally alien to the NT, and expect to reintrepret the Christian position in the light of this. *Cf.* T. Oglethorpe, *The 'Death of God' Controversy* (1966); L. Morris, *The Abolition of Religion* (1964).

[102] For a useful account of the OT evidence as a background for the NT view, *cf.* G. A. F. Knight, *A Biblical Approach to the Doctrine of the Trinity* (1953). Behind the strong monotheism there were other factors which prepared the way for the later NT revelation. E. J. Fortman, *The Triune God* (1972), p. 9, does not admit even of the existence of 'veiled signs' of a trinity of persons in the OT, but concedes that the OT gives the words (Father, Son, Word, Wisdom, Spirit) which the NT uses.

guished from Yahweh (Ex. 33:2,3). It is certainly significant for the NT teaching about the trinity.

An entirely new factor was nevertheless introduced with the emergence of the Christian gospel, which led to a development of the monotheistic approach and ultimately to the doctrine of the trinity.[103] Of the trinity there are many adumbrations in the NT, although it cannot be said that the doctrine is expounded. Indeed it is significant that none of the NT writers sees the need to speculate about such a doctrine. They are content to present data which imply the divine nature of both Christ and the Spirit and which naturally give rise to reflections about the unity of God. In drawing attention to the trinity at this early stage in our examination of NT thought, we must unavoidably anticipate our later discussion on the deity of Christ and on the person and activity of the Holy Spirit. Yet no presentation of the NT view of God would be complete without some section on trinitarian developments.

The NT evidence may be summarized under four different types of passages. First, there are a few passages where deliberate trinitarian formulae are used. In Matthew 28:19 the name of the Father, the Son and the Spirit occurs in the baptismal formula. Problems have arisen over this formula, because in the book of Acts baptism is carried out only in the name of Jesus. Even if the trinitarian formula in Matthew is a development from the Acts type of formula, it is clear evidence of an early recognition that the names of the Father, Son and Spirit are inextricably linked.

Another such passage is 2 Corinthians 13:14, where Paul adds a benediction involving God, the Lord Jesus Christ and the Holy Spirit.[104] No distinction is made between them and it is a reasonable assumption that Paul regarded them as co-equal Persons.[105] A similar form of greeting is found in Revelation 1:4 which refers to God as the one who is and who was and who is to come, to the Spirit as the 'seven spirits' and to the Son as Jesus Christ.

The second group of passages are those cast in triadic form. In Ephesians 4:4–6, Paul speaks of 'One Spirit . . . one Lord . . . one God and Father.

---

[103] For a study of the biblical evidence which contributes to a doctrine of the trinity, cf. A. W. Wainwright, *The Trinity in the New Testament* (1962); L. Hodgson, *The Doctrine of the Trinity* (1943), pp. 38–84; E. J. Fortman, *The Triune God* (1972), pp. 3–33.; A. W. Argyle, *God in the New Testament*, pp. 173–181. An older work, but still worth consulting is J. S. Candlish, *The Christian Doctrine of God* (n.d.) especially pp. 102ff. A popular but valuable survey of the evidence is R. T. France's *The Living God* (1970).

[104] On this passage, A. W. Argyle, *op. cit.*, p. 175, comments that it is the same God who works as Father, Son and Holy Spirit. Expressed in this form it sounds Sabellian, but Argyle is concerned to point out that the setting alongside each other of Father, Son and Spirit suggests three co-equal persons.

[105] When speaking of personality in God, care must be taken not to suppose that the human pattern is adequate. As D. M. Baillie points out, 'Personality in God must be a very different thing from personality in us', *God was in Christ* (²1955), p. 143. It should be noticed that 'person' is not an NT term. When theologians use it has a different sense when referring to 'personality' in God and when applied to the three 'Persons' of the trinity, two senses which are barely compatible.

The threefold form occurs also in 1 Corinthians 12:3–6, where each Person is introduced with the adjective 'same' in the sequence Spirit, Lord and God, as in Ephesians 4. Under this category may be included 1 Peter 1:2, where the words occur: 'chosen and destined by God the Father and sanctified by the Spirit for obedience to Jesus Christ'. In a rather more indirect way the three persons are mentioned in the extended passage, Ephesians 1:3–14.

The third type consists of passages where the three Persons are mentioned together, but without any clear triadic structure. Samples of such passages are Galatians 4:4–6 ('God has sent the Spirit of his Son into our hearts'), Mark 1:9–11 (the baptism of Jesus, in which the Father and the Spirit were also involved), Romans 8:1ff.; 2 Thessalonians 2:13f.; Titus 3:4–6; Jude 20f. The close linking of Father, Son and Spirit in these passages cannot be regarded as accidental.

The remaining group of passages is probably the most significant in that it brings out the relationship between the different Persons of the trinity. The passages are all from John's gospel (14:26; 15:26; 16:15 and perhaps 14:6). It is the Father who sends the Spirit in the name of the Son. Indeed, the Son also sends the Spirit who proceeds from the Father. All three Persons are involved in the declaration of the truth to man. There is no denying that the contribution of these passages to the NT testimony regarding the trinity is unique.

If we add to these texts the passages where actions which are normally attributed to God are ascribed to Christ (such as creation) or to the Spirit (*e.g.* acts of power), we add further dimension to the NT evidence. Whereas no formal trinitarian doctrine is stated, the NT furnishes several hints which point in that direction. None of the writers, however, gives a formal definition of the precise relationship which exists between the three Persons of the Godhead. The problems which confronted later theologians do not seem to have occurred to the NT writers. It is John who comes nearest to an awareness of the problem, since in his writings is presented in the clearest way the personality of the Spirit, his distinctness from both the Father and the Son and the relationship between them. These aspects are of utmost importance in evaluating the NT view of God.

We have been discussing the adumbrations of the trinity, but it is under the general heading of the unity of God and some comment must be made concerning this. It must at once be noted that nowhere in the NT is any concern shown over purely speculative ideas about unity. A statement can be found like 'I and the Father are one' (Jn. 10:30) without any apparent blurring of the distinction between them in the context. Undoubtedly there are deep mysteries in the NT conception of God, but what must strike the thoughtful reader is the complete absence of any attempt to explain the mysteries. Christian convictions were strong enough to maintain the divine nature of both Jesus Christ and the Spirit without falling into the trap of postulating three gods.[106] The conviction that God was active in Christ and in the Spirit prevented this from happening. It may be said that the NT writers do not work with a conceptual framework which would lead naturally to speculations about the essence of God. In a study of NT theology we cannot go further than the evidence we find. Nevertheless the evidence lays foundations for the later developed doctrine.[107] The problems which that later doctrine grappled with had their roots in the NT itself. Although the NT concentrates more on functions[108] than relationships, the latter aspect is certainly not lacking.

SUMMARY

Our brief survey of the NT presentation of God has done no more than erect signposts towards an understanding of what must always retain an air of profound mystery. No outline of names or qualities can present a total picture. But the NT gives abundant indication that what is necessary to know about God can be known. Indeed, this is a basic assumption which colours the whole NT revelation.

Enough has been said to demonstrate the basic unity of the NT view about God. While some parts emphasize certain aspects more than others, there is no suggestion of contradictions. The combination of Creator, Father and King provides a wide spectrum of ideas about God, but one aspect is never set against another. The Creator is both fatherly and kingly. The King never acts in a tyrannical way because he is also a Father.

Moreover, both in the titles and attributes of God found in the NT, there is a remarkable combination of what might at first appear to be opposites. The paradox of the love and wrath of God, his kindness and severity, his mercy and judgment are examples of apparent antitheses which nevertheless are perfectly balanced in the character of God. What in man would be regarded as real antitheses are postulated in God in a way which shows no awareness of any problem.

Another remarkable fact about the NT evidence is that it includes both transcendent and immanent aspects without any tendency to lay an over-emphasis on either. There are no signs, in fact, that the problems which

---

[106] Wainwright points out (op. cit., p. 249), that the real problem did not arise over the person of the Spirit, but over the deity of Christ. It is because Christ had appeared as a man and could not possibly be conceived as an emmanation of the deity.

[107] Wainwright (ibid., p. 267) concludes his study with the comment that the NT writers 'did not make it their chief aim to unravel all the complexities of the divine nature. Their chief aim was to show God as revealed in Christ and as present in the Spirit'.

[108] The functional aspect comes particularly to the fore in the NT teaching on the Spirit. Cf. G. S. Hendry, The Holy Spirit in Christian Theology (1957), pp. 30ff., for a brief discussion of the close relation between Father, Son and Spirit in their activities. 'The worship of God in spirit and truth . . . is to worship God through Jesus Christ, in the Holy Spirit' (p. 32).

arise from such an over-emphasis ever bothered the minds of the early Christians. God was at the same time both majestic and concerned about man's condition. He is never remote, but is at the same time apart from his own creation.

The relevance of a right doctrine of God for an approach to NT theology may be illustrated as follows. A God who cares for his creatures is the God who acts to redeem them. A true understanding of the incarnation and therefore of the person of Christ is impossible if a wrong notion of God is maintained. Similarly if God were an angry deity who needed to be placated this would naturally colour any approach to the doctrine of the mission of Christ. Some indication of the havoc which can be caused within a theology based on wrong assumptions about God can be seen in the 'death of God' school which all but annihilated the Christian content of NT theology altogether.

Chapter 2

Man and his world

There is no formal systematic doctrine of man in the NT. The writers were not interested in the study of man for his own sake. Their concern was for man in relation to God. It is for this reason that the NT teaching about man is continually relevant, in spite of the advance of scientific knowledge and sociological theories. The environment of modern man is essentially different from that of first-century man, but the same problems arise in relation to God. Since these problems are not environmental as is sometimes supposed, what the NT says about man cannot be considered to be obsolete. Our survey of the NT evidence will be preceded by a brief statement on the OT, Judaistic and Greek background.

BACKGROUND

Old Testament

In the previous section on the doctrine of God, it has been pointed out that the NT takes over without challenge the OT view of the creatorship of God.[1] Man is thus viewed as a creature of God. The basic OT view of man begins with this assumption. Man was created with a physical body. He is described as dust (Gn. 2:7; 3:19). He received his life from the breath of God (cf. Gn. 2:7), as did the animals (cf. Gn. 7:15, 22). But the OT leaves no doubt about the superiority of man to the animals.[2] Only of man is it said

---

[1] For a discussion of the OT view of the world and man, cf. E. Jacob, *Theology of the Old Testament* (Eng. trans. 1958), pp. 151–182.; W. Eichrodt, *Theology of the Old Testament* 2 (Eng. trans. 1967), pp. 93–150; *idem, Man in the Old Testament* (Eng. trans. 1951); T. C. Vriezen, *An Outline of Old Testament Theology* (Eng. trans. ²1970), pp. 404–429; C. Ryder Smith, *The Bible Doctrine of Man* (1951), pp. 3–64.; H. Wheeler Robinson, *The Christian Doctrine of Man* (³1926), pp. 4–42.; H. W. Wolff, *Anthropology of the Old Testament* (Eng. trans. 1974).

[2] As compared with ancient attempts to suggest a suitable origin for man, the biblical revelation alone invests man's appearance with dignity and splendour. *Cf.* the brief study of the Catholic writer Nicolas Corte, *The Origin of Man* (1959). He examines the subject against the background of mythological and philosophical views of man.

that he bore the 'image of God' (Gn. 1:26).[3] This constitutes man as God's greatest creative work, the only part of the created order capable of entering into fellowship with the Creator. It is man who names the animals and exercises dominion over them. This draws attention to an essential difference between them, *i.e.* that man uses language, which is both a creation of his own and also a powerful influence affecting his behaviour. Whatever view modern man takes of the evolutionary process, the OT testimony is clear that man has a distinctive superiority over the animal creation. The Hebrews never conceived of man as merely animal in his constitution. He had the power of observing relationships, *i.e.* the power of reason. Man was regarded as possessing both body and 'soul' (Hebrew *nepeš*),[4] *i.e.* he was regarded as a person (*cf.* the use of the word in Gn. 12:5). The body was distinct from the personality (*cf.* Ps. 63:1; 73:26).[5] For this reason it was proper to speak of a dead person (*cf.* Nu. 6:6), to differentiate the person from the physical corpse. But the body itself is essentially mortal. Death is inescapable, and by way of contrast God is eternal (*cf.* Is. 44:6; 45:5).

Another feature of the OT conception of man is his corporate aspect. Woman was the only appropriate helpmeet for man. The family concept was seen to be essential to the development of the race. Moreover the family concept was extended to include many who were not blood relations.[6] The individual emphasis must be balanced against the idea of solidarity.[7] Not only is this seen in the family, but also in the nation of Israel. The fact that the people were known as 'the children of Israel' shows a strong sense of solidarity within the nation,[8] based on an extension of the

[3] Eichrodt, *Theology of the Old Testament* 2, pp. 120ff., argues that the expression 'image and likeness of God' excludes the view that man was simply a copy of God. The expression denotes a correspondence between man and God which is figuratively described as an 'image'. *Cf.* D. J. A. Clines' article 'The Image of God in Man', *TB* 19, 1968, pp. 53–103, for a careful discussion of 'image' in the Genesis account. He suggests that the 'image' includes the idea of God's representative, as one who rules the rest of creation as God's viceroy. This enhances the view that man as a creature has a unique dignity.

[4] For a discussion of the various terms used in OT psychology, *cf.* H. W. Robinson, *op. cit.*, pp. 11ff.; E. C. Rust, *Nature and Man in Biblical Thought* (1953), pp. 101ff.

[5] The importance of the individual emphasis in OT thought linked with the community idea is well brought out by E. F. Scott in his *Man and Society in the New Testament* (1947), pp. 23–36. He nevertheless rightly notes that it is the communal aspect which is dominant.

[6] Vriezen, *op. cit.*, p. 411, points out that the Genesis account supports not only monogamy, but also a high regard for the miracle of reproduction. There is no support in the OT for the widely held view in pagan society that parents might dispose of their children. Vriezen, however, does not consider this feature to be primitive, but what he calls 'a spiritually purified element of Yahwism' (p. 411).

[7] H. W. Robinson, *op. cit.*, pp. 27ff., strongly argues for the idea of corporate personality in OT thought. He claims, 'whether in relation to man or to God, the individual person was conceived and treated as merged in the larger group of family or clan or nation' (p. 27). Nevertheless he admits that in the prophetic period there was much more stress on individualism, although he notes, 'The individualism of the Old Testament is usually, if not always, conceived as realized in and through the society which is based upon it' (p. 34). But see next footnote for two recent writers who have cautioned against Robinson's corporate personality idea.

[8] J. W. Rogerson, 'The Hebrew Conception of Corporate Personality: A Re-examination', *JTS* n. s. 21,

family idea. The father-image is extended to the leader-image. This sense of the solidarity of the race plays an important part in Paul's view of man and this will be discussed in some detail below.

The major fact which emerges from the OT data is the universality of man's sin. The account in Genesis 3 shows sin to be a violation of God's commandment.[9] It is essentially a deeply religious concept. This is clear whatever view we take of the nature of the narrative. The account of the fall of Adam and its consequences puts in succinct form the common experience of mankind.[10] With Adam's fall, there follows almost immediately the disruption of family solidarity in the murder of Abel by his brother (Gn. 4:1–15). Lot selfishly takes advantage of his uncle Abraham (Gn. 13). Moreover Jacob does not hesitate to defraud his brother Esau (Gn. 25:29ff.). This breakup of the solidarity of the family affected the wider community, as the whole of the OT testifies. The deterioration of morality among the nations is evident. Power-blocks hold the ascendancy. The weak are oppressed, particularly economically. Even Israel, the people of God, sins against God and pays the penalty in national disaster and exile. The message of the prophets can be understood only against this background of personal and national sin against God.[11]

As an introduction to the NT doctrine of sin, it is necessary to summarize the main OT words used to describe sin and these may be characterized as follows.[12] One word (*hātā'*) means to miss the mark, but is used in a more general way of personal sinning. In the majority of cases it is sin against God rather than sin against man. Another word for sin (*pāša'*) is used for offences, both against man and against God, more frequently the latter. The third word (*'āwôn*) again is almost always used of sin against God. This evidence shows that the greater emphasis in the OT is on sin against God rather than sin against man, and this supports the essentially religious approach to sin in the OT. The outworking of this revolt against God is seen in a variety of different ways affecting man's approach. It is expressed

---

1970, pp. 1ff.; J. R. Porter, 'The Legal Aspect of the Concept of "Corporate Personality" in the Old Testament', *VT* 15, 1965, pp. 361–380.

[9] For an outline of the theological implications of the Gn. 3 account of sin, *cf.* S. Lyonnet in *Sin, Redemption and Sacrifice* (ed. S. Lyonnet and L. Sabourin, 1970), pp. 5ff. Although E. Brunner, *The Christian Doctrine of Creation and Redemption* (Eng. trans. 1952), p. 90, dissociates the doctrine of the fall from the Genesis 'myth', he nevertheless affirms that it is impossible to understand redemption apart from the doctrine of fallen humanity.

[10] The OT does not support the view that when man sinned he lost the 'image of God' (*cf.* Vriezen, *op. cit.*, p. 413). Nevertheless, if image has to do with relationship between God and man, that relationship was definitely marred by man's sin. Having set his will at variance with God, man could not continue in the same way to be a true representative of God (*cf.* Jacob, *op. cit.*, pp. 166ff.). *Cf.* Clines, *art. cit.*, pp. 99ff.

[11] W. Eichrodt, in his monograph, *Man in the Old Testament* (1951), finds in the OT the dominant view that man's true destiny is to fulfil the sovereign will of God. It follows, therefore, that the basic concept of sin is seen as rebellion against God.

[12] For further discussion of this terminology, see H. W. Robinson, *op. cit.*, pp. 42ff.

as provoking God to 'anger' (Dt. 4:25; 32:21f.), as that which detracts from him in the sense of contempt (*cf.* Nu. 14:11; Dt. 31:20; 1 Sa. 2:30; 2 Sa. 12:9), as a despising of God and his precepts (Je. 7:19; Jb. 35:6–8). Sin is definitely an offence against God,[13] which incurs his judgment.

The idea of divine judgment carries with it the notion of guilt (*cf.* Ps. 51:4). It is this situation of guilt which comprises man's greatest problem. The OT consistently shows man's inability to deal with this problem. Although provision was made through the sacrificial system for atonement to be made, this did not remove man's awareness of guilt. His basic problem was still unresolved until in the NT a better way was provided. It is, in fact, the religious conception of sin which is taken over in the NT. The OT background is frequently assumed in NT statements, although there is often a development of the meaning of the key concepts, particularly in the epistles of Paul.

Judaism

The previous brief account of man in the OT has concentrated on the past and present. The OT has little to say about man's individual destiny. It consists of a rather shadowy existence, with here and there brief flashes of more solid hope. But the intertestamental period shows a development here (see pp. 820ff.). It is, however, in the doctrine of sin that this period makes a distinctive contribution, particularly because it serves to bring into focus the problem of man's responsibility. Sin is viewed as an evil tendency (*yēṣer hārā‘*) which existed in man at the beginning (Ecclus. 15:14–15). But man, if he so wills, is able to keep God's commandment. By his free will, he is able to overcome the adverse influence of the *yēṣer hārā‘* within him. Ben-Sira appears to attribute the creation of this evil principle to God (37:3), although he does not push this to its logical conclusion. This came to expression in later midrashim, in which God is viewed as the creator of the *yēṣer hārā‘* and the Law was considered to be an escape from its power (Babylonian Talmud).[14] In another passage Ben-Sira seems to equate Satan with the man himself (21:27), which would firmly maintain that man is the origin of his own sin. And yet man's frailty is cited as an excuse for his being unable to overcome the *yēṣer hārā‘* (17:31; Syriac Vs). The Tannaim maintained that man was created with a good impulse (*yēṣer hāṭôb*) as well as an evil impulse, and that there was a tension between the two impulses.[15] Something of this kind of tension comes over in Paul's wrestling with the

---

[13] C. Ryder Smith has a full treatment of the OT view of sin in his *The Biblical Doctrine of Sin* (1953), pp. 7ff.

[14] H. M. Hughes, *The Ethics of Jewish Apocryphal Literature* (n.d.), shows that the *yēṣer* idea appears in many of the intertestamental books.

[15] For a full discussion of the *yēṣer* principle in Tannaitic literature, *cf.* G. F. Moore, *Judaism* 1, pp. 474ff. On Adam's fall and Jewish theology, *cf.* the note in F. Prat, *The Theology of St Paul* 1 (1933), pp. 440–2. *Cf.* also R. Scroggs, *The Last Adam* (1966), pp. 16ff.

problem of sin in Romans 7 (see discussion of this on pp. 204f.).[16]

Some comment must be made on the contribution of the Qumran view of man and sin to our understanding of the background notions of Judaism at the time of Jesus. Sin, represented symbolically as the angel of darkness, is diametrically opposed to the spirit of truth. This strong dualism can be illustrated from *The Rule of the Community* (1 QS III, 17–23) and from the *Psalms of Thanksgiving* (1 QH XIV, 15, 26; XV, 25). There is a vivid realization of the power of the kingdom of darkness, which is nevertheless an abhorrence to the Lord.[17] Some references are found to the remedy for this powerful influence in the promise of a spirit of holiness.[18]

Hellenism

When we consider the Greek view of man, we are faced with a totally different kind of dualism, of which the key is found in Plato's theory of ideas.[19] This kind of dualism was still exerting considerable influence on Greek thought during the period in which the Christian church was established and was a vital factor in the developed forms of gnosticism in the second century AD. It is important, therefore, to note the dominant features of Greek dualism for a right appreciation of NT thought, even if it is more often at variance with, rather than in conformity to, that thought.

Plato's dualism is seen clearly in his idea of two worlds, the visible and the invisible or spiritual world. The real world was the unseen in which alone man could discover his true self. Hence the physical body was a hindrance, even at times being likened to a prison.[20] Man's soul moreover consists of three parts, according to Plato,[21] of which only the highest part is immortal and pre-existed the body. Man's struggle may therefore be regarded as a struggle between his mind and the rest of his constituted parts. Although Plato did not go as far as the gnostics in regarding all matter as evil, he nevertheless considered that the body was a mass of

---

[16] For a discussion of the relationship of the two impulses to Paul's teaching on sin, *cf.* W. D. Davies, *Paul and Rabbinic Judaism* (1948), pp. 7ff.

[17] The idea of the two spirits, Belial, the Angel of Darkness and his spirits of wickedness against the Spirits of Truth and Light, was particularly in evidence in Qumran (see 1 QS III 13 – IV 26). There is clearly some parallel between this idea and the Rabbinic 'two impulses' (*cf.* J. T. Milik, *Ten Years of Discovery in the Wilderness of Judea* (Eng. trans. 1959), pp. 118f. *Cf.* also M. Mansoor, *The Thanksgiving Hymns* (1961), p. 56 n.1; J. P. Hyatt, 'The View of Man in the Qumran Hodayot', *NTS* 2, 1955–6, p. 281. In the article on 'Light from Qumran upon some aspects of Johannine Theology', in *John and Qumran* (ed. J. H. Charlesworth, 1972), J. L. Price points out, 'Belief in the God of Israel as Creator led the sectarians to espouse a "modified dualism", or perhaps one should say, a qualified or relative system' (p. 15).

[18] It should be noted that although the Qumran community has a decidedly dualistic outlook, it does not go beyond a monotheistic view of God – 'it is God who will bring about the final victory of Good over Evil', Milik, *op. cit.*, p. 118.

[19] For an excellent, succinct account of Greek views of man and his world, *cf.* G. E. Ladd, *The Pattern of New Testament Truth* (1968), pp. 13–31. *Cf.* also E. F. Scott, *Man and Society in the New Testament* (1947).

[20] *Cf. Phaedo* 82 E; 62 B.

[21] *Cf. Timaeus* 69 D – 70 A; *Republic* 439–441; *Phaedo* 72 E.

evil.[22] This led him to think of salvation as cultivation of the mind.[23] Naturally under this system the philosopher has a great advantage over all others.

Closely akin to Plato's view was that advanced by Plutarch,[24] who reckoned the mind to be the only immortal part of man, but that after death it had to be purified from the pollutions contracted from the body. Because this latter process was not always successful, Plutarch advanced the theory of a return to earth for rebirth.[25] It is only when a person escapes from this cycle of birth that he becomes secure. Those who have succeeded in purifying the pollutions of the body become daemons (*i.e.* pure spirits), a very different idea from the demons (*i.e.* agents of evil) of the non-Greek world.

Philo, the leading exponent of Hellenistic Jewish ideas, was clearly in-debted to Plato's theory of ideas.[26] In fact, he was decidedly syncretistic in his attempt to commend Judaism to the Greek world. To further this end Philo resorted to allegory to demonstrate that a dualism between mind and body could be traced to the Mosaic Law. He maintained that souls were pre-existent and immortal, and yet following the creation of the body the soul possessed a lower part which is irrational. Like Plato, Philo regarded the body as a prison house of the soul, but did not pronounce all matter as evil.[27] Since the soul is so clearly linked with mind, salvation is a matter of knowledge.

It will be seen that there is a marked distinction between the Greek and Hebrew view of man. The dualism which seems on the surface to be parallel is nevertheless approached from essentially different viewpoints. It will become evident as we examine the NT that Greek influences are far less pronounced than Jewish.

THE WORLD

The belief that God is the Creator and that the natural world is his handi-work is accepted without question by all the NT writers. It is in line with

[22] *Cf. Phaedo* 66 B.

[23] *Cf. Theatetus* 176 A; *Phaedo* 65 B.

[24] For Plutarch's views, *cf.* M. Nilsson, *Geschichte der griechischen Religion* (in *Handbuch der Altertumswissenschaft* 5) II (1949), pp. 402f.; T. R. Glover, *The Conflict of Religions in the Roman Empire* ([12]1932), pp. 75–112.

[25] *Cf. Face of the Moon* 940 F – 945 D; *Divine vengeance* 560 F – 567 E; *The Sign of Socrates* 590 A – 594 A.

[26] For a discussion of Philo's views, *cf.* E. R. Goodenough, *An Introduction to Philo Judaeus* ([2]1962); idem, *By Light, Light. The Mystic Gospel of Hellenistic Judaism* (1935); H. R. Willoughby, *Pagan Regenaration* (1929), pp. 225–262. For studies relating Philo's view to NT books, *cf.* C. H. Dodd, *The Interpretation of the Fourth Gospel* (1953), pp. 54–73; R. Williamson, *Philo and the Epistle to the Hebrews* (1970); C. Spicq, *Hébreux* 1 (*EB*,[2] 1952), pp. 39–87.

[27] R. M. Wilson, *The Gnostic Problem* (1958), pp. 44f., commenting on Philo's view of the world, says that it 'almost seems that Philo regards matter as evil'. Wilson, nevertheless, considers that Philo is not consistent.

the OT and Jewish beliefs. It colours the whole NT conception of man if man is regarded as a special creation of God. In view of evolutionary theories of man's origin, it may at once be questioned how relevant the NT evidence is on this theme, and some justification is needed. Since our purpose is to present NT theology, it would be out of place here to discuss the full implications of modern scientific theories of the origin of man. Nevertheless if the scientific method had so radically affected man's approach to himself as to make the NT teaching on man obsolete, the NT theologian would be obliged to do a considerable amount of reinterpreting. But certain important considerations must be borne in mind. The first is that the NT is a religious and not a scientific account of man and his world.[28] Indeed, the religious interest is so strong that little attention is given to psychological aspects and no attention at all to the relation of man to the rest of animate creation. The second consideration is that the scientific method cannot be said to be necessarily in conflict with the biblical view of creation, for whereas some would maintain it is, others would take the contrary view.[29] There is, in short, no conclusive position. We shall need to assess what the NT says about the world, therefore, from an essentially religious point of view.[30]

The synoptic gospels

In these books the word *world* (*kosmos*) is used either of the material earth as, for instance, in the reference to coming tribulation which is described

---

[28] Many scholars treat the NT view of the world as essentially mythological. This is especially so in the case of Bultmann. This is brought out in the following statement from *Jesus Christ and Mythology* (Eng. trans. 1960), p. 15, 'The whole conception of the world which is presupposed in the preaching of Jesus as in the New Testament generally is mythological; i.e. the conception of the world as being structured in three stories, heaven, earth and hell; the conception of the intervention of supernatural powers in the course of events; and the conception of miracles, especially the conception of the intervention of supernatural powers in the inner life of the soul, the conception that men can be tempted and corrupted by the devil and possessed by evil spirits'. This view of Bultmann's was first advanced by him in an essay entitled *Neues Testament und Mythologie*, published in 1941. For a concise summary of this essay and a critique of Bultmann's position, *cf.* I. Henderson, *Myth in the New Testament* (1952). *Cf.* also J. Marquarrie, *An Existentialist Theology* (1955), for a discussion of the philosophical issues involved. Bultmann's *a priori* rejection of the supernatural on the grounds that it is incompatible with the modern scientific view of the world naturally leads him to a reinterpretation of the NT evidence (*i.e.* an existential approach). But Bultmann's criticism of the NT world view is based on the acceptance of a scientific closed system view of the world, which is increasingly under attack even within the scientific world.

[29] *Cf.* the brief but perceptive article by Mary Hesse, 'On the alleged incompatibility between Christianity and Science', *Man and Nature* (ed. H. Montefiore, 1975), pp. 121ff., who responds from a philosophical point of view to the view of Jacques Monod (*Chance and Necessity*) that modern biology is incompatible with what he calls the 'anthropocentric illusion'. She shows that Monod's theory is not based wholly on objective scientific knowledge.

[30] R. Bultmann, *Jesus Christ and Mythology*, p. 69, will not accept as legitimate statements which speak of God's actions as cosmic events. Instead he considers only a personal confession that I understand myself as a creature which owes its existence to God as legitimate. But the sense of God's creativity cannot be reduced to a subjective experience, although an element of this is indispensable. The NT evidence shows that the early Christians did not hesitate to think of God's acts as cosmic events.

as being unparalleled since the beginning of the world (Mt. 24:21); or, of the world of men. In the latter sense, such references as 'the kingdoms of the world' (Mt. 4:8) or the 'nations of the world' (Lk. 12:30) must be understood. It naturally comes to stand for a materialistic approach to life, as in the Luke 12:30 reference, where it is contrasted with the kingdom of God (Mt. 16:26). At the same time the whole world presents the challenge for the preaching of the gospel (Mt. 28:19; *cf.* Mk. 16:15). In the parable of the tares, the field is the world (Mt. 13:38). Disciples, moreover, are to be lights in the world (Mt. 5:14). The 'world', therefore, stands for a universal need and therefore a universal challenge.

There is a complete absence of the idea that the world is in itself evil. However, in the temptation of Jesus, Satan offers to give him 'all the kingdoms of the world' (Mt. 4:8), which supports the view that the world is under evil domination. But this is a different concept from the gnostic belief that matter itself is evil.[31] Because the world is under Satan's influence, it can become a source of temptation to sin (Mt. 18:7), but a woe is pronounced against it for this reason. At his temptation Jesus strongly resisted the tempter's offer.

The dominance of satanic influence over the world of men leads to a consideration of the *spirit world*. This is another sphere in which modern opinion often conflicts with the NT records, leading to the conclusion that the evangelists have used the categories of their own time to express phenomena which are now capable of being described in psychological terms. Undoubtedly there are cases related in the gospels which bear resemblance to certain modern psychiatric conditions, but this does not justify the wholesale excision of all cases of exorcism from the gospels. There is no support for the view that belief in the spirit world is outmoded, for it is an acute expression of the acknowledged clash between good and evil affecting human lives.[32] If all trace of this conflict is removed from the gospels, it would result in a misunderstanding of the mission of Jesus. His work was conducted against the background of spiritual agencies.

In the birth narratives of both Matthew and Luke the activity of *angels* played an important part. Such activity is in line with OT evidence.[33] In the intertestamental period interest in angels intensified and went hand in hand with the emphasis on the remoteness of God, which increased the need for

---

[31] *Cf.* R. M. Wilson, *The Gnostic Problem*, p. 70.

[32] R. Bultmann, *TNT* 1, pp. 172ff., traces the view that demonic world-rulers controlled the world to gnostic influences. But he gives inadequate weight to the fact that belief in spiritual forces was already current in Judaism. He tends to ascribe all traces of dualism to gnostic origins. Paul may certainly use concepts that were also used by gnostics, but this is no proof that he was indebted to them.

[33] For a study of angels in the OT, *cf.* W. Grundmann, *angelos, TDNT* 1, pp. 76–80; H. Bietenhard, 'angel', *NIDNTT* 1, p. 101. On the intertestamental period, *cf.* H. B. Kuhn, 'The Angelology of the Non-Canonical Jewish Apocalypses', *JBL* 67 (1948), pp. 217–232.; Y. Yadin, *The Scroll of the War of the Sons of Light against the Sons of Darkness* (1962), pp. 229–242.

adequate mediators. Yet in the remaining parts of the synoptic gospels the reference to angels is, by contrast, reserved.[34] The angel participants in the birth narratives underline the view that the incarnation was a direct intervention of God into human life. The angelic messages were the messages of God to the active participants in the events. It was natural for the evangelists to express themselves in this way because the existence of good angelic agencies was everywhere accepted. But did Jesus himself believe in angels? According to Mark 12:25, Jesus answers a quibble of the Sadducees about marriage and the resurrection by pointing out that the angels in heaven neither marry nor are given in marriage. There is not only a clear statement here of a distinction between angels and men, but also an unmistakable assertion that Jesus accepted their existence – unless, of course, the words are regarded as a reading back by the community. Yet the way in which Jesus turned the tables against the Sadducees is thoroughly characteristic of his method. Moreover, in Gethsemane Jesus claimed to be able, had he so willed, to command twelve legions of angels to come to his assistance (Mt. 26:53). But is this reference to be taken literally or in a symbolic way? There is room for difference of opinion here, but if it had been intended symbolically Jesus would surely have spoken of the power of God instead of angels (cf. Mt. 22:29ff. where 'the power of God' is spoken of in the same context as angels).

In some cases the angels are specifically mentioned to indicate the presence of God, as in Luke 12:8 ('the Son of man also will acknowledge before the angels of God'; cf. Mt. 10:32) and Luke 15:10 ('joy before the angels of God'). In these cases the phrase 'before the angels' seems to mean 'before God'. The transference from one to the other would be most natural if angels were thought of as beings who are constantly in the presence of God.[35] The most specific statement about the duties of angels is found in Matthew 18:10 where Jesus urges respect for little ones, 'for I tell you that in heaven their angels always behold the face of my Father who is in heaven'. Jesus is here commending the guardian care of God, but he does it in terms of angelic agencies. He certainly seems to imply that angels have a providential function, whether the little ones (mikroi) are understood figuratively or as children. It is difficult to believe that Jesus would have spoken in these terms had he considered that angels were non-existent.

---

[34] K. Barth, Church Dogmatics III 3, maintained that angels were an indispensable aspect of Christian theology. Cf. W. A. Whitehouse's summary in SJT 4, 1951, pp. 376–382.

[35] Strack-Billerbeck, 1, on Mt. 18:10, points out that it was not a rabbinic belief that angels see God. W. D. Davies, The Setting of the Sermon on the Mount (1964), p. 226, draws attention to other NT passages in which angels are connected with church activity. He interprets the 'little ones' as 'church members'. E. Schweizer, Matthew (Eng. trans. 1976, from NTD, 1973), ad loc., considers that the lack of parallels (except in later Jewish writings) to guardian angels makes Matthew's reference here doubly significant. He regards the angels here as cosmic powers through whom God rules the world, or intercessors with God on behalf of the weak.

At the temptation of Jesus, the devil cites the OT passage about God giving his angels charge over him (Ps. 91:11–12, *cf.* Mt. 4:6; Lk. 4:10). Jesus accepts the challenge implied in the temptation, by citing Deuteronomy 6:16 in reply. After the temptation, according to both Matthew 4:11 and Mark 1:13, angels ministered to Jesus, but Luke omits this detail. In Gethsemane at the hour of his agony Jesus was assisted by an angel, according to one reading of Luke 22:43, which, however, might not be original. In view of the temptation narratives, it would not be out of keeping if Luke 22:43 were the original reading. If angelic beings exist, they may be expected to have had the keenest interest in the crises of the messianic mission. It is not surprising, also, to find an angel mentioned at the tomb (Mt. 28:2f.), although Mark's record mentions only a young man (Mk. 16:5). The report of the two on the Emmaus road mentions that the women had seen a vision of angels at the tomb (Lk. 24.23).

When Jesus was teaching about his future coming, he said he would come with angels (Mt. 16:27; 25:31; Mk. 8:38). This was a feature of current apocalyptic imagery, and Jesus' use of it puts his own *imprimatur* upon it. In two of the parables angels appear as the reapers in the final harvest (Mt. 13:39f. (the tares) and Mt. 13:49 (the drag-net)). Mark has the same idea, but in a different context (Mk. 13:27). When speaking of the future coming Jesus links the ignorance of the angels regarding the time with the ignorance of the Son (Mt. 24:36), which shows the high respect given to the angels. One other reference which is worth mentioning is the angels' function in carrying Lazarus to Abraham's bosom (Lk. 16:22). Admittedly this is in a parabolic form and cannot be depended on to supply historic information, but it does reflect current ideas, which Jesus appears to endorse.

It is against this strongly attested evidence for the existence of good spirits that we must consider the *world of demons* which we frequently meet in the synoptic gospels.[36] We begin by noting that evil is personified in a

[36] Bultmann demythologized the references to demons, but it has been recognized by many others that this removes an essential element for a right understanding of the gospel. *Cf.* A. Fridrichsen, 'The conflict of Jesus with the unclean spirits', *Theology* 22, 1931, p. 122; J. S. Stewart, 'On a neglected emphasis in NT theology', *SJT* 4, 1951, pp. 292–301; W. Manson, (Principalities and Powers: the Spiritual background of the work of Jesus in the Synoptic Gospels', *Studiorum Novi Testamenti Societas*, Bulletin 3 (1952), 15. E, Brunner, *The Christian Doctrine of Creation and Redemption*, p. 136, points out that in contrast to Zoroastrianism the biblical view of the devil is that he is not equal to God, although his immense power is admitted. He is regarded as an already defeated foe. *Cf.* W. Manson, *op. cit.*, for a discussion of the importance of a study of these spiritual dimensions for a right understanding of the ministry of Jesus. For further studies in demonology, *cf.* E. Langton, *Essentials of Demonology* (1949); R. Bultmann, *Jesus and the Word* (Eng. trans. 1935), p. 56; *idem, Jesus Christ and Mythology* (Eng. trans. 1946), pp. 13ff.; G. Bornkamm, *Jesus of Nazareth* (Eng. trans. 1961), pp. 60, 63, 130f., 149; V. Taylor, *Mark* (²1966), 239ff.; A. M. Hunter, *Introducing New Testament Theology* (1957), pp. 28ff.; H. Riesenfeld, *The Gospel Tradition* (Eng. trans. 1970), pp. 84f.; J. Reumann, *Jesus in the Church's Gospel* (1968), pp. 199ff.; E. Schweizer, *Jesus* (Eng. trans. 1971), pp. 43ff.; R. Otto, *The Kingdom of God and the Son of Man* (Eng. trans. 1938), pp. 101f.; C. K. Barrett, *The Holy Spirit and the Gospel Tradition* (1947), pp. 68, 92; L. E. Keck, *A Future for the Historical Jesus* (1972), pp. 126, 183.

single person, *Satan*,[37] in agreement with OT belief.[38] At the temptation of Jesus, the conflict is between this personification of evil, the devil, and Jesus himself. It is clear from both Matthew's and Luke's account that the function of tempting people with a view to persuading them to commit a moral offence is integral to the activities of the devil. He is by nature a tempter, as the Genesis account shows. But more than that he claims a dominating influence over the world, which Jesus does not dispute. Since the temptation occurs at the commencement of the ministry, it may be seen as symbolic of the spiritual conflict which surrounded Jesus throughout his mission. But did Luke intend us to understand it otherwise when he noted that the devil 'departed from him until an opportune time' (Lk. 4:13)? Does this, in fact, mean that in Luke's view the ministry was a period of satanic inactivity?[39] In view of the fact that Luke records instances of the confrontation of Jesus with demons, he cannot have meant complete withdrawal. The messianic mission of Jesus is misrepresented by the devil as a major temptation and we cannot suppose that Jesus was exempt from this temptation to fulfil popular expectations at various points during the ministry. Moreover, it is significant that Luke, the physician, records that Satan had bound a woman for eighteen years (13:16).[40] When confronted with Jesus the woman was at once delivered. There is a striking contrast between the crippling act of Satan and the releasing act of Jesus. Moreover it is Luke who comments that Satan entered into Judas before his consultation with the chief priests to betray Jesus (Lk. 22:3). Since neither Mat-

[37] There are more references to Satan and demons in the NT than in the OT. Satan is, in fact, referred to only three times in the OT, *i.e.* in Zc. 3:1 and Job 1—2, where the word is used as a title (=the Adversary) and in 1 Ch. 21:1 in a form without the article. For an account of Satan in Jewish apocalyptic literature, *cf.* E. Langton, *op. cit.*, pp. 107–144. E. Jacob, *Theology of the Old Testament* (Eng. trans. 1958), pp. 70ff., is in agreement with the suggestion of A. Lods that the Satan idea developed from the lawsuit customs of the Israelites and the police methods of Persian kings. The origin of the name is less important than the conviction that a powerful accuser was acting against men before God. It is true that Satan is represented in Jb. 1:6 as enjoying special privileges at the court of God, but the over-all impression is that his function is to bring accusations. It is a short step from Accuser to Destroyer. As J. Kallas, *The Significance of the Synoptic Miracles* (1961), p. 50, remarks on the Job passages, 'Satan already, despite his role as servant of God and restrained by God's orders, seems on the brink of a metamorphosis towards evil'.

[38] For a survey of demonology in the OT, see the article of T. H. Gaster, 'Demon', *IDB* 1, pp. 817–882. He maintains that daimonism represents an externalization of human experiences. He goes on to suggest that in the Bible there is an ambivalence of expression in which it is not always clear whether the objective or subjective interpretation is in mind (p. 818). For a more comprehensive study of the background to biblical demonology, *cf.* E. Langton, *Good and Evil Spirits* (1942).

[39] H. Conzelmann, in his book *The Theology of St Luke* (Eng. trans. 1960), considered that a distinction should be drawn between the time of Jesus and the time of the Church in Luke's approach to history, since the former was a period free from the activity of Satan (*cf.* pp. 170ff.). But this view is challenged by E. Ellis, *Luke* (NCB, 1966), pp. 15f. Ellis maintains that Satan was active in the pre-resurrection period and that the ministry of Jesus continued in the post-resurrection period according to Acts.

[40] R. Leivestad, *Christ the Conqueror* (1954), pp. 42ff., suggests that two patterns regarding Satan occur in the NT, one connecting him directly with sin, and the other, through demons, connecting him indirectly with disease, with 'possession', and death. In the case of Lk. 13:16 there is a direct linking of satanic influence with physical sickness. Acts 10:38, where oppression by the devil is mentioned, may possibly include physical sickness, although this is not specifically mentioned.

thew nor Mark mention this (Mt. 26:14; Mk. 14:10), it is clearly Luke's own conviction that the details which brought about the arrest and crucifixion of Jesus were the design of the devil. On the other hand Matthew's parable of the weeds attributes the weeds (the direct counterpart of the good seed, Mt. 13:38) to the sons of the evil one. Not only is Satan represented as counterfeiting the good, but also as snatching away the good seed to prevent growth (Mk. 4:15; Mt. 13:19; Lk. 8:12). Since it is highly probable that in this parable Jesus is symbolically representing the various reactions to his own ministry, this is further evidence of Satan's consistent opposition to the messianic mission.

Perhaps the most vivid occasion when a confrontation between Jesus and Satan occurred was the occasion, noted by Matthew and Mark (Mt. 16:23; Mk. 8:33) when Jesus said to Peter, 'Get behind me, Satan.'[41] This recognition of Satanic activity in one of the closest disciples shows how lonely the conflict was for Jesus. Of all people he alone could resist the devil. He was the only one who could tackle the 'strong man' (the devil) in his house (this age) (Mt. 12:29). It must also be noted that only the prayer of Jesus kept Peter from succumbing to Satan (Lk. 22:31). The synoptic gospels everywhere present Satan as a powerful personal agency of evil, in whom is concentrated intense opposition to the mission of Jesus. We shall discover later that this intense spiritual conflict appears in essentially similar form in all the major NT writings. It must be noted, however, that in the evidence so far considered there is no suggestion of the Greek type of dualism, for Satan is never absolute in his power. Whatever demands he makes, he can never exceed the boundaries set for him by God. There is, moreover, here as in the OT, no attempt to discuss the origin of Satan or to suggest a reason for his existence. The nearest is the statement of Jesus on the return of the seventy – 'I saw Satan fall like lightning from heaven' (Lk. 10:18).[42]

Our attention must now be turned to *demons* generally. It follows logically that if a supreme agent of evil exists, there will also be an army of lesser spirits. The synoptic gospels are so full of exorcisms of demon-possessed people that no true estimate of the ministry of Jesus can be given without taking full account of evil spirits.[43] Jesus came into a world in

---

[41] A. E. Osborne, 'Peter: Stumbling-block and Satan', *NovT* 15, 1973, pp. 187–90, interprets Mk. 8:33 in the light of rabbinic teaching on the *yēṣer*. The stumbling block is the evil *yēṣer*. Hence the contrast between the thoughts of men and the thoughts of God corresponds to the evil *yēṣer* and the good *yēṣer*.

[42] For a summary of various interpretations of Lk. 10:18, *cf.* R. Leivestad, *op. cit.*, pp. 48ff. He takes the words in a symbolic sense of the present certainty of Satan's defeat, although the final victory will not take effect until the judgment. If this interpretation is correct the statement tells us nothing about Satan's origin. R. Otto, *op. cit.*, p. 103, also takes it in a present sense of Satan's kingdom crumbling before the eyes of Jesus. On the other hand E. Langton, *Essentials of Demonology*, p. 170, is similar to Leivestad in assuming a future fact as if it were an accomplished fact in the present.

[43] In an interesting study of Mark's exorcism accounts, H. C. Kee, 'The terminology of Mark's exorcism stories', *NTS* 14, 1968, pp. 232–246, notes that the word which he uses (*epitimaō*) does not occur in the Great Magical Papyrus of Paris (*cf.* A. Deissmann, *Light from the Ancient East* (Eng. trans. 1927), pp.

which the adverse activities of evil spirits was everywhere acknowledged. All the cases of demon possession in the synoptic gospels are seen as specific instances of satanic activity. On occasions the spirits are described as 'unclean' (Mk. 1:23), or as 'evil' (Mt. 12:45).[44] At other times they are described by the effects they produce as, for instance, a 'dumb spirit' (Mk. 9:17) or a 'blind and dumb' demoniac (Mt. 12:22). The physical effects of the possession of the Gerasene demoniac (Mk. 5:1ff.) are vividly noted, particularly the uncontrollable violence. The daughter of the Syro-Phoenician woman is said to have been severely possessed (Mt. 15:22). It is further to be noted that Matthew records a saying of Jesus that it is by the Spirit that demons are cast out (Mt. 12:28).[45]

These instances, in all of which the removal of the demon also removed the physical features associated with the possession, might be identified with known medical or psychiatric conditions. Because of this it has been thought possible to explain away the accounts of demon possession by regarding it as a first-century mode of expression which has now become out-dated.[46] It is not surprising that demon possession has been a subject for demythologization. But the question arises whether the mere substitution of medical terminology is a sufficient explanation of the many instances of demon possession in the synoptic gospels.[47] These cases are not simply presented as illnesses. Indeed there is a clear distinction in the gospels between illness and possession (cf. Mk. 1:32,34; Lk. 13:32; cf. Acts 8:7). Moreover, healing of demon possession was almost always by a word of command, with the patient passive, in contrast to the healing of illnesses. There is a close tie-up between the spiritual conflict of Jesus and his commanding power over the demon world. A reinterpretation of the gospel exorcisms in psychiatric terms cannot satisfactorily explain the important place that this conflict had in the messianic mission of Jesus. It does not,

---

254ff.), nor in the leaden tablet from Hadrumetum (cf. A. Deissmann, Bible Studies (1901), pp. 273–293). He therefore distinguishes between Mark's use of exorcism stories (not intended to glorify the exorcist) and Hellenistic accounts (which glorified the heroes as wonder-workers). Kee thinks that only in the later stage in the development of the tradition did the question, 'who is this?' arise.

[44] T. Ling, The Significance of Satan (1961), pp. 14ff., maintains that Mark emphasizes that the demonic is essentially unclean.

[45] Some exegetes see demonic activity in the narrative where no mention of demons is made, as for instance F. W. Danker, 'The Demonic Secret in Mark: A Re-examination of the Cry of Dereliction (15:34)', ZNW 61, 1970, pp. 48–69. He sees the cry as a demonic attempt to discredit Jesus, but suggests that the subsequent and final cry expelled the demon. According to this theory, the resurrection shows that Jesus was not left to the demonic forces. J. Kallas, The Significance of the Synoptic Miracles, pp. 95ff., brings in the withering of the fig tree and suggests apocalyptists attributed soil sterility to the works of the devil.

[46] E. Brunner, The Christian Doctrine of Creation and Redemption, p. 135, in commenting on the 'powers of darkness' rejects the view that to believe in the agencies would be to revert to the darkness of the Middle Ages, on the grounds that modern acts of diabolical wickedness have made people more disposed to believe in agencies of evil.

[47] S. V. McCasland, By the Finger of God (1951), interprets demon possession in terms of mental sickness (as noted by G. E. Ladd, TNT, p. 53).

for instance, avoid the conclusion that Jesus himself accepted demon possession as a fact, and must, therefore, have either been mistaken or adapted himself to the level of understanding of his contemporaries.[48] Yet neither of these alternatives is wholly satisfactory. The 'mistaken' view clearly impinges on our understanding of the person of Christ, and raises more acute problems than it solves. The 'adaptation' view assumes that Jesus used contemporary concepts as symbols and that the symbols may be reinterpreted without loss to the authority of Jesus. Although this view raises fewer objections than the first, it is nevertheless no more acceptable as an adequate understanding of the mission of Jesus, for the gospel records give no indication that the demons were anything other than real.[49] Moreover, if the temptation of Jesus resulted from a real conflict between himself and the chief agency of evil, it would have been strange if he had had no confrontations with demons.[50]

Modern rejection of the synoptic exorcisms is not based on a study of the text but rather on *a priori* considerations. Medical science classifies in accordance with well defined scientific principles, which make no allowance for spiritual forces as explanation of physical phenomena. Belief in demons and their harmful effect on human life is *ipso facto* excluded. But this in itself is no conclusive proof that demons do not exist. The NT theologian cannot easily dismiss the significance of the accounts of exorcism. He is confronted with the inescapable fact that the gospels portray the demons meeting with defeat when confronted with the personality of Jesus. He is bound to face the question whether any theory of man which fails to take account of adverse spiritual forces outside of man himself is closer to the truth than the view set out in the NT. It is no less credible to maintain such agencies than to deny them. At all events, they are indisputably attested in the synoptic gospels.

One important feature of the confrontation between Jesus and demonic forces is the spontaneous way in which evil spirits at once recognize the dignity and power of Jesus. Mark, in recording the casting out of demons by Jesus, comments that he would not permit the demons to speak 'because they knew him' (Mk. 1:34). In an early case of demon confrontation

---

[48] G. B. Stevens, *TNT* (²1918), considered that Jesus spoke in terms which were current in his age, but he did not concede that this limits the authority of his teaching (pp. 90f.). E. Langton, *Essentials of Demonology*, pp. 173ff., maintains that there is no doubt that Jesus accepted the beliefs of his age in the existence of demons and Satan and that theories of accomodation cannot fully explain the evidence.

[49] J. Kallas, *op. cit*, p. 67, says that Jesus did not merely accommodate himself to contemporary thought, but deepened the concepts of his day concerning demons. He showed the fallacy of the Jewish belief that one demon could cast out a weaker demon, as if the whole world was in a chaotic state.

[50] R. Otto, *The Kingdom of God and the Son of Man* (Eng. trans. 1938), p. 106, considered that exorcism of demons was the centre of Jesus' message, although he interpreted the exorcisms as psychological phenomena. Kallas, *op. cit.*, p. 87, claims that such a view denies all external power to the demon world. It reduces Jesus 'to a rather befuddled do-gooder who spent all his time chasing harmless spectres who existed only in the imagination of the self-styled afflicted!'

recorded by Luke, the unclean spirit says, '. . .Have you come to destroy us? I know who you are, the Holy One of God' (Lk. 4:34), and is at once rebuked. A similar assertion was made by the Gerasene demoniac (Mk. 5:7), where the demon further expresses fear of torment, as if the very presence of Jesus constitutes torment for the demon world. Another feature of this incident is the request of the demons (Legion) to be sent into the herd of swine (Mk. 5:12). Whatever the explanation of this might be, there seems to be a suggestion that demons prefer some kind of embodiment. It would, however, be precarious to deduce too much from this regarding the manner of existence within the demon world. The gospels are not treatises on mental illnesses or on demonology, but accounts of what actually happened when Jesus ministered to people's needs. The important aim was not to demonstrate that Jesus had the power of exorcism, but to show unmistakeably that perfect goodness could not fail to arouse the activity of opposing evil forces, which had no alternative but to yield in face of superior power. This is more far-reaching than mere exorcism, for others could exorcize. The Jews practised exorcism[51] (cf. Mt. 12:27; Acts 19:13). Among other people it was often connected with magical incantations (cf. Acts 19:19). But what distinguished the exorcisms of Jesus was the sheer authority and total success with which he performed them. At the same time he accepted what others performed in his name (cf. Mk. 9:38ff.). The whole range of exorcisms appear to be an essential feature of the messianic mission.[52] When the twelve were commissioned they were given authority over demons (Lk. 9:1), and when the seventy returned from their preaching mission, they were overjoyed because the demons were subject to them (Lk. 10:17).[53] The name of Jesus was as powerful as his presence.

The Johannine literature

The concept of the *world* (*kosmos*) in John's gospel plays a more important

---

[51] Cf. Josephus, *Antiquities* VIII 2.5; G. Vermes, *Jesus the Jew* (1973), pp. 63ff.

[52] J. Kallas claims that the demonological motif is the key to the understanding of the mission of Jesus. His conclusion is that anyone who does not take this motif seriously, not only obscures the miracles, but makes the resurrection insignificant (*op. cit.*, p. 102). Even if Kallas is inclined to overstate his case, there is no doubt that he has rightly drawn attention to a generally neglected feature of the work of Christ. R. H. Hiers, 'Satan, Demons and the Kingdom of God', *SJT* 27, 1974, pp. 35–47, maintains that demon exorcism in the ministry of Jesus was an essential preparatory activity before the coming of the kingdom, which in his view is wholly future. *Cf.* also O. Betz, 'Jesus Heiliger Krieg', *NTS* 2, 1958, pp. 116–137: J. Weiss, *Jesus' proclamation of the Kingdom of God* (1892, Eng. trans. 1971), pp. 74–81.

[53] It is important to recognize that Christian exorcism was a powerful method for early Christian mission. As A. Harnack, *The Expansion of Christianity* 1 (Eng. trans. 1904), p. 161, points out: 'The whole world and the circumambient atmosphere were filled with devils; not merely idolatry, but every phase and form of life was ruled by them.' In such a milieu, the power to exorcize demons joined with a proclamation of liberty through Christ paved the way for the spread of the gospel.

part in the presentation of Jesus than in the synoptic gospels. It is complicated by the fact that John uses the word with a variety of meanings.[54] In
some cases the word means the created order (as Jn. 17:5; 1:10; *cf.* 1:3ff.).
But generally something more than the creation itself is intended, for the
word comes to stand for the whole order of existence into which men are
born (6:14). Jesus speaks of his own incarnation in terms of coming into
the world (Jn. 9:39; 18:37). In the latter reference it is paralleled with being
born. Martha, in John 11:27, speaks of the Christ, the Son of God, as 'he
who is coming into the world.' Clearly in these cases the 'world' is a
synonym for the present world of men. Hence Jesus can refer to his human
life as being 'in the world' (Jn. 9:5), and his death as departing out of the
world (13:1). When this happens the world will see him no more (Jn.
14:19). Departing from the world is, moreover, linked with going to the
Father (Jn. 16:28). We note, therefore, that in the statements just quoted
there are two important factors which can be observed. The first is that
the world was created by God and is still regarded as being his. The second
is that Jesus in his incarnation came into this created order.[55] So far we
have not considered any instances in which 'world' stands for something
evil. Before doing this, however, we need to note the personal use of the
term.

When God is said to love the world it clearly means the world of men,
who are capable of believing in him (Jn. 3:16). The Pharisees complained
that the 'world' had gone after Jesus (Jn. 12:19). Jesus himself tells the high
priest that he has spoken openly to the world (Jn. 18:20). His brothers urge
him to show himself to the world (Jn. 7:4). Obviously in these last three
instances John does not intend us to understand everyone in the world.
The word is almost a synonym for people in a generic sense. Presumably
we are to understand, however, that in this sense 'world' stands for a
considerable number of people. In the case of John 3:16 it may not be
thought unreasonable to suppose that God's love embraces everyone in the
world, although this raises some problems over the statement in John 3:17
that God sent his Son 'that the world might be saved through him', since
immediately afterwards salvation is restricted to those who believe. This
implies that caution should be used before assuming that the 'world' means

---

[54] A. E. Brooke, *The Johannine Epistles* (*ICC*, 1912), p. 47, regards the basic meaning of *kosmos* in John
to be 'the whole system considered in itself apart from its Maker, though in many cases the context shows
that its meaning is narrowed down to humanity'. For a study on the Johannine *kosmos*, *cf.* R. Bultmann,
TNT, 2, pp. 50ff.

[55] It is clear that the words in Jn. 1:9, which speaks of the true light 'coming into the world' (*eis ton
kosmon*), are intended to imply more than that Jesus came among men. There is some rabbinic support for
the expression referring to men in general (*cf.* Strack-Billerback, 2, p. 358; H. Sasse, *kosmos*, *TDNT* 3, pp.
889f.). But in the context of John's prologue it must refer rather to the sphere of operation for the mission
of Jesus, *i.e.* the theatre for the drama of redemption; *cf.* F. M. Braun, *Jean le Théologien: Le mystère de
Jésus-Christ* (1966), pp. 26ff.

everyone. The general title 'Saviour of the world'[56] is used of Jesus in John 4:42 and since this is recorded of Samaritans it may well be intended to indicate the universal scope of the salvation brought by Jesus, *i.e.* in the sense of extending to all nationalities in the world. The mission of Jesus is also related to the world in John 1:29 and 6:33.

More distinctive of John's gospel is the use of *kosmos* of the sinful world which is in conflict with God.[57] The reader of the gospel is prepared for this in the prologue where the statement about the Word being in the world is followed by the emphatic assertion that 'the world knew him not' (Jn. 1:10). Also in the prologue is the antithesis between light and darkness,[58] which links with the later statement of Jesus claiming to be the light of the world (Jn. 8:12; 9:5; *cf.* 12:46). Apart from him the *kosmos* is in a state of spiritual darkness. Indeed the *kosmos* is antagonistic to Jesus (Jn. 7:7). He came into an alien setting (*cf.* Jn. 8:23). It is an alien setting, not because it is intrinsically evil, but because it is dominated by the powers of evil.[59] Jesus sees his hour as the hour when the ruler of this world would be cast out (Jn. 12:31). The passion is a confrontation of Jesus with this ruler (Jn. 14:30), as a result of which this personification of evil is judged (Jn. 16:11). In this sense, therefore, the world stands for a system directly opposed to God,[60] which nevertheless has met its match in Christ (Jn. 16:33).

In view of the antithesis between Christ and the world dominated by Satan, it is not surprising that the disciples are also set in contrast with the world. In his prayer in John 17 Jesus declares that the disciples are not of the world even as he is not of the world (Jn. 17:14, 16). This section is particularly rich in references to the *kosmos* in this sense. The disciples are

---

[56] It is maintained by W. Bauer, *Das Johannesevangelium* (*LHB*, [2]1925), p. 71, that the title 'saviour of the world' is taken over from emperor worship. Whereas there is evidence for its use elsewhere, it nevertheless fits into John's world view and there is no reason to suppose that it does not represent genuine tradition.

[57] For a detailed list of the use of *kosmos* in John, *cf.* N. H. Cassem, 'A Grammatical and Contextual Inventory of the use of *kosmos* in the Johannine Corpus with some implications for a Johannine Cosmic Theology', *NTS* 19, 1972, pp. 81–91. He sees a different emphasis in Jn. 1–12 from Jn. 13–21.

[58] Bultmann, *TNT* 2, p. 17, sees these antitheses as derived from gnostic dualism, but John's type of dualism is different in that he never suggests that light and darkness and the other antitheses exist with equal rights. Bultmann does not take sufficient account of the Jewish background of Johannine ideas. W. G. Kümmel, *TNT*, p. 289, also attributes the Johannine understanding of the world to gnostic influence and suggests that John thought of salvation as liberation from the world of matter. Yet he acknowledges that John's use of the concept 'world' is thoroughly anti-gnostic.

[59] According to Bultmann, *TNT* 2, p. 16, for John *kosmos* is in essence existence in bondage. Although Bultmann thinks it is very doubtful whether for John the devil is a reality even in the mythical sense, he agrees that he represents 'the power to whose domination the world has surrendered itself: the power of darkness and falsehood, the power of sin and death' (p. 17).

[60] When Kümmel, *Man in the New Testament* (Eng. trans. 1963), p. 75, claims that John's *spatial* understanding of *kosmos* is derived from gnosticism, he goes beyond the evidence. He cites W. Bauer, *Das Johannesevangelium* ([3]1933), pp. 19f., and H. Jonas, *Gnosis und Spätantiker Geist* 1 (1934), pp. 146ff., in support, but parallels do not establish derivation, especially where a fundamentally different theological milieu is in mind (*cf.* the similar comment in n. 32 in this chapter).

deliberately distinguished from the world (17:9). Nevertheless Jesus does not pray for them to be taken out of the world (17:15).[61] On the contrary they are to be sent into the world precisely as he had been (17:18). The apostolic mission was in fact designed to bring faith and knowledge to the world (17:21, 23).

Although a dualism comes more sharply into focus in John's gospel than in the synoptic gospels, it is not an unbreakable dualism.[62] In spite of the antagonism and hatred, the *kosmos* is not sovereign. The same ideas occur in 1 John. Christians are warned not to love the world (1 Jn. 2:15), which is equated with 'the lust of the flesh and the lust of the eyes and the pride of life' (1 Jn. 2:16).[63] It is passing (1 Jn. 2:17); it does not know God (1 Jn. 3:1); it hates Christians (1 Jn. 3:13); it receives false prophets (1 Jn. 4:1); it harbours the spirit of antichrist (1 Jn. 4:3); it listens to its own people (1 Jn. 4:5); it is in the power of the evil one (1 Jn. 5:19).[64] There is therefore in 1 John a strong parallel between the 'world' and the 'devil'. Yet there is a careful distinction between them. Christians know that Jesus is the Saviour of the world (1 Jn. 4:14), and therefore faith in him can overcome the world (1 Jn. 5:4,5).

The Johannine literature is entirely in line with the synoptic gospels in portraying the activity of *Satan*. His existence is assumed. Moreover, his power over the world is focused in the expression 'the ruler of this world' (Jn. 12:31; 14:30; 16:11), which attributes to him a position of considerable status.[65] He is in fact the arch-enemy of God. He is also called 'the father of lies' and a 'murderer' (Jn. 8:44). He is therefore the antithesis of truth and life. When Jesus charged his Jewish opponents with being children of the devil (Jn. 8:44),[66] he was putting the position strongly. Some think this was too anti-Jewish to be genuine, but Jesus is commenting on their attitude to the truths he had just declared.[67] Their opposition reflected an alignment

[61] The distinction which comes out clearly in Jn 17:15 between being 'in the world' and yet not 'of the world', shows conclusively that Jesus did not consider that being in the world was evil, as the later gnostics did. *Cf.* Kümmel, *TNT*, pp. 289f.

[62] It is essentially an ethical and not an absolute dualism. *Cf.* E. K. Lee, *The Religious Thought of St John* (1950), pp. 109f. For comments on an aspect of dualism in some Qumran literature, *cf.* H. Hübner, 'Anthropologischer Dualismus in den Hodayoth', *NTS* 18, 1972, pp. 268–284.

[63] This at once suggests that Christians are intended to show detachment towards the world (*cf.* W. N. Pittenger, *The Christian Understanding of Human Nature* (1964), pp. 162ff.).

[64] There is in this context of 1 Jn. 5:19 a contrast between believers being 'from' (*ek*) God and the world lying 'in' (*en*) the evil one. T. Ling, *The Significance of Satan*, p. 34, points out that although in John's prologue all things are said to be from (*ek*) God, yet in its present fallen condition the world is in the evil one. 'The devil is the world's personality in a *qualified and temporal sense*'. *Cf.* B. F. Westcott, *The Epistles of St John* (³1892), *ad loc.*, on the contrast implied in the *ek* and *en* in 1 Jn. 5:19.

[65] It is worth noting that a similar title to 'the ruler of this world' is found in some of the apocalyptic writings (Martyrdom of Isaiah and 3 Enoch).

[66] R. M. Grant, *An Introduction to New Testament Thought* (1960), p. 94, expresses himself strongly on this matter. He treats John's gospel as a dramatization of the meaning Christ had come to have for the church, which reflects bitter feelings between church and synagogue.

[67] As L. Morris, *John* (*NICNT*, 1971), pp. 463f., says, 'Satan has no interest in them or in the truth. His

with the aims of the devil.[68] If Jesus could rebuke the Satan in Peter (Mt. 16:23), he could certainly use similar language of the Jews who were opposing him. There is no reason to suppose that these words were not original.[69]

Whereas Luke notes that Satan entered into Judas Iscariot at the time that the chief priests were plotting against Jesus (Lk. 22:3), John uses the same expression of the prompting of Judas to withdraw from the passover meal in order to betray Jesus (Jn. 13:27). Both are agreed that an action like the betrayal could be explained only on the assumption of satanic intervention. Judas seems almost to be a mere tool in his hands. There is a marked connection between the antagonism of the personification of evil and the antagonism of the *kosmos*. Satan has made himself king of his domain as a parallel to the kingdom of God. This may be called a dynamic dualism.[70]

It is only at the tomb of Jesus that *angels* appear in John's gospel (Jn. 20:12). In this feature John's account is in line with the synoptic accounts. Belief in angels and their possible intervention in human affairs is assumed in the reaction of some of the populace to Jesus. Their interpretation of thunder was that an angel had spoken (Jn. 12:29). But interest in angels was not strong in John's mind.

When we consider the approach in John's gospel to *demons*, we are immediately struck by the absence of any cases of exorcism.[71] In view of the many instances in the synoptics this raises questions. Did John dismiss the idea? This may be rejected on the grounds that belief in Satan was accepted, as demonstrated above. What then is the explanation? Since John is sparse in his narrating of healing miracles, his selective procedure caused him to exclude altogether many aspects of Jesus' ministry which did not immediately fit into his purpose. Moreover, he includes the occasion when Jesus was charged by some of the Jews with being demon-possessed (Jn. 10:19ff.). It is possible that John did not include exorcisms in his account of the ministry because he did not regard these as 'signs'. Such exorcisms were common in Judaism. Victory over the forces of darkness is nevertheless demonstrated in a more theological way (the ruler of this world has no power over Jesus, Jn. 14:30) than in the synoptic gospels. But John no less

---

habitat is falsehood'. Satan in John's gospel stands over against the Spirit of Truth.

[68] *Cf.* W. F. Howard, *Christianity According to St John* (1946), p. 89, 'Their attitude to him in resisting the truth which he revealed to them from the Father, and in resolving to put him to death, was quite consistent with the character of their father, the Devil.'

[69] Some scholars treat the references to Satan in John's gospel as symbolic (*cf.* J. H. Charlesworth in *John and Qumran*, pp. 92ff.).

[70] On the subject of Johannine dualism, see the excellent summary in G. E. Ladd's *TNT*, pp. 223–236. *Cf.* also J. H. Charlesworth, *op. cit.*, pp. 89ff., who includes a comparison with Qumran dualism.

[71] According to Fridrichsen, *Theology* 22, 1931, p. 127n., all demonism is condensed in the fourth gospel in the 'darkness' and the 'world'. T. Ling, *op. cit.*, pp. 28ff., in discussing the Johannine literature, considers that John's emphasis falls 'upon the total corpus of evil, rather than upon its local or temporary manifestation' (p. 36).

than the synoptics has no doubt about the reality of the unseen world of evil spirits.

Acts

It is not surprising to find precisely the same assumptions in Acts as in the synoptic gospels regarding the *created world*. When the Christians prayed to God, they addressed him as Creator (Acts 4:24). When Paul and Barnabas were hailed as gods, they not only claimed to be men like their hearers, but contrasted the practice of worshipping false gods with the worship of the living God 'who made the heaven and the earth and the sea and all that is in them' (Acts 14:15). This strongly brings out the distinction between Christian and pagan cosmology. Moreover in the same context the Creator's control over providence in providing food and 'gladness' is stressed (Acts 14:17). His further control of history is seen in his permitting the nations to pursue their own will. It is taken for granted, even in speeches addressed to pagan audiences, that God's absolute control of his universe would not be challenged.

An even clearer example of the same basic assumption is found in Paul's Aeropagus address (Acts 17:24ff.).[72] He identifies the Athenians' 'Unknown God' as Creator and names him 'Lord of heaven and earth'. Everything is attributed to him. He is the source of man's life and breath.[73] Paul even appeals to some words of Epimenides in support, which shows he did not expect the Athenians to be ignorant of God's presence in the world (Acts 17:28).[74] Again the divine control of history is especially brought out in the words 'he made from one every nation of men to live on all the face of the earth, having determined allotted periods and the boundaries of their habitation' (Acts 17:26) (see further the section below on man, pp. 162f.).

[72] For a discussion of the world view in the Areopagus speech, *cf.* N. B. Stonehouse, 'The Areopagus Address', in *Paul before the Areopagus and other Studies* (1957), pp. 1–40; B. Gärtner, *The Areopagus Speech and Natural Revelation* (Eng. trans. 1955); M. Dibelius, *Studies in the Acts of the Apostles* (Eng. trans. 1956), pp. 26–77; W. Eltester, 'Gott und die Natur in der Areopagrede', *Neutestamentliche Studien für Rudolf Bultmann* (ed. W. Eltester, ²1957), pp. 202ff.

[73] N. B. Stonehouse, *op. cit.*, p. 26, points out that Paul is here reflecting ot language, although he does not appeal to the text. The view of the created world which he here presents is thoroughly biblical and cannot be attributed to Hellenistic motifs. M. Dibelius, *op. cit.*, sees more contact with Hellenistic thought, but not with ot thought. For a thorough study of the speech, *cf.* B. Gärtner, *op. cit.* W. Eltester, in his article 'Schöpfungsoffenbarung und natürliche Theologie im frühen Christentum', *NTS* 3, 1956–7, p. 101, agrees with Dibelius in seeing in this speech alliance with Natural Theology and not ot thought. But this view is criticized by Gärtner (*op. cit.*, pp. 167ff.).

H. P. Owen, 'The Scope of Natural Revelation in Rm. i and Acts xvii', *NTS* 5, 1958–59, pp. 133–143, considers that the gist of what Paul is saying in this address is that Gentiles who are ignorant of God as Creator of the world may now be introduced to him. It is in this sense that he has been the unknown God.

[74] It should be noted that the idea of creation was absent among the Greeks (*cf.* E. L. Mascall, *Existence and Analogy* (1949), pp. 1–17). The Athenians would not have been familiar with the form in which Paul spoke of the created world. Current ideas, especially in Stoicism, were dominated by an immanent idea of God. *Cf.* the comments of H. P. Owen, *op. cit.*, p. 139, n. 1.

It is worth noting that Acts 17:24 is the only place in Acts where the word *kosmos* is used.

The activity of *angels* is seen in several Acts events. An angel of the Lord is the agent who released the apostles from prison (Acts 5:19). The same expression is used in Acts 8:26 in describing the one who gave instructions to Philip, and in Acts 10:3ff. (*cf.* also 10:22; 11:13) the one appearing in a vision to give instructions to Cornelius. An angel of the Lord figures in the release of Peter in Acts 12:7–11, and in the judgment on Herod in Acts 12:23. Stephen alludes to the Exodus narrative in which the appearance and voice at the burning bush are attributed to an angel (Acts 7:30,35,38)[75] and also mentions that the law came by angels (Acts 7:53). A curious remark of the disciples to Rhoda, while Peter was locked out, *i.e.* 'It is his angel' (Acts 12:15), seems to suggest some idea of a guardian angel who could assume the bodily form of the person he represents.[76] In this case it is reminiscent of the reference in Matthew 18:10. During the storm at sea Paul claims to have received a message from an angel (Acts 27:23). In spite of this strong evidence for widespread belief in angelic activity in the early church, there was one group of their contemporaries who did not believe in angels, *i.e.* Sadducees (Acts 23:8), whose opinion was combated by Pharisees (23:9).

As in the synoptic gospels the existence of an adverse spirit-world is accepted without question. *Satan* is mentioned twice (Acts 5:3; 26:18) and the devil once (13:10). Ananias is seen as a man whose heart Satan had filled, with the result that he lied against the Holy Spirit (Acts 5:1ff.). There is no question here of Ananias being absolved from moral responsibility because he was indwelt by Satan. This kind of Satan possession[77] must be distinguished from the demon possession in the synoptic gospels where there is no suggestion of any special wickedness on the part of the person possessed. In his address before Agrippa, Paul describes how he was called to turn people from 'the power of Satan to God' (Acts 26:18). This description reflects an important factor in the conception of the mission of the early church. Those outside the church were regarded as being in the grip of satanic power, an idea which is echoed in the Pauline epistles. Both Luke and Paul clearly see Satan as possessing power, although the power is limited. The clash between good and evil power is especially seen in the exorcisms.

There are several cases of *demon* possession reported in Acts, although

[75] The angel in this case clearly refers to the special representative known as the Angel of the Lord. In the Exodus passage to which Stephen alludes, the one who speaks is described not only as the Angel of the Lord, but also as God and as Lord. *Cf.* F. F. Bruce, *The Acts of the Apostles* (²1952), p. 170.

[76] *Cf.* J. H. Moulton, *JTS* 3, 1902, pp. 516f.

[77] E. Langton, *Essentials of Demonology*, p. 182, well brings out this distinction when he says that 'in those cases in which Satan is said to enter into a man, the possession is not supposed to be forcibly effected, and the man is held to be blameworthy for allowing Satan to enter into his life'.

far less than in the synoptic gospels. Nevertheless, people continued to be liberated as they had been in the ministry of Jesus. The exorcisms were performed by the apostles (Acts 5:16), by Philip (8:7) and by Paul (16:16ff. and 19:12ff.). They were carried out in widely distributed places (Jerusalem, Samaria, Philippi, Ephesus), and may be regarded as samples of the general confrontation with evil which the apostles encountered on both Jewish and Gentile missions.

Paul

In view of his strong indebtedness to the OT it is not surprising that the apostle shared the Hebrew view of the *world*. In some cases *kosmos* means the earth as in Romans 1:20 where the creation of the world is mentioned. Paul's view of creation is that God is himself the Creator (Rom. 1:25; Eph. 3:9). But he goes further and links Christ as also an agent in creation (Col. 1:15ff.). In this Paul's idea is parallel with the view found in John 1:3ff. and Hebrews 1:3. In fact he sees creation as made not only by Christ but also for him.[78] Paul sees the physical world from a Christocentric, not an anthropocentric point of view. Since *kosmos* is used in this physical sense, it is often applied to the sphere of human life, as for instance in 1 Timothy 6:7 ('we brought nothing into the world'). Paul can also refer to the different languages in the world (1 Cor.14:10), *i.e.* in the sense of the world of men. This use of *kosmos* for the world of men is characteristic of the NT. It is this sense which is most in mind when Paul speaks of Christ coming into the world to save sinners (1 Tim. 1:15), or when he speaks of the behaviour of himself and his companions 'in the world' (2 Cor. 1:12). Similarly he can speak of sin coming into the world (Rom. 5:12).

In some occurrences *kosmos* is distinguished from men (as in 1 Cor. 4:9) in which case it seems to refer to the physical environment. At the same time, it is difficult to see how Paul and his companions could be a spectacle to the non-human world,[79] and it is perhaps better to regard the conjunctions as explanatory, with the meaning 'the world, even angels and men'. Abraham and his descendants were promised that they should inherit the world (Rom. 4:13) and again the physical sense seems dominant here.

As in other NT writings, *kosmos* in Paul's letters more often has a moral

---

[78] There is clearly some similarity between Paul's view that Christ was that agent of creation and the Hellenistic Jewish idea that wisdom had a share in creation (*cf.* R. P. Martin, *Colossians and Philemon* (NCB, 1974), pp. 57f). Philo even calls God's partner in creation 'the first-born son' (*Conf. Ling* 146; *Agric.* 51; *Som.* i.215). But Paul's view that creation was made 'for him', so that the whole creation centres around Christ, is unique. The force of *eis auton* (for him) in Col. 1:16 is that Christ is seen as the goal of creation; *cf.* E. Lohse, *Colossians and Philemon* (Eng. trans. *Hermeneia*, 1971, from *KEK*, 1968), pp. 51f.

[79] The Stoic could think of himself as a 'spectacle' to the gods (*cf.* Seneca, *De Providentia* ii.9). *Cf.* H. Conzelmann, *I Corinthians* (Eng. trans. *Hermeneia*, 1975, from *KEK* 1975), p. 88 n. 36. Yet as C. K. Barrett points out there is a profound difference between the Stoic and Paul (*1 Corinthians* (BC, ²1971), 110). The former was proud of being a spectacle, but for Paul the word is used in a derogatory sense – he glories in his humiliation.

connotation, referring to the world at variance with God.[80] The whole world is accountable before God (Rom. 3:19). It has fallen under the judgment of God (Rom. 3:6; 1 Cor. 6:2; 11:32).[81] Hence the wisdom of the world is contrasted with the wisdom of God (1 Cor. 1:20; 3:19) and the spirit of the world stands over against the Spirit of God (1 Cor. 2:12). The world on its own is without hope and without God (Eph. 2:12).[82]

Yet Paul did not support the view that the world of matter was in itself evil. He sees Christians as lights among a perverse generation which dwells in the world (Phil. 2:15). He admits however that an alien force operates in the world – 'the course of this world' is equated to 'following the prince of the power of the air' (Eph. 2:2). Nevertheless, there is hope because Christ has reconciled the world (2 Cor. 5:19). This leads for the Christian to a totally new way of living in the world, *i.e.* living in it although not belonging to it (Col. 2:20). Indeed, instead of belonging to it, the Christian is thought of as possessing the world (1 Cor. 3:21–22).[83] The Christian must never forget, however, that the form of this world is passing (1 Cor. 7:31).

In the Pauline epistles, there are far fewer allusions to *angels* than in the gospels, but there are sufficient to show that they held a significant place in Paul's idea of the unseen world. A belief in their existence is undoubted. When Paul speaks of being a spectacle, he links angels with men as the audience (1 Cor. 4:9). He can refer to the tongues of angels in a way that suggests the quintessence of eloquence (1 Cor. 13:1). He rejects any other gospel but the apostolic gospel, even if it were proclaimed by 'an angel from heaven' (Gal. 1:8). When writing to the Colossians, he specifically forbids the worshipping of angels, which some had been urging on the group (Col. 2:18). In what appears to be part of a Christian hymn in 1 Timothy 3:16, Christ is said to have been 'seen by angels'; in this case angel attestation seems to be cited in support of the resurrection of Jesus.[84]

---

[80] There are several instances in which Paul uses *kosmos* in connection with 'this age' (*aiōn houtos*), *e.g.* 1 Cor. 3:19. 5:10; 7:31). This usage clearly merges into that which sees this age as alienated from God. *Cf.* H. Sasse, *kosmos, TDNT* 3, p. 885.

[81] The particular contribution which Paul makes towards the understanding of the *kosmos* is that he brings out most clearly that *kosmos* is the sphere of salvation history, which is not, in fact, confined to the world of men, but embraces the whole universe (Rom. 8:22, Col. 1:16). As Sasse, *op. cit.*, p. 893, says, 'The *kosmos* is the sum of the divine creation which has been shattered by the fall, which stands under the judgment of God, and in which Jesus Christ appears as the Redeemer'.

[82] In his article '*Oikoumenē* and *kosmos* in the New Testament', *NTS* 10, 1963–4, pp. 352–360, G. Johnston maintains that the NT view of the world has very definite limitations, and requires a reinterpretation. He does not, however, seem to give enough weight to the adverse spiritual influences which are unquestionably at work in our secularized society. He disposes too easily with what he calls mythological explanations.

[83] This conception of being in but not of the world is wholly in line with the Johannine view. *Cf.* above, n. 60.

[84] There is difference of opinion over the interpretation of the phrase 'seen of angels'. It has been suggested that 'angels' should bear its primary meaning of 'messengers' and relate to the witnesses of

When Paul speaks of the way he was initially received by the Galatians, he suggests that they could not have been more hospitable to an angel of God (Gal. 4:14). Moreover, when he wishes to deliver a solemn charge to Timothy he does so in 'the presence of God and of Christ Jesus and of the elect angels' (1 Tim. 5:21).[85] These statements are sufficient to show that Paul accepted without question the existence of an angel hierarchy which consisted of beings who were exalted and good.

There are a few particular statements which need special comments. One is Galatians 3:19 where Paul speaks of the law as having been 'ordained by angels through an intermediary.' Here he is reflecting a Jewish belief. The only OT basis for the idea of angels being concerned with the giving of the Law is in Deuteronomy 33:2 (LXX). The meaning in Galatians 3:19 is that the law came through secondary agencies as contrasted with the 'promise' which came direct from God.[86] Whatever the reason for the mention of the angels here (*cf.* also Acts 7:53 and Heb. 2:2), their participation is clearly intended to add authority and dignity to the occasion, although direct revelation is seen to be superior.[87]

The part of angels in the parousia is clearly brought out in 2 Thessalonians 1:7 where the coming judgment is accompanied by 'flaming fire'. This gives some insight into the function of angels as carrying out the commands of a holy God. This status is the exact antithesis of the fate awaiting the devil and his angels as predicted in Matthew 25:41. In 1 Corinthians 6:3 Paul mentions that Christians are to judge angels which suggests that angels are seen as actual beings.[88]

A more difficult exegetical problem is raised by 1 Corinthians 11:10f. when Paul says that a woman ought to have authority on her head 'because

---

Christ's resurrection, but a more likely interpretation is that spiritual beings are in mind, either bad angels or good. The latter seems most appropriate and could imply that the worshipping good angels rejoiced at the exaltation of Christ, in conformity with the idea in 1 Pet. 1:12 *Cf.* my *The Pastoral Epistles* (*TNTC*, 1957), *ad loc.*; J. N. D. Kelly, *The Pastoral Epistles* (*BC*, 1963), *ad loc.*; C. K. Barrett, *The Pastoral Epistles* (1963).

[85] The description of the angels here as 'elect' is intended to differentiate them from the fallen angels. A similar description is given in Enoch 39:1 and Odes of Solomon 4:8. The idea that angels will take part in the final judgment is found in Mt. 25:31; Mk. 8:38; Lk. 9:26; Rev. 14:10 (*cf.* Kelly, *op. cit.*, p. 127). M. Dibelius and H. Conzelmann, *The Pastoral Epistles* (Eng. trans. *Hermeneia*, 1972, from *LHB*, [4]1966), p. 80, suggest that the words may perhaps be part of a liturgical formula, but they do not attribute the words to Paul, *ad loc.*

[86] A different interpretation of Paul's intention here is given by R. A. Cole, *Galatians* (*TNTC*, 1965), *ad loc.*, who suggests that Paul is admitting the Jewish claim of angelic mediation of the law in order to go beyond it and show that angels also had a part in the revelation of Christ (in view of the angel visitations in the gospels). But if this was in Paul's mind he does not state or allude to it. *Cf.* my further comments in *Galatians* (*NCB*, 1969), *ad loc.*

[87] R. Bring, *Galatians* (Eng. trans. 1961), pp. 160f., considers that the reference to the mediation of angels 'suggests that God's highest revelation was not given in and through the law . . . Paul held fast to the holiness of the law, but the gospel represented a greater glory'.

[88] *Cf.* C. K. Barrett, *1 Corinthians*, pp. 136f.

of the angels'.[89] It seems best to regard the angels here as a guarantee or guardian of order in public worship, which finds some support from Qumran evidence.[90] It has been argued, in view of the contemporary nature of the problem with which Paul is here dealing, that the angels are considered to be guardians of the existing social order to ensure a stable society.[91] Under this view angels are not necessarily good agencies for they may be considered as upholding a corrupt society. Whatever the true meaning, there can be no denying that behind the existing order are powerful spiritual agencies whose presence cannot be ignored (see pp. 177f. for further discussion of Paul's view on the subordination of women).

Two other statements show decisively that Paul uses the word angel in both a good and a bad sense. Satan is said to disguise himself as an angel of light (2 Cor. 11:14f.). In Romans 8:38 angels are listed with principalities and powers as among the agencies which could not separate Christians from the love of God in Christ Jesus our Lord. Angels in this sense must be adverse agencies.

We come next to consider Paul's conception of *Satan*. Again there is no doubt that he was acutely conscious of the existence of this agent of evil.[92] He speaks of him under the two main terms *Satanas* and *diabolos*. Whatever the earlier history of Satan the adversary might be, in the Pauline epistles he represents, as in the gospels, the embodiment of antithesis to the will and purpose of God. Satan is seen as a hindrance in the apostolic mission (1 Thes. 2:18). He seeks to take advantage over Christians through tensions which arise in church life (2 Cor. 2:11). He tempts Christians to forfeit their self-control (1 Cor. 7:5). He uses various means to harass God's people, as in the case of Paul's thorn in the flesh (2 Cor. 12:7). In two passages Paul attributes to Satan activities which can result in good for people, as when he delivers to Satan the man who had committed incest 'for the destruction of the flesh' in order that his spirit may be saved (1 Cor. 5:5). The other passage is where Hymenaeus and Alexander are

---

[89] M. D. Hooker, in her discussion of this in her article, 'Authority on her head: an examination of 1 Cor. xi. 10', *NTS* 10, 1963–4, pp. 410–416, takes the reference to angels to draw attention to the worship of God. In her view the statement that Paul makes gives the woman 'authority', *i.e.* 'in prayer and prophecy she, like the man, is under the authority of God' (p. 416).

[90] *Cf.* J. A. Fitzmyer, 'A feature of Qumran angelology and the angels of 1 Cor. xi. 10', *NTS* 4, 1957–8, pp. 48–58. This author shows that evidence from Qumran suggests that any defilements (bodily as well as moral) were considered to be an offence to the angels, and he goes on to suggest that a woman with head uncovered was considered by Paul similarly to be a defect. Without conceding this latter point, we would agree that angels as guardians of order in worship was a current notion which may have influenced Paul.

[91] *Cf.* G. B. Caird, *Principalities and Powers* (1956), pp. 20f.

[92] R. Leivestad, *Christ the Conqueror*, p. 85, maintains that the devil plays no central part in Paul's theology. In this he agrees with M. Dibelius, *Die Geisterwelt im Glauben des Paulus* (1909), p. 191. Nevertheless the spiritual conflict between God and Satan forms an essential part of the background to Paul's thought.

similarly delivered to Satan so as to learn not to blaspheme (1 Tim. 1:20).[93] These cases appear to be an acknowledgment of Satan's dominion in the sphere outside of the church, but they also show that his power is not absolute and that God can turn his activities to good account. This idea that Satan is set over against God is reflected in the statement in 1 Timothy 5:15 that some had already strayed after Satan.

The astuteness of the adversary is brought out in Paul's assertion, mentioned above, that Satan can transform himself into an angel of light (2 Cor. 11:14). Since earlier in the same letter the apostle referred to the activity of the god of this world blinding men's eyes lest they should see the light of the gospel (2 Cor. 4:4), it is evident that the nature of Satan is darkness and his subterfuge in pretending to be light must be seen against this background. When speaking of the coming lawless one, Paul says he will come 'by the activity of Satan' (2 Thes. 2:9), thus focusing on the future designs of the adversary. Nevertheless Paul is convinced of the ultimate crushing of Satan by God (Rom. 16:20).

There are some instances where he uses *diabolos* instead of Satan, but these are fully in harmony with the concept of Satan outlined above. In Ephesians, Christians are urged to give no opportunity to the devil (Eph. 4:27) and to stand against his wiles (Eph. 6:11). In 1 Timothy 3:6 Paul warns against falling into the condemnation of the devil, *i.e.* the condemnation which the devil has incurred. In 1 Timothy 3:7 and 2 Timothy 2:26, he refers to the 'snare' of the devil, which is in line with Ephesians 6:11 in focusing on Satan's guile.[94]

In view of this emphasis on the chief agent of evil, it is not surprising to find evidences in Paul of *other agencies of evil* as a background against which man's salvation must be viewed. In line with the idea of Satan having an effect on human affairs is the concept of adverse spiritual agencies which are actively behind the rulers of this world, where these are at variance with God. Paul's most characteristic expression is 'principalities and powers' (*archai* and *dynameis*) or 'principalities and authorities' (*exousiai*). Other expressions linked with them are 'dominions' (*kyriotētes*) and 'world rulers' (*kosmokratores*). We shall also need to take into account such terms as 'the rulers of this age' and 'elemental spirits' (*stoicheia*). Over some of these terms there has been dispute whether they in fact refer to spiritual agencies at all. A good case can be made out for the view that the political authorities were regarded in some ways in the contemporary world as

---

[93] T. C. G. Thornton, in his article, 'Satan – God's agent for punishing', *ExT* 83, 1972, pp. 151f., departs from the usual interpretation and suggests that God uses Satan for disciplinary purposes.

[94] In addition to the names of *Satan* and *Diabolos*, mention should be made of *Beliar* which Paul uses in 2 Cor. 6:15, since this name was used in Jewish apocalyptic literature as synonymous with Satan (*cf.* H. H. Rowley, *The Relevance of Apocalyptic* (1944), p. 62). In the Testaments of the Twelve Patriarchs, *Beliar* is regarded as the personification of iniquity, who is the antithesis of God.

representatives of the demonic powers, which were believed to be the real authorities behind human affairs.[95] A proper understanding of these terms is essential for a true grasp of Paul's teaching on the Christian approach to the state (see later section pp. 947f.).

Paul includes principalities and powers in the list of those things which could not separate us from the love of God (Rom. 8:38,39). They are presumably regarded as potentially adverse. In 1 Corinthians 15:24, they are to be destroyed when Christ delivers the kingdom to the Father. They are already disarmed and defeated through the cross of Christ (Col. 2:15). Yet the Christian is in a constant conflict with them (Eph. 6:12). The superiority of Christ over the principalities and powers is vividly brought out in Ephesians 1:21, where he is said to sit far above these powers.[96] There are two passages which suggest a rather different approach. Ephesians 3:10 suggests that the church is to be made known to the principalities and powers 'in the heavenly places', but the purpose of this demonstration is not stated. In Colossians 1:16, Christ is seen as creator, not only of the material world, but also of the principalities and powers. The advice to be submissive to the state (Rom. 13:1; Tit. 3:1) uses the same word for 'authorities' and shows that a close connection must have existed in Paul's mind between the State and the spiritual agencies.[97]

In addition to the expressions which have demonic implications there are a few direct references to demons in Paul's letters which warrant our attention. In 1 Corinthians 10:19ff., Paul implies that Gentiles sacrifice to demons, which shows that, having declared idols to be nothings (1 Cor. 8:4ff.), he is not unmindful of the powerful forces behind them. He may have had the words of Deuteronomy 32:17 in mind when writing this passage.[98] Similarly, in 1 Timothy 4:1, when Paul speaks of 'doctrines of demons' and connects this expression with seducing spirits, he is clearly thinking of the activity of adverse spirits in teaching error.[99] He sees in the false teachers more than just purveyors of wrong teaching: he sees the powerful agencies of evil which are bent on perverting the people of God if at all possible.

[95] G. B. Caird, *Principalities and Powers*, pp. 1–70, has a full discussion of the NT approach to the political powers. *Cf.* also J. Y. Lee, 'Interpreting the Demonic Powers in Pauline Thought', *NovT* 12, 1970, pp. 54–69.

[96] On this passage, *cf.* T. Ling, *The Significance of Satan* (1961), p. 72. He interprets the powers here in relation to the law and sees Christ's exaltation over them as symbolic of his superiority over legalistic religion.

[97] This theme is strongly maintained by C. Morrison, *The Powers That Be* (1960). He shows that the association of civil authorities and spiritual powers was not only found in Jewish apocalyptic, but was also generally accepted in the Graeco-Roman world. Morrison develops his interpretation of Rom. 13:1 on the strength of this.

[98] So E. Langton, *Essentials of Demonology*, p. 185.

[99] *Cf.* my *The Pastoral Epistles, ad loc.*, It is not likely that the expression 'doctrines of demons' means doctrines about demons. In view of the link with seducing spirits, it must mean 'doctrines taught by demons'.

Linked with this idea is the view expressed in Ephesians that the Christians were formerly under the influence of the prince of the power of the air (Eph. 2:2). Their experience in Christ has therefore liberated them from the thraldom of demonic powers.

From the above evidence we may deduce certain features. (i) The world into which Christ came is seen to be so dominated by demonic agencies that the rulers can only be regarded as their tools. This does not mean to say that Paul was disclaiming the possibility of good rulers. What he is maintaining is that powerful spiritual forces lay behind the 'world' rulers generally. It is significant that Paul describes Satan in 2 Corinthians 4:4 as 'the god of this world', which powerfully brings out the dominant force of evil behind world affairs.[100] (ii) It is implied that dominion belongs to God and can be exercised by man only in a delegated way. If it becomes used by man in an absolute way (*i.e.* independent of God), it at once becomes a tool of demonic forces. (iii) The only real way out of this stranglehold is through Christ, whose power is greater than the opposing forces. This introduces an aspect of some significance for our understanding of the work of Christ (see pp. 476ff.). It also explains Paul's statement in 1 Corinthians 2:8, 'None of the rulers of this age understood this; for if they had, they would not have crucified the Lord of glory.'[101] Although the political officials (Pilate, Herod, Caiaphas) are primarily in mind, Paul's statement here must be interpreted via 1 Corinthians 15:24, where clearly the underlying spiritual powers are in mind. (iv) Some identify the principalities and powers with the existing fabric of society and suppose that Christian duty is to avoid weakening that fabric.[102] But Paul's approach seems to suggest that the principalities and powers will continue to be adverse to the Christian church. (v) Paul's view ties in with the extensive emphasis on exorcisms and demon possession in the synoptic gospels.[103]

---

[100] R. Bultmann, *TNT* 1, p. 172, contends that Paul is using gnostic language when he uses such expressions of Satan as 'the god of this world', and 'the prince of the power of the air' (Eph. 2:2). This usage is also found in Jn. 12:31; 14:30; 16:11. It is reasonable to suppose that both Paul and the gnostics based their terminology on the conviction held throughout the Graeco-Roman world that evil influences were at work in the world which are beyond man's control (see earlier comment in n. 32).

[101] There are different opinions over the right interpretation of the expression 'rulers of this age'. For an understanding of it as 'spiritual powers', *cf.* W. G. Kümmel, *TNT*, pp. 188f.; V. Furnish, *Theology and Ethics in Paul* (1968), p. 116. C. K. Barrett, *1 Corinthians*, p. 70, regards the rulers of this age as supernatural beings, but thinks that Paul, 'not merely permits but encourages the demythologizing of the primitive Christian beliefs, in part – but only in part'. This demythologizing according to Barrett is through Paul's conviction that the 'rulers' were being brought to nothing.

But against this view, *cf.* G. Miller, ' "*Archontōn tou aiōnos toutou*" – a new look at 1 Corinthians 2:6–8', *JBL* 91, 1972, pp. 522–528. J. Young, 'Interpreting the Demonic Powers in Pauline Thought', *NovT* 12, 1970, pp. 54–69, gives more weight to spiritual powers.

The most recent discussion is to be found in Wesley Carr's article 'The Rulers of the Age – 1 Corinthians II.6–8', *NTS* 23, 1976, pp. 20–35. This author maintains that the expression must be interpreted according to Jewish wisdom literature, in which the archons would be human rulers.

[102] See G. B. Caird's discussion, *op. cit.*, pp. 22ff.

[103] H. Schlier, *Principalities and Powers in the New Testament* (Eng. trans. 1961), pp. 14f., identifies the

It underlines his spiritual rather than political approach to the world around him.

The teaching in Paul's epistles on demonic agencies has a direct bearing on his doctrine of sin which will shortly be considered (pp. 200ff.). We must now, however, examine the meaning of the word *stoicheia*. The word occurs in two passages in Paul (Gal. 4:3,9; Col. 2:8,20),[104] but there is dispute over its meaning in both cases. Some regard it as relating to 'elemental spirits' although the root meaning of the word is simply 'elements'. There are no parallels to its use as 'spirits' and this presents some difficulty for this interpretation. The alternative is to take it to mean 'elementary teaching'.[105] In this case it may refer to elementary truths of natural religion, or to the whole system of earthly human relationships (derived from the use of *kosmos* in the same expression)[106] or to precepts. The major crux is the use in Galatians 4 where it occurs in a context which speaks of Jewish observances (*cf.* Gal. 4:10) and which some think excludes the reference to 'spirits', since it is difficult to believe that Jews could ever be thought to return to the beggarly spirits. On the other hand this is not a conclusive objection, for if the Judaizers were attempting to foist Jewish festivals on Gentile converts, for them in Paul's view it would amount to reverting to a state similar to that of their pagan background in which they relied on their own achievements to gain divine favour. In the parallel ideas expressed in Colossians 2 it is possible to understand the term in either sense, but the interpretation as elemental spirits makes good sense, as these are contrasted with Christ (Col. 2:8). The Christian has died with Christ to the elemental spirits (Col. 2:20), which means that they no longer have any jurisdiction or power over him.[107]

We may conclude that in Paul's view the coming of Christ has effected

---

demons of the synoptic gospels with the cosmic powers of the Pauline epistles, but G. H. C. Macgregor, 'Principalities and Powers: the Cosmic Background of Paul's Thought', *NTS* 1, 1954, p. 19, is not so certain. H. Weiss, 'The Law in the Epistle to the Colossians', *CBQ* 34, 1972, pp. 294–314., criticizes Schlier and strongly contends that the *stoicheia* are precepts.

[104] For a discussion of the meaning of *stoicheia* in Gal. 4:3, 9, *cf.* my *Galatians, ad loc.*; R. Bring, *Galatians*, pp. 188ff.

On the use of the term in Colossians, *cf.* C. Masson, *Colossiens* (*CNT*, 1950), pp. 122f.; E. Lohse, *Colossians and Philemon*, pp. 96ff. R. Leivestad, *Christ the Conqueror* (1954), pp. 95f., sees strong parallels between statements relating to the law and statements about the *stoicheia* in Galatians, which leads him to the conclusion that the *stoicheia* are not essentially evil. Yet they become a hindrance to salvation.

On *stoicheia* both in Gal. 4:3, 9 and Col. 2:8, 20, *cf.* A. T. Hanson, *Studies in Paul's Technique and Theology* (1974), pp. 7ff.

[105] Consult G. H. C. MacGregor, *op. cit.*, pp. 18f.

[106] This view is maintained by G. E. Ladd, *TNT*, pp. 402f. He contends that the use of *stoicheia* of astral deities is much later than the first century. C. E. B. Cranfield, *New Testament Issues* (ed. R. Batey, 1970), pp. 164ff., also rejects the 'spirit' interpretation. *Cf.* also H. Weiss, *op. cit.* (see above, n. 103).

[107] There is much difference of opinion over the real significance of the cosmic powers. Bultmann resorts to demythologization, but some who do not follow his existential reinterpretation nevertheless suggest their own interpretation which removes from the concept the 'demonic' element. MacGregor, *op. cit.*,

a remarkable transformation in the world-view of the Christian.[108] The world of adverse spiritual influences has been conquered.

Hebrews

The writer of this epistle has a strong belief in the OT doctrine of creation. He uses two different words to describe the creation, *kosmos* and *aiōn* (in the plural). The first of these is sometimes used to describe the world of men, as when Christ is said to come into the world (Heb. 10:5). The same sense is seen in the remark that the world was not worthy of the heroes of faith (Heb. 11:38). It is specifically used of the created world in Hebrews 4:3 and 9:26. On the other hand it is used in Hebrews 11:7 to describe the world over against God, where it is said that Noah condemned the world and inherited righteousness. This dualistic view, however, is not strong in Hebrews.

The word *aiōn* (literally 'age')[109] occurs in two places where creation is in mind. The writer begins with a high concept of Christ as Creator (Heb. 1:2) and maintains that he upholds all things by the word of his power (1:3). This is what we might call a Christological cosmology. A similar view is possible from Hebrews 2:10, although 'he, for whom and by whom all things exist' in this context most probably refers to God.[110]

The author assumes, without seeking to prove, the creative activity of God. In fact, he recognizes that man's understanding of that creative activity is an act of faith (Heb. 11:3).[111] It should be noted that the creative Word comes into focus here, as the upholding Word does in 1:3.

This epistle has much to say about *angels*. It was clearly important for evidence to be provided for Christ's superiority to angels, presumably because some were giving too much attention to them (*cf.* Col. 2:18). Since the writer nowhere calls in question their existence, he deduces evidence from OT citations to illustrate their true status. He sees the exalted position

---

p. 27, treats the cosmic powers as world problems (economic, political, military), while M. Barth, *The Broken Wall: A Study of the Epistle to the Ephesians* (1959), p. 90, considers them to represent the axioms and principles of world politics, ethics, culture. But Paul's own view of the principalities and powers as agencies which separate man from God is a more satisfying position, for this could account for anything which is opposed to God. Whereas he affirms that Christ has conquered the cosmic powers, Paul does not suggest that they are not still active. As A. Richardson points out, we see here the polarity of the 'even now' and the 'not yet': *An Introduction to the Theology of the New Testament* (1958), p. 214.

[108] J. Y. Lee, 'Interpreting the Demonic Powers in Pauline Thought', *NovT* 12, 1970, pp. 54ff., sets Paul's usage against Jewish and gnostic beliefs. He favours the view that God's redemptive purpose in Christ embraced the cosmic powers so that they, as well as man, will be restored. For a similar view, *cf.* A. Richardson, *op. cit.*, pp. 213f.

[109] F. F. Bruce, commenting on *aiōn* in this context, considers that although it primarily means 'age', it cannot be so restricted here. It refers to the whole created universe of space and time (*NICNT*, 1965), p. 4.

[110] *Cf.* J. Héring, *Hebrews* (Eng. trans. 1970), *ad loc.*

[111] *Cf.* K. Haacker, 'Creatio ex auditu. Zum Verständnis von Hbr. 11:3', *ZNW* 60, 1929, pp. 279ff.

of Christ as superior (Heb. 1:4). He distinguishes angels as of lesser status than God's Son (Heb. 1:5ff.). He maintains that the task of angels is to worship (1:6). In two statements something is said about their function. In Hebrews 1:7 angels are compared with 'winds' and 'flames of fire' (from Ps. 104:4), and are regarded as servants. This is reiterated in Hebrews 1:14: 'Are they not all ministering spirits sent forth to serve, for the sake of those who are to obtain salvation?' This function in the whole plan of salvation is not enlarged on in the epistle. It is introduced almost incidentally. In fact, apart from the section devoted to demonstrating Jesus' superiority to angels, angels are mentioned again only in 12:22, where an innumerable company of angels are linked with Mount Zion and the heavenly Jerusalem,[112] and in 13:2, where there is a reference to entertaining angels unawares (an allusion possibly to Gn. 18:1–8; 19:1–3).

If there is much on good spirits in Hebrews, there is little on bad spirits. Once only the *devil* is mentioned – as the one who had 'the power of death (Heb. 2:14), but at once his destruction through the death of Christ is noted. This is the only direct NT reference to the devil having the power of death, although John 8:44 implies it. Hebrews is not concerned so much with spiritual conflicts as with the major problem of approach to God. The writer concentrates on man's need and God's answer, without speculating on the spiritual forces involved. It should be noted that he twice refers to the temptations of Jesus (Heb. 2:18; 4:15), without referring to the tempter, although he could not have been ignorant of the source of the temptations. He has a pragmatic rather than speculative approach.

The rest of the New Testament

In the epistle of *James* there is one statement in which man is said to have been brought forth 'by the word of truth' (Jas. 1:18). Some echo of the Genesis account is here unmistakeable. A rather different approach to human affairs is expressed in James 2:5, where God is said to have chosen those who are poor in the world and promised them a rich inheritance.[113] There is no need to suppose that James believed that God's choice was affected by a person's social conditions. He is rather setting God's concern in contrast to the lack of concern shown by the rich, in order to show the unacceptable nature of any partiality shown to the rich in the assembly. A passing allusion is made to man being made in the image of God (Jas. 3:9)

---

[112] F. F. Bruce, *Hebrews*, p. 375, finds parallels in Dt. 33:2 and Dn. 7:10 to the multitude of angels. He points out that the Qumran community did not go as far as Hebrews, although there are some parallels to the idea of a heavenly assembly. *Cf.* J. Strugnell, 'The Angelic Liturgy at Qumran', *VT Supplement* 7 (1960), 318ff.

[113] An alternative reading has the dative with the sense 'poor to the world' (*i.e.* in the judgment of the world). In that case *kosmos* is set over against the poor in spirit. *Cf.* R. V. G. Tasker, *James* (1956), *ad loc.* For a discussion of the use of *kosmos* in James, *cf.* B. C. Johanson, ' "Pure Religion" in James 1', *ExT* 84, 1973, pp. 118ff.

(see next section, pp. 187ff.). Some indication of God's providential care is seen in James 4:14f. where James says that life is like a vapour and that the terms of its continuance depend on the divine will. Nature is recognized as working to a pattern, as the expression 'cycle of nature' or 'wheel of birth' shows (Jas. 3:6). James thinks of the world in an adverse sense in 1:27 and 4:4, but he does not regard the *kosmos* as itself evil, but rather thinks of it as representative of all that is at enmity with God.

The spiritual world is not much in prominence. Indeed the only allusions are an exhortation to resist the devil (Jas. 4:7)[114] and an assertion that demons believe and tremble (2:19).[115] There is an absence in James of that sense of spiritual conflict that plays an important part in Paul's understanding of the world. Nevertheless the existence of adverse spiritual forces is assumed.

In *1 Peter* God is specifically called 'a faithful Creator' (1 Pet. 4:19) and on three occasions mention is made of God's will which extends to various aspects of life – in the realm of suffering (3:17; 4:19), in the Christian life generally (4:2) and in social life (2:15). The Creator has not only created but maintains a continued concern for human affairs. The word *kosmos* is not used in 1 Peter in the moral sense.

The existence of angels is admitted (1 Pet. 1:12). Not only so, but Peter considers that they have a real interest in man's salvation. In linking them in 1 Peter 3:22 to authorities and powers which are now subject to Jesus Christ, he may be thinking of adverse angelic agencies. But since Peter gives no indication that they are evil forces, it may be better to regard them as good but under the control of Jesus Christ at the right hand of God. In one case, however, Peter urges resistance to the devil whose adverse intentions against man are symbolized as of a roaring lion (1 Pet. 5:8),[116] which implies his strength and destructiveness. If the obscure reference to 'spirits' in 1 Peter 3:19[117] refers to fallen angels, it should also be included here, but many exegetes do not take it in this sense.

In *2 Peter* reference is made to creation (2 Pet. 3:4ff.) and this is attributed

---

[114] Resistance to the devil, which is urged here in Jas. 4:7 and also in 1 Pet. 5:8, can be paralleled in the Testament of the Twelve Patriarchs (*cf.* Test. Simeon 3:4f.; Test. Iss. 7:7; Test. Dan. 5:1; Test. Naph. 8:4). This shows that the idea would probably have been familiar to Jewish Christians.

[115] Jas. 2:19 implies that demons possess intelligence to recognize their fearful destiny before God. This fear motif is also found in the synoptic gospels when demons come face to face with Jesus (*cf.* Mk. 1:24; 5:7; Mt. 8:29). There is ancient testimony to the belief that demons trembled at the names of the great gods (*cf.* E. Langton, *Essentials of Demonology*, pp. 26ff.; A. Deissmann, *Bible Studies* (1901), p. 228).

[116] It was a common belief that demons could assume animal forms (*cf.* Langton, *op. cit.*, p. 202), but there is no need to suppose that Peter is thinking in such terms. Similar language is used by the psalmist of his enemies in Ps. 22:13.

[117] The interpretation of 1 Pet. 3:19 is a well-known crux. For a full-scale examination of this passage and the problems it raises, *cf.* Bo Reicke, *The Disobedient Spirits and Christian Baptism* (1946). *Cf.* also E. Best, *1 Peter* (NCB, 1971), *ad loc.*; J. N. D. Kelly, *Peter and Jude* (BC, 1969), *ad loc.*; W. J. Dalton, *Christ's Proclamation to the Spirits* (1965). The latter book is the most important recent discussion. See also R. T. France's article in *New Testament Interpretation* (ed. I. H. Marshall, 1977), pp. 268ff.

147

to the Word of God. There is a clear allusion to the Genesis account in the fact that the earth is said to have been formed 'out of water and by means of water'. This comment on its beginnings is then immediately linked with the final destruction of the heavens and earth. The latter will occur only at the day of the Lord (2 Pet. 3:10, 12). In other words the beginning and end of the present material creation is wholly determined by God. The means for destruction is mentioned as fire (2 Pet. 3:7, 10, 12), a characteristic symbol of divine judgment. In two passages (2 Pet. 1:4; 2:20) the *kosmos* is specifically connected with corruption or defilement.

The only mention of angels in 2 Peter refers to fallen angels whom God had cast into hell (Gk. *tartarys*) (2 Pet. 2:4),[118] but nothing is said of the activity of these creatures among men. Indeed, it might have been expected in the list of sinful deeds and attitudes in 2 Peter 2, but there is no acute awareness of spiritual conflict. Satan and his legions are clearly regarded as defeated foes. In *Jude*, in addition to fallen angels (verse 6),[119] there is a special mention of the archangel Michael contending with the devil for Moses' body (verse 9).[120]

The book of *Revelation* is notable for its demonstration of the absolute power which God exercises over the world. The only time the actual word *kosmos* is used it is applied to the kingdom which has now become the kingdom of our Lord and of his Christ (Rev. 11:15). In this case it carries the meaning of the world inhabited by men estranged from God. At the same time there is no suggestion that the world has any other origin than God. In the liturgical passage in Revelation 4, the elders give praise to God who created all things – 'by thy will they existed and were created' (Rev. 4:11). This book shares the same conviction as the rest of the NT books that God created heaven, earth and sea (Rev. 10:6). The introduction to the message to the church at Laodicea speaks of Christ as the Amen, the beginning of God's creation (3:14).

In addition to this view of the world as created is the view of the Creator as Almighty (Rev. 1:8; 4:8; 11:17; 15:3; 16:7,14; 19:6,15; 21:22). This view

[118] The idea of Tartarus, as a place of punishment for the spirits of the wicked, is found in Greek mythology (*cf.* T. F. Glasson, *Greek Influence in Jewish Eschatology* (1961), pp. 62ff., who discusses the relation between the Titans and the fallen angels). *Cf.* E. M. B. Green, *2 Peter and Jude* (*TNTC*, 1968), *ad loc.*; C. Spicq, *Les Épîtres de Saint Pierre* (1966), *ad loc.*

[119] E. M. B. Green, *op. cit.*, p. 165, suggests that Jude may be using here the current language and thought forms of his day to teach the perils of lust and pride. In referring to the fallen angels, he is, however, introducing an idea akin to Jesus' reference to seeing Satan fall from heaven. R. T. France, *op. cit.*, pp. 269f., notes how popular the theme of the fall and the punishment of angels was in Jewish literature and thinks that 1 Peter, 2 Peter and Jude have all used this popular motif for their own purposes.

[120] Only in Jude 9 and 1 Thes. 4:16 is the title 'archangel' found in the NT. Michael is mentioned several times in Jewish literature (Dn. 10:13, 21; 12:1; 1 Enoch 20:5; 40:4–9; 2 Enoch 22:6; 33:10; Ass. Moses 10:2). He also features in Rev. 12:7. In the Jewish literature he is the guardian angel of the Jewish people and in Rev. 12:7 of the church. He is the opposer of the devil. *Cf.* J. N. D. Kelly, *op. cit.*, *ad loc.*, on the Michael legend referred to in Jude.

of God reflects on the utter dependence of all creation upon him. He is, throughout the book, on the throne. Even the activities of the enemy are only with his permission (*cf.* Rev. 17:17). The whole created order is expected to praise God and the Lamb (5:13). In the end, the creation itself is replaced by something infinitely better than the existing order (Rev. 21:1f.). The reader is never left in doubt about the final victory of God in his own world.

There is strong stress on supernatural agencies. The world of the book of Revelation is a world in which *angels* are busy carrying out the commands of God. The contents of the book are said to be made known through an angel (Rev. 1:1). In the vision from heaven in 5:2 an angel proclaims with a loud voice, a feature which is several times repeated (*cf.* Rev. 10:1; 18:1; 19:17). Angels are powerful creatures (*cf.* Rev. 10:1; 18:21). They are robed in white, symbol of purity, and are honoured with girdles of gold at their breasts (15:6). All the important actions of judgment are performed by angels (with trumpets, 8:2; with plagues, 15:1; with bowls, 16:1). (*Cf.* also Rev. 8:3; 14:6, 8, 15, 17, 18). They form the courtiers around the throne of God (Rev. 5:11; 7:11). One of them holds the keys to the bottomless pit (20:1). The leading archangel as in Jude is named 'Michael' who wars against the dragon.

If the good angels are portrayed as powerful agencies for the carrying out of God's will, the book also shows an impressive army of evil agencies who counterfeit the activities of those good angels. *Satan* appears under various names. The name Satan appears in Revelation 2:9, 13, 24; 3:9; 12:9; 20:2, 7. But he is identified also as the Devil (*diabolos*) (Rev. 2:10; 12:9, 12; 20:10), as the dragon (12:3f.; 13:2; 20:2), as that ancient serpent (12:9, 14–15; 20:2), as the deceiver of the whole world (12:9) and as the accuser of the brethren (12:10).[121] He has his counterfeit angels (12:9). He even counterfeits the divine trinity by exercizing his authority through a second beast from the pit and a false prophet (chapter 13). The dragon claims absolute homage from his followers in worship (13:4) and causes his mark to be impressed on their foreheads (13:16).

Among the devices used by the forces of evil are foul demonic spirits who influence the nations of the world to gather at Armageddon (16:13ff.; *cf.* also 18:2). The world of demons is very much a reality for the writer of this book[122] and the final triumph is not achieved until the overthrow of all these adverse agencies in chapter 20. The end of this book is a fitting

---

[121] T. H. Gaster, in his article 'Demon' in *IDB* 1, p. 823, maintains that Apollyon or Abaddon in Rev. 8:11 is an angel, not a demon. This seems strange since he admits that an angel is an agent of, not a rebel against, the power of God.

[122] E. Langton, *Essentials of Demonology*, p. 204, sees in the masses of horseman in Rev. 9:17ff., not a reference to a Parthian invasion, but a reference to demonic hordes. He thinks the bizarre features support this view.

conclusion to the account of the spiritual conflict which is hinted at throughout the other NT books. The final destruction of Satan marks the final triumph of God over all the forces of evil.[123]

Summary of ideas of the created world

In the preceding discussions we have discovered a wide measure of agree-ment in the different NT witnesses over the material and spiritual world. There is a general belief that although the *kosmos* is God's world, it is under the influence of evil to such an extent that the word itself can be used of mankind at enmity with God. An impression of dualism is unavoidably created by this means, but it is never a metaphysical dualism, only an ethical. It comes out most clearly in John and Paul.

There is also general agreement that spiritual agencies have a powerful influence. Angelic agencies for good figure in many of the NT books, and no account of the world of the NT would be complete without them. They are servants of God whose main task is to communicate the message of God to men.

Of greater significance for an appreciation of the mission of Jesus is an understanding of the background of spiritual forces of an adverse kind. Demonology pervades the NT literature and the activities of the demonic world were seen as hostile to the propagation of the gospel. Powerful forces are pitted against the power of the Spirit of God. There are constant evidences of the clash between God and Satan, but never any doubt about the ultimate issue. What is adumbrated in other NT books comes to expres-sion in the ultimate overthrow of Satan in the book of Revelation.

MAN IN HIMSELF

The most important part of the created order according to the NT is man, a view wholly in line with OT teaching. Indeed, the alienation which led to the redemptive activity of Christ is seen to be man's responsibility.[124] We must consider various aspects of the NT idea of man to provide an adequate comparison with modern views of man as well as supplying an intelligible guide to the approach of Jesus and the early Christians. Al-though the NT does not set out to answer the question 'What is man?', it provides some valuable insights which make its teaching particularly rel-

---

[123] E. Langton, *ibid.*, p. 218, considers that in portraying the doom of Satan, the Seer is following the forecasts of earlier apocalyptists. Yet the distinctive feature about the book of Revelation is that the agent of the final overthrow of evil is the Lamb, which links it with the total redemptive purpose of God in Christ.

[124] C. Spicq, *Dieu et l'Homme selon le Nouveau Testament* (1961), says 'La valeur de l'homme n'est plus appréciée en fonction de son origine, mais en relation avec sa destinée' (p. 114). Spicq maintains that man's greatness, according to the NT, is less as a creature of God than an object of divine love. This view represents man as he is seen in the plan of salvation.

evant in the modern debate. Much that humanism claims to be desirable in its definition 'human' will be seen to find a counterpart in NT theology, but without the weaknesses of humanism. Similarly existentialism, emphasizing a view of the meaninglessness of man, finds echoes in the NT's realistic presentation of man's plight, but again without its weaknesses. It is striking that the Christian view of man as expounded in the NT may be seen to speak to the ever changing world in which man finds himself, because it not only faces us with a brutally realistic view of man (as existentialism does), but also offers a completely satisfying solution to man's need. Our present task is to consider the NT teaching to provide a basis for a true assessment of man in any age.[125]

The synoptic gospels

Our starting point in considering man is that the human Jesus shows *par excellence* what man *ideally* is. The evidence for the true humanity of Jesus will be considered in the section on Christology (pp. 221ff.), and will not be examined here. Nevertheless, the salient features of Christ's humanity must be noted – his powerful impact on others, his concern and compassion for needy people, his kindness, especially to children, his utter selflessness and sacrifice, his evaluation of spiritual as superior to material possessions. In the gospel records he stands out above other people as unique. He provides a pattern against which all other humanity may be assessed. Because the evangelists are essentially concerned with the human life of Jesus and because they share with the other NT writers the conviction that Jesus was without fault, the idea cannot be dismissed that we are intended to see in Jesus a perfect picture of what man should be. The NT presentation of true humanity is radically different from those modern definitions of man which exclude *a priori* all reference to the supernatural (such as humanism, existentialism, Marxism). Jesus is never seen by the synoptic writers as totally self-sufficient. His perfect humanity is always seen in relation to God. The Johannine portrait, with its constant reference to the communication between the Father and the Son, brings this out more vividly, but it is not absent from the synoptics, as Matthew 11:25ff. shows.

We may deduce certain features from these gospels which will enable us to piece together something of a doctrine of man.

THE SUPERIORITY OF MAN OVER THE ANIMAL WORLD
While there is little specific teaching on this, it is the basic assumption.

---

[125] The importance of the doctrine of man for a right understanding of NT theology cannot be ignored, but care must be taken not to give it too much emphasis. R. Bultmann, for instance, places anthropology and especially individualism at the centre of his exposition of Paul's theology (*cf. TNT* 1, p. 91, and the fact that he devotes so much space to man in this section of his book). This results in an anthropocentric approach to Paul's teaching, which affects adversely its revelatory character. Bultmann's view is criticized by his own pupil E. Käsemann in his *Perspectives on Paul* (1971), pp. 1–31, 114, 135.

When Jesus said, 'You are of more value than many sparrows' (Mt. 10:31), he introduced a comparison which was beyond dispute. The same assumption lies behind Jesus' criticism of those who quibbled over the healing of a man on the sabbath, but who would nevertheless save their own animals on the sabbath if they had fallen into a ditch (Mt. 12:10f.).[126] This leads to the next observation.

THE INFINITE VALUE OF MAN TO GOD

In the same context as the 'sparrows' saying, Jesus mentions that the hairs of an individual's head are numbered (Mt. 10:30), a striking way of emphasizing, not only the providential care of God, but also the value of man. Yet we need to enquire in what sense this value is to be understood. Is it to be regarded that all people, whatever their condition and whatever their attitude to God, are equally valued by God? Those who have maintained a doctrine of the universal fatherhood of God have answered strongly in the affirmative.[127] But this goes beyond the teaching of Jesus, who did not speak of God as 'Father' of all men.[128] The conditions of repentance and faith by which people become 'sons of God' must be limiting. God is Father of all only perhaps in a creative sense (see pp. 78f.); nevertheless even this limited sense is testimony to the potential in man. There is a difference between potentiality and self-sufficiency. The teaching of Jesus in the synoptic gospels lends no support to the view that man is so superior he can do without God's aid in the business of living. There is also a difference between potentiality and destiny. Jesus gives no over-optimistic view that what man is capable of he must fulfil. The fact of sin (see below) shatters all illusion in that direction.

Other aspects of the value of man can be seen in such statements as the disaster of losing one's self even after gaining the world (Mk. 8:37; Mt. 16:26; Lk. 9:25).[129] This sets out man's value over against his achievements, his possessions, his power. Jesus is more concerned about what man *is*

---

[126] E. Schweizer, *Matthew*, p. 280, comments that Jesus' interpretation of the law differed from the view of the rabbis and the Essenes, who allowed men to be rescued when in peril of their lives, and animals to be helped to permit them to escape themselves. Jesus' approach enhances the dignity of man. 'Man can be seen in this light only from the perspective of faith in his creator'.

[127] A. Harnack, in his book *What is Christianity?* (Eng. trans. [5]1958), pp. 54ff., combines the fatherhood of God, providence, the position of men as God's children and the infinite value of the human soul as expressing the whole gospel. Although this leaves out the essential redemptive element in the gospel and must therefore be regarded as totally inadequate, Harnack is right in seeing that recognition of God as Father of us all brings with it a real reverence for humanity, even if the fatherhood of God is seen only in a creative sense.

[128] H. W. Robinson, *The Christian Doctrine of Man*, p. 82, admits that it is not explicitly declared that God is Father of all men, but he has little doubt that this is implied. He speaks of a 'real universal Fatherhood' and an 'ideal universal sonship'. It could be reasonably said that the 'ideal' sets out the value of man, but the 'actual' must take account of man's present plight apart from Christ.

[129] V. Taylor, *Mark*, p. 382, compares this saying in Mk. 8:37 with the statement in Ecclus. 26:14 which he translates, 'nothing can buy a well-instructed soul'.

rather than what he *has*. This must not be regarded as implying that Jesus is unconcerned about man's present environment. What he is pointing out is the principle of priorities – that man matters more than things. There is nothing to suggest that Jesus would have supported the view that a perfect environment would lead to a full realization of man's potential. The mission of Jesus was geared to a more realistic view of man's present condition. When he said that a maimed body [130] was preferable to a forfeited life (Mk. 9:43–47), he had in mind the view that it was worth any cost to secure the true fulfilment of man, but that this would not necessarily presuppose ideal physical conditions. In other words, spiritual values take precedence over physical.

JESUS' VIEW OF THE FLESH

There is no suggestion of gnostic dualism in which the physical was considered to be essentially evil. There is, moreover, a notable absence of asceticism in the example of Jesus (Mt. 11:19). Indeed he was criticized for his lack of it. What defiled a man, however, was what came from inside and not what came from outside (Mk. 7:14ff.).[131] The defilement had its origin in man's mind, not in his flesh. Nevertheless, the flesh itself was seen as a willing servant of the mind, because of its weakness (Mt. 26:41; Mk. 14:38). 'Flesh and blood' is sometimes used as a synonym for man without any moral connotation (*cf.* Mt. 16:17 and Mk. 13:20). Moreover, 'flesh and bones' distinguishes the risen Lord (in human form) from a 'spirit' (Lk. 24:39) according to Luke's record.[132]

JESUS' VIEW ABOUT MAN IN SOCIETY

Not only by his own example, but also through his specific teaching, he made it clear that man was never intended to be an individualist with concern for no-one beyond himself. He thoroughly endorsed the OT view of human solidarity, involving a spreading of responsibility. Social concern will be included in the later section on ethics (see pp. 935ff.), but here it is necessary to draw attention to man as a social creature. Jesus himself was concerned about those who were socially deprived, the poor and needy,

---

[130] This statement must not be regarded as a recommendation of self-mutilation. Jesus is following the Jewish practice of referring to the member of the body responsible for an action rather than to an abstract idea, *cf.* W. Lane, *Mark*, (*NICNT*, 1974), pp. 347f., H. Anderson, *Mark* (*NCB*, 1976), p. 238.

[131] On Mk. 7:14, *cf.* C. E. Carlston, 'The Things that Defile (Mark vii:14) and the Law in Matthew and Mark' (*NTS* 15, 1968–9), pp. 75–96. *Cf.* also A. W. Argyle, ' "Outward" and "Inward" in Biblical Thought', *ExT* 68, 1957, pp. 196ff. S. Johnson, *Mark* (*BC*, 1960), pp. 133f. comments that the principle expressed in Mk. 7:14 sweeps away hundreds of traditions in the Talmud and also in parts of the OT Law. But Jesus is here putting food and ritual requirements in their true perspective.

[132] There may be a good reason why Luke includes this flesh and bones saying of Jesus to refute any suggestion that the risen Lord was no more than a phantom. G. B. Caird, *Luke* (²1968), pp. 260f., suggests a possible anti-docetic apologetic. E. Ellis, *Luke*, p. 279, considers that Lk. 24:39 and Acts 2:31 'underscore Luke's affirmation of the resurrection of the flesh of Jesus'.

the deaf, the blind, the lame (Mt. 11:4ff.). He mixed with despised groups such as tax-collectors and sinners (Mt. 11:19) and sought to bring them into the kingdom (Mt. 21:31). The Sermon on the Mount contains many injunctions which would make no sense if man was merely answerable for himself. He must be merciful to others (Mt. 5:7), be a peacemaker (Mt. 5:9), be a light to illuminate others (Mt. 5:16), avoid anger or insult against a brother (Mt. 5:22ff.), avoid adultery or divorce (except on the ground of adultery) (Mt. 5:27ff.), be absolutely truthful (Mt. 5:33ff.), share his cloak with someone more needy (Mt. 5:40), even love his enemies (Mt. 5:44), and refrain from a critical spirit (Mt. 7:1f.). It is assumed without being specifically stated that a person's attitude and actions must take into account his responsibilities within the community (*cf.* Mt. 25:31ff.). If the teaching of the Sermon on the Mount appears impossible because too idealistic, it must still be regarded as indisputable proof that man's true destiny is to act responsibly in a social situation, in addition to being individually answerable to God for his religious life.[133] The teaching of Jesus on this theme is seen to be diametrically opposed to the self-centred and subjective view of man so frequently presented by modern existentialism.

THE PERSONAL RESPONSIBILITIES WHICH FALL ON MAN

As creature, man is expected to obey the ordinances of God. Such OT injunctions as the commitment of husband to wife and vice versa are assumed to apply to people generally, because they are part of God's creation ordinances (*cf.* Mt. 19:3ff.). The sanctity of the family is accepted without question as applicable to Jesus' contemporaries, but it is important to note that the reason given is the authoritative command of God. Similarly the rich young man was ordered to keep the commandments of God (Mt. 19:16ff.). Man is expected to obey. He is not given the opportunity to decide for himself. This hard line view of external supernatural authority is resented by modern humanists and existentialists alike, because it interferes with man's freedom of choice.[134] But is Jesus' view of man's accountability to God so totally unacceptable and therefore irrelevant for our present age? It was not palatable in his own time. It required total commitment, nothing less than taking up a cross (Mt. 10:38; 16:24). If man were to please himself he could never do this. The obedience that Jesus demands is not a shackle placed on the free spirit of man, but a wholehearted commitment to the perfect will of God. This is not a limiting process, but is seen as the ideal for which man was made in the image of

---

[133] It was this aspect of the teaching of Jesus which fixed the doctrine of the universal brotherhood of man (*cf.* H. W. Robinson, *The Christian Doctrine of Man*, pp. 87ff.).

[134] For a brief account of the modern humanist and existentialist view of man, *cf.* T. M. Kitwood, *What is Human?* (1970); J. W. Sire, *The Universe Next Door* (1977). Both evaluate these movements from a Christian point of view.

God. Jesus himself was the perfect example of this complete obedience to God. He carried his own cross both literally and spiritually. Those who do not like the imposition of a greater and nobler authority than man himself must part company with the view held by Jesus.[135] Luke records a saying of Jesus which sums up the point we are here making: 'When you have done all that is commanded you, say "We are unworthy servants; we have only done what was our duty" ' (Lk. 17:10).[136]

In the view of Jesus, therefore, man's true self is found in a life of obedience to God, because God knows what is best for him. Man is dependent upon God. He is taught to pray 'Give us this day our daily bread' (Mt. 6:11). There is no room for boasting in man's own achievements, for it is the meek who will inherit the earth (Mt. 5:5).[137] Again this view of man may seem unacceptable in an age of science in which man's achievements have made him think that nothing is beyond his capacity. But the words of Jesus do not refer to man's capacity for knowledge and ingenuity, but to his status before God. Whatever man does he is still creaturely, still dependent on God's provision. With all his ingenuity man has not yet created worlds, and until he does the approach of Jesus will remain relevant. Meekness was no more acceptable in the time of Jesus than it is today. Indeed, it is the very absence of this quality which precipitated the first rebellion against God, and has maintained it.

THE RELATION OF MEN AND WOMEN

In what has so far been said about man, we have used the term 'man' in a generic and not an exclusively masculine sense. Some comparison must be made between the attitude and teaching of Jesus affecting women and that of the Jewish world of his time. Judaism was certainly male-dominated and gave little respect to women. The distinction between men and women was so great that there was no provision in religious education or in worship for women to join with men on equal terms. In the pagan world, with few exceptions, the female was regarded as inferior to the male. We

---

[135] In a comment on Lk. 17:10, Kümmel, *Man in the New Testament*, p. 27, says that this shows that 'man was never anything other than a slave intended for God's service'. Man according to Jesus is under total obligation to God. This naturally sets out man as he should be.

[136] A Jewish saying (*Aboth* 2:8) applies a similar idea to whole-hearted commitment to the law – 'If thou has wrought much in the Law claim no merit for thyself, for to this end wast thou created' (Danby's translation, *The Mishnah*, p. 448). But this saying must be judged by its immediate context, which lauds the wisdom of certain rabbis. This is very different from the saying of Jesus.

[137] It is important to note the distinction between the Greek approach to humility and the virtue being extolled in Mt. 5:5. The former recognized the value of its wise men and philosophers avoiding presumption (*cf.* E. Schweizer, *Matthew*, *ad loc.*,). But Jesus' demand for meekness was more radical than that, in that he wished his followers to have no dependence upon themselves. Some see this beatitude as an assimilation to the LXX text, Ps. 37 (36): 11 (*cf.* J. H. Moulton, *The Expositor*, 7th series, 2, 1906, p. 2). But R. H. Gundry, *The Use of the Old Testament in St Matthew's Gospel* (1967), 132f., suggests that Jesus himself may have modelled the beatitudes after OT passages. There seems no good reason to deny that the words accurately represent the thought of Jesus on the value of humility.

shall note with special interest the approach of Jesus, because it not only affects our understanding of his mission but also paves the way for a more radical appreciation of the true place of sexual distinctions in the NT view of man.

There is ample evidence to show what might be called the humanizing of men's attitudes to women in the synoptic accounts of the ministry of Jesus. Matthew and Luke have rather more on this theme than Mark. Our concern will be to collect evidence which shows that both Jesus and the evangelists recognized the rights of women as much as the rights of men. The birth narratives of both Matthew and Luke focus on a virgin birth, which places a woman, Mary, in the place of highest honour (cf. Lk. 1:28ff. especially). She became the instrument of the incarnation. God could certainly have chosen another way; but Jesus entered humanity, as all other people do, via a woman's womb, as an indisputable proof that he was truly man. Indeed Luke's birth narrative is dominated by the women Mary and Elizabeth. All the synoptic accounts stress the importance of women in the passion and resurrection narratives. It is as though Luke especially wanted to highlight the place of women in the mission of the Messiah.

No distinction is made in the healing works of Jesus. Such summaries as Matthew 4:23ff.; 9:35ff.; 14:14ff.; Mark 1:32f. speak of people in general being healed. In addition several instances of women being healed are specifically mentioned – Peter's mother in law (Mt. 8:14f.; Mk. 1:29f.; Lk. 4:38f.), the Jewish ruler's daughter and the woman with haemorrhage (Mt. 9:18ff.; Mk. 5:21ff.; Lk. 8:40ff.), the daughter of the Canaanite woman (Mt. 15:22ff.; Mk. 7:24ff.), and the woman with a spirit of infirmity (Lk. 13:10ff.). Jesus allowed himself to be anointed with ointment by a woman and his feet washed with tears and wiped with her hair, and he defended her action in face of Pharisaic criticism (Lk. 7:36ff.).[138] Perhaps the most significant feature of this incident is Jesus' parting comment that her faith had saved her. Messianic salvation was certainly not to be restricted to men, and faith was seen to be available irrespective of sex.

Although all the apostles appointed by Jesus were men, the band of supporters who went with Jesus included women. In fact Luke makes a point of mentioning a preaching tour in which Jesus was accompanied by the twelve with several women, some of whom had been delivered from evil spirits and infirmities, but all of whom provided financial backing for the mission (Lk. 8:1–3). It is significant that none of the evangelists mentions any other source of support. Moreover the home of the two sisters in Bethany had a special importance for Jesus (Lk. 10:38ff.). It must further be pointed out that no opposition to Jesus on the part of women is recorded

---

[138] Note further that it was because of Jesus' compassion for the widow at Nain that he raised her son from the dead (Lk. 7:11).

in any of the gospels. Jesus quoted the OT basis of marriage as male and female becoming one flesh (Mt. 19:4ff.; Mk. 10:6ff.), which sets the marriage bond on a permanent footing and acknowledges the equal status of women (see later section on marriage and divorce, pp. 948ff.). Within households, Jesus admitted that his coming would cause tensions, which would affect daughters as well as sons (Mt. 10:35; Lk. 12:51–53; *cf.* Mt. 10:21; Mk. 13:12). Mothers were to be honoured as much as fathers in conformity to the commandment (Mt. 15:4ff.; *cf.* Ex. 20:12; Dt. 5:16). The importance of women in the family setting would be valued by Jesus, who had a special concern for his mother (*cf.* Jn. 19:27) and who was brought up in the company of sisters as well as brothers (Mt. 13:56; Mk. 6:3). When Jesus wanted to describe the wider family of his disciples, he included brother, sister and mother (Mt. 12:50).

When Jesus was led away after his trial, the only recorded expression of lament or sorrow was that of the women in the multitude that followed him (Lk. 23:28). Moreover, it was the women who stayed at the cross (Lk. 23:49), who noted the tomb where Joseph of Arimathea had laid the body and brought spices for embalming (Lk. 23:56), and who were present at the tomb when the first news of the resurrection was given (Lk. 24:1).[139] Twice Luke describes these women as having come with Jesus from Galilee (Lk. 23:49, 55; *cf.* also Lk. 24:22). Both Matthew and Mark record the presence of the women at the cross and at the tomb (Mt. 27:61; 28:1ff.; Mk. 15:40f.; 16:1ff.); indeed if Mark 16:8 was the original ending, Mark ends his gospel with an account of the women's reactions.

In view of all this, there is no basis for supposing that Jesus shared the contemporary Jewish view of women's place in the world. His liberated approach was quite revolutionary.

JESUS' APPROACH TO CHILDREN
Again Jesus reflects a human and tender approach compared with his contemporaries. It was one of the greatest scandals of the ancient world that unwanted children could be brutally exposed as a means of disposing of them. But Jesus' approach was utterly different. He welcomed children and criticized the disciples for not allowing them near (Mt. 19:13ff.). Moreover, he maintained that the kingdom belonged to such as them. His meaning is clarified by the passage in which he used a child as an example of humility (Mt. 18:1ff.). He pronounced strong judgment on any who caused a child to sin (Mt. 18:6). Special protection is provided for by God (Mt. 18:10,14). In this teaching Jesus shows the high importance he attached to the child, a factor which must be given full weight in any total pres-

---

[139] That women were regarded as witnesses of the resurrection runs counter to the Jewish ideas of the invalidity of women's testimony.

157

entation of his doctrine of man. It is significant that after the entry of Jesus into Jerusalem, it was children who cried hosanna in the temple, an act which Jesus himself recognized to be in fulfilment of Psalm 8:2 (Mt. 21:15f.).

The Johannine literature

The doctrine of man in John's gospel is inextricably bound up with the strong antithesis between God and the world. As already noted (pp. 130f.) the *kosmos* represents among other ideas the world of men alienated from God. Yet the central idea in John as in the synoptics is that man is a creature created by God. God is the source of his life and light (Jn. 1:4). There is, in fact, only one true light (Jn. 1:9). Those who do not possess that light are not enlightened. So John in his prologue leads into his account of the man *par excellence*, who was full of grace and truth (1:17). Moreover, John's portrait of Jesus was of man at his most glorious ('glory as of the only Son from the Father', 1:14).

It has a direct bearing on John's doctrine of man that he presents more specific comments than the synoptics on the perfect humanity of Jesus. He could be weary (Jn. 4:6); he could thirst (4:7; *cf.* 19:28); he could be disturbed and weep (11:33ff.); he could stoop to do menial tasks (13:1ff.). He is presented as a perfect man. Moreover, Jesus is declared to know all men, even to the point of knowing what was in them (Jn. 2:25), presumably referring to their motives. This makes his teaching on man's nature and destiny of vital importance for a true understanding of humanity.

If we take John's presentation of Jesus as the perfect pattern of manhood it throws light both on ideal humanity and, by way of contrast, on man's present deficiency. We note first the absolute dependence of Jesus on God. John's gospel is full of this theme. Jesus was sent from God (Jn. 3:16, 34); his working is the Father's working (5:17, 19); he shares the life of the Father (5:26); he came in the Father's name, not his own (Jn. 5:43; 10:25); he does the Father's will (6:38); he did not speak on his own authority (7:17; 8:28); he is one with the Father (10:30). The farewell discourses contain many allusions to the same theme. Since John is presenting Jesus as the Word become flesh (1:14), he intends us to see what kind of man Jesus turned out to be. Admittedly he is presenting Jesus the man as also Jesus the Son of God, but if Jesus was a real man his type of manhood must be a perfect representation of what humanity can be. Indeed there are many instances in John where the experience of Jesus is held up as an example for the disciples (*cf.* 17:11, 14, 18, 21, 22, 23; *cf.* also 13:15).

On this showing a true humanity must exclude all notions of man's independence. Views of man which dispense with God are diametrically opposed to the humanity of Jesus. If it is contrary to true humanity for man to be dependent on supernatural forces outside himself as modern existentialists like Jean-Paul Sartre believe,[140] then John's portrait of Jesus shows *par excellence* what Sartre would call an unauthentic man. But the portrait which John paints is not based on such existential concepts. No stronger picture of a real human person who faces the grim reality of his own situation with amazing dignity, because he lives in utter dependence on God, has ever been given than John's account of Jesus. It is in line with the synoptics, but more explicit. We may deduce as an absolute principle that man is only really man when he lives in complete fellowship with God, as Jesus did.

We may also note the particular attitudes towards people which Jesus shows in John's account. His human concern for others is as marked as in the synoptic gospels, although more selectively illustrated. If the element of Jesus' compassion is not as explicitly stressed, his desire to alleviate suffering is nonetheless present (Jn. 4:46ff.; 5:1ff.; 9:1ff.; 11:1ff.). Although John sees these miracles more as signs than as works of compassion, he highlights Jesus' concern for those with particular human problems (*cf.* Jn. 5:14; 9:35ff.). He has feeling for the family at Cana with problems at a rural wedding (Jn. 2:1ff.); he is prepared to talk with Nicodemus at night (3:1ff.); and the Samaritan woman at high noon (4:6); he looks at the hungry multitude and decides to take action (6:5ff.); he sends for Mary before raising her brother to life (11:28) and then weeps with her; he later defends her after she has anointed him (12:1ff.); he washes his disciples' feet (13:4ff.); he earnestly prays for his disciples (17:6ff.); and he commends his mother to John while being crucified (19:27). The risen Lord speaks tenderly to Mary Magdalene (20:11ff.), to the doubting Thomas (20:27) and to Peter (21:15ff.). He also provided breakfast for the disciples (21:12ff.). The conclusion is inescapable that Jesus, as perfect man, was deeply concerned for other people and reflects an attitude of compassion which leads to action. It involves a societal concept of humanity.

Another aspect of the ideal man seen in the teaching of Jesus in John is the superiority of spiritual over physical concern. Although John does not relate the fasting of Jesus in the wilderness, he includes a significant statement of Jesus to the effect that his food was to do the will of him who sent him and to finish his work (Jn. 4:32–34).[141] This cannot be regarded as a lack of concern for necessary food, but rather as an indication of priorities. It shows a non-materialistic, non-grabbing approach to life.[142] The work in this case involved other people (the Samaritans) whose spiritual hunger

---

[140] 'Total responsibility in total solitude – is not this the very definition of liberty?' J.-P. Sartre, *Situations* 3 (1949), p. 13.

[141] As L. Morris points out (*John*, p. 277), the disciples' misunderstanding opens the way for Jesus to impart valuable truths. To press on with the Father's will, ignoring all other pressures, requires great single-mindedness.

[142] The Johannine evidence for the true manhood of Jesus refutes any suggestion of docetism, as advanced, for instance, in E. Käsemann's *The Testament of Jesus*.

took precedence over Jesus' own immediate needs. A perfect man must be utterly unselfish.

When we turn to consider what John records about the constitution of man, we find the evidence is sparse. Various words are used to describe man. It is valuable to note the different senses in which these are used. The word *anthrōpos* is frequently used of man in a general sense (Jn. 1:4, 9; 2:25; 7:22–23; 8:17; 11:50; 16:21; 17:6; 18:17; 19:5), in some cases reflecting the opinion of others about Jesus. It is not used in these instances with any special significance.[143] In other references, however, there is a more specific distinction between man and God (Jn. 3:27; 5:34, 41; 10:33; 12:43; *cf.* 1 Jn. 5:9). According to John 3:19 men loved darkness rather than God, *i.e.* *anthrōpos* was in opposition to God (*cf.* also 9:16, 24). The word used for a man's life is usually *psychē* (Jn. 12:25; 13:37; 15:13; 1 Jn. 3:16). Only in John 10:24 and 3 John 2 is it used of a man's inner self. The inner disturbance of Jesus is referred to his *pneuma* (spirit) (Jn. 13:21), and the same word is used in contrast to *sarx* (flesh) (Jn. 6:63). This contrast of *sarx* with spirit is also found in other statements (as also in Jn. 3:6) or contrasted with God (Jn. 8:15; 1 Jn. 2:16). It will be seen therefore, that *sarx* in the Johannine literature (as in Paul)[144] sometimes stands for man apart from the Spirit of God. It is also used, however, of the human life of Jesus (Jn. 1:14; 6:51–56; 1 Jn. 4:2; 2 Jn. 7). The word for 'body' (*sōma*) is not used in a sacramental sense as in the synoptic gospels, but only of the body of Jesus that was crucified (Jn. 2:21; 19:38; 20:12).[145]

It is clear from the Johannine literature that man, in spite of his present state of antagonism to God, is nevertheless of high value in the sight of God. The incarnation is in itself a sufficient warrant for this. The becoming of the Word in flesh was the result of God's great love for man. Indeed, the whole mission of Jesus underlines man's worth in God's sight. Throughout there is the contrast between what man ought to be and what he is. Man's fallen state will be discussed in the next section, but the gist of Jesus' message in John's gospel is that opportunity is open for man to find his true fulfilment by faith in him. There is a paradoxical alternation of God's action and man's response. The Father 'draws' (Jn. 6:44; *cf.* 6:37, 39; 17:2, 6, 9, 12, 24), but man must believe (Jn. 5:24; 6:35). The main point we wish to stress at the moment is that it is clearly the intention of God that man should not be closed up to the present world (*kosmos*) system,[146] but that a way should be provided for a restitution of man to

[143] *Cf.* F. M. Braun, *Jean le Théologien: Le Christ, notre Seigneur* (1972), p. 205.
[144] See W. G. Kümmel's note on *anthrōpos, sarx* and *sōma* in John's gospel, *Man in the New Testament*, p. 74, n. 84. Kümmel considers that 'man for John as for Paul always stands over against God and from this he derives his characteristic stamp' (p. 74). Nevertheless Kümmel agrees that John did not see man bound in inextricable opposition to God as in metaphysical dualism.
[145] *Cf.* W. G. Kümmel, *op. cit.*, 74 n. 84.
[146] *Cf.* R. Bultmann, *TNT* 2, pp. 21f., for a discussion of Johannine determinism.

his full capacity as a human being. It is in this sense that the doctrine of re-birth is so important (see later section pp. 585ff.).

Acts

There are a few distinctive features in the doctrine of man in Acts as compared with the synoptic gospels. The human life of Jesus is mentioned both in Acts 2:22 and 10:38f., but the focus of attention in the speeches is not on Jesus as the ideal man, but on the man who was crucified.

Man is seen as a creature who owes obedience to God (Acts 5:29, 32). The disciples had grasped this obligation and were implying that the religious authorities were failing to do so. Peter and John put the choice clearly when they challenged the council to judge whether they should take them or God as their guide in determining what is right (Acts 4:19). The earliest Christian ethic was based on the unshakeable belief that God's commands for men were authoritative. Even among the more thoughtful members of the Jewish hierarchy there was a strong fear that they might be opposing God (Acts 5:39). The Israelites' disobedience to God was one of the main themes of Stephen's speech (Acts 7:39) and he charged his hearers with continually resisting the Holy Spirit (Acts 7:51—'as your fathers did, so do you'). This is not based on the concept of collective responsibility, but on the repetition of history. Failure in the past and present to achieve this ideal of obedience only highlights the real pattern for which man was created.

One of the most distinctive features in Acts is the realization that all men, Jew and Gentile, were on an equal footing before God. This did not come easily in the first century AD, especially in a strongly Jewish milieu. It required a direct vision from God to convince the leading apostle of it (Acts 10 and 11). The inclusion of the Gentile Cornelius and his household into the Christian church on equal terms (demonstrated by the descent of the Holy Spirit) marked a vital development in the early Christian doctrine of man. This was further established by the far-reaching decision of the Jerusalem church not to require Gentiles to be circumcised. When Peter said that the Holy Spirit 'made no distinction between us and them' (Acts 15:9), he enunciated a principle which the apostle Paul was specifically to stress in his letters (*cf.* Gal. 3:28). Racial barriers were swept away and man was seen as man rather than as a member of an ethnic group.

Another distinctive feature in Acts is the way in which man is recognized in his social aspect. Although the earliest experiment in communal living was not continued (4:32f.), it bears testimony to the strong social feelings of the early Christians. They did not regard their lives from a purely selfish point of view. There was a sense of solidarity which made many desire to share all their possessions, although this was entirely voluntary. This corporate concept of man also led to other acts of relief within the Christian community, as when the widows were cared for (6:1ff.) or when relief was sent from Antioch for famine-stricken Christians in Judea (11:29). Even before his conversion to the Christian faith, Cornelius was renowned for his public-spirited generosity towards the people, which received commendation from Luke in narrating it (10:2). In his address to the Ephesian elders Paul concludes by urging help to the weak, citing words of Jesus about giving, which are not recorded in the gospels (20:35). There is a strong community spirit running through this book.

Following on the synoptic evidence of the place of women in the ministry and teaching of Jesus, we are not surprised to find a similar emphasis in Acts. In the upper room women were present with the men (Acts 1:14), and equally received the Holy Spirit on the day of Pentecost without any distinction. Indeed in citing Joel's prophecy, Peter included both 'sons' and 'daughters' in the act of prophecy (2:17). 'All flesh' is thus explicitly defined as including both sexes on equal terms in the age of the Spirit. When the full fury of Saul's persecution burst on the church, no distinction was made between men and women (Acts 8:3). At Philippi two women (Lydia and the slave girl) were among the first to be influenced by the Christian gospel (16:14ff.). Also Luke specially mentions that at Thessalonica several leading Greek women believed (17:4). The same happened at Beroea, where many high ranking Greek women were among the believers (17:12). It should be noted that Macedonia, where all these places were situated, had a particularly enlightened attitude towards women, which few of their pagan contemporaries shared. It is not surprising that the gospel, with its view of the essential equality of men and women in the sight of God, found a ready response in such an environment. Some prominence is also given to Priscilla among the associates of Paul (18:2, 26).

One further feature must be noted – the joint responsibility of Sapphira with her husband Ananias for their lying to the Holy Spirit (Acts 5:1ff.). In this case they had consented together and were therefore jointly responsible and consequently shared the same fate.

There is one passage in Acts which is reckoned by some to present a different view of man from the NT as a whole (except 2 Peter 1:4). The Areopagus address of Paul in Acts 17 contains a statement which is claimed to present a Hellenistic view of man. People are urged to seek God on the grounds that he is not far from any of us and one of the Greek poets is quoted as saying, 'We are his offspring' (Acts 17:27–29).[147] The Stoics advanced the idea of man's kinship to God and of the existence of the world in God, ideas admittedly alien to the NT generally. Since the text of Acts specifically attributes the ideas mentioned to a Greek poet and has

---

[147] Kümmel, *op. cit.*, p. 87, finds only two exceptions within the NT to the idea that man is tied to history and can be delivered only by a change in that historical context. One such passage is Acts 17:27–9, which Kümmel sees as Stoic in origin. The other passage is 2 Pet. 1:4. *Cf.* also M. Dibelius, *Studies in the Acts of the Apostles* (Eng. trans. 1956), pp. 26ff., who takes a similar view.

probably derived the saying, 'in him we live and move and have our being', from a similar source, it is not surprising to find a strongly Greek view of man being expressed. Some think that the Areopagus address is incomplete and that Paul was interrupted (Acts 17:32).[148] It would be precarious in that case to base the view of man set out in this speech solely on statements which the speaker himself does not claim to be original and which are not therefore purporting to be specifically Christian.[149] But the basic doctrine of man expressed in this speech is no different from that found in other biblical evidence, and there is therefore no need to isolate it. The facts are expressed in a unique way, but there is insufficient support for the view that it represents a different school of thought compared with the mainstream of NT thought about man.[150]

Paul: preliminary remarks

Of all the NT writers, Paul gives the fullest expression to a doctrine of man.[151] In fact, many theological treatments of the theme concentrate wholly on the terms which Paul uses to describe the constitution of man. While these terms are of great importance and must be carefully considered, they cannot be regarded in isolation from the rest of the NT evidence. Moreover, the terms themselves are variously used by Paul and it is therefore difficult to build up a consistent picture. The apostle does not present a careful definition of his terms. Although we may discover some light on them by examining contemporary usage, this usage must be viewed with caution, since Paul's approach has its own distinctive features. It must further be noted that there are other aspects of Paul's doctrine of man which are not contained within an examination of the terms he uses, and these must be brought in to give a balanced picture.

The Pauline anthropological terms

The main ideas which Paul uses to describe various aspects of man are soul (*psychē*), spirit (*pneuma*), flesh (*sarx*), body (*sōma*), heart (*kardia*) and mind

---

[148] Luke, of course, does not specifically say that Paul was interrupted. He presents the speech in a way that suggests that Paul had finished, but that the resurrection, the key factor in a radically Christian approach, met with obdurate resistance. *Cf.* N. B. Stonehouse, *Paul before the Areopagus*, pp. 36ff., on the ending and its implications.

[149] For a defence of the Pauline origin of the Areopagus speech, *cf.* B. Gärtner, *The Areopagus Speech and Natural Revelation* (1955).

[150] *Cf.* H. P. Owens, 'The Scope of Natural Revelation in Rom. I and Acts XVII', *NTS* 5, 1958–9, pp. 133–143, for an interpretation of Acts 17 in the light of Rom. 1. (See above, n. 73). T. D. Barnes, 'An Apostle on Trial', *JTS* 20, 1969, pp. 407–419, maintains that Paul was put on trial and that his speech in Acts 17:16–34 was his defence.

[151] For studies on Paul's view of man, *cf.* E. D. Burton, *Spirit, Soul and Flesh* (1918), pp. 186–198; H. W. Robinson, *The Christian Doctrine of Man*. pp. 104–135; W. D. Stacey, *The Pauline View of Man* (1956); W. G. Kümmel, *Man in the New Testament*, pp. 38–71; R. Bultmann, *TNT* 1, pp. 190–245; H. Conzelmann, *TNT*, pp. 173–183; H. Schlier, 'Vom menschenbild des Neuen Testaments', in *Der Alte und Neue Mensch* (G. von Rad, *et al.*); *Beiträge zur Evangelischen Theologie* VIII (1942), pp. 24ff.; C. Spicq, *Dieu et l'Homme selon le nouveau Testament*, Lectio Divina (1961), pp. 147–177.

(*nous*).[152] To these may be added the important concept of conscience (*syneidēsis*) and the characteristically Pauline idea of the inner man. A brief summary must be given of each of these terms to demonstrate the rather loose way in which Paul uses them. Taken separately they can lead to considerable confusion, as they frequently overlap in their meaning, but taken together they provide a valuable insight into the apostle's understanding. It is essential, when considering these terms, to bear in mind that Paul views man's constitution from God's standpoint, which means that his statements often involve a merging of the non-Christian state of man with the potentials of the Christian ideal. In this section our focus will be on the non-Christian state, since Paul's teaching about the new man in Christ will be considered in a later section (see pp. 641ff.).

SOUL

This is the least important of Paul's terms. He uses it only thirteen times. It is completely overshadowed by the word 'spirit'. When 'soul' is used, it mainly indicates a man's life (Rom. 11:3; 16:4; Phil. 2:30). It involves a little more than this in 1 Thessalonians 2:8, where it seems to mean 'self'. Since Paul uses the adjective 'lifeless' (*apsychos*) as a term for inanimate objects, the general force of 'soul' for 'life' becomes clear (*cf.* 1 Cor. 14:7). Man as a living creature is very much tied up with his 'life'. In 2 Corinthians 1:23 Paul calls God to witness on his *psychē*, when he wants to emphasize the truth of his words. Contemporary usage sometimes invested the word with the sense of 'will', but the only support in Paul for this meaning is in Colossians 3:23 and Ephesians 6:6. In Philippians 1:27 it may have this sense or alternatively it may mean 'desire'.[153] On the other hand *psychē* is so closely linked with *pneuma* in this passage, that Paul's distinctive use of 'spirit' (see next section) has clearly led him to his own modification of the use of 'soul'.

In one instance Paul links man's soul with the agency of evil (Rom. 2:9). There is no suggestion here, however, that the soul is evil in itself, but since it is part of the whole man it must be implicated in man's general sinful condition. A similar usage is found in Romans 13:1 where, although reference to sin is absent, the *psychē* again refers to the whole man (*cf.* also 2 Cor. 12:15). In 1 Corinthians 2:14 *psychikos* (unspiritual, natural) is used of unregenerate man in antithesis to *pneumatikos* (spiritual); this is a some-

---

[152] For word studies on these terms, see *kardia*, TDNT, 3, pp. 605ff. (J. Behm); *nous*, 4, pp. 951ff., (J. Behm); *pneuma*, 6, 332ff., (H. Kleinknecht, F. Baumgärtel, W. Bieder, E. Sjoberg, E. Schweizer); *sarx*, 7, pp. 98ff., (E. Schweizer, R. Meyer); *sōma*, 7, pp. 1024ff. (E. Schweizer, F. Baumgärtel); *psychē*, 9, pp. 608ff., (G. Bertram, A. Dihle, E. Jacob, E. Lohse, E. Schweizer, K. W. Tröger). On *sōma*, *cf.* also R. H. Gundry, *Sōma in Biblical Theology* (1976). On *sarx*, see also works cited in n. 169 below. For an over-all survey, *cf.* R. Jewett, *Paul's Anthropological Terms: A Study of their Use in Conflict Settings* (1971).

[153] H. W. Robinson, *op. cit.*, p. 108, prefers the sense 'desire', but C. Ryder Smith, *The Bible Doctrine of Man* (1951), p. 138, considers it here means simply man's life.

what different use of the term, but again does not imply that *psychē* is necessarily evil.

One Pauline use of 'soul' (in 1 Thes. 5:23) has given rise to much debate over whether Paul viewed man as a triad, since *psychē* is linked in this passage with body and spirit. If he is here giving his own opinion that man is tripartite, it is the only occasion on which he does, and it seems highly unlikely that the statement should be considered as a careful description of the constitution of man. If the apostle's use of the terms elsewhere had been uniform there might well have been some support for the triad view. Since in this passage Paul is concerned with the preservation of the whole man, it would seem reasonable to suppose that the piling up of terms is for emphasis rather than for definition.[154] In this case it would be in line with the OT view of man as a unity. It has been supposed, however, that this would conflict with the antithesis between *psychikos* and *pneumatikos* in 1 Corinthians 15,[155] but in the latter case Paul is contrasting the non-Christian with the Christian, whereas in 1 Thessalonians 5:23 his prayer relates to Christians only. Admittedly there is lack of uniformity in Paul's terms, but there is also lack of uniformity in his purpose.

We should note the complete absence in Paul's epistles of any suggestion of the Hellenistic notion of the soul's pre-existence before the existence of the body.[156] The one cannot exist without the other. Indeed Paul never links the two ideas in a description of a person, since either covers both, *i.e.* the whole person. As contrasted with the lofty Greek view of the soul, Paul's view of it is always linked with man in his position of inferiority. Moreover, the Platonic ideal was centred on the deliverance of the soul from the body, but this is entirely alien to Paul's way of thinking. In the Christian doctrine of man the central idea is not *psychē* but *pneuma*. In Paul's exposition of it he modifies the OT emphasis on *nepeš* (LXX *psychē*) and switches to *pneuma* because he at once considered man from the view-point of his experience of Christ.

SPIRIT

Although the word *pneuma* is used many times by Paul in relation to the Holy Spirit (see section on the Holy Spirit, pp. 549ff.), there are various other applications of the term, some of which are important for our purpose. We are not here concerned with the idea of *pneuma* as a description of spiritual influences or gifts in the lives of believers. In this sense *pneuma* describes a specifically Christian state. It separates the Christian person

---

[154] *Cf.* J. A. T. Robinson, *The Body* (1952), p. 27.

[155] W. D. Stacey, *The Pauline View of Man*, p. 123, affirms that 1 Cor. 15 here conflicts with 1 Thes. 5, but explains that the 1 Cor. reference represents his more mature view of the resurrection.

[156] *Cf.* H. Lüdemann, *Die Anthropologie des Apostles Paulus und ihre Stellung innerhalb seiner Heilslehre. Nach den vier Hauptbriefen* (1872), p. 4.

from the non-Christian, because the latter is not in possession of it. In this use, in fact, it stands in direct contrast with flesh (*sarx*), as will become clear in the next section. Our aim here is to discover in what sense, if any, Paul can think of *pneuma* as applicable to both Christian and non-Christian. Yet to do this we are bound to consider the various nuances in the other uses of the term, since in Paul's mind no clear-cut distinctions are maintained and one usage merges into another.

The most important influence on the term undoubtedly comes from the powerful operation of the Spirit of God at conversion and in the Christian life. This brought a new dimension into human affairs. Man as a result became a new creature (2 Cor. 5:17). But the Spirit of God works in and through human personalities. He witnesses to man's spirit, to that part of man which is capable of responding to divine influences (Rom. 8:16). There is a clear distinction between the Holy Spirit and man's spirit. The real problem is the extent to which it is legitimate to speak of *pneuma* as a general constituent of man's nature. For the believer, *pneuma* seems to mean the whole man committed to God. It is man moved and motivated by God. It is man in fellowship with God. Non-Christians cannot have fellowship with God, for the natural man cannot discern the things of God (1 Cor. 2:6ff.). What then does Paul mean by 'the spirit of the man which is in him' (1 Cor. 2:11)? Some light may perhaps be shed on this by 1 Corinthians 15:45 where Adam's *psychē* is compared and contrasted with Christ's life-giving *pneuma*. Does this support the view that Adam had no natural *pneuma*? Such a view would read too much into the context. What is more important is whether, when he operates in man, the Holy Spirit transforms man's natural *pneuma* and then makes him a new creature; or whether the Spirit gives to man a *pneuma* at conversion which he did not previously possess.

It is difficult to conceive of *pneuma* as something added to man's existing state. It is more reasonable to consider that man's natural spirit, which in his unregenerate state is inactive, is revived at conversion by the Spirit of God.[157] If this is so a distinction must be made between man's natural *pneuma* and his Christian *pneuma*, although the connection between them is close. Where Paul speaks of his spirit being refreshed, he is using the term in a general way which could be equally applicable to non-believers (*cf.* 1 Cor. 16:18; 2 Cor. 2:13; 7:13). The *pneuma* in this sense virtually stands as equivalent to 'self'. It was the whole man who was refreshed and no mention is made of the Spirit of God. Here 'spirit' seems to be used in the sense of 'mind'. Paul does not use the word *pneuma* in the sense of 'wind' or 'breath', nor does he use it of animals. It represents man's higher nature which of itself is neither good nor evil. It is capable both of defile-

---

[157] *Cf.* W. Sanday and A. C. Headlam, *Romans* (*ICC*, 1895), p. 196.

ment (2 Cor. 7:1) and of consecration (1 Cor. 7:34). It takes on the flavour of the dominant influence. There can be no question that for the apostle the *pneuma* of the Christian must be dominated by the Spirit of God. At times, therefore, Paul uses this word in an almost identical way as he sometimes uses *psychē*.

If we enquire more closely into the origin of Paul's ideas regarding man's *pneuma*, we discover a great similarity between the OT doctrine of man and the Pauline doctrine.[158] There are no contradictions, although several developments and modifications. We need to note that scholars have appealed rather to Hellenistic than to Jewish origins, but their contentions are not convincing. The 'history of religions' school maintained that among the contemporary cults, the notion that the 'spiritual' person (*pneumatikos*) was superior to others prevailed, as in Pauline thought.[159] But a fundamental difference remained. Unlike the 'spiritual' man in the mystery religions, the *pneumatikos* in Paul's thinking remains wholly dependent upon God. The new revelation he has received makes him more humble rather than more proud. There is never in Paul any confusion between the human and the divine as there is both in the mystery religions and in the Hermetic literature. In the latter, man's spirit can be absorbed into the Divine Spirit and therefore loses the personal element.

Mystical religious experience was not generally linked with moral obligations, and this supplies another marked contrast with Paul's view of *pneuma*. In the mystery religions, redemption was centred in a single ecstatic temporary experience, whereas in Christianity, as Paul expounds it, redemption involves a continuous sanctifying process. Furthermore the mysteries concentrated on taking the *pneumatic* into a world other than his own, whereas Paul was quite clear that Christians, though not of this world, are nevertheless in the world and cannot avoid meeting its challenge. Another contrast is the lack of any idea of the immortality of the spirit apart from the body in Paul's teaching, although it is present in the Orphic mysteries. One concluding observation is that *pneuma* and *psychē* are never identified in Paul when referring to the higher life, although they are in the mysteries.

We may conclude that Paul's wider use of *pneuma* rather than *psychē* was dictated by his conversion experience in which God had so clearly taken the initiative. *Psychē* was traditionally too man-centred to serve as a suitable term for his purpose.

HEART

There is a strong indebtedness to OT thought in cases where organs of the

---

[158] W. D. Stacey, *op. cit.*, p. 138, considers that Paul's view of *pneuma* owes much to the OT and intertestamental literature and departs in several ways from the rabbis. Cf. E. Sjöberg's '*rûaḥ*' in Palestinian Judaism, in *TDNT*, 6, pp. 375–389.

[159] So R. Reitzenstein, *Die hellenischen Mysterionenreligionen* ([3]1927, r.p. 1956). *Cf.* also the comments of H. A. A. Kennedy, *St Paul and the Mystery Religions* (1913), p. 141.

body are used to express emotions. In fact, in only one instance does Paul use the term (*kardia*) of the centre of life (2 Cor. 3:3), but even here it is used metaphorically (of the writing by the Spirit of God on human hearts).

In some cases *kardia* is used of the whole inward man. Paul sees the heart as the exerciser of faith (Rom. 10:10), which shows commitment of the whole person to Christ. It is into the heart that God has shone 'to give the light of the knowledge of the glory of God in the face of Christ' (2 Cor. 4:6; *cf.* also Eph. 1:18). A comparison of 2 Corinthians 1:22 with 2 Corinthians 5:5 shows that the guarantee of the Spirit in our hearts is the same as the guarantee in us, indicating that 'heart' stands for the whole person. Christ is said to dwell within the heart (Eph. 3:17), the Spirit is sent into the heart (Gal. 4:6), the peace of Christ, for the Christians, rules the heart (Col. 3:16).

Because the *kardia* in its natural state is not devoted to God, it is not surprising to find statements which speak of the corruption of the heart. Gentile lust was attributed to their hearts (Rom. 1:24). The heart can be hard and impenitent, in which case it stores up wrath against itself (Rom. 2:5). Nevertheless, the heart is not considered to be inherently bad. It can become obedient as well as disobedient (Rom. 6:17). Paul expresses his own strong longings for his own people as his heart's desire (Rom. 10:1). The heart is, therefore, conceived as the seat of the emotions. The apostle speaks of his great affliction and anguish of heart over the Corinthians (2 Cor. 2:4). When Paul uses the adjective 'senseless' of the hearts of the Gentiles in Romans 1:21, he is not meaning to suggest that the 'heart' is naturally senseless, but that through moral failure the heart was acting in a state of moral stupor. The heart in fact sometimes stands for the 'will' (as in 1 Cor. 4:5), where the Lord is said to plan to disclose the purpose of men's hearts (*cf.* also 1 Cor. 7:37).

When in 2 Corinthians 7:2 Paul urges the Corinthians to open their hearts to him and his companions, he is using the term *kardia* of the seat of Christian affection, the same sense which occurs in Philemon 7, 20, although here *splanchna* is used in place of *kardia*, following Hebrew influence. To refresh the heart means to refresh the whole person.

Enough has been said to show that again Paul is not restrictive in his use of physical terms in a metaphorical way. The terms, however, are used mainly to describe emotional and volitional aspects. These must be set over against 'mind' (*nous*) which will next be considered and which is reserved for mental activities.

MIND

The word for 'mind' (*nous*) had very definite connotations in the Greek world and yet when Paul uses it he transfers it to a typically Hebrew approach. In Paul it is never conceived of in a way distinct from man himself. If the apostle singles it out, he does not do so to propound 'mind' as a special faculty.[160] In Hebrew fashion, he means the whole thinking man, man as a creature capable of understanding. In no sense, therefore, can the intellect be exalted above the rest of man as it so often was in Greek thought. The very fact that Paul can speak of 'the mind of the flesh' (Col. 2:18), or 'sensuous mind' (as RSV) shows how closely linked the mind is with the *sarx* (see next section). Moreover, 'mind' extends over the whole mental activity of man, not simply the purely contemplative.

We note next that *nous* is a universal aspect of man. This is implied in the statement that God's peace surpasses *all* understanding (Phil. 4:7). *Nous* is not in itself either good or bad. Its moral standing is determined by what is dominating it, either the Spirit of God or the flesh. In 1 Corinthians 14:14, the mind stands over against the spirit and is certainly not included in the gifts bestowed on the believer. In this latter case ecstasy of spirit (*pneuma*) is regarded as of little value unless the mind is enlightened. Again Paul is concerned about the whole man. Emotional experiences must be linked with understanding.

When the mind does not acknowledge God, it becomes base (*adokimos*), a state which leads to improper conduct (Rom. 1:28). Paul dares to say that God gave men up to such a mind. This seems to mean that refusal to acknowledge God has an adverse effect, which makes it harder for the mind to receive subsequent revelations of God. Elsewhere, when Paul speaks of the minds of unbelievers, he maintains that they have been blinded by Satan (2 Cor. 4:4). Yet for believers the mind is not only enlightened (2 Cor. 4:6), but can be renewed (Rom. 12:2).

For a proper understanding of *nous* as God intended it to be, we must take into account that Paul can speak of the mind of God (*cf.* Rom. 11:34, a quote from Is. 40:13ff.). He sees it as desirable that the human *nous* must be conformed to the mind of God (1 Cor. 2:16). The mind of man functions properly only when fulfilling the will of God. It is through the mind, moreover, that man can perceive the works of God in creation. The mind of the Christian performs an important function in discerning the will of God, although it does not necessarily follow that an understanding of God's will enables man to perform it.[161] It seems to follow from Romans 12:2 that the renewal of mind which accompanies Christian conversion equips the believer with a sharper means of discernment than he had before (he can prove God's good, acceptable and perfect will). The difference between the Christian and non-Christian *nous* is vividly brought out in Romans 7; although this passage shows Paul finally serving the law of God with the

---

[160] Bultmann, *TNT*, 1, p. 213, claims that *nous* is not a higher principle in man, any more than *psychē* or the human *pneuma*.

[161] Stacey, *op. cit.*, p. 201, says '*nous* approves the course of action but *pneuma* supplies the energy to perform it'.

mind (7:25), it nevertheless portrays a conflict. This will be dealt with in the section on flesh, but it is necessary here to note the expression 'the law of my mind', which Paul uses in verse 23. Since this is at variance with another law which makes him captive to the law of sin, by 'the law of my mind' Paul must have meant the true function of the mind which desires to serve God.[162] Nowhere do his writings suggest, however, that the natural man, by means of *nous* and unaided by the Spirit of God, could effect his own salvation. When *sarx* is corrupted the whole person is corrupted, including his mind.

A distinction must be drawn between the *nous* and the *pneuma*, although their functions frequently overlap. If *nous* is the thinking and willing aspect of man, *pneuma* is man under the influence of the Spirit. Full harmony is reached only when they pull together. 1 Corinthians 14:14 is an example of what happens when the *pneuma* is not in line with the *nous*. Paul points out the possibility that it might prove unfruitful. In the Spirit-dominated life, the Holy Spirit takes control of the *nous*.[163] The Christian indwelt by the Spirit finds his mind increasingly conformed to the mind of the Spirit.

CONSCIENCE

Closely linked with mind is the concept of 'conscience'. No specific word for this existed in Hebrew thought, where the word 'heart' (*lēḇ*) included the general function of what the Greeks came to know as *syneidēsis*.[164] The root meaning of the word seems to be a knowledge of an act, together with reflective judgment upon it. Hence it differs from *nous* in that it does not involve the exercise of the will. The conscience shows man as aware of himself as a rational being.

In the Pauline epistles various uses of the word 'conscience' are found. (i) In Romans 2:15, Paul implies that conscience is universal, since he maintains of the Gentiles that 'their conscience also bears witness and their conflicting thoughts accuse or perhaps excuse them'. On the basis of this statement it seems that Paul considered that all people had the capacity to determine what was right, although he gives no indication of the standards by which this was done. It could not have been by reference to the law, as was the case among the Jews as a result of the Mosaic legislation. Yet the patriarchs were in the same position, prior to the giving of the law.

---

[162] Stacey, *op. cit.*, p. 201, puts it in this way: 'So concerned is *nous* with God's Law that the phrase "the law of my mind" can be used as synonymous with the Divine Law'.

[163] *Cf.* Kennedy, *St Paul and the Mystery Religions*, p. 139.

[164] In his careful study, *Conscience in the New Testament* (1955), C. A. Pierce gives a survey of the pre-NT use of the term and concludes that it was taken over from Gk. not Heb. sources. He shows, moreover, that in the Greek world it almost always had the sense of a *guilty* conscience. It comes from ordinary Greek speech with its own connotation, 'basically, the pain suffered by man, as man, and therefore as a creature involved in the order of things, when, by his acts completed or initiated, he transgresses the moral limits of his nature' (p. 54).

Conscience must be aware of what is right, independent of man's own standards. No authority is vested in man himself.[165] He does not decide his own standards. (ii) In Romans 9:1 and 2 Corinthians 1:12, Paul calls on his conscience as an additional witness, but this is purely for emphasis. He is affirming the essential truth of his own words. His conscience would have accused him had his words been insincere. In 2 Corinthians 4:2 his aim is to commend himself to every man's conscience in the sight of God. A similar thought occurs in 2 Corinthians 5:11. (iii) The function of the conscience, although clear, is not to acquit itself, for it is the Lord who judges (1 Cor. 4:4). On the other hand, the conscience, if disobeyed, can become defiled, as in the case of the weaker person confronted with the problem of food offered to idols (1 Cor. 8:7; *cf.* also 10:25). If conscience is persistently disobeyed, it becomes hardened. In 1 Timothy 4:2 it is spoken of as 'seared'[166] among those who had been deceived by those advocating doctrines of demons.

As for the origin of Paul's idea of conscience, there can be little doubt that he shows some indebtedness to Stoic concepts. Among the Stoics, law was considered to be the law of nature immanent in man (*empsychos nomos*). Although this may have contributed in some ways, it is more likely that Paul is indebted to the popular use of the word 'conscience'. But neither source accounts for the specifically Christian use of the term in Paul's epistles. The apostle did not see man's best actions as conformity to nature, but conformity to the will of God, an idea equally absent from Stoic thought[167] and from popular usage. Moreover, Paul sees the indwelling Spirit as the quickener of man's consciousness, and therefore views the Christian conscience as more perceptive than the conscience of the natural man.

FLESH

For an understanding of man's basic need, a study of Paul's use of the word *sarx* (flesh) is indispensable.[168] But such a study is fraught with

[165] Stacy, *op. cit.*, p. 208, criticizes the view of conscience which sees authority as vested in man. He particularly refutes the view of O. Pfleiderer, *Paulinism* (Eng. Trans. 1877), 1, p. 63.

[166] The force of the word rendered 'seared' here seems to be that as the nerve ends are dulled in an act of cauterizing, so the conscience becomes incapable of discernment between right and wrong. This seems more applicable than the view that the false teachers are regarded as branded with their owner's name (*i.e.* Satan), so C. Spicq, *Les Épîtres Pastorales* (EB, ²1947) *ad loc.*

[167] C. A. Pierce, *op. cit.*, pp. 13–20, has a chapter on the fallacy of Stoic origin for the NT usage, which speaks for itself that Pierce considers a Stoic origin is unfounded.

[168] Some have considered Paul's usage to be influenced by the kind of developments found at Qumran in the use of 'flesh'. *Cf.* K. G. Kuhn, 'New Light on Temptation, Sin and Flesh in the New Testament', *The Scrolls and the New Testament* (ed. K. Stendahl, 1958), pp. 94–113; W. D. Davies, 'Paul and the Dead Sea Scrolls: Flesh and Spirit', *idem*, pp. 157–182. *Cf.* also J. Pryke, ' "Spirit" and "flesh" in the Qumran Documents and some New Testament Texts', *RQ* 5, 1965, pp. 345ff. But the points of comparison are outweighed by the differences and are insufficient to establish any kind of dependence.

difficulties because of the variety of ways in which the term is used.[169] Whereas people, animals, birds and fish all share *sarx*, Paul makes a distinction between them (1 Cor. 15:39). In this case *sarx* refers simply to bodily substance. The term came to denote the natural man in his earthly origin (*cf.* 1 Cor. 1:29; Rom. 1:3; 3:20;[170] Gal. 1:16). Because this sense of creatureliness is strong, *sarx* came naturally to represent man in his weakness. This idea of flesh is indebted to the Hebrew idea that the creature is always weak as compared with the power of the Creator.

The word can also be used of what relates to oneself, as in the statement of Paul that 'no man ever hated his own flesh' (Eph. 5:29). So far, the uses mentioned do not imply any moral meaning. This is important because it shows that Paul did not share the current Greek conception of the essential evil of matter, and particularly of the flesh. Nevertheless *sarx* generally stands over against God. It is often in Paul the opposite of spirit (*pneuma*), but this applies only to the Christian idea of man (*cf.* Gal. 5:17). In reference to the natural man *sarx* denotes not so much the lower nature of man as contrasted with the higher, but the whole man in his state of alienation from God.

There is in the use of *sarx* in Paul's epistles a double aspect in relation to sin.[171] Sometimes it denotes no more than a general relationship to sin as in such terms as *en sarki* (in flesh), *kata sarka* (according to the flesh), or the 'mind of the flesh'. In 2 Corinthians 10:3 Paul draws a distinction between the first two expressions – we walk *in flesh*, but we do not carry on warfare *according to flesh*.[172] The flesh is still the sphere of the Christian's activity, but is no longer the dominant pattern for his actions. Here a distinction is seen when Paul's view is compared with the contemporary Hellenistic idea of the antithesis between the inner and outer man, for Paul's idea of the inner man is essentially man as he is renewed (2 Cor. 4:16). Moreover, it is a continual process. This suggests also that Paul did not think in terms

---

[169] *Cf.* R. Bultmann, *TNT*, 1, pp. 232–239 for a discussion of Paul's view of *sarx*. *Cf.* also W. D. Stacey, *The Pauline View of Man*, pp. 154ff.; E. Schweizer, *TDNT*, 7, pp. 125ff. H. Ridderbos, *Paul*, (Eng. trans. 1975), pp. 101ff., criticizes Bultmann's view that flesh typifies man's total mode of existence. 'What is deceptive in Bultmann's interpretation is that with the idea of sin as "flesh" he starts once again from the flesh as humanly limited, etc., as though it were especially therein that the point of contact for sin lay; whereas for Paul "flesh" denotes sin in the whole of its purport as turned away from and averse to God' (p. 103). *Cf.* also A. Thiselton, 'The Meaning of *Sarx* in 1. Cor. 5:5: A Fresh Approach in the Light of Logical and Semantic Factors', *SJT* 26, 1973, pp. 204–228; A. Sand, *Der Begriff 'Fleisch' in den paulinischen Hauptbriefen* (1967).

[170] For a discussion of *kata sarka* in relation to *kata pneuma hagiōsynēs*, both applied to Christ in Rom. 1:3, 4, *cf.* B. Schneider, *Bib.* 48, 1967, pp. 359–387.

[171] See H. W. Robinson, *The Christian Doctrine of Man*, pp. 119ff.

[172] In 2 Cor. 10:3 there is clearly a double sense of the word *sarx*, since *en sarki* is neutral whereas *kata sarka* is not. *Cf.* P. E. Hughes, *2 Corinthians NICNT* (1962), pp. 348f. There is a powerful difference between the two uses, one expressing present human frailty, the other a principle of life dominated by wrong moral standards. C. K. Barrett, *2 Corinthians* (*BC*, 1973), p. 250, points out that Paul is not consistent in his use of *en sarki* as a comparison of this passage with Rom. 8:9 and Gal. 2:20 shows.

of Hellenistic dualism. He recognized as a fact of history that *sarx* in its natural state is closely allied to sin.

But Paul went further than this and saw *sarx* as the seat of an activity which resulted in sin, even encouraging its production. Hence flesh is closely allied to lust as if it had become the natural thing for *sarx* to lust. Paul speaks of 'the desires of the flesh' (Gal. 5:16) and then goes on to give an unenviable list of the 'works of the flesh' (Gal. 5:19). He selects fifteen sins to serve as representative of what follows from the flesh. The fact that they exclude people from entry into the kingdom shows that there is a strong antithesis between *sarx* and the kingdom.

We shall next examine the key passage in our discussion, *i.e.* Romans 7. In this section in which Paul sets out a strong inner conflict, *sarx* plays an important part. The setting of the pre-Christian state is expressed in verse five, 'while we were living in the flesh, our sinful passions, aroused by the law, were at work in our members to bear fruit for death'. In the pre-Christian state *sarx* is clearly dominating.[173]

In the ensuing discussion, the conflict is mainly between the *ego* affected by sin and the *ego* desiring to do the will of God. It reaches its climax in the statement, 'For I know that nothing good dwells within me, that is, in my flesh. I can will what is right, but I cannot do it' (Rom. 7:18). 'Flesh' here demonstrates powerfully the hampering effect of the natural man when the apostle was faced with a recognition of what is right. Although not evil of itself, *sarx* prevents the good and therefore encourages evil. Flesh is also contrasted with the 'inmost self' (*esō anthrōpos*) (Rom. 7:22).

It is of some importance to determine whether this passage relates to Paul himself as a Christian, or to himself or to others as non-Christians.[174] If the former, the passage would relate to the Christian's continuing strug-

---

[173] As C. E. B. Cranfield, *Romans* (*ICC*, 1975), 1, p. 337, remarks of Christians, 'They are no longer in the flesh in the sense of having the basic direction of their lives determined and controlled by their fallen nature'. *Sarx* is nevertheless still 'a far from powerless element' in their lives. C. K. Barrett, *Romans* (*BC*, 1957), pp. 137, 416, commenting on Rom. 7:5f., notes that Paul uses *sarx* in two different senses – *i.e.* sometimes physical and sometimes in the sense of a proclivity to sin.

[174] For the view that Rom. 7 refers to Paul's own pre-Christian experience, *cf.* G. W. Buchanan, *The Consequences of the Covenant* (1970), p. 183, who relates it to the time before the *bar mitzvah*. *Cf.* also W. D. Davies, *Paul and Rabbinic Judaism*, pp. 24, 30; S. Sandmel, *The Genius of Paul* (²1970), pp. 24f.; J. Knox, *Chapters in a Life of Paul* (1950), pp. 153f.; H. Schoeps, *Paul: The Theology of the Apostle in the Light of Jewish Religious History* (Eng. trans. 1961), pp. 184f. Against the view that Paul is referring to his own experience, *cf.* W. G. Kümmel, *Römer 7 und die Bekehrung des Paulus* (1929); R. Bultmann, 'Romans 7 and the Anthropology of Paul', *Existence and Faith* (Ed. S. M. Ogden, 1960), pp. 147–157; J. Dupont, 'La conversion de Paul', *Foi et Salut selon S. Paul* (M. Barth *et al.*, 1970), pp. 67–88, esp. 75.

For other treatments of the passage, *cf.* J. I. Packer, 'The "wretched man" of Romans 7', *Studia Evangelica*, 2 (ed. F. L. Cross, 1964), pp. 621–627; K. Kertelge, *ZNW* 62, 1971, pp. 105–114; C. L. Mitton, *ExT* 65, 1953–4, pp. 78ff., 99ff., 132ff.; E. Fuchs, 'Existentiale Interpretation von Röm. 7:7–12 und 21–23', in his *Glaube und Erfahrung* (1965); J. M. Bover, *Bib* 5, 1924, pp. 192ff.; H. Ridderbos, *Paul*, pp. 126ff.; J. Dunn, *ThZ* 31 (1975), pp. 257–273. H. Conzelmann, *TNT*, p. 181, maintains that Paul does not teach that the *nous* is free and good. Rom. 7, therefore, merely shows that man has totally lost his freedom.

gle with the old nature.[175] But many deny this interpretation and maintain that a conflict within a non-Christian is in mind, in which case the passage could refer to human experience in general. In that case *sarx* will have its usual meaning of human nature in its weakness. The man knows God's demands and wants to fulfil them (verses 15, 18, 19, 21, 22). But the *sarx* sins, because sin takes advantage of it. In a sense *sarx* is set over against *nous*. The latter serves or seeks to serve God, but the former does not. An objection has been raised that it is only in the Christian that *nous* desires to serve God and therefore the passage must relate to Christian experience. But no wedge must be driven between 'flesh' and 'mind'. Both are aspects of the whole man. It must be remembered that the non-Christian experience is seen in this chapter through Christian eyes.[176] The conclusion is that man's position is hopeless (Rom. 7:24). The non-Christian, while in the throes of this conflict, utterly fails to understand what is going on (7:15). *Sarx* is in control. The apostle is not, however, giving in this passage a full exposition of either *sarx* or *nous*. He is wanting to show that the guilt of sin does not fall upon the Law. Man in his *sarx* is responsible for his own sin.

Some comment is needed on the relationship between *sarx* and *sōma* (body). In the physical sense there is no distinction between these words, but they are used differently in an ethical sense. It has been maintained that the body is thought of as under the sway of the flesh,[177] but this is an oversimplification which does less than justice to the most extensive meaning of 'body' in Pauline thought. Nevertheless at times the ethical implications of the flesh are transferred to the body (*cf.* Rom. 8:1–11).

Man seen as *sarx* is man in his membership of this present evil age (Gal. 1:4). The word does not describe his fundamental nature.[178] Paul's view of salvation includes deliverance from the present age, from the view of man as *sarx* to the view of man as spirit (*pneuma*). But naturally the Christian is not all at once delivered from the adverse effects of *sarx*. Paul's approach to salvation is therefore of a continuous process of overcoming the adverse

---

[175] More will be said on the interpretation of Rom. 7 when discussing Paul's approach to the law (see below, pp. 687ff.).

[176] W. G. Kümmel, *TNT*, p. 177, argues that in Rom. 7 Paul sees man 'in the flesh' as a Christian sees him. 'Thus even here, in spite of the dualistic-sounding terminology, man is seen as a unity, as "fleshly, sold under sin" (verse 14)' '. *Cf. idem, Man in the New Testament*, pp. 60f. R. Harrisville, *The Concept of Newness in the New Testament* (1960), p. 86, argues that the struggle must be of the new man, since the old man would be unable to recognize the conflict because he is wholly under the domination of this age.

[177] *Cf.* R. Bultmann, *TNT*, 1, p. 197, who argues from Rom. 8:13 that *sōma* is seen as 'under the sway of an outside power. . . The context shows that the outside power is "the flesh", for the "deeds of the *sōma*" correspond to "living according to the flesh".' But Bultmann's inadequate view of the 'flesh' must here be borne in mind (*cf.* n. 169).

[178] Kümmel, *Man in the New Testament*, p. 63, says 'In so far as man lets himself be determined by the reality of "this age" (*aiōn houtos*), and thereby denotes that he is yet *sarx*, so far is he "a slave of sin and death" (Rom. 6:16).'

effects of *sarx*. This is where salvation merges into sanctification. More will be said later on the relation between *sarx* and sin (see pp. 206ff.). Our next consideration is the body distinct from *sarx*.

BODY

Unlike *sarx*, the body is capable of being transformed. It is described as mortal (Rom. 8:10, 11), but God can give life to it through his Spirit. Moreover, the body is not meant for immorality (1 Cor. 6:13). Anyone who commits immorality sins against his own body (1 Cor. 6:18). The real purpose of the body is to be a temple of the Holy Spirit (1 Cor. 6:19). Because of this God can be glorified in the body (1 Cor. 6:20). This at once sets 'body' (*sōma*) apart from 'flesh' (*sarx*) and shows its superiority.[179] In every way, the body in its true state is meant 'for the Lord' (1 Cor. 6:13).

The body is due for resurrection and redemption (Rom. 8:23). What is now limited through the domination of the flesh will be renewed. Our lowly body will be changed to become like Christ's glorious body (Phil. 3:21). These statements give some insight into the dramatic change in the body which is in store for the Christian. By implication the non-Christian, still dominated as he is by the flesh, has no such hope that his body will be delivered from its mortality (see further discussion on pp. 207ff.).

Another feature of Paul's doctrine of the transformation of the body is its gradual character. As the mind (*nous*) is renewed by a gradual process, so it is linked with the dedication of the body (Rom. 12:1–2). Although ultimately the old must give place to the new, the change is not cataclysmic, but progressive.

It has been pointed out that when Paul speaks of the body he is thinking in corporate terms.[180] Hence the mortal body or body of death stands for the solidarity of all men belonging to a race in which death is inescapable.[181] It is this idea of solidarity that Paul so effectively uses when applying the metaphor of the body to the church (see the section on the church, pp. 742ff.).

At the same time there are some statements in Paul which show that he recognized the sinful character of the body. In Romans 6:6 he uses the expression 'sinful body' (*to sōma tēs hamartias*)[182] and speaks of its destruction

---

[179] J. A. T. Robinson, *The Body*, p. 31, brings out the important distinction between *sarx* and *sōma*: 'While *sarx* stands for man, in the solidarity of creation, in his distance from God, *sōma* stands for man, in the solidarity of creation, as made for God'.

[180] *Cf.* J. A. T. Robinson, *op. cit.*, pp. 73ff.

[181] R. H. Gundry, *Sōma in Biblical Theology*, pp. 217f., criticizes Robinson's view (*op. cit.*, p. 15) that Paul used *sōma* in the Heb. sense of somatic socialism. He suggests that in the OT there is support for both solidarity and individualism.

[182] Gundry, *op. cit.*, pp. 57ff., includes a brief excursus on Rom. 6:6a, in which he maintains that the phrase *to sōma tēs hamartias* 'does not refer to an abstract mass of sin, to the system of sinful desires, to sin

so that we might no longer be enslaved to sin. At the conclusion of his passage on the inner tensions which result from sin, Paul asks a rhetorical question, 'Who will deliver me from this body of death?' (Rom. 7:24). Here the expression is again genitival, in which the genitive gives the description of the body in a qualitative sense, *i.e.* a body destined for death. The deeds (*praxeis*) of the body need to be put to death, according to Romans 8:13. Another expression is 'body of flesh' which occurs in Colossians 2:11, also used in an adverse sense. These statements remind us of the basic condition of man brought about through sin, which will be more fully discussed later (see pp. 187ff.).

Some theologians have obscured Paul's teaching about the body by adopting the view that for Paul 'body' stands for the whole person (what has been called the holistic view).[183] According to this view 'body' does not refer to the physical body. But a careful examination of the evidence does not support this view.[184]

Other features in Paul's view of man

The foregoing evidence has demonstrated the wide variety of Paul's terms for aspects of man and the impossibility of constructing a consistent psychology. Indeed psychology is the wrong word to use, since Paul is so strongly influenced by the Hebrew idea of the whole man that Greek notions of separate functions have only a minimum impact on Paul's thinking. We may summarize his approach in the following ways.

(i) Paul sees man as a creature, but nevertheless a creature made in the image of God. This strongly OT view of the origin of man is specifically stated in 1 Corinthians 11:7 (see further comments under Paul's approach to creation on pp. 209ff.).

(ii) Man in his totality was expected to honour God. In company with other parts of the NT, the Pauline epistles regard man in his natural state as having dishonoured God (Rom. 1:21).

(iii) Nevertheless man cannot disclaim responsibility for his rejection of God, since God has given him the capacity to understand. The classic passage in this respect is Romans 2:14, 15, in which Paul demonstrates that Gentiles, although not having the Jewish law, nevertheless have the capacity for discernment. Paul is referring to natural revelation which demonstrates 'the great distance from Him in which the *whole* man stands'.[185]

---

personified as a sphere of power in the old Aeon, or to the sinful personality, but concretely to the physical body which has been dominated by sin, is doomed to destruction and will receive resurrection' (p. 58).

[183] This view is central to Bultmann's exposition of Paul's thought, *TNT*, 1, pp. 192–203. It is followed up also by J. A. T. Robinson, *The Body*, especially in its application to the church.

[184] *Cf.* R. H. Gundry, *op. cit.*, who gives a detailed examination of all the usages in OT, intertestamental and NT literature and concludes that a dualistic view consistently explains all the evidence.

[185] W.G. Kümmel, *Man in the New Testament*, p. 49.

(iv) Paul draws a distinction between the natural and spiritual man.[186] He uses the adjectives *psychikos* (natural) and *pneumatikos* (spiritual) in rather different ways from the nouns *psychē* and *pneuma*, already considered. The spiritual man is man in possession of *pneuma* which the natural man does not possess. The former derives life from the Holy Spirit, whereas the latter derives life only from an earthly source (*choïkos*). The 'spiritual' man may at times refer to all believers, but at other times be restricted to those who possessed special gifts (*cf.* 1 Cor. 14:37; 2:15; 3:1; and Gal. 6:1). The idea of 'spiritual' is certainly not reserved for an élitist class of Christians. What is most important is that in Paul's mind the natural man is unspiritual.[187] He is deficient in an aspect which can be supplied only by the Spirit of God.

(v) Nowhere else in the NT does the basic equality of all people before God come so vividly into focus as with Paul. Not only is man's sin universal, but all distinctions of sex and nationality and social status are swept away. Admittedly this happens only in Christ, but the fact that it happens points to an important element in Paul's basic conception of man. Such distinctions were powerful divisive factors in Paul's world, but he recognized them as unacceptable. In this he showed remarkable insight into the true nature of man, which had become blurred through human prejudices.

(vi) The problem as to whether Paul regarded man as a monad, dyad or triad is somewhat academic, but we may say that the evidence for the tripartite nature of man is confined in Paul to 1 Thessalonians 5:23 which is capable of alternative interpretations (see earlier section under 'soul', p. 164f.). Since man as a unity is in line with Hebrew thought, this seems most basic to Paul, but when he introduces the spiritual element he does so in a way unknown to Hebrew thought and thus introduces a dual idea.

Our survey of Paul's view of man would not be complete without some reference to the relationship between man and woman. We shall deal with this subject here in a general sense, but we shall need to return to it in a particular sense when considering the church (see pp. 774ff.).

We begin by focusing on Adam, who is used in a special theological sense in two passages (Rom. 5:12ff. and 1 Cor. 15:22, 45ff.) and is mentioned in a third (1 Tim. 2:13, 14). In the first two cases, Adam clearly

---

[186] There is a useful discussion of the natural and spiritual in Stacey, *The Pauline View of Man*, pp. 146-153. He agrees with H. A. A. Kennedy, *St Paul's Conceptions of the Last Things* (1904), p. 251, that although the OT throws light on Paul's use of *psychē* and *pneuma*, the apostle's own experience contributes the element of originality in his teaching. On *pneuma*, Stacey says 'the word is Paul's word, and the force and effect of the contrast must be largely attributed to his own religious insight' (p. 153).

[187] R. Bultmann, *TNT* 1, p. 174, argued that Paul's use of the distinction between natural and spiritual can be explained only from gnostic anthropology. But gnostic anthropology did not, as Paul does, attribute the spiritual life to the activity of the Spirit of God. For a summary of gnostic views of *pneuma*, *cf.* E. Schweizer, *TDNT*, 6, pp. 392ff. *Cf.* also B. A. Pearson, *The Pneumatikos-Psychikos Terminology in 1 Corinthians. A Study in the Theology of the Corinthian Opponents of Paul and its relation to Gnosticism* (*SBL* Dissertation Series 12, 1973).

stands as representative of the whole race. Paul sees mankind as 'in Adam' in the same mystical way as he sees all Christians as 'in Christ'. In a later section we shall be discussing Romans 5:12ff. in its relation to Paul's doctrine of sin (pp. 209ff.), but our purpose here is to demonstrate that at times Paul's arguments depend on a corporate conception of mankind. Basic humanity, which all people share, may in this way be represented by Adam, the first man. There is no distinction in this sense between man and woman. Adam stands not for the male over against the female, but for mankind, incorporating both sexes.

In the Corinthians passage (especially 1 Cor. 15:45ff.), the first man Adam is again set over against Christ as the last Adam. What is most significant here is the introduction of the 'image' idea, reminiscent of the Genesis passage, but applied in a different way. Here Paul shows that as people have borne Adam's image, so they will bear Christ's. There is no question that Paul accepts the authenticity of the Genesis account, for his whole theological argument depends on it. Adam is again considered as in some way the representative of mankind as a whole.

It is in the 1 Timothy passage that a different slant on the Adam saga is introduced, for in this case Adam is contrasted with Eve. Although the main argument in this passage is based on Adam's priority in the order of creation, yet the secondary point is that Eve's fall has placed all her female descendants in a subordinate position. It must, of course, be borne in mind that in the contemporary Jewish world the subordination of women to men was not only taken for granted, but actively propagated by the customs of society. Moreover, in few places in the Gentile world were women regarded as possessing independent rights or influences (Macedonia was one of the exceptions). In this passage in the Pastorals, therefore, Paul is reflecting the almost universal approach of the ancient world. We shall need to see how he applies this contemporary approach to women in the church (see pp. 774f.). He makes a significant contribution towards challenging contemporary patterns when he maintains that in Christ there is neither male nor female (Gal. 3:28). The fact that he links this with the abolition of the slave/freeman distinction suggests that he sees a vital difference between humanity in the non-Christian world and in Christ. This does not suppose that he visualized an immediate sweeping away of all social distinctions, but he recognized that ideally in Christ things could be totally different. There is no suggestion in Paul's epistles that man's standing before God was any different from woman's. Both need salvation in the same way and on the same terms.

We may further note that Paul takes for granted, in accordance with the strong Jewish practice of the time, that marriage was a natural procedure between men and women. He has advice to give to Christians on the subject of the sanctity of marriage and this will be discussed in the section on marriage (pp. 948ff.). In one passage, however, (Rom. 1:26, 27), Paul speaks of the relationship between the sexes in the non-Christian world, commending natural relations and condemning unnatural (*i.e.* between those of the same sex). This is sufficient to show that in Galatians 3:28 Paul is not seeking to abolish the distinction between the proper function of the respective sexes.[188]

Because of his remarks in 1 Corinthians and 1 Timothy about the relationships between Christian men and women and their roles in the church (see pp. 774f.), some have supposed that Paul was a misogynist, but this cannot be sustained. He is deeply concerned with orderliness and it is in this context that he gives his advice. The fact that he numbers some women among his associates shows that the charge of misogyny is baseless. It must be recognized that the placing of men and women on an equal footing in their need of salvation gives some indication of his basic approach to men and women in general.

One other passage which may have relevance is 1 Timothy 5:2–3, where Timothy is advised to treat older women like mothers and younger women like sisters. Real widows are singled out for special honour. There is no suggestion here of male domination. This basic approach must be taken into account when considering what Paul says about women in the Christian church.

Some scholars maintain that Paul's use of the Genesis creation narrative (in 1 Corinthians 11:8–9) shows that he accepted a hierarchical relationship, with man as the dominant sex.[189] But it cannot be maintained that the Genesis narrative requires such an interpretation. When 1 Corinthians 11:8–9, in which Paul stresses that the woman gives herself for the man, is compared with Ephesians 5:31, which stresses the reverse, it will be clear that Paul is not assuming a sexual hierarchy, but holds that the sexes complement one another. Indeed he states that 'in the Lord' man and woman are dependent on each other (1 Cor. 11:11–12).

Some discussion has arisen over whether 1 Corinthians 11:7, in referring to the 'image of God', applies it only to the man[190] or whether it also includes the woman.[191] In view of the fact that Paul does not say that the woman is the image of the man (he substitutes the word 'glory'), the

[188] L. Scanzoni and N. Hardesty, *All we're Meant to Be* (1974), maintain that Gal. 3:28 removes all role distinctions. *Cf.* also J. Harper, *Women and the Gospel* (Christian Brethren Research Fellowship Occasional Paper 5, 1974). But *cf.* M. Boucher, 'Some unexplored Parallels to 1 Corinthians 11:11-12 and Galatians 3:28', *CBQ* 31, 1969, pp. 50ff.; G. B. Caird, 'Paul and Women's Liberty', *BJRL* 34, 1972, pp. 268–281. *Cf.* also D. S. Bailey, *The Man-Woman Relation in Christian Thought* (1939).

[189] *Cf.* for instance J. B. Hurley, 'Did Paul require Veils or the Silence of Women?, *WTJ* 35, 1972-3, pp. 190–220.

[190] *Cf.* A. Robertson and A. Plummer, *1 Corinthians* (ICC, 1911), *ad loc.*; J. Héring, *1 Corinthians* (Eng. trans. 1962), *ad loc. Cf.* also J. Jervell, *Imago Dei* (1960), pp. 299f.; S. V. McCasland, ' "The Image of God" according to Paul', *JBL* 69, 1950, pp. 85f.

[191] *Cf.* J. B. Hurley, *op. cit.*; F. F. Bruce, *1 and 2 Corinthians* (NCB, 1971), *ad loc.*

second interpretation is undoubtedly correct. But our concern here is to note in what sense mankind may be said to bear the image of God. The fact that the woman is said to be the glory of the man has a direct bearing on our interpretation of the 'image'. The two ideas must be closely connected, although they are also distinguished. Glory has been forfeited by men because of sin, but the 'image' has not been entirely erased. This conforms well with Paul's argument in Romans 1 where he charges the pagan Gentiles with having exchanged God's glory for creaturely images (verse 23).

That it is right to interpret 'image' through its close connection with glory is seen when 'image' is applied to Christ himself as in 2 Corinthians 4:4; there he is said to be 'the image of God' (or the likeness of God), and the concept of glory clearly comes into focus. A similar idea, although without the mention of glory, comes to expression in Colossians 1:15ff. At no time does Paul suggest that Christ needed the image of God to be restored to him. He already was that image. But Paul recognizes the process in the new man in Christ of being conformed to that image (Col. 3:10). He goes one step further in Romans 8:29; 1 Corinthians 15:49; 2 Corinthians 3:18, where the 'image' is described as the image of Christ.

Undoubtedly Paul puts his own interpretation on an idea which is derived from Genesis 1.[192] He does not, in fact, discuss to what extent man in general still bears the image of God, but since he sees the process of salvation as a process of conformity to that image, this suggests that man apart from Christ does not reflect that image as he did before the fall. Nevertheless the 'image of God' in the creation account set man apart from the animal world, and there is no reason to suppose that he lost this distinction as a result of sin. Only man has the capacity for a personal relationship with God. Paul gives no support, however, to the view that man in his fallen state still has a spark of divinity in him which needs only to be fanned into a flame.[193] His view of sin is much more radical than that (see next section, pp. 200ff.).

Hebrews

It has been shown that this epistle strongly presents the doctrine of creation by God (see pp. 79f.) and the crown of that creation is man. Psalm 8 is cited in support of the view that God made man only a little lower than the angels and gave him dignity (Heb. 2:6ff.). He is crowned with glory and honour and everything is put in subjection to him. This shows man in his ideal state, a state which has been fulfilled only by Jesus. In a few

---

[192] It is worth noting that among Jewish exegetes there was no common interpretation of the 'image' idea in Genesis 1. It is abundantly clear that Paul did not inherit much from this source. He seems to have developed the idea as a result of his own experience in Christ.

[193] *Cf.* below, n. 288.

words, therefore, the writer shows what dignity man might have had, in order to highlight man's weakness, which comes out so vividly in the rest of the epistle.

Man is described corporately by the term *anthrōpos*, as in Paul's epistles. In spite of his high status within creation, man is mortal. He is appointed to die (Heb. 9:27), and in fact lives his life in fear of death (Heb. 2:14). In this respect man is seen to be in the grip of Satan who has the power of death. Moreover, man's state is described as weakness (Heb. 4:15; 7:28). The whole burden of the epistle is that man is incapable of coming to God and incapable of saving himself. This is the nature of his weakness.

There is some use of the word *psychē* (soul). Christians are said to have an 'anchor of the soul' (Heb. 6:19), which means a security for the whole person.[194] The word occurs in Hebrews 10:38 in a quotation from Habakkuk 2:3, 4 where 'soul' stands for 'self' ('my soul has no pleasure in him'). It also occurs in Hebrews 13:17, which refers to leaders as 'keeping watch over your souls',[195] where the word again seems to be used of the whole person. But a problem arises over the author's statement that the word of God could pierce 'to the division of soul (*psychē*) and spirit (*pneuma*)' (Heb. 4:12). Whatever the meaning of the statement, it would seem that some distinction is being made between soul and spirit, but it is not easy to determine the nature of that distinction.[196] If 'spirit' denotes the whole person in relation to God and 'soul' the whole person without relation to God, the division through the word of God becomes intelligible. But is this interpretation of *pneuma* supported elsewhere in the epistle? On most of the occasions when *pneuma* is used, it is applied to the Holy Spirit, but there are two instances where it is not. In Hebrews 12:9 God is described as 'the Father of Spirits', a title which draws special attention to the spiritual nature of God. The other instance is in the expression 'the spirits of just men made perfect' (Heb. 12:23), and in this case the idea of relation to God belongs essentially to the context. According to this view the writer uses the word *pneuma* in a distinctively Godward sense and distinguishes it from 'soul'.[197] The words would then mean that it is only through the Word of

[194] H. W. Montefiore, *Hebrews* (BC, 1964), p. 116, rightly says, 'This is not just a sheltered mooring for that most precious part of human personality which is commonly called the soul. On the contrary, it is an anchor which guarantees inner peace and security for the whole of life.'

[195] The expression 'those who have faith and keep their souls' in Heb. 10:39 is a variant form of Habbakuk's living by faith. Cf. F. F. Bruce, *Hebrews*, p. 275 n. 206.

[196] Montefiore, *op. cit.*, p. 88, understands the expression to mean that the Word of God can penetrate 'to the very ground of a man's being'. It is certain that the words are no guide to the writer's understanding of human psychology. A. B. Davidson thinks that the accumulation of terms expresses man's whole mental nature, *Hebrews* (ICC, 1882), p. 96. Some, however, see a Philonic dichotomy between soul and spirit, *cf.* C. Spicq, *Hébreux*, 1, pp. 52f. F. F. Bruce, *Hebrews*, p. 82, sees a judicial function attributed to the Word in this passage.

[197] It should be noted that there is a parallel to the expression 'the spirits of just men' in Wisdom 3:1 which speaks of 'the souls of the righteous'. Bruce, *op. cit.*, p. 378, thinks no distinction between the two can be pressed. But it is reasonable to conclude that the choice of 'spirits' in Heb. 12:23 is not accidental.

God that such a distinction is recognizable. Alternatively it is possible that the expression in Hebrews 4:12 is no more than figurative language for penetration in depth, in which case it tells us very little about *pneuma*.

There is an absence of the sharp antithesis between spirit and flesh (*sarx*) which is found in Paul's epistles. The expression 'flesh and blood' which occurs in Hebrews 2:14 is applied to human nature which all men share and which Jesus also took at his incarnation. There is clearly no thought here of the evil character of flesh in the Greek sense. The same may be said of the words 'in the days of his flesh' (Heb. 5:7), referring to the human experience of Jesus. Indeed, the writer thinks of Jesus' human flesh as a kind of veil through which he has opened a way of access to God (Heb. 10:20).

Nevertheless *sarx* has become affected by sin since it needs purification (Heb. 9:13). The same is probably implied in the 'regulations of the flesh' mentioned in Hebrews 9:10. It would seem, therefore, that this writer thinks of 'flesh' in terms of man's earthly existence (Heb. 12:9), without attaching any moral aspect to *sarx*, except in so far as it is part of the whole man, whose sinful condition is never disputed (see below, pp. 213ff.).

It remains only to observe that the writer's use of 'heart' (*kardia*) follows the usual Hebrew pattern. In fact, the refrain 'harden not your hearts' is taken from Psalm 95:11 which is cited in Hebrews 3:8; 4:7, and echoed in 3:15. Part of the same citation declares of the Israelites that 'they always go astray in their hearts' (Heb. 3:10). In Hebrews 4:12, in addition to the reference to 'soul' and 'spirit', mention is made of the 'thoughts and the intentions of the heart'. In the extensive quotation from Jeremiah 31, the laws of God would be put in men's minds (*dianoia*) and written on their hearts (Heb. 8:10; *cf.* 10:16 where the two words are reversed). There is a strange combination of heart and conscience in Hebrews 10:22, which shows that what affects one affects the other. In all these references it is clear that 'heart' in this epistle performs the functions mainly denoted by 'mind' in Paul's epistles.

Reference has to be made to 'conscience' (*syneidēsis*) which plays some part in the ideas of the writer. He concedes that the old ritual could not perfect the conscience (Heb. 9:9), which shows that in its natural state it is in some sense imperfect (*cf.* Heb. 10:2). Indeed in Hebrews 10:22 it is specifically described as 'evil'.[198] The whole function of Christian living is a matter of keeping a 'clear' conscience (Heb. 13:18). It is for this reason that the value of the blood of Christ is seen to 'purify your conscience from dead works' (Heb. 9:14). There is here a less developed idea of conscience

---

[198] Heb. 10:22, in calling the conscience 'bad' (*ponēra*), is not implying that in itself it is evil, but that for the non-Christian it always has bad effects. The benefits of the passion of Christ as set out in this epistle include a cleansing of the conscience, *i.e.* in delivering it from its former enslavement.

than in the Pauline epistles,[199] but basically it is the same usage. Conscience reveals to man his own imperfections, but this writer gives no indication of how this is done. The designation of the conscience as 'evil' is, of course, a Christian commentary. There is no suggestion that conscience pronounces this judgment on itself. It is when it has been cleansed that its former character is understood. Nevertheless conscience does seem to recognize the essential need for some adequate mediation between man and God.

The rest of the New Testament

In the letter of *James* there is little information on the constitution of man. The most explicit is James 3:9 where man is said to have been made in the image of God, in a way which echoes the Genesis 1:27 account, but does not enlarge upon it. James does not mention the spoiling of the image through sin, but he has no doubt of the reality of sin, as will be seen later (pp. 215ff.). There is no support from James for the view that every man bears the image of the heavenly Son of man, or that man is naturally like God because he belongs to the heavenly Archetypal Man. The NT view is that the 'image' was marred at the fall and can be restored only through Christ.[200] There is in James an implied conflict between man as he was created and man as he is now. Yet even as he now is, he still shows traces of the image of God. The readers are reminded to put away filthiness and wickedness and to receive the implanted word, which can save their souls (Jas. 1: 21). James throughout is more concerned with man's practical behaviour than with speculative matters of man's constitution. When he speaks of a man's soul (*psychē*) being saved from death (Jas. 5:20), he is clearly using the word of the person apart from the flesh, which is mortal. The word seems to be used here in a sense almost equivalent with *pneuma*. In fact, James cites a saying about God jealously yearning over the spirit he has made to dwell in us (Jas. 4:5), which if it refers to man's human spirit would denote that part of him which has direct reference to God.[201] In another statement James differentiates between spirit and body, but maintains that both are necessary for life (Jas. 2:26). Man conceived of as simply body, according to James, would be dead, and it is clear that he

---

[199] C. A. Pierce, *Conscience in the New Testament*, pp. 101f., sees five stages in the author's use of *syneidēsis*. The climax is reached in 13:18 where the author speaks of having a clear conscience 'desiring to act honorably in all things'. Pierce suggests that this is 'of intention and aspiration, rather than of accomplishment' (p. 103).

[200] *Cf.* J. Héring, *Die biblischen Grundlagen des christlichen Humanismus* (1946), cited by and refuted by W. G. Kümmel, *Man in the New Testament*, p. 86 n.96a. The latter argues that the NT view is that the image of God does not belong to man's nature, but is given as a gift. The fall robbed man of the gift. Moreover, Kümmel asserts that the Archetypal Man is not a heavenly being.

[201] R. V. G. Tasker, *James* (TNTC, 1956), *ad loc.*, takes *pneuma* here to relate to the Spirit of God, not to the human spirit.

assumes his readers would accept this conclusion without question.

A similar position is reflected in the *Petrine epistles*, although there are some interesting variations. One of the most striking is that which speaks of the passions of the flesh (*sarx*) warring against the soul (*psychē*) (1 Pet. 2:11).[202] There is an echo here of the familiar Pauline antithesis between *sarx* and *pneuma*, but it does not feature so prominently in Peter.[203] In setting out the example of Christ, Peter speaks of him 'being put to death in the flesh but made alive in the spirit' (1 Pet. 3:18), where the antithesis is between mortal *sarx* and living *pneuma* (*cf.* also 1 Pet. 4:6, where these concepts are again contrasted). It should be noted, however, that *sarx* and *pneuma* in this context denote not two parts of Christ, but two different spheres of existence.[204] Salvation is related to the soul (1 Pet. 1:9).[205] The soul is capable of being purified (1 Pet. 1:22). Jesus can be described as Shepherd and Guardian of the soul (1 Pet. 2:25). Sufferers are urged to entrust their souls to God (1 Pet. 4:19). In all these instances 'soul' stands for persons, especially in their spiritual capacity, *i.e.* the whole man. It is very close to the frequent use of 'spirit' in Paul. The latter word is used of the inner life in 1 Peter 3:4. But it has a different use in 1 Peter 3:19, where it relates to spiritual beings in prison, a statement which has caused considerable debate. In the same passage the word 'soul' (*psychē*) is used in the sense of 'persons', obviously intended to differentiate them from the 'spirits'. Again, in 2 Peter 2:8 Lot is vexed in soul, while the false teachers are enticing the souls of the unsteady (2 Pet. 2:14), which shows a further extension of the idea of 'soul' to include the mind. None of these general epistles uses the word 'mind' (*nous*).

There are three occurrences in *syneidēsis* in 1 Peter, which must be noted (1 Pet. 2:19; 3:16, 21). In the first, the word should not be translated 'conscience', since it occurs followed by the genitive 'of' or 'towards God'. There are no parallels to this kind of construction and it would differ from normal usage if *syneidēsis* were used in this sense. The RSV 'mindful of God' is to be preferred. But in the other two cases the meaning 'conscience'

---

[202] Some exegetes have seen in 1 Pet. 2:11 evidence for the view that the natural man stands in antithesis to the soul, as the immortal, divine part of man (so E. G. Selwyn, *1 Peter*, 1946, pp. 169f.; E. Schweizer, *ZNW* 48, 1957, p. 251; *idem*, *TDNT* 7, p. 144). W. G. Kümmel, *Man in the New Testament*, p. 84 n. 95, objects that the text does not suggest any opposition between the inner and outer man. Man in 1 Peter, as in the NT generally, is regarded as a whole. In this case Peter seems to use *psychē* in the sense that Paul uses *pneuma* to express the inner warfare in man.

[203] F. W. Beare, *The First Epistle of Peter* (²1958), pp. 110f., denies that Peter uses *psychē* in the sense of Paul's *pneuma*. He claims that for Peter *psychē* is 'the essential being of man'. In view of the flexibility in the use of the NT words describing the nature of man, it is reasonable to see general agreement, although not a precise parallel.

[204] For a recent discussion of the relation between *sarx* and *pneuma* in 1 Pet. 3:18, *cf.* R. T. France in *New Testament Interpretation* (ed. I. H. Marshall, 1977), p. 267.

[205] The expression 'the salvation of souls' in 1 Pet. 1:9 embraces whole persons. *Cf.* E. Best, *1 Peter* (*NCB*), p. 80. Peter's usage is somewhat different from Paul's, since the latter uses it generally of unredeemed man.

is undeniable. In 1 Peter 3:16 it is used in a negative sense of the avoidance of conscious sin, to prevent non-believers from finding fault and therefore hindering faith. 1 Peter 3:21 is a notable crux. The reference to a 'clear conscience', however, is in line with other NT usage. In an unmistakable way initiation into the Christian church separates the Christian from the non-Christian in the sphere of conscience. What was 'bad' (*ponēra*) now becomes 'clear' (*agathēs*), *i.e.* free of guilt feelings about the past.

Some have found difficulty with 2 Peter 1:4, which, they maintain, presents a decidedly Hellenistic view of man, at variance with that given in the rest of the NT. A similar contradiction is seen in Acts 17:27–29. The crux of the 2 Peter statement lies in its conclusion, 'that you . . . may become partakers of the divine nature'. This is thought to imply that man in his natural state does not possess the divine, but is wholly cut off from God. Undoubtedly Peter here uses current Hellenistic terminology which is strongly attested in Philo and Josephus. It is a different way of putting the idea from Paul's imagery of sonship.[206] But can this be said to be contradictory? It would be so only if Peter were using the expression 'partakers of the divine nature' in a typical Hellenistic sense,[207] in which it was regarded as the means of escape from the corruption of the material world. But Peter is careful to define the nature of the corruption he has in mind, *i.e.* corruption that is in (*en*) the world because of (*en*) passion. There is a deliberate avoidance of the concept that the material world is itself evil. Moreover, Peter makes clear that no sharing of the divine nature is possible unless God himself takes the initiative (in granting 'his precious and very great promises'). This is very different from the deification of man held out as a goal in the contemporary mystery religions and in popular philosophic ideas (as in the Hermes tracts). In fact, sharing the divine nature in a Christian sense is the beginning not the end. The people whom Peter addresses have already 'obtained a faith of equal standing with ours in the righteousness of our God and Saviour Jesus Christ' (2 Pet. 1:1). In spite of the unusual wording which Peter selects to communicate with his contemporaries, it is not unreasonable to interpret the words in a sense akin to other NT writers like Paul (Rom. 5:2ff.; 8:14–21; Gal. 4:5, 6), John (*cf.*1 Jn. 2:29—3:2) and the writer to the Hebrews (*cf.* Heb. 3:14).[208] To share with Christ means to share what is characteristic of divine nature, without becoming divine and thus losing true humanness.[209]

In the *Revelation* of John there are no fundamental differences, but some

---

[206] *Cf.* J. N. D. Kelly, *The Epistles of Peter and Jude*, p. 303.

[207] Kümmel, *op. cit.*, pp. 92f., sees 2 Peter 1:4, together with Acts 17:28, as contradictory when compared with the teaching of the NT elsewhere. He finds here 'a definite expression of the Hellenistic view of man which presupposes the dualism between the earthly, material world and the divine spiritual world'.

[208] *Cf.* E. M. B. Green, *2 Peter and Jude* (*TNTC*, 1968), pp. 64ff.

[209] *Cf.* C. E. B. Cranfield, *1 and 2 Peter and Jude* (1960), pp. 175ff.

minor shifts of emphasis are worth noting. The various anthropological terms are all found, but not in the same distinctive manner as in Paul. The word *pneuma* is used mainly for the Holy Spirit, but does occur in a few other usages. Twice it is used in the sense of breath, as in Revelation 11:11 of the reviving of the two witnesses, and in Revelation 13:15 of the breath allowed to be given to the image of the beast. In two other cases the word describes the spiritual gift of prophecy (Rev. 19:10; 22:6). In other instances the word is applied to demonic spirits (see above, p. 149). When the whole man is described in this book the word 'soul' (*psychē*) is used, whether of those who are still alive, or of the righteous dead. Those under the altar who had been slain for the word of God (Rev. 6:9) are so described. The martyrs are, however, said not to have loved their own lives (or souls) even unto death (Rev. 12: 11), which suggests that *psychē* is here regarded as earthbound. But again those beheaded for their testimony are described as 'souls' at the last judgment (20:4). In the general sense of 'people' it occurs in Revelation 16:3, 18:13, 14. It is evident therefore that the use of neither 'spirit' nor 'soul' in this book tells us anything about the constitution of man. Moreover, the word 'body' occurs only once (in Rev. 18:13) and is there used in conjunction with *psychē* (RSV renders it 'slaves').[210]

It is significant that the notion of mind (*nous*) occurs only in Revelation 13:18 and 17:9, in both cases to indicate the need for particular understanding of difficult interpretations (the number 666 and the seven hills). It stands for the capacity for special wisdom and not for the natural understanding of man. The choice of word has no anthropological significance.

The book as a whole divides mankind between those who own allegiance to the Lamb and those who are dupes of the devil. The action centres on spiritual forces rather than on merely human confrontation. People almost become puppets to be manipulated in the general struggle. Nevertheless, the author stops short of asserting that people are mere tools in the hands of unseen forces, for the challenge to repentance is constantly heard. People have the option whether to bear the mark of the beast or the mark of the Lamb (Rev. 13 and 14).

Summary of ideas about man

The NT view of man must be deduced from a wide range of apparently disparate material. In fact, the NT does not set out in so many words what man is. It does not supply a psychological account. Paul gets closest to this, but he presents no systematic view. There is little support for an analytical approach to man's nature. Such distinctions as are made concern man's relation with God. Man's whole being is either in communication

---

[210] In this instance 'bodies' appear to be distinct from, although closely allied to, the 'souls' of men. R. H. Gundry, *Sōma in Biblical Theology*, pp. 26f., suggests that slaves are here called 'bodies' precisely because they are not treated as persons.

with God (*i.e.* spiritual) or not in communication with God (*i.e.* carnal).

It is this distinction which leads to the NT teaching about sin which will be explored more fully in the next section. But the major factor about the NT view of man is that in his present state, apart from the grace of God in Christ, he is no longer a true reflection of his Creator. The whole plan of salvation as expounded in the NT is aimed to rectify this lack. Man is definitely superior to the animal creation and is capable of glorifying God.

The relation between the sexes is clearly stated in the NT, and while there are some indications (especially in Paul) that the male is dominant, yet the NT view is radical when compared with the general viewpoint and practice of the world in which the Christian church developed. The view of Jesus was revolutionary in giving women a place of respect, and Paul's doctrine of the abolition of any distinction between men and women in the plan of salvation adds support to this view. This did not eliminate differences of role, but paved the way for a reappraisal of current attitudes.

It has further been noted that Jesus himself appears to be presented in the NT as the ideal or perfect man. This feature is bound up with Christology and will need further comment in the later section on the humanity of Jesus. But it is clear that Jesus alone has perfectly fulfilled the divine intention for manhood.

MAN IN RELATION TO GOD

In our survey of the attitudes, actions and teachings of Jesus we have been looking at the ideal. Yet everywhere there is the consciousness of failure to match up to that ideal.[211] The exemplary life of Jesus highlights the deficiency of man. This leads into the study of man in relation to God and consequently of sin and guilt. This subject is more specifically presented in other NT books, including John's gospel, than in the synoptic gospels. But there are some important features in the synoptic gospels which point the way to an understanding of the NT doctrine.

The synoptic gospels
THE VARIETY OF ASPECTS WITHIN THE IDEA OF SIN
AS SEEN IN THE TERMS USED
The general word for sin (*hamartia*) occurs several times in the synoptic gospels, most often in connection with confession of sins (Mt. 3:6; Mk.

---

[211] For general literature on the NT approach to sin, *cf.* F. Greeves, *The Meaning of Sin* (1956), esp. pp. 100–124; J. S. Candlish, *The Biblical Doctrine of Sin* (n.d.); H. T. Powell, *The Fall of Man: Its Place in Modern Thought* (1934), pp.1–31; J. L. Houlden, 'Man : His nature, predicament and hope (2) The New Testament', in *Man, Fallen and Free* (ed. E. W. Kemp, 1969), pp. 120–141; C. Ryder Smith, *The Bible Doctrine of Sin* (1953); H. Wheeler Robinson, *The Christian Doctrine of Man* (³1926). pp. 91ff., 112ff., 138ff. For discussions on the fall of man in the teaching of Jesus, *cf.* H. T. Powell, *op. cit.*, pp. 1-15; J. Tulloch, *The Christian Doctrine of Sin* (1876) pp. 98–134.

1:5) or forgiveness of sins (twenty-one times). Its basic meaning is failure to hit the mark. Some consciousness of this is essential if confession is to be made. But it implies an awareness of what is expected and the conviction that one's best efforts have failed to achieve it.[212] When John the Baptist preached repentance, he did not need to explain what sin was. No Jew familiar with his nation's history in the OT would be ignorant of the fact that sin was an offence against God and called for repentance. The insistence on repentance by both John the Baptist and Jesus points to a fundamental need on man's part (cf. also Lk. 13:3; 15:7, 10). Since hamartia (with one exception) is used in the plural, 'sinful acts' are clearly in mind, rather than sin in the abstract. Matthew comments that Jesus came to save his people from their sins (Mt. 1:21). All the synoptic gospels relate the incident in which the paralytic is not healed until his sins have been forgiven (Mt. 9:1–8; Mk. 2:1–12; Lk. 4:17–26; this incident accounts[213] for eleven occurrences of the word). Jesus reminds Simon the Pharisee that the sins of the woman who had anointed him, though many, were forgiven (Lk. 7:47). The same word is used in Luke's version of the Lord's prayer (Lk. 11:4). At the last supper, according to Matthew's record, the cup relates to the blood poured out 'for the remission of sins' (Mt. 26:28).[214] The great importance of the theme of forgiveness of sins is stressed in the final words of Jesus to his disciples according to Luke's gospel (Lk. 24:47). In the one case of the concept in the singular it is linked with blasphemy against the Holy Spirit (Mt. 12:31; Mk 3:29 uses the cognate hamartēma in the singular).

Another word used is paraptōma (trespass), which again is linked with forgiveness on the occasions when it occurs. In Mark 11:25 and Matthew 6:14 it is used in the plural and has the sense of acts which deviate from the standard. Again Jesus does not need to demonstrate that man has trespassed. He not only takes this for granted, but assumes also that all who have a disquiet over their trespasses will desire forgiveness.

A change in terminology is seen in the suggestion of man's indebtedness. Matthew's account of the Lord's Prayer includes the request 'forgive us our debts' (Mt. 6:12). The word used in this case (opheilēma) is most rare in the NT (elsewhere only in Rom. 4:4), but the idea of indebtedness nevertheless occurs in other contexts in the synoptic gospels. Indeed, in

---

[212] G. Aulén, in The Faith of the Christian Church (²1961), pp. 231ff., makes the point that the category of sin is irrelevant outside the religious sphere. All sin is sin against God. Sin would, therefore, have no meaning in purely ethical discussion.

[213] V. Taylor, Mark, ad loc., commenting on this incident points out that although Jesus did not believe that sin was the sole cause of the affliction, 'He could not fail to observe how closely mental, spiritual, and physical conditions are connected'.

[214] Those who regard this phrase as an addition by Matthew generally consider that he was influenced by the servant concept (Is. 53:12) (so A. H. Neile, Matthew (1915), p. 383; E. Schweizer, Matthew, p. 491). Since the old covenant is clearly in view, the idea that Jesus was doing something about sins would not be an alien concept. See further discussion, pp. 442ff.

Luke's account of the Lord's Prayer a distinction is made between sin and debt ('forgive us our sins, for we ourselves forgive every one who is indebted to us', Lk. 11:4),[215] sin relating to God and debt relating to other people. The train of thought seems to proceed from the idea of debt, which arises as a matter of experience in communities and which gives rise to a position of power over the debtor, to the idea of general sin against God. The idea of debt is not intended to reduce sin to commercial terms, but rather to transfer the idea of material indebtedness to spiritual obligation. Matthew includes a similar idea in a comment of Jesus on the Lord's Prayer (Mt. 6:14, 15).[216] The same evangelist includes the parable of the unforgiving debtor (Mt. 18:21ff.).

A third term which is equally important is *anomia* (lawlessness). This is used only by Matthew among the gospels and more specifically refers to hostility towards God, the antithesis of what is right and good. In Matthew 7.22, 23, the evildoers are contrasted with those who do the will of God. This suggests that anyone who does not fulfil God's will is guilty of *anomia*.[217] In the explanation of the parable of the tares, those excluded from the kingdom are described as evildoers (*tous poiountas tēn anomian*) (Mt. 13:41). In this context the word is linked with *skandala* (literally, traps which cause sin). In Matthew's eschatological discourse a time is foreseen when lawlessness (*anomia*) will be multiplied and people's love will grow cold (Mt. 24:12). The same word is linked with hypocrisy as a contrast to pretended righteousness among the scribes and Pharisees (Mt. 23:28). Wickedness, in this case, is an inward condition.[218] So strong is Jesus' condemnation of those who are not what they pretend to be that he asks the question, 'How are you to escape being sentenced to hell (Gehenna)?' (Mt. 23:33).[219]

---

[215] The fact that Luke has 'sins' and Matthew has 'debts' (*opheilēma*) in their respective versions of the Lord's prayer does not materially affect the meaning. The linking of debt with sin is familiar in the OT (*cf.* P. Bonnard's comments, *Matthieu* (CNT, 1963), p. 86). E. Schweizer, *Matthew*, p. 155, reckons 'debts' to be the earlier term, but since the idea of indebtedness is still present in Luke, the distinction should not be over-emphasized. Indeed both sin and debt are variant translations of the Aramaic *hôbā'*, which literally means debt and metaphorically means sin.

[216] In this case the word used is *paraptōmata*, not *opheilēma* as in the prayer. Although the distinction between the words must be preserved, their juxtaposition in Matthew is significant. Sin was too big to be confined to one expression.

[217] This sense of *anomia* is akin to the OT idea of it as doing what is forbidden in the law, but is an extension of it in that the law is reinterpreted in the Sermon on the Mount. Schweizer, *op. cit.*, p. 189, considers that the major prohibition in the law which is in mind is cooling of love to one's neighbours. Hence, even those upholders of the law, like Pharisees, could be guilty of 'lawlessness'.

[218] In this context *anomia* is linked with 'hypocrisy'. RSV renders it 'iniquity' to bring out more forcefully this inward state. Nevertheless, the concept of lawlessness, when applied to those who sit on Moses' seat (Mt. 23:2), is striking and cannot be altogether eliminated.

[219] F. Greeves, *The Meaning of Sin*, p. 103, makes the point that it is impossible to give a clear picture of what sin meant to Jesus if we limit ourselves to the synoptics' record of his teaching about sin. But nevertheless he goes on to say that we learn more about sin from Jesus than from any other teacher, and that is through noting his dealing with sinners.

OTHER INDICATIONS THAT MAN IS NOT WHAT HE OUGHT TO BE

In the parable of the Pharisee and tax-collector, Jesus contrasted the self-righteous attitude of the one with the other's confession that he was a sinner (Lk. 18:9ff.). This gives a clue to Jesus' understanding of man. No doubt the Pharisee sincerely desired to be righteous, but his great mistake was to imagine that he was capable of achieving it through his own efforts. It would have been deeply perplexing to him to discover his whole approach to be wrong, especially as he followed a strong religious tradition. The other man was more realistic, seeing himself gripped by a need which he could do nothing to alleviate. It is clear that the Pharisee had an over-optimistic view of human nature, and that the tax-collector, although thoroughly pessimistic, was nevertheless nearer to man's common experience. He could do nothing but throw himself on God's mercy. It should be noted that Jesus gives no support to any view that sees man as self-reliant.

In the teaching of Jesus the most devastating condemnation of self-righteousness occurs in Matthew 23. There is good reason to believe that the presentation of Pharisaism was not typical of all Pharisees. But the abuses to which man's over-confidence in his own ability can lead are stressed so as to draw sharper attention to the inevitable judgment. Jesus was addressing those who were blind guides (Mt. 23:19, 24, 26). He saw in them descendants of those whom the prophets were sent to challenge. Thus the leaders of religious thought among Jesus' contemporaries were condemned because they depended on their own achievements, rather than on the mercy of God. We may also note Jesus' statement that he had come to call sinners, not righteous people (Mk. 2:17), *i.e.* those who considered themselves righteous.[220]

One statement of Jesus has occasioned much discussion. Both Matthew and Luke record it in almost identical words (Mt. 7:11; Lk. 11:13): 'If you then who are evil, know how to give good gifts to your children. . . ' . In what sense did Jesus mean that man was evil? Those who believe in the inherent goodness of man (influenced by evolutionary ethics) have sought to avoid the conclusion that Jesus meant to say that the race is evil.[221] There is no reason to suppose that Jesus is disputing man's ability to choose between good and evil, but he was certainly affirming an evil bias which marked all people in contrast to the perfectly good intention of God the heavenly Father. This is a devastating comparison, but it should be observed that Jesus is commenting not so much on the sinful nature of man,

---

[220] Kümmel, *Man in the New Testament*, pp. 19ff., says of Jesus' opponents that their mistake 'lies in the fact that they exclude themselves from insight into their own sinfulness, whereas Jesus presupposes that all men, including these "righteous ones", are sinful'.

[221] The same would be true of those who approach man from an exclusively psychological point of view (*cf.* E. H. Robertson, *Man's Estimate of Man* (1958), pp. 36ff.).

which is taken for granted, as on the superior generosity of a heavenly Father over an earthly father.[222]

We have already noted some evidence that sin was regarded as a debt, and this is borne out further by the parable of the unmerciful servant (Mt. 18:21ff.). This was told to elucidate Jesus' comment to Peter that he should place no limit on forgiveness (as 'seventy times seven' implies, Mt. 18:21, 22). In the parable an enormous debt is forgiven by the master, while a trivial debt remains unforgiven by the servant. The context seems to suggest that the focus is on forgiveness rather than on the differential in the size of debt, as the concluding saying shows (Mt. 18:35).

The most poignant example of disaster which overtook one man through sin is Judas Iscariot. Jesus' comment on his intention to betray him is laconic and devastating – it would have been better if he had never been born (Mk. 14:21; Mt. 26:24; Lk. 22:22).[223] Since Judas' sin was a direct opposition to Jesus himself and to God's purpose through him, this suggests that a man's attitude to Jesus constitutes an important aspect of sin.

Some indication that sin is regarded as lawless action through sheer disobedience is seen in the parable of the two sons (Mt. 21:28–32), in which it was the final action, not the initial verbal response, which came in for condemnation ('He answered, "I go, sir," but did not go').

SUMMARY OF JESUS' ESTIMATE OF MAN'S SIN IN THE SYNOPTIC GOSPELS
It will be clear from the preceding evidence that certain conclusions may be drawn about Jesus' teaching on sin.

(i) Sin is universal. There is no suggestion that part of the race is exempt. What applies to one man applies to all. We may justly claim that Jesus was a realist in his estimate of man; that side by side with his assessment of the tremendous worth of man in the eyes of God, he takes it for granted that all have failed to reach their potential because of sin.[224]

(ii) Sin is internal. Although much of the teaching centred on external acts, the root cause was seen to be much deeper. It is what comes out of

---

[222] Schweizer, *op. cit.*, 173f., argues that Jesus bases his statement on the assumption that earthly fathers reflect something of the fatherhood of God. Nevertheless he acknowledges that human maliciousness is here presupposed.

[223] There is no suggestion that Judas' action could be excused because he was a blind instrument of fate (*cf.* V. Taylor, *Mark*, p. 542), in spite of the fact that the destiny of the Son of man is seen to be in accordance with the divine purpose (*cf.* K. Stendahl, *Matthew*, Peake, p. 693g).

[224] W. G. Kümmel, *op. cit.*, pp. 18ff., agrees that the call to conversion is addressed to all mankind, and deals with the main objections. (i) The claim that in Mk. 2:17b and Lk. 15:7 Jesus acknowledged the existence of a righteous people. Kümmel dismisses Bultmann's view that we are dealing with a secondary application. He maintains that Jesus is not obviating the distinction between 'good' and 'bad', but desires that those who consider themselves to be blameless should become aware of their guilt.

(ii) The second objection is based on Jesus' view of the infinite value of man (as in Mk. 8:36). But Kümmel rightly points out that this passage shows the superiority of heavenly life over earthly and therefore does not conflict with the view that Jesus saw all men as sinners.

man that defiles. Other evidence from the NT highlights this inner nature, particularly in the Pauline epistles, but it is nevertheless present in germ in the teaching of Jesus.

(iii) Sin is enslavement. When seen against the background of adverse satanic forces, man in his sinful state is seen to be in the grip of Satan. This is indirectly assumed in the ransom concept of the work of Christ (see pp. 440ff.). Delivery can come only to those who are already bound, an idea again further expounded by Paul (see pp. 476ff.).

(iv) Sin is rebellion. In the parable of the prodigal son (Lk. 15:11ff.) the critical turning point comes when the younger son reaches the conclusion that he has sinned against God and against his father (verses 18, 21). Sin is not the squandering of the family property, although this is not condoned. It is rather a refusal to act as a son, which in effect amounted to rebellion against the father.[225] The elder son's idea of his brother's offence is, however, tied up with the property. The rebellion could be overcome by a change of attitude, but the property could not be so easily restored. The elder brother's anger reflects a too superficial understanding of the nature of sin. Restoration, the overcoming of alienation, is based on grace not merit.

(v) Sin merits condemnation. The teaching of Jesus about the day of judgment will be considered more specifically when dealing with the future life (see pp. 849ff.), but it is essential to note here that man is seen to be under the judgment of God. Everyone will render account before God, even for careless words which have been uttered (Mt. 12:36).[226] Punishments are regarded as necessary, but are graded to fit the crime (cf. Lk. 12:47, 48; Mt. 11:20–24). This aspect of man's accountability before God is developed also in Paul's writings, but it must be recognized as an essential feature in the background to the mission of Jesus. Although alienation from God[227] is seen to be the common lot of all, only in the case of blasphemy against the Holy Spirit (Mk. 3:28ff.; Mt. 12:31, 32; Lk. 12:10) is sin declared to be unpardonable.[228] Indeed the repeated calls for repentance show that the synoptic gospels in no sense adopt a fatalistic approach to man's sinful condition.

[225] Cf. S. Lyonnet, in Sin, Redemption and Sacrifice, p. 37.

[226] It was believed by the rabbis that the heavenly record included words as well as deeds (see Strack-Billerbeck 1, pp. 639f.). The idea which Jesus expressed may not have been unfamiliar to his hearers. McNeile, Matthew, p. 180, reckons that a careless word (rhēma argon) is one that does not, and is not intended to, effect anything.

[227] In the matter of alienation, non-Christian existentialism sees no way of escape, thus standing in direct contrast to the Christian position.

[228] W. Lane, Mark (NICNT 1974), pp. 144ff., rightly points out that this unpardonable sin must not be divorced from the context in which Jesus' opponents were denying God's action through him. 'In this historical context, blasphemy against the Holy Spirit denotes the conscious and deliberate rejection of the saving power and grace of God released through Jesus' word and act'. Cf. O. E. Evans, 'The Unforgivable Sin', ExT 68, 1957, pp. 240ff.

The Johannine literature
CONCEPTS OF SIN

Sin plays an important part in the teaching of Jesus in John's gospel, although it is approached from a point of view slightly different from that in the synoptics. The general word for sin (*hamartia*) is almost always used in the singular and sums up the idea of sinfulness rather than individual sins. We are first introduced to it in John the Baptist's statement about Jesus in John 1:29 ('Behold, the Lamb of God, who takes away the sin of the world'). The concept of the world's sin is assumed rather than demonstrated. In the prologue we meet with darkness as the antithesis of light, but the darkness is not linked with sin (Jn. 1:5). It is, however, linked with ignorance of God (Jn. 1:10) (see section (iii) below). The significance of the bearing away of sin will be discussed more fully under the mission of Christ (see pp. 450ff.). This early focus on sin supplies one of the important clues to an understanding of the mission of Jesus as it is presented in John's gospel.

The linking of sin with death is found in such an expression as 'you will . . . die in your sin' (Jn. 8:21) or 'in your sins' (Jn. 8:24), an expression which may be derived from Ezekiel 3:20 (LXX). Sin is seen as a slave-master (in Jn. 8:34), as sometimes in Paul's epistles. In debates with the Jews Jesus challenged them, 'Which of you convicts me of sin?' (Jn. 8:46), implying that no-one could. In this case Jesus separates himself from others.[229] The Pharisees considered that the man born blind, whose sight had been restored, was born in sin (Jn. 9:34) and they therefore excommunicated him. Jesus, however, took a totally different approach to the man and at once challenged him to faith. It is clear that in this case 'sin' is used with a connotation which was highly questionable, arising from the mistaken view that the man's blindness was directly due to sin, a view which even the disciples shared (Jn. 9:2, 3), but which Jesus emphatically dismissed.

Sin as alienation from God. The fourth gospel is a book of antitheses. The contrast between light and darkness noted above is in line with other contrasts like truth and error, the world and God, life and death. The negative aspects of these contrasts contribute to the flavour of sin as set out in the whole book. Sin is opposition to God, a denial of all that is best for man. 'He who . . . believes . . . does not come into judgment, but has passed from death to life' (Jn. 5:24), which clearly links judgment with

---

[229] Bultmann, *John*, p. 323, denies that this question refers to the personality of Jesus, but affirms that it relates to him as Revealer. 'It is the character of his word, which, as the word of revelation, forbids all critical questions.' This is Bultmann's interpretation of the implication of Jesus' 'sinlessness' in this context. It still follows, in any case, that Jesus is distinguishing himself from other men. See the section on the sinlessness of Jesus, pp. 228ff.

death. This further supports the view that in John sin is connected closely with unbelief (see below).

We have already seen that 'the world' (*kosmos*) in John's gospel is described as actively hostile to God, which illustrates sin as enmity. Jesus explained that the reason the world hated him was that he testified to its essentially evil nature (Jn. 7:7). The hatred of the world is therefore assumed by Jesus, who warned the disciples to expect it (Jn. 15:18–19). 'The ruler of this world', who is judged and cast out at the 'hour' of Christ, has clearly usurped the place of God and has brought men into a similar alienation (Jn. 12:31; 14:30; 16:11).

Since the disciples of Jesus are distinguished from the world even though they live in the world (Jn. 15:19, 17:14), it is evident that Jesus himself is the key to the division. Man's attitude to him profoundly affects his position in the world, *i.e.* whether or not he becomes a target for hate. This demarcation between God and the world, while implicit in the synoptic gospels, becomes quite explicit in John's gospel. It becomes even more so in the appearance of antichrist in 1 John 2:22; 4:2f.

Sin as unbelief. We have noted above the statement from John 5:24 which connects unbelief in Jesus with condemnation. This is characteristic of John's gospel, but it must not be supposed that this exhausts his view of sin. There are two sayings in John 15 which suggest that the coming of Jesus (verse 22)[230] and the works of Jesus (verse 24) are the basis on which sin is estimated. If Jesus had not come and performed works, they (*i.e.* the world) would not have sin. Obviously the sin in question is of a special kind, *i.e.* connected with their attitude to Jesus.[231] A similar idea seems to be present in John 9:41, when Jesus answered the Pharisees' question, 'Are we also blind?', by saying, 'If you were blind, you would have no guilt (*hamartia*); but now that you say, "We see", your guilt remains.' It was the Pharisees' refusal to recognize that their true attitude to Jesus was spiritual blindness which constituted their sin.

Condemnation is unequivocally pronounced against unbelief in God's Son (Jn. 3:18). Moreover, the cause of unbelief and its consequent darkness is found in the evil character of men's deeds (Jn. 3:19), since the deeds reflect the real nature of the persons doing them. Unbelief is also linked with disobedience, for it is on the man who disobeys the Son of God that the wrath of God rests (Jn. 3:36). In his comment on the convicting work of the Holy Spirit, Jesus declared that the Spirit would convict the world

---

[230] *Cf.* C. K. Barrett, *John*, p. 401, who says, 'The coming of Jesus makes possible the ultimate and unmistakable manifestation of sin, which is disbelief in him (16.9)'.

[231] It must be noted that where sin is seen as unbelief, it is being contrasted with faith as a commitment of oneself to the cause of Christ. It would be difficult to attach any meaning to it as a definition, if sin were conceived of as an absence of intellectual belief. But Jesus called for a radical faith. To decline to accept the challenge means to oppose the will of God.

of sin 'because they do not believe in me' (Jn. 16:9). This linking of unbelief with sin is significant in view of the frequent emphasis on faith in this gospel. Since in fact the purpose was to lead men to believe in Jesus Christ, it is not surprising that unbelief is so emphatically described as sin.[232] Whereas the world was dark when Christ came, his coming introduced a new challenge, and failure to meet that challenge intensified men's condemnation.

Sin as ignorance. Because some scholars consider that the major work of Jesus was revelation,[233] some attention must be given to the complementary view that man's chief need is for knowledge. In this case the Johannine concept of sin would be ignorance. There is some evidence which could be made to support this. If darkness is construed as lack of light, then Jesus, coming as Light (Jn. 1:4, 5, 9; 8:12; 1 Jn. 2:8ff.) which dispels the darkness, meets man's deepest needs. If this were the whole story, people could hardly be blamed for the lack of light. It is not, however, the whole story. It is only part of it. Knowledge is necessary, but the NT does not fall into the trap of gnosticism in thinking that knowledge is all that is needed. Faith is never confused with knowledge, any more than sin is confused with ignorance. The strong presentation in John's gospel of the world in the grip of evil forces is sufficient to show that more is needed to deliver man than further illumination. In line with this, we should note that Jesus did not excuse the Pharisees when he charged them with being blind (Jn. 9:41).[234]

Sin as mortal. The connection between sin and death which is strongly brought out in Paul's epistles is present only indirectly in the Johannine literature. It is implicit in the antithesis between life and death. The view of salvation presented may be summed up as 'eternal life', which presupposes the opposite for those who do not believe (Jn. 3:16f.; 1 Jn. 2:25). Faith enables a person to pass from death to life (Jn. 5:24; *cf.* 1 Jn. 3:14), which implies that the natural man, before faith, is in a state of death.

---

[232] *Cf.* Kümmel, *Man in the New Testament*, p. 78, who says that 'rejection of Jesus denotes man's attempt to set himself up against God, to assert himself'.

[233] Bultmann, *John* (1971), divides the whole book into two main parts, 'Revelation to the world' and 'Revelation to the community'. He is fond of the expression 'the Revealer' when referring to Jesus. *Cf.* also J. Painter, *John, Witness and Theologian* (1975), who takes revelation to be the key to Johannine theology. J. T. Forestell, *The Word of the Cross: Salvation as Revelation in the Fourth Gospel* (1974), takes a similar position.

[234] To maintain, as F. R. Tennant, *The Concept of Sin* (1912), p. 31, does, that this statement in Jn. 9:41 means that if the Pharisees could have pleaded blindness they would not have been sinners, is to miss the point. F. Greeves, *The Meaning of Sin*, p. 107, contends that this passage shows that at the root of all sin is ignorance. This does not mean, however, that sin *is* ignorance. Bultmann, *op. cit.*, p. 341, comments that 'blindness' is 'no longer simply a wandering in the dark, which can always become aware that it is lost, and so have the possibility of receiving sight; for now it has forfeited this possibility'.

Moreover, there is a distinction between those destined to the resurrection of life and the resurrection of judgment (Jn. 5:29), which again suggests that evil is linked with the absence of life, *i.e.* death. Of course, in these instances 'life' and 'death' are thought of in spiritual terms.

One passage in 1 John has caused difficulty because of the mention of 'mortal sin' (1 Jn. 5:16–17). The expression used is *hamartia thanatēphoros* (literally 'death-carrying sin'). There seems little doubt that John is suggesting two types of sin, one death-bearing, the other not. Since he does not enlarge on the death-bearing type, this can be deduced only from the context. The statement comes immediately after the statement of the purpose of the epistle (1 Jn. 5:13), in which a knowledge of eternal life is desired for the readers. Those who have such a knowledge may sin, but prayer may be made for them. But the death-bearing sin is different. Is this the sin of rejecting Christ, a deliberate sinning against the light? It may well be so. John concludes that all wrongdoing is sin, but there is a sin which is not mortal (1 Jn. 5:17).

Sin as universal. Whereas this is implicit in the gospel, it becomes explicit in 1 John. Those who deny that they have sin are self-deceived (1 Jn. 1:8). Moreover, such people make God a liar (1 Jn. 1:10). When speaking of Jesus Christ, John notes the effectiveness of his self-offering for the sins of the whole world (1 Jn. 2:2; *cf.* Jn. 1:29). He can further say that 'all that is in the world . . . is not of the Father' (1 Jn. 2:16). He describes this alien element in terms of lust and pride, and has no doubt that all men are implicated. This universalism is demonstrated by the fact that the world is in the grip of the evil one (*cf.* Jn. 14:30; 1 Jn. 5:19). The only exceptions to this are those who belong to God.

Sin as lawlessness. There is yet one other aspect, which comes out clearly in 1 John 3:4, and that is the definition of sin as lawlessness (*anomia*).[235] This is a deliberate rejection of God's standards and a resort to one's own desires. Whereas the Christian has a restraint against deliberate sinning of this nature (*i.e.* abiding in Christ), the world has no such restraint. In fact, those not abiding in Christ are in the devil's domain. Hence John can say, 'He who commits sin is of the devil; for the devil has sinned from the beginning' (1 Jn. 3:8). The children of the devil are those who do not do right (1 Jn. 3:10).

The origin of sin. This problem is never overtly mentioned in John's gospel. There is no attempt to trace it back to Adam. Nevertheless there is nothing

---

[235] I. de la Potterie has maintained that *anomia* in this context refers to eschatological rebellion against God and not to 'lawlessness'. *Cf.* I. de la Potterie and S. Lyonnet, *The Christian Lives by the Spirit* (1971), pp. 79–143.

to suggest an alternative idea which would conflict with this essentially OT view. It was during the dialogue over Abraham and his seed that Jesus accused his Jewish contemporaries of being 'of your father the devil' (Jn. 8:44).[236] There is everything in John's gospel to suggest that Jesus himself traced evil back to its source in Satan. But this does not absolve men from responsibility. The Jews in question were palpably guilty because they had not believed in Jesus (Jn. 8:45). Nevertheless, Jesus looked back to the ultimate source of sin. The statements in 1 John 3:8, 10, already mentioned above, also trace the cause of sin to the devil. Despite the absence from John's gospel of the synoptic narratives of the temptation of Jesus, it is significant that the book nevertheless makes a close connection between sin and the devil.

JOHANNINE DUALISM

It has been maintained that a different kind of dualism is found in John when compared with the synoptics.[237] Whereas the latter are concerned with a horizontal dualism (this age and the age to come), the former has a vertical view (the world above and the world below). In so far as much of this discussion affects the various end-time teachings, it will mainly be dealt with under the future life (see pp. 790ff.). But since the doctrine of sin raises the problem of dualism, it must be mentioned here.

The whole problem of man is viewed in dualistic terms so far as the world is set over against God. The various antitheses all illustrate this. Light, truth, life all come from above; darkness, falsehood, death, belong to the world below. This is presented in the prologue and supported by many of the sayings in the gospel.[238] The sphere above is the sphere of the Spirit, that below is the sphere of the flesh.

Nevertheless it would not be correct to drive too strong a wedge between the vertical and horizontal views in considering John's dualism. The so-called horizontal view which presupposes some progression in history is by no means absent. If the Logos pre-existed in the world above, he had to come into human history to effect salvation. With all its vertical emphasis John's gospel nowhere supposes that God's saving work could actually take place anywhere other than in the world below. There is, therefore, no essential clash between the two views.

It is against this background of both horizontal and vertical dualism that views greatly emphasizing the influence of gnostic[239] or Platonic patterns

---

[236] The construction could be rendered, 'You are of the father of the devil,' but the context is contrasting the devil's children with God's (*cf.* C. K. Barrett, *John*, p. 289, B. Lindars, *John*, pp. 328f.).

[237] For a discussion of John's dualism and its implications for the doctrine of sin, *cf.* G. E. Ladd, *TNT*, pp. 223–36; F. M. Braun, *Jean Le Théologien. Sa Théologie* III, 1*EB* (1966), pp. 43–47; R. Bultmann, *TNT* 2, pp. 15ff.

[238] *Cf.* R. E. Brown, *John*, (1966), 1, p. cxv.

[239] Bultmann, *TNT*, 2, 21, states categorically that the language of John's dualism is that of gnosticism.

of thought must be examined. Bultmann's contention that the fourth gospel has taken gnostic dualism and converted it into a gospel of decision has concentrated on one line of evidence to the exclusion of the other.[240] Dodd did a similar thing with his appeal to Platonic dualism[241] (the antithesis between the real and apparent world), but he also gave insufficient attention to the importance of history in the Johannine presentation of the mission of Jesus.

It is one thing to note parallels with gnostic thought, but quite another to establish that John's presentation is derived from such a source. The danger of maintaining this lies in then supposing that gnostic terminology must be understood in a gnostic sense. But the strong strand of historical development in John's gospel, particularly the unfolding of the 'hour' throughout the book and the climax reached in the passion story, is more than enough to rule out a gnostic source for John's dualism. In addition the attention given to OT fulfilment in this gospel amply demonstrates the conviction of continuity between the OT order and the ministry of Christ,[242] which is strongly in harmony with the similar emphasis in the synoptic gospels. There is no justification for supposing that a different approach to history is being maintained.

In support of a Jewish emphasis in the dualism of the fourth gospel the evidence from Qumran may be noted.[243] This presents a clash between the spirit of truth and the spirit of perversity, between the children of light and the children of darkness, between the Teacher of Righteousness and the Wicked Priest. There is some echo of the rabbinical idea of the two impulses within men (yēṣer haṭôḇ and yēṣer hārā') since the two spirits of the Qumran literature contest for the dominant influence over the hearts of men.[244] There is also a cosmic aspect,[245] for the overthrow of the spirit of perversity is predicted for the day of judgment.[246] The spirit of truth, however, resides in the meantime in those who are obedient to the law. In spite of certain apparent similarities between Qumran and John's gospel, there are important differences. The main clash in John is between Jesus Christ, the incarnate Word, and the world-system under the domination

---

[240] *Cf.* Kümmel's criticism of Bultmann's rejection of the temporal eschatological expressions in Jn. 5:28-29; 6:39,40,44,54. He says, 'The temporal expressions about creation and fulfilment are quite indispensable'. *Man in the New Testament*, p. 80 n. 93.

[241] *The Interpretation of the Fourth Gospel*, p. 143.

[242] *Cf.* R. Morgan, 'Fulfilment in the Fourth Gospel', *Int* 11, 1957, pp. 155–165.

[243] J. Jeremias, *The Central Message of the New Testament* (1965), p. 83, maintains that John's dualism is Palestinian. He claims that its monotheism, ethics and eschatology are all non-gnostic. They are paralleled in Qumran literature.

[244] For a discussion of the *yēṣer* principle in relation to Paul's theology, *cf.* W. D. Davies, *Paul and Rabbinic Judaism* (1948), pp. 20ff.

[245] According to H. Odeberg, *The Fourth Gospel* (1929), p. 300, in rabbinic opinion the *yēṣer-hārā'* was connected with and even identified with Satan. Sinfulness is slavery to the *yēṣer-hārā'*.

[246] This conflict is described in detail in 1 QM.

of the spirit of evil. Instead of observance of the law as the condition on which men become children of light, John shows faith in Christ as the only way. In John and in the teaching of Jesus which he records, the darkness is universal until the shining of the light. There is no division of people into two classes according to the dominance of two spirits. In John's gospel the prince of this world is already a defeated foe, although all unbelievers are still under his influence. The fundamental difference between the dualism of Qumran and the dualism of John is the centrality of Christ in the latter, which is naturally absent from the former.[247]

Acts

Man's failure to match up to God's pattern for him has already been noted in Acts when commenting on man (see pp. 161ff.), but it is necessary to see how the Christians conceived of the needs of the world and how they related their message to it. The call to repentance is as strong as in the ministries of John the Baptist and Jesus. Peter, in his Pentecost sermon, urges repentance leading to forgiveness of sins (Acts 2:38). The same idea comes in Acts 3:19 and in 17:30. The latter reference is noteworthy because it is addressed to an Athenian audience. Both Jew and Gentile are seen to be equally in need of repentance (*cf.* Acts 11:18; 26:20). It is against the basic assumption that all are equally afflicted with the same malaise of sin that the gospel of Christ was preached. There had to be a recognition of need in response to the challenge to repent. Peter summed up his contemporaries as 'this crooked generation' (Acts 2:40).[248]

As in the synoptic gospels, the general word for sin (*hamartia*) is used in the plural in descriptions of the purpose of the gospel, always linked with forgiveness or blotting out or cleansing (Acts 2:38; 3:19; 5:31; 10:43; 13:38; 22:16; 26:18). It is also used once in the singular of the sin of Stephen's death (7:60). Other concepts found in Acts are those denoted by the words for 'wickedness' (*ponēros*) or 'evil' (*kakos*). The former occurs in Acts 17:5; 18:14; 25:18; 28:21, but relates more to crimes than general sinfulness. The second word is also used specifically of Saul's persecution (9:13) or of general harm (16:28; 28:5) or of crime (23:9). The cognate *kakia* occurs only in Acts 8:22 as the evil from which Simon the magician is called to repent. It will be seen therefore that sin in the sense of 'sinful acts' is everywhere assumed, and represents the need of man which can be met by Christ alone.

Luke gives no indication that sin is a violation of the law of God, but he records sayings about the day of judgment, as for instance in the Areopagus

[247] For a detailed study of Qumran dualism and John's dualism, *cf.* J. H. Charlesworth's article in *NTS* 15, 1969, pp. 389–414, reproduced in *John and Qumran* (ed. J. H. Charlesworth, 1972), pp. 76–106.

[248] This expression (*genea skolia*) is derived from Dt. 32:5 and Ps. 78:8. Jesus had already used similar words in Lk. 9:41; 11:29; 17:25.

address (Acts 17:31).[249] Paul spoke about justice and future judgment before Felix (Acts 24:25). The judgment idea was presumably taken over by the early church from the OT (see pp. 848ff.).

Paul

Undoubtedly of all the NT writers, Paul approaches nearest to working out what might be called a theology of sin.[250] Nevertheless the basis on which he builds is the same basis as we have already seen in the gospels. Our procedure will be to note first the various concepts by which Paul expresses the idea of sin,[251] and then to discuss such themes as personification and universality. Next we shall consider Paul's teaching on the relation between sin and flesh, sin and death, responsibility, punishment and original sin. By this means we shall discover his idea of man's basic needs.[252]

CONCEPTS OF SIN

As with so many other of Paul's concepts, a wide variety of words is used to describe the nature of sin. We need to note these terms, but Paul's doctrine of sin has a broader basis than his use of terminology. Indeed, the terminology gives only the general drift of his ideas, which are more fully explored in other ways.

The word *hamartia* is the general word for sinful acts and is used both in the plural and the singular. When used in the plural it frequently occurs in OT citations (as *e.g.* Rom 4:7; 11:27; *cf.* also 1 Thes. 2:16 and 1 Cor. 15:17). It also occurs in several statements linking Christ's death with man's sin as in the kerygmatic passage in 1 Corinthians 15:3. Where the phrase 'remission of sins' is used by Paul (as in Col. 1:14) or the idea of deliverance from sins (as in Gal. 1:4), the plural *hamartiai* expresses the general accumulation of sins (*cf.* also Eph. 2:1).

---

[249] B. Gärtner, *The Areopagus Speech and Natural Revelation*, p. 230, raises the question that a hearer of Paul's might have asked, *i.e.*, Why should this other (Christ) judge us? Gärtner sees the answer in the fact that Christ has been ordained (*horizein*) by God. Paul assumes that by virtue of who God is he has a right to judge.

[250] On the fall of man in the teaching of Paul, *cf.* H. T. Powell, *The Fall of Man*, pp. 17–31, D. E. H. Whiteley, *The Theology of St Paul*, pp. 45ff. *Cf.* H. Ridderbos, *Paul*, pp. 91ff.

[251] The question has been raised whether awareness of sin is the real starting point of Paul's theology. Bultmann, *TNT* 1, p. 249, maintains that it is. He considers that Paul's position was that man encounters the Torah and becomes aware of his sin. But E. P. Sanders, *Paul and Palestinian Judaism*, p. 475, denies this and suggests that Paul's conviction that all have sinned arises from his conviction that God has acted to save. Therefore all need salvation. According to this view, Paul's understanding of the solution preceded an understanding of the plight. Yet what significance could salvation have without a sense of sin?

[252] When dealing with Paul's concept of sin, W. Grundmann in *TDNT*, 1, pp. 308f., considers that it is essential for a right understanding of this subject to recognize two propositions. '1. The Christ event comes upon man in a specific reality, i.e. his reality as a sinner. 2. It comes upon him as an event which rescues him from this reality and reconstitutes him.' It is therefore maintained that what Jesus saw as an event is in Paul described and developed. This highlights the difficulty of dealing with the subject of sin apart from God's answer to it.

When the word is used in the singular, it almost always describes not an individual act of sin, but a state of sinfulness. Hence Paul can speak of the power of sin (Rom. 3:9), knowledge of sin (Rom. 3:20), increase in sin (Rom. 5:20), slaves of sin (Rom. 6:16), wages of sin (Rom. 6:23). He can even personalize sin (as in Rom. 7). With so great a variety of uses for the word it will be necessary to attempt some kind of classification of Paul's ideas.

In addition to this general word for sin, Paul uses four others which convey specific aspects of his doctrine. One is a derived form (*hamartēma*) which means practically the same thing (*cf.* Rom 3:25; 1 Cor. 6:18). Other words, however, have their own particular sense. One represents trespass (*paraptōma*), a word which means a false step in contrast to a true one. Examples of the use of this term are Romans 4:25 and Galatians 6:1. In one instance it is used linked with sins (*i.e. hamartiai*), Ephesians 2:1, in which it gives a specific edge to the more general word. Another term, *parabasis*, conveys the idea of a stepping aside, *i.e.* a deviation from the true path, usually translated 'transgression' (*cf.* Rom. 2:23; 4:15; Gal. 3:19).[253] Somewhat allied to this idea is the word *anomia*, which means lawlessness or iniquity (*e.g.* 2 Cor. 6:14, 2 Thes. 2:3). Common to all these words is the notion of failure to match up to what is required. In the Pauline epistles particularly, all the phases of sin are seen against righteousness (*dikaiosynē*), which is not only the aim of salvation, but is also seen to be the original pattern.

Sin as debt. We come now to think of the various aspects of sin which find expression in Paul's letters and we begin with the idea of debt.[254] The idea of sin as debt which has to be settled by the accrual of merit is wholly absent from Paul. In fact, it is entirely nullified by his doctrine of grace. Nevertheless the very fact that much is made of the forgiveness of sins (*aphesis*) (*cf.* Col. 1:14; Eph. 1:7) shows a sense of man's obligation which he himself could not meet.

It must be noted that the idea of sin as debt is far less prominent in Paul than in the synoptic gospels, perhaps because of his acute awareness of the dangers caused by the idea in Jewish thought. It contributed in the later church to certain commercial theories of the atonement, but there is no warrant for this either in Paul or in the rest of the NT. In one passage, Colossians 2:14, Paul uses a word (*cheirographon*) which may refer to a 'certificate of indebtedness'. If this is a right interpretation, he is representing God as cancelling our debts through Christ.

---

[253] In all these cases, the *parabasis* is directly linked to the law, which becomes the standard by which the transgression is assessed. *Cf.* J. Schneider, *TDNT*, 5, pp. 739f.

[254] *Cf.* S. Lyonnet, *Sin, Redemption and Sacrifice*, pp. 47f., for comment on sin as debt in Paul.

Sin as deviation. If we note the occasions when Paul uses the word *parabasis* (five times), we gain some impression of sin as a swerving from a straight path. Romans 2:23 makes clear that the Jews transgressed through breaking the law. The law had set a standard and the Jewish people had fallen short. Earlier in the same passage Paul had maintained that in some sense even Gentiles were conscious of a law which served as a standard by which the conscience could either accuse or excuse (Rom. 2:14, 15). Indeed, so essential is a standard by which to judge, that Paul can say in Romans 4:15 that 'where there is no law there is no transgression'.[255] This particular view of sin makes no sense unless there is a recognized standard by which the deviation can be measured. At the same time, the word is used of Adam's transgression (Rom. 5:14), which was occasioned by a refusal to obey a divine prohibition. The same is said of Eve's sin (1 Tim. 2:14).[256] It was, therefore, as much a deviation from moral duty as a failure to observe the Mosaic law. All the law could do in any case was to identify the transgressions (*cf.* Gal. 3:19). It could do nothing to check them.

Sin as lawlessness. If sin is a deviation from a known path, it can degenerate into an attitude of lawlessness,[257] as is seen especially in the use of *anomia*. In Romans 6:19 Paul reminds his Christian readers that they once yielded their members to impurity and greater and greater iniquity (*anomia*),[258] as if it had an accumulating effect. According to the most accepted reading of 2 Thessalonians 2:3, the anticipated personification of evil is named as 'the man of lawlessness' who usurps the place of God. Lawlessness leads to rebellion. In 2 Corinthians 6:14 *anomia* is directly contrasted with righteousness, which is linked with the idea that believers are the temple of the living God. Anything which contravenes God's rights is lawlessness or iniquity.[259]

[255] C. E. B. Cranfield, *Romans*, 1, p. 241, says on Rom. 4:15 that Paul's statement about the consequences of the absence of law was 'to suggest the process (the conversion of sin into conscious transgression) by which the law's advent works wrath'. *Cf.* also C. K. Barrett, *Romans, ad loc.*

[256] There is some dispute over 1 Tim. 2:14 on the grounds that it does not attribute the first transgression to Adam, but to Eve. *Cf.* A. T. Hanson, *Studies in the Pastoral Epistles* (1968), pp. 65-77, who comes to the conclusion that someone other than Paul must have written 1 Tim. 2:14. But could not the passage mean that Adam was not deceived, because he well knew what he was doing? (*cf.* my *The Pastoral Epistles*, p. 77). Hanson argues that for the Pastorals the root sin was sexual, on the basis of a Jewish legend, but he contends that Paul used the legend in 2 Cor. 11:1-3, 14, without such implication. But the argument is not convincing. Another possibility is to connect the previous *prōtos* with the deception, and to regard the meaning to be that Adam was not the first to be deceived.

[257] There is a close connection between the idea of 'guilt' and Paul's idea of sin as lawlessness. Whiteley, *op. cit.*, p. 47, maintains that 'guilt' is a concept derived from law. He rightly says that Paul does deal with a guilt situation, because he deals with the fact that we are all sinners.

[258] The repetition of the word *anomia* in Rom. 6:19 is generally understood in an intensifying sense. But F. J. Leenhardt, *Romans* (Eng. trans. 1961 from *CNT*, 1957), p. 173, suggests that the first *anomia* refers to the actual concrete disobedience of man and the second to the state of disobedience as judged and condemned by God. But the distinction is too fine to be convincing.

[259] On the radical opposition between righteousness and lawlessness, *cf.* P. E. Hughes, *2 Corinthians*, pp. 246f.

202

This idea of rebellion is brought out in various ways. In Romans 11:30 the Gentiles are declared to be 'disobedient to God'. Those who follow the prince of the power of the air are called 'sons of disobedience' in Ephesians 2:2 (*cf.* also Eph. 5:6; Col. 3:6, in some ancient texts).[260] The cleavage between Christians and non-Christians in Paul's view is the difference between obedience and disobedience to God's demands. The best of men who are living according to their own efforts fall far short of the requirements of God. It is taken as axiomatic that men ought to obey the gospel, and those who fail to do so class themselves among the children of disobedience. Iniquity or lawlessness is a habit of mind from which we can be released only through Christ's act of redemption (Tit. 2:14).

Sin as both external acts and internal attitudes. Paul shares with the contemporary Hellenistic world a fondness for producing lists of sins,[261] in which there is a mixture of both acts and attitudes. This shows the breadth of his interpretation of sin. The list in Romans 1:29–31 well illustrates the external and internal combination. Some items in the list are acts which can be objectively verified, such as murder, strife, gossipping. But others like envy, foolishness, faithlessness, heartlessness, ruthlessness, are attitudes rather than acts, although they undoubtedly found expression in acts. Other lists of a similar kind are to be found in Romans 13:13; 1 Corinthians 5:10f.; 6:9f.; 2 Corinthians 12:20f.; Galatians 5:19–21; Ephesians 4:31; 5:3–5; Colossians 3:5–8; 1 Timothy 1:9f.; 2 Timothy 3:2ff.; Titus 3:3; It is abundantly clear that Paul wished to show the true nature of sin in specific terms. He was also concerned to demonstrate that no essential difference existed between the wide range of sins stretching from extreme criminal acts like murder to attitudes of mind like jealousy or hatred. This clearly shows that for him sin was interpreted far more widely than in merely forensic terms. The inward nature of sin may not always be easily detected by man, but God knows and judges the inward desire as well as the outward act. It is because of this that he pours out his wrath (Col. 3:6).

Sin as task-master. In Romans Paul uses the expression 'slaves of sin' (Rom. 6:16, 17) to describe the state of bondage in which people are held.[262] But

---

[260] It is most probable that the shorter text of Col. 3:6, which omits the expression, is original and that the other MSS have been influenced by Eph. 5:6.

[261] Such lists were widely used in the ancient world. They were popular among Stoics and are found in the intertestamental literature. For studies on these lists, *cf.* A. Vögtle, *Die Tugend- und Lasterkataloge im Neuen Testament* (1936); S. Wibbing, *Die Tugend- und Lasterkataloge im Neuen Testament und ihre Traditionsgeschichte unter besonderer Berücksichtigung der Qumran-Texte* (1959); B. S. Easton, 'NT Ethical Lists', *JBL* 51, 1952, pp. 1–12. For a special study on Rom. 1:28-31, *cf.* J. Lagrange, *RB* n.s. 8, 1911, pp. 534–549. *Cf.* also O. J. F. Seitz, *IDB* 2, pp. 138f.

[262] Paul's position here can be paralleled in Jn. 8:34. J. Murray, *Romans*, p. 231 points out that 'we are bondslaves of that to which we present ourselves for obedience'. Hence if we obey sin, we are expressing a direct disobedience to God.

the slaves of sin are contrasted with the slaves of obedience, which suggests that here also sin is thought of in terms of deliberate disobedience to God. In the same vein is Paul's exhortation to Christians not to let sin reign over them (Rom. 6:12, 14). For the believer, sin ceases to have any rights, and if it continues to exert dominion, it must be regarded as a usurper.[263] In this sense sin seems to be personified, as it is in other cases to be considered below.

Sin as falsehood. Although there is not in Paul the same sharp antithesis between truth and error as in the Johannine writings, it is nonetheless present. In Romans 1:18 wickedness is defined in terms of suppression of the truth.[264] Moreover, the wicked have exchanged the truth about God for a lie and have worshipped the creature rather than the Creator (Rom. 1:25).[265] When speaking of the putting off of the old nature Paul draws special attention to the putting away of falsehood (Eph. 4:25). In the prediction of the coming of the lawless one, he points out how easily some will be deceived 'because they refused to love the truth' (2 Thes. 2:10). Indeed God sends them a strong delusion to make them believe what is false (2 Thes. 2:11–12).

God's wrath is declared against those who do not obey the truth (Rom. 2:8), but God's desire is that all should come to a knowledge of the truth (1 Tim. 2:4).[266] The man of God seeks to lead people to repent and come to know the truth (2 Tim. 2:25). A strong criticism is made of those who are 'depraved in mind and bereft of the truth' (1 Tim. 6:5; *cf.* 2 Tim. 3:8). The false teachers who were advocating myths were positively rejecting truth (Tit. 1:14).

The apostle sees the world apart from Christ as a world in which falsehood is dominant, since he understands falsehood as a negation of God and his plans for men.

THE PERSONIFICATION OF SIN

When Paul personifies sin[267] he draws vivid attention to its dangerous

---

[263] According to E. P. Sanders, *Paul and Palestinian Judaism*, pp. 546ff., Judaism universally regarded sin as 'transgression', but did not, as Paul did, see it as a power from which man must be freed to be saved.

[264] The word Paul uses, *katechein*, could have the meaning 'possess' or 'hold fast', but this would be foreign to the context. As Cranfield, *op. cit.*, p. 112 n. 5, points out there is nothing in Paul's treatment of his subject to suggest that he thinks of people combining orthodox belief with unrighteousness of life. *Cf.* also C. K. Barrett, *op. cit.*, p. 34, who translates the phrase as 'hold the truth imprisoned'.

[265] M. D. Hooker, 'A Further Note on Romans 1', *NTS* 13, 1966–7, pp. 181ff., considers that the background to Rom. 1 is Adam's fall in Gn. 1–3 and that the language is indebted also to Ps. 106. The nature of man's sin is essentially disobedience and rebellion against God.

[266] 'Knowledge of the truth' means more than simply intellectual grasp. It involves acceptance by faith. The phrase itself is peculiar to the pastorals in Paul's writings, *cf.* J. N. D. Kelly, *The Pastoral Epistles*, p. 62.

[267] On personification, *cf.* S. Lyonnet, in *Sin, Redemption and Sacrifice*, pp. 54ff.

qualities.[268] This comes out strongly in the passage in Romans 7, although it also occurs elsewhere. We have already noted sin portrayed as a tyrant. In addition, sin pays wages, *i.e.* death (Rom. 6:23). Paul can speak of the body as if it had become the possession of sin (Rom. 6:6). Sin in the singular is therefore a more potent factor than acts of sin. In fact, the distinction is between sinfulness as an active principle and sin as a specific act against a known standard.

In Romans 7:8 Paul speaks of sin finding opportunity in the commandment,[269] as if sin were scheming to take advantage in order to produce 'covetousness'. The commandment awakened desire for mental acts of sinfulness. In addition sin works death in man (Rom. 7:11, 13). Since sin deceives it effects death while purporting to give life. The further expression 'sold under sin' (Rom. 7:14) shows sin in a commercial role, exploiting its dupes.[270]

The apostle is deeply conscious of the power of sin. He mentions almost incidentally in 1 Corinthians 15:56 that the sting of death is sin,[271] and the power of sin is the law. In Romans 7:17 he seems to set the power of sin over against the impotence of the self. This raises the question whether Paul is disclaiming the self's responsibility for the sin and this will need further comment below (see pp. 207ff.); but his main purpose in this passage is not to absolve self from accountability, but to demonstrate sin's stranglehold until Jesus Christ gains victory over it. Paul speaks of sin dwelling within him in a personal sense.[272]

THE UNIVERSALITY OF SIN

There is never any suggestion in Paul's epistles that sin has by-passed anyone, either as individuals or in groups.[273] The classic statement of the case is found in Romans 1–3. Although it may be thought that Paul exaggerates in enumerating the types of sin to which people are prone, he is setting out the most obvious cases in contemporary Gentile life in order to be all-inclusive. It is certainly not necessary to suppose, nor is it implied, that all Gentiles were guilty of all the sins in the list. But Paul does not

---

[268] Paul did not originate the idea of the personification of sin. Stählin, *TDNT*, 1, p. 296, mentions instances from Judaism and from the Paris magic Greek papyrus.

[269] The commandment possibly became for Paul 'the psychological means by which sin was stirred to activity within his own experience' (C. K. Barrett, *Romans*, p. 143). Prohibition often encourages the pursuit of the prohibited thing.

[270] There is some support for the view that the verb used here implies the idea of being sold as slaves, in which case sin is seen to possess the authority to treat its victims in this way. *Cf.* C. E. B. Cranfield, *Romans, ad loc.*; C. K. Barrett, *Romans, ad loc*; and H. Schlier, *Der Römerbrief* (1977), *ad loc.*

[271] C. A. A. Scott, *Christianity according to St Paul* (1927), p. 51, interprets Paul's words to mean that 'death employed sin to stab for itself an opening into human nature'.

[272] This personifying of sin is much more expressive than treating sin as a sinful status. As C. A. A. Scott says, 'it is a power invading, attacking, subjugating men from without' (*op. cit.*, p. 47).

[273] On the universality of sin, *cf.* H. Ridderbos, *Paul* (Eng. trans, 1975), pp. 93ff.

give any indication that any Gentiles had escaped the taint of sin.

When he goes on to discuss the Jewish position, he is quite specific and shows that Jews as well as Gentiles are equally under the power of sin (Rom. 3:9). This conclusion is supported by a sequence of OT citations, which are emphatically introduced by the statement 'None is righteous, no, not one; no one understands, no one seeks for God' (Rom. 3:10, 11). He further maintains that the whole world is held accountable to God (Rom. 3:19).[274] It is, indeed, on the basis of the universality of sin that Paul builds his doctrine of justification through Christ. There is no distinction – all have sinned (Rom. 3:23).

Another specific statement in the same epistle asserts the universality of sin (Rom. 5:12). Whatever the interpretation of Paul's view of Adam's part in human sin (see section on original sin, pp. 210ff.), there can be no denying that he accepts without question, not only that all without exception have sinned, but also that universal death is the result of universal sin. These propositions might be said to be deducible from observation. Paul regards them as too obvious to require demonstration.

In this respect the apostle is in line with other parts of the NT where the truth of sin's universal dominion is everywhere assumed.

SIN AND FLESH

We have already discussed Paul's use of *sarx*, but we need now to note the precise relationship between sin and *sarx*.[275] Paul frequently refers to 'the desires of the flesh'[276] (Gal. 5:24; Rom. 13:14; Eph. 2:3) or to the desires of the mortal body (Rom. 6:12). Since desire is a prelude to action, it may be said that Paul views the flesh as in some way a source of sins. While a man is alienated from God, his *sarx* has taken on a sinful bias, which it did not naturally possess. Paul does not maintain that all matter including flesh is evil and is therefore the source of sin, for the very expression 'desires of the flesh' implicates the whole man. Nevertheless since *sarx* has become conditioned by sin, it cannot avoid promoting sin. It is for this reason that Paul is so radical in his conviction that those who are in the flesh cannot please God (Rom. 8:8).[277] He maintains, in fact, that 'the mind that is set

---

[274] According to Cranfield, *op. cit.*, p. 197, the word Paul uses in this statement (*hypodikos*) conveys the idea of people standing at God's bar, their guilt already proved and awaiting condemnation. Sanday and Headlam, *Romans* p. 80, suggested 'answerable to God', but Cranfield thinks this says too little. The reference to the whole world certainly shows the universality of guilt.

[275] For a discussion of sin and flesh in Paul, *cf.* D. E. H. Whiteley, *The Theology of St Paul*, pp. 39f.; R. Bultmann, *TNT* 1, pp. 239–246. So close is the connection between sin and flesh that Ridderbos (*Paul*, p. 103) makes the claim that 'flesh' is a description of sin itself in the most inclusive sense of the word.

[276] *Cf.* my *Galatians, ad loc.* The word used for passions (*pathēma*) is in itself neutral, but the moral quality is indicated by the *sarx*.

[277] C. K. Barrett, *Romans*, p. 158, maintains that in this context for the flesh to be obedient to God would be a contradiction in terms. He paraphrases Rom. 8:8 'Those who are living to please themselves (not simply in a "carnal" sense) cannot also please God.'

on the flesh is hostile to God' (Rom. 8:7), an expression which shows that the whole man is intended. In the difficult statement in 1 Corinthians 5:5, where Paul advises that a moral offender should be delivered to Satan for the destruction of the flesh, there is an unmistakable connection between sin and flesh. It is most likely that in this case *sarx* does not convey a purely physical sense.[278]

SIN AND HUMAN RESPONSIBILITY

The evidence adduced so far has been sufficient to show that Paul assumes that man is responsible for the sin he commits. The idea of man as the hapless tool of an inevitable fate[279] nowhere finds expression in Paul's epistles. The accountability of man before God (Rom. 3:19), which Paul specifically asserts, reflects his belief that man must take responsibility for his sin, especially that aspect of it that is viewed as rebellion against God. This is not nullified by the statements in Romans 7 which might suggest that sin takes responsibility, for responsibility can be attributed only to a person, not to an abstract principle, even if personified.[280] The sin principle would be powerless without the cooperation of the person. The terms used require the involvement of man's will.

If man is now without excuse and must accept responsibility for his sin, this leads into the Pauline teaching on punishment against sin which will be discussed below. In Paul's doctrine responsibility in the believer came to be linked with predestination (as in Rom. 8:28f.), and raised what has remained a paradox. Although the apostle does not attempt to resolve the paradox, he had no intention of lifting from man himself the responsibility for his own actions. The problem of predestination belongs properly to the discussion on salvation and grace and will be dealt with then (pp. 620ff.).

SIN AND PUNISHMENT

We have considered the many facets of Paul's view of sin. We must now note its consequences. When the apostle mentions God's wrath, he means God's wrath against sin. God's wrath is revealed alongside his righteousness

---

[278] *Cf.* A. C. Thiselton, 'The Meaning of *sarx* in 1 Cor. 5:5: A Fresh Approach in the Light of Logical and Semantic Factors', *SJT* 26, 1973, pp. 204–228. He argues for an open-endedness in the understanding of Paul's language, and points out the difficulties in understanding *sarx* here in a physical sense. He contends that the punishment of the offender *may or may not* have included physical suffering in its outworking. He thinks there is something to be said for *sarx* meaning 'self-satisfaction' in this context (as in 3:1ff.).

[279] This is characteristic of gnostic ideas, but is alien to Paul's theology. See J. Zandee, 'Gnostic Ideas on the Fall and Salvation', *Numen* 2, 1964, pp. 34–41. Man's defect, in gnostic thought, is due to external powers and is not therefore his own responsibility. Also against a gnostic background for Rom. 5:12ff., *cf.* A. J. M. Wedderburn, 'The Theological Structure of Romans v. 12', *NTS* 19, 1979, pp. 342ff.

[280] J. S. Stewart, 'On a neglected emphasis in NT Theology', *SJT* 4, 1951, p. 293, sees in Rom. 7 a struggle between the forces of evil and the kingdom of Christ. It is not concerned therefore about a struggle between a higher and a lower self. There is no question of a lessening of responsibility.

(Rom. 1:17–18),[281] and is directed against 'all ungodliness and wickedness of men'. Paul anticipates a day of wrath when God's righteous judgment will be revealed (Rom. 2:5) and warns against a hardness of heart that could store up wrath. Paul adds that God 'will render to every man according to his works' (Rom. 2:6). For the disobedient, wrath and fury are in store (Rom. 2:8; Eph. 5:6). When God inflicts wrath it is never unjust (Rom. 3:5, 6). The apostle sees salvation as being 'from the wrath of God' (Rom. 5:9; 1 Thes. 5:9), *i.e.* in its negative aspect. When thinking of the sovereignty of God in the remarkable illustration of the potter and his clay, he claims that God has complete power in the exercise of his wrath (Rom. 9:22).[282]

Paul sums up the precarious position of the natural man in the words in Ephesians 2:3 – 'So we were by nature children of wrath', *i.e.* people who are destined to receive God's wrath.[283] Moreover, 'the rest of mankind' is included in this description. What is clear is the marked divide between those outside of Christ and those who have become children of God. Unless this cleavage is clearly recognized, Paul's statements about the mission of Christ will make no intelligible sense. It is important to note that Jews as well as Gentiles are included under God's wrath (1 Thes. 2:16).

Paul has much to say about the judgment of God (Rom. 2:2f; 5:16; 1 Cor. 11:29, 34). That judgment results in the condemnation of the sinner.[284] The disobedient are under sentence and apart from Christ there is no reprieve.[285] Moreover there is nothing arbitrary about God's judgments. They are always just (2 Thes. 1:5). As no-one is exempt from the general condition of sinfulness, so no-one is exempt from the consequences of that sinfulness.

The consequence that Paul mentions most is death. Death is regarded as man's last enemy (1 Cor. 15:26). The string of death is sin (1 Cor. 15:56). In his exposition in Romans 5–7, Paul many times establishes a direct

[281] Conzelmann, *TNT*, p. 240, rejects the timeless juxtaposition of wrath and righteousness in Rom. 1:17, and maintains that Rom. 3:21 shows that they are two stages in salvation history. Conzelmann identifies God's wrath with his judgment, rather than regarding it as a property of God. But Paul's language in Rom. 1:17 contains more of an objective element than Conzelmann allows (see p. 100 for a discussion of this).

[282] *Cf.* G. H. C. Macgregor, 'The concept of the wrath of God in the NT', *NTS* 7, 1960–1, pp. 101–109. Macgregor rightly rejects the view that God is waiting to vent his anger against the sinner in exacting punishment, but he empties the concept of wrath of any real connection with God. While admitting that for Paul in Rom. 9:22 wrath is an attribute of God, he considers it to be an attribute held in reserve.

[283] There is some debate about the meaning of the phrase 'by nature' (*physei*). *Cf.* M. Barth, *Ephesians 1— 3* (*AB*, 1974), p. 231, who contends that there is here 'no hint of a fall of nature, or of a timeless fallenness, but there is full consciousness of the historic corruption of the flesh.' Paul is not debating the origin of sin, but the vast difference between what Christians were and what they are now. Barth firmly denies the doctrine of innate sin. *Cf.* J. Armitage Robinson's discussion of this verse, *Ephesians* (²1904) *ad loc.*

[284] For the place of judgment by works in the theology of Paul, *cf.* E. P. Sanders, *Paul and Palestinian Judaism*, pp. 515ff.

[285] D. E. H. Whiteley, *The Theology of St Paul*, pp. 46ff., distinguishes between sin and guilt. He concludes that Paul deals with what he calls 'a guilt situation' (see above, n. 257).

connection between sin and death.[286] The classic passage is again Romans 5:12ff., which begins with the assertion that death came into the world through sin and that it reigned from Adam to Moses. It continued to reign until the one man Jesus Christ, through his own death, turned the tables and brought the free gift of grace. Whereas sin reigned in death, grace reigns in righteousness (Rom. 5:21). Using the metaphor of baptism Paul speaks of believers as baptized into Christ's death, as a result of which they are dead to the power of sin, and should consider themselves so (Rom. 6:2, 6, 10, 11). He points out that the wages of sin is death (Rom. 6:23). Again, sin works death (Rom. 7:13) and turns the whole body into a 'body of death' (Rom. 7:24; *cf.* 8:10). Paul is therefore under no delusion about the serious consequences of sin. He is not, of course, expressing a new truth in linking death with sin, but he is expressing it as seen from the Christian standpoint. The death which is the only end of sin (Rom. 6:21) is in stark contrast to the life which comes as a gift through Christ.

Another inevitable consequence of sin is alienation from God. Paul describes the pre-Christian state as enmity (Rom. 5:10). The Gentiles are without hope and without God in the world (Eph. 2:12). The wrath of God puts us at a distance from him. It is this deep sense of alienation which gives meaning to Paul's doctrine of reconciliation (see pp. 486ff.). He is convinced that the natural man is estranged from God and needs the restoration of a right relationship.

THE ORIGIN OF SIN IN MAN

It certainly would not be true to say that Paul expounds a doctrine of original sin, but there are indications that he may have held it.[287] By 'original sin' in this context is meant the passing on through heredity of the bias towards sin. It naturally affects the problem of how sin originates in each individual. The key passage is Romans 5:12ff., but even this does not discuss any theory of the origin of sin. What Paul says is incidental to his main purpose to contrast death with life and condemnation with righteousness. Before considering this passage there are a few general observations which need to be made in order to set the discussion in its right perspective.

(i) Paul certainly did not hold that man was created with sin. He maintained the OT view that man was made in the image of God (1 Cor. 11:7), which must have precluded the presence of evil. The image denotes the

---

[286] *Cf.* T. Barosse, 'Death and Sin in St Paul's Epistle to the Romans', *CBQ* 15, 1953, pp. 438–459. *Cf.* also H. Ridderbos, *Paul*, p. 113.

[287] W. N. Pittenger, *The Christian Understanding of Human Nature* (1964), p. 95, favours the phrase 'originating sin', after R. M. Frye, *Perspective of Man* (1961), pp. 122f. Pittenger takes 'originating sin' to be the creature's will to exist as his own god, but it should be noted that Pittenger approaches the matter from the viewpoint of man in community, not man simply as an individual. G. Aulén, *The Faith of the Christian Church* (²1961), p. 241, also regards original sin as a 'solidary interrelationship'.

moral character of God. The entrance of sin into the world resulted in the spoiling of the image; hence in the plan of salvation the restoration of the image comes through the believer being conformed to the image of God's Son (*cf.* Rom 8:29).[288] It should be noted, however, that Paul does not support the view that no vestige of the original image remains. If man is still the image and glory of God, some distinguishing marks of his origin must still be visible. Indeed, the fact that man is a moral creature separates him from other creatures, in spite of the fact that he has corrupted his moral nature.

(ii) We have already adduced ample evidence to show that man universally is sinful. The apostle is concerned more with sin and sinfulness as an established fact than with its origin or transmission. Although he maintains that sin entered through Adam (Rom. 5:12ff.; 1 Cor. 15:21–22), he does not argue from the one to the many, as if he were heaping the responsibility of everyone's sins on Adam's head. He is rather beginning from the established fact that sin is present in every man. The concentration on Adam may be attributed to the background of Jewish ideas of solidarity. Because of this, Adam can stand as representative of all his seed.

(iii) The close connection between sin and death (noted above, pp. 208f.) has some bearing on Paul's arguments, for death is seen as an adverse factor which has affected man's nature. Since it has come through sin, the universality of death in Paul's mind must in some way be connected with Adam's sin (Rom. 5:12). Although we cannot be certain whether Paul was influenced by the intertestamental view of the 'evil impulse' (*yēṣer hārā'*),[289] it is not impossible that he was. The rabbis maintained that this impulse became evil only when yielded to (see p. 119f.). Some think that the 'other law' (Rom. 7:23) may be an allusion to this impulse.[290] What is clear is that Paul nowhere suggests that man's responsibility is lessened by any adverse impulse present within him.

(iv) We have noted Paul's strong belief in the existence of adverse spiritual agencies and the influence of these must be taken into account in discussing Adam's fall. In one place Paul mentions that Eve was deceived by the serpent (2 Cor. 11:3), but this occurs in a context which is dealing generally with deception, not with the origin of sin. Nowhere in Paul's letters does he attribute the impetus to sin to these evil forces, but his acceptance of the Genesis account would predispose him to do so. This would not, of course, throw light on his views about the transmission of sin.

[288] There is no NT support for the view that the image of God is man, and that man has therefore a divine spark which is capable of being fanned into a flame. For an exposure of this view, *cf.* D. Cairns, *The Image of God in Man* (1953), who examines all the NT occurrences of the 'image' idea. *Cf.* also E. H. Robertson, *Man's Estimate of Man* (1958), pp. 80fff.

[289] *Cf.* the discussion of *yēṣer* on pp. 119ff.

[290] *Cf.* H. A. A. Kennedy, *The Theology of the Epistles* (1919), p. 40.

(v) Strictly speaking, the statements in the passage (Romans 5:12ff.)[291] impinging on original sin are incidental to the main argument, which centres on the extension of the work of Christ to others.[292] This is achieved by means of comparison (verses 12–14) and contrast (verses 15–19).

The first problem is grammatical. Having stated that sin and death had come into the world, Paul adds 'and so death spread to all men because (*eph' hō*) all men sinned.' The words translated 'because' could conceivably be rendered 'in whom',[293] which would then mean that all men sinned 'in Adam'. But apart from the fact that a different preposition (*en*) would normally be used for this idea of 'in', the notion of sinning 'in Adam' finds no parallels elsewhere. The sense of 'because' or something akin to it, like 'on this condition, that', is therefore to be preferred.[294]

The next question which arises is whether Paul is maintaining here that all people are affected adversely because of one man's sin. He is confronted with certain indisputable facts. He knows that all have sinned. He knows also that all die. He further knows that historically Adam was the agency through whom sin first entered (according to the Genesis account). Combining these three facts he sees a line of connection between them all. He can maintain a link between universal sin and Adam's sin only because he believes in the solidarity of the race. There is no justification for supposing that Paul would have supported the view that any of Adam's seed could be held responsible for Adam's sin, since he so clearly supports the accountability of people for their own sins. Some notion of the solidarity of the race with Adam is, however, necessary to make intelligible Paul's statements about grace through Christ. What he seems to be saying is, that as the whole race shares the disastrous results of Adam's sin, so the whole race may be affected by the abundance of grace and the free gift of righteousness.[295]

---

[291] For special studies on this passage, *cf*, C. E. B. Cranfield, 'On Some of the Problems in the Interpretation of Rom. 5:12', *SJT* 22, 1969, pp. 330–340; F. W. Danker, 'Rom. v. 12: Sin under Law', *NTS* 14, 1967–8, pp. 435ff.; S. Lyonnet, 'Le sens de *eph' hō* en Rom. 5.12 et l'exégèse des pères grecs', *Bib* 36, 1955, pp. 436–456.; J. Cambier, 'Péchés des hommes et péché d'Adam en Rom. v. 12', *NTS* 11, 1964–5, pp. 20f.; A. J. M. Wedderburn, 'The Theological Structure of Romans v. 12', *NTS* 19, 1973, pp. 339–354.

[292] Conzelmann, *TNT*, p. 197, argues that in Rom. 5:12ff., Paul begins from the idea of representation (the tribal ancestor including posterity within himself, a Jewish idea), but he comes to a new conclusion, *i.e.* *eph' hō pantes hēmarton*, in the sense, 'I always already have the fall behind me'.

[293] It should be noted that the dispensing with the grammatical rendering 'in whom' does not obliterate all idea of solidarity. As F. F. Bruce, *Romans* (*TNTC* 1963), p. 130, points out, this may be a mistranslation, but a true interpretation. He further maintains that for Paul Adam *is* mankind.

[294] Cf. A. M. Dubarle, *The Biblical Doctrine of Original Sin* (Eng. trans. 1964), pp. 142–184, for a discussion of the whole passage. On *eph' hō*, he agrees with S. Lyonnet's conclusion that it means 'on this condition, that' (p. 149 n. 3). It should be noted that there is a tendency among Roman Catholic scholars to prefer some kind of 'solidarity' interpretation, following Augustine's view of it. But the idea of sinning 'in Adam' is not confined to Catholic exegetes. *Cf*. also A. Nygren, *Romans* (Eng. trans, 1952), pp. 214f, who maintains that Paul's argument would be weakened if this is denied.

[295] Karl Barth, *Christ and Adam: Man and Humanity in Romans 5* (Eng. trans. 1956), contends that Christ's

Although it seems inescapable that Paul accepts that mankind inherited a sinful bias through Adam, what might be called 'a bent towards sinfulness', yet it is the definite committing of sin which brings condemnation.[296] Paul's whole approach to the subject of sin elsewhere would not support the view that any man is held responsible for the sinful bias he has inherited.[297] But does this mean that man can claim that his will is shackled and that consequently it would be unjust to hold him responsible for his own actions? This question never seems to have arisen in Paul's mind. He described in Romans 7 a typical struggle in which what he wanted he could not achieve (Rom. 7:18), but he does not absolve himself from the responsibility of doing what is right.[298] The discussion in Romans 5:12ff. must therefore be approached from the same point of view.

(vi) In a passage which also contrasts Adam with Christ in 1 Corinthians, Paul mentions the coming of death to all through Adam (1 Cor. 15:21ff.), but makes no mention of sin.[299] This is no doubt because his immediate purpose is to set out the theme of resurrection life. He is not in this context concerned with the relation between death and sin. Nevertheless, he does ascribe to Adam the coming of death to all, and contrasts this with the life which comes in Christ through his resurrection. Paradoxically he goes on in the same chapter to use the metaphor of the seed, which must necessarily die before it can germinate. In this case death is seen as a natural process. Although paradoxes of this kind are often unacceptable to cold logic, they are not unacceptable to Paul. He did not debate the question whether death was introduced into the race by Adam, or whether it is the result of the inevitable course of nature. The solidarity of the race was sufficient to support both contentions at once, without any attempt to resolve them. It must also be noted that it is by no means certain that Paul always means precisely the same thing when he refers to death. Sometimes he means cessation of life, but at other times he means separation from God. Clearly

---

humanity is prior to Adam's. Adam's sin, therefore, affects humanity until it is restored in Christ. R. Bultmann criticized Barth's exegesis in his article, 'Adam and Christ according to Rom. 5', *Current Issues in New Testament Interpretation* (ed. W. Klassen and G. F. Snyder, 1962).

[296] A. J. M. Wedderburn, *NTS* 19, 1973, pp. 351f, strongly argues that the words *pantes hēmarton* in this passage refer to the responsible, active, individual sinning of all men.

[297] Bultmann confuses the issue when he says, 'Nevertheless, it cannot be denied that in Rom. 5:12ff., the sin of humanity after Adam is attributed to Adam's sin and that it therefore appears as the consequence of a curse for which mankind is not itself responsible' (*TNT* 1, p. 251). Paul shows no awareness of exempting people from responsibility for their own actions, however clearly he recognizes that mankind was implicated in Adam's sin. Bultmann does admit that every one is born into a world guided by a false striving.

[298] E. Brunner, *Romans*, (Eng. trans. 1959), p. 59, rightly remarks that the apostle in Rom. 7 'is not concerned with a psychology of sin, though he certainly begins with a psychological observation; his glance penetrates deeper into the secret of the origin of sin'. Brunner says that Paul passes from the merely psychological to the historical aspect and takes up in Rom. 7 what he has earlier expounded in Rom. 5:12ff. by means of referring to his own history.

[299] For a concise treatment of this passage, *cf.* R. Scroggs, *The Last Adam*, pp. 82ff.

when Christ gave life instead of death to those who believe he did not exempt them from physical death, but he did exempt them from spiritual death. This is what Paul means by referring to all being made alive in 1 Corinthians 15:22.[300]

From this brief survey of original sin in Paul's teaching we must conclude that he saw the human race as affected by Adam's sin, but gives no indication of how this worked out apart from the universality of sin and death. If the gist of Paul's argument polarizes all the sinfulness under Adam and all the righteousness under Christ, this is for the sake of demonstrating the breadth of application of the salvation which Christ has effected. The doctrine of original sin as it has been traditionally expounded is frequently rejected because it is said to conflict with man's consciousness of freedom of action. But the doctrine preserves another consciousness in man – that of his own inner conflicts with his nobler ideas, which has never been better expressed than in Romans 7.[301]

Hebrews

In an epistle devoted to expounding the Christian approach to God, it is not surprising to find that considerable attention is paid to man's need. It is against the background of the levitical sacrificial system that the superiority of Christ as high priest is seen, and therefore the OT recognition of sin is taken over without discussion. We shall note especially those features which are highlighted through the exposition.

SIN AND SINS

It is significant that although the plural 'sins' (*hamartiai*) is generally used in relating the sacrificial system to man's need,[302] there are two instances (Heb. 9: 26; 13:11) where the singular is used in precisely the same sense (*cf.* for instance Heb. 13:11 with 10:12). There would not appear to be any vital difference between the two forms and it must be concluded, therefore, that the writer did not draw any important distinction between sinful acts and the state of sin. He can speak of purification for sins (Heb. 1:3), of expiation for sins (2:17), of an offering to bear the sins of many (9:28), of sacrifices for sins (5:1; 7:27; 10:4, 12, 26). He is dealing with the needs of a sinful people who are aware of their constant committing of sins. On the

---

[300] Some have found the Adam theme in Rom. 1 and if their arguments hold there would be a closer connection with sin than in the case of 1 Cor. 15. *Cf.* M. D. Hooker, 'Adam in Romans I', *NTS* 6, 1959–60, pp. 297–306; J. Jervell, *Imago Dei* (1960), pp. 312–331.

[301] E. Brunner, *Man in Revolt* (Eng. trans. 1939), pp. 383f., discusses the connection of modern theories about heredity and original sin. He points out that character-dispositions may be inherited, but never the character itself. *Cf.* also *idem*, *The Christian Doctrine of Creation and Redemption*, pp. 140f., where he links 'original' sin with the condition of man under a wicked spell, which results in a sense of impotence without removing man's responsibility.

[302] On 'sin' in Hebrews, *cf.* C. Spicq, *Hébreux* 1, pp. 284ff.

other hand he can refer to 'consciousness of sin' (Heb. 10:2), to the 'fleeting pleasures of sin' (11:25), to sin that clings (12:1),[303] to the struggle against sin (12:4), and to the deceitfulness of sin (3:13). In this general sense of a sinful disposition, which includes acts which result from it, he can pronounce that Jesus was without sin (Heb. 4:15). All this shows a marked divide between man and God, with Jesus as the only exception. Not even the high priest was exempt from offering sacrifice for his own sin (Heb. 7:27). There is no doubt that the writer regards sin as universal.

SIN AS UNBELIEF AND DISOBEDIENCE

In the discussion on 'rest' in which the Israelites' failure to enter the promised land is the main theme, that failure is specifically ascribed to unbelief (Heb. 3:19).[304] The writer is concerned lest his readers should have 'an evil, unbelieving heart' (3:12). Unbelief arose out of disobedience (3:18; 4:6). It was a failure to take seriously the commands of God. The writer quotes the passage from Psalm 95: 7–11 in which God says that his people have strayed and not known his ways (Heb. 3:10). He sees the Israelites' type of disobedience as a basis for exhorting his readers to avoid it (Heb. 4:11). He clearly assumes they will be sufficiently familiar with the disastrous consequences of the Israelites' disobedience to recognize the seriousness of giving way to similar disobedience themselves. The whole passage does not define any particular judgment of God on their sin, apart from the fact that they missed out on their inheritance (the 'rest'). In Hebrews 2:2 however a hint is given on the just retribution on disobedience.

SIN AS LAWLESSNESS

Closely linked with the last theme is the theme of rebellion (cf. Heb. 3:8, 15–16). This draws out in a more dynamic way the deliberate and indeed defiant character of disobedience. It involved a direct rejection of God's plans. In Hebrews 1:9, the statement from Psalm 45:6–7 is cited with approval to the effect that God 'hated lawlessness' (anomia). The great value of the work of Christ is that under the new covenant God says 'I will remember their sins and their misdeeds (anomiai) no more' (Heb. 10:17).

Under this section some reference should be made to the apostasy passages (Heb. 6:6f.; 10:26f.),[305] which show the extreme seriousness of a

---

[303] The reference in 12:1 is not to some particular sin that clings, but sin itself. It is a constant hindrance to the athelete's progress (cf. H. Montefiore, Hebrews, p. 214). There is difference of opinion over the meaning of the word euperistatos, but some notion of wrapping round or clinging would seem to be preferable; cf. Bruce, Hebrews, pp. 349f., who cites E. K. Simpson, Words Worth Weighing in the Greek New Testament (1946), pp. 26f.

[304] For comments on unbelief and disobedience in Heb. 3 and 4, cf. S. Kistemaker, The Psalm Citations in the Epistle to the Hebrews (1961), pp. 108ff.

[305] W; Grundmann, TDNT 1, p. 314, comments on the sin in 10:26 that it is a rather different concept from the sin against the Holy Spirit in the synoptic gospels. He sees emerging in this passage 'the readiness for martyrdom which characterizes primitive Christianity'. But this is reading too much into the passage.

rejection of what God has done in Christ. The passages are directed to those who have become Christians and in this respect throw little light on the general sinfulness of man. Nevertheless the possibility of re-crucifying the Son of God or of profaning the blood of the covenant shows the extent to which man's rejection of God's methods can stretch (see pp. 630ff. for a further discussion of these passages).

OTHER ASPECTS OF SIN

In one instance the high priest's work is said to be 'for the errors of the people' (Heb. 9:7), *i.e. agnoēmata*, the only place in the NT where this word is used. It refers to sins of ignorance,[306] but this idea is not enlarged on elsewhere in the epistle.[307] The deceitful character of sin is brought out in Hebrews 3:13. In the case of Esau's failure, his sin is described as 'immoral and irreligious' (Heb. 12:16). All of these aspects seem to be incidental to the main characteristics mentioned above, but one aspect which is somewhat more stressed is the idea of sin as 'evil'. As *kakos*, it is contrasted with good (Heb. 5:14), and is described as *ponēros* in the expressions 'evil heart' (Heb. 3:12) and 'evil conscience (10.22).

The rest of the New Testament

Of the general epistles, *James* and *1 Peter* both have some significant sayings about sin, generally under the term *hamartia*. James, in fact, suggests that sin arises from desire and that sin, when developed, brings death (Jas. 1:15). This is tied up with the reflection that desire plays an important part in temptation. James shows the distinction between God and man, since God cannot be tempted through wrong desires. In James 2:9 sin is viewed from a legal point of view and is described in terms of transgression of the law. It is a failure to do right when the right way is known (Jas. 4:17). Some connection between sins and sickness is implied in James 5:15, but this theme is not developed. It is not necessarily suggested that sickness is the direct consequence of sin, although forgiveness is assured to those who confess. James concludes by expressing concern that his readers should turn sinners from the error (*planē*) of their ways, and by giving the assurance that anyone who does this will cover a multitude of sins (Jas. 5:20). This looks at first sight as if man through his own effort can deal with sin; but in this essentially practical epistle the comment is not theological. James is more concerned with preventing sin in others than explaining how one's

---

To apostatize was a sin against the Spirit in the sense of being a rejection of the whole mission of Jesus, in precisely the same sense as those who charged Jesus with being in league with Beelzebub.

[306] As in the OT, so at Qumran there was a distinction between inadvertent sins and deliberate sins (*cf.* 1 QS 9.1f.).

[307] The 'ignorant and erring' are referred to in Heb. 5:2 (*tois agnoousin kai planōmenois*), which F. F. Bruce (*Hebrews*, p. 91) takes to mean 'those who go astray through ignorance', an idea closely akin to Heb. 9:7.

own sin is covered, although he is convinced that the one will lead to the other.

Other aspects of sin found in James are evil (*kakos*, Jas. 1:13; 3:8; 4:11, and *poneros*, Jas. 2:4; 4:16, in which the evil consists more in wrong thought than action), wickedness (Jas. 1:21), deceit (1:22, 26), partiality (2:9), and transgression (2:9, 11).

In the Petrine epistles we meet with the same mixture of plural and singular in the use of the word 'sin' (*hamartia*). Christ is said to have died for sins (1 Pet. 3:18) and the believer is reminded that he has been cleansed from his old sins (2 Pet. 1:9). The singular, however, is used in 1 Peter 2:22, 4:1; 2 Peter 2:14. One saying about covering a multitude of sins (1 Pet. 4:8) is parallel to James 5:20, only here the effective tool is love. When Peter says that whoever has suffered in the flesh has ceased from sin (1 Pet. 4:1), he clearly means that anyone who has sufficiently identified himself with Christ has ceased from a life dominated by sin. Peter shares with the other NT writers the conviction that sin is universal and the only escape is through faith in Christ. He is at pains to point out, however, that Christ himself was without sin (1 Pet. 2:22).

Four times 1 Peter speaks of 'evil' (*kakos*). Do not return evil for evil (1 Pet. 3:9); do not speak evil (1 Pet. 3:10); turn away from evil and do right (1 Pet. 3:11), and the face of the Lord is against evil (1 Pet. 3:12). The last three occurrences are in the quotation from Psalm 34:12–16.

We may sum up this epistle's estimate of sin as the very antithesis of righteousness, a contrast brought out vividly in 1 Peter 2:24.

For a record of the possible manifestations of sin, *2 Peter 2* would be hard to beat. It illustrates what happens when people are 'insatiable for sin' (2 Pet. 2:14). Such people are called 'slaves of corruption' (2 Pet. 2:19), although they think they are free. What strikes one most about the list is the distortion which is everywhere apparent. It is summed up as rebellion against God's commandment (2:21).

The epistle of *Jude* is so close in content to 2 Peter that little more needs to be said. Jude cites a prediction which sums up the false teachers as 'scoffers following their own ungodly passions' (Jude 18). They are, moreover, 'worldly people, devoid of the Spirit' (Jude 19).

The book of *Revelation* records in symbolic language the distinction between the followers of Christ and the rest of mankind. The former know they have been released from their sins (Rev. 1:5). By way of contrast the sins of Babylon the great are heaped high as heaven (Rev. 18:5). The climax of the book is the impending day of wrath. It is inescapable for those who are not the followers of the Lamb. The build-up of the whole book depends on the recognition of the universality of sin and the inevitability of God's judgment upon it. People's reactions to the plagues are typical of man's general refusal to repent (*cf.* Rev. 16:9, 11, 21).

The theme of judgment against all that is opposed to God dominates the book. The final triumph of right over wrong is typified by the triumph of the Lamb over all the agencies of evil. In the vision of the New Jerusalem, there is a specific exclusion of all uncleanness, abomination or falsehood (Rev. 21:27). All that mars the perfect plan of God is incompatible, and the Lamb himself is the lamp, the guiding principle of the new society. So great is the contrast between the ideal and the actual that it may be said that this book describes more vividly than any other NT book the destiny of man apart from God.

Summary of ideas on man in relation to God

It has become clear from the preceding survey that the one fact that stands out is that man is not what he ought to be. The precise nature of the fault is variously explained. In different parts of the NT evidence the emphasis falls in different places. There is general agreement, however, on a number of features. The universality of sin is undisputed, although it comes to clearest expression in Paul. Emphasis on the inward character of sin as distinct from external acts is summed up in the view of Jesus that it is what comes out of a man that defiles him.

Not all the NT literature presents as clearly as Paul's epistles the wide variety of forms which sin takes – debt, deviation, lawlessness, slavery, falsehood – but the total presentation is unmistakable. Man has rebelled against God. He has disobeyed God's law. He has allowed himself to come into a bondage to sin, from which, through his own efforts, he cannot escape. This picture of man sees him as blinded to his own original potential. Sin has placed him in a position of ignorance of God and of a true estimate of himself. In both the Johannine and Pauline literature sin is more specifically seen as unbelief, which places the responsibility fairly and squarely on man's shoulders. The unbelief is expressed as a refusal to believe in Christ.

There is no formal discussion of original sin. But there is no reason to suppose that any of the NT writers did not assume the fallenness of man. It is treated as a historical fact rather than discussed in a theoretical manner. It is Paul who says most on this subject, especially when bringing out the basic sinfulness of man in the course of his Adam teaching.

Another aspect of sin which becomes clear from the NT is the fact that it merits punishment. This will be dealt with more fully when discussing judgment (see pp. 848ff.), but the condemnation of sin by a righteous God is an integral assumption behind the NT teaching on salvation and must be borne in mind if the mission of Jesus is to be rightly understood. Indeed, many of the particular facets in which sin is presented in the NT contribute to the different interpretations of the work of Christ. If sin is enslavement, Christ brings deliverance. If it is falsehood, Christ presents truth. If disobedience, Christ shows the way of obedience. If deviation from the will of God, Christ sets the perfect example of righteousness.

Chapter 3
Christology

INTRODUCTION

Anyone who attempts to assess the place of Jesus Christ within NT theology must first make clear his position relative to the modern debate over the Christ of faith and the historical Jesus. It is impossible to set out the issues in a brief compass, and in any case such a survey would not be in place here. The position adopted over this issue affects all aspects of NT theology, but it is of particular significance for Christology. The stance adopted will determine whether any evidence exists for determining what Jesus thought about himself.

The extent of the differences of opinion over this issue can be gauged by the fact that they range from an almost total scepticism about the possibility of any historical knowledge to an acceptance of the full historicity of the words and works of Jesus. Many, for instance, would strongly reject scepticism, but would nevertheless want to maintain some modifications of the facts in the course of the transmission of the tradition. The extreme sceptical position maintains that since practically all of the material in the gospels is considered to represent the theological stance of the early church, it naturally follows that the gospels are almost valueless for arriving at a true assessment of the historical Jesus. On the other hand it is possible to recognize that the records have come to us through Christian writers who held definite beliefs about Jesus Christ, without calling in question the reliability of the records. In face of the wide diversity of opinions, all that is possible for the New Testament theologian is to state his own view and to take note in the following discussions of views which proceed from different presuppositions.

In the following survey of evidence we shall regard the gospels as records which enable us to ascertain in a dependable way what Jesus thought about himself, as the NT has presented the evidence. We shall also examine what others thought about him. It will be necessary to consider the relationship between these two sources of evidence.

Our survey will begin with Jesus the man. We shall then examine what he called himself and what others called him. This approach to the subject by means of the Christological titles will provide valuable insights. Nevertheless, it will be necessary to compare this evidence with that from the so-called Christological hymns, which show something of the profound reflections on the person of Christ in the early church. This will be followed by an examination of the three important Christological events – the virgin birth, the resurrection and the ascension – to discover what light these throw on the person of Christ and to consider their theological implications. Our survey will conclude with a brief summary of the problems raised by the evidence.

In the following discussions we shall not deal with the subject of the origins of Christology, because such a study does not strictly belong to the field of NT theology. We shall be concentrating on what Christology the NT writers present to us rather than on the processes of growth. Valuable as the search for origins is, the NT theologian is concerned about the whole rather than the parts. In the field of Christology this is particularly important, for the aim must be to show the rich variety of interpretations of the person of Christ, rather than to attempt to chronicle the way in which Christians came to believe what they did. Too often theories of development have been imposed on the evidence with a consequent distortion of the facts. It is almost certain that many of the ideas existed side by side, with no clear line of development between them.

JESUS AS MAN

In approaching an examination of the NT teaching about Jesus Christ, it is natural first to draw attention to those evidences which show that he was truly man. We could have dealt first with those evidences which point to him as more than man, but these will have greater point if studied against the background of his real manhood. It may seem unnecessary to set out the evidence on this theme, but in view of the tendency which developed in early Christian times to overplay the divine nature of Jesus against his human nature (as the docetists did), it is essential to establish that the person who came to be regarded in a variety of exalted ways was nonetheless a real man.[1]

---

[1] J. Knox, *The Humanity and Divinity of Christ* (1967), pp. 5ff., may be right in suggesting that no-one would have asked the question at first, Why was Jesus human? This may, indeed, account for the almost incidental way in which the NT writers present the humanity. Nevertheless, in assessing the evidence, we cannot avoid enquiring how the Christians understood the humanity. Knox may be questioned when he suggests that the earliest Christology was adoptionist, on the strength of which he claims that the humanity of Christ as first presented no problem (*cf.* S. S. Smalley, 'The Christology of Acts', *ExT* 73, 1962, pp. 358ff., for an objection to the adoptionist view).

In adopting this method, we must guard against any attempt to discuss Christology from a purely manward point of view. Our concern will be to examine the NT texts in order to discover what the different writers thought about Jesus, and to what extent many of their views are inexplicable as deductions from the life of even a perfect man.

Our study in this opening section will centre on two aspects, the humanity and the sinlessness of Jesus.

THE HUMANITY OF JESUS

The synoptic gospels

We have in our synoptic gospels three portraits of Jesus of Nazareth, which although differing in many details, are all concerned with the same person. It is only Mark, of the three, who in the opening words gives an indication that he is introducing more than a man, and yet he, more than the others, concentrates on the human Jesus. On the other hand, it is Matthew and Luke who, by including birth stories, focus on the beginnings of the human life of Jesus (see the section on the virgin birth, pp. 365ff.). The birth details represent Jesus in an ordinary human home, subject to all the normal pressures that this involves.[2] The one childhood incident which is related shows something of the humanness of the family situation with the parental anxiety over the missing boy. But Luke's comment that Jesus was obedient to his parents sums up the whole period of his growing up (*cf.* Lk. 2:51). His further comment that Jesus increased in wisdom and in stature (Lk. 2:40, 52) suggests a development under normal laws of human growth. There is nothing to suggest any fantastic developments.

All the gospels centre the commencement of his ministry on the baptism. This is intended to show the identification of Jesus with the people who were flocking to John's baptism.[3] At the same time the heavenly voice clearly distinguishes Jesus from his contemporaries. The subsequent temptations are again intended to show fairly and squarely that Jesus, like all people, was exposed to moral testings. If the sample temptations recorded are regarded as real[4] – and the records give no indication to the contrary

---

[2] H. Johnson, *The Humanity of the Saviour* (1962), p. 44, takes the view that the virgin birth does not exclude the idea that Jesus inherited fallen human nature. Although he maintains this, he also adheres to the NT view of the sinlessness of Jesus.

[3] *Cf.* J. W. Bowman, *The Intention of Jesus* (1945), pp. 36ff, who suggests that for Jesus it was not repentance, but a moral act of commitment to God's call. *Cf.* H. Johnson, *op. cit.*, p. 47, who considers both of these views to be inadequate, and favours some idea of Christ's self-identification with those he came to save.

[4] The temptations of Jesus must be regarded as real temptations if the true humanity of Jesus is to be preserved. In NT usage temptations are essentially testings. The sinlessness of Jesus does not rule out the possibility of real temptation, *cf.* L. Morris, *The Lord from Heaven* (1974), pp. 50ff. W. Temple, *Christus Veritas* (1925), p. 217, comments that a man of high moral character needs to exert effort to overcome temptation, but the effort will be made because of the character of the person. O. Borchert, *The Original*

– they will suggest that Jesus was a real man. But there is a difference in that the temptations of Jesus came to him in the context of his messianic mission, the kind of temptations which were peculiar to him. Neither evangelist implies that the temptations of Jesus were exemplary (as Heb. 4:15 does).[5]

All the synoptic gospels present Jesus against a background of Judaism. He is portrayed in a world of scribes and Pharisees, Sadducees and Hero-dians. His life span belongs essentially to first-century Palestinian life. The people he healed and taught were men and women facing the same social and political tensions that he faced. Such mundane features as eating meals in people's houses, manoeuvering fishing boats, paying taxes, talking among various types of people, are all evidence that the evangelists portray Jesus as essentially a man among men, doing things that ordinary people do. They all note his deep compassion for the socially deprived, his criti-cism of hypocrisy, his dialogues with the religious leaders. They mention his distress in the garden of Gethsemane, Luke especially drawing attention to the sweat of blood, indicative of an intense human conflict which cannot be glossed over. Matthew and Mark insert the cry of abandonment on the cross. And yet with all this, there is an essential difference between Jesus and other men. Each evangelist brings it out in his own way, but the man Jesus makes the most incredible claims for himself. He claims authority to go beyond the law, to forgive sins, to command nature, to exorcize de-mons. He is transfigured before three of the disciples in a way that no other living person could be. He uses and accepts titles which place him in a class of his own.

None of the synoptics makes any attempt to resolve the problem of the tension between his identity with man and his distinctiveness from men. Indeed none of them seems aware of the tension.

The Johannine literature

It is striking that this gospel which presents so much more than the synoptic gospels evidence of a divine Person, commencing with his pre-existence, also contains strong features in support of his humanity. The statement in John 1:14 that 'the Word became flesh and dwelt among us . . . and we beheld his glory', while stressing the sonship manifested in the incarnation,

---

Jesus (Eng. trans. 1933), p. 343, claims that the temptations of Jesus were on a higher level than ours. 'His heart was pure and therefore could not be assailed by temptation to impurity'. Nevertheless, the temptations were of a real man.

[5] E. J. Tinsley, *The Imitation of God in Christ* (1960), pp. 73–80, sees both the baptism and the temptation of Jesus in terms of Israel. The temptations were, therefore, a re-enactment of the temptations of Israel. Jesus is seen as the exemplar of the new Israel and his disciples are expected to imitate him (see p. 81). On the background to the temptation narratives, *cf.* J. Dupont, 'L'Arrière-fond Biblique du Récit des Tentations de Jésus', *NTS* 3, 1956–7, pp. 287–304.

nevertheless suggests a humanity similar to ours which could be seen (see later section on the Logos, pp. 326f.). At the same time the distinctiveness of Jesus is even more apparent. John the Baptist's two followers and Nicodemus and others regarded him as a rabbi (Jn. 1:38; 3:2; 9:2; 11:8). He was wearied with his journey to Sychar (Jn. 4:6) and also experienced thirst (Jn. 4:7; 19:28). He several times aroused the hatred of the Jews (*cf.* 7:44; 10:31ff.; 11:57). At the grave of Lazarus he was deeply disturbed and wept (11:33–35). He was again troubled after his entry into Jerusalem (12:27ff.). He washed his disciples' feet (13:1ff.). In the account of one of the resurrection appearances, he prepares a meal on a charcoal fire (21:9).

There can be no doubt that John wishes to create the impression that when the Logos became flesh, it was real flesh. The pre-existent Word took on true humanity. Nevertheless that humanity could not obscure the equally strong impression that Jesus as a man was unique. The question arises whether in this gospel the evangelist is combatting docetism as seems to be the case in the Johannine epistles (see below). It may well be that the clear indications of the real humanity of Jesus are intended to offset the over-emphasis on the divine nature of Jesus, which was the basic error of the docetic view (*i.e.* that the heavenly Christ only appeared to be identified with the human Jesus).[6] Lack of sufficient attention to the humanity of Jesus in John's account has led some to conclude that the Johannine Christ is mildly docetic.[7] A true assessment of all the evidence does not support this, and we must conclude that, although there is strong evidence of what has been called 'the Christology of glory',[8] there is no evidence that John did not hold in balance that Jesus was a real man as well as being the Son of God.

The opening of 1 John is notable for its insistence on what has been heard, seen, and even touched, of the Word of life (1 Jn. 1:1). This is a

[6] J. Knox, *The Humanity and Divinity of Christ*, p. 26, suggests that the fourth gospel goes as far as it was possible to go without actually embracing docetism. Yet at the same time he admits that no-one in the NT 'affirms the reality of the humanity more unequivocally than he'.

[7] E. Käsemann, *The Testament of Jesus* (1968), p. 26, denies that John's gospel is anti-docetic, but proposes instead that on the question of Christology 'we have to recognize that he (John) was able to give an answer only in the form of a naïve docetism.' *Cf.* also R. Bultmann, *John* (Eng. trans. 1971), p. 13. Against this view, *cf.* F. J. Moloney, *The Johannine Son of Man* (1976), p. 214, who considers that it does violence to the evidence from the gospel.

[8] Käsemann, *op. cit.*, uses this expression. He sees the whole of John's presentation as intended to present the glory of Christ. He writes, 'His dominant interest which is everywhere apparent is that Christ himself may not be overshadowed by anything, not even by his gifts, miracles and works' (p. 21). Käsemann's opinion is that John uses the earthly life of Jesus 'merely as a backdrop for the Son of God proceeding through the world of man and as the scene of the inbreaking of the heavenly glory' (p. 13). W. Thüsing, *Die Erhöhung und Verherrlichung Jesu im Johannesevangelium* (²1970), examines the glorification theme in John's gospel, especially the fact that in one sense glory is perfectly manifested only in the passion. Käsemann's view is criticized by G. Bornkamm, 'Zur interpretation des Johannesevangeliums. Eine Auseinandersetzung mit E. Käsemanns Schrift "Jesu letzter Wille nach Johannes 17" ', *EvT* 28, 1958, pp. 8–25, and in *Geschichte und Glaube*, Aufsätze 3, 1968, pp. 104–121.

prelude to the specific condemnation of those who denied that Jesus is the Christ (2:22) and of those who denied that Jesus Christ had come in the flesh (4:2–3; 2 Jn. 7). Most exegetes agree that some form of docetism, which denied the reality of the incarnation, is being combatted. If a distinction was drawn between the heavenly Christ and the human Jesus, and the former favoured at the expense of the latter, not only would this be an inadequate Christology, it would be nothing short of 'antichrist', as all the statements above affirm. There can be no doubt therefore that, at the time these letters were written, there was a pressing need to assert the real humanity of Christ because this was being undermined.

Acts

In turning from the gospel accounts to the testimony of the early preachers we note at once how Jesus was introduced into the speeches. Acts 2:22 speaks of Jesus as 'Jesus of Nazareth, a man attested to you by God with mighty works and wonders and signs'. The first healing miracle was performed in the name of Jesus of Nazareth (Acts 3:6). In Acts 4:10 he is called 'Jesus Christ of Nazareth'. The description 'Jesus of Nazareth' is taken up by the false accusers against Stephen (Acts 6:14). The same name is used by Peter in his speech to Cornelius and his household (Acts 10:38ff.). In Paul's account of his conversion in Acts 22:8 the risen Lord introduces himself as Jesus of Nazareth. Paul uses the same name in addressing Agrippa (Acts 26:9). These are unmistakable references to the historical Jesus who had lived as a man in the village of Nazareth. It must be admitted, however, that Acts focuses greater attention on the exalted character of Jesus.

Paul

Our discussion of the humanity of Jesus in Paul's letters is naturally connected with the problem of whether Paul knew much about the historical Jesus.

There is a striking paucity of allusions to this subject but the lack of evidence has often been exaggerated. It has seemed to support the claim that Paul had no interest in the historical Jesus. This, however, cannot be sustained. Paul knew that Jesus was of the line of David (Rom. 1:3). Indeed he belonged to Israel according to (*kata*) the flesh (*sarka*) (Rom. 9:5). He had been sent by God at a specific time to be born of a woman and to live under the law (Gal. 4:4). Paul knew something of the family of Jesus for he refers to James as the Lord's brother (Gal. 1:19). When he wanted an example to set before the Corinthians to urge them to give, he made allusion, quite incidentally, to the poverty of Jesus (2 Cor. 8:9). He may well have known that the Son of man had nowhere to lay his head. He certainly knew of the twelve disciples (1 Cor. 15:5); however, since this reference comes in a passage based on early tradition, it is difficult to know how much knowledge he had of Jesus' ministry to and through the disciples. Since Paul met the apostles in Jerusalem (*cf.* Acts 9:26) he must have received many details of incidents in which Jesus and the twelve were involved. The absence of any references to such events is at first perplexing, but may be satisfactorily accounted for by the didactic character of the epistles, the particular style of the apostle lending itself only rarely to illustrative material. The most specific event mentioned by Paul, apart from the crucifixion, burial and resurrection (1 Cor. 15:4), was the institution of the Lord's Supper (1 Cor. 11:23ff.). Even then the historical details are kept to the barest minimum in spite of the importance which Paul attached to the observance of the supper in the right way.

Again, although the apostle does not give a pen portrait of the personality of Jesus, any more than the evangelists do, he is aware of certain facets of the person of Jesus which are valuable for our purpose. He speaks of the meekness and gentleness of Christ (2 Cor. 10:1). Did he know of the saying of Jesus recorded in Matthew 11: 29? He also knows of the grace of the Lord Jesus Christ, seen especially in his approach to his poverty (2 Cor. 8:9). These are attitudes of mind which could have been observed. Yet they were qualities utterly at variance with current expectations about the Messiah. Other aspects of Jesus which exercised a profound effect on Paul's Christology were his righteousness (Rom. 5:18) and sinlessness (2 Cor. 5:21), for on these he built up his exposition of the Christian's attainment of righteousness. Another feature which Paul endorsed was the humility of Jesus in his great Christological passage in Philippians 2:6ff. In 2 Thessalonians 3:5 Paul mentions the steadfastness of Christ. For these allusions the apostle must have been drawing on wide traditions about the historical Jesus. The evidence, though sparse, is sufficient to show that he was not unmindful of the importance of the historical Jesus.

There are several passages in Paul's epistles which stress the manhood of the historical Jesus. Some will be mentioned in other connections, but it is impressive to gather the united testimony here. The discussion in Romans 5:12ff. depends for its force on Christ being a man, just as Adam was (note especially 'the one man Jesus Christ', 5:15). The same emphasis is found in 1 Corinthians 15:21f. (by a man came the resurrection of the dead), another Adam passage. In 2 Corinthians 5:14 Paul asserts that one has died for all. His similarity to his brethren is alluded to in the expression 'first-born among many brethren' in Romans 8:29. To these references must be added Romans 8:3 ('in the likeness of sinful flesh'; but see the section on sinlessness, pp. 231ff.).

It must be frankly admitted that Paul has more to say about the divine nature of Christ than about his humanity. But the latter is nonetheless present. In the Philippians 2 passage Jesus takes the form of a servant (see pp. 345ff.). If, as C. F. D. Moule[9] argues with some cogency, the passage means that Christ considered that equality with God meant not snatching, but giving, this must have involved some self-limitation. The form of a servant (*i.e.* a real manhood) expresses the boundaries of that limitation. All that Jesus did during his earthly ministry was governed by that limitation. Anything less than real humanity would detract from the value of the cross and of the striking character of the humiliation theme which is the main point of the passage. Moreover, the exaltation is affected by whether Jesus was really man, because if he was a true man his humanity is combined with his Lordship in his exalted position.

When Paul says in 2 Corinthians 5:16 that we no longer regard Christ from a human point of view, his words may imply the humanity of Jesus, unless he is meaning that we now approach Christ from a spiritual point of view. The understanding of this passage is enigmatic (see the discussion on pp. 248f.), but in the same epistle Paul refers to the poverty of Christ (2 Cor. 8:9), a clear allusion to the humble conditions into which he came.

In the pastoral epistles there is one passage in which the mediator between God and man is described as 'the man Christ Jesus' (1 Tim. 2:5). It is all the more striking because this man gave himself as a ransom, an echo of the words of Jesus in Mark 10:45.

Because these references to the humanity of Jesus are mostly incidental, it may at first seem that Paul had little interest in this subject, but this would be a wrong deduction. He rather assumes the humanity, because without it neither the work of Christ on the cross, nor his glorious exaltation, would make sense.

Hebrews

After introducing Jesus as the exalted Son in Hebrews 1:3, the writer brings out the following details of his human nature.

(i) First, he was lower than the angels and was concerned with men, not angels, in his mission (2:9, 16). (ii) He shared flesh and blood like his brethren (2:14). (iii) While in the flesh, he was subject to temptation (2:18; 4:15). (iv) He prayed and offered supplications with loud cries and tears, a reference to Gethsemane (5:7).[10] (v) He learned obedience through suffering as a result of which he is said to have been made perfect (2:10; 5:8–9). (vi) He knew what it was to experience godly fear (5:7). (vii) He regarded death as an inescapable part of his mission (2:9, 14).

---

[9] C. F. D. Moule, 'Further reflexions on Phil. 2:5–11', *Apostolic History and the Gospel* (ed. W. W. Gasque and R. P. Martin), pp. 264ff.

[10] *Cf.* A. E. Garvie, 'The Pioneer of Faith and Salvation', *ExT* 26, 1914–15, p. 549, on Heb. 5:7. *Cf.* also M. Rissi, 'Die Menschlichkeit Jesu nach Heb. 5:7 und 8', *ThZ* 11, 1955, pp. 28ff.; E. Brandenburger, 'Text und Vorlagen von Heb. v. 7–10. Ein Beitrag zur Christologie des Hebräerbriefes', *NovT* 11, 1969, pp. 190–224. O. Cullmann, *The Christology of the New Testament* (Eng. trans. ²1963), p. 95, maintains that the words 'without sin' in Heb. 4:15 go far beyond the synoptic temptation narratives.

In the subsequent discussion in the epistle of the qualifications of Christ's high priesthood, the humanity of Jesus is seen to be indispensable to the idea of his offering himself as a willing sacrifice, which he did through the eternal Spirit (9:14; 9:26f.). Moreover, that offering is specially connected with the human body of Jesus (10:10; *cf.* 10:20). There could have been no access for men if Jesus the man had not first blazed the way.

This writer nowhere displays any tension over the parallel concepts of divine sonship and perfect humanity. He can present at the same time the Son who reflects the glory of God and the man who can be tempted as we are, and can identify them in the person of Jesus Christ. In this he is in line with the other evidence so far considered.

The Petrine epistles

In 1 Peter the true humanity of Jesus is assumed rather than expressed. His death was a bearing of our sins in his body on the tree (1 Pet. 2:24). It was because of this that he qualified to be an example for us (1 Pet. 2:21), which he could not have been if he had not shared our common humanity. Peter points out that it was 'in the flesh' that Christ was put to death for our sins (1 Pet. 3:18). In fact, in writing to Christians threatened with persecution, Peter can meaningfully speak of them sharing Christ's sufferings (1 Pet. 4:13). What he suffered he suffered as a man whose example could inspire others, although his death has profoundly deeper consequences than this. Peter claims to have been a witness of the sufferings of Christ (1 Pet. 5: 1).

In 2 Peter 1:16ff. there is a direct appeal to the transfiguration from an eyewitness account, although the reference could not be considered to be evidence of complete humanity since it is cited to prove the majestic glory of Christ. What is most significant here is that the glory is seen in an earthly setting.

Revelation

In this book, since it centres on the heavenly risen Christ, there is little stress on his humanity. But even in the vision of the ascended Lord in Revelation 1:13, the description is of 'one like a son of man' (echoing the language of Dn. 7). There are references to his actual death (Rev. 1:7; 1:18). The humanity also comes out in the references to the wounded Lamb. These allusions are sufficient to identify the triumphant Lamb with him who lived on earth and died a redeeming death.

Summary

Our survey of the evidence for the humanity of Jesus has clearly shown that whatever exalted view of Jesus the early church had, they had no doubt that he was a real man.[11] There is nowhere in the NT any suggestion that he was so exalted a being that it would not be meaningful to speak of his humanity. Yet because of the exalted nature and status of Jesus according to the evidence from the NT discussed in the following sections, the conclusion is inescapable that as man Jesus was unique.[12]

THE SINLESSNESS OF THE MAN JESUS

In order rightly to assess the human nature of Jesus, account must be taken of the clear NT testimony to his sinless character. This conviction is seen in several strands of NT evidence as set out below.[13]

The synoptic gospels

Whereas there are no specific records in the synoptic gospels of a claim by Jesus himself to be sinless, there are indications which would support such a view of him.[14] Indeed it may at once be asserted that there is no evidence which makes the later apostolic testimony to his sinlessness incongruous. Never at any time did Jesus make any confession of sin. He began his ministry with a call to repentance, although he never revealed in himself any need to repent. When he submitted to John's baptism, it was with some hesitation (according to Matthew's account, Mt. 3:14) that John finally agreed to the baptism. Jesus declared that it was 'to fulfil all righteousness', not to signify repentance from sin.[15]

The fact that Jesus showed such sensitive resistance to evil when, for

---

[11] For a recent book which attempts a modern assessment of the humanity of Jesus, cf. J. A. T. Robinson, *The Human Face of God* (1973). Robinson speaks of three representations of reality – mythological, ontological and functional – and prefers the latter for modern understanding. But our purpose has been to discover the NT view and it is questionable whether these distinctions have meaning for first-century thought.

On the religious and moral personality of Jesus, cf. O. Bochert, *The Original Jesus*, pp. 209ff. Cf. also S. W. Sykes, 'The Theology of the Humanity of Christ', in *Christ, Faith and History* (ed. S. W. Sykes and J. P. Clayton, 1972).

[12] In a psychological approach to the humanity of Jesus, Romani Guardini, *The Humanity of Jesus* (Eng. trans. 1964), pp. 48ff., shows an important distinction between Jesus as man and other men in that Jesus everywhere met with a lack of understanding. Guardini believes that in a sense this isolated Jesus from other men without in the least degree diminishing his true humanity.

[13] For an older contribution on this theme, cf. Carl Ullmann's *The Sinlessness of Jesus* (Eng. trans. from 7th edn. 1901). This book is structured on an apologetic approach, but still has some valuable insights.

[14] Some have discussed the virgin birth in relation to the sinlessness of Jesus, and in order to safeguard the latter have proposed the doctrine of the immaculate conception. This is the Roman Catholic view. It cannot be maintained that the virgin birth is necessary to support the sinlessness of Christ, for it does not in itself prove it. In fact, all that could be said is that a miraculous birth predisposes towards an exceptional person in respect of whom sinlessness would not be out of place. See comment on p. 374.

[15] One explanation of the hesitation of John is that the problem was one of inferiority-superiority, that is that John recognized that Jesus should baptize him with the Spirit; cf. D. Hill, *Matthew* (NCB, 1972), p. 96, who goes on to explain 'righteousness' as 'righteousness of life'. Cullmann (*Baptism in the New Testament* (Eng. trans. 1950), pp. 18f.) on the other hand interprets it in the Pauline sense of Jesus acquiring righteousness for all.

instance, he rebuked Peter's wrong attempt to deflect him from the consequences of his messianic mission, suggests the absence of any consciousness
of evil within himself (Mt. 16: 23). Indeed, the terms of the rebuke – 'Get
behind me, Satan' – show an acute reaction to the presence of Satan,
especially when present in the words of one of his closest disciples.[16] In the
accounts of the temptations both Matthew and Luke leave a strong impression of the complete victory of Jesus. There is no suggestion that Jesus
even wavered in his attitude towards the tempter. Since these temptations
may be regarded as samples of what was true throughout the ministry, this
triumph over evil may be extended to cover the whole life of Jesus. It
should be noted, of course, that the temptations recorded have special
relevance to the commencement of the ministry, but they set the tone for
the whole.

The strong condemnation of the scribes and Pharisees for hypocrisy and
the absence of any counter-condemnations against Jesus support the view
that no-one could lay the charge of hypocrisy against him. What he expected of others may be accredited to himself. In urging people to be
perfect as their heavenly Father is perfect (Mt. 5:48), Jesus would have been
guilty of hypocrisy if there had been any doubt about his own perfection.
Had he included himself in the exhortation, the question of his own need
to be more perfect might have been implied. But the exhortation is addressed to others, not to himself. The whole teaching of Jesus in the
synoptic gospels is set on a consistently high moral tone and none of his
hearers ever charged him with not living up to his own teaching. When he
mentioned that his hearers, though evil, know how to give good gifts to
their children, he was differentiating himself from them (Mt. 7:11; Lk.
11:13).

A few instances in the synoptic gospels have raised problems of a moral
kind. Was Jesus too harsh in his denunciation of the scribes and Pharisees?
He certainly did not mince his words, but this would not involve moral
blame unless the criticisms can be shown to be unfounded. Despite the
claims of some scholars that Jesus exaggerated the hypocrisy[17] and gives
no credit to the scribes and Pharisees for their good qualities, there is no
certain evidence that Jesus was unfair. Indeed, in view of the deliberate
rejection by the scribes and Pharisees of his messianic claims and of their
active part in the crucifixion, it is clear that Jesus was justified in his opinion
of them. The basis of their religious beliefs was diametrically opposed to
his teaching, which stressed the importance of man's personal relation to
God, rather than the observance of ritual demands. The strong tone of

---

[16] It is probably preferable to interpret the rebuke to mean that Peter was behaving in the manner of
Satan rather than to suppose that Satan was possessing Peter, *cf.* E. Best, *The Temptation and the Passion:
The Markan Soteriology* (1965), p. 29.

[17] *Cf.* C. Montefiore, *Rabbinic Judaism and Gospel Teachings* (1930). *Idem, The Synoptic Gospels* (1909).

criticism cannot be condemned as unworthy of a perfect man, but it demonstrates the validity of righteous anger against abuses.[18]

A statement which has caused difficulty is Jesus' word to the young ruler who addressed him as 'Good Teacher' (Mk. 10:17–18; Lk. 18:18–19). In affirming that one only was good, *i.e.* God, did Jesus imply that he was not himself good?[19] Some have supposed that Jesus as man was disclaiming the absolute goodness of God which cannot be exposed to temptation. Contrasted with this was the goodness in Jesus which was the result of successful resistance to temptation and perfect obedience which involved suffering. But such a view supposes degrees of goodness, which clouds the issue.[20] It is better to suppose that Jesus was challenging the young man about the basis of his assessment of goodness in order to set his appreciation of Jesus himself in its right perspective.[21] In other words the question, 'Why do you call me good?', is intended to draw out a reason. Matthew's account, which has, 'Why do you ask me about what is good?' (Mt. 19:16), shifts the emphasis and lessens the supposed moral difficulty. The notion of goodness is not discussed in any of the accounts and serves only as an introduction to a direct challenge to the young man about the commandments.

We may conclude that the presentation of Jesus in the synoptic gospels, although not explicit about his sinlessness, prepares us for the more specific account in John's gospel and for the confident assertions of the epistles.

The Johannine literature

John's account, with its portrait of Jesus as both Son of God and yet truly man, presupposes sinlessness. In John 8:44 Jesus charges the Jewish hearers with being of 'your father, the devil', and this is followed up by the direct challenge, 'Which of you convicts me of sin?' The retort was not evidence of Jesus' sin, but an emotional outburst, 'Are we not right in saying that you are a Samaritan and have a demon'? (Jn. 8:48). Moreover, the astonishing claims that Jesus made for himself in this gospel (*e.g.* 'I am the light of the world', Jn. 8:12) would be total arrogance if his moral status did not

---

[18] D. Bonhoeffer, *Christology* (Eng. trans. 1966), p. 112, asserted that Jesus was not a perfectly good man, because he was angry, harsh to his mother, evaded his enemies, broke the law, stirred up revolt. But Bonhoeffer is collecting evidence which can be effectively explained without implying sinfulness. Admittedly he goes on to qualify his statement in the light of who it was who was acting in such a way, for he still affirms that Jesus was without sin.

[19] *Cf.* B. B. Warfield's essay on this passage, 'Jesus' Alleged Confession of Sin', in his collected essays, *Christology and Criticism* (1929), pp. 97–143. H. B. Swete, *Mark* (³1913), *ad loc.*, points out that the stress falls on the adjective and not on the pronoun. This focuses on the meaning of goodness and does not suggest any contrast between Jesus and God.

[20] *Cf.* H. R. Mackintosh, *The Doctrine of the Person of Jesus Christ* (³1914), who, in his note on the sinlessness of Jesus (pp. 35ff.), writes, 'What Jesus disclaims, rather, is *God's* perfect goodness.'

[21] On Mk. 10:18, R. P. Martin, *Mark: Evangelist and Theologian* (1972), p. 124, suggests that Jesus' reply to the rich young ruler points out that 'good' should not be used as a flippant gesture of praise.

match it. It was not on the grounds of inconsistency between his words and actions that his enemies plotted against him, but on the grounds of their jealousy (*cf.* Jn. 12:10–11). Jesus frequently claimed to do the will of God in terms which suggest that it was unthinkable to him to do otherwise (*cf.* Jn. 10:37f.; 14:10–11; 14:31; 15:10; 17:4). He could hardly have claimed to be one with the Father (10:30; 17:22), had there been any awareness of sin in him. The presentation of Jesus in John's gospel assumes for him the highest moral level and there is nowhere any suggestion of fault or failure in him, except in the false accusations of his enemies (18:30), although even here no specific charge was brought. His moral purity is inviolable.

In the Johannine epistles an equally specific claim to sinlessness in respect of Jesus Christ is found (1 Jn. 3:5, 'in him there is no sin'. He came, in fact, to take away sin). It is also in 1 John that our advocate with the Father is described as 'Jesus Christ the righteous' (1 Jn. 2:1). He is clearly distinguished from the rest of us, for if we say that we have no sin, we deceive ourselves (1 Jn. 1:8).

Acts

Again the sinlessness is more implicit than explicit. In Peter's Pentecost speech the description 'the Holy One' from Psalm 16 is applied without hesitation to Jesus (Acts 2:27). A similar idea occurs in Peter's second speech in Acts 3:14, where the audience is charged with having denied 'the Holy and Righteous One'. In the disciples' prayer in 4:24ff., reference is made to 'thy holy servant Jesus' (verse 30). Stephen in his speech referred to Jesus as 'the Righteous One' (7:52). In his Areopagus address Paul refers to God judging the world in righteousness by a man whom he has appointed (Acts 17:31) without specifying further. In fact his address was abruptly curtailed. Since the amount of Christological material in Acts is severely limited by the author's purpose, it is not surprising that no more is said explicitly about the sinlessness of Jesus. But there seems little doubt that it is implied.

Paul

In his letter to the Romans Paul states that God sent 'his own Son in the likeness of sinful flesh' (Rom. 8:3), a remark which has occasioned much discussion. Does he mean that the flesh that Jesus took was flesh of a different kind from other men? Or does he mean that Jesus shared precisely the same nature of man including its inherent self-centred bias? The answer hinges on the sense of 'likeness' (*homoiōmati*).[22] It has been understood in

---

[22] D. Bonhoeffer, *op. cit.*, p. 113, argues for a paradox in his discussion of the phrase 'likeness of flesh'. He distinguishes between Christ and the flesh and relates the phrase only to the former. This lands him with the paradox of saying that Jesus' deeds are not sinless, but Jesus himself is. To assert that Jesus' acts are sinless, he thinks is a statement of belief. But it is confusing to draw such a distinction between Jesus' acts and himself.

the sense of 'identity of form', which would support the second alternative, or in the sense of 'analogy' which would support the first. The expression 'in the likeness of' (*en homoiōmati*) occurs in a Christological statement in Philippians 2:7, where Christ is said to have been born 'in the likeness of men'.[23] Here the sense seems to require identity of form, although it should be noted that the identity is with humanity as compared with deity. It is not, therefore, a precise parallel with Romans 8:3.[24] The same word (*homoiōmati*) occurs in Romans 5:14 where it is used of the transgression of Adam. It is difficult from an exegetical point of view to reach any conclusion, but there is nothing in the statement in Romans 8:3 which requires the view that in his human nature, Jesus had inherited a sinful bias.[25] Indeed, the additional statement 'for sin' (*peri hamartias*), which could mean 'for a sin offering', and the further comment that 'he condemned sin in the flesh', support the view that it was only because he himself was without sin that he could condemn it 'in the flesh'. The question whether he was born without sin is not discussed by Paul. If Christ did not sin it is impossible to suggest that he was born with sin, in the sense of original sin. The NT is nowhere speculative about possibilities. It simply asserts as an accepted fact that Christ was sinless.

This is brought out particularly in 2 Corinthians 5:21, where Paul says 'For our sake he made him to be sin who knew no sin'. Sinlessness here is explicit, in spite of the profound problem involved in his being 'made sin' (for which see the discussion on pp. 465f.). He could be 'made sin' only if he was without sin. Again the focus falls on the fact that he *did* (or *knew*) no sin. The sinless life was the necessary prelude to the identification of Christ with those he had come to save from sin. A similar idea occurs in Galatians 3:13 where Paul declares that Christ became a curse for us, again implying that he was not under a curse for himself.

Hebrews

In setting out the qualities of Jesus as a sympathetic high priest, a comparison is made between his temptations and ours with the significant proviso, 'yet without sinning (Heb. 4:15).[26] Again, the possibility of falling is not

[23] R. P. Martin, *Philippians* (*NCB*), p. 98, recognizes that *homoiōmati* here has within it the sense of being marked out from men.

[24] R. Jewett, *Paul's Anthropological Terms* (1971), pp. 151f., criticizes J. Schneider, *TDNT* 5, p. 196, for maintaining a double sense in *homoiōma* in Rom. 8: 3 and Phil. 2:7. Jewett contends that Jesus actually became flesh and sin. Without committing ourselves to a double sense which is contradictory, we must note that in common usage 'like' involves both similarity and distinction, thus excluding identity. This is supported by the use of the word in Heb. 4: 15.

[25] For an exposition of Rom. 8:3 in support of the view that Christ assumed fallen human nature, *cf.* H. Johnson, *The Humanity of the Saviour*, pp. 107ff. For the converse view that Christ did not take fallen human nature, *cf.* C. H. Dodd, *The Epistle to the Romans* (1932), pp. 119f., who points out that fallen humanity in Adam is not the only humanity.

[26] R. Williamson, 'Hebrews 4:15 and the sinlessness of Jesus', *ExT* 86, 1974, pp. 4ff., suggests that Jesus participated in the actual experience of sinning.

discussed, but the resultant fact of sinlessness is affirmed.[27] The proviso seems to make a distinction, however, in the parallelism of the temptations. Sympathy of understanding is based on similar exposure to testing. Yet the whole of this epistle does not conceal the fact of the essential difference in nature between our high priest and ourselves.[28]

The Petrine epistles

In a striking passage in which ethical exhortation is merged with doctrinal affirmation, Peter maintains that Christ committed no sin (1 Pet. 2:22), while at the same time affirming that he bore our sins that we might die to sin (1 Pet. 2:24). There is undoubtedly here a direct echo from the Servant Song of Isaiah 53, in which the Servant's identification of himself 'with the transgressors' is mentioned. Whereas the Servant's sinlessness is not explicitly stated in Isaiah 53, Peter does not hesitate to make this assertion of Jesus, whom he sees as the fulfilment of the Isaianic Servant passage. Jesus' blood is described in terms of a lamb without spot or blemish (1 Pet. 1:19), another allusion perhaps to Isaiah 53.

This is further supported by the statement in 1 Peter 3:18, which declares of Christ that the righteous died for the unrighteous. In both these references the major matter of importance is the death of Christ and it is clear that the sinless quality of his life was regarded as a vital factor in the meaning of his death.

Revelation

With the emphasis shifted to the exalted Christ there is no occasion in this book for reference to the sinlessness of Jesus, but it should be noted that the righteousness of the risen Lamb is never in dispute. At the climax of the book judgment is in the hands of him who is called Faithful and True (Rev. 19:11). There is no incongruity between this view of the heavenly Christ and the purity of the earthly Jesus, for had there been the validity of the whole vision would have been in question.

Its theological significance

The evidence set out above shows the wide distribution of the conviction

---

[27] Montefiore, *Hebrews*, p. 91, comments on the ambiguity of the Greek words in Heb. 4:15, where 'yet without sin' could be understood in the sense that Jesus was tempted exactly as we are and yet did not succumb; or that he was tempted as we are except for those sins which result from previous sins. It may be that the writer intended to be ambiguous. He certainly does not appear to be aware of raising problems with the words 'yet without sin'. The almost incidental way in which the words are introduced suggests, moreover, that he expected his readers to receive them as acknowledged fact.

[28] The problem arises whether or not the author of Hebrews considered that Jesus took sinful human flesh, especially in view of Heb. 2:17–18. H. Johnson, *op. cit.*, pp. 116ff., maintains that it must mean that Jesus assumed a human nature affected by the fall. *Cf.* also J. Knox, *The Humanity and Divinity of Jesus*, p. 49. But the writer carefully safeguards the sinlessness of Jesus and this is clearly his dominant concern, while at the same time maintaining his true humanity. *Cf.* L. Morris, *The Lord from Heaven*, pp. 85f.

that Jesus did no sin.[29] The breadth of evidence excludes any suggestion that belief in the sinlessness of Jesus was a later accretion. It would not have developed at all if it had not been firmly rooted in historical evidence. It is a striking fact that no report was recorded which was at variance with the conviction that Jesus was sinless; this must be taken into account in assessing its importance.

One problem which has been raised is whether the sinlessness of Jesus is in conflict with the doctrine of original sin, since if the latter doctrine is correct (see pp. 209ff.) Jesus could not have become true man without being predisposed to sin as all others are.[30] The problem is more apparent than real, for it is built on the presupposition that fallen humanity was the only kind of humanity that Jesus could share. But the biblical view is that fallen humanity is a corruption of what was intended, which means that Jesus' sinlessness shows God's true ideal for man. Admittedly this does not touch the question of how Jesus entered the stream of life without being affected by the sinful bias. The NT does not discuss the problem, but presents some evidence of a virgin birth (see pp. 365ff.) as at least a contributory factor. Even this, however, does not explain how conception through the Spirit in a human person absolved Jesus from all taint.[31] Indeed, many theologians resolve the problem by denying the virgin birth and the doctrine of original sin. In this case sinlessness is wholly the result of the morality of Jesus, demonstrated by his integrity. But this line of approach fails to take account of the true nature of sin (see pp. 187ff.), which has had a more radical effect on the human race in pre-conditioning the human will.

The significance of the sinlessness of Jesus lies in its relation to the incarnation. If Jesus became man in a form which was purged of all bias to sin, could he then be said to have become man like other men? Could he then be identified with those he came to redeem? The answer lies partially in the understanding of Christ's work of redemption. Nowhere does the NT suggest that Christ had to become identical to man in his fallen state. In each case where he is identified with man's sin the proviso is added that he was without sin. The assumption is that he was obliged to become man to save man, but there is no suggestion that he must become implicated in man's sin. Pannenberg[32] rejects the view that Jesus shared uncorrupted, but not corrupted, humanity on the grounds that it contradicts 'the anthropological radicality of sin', and is contrary to the NT (and early Christian) view that the Son of God assumed sinful flesh and in sinful

---

[29] On the significance of the sinlessness of Jesus, cf. L. W. Grensted, *The Person of Christ*, Appendix, pp. 279ff. On the problem raised by it, cf. J. Knox, *op. cit.*, pp. 39–52. J. A. T. Robinson, *The Human Face of God*, pp. 88f., maintains that the statement that Jesus never sinned was a theological and not a historical observation, since no-one could prove a universal negative.

[30] Cf. W. Pannenberg, *Jesus – God and Man* (Eng. trans. 1968), p. 361.

[31] Hence the development of the Roman Catholic view of the immaculate conception; see above, n. 14.

[32] Cf. Pannenberg, *op. cit.*, p. 362.

flesh overcame sin. But he is basing his observations on a particular understanding of Romans 8:3 which is open to challenge. If, of course, 'sinful flesh' means flesh like other men's flesh, which in them always results in sin but in Jesus never did, there would be less difficulty. Even if Jesus differs from us in that he never yielded to temptation, he cannot be so entirely different that his example could not provide an encouragement to us. Moreover, the NT concept that fallen man cannot please God (Rom. 8:8), would seem to be irreconcilable with the view that Jesus took sinful flesh.

Whatever subsequent debates have arisen over the explanation of the sinlessness of Jesus, we may confidently affirm that the NT has no doubt that Jesus became truly man and equally no doubt that he was sinless. To make him take on corrupt human nature would not make him more of a true man, but less. Those who have maintained that what is not assumed cannot be redeemed[33] have gone beyond NT teaching, for God's method of redemption is to use the agency of a sinless man, his own Son, to redeem a race of sinful men.

In conclusion, we may note that any discussion over whether the sinlessness of Jesus means that he could not sin (*peccare non potuit*) or that he was able not to sin (*potuit non peccare*) is not foreshadowed in the NT. The question is speculative. The latter alternative assumes that sinlessness is equated to obedience. But in itself this would not go far enough in understanding the NT concept of sinlessness. There is a sense in which the perfect will of God so completely represented the perfect will of Jesus that any act or even desire short of that perfect will was unthinkable to him.

THE CHRISTOLOGICAL TITLES: INTRODUCTORY COMMENTS

Our next consideration is to discover how Jesus thought of himself and how the early Christians came to think of him. We will seek an answer to this enquiry by first examining the meaning and significance of the various titles which either Jesus himself used or others came to use of him. Although this survey will by no means exhaust the NT evidence on the person of Christ, it will present a wide spectrum in a manageable form.[34] It will

---

[33] This was a familiar idea among patristic writers. K. Barth, *Church Dogmatics*, I, 1, pp. 153ff., strongly maintained the sinlessness of Christ, but nevertheless insisted that the Word assumed our human existence, *i.e.* our fallen nature.

[34] It is not to be thought that an adequate Christology could be deduced from the titles alone, but they undoubtedly make an important contribution towards it. J. Jeremias, *NTT*, 1, pp. 250ff., attaches more significance to the emphatic *egō* passages. His distrust of the titles is on the grounds that all but one are post-Easter. He thinks, on the other hand, that pictures like messenger of God, physician, shepherd, master builder and father are pre-Easter (p. 251). H. Conzelmann, *Jesus* (Eng. trans. 1978), p. 49, maintains that the Christological titles can tell us nothing about Jesus' self-consciousness.

be complemented by a following discussion of the so-called Christological hymns, which set out what Christians thought about Jesus as they came to worship him.

The titles have each a specific background which shows that they were not created out of nothing. It will clearly be important to consider what meaning the various terms would have had in contemporary understanding, although it must always be recognized that any term applied to Jesus may have been considerably modified compared with the meaning it had in its contemporary usage.

A rough division may be made between those titles which possessed messianic connotations and those which did not. In this context the word 'messianic' is understood to relate to the deliverer-figure who was anticipated in the Jewish world, and who would be God's agent for the inauguration of a new age for his people. The word 'messianic' comes from the Hebrew word 'Messiah', for which the Greek equivalent is 'Christ'. Both terms are derived from roots meaning 'to anoint', from which it may be seen that Jesus was regarded as being specially set apart for a specific task.

MESSIAH

It is logical in discussing Christology to begin with 'Messiah', since the Greek term *Christos* (the anointed one) has provided the Christian church with its most widely used term. Indeed the fact that the believers in Jesus were at an early stage described as 'Christians' is eloquent testimony to the importance of the concept in their minds. They were so convinced that Jesus was the Messiah and were so open in announcing it that others tagged on to them the description of 'Christ's people'. That this first happened at Antioch is significant for it was there that the church first had an impact on Gentiles (Acts 11:26). Jews would never have described believers as Messiah's people, for they never recognized that the church had any right to apply the term to Jesus. But Gentiles would have no such inhibitions and would in fact be ignorant of the implications of the name. Constant use of the word 'Christ' would seem to them meaningless. It is, in fact, to Jewish sources that we must look for light on its significance for Jesus and his contemporaries. Only then will the evidence of the gospels be properly understood.

The Jewish background

It is possible to give only the briefest summary of the Jewish idea of Messiah. We should, in fact, speak of a variety of ideas, for there was certainly no unified concept about the one who was to inaugurate the coming age. Some indication must be given about the idea of Messiah in the four main sources for contemporary Judaism – the Old Testament, the

Apocryphal and Pseudepigraphical literature, the Qumran scrolls and the rabbinical writings.

In the Old Testament much is said, especially in the prophets, about the coming messianic age which offered bright prospects to the people of God (*cf.* Is. 26–29; 40ff.; Ezk. 40–48; Dn. 12; Joel 2:28–3:21), but little is said about the Messiah. The title is nowhere used of the coming deliverer. Indeed, the agent for inaugurating the coming age was God himself. But although the absolute use of the term 'Messiah' does not occur, there are various uses of the word in a qualified way, such as the Lord's Messiah (*i.e.* anointed one). The idea of anointing a person for a special mission appears in a variety of applications, but mainly of kings and priests (Lv. 4:3ff.), also of prophets (1 Ki. 19:16) and patriarchs (Ps. 105:15) (*cf.* 1 Sa. 24:6ff.; 26:9ff.), and even of a heathen king, Cyrus (Is. 45:1). This use of anointing to indicate a specific office became later applied in a more technical sense of the one who, *par excellence*, would be God's chosen instrument in the deliverance of his people. The OT without doubt prepares the way for the Messiah and many OT messianic passages are cited in the NT.

During the intertestamental period, the meaning of the term underwent some modifications, in which the technical sense of the Lord's anointed one becomes more dominant (*cf.* Psalms of Solomon 17–18). The hope of the coming Messiah took many different forms, but the predominant one was the idea of the Davidic king, who would establish an earthly kingdom for the people of Israel and would banish Israel's enemies. The Messiah was to be a political agent, but with a religious bias. The concept was a curious mixture of nationalistic and spiritual hopes.[35]

It is generally supposed that in the Qumran literature there are two Messiahs, one of Aaron and one of Israel (*cf.* 1 QS 9:11).[36] Since the Qumran sect was a priestly community, it is not surprising to find that the Messiah of Aaron took precedence over the Messiah of Israel.[37] To what extent this diversified view of Messiahship is significant for a determination of NT usage is debatable, but it at least testifies to the fact that there were divergent views concerning the precise nature of the messianic office.[38]

---

[35] *Cf.* R. N. Longenecker, *The Christology of Early Jewish Christianity* (1970), pp. 63f., who points out that the Semitic mind prefers to think of functions rather than persons, which may explain the greater emphasis on the messianic age.

[36] *Cf.* the discussion on the messianic hope at Qumran in F. F. Bruce's *Second Thoughts on the Dead Sea Scrolls* (1956), pp. 70–84.

[37] Note that in the Damascus document the royal and priestly concepts seem to be combined in one (*CDC* 19:11; 12:23 – 13:1; 14:19; 20:1).

[38] D. E. Aune, 'A Note on Jesus' Messianic Consciousness and 11 Q Melchizedek', *EvQ* 45, 1973, pp. 161ff., maintains that the Qumran fragment is the earliest evidence that the proclamation of glad tidings could be part of the expected Messiah's task.

There is little doubt that Ps. 2:7 was read and expounded in a messianic sense at Qumran. *Cf.* E. Lohse, *TDNT* 8, p. 361, who suggests that a fragmented text, 1 Q 28a (1 Q Sa) 2:11f., may refer to God begetting the Messiah. Both Ps. 2:7 and 2 Sam. 7:14 were used messianically in 4 Q Flor. *Cf.* also Ps. Sol. 17:26 and perhaps 17:36; 18:6, 8, for a similar use of Ps. 2.

It is of some importance to note that there is no evidence that the rabbis before AD 70 used the term 'the Messiah', but information regarding rabbinic teaching of this period is scarce.[39] The term, moreover, was understandably never used by Josephus in his attempt to make Judaism more acceptable to the Romans. In the Apocalypses of Ezra and Baruch, both of which were contemporary with the emerging church, the term occurs, and as in the intertestamental period seems to be linked with the idea of the Davidic son, specifically so in 4 Ezra 12:32–34.[40] In the Targums there is a frequent technical use of the word meṣīa', although in view of the difficulty of dating, the value of this evidence is doubtful.

From this brief survey of the background, it becomes clear that whereas the idea of a coming Messiah was widespread among the Jews, the origin and character of the coming Messiah was not clearly understood. Different groups tended to visualize a Messiah who would be conducive to their own tenets – priestly groups like Qumran in priestly terms, nationalist groups in political terms. In determining the approach of Jesus to the term 'Messiah' we must bear in mind that he would be concerned with the most popular understanding of the term and there is little doubt that popular opinion leaned heavily towards hope of a coming political leader who would deliver the Jewish people from the oppressive Roman yoke.[41] When seen against this prevalent notion, it is understandable why Jesus avoided the use of the term.

The synoptic gospels

We shall next list any evidence from the synoptic gospels which gives an indication of Jesus' approach to the messianic office. By way of introduction to this discussion, it must be noted that the gospels supply definite information regarding current messianic expectations. Matthew reports that Herod's Jewish counsellors were able at once to tell him that the Messiah was to be born in Bethlehem (Mt. 2:3–5). Luke records the confusion of the populace over whether John the Baptist was the Messiah (Lk. 3:15), which bears strong testimony to their expectation. Even more specific is the evidence from John's gospel, where it is said that John the Baptist emphatically denied that he was the Messiah (Jn. 1:20) and where the first disciples of Jesus on their initial encounter with him believed they had

---

[39] Cf. G. E. Ladd, TNT p. 138. He adds that 'in Rabbinic literature as a whole the Davidic kingly messiah becomes the central figure in the messianic hope, while the Son of Man drops out of usage'. He refers to J. Klausner, The Messianic Idea in Israel (1956), pp. 458–469.

[40] K. Berger, in his examination of 'Die Königlichen Messiastraditionen des Neuen Testaments', NTS 20, 1974, pp. 1–44, finds connections with the wisdom literature, and thinks that this is significant in the interpretation of titles like 'Son of David' and 'Son of God'.

[41] For a discussion of the Jewish background to the main titles, especially Messiah, as they developed in the Christian church, cf. K. Berger, 'Zum traditionsgeschichtlichen Hintergrund christologischer Hoheitstitel', NTS 17, 1970, pp. 391–426.

found the Messiah (Jn. 1:41), whatever they understood by the term.

Although the Johannine account has been questioned because of this early recognition, it is not out of harmony with other evidence of popular expectations that the disciples should have been looking for someone to identify as the coming Messiah. Even among the Samaritans some kind of messianic expectation was common (Jn. 4:29ff.). John also reports that confusion arose in the minds of some people in Jerusalem because of the tradition that Messiah's origin would be unknown, whereas the origin of Jesus was known (Jn. 7:26ff.). Moreover, there was a popular belief that Messiah would perform signs and this led others to believe in Jesus, presumably as Messiah (Jn. 7:31). This connection between 'signs' and the Messiah seems to have resulted in the apprehension of the hierarchy about the actions of Jesus, which led them to plan to put him to death (Jn. 11:45–53). It is further noteworthy that John's account of the feeding of the multitude is the only one which links it with popular clamour to make Jesus king and with his escape from such a design (Jn. 6:15). That many of those who had previously followed Jesus immediately withdrew their support (Jn. 6:66) is further evidence that a political Messiah was the predominant idea in popular conceptions. When false accusations were sought in order to incriminate Jesus before the Roman authorities, among them was the statement that Jesus had claimed to be Messiah a king (Lk. 23:2). Pilate referred to Jesus as the one 'who is called Messiah' (Mt. 27:17) and the mockers at the cross used the same title in their jibes.

It remains to question, in view of this background of popular expectation, what Jesus himself thought about the messianic office. That there is an enigmatic character about the answer is undeniable, since Jesus himself was reticent to acknowledge himself publicly as Messiah, and since the gospels (Mark in particular) record several occasions when Jesus commanded secrecy regarding his mission.

The latter point gave rise to the theory that Mark had imposed his own idea of the 'messianic secret' on the true facts of the historical Jesus and that in reality Jesus never thought of himself as Messiah (Wrede).[42] According to this theory it was only later that the Christian church came to think of Jesus as Messiah, and Mark's 'messianic secret' is regarded therefore as a device to explain why Jesus said so little about messiahship and

---

[42] For a brief discussion of this theory, *cf.* G. E. Ladd, *TNT*, p. 169. W. Wrede's book, published in 1901, was entitled *Das Messiasgeheimnis in den Evangelien*. It has now been published in English as *The Messianic Secret* (1971). For fuller discussions in recent publications, *cf.* D. E. Aune, 'The problem of the Messianic Secret', *NovT* 11, 1969, pp. 1–31; B. G. Powley. 'The Purpose of the Messianic Secret. A Brief Survey', *ExT* 80, 1969, pp. 308ff.; R. N. Longenecker, 'The Messianic Secret in the light of Recent Discoveries', *EQ* 41, 1969, pp. 207ff.; J. D. G. Dunn, 'The Messianic Secret in Mark', *TB* 21, 1970, pp. 92–117. Dunn concludes his study with the statement that the so-called 'messianic secret' originated in the life situation of Jesus and is in essence at least wholly historical. G. M. de Tilesse, *Le secret messianique dans l'Évangile de Marc* (1968), on the other hand, attributes the idea of the messianic secret to the evangelist.

why the Jews did not acclaim him. Many followers of Bultmann, with their predisposition towards a church-created tradition, have embraced Wrede's basic idea.[43] But this is not the only way to understand the injunction to secrecy, nor is it the most probable.

If the messianic office was popularly considered to be political, it is highly probable that Jesus would have enjoined silence until after it became clear that he was no political leader (*i.e.* after the crucifixion).[44] It certainly makes better sense to suppose that Jesus was not acknowledging a particular kind of messiahship than to suppose that he never thought of himself as Messiah at all. In the latter case it is impossible to give an adequate explanation of the church's notion that Jesus was, in fact, the promised Messiah. All the circumstantial evidence of the passion would be against the development of a messianic belief *ex nihilo*, since no-one would have pronounced a crucified man as Messiah. It is more intelligible to suppose that Jesus consciously came to fulfil the messianic office,[45] but interpreted that office in a way differing radically from current expectations. This is borne out by the most probable interpretation of the main passages in the synoptic gospels which bear on the matter.

First, we must consider Peter's confession (Mt. 16:13–20 = Mk. 8:27–30 = Lk. 9:18–21), 'You are the Christ'. All the synoptics give the confession as a sequence to the question of Jesus regarding popular ideas of his identity and an answer to the enquiry about their own view. Mark and Luke record the question in the form 'who do men say that I am?' and Matthew has 'Son of man' in place of 'I'. That the confession was explicitly drawn out by Jesus has an important bearing on our understanding of his messianic consciousness. But a two-fold difficulty arises over the interpretation of Peter's confession. The first problem is that the form of it is differently expressed in the respective gospels. Mark has simply, 'You are the Christ' (Mk. 8:29), Luke has 'The Christ of God' (Lk. 9:20) and Matthew has 'You are the Christ, the Son of the living God' (Mt. 16:16). Some scholars regard the Markan saying as the only genuine one and the other forms as later adaptations. But the additions are no more than explanations of the par-

---

[43] For recent works reflecting Wrede's influence, *cf.* G. Bornkamm, *Jesus of Nazareth* (Eng. trans. 1960), pp. 171ff.; N. Perrin, *JR* 46, 1966, pp. 296ff.; H. Conzelmann, *ZTK* 54, 1957, pp. 293ff. In an article in *Int* 27, 1973, pp. 10–30, W. C. Robinson, Jnr, discusses 'The Quest of Wrede's Secret Messiah' and considers the current influence of the theory to be unwarranted.

[44] Against Wrede's view, *cf.* E. Hoskyns and N. Davey, *The Riddle of the New Testament* (1931), pp. 105ff., who deny a non-messianic tradition; T. W. Manson, 'The Life of Jesus: Some Tendencies in Present-Day Research', in *The Background of the New Testament and its Eschatology* (ed. W. D. Davies and D. Daube, 1964), pp. 211–221. *Cf.* also G. H. Boobyer, 'The Secrecy Motive in Mark's Gospel', *NTS*, 6, 1960, pp. 225–235; J. C. O'Neill, 'The Silence of Jesus', *NTS* 15, 1969, pp. 153–167. O'Neill claims that of the succession of Jewish revolutionaries, none of them called himself Messiah. In his view Jesus was charged with blasphemy because he was alleged to have claimed to be Messiah; for the Jews believed that the prerogative for announcing the Messiah belonged to God alone.

[45] *Cf.* R. N. Longenecker, *EQ* 41, 1969, pp. 207–215, who denies that the messianic secret can be appealed to in order to dismiss Messiahship as a foundational element in early Christology.

ticular sense in which the messianic title should be understood. The title 'Messiah' alone could be misunderstood in a political sense, whereas the additions make this less probable, because they introduce spiritual concepts.

Some, however, have put a different construction on the variations in the synoptic accounts. Cullmann,[46] for instance, considers that the confession was a simple statement as in Mark, and that Matthew's addition comes from a different context. Bultmann,[47] on the other hand, rejects altogether the genuineness of the confession in its context. But there are no sufficient grounds for supposing Matthew to be unhistorical in linking Messiah and Son of God as part of Peter's confession. Peter undoubtedly misunderstood the real nature of the messianic office, as his subsequent rebuke of Jesus for his prediction of the passion shows (Mt. 16:21ff.); but this does not eliminate the possibility that he had seen in Jesus more than a merely human Messiah. It is not necessary to suppose with Cullmann that Peter had misunderstood Messiah in a wholly political sense. Indeed had this been so it is incredible that Jesus did not specifically reject the ascription rather than merely enjoin the disciples to silence. It was the idea of a suffering Messiah which proved a stumbling block to Peter.[48]

This highlights the second problem about Peter's confession, *i.e.* what does it tell us about Jesus' own messianic consciousness? There is no reasonable doubt that Jesus rejected the idea of political messiahship. His teaching regarding his mission was not cast in this mould. He eschewed the idea of violence and advocated an approach which would obviously have been a political non-starter.[49] No political revolutionary would ever have exhorted people to love their enemies. The Sermon on the Mount is intelligible as a spiritual directive, but makes nonsense as a political manifesto.

In what sense therefore did Jesus consider himself to be Messiah?[50] The answer lies mainly in his consciousness of OT fulfilment – the consciousness

---

[46] *Cf.* O. Cullman, *Peter: Disciple, Apostle, Martyr* (Eng. trans. 1953), pp. 170ff. He considers that the saying in Mt. 16:17ff., belongs to the Passion story. His main reasons for this transposition are based on the exegetical difficulties which he finds in the existing context.

[47] R. Bultmann, *TNT* 1, pp. 26f. He states categorically that Peter's confession was an Easter-story projected backwards into the life of Jesus. He gives no supporting evidence for this view.

[48] R. H. Fuller, *The Foundations of New Testament Christology* (1965), p. 109, declares that 'Jesus rejects Messiahship as a merely human and even diabolical temptation'. But he bases this view on his own re-editing of the text of the passage (he removes verses 30–32a, which leaves only the statement 'you are the Christ' and the rebuke of Peter for making it).

[49] *Cf.* M. Hengel, 'Was Jesus a Revolutionist?' (Eng. trans. 1971); *idem, Victory over Violence* (Eng. trans. 1975). See the further discussion of this in the section on ethics and social responsibility below, pp. 947f.). In his book *Christ the Conqueror* (1954), pp. 27–40, R. Leivestad denies any appreciable connection between Christ and zealotic messianism, after examining the synoptic texts which might suggest it. He sees the conflict motive as connected with demons (pp. 40–50.).

[50] *Cf.* G. E. Ladd, *TNT*, p. 142; R. N. Longenecker, *The Christology of Early Jewish Christianity*, p. 70. Longenecker pertinently asks how Jesus would ever have aroused such intense opposition if he had not made any messianic claim and had done nothing distinctive.

that he was God's agent for the redemption of his people, interpreted in a spiritual and not a nationalistic sense. It must have been the political overtones of the title Messiah which led to Jesus' reticence in acknowleding the ascription and which caused him to urge silence on his disciples (*cf.* Mk. 8:30). This would satisfactorily account for his acceptance of the idea under certain circumstances, when the political motif was not in question. (*e.g. cf.* Lk. 24:26). In the case of Peter's confession, if Matthew's additional section (Mt. 16:17ff.) belongs to its present context (and there is no conclusive reason for supposing that it does not, see discussion on this on pp. 710ff.), Jesus clearly recognized that Peter was using more than human deduction or intuition in ascribing Messiahship to Jesus. The spiritual insight necessary for recognizing the true nature of the messianic office of Jesus was God given. This is a clear admission that in popular opinion no such concept of the office would be held, which sufficiently justifies the charge to silence.

A more radical interpretation of the confession passage is to suppose that Jesus never considered himself to be Messiah, but only 'Messiah-designate', and that he expected another, the Son of man, to fill the office more fully (so Bultmann).[51] But this is based on a particular view of the Son of man passages which will be discussed later and shown to be unacceptable.

The second passage to be considered centres around Caiaphas' question, 'Are you the Christ?' (Mt. 26:57–68; Mk. 14:53–65). Here again there is a slight difference in the two accounts, Matthew has 'the Son of God' after Christ, and Mark has 'Son of the Blessed' (*eulogētos*). The latter is a Jewish periphrasis for God, and both forms of the question, therefore, mean the same thing. What is significant here is that Caiaphas links the messianic idea with the title Son of God. It is not clear whether he did this because he knew the latter to be a current designation for the Messiah. What evidence there is does not suggest that it was widely known.[52] It is possible that a report had reached Caiaphas that some people were making assertions about Jesus which linked the two (which would support Matthew's version of Peter's confession). There is some difference in Mark's text over Jesus' reply to Caiaphas' question. The most probable reading has 'I am', an affirmative followed immediately by a statement about the Son of man, which shows the non-political sense in which the affirmation was made. A less well-supported reading[53] has 'You have said that I am', which is somewhat similar to Matthew's 'You have said so', and provides a less specific response.[54] If this second reading were correct, it may be a case of

[51] R. Bultmann, *TNT*, 1, pp. 26f. *Cf.* also F. Hahn, *The Titles of Jesus in Christology* (Eng. trans. 1969), pp. 159f.; R. H. Fuller, *Foundations of New Testament Christology* (1965), pp. 109f. According to this view it was the early church, not Jesus, which spiritualized the term 'Messiah' (*Christos*).

[52] See the evidence cited above in footnote 38.

[53] *Cf.* V. Taylor, *Mark* (²1966), *ad loc.*

[54] O. Cullmann, *The Christology of the New Testament*, p. 118, supports the interpretation which favours

Mark's text having been adapted to conform with Matthew's, but if the former reading is right, it would indicate that Jesus was no longer reluctant in the light of his passion to acknowledge messiahship.

What is at first enigmatic is why Jesus' answer drew out an immediate charge of blasphemy from the high priest.[55] Caiaphas would have recognized that the words implied an identification with Daniel's son of man passage. What was evidently considered blasphemy was the implication that he would sit at the right hand of the power of God (Lk. 22:69), which must have been treated as tantamount to blasphemy.[56] Nevertheless the official charge before Pilate was that Jesus had claimed to be a kingly Messiah (Lk. 23:2), and the official inscription on the cross described him as king of the Jews (Mk. 15:26). In response to Pilate's question he had used the same circumlocution ('You have said so', Mt. 27:11; Mk. 15:2; Lk. 23:3) as before the high priest.

When the reluctance of Jesus to use the title, or to acknowledge it is set over against the statements in Luke's resurrection accounts that Jesus expounded from the Scriptures the necessity for a suffering Messiah, some explanation is needed.[57] Why was there a sudden switch from reluctance in the pre-resurrection period to deliberate exposition after the passion and resurrection? The answer must lie in the fact that the crucifixion and resurrection of Jesus had now rendered impossible a purely political interpretation of the messianic mission. Jesus himself appeals to an accomplished event (the passion) as the basis for the messianic claim. This would be in harmony with the view that in Jewish thought a claim to messiahship would not be expected until the messianic mission was finished. Neither the Teacher of Righteousness at Qumran nor Simeon ben Kosebah at Murrabba'at called themselves Messiah, although they considered themselves to be doing a messianic type of work.[58]

The Johannine literature

Unlike the synoptic gospels, John's gospel mentions two specific occasions when the title Messiah is applied to Jesus, on both occasions early in the

---

a more evasive answer. *Cf.* also J. Héring, *Le royaume de Dieu et sa venue: étude sur l'espérance de Jésus et de S. Paul* (1937), pp. 112f.

[55] On the interpretation of these words, *cf.* D. R. Catchpole, 'The Answer of Jesus to Caiaphas (Matt. xxvi. 64)', *NTS* 17, 1971, pp. 213–226, who concludes that the formulae used in both Matthew's and Luke's narratives are 'affirmative in content and reluctant or circumlocutory in formulation'. *Cf.* also *idem, The Trial of Jesus* (1971), pp. 126–148.

[56] *Cf.* D. Hill, *Matthew, ad loc.*

[57] *Cf.* I. H. Marshall, *Luke: Historian and Theologian* (1970), p. 128 n. 5, who points out that Luke's use of *Christos* shows three facets: he identifies Jesus with the Messiah, he reproduces the questions and problems regarding the Messiah, and he allows the risen Jesus to speak of himself as Messiah.

[58] *Cf.* R. N. Longenecker, *The Christology of Early Jewish Christianity*, p. 73.

ministry.[59] Moreover John preserves the Aramaic form and at the same time gives the Greek translation (Jn. 1:41; 4:25). A problem arises over the fact that John's record supposes that the first disciples at once recognized the messianic status of Jesus, whereas the synoptic gospels show no awareness of this until the confession at Caesarea Philippi. One solution is to suppose that John's record in these places is not presenting authentic tradition, but is an interpretation superimposed on the tradition. But the use of the messianic title by the woman at Samaria (Jn. 4:25) is intelligible because for Samaritans the title would not be subject to the same political misunderstandings as for the Jews. Indeed, it is certain that the woman's idea of the term 'Messiah' would have been very general, since the Samaritans thought of a coming restorer, but were vague about the form that any restoration would take.[60]

On the other occasion where the term is introduced, it is found on the lips of Andrew, who tells his brother Peter, 'We have found the Messiah' (Jn. 1:41). Immediately afterwards Philip tells Nathanael, 'We have found him of whom Moses in the law and also the prophets wrote.' This suggests that messiahship among these early disciples was understood against its OT background. There is no reason to suppose that this early impression was anything but a glimpse at a truth that would take some time to dawn on their minds with any clarity.[61] John is giving an insight into first impressions, which the synoptic gospels omit.

It must be remembered that John's purpose for writing is that his readers might believe that Jesus is the Christ, the Son of God (20:31).[62] This aim, therefore, was responsible for his selection and arrangement of material.

[59] For a treatment of the Messiah theme in John's gospel, *cf.* C. H. Dodd, *The Interpretation of the Fourth Gospel* (1953), pp. 91ff; N. A. Dahl, 'The Johannine Church and History', in *Current Issues in N.T. Interpretation* (ed. W. Klassen and G. F. Snyder, 1962), pp. 124–142; R. Schnackenburg, 'Die Messiasfrage im Johannesevangelium', in *Neutestamentliche Aufsätze: Festschrift für J. Schmid* (ed. J. Blinzler, O. Kuss and F. Mussner, 1963), pp. 240–264.

[60] M. de Jonge, in an appendix to his article: 'Jewish Expectations about the "Messiah" according to the Fourth Gospel', *NTS* 19, 1973, pp. 246–270, discusses the statement concerning the Messiah in Jn. 4:25. He claims there is no evidence from Samaritan sources that the Samaritans used the title Messiah before the sixteenth century, citing H. G. Kippenberg, 'Garizim und Synagoge. Traditionsgeschichtliche Untersuchungen zur samaritanischen Religion der aramäischen Periode', *Religionsgeschichtliche Versuche und Vorarbeiten* 30 (1971), p. 303 n. 218. *Cf.* also W. A. Meeks, *The Prophet-King*, pp. 216–257. The Samaritans thought somewhat generally of one who was to come, the *Taheb*, Restorer. For a full discussion of Samaritan theology, *cf.* J. Macdonald, *The Theology of the Samaritans* (1964). He especially brings out the importance of Moses in Samaritan thought. It should be noted, however, that the sources on which reconstructions of Samaritan theology are made are mostly too late to inspire much confidence in their correctness.

[61] It is noticeable that misunderstandings on the part even of the disciples of Jesus are a distinctive feature of this gospel (see 2:22; 12:16; 13:36; 20:25). *Cf.* M. de Jonge, 'Nicodemus and Jesus: Some observations on misunderstanding and understanding in the Fourth Gospel', *BJRL* 53, 1970–1, pp. 337–359.

[62] It should not be supposed that Nathanael, in using the title 'Son of God', means to express divine nature. Indeed, the order of words in this context shows that it really qualified the expression *King of Israel*. What is clear is that Nathanael was thinking of kingship in a special way, *cf.* L. Morris, *John* (NICNT, 1971), pp. 167f.

Not only does he note the case of the first disciples and of the Samaritans, but also the confession of Martha (Jn. 11:27). In the latter case messiahship is linked with the title Son of God, as it is in 20:31 (*cf.* also 1:49). This conditions the view of messiahship which John presents, a view certainly far removed from any political concept. It was after the miracle of the feeding of the multitude that the people wanted to make Jesus king (6:15), and his rejection of this move clears away the political possibilities.

The expression 'King of the Jews (or of Israel)' would certainly have had messianic connotations in John's mind. Nathanael used the expression (1:49). It is used, moreover, by John in his record of the acclamation of the crowds on the entry of Jesus into Jerusalem (12:13), although not recorded in this form in the synoptic gospels. The expression 'King of the Jews' further occurs in John 19:3, 19, both times in mockery.

On two occasions John gives information about current views of the Messiah. Some believed he would make a sudden appearance from a secret origin (Jn. 7:27) and some that he would perform signs (7:31).[63] Others understood from the law that Messiah would continue for ever (12:34), evidently understanding the 'law' here of the general import of current messianic interpretations of the OT.[64] The first popular belief would exclude Jesus on the grounds that his origins (from Nazareth) were known. The second would equally exclude a Messiah who was predicting his own death. In recording these dialogues, John evidently intends to justify his contention that Jesus is the Messiah by recording the answer of Jesus himself to the questions raised. In the former case he appeals to his heavenly origin ('I know him, for I come from him, and he sent me', 7:29) and in the latter he points out that Jesus as light throws light on the darkness of their minds (12:35ff.), which means that belief in a suffering Messiah needs spiritual insight.

Although the gospel of John is dominated more by the concept of Jesus as Son of God, the messianic presentation plays an important part. The over-all impression of the gospel is that Jesus is the Messiah, not in the sense of current speculations, but in a new spiritual sense which is unintelligible apart from the filial consciousness of Jesus.

In the Johannine epistles Messiah has become an accepted title. The combination 'Jesus Christ' occurs in 1 John 1:3; 2:1; 3:23; 4:2; 5:6; 5:20; 2 John 7. But the most important testimony in 1 John concerns those who were denying that Jesus is the Messiah (2:22; 4:3, *cf.* also 2 Jn. 7). Most exegetes think that some early form of docetism is here in view which distinguished the human Jesus from the heavenly Christ and centred faith

---

[63] It is widely disputed that the Jews expected the Messiah to perform signs. *Cf.* J. L. Martyn's discussion of this in his *History and Theology in The Fourth Gospel* (1968), pp. 81ff.

[64] W. C. van Unnik, 'The quotation from the Old Testament in John 12:34', *NovT* 3, 1959, pp. 174ff, concludes that the nearest OT parallel is Ps. 89:37. It is not, however, a direct quotation.

in the latter. John is clear that such a distinction is not only not permissible, but is an evidence of antichrist (4:3). He insists that it is integral to Christian faith to accept that Jesus is the Messiah (5:1). His Christology is in line with the other strands of early Christian thought, as will be clear in the following discussions. Linked with the messianic concept, there is the same emphasis on the Son of God in 1 John as seen above in the gospel (*cf.* 1 Jn. 1:3; 2:22ff.; 3:8; 3:23; 4:15; 5:10, 13, 20).

Acts

The first pronouncement in the early church on the day of Pentecost reached its climax in the assertion that 'God has made him both Lord and Christ, this Jesus whom you crucified' (Acts 2:36). The importance of this is obvious since it is the first public announcement since the resurrection which bears on the person of Christ. The linking of lordship with messiahship is significant, for it shows that in the initial stages of the Christian church one title was not considered sufficient as a description of the present status of Jesus.

But a problem has been raised over the interpretation of this verse. Did it mean that Jesus became Messiah only at his resurrection? Those who maintain this interpretation [65] advance an 'adoptionist' Christology as being the main emphasis in the primitive period. But it rests on a misunderstanding. The fact that in the gospels Jesus and others spoke in terms of his messianic office is sufficient to raise a major objection against the adoptionist theory. Naturally if the gospels are treated as church creations in which the messianic idea was imposed on the facts, some explanation would have to be given for the development of the idea, and Acts 2:36 would lend itself to adaptation in this direction. But it would still be mysterious how the post-resurrection community would have come to so widespread and unanimous a conviction that Jesus was Messiah, if he had never actually acknowledged himself to be so to his disciples.

The words of Acts 2:36 must mean that since the death and resurrection of Jesus, God has exalted him and declared him to be not only Messiah, but a Messiah-Lord, *i.e.* an enthroned Messiah as contrasted with a suffering Messiah. Peter and other early Christians learned with astonishing rapidity the real difference that the resurrection had made for the understanding of Jesus. Addressing an audience, many of whom were probably witnesses of the crucifixion, Peter dared to do what Jesus himself had not done in his ministry, *i.e.* proclaim that Jesus was Messiah. There was no fear that the claim would be understood politically, since a crucified Christ could not be considered a potential political power.

---

[65] *Cf.* J. Weiss, *The History of Primitive Christianity* 1 (Eng. trans. 1937 r.p. 1970), pp. 118f.

Another statement which has also raised problems is Acts 3:20, 'that he (*i.e.* the Lord) may send the Christ appointed for you, Jesus'. Does this refer to the future (*i.e.* the return from heaven) and not to the past? If it does, there might be some justification in the contention that a more primitive theology than the adoptionist theology is here in mind,[66] that is that Jesus will become Messiah only in the future. But another interpretation is possible and indeed more probable, for the appointing need not coincide with the sending. It could refer to a coming in the future of one who is already appointed Messiah (*prokecheirismenon*).[67] There are numerous other references to 'Christ' in Acts, mainly used as a title. Healings were performed 'in the name of Jesus Christ' (3:6; 4:10). OT prophets foretold the sufferings of Christ (3:18). In Acts 4:26 a citation is given from Psalm 2:2 in which the expression 'his Messiah' (RSV has 'Anointed') occurs. This Messiah is immediately identified as 'thy holy servant Jesus, whom thou didst anoint'. Further comment will be made on the servant aspect in a later section, but the important aspect here is the anointing. Since the anointing is mentioned in Luke 4:18 in the passage from Isaiah 61:1,2 quoted by Jesus and applied to himself, it clearly formed part of his consciousness of his calling to the messianic office.[68]

During the earliest period of Christian preaching and teaching, the theme is summed up as preaching 'Jesus as the Christ' (5:42).[69] The apostles recognized this as their mission. It clearly did not exhaust their view of Christ, but was a basic constituent. The same is said of Philip's preaching at Samaria (Acts 8:5; *cf.* 8:12), and of Paul's first testimony at Damascus (9:22). In Peter's speech to Cornelius he refers to Jesus Christ as Lord of all, as well as mentioning God's anointing of Jesus of Nazareth (10:36, 38). In reporting the incident to the Jerusalem church, Peter affirms that God gave the same gift (*i.e.* the Holy Spirit) to us 'when we believed in the Lord Jesus Christ' (11:17). Although in the form of a title, the name here clearly involves the dual concept of Lordship and Messiahship as a confession of faith (*cf.* 24:24). The Messianic theme occurs in Paul's pronouncements at Thessalonica (17:3) and at Corinth (18:5). The same is said of the preaching of Apollos (18:28). It is significant that the audiences in these Acts passages were Jews, for whom the Messianic theme would be particularly relevant. The book ends with Paul preaching the Kingdom and teaching about the Lord Jesus Christ – the two themes evidently closely linked together (Acts 28:31).

---

[66] *Cf.* J. A. T. Robinson, *Twelve New Testament Studies* (1962), pp. 139ff.

[67] According to Bultmann, Jesus' Messiahship was believed by the early church to date from the resurrection (*TNT* 1, p. 27). But it is not surprising that he makes such an assertion, since he has already attributed the Messianic concept to the early church.

[68] *Cf.* W. C. van Unnik, 'Jesus the Christ', *NTS* 8, 1962, pp. 113ff.

[69] *Cf.* R. N. Longenecker, *The Christology of Early Jewish Christianity* p. 79.

Paul

We note first that 'Messiah' (Christ) in the epistles of Paul has now become a proper name. It is probable that Romans 9:5 is the only instance where *Christos* is used specifically in the sense of 'the Messiah'. But the forms 'Jesus Christ' or 'Christ Jesus' or 'Lord Jesus Christ', which occur in all Paul's epistles show how basic the Christ concept was in the apostle's thought. He has no doubt that Jesus is the Messiah. He does not need to demonstrate it. In the Acts record Paul, soon after his conversion, not only recognized that Jesus was Messiah, but actually proved it to the Damascus Jews. The recognition of the Messianic role of Jesus clearly played an important part in his conversion. He had had direct contacts with many early Christians and would certainly have heard of the consistent claim that Jesus was the Messiah (*cf.* Acts 5:42). This was not only one of the major themes of early Christian teaching and preaching, but was also the main cause of Jewish opposition. It was an important factor in the opposition of Saul of Tarsus to the Christian faith. His conversion involved a *volte-face* in his approach to the messianic claims of Jesus.

Paul's presentation of Jesus differs in a radical way from the presentation in the gospels. The vital difference was made by the resurrection of Jesus. The unfolding of the suffering Messiah in the gospels becomes the triumphant living Christ of the epistles, but he is no less Messiah. The title Jesus Christ or Christ Jesus is after all only a stylized form of Jesus the Messiah. When Paul writes, the messianic mission has been accomplished. He develops his own reflections on the new-look messianic concept, which found fulfilment in the risen Christ, who inaugurated a spiritual kingdom.

If, of course, the resurrection of Jesus is interpreted as an experience rather than a fact, a much more radical reinterpretation of Jesus of Nazareth will be involved, and the messianic concept will be replaced by theories of a Hellenistic origin of the exalted Christology of Paul. But any approach to these great Christological themes from the point of view of their close connection with what Jesus himself said and did is to be preferred. This is not, however, the position adopted by the 'Jesus of history' school, which regarded Paul's developments as perversions of the original simplicity of Jesus. It might justly be said that the 'simplicity' suggested is itself a figment of the imagination.

An important passage which throws light on Paul's approach to the historical Jesus is 2 Corinthians 5:16. 'From now on, therefore, we regard no one from a human point of view (*kata sarka*); even though we once regarded Christ from a human point of view, we regard him thus no longer.'[70] Interpreters have differed widely over the meaning of this statement, which has then affected their approach to Paul's Christology.

---

[70] For a detailed discussion of the meaning of this verse, *cf.* J. W. Fraser, 'Paul's Knowledge of Jesus: II Corinthians v. 16 once more', *NTS* 17, 1971, pp. 293–313.

The crucial question is whether Paul is discounting the historical Jesus in favour of a spiritual appreciation of Christ. Those who maintain a lack of continuity between the historical Jesus and the kerygmatic Christ see in this statement support for their view.[71] It is claimed that Paul is drawing a distinction between Christ *kata sarka* (*i.e.* the historical Jesus) and Christ *kata pneuma* (*i.e.* the kerygmatic Christ).

But this interpretation is based on a misunderstanding. Our first consideration must be to decide why Paul used the title 'Christ' if he was referring to the historical Jesus. Admittedly he uses both 'Jesus' and 'Christ' in this epistle as variants for no obvious reasons, but since he uses the simple name 'Jesus' seven times elsewhere in the epistle, it is surprising that he uses 'Christ' here, if the expression is intended to describe the historical Jesus. Moreover, the words *kata sarka* do not describe Christ, but the way in which Paul looks at Christ. The phrase may, therefore, mean that he has come to look at the Christ (Messiah) in a new way. No doubt as a Jew he had shared the same views about the coming Messiah as his fellow Jews, *i.e.* with a strong materialistic political slant. He certainly had to relearn a true approach to messiahship as expounded by Jesus himself [72] and he did not do this *kata sarka* – it required a dynamic vision. There is no basis, therefore, for the view that Paul is here renouncing all interest in the Jesus of history.

The question has been raised whether Paul had actually known Jesus in the flesh[73] and is here refusing to claim any advantage for having done so. While the possibility cannot be ruled out, there are no supporting evidences for it.[74] The apostle's experience of Christ has come through revelation. He may here be combatting the claims of the Christ party at Corinth (1 Cor. 1:12), who may have been critical of Paul because he had not had any contact with Jesus *kata sarka*.[75]

The rest of the New Testament

In a letter addressed to *Hebrew* Christians we might have expected that

[71] *Cf.* R. Bultmann, *TNT*, 1, p. 239; see also his *Faith and Understanding* 1, (1933, Eng. trans. 1960 from ⁶1966), pp. 95–115, where he rejects the view that past history contributes to present faith.

[72] *Cf.* P. E. Hughes, *2 Corinthians* (*NICNT*, 1977) pp. 198f.

[73] *Cf.* C. A. A. Scott, *Christianity according to St Paul* (1932), pp. 12ff. He maintains that Paul shows knowledge not only of the character of the human Jesus, but also of his teaching. This is not to say, however, that Paul's knowledge was firsthand knowledge, although there is reason to believe that he must have received information from firsthand sources.

[74] *Cf.* also R. Bultmann, 'The Primitive Christian Kerygma and the Historical Jesus', in *The Historical Jesus and the Kerygmatic Christ* (ed. C. E. Braaten and R. A. Harrisville, 1964), pp. 15–40; A. Oepke, 'Irrwege in der neueren Paulusforschung', *ThLZ* 77, 1952, pp. 149ff. Bultmann discusses the continuity-discontinuity question, but because he does not admit continuity in any real sense he naturally attaches no importance to any hints of historical knowledge on Paul's part.

[75] See the discussion of 2 Cor. 5:16 by P. E. Hughes, *op. cit., ad loc.* A. Schlatter, *Paulus der Bote Jesus: Eine Deutung Seiner Briefe an die Korinther* (²1956), pp. 559ff., applies *kata sarka* to Paul's former way of thinking. He no longer thinks in this way.

some space would be devoted to demonstrating the Messianic claims of Jesus. Instead we find an exposition of the high-priest theme and the frequent occurrence of the absolute use of 'Christ' as a title for Jesus. This usage links the messianic function with the mediatorial work. This epistle is therefore in line with the other NT evidence in its messianic teaching. The one peculiarity is the Melchizedek theme (see on high priest, pp. 482ff.), which gives some support to the idea of a priestly Messiah.

In *1 Peter*, as in the Pauline epistles, 'Christ' has become exclusively a title, but the frequency of the combination 'Jesus Christ' suggests that it rests on solid grounds of early Christian usage.[76] It is noticeable that in this epistle the title 'Christ' is used in conjunction with the sufferings of Jesus (1 Pet. 1:11, 19; 2:21; 3:18; 4:1, 13; 5:1) and in view of the further clear allusion to the suffering Servant (1 Pet. 2:21–25), the belief in Jesus as a messianic figure, who purposely accepted suffering, is inescapable. However, equally emphasized is the resurrected Messiah (*cf.* 1 Pet. 1:3; 3:21), who has conquered suffering and death.

There is little to add from *2 Peter* and *Jude* except to note that the use of the messianic title is found throughout in the form Jesus Christ, mostly linked with Lord. There is, in fact, only one reference to Jesus which does not include the title 'Christ' (*i.e.* 2 Pet. 1:2). The messianic office is certainly never in question, even if the form has become stereotyped.

The *Revelation* of John contains only three references under the title Jesus Christ (Rev. 1:1, 2, 5). Jesus is presented under other names. The messianic view does not come to the fore even in the consummation of the present age, although there is no doubt that the victorious Lamb performs the functions of the victorious Messiah. What is particularly dominant is the idea of antichrist, who appears unders several names and represents the whole spirit and power of evil which operates in the world. The conflict between the Lamb and Satan is a conflict between Messiah and anti-Messiah. The kingdom of God is confronted with a pseudo-kingdom of evil. The messianism of Revelation reaches its climax in the establishment of the New Jerusalem (see p. 887).

The significance of the title

We have seen, from the preceding survey of the ascription to Jesus of the messianic title, the confirmed belief of the NT church that he was the fulfilment of the long awaited hopes of a deliverer. We have noted, however, that in the process of being the 'fulfilment' Jesus considerably modified the concept. There is nothing to suggest that Jesus as Messiah was ever thought of by Christians in a political sense, and this at once modified

---

[76] W. Kramer, *Christ, Lord and Son of God* (Eng. trans., 1966), p. 68, maintains that the double name 'Jesus Christ' is of Hellenistic origin. But *cf.* Longenecker's caution (*The Christology of Early Jewish Christianity*, pp. 126f.). He regards 1 Peter as Jewish Christian.

many current messianic hopes. Indeed this accounts for the fact that Jesus himself did not use the title Messiah. Yet the Christian recognition of him as Messiah and the title's Jewish background share the common conviction that Messiah was God's agent. He was the one through whom God would break through into the present for the salvation of his people.

In addition to the use of the title Messiah there are two other considerations which must be borne in mind. The first arises from the question whether Jesus' actions confirm the early Christian conviction that Jesus was Messiah. Does the record of his ministry portray him as fulfilling the role of Messiah? A concise answer may be found in Jesus' response to the enquiry of John the Baptist whether he was the Coming One (Mt. 11:3ff.). Jesus contented himself with reminding John the Baptist of his healing work, his raising the dead, and his preaching to the poor. In effect Jesus' answer is indirect. The ministry of Jesus was known already to John, a ministry of compassion, very different from the political aspirations in much current speculation. Jesus was, therefore, probably saying to John that he should revise his view of messiahship. Since the acts and teaching of Jesus in the gospel records can be summed up in terms of a ministry for others, his intention must be to set the messianic office in its true light. It was this kind of Messiah which formed the basis of the early Christians' acceptance of him as 'the Christ'; but the term was considerably extended to include within it the concept of suffering for others, which became powerfully evident in the passion. It would be true to say, therefore, that the early Christians' belief in the messianic office of Jesus was brought about by a combination of his messianic acts and his messianic death, both of which had demanded a considerable modification of what was generally expected from the Messiah.

The other important consideration is the part played by Jesus' implicit rather than explicit claims to messiahship. While these are not directly concerned with the title, they have a bearing on the total significance of Jesus as Messiah and deserve some mention here. The most powerful evidence which can be adduced in this connection is the influence of the OT on the thoughts and words of Jesus. Indeed, the passage cited above is a case in point, since the reply to John the Baptist is couched in language indebted to some passages in Isaiah (35:5, 6; 61:1, cf. also 26:19). In a wide variety of instances Jesus used OT language in a way which showed his acute awareness that he was fulfilling what the OT had predicted.[77] This feature added considerable strength to the Christian conviction that Jesus was the 'fulfilment' of messianic hopes.

---

[77] For a detailed discussion of Jesus' use of the OT, cf. R. T. France, *Jesus and the Old Testament* (1971). He particularly brings out the fact that almost all the OT predictions used by Jesus looked forward to the day of Yahweh, the end of the present order of things. Hence the earthly life as well as the future glory of Jesus is presented as the fulfilment of the OT hopes of the day of Yahweh (pp. 160f.).

The fulfilment motif is particularly significant in those instances where passages which were currently accepted as being messianic are applied to Jesus, either by himself or by others. The way in which in almost all the NT books the OT is cited in support highlights the powerful influence that this consideration had on the Christological views of the early Christians. Since the Messiah concept has such strong roots in the OT, it is not surprising that Jesus came to be known so universally as the Christ.

SON OF DAVID

Closely connected with the title of Messiah is the title Son of David. The title itself occurs several times in the NT, and there are additional indications that the early Christians recognized the significance of the Davidic origin of Jesus. It is necessary to set the NT evidence against the background of the Jewish understanding of the idea.

The background

The idea that Messiah would be a king of the Davidic line can be traced back to the statement in 2 Samuel 7:16 containing God's promise to David, 'And your house and your kingdom shall be made sure for ever before me; your throne shall be established for ever.' This promise is basic to the prophetic predictions regarding the messianic kingdom. It explains how the messianic hope of a restored kingdom was seen to be a fulfilment of the divine promise to David.[78] The prophets looked for a descendant of David, not for a heavenly being. He is frequently called 'David' (Je. 30:9; Ezk. 34:23f.; 37:24; Ho. 3:5) after the Hebrew pattern of seeing an ancestor in his descendants. In line with this is the idea of a coming 'Branch' for David (as in Je. 33:15). It is with David that God will make a covenant.[79] 'David' came to represent a restored Israel. The idea of a Davidic king is, therefore, not unconnected with a political Messiah, but OT prophecy places most emphasis on the religious aspect.

In the intertestamental period the Davidic origin of the Coming One is frequently found, as in Ecclesiasticus 47:11,22; 1 Maccabees 2:57. It has already been noted that Messiah was to be Son of David according to Psalms of Solomon 17, and here again the political and religious elements are inextricably mixed. When the notion of a priestly Messiah developed, as in the Qumran community, the Davidic origin continued to be maintained by postulating two Messiahs, that of Israel being the Davidic figure

---

[78] Cf. S. Mowinkel, He that Cometh (Eng. trans. 1954), pp. 155ff., who discusses the OT expectation of a future Davidic King. Cf. also C. Burger, Jesus als Davidssohn: Eine traditionsgeschichtliche Untersuchung (1970), who surveys the Jewish background as well as the NT occurrences of the Son of David concept. Cf. also Burger's art. in ThLZ 95, 1970, pp. 311f., in which he gives a summary of his book.

[79] Cf. J. Pedersen, Israel: Its Life and Culture 3/4 (²1959), pp. 89ff. Pedersen remarks that only with David's line does the true history of Israel begin.

and that of Aaron being the priestly. It is significant that the Davidic Messiah was too strong to be dropped even in a predominantly priestly movement.

The first century Jewish apocalypse, 4 Ezra, preserves the hope that a Messiah would arise from the seed of David (12:32–34).[80] It is, therefore, indisputable that the coming Messiah was believed to be closely connected with David in contemporary Judaism in the time of Jesus and the development of the Christian church.

The synoptic gospels

In the light of these expectations we can now evaluate the references to the title Son of David and kindred ideas in the NT. The passages of relevance in the synoptic gospels are the genealogies, the Benedictus, passages recording popular use of the title, the discussion over Psalm 110, and the entry of Jesus into Jerusalem.

The tracing of the origin of Jesus from David occurs in both Matthew's and Luke's genealogies, but more prominently in the former. Indeed, it may be noted that David is one of the key figures in Matthew's three-fold division of his genealogy, for he introduces the second section. He also is linked with Abraham in the superscription, which at once brings the Davidic descent into prominence. Many scholars consider that these genealogies were worked over and they are inclined to minimize the significance of the Davidic ascription.[81] But in view of the strong Jewish link between Messiah and David, it is natural to suppose that the early Christians came to regard Jesus as the Son of David. It may be true that the precise title occurs only in Psalms of Solomon 17:21 in a pre-Christian work, as Hahn maintains,[82] but the Jewish expectation of a Davidic king was far too strong to make the rise of the title questionable. The need for the genealogies testifies to the concern of Christians that Jesus fulfilled the necessary qualifications for the Messianic office. Indeed, as Dalman pointed out,[83] the opponents of Jesus would have made much of Jesus' ineligibility for the messianic office if his Davidic descent had been in doubt. The genealogies are therefore an important witness to Jesus as 'Son of David'.

In considering the evidence from the Benedictus (Lk. 1:68ff.), which declares that God 'has raised up a horn of salvation for us in the house of

---

[80] R. Leivestad, *Christ the Conqueror*, p. 9, remarks, 'The Messiah of the apocalypses usually belongs to the Son-of-David type, even though his attributes, partly due to the influence of the Son-of-Man type, may be superhuman and fantastic'. On the contrary, in the Son of man passages, conflict centres on forensic scenes. The Son of man is not an earthly conqueror.

[81] Cf. F. Hahn, *The Titles of Jesus in Christology*, pp. 240ff.

[82] Cf. F. Hahn, *ibid.*, f. 242.

[83] G. Dalman, *The Words of Jesus* (Eng. trans. 1902), 319ff. He says, 'The proper conclusion, therefore, is to maintain, with Paul, the Davidic descent of Jesus, although the continuity of the divine revelation in the Old and the New Testaments does not depend upon it' (p. 321).

his servant David', we observe a strong flavouring of the OT prophetic hope. There is the same mixture of political and religious elements, although the Christians came to interpret the Song in an essentially spiritual sense. Even if the form of the Song is pre-Christian we need not suppose with Hahn[84] that it has been appropriated by the church. It is more reasonable to suppose that Zechariah would have understood it in an OT sense, but that its meaning had been more fully appreciated by the time it was included in Luke's account. This seems probable in the light of the Christian understanding of Jesus as 'horn of salvation' and thus the true Son of David.[85] It should be noted that Luke records a similar idea in the angelic announcement to Mary that her son should be given 'the throne of his father David' (Lk. 1:32).

The evidence for the popular use of the title Son of David comes mainly in Matthew.[86] There is no doubt that he brings out its importance more clearly than the other synoptic writers, but this was determined by his purpose, *i.e.* to expound in a meaningful way to a Jewish audience how Jesus was identified with the coming Messiah. On three separate occasions, according to Matthew, Jesus was popularly referred to as 'Son of David'. The blind man at Jericho (Mt. 9:27; *cf.* Mk. 10:47; Lk. 18:38),[87] the Canaanite woman near Tyre and Sidon (Mt. 15:22) and the people in their questioning after the healing of a blind and dumb demoniac (Mt. 12:23) all use the title.[88] The widespread hope of a Son of David to come may have led those healed and those who observed an act of healing to conclude that Jesus was powerful enough to be the coming deliverer, but it cannot be supposed that the people mentioned by Matthew had any clear notion of identifying the Son of David as Messiah. The Canaanite woman's use of the title is interesting since the title would not convey much to her as a Gentile. She seems in this case to be echoing popular Jewish usage, pre-

[84] *Cf.* Hahn, *op. cit*, p. 243. Hahn sees the Benedictus (Lk. 1:68–75), in which hope is centred on a successor to David, as in essence a pre-Christian hymn. He takes a similar view on Lk. 1:32f.

[85] For an exposition of Luke's theology as a theology of salvation, *cf.* I. H. Marshall, *Luke: Historian and Theologian*, pp. 77ff. Marshall regards the expression 'horn of salvation' as tantamount to 'a mighty Saviour' (p. 99). Salvation is linked closely with a Davidic Messiah in Luke's nativity narratives.

[86] For an examination of this evidence, *cf.* J. M. Gibbs, 'Purpose and Pattern in Mt's use of the title "Son of David" ', *NTS* 10, 1963–4, pp. 446–464. He thinks Matthew uses the material to bring out the following points: (i) Jesus was the messianic Son of David; (ii) His messiahship was so apparent that Gentiles could recognize it; (iii) Gentiles could come to faith through the Jewish Messiah; (iv) The mass of Jews were moving towards accepting Jesus, but were prevented by the opposition of the Jewish leaders; (v) Matthew lays aside the title 'Son of David' in favour of Jesus as Son of God.

[87] V. K. Robbins, 'The Healing of Blind Bartimaeus (10:46–52) in the Marcan Theology', *JBL* 92, 1973, pp. 224–243, maintains that Mark inserted 'Son of David' into the Bartimaeus story. He thinks his reason was to present Jesus as entering into Jerusalem as Son of David, with the relevant authority. He concludes that it is unlikely that Mark has rejected the conception of Jesus as Son of David. He has christianized it to include the idea of Son of God.

[88] *Cf.* Hahn, *op. cit.*, p. 255, who thinks that in the address to the Son of David we have 'the influence of a specific tradition'. He bases this on the evangelist's fondness for the *kyrie* form of address.

sumably because she is addressing a Jew.[89]

Of special importance in the present discussion is the question which Jesus posed for the Jewish leaders. All the synoptists record the incident. The question is stated by Mark in the form, 'How can the scribes say that the Christ is the Son of David?' which is paralleled in Luke, although Matthew says that Jesus elicited from his hearers the statement that the Christ is the Son of David (Mk. 12:35–37; Mt. 22:41–46; Lk. 20:41–44). All are agreed therefore that the religious leaders accepted the identification of Messiah with Son of David. The enigma which Jesus posed was based on the fact that Psalm 110 begins with the words, 'The LORD said unto my Lord'; since this was acknowledged to be a Davidic and also messianic Psalm, it involved David in addressing the Messiah as Lord. The implication is that lordship places the Messiah in a superior status to David, whereas the title Son of David suggests the opposite.

Various interpretations have been assigned to this passage. Some have considered the incident to show that the Davidic descent of the Messiah is being rejected (so Wrede).[90] Others consider that the political aspect is being denied, but the actual descent is being accepted (Cullmann).[91] Yet others consider that the passage presents a two-stage Christology, 'Son of David' for the span of his human life and messianic lordship for the risen Lord (Hahn).[92] Dispute has also arisen over the Davidic origin of Psalm 110, but whatever the answer to that debate it cannot be denied that both Jesus and his contemporaries accepted the Davidic authorship and the force of the question must be judged accordingly. The enigma is allowed to stand without any comeback from the religious leaders. It must be supposed that Jesus saw the application of the words to himself. Yet on this occasion he said nothing publicly to identify himself with the Son of David.[93] It should be noted in passing that Psalm 110 played an important part in later

---

[89] O. Cullmann, *The Christology of the New Testament*, pp. 128f., gives reasons for believing that Jesus' Davidic descent was generally known.

[90] W. Wrede, *The Messianic Secret* (Eng. trans. 1971), p. 46, considers that the title Son of David was being challenged, which raises the question, whether this was because the title was taken to be a perverse opinion on how the Messiah was to come, or whether it arose from too low a view of Messiah. Wrede does not see in the title any anti-political bias. B. E. Meyer, *Ursprung und Anfänge des Christentums* 2 (1921), p. 446, takes it for granted that Jesus is expressly denying his Davidic sonship.

[91] O. Cullmann, *op. cit.*, pp. 131f., suggests that what Jesus is arguing against is that Messiah must be of the physical lineage of David. The implications of the passage are that Messiah must be greater than David to be addressed as Lord by him. Cullmann thinks that an appeal to Davidic origin would suggest political aspirations which Jesus refutes. *Cf.* G. Schneider's discussion of this passage, 'Die Davidssohnfrage (Mk. 12:35–37)', *Bib* 53, 1972, pp. 65–90.

[92] F. Hahn, *The Titles of Jesus in Christology*, pp. 247f. In Hahn's view the title 'Son of David' denotes the Messiah in his humanity and lowliness. In this he echoes the view of G. Bornkamm, *Jesus of Nazareth*, p. 228. Bornkamm treats the title Son of David as not referring in a typical Jewish sense to the Messiah.

[93] The distinction between the Son of David and the Son of Man which arises from Mark's use of the passage is discussed by F. Neugebauer, 'Die Davidssohnfrage (Mark xii. 35–7 parr) und der Menschensohn', *NTS* 21, 1974, pp. 81–108. He points out that as Son of man Jesus is presented as interpreter of the law, but 'Son of David' in Jewish thinking was bound by the law.

Christian thinking on the messianic theme (particularly in the epistle to the Hebrews).

Prior to this incident Jesus was nevertheless acclaimed, as he entered Jerusalem with the words 'Hosanna! Blessed be he who comes in the name of the Lord! Blessed is the kingdom of our father David that is coming! Hosanna in the highest!' (Mk. 11:9). Matthew's account is more concise, summing up the clamour as 'Hosanna to the Son of David' (Mt. 21:15). Luke omits the reference to David and expresses it as 'Blessed is the King who comes in the name of the Lord' (Lk. 19:38). There is no doubt that the crowd's cry presupposes that they saw, however temporarily, Jesus as a Davidic king. In considering the consciousness of Jesus regarding his office, the significant feature in all the accounts is that Jesus did not reject the ascription, although directly challenged to do so by his critics. It is only Matthew, incidentally, who links the Davidic kingship with OT prediction (Zc. 9:9).[94]

John

In the Johannine account of the entry into Jerusalem there is no mention of David, but of him 'who comes in the name of the Lord, even the King of Israel'. (Jn. 12:13). The same passage from Zechariah is cited as in Matthew's account and there can be no doubt that Davidic kingship is implied. There is, however, one passage in John which bears on the idea of Jesus as Son of David, although the title is not used. Some of the people in discussing the position of Jesus were asking, 'Has not the scripture said that the Christ is descended from David, and comes from Bethlehem, the village where David was?' (Jn. 7:42). The question itself reveals popular ignorance about the birthplace of Jesus, which is not surprising. But it accords well with the synoptic evidence that Jesus was born in Bethlehem and with the Davidic origin of the Messiah. The fact that some wanted to arrest Jesus on the grounds that he might after all be the Messiah shows their fears that he might fulfil the conditions. It is not improbable that some reports were circulating about his origins.

Acts

In the account of Paul's speech at Antioch in Pisidia in Acts 13:22ff., an assertion is made about the Davidic origin of Jesus. After a reference to the OT story of God's choice of David as king, Paul is recorded as saying, 'Of this man's posterity God has brought to Israel a Saviour, Jesus, as he promised.' Davidic descent was again regarded as important, presumably

---

[94] It should be noted that at the trial of Jesus, the charge that he claimed to be Son of David in a messianic sense did not form part of the accusation. It would not in itself be regarded as blasphemous (cf. F. F. Bruce, *This is That* (1968), p. 81). In using the language of Daniel at his trial (Mk. 14:62), Jesus went beyond the Son of David claim.

because it carried with it the promise and fulfilment motif which was a powerful apologetic in the Christian approach to the Jews. In the earliest speech in Acts, much is made of David (2:25ff.), and the same passage from Psalm 110 is cited as was used by Jesus himself (2:34ff.).[95] In this case Jesus is specifically identified as David's Lord.

Paul

The Son of David motif is not prominent in Paul's letters, nor indeed in the rest of the NT. But there are a few indications. In the introduction to his Roman letter, where Paul is thought by some to be including a primitive statement of theology (so Dodd),[96] he refers to 'the gospel concerning his Son, who was descended from David according to the flesh' (Rom. 1:3).[97] The words 'according to the flesh' (*kata sarka*) in this statement draw attention specifically to human descent, and are in line with Paul's assumptions elsewhere about the perfect humanity of Jesus.[98] It seems probable that the 'seed of David'[99] was an important part of the earliest Christian approach to an understanding of Jesus. As a Jew Paul would recognize that messianic status was implied in a belief that Jesus was descended from the royal line of David.[100] The kingship motif is developed in other ways, but the basis is found in the fulfilment of the prophetic hope in a coming scion of the house of David.[101]

In another passage of a credal type (2 Tim. 2:8), a similar emphasis on Davidic descent is found and is stated to be an integral part of the gospel. It is certainly significant that in this passage the two prongs of the gospel

[95] It should be noted that if those scholars are right who see the resurrection of Jesus as an enthronement (*cf.* J. H. Hayes, 'The Resurrrection as Enthronement and the earliest church Christology', *Int* 22, 1968, pp. 342ff., it would carry with it more indirect connections in Acts with the royal messianism theme. *Cf.* also E. Schweizer, 'The Concept of the Davidic "Son of God" in Acts and its Old Testament background', in *Studies in Luke-Acts* (ed. L. E. Keck and J. L. Martyn, 1966), pp. 186ff.

[96] C. H. Dodd, *The Apostolic Preaching and its Developments* ([2]1963), p. 14. Dodd argues that the language is unlike that of Paul elsewhere and he therefore finds it hard to believe that Paul coined the passage.

[97] On Rom. 1:3ff, see E. Schweizer, 'Rom. 1:3f. und der Gegensatz von Fleisch und Geist vor und bei Paulus', *EvT* 15, 1955, pp. 563–571; E. Linnemann, 'Tradition und Interpretation in Rom. 1:3ff.', *EvT* 31, 1971, pp. 264–275.

[98] In his article, 'Jesus – Flesh and Spirit: An Expositon of Romans i. 3–4', *JTS* 24, 1973, pp. 40–68, J. D. G. Dunn argues that *kata sarka* means that Paul treats Davidic sonship in a somewhat pejorative manner as a defective understanding of Jesus. He further maintains that Jesus became Son of God through the Spirit.

[99] The form *ek spermatos Daveid* follows the ancient traditional pattern in genealogies (*cf.* Hahn, *The Titles of Jesus in Christology*, p. 247).

[100] D. C. Duling, 'The Promises to David and their Entrance into Christianity', *NTS*, 20, 1973, pp. 55–77, discusses the significance of the promises found in OT and in late Jewish literature and finds echoes of the idea in the NT. According to him the point of entry of the promise tradition into early Christianity is Rom. 1:3–4. He finds evidence of it in 2 Cor. 6:4–7:1, although David is not mentioned. But 2 Sa. 7:14 lies behind the passage. Duling regards 2 Tim. 2:8 as later Christian tradition.

[101] F. J. Leenhardt, *Romans* (Eng. trans. 1961 from *CNT*, 1957), p. 36, considers that the Davidic origin of the Messiah was a postulate of faith. According to him, 'the name of David sums up the whole history of Israel and expresses the hope that one day it will find a glorious fulfilment'.

are said to be that Jesus was (i) risen from the dead and (ii) descended from David.

The rest of the New Testament

In the letter to the *Hebrews*, the writer assumes that his readers will know that Jesus was descended from Judah, since this is why he goes to such lengths to expound another order of priesthood which did not depend on Aaronic descent (Heb. 7:14). It is in *Revelation* that Davidic descent is again specifically implied in the title 'Root of David' which is applied to Jesus (Rev. 5:5; 22:16).[102] In the first of these occurrences the name comes in a liturgical passage and is linked with the title 'Lion of the tribe of Judah'. Since in this case the conquering aspect is stressed, the Davidic kingship is unmistakable. In the message to one of the seven churches Jesus is introduced as 'the true one, who has the key of David' (Rev. 3:7), which must be understood as expressing his royal authority.

SERVANT

Although the title 'Servant of God' was never used by Jesus and is never attributed to him by the evangelists, it seems to have become a conviction in early Christian belief and must therefore be considered as a contribution to Christology. Reference will be made to the suffering servant idea in the discussion on the meaning of the Son of man title, but it is necessary here to examine the probability that Jesus was conscious of fulfilling the role of the servant. In this section our main concern will be to focus on the servant concept itself. The suffering aspect will be more fully dealt with in the section on the work of Christ.

The Old Testament background

Since the idea of the servant of God comes directly from the servant songs in Isaiah, these are the obvious passages to comb for background information, but there are some preliminary considerations to take into account. The Greek expression *pais Theou* can mean either 'child of God' or 'servant of God', the latter being the meaning in the majority of cases in the intertestamental period. This carries on the strongly attested OT usage of *'ebed* or *'ebed Yahweh*, i.e. the use of 'servant' in a religious sense. Zimmerli[103] gives five different OT uses: (i) the humble self-description of the pious in the presence of God, (ii) 'servants of Yahweh' in the plural as denoting the pious, (iii) *'ebed Yahweh* in the singular as a description of

---

[102] In discussing the references to David in the book of Revelation, Hahn considers the statements to refer to the future office of Jesus (*op. cit.*, pp. 244ff.). But he comes to this conclusion only by setting aside the reference to the slain lamb. There is, however, no justification for doing this.

[103] *Cf.* W. Zimmerli and J. Jeremias, *The Servant of God* (Eng. trans. 1957), pp. 44ff.

Israel, (iv) *'ebed Yahweh* as a title for specially distinguished instruments of God, and (v) the servant of God as denoting Messiah, which is found only in the form 'my servant' where God is the speaker. These different uses prepare the way for an understanding of the Isaianic servant passages.[104] As a background to the NT use we are concerned with this special OT person who is referred to in the songs known as the servant songs (Is. 42:1–4; 49:1–6; 50:4–9; 52:13—53:12). There has been much debate over whether the servant in these songs is an individual or represents Israel collectively. It is beyond our purpose here to examine the matter and we must be content to observe that both interpretations are possible and would have been compatible in Hebrew thought. Both aspects may have contributed to the NT application of the passages to Jesus Christ, although the individual concept seems more probable. Certainly the task of the servant in these passages is more intelligible if an individual who is called by God and endowed with his Spirit is in mind. He is to restore Israel and will establish justice among the people. Moreover his mission will be universal (*cf.* Is. 49:5ff.), to declare his judgment among the nations. To achieve his end he must expect suffering which is, however, vicarious in nature.

We need to enquire to what extent the later Jews appreciated the significance of the coming servant of the Lord. There is difference of opinion over whether they conceived of a suffering servant, but the evidence does not support a general expectation of a suffering Messiah.[105] That suffering, if sent by God, had atoning value was acknowledged in the Talmud.[106] But this idea was never specifically ascribed to the Messiah in pre-Christian times. Indeed there is a striking absence of the use of the title 'servant of God' of the Messiah in late Jewish literature. He is, however, addressed a few times by God as 'my servant'.[107] Jeremias[108] makes three points in summing up the messianic interpretation of the Isaianic servant in Palestinian Judaism. (1) It was limited to Isaiah (42:1ff., 43:10; 49:1f., 6f.; 52:13ff.). (ii) In the case of 42:1ff. and 52:13ff. messianic interpretation is constant from pre–Christian times. (iii) 'As far as the messianic interpretation of the 'suffering' in Isa. 53:1–12 is concerned, this can again be traced back with

---

[104] Zimmerli, *op. cit.*, p. 50, concludes that 'servant of God' as a real title for the Messiah never existed in Judaism.

[105] *Cf.* E. Lohse, *Martyrer und Gottesknecht*, *FRLANT*, n.f. 46 (1955), pp. 64ff, who admits some idea of an atoning significance in death, because such an idea had a connection with Is. 53.

[106] *Cf.* W. D. Davies, *Paul and Rabbinic Judaism* (1948), pp. 262ff. He points out that passages attesting the atoning efficacy of suffering are plentiful in rabbinic writings. E. P. Sanders, *Paul and Palestinian Judaism*, p. 170, states that although sacrifices may atone for sins, suffering is more effective because it is more costly. It should be noted, however, that suffering and punishment were also linked in Rabbinic thought. For a similar idea of Qumran literature, *cf.* 1 *QS* 8:3f.

[107] *Cf.* Ezk. 34:23f.; 37:24f.; Zc. 3:8; 4 Ezr. 7:28; 13:32; 37:52; 14:9; 7:28; Syr. Bar. 70:9; Targ. Is. 42:1; 43:10; 52:13; Targ. Zc. 3:8; Targ. Ezk. 34:23f.; 37:24f.

[108] In W. Zimmerli and J. Jeremias, *op. cit.*, p. 77.

great probability to pre-Christian times.' Jeremias[109] cites several passages from Jewish writings in support of the view that the Messiah suffers vicariously to expiate the sins of Israel. But the third point has been vigorously challenged.[110]

The evidence from Qumran, while not explicit, suggests a continuing belief in the inevitability of suffering linked with echoes of the servant songs of Isaiah. Longenecker[111] makes the following three points: (i) The psalmist in the Hymns of Thanksgiving (The Teacher of Righteousness) was conscious of being God's servant. (ii) In pursuing the divine will, the Teacher and the community recognized that persecution and suffering were their lot. (iii) They often expressed themselves in the language of the servant songs.[112]

The synoptic gospels

There is evidence to show that the early church came to regard Jesus as the servant (cf. Acts 3:13, 26; 4:27–30). But the prior question is whether Jesus thought of himself in terms of the servant and whether his contemporaries would have recognized it. We have seen good grounds for supposing that there was no clear background of a suffering Messiah. Nevertheless Matthew seems to have regarded Jesus in this light. We will first examine passages in which citations from the servant songs are applied to Jesus.

(i) After the healing of Peter's mother-in-law and many others, Isaiah 53:4 is cited by Matthew with one of his special introductory formulae stressing fulfilment (Mt. 8:17). This quotation is not made by Jesus, but it

---

[109] W. Zimmerli and J. Jeremias, *op. cit.*, p. 78. Among the passages cited are Test B 3:8; Siphre Lev; B. Sahn 98b; Midr. Sam. 19:1; Pesiqt R. 31 and 36.

Some comment must be made in this context on the connection between the suffering servant theme and the binding of Isaac in Jewish writings. *Cf.* N. Hillyer, 'The Servant of God', *EQ* 41, 1969, pp. 143–160. He produces evidence from both Jewish literature and the NT to support a strong connection between the two themes. He does not consider that the absence from the NT of clear-cut references to the binding of Isaac as an explanation of the atonement is a barrier. He thinks there is reason to suppose that Jesus may have been responsible for revealing the sacrifice of Isaac as a factor in the servant Christology. He finds some striking parallels between Gn. 22 and 1 Pet. 1:1–12. For the idea of the suffering servant of Is. 53 as viewed as a new Isaac, *cf.* R. A. Rosenberg, 'Jesus, Isaac and the Suffering Servant', *JBL* 84, 1965, pp. 381ff. He suggests that the background might be the ritual of the humiliation of the king known to have been practiced in Babylon and Syria. *Cf.* also H. J. Schoeps, 'The Sacrifice of Isaac in Paul's theology', *JBL* 65, 1946, pp. 385ff; *idem, Paul: the Theology of the Apostle in the Light of the History of Jewish Religion* (Eng. trans. 1961), pp. 141ff. J. E. Wood, 'Isaac Typology in the New Testament', *NTS* 14, 1968, pp. 583ff., sets out the possible allusions to this motif in the NT.

[110] *Cf.* M. Rese, 'Überprüfung einiger Thesen von Joachim Jeremias zum Thema des Gottesknechtes im Judentum', *ZTK*, 60, 1963, pp. 21–41. Rese considers that Jeremias has combined the concept of the suffering servant with the Davidic Messiah and has not sufficiently shown that suffering formed an essential part of Messiah's office.

[111] R. N. Longenecker, *The Christology of Early Jewish Christianity*, p. 105.

[112] For a fuller treatment of the Qumran evidence on the servant theme, *cf.* W. H. Brownlee, *BASOR* 132, 1953, pp. 8ff.; 135, 1954, pp. 33ff.; F. F. Bruce, *This is That*, pp. 91ff.

reflects Matthew's own awareness of a messianic fulfilment. Because there is no mention here of expiation from sins, M. Hooker[113] denies that Jesus or his earliest followers identified Jesus as the servant. But even without the expiatory element, the connection between the servant's work and sicknesses is clearly reflected in the healing ministry of Jesus. That healing ministry was not considered to be expiatory in early Christian thought.

(ii) Another quotation included by Matthew, introduced by the same formula as the previous one, is found in Matthew 12:18–21. It is an extensive passage from Isaiah 42:1–4. It follows the statement that Jesus exhorted his followers whom he had healed not to make him known. The servant passage speaks of the refusal of the servant to wrangle or cry aloud. Admittedly there is again no emphasis on suffering, but it seems undeniable that Matthew was identifying Jesus in his mind with Isaiah's servant.[114]

It is clearly important to consider whether Jesus thought of himself in terms of the Isaianic servant of the Lord. In his teaching recorded in the synoptic gospels the only direct quotation from the servant songs is found in Luke 22:37; here Jesus appeals to Isaiah 53:12, with a strongly worded fulfilment formula, which is emphasized by reiteration. This strong fulfilment motif suggests a firm consciousness on Jesus' part that the OT servant figure was in some way being fulfilled in him. Admittedly the context is difficult, for Jesus suggests that the disciples should prepare for other more violent tactics to be used against them. He himself would soon be numbered among the transgressors, precisely as the servant of the Lord in Isaiah. But was he advocating armed resistence? This is so totally alien to his teaching in general that either the saying must be considered unauthentic[115] or else must be interpreted in a metaphorical way.[116] This latter must be considered more probable, since the former explanation would itself raise an insoluble problem over why the Christian tradition ever preserved so enigmatic a saying. Those who adopt the former alternative then claim to have removed all trace that Jesus ever thought of himself as the servant.

But not all of those who accept the authenticity of the saying agree that the citation shows that Jesus saw his role as the servant as involving vicarious suffering. If it is maintained that only passages which connect the servant songs with vicarious suffering are to be regarded as valid evidence that Jesus was claiming to fulfil the Isaianic servant, Luke 22:37 would have

---

[113] M. Hooker, *Jesus and the Servant* (1959), p. 83. She maintains that Mt. 8:16–17, far from proving that Jesus was thought of as one who suffered for the sins of others, points in the opposite direction.

[114] For a general view of Jesus as Servant, *cf.* B. Gerhardsson, 'Gottes Sohn, als Diener Gottes. Messias, Agape und Himmels – herrschaft nach dem Matthäusevangelium', *StTh* 27, 1973, pp. 73–106.

[115] *Cf.* J. M. Creed, *Luke* (1930), p. 270.

[116] F. F. Bruce, *op. cit*, p. 95, expresses the situation as follows: 'Their Master was about to be condemned as a law-breaker and they would find themselves outlaws . . . they might as well act the part properly; hence His reference to a sword.' When the disciples took the words too literally Jesus dropped the subject. *Cf.* also F. C. Burkitt, *The Gospel History and its Transmission* (1906), pp. 140ff.

to be ruled out.[117] But this is an unreasonable demand. The fact that Jesus applied any part of Isaiah 53 to himself raises a strong probability that he saw himself as fulfilling the whole role including the vicarious suffering. It cannot be said that the absence of mention of the suffering element is a bar to the self-identification of Jesus with the servant.[118] It would seem that Luke 22:37 is a definite witness to the fact that Jesus thought of himself in such terms.

In addition to this citation there are certain allusions which must also be taken into account. Some of these belong to the discussion of the mission of Christ and will be mentioned again in the section on that theme. But the evidence has some bearing on Jesus' awareness of his own person and must be considered here. Some appeal strongly to Mark 10:45/Matthew 20:28 to support the servant concept, although it is strongly disputed by others.[119] The idea of serving would naturally link with the Isaianic figure. Nevertheless there is a difference in that Isaiah's servant is servant of God, and Son of man in the Markan saying speaks of service to men. It would be safe to conclude that although Mark 10:45 does not demand the servant background, it makes good sense to see it there. There is, of course, no mention of ransom (*lytron*) in Isaiah 53, but there is a close connection between ransom and vicarious suffering. There is no great step from the servant making himself an offering (*āšām*) for sin (Is. 53:10), and the Son of man giving his life as a ransom (or equivalent substitute). Yet another pointer in the same direction is the use of 'many' both in Isaiah 53:12 and in Mark 10:45.

Some reference must be made to the possibility of an allusion to the servant concept in the words of institution at the last supper (Mk. 14:24 *et par*). Although the major background is clearly Exodus 24 and Jeremiah 31, it is possible that Isaiah 53 may also have contributed. The references to the covenant, to the 'pouring out', and to the 'many' all find parallels in the servant songs. It is not too much to claim that Jesus is here giving a definite theological explanation of his own.[120] His statement is a contribu-

---

[117] *Cf.* M. Hooker, *op. cit.*, p. 86. The latter takes an opposite line from J. Jeremias, '*pais Theou*', *TDNT* 5, p. 716; W. Manson, *Jesus the Messiah* (1943), pp. 111,132; V. Taylor, *Jesus and His Sacrifice* (1937), pp. 190ff.

[118] *Cf.* R. T. France, 'The Servant of the Lord in the Teaching of Jesus', *TB*, 19 (1968), pp. 26–52 (esp. 30–32), who argues from the use of Jesus in Lk. 22:37 of the Isaianic phrase 'was numbered with the transgressors' that the idea of vicarious suffering could not have been absent from the mind of Jesus. Moreover, the strong 'fulfilment' formula which introduces the citation suggests that Jesus identified himself with the one spoken of, *i.e.* the suffering servant.

[119] There has been much discussion over the relevance of Mk. 10:45 to the servant discussion. C. K. Barrett, 'The Background of Mark 10:45', in *New Testament Essays: Studies in Memory of T. W. Manson* (ed. A. J. B. Higgins, 1959), pp. 1–18, argues for Dn. 7. But R. T. France, *Jesus and the Old Testament*, pp. 116ff., criticizes Barrett and concludes for Is. 53 as background to the saying.

[120] For a succinct statement of views on this, *cf.* R. T. France (*TB* 19, 1968, pp. 37ff.). He concludes that we have here 'a deliberate theological explanation by Jesus of the necessity for His death, and it is not only

tory factor in our understanding of his function as servant of Yahweh.

Less certain, but nevertheless of some significance, are the predictions by Jesus of his sufferings (Mk. 9:12 and parallels). It cannot be maintained that all references to the suffering of Christ are indirect testimony to him as suffering servant, but where there is a specific reference to OT fulfilment ('it is written'), it is not unreasonable to see an awareness on Jesus' part that the coming passion was predicted in Isaiah 53. A similar background of the Isaianic servant can be seen in the heavenly voice at the baptism of Jesus (Mt. 3:17, Mk. 1:11, Lk. 3:22), particularly in the expression 'My Son the Beloved' (*ho huios mou ho agapētos*)[121] which may well be an echo of Isaiah 42:1.[122]

From the above evidence one other feature of the Servant concept may be noted, and that is the alignment with the Son of man. Special consideration will be given in a later section (pp. 276ff.) to the suffering aspect of the Son of man,[123] but there can be no doubt that the parallels with the suffering servant idea are significant.[124] There is no reason to think that the two ideas are mutually exclusive. They are, in fact, complementary.

John

Only one passage in the fourth gospel (*i.e.* 12:38) directly cites the servant songs. John is commenting on the people's lack of belief in Jesus in spite of the signs performed among them, and relates this lack of response to Isaiah 53:1, which he quotes verbatim from the LXX text. The context in which John places it contains no reference to suffering, but only to the obdurateness of the hearers. Does this mean that the passage can be discounted as evidence that Jesus was thought of in terms of the servant?[125] It might well be so if there were no supporting clues. The idea of Jesus'

---

drawn from Is. 53, but specifically refers to the vicarious and redemptive suffering which is the central theme of that chapter'.

[121] In an article, 'Son of God or Servant of Yahweh? – A Reconsideration of Mark 1:11', *NTS* 15, 1968–9, pp. 326–336, I. H. Marshall refutes the view that in the baptismal account an original *pais* has been replaced by *huios* (see next note). He considers that it is more correct to say that Jesus is the Messiah because he is the Son of God, not vice versa.

[122] M. D. Hooker, *Jesus and the Servant*, pp. 70ff, denies the allusion to Is. 42:1 on the grounds of its disagreement with the LXX. But see R. T. France's criticism of this view, *op. cit.*, p. 40 n. 74. Jeremias, (*The Servant of God*, W. Zimmerli and J. Jeremias, p. 81), considers that the voice at the baptism was originally purely an echo of Is. 42:1. Many scholars link it with Ps. 2:7, but Jeremias thinks that before Mk. wrote, the *pais mou* of Is. 42:1 became clarified as *huios mou* on Hellenistic territory.

[123] F. F. Bruce, *This is That*, pp. 97ff., maintains that the influence of the fourth Servant Song is seen in the gospels interwoven in large measure with the evidence for Jesus' use of the expression Son of man.

[124] In spite of the claim by R. H. Fuller, *The Foundations of New Testament Christology*, pp. 118f., that H. Tödt and M. D. Hooker have demolished the thesis that Jesus thought of himself as the servant of the Lord. In this work, Fuller expresses a different opinion from that advocated in his *The Mission and Achievement of Jesus* (1954), pp. 55ff.

[125] *Cf.* M. Hooker, *op. cit.*, p. 106, who says of Jn. 12:38, 'There is no indication that the author intended any identification of Jesus with the Servant'. She regards the passage as no more than a proof-text.

lifting up being a glorification, which features in the immediately preceding passage (12:20–36), may well be indebted to the servant songs (cf. Is. 52:13).[126] It cannot be maintained that the context of the citation is in no way connected with the theme of the passion. It might even be claimed that it is set where it is to act as a kind of prelude to the passion story.[127]

The baptism narrative in John (1:24ff.), as in the synoptics, may furnish other allusions to the servant theme. If the correct reading in John 1:34 is 'the chosen of God' (*eklektos*), attested as it is by some old MSS, it would in all probability depend on Isaiah 42:1.[128] But most editors prefer 'Son' as the more likely reading, in which case Psalm 2 is a more probable parallel. Greater weight can be given to the statement of John the Baptist in John 1:29, 36, where Jesus is declared to be the Lamb of God, a description which he did not deny. Since the Isaianic Servant was described in terms of a lamb (Is. 53:7), there is some probability that a connection of thought existed. Admittedly it is difficult to maintain that 'the Lamb of God' as a title was recognized as being equivalent to 'the servant of God'; but it is equally difficult to avoid the conclusion that the reference to the Lamb by John the Baptist carried overtones of the suffering servant of Isaiah.[129]

Acts

The three passages in Acts where the word 'servant' is used as a description of Jesus (3:13, 26; 4:27–30) would seem to show the strong belief of the primitive community in the identification of Jesus as the servant of Isaiah.[130]

---

[126] R. E. Brown, *John* (*AB*, 1966), p. 146, remarks that the statement that the Son *must* be lifted up (cf. Jn. 3:14) reflects the theme that the lifting up of Jesus was predicted in Scripture, especially in Is. 52–53. Brown considers that the use of Is. 53:1 in Jn. 12:38 explains the rejection of Jesus, on the grounds that Is. 53 is the song *par excellence* of the rejected and despised.

[127] M. Hooker, *op. cit*, p. 106, although considering the lifting-up theme in Jn. 3:14; 8:28; 12:32, minimizes its importance by commenting that it reflects the meditation of a mystic and tells us nothing about the use of the servant theme in the early church.

[128] Cf. Jeremias, (*The Servant of God*, W. Zimmerli and J. Jeremias, p. 82), who cites Jn. 1:34 in support of his contention that *pais* was the original form of the words in the baptismal saying from heaven. Both Lindars, *John* (*NCB*, 1972), p. 140, and Marshall, *NTS* 15, 1968–9, p. 330, criticize Jeremias' use of the evidence.

[129] It must be noted that *amnos*, the word used for lamb in both Is. 53: 7 (LXX) and in Jn. 1:29 is not used elsewhere in the NT as a title for Christ. On the other hand, in the Apocalypse of John the word *arnion* is used repeatedly as a title for Christ. M. Hooker, *op. cit.*, pp. 103ff., maintains that since *amnos* is not used elsewhere as a title for Christ, it is improbable that it is so used in Jn. 1:29 as an equivalent for servant. Jeremias (*The Servant of God*, W. Zimmerli and J. Jeremias, pp. 82f.), takes a different view, seeing the Aramaic *talyâ* behind *amnos* and then maintaining that its meaning is ambiguous, (*i.e.* lamb, boy or servant). There is a difference between Isaiah's lamb which is shorn and Jn. 1:29 where the lamb is clearly sacrificial in that it bears away sin, but there are certainly sacrificial features about the servant concept in Is. 53. For other comments on the linguistic debate over Jn. 1:29, cf. C. F. Burney, *The Aramaic Origin of the Fourth Gospel* (1922), pp. 104ff; and C. H. Dodd, *The Interpretation of the Fourth Gospel*, pp. 235f.; C. K. Barrett, *John* (²1978), *ad loc.*, idem, 'The Lamb of God', *NTS* 1, 1955, pp. 210ff.

[130] For some who have supported this understanding of *pais*, cf. F. F. Bruce, *The Acts of the Apostles* (1951), pp. 107f.; V. Taylor, *The Atonement in New Testament Teaching* (²1945), pp. 18f.; J. Jeremias, *TDNT*, 5, pp. 705ff.

The idea of *pais Theou* appears to be essentially Jewish and is therefore in keeping with early Jewish Christian usage in these Acts passages. But the identification with the servant songs has been disputed on the grounds that the word 'servant' is applied to David in Acts 4:25, as well as being applied to Jesus in 4:27, thus showing a general rather than a specific use (*cf.* also Lk. 1:69, where *pais* is also used of David).[131] But since *pais* is twice used of Jesus in Acts 3, both times in the sense of a person whom God has specifically exalted, the conclusion is inescapable that Luke is recording a specific identification and not merely a general use. The reference in 3:13 (which contains an allusion to the exaltation of the servant in Is. 52:13), is to the suffering of Jesus at his trial, while that in 3:26 is to the servant's mission in turning people away from wickedness. Apart from these specific references to *pais*, Acts 8:32f. (= Is. 53:7–8) contains a direct quotation which is applied specifically to Jesus, although no indication is given of how it was applied. No reference is made to sins. Taking a broad view of the evidence, it is not unreasonable to see in Acts an early recognition of the appropriateness of the servant idea as a description of Jesus. Having admitted this, however, an enigma remains. Why does the title Servant occur only in the first part of Acts? Moreover, why did it fail to capture the attention of other NT writers? Some suggestions will later be given on this point.

Paul

Several passages are of value in enabling us to determine to what extent Paul thought of Jesus as the suffering servant. He had received a tradition which directly linked the death of Christ with people's sins (1 Cor. 15:3), in precisely the same way as the suffering servant. Moreover, the phrase 'according to the scriptures' (*kata tas graphas*) stresses that it is an OT fulfilment. Similarly the tradition of the institution of the last supper (1 Cor. 11:23–25) shows the link between the passion of Jesus and the broken bread and poured out wine. In such a passage as Philippians 2:6–11 some background of the suffering servant may be detected,[132] particularly in his humiliation and obedience. Nevertheless no specific identification is made.[133] There is however a close similarity between the Hebrew text of Isaiah 53 and the Philippian passage (see further discussion on pp. 345ff.).

---

[131] *Cf.* M. D. Hooker, *op. cit.*, p. 109: 'The fact that in Acts the title is used first of David and then of Jesus, suggests that no particular reference is intended.' This statement is true of Acts 4, but does not take into account Acts 3.

[132] A. Feuillet, *RB* 72, 1965, pp. 325–360; 481–507; W. Zimmerli and J. Jeremias, *The Servant of God*, p. 97. This view is also advocated by J. T. Sanders, *The New Testament Christological Hymns* (1971), pp. 58ff. Jeremias sees the expression *heauton ekenōsen* in Phil. 2:7 as directly related to Is. 53:12.

[133] O. Cullmann, *The Christology of the New Testament*, pp. 76f., discusses why Paul does not use the servant title for Jesus. He explains it by mentioning that the servant concept primarily relates to Christ's earthly work, whereas Paul's interests include Christ's exaltation. Hence his preference for *kyrios*.

It is totally unacceptable to explain away this allusion to the suffering servant by maintaining that no mention is made of vicarious suffering nor of forgiveness of sins. It was common knowledge that Jesus in his death had suffered. Indeed, if this were not a well-known fact, we should have expected some explanation. In any case death on a cross is the supreme form of suffering. Admittedly no reference is made to forgiveness of sins, but the whole point of the passage is to promote humility, not to expound the atonement.

In two passages in Romans (4:25 and 8:32–34) similar ideas to the servant songs occur. In Romans 4:25 Jesus is said to be delivered (*paredothē*) for our trespasses and raised for our justification, and in 8:32 God is said to have given up (*paredōken*) his Son. In both cases the same verb is used as that found in Isaiah 53:6 (LXX). It is highly probable that Paul has been influenced in his language by his familiarity with Isaiah's servant songs. It is not necessary to suppose that had this been the case he would have been more specific in his use of the suffering servant concept. It should be noted that the one definite quotation in Paul's epistles from the servant songs occurs in Romans but is used in a non-Christological way (Rom. 15:21 = Is. 52:15 LXX).

The rest of the New Testament

In the letter to the *Hebrews* an allusion to Isaiah 53:12 (LXX) occurs in 9:28. The statement that Christ was offered once 'to bear the sins of many' is certainly reminiscent of Isaiah's language. It comes towards the end of the long section portraying Christ as high priest, who is also the victim. His death as a sacrificial offering has just been mentioned (9:26). The view of Jesus here is therefore of a suffering saviour.[134] The idea behind the whole passage is clearly of the suffering servant as well as the high priest.

A more direct allusion to the suffering servant, identifying him with Jesus, is found in *1 Peter* 2:21–25. In this passage there are many allusions to Isaiah 53 (LXX); 1 Peter 2:22 = Isaiah 53:9; 1 Peter 2:24a = Isaiah 53:12; 1 Peter 2:24b = Isaiah 53:5; 1 Peter 2:25 = Isaiah 53:6. Although the order of the citations is changed there is no doubt that Peter must have had the Isaiah passage in mind in speaking of the sufferings of Christ.[135] The whole passage is intended to illustrate the supreme example of suffering. This is a remarkable case of a practical problem (suffering) which led into a doctrinal statement, expressed almost wholly in OT language and reaching its climax in an explanation which is removed from the original theme. The

---

[134] *Cf.* M. Hooker, *Jesus and the Servant*, p. 124, who concludes that the concept of Is. 53 'very probably' lies behind this passage.

[135] *Contra cf.* M. Hooker, *op. cit*, p. 125, who does not doubt that this passage is based on Is. 53, but who contends that the author first recalls the humiliation of Christ and this then leads on to an expositon of Christ's sufferings in relation to sin.

sufferings of Christ, although an example for all believers, are nevertheless differentiated from the sufferings of believers in being vicarious ('he bore our sins in his body on the tree'; see the section on the work of Christ, pp. 474ff.). Another passage in this epistle which is along similar lines is 1 Peter 3:18 ('he died, the just for (*hyper*) the unjust'). With this may be linked 1 Peter 1:10, 11 where the prophets are said to have been led by the Spirit when predicting the sufferings of Christ and the subsequent glory. There is no prophetical passage which does this more superbly than Isaiah 53, and it is therefore not surprising to find allusions to this chapter in subsequent sections of the epistle.

In the remaining NT books there are no allusions to the servant idea.[136] The foregoing brief survey has shown that, although the idea seems to have played an important part in the consciousness of Jesus, it was not as dominant in early Christian thought. In later developments it gave way to other titles like 'Lord' and 'Son of God'. Yet it is sufficiently important for us to enquire into the significance of the servant idea for an understanding of NT Christology.

Its significance for Christology

The suffering servant clearly plays an important role in our understanding of the work of Christ, but our present purpose is to discover its function for the person of Christ. Some go as far as to speak of a servant Christology, but this tends to become restricting. It is better to speak of the contribution which the servant theme makes to the many facets of early Christology. Jeremias[137] finds the following predicates made about Jesus from the servant theme: *ho pais* (the Servant), perhaps *ho huios tou Theou* (the Son of God), *ho amnos tou Theou* (the Lamb of God), *to arnion* (the Lamb), *ho eklektos*, *ho eklelegmenos* (the Chosen One), *ho agapētos* (the Beloved), and *ho dikaios* (the Just). These are all descriptive names which may be derived from the servant songs. To these Jeremias adds *hilasmos* (propitiation or expiation, as in 1 Jn. 2:2; 4:10) from Isaiah 53:10, and the description of the servant as an intercessor. It may well be that Jeremias has claimed too much, but the contribution of the servant concept to the Christological theme is impressive. The derived titles are wholly in harmony with the view that both Jesus and the earliest Christians recognized Jesus as the servant, but at the same time recognized that this concept on its own would never have been adequate for a full expression of the identity of Jesus. It rapidly gave rise to other ideas.

[136] It has been maintained that the Lamb idea in Revelation is derived from Is. 52:13ff., although a different Greek word is used. *Cf.* V. Taylor *The Atonement in New Testament Teaching* ([3]1958), p. 36; J. Jeremias, *TDNT*, pp. 338ff. Against this view, *cf.* M. Hooker, *op. cit.*, p. 126. H. B. Swete, *The Apocalypse of St John* ([2]1907), p. 78, suggested that a non-LXX text of Isaiah may have been used, which could account for the different word for 'lamb'.

[137] *Cf.* Jeremias (*The Servant of God*, W. Zimmerli and J. Jeremias), pp. 94f.

Some attention must be given to the probable reason for the fewness of the texts relating to the servant. It has been maintained that Jesus 'only allowed himself to be known as the Servant in his esoteric and not in his public preaching'.[138] This is probably true, but it does not explain why the servant concept is not more evident in the NT epistles. Another explanation is that it was a reaction to the redemptive idea of salvation in the contemporary world. 'Probably, therefore, ideas current within both Judaism and Grecian religious philosophy regarding the nature of divine salvation must be credited in large measure for the muting of a suffering servant motif in the church' (Longenecker).[139] It is certainly probable that Christians with a Gentile background would be less able to appreciate the significance of the servant concept, and that other ideas would be sought that could express the same truth in ways more readily understood.[140] Although this explanation has much to commend it, Gentile Christians for whom the LXX was sacred scripture would surely not be unmindful of the significance of the servant songs. The cross might be foolishness to the unconverted Greek mind, but this cannot be postulated of Gentile converts.

One of the main problems of a discussion of this sort is that too much emphasis tends to be placed on a quantitative assessment of evidence.[141] But in the case of the servant concept this may lead to misleading conclusions. It must always be remembered that it is unreasonable to expect that all concepts will continually recur throughout the NT literature. In view of the comparatively small quantity of apostolic writings, quantitative evaluations of theological ideas are precarious. It is better to regard the servant concept as one of the many facets of the rich Christology of the early church, which particularly, although not exclusively, manifested itself among Jewish Christians. More will be said about the suffering servant later, for the idea is closely linked with the general idea of suffering (see pp. 440ff., 451, 461f.).

Another factor which might be mentioned is that where echoes of the servant Christology occur in Paul, they are mainly in traditional or confessional passages. This also seems to apply to the writings of the apostolic fathers. At least this line of evidence excludes the possibility of a Hellenistic provenance for the idea.

---

[138] Jeremias, *op. cit.*, p. 104, citing M. Buber, 'Jesus und der Knecht', in *Pro Regno, pro Sanctuario* (Festschrift G. van der Leeuw, 1950), p. 74.

[139] *Cf.* R. Longenecker, *The Christology of Early Jewish Christianity*, p. 108. He views it against the scandal which the cross was to Jews and the foolishness to Greeks (1 Cor. 1:23).

[140] Note that M. Hooker explains the absence of identification of Jesus as the servant, which she virtually claims for the whole NT, by simply declaring that the approach which presupposes the existence of a 'servant' is fundamentally false (*op. cit.*, p. 158).

[141] *Cf.* Longenecker's criticism of Hooker's method (*op. cit.*, p. 106 n. 191). He bases his criticisms on the grounds of atomistic exegesis, a failure to see significance in the use of Is. 53 unless a suffering element is present, and neglect of circumstantial factors in explaining the lack of sustained interpretation of Is. 53.

JESUS AS PROPHET AND TEACHER

The idea of a coming prophet was strong in Jewish belief. It was based on Deuteronomy 18:15 which declares that the Lord will raise up a prophet like Moses.[142] It is not surprising that the coming prophet came to be thought of in some circles as Moses *redivivus*. Running parallel to this was a belief in the return of Elijah. These ideas developed further into the belief that two prophets would come – Enoch and Elijah or Moses and Elijah.[143] Such expectations together with one connected with the name of Jeremiah would explain the popular ideas about Jesus mentioned in the gospels.

It is not surprising in view of such a background that John the Baptist was regarded as a prophet, but the question arises whether he was considered to be 'the eschatological prophet'. Since Jesus identified John the Baptist as the expected Elijah (Mt. 11:7f.)[144] it is clear that he regarded John as a special prophet (*i.e.* more than *a* prophet). In this case the prophetic office was considered to involve not only the proclamation of the kingdom, but also the preparation for the Messiah. The gospels present John the Baptist in the role of the forerunner.

In considering the prophetic role of Jesus, we note several features which support the view that he was popularly regarded as fulfilling such a role. He was variously identified with John the Baptist, Elijah, Jeremiah, one of the prophets (Mk. 8:27f. = Mt. 16:14f. = Lk. 9:18f.).[145] In Luke 4:24 Jesus indirectly applies the title to himself. There is much in the ministry of Jesus that fits into the prophetic role. His teaching ministry centred around the proclamation of the kingdom. He was addressed as rabbi, which showed that he was popularly regarded as an authoritative teacher, even although he was not officially recognized as such. Yet in his teaching ministry he went beyond the function of proclamation which the old prophets exercized. He was himself the eschatological prophet, the one who inaugurated a new era.

There are many reasons why the concept of prophet ceased to play a part in the post-Easter development of Christology. It proved an inadequate basis. Cullmann[146] gives four reasons. (i) The prophet concept is one-sided

---

[142] The importance of this passage for the early Christians is seen from the quotation of it by Peter in Acts 3:22 and by Stephen in Acts 7:37. In both places it is implied that Jesus is the coming prophet.

[143] For details of these expectations, *cf.* O. Cullmann, *Christology of the New Testament*, pp. 16ff. For other discussions on Jesus as a prophet, *cf.* C. H. Dodd, 'Jesus as Teacher and Prophet', *Mysterium Christi* (ed. G. K. A. Bell, and A. Deissman, 1930), pp. 53–66; F. V. Filson, *Jesus Christ the Risen Lord* (1956), pp. 137ff.; R. Meyer, *Der Prophet aus Galiläa* (²1970).

[144] *Cf.* Cullmann, *op. cit.*, p. 28, who maintains that although the fourth gospel shows John the Baptist as refusing to be identified with the coming eschatological prophet (*i.e.* Elijah, *cf.* Jn. 1:21), there is no real disagreement with the synoptics. Cullmann thinks that the evangelist is discouraging a wrong opinion of John the Baptist, *i.e.* as the final eschatological prophet, for if this opinion were true it would make the work of Messiah unnecessary.

[145] *Cf.* also Mk. 6:15 (=Mt. 14:1–2=Lk. 9:7–8), where reports are given to Herod.

[146] *Cf.* Cullmann, *op. cit.*, pp. 45ff.

in that it emphasizes the preaching ministry at the expense of other even more important aspects, especially the atoning death of Christ. The suffering servant idea is more expressive of the main purpose of the coming of Christ. (ii) The prophet idea does not admit of an interval of time between the earthly activity and the parousia. The Jewish coming prophet would inaugurate the kingdom after his preaching of repentance. The work of Jesus does not fit into that category. (iii) The prophet concept further does not fit into the framework of Jesus' future work. The prophet's work ceased when he had proclaimed the inauguration of the kingdom, but Jesus' present activity was inextricably linked with his future work, as completer of the kingdom. (iv) The prophet concept can take no account of Christ as a pre-existent being. For these reasons the concept of prophet (as also teacher) plays no significant part in NT Christology. The nearest approach is the Johannine Logos.

SON OF MAN

The synoptic gospels

Of all the titles appearing in the synoptic gospels 'Son of man' is both the most significant and the most enigmatic. It is moreover used only by Jesus himself, and the problem immediately arises over what he meant by it. A more basic consideration even than this arises from the view of some scholars that some or all of the statements in the gospels cannot be regarded as authentic.[147] If this kind of approach is valid, the use of the title Son of man can tell us nothing about Jesus' view of himself, only about how the early church came to describe him. An intermediary view is that the sayings are authentic, but refer to someone other than Jesus.

Emerging from the continuous debate and the massive amount of literature are five possible approaches to the Son of man designation. (i) The Son of man sayings in each category (listed on pp. 275ff.) may be authentic and therefore reveal Jesus' view of his own identity.[148] (ii) The Son of man

---

[147] For useful surveys of discussion on the Son of man question, cf. C. C. McCown, 'Jesus, Son of Man: A Survey of recent discussion', JR 28, 1948, pp. 1–12. A. J. B. Higgins, 'Son of Man – Forschung since "The Teaching of Jesus" ', New Testament Essays: Studies in Memory of T. W. Manson (ed. A. J. B. Higgins), pp. 119–135; R. Marlow, 'The Son of Man in Recent Journal Literature', CBQ 28, 1966, pp. 20–39; I. H. Marshall, 'The Synoptic Son of man Sayings in Recent Discussion', NTS 12, 1966, pp. 327–351; F. H. Borsch, The Son of Man in Myth and History (1967), pp. 21–34; O. Michel, 'Der Menschensohn. Die eschatologische Hinweisung. Die apokalyptische Aussage. Bemerkungen zum Menschensohn – Verständnis des N.T.' ThZ 27, 1971, pp. 81–104. J. N. Birdsall, 'Who is the Son of Man?', EQ 42, 1970, pp. 7–17, gives a useful review of the studies of H. E. Tödt, The Son of Man in the Synoptic Tradition (Eng. trans. 1965); A. J. B. Higgins, Jesus and the Son of Man (1964), R. H. Fuller, The Foundations of New Testament Christology (1965); M. Hooker, The Son of Man in Mark (1967); and F. Borsch, The Son of Man in Myth and History. Cf. also C. F. D. Moule's review of Tödt's book in Theology 69, 1966, pp. 174ff.

[148] So O. Cullmann, The Christology of the New Testament, pp. 137–192; V. Taylor, The Names of Jesus (1953), pp. 25–35; C. E. B. Cranfield, Mark (CGTC, 1959), pp. 272ff.; I. H. Marshall, 'The Son of Man in Contemporary Debate', EQ 42, 1970, pp. 67–87; idem, NTS 12, 1966, pp. 327–351.

sayings are all community products and do not reflect Jesus' view of himself.[149] (iii) The Son of man sayings which refer to the future are alone authentic, but these refer to someone other than Jesus.[150] (iv) The Son of man sayings which refer to the future are alone authentic, but Jesus thought of himself as the heavenly Son of man to be revealed at the consummation of the present age.[151] (v) The Son of man sayings which refer to Jesus' earthly life are alone authentic.[152] It will at once be seen that these views differ according to the different views about the authenticity of the whole or part of the traditions.

These differences are generally determined not so much by scientific exegesis of the texts, as by the view of early Christian history held by the various scholars. If, for instance, it be maintained that the Christian church created the sayings, this opinion will clearly govern the interpretation of the texts. But the theory that Christians themselves started thinking of Jesus as Son of man runs into considerable problems; for in that case there is no reasonable explanation of the fact that the title drops out of the names for Jesus used by the apostles and was, therefore, not dominant in early Christian traditions. It is incredible that the early Christians should invent a name for Jesus himself to use and then never use it themselves as an appellative for him. It makes better sense to maintain that the title was used by Jesus as recorded in the synoptic gospels, but was displaced by other titles in early Christian thought.[153] Two possible reasons have been given for such displacement: (i) because in the Greek world the title could mean only the humanity of Jesus, and (ii) because of the possible inappropriateness of the title until the Son of man's work was finished (*i.e.* at the end of the age).[154] On the other hand the words might well have been regarded as meaningless. In the following survey of the evidence we shall discuss the linguistic problem, the probable origin of the idea, the grouping of the sayings, their consistency, and their most likely meaning for the mind of Jesus.

[149] So P. Vielhauer, 'Jesus und der Menschensohn', *ZTK* 60, 1963, pp. 133–177; H. M. Teeple, 'The Origin of the Son of Man Christology', *JBL* 84, 1965, pp. 213–250; N. Perrin, *Rediscovering the Teaching of Jesus* (1967), pp. 164–199.

[150] So R. Bultmann, *TNT* 1, pp. 28ff.; G. Bornkamm, *Jesus of Nazareth* (1960), pp. 228ff.; H. E. Tödt, *op. cit.*; F. Hahn, *The Titles of Jesus in Christology* pp. 15–53; A, J. B. Higgins, *op. cit.*

[151] A. Schweitzer, *The Quest of the Historical Jesus* (1906, Eng. trans. ³1954); J. Jeremias, *NTT* 1 (1971), pp. 257–275.

[152] E. Schweizer, 'Der Menschensohn', *ZNW* 50, 1959, pp. 185–209; *idem*, 'The Son of Man', *JBL* 79, 1960, pp. 119–129; *idem*, 'The Son of Man Again', *NTS* 9, 1963, pp. 256fff.

[153] It has been argued by W. Stott, 'Son of Man' – A Title of Abasement', *ExT* 83, 1972, pp. 278ff., that it was because the title was not a title of honour that the early Christians dropped it, out of reverence for Jesus.

[154] *Cf.* Longenecker, *The Christology of Early Jewish Christianity*, pp. 91f. He says, 'It is only in those portions where suffering and glory are brought together on the part of his people, and Jesus is portrayed as standing with his afflicted saints (*i.e.* Acts 7:56; Rev. 1:13; 14:14), that he is spoken of in terms of the Son of Man.'

The linguistic problem. The probable Aramaic basis for the title would be *bar ᵉnāš* (or *bar ᵃnāšā*).[155] This would, however, generally denote 'man', but could be an alternative usage for the first person. If the Aramaic meant no more than man in general, the phrase could not have been used by Jesus in the sense of a particular man, whether himself or someone else. Although there are a few of the sayings in the gospels which could conceivably be understood as referring to mankind in general, however, the majority could not possibly be taken in this way.[156] In this case it is clear that an attempt to prejudge the issue on purely linguistic grounds is unsatisfactory. The suggestion that in Aramaic the phrase would simply mean 'I' is more easily applied to the sayings in the gospels and would support the view that in every case Jesus was referring to himself. In this case the use by Jesus of the title would mean that he was referring to himself in an exclusive sense – he and no-one else among men.[157]

Another possibility is that the original form of the phrase would draw attention both to man in general and to a particular representative.[158] In this case its use by Jesus would focus attention on himself as the representative man. Many scholars, who consider that behind the usage of Jesus is an apocalyptic Son of man, trace this idea back to Daniel 7:13.[159] It could be maintained that in apocalyptic contexts[160] the phrase may have had a titular usage which it would not otherwise have had.

The linguistic usage is not conclusive. Although no firm basis exists for maintaining that the title could have been used in an Aramaic form, it is valuable to note that the phrase would predominantly denote a person *as* man. This representative character of the phrase is of particular importance in deciding its probable meaning in the mind of Jesus.[161] At the same time it must be recognized that Jesus was saying things which were true for himself as man, which did not apply to man in general.

---

[155] *Cf.* the appendix by G. Vermes, in M. Black's *An Aramaic Approach to the Gospels and Acts* (³1967), pp. 310–328. M. Black (p. 328) does not agree with Vermes that the Aramaic *barnash* is not suitable for messianic use. *Cf.* also R. E. C. Formesyn, 'Was there a pronominal connection for the "barnasha" selfdesignation?', *NovT* 8, 1966, pp. 1–35.

[156] *Cf.* M. Black, 'The "Son of Man" Passion Sayings in the Gospel Tradition', *ZNW* 60, 1969, pp. 1ff.; *idem*, 'The Son of Man Problem in Recent Research and Debate', *BJRL* 45, 1963, pp. 305–318.

[157] *Cf.* Vermes, *op. cit.*, pp. 316ff.

[158] *Cf.* J. Jeremias, 'Die älteste Schicht der Menschensohn-Logien', *ZNW* 58, 1968, p. 165 n. 9; A. Gelston, 'A Sidelight on the "Son of Man" ', *SJT* 22, 1969, p. 189 n. 2.

[159] C. F. D. Moule, *The Origin of Christology* (1977), pp. 12ff, argues strongly from the invariable use of the article with the Son of man in the gospels that it must point to some particular Son of Man, *i.e.* the one mentioned in Dn.. 7.

[160] For a study of the Son of man in Jewish apocalyptic, *cf.* C. Colpe, *TDNT*, 8, pp. 420–430. Colpe points out that Judaism interpreted the Son of man in Dn. 7 messianically, although the title was changed usually to Son of the Clouds. *Cf.* also G. Dalman, *The Words of Jesus*, pp. 234ff.

[161] *Cf.* Longenecker, *op. cit*, pp. 85f., who agrees with Vermes' conclusions except his view that Son of man could not have been used with messianic import in pre-Christian times. In this he sides with M. Black, citing the latter's conclusion that the term was fitted both to conceal and to reveal (*cf.* M. Black, *op. cit.*, p. 329).

The probable origin. There are a variety of theories about the pre-Christian use and significance of the title Son of man.[162] The importance of such a discussion is the contribution it can make to our defining the contemporary understanding of the term in the time of Jesus. Since it was a term which he so deliberately chose to use and used so frequently when addressing popular audiences, or his disciples or even his enemies, it is essential to enquire not only what it meant to himself, but also what it meant to his hearers. It is usual to find evidence of the background in three main Jewish sources – Daniel 7, the Similitudes of Enoch,[163] and the Apocalypse of Ezra. It should be noted that the phrase 'son of man' is used many times in addressing Ezekiel, but this is not significant in relation to the synoptic usage.[164] Similarly the reference to 'son of man' in Psalm 8:4–6 is parallel to 'man' and is used to contrast man in his weakness with the power of God,[165] who nevertheless has crowned man with glory (*cf.* also Ps. 80:17–19).[166]

Of the three main sources, the evidence from 4 Ezra 13 can be discounted for our purpose since it is not pre-Christian in date. The Enoch passage in which the title appears (37–71) is in all probability not pre-Christian since there is no evidence for these sections in the extant portions of Enoch found in the Qumran library. It is precarious therefore to place weight upon them for the interpretation of the synoptic usage. This leaves us with Daniel 7 as the sole pre-Christian source, but there has been much debate about the significance of this reference. In the passage itself 'son of man' stands in direct relationship to 'the saints of the Most High'. The latter phrase is generally taken to refer to the pious in Israel, but the alternative

---

[162] *Cf.* P. C. Hodgson, 'The Son of Man and the Problem of Historical Knowledge', *JT* 41, 1961, pp. 91–108; J. A. Emerton, 'The Origin of the Son of Man Imagery', *JTS*, n.s. 9, 1958, pp. 225–242; S. S. Smalley, 'The Johannine Son of Man Sayings', *NTS* 15, 1968–9, pp. 278–301; W. O. Walker, 'The Origin of the Son of man concept as Applied to Jesus', *JBL* 91, 1972, pp. 482ff.; O. Michel, 'Der Menschensohn. Die eschatologische Hinweisung. Die apokalyptische Aussage. Bemerkungen zum Menschensohn-Verständnis des N.T.', *ThZ* 27, 1971, pp. 81-104.

[163] O. Cullmann, *The Christology of the New Testament*, pp. 140f., gives some credence to the connection of the Son of man with the occurrence of the expression in Enoch, and concludes that it was known in esoteric Jewish circles, He recognizes, nonetheless, that this evidence is late.

[164] Yet compare G. S. Duncan, *Jesus, Son of Man* (1947), pp. 145f. C. H. Dodd, *According to the Scriptures* (1952), p. 117 n., does not include Ezekiel in the testimonia. But A. Richardson, *TNT*, pp. 128f., includes the Ezekiel evidence as a contribution to the understanding of Son of man.

[165] W. O. Walker, Jr, 'The Origin of the Son of Man Concept as applied to Jesus', *JBL* 91, 1972, pp. 482ff., discusses the contribution, not only of Ps. 8, but also of Ps. 110. *Cf.* also J. Bowker, 'The Son of Man', *JTS*, n.s. 28, 1977, pp. 19–48, for a discussion of the possible sources of Son of man in the sayings of Jesus. He inclines to the meaning 'man subject to death'.

[166] For the view that Ps. 80 was the 'catalyst' in the development of the Son of man concept rather than Dn. 7, *cf.* O. J. F. Seitz, 'The Future Coming of the Son of Man: Three Midrashic Formulations in the Gospel of Mark'. *StEv* 6, 1973, pp. 478ff. C. H. Dodd, *According to the Scriptures*, pp. 101f., expresses a similar view. But C. F. D. Moule, *The Origin of Christology*, pp. 25f., is not convinced by Seitz's argument and still maintains that Dn. 7 is more likely. *Cf.* D. Hill's discussion of the Ps. 80 passage in ' "Son of Man" in Ps. 80: 17', *NovT* 15, 1973, pp. 261ff.

view has been put forward that they were angelic beings.[167] The former is more natural, but raises the question in what sense 'son of man' can be understood corporately. Does the Daniel passage rule out an individual? Again, opinions differ, but since the title undoubtedly later came to be interpreted in an individual sense, it seems likely that the Daniel passage was not intended in an exclusively corporate sense. The son of man here seems to be representative of the people of God; if this is correct it has a bearing on the synoptic usage, but is clearly less than a developed messianic use of the title.

It has been suggested that Daniel's usage was influenced by non-biblical ideas, mythological and speculative.[168] But the evidence appealed to in the Avestas, in Babylonian and Egyptian mythology, in rabbinic theologizing on the Adam theme or gnostic speculation about the primal man is far removed from Daniel's son of man. So also is the idea that it is derived from Canaanite Baal worship.[169] There is no hope that the introduction of such obscurities may shed light on the meaning of the synoptic Son of man. It is better to suppose that Jesus himself invested the term with his own interpretation of Daniel's usage.

One facet of Daniel's vision which is important is the statement that the Son of man came on the clouds of heaven to the Ancient of Days. Does this mean that a heavenly figure is in mind? By the time of the *Similitudes of Enoch*[170] 'son of man' is conceived of as a pre-existent heavenly figure who will come to judge and overthrow the enemies of God, which shows that Daniel's term was then understood as a heavenly and not an earthly figure. The problem is that no evidence exists that these Similitudes reflect the general interpretation at the time of Jesus and his contemporaries. It is probable that they represent a restricted viewpoint. In short, it is clear that background studies, apart from Daniel, provide little positive guidance about the real significance of the synoptic Son of man. The two aspects

[167] *Cf.* M. Hooker, *The Son of Man in Mark*, p. 13, who discusses the proposal of R. H. Charles that 'the saints' refer to the faithful in Israel who are to be transformed into supernatural beings, (*cf.* his commentary on Daniel, *A Critical and Exegetical Commentary on the Book of Daniel* (1929), p. 187). In a detailed footnote (n. 3), Morna Hooker discusses M. Noth's view that the 'saints' are not Israelites but heavenly beings, but concludes that in its present form Dn. 7 seems to use the term 'saints of the Most High' to refer to the righteous within Israel. *Cf.* also D. S. Russell, *The Method and Message of Jewish Apocalyptic* (1964), pp. 324ff.

A more recent writer, J. J. Collins, has maintained that the 'one like a son of man' in Dn. 7 primarily symbolizes the angelic host and its leader, although including faithful Jews in so far as they are associated with the heavenly host in the eschatological era, 'The Son of Man and the Saints of the Most High in the Book of Daniel', *JBL* 93, 1974, pp. 50–66.

[168] See Colpe's examination, *TDNT*, 7 pp. 408ff. Colpe classes all these suggestions under the general heading of untenable hypotheses, except the Canaanite theory which he favours.

[169] J. A. Emerton, *JTS* n.s. 9, 1958, pp. 225–242, interprets the Dn. 7 passsage in terms of enthronement, and sees in this some Canaanite influence. He thinks this explains the eschatological role of the Son of man.

[170] Sim. Enoch 46:48. 62:6–16; 69:26–29.

which are of some importance in Daniel's vision are the future coming on the clouds (which finds parallels in the synoptic sayings about the future) and the fact that 'saints' are first afflicted before being glorified (a motif which occurs in the Son of man sayings about the passion).[171]

Classification of the synoptic Son of man sayings. It is usual to group the sayings according to their reference (i) to the work of the Son of man on earth, (ii) to the suffering of the Son of man, and (iii) to the future glorification of the Son of man. Although this classification is not fool-proof[172] and can in fact lead to an over-analytical approach to the evidence, it is helpful to use some kind of grouping to reduce the evidence to manageable proportions.

(i) The first group consists of the following passages: Mark 2:10 (= Mt. 9:6; Lk. 5:24) and Mark 2:28 (= Mt. 12:8; Lk. 6:5).[173] In Mark 2:10 the Son of man claims authority to forgive sins, and in Mark 2:28 he claims authority to be Lord of the sabbath. In both cases Jesus faced criticism from the religious leaders, who must have recognized that he was referring to himself in claiming this authority.

Other cases where the title is used in describing Jesus' manner of living are Matthew 11:19 (= Lk. 7:34), where his special habits are mentioned (eating and drinking with others), and Matthew 8:20 (= Lk. 9:58), where the Son of man has nowhere to lay his head (*i.e.* no settled dwelling place). Again these sayings are intelligible only when seen as a description of Jesus himself. In the Beelzebub controversy, Jesus says that a word against the Son of man will be forgiven, but not against the Holy Spirit (Mt. 12:32 = Lk. 12:10) and the context shows that Jesus himself must have been intended by the title. In the explanation of the parable of the sower (or soils), the sower is identified as the Son of man who sows his seed in the world (Mt. 13:37). In Jesus' answer to Zacchaeus' offer to restore four-fold what he had falsely taken, he makes the significant statement that the Son of man came to seek and to save the lost (Lk. 19:10), which must refer to the earthly mission of Jesus. Luke also records the question of Jesus to

---

[171] For a full discussion of this theme, *cf.* A. J. B. Higgins, *Jesus and the Son of Man.* (1964). *Cf.* also *idem*, 'Son of Man.' Forschung since "The Teaching of Jesus" ', *The New Testament Essays: Studies in Memory of T. W. Manson* (ed. A. J. B. Higgins, 1959), pp. 119ff. *Cf.* also C. F. D. Moule, *Theology* 69, 1966, p. 174. *Cf.* R. Leivestad, 'Exit the Apocalyptic Son of Man', *NTS* 18, 1972, pp. 243–267, who accepts that 'Son of man' was not a Jewish title. He regards it as always a self-designation. But see B. Lindars' article, 'Re-enter the Apocalyptic Son of Man', *NTS* 22, 1975, pp. 52–72. He maintains that the apocalyptic Son of man, 'retains its value as a very convenient summary of what Jesus actually thought about himself, and is the proper starting point for an historical approach to Christology.'

[172] *Cf.* for instance, C. K. Barrett, *Jesus and the Gospel Tradition* (1967), pp. 32, 79ff., on Mk. 8:38. Barrett regards this verse to be of crucial importance because it cuts across the usual three-fold division of the Son of man sayings. The three-fold division must, in fact, be considered approximate.

[173] For a discussion of these two sayings in Mk., *cf.* L. S. Hay, 'The Son of Man in Mk. 2:10 and 2:28', *JBL* 89, 1970, pp. 69ff.

Judas, 'would you betray the Son of man with a kiss?' which in the context relates to the immediate approach of Judas to Jesus (Lk. 22:48).

There are two other passages which must be included here – Matthew 16:13 and Luke 6:22. In both the corresponding passages (Mk. 8:27 and Mt. 5:11) the use of the title is not recorded and this has led some to regard these as editorial additions. The first is of particular interest, for Matthew has 'Who do men say that the Son of man is?', whereas Mark has 'I' instead of 'Son of man'. The difference in the texts is itself striking testimony that the title was understood to relate to Jesus himself. The second passage is a similar testimony, since Luke's 'on account of the Son of man' is parallel to Matthew's 'on my account'.

In the light of this evidence there seems no alternative but to maintain that the synoptic writers understood Jesus to mean himself when he used the title in the above group of sayings. We shall discuss below the reasons that have led some scholars to question whether these sayings can be regarded as authentic.[174]

(ii) The second group, relating to the sufferings of the Son of man, consists of nine sayings.[175] We begin with those which predict the death and resurrection of the Son of man. It was immediately following Peter's confession at Caesarea Philippi that Jesus began to make such predictions (Mk. 8:31 = Lk. 9:22) under the title Son of man (Matthew is more direct and refers to Jesus, rather than to the Son of man, cf. Mt. 16:21). The fact that Peter immediately rebuked Jesus for his defeatist attitude shows clearly that he understood that the 'Son of man' was Jesus himself. After this prediction Jesus again refers to the Son of man's rising from the dead (Mk. 9:9 = Mt. 17:9). Similar predictions are made in similar terms in Mark 9:12 (= Mt. 17:12) and Mark 9:31 (= Mt. 17:22; Lk 9:44) and Mk. 10:33 (= Mt. 20:18; Lk. 18:31). In the latter case, the wording explicitly identifies Jesus – 'we are going up to Jerusalem; and the Son of man will be delivered'.

In addition to these plain predictions of the passion, there is one statement recorded by Mark (10:45) and Matthew (20:28) in which Jesus uses the title Son of man to give the significance of his death, i.e. as a ransom for many. The precise significance of this will be discussed in the section on the work of Christ (pp. 440f.), but it is plain that a redemptive meaning was attached to the figure of the Son of man in the mind of Jesus. Mark has two other Son of man passion sayings – Mk. 14:21 (= Mt. 26:24; Lk. 22:22) predicting the betrayal and expressing woe to the betrayer, and Mk. 14:41 (= Mt. 26:45) which again mentions the approaching betrayal. To complete this

---

[174] For a special study of Mark's Son of man sayings, cf. M. D. Hooker, *The Son of Man in Mark*. For Matthew's use, cf. J. D. Kingsbury, 'The title "Son of Man" in Matthew's gospel", *CBQ* 37, 1975, pp. 193fff.

[175] M. Black discusses these passages in his article, 'The "Son of Man" Passion Sayings in the Gospel Tradition', *ZNW* 60, 1969, pp. 1ff., and contests the minimizing of Isaianic influence in these (*contra* Tödt).

section Matthew 12:40 (= Lk. 11:30) must be included, which compares the Son of man to Jonah in being three days and nights in the earth. This latter reference is not as clearly identified with Jesus as the former statements, but in the light of them could hardly refer to anyone else.

(iii) The third group, in which the Son of man is mentioned in his future glorification, contains more passages than the other groups, and certainly more which are recorded in only one gospel. There are three sayings which all the synoptic gospels include: Mark 8:38 (= Mt. 16:27; Lk. 9:26), Mark 13:26 (= Mt. 24:30; Lk. 21:27), Mark 14:62 (= Mt. 26:64; Lk. 22:69). All speak of the coming in glory: the first followed immediately after the first prediction of the passion, the second is in the so-called eschatological discourse and the third is a saying made by Jesus before the high priest. Three other sayings are shared by Matthew and Luke, all of which are in Matthew's eschatological discourse: Matthew 24:27 (= Lk. 17:24), Matthew 24:37–39 (= Lk. 17:26–27) and Matthew 24:44 (= Lk. 12:40). These sayings focus on the rapidity and unexpected character of the coming. In the same discourse, Matthew has a saying about the sign of the Son of man (Mt. 24:30), and another about his coming glory (Mt. 25:31). In the interpretation of the parable of the tares in Matthew, it is the Son of man who will superintend the final harvest (Mt. 13:41). Matthew also has a saying about the enthronement of the Son of man (Mt. 19:28) and two enigmatic sayings (Mt. 10:23 and 16:28), which may or may not refer to the future coming.

Luke has a few of his own Son of man sayings. Luke 12:8 speaks of the Son of man acknowledging men before the angels of God (Matthew in his parallel saying, (Mt. 10:32), has 'I' instead of 'Son of man'). He also includes a prediction that the disciples would desire to see one of the days of the Son of man (Lk. 17:22), and a prediction of a judgment like that suffered by Sodom (Lk. 17:29–30). Luke alone includes the poignant saying, 'Nevertheless when the Son of man comes, will he find faith on earth?' (Lk. 18:8), and an exhortation to pray for strength to stand before the Son of man (Lk. 21:36).

This survey of the evidence shows how powerfully the idea of a future coming in glory of the Son of man dominated the mind of Jesus. It is in fact this third group which has appealed most strongly to those scholars who interpret the whole mission of Jesus in eschatological terms. When the total evidence for the use of the Son of man title is surveyed it is striking that the sayings are distributed over the whole period of ministry, although the second and third group understandably are concentrated in the post-Caesarea-Philippi section. It is important to note that Jesus did not restrict the use of the title to sayings addressed to his disciples. It appears to be part of his consciousness at all times. It is for this reason that its meaning for him is so important in discussions of NT Christology.

The consistency of the Son of man sayings. The debate over the meaning of the title for Jesus is largely influenced by the different views which have been maintained over the matter of formal consistency. If it is supposed that the three groups present contradictory presentations of the Son of man figure, there would be no alternative for the theologian but to select one and reject the rest. Bultmann, for instance, maintains that the third group of sayings, which he accepts, relates to a Son of man who is not identified with Jesus; but the other groups, which identify Jesus as Son of man, he claims are inconsistent with the former, and must therefore be rejected. On the other hand Vielhauer finds inconsistency on somewhat different grounds. His point is that there is inconsistency between the Son of man sayings and the kingdom sayings. Since he finds no link between these, he regards only one group as authentic and consequently rejects the former.[176] But such an approach is unsatisfactory because of the arbitrary interpretation of 'inconsistency'. There is no logical reason why Jesus should not have used the title in a variety of different ways.[177] It is, in fact, unnatural to suggest that it would have referred exclusively to the future rather than the present or vice versa. If, as seems highly probable, Jesus used it to denote something of his own consciousness within his mission, it must have spanned both the present and the future, and have taken into account the intervening passion.[178]

One aspect of this consistency problem which is often overlooked is that the above grouping takes no account of the contexts in which sayings from different groups occur together. The close connection between the passion predictions and the glory predictions (as in Mk. 8 and 9) cannot be dismissed as editorial. The fact that the passion is never predicted without a corresponding prediction of resurrection paves the way for the sayings about the Son of man in glory. We must seek some solution to the meaning of the title which allows for the possibility that all three groups are authentic and contribute to a total understanding of the title.

The meaning of the Son of man title. Several considerations must be taken into account if a true assessment of the significance of the title is to be made.

---

[176] *Cf.* Bultmann, *TNT* 1, pp. 28ff. P. Vielhauer, 'Gottesreich und Menschensohn in der Verkündigung Jesu', in *Festschrift für Günther Dehn* (ed. W. Schneemelcher, 1957), pp. 51ff. *Cf.* also W. Bousset, *Kyrios Christos* (Eng. trans. 1970), pp. 40ff., who regarded most, if not all, of the Son of man sayings as community tradition.

[177] *Cf.* I. H. Marshall, 'The Synoptic Son of Man Sayings in Recent Discussion', *NTS* 12, 1966, p. 338. He says, 'Moreover, if the early church could hold together statements in which Jesus was clearly identified with the Son of Man along with others which might give a different impression . . . we might well ask why its Master was not permitted to behave in the same way.' *Cf.* also *idem*, *EQ*, 1970, pp. 67–87.

[178] *Cf.* M. D. Hooker, *The Son of Man in Mark*, pp. 178ff., who shows that there are common factors in the three groups of sayings in Mark. She sees Mark's pattern as a logical and coherent whole.

(i) All the sayings in the synoptic gospels are sayings of Jesus, who alone used the title.

(ii) This is equally true of the Johannine sayings (see below).

(iii) Apart from these books, the title occurs only in Acts 7:56 (on the lips of Stephen and referring to a glorified person at the right hand of God). It is used in a non-titular sense in Hebrews 2:6–8 (in a quotation from Ps. 8:4–6) and in Revelation 1:13; 14:14 (in a description of one like a son of man).

(iv) The use of the title by Jesus was, therefore, of sufficient importance for all the evangelists to record many such sayings, but it was evidently displaced by other titles in the use of the church.

(v) Theories which maintain that the church attributed the title to Jesus do not accord with the fact of its complete displacement in all other early Christian literature.[179]

(vi) The Daniel passage is the main pre-Christian passage which furnishes a clue to the meaning of the phrase Son of man on the lips of Jesus. Since this passage links suffering and glory, it is highly probable that Jesus had this combination in mind in his own use of the title.

(vii) Since the Daniel passage was later interpreted in a messianic way it is not improbable that Jesus used it with some understanding of his messianic office, while its veiled character would be suitable to his present purpose. Indeed, it is highly probable that the ambiguity of the title was part of the reason for its use.[180]

(viii) In view of the possible corporate element in both Daniel 7 and in the Isaianic Servant idea (especially Is. 52—53), it is just possible that such a synthesis was present in the mind of Jesus,[181] but it can hardly be supposed that his varied audiences would have appreciated this.[182]

(ix) There are no grounds for supposing that Jesus was thinking of an apocalyptic Son of man distinct from himself who would later vindicate his mission.[183] All the sayings listed above are capable of being understood without such an interpretation.

(x) Nevertheless, the heavenly origin of the Son of man could not have

---

[179] *Cf.* E. Schweizer, 'The Son of Man Again', *NTS* 9, 1963, p. 257 n. 3. Schweizer criticizes Conzelmann and Tödt for the view that 'Son of Man' was not part of the creed, but was introduced by Christian prophets. He rightly asks why the church was so careful to introduce the title only into the sayings of Jesus and so inventive to create words like Lk. 12:8, although there was no more distinction between Jesus and the Son of man. It is G. Bornkamm, *Jesus of Nazareth*, p. 176, who places special emphasis on Lk. 12:8f. as showing that Jesus thought of the Son of man as distinct from himself. According to him only these sayings are to be regarded as authentic and the rest are creations of the church.

[180] G. Dalman, *The Words of Jesus*, p. 259, suggests that the enigma attached to the title was intentional so as to encourage reflection on the mystery of the personality of Jesus.

[181] *Cf.* Longenecker, *The Christology of Early Jewish Christianity*, p. 91, who contends that in using this title Jesus possessed a title which combined the elements of suffering and glory.

[182] *Cf.* T. W. Manson, *The Servant Messiah* (1953), pp. 72ff.

[183] *Cf.* R. Leivestad, *NTS* 18, 1972, pp. 243ff. See n. 171 above.

been absent from the consciousness of Jesus.

A summary of the character of the Son of man in the synoptics. On the assumption
that the Son of man passages may all be regarded as referring to Jesus
himself, there are certain features which may be noted about his character.
He certainly conceived of himself as possessing *authority*. This is seen both
in his earthly ministry and in his heavenly status. In the former, his claim
to forgive sins (Mk. 2:10) carried with it sufficient authority for his critics
to charge him with blasphemy. They clearly did not interpret the saying
in the sense that all men have power to forgive, since the forgiveness of
sins (as distinct from a forgiving attitude towards people) was regarded as
a divine prerogative. Jesus as Son of man was exercising authority which
he himself knew was legitimate only for God. Furthermore, the claim of
Jesus that the Son of man has authority over the sabbath (Mk. 2:27, 28)
certainly implies more than that man can treat the sabbath as he wishes.
Not man in general, but the Son of man in the person of Jesus has that
power. It is clear from his statement about the sabbath that, in his capacity
as Son of man, Jesus would superintend the sabbath for man's good, and
not in the legalistic manner of the Pharisees. Since it was God who instituted the sabbath, the claim of Jesus to be Lord of the sabbath was another
claim to exercise divine authority. This idea of authority is also linked to
the sayings which predict the part of the Son of man in the coming
judgment. Authority is epitomized in the throne saying of Matthew 19:28
(*cf.* also Mt. 26:64), and in the Son of man acknowledging men before the
angels (*i.e.* before God) in Luke 12:8. There is no break in the continuity
between the authority exercised by the Son of man on earth and that
exercised in heaven.

Closely linked to the authority theme is the *glorification* theme. While all
the passages which speak of glory link it with the future coming, this
essential glory of the Son of man clearly played an important part in the
consciousness of Jesus during his earthly ministry. The approaching passion
must in fact be seen against the background of the certainty of glory to
follow. There is no suggestion that Jesus ever thought of his sufferings as
anything other than a pathway to future glory.

Another theme which stands out is the *humiliation* of the earthly life of
the Son of man. The fact that he has nowhere to live seems incongruous
(Mt. 8:20; Lk. 9:58) in the light of the coming glory. But the title was not
used here without significance. It was not merely that Jesus as a man
possessed no earthly home. It was intended to show that he, even knowing
himself to be the Son of man, was not enjoying any material advantages
of his office, and did not expect his followers to do so either. In no clearer
way could Jesus dissociate himself from a materialistic conception of his
mission.

It is not surprising that many of the sayings focus on *suffering and death*. Jesus had no doubt that he had come to die. The significance of his death in his own thinking will be discussed later under the section on the mission of Christ (pp. 436ff.); for our present purpose we note that the Son of man and suffering are inextricably connected. This introduces an element which was implicit in Daniel's vision, but which was never grasped in Jewish messianic expectations. As Son of man, Jesus knew he would not be exempt from death, but he knew also that he would triumph over it in resurrection. We might note that the only Son of man saying which gives any clue of the meaning of the death of Jesus is Mark 10:45 (= Mt. 20:28), where Jesus speaks of giving his life as a ransom. There can be no doubt that he never for a moment approached the passion as if it were a ghastly accident. There is a strong consciousness that it was part and parcel of his office as Son of man.

One statement brings out something of the relationship between the Son of man and *the Holy Spirit* (Mt. 12:32 = Lk. 12:10), where a distinction is made between a word against the Son of man as being forgivable and an attitude against the Spirit as being unforgivable. At first glance it may seem that Jesus is distinguishing his own work from that of the Spirit; but, in fact, he is showing that his own work, as Son of man, is in the power of the Spirit. Anyone attributing the work of the Son of man to evil forces was blaspheming the Holy Spirit at work in him. This is, therefore, an important passage for an understanding of the Spirit's activity in the mission of Jesus.

The mission of Jesus in the Son of man passages is directly related to the *salvation* of men (Lk. 19:10). The Son of man has an awareness of man's lost condition and aims his mission to meet that need. His mission is dominated by this spiritual purpose (see the later section on the mission of Christ).

Conclusion. It will be seen that the title Son of man was associated in the mind of Jesus with a variety of factors which make sense on only one supposition: that Jesus thought of himself in terms of a heavenly Messiah fulfilling on earth a ministry on men's behalf which would culminate in scenes of final glory. It can be well understood in the light of this why Jesus did not use the title Messiah to describe his mission, since his work was not political but spiritual.

Furthermore, in view of the inherent difficulty of any concept of a suffering Messiah in contemporary thought, and Jesus' own awareness that his spiritual mission could be accomplished only through suffering and death, it seems reasonable to suppose that he identified himself inwardly with the idea of the suffering servant. It must be supposed that he used the Son of man title, not so much for the benefit of his hearers as to combine in his own mind several strands which made his mission unique.[184] He was in fact reinterpreting the concept of messiahship until his own disciples would identify the Son of man with Jesus the Messiah.

John's gospel

There are several passages in John's gospel which preserve the title Son of man,[185] and these are important for two reasons: (i) they show substantial agreement with the synoptic sayings, and (ii) they contribute some features more explicitly. The fact that such sayings are preserved at all in a gospel which differs both structurally and thematically from the synoptic gospels is a remarkable testimony to the authentic nature of the sayings. If the Johannine account was later than the synoptic gospels and is independent of them (as is most probable), these Son of man sayings must have been preserved because they were considered significant.

The passages. (i) The first passage is one of the most distinctive: John 1:51 which speaks of the angels of God ascending and descending upon the Son of man.[186] Most exegetes agree that this is an allusion to Jacob's ladder, but its significance for the Son of man concept lies in its clear assumption that the Son of man is a pre-existent figure. It is, however, enigmatic and will be further mentioned below.[187]

(ii) The second passage contains two sayings in the Nicodemus section. One saying speaks of the ascent and descent of the Son of man (Jn. 3:13),[188] and the other saying mentions the necessity for the lifting up of the Son of man as a means by which men may acquire eternal life (Jn. 3:14).

[184] L. Morris, *The Lord from Heaven*, p. 28, gives four reasons why Jesus adopted the term Son of man: (i) because of its rarity and non-nationalistic associations; (ii) because it had overtones of divinity: (iii) because of its societal implications: (iv) because of its undertones of humanity.

[185] For a full discussion of John's Son of man sayings, *cf.* F. J. Moloney, *The Johannine Son of Man* (1976), *Cf.* also E. Kinniburgh, 'The Johannine Son of Man', *StEv* 4, 1968, pp. 64ff.; S. S. Smalley, 'The Johannine Son of Man sayings, *NTS* 15, 1968–9, pp. 278–301; E. M. Sidebottom, 'The Son of Man in the Fourth Gospel', *ExT* 68, 1956–7, pp. 231ff, 280ff.; B. Lindars, 'The Son of Man in the Johannine Christology', *Christ and Spirit in the New Testament*, (ed. B. Lindars and S. S. Smalley, 1973), pp. 43–60.

[186] It is important to note that the saying in 1:51 is introduced by the double *amēn* which is a characteristic of the sayings of Jesus in this gospel. J. N. Sanders and B. A. Mastin, *John* (BC, 1968), p. 105, regard the Johannine *amēn* sayings as suggesting the prophetic activity of the evangelist or his authority, R. Schnackenburg, *John* 1 (Eng. trans. 1968), p. 320, remarks that the double *amēn*, although peculiar to Jesus in John's gospel, is found in a liturgical form in Qumran texts.

[187] B. Lindars, *Behind the Fourth Gospel* (1971), regards this Son of man saying as having been added to the original context by John, (pp. 53f.). A similar view is maintained by R. E. Brown (*John* pp. 88ff.), who nevertheless recognizes that in its present context it must have made sense to somebody. He points out that 'Son of man' is the only title in Jn. 1 which Jesus uses of himself and considers that this may reflect historical reminiscence that Jesus did use the title. There is no reason to dispute that John is here recording a genuine saying.

[188] R. H. Fuller, *The Foundations of New Testament Christology*, pp. 229f., treats Jn. 3:13, together with Jn. 6:62, as belonging to the *katabasis-anabasis* Christology of the Hellenistic church, but R. N. Longenecker, 'Some Distinctive Early Christological Motifs', *NTS* 14, 1967–8, pp. 524f., finds similar ideas in an early Palestinian Jewish Christian milieu.

(iii) In a passage which has much to say about Jesus as the Son of God, there is a reference to the authority of the Son of man to execute judgment (Jn. 5:27).[189] This authority is a derived authority, given by the Father. Here there is a closer connection with the future status of the Son of man in the synoptic gospels.[190]

(iv) In the discourse on the bread, it is the Son of man who gives food which endures to eternal life (Jn. 6:27).[191] Since it is also stated that the bread comes from heaven and is given by the Father (6:32), the close connection between the Father and the Son of man is unmistakable. What the Son of man does is, in effect, the Father's work. This accords with Jesus' statement that he comes to do the will of the Father (6:38).

(v) At the conclusion of the same discourse occurs the remarkable saying about eating the flesh of the Son of man and drinking his blood (6:53). This is immediately identified as signifying 'my flesh' (6:54). There must have been some reason for the special use of the title here. It recurs again in 6:62 in reference to the ascending of the Son of man.

(vi) In Jesus' dialogue with the Jews, he announces that when they have lifted up the Son of man they would know that Jesus was he (Jn. 8:28).

(vii) After the blind man is healed and is sought out by Jesus, he is asked, 'Do you believe in the Son of man?' (Jn. 9:35). The question is at first sight

---

[189] F. J. Moloney, *op. cit.*, p. 84, points out that in this statement Jesus not only *has* 'judgment' because it is given by the Father, but *exercises* judgment by virtue of his status as Son of man. He writes, 'The Johannine Son of Man is "where judgment takes place" in the manner described in vv. 24–25' (p. 85). He agrees with W. H. Cadman, *The Open Heaven* (1969), p. 34, who says there is no question here of a pre-existent Son of man. Cadman sees the human figure to whom authority is granted. But the Son of Man sayings as a whole imply a pre-existent figure.

[190] S. S. Smalley, *op. cit.*, p. 293, speaks of this statement as 'harmonizing with the quintessential pattern of the Son of man tradition outside John'. He sees the saying as belonging both to the present and to the exalted authority of the Son of man. Nevertheless, the emphasis is clearly more on the future status. There has been some debate over whether the Jn. 5 reference is indebted to Daniel. A. J. B. Higgins, *Jesus and the Son of Man*, pp. 165f, and F. H. Borsch, *The Son of Man in Myth and History*, p. 294, see no connection, but against this, *cf.* J. L. Martyn, *History and Theology in the Fourth Gospel*, pp. 129ff.; R. G. Hamerton-Kelly, *Pre-existence, Wisdom and the Son of Man* (1973) pp. 235f., and C. F. D. Moule, *The Phenomenon of the New Testament* (1967), p. 92. One writer, B. Vawter, 'Ezekiel and John', *CBQ* 26, 1964, pp. 450ff, sees a connection between Jn 5 and Ezekiel rather than Daniel.

[191] Many scholars regard Jn. 6:27 as redactional – *cf.* R. Bultmann, *John* (1971), p. 225 n. 1., who maintains that 6:27b accords ill with the other Johannine Son of man sayings. *Cf.* also S. Schulz, *Untersuchungen zur Menschensohn – Christologie im Johannesevangelium. Zugleich ein Beitrag zur Methodengeschichte der Auslegung des 4 Evangeliums* (1957), p. 115, who considers the addition was made before the evangelist used it as a source.
Both C. K. Barrett, *John*, p. 238. and R. H. Strachan, *The Fourth Gospel: Its Significance and Environment* (³1941), pp. 185f., connect this passage with the 'heavenly man' speculation. Several other scholars, however, see the Son of man figure here as representing the perfect man (*cf.* B. F. Westcott, *John* (1887), p. 100; G. H. C. Macgregor, *John* (MNT, 1928), p. 138. S. S. Smalley, *NTS* 15, 1968–9, pp. 293f., notes that this saying stands in a context of conflict. Although admitting the Johannine flavour of Jn. 6:27, 53, Smalley does not think that this demonstrates the unauthenticity of the sayings. In his monograph, *Bread from Heaven. An Exegetical Study of the Conception of Manna in the Gospel of John and the writings of Philo* (1965), P. Borgen claims that this is based on midrashic tradition and that 'bread from heaven' is identified as 'Wisdom' and 'Torah',

surprising. The man had no idea of the identity of the Son of man, which suggests that Jesus posed an enigma to challenge him to reflect on the person of Jesus, something he had clearly never previously done.[192]

(viii) In the passage describing the encounter of Jesus with various Greek enquirers, two Son of man sayings occur. The first announces that the hour for Jesus to be glorified has arrived (Jn. 12:23), and the second gives the question which the crowd puts to Jesus – 'How can you say that the Son of man must be lifted up?' (12:34). The latter seems to be a popular taking up of the title used in the former statement. The obvious confusion among the hearers shows that the term had no precise connotation in their minds.

(ix) The idea that the time for the Son of man to be glorified had arrived occurs again in John 13:31[193] in a statement to the disciples in the upper room, but seems to have met with no more understanding than before.

The different uses of 'Son of man'. It needs to be pointed out that in some of the above passages 'Son of man' is used as an alternative for the first person, as for instance in John 6:27, which may be paralleled with 6:51 where 'I' replaces 'Son of man' as giver of heavenly bread. This may also be illustrated from a comparison between the Son of man sayings and the Son (of God) sayings in 5:25ff., where both concepts are used, apparently interchangeably, with reference to Jesus.[194] Although this may be regarded as a characteristic of John's style, it is not possible to exclude the Son of man on this score. Indeed, this use of Son of man as equivalent to 'I' is fully in accord with some of the synoptic sayings. Other passages contain the same usage – John 6:53f., where 'Son of man' and 'my' are interchanged; 8:28, where 'Son of man' and 'I' stand in juxtaposition; and 9:35ff., where 'Son of man' is introduced as 'he who speaks to you' (*cf.* a parallel style in 4:25f.).

We need to set over against these instances others where no clear identification is given. Although the Son of man mentioned in 1:51 and 3:13f.,

---

[192] Some see the description of the man's reaction in Jn. 9:35 as a later addition to the text. *Cf.* R. E. Brown, *John*, p. 375; C. L. Porter, 'Jn. 9:38, 39a: A Liturgical addition to the Text', *NTS* 13, 1966–7, pp. 387ff.; B. Lindars, *John*, p. 351. C. H. Dodd, *Historical Tradition in the Fourth Gospel* (1963), p. 114, regards it as confessional. *Cf.* also C. F. D. Moule, *The Birth of the New Testament*, pp. 94f. But see S. S. Smalley, *NTS* 15, 1968–9, p. 296, maintains that the form in Jn. 9:35 does not fit into the form of other NT confession.

[193] The glorification appears to be centred in both the passion and exaltation of Jesus. *Cf.* Moloney's discussion here, *The Johannine Son of Man*, p. 195. The *oun* suggests a close connection between what has just been referred to and what follows. Bultmann, *John*, pp. 461ff., obscures the connection by placing Jn. 17 between 13:30 and 13:31. But see D. M. Smith's criticisms of Bultmann's reconstruction, *The Composition and Order of the Fourth Gospel* (1965), pp. 168ff.

[194] *Cf.* E. D. Freed, 'The Son of Man in the Fourth Gospel', *JBL* 86, 1967, pp. 402ff, who regards 'Son of man' as simply a variant of 'Son' or 'Son of God'. The various titles, according to him, are all used as variations of the name Jesus. Most scholars would, however, regard 'Son of man' as in some sense a title, or at least as conveying some distinctive significance in John as in the synoptics.

both referring to ascending and descending, could possibly be considered to be another person, the context does not support this. The same may be said of John 6:62. Again, in the passage in 12:23ff., the identification is more implicit than explicit; nevertheless, having heard Jesus say that he would be lifted up (12:32), the audience immediately asked a question about the 'Son of man' being lifted up, which shows that the hearers made some sort of identification of the title with Jesus. The question, 'Who is this Son of man?' is to be understood in the sense, 'Who is this Son of man whom you are claiming to be?'

The characteristics of the Son of man in John's gospel. Although there is much continuity between the synoptic and Johannine sayings about the Son of man, those in John bring out more explicitly features in the synoptic gospels, as well as presenting additional features. In view of John's declared theological purpose, it is not surprising that theological aspects of the Son of man sayings made a special appeal to him. These aspects may be grouped under the following headings.

(i) Statements about the *origin and destiny* of the Son of man. Perhaps the most significant feature which John focuses on is the *descent and ascent* of the Son of man (Jn. 1:51; 3:13).[195] The fact of the descent is integral to John's whole approach to Jesus as the connecting link between earth and heaven. It at once differentiates Jesus from the pre-Christian Jewish idea of Son of man, where the idea of descent is wholly absent.[196] It allows for the idea of incarnation, of which John makes a special point in his Logos doctrine (see later section, pp. 328f.). While the concept of 'descent' owes something to the spatial idea of heaven being above the earth, it is a vivid expression of the breaking in of the Son of man from the spiritual world of God to the material world of men. It reveals, moreover, an important consciousness in the mind of Jesus of his having been sent by and from God. The corresponding idea of ascent (*cf.* also 6:62) is important because it makes clear that the real sphere of the Son of man is in heaven and not earth.[197] Once his earthly mission is accomplished he returns to God. Ascension is therefore an integral part of the Son of man consciousness.

Closely allied to this and indeed an essential facet of it is the emphasis on the *pre-existence* of the Son of man. In addition to the above references,

---

[195] *Cf.* E. M. Sidebottom, *The Christ of the Fourth Gospel* (1961), pp. 112f. *Cf.* also *idem*, 'The Ascent and Descent of the Son of Man in the Gospel of St John', *ATR* 2, 1957, pp. 115ff.

[196] According to W. A. Meeks, 'The Man from Heaven in Johannine Sectarianism', *JBL* 91, 1972, pp. 44–72, the ascending-descending Son of man is the product of the sociological situation of the community (*i.e.* as alienated from the world). *Cf.* also Meeks' *The Prophet-King* (1967), pp. 292f., 318f.

[197] W. H. Cadman, *The Open Heaven*, pp. 26–42, puts a different construction on the descending-ascending theme. He reckons that Jesus entered so fully into knowledge of his own heavenly origin that he could be said to have ascended into heaven and to be in heaven. He takes the expression 'The Son of man in heaven', therefore, in a metaphorical sense.

John 6:62 brings this out – 'Then what if you were to see the Son of man ascending where he was before?'[198] Here then the pre-existence theme becomes explicit, while it is no more than implicit in the synoptic gospels. It is not only in such sayings, moreover, that the pre-existence of Jesus comes to the fore in John's gospel, for it is maintained in such passages as 1:1–14 (the Logos section) and 17:5. Indeed John's whole approach demands that his portrait of the historical Jesus should be viewed from the standpoint of his pre-existence.[199] Such a Son of man must be more than a man and the significance of the title cannot, therefore, be restricted to his humanity.

Another feature is that of the *glorification* of the Son of man which occurs in 12:23 and 13:31. The glorification begins on earth, but continues beyond. It is a specific way of describing the passion in terms of its ultimate consequences. The Son of man's glorification involved a cross, but the glory was more important to Jesus than the shame. It is worth noting that the theme of glory plays an important part in John's gospel, for not only is the Son of man glorified, but John claims in his prologue that 'we have beheld his glory, glory as of the only Son from the Father' (1:14) and the theme is frequently echoed elsewhere (*e.g.* 2:11; 5:41f.; 7:18; 8:50f.; 11:4; 12:41; 17:1f.; 17:22, 24).[200]

(ii) Statements showing the *authority* of the Son of man. Those passages which describe activities of the Son of man parallel to those attributed to God (as in 6:27) imply that there is no difference in authority between God the Father and the Son of man. In John 8:28 Jesus makes the assertion that he can do nothing on his own authority, but claims nevertheless to act on the authority of the Father. There is, therefore, an intimate connection between the mission of the Son of man and the will and plan of God.

It is, moreover, the Son of man who bestows eternal life on believers (*cf.* 3:14,15; 6:27). This activity of the Son is also linked to two other descriptions of Jesus used in John's gospel – Messiah and Son of God (see 20:31). The benefits of the mission of the Son of man are spiritual and require therefore a spiritual authority to bestow them. The portrait of Son of man in John's gospel is of one who possesses such authority.

---

[198] F. J. Moloney, *The Johannine Son of Man*, p. 123, in commenting on Jn. 6:62, rejects the view that this refers to the ascension. He thinks it refers to the Son of man's origin with God. 'It is because of his origin "with God" that his revelation is true; he has no need to ascend'. *Cf.* also C. H. Dodd, *The Interpretation of the Fourth Gospel*, p. 341.

[199] R. G. Hamerton-Kelly, *Pre-existence, Wisdom and the Son of Man*, p. 234, considers that both Jn. 12:23 and Jn. 13:31 emphasize that the exaltation of the Son of man is a return to pre-existence. Note that S. Schulz, *op. cit.*, pp. 120ff., considers that Jn. 13:31–32 is a pre-Johannine hymnic fragment based on 1 Enoch 51:3. But this is based on the dubious assumption that 'glorification' refers to the enthronement of the Son of man.

[200] For the significance of the use of the theme 'the glory of God', *cf.* G. B. Caird, 'The Glory of God in the Fourth Gospel: An Exercise in Biblical Semantics', *NTS* 15, 1968–9, pp. 265–277. He thinks that when John wrote *ho Theos edoxasthe en autoi*, he meant that God had fully displayed his glory in the person of the Son of man.

A further aspect of this authority is related to judgment. It is precisely because Jesus is Son of man that he has been given authority to execute judgment (5:26f.), a clear indication that his mission involved condemnation as well as salvation. Since judgment is the prerogative of God, the conclusion is inescapable that Jesus was deeply conscious of divine authority even during his earthly ministry. The hour for the exercise of that judgment is, however, not yet.

(iii) Statements predicting a *lifting up* of the Son of man. There are three passages in which a lifting up (*hypsoō*) is mentioned – John 3:14; 8:28; 12:32–34. In 12:33 the lifting is explained by an editorial comment: 'He said this to show by what death he was to die.' In John's mind the uplifting, therefore, referred to the raising of Jesus on a cross. This is equally clear from the analogy of Moses' lifting up of the serpent (3:14) and of Jesus' statement to the Jews that they would lift him up, both allusions to the coming passion (8:28). These statements are important for two reasons. They rule out the idea that John's gospel presents a heavenly Son of man Christology unrelated to the passion; and they accord completely with those synoptic predictions of the suffering Son of man. It is not, however, without significance that John prefers sayings which have a two-fold meaning. The idea of *hypsoō* is ambivalent.[201] While primarily referring to the passion, it nevertheless retains the overtone of coming exaltation through the passion and accords with the glorification motif mentioned above.[202]

In summing up the Johannine Son of man teaching, we must note that it accords completely with the synoptics' presentation, that it presents both heavenly and earthly aspects, that all the passages undoubtedly refer to Jesus and not to another, and that it is in harmony with other expressions of Christology in the gospel.[203] In itself it is an important link in the view that a basic unity exists between the synoptic and Johannine approach to Christology.

Additional note on the Son of man in John. As in the case of the synoptic Son of man sayings, so in the Johannine occurrences of the title, there is a wide variety of opinions regarding the significance of the evidence. There is

---

[201] C. H. Dodd, *The Interpretation of the Fourth Gospel*, pp. 377f., traces the *hypsoō* reference in Jn. 8:28, not to Is. 52:13, but to the play on words in the narrative of Gn. 40:13, 19, where 'lifting up' has the double meaning of hanging and exalting.

[202] Hamerton–Kelly, *op. cit.*, pp. 231ff., discusses the significance of the exaltation and glorification themes for the pre-existence of the Son of man. He points out, particularly on the basis of Jn. 3:14, that the return of the Son of man to pre-existence is by way of the cross. The lifting up refers, therefore, both to the passion and to future exaltation.

[203] F. J. Moloney, *op. cit.*, p. 215, speaks of 'a johannisation of a traditional theme' when he notes that the synoptic Son of man future sayings compare with the Johannine view that judgment takes place already in the person of Jesus as Son of man. R. Maddox, 'The Function of the Son of Man in the Gospel of John', in *Reconciliation and Hope* (ed. R. J. Banks, 1974), pp. 186–204, admits differences in vocabulary and imagery, but maintains there is no difference in fundamental significance.

divergence of opinion regarding the origin of the sayings. Some have traced the title back to pre-Christian Jewish or Hellenistic sources and seen the key to the understanding in some kind of ideal man. These have supposed that, through his use of the title, John has expressed his own belief in the representative character of Jesus. There is a tendency in these views to overlook the essentially incarnate character of the Son of man in John's gospel. Dodd (*The Interpretation of the Fourth Gospel*, p.249), admittedly recognizes the new slant which John gives to the Hellenistic 'heavenly man' by presenting him as a historical figure, but he does not do justice to the use of the title on the lips of the earthly Jesus, nor give sufficient weight to Jewish influences (like Dn. 7).

Another view, which regards the Johannine presentation as a theological rehabilitation of the title in new dress, is advanced in various guises. E. Kinniburgh ('The Johannine Son of Man', *StEv* 4, 1968, pp.64ff.), also denies that the Son of man is a future figure, but sees the title as referring to the death of Christ, which was his claim to glory. J. L. Martyn, *History and Theology in the Fourth Gospel* (1968), sees the 'Son of man' as the result of midrashic discussion between the church and synagogue, although Jesus himself is presented as a Mosaic Messiah, the one level leading to the other. There is much speculation in Martyn's views, because of his basic assumption that church and synagogue were separated under Gamaliel, which seems highly improbable. W. A. Meeks (*JBL* 91, 1972, pp.44–72) goes further and sees the Johannine Son of man sayings as a theologizing of a particular sociological situation, *i.e.*, the rejection of believers because they are 'not of this world'. Hence the descending and ascending Son of man provided the encouragement which these believers needed in their quest to attain to union with God. It is to be seen that this kind of interpretation supposes no continuity with the synoptic accounts, nor with the actual teaching of Jesus.

Many scholars would wish however to maintain a much closer link with the synoptic tradition, while admitting some significant differences in expression. *Cf.* J. H. Bernard, *John* (*ICC*, 1928), pp.cxxxiif.; W. F. Howard, *Christianity According to St John* (1943), pp.110ff.; L. Morris, *John* (*NICNT*, 1971), pp.172f.; E. K. Lee, *The Religious Thought of St John* (1962), pp.138–145. M. Black (*ZNW* 60, 1969, pp.5ff.) connects the Johannine usage, as in the synoptics, with the servant songs, although he notes the addition of the exaltation and glorification themes. Another scholar, S. S. Smalley, has argued that John's usage is firmly linked with the synoptic traditions, particularly in the influence of OT ideas, including an Adam theology (*NTS* 15, 1968–9, pp.278–301.). He sees the Johannine sayings as mainly authentic, but modified in their form.

Others admit that John knows of the synoptic traditions, but considerably reinterprets the Son of man idea. B. Lindars ('The Son of man in the

Johannine Christology', *Christ and Spirit in the New Testament* (ed. B. Lindars and S. S. Smalley, 1973), pp.43–60), who maintains a two-edition form of the gospel, thinks that John has modified the tradition to express the relationship between Jesus and God. R. Schnackenburg also sees some developments in John's use of the synoptic Son of man traditions (*John* 1 (Eng. trans. 1968), pp.529–542), which have been modified in the interests of his Christology. *Cf.* also his article, 'Der Menschensohn im Johannesevangelium', *NTS* 11, 1964–5, pp. 123–137. A. J. B. Higgins, *Jesus and the Son of Man* (1964), pp.153–184, considers the Son of man passages to be the central theme of John's Christology. He thinks the sayings come from an extensive source, probably liturgical, although he does not consider any of John's passages to refer to the earthly Son of man. This latter assumption is not supported, however, by a study of the passages in their existing context (*e.g.* the lifting-up passages).

Yet another approach is that which virtually identifies the Son of man passages with the Johannine Logos theme, and sees nothing distinctive about the Christology of the former. According to this view it is a misnomer to speak of a Son of man Christology in John. Among adherents of this view may be mentioned O. Cullmann (*The Christology of the New Testament*, pp.184f.). The Son of man presentation is linked for him with the pre-existence theme. E. D. Freed, (*JBL* 86, 1967, pp.402ff.) regards 'Son of man' in John as a variation of 'Son of God' and 'Son'. A similar view was maintained by W. Bousset, *Kyrios Christos*, pp.52f., 211ff. All the sayings except Jn. 1:51 are regarded as non-genuine by J. Jeremias (*ZNW* 58, 1967, pp.163f., 170f.) and as a Johannine elaboration with no special theological point.

In the above-mentioned views, there is a marked distinction between those which treat the sayings as John's own method of expressing a specific theological point of view, and those who are prepared to see them as based on genuine tradition of the teaching of Jesus. In view of the many close parallels in thought between the synoptic and Johannine sayings, it seems most reasonable to accept that John is presenting genuine traditions. In view of the total absence of the use of the title Son of man by anyone in the epistles, it is inconceivable that the Christian church invented it, and as inconceivable that John would have invented sayings which had no basis in fact. There is no more reason to suppose that John attributed Son of man sayings to Jesus to express his own assessment of him, than to suppose that Jesus himself made the statements in the context of his own dialogue with various people in his time. This is not, of course, to deny that the full import of the sayings did not become intelligible until later, and to this extent the Johannine setting of the sayings in the total context of his Christological presentation has particular significance.

Cf. E. M. Sidebottom, *The Christ of the Fourth Gospel*; C. K. Barrett,

John, (²1978); P. Ricca, *Die Eschatologie des vierten Evangeliums* (1966), for Jewish sources, and C. H. Dodd, *The Interpretation of the Fourth Gospel* (1953); R. G. Hamerton-Kelly, *op. cit.*, pp.271ff. for Hellenistic sources.

The rest of the New Testament

The fact that all the evidence about the Son of man outside the gospels can be reduced to one brief section highlights the almost complete replacement of the title in early Christian theology. It is strange that in the description of Stephen's death in *Acts*, Luke reports the statement, 'Behold, I see the heavens opened, and the Son of man standing at the right hand of God' (7:56), whereas there are no other occasions in Acts where the title is used.[204] Some significance must be attached to the title here, since Stephen's use of it cannot be regarded as accidental. The use bears a strong resemblance to Daniel's vision (Dn. 7:13f.), which may suggest that Stephen had seen the fulfilment of that vision in Jesus as Son of man in a unique sense. The exalted position of the Son of man at the right hand of God may also be indebted to Psalm 110:1. The understanding of the Son of man here in his status of glorious sovereignty is in line with the synoptic view of him in his future glory. There is a striking parallel also with the language of Mark 14:62. There is, in fact, a continuity between Stephen's use of the title and that of Jesus himself. One special feature of Stephen's vision is the standing position of the Son of man, since elsewhere in the NT the exalted Messiah is seated. It has been variously interpreted as indicating Jesus' welcome to the first Christian martyr, or of his testifying as a witness on his servant's behalf, or of his readiness for his return.[205] But whatever the explanation it is inescapable that Stephen viewed Jesus as having a position of particular authority.[206]

There is one reference to the Son of man in *Hebrews*, in a citation from Psalm 8:4–6 (Heb. 2:6–8) which is less significant, for the words are repeated precisely in their OT context without any independent use of the title. It is, of course, clear that the writer identifies the Son of man as Jesus, who is also referred to as Son of God. But the Son of man concept plays no part in the main doctrinal part of the letter. The citation comes in that

---

[204] G. E. Ladd, *TNT*, p. 337, criticizes those who maintain on the basis of Acts 7:56 that it was the primitive church who identified the exalted Jesus with the eschatological Son of man. He rightly points out that the NT does not contain evidence that the early church ever called Jesus Son of man.

[205] *Cf.* F. F. Bruce, *The Book of the Acts* (*NICNT*, 1954), pp. 165ff. W. Manson, *Hebrews* (1951), pp. 31f., in commenting on the Stephen passage in the Acts, sees the significance of Stephen's use of the Son of man title as being that 'Stephen grasped and asserted the more-than-Jewish-messianic sense in which the office and significance of Jesus in religious history were to be understood.'

[206] E. P. Blair, *Jesus in the Gospel of Matthew* (1960), pp. 142ff., discusses similarities between Mt's presentation and that in Stephen's speech in Acts 7, among which is the mention of the Son of man. Blair sees Stephen's use of the title as indicating the Son of man's role as coming judge. *Cf.* also H. P. Owen, 'Stephen's Vision in Acts 7:55, 6', *NTS* 1, 1955, pp. 224ff.

part which establishes the humanity of Jesus as an essential characteristic of our great high priest.

The two occurrences of Son of man in the book of *Revelation* (1:13f.; 14:14f.), are not strictly used as a title. In both cases the person of Christ is described as one 'like a son of man', after the pattern in Daniel 7. It is, therefore, descriptive of a person in human form rather than a specific reference to an apocalyptic figure. Nevertheless the man-like person possesses remarkable qualities, which show him to be divine. It is, for instance, he who is responsible for the final harvest of the world (Rev. 14:14f.). It is from his mouth that a sharp two-edged sword comes, symbol of his authority in judgment.

It would seem from this evidence that the title Son of man applied to Jesus made no important impact on early Christian theological thinking and that there is no evidence of a Son of man Christology.[207] Those distinctive features of the title in the synoptic gospels and John found different expressions in the rest of the NT. The title itself was displaced, but the basic ideas it was intended to express lived on in other forms.

LORD

The word *kyrios* (lord) was used as a title of respect in the world of the NT period. It was a title of courtesy when addressing a superior. An extended use of it was in addressing the Roman emperor or a pagan deity (such as Sarapsis or Isis). It was therefore widely used in the Gentile world. But it also carried with it particular connotations for Jewish people in that it was frequently used in the LXX as a rendering for the Hebrew *Adonai*, which was in turn used as a substitute for Yahweh. In view of this LXX usage some overtone of divine character would at times quite naturally be implied when the title was applied to Jesus, although by no means on every occasion.

Much debate has surrounded the origin of the use of the title in Christian thought. Some have maintained that it was due to the exposure of the Christian church to Hellenistic cultural usage.[208] Hence it has been main-

---

[207] It could, of course, be argued that the preservation of the Son of man sayings points at least to a continued interest in the theme, even if no specific Son of man Christology can be isolated. But the absence of the theme from the epistles corroborates the lack of a specific Son of man Christology. The preservation of the sayings requires another explanation – an over-riding desire to preserve the teaching of Jesus because of its authority.

[208] W. Bousset, *Kyrios Christos*, builds his thesis on this assumption. *Cf.* V. Taylor, *The Names of Jesus*, pp. 38ff., who takes a different line and maintains that we do not need to step outside Palestine to account for the confession 'Jesus is Lord' (see p. 51). For a discussion of the application of the title in emperor worship, *cf.* A. Deissmann, *Light from the Ancient East* (Eng. trans. 1927), pp. 338ff.; K. Prümm, 'Der Herrscherkult im Neuen Testament', *Bib* 9, 1928, pp. 1ff.

For recent assessments of Bousset's work, *cf.* N. Perrin, 'Reflections on the Publication in English of

tained that the earliest Gentile confession was that Jesus is Lord. But in that case it does not necessarily follow that it originated in such an environment. An examination of the NT evidence does not, in fact, support a later Hellenistic origin for the term.

The synoptic gospels

Many of the occurrences of *Kyrios* applied to Jesus in the synoptic gospels are instances where the vocative stands for a title of respect, rather similar to the familiar 'Sir' in popular usage. These instances are of little importance in discussing the theological use of 'Lord' as a revelation of the nature of Jesus.[209] They may in some cases imply more than respect in view of the early Christian use of Lord as a specific title for Jesus. Indeed, there are instances where 'the Lord' (*ho kyrios*) is used by the evangelists in referring to Jesus, no doubt because of the established usage at the time of writing. It seems reasonable to suppose therefore that *ho kyrios* was used of Jesus only after the resurrection. Luke is particularly fond of describing Jesus in this way (Lk. 7:13, 19; 10:1, 39, 41; 11:39; 12:42; 13:15; 17:5–6; 18:6; 19:8; 22:61 (twice); 24:34). It suggests that for him 'the Lord' had become a familiar and favourite way of referring to Jesus. Indeed, Luke's recording of the two disciples' words in the post-resurrection scene in 24:34, 'The Lord has risen indeed', furnishes a cue for the origin of his own usage. It is further noted that Luke's birth narrative abounds with instances where God is described as Lord (1:9, 11, 15ff., 25, 32, 38, 45, 46, 58, 66, 68, 76; 2:9, 22, 23, 24, 29, 39). In view of this, the angelic identification of the Saviour born in Bethlehem as Christ the Lord must convey some connotation of divine lordship. There can be no doubt that Luke would understand it in this way in view of the powerful influence of the LXX upon him in these birth narratives.

There are one or two other passages which call for special mention. When in the conclusion of the Sermon on the Mount Jesus defines those who qualify for entry into the kingdom, he differentiates between those who merely call him Lord and those who do the Father's will (Mt. 7:21). He implies that all should recognize his lordship, but that this recognition carries with it obligations. While this passage does not define what Jesus meant by Lord here, it certainly implies that it is more than a courtesy title. Another passage which carries with it an implicit acceptance of lordship on the part of Jesus is the discussion concerning Psalm 110, which has already

---

Bousset's *Kyrios Christos' ExT* 82, 1970–1, pp. 340ff.; I. H. Marshall, *The Origins of New Testament Christology* (1976), pp. 15ff.; F. H. Borsch, 'Forward and Backward from Wilhelm Bousset's *Kyrios Christos*', *Religion* 3, 1973, pp. 66ff.

[209] *Cf.* C. F. D. Moule, *The Origin of Christology* (1977), pp. 35f., who dismisses the vocative uses of *kyrios* as of no importance for Christology. *Cf.* J. D. Kingsbury, 'The Title "*Kyrios*" in Matthew's Gospel', *JBL* 94, 1975, pp. 246ff., who includes the vocative instances when reckoning the number of occurrences.

been mentioned in the section on 'The Son of David' (Mt. 22:41f. = Mk. 12:36f. = Lk. 20:42–44). If Jesus acknowledged himself to be Messiah, and admitted in the course of the dialogue that the psalmist addresses the Messiah as Lord, it is tantamount to recognizing the title as applicable to himself. The content of the title must again be determined by normal LXX usage. Some have supposed that the synoptic accounts of this discussion reflect later Christian deductions through the application of Psalm 110 to Jesus.[210] Even so the lordship is claimed to be used in an adoptionist and functional sense. It is further maintained that the second title 'Lord' did not originally express divinity.[211] Nevertheless, the word has considerable importance in denoting the dignity of the messianic office. In the context of the question over Psalm 110, however, the point in question is the superiority of Messiah to David.

The only other synoptic passage which might contribute anything to our present discussion is Matthew 21:3 (= Mk. 11:3 = Lk. 19:31), where Jesus instructs his disciples to tell the owner of the colt, 'The Lord has need of him.' The statement may suggest that Jesus was known as 'the Lord' in his lifetime, but it is more likely that the disciples would have regarded this as no more than a title of respect. It seems highly probable, for instance, that the owner of the colt had had previous contact with Jesus. In this case 'the Lord' may here be equivalent to 'the Master'.

The Master-disciple relationship, which is so strong in the synoptic gospels, would owe much to the Jewish idea of the teacher (*didaskalos*) and his pupils, but it is significant that the use of *kyrios* extends beyond this. Whereas undoubtedly the early Christian use of the title infused considerably more content into it, its tacit acceptance by Jesus prepared the way for that development.

The Johannine literature

The fourth gospel reflects a similar basic pattern of the non-theological use of the title before the resurrection and the theological use after. There are three occasions on which John describes Jesus as *ho kyrios* in narrative (4:1;[212] 6:23; 11:2). These instances are frequently regarded as editorial or textual glosses, in which case they are excised from the evidence. But if the words are authentic, John's usage is in line with Luke's. The title became a normal way of describing Jesus after the resurrection. It is strange

---

[210] *Cf.* Hahn, *The Titles of Jesus in Christology*, p. 113. He says that the concept of Messiah was applied to denote 'an independent heavenly office of Jesus' and the *kyrios* title was linked to this on the basis of Ps. 110:1.

[211] Hahn, *ibid.*, pp. 105ff.

[212] In the case of Jn. 4:1, J. H. Bernard, *John* 1, p. 132, prefers the reading which has *ho Iēsous*. He also regards 6:23 as a gloss. C. K. Barrett, *John*, thinks this is unnecessary, but he treats the occurrence of *kyrios* as a gloss. *Cf.* B. Lindars, *John*, p. 177, on Jn. 4:1, which he prefers to understand as originally not using the title Lord.

that John did not use it more. It may have slipped into his narrative without apparent reason. In chapters 20 and 21 the title is used to refer to the risen Lord. The most striking instance is in Thomas's confession where it is linked with God (Jn. 20:28). In the Johannine epistles there is no occurrence of the title.

Acts

The title Lord is a particular favourite with Luke in narrating the deeds and teachings of the early church. The application of the title to Jesus is immediate and almost automatic. The disciples, in putting the question about the restoration of the kingdom instinctively address the risen Jesus as Lord (Acts 1:6) and this is frequently continued in direct prayers included in this book (cf. 1:24; 4:29; 9:5; 10:4, 14; 22:8,19). As in most of these cases there is no indication that Jesus is being addressed, it cannot be ruled out that 'Lord' may be an address to God. Where Saul of Tarsus addresses the risen Christ as Lord, he uses the title before discovering the identity of the voice. The use of kyrios for God is so frequent that it is all the more remarkable when the title is undoubtedly used of Jesus. There are several instances where 'Lord Jesus Christ' or 'Lord Jesus' occurs (cf. 1:21; 4:33; 7:59; 8:16; 11:17; 11:20; 15:11; 15:26; 20:21, 24, 35; 28:31). There are a few instances of these titles being used with the personal pronoun 'our' (cf. 15:26; 20:21). These are sufficiently numerous to show how natural it was for the Christian church to refer to Jesus in this exalted way.

One of the most significant statements in Acts is in Peter's first sermon. The climax was reached with the declaration in 2:36 that 'God has made him both Lord and Christ, this Jesus whom you crucified'. The linking of lordship with messiahship is important, especially at this early stage. Lordship here is undoubtedly an ascription of sovereignty in vivid contrast to the crucified Jesus. It was this contrast which caused the strong reaction among the hearers. In the account of Saul's conversion, Ananias identifies the Lord who had spoken to him and sent him to Saul as the Jesus who had appeared to Saul on the road (Acts 9:17). It is significant that Saul's first question in answer to the heavenly voice was, 'Who are you, Lord?' (Acts 9:5).[213] It was instinctive to connect lordship with a situation in which a revelation comes in the form of a vision. There can be no doubt that this experience played a vital part in Paul's subsequent understanding of Jesus as Lord. In Peter's speech to Cornelius the statement is made about the preaching of peace by Jesus Christ ('he is Lord of all') (Acts 10:36).[214] This

---

[213] Some exegetes prefer to see in the form of address 'Lord', no more than a polite form of address (i.e. 'sir'). Cf. F. F. Bruce, The Book of the Acts (1954), p. 195. But the extraordinary character of the revelation demands more than this. We need not, of course, suppose that Saul of Tarsus had any appreciation as yet of the full implications of the title for Christ.

[214] E. Haenchen, Acts (Eng. trans. 1971), p. 352, points out that 'Lord of all' is properly a pagan predicate of God. But when applied to Christ the pantōn is meant personally in the sense of lordship over both Jews and Gentiles.

is a remarkably comprehensive view of the lordship of Jesus, implying full sovereignty.

The evidence from Acts shows that the lordship of Christ carried with it implications of Godhead. In many cases where *kyrios* is used in Acts it comes in OT (LXX) citations, which shows that it is right to use the OT background for the interpretation of the word in early Christian thought (*cf.* for instance 2:20–21, 25, 34 from Peter's first sermon).

Paul

Among the many occasions when Paul attributes lordship to Jesus there are in the main two lines of evidence. There are several instances where the apostle may well be echoing traditional material, and in these cases we shall discover a close link with primitive thought. We shall consider this strand of evidence first and then lead into a consideration of Paul's own distinctive developments.

The marana tha *saying in 1 Corinthians 16:22.* The form *marana tha* is Aramaic [215] and is generally translated 'Our Lord, come', but it has raised many difficulties of interpretation.[216] To begin with it is not certain whether *marana tha* is the right division in Aramaic, since the form could have been *maran atha*. If the latter is correct, the translation would be 'Our Lord comes' (future) or 'Our Lord is here' (perfect). If the similar formula in Revelation 22:20 ('Come Lord Jesus') is taken as the key to the understanding of 1 Corinthians 16:22, it would favour the former of the two propositions mentioned above, *i.e.* the view that regards it as a prayer rather than an announcement. Whichever interpretation is followed, it would not affect the ascription of lordship to Jesus, unless it be maintained that God and not Jesus is being referred to in this statement.[217] The context, however, would strongly support the view that Jesus is here in mind (as verses 23 and 24 both show). What is of particular interest is that an Aramaic form should be repeated, without a Greek translation, to a Greek-speaking church like Corinth. There can be only one satisfactory explanation, *i.e.* that the form represents an early Jewish Christian saying which had already

---

[215] For detailed discussions on the *Marana tha* form, *cf.* F. Hahn, *op. cit.*, pp. 89–99; C. F. D. Moule, *op. cit.*, pp. 36ff.; R. N. Longenecker, *The Christology of Early Jewish Christianity*, pp. 121ff. O. Cullmann, *The Christology of the New Testament*, pp. 208ff., considers the correct form to be a prayer. He sees it in a eucharistic setting and concludes that the ascription of lordship to Jesus arose in a worship context.

[216] On the context of this *Maranatha* passage, *cf.* C. F. D. Moule, 'A Reconsideration of the Context of Maranatha', *NTS* 6, 1960, pp. 307ff. *Cf. idem*, 'The Distinctiveness of Christ', *Theology* 76, 1973, pp. 564f. On this passage, *cf.* also M. Black, 'The Maranatha invocation and Jude 14, 15 (1 Enoch 1:9)', in *Christ and Spirit in the New Testament* (ed. B. Lindars and S. S. Smalley), pp. 189ff., who prefers a future reference equivalent to a prophetic perfect.

[217] *Cf.* W. Bousset, *op. cit.*, p. 22f. in the 1916 edition, although he abandoned this position in his 1921 edition. It has been more strongly advocated by Bultmann, *TNT* 1, pp. 51f.

become a kind of stock expression among Gentiles.[218]

Another problem arises over the precise meaning of *mara*. Does it carry with it the full meaning of the Greek *kyrios*, or is it a title with little if any religious overtones? One theologian distinguishes between what he calls a *mare-kyrios* ascription and an acclamation–*kyrios* title, the latter developing through the influence of Hellenism.[219] This may be criticized on the ground that no basis exists for supposing that the *kyrios* title could not have been applied to Jesus in Jewish Christian circles (on the contrary, *cf.* Acts 2:36). It must also be pointed out that the theory makes too sharp a cleavage between Judaic and Hellenistic Christianity.[220] It will not do to dispense with this evidence by maintaining that the early Jewish Christians did not at first attribute present lordship to Jesus, believing that this would be bestowed only at the parousia. Our investigations of the gospels material would not, however, support this view. Of particular value here is the debate over Psalm 110.[221] There seems no reason to doubt that those who used the *marana tha* form would not think it strange to link it with the *kyrios* ascription.

An early confessional formula (Rom. 10:9; 1 Cor. 12:3). The first of these passages shows that salvation is available to the one who confesses (*homologēsēs*) that 'Jesus is Lord' and believes that God raised him from the dead. Some have supposed this to mean that the only creed required was this statement about the lordship of Christ rather than an affirmation of Christ as Saviour. But this interpretation does less than justice to Paul's gospel. The apostle is concerned in this passage with the relation of confession to faith, not with a definition of the creed. He is deeply aware that anyone who has come to acknowledge the lordship of Jesus has seen him in an exalted light, and such a confession naturally goes hand in hand with faith in a risen Lord. Lordship would make no sense apart from the resurrection.[222] In the same passage (Rom. 10:12) Paul asserts that 'the same Lord is Lord of all' (*i.e.* both Jew and Greek).[223] Any attempt to drive a wedge

---

[218] O. Cullmann, *The Christology of the New Testament*, p. 214, regards the retention of words in Aramaic as due to respect for the Jerusalem church, where the expression was believed to have originated.

[219] W. Kramer, *Christ, Lord and Son of God*, pp. 101f., complains that confusion arises because of a blurring of the two *kyrios* uses. *Cf.* Longenecker's criticisms of this view, *op. cit.*, p. 123.

[220] *Cf.* I. H. Marshall, 'Palestinian and Hellenistic Christianity: Some Critical Comments', *NTS* 19, 1972-3, pp. 271-287.; *idem, The Origins of New Testament Christology* (1976), pp. 32ff. The sharp distinction between Judaistic and Hellenistic Christianity was strongly advocated by W. Bousset, and the *Religionsgeschichte* school. Their opinions have exerted a powerful influence on Bultmann and many of his followers.

[221] *Cf.* O. Cullmann, *The Christology of the New Testament*, p. 223. He writes, 'Scholars do not usually attribute sufficient importance to the fact that statements about the exaltation of Christ to the right hand of God (which were very early included in the creed) formally go back to this psalm'.

[222] As F. J. Leenhardt, *Romans*, p. 271, affirms, 'Lordship and resurrection are inseparable. It is the resurrection faith which provides the basis for the confession of Christ's Lordship.'

[223] That 'Lord' here must refer to Christ is clear from the context as well as from Paul's general usage. *Cf.* J. Murray, *Romans* 2 (*NICNT*, 1967), p. 57.

between Jewish and Gentile Christology on the ground that the latter, not the former, confessed lordship falters on Paul's claim that lordship is common to both. What is more, anyone to be saved is required to call on the name of the Lord (*i.e.* both Jew and Greek). The second passage (1 Cor. 12:3) contains the same confession 'Jesus is Lord', but here Paul is concerned with the essential aid of the Spirit if anyone is to make such a confession.[224] We shall need to discuss later the content of lordship in Pauline thought.

A general confession of lordship (Phil. 2:11). At the conclusion of the great Christological hymn (Phil. 2:6ff.) the climax is reached with everyone confessing that 'Jesus Christ is Lord, to the glory of God the Father'. The wording of the confession is allied to the last two passages except that here the double name Jesus Christ is used. Some see this as a more developed form originating from a Hellenistic environment and therefore less early.[225] But again the evidence does not support so sharp a distinction in the use of 'Jesus' and 'Jesus Christ'. Since most scholars regard this Philippians passage as an early Christological hymn which Paul has adapted for his own purpose,[226] it is highly probable that the confession of lordship here reflects a conviction that at once sprang up in the Christian church. What is most significant is the fact that the confession in this case is based on a new name given to Jesus (presumably that of Lord, *kyrios*).[227] The confession therefore involves the acknowledgment of the universal sovereignty of Jesus.[228] But when can this confession be expected to be fulfilled? Certainly every knee has not yet bowed at the name of Jesus and every tongue has not yet confessed his sovereignty, although he has already been highly exalted.[229] There is a drawing together here of a present acknowledgment of the lordship of Jesus among Christians (see Phil. 2:5) and the prospect of universal acknowledgment in the future. But the future scene of confession need not be a confession of faith, for Paul does not support such a view of universal faith, but it means a recognition by everyone of what Christians aided by the Spirit have already confessed (see the further discussion of this passage later, pp. 344ff.).

[224] O. Cullmann, *The Christology of the New Testament*, pp. 219f., sees 1 Cor. 12:3 in the context of emperor worship and persecution, not in the context of *glossalalia*. On the same passage, *cf.* T. Holtz, 'Das Kennzeichen des Geistes (1 Kor. XII: 1–3)', *NTS* 18, 1971–2, pp. 365–376.

[225] So W. Kramer, *op. cit.*, p. 68. He claims that only in a Hellenistic setting was Jesus Christ regarded as a double name. But see R. Longenecker's criticism of Kramer's position (*The Christology of Early Jewish Christianity*, pp. 126f.).

[226] *Cf.* R. P. Martin, *Carmen Christi* (1967). A thorough presentation is given of the various arguments affecting the authorship of this hymn. Martin concludes for a non-Pauline origin.

[227] J. Behm (*TDNT*[3], p. 1089) says, 'The name of *Kyrios* thus designates the position of the Risen Lord.'

[228] *Cf.* R. H. Fuller, *Foundations of New Testament Christology*, p. 213.

[229] *Cf.* R. P. Martin, *An Early Christian Confession* (1960), pp. 36f. Martin comments, 'From a cultic standpoint, then, which views His glory *sub specie aeternitatis*, His dominion is already acknowledged and His triumph over all his foes complete'.

297

Other evidence from Paul's epistles. In writing to the Corinthians Paul describes what he preached as 'Jesus Christ as Lord' (2 Cor. 4:5), which sums up what he has just called 'the gospel of the glory of Christ'. Any gospel which did not acknowledge the sovereignty of Jesus Christ would be out of step with Paul's gospel. This statement pours into the title Lord the profound truths of Paul's Christology. It was clearly infinitely more than a formal name – it conveyed with it the nature of sovereignty. Thus the apostle identifies himself in his preaching with the primitive confessions of faith.

In his former letter to the same church, Paul includes a passage which contains some basic facets of belief – 'Yet for us there is one God, the Father, from whom are all things and for whom we exist, and one Lord, Jesus Christ, through whom are all things and through whom we exist' (1 Cor. 8:6).[230] The lordship here is identified with the same creative and sustaining functions as God the Father. In no clearer way could Paul bring out the exalted nature of the Lord. It is perhaps worth noting that in both these Corinthian passages the double name Jesus Christ is found, as in the Philippian passage. Moreover in the case of 1 Corinthians 8:6 the unique lordship is specifically brought out, thus excluding comparisons with any other kind of lordship.[231]

In a passage of practical importance (Rom. 14), Paul discusses the observance of festival days and food taboos with reference 'to the Lord' The use of the title Lord here is not accidental. It occurs seven times in verses 5–9 reaching the climax 'that he (Christ) might be Lord both of the dead and of the living' (verse 9). Clearly Christ is being identified through the title which brings out the idea of his sovereignty over all Christians, as the context shows. The lordship, moreover, is not confined to the sphere of this life.

Add to the evidence already cited the numerous occasions when Paul uses such expressions as 'Our Lord Jesus Christ', 'Our Lord Jesus' or 'Jesus Christ our Lord'; all of which specify a personal relationship with believers. The total picture emphasizes the great importance of the concept of lordship in the apostle's approach to the person of Christ.

But we have yet to discuss what lordship meant in the mind of Paul.

---

[230] H. Conzelmann, *1 Corinthians* (Eng. trans. *Hermeneia*, 1975, from *KEK*, 1969), p. 144, considers that *Kyrios* in 1 Cor. 8:6 is deliberately set in contrast to *Theos*, as is seen by the use of the preposition *dia*. That a distinction is being made is undeniable, but it is equally clear that the relation between God and Christ is intended to be close (*cf.* C. K. Barrett, *The First Epistle to the Corinthians* (BC, ²1971), p. 193). H. Langkammer, 'Literarische und theologische Einzelstücke in 1 Kor. viii. 6', *NTS* 17, 1971, pp. 193ff., considers that a pre-Pauline form of this statement was 'one God the Father and one Lord Jesus Christ'.

[231] The strong contrast between the many lords of the non-Christian world and the one Lord over all creation heightens the emphasis on the uniqueness of the lordship of Christ. E. -B. Allo, *Première Épître aux Corinthiens* (EB, ²1956), p. 201, rightly points out that the incidental way in which Paul refers to Christ's part in creation suggests that he is not expounding a new doctrine. He claims that from the beginning Paul must have been in possession of such a Christology.

Since he was strongly conditioned by an OT background of thought, it is certain that for him the title *kyrios* would be influenced by its LXX use in reference to Yahweh.[232] Although this cannot be demonstrated to mean that Lord when applied to Jesus signified God, yet other considerations show that this would not be an unreasonable deduction. Functions which in the OT are ascribed to God are in Paul's epistles attributed to Jesus Christ. For instance, salvation in the OT is for those who call on the name of Yahweh, but in Paul's epistles for those who call on the name of Jesus as Lord (*cf.* Rom. 10:13). The Lord Jesus shares the same creative functions as God (1 Cor. 8:6).[233] The transfer of functions from God to Christ is quite natural, because of the ascription of lordship (in a divine sense) to Christ. The frequently predicted day of the Lord in the OT often becomes the day of Christ in Paul's letters (*cf.* 1 Cor. 1:8; Phil. 1:6, 10; 2:6; *cf.* 2 Cor. 1:14). Indeed, the frequent difficulty of deciding whether Paul means to refer to God or to Jesus in using *kyrios* shows its exalted connotation.

There is a continuity between the gospels, Acts and Paul's epistles in the unhesitating acceptance of the title Lord as applied to Jesus. It is a title which made sense to both Jews and Gentiles, although the overtones for each group would be different. But the common denominator is the notion of divine sovereignty.

The rest of the New Testament

Most of the occurrences of Lord in *Hebrews* are in OT quotations (1:10; 7:21; 8:8; 10:30; 12:5, 6; 13:6). Against this background it is significant that Jesus is referred to as 'our Lord Jesus' (13:20), as simply 'the Lord' (2:3) and as 'Our Lord . . . descended from Judah' (7:14). Moreover, the promise of the new covenant that people would no longer have to teach 'Know the Lord', is directly applied to Jesus Christ (*cf.* 8:8ff.). If this theme of lordship is not dominant because of other themes, yet it is present in the background. Focus falls rather on divine sonship and priesthood.

Although only once in *1 Peter* is the full title 'Lord Jesus Christ' used (1:3), this does not mean a playing down of lordship, as 3:15 in a practical way shows: 'reverence Christ as Lord'.[234] Since this advice is intended for

[232] F. F. Bruce, 'Jesus is Lord', in *Soli Deo Gloria* (ed. J. M. Richards, 1968), pp. 23ff., maintains that since Jesus was thought of as *Kyrios par excellence*, it was easy for Christians to think of him in the LXX sense of *Kyrios* (*i.e.* as Yahweh). *Cf. idem, This is That* (1968), p. 36.

[233] Note that when Paul says there is *one* Lord Jesus Christ (1 Cor. 8:6), he may be reacting against the view that the deity of Christ clashes with Jewish monotheism. Longenecker, *The Christology of Early Jewish Christianity*, p. 135, however, is probably right when he claims that for the earliest Jerusalem believers 'the implications of deity contained in the ascription as yet lay in the substratum of thought'. In that case the title of Lord did not at that time pose any overt threat to Jewish monotheism.

[234] E. G. Selwyn, *1 Peter* (1946), p. 193, comments that what is enjoined 'is not merely a devotional love of Christ, but such a love inspired by a right theology, which at once invests Christ with the OT attributes of Jehovah as "Lord", and Christ's death, which was outwardly a judicial murder, with atoning significance'. E. Best, *1 Peter*, p. 133, notes that the expression could be rendered, 'Reverence the Lord

those who suffer for righteousness' sake, it demonstrates the encouragement which comes from accepting the over-all sovereignty of Jesus Christ. The same epistle contains two OT citations which use the title Lord as applied to God (1:25; 3:12), and point to the sense in which it is applied to Christ.

In *2 Peter* there are more uses of Lord in the titles of Jesus: 'Lord Jesus Christ' (three times), and the expression 'Lord and Saviour Jesus Christ' (three times; 1:11; 2:20; 3:18. *Cf.* also 3:2),[235] as well as the form 'Jesus our Lord.' Again the Christology is of a high order.

In an epistle which is notorious for its paucity of references to Jesus Christ, it is highly significant that *James*, in the only two instances of specific mention, uses the form 'Lord Jesus Christ' (1:1; 2:1). In the second instance the lordship theme is enlarged on by the further description 'the Lord of glory'. This must refer to the risen and exalted Lord and is therefore an indirect testimony to the resurrection of Jesus. James is wholly in line with the rest of the NT in ascribing lordship to Jesus. It is strange that he says so little, but the firm conviction of lordship lies behind the essentially practical teaching in this letter.

Jude, like 2 Peter, uses the title 'Lord Jesus Christ' (verses 17, 21, *cf.* verse 25). The false teachers, whom he condemns, were those who were denying 'our only Master and Lord, Jesus Christ' (verse 4),[236] so there is no doubt about the importance in Jude's mind of the concept of lordship.

In the book of *Revelation*, however, the title is generally applied to God (*cf.* 1:8; 4:8, 11; 11:15, 17; 15:4; 16:7; 18:8; 19:6; 22:5–6), mostly in liturgical passages. But on three distinct occasions it is used of Christ. In 11:8 the expression 'where their Lord was crucified' clearly identifies Christ as Lord, and in 17:14; 19:16, the full expression 'Lord of lords' is applied to the conquering Lamb (an expression which occurs in Dt. 10:17 applied to Yahweh). At the consummation there is no doubt that Jesus Christ is entitled to the same ascriptions of sovereignty as God himself. In the New Jerusalem the throne is described as the throne of God and of the Lamb (22:1, 3).

Conclusion

The ascription of lordship to Jesus Christ, which occurs in all the different literary groups, makes a distinctive contribution to the total NT doctrine

---

who is Christ.' It does not materially affect the notion of lordship here. A. M. Stibbs, *1 Peter* (*TNTC*, 1959), p. 135, prefers the predicative force for 'Lord'.

[235] These are the only occasions in the NT where the expression occurs. It makes doubly clear that sovereignty includes also salvation. In 2 Pet. 1:11, the kingdom is referred to Christ in a manner similar to Paul's usage (*cf.* J. N. D. Kelly, *Peter and Jude*, BC, 1969, p. 310).

[236] Or the 'our' could be restricted to 'Lord', as in RSV mg.

about the person of Christ for the following reasons:

(i) Absorbed into the current title of Jesus Christ, it denoted an acknow-ledged understanding of the dignity of Jesus.

(ii) In view of the frequent use of the title in OT citations, it is probable that the LXX usage of *kyrios* should be regarded as a key to an understanding of the term when applied to Jesus (*i.e.* as an appelative for God).

(iii) In NT usage the implication is that the same functions assigned to God are assigned to Christ.

(iv) The lordship is closely linked to the resurrection of Jesus and sym-bolizes his conquest over death.

(v) There is no suggestion in the NT that the title Lord was not an entirely appropriate ascription to Jesus. Neither is there any suggestion that the early church developed the idea of lordship when Christianity spread to a Hellenistic environment. It appears in the most primitive strata of Christian tradition. It makes better sense of the total NT Christology to maintain that lordship is a necessary accompaniment of belief in a risen Christ.[237]

(vi) In the Christian use, it implied the absolute sovereignty of Jesus over all aspects of faith and life.[238] He had become Lord and Master and his followers willing bond-slaves.[239]

SON OF GOD

There can be no doubt of the importance of the consideration whether Jesus thought of himself as Son of God. This will be the chief aim of our investigation of the evidence of the gospels. Certainly the early Christians in their reflection about the person of Jesus were convinced that he was the Son of God. It will be necessary to consider first the background to the use of the title in view of conflicting opinions over its origin and its part in the consciousness of Jesus. If Jesus was the Son of God in a unique sense this consideration will affect our approach not only to his teaching but to all that he did.

The background

We begin with the OT. It is noticeable at once that the idea of divine sonship is applied in a number of different ways.

[237] O. Cullmann, *The Christology of the New Testament*, p. 235, maintains that in the NT the deity of Christ is set out in connection with faith in the lordship he exercises. It is distinguished therefore from the later Greek discussions over the two natures. *Cf.* E. Stauffer, *NTT*, p. 114, who considers the title Lord to be the richest of the Christological titles.

[238] Longenecker refers to Paul's doctrine of *en Kyriō* as a distinctive feature of his own development of the lordship theme (*op. cit.*, p. 135). C. F. D. Moule, both in his book, *The Phenomenon of the New Testament* (1967), and in his more recent *The Origin of Christology* (1977), places much stress on the concept of what he calls the corporate Christ.

[239] Cullmann, *op. cit.*, p. 233, maintains that since there is no Christological vacuum between the resurrection and parousia of Christ, the *kyrios Christos* confession has particular significance.

(i) Angelic beings are described as sons of God (as in Gn. 6:1–4; Job 1:6; 2:1). This usage has frequently been called mythological, largely because angels are considered to be mythological beings. But there are no grounds for disputing the existence of such beings and the description of them as sons of God would denote their spiritual nature.

(ii) This is also the basis on which Adam can be described as a son of God (*cf.* Lk. 3:38).

(iii) In a more particular sense Israelites are called sons of God (*e.g.* Dt. 14:1–2; Je. 3:19–20; Ho. 1:10; *cf.* also Ecclus. 4:10; Wisdom of Solomon 2:18; Psalms of Solomon 13:8; 18:4). This suggests a more intimate sense in which Israelites as distinct from the people of the surrounding nations were regarded as God's chosen people. It was, therefore, a collective and not an individual sense.

(iv) What was true of the people individually was then applied to the nation corporately as is evident from the statement in Hosea 11:1, 'out of Egypt I called my son', in which the whole nation has a father-son relationship to God, which in Christian thought became personalized in the person of Jesus, as Matthew 2:15 shows.

(v) Even in OT times, the idea of sonship was applied in a special sense to the theocratic king. 2 Samuel 7:14 is a direct promise to David's son that God would be his father and he would be God's son. The promise was not restricted to Solomon, but was extended to his successors. It later came to be applied to the Messiah as Son of David. In line with this is the statement in Psalm 2:7, which is quoted more than once in the NT in reference to Jesus. We shall discuss below whether in pre-Christian times Messiah was ever described as Son of God.

We must give some consideration to the evidence from the intertestamental period, and this falls into two sections. The references to divine sonship are admittedly slight in both apocalyptic Judaism and in the Qumran literature.[240] In fact the only use of the idea in the former comes in Enoch 105:2 ('and my son will be united with them for ever'), although even here there is doubt about the pre-Christian date of this passage since it does not occur in the Greek version (in the sixth-century Chester Beatty papyrus).[241] In the later Apocalypse of Ezra there is a clearer identification of Messiah as God's Son (7:28f.; 13:32, 37, 52; 14:9), but since this apocalypse is dated late in the first century, it can make little contribution to our understanding of the use of the title in Judaism in the time of Jesus and the emergent Christian church. The evidence from the Qumran literature is more relevant, although even here the amount of evidence is slight. In 4Q

---

[240] For a brief statement of the idea of 'Son of God' in late Judaism, *cf.* B. Gerhardsson, *The Testing of God's Son* (Eng. trans. 1966), pp. 20ff. *Cf.* also E. Lohse, *TDNT* 8, pp. 357ff.

[241] For a discussion of the text of the Greek Enoch, *cf.* A. M. Denis, *Introduction aux Pseudépigraphes Grecs d'Ancien Testament* (1970), pp. 15–50.

Florilegium, the text of 2 Samuel 7:14 is applied to the Branch of David.[242] Although it is not conclusive that this means that 'Son' was used as a title, it may point to such a usage, in which case this text is evidence that Son of God was beginning to be thought of in a messianic sense.[243]

Some scholars, however, have appealed to Hellenistic sources for an understanding of the NT use of Son of God on the supposition that it is derived from the Greek idea of divine men, as for instance the concept of kings as divine (*theioi andres*).[244] But this is widely removed from the use of Son of God in the gospels. The Greek divine men [245] exercised their authority in a very different way from Jesus, and in view of the basically Jewish background of Jesus and the disciples this theory introduces an alien concept. It is a legacy from the school of thought which traced most ideas in the NT to Hellenistic sources in the interests of a history of religions approach to Christian origins.

The synoptic gospels

In considering the fatherhood of God, some discussion was included on the special sense in which Jesus addressed God as Father (pp. 81ff.). This general understanding of God as Father implies the divine sonship of Jesus and should be considered as a necessary prelude to the more specific use of the title. On numerous occasions Jesus spoke of God as 'the Father', 'my

---

[242] *Cf.* above, n. 38, for comments on this.

[243] *Cf.* R. H. Fuller, *The Foundations of New Testament Christology*, p. 32; R. N. Longenecker, *The Christology of Early Jewish Christianity*, p. 95. Against this view, *cf.* J. Jeremias, *The Prayers of Jesus* (1967), p. 40.

[244] R. Bultmann, *TNT* 1, p. 130. There has been much appeal to the idea of divine men in Greek usage, but W. von Maritz, *TDNT* 8, pp. 335ff., claims that the phrase 'divine man' is of modern origin. *Theios* was used predicatively, not as an attribute.

[245] M. Smith, 'Prolegomena to a Discussion of Aretalogies, Divine Men, the Gospels and Jesus', *JBL* 90, 1971, pp. 174–199, gives a survey of studies which have taken into account the evidence of divine men in the Graeco-Roman world. He makes much of parallels and suggests that Jesus was at first primarily seen as a miracle worker. He claims that the gospels are nearer to the accounts of divine men in the Graeco-Roman world than to any other known non-Christian works. The significance of this for M. Smith lies in his prior rejection of the close continuity between the OT and NT.

Smith mentions L. Bieler's study *THEIOS ANĒR das Bild des 'göttlichen Menschen' in Spätantike und Frühchristentum*, 2 vols. (1935–6, r.p. 1967), as the fullest analysis of a large selection of material on this subject. He also mentions G. P. Wetter's earlier work, *Der Sohn Gottes* (1916), among other works exploring the non-Christian parallels. P. J. Actemeier, 'Gospel Miracle Tradition and the Divine Man', *Int* 26, 1972, pp. 174–197, discusses the rabbinic and Hellenistic parallels and thinks the NT miracles approximate nearer to the latter than the former.

The Hellenic idea of *theios anēr* has been particularly taken into account in explaining the Christology of Mark. For a criticism of this, *cf.* O. Betz's study, 'The concept of the so-called "Divine Man" in Mark's Christology', in *Studies in New Testament and Early Christian Literature: Essays in Honour of A. P. Wikgren* (ed. D. E. Aune, 1972), pp. 229–240. He sees very little evidence of the existence of such a person as *theios anēr* and finds no reason for accepting the concept in relation to Jesus. *Cf.* W. Lane's critique in *New Dimensions in New Testament Study* (ed. R. N. Longenecker and M. C. Tenney, 1974), pp. 144–161. *Cf.* also the brief critique of Bieler's theory by C. F. D. Moule, 'The Distinctiveness of Christ', *Theology*, 76, 1973, pp. 563f.

Father', 'my heavenly Father' and 'your heavenly Father' – fifty-one times in all. Matthew includes more instances of this usage than his fellow synoptists. The evidence suggests that Jesus' naming of God as Father was part of his constant awareness of God's fatherly concern for him and his mission. His use of *Abba* in addressing God is striking when considered against the background of Jewish transcendentalism, and made so deep an impression on the early disciples that the Aramaic form was preserved, even in Greek-speaking circles (Rom. 8:15; Gal. 4:6). It came to be used by Christians in their own approach to God.[246]

This latter observation raises an important question. Did Jesus consider that God was his Father in precisely the same sense in which it can be maintained that he was Father of all? Although there are differences of opinion on this matter, the evidence supports most strongly the view that Jesus was conscious of a relationship to his Father which was unique. Some suppose that he regarded all men as sons of God by virtue of creation, whether actually[247] or potentially.[248] But all the sayings are addressed to the disciples, with the possible exception of those contained in the Sermon on the Mount, and even there it is questionable whether this teaching was intended to apply to all men irrespective of their relationship to Jesus. In no case does Jesus link himself with his disciples in saying 'Our Father', for the use of that phrase in the pattern prayer was given specifically to the disciples (Mt. 6:9).[249] Moreover, people may become sons of God (Mt. 5:45), a sense which is never applied to Jesus himself. Our approach to the synoptic evidence must, therefore, recognize at the outset a distinction between God as Father of Jesus, and God as Father of the disciples;[250] the distinction becomes even more specific in John (20:17).

Another important preliminary question is whether 'Son of God' is always equivalent to 'Son', or whether, as some have maintained, two distinct Christological titles are in mind. The debate revolves around the allegation that the absolute use of 'Son' is alone linked with a corresponding use of 'Father', whereas 'Son of God' never is.[251] According to this theory it was only in later developments that 'Son of God' came to be used as a title, but in any case it is denied that it could have been derived from the absolute use of 'Son'. But this attempt to draw a sharp distinction between

[246] *Cf.* J. Jeremias, *The Central Message of The New Testament* (1965), pp. 9–30. Jeremias comments, 'We are confronted with something new and unheard of which breaks through the limits of Judaism' (p. 30).

[247] *Cf.* H. Montefiore, 'God as Father in the Synoptic Gospels', *NTS* 3, 1956, pp. 31–46.

[248] B. M. F. von Iersel, *Der Sohn in den synoptischen Jesusworten* (1961).

[249] *Cf.* T. W. Manson, *The Teaching of Jesus* (²1935), pp. 89–115. In this section Manson examines all the evidence in the synoptic gospels for God as Father. He pays particular attention to the form in which fatherhood is spoken of, *i.e.* whether 'my' or 'your'.

[250] *Cf.* I. H. Marshall, 'The Divine Sonship of Jesus', *Int* 21 (1967), p. 90, who thinks that the absence of any record of Jesus using the form 'our Father' to include himself as well as his disciples suggests there is a difference in status which is not accidental.

[251] So F. Hahn, *The Titles of Jesus in Christology*, pp. 279f.

the two is unsatisfactory for the following reasons.[252] The two forms are used by both Mark and John, who were clearly unaware of any distinction between them. It is moreover not established that 'Son' always occurs in conjunction with 'Father' (*cf.* Mk. 1:11; 9:7; 12:6). It seems arbitrary in the extreme to drive a wedge between two forms which both depend on a filial relationship. There is no doubt that the theory rests too heavily on the view that Son of God is derived from the Greek notion of divine man. It should also be observed that this is an example of speculation about comparative sources being used to dominate the exegetical question of what the term 'Son' meant for Jesus. Whatever its origins, room must be left for Jesus himself to use the term in his own unique way, which can be determined only by an exegetical examination of the contexts.

Passages in which 'Son of God' is used with 'Messiah'. Even if the pre-Christian Jewish literature cannot provide evidence of the fully developed use of Son of God as a title for the expected Messiah, there are three passages in the synoptic gospels where the two titles are linked and it would be valuable to begin with these passages.

The most important is Peter's confession (Mt. 16:16; *cf.* Mk. 8:29; Lk. 9:20), although this is not recognized by those scholars who regard the words 'Son of the living God', after 'you are the Messiah', as unhistorical. It is true that Mark has only 'you are the Messiah', but before we dispense with Matthew's further words as unoriginal, we need to enquire whether there are any grounds for supposing that Peter could not have uttered them in his confession. Naturally if it be supposed that Son of God was a Hellenistic concept, it is easy to claim that the Jewish Peter could not have used it. But we have already seen that Jewish parallels are closer than Hellenistic to the gospel usage, which means that the combination of Messiah and Son of God is not impossible in a Jewish context. It is, moreover, not self-evident that Matthew's addition must be discounted, simply because it is peculiar to him. Both Mark and Luke record the application of the title Son of God to Jesus in other contexts. The distinctive aspect of this confession in Matthew is, therefore, that it represents an awareness on Peter's part that the Messiah had come from God and had a special relationship to God. In view of the numerous occasions on which Jesus called God his Father it would have been extraordinary if none of the disciples had recognized him in a special sense as Son of God and confessed him as such. In the absence of any good grounds for denying the validity of Matthew's addition, we may regard Peter's confession as a significant stepping stone in the development of early Christian awareness of the

[252] Marshall, *art. cit.*, p. 88, maintains that the alleged distinction is not well-founded exegetically. The whole article (pp. 87–103) shows that there is a firm basis for the view that Jesus spoke of God as Father and himself as Son.

nature of Jesus the Messiah as Son of God.

Another passage is that of Matthew 26:63f. (= Mk. 14:61f.; Lk. 22:66f.) in which Caiaphas puts the direct question, 'Tell us if you are the Christ, the Son of God.' (Mark has 'Son of the Blessed,' and Luke splits the question into two). In all the accounts Jesus answers in the affirmative with sufficient clarity for action to be taken against him for blasphemy (according to Matthew and Mark). The title must certainly have conveyed more than a courtesy title for it to create such a strong reaction. Mark's 'Blessed' is a periphrasis for God and we may therefore note that there is no essential difference between the accounts. Even Luke's splitting of the questions does not introduce a significant variation, although it makes more clear that it was the admission of divine sonship which the hierarchy could not tolerate.

The other synoptic passage which links Son of God with Messiah is Luke 4:41, where demons say to Jesus, 'You are the Son of God', and Luke comments, 'But he rebuked them, and would not allow them to speak, because they knew that he was the Christ.' Some messianic connotation must, therefore, have been linked with the title 'Son of God'. It is significant that Jesus declined demonic testimony to his sonship, although he accepted the testimony of Peter.

Passages where Jesus' consciousness of sonship comes into focus. We turn now to the key passage in the synoptic gospels on Jesus' consciousness of his divine sonship (Mt. 11:25f.; Lk. 10:21f.).[253] This passage is remarkably parallel to many statements in John's gospel, which has caused it to be described as 'a bolt from the Johannine blue'.[254] It is the most important link between the synoptic and Johannine presentations of Jesus. There has been much debate about this key passage, but it will be possible here only to give a brief account of the salient features of the debate.[255]

It combines a prayer of Jesus with a statement by Jesus. The prayer is addressed to God as Father, which title is included twice. By way of

[253] Some of the debate over this passage concerns textual matters. These were debated in detail by P. Winter, 'Matthew x. 27 and Luke x. 22 from the First to the Fifth Century: Reflections on the Development of the Text', *NovT*, I, 1956, pp. 112ff., who concluded that the tradition was preserved only in a corrupt form. But M. J. Suggs, *Wisdom, Christology and Law in Matthew's Gospel* (1970), pp. 71ff., criticizes the basis of Winter's arguments.

[254] As T. W. Manson, *op. cit.*, p. 110, pointed out there is no reason to doubt the authenticity of this saying on the grounds that it has Johannine parallels. See also J. Jeremias, *The Prayers of Jesus*, p. 51, and *NTT* 1, p. 57, and I. H. Marshall, *Int* 21, pp. 91f., both of whom comment on the objections to the sayings.

[255] J. Zahrnt, *The Historical Jesus* (1963), p. 142, maintains that the understanding of Jesus as Son of God does not involve anything supernatural or unnatural. Sonship is defined in terms of allowing God really to be his Father. J. D. G. Dunn, *Jesus and the Spirit*, p. 37, claims that the evidence does not assert with any certainty the uniqueness of Jesus' sense of sonship. *Cf.* R. E. Brown, 'How much did Jesus know?' *CBQ* 29, 1967, pp. 337f., who considers that the evidence shows that Jesus claimed a special relationship with God.

definition the Father is described as Lord of heaven and earth. But the most significant feature of the prayer is that it concerns revelation. It is not, however, simply a Hellenistic idea.[256] The contrast between the 'babes' and 'the wise and understanding' finds parallels in the Qumran literature.[257] Even Hahn[258] recognizes here a Jewish type saying. The prayer section does not, however, specify what 'these things' are which are the subject of revelation. It is necessary to look at the explanatory statement which follows.

Here Jesus refers to God as both 'my Father' and 'the Father', but uses the absolute form 'the Son' as a self-description. We may dismiss as arbitrary the contention that Jesus never uses elsewhere the expression 'my Father' in addressing God and that therefore the first part of the statement must be considered unauthentic.[259] There is no reason why Jesus could not have said 'my Father', even if this is the only record of it. We may equally reject the contention that this saying is too closely parallel to Matthew 28:18f., where, as here, Father and Son are linked, to be considered authentic. This is because both are supposed to be a developed form in which authority and power are claimed by the Son. But again, there is not only no reason to deny such exercise of power to Jesus, but also no reason to maintain that Matthew 11:25f. deals with authority anyway. The theme is revelation passed on from the Father to the Son who is the sole agent for revealing it to others.[260] This revelation seems to include the unique filial relation between Jesus and God. There can be no doubt that Jesus was conscious of that relationship.[261]

An important consideration here is whether the statement in Matthew 11:27 implies the limitation or inferiority of the Son to the Father.[262] The

---

[256] *Cf.* R. Bultmann, *History of the Synoptic Tradition* (Eng. trans. 1963) p. 160, who regards it as a Hellenistic revelation saying. W. G. Kümmel, *Promise and Fulfilment* (Eng. trans. 1957), p. 41, maintains that the function of the Son as revealer rests on the Father's recognition of him, an idea of Hellenistic mysticism.

[257] E. Sjöberg, *Der verborgene Menschensohn in den Evangelien* (Humaniorum Litterarum Lundensis, 53, 1955).

[258] Hahn, *The Titles of Jesus in Christology*, p. 309. W. D. Davies devotes a chapter to this passage in his *Christian Origins and Judaism* (1962), pp. 119–144, and concludes for a definitely Jewish milieu for the logion.

[259] *Cf.* Hahn, *op. cit.*, 308ff., who gives serious consideration only to Mt. 11:27 (= Lk. 10:22), but even this he does not treat as authentic. He finds in the passage a Christological narrowing. 'Originally every one could say "Father", now access to the Father is tied to Jesus' (p. 312). The accuracy of this statement is dubious. Nevertheless, when Jesus says 'my Father' he uses the expression in a unique sense.

[260] Jeremias, *NTT* 1, pp. 59f., treats the father-son language in Mt. 11:25ff. as a parable of sons and fathers in general. Yet this does not explain why Jesus would want to use such a parable if it were not to imply some Christological relationship.

[261] *Cf.* I. H. Marshall, *Int* 21, 1967, p. 93, who contends that Jesus' self-understanding was grounded in his filial relationship to God on the basis of which the tasks of Messiah, Son of man, and servant to God were carried out.

[262] *Cf.* F. Hahn, *op. cit.*, p. 311. He relates this subordination, however, to the unity of purpose between Father and Son. He agrees that in his authority the Son altogether represents the Father.

reciprocal 'no one knows the Son except the Father' and 'no one knows the Father except the Son' does not, however, suggest inferiority. The fact that the Father delivers (*paradidōmi*) all things to the Son seems to be meant in the sense of the process of revelation.[263] It is the Son who chooses to whom he will make the revelation.

Another statement of Jesus which is not without its enigmatic difficulties is Mark 13:32 (= Mt. 24:36). The Markan text reads as follows: 'But of that day or that hour no one knows, not even the angels in heaven, nor the Son, but only the Father.' The statement supports the close filial relationship between Jesus and God, but it raises the difficulty of the seeming ignorance of the Son.[264] Does this imply inferiority? Some have supposed the exceptive clause to have been added by the church to explain difficulties over the delayed parousia. But it is inconceivable that the Christians would create such a difficult saying to explain a less difficult problem, or would distort an original saying to make it mean something different.[265] It certainly, as it stands, implies some limitation on the Son as compared with the Father, and this must be taken into account in considering the nature of the Sonship of Jesus in the gospels. It has alternatively been suggested that in this statement 'Son' stands for an original 'Son of man';[266] but unless 'Son of man' refers to someone other than Jesus, which is highly improbable in the present context, there is no essential difference in meaning.

We turn next to the accounts of the baptism, temptation and transfiguration of Jesus, in all of which his sonship plays an important role. The *baptism* is significant as marking the inaugural act of the mission with the heavenly voice setting a divine seal on that mission. The words, 'Thou art my beloved Son; with thee I am well pleased' (Mk. 1:11; *cf.* Mt. 3:17; Lk. 3:21–22) certainly identify Jesus as God's Son, but in what sense? Does the saying imply that only at this moment Jesus became God's Son?[267] There is no reason to suppose from the words themselves that sonship was a new experience for Jesus. Both Mark and Luke record the saying as a direct address to Jesus using the present tense, whereas Matthew puts it in the

---

[263] According to A. von Harnack, *What is Christianity?* (Eng. trans. 1901, [5]1958), p. 97, when rightly understood the name of Son means nothing but the knowledge of God. But this understanding is inadequate because it does not do justice to the question of relationship. In Harnack's treatment, the focus falls on Jesus' consciousness and this must be regarded against the background of the quest for the historical Jesus, now so widely regarded as unacceptable.

[264] *Cf.* I. H. Marshall, *op. cit.*, pp. 94f. He points out that if a saying existed which made no reference to the ignorance of the Son 'it is hard, if not impossible, to conceive of the early church's proceeding to transform an unexceptional saying into a "hard" one' (p. 94).

[265] *Cf.* the comments on the wording of this passage by G. Dalman, *The Words of Jesus*, p. 194; W. G. Kümmel, *Promise and Fulfilment*, pp. 40ff.; R. Schnackenberg, *God's Rule and Kingdom* (Eng. trans. 1963), p. 210. Schnackenberg accepts the authenticity of Mk. 13:32.

[266] *Cf.* R. H. Fuller, *The Foundations of New Testament Christology*, p. 114. E. Lohmeyer, *Das Evangelium des Markus* ([15]1959), p. 283, accepts the clause as genuine.

[267] *Cf.* B. H. Branscomb, *Mark* (*MNT*, 1937), pp. 16ff. F. Hahn, *op. cit.*, p. 293, considers that on the basis of the Spirit's descent, Jesus 'obtains the messianic dignity of the Son of God'.

third person. The most natural interpretation of these words is to regard them as a heavenly declaration of what was already in the consciousness of Jesus. There would be added point in the declaration if Son of God is connected with messiahship. There is a high probability that in the mind of Jesus filial consciousness and messianic consciousness were inextricably linked.

Two other features deserve mention. There is an echo from both Psalm 2:7 and Isaiah 42:1 in the words of the heavenly voice. The latter is significant because it refers to God's choice of his servant.[268] The passage would certainly have been familiar to Jesus and must have coloured his own understanding of the words 'with thee I am well pleased'. The other factor is the use of the word 'Beloved' (*agapētos*),[269] which can either be regarded as an adjective or as a title. If the former, it may be understood in the sense of 'only' (as in the LXX in Gn. 22:2, Je. 6:26; Am. 8:10) and therefore equivalent to the Greek *monogenēs*. This would support the interpretation mentioned above of the pre-existent Sonship of Jesus. If the word is taken as a title, it would draw attention to sonship of a unique kind.

The *temptation* narrative records the twice-repeated challenge of Satan, 'If you are the Son of God. . .' (Mt. 4:3, 6; Lk. 4:3, 9), which focuses the main thrust of the temptation on the filial consciousness of Jesus. Although the challenge is expressed as an if-clause, the Greek makes clear that there is no casting of doubt on the sonship of Jesus.[270] What is in mind is the way in which the privileges of sonship should be used. Satan is seen as accepting without question that Jesus was Son of God. This narrative is in harmony with that already mentioned in the demons' acknowledgement in Luke 4:41. The close connection in both Matthew and Luke between the baptism and the temptation narratives means that each must be interpreted in terms of the other and since both focus on sonship, it must be intended that at the commencement of the mission, the declaration of Jesus as Son of God and its consequences should be clearly understood. The

---

[268] *Cf.* C. E. B. Cranfield, *Mark*, 55; *idem*, 'The Baptism of our Lord – A Study of Mk. 1:9–11, *SJT* 8, 1955, p. 62. In the latter article, Cranfield remarks, 'In response to his self-dedication to the mission of the Servant, made when He submitted to the baptism of repentance, He is given a confirmation of His own consciousness of being the Son of God that is at the same time a consciousness of His Servant-vocation, as the echoes of Isa. 42:1 indicate'. *Cf.* also O. Cullmann, *The Christology of the New Testament*, p. 66; *idem, Baptism in the New Testament* (Eng. trans. 1950), pp. 16ff.; C. Maurer, 'Knecht Gottes und Sohn Gottes im Passionsbericht des Markusevangeliums', *ZTK*, n.f. 50, 1953, pp. 30ff. *Cf.* also I. H. Marshall's article cited in n. 121.

[269] G. Schrenk, *TDNT* 2, pp. 740f., considers that this expression implies sonship in the sense of an only Son. O. Cullmann, *The Christology of the New Testament*, p. 284, sees it as a combination of Son of God with *'Ebed Yahweh*. T. F. Glasson, 'The Uniqueness of Christ: The New Testament Witness', *EQ* 43, 1971, pp. 25–35, appeals to *agapētos* as evidence for the uniqueness of Christ (see p. 27).

[270] *Cf.* Hahn's discussion, *The Titles of Jesus in Christology*, p. 295. He sees the temptation narrative, especially in the first two temptations in Matthew, as the 'warding-off of a falsely understood Son of God concept'.

synoptic gospels present a Messiah who was fully conscious of his special relationship to God as Son.

Because of the heavenly voice in the *transfiguration* narrative, there are certain parallels to the baptism narrative which are worth considering[271] (Mk. 9:2ff.; Mt. 17:1ff.; Lk. 9:28ff.). In Matthew's account the idea of sonship is linked again with 'Beloved' and the same expression of divine pleasure is given. The expression of pleasure is, however, omitted in Mark and Luke, and the word 'Chosen' is substituted for 'Beloved' in the best texts of Luke. All the accounts contain an exhortation to the hearers to listen. What is most significant about this incident is that sonship is here linked with transformation. Some scholars have considered this account of sonship to be different in that the reference is to 'being'.[272] This is then considered to be Hellenistic, and therefore a later development. Or else the story is claimed to be an Easter story read back into the life of Jesus and therefore not to be regarded as historical.[273]

The transformation theme may, however, be otherwise understood.[274] It is not without importance that the synoptic accounts of the transfiguration place it after Peter's confession at Caesarea Philippi. It must, therefore, be seen against this background. If Matthew's account is followed and Jesus' comment that flesh and blood did not reveal the identity of Jesus to Peter is accepted as belonging to this context, the supernatural unveiling at the transfiguration falls into place. What Peter had previously declared is visually and orally attested in a supernatural way. It is clear from the transfiguration accounts that the disciples recognized that Jesus was more than purely human, although the full wonder of the event did not become intelligible until after the resurrection.[275] It is not surprising that a charge to secrecy was given immediately following this event. It would have been easy for the disciples to misconstrue the significance of the transfiguration before the full realities of the passion had been faced. But the account undoubtedly focuses on the special sonship of Jesus. The transfiguration sets him apart from other men in his unique relation to the Father. This explains his superiority to both Moses and Elijah (who may be legitimately

---

[271] For separate studies of the transfiguration, *cf.* G. H. Boobyer, *St Mark and the Transfiguration Story* (1942); H. Riesenfeld, *Jésus Transfiguré* (1947); A. M. Ramsey, *The Glory of God and the Transfiguration of Christ* (1949), pp. 101–147.

[272] *Cf.* Hahn, *op. cit.*, p. 300, who sees a development in a Hellenistic direction from a divine sonship that was messianically and therefore functionally determined to one of being.

[273] S. J. Wellhausen, *Das Evangelium Marci* (²1909), p. 71; R. Bultmann, *TNT* 1, p. 50; *idem, The History of the Synoptic Tradition*, p. 259.

[274] O. Cullmann, *The Christology of the New Testament*, p. 285, mentions Harnack and Meyer as opposing the reading-back theory. *Cf.* also E. Lohmeyer, *ZNW* 21, 1922, pp. 185ff., who did not regard the account as historical, but traces it to a Jewish origin.

[275] *Cf.* R. H. Gundry, 'The Narrative Framework of Mt. 16:17–19', *NovT* 7, 1964, pp. 1ff. Von Iersel, *Der Sohn in den synoptischen Jesusworten*, p. 176 n. 5, does not include this passage in his discussions because he thinks its *Sitz im Leben Jesu* is doubtful. But *cf.* I. H. Marshall, *Int*, 21, 1967, pp. 95f.

regarded as representatives of the law and prophets), neither of whom had such transfiguration in their lifetime.

There are two passages in which Jesus confronts the Pharisees which have a bearing on his consciousness of sonship. They occur in all the synoptic gospels. The first is the parable of the vineyard (Mk. 12:1–12; Mt. 21:33–43; Lk. 20:9–19), where the wicked tenants kill the owner's son. The important feature here is that other missions to the tenants have been unsuccessful and the focus falls on the special mission of the son to receive the inheritance. Sonship is therefore seen to be an essential qualification. Since the parable clearly relates to the treatment of Jesus by the religious leaders, it involves prediction of his own death at their hands. His position as Son is seen to be an important factor in the precipitation of his passion. So familiar was the vineyard imagery of Israel (*cf.* Is. 5:1–7) that the hearers readily detected that the message was against themselves (Mk. 12:12).[276]

The other passage also appears in all three gospels subsequent to the vineyard parable. The initiation of the debate with the Pharisees over David's Son was through a question put by Jesus himself (Mk. 12:35–37; Mt. 22:41–46; Lk. 20:41–44) – 'How can the scribes say that the Messiah is the Son of David?' This passage has already been discussed under the title Son of David (pp. 255f.). It has been suggested that Jesus' use of Psalm 110 implies that he is both Son of David and Son of God. Yet although it is clear that Jesus is claiming sonship of a different kind from current speculations regarding the Messiah, it is not certain that Jesus was here thinking of himself as Son of God. If he was, it has further been suggested that the words imply that Jesus was pre-existent for David to call him Lord.[277]

One concluding passage[278] may be considered: Luke 22:29, 'As my Father has appointed a kingdom for me, so do I appoint for you.' Before this statement can be taken in evidence, mention must be made of the view that it is not an authentic saying. On the assumption that it is a parallel to Matthew's Son of man saying about the twelve thrones (Mt. 19:28), it is maintained that Luke's 'my Father' cannot be regarded as original.[279] But there is no reason to suppose that it is the same saying. In any case it is more likely to have been a genuine saying of Jesus than a creation of the

---

[276] *Cf.* J. Jeremias, *The Parables of Jesus* (Eng. trans. ²1963), pp. 70ff., who recognizes that for the mind of Jesus the sending of the son was connected with his own sending, although the mass of the hearers would not have linked Son of God with Messiah.

[277] J. Schniewind, *Das Evangelium nach Matthäus* (*NTD*, 1960), p. 225, thinks that pre-existence may be in mind here. G. E. Ladd, *TNT*, p. 168, comments, 'The Messiah is at the same time an earthly man of Davidic descent and the coming world Judge – David's Lord and Judge.'

[278] F. W. Beare, *The Earliest Records of Jesus* (1962), pp. 227f., regards Lk. 22:28–30 as 'a theological construction of a subsequent age'. But see I. H. Marshall's criticisms of Beare's objection to authenticity (*Int* 21, 1967, p. 97).

[279] H. Schürmann, *Jesu Abschiedsrede, Lk. 22:21–38* (1957), pp. 37–54, rejects the view that this passage is Luke's own composition. He claims that the expression 'My Father' (v. 29) is pre-Lukan.

community, since the appointment of the disciples to a kingdom does not figure in later Christian thought. There is, moreover, no reason to suppose that Jesus did not use the expression 'my Father', which is in line with the evidence of his filial consciousness elsewhere.[280]

The Johannine literature

Since the purpose of the gospel of John is specifically stated to be that the readers might believe that Jesus is the Son of God (Jn. 20:31), it is not surprising to discover considerably more emphasis on this concept than on Son of man. The title itself occurs several times, but even more significant is the absolute use of the Father-Son relationship which permeates the words of Jesus in this gospel. There are more than a hundred occasions on which Jesus speaks of God as Father, distributed throughout the public ministry and not confined to any particular type of audience. The consciousness of sonship was present wherever he was. This indeed is the dominant feature in John's Christology and distinguishes it from that of the synoptic gospels. It has the same basis but focuses on the relationship of Jesus to God as Father in a manner so striking that the reader is left with the impression that he is being allowed a glimpse at what it means to be in a unique sense the Son of God.[281] The widespread occurrences of the sonship idea in John can be explained only on the assumption that this theme had come to have an absorbing interest for this evangelist.

The uniqueness of Jesus as Son of God. There are four occasions in John where Jesus is described as the 'only (*monogenēs*) Son' (*i.e.* 1:14, 18; 3:16, 18). There are different opinions regarding the meaning of the adjective;[282] it

[280] Some comment is needed on the centurion's confession in Mk. 15:39, which RSV renders, 'Truly, this man was a son of God.' W. L. Lane, *Mark*, (NICNT, 1974), p. 576, interprets this confession in two ways – what it meant to the centurion and what Mark intended it to mean for his readers. The centurion probably thought of son of God in terms of the Greek idea of a divine man or deified hero. But Mark himself saw significance in the fact that a Roman had confessed Jesus in a form which could convey a genuine Christian confession. 'Most effectively, therefore, Mark reports that the centurion proclaimed that the crucified Jesus (and not the emperor) is the Son of God.'

V. Taylor, *Mark* ([2]1966), p. 597, thinks it more probable that Luke's *ontōs ho anthrōpos houtos dikaios ēn* is more primitive, although he notes A. Plummer's view (*Luke*, ICC, [5]1922, p. 539) that there is little difference in meaning. Some importance must surely be attached to the fact that Mark opens and closes his gospel with references to Jesus as 'Son of God'. H. Anderson, *Mark*, (NCB, 1976), p. 348, rightly remarks that for Mark it was crucial that the centurion's believing should be seen to arise out of what Jesus' death accomplished. *Cf.* P. H. Bligh, 'A Note on *Huios Theou* in Mark 15:39', *ExT* 80, 1968, pp. 51ff.; T. F. Glasson, 'Mark xv. 39. The Son of God', *ExT* 80, 1969, p. 286.

[281] *Cf.* R. H. Lightfoot, *History and Interpretation in the Gospels* (1935), p. 224. He comments that in John, he who speaks and acts on earth is always at the Father's side. He nevertheless finds what he calls 'a kind of luminous haze' surrounding Jesus and other speakers in this gospel. This is not surprising in view of the fact that in all the gospels, Lightfoot could find little more than 'a whisper of the voice of Jesus' (p. 224).

[282] It is probable that Jn. 1:18 should read 'only God' (as RSV mg.). *Cf.* R. E. Brown's discussion of the textual evidence, *John, ad loc.* It occurs in the Bodmer papyri, whereas the alternate reading has only late Greek support, although it is found in Latin and Curetorian Old Syriac versions. For a comparison of the

seems most reasonable to suppose that its meaning in these contexts is 'alone of its kind', and in this case it draws attention to the unique kind of sonship which Jesus possessed. In all probability, John 1:18 should read 'only God' instead of 'only begotten Son' (or only Son), in which case it does not contribute to our present discussion.[283] The uniqueness of the sonship of Jesus is supported by the clear statement of the risen Jesus in John 20:17, when he made a distinction between 'my Father[284] and your Father' and 'my God and your God'. The distinction is of great importance because it rules out the view that Jesus' sonship was of the same kind as man's, but developed to a greater intensity. Others may be given power to become sons of God (1:12), but Jesus has no need for this since he is Son of a different kind, *i.e.* he is essentially a son. It is highly unlikely that *monogenēs* contains the idea of birth, as some have maintained.[285] But, even if it did, the emphasis would still be on the unique position that Jesus held.

Various testimonies to Jesus as Son of God. John is at pains to give specific instances of various people who recognized Jesus as Son of God. John the Baptist (1:34), Nathanael (1:49), and Martha (11:27) all make precise announcements to this effect.[286] Of even greater importance is the occasion when Jesus specifically laid claim to the title Son of God in a dialogue with his critics who were bringing a charge of blasphemy against him (10:36). In this case Jesus appealed to his works as evidence of his sonship (10:37 speaks of 'the works of my Father'). In line with this is the statement in 11:4 that Lazarus' illness was not unto death 'so that the Son of God may be glorified by means of it.' Moreover, the accusers of Jesus before Pilate brought the charge against him that he called himself the Son of God (19:7). Some clearly recognized the claims of Jesus, whereas others considered them to be fantastic and even blasphemous.

The special characteristics of Jesus as Son of God. It is impossible to present an adequate interpretation of the meaning of sonship for Jesus without taking into account the evidence of the whole gospel. What is important is to

---

text of the Bodmer papyri P 66 and P 75, and the earliest Alexandrian and other MSS relating to Jn. 1:18, *cf.* J. Finegan, *Encountering New Testament Manuscripts* (1974), pp. 111–177. He agrees with the reading *monogenēs Theou*, but thinks the best translation is as GNB, 'the Only Son who is the same as God'.

[283] *Cf.* D. Moody, ' "God's only Son", the translation of John 3:16 in RSV,' *JBL* 72, 1953, pp. 213ff.

[284] Jesus says 'My Father' nearly thirty times in John's record.

[285] *Cf.* F. Büchsel, *monogenēs*, *TDNT* 4, p. 741, who thinks a reference to birth is probable. R. E. Brown, *John*, pp. 13f., states that *monogenēs* describes a quality of Jesus, his uniqueness, not his 'procession' as in trinitarian theology.

[286] Some reference should be made to the variant reading in Jn. 6:69 which has 'Son of God' in place of 'Holy One of God'. Most textual editors prefer the latter because of its more unusual character. According to R. Bultmann, *John*, *ad loc.*, both titles are non messianic, but this opinion is disputed by G. Friedrich, *ZTK* 53, 1956, pp. 275ff., who sees both descriptions as relating to Jesus as messianic high priest. Whichever is the correct reading, the statement is significant as it occurs in Peter's confession of faith.

single out the most striking features. The first is that *the Son is sent by the Father*. So characteristic is this of John's gospel that God is at times referred to as the one who has sent Jesus (*cf.* 3:34; 5:36, 38; 7:29; 11:42). There are implications in this for the pre-existence of Jesus, for he could not be sent unless he was pre-existent. The relationship between Father and Son is seen as a continuation of that which existed before the incarnation (*cf.* Jn. 17:4, 5). This concept of the Son is identical to that of the Logos doctrine of the prologue (see the separate section on this, pp. 321ff.).

The second important feature is *the love of the Father for the Son*. This is brought out in 5:20, where the Father's love for the Son leads him to show the Son all that he is doing; in 3:35, where that love results in his giving all things into the Son's hand; in 10:17, where the Father's love is intensified by the Son's voluntary laying down of his life; and 17:24 where the Father's love for the Son is said to have existed before the foundation of the world. John reflects the deep conviction of Jesus that he was the object of the Father's love, a love of a wholly different kind from that between two human beings. There is no suggestion in this gospel that anything ever marred the relationship of loving understanding. What is most significant is that the Father's love for the Son is the pattern for the Father's love for those who believe in Jesus (17:23). It is the same quality of love. Similarly the love of the Son for his people is set out as the pattern for their love for each other (13:34). This is a fine example of the way in which a high Christology is seen to have practical implications of a far-reaching nature.

Another factor is *the dependence of the Son on the Father*. In John 5:19 Jesus makes the statement, 'The Son can do nothing of his own accord, but only what he sees the Father doing.'[287] In 5:30, 'I can do nothing on my own authority . . . I seek not my own will but the will of him who sent me' (*cf.* also 14:31; 15:10). These statements sum up the perfect obedience of the Son to the Father's will, and explain the unambiguous assertion in 14:28, 'My Father is greater than I.' It is not surprising that some see in this the inferiority of the Son to the Father, but it must be recognized that Jesus is contrasting the heavenly state with the earthly. The dependence of the Son on the will and power of the Father demonstrates, not the inferiority of the Son, but the identity of purpose between the Father and the Son (*cf.* 14:20). The absolute unity of Father and Son (10:30; 17:11; *cf.* 14:11, 20) is as important as the dependence of the Son on the Father. These two concepts are different facets of one truth and neither can be separated from the other. John, in recording them, evidently saw no contradiction between them.[288] The paradox is the mystery of incarnation. Indeed, a passage like John 5:19ff. is remarkable for its testimony to the complete harmony

---

[287] As L. Morris, *John*, p. 312, comments, the Son cannot act in independence of the Father.

[288] It is worth noting that those books of the NT which have the most explicit teaching on the subordination of the Son (especially John and Hebrews), have the highest Christology.

between the Father and the Son, and this is reflected throughout the gospel.

John's gospel is notable for the times that Jesus as *Son prays to the Father*. At the grave of Lazarus Jesus prays, 'Father, I thank thee that thou hast heard me' (11:41). In the Johannine account of the soul-agony of Jesus, the Son shares his tension with the Father, but triumphantly concludes, 'Father, glorify thy name' (12:28). But it is John 17 where the quintessence of Jesus' prayer approach to God is found and where six times within the prayer Jesus expressly addresses God as Father (verses 1, 5, 11, 21, 24, 25). Nowhere else in the gospels is the mind of Jesus in his filial consciousness so vividly presented. The major element of the prayer is wholly outgoing, concentrated on the needs of the disciples. The whole approach exemplifies in a remarkable way the approach in the prayer that Jesus taught his disciples, with the important difference that Jesus never addresses God as 'our' Father, but draws a distinction between his own sonship and that of others. This is especially clear in John 20:17 where the risen Christ is addressing Mary.

Jesus as Son makes the claim to be the exclusive *revelation of the Father*. He alone has seen the Father (6:46). He therefore is the sole medium by which men may come to know him. When the Pharisees asked, 'Where is your Father?', Jesus pointed out, 'If you knew me, you would know my Father also' (8:19). A similar response was given to Philip's request, 'Show us the Father,' for Jesus puts the question, 'Have I been with you so long, and yet you do not know me, Philip?' (14:8–9). In no clearer way could he have claimed to be the perfect revelation of the Father. There is a complete understanding between the Father and the Son – 'as the Father knows me and I know the Father' (10:15). The theme of revelation is prepared for in the prologue, since the Logos is there identified as light.

Closely akin to this point is the fact that the *Son speaks the words of the Father*. Not only works but words are vehicles of the Father's activity. Jesus had received a 'charge' from the Father (10:18). He calls his disciples 'friends' and then adds, 'for all that I have heard from my Father I have made known to you' (15:15). He declines to speak on his own authority; it is the Father who has 'given me commandment what to say and what to speak' (12:49f.). In the farewell discourse the same thought is reiterated – 'The word which you hear is not mine but the Father's who sent me' (14:24). As yet, however, much of what is said is necessarily veiled, but Jesus promises to speak of the Father no longer in figures but plainly (16:25). These passages bring out vividly the firm conviction of Jesus that his mind and words are wholly dominated by his consciousness of God.

With regard to the future the evidence is equally explicit. *The Father has given all things into the Son's hands*. In John's account of the upper-room discourses, there is a remarkable statement that Jesus knew 'that the Father had given all things into his hands, and that he had come from God and was going to God' as a prelude to the feet-washing episode (13:3ff.). This is the evangelist's comment to highlight the condescension of Jesus, but it is in line with Jesus' own claim as 16:15 shows ('All that the Father has is mine'). Moreover, the Son shares with the Father in the judgment (8:16). It should also be remembered that included in what the Father had given the Son was a 'cup' (18:11).

Several times Jesus speaks of *returning to the Father*, especially in the farewell discourses when it was clearly most in his mind. He expects the disciples to rejoice because he goes to the Father (14:28). He looks beyond the cross to the triumphant ascension. The disciples were, however, perplexed over this kind of talk (see 16:16ff.), for they could not understand it at this stage. For other similar references to going to the Father, see 14:12; 16:10 and 16:28. In the post-resurrection appearance to Mary, Jesus announces his ascension (20:17). For him to go to the Father was to go where he belonged. In line with this is the conviction that the Father will glorify the Son (8:54), which shows that the consummation of the mission will be the exaltation of the Son, whatever intervening suffering may lie immediately ahead.

The theme of Jesus as God's Son is particularly emphasized in 1 John. Indeed the central confession expected of believers is that Jesus is the Son of God (1 Jn. 2:22, 23; 3:23; 4:15; 5:5, 10, 12–13). The believer's fellowship is with the Father and with his Son Jesus Christ (1:3). The sending of the Son comes into prominence in 4:9–10, 14. The saving activity of God is expressed in the words 'the blood of Jesus his Son cleanses us from all sin' (1 Jn.1:7). The mission of the Son is also described as a victory over the devil (1 Jn. 3:8). It is the Son who makes expiation for our sins (4:10). It is the Father who bears testimony to the Son (5:9) as the source of eternal life (5:11). The whole aim of this brief letter is that the readers, who believe in the name of the Son of God, may know that they have eternal life (5:13). It is the Son who gives us understanding (5:20). In this letter there are no fewer than twenty-one mentions of the Son, a clear indication of the importance of the theme for the writer. This is one of the strongest confirmations that the epistle is written by the same person as the gospel. Both books present a high Christology.

Acts

After turning from the Johannine literature to Acts, the investigator is struck by the small part the divine sonship of Jesus plays in the primitive proclamations. Indeed there is no indication of the importance of the theme until Acts 9:20, where Luke records that Paul (Saul) proclaimed of Jesus that 'he is the Son of God'. Does this give any support for the view that this was a particular Pauline deduction? Since it took place so soon after Paul's conversion it is incredible that he was following a line of his own.

Indeed the Son of God theme was linked with the messianic theme (9:22), which shows his indebtedness to the general messianic beliefs of the early church.[289] Saul of Tarsus must have received traditions about the sonship of Jesus even although it took the Damascus experience to convince him that they were true.

In his speech at Pisidian Antioch Paul cites the well-known messianic Psalm (2), 'Thou art my Son, today I have begotten thee,' and applies it to Jesus (13:33). The theme is not developed in Luke's record, but there is little doubt that this quotation from Psalm 2 reflects early Christian conviction that Jesus was Son of God.[290]

Paul

In the Pauline epistles the concept of Jesus as the Son of God plays an important part in the total presentation of Christ. Yet nowhere does Paul attempt to demonstrate the divine sonship of Jesus. He everywhere assumes it. It comes out quite naturally in many of his epistles.

It has already been noted that many scholars regard Romans 1:1–4 as a piece of traditional material which Paul has taken over (see p. 257). If it is, Paul has lent the weight of his authority to it and it may therefore be regarded as expressing his view. It affirms that God's Son was 'designated (*horizō*) Son of God in power according to the Spirit of holiness by his resurrection from the dead' (Rom. 1:4).[291] But the affirmation is not without its difficulties. Can this be construed to mean that prior to the resurrection Jesus was not Son of God?[292] Assuming that Paul would not have quoted a traditional statement with which he did not agree, it is reasonable to interpret this in the light of other statements of his, and nowhere does he suggest that the pre-existent status of Jesus was as a man, although he emphatically maintained pre-existence (*cf.* Phil. 2).[293] This affirmation must mean, therefore, that the resurrection declared and delineated what was already an established fact. It confuses the whole concept of sonship if it is affected by events in time. Sonship is an essential relationship which

---

[289] *Cf.* E. Schweizer, 'The Concept of the Davidic "Son of God" in Acts and its Old Testament Background', in *Studies in Luke-Acts* (eds. L. Keck and J. L. Martin, 1966), pp. 186–195. He suggests that there were two streams of Davidic prophetic interpretation – one a messianic figure (God's Son of Davidic descent) which he finds referred to in Acts 2:30; 13:33, as well as Lk. 1:32–33; Rom. 1:3–4 and Heb. 1:5–13; 5:5. The other stream stresses the divine sonship of eschatological Israel.

[290] Note that Ps. 2 is cited in Acts 2 and in Heb. 1 in relation to Christ.

[291] C. K. Barrett, *Romans* (*BC*, 1957), pp. 18ff., maintains that Paul has taken over a pre-Pauline formula, but has adapted it by the addition of *en dynamei* to avoid the suggestion of naïve adoptionism.

[292] *Cf.* W. C. van Unnik, 'Jesus the Christ', *NTS* 8, 1962, p. 108, 'The Resurrection did not *make* Jesus "the Son of God": He was it already as a descendant of David, but this fact was powerfully marked out by the resurrection.' On the meaning of the verb, *cf.* L. C. Allen, 'The Old Testament Background of (pro)*horizein* in the New Testament', *NTS* 17, 1970, p. 104ff. He traces both the verb and the use of the title here to Ps. 2.

[293] *Cf.* I. H. Marshall, *Int* 21, 1967, p. 102. Commenting on Phil. 2:5–11 he says, 'As in Romans 1:3f., the Resurrection confirms and manifests an existing position.'

could not be altered by incarnation, and the evidence of the gospels supports this view. Another important facet of this passage is the linking of the Spirit to the declaration of sonship. It has been suggested [294] that in his earthly life Jesus was dependent on the Spirit whereas at his resurrection he fully took over the Spirit and so was installed as Son of God in power. But again confusion will arise if a distinction is made which suggests that he was not Son of God before the resurrection. Certainly after the resurrection the disciples came to have a better appreciation of Jesus as Son of God.

When speaking of God, Paul frequently goes on to speak of his Son (it occurs ten times in his epistles). He speaks of the gospel of his Son (Rom. 1:9), of the knowledge of his Son (Eph. 4:13), of the Spirit of his Son (Gal. 4:6), of the image of his Son (Rom. 8:29), of the kingdom of his beloved Son (Col. 1.13). The full expression 'Son of God' occurs only three times apart from the instance in Romans 1:4. In writing to the Corinthians Paul speaks of having preached to them 'the Son of God, Jesus Christ' (2 Cor. 1:19), which leaves no doubt that he was accustomed to include this theme in his kerygma. He did not reserve it for those already initiated into Christian truth. The Son of God is seen, moreover, as the object of faith (Gal. 2:20), and as the content of the Christian's quest for knowledge (Eph. 4:13). Christians are also called into the fellowship of his Son Jesus Christ our Lord (1 Cor. 1:9).

Sonship in Paul's theology is tied up with the whole mission of Jesus. When God acted to redeem man he sent his Son (Gal. 4:4). Paul goes further in a notable statement in which he links sonship with the coming of Jesus in the likeness of sinful flesh (*en homoiōmati sarkos harmartias*). He could not have expressed more clearly the idea of the pre-existent Son entering the sphere dominated by sin (Rom. 8:3). A strong contrast is intended between the status of Son and the environment of sinful flesh.

Another passage possessing great Christological significance is 1 Corinthians 15:28 which reads, 'When all things are subjected to him, then the Son himself will also be subjected to him who put all things under him, that God may be everything to everyone'. The passage makes clear the sonship of Jesus, and suggests the subordination of the Son to the Father. Paul's meaning here must be carefully weighed. He is not implying that the present plan or mission of the Son differs in any way from the plan or mission of the Father. That would be unthinkable. In the sense that the Son is committed to the will of the Father both before and after all things

---

[294] Cf. J. D. G. Dunn, 'Jesus – Flesh and Spirit: An Exposition of Rom. 1:3–4', *JTS* n.s. 24, 1973, pp. 40–68, contends that in this and other passages it is the 'continuity and difference between historical and exalted Jesus in terms of the Spirit' which finds expression (p. 67). According to Dunn it is because Jesus lived on the level of the Spirit that he manifested that he was indeed the Son of God and proved his right to be installed as Son of God in power as from the resurrection (*cf.* p. 57).

are subjected to him, the future subjection of the Son is intended to mark the demonstration of the perfect harmony of all things in God. The Son has no other desire than that the Father might be everything to everyone. Paul is not discussing the nature of God, but the perfect submission of the Son in service in the interests of the mission.[295]

The Father has transferred us from the dominion of darkness to the kingdom of the Son of his love (Col. 1:13). It is noteworthy that what is described as the kingdom of God in the teaching of Jesus has become here the kingdom of the Son, another indication of the special divine status of the Son. It is the Son, Jesus, for whom believers wait at the time of the parousia (1 Thes. 1:10).

Is it possible to see any development between the later Pauline epistles and the former? Some have regarded the emphasis on knowledge of the Son in Ephesians 4:13 as such a development. The idea does not occur elsewhere and may be intended to offset gnosis-type movements in which pursuit of knowledge was regarded as meritorious. On the other hand an increasing awareness of the importance of the divine sonship of Jesus is one of the main evidences of Christian maturity, according to the context of this passage.

One aspect of the sonship of Jesus which is important is the effect it has on believers. When Paul discusses the Galatians' position as sons of God, he reminds them that God has sent the Spirit of his Son into our hearts, crying 'Abba, Father' (Gal. 4:6; *cf.* also Rom 8:15). This gives some insight into the intimate nature of the relationship between Father and Son which serves as a pattern for his people. The 'Abba, Father' is particularly significant because Jesus used it in his Gethsemane prayer (Mk. 14:36).

Hebrews

As compared with the almost incidental references to Son of God in Paul's letters, there is a more deliberate exposition of the theme in the epistle to the Hebrews. In fact Hebrews 1 concentrates on the significance of the Son and this is reinforced by other references which occur in the process of the argument. Divine revelation had used various means in the past, but now God has spoken by means of a Son (Heb. 1:1). The Son is not at first identified with Jesus, but there is an initial build-up which impressively presents the Son's exalted status.[296] He is heir of all things, creator, reflector

---

[295] On 1 Cor. 15:28, Cullmann, *The Christology of the New Testament*, p. 293, says, 'It is only meaningful to speak of the Son in view of God's revelatory action, not in view of his being'. Although Cullmann adds that Father and Son are one in this activity, Paul's words cannot be emptied of all ontological meaning.

[296] M. Hengel, *The Son of God* (Eng. trans. 1976), p. 87, cites approvingly the view of E. Lohmeyer (*Kyrios Jesus : Eine Untersuchung zu Phil. 2:5–11* ([2]1961, pp. 77f.) that Heb. 1:1ff. makes the Christological outline of Phil. 2:5ff. more precise. Hence 'Son' is more precise than 'being in the form of God'. Hengel says, 'One might almost regard the whole of Hebrews as a large-scale development of the Christological theme which is already present in the Philippian hymn.'

of God's glory; he bears the stamp of God's nature, upholds the universe by his power, has purged sins and has been enthroned at God's right hand (see the later section on Heb. 1:1–3, pp. 360ff.). Such an exalted character is the focus of attention in the whole epistle, but is not connected with Jesus until 2:9. The Son performs functions which are prerogatives of God as well as being the perfect means for making him known. It is not surprising in view of this that several OT passages are cited in the first chapter. Psalm 2:7 and 2 Samuel 7:14, well-known messianic passages, are cited (1:5) in support of the Son, but the most remarkable is the application of Psalm 45 to the same Son with the words, 'Thy throne, O God, is for ever and ever' (Heb. 1:8). In citing this Psalm in this way, the writer shows that there was no incongruity in speaking of the Son as God (see later section on Jesus as God, pp. 340f.).

In contrast to Moses, a servant, Christ was faithful over God's house as a son (Heb. 3:6), which brings out his superior status. This is further echoed in the second preliminary introduction of the high priest theme in 4:14, where he is called 'Jesus, the Son of God' (*cf.* 2:17). The 'son' theme from Psalm 2:7 occurs again in 5:5, and in the same context the Son (*i.e.* Jesus) is said to have learned obedience through what he suffered (5:8). The allusion to the earthly life of Jesus (the agony in Gethsemane) is linked to his sonship. It is in harmony with this emphasis on Jesus as Son of God that Melchizedek, who is clearly regarded as a type of Christ, is described as 'resembling the Son of God' (7:3). Even more striking is the fact that in the two apostasy passages (6:6; 10:29), it is the Son of God whose position would be undermined ('crucified afresh', 'spurned'). The writer is conscious throughout of the importance of this theme. His presentation is wholly in line with the other NT evidence already considered.[297]

The rest of the New Testament

The sonship theme is absent from *James* and *Jude* and occurs only incidentally in the *Petrine epistles*. God is called the Father of our Lord Jesus Christ in 1 Peter 1:3, and the heavenly voice at the transfiguration of Jesus is recalled in 2 Peter 1:17. In neither case does it play a major role in the teaching of the epistles.

In *Revelation* only one mention is made of Jesus as Son of God, in the introduction to the message to the church at Thyatira (2:18). The flaming eyes and burnished feet in the description of him go back to 1:17–18, where he is nevertheless described as 'one like a son of man'. The Lamb theme

---

[297] C. Spicq, *L'Épître aux Hébreux* 1 (1952), 288 n.8, summarizes the use of the title in Hebrews as follows: (i) Without the article: 3 times in OT citations; 4 times to stress the quality of the mediator (1:2; 3:6; 5:8; 7:28). (ii) With the article as an affirmation of divinity: 4:14; 7:3 in relation to Christ's priesthood, and 6:6; 10:29 in relation to apostates.

becomes more dominant, but the exalted position of the Lamb is fully in accord with the status of sonship.

LOGOS

The Johannine literature

One of the distinctive terms used in John's gospel is the Greek *logos*, normally rendered 'word' in English. In view of the rich cluster of concepts behind the original term, which we are about to consider, it is preferable to retain the Greek word in this discussion. The writer uses *logos* in this gospel to denote sometimes the message of Jesus and sometimes the divine word about Jesus. It may be said that the ordinary use of *logos* in John, as distinct from the Christological, shows Jesus as proclaiming the *logos*.[298] This is more than the words spoken; it implies the need for hearing and understanding (*cf.* 8:31, 51; 5:24).[299] But the distinctive feature of John's gospel is the use of *logos* in the prologue (1:1–18) in what appears to be a more technical sense as a designation of Jesus. This merits careful examination as a contribution to Christology.

The background to the idea. 1. Greek sources. The use of *logos* in a philosophic sense had a long history before its use in John's gospel. It is one thing, however, to outline the development of the idea and to consider its various facets, but quite another problem to decide how far John is indebted to any of these ideas. It is important to consider both Hebrew and Greek backgrounds to enable a decision to be reached regarding the theological significance of the title.

We begin with the Greek usage. The earliest Greek writer to give expression to a *logos* principle was Heraclitus (*c.* 500 BC) who was concerned to establish some abiding principle in a world which was continuously subject to change; he called this principle *logos*. It was, in fact, his philosophical explanation of God. *Logos* was the unifying principle, the Law or Reason which accounted for the stable pattern in the ever changing world. Man's quest must be to become aware of this *logos* principle. There was no concept of transcendence, for *logos* pervades everything. In fact *logos*, fire and God were identical.

---

[298] Bultmann makes much of the revelatory character of the Word and thinks this everyday meaning of *logos* is present in the evangelist's mind, *TNT* 2, p. 64. The significance of the general use of *logos* in relation to the specific use in John's gospel is well brought out by J. M. Boice, *Witness and Revelation in the Gospel of John* (1970), pp. 65ff. He finds four uses of *logos* in the Gospel. (i) The common use of a word spoken and then heard by someone. (ii) A theological and religious use in which the words of Jesus take on a character impossible to men's words. (iii) A use which denotes the sum total of Jesus' teaching. (iv) A use in which *logos* is applied to Christ himself (in the prologue).

[299] O. Cullmann, *The Christology of the New Testament*, p. 260, remarks that 'a direct line leads from the theologically charged concept of the proclaimed word to the Logos who became flesh in Jesus'.

In Anaxagoras, *logos* performs more of a mediatorial function, because God is conceived of as transcendent rather than immanent. While Plato did not expound a *logos* principle, his theory of ideas in some ways prepared for the later Stoic ideas by providing a framework of distinction between an idea and its expression, which may be said to parallel reason and its expression or verbalization (word). The Stoics were successors to Heraclitus in so far as they conceived of ethereal fire as the primordial source of all things. The fire, which was creative, was known as *logos spermatikos* (*i.e.* the Seminal Reason). Thus the *logos* pervaded all things, as in Heraclitus' system. This lead the Stoics into 'theoretical pantheism'.[300] It is important to note that they did not think of a single *logos* but rather of *logoi spermatikoi*, which were forces responsible for the creative cycles in nature. These principles provided a standard by which the Stoics claimed to order their lives. Reason was thus closely identified with nature. Later Stoics considered the *logos* to be the world soul, again highly pantheistic.

The teaching of the Alexandrian Jew Philo, who was influential in Hellenistic thought at the same time as Jesus was teaching in Palestine, widely develops a *logos* doctrine.[301] It forms an important key to his system of thought. His is the most articulate attempt to trace Greek ideas to a Semitic context. His highly developed allegorization enabled him to find current Greek ideas in an OT setting, but he sacrificed any historical approach in doing so. He was influenced by Plato's theory of ideas in formulating his *logos* doctrine. While he considered the *logos* belonged to the world of ideas, he nevertheless also linked *logos* with the expression of the idea. He was, in fact, influenced by both his Hebrew and Greek background. Five points may be noted about Philo's *logos* doctrine.

(i) The *logos* has no distinct personality. It is described as 'the image of God . . . through whom the whole universe was framed'.[302] But since it is also described in terms of a rudder to guide all things in their course, or as God's instrument (*organon*) for fashioning the world, [303] it seems clear that Philo did not think of *logos* in personal terms.

(ii) Philo speaks of the *logos* as God's first-born son (*prōtogonos huios*),[304] which implies pre-existence. The *logos* is certainly regarded as eternal. Other descriptions of the *logos* as God's ambassador (*presbeutēs*), as man's advocate (*paraklētos*) and as high priest (*archiereus*), although offering interesting parallels with Jesus Christ, do not, however, require pre-existence.

(iii) The *logos* idea is not linked with light and life in Philo's doctrine as

---

[300] So W. F. Howard, *Christianity according to St John* (1943), p. 35. He cites E. Bevan's *Later Greek Religion*, p. xv, to the effect that in the old Stoic books the idea always occurs in the plural.

[301] For a discussion of Philo's Logos doctrine, *cf.* C. H. Dodd, *The Interpretation of the Fourth Gospel*, pp. 66ff.; 276ff.; W. F. Howard, *op. cit.*, 34ff.; E. K. Lee, *The Religious Thought of St John*, 87ff.

[302] *Cf.* Philo, *De Somm.* ii. 45.

[303] *Cf.* Philo, *De migr.Abr.* 6.

[304] *Cf.* Philo, *De agr.* 51.

it is in John's, and the combination cannot have been derived from him, although it would have been congenial to him.

(iv) There is no suggestion that the *logos* could become incarnate. This would have been alien to Greek thought, because of the belief in the evil of matter.

(v) The *logos* definitely had a mediatorial function to bridge the gap between the transcendent God and the world. It can be regarded as a personification of an effective intermediary, although it was never personalized.[305] Philo's *logos* has, therefore, both parallels and differences from John's *logos* as the following section will show.[306]

Some mention must be made of the Hermetic literature because some have appealed partly to this to explain the *logos* doctrine (as, for instance, Dodd).[307] The Hermetica were speculative philosophical writings belonging to the second and third centuries AD. It may be supposed that some of the literature depended on earlier ideas which might have been contemporary with John's gospel. But the evidence from this source must clearly be used with some reserve. The discourses of Hermes Trismegistus show a blending of Greek philosophy and Hellenistic Jewish mysticism. The tractate *Poimandres*, which speculates on the cosmogony of Genesis, frequently used the *logos* idea, but in a way that shows no Christian influence. According to Dodd[308] what parallels there are with Johannine thought are explicable 'as the result of minds working under the same general influences'. Yet whereas the Greek mind sought knowledge of God and communion with him through nature, the Christian approach to God is through Christ, which marks a fundamental distinction.

Although there are some striking verbal parallels between the Johannine prologue and the Mandaean liturgies in such phrases as 'I am a Word', 'the Word of life', 'the Light of Life', it is unsatisfactory to claim any Mandaean influence on John since the evidence for the liturgies is very late.[309] Only if chronological considerations are played down can any literary connection be claimed. If there is any influence it is more reasonable to suppose that the Mandaean liturgies have absorbed ideas from Christian sources. We may dispense with these, therefore, as a probable source of information for the understanding of John's Logos doctrine.

2. Jewish sources. There has been a definite shift of emphasis from

---

[305] *Cf.* Howard, *op.cit.*, p. 38, who sums up Philo's *logos* in the following way. 'Philo uses the term Logos to express the conception of a mediator between the transcendent God and the universe, an immanent power active in creation and revelation, but though the Logos is often personified, it is never truly personalized'.

[306] For a useful survey of views, *cf.* E. M. Sidebottom, *The Christ of the Fourth Gospel* (1961), pp. 26ff.

[307] On the Hermetic literature, *cf.* C. H. Dodd, *The Interpretation of the Fourth Gospel*, pp. 10–53.

[308] C. H. Dodd, *The Bible and the Greeks* (1935, ²1954), p. 247.

[309] *Cf.* R. Bultmann, *The Gospel of John*, p. 8. He claims that John is particularly indebted to the gnostic Odes of Solomon and the letters of Ignatius, which he considers were influenced by Syrian gnosticism.

323

Greek to Hebrew sources for the interpretation of the fourth gospel as a whole, and this applies to the prologue in particular. There are four main lines in which Hebrew ideas have been claimed to throw light on John's usage.

The most obvious line is to investigate *the OT background*. Creative power is attributed to the Word of God in several passages, notably Genesis 1 and Psalm 33:6, 9. This Word is clearly invested with divine authority. But not only is the Word creative: it is also sustaining. Such passages as Psalm 147:15–18; 148:8 show God's providential care for his creation through his powerful Word. Indeed that Word is so powerful that it cannot fail to accomplish its purpose in the world (Is. 55:11; Ps. 147:15). Moreover, judgment is executed by the Word of God (Ho. 6:5). In these senses the Word of God is seen as the powerful agency of God.

Yet the more frequent idea of the Word in the OT is as the means of revelation.[310] In the work and writings of the prophets, the expression 'Thus says the Lord' or similar words abound. Each prophet was conscious of being the mouthpiece of God. The divine message is spoken of by Jeremiah as a fire in his bones (Je. 20:9). Similarly Ezekiel (Ezk. 33:7) and Amos are men under compulsion to proclaim the oracle of God. A development from this prophetical idea is when the 'Word' came to sum up the whole message of God to man as in Psalm 119:9, 105. It is virtually identified with the law, but the important feature is the emphasis on the divine revelation in its application to the psalmist's way of life.

Another OT concept which has some bearing on the *logos* idea is that of wisdom.[311] The wisdom literature plays a significant part in the presentation of OT theology and there is no doubt its influence was strong during the intertestamental period. As with the revelatory character of the Word, so with wisdom the initiative is from God (*cf.* Job 28:12–19, which shows that creation itself cannot produce it). The gift of wisdom was specifically given to Solomon in response to his own request, and this idea is carried on in the wisdom literature where wisdom is never a possession which can be worked up by man. The most important OT passage for our purpose is Proverbs 8, where a personified Wisdom speaks of having been present at the creation of the world (8:27ff.). Nevertheless Wisdom speaks of its own creation in Proverbs 8:22, and this must modify the understanding of the sense in which Wisdom can be said to be pre-existent. Undoubtedly the Proverbs passage provides some remarkable parallels with the Johannine

---

[310] P. Borgen, 'Logos was the true Light. Contributions to the Interpretation of the Prologue of John', *NovT* 14, 1972, pp. 115–130, approaches the prologue from the point of view of Jewish ideas of the close connection between the Word and Light. He views Jn. 1:1–18 as a unity on the basis of its structure.

[311] For a useful survey of the evidence from the OT and later Jewish sources on the theme of Wisdom, *cf.* A van Roon, 'The Relation between Christ and the Wisdom of God according to Paul', *NovT* 16, 1974, pp. 207–219.

prologue and is probably the closest OT parallel to be found.[312]

Similar ideas are found in *other wisdom literature*. In the apocryphal Wisdom of Solomon, Logos ('thy all-powerful Word') leapt down from heaven as a warrior (18:15–16) in a way reminiscent of the warrior Word of God in Revelation 19:13; but the idea is not closely linked to the coming of the Logos in John's prologue. It is clear however that Logos, as Wisdom itself, is for the writer personified, although not personalized. That is to say, it can be spoken of in personal terms without being identified as a person. Wisdom is said to penetrate all things because she is the breath of the power of God (Wisdom 7:24), a significant linking of Logos and Spirit (= breath), which may be paralleled in the creation account. In this same passage Wisdom is said to be the image of God's eternal light (Wisdom 7:26). Similarly in Ben-Sira's writings there is a passage which personifies Wisdom as having 'come forth from the mouth of the Most High and covered the earth like a mist' (Ecclus. 24:1ff.). In this writer there is a close connection between Wisdom and law.

The third Jewish source which has sometimes been appealed to is *the rabbinic idea of the Torah*, which was regarded as an intermediary between God and the world. There are several parallels between this and the Logos of John's prologue.[313]

First, the Torah was believed to have been created before the foundation of the world; in other words, its pre-existence is asserted. Secondly, the Torah lay on God's bosom. Thirdly, 'my daughter, she is the Torah.' Fourthly, through the first-born, God created the heaven and the earth, and the first-born is no other than the Torah. Fifthly, the words of the Torah are life for the world.

In John's prologue, however, the superiority of Jesus Christ, as the divine Logos, to Moses the law-giver is expressly brought out (Jn. 1:17). Moreover, whereas the law was 'given' through Moses, 'grace and truth', the distinguishing marks of the new law, 'came through Jesus Christ'. In other words John's assertions go beyond the assertions of the rabbis.[314] Jesus more than fulfilled the function of the pre-existent Torah.[315]

[312] For recent writers who have stressed the connection between Logos and Wisdom, *cf.* R. E. Brown, *John* 1, pp. 520ff.; F. M. Braun, *Jean le Théologien: 2. Les grandes traditions d'Israël* (EB, 1964), pp. 137–150. But R. Schnackenberg, *John* 1, (Eng. trans. 1968), pp. 481–493, while acknowledging Jewish links, still prefers to think of John's Logos concept as basically Greek, but worked over to include Jewish notions.

[313] *Cf.* W. F. Howard's summary, based on Strack-Billerbeck and *TDNT*, *Christianity according to St John*, pp. 50f.

[314] T. W. Manson, *On Paul and John* (1963), p. 146, draws attention to the fact that one of the favourite periphrases for the divine name was 'He who spoke, and the world came into being', which shows some parallel with the creative Logos of John's gospel.

[315] It has sometimes been claimed that *memra* (an Aramaic word used in the Targums) may be seen as an antecedent to the Johannine Logos. But G. F. Moore considered that *memra* was simply a phenomenon of translation, *i.e.* a formal substitute for the sacred tetragrammaton; *Judaism* 1 (1927, pp. 417ff.). C. K. Barrett, *John*, p. 128, calls the appeal to *memra* a 'blind alley'. R. E. Brown, *John* 1, p. 524, regards *memra* as a surrogate for God himself. 'Memra serves as a buffer for divine transcendence.'

The fourth Jewish line of evidence is *the Qumran literature*, which does not explicitly contribute to the discussion, but provides a background which lessens the impact of Hellenistic claims.[316] The scrolls bear testimony to many aspects which were for long assumed to belong to a Hellenistic milieu. Of particular importance for our purpose is the underlying Qumran dualism[317] which approximates more closely to John's background in his Logos doctrine than does the gnostic dualism which Bultmann stresses so strongly.[318] Indeed, the Qumran dualism, like John's, is monotheistic, ethical and eschatological. It makes far better sense to see parallelism within a Jewish framework than to force John into a gnostic mould which is alien to his purpose.

The interpretation of Logos in John's gospel. Having narrowed the probable background to mainly Jewish sources, with Hellenistic parallels, we must next consider why John chose to call Jesus the Logos and precisely what he meant by it. No explanation is valid which does not do justice to the fact that after the prologue the actual title is dropped. This fact raises two closely linked questions —Why did he introduce the name Logos at the beginning of his gospel, and what bearing did it have on his subsequent account of Jesus?

The first question demands an answer that links John's purpose with his readers. Since he gives no explanation of the Logos, he assumes that the readers will identify his idea. Greek readers would presumably think he was talking about the rational principle of the universe and would be amazed at his statement that that principle became not only personalized but incarnate. Jewish readers on the other hand would not find the transference of thought so alien,[319] for their minds would at least be prepared for some kind of personified pre-existent Wisdom who could operate in the world of men. Nevertheless, they too would be amazed at some of the statements that John makes, again especially the personal attributes and the incarnation in flesh. It seems reasonable to suppose that John wants to present Jesus as the true Logos in order to prepare the way for his own presentation of Jesus Christ as the Son of God.

For an approach to the Logos doctrine from the point of view of Jewish midrashic interpretation, *cf.* P. Borgen, 'Observations on the Targumic Character of the Prologue of John', *NTS* 16, 1969–70, pp. 288ff. *Cf.* also M. McNamara, 'Logos of the Fourth Gospel and Memra of the Palestinian Targum (Ex. 12:42), *ExT*, 79, 1968, pp. 115ff.

[316] It does this by showing that many facets previously thought to be exclusively Hellenistic were present in the literature of this Jewish sect.

[317] For a discussion of Qumran dualism, *cf.* R. E. Brown, *New Testament Essays* (1965), pp. 102–131.

[318] J. Jeremias, *The Central Message of the New Testament*, p. 82 n. 1, points out that Bultmann's work on John would have been considerably modified had the results of the Qumran researches been more available when he wrote his commentary.

[319] In the Manual of Discipline 11.11 the idea occurs of divine thought as the origin of all. Longenecker, *The Christology of Early Jewish Christianity*, p. 146, appeals to this evidence.

Important though it is, the Logos doctrine is almost incidental to his main thrust. There is much to be said for the view that the prologue was tacked on after the body of the gospel was written. But this view may not do justice to the clear links in the prologue with leading ideas in the rest of the gospel (such as light, life, truth). It seems better, therefore, to regard the prologue as essentially introductory, giving some flashes of insight into the kind of person to be introduced in the following narrative. There is no denying that the Logos doctrine raises an expectation that the presentation of Jesus will be of a person who is both God and man.

We may note three main characteristics of Jesus Christ as seen in his Logos role. First, to describe his relation to the Father, John goes back in thought to the pre-creation state. The Word was with God (*pros ton Theon*). Since the beginning is expressed in the same formula as Genesis 1:1, there is clearly a reference to the pre-existence of the Word.[320] The further statement that the Word was God explicitly states the deity of the Word, without blurring the distinction between the personal quality of the Word and the personal quality of God. The absence of the article with *Theos* has misled some into thinking that the correct understanding of the statement would be that 'the Word was a God' (or divine),[321] but this is grammatically indefensible since *Theos* is a predicate.[322] There can be no reasonable doubt that John intended his readers to understand that the Word had the nature of God. He did not mean, moreover, that the Word and God were interchangeable terms, since the previous statement so clearly distinguishes them. The meaning must be that although the Word is God, the concept of God is more embracing than the Word.[323] John does not pause to elucidate. He assumes no further explanation is needed. He has with few words created an impression of the divine character and dignity of the Word, eternally with God.

Secondly, John gives some indication of the relationship between the Logos and the world. His part in the creation is specified: 'all things were made through him, and without him was not anything made that was made' (Jn. 1:3). In no clearer way could his unique part in creation be stated, although it is not as full as in Colossians 1:15. There is no distinction here between the creative power of the Logos and the creative power of God. Moreover he is clearly distinguished from creation. The use of a

[320] According to G. B. Caird, 'The Development of the Doctrine of Christ in the New Testament', *Christ for Us Today* (ed. N. Pittenger, 1968), pp. 66–80, the Jews believed in the pre-existence of a personification, but never of a person. He claims that neither the fourth gospel nor Hebrews compels us to regard either Word or Wisdom in personal terms. Cf. also J. A. T. Robinson, *The Human Face of God*, p. 178 n. 182, for a similar view.

[321] An early example of this is Origen, *In Jon* 2:2. Cf. T. E. Pollard, *Johannine Christology and the Early Church* (1970), pp. 86–105.

[322] Cf. E. C. Colwell, *JBL* 52, 1933, p. 20.

[323] B. A. Mastin, 'A Neglected Feature of the Christology of the Fourth Gospel', *NTS* 22, 1975, pp. 32ff., says, 'It is . . . overwhelmingly probable that Jn. 1:1 describes the pre-existent Logos as God'.

different verb – 'to be' (for the Logos) and 'to become' (for the creation) – underlines this distinction.

The third characteristic is the relation of the Logos to men. This is summed up in the incarnation of the Logos, who became flesh (Jn. 1:14).[324] There is no parallel to this in the widespread use of Logos in the Greek world. In fact the idea as we have seen would have been alien to Greek modes of thinking, according to which there must always be a gap between God and man. Any idea of an incarnate Logos would not fit into such a view. For this reason John's statement is startling. It focuses what was previously a theoretical idea into a person. Moreover, the person became 'flesh' (*sarx*), *i.e.* of the same nature as man. The word 'flesh' is not used here in the way in which Paul sometimes uses it of 'sinful flesh', because John's whole presentation of Jesus would not support such a view. 'Flesh' indicates for him the complete manhood of the Logos. John's statements about Logos therefore combine the greatest possible exaltation with the humiliation of incarnation. This sums up his basic Christology. His gospel, moreover, links the Logos at the beginning with the Messiah and Son of God at the end (Jn. 20:31). Although he is distinctive in the use of the former title, he shares a similar view to the synoptics in the latter titles.

We have still to discuss what relationship the introductory Logos doctrine has to the remaining part of the gospel, for only when this can be demonstrated can the real place of the Logos be assessed.[325] Those who saw the Logos doctrine as wholly Hellenistic[326] were obliged to hold that it was superimposed on the Jesus of history. Yet this is untenable because of the essentially Jewish character of the presentation of Jesus in the main body of the gospel. The same objection stands whether the supposed source is Philo's doctrine[327] or some gnostic view.[328] The Logos doctrine does not

---

[324] G. Richter, 'Die Fleischwerdung des Logos im Johannesevangelium', *NovT*, 14, 1972, pp. 257f., does not consider that Jesus' becoming man and humbling himself is a central theme of this gospel. He considers Jn. 1:14 is not a part of the original hymn and is anti-docetic in character. Another who regards Jn. 1:14a as a later gloss is J. C. O'Neill, 'The Prologue of St John's Gospel', *JTS* 20, 1969, pp. 41–52. Verses 6–9 and 15a are also treated as glosses.

[325] *Cf.* M. D. Hooker, 'The Johannine Prologue and the Messianic Secret', *NTS*, 21, 1974, pp. 40–58, who discusses the prologue's significance for the structure of the gospel, comparing it with Mark's prologue.

[326] E. Käsemann, 'The Structure and Purpose of the Prologue to John's Gospel', *New Testament Questions of Today* (1969), pp. 138–167, concludes that the prologue is neither a summary of the gospel nor a pedagogic introduction for the Hellenistic reader. He thinks it must be theologically understood. 'It bears witness to the presence of Christ, whose earthly history lies now nineteen hundred years in the past, as the Creator of eschatological sonship to God and of the new world'. He takes *sarx* in Jn. 1:14a in the sense of humanity over against God.

[327] *Cf.* E. F. Scott, *The Fourth Gospel: Its Purpose and Theology* (1908), stresses John's indebtedness to Philo's ideas, although he concedes that they have been modified. He thinks that John 'rests his account of the Christian revelation on a speculative idea, borrowed, with whatever differences, from Philo'. He gives weight to the OT background as well as the synoptic gospels as sources of the gospel, but gives less weight to Jewish ideas behind the prologue.

[328] R. Bultmann, *John*, pp. 9ff., gives weight to gnostic influence on John's language, while E. F. Scott, *op. cit.*, appeals more to Philo.

remove Jesus from history and set him up as a divine being in constant and eternal communion with God. It sets Jesus firmly in history as one who is nevertheless divine. This is the paradox which is at the heart of John's gospel.

In all probability the Christology of the gospel, with its combination of true humanity with divine nature, was expressed in contemporary terms with a view to offsetting the docetic-type over-emphasis on the divine at the expense of the human, a real danger to the stability of early Christian Christology. A Logos doctrine on its own might have been construed to support the docetic notion,[330] but in connection with the rest of the gospel, which stresses even more clearly than the synoptics the human characteristic of Jesus, the 'becoming flesh' becomes diametrically opposed to docetism.

Some references must be made to the other Johannine literature. In 1 John the Logos becomes the Logos of life (1 Jn. 1:1), but still refers to Christ.[331] The Word gives life in the same sense that life is introduced into the Logos passage in John 1. That there is a close connection between Logos (as revelation) and Christ cannot be denied. The importance of the statement in 1 John 1:1f. particularly lies in the fact that the Logos is firmly set in history supported by eyewitnesses. He is an objective reality which had been heard, seen and touched.

The rest of the New Testament

Although there is not the same distinctive emphasis in *Paul's epistles* on Logos as a title, there are several aspects which are parallel. For him, as for John, Christ is pre-existent, is the agent of creation, and became incarnate (*cf.* Col. 1:15ff.; Phil. 2:5ff.). Certainly, although Paul does not describe Jesus Christ as Logos, he recognizes that Christ possesses to the full those characteristics which the Logos possesses. Indeed, we may note that Paul specifically presents Christ as Wisdom (1 Cor. 1:30ff.), and there is strong kinship between this and John's Logos.[332] John's high Christology is not an isolated phenomenon in NT thought.

---

[329] H. Schneider, ' "The Word was made Flesh". An analysis of the Theology of Revelation in the Fourth Gospel', *CBQ* 31, 1969, pp. 344–356. This author maintains that John's theological answer to the problem why Jesus, the Word, was rejected was that only by faith, a God given gift, could the revelation be accepted. This explains why Jesus was still rejected by some after his glorification. Schneider maintains in any case that Jesus could only communicate himself fully when he had perfectly realized in the flesh his divine sonship.

[330] In considering the distinctive contribution of Christianity, C. F. D. Moule, *Theology* 76, 1973, pp. 562–572, comments that the appropriation of *logos* and *sophia* but the rejection of *pneuma* was distinctive of the Christian response to events (p. 569), in contrast to docetism which merged all three.

[331] R. Law, *The Tests of Life* (1909), pp. 44f., 370, takes *logos* in this sense. But *cf.* Westcott, *The Epistles of St John* (³1892), *ad loc.*, who considers *logos* here means revelation.

[332] For a discussion of the Wisdom theme, *cf.* H. Ringgren, *Word and Wisdom* (1947); A. Feuillet, *Le Christ sagesse de Dieu d'après les épîtres pauliniennes* (EB, 1966).

In the book of *Acts* there are many instances where *logos* stands for the message about Christ, which at times becomes almost personified (*cf.* Acts 2:41; 4:4; 6:7). Everywhere the Christians proclaimed 'the word', which was identical to the idea of preaching Jesus (*cf.* 6:2 with 8:35). It is highly probable that Luke regarded Jesus Christ as so closely identified with the 'Word' that he made no explicit distinction between them. What is specifically expressed in John is implied in the whole concentration of early Christian preaching on Jesus.[333]

The epistle to the *Hebrews* begins with a statement about the revelatory character of the Son (Heb. 1:1ff.). It was through him that God had now spoken. Moreover, the salvation which the whole epistle is commending has been 'declared' by the Lord (Heb. 2:3). A more specific reference to Logos is found in Hebrews 4:12, where its penetrating character is particularly brought out, although it is not so much viewed as personal (as in John's prologue) as in the metaphor of a sharp sword.

In the book of Revelation we again meet with Logos in the Johannine sense, since Christ is called the Logos of God (Rev. 19:13). This shows a close link between Revelation and the fourth gospel and is one of the indications of possible common authorship. We may conclude therefore that Logos is an essentially Johannine concept in the NT, but with some support from other sources.[334]

THE 'I AM' SAYINGS

John's gospel

An important group of sayings, which are peculiar to John's gospel, have a significant function in Christological discussions.[335] Since these are statements in the first person which attribute certain predicates to Jesus, they are, if authentic, invaluable as revelations of his self-consciousness. Not all scholars will attach to these statements the same significance as is assumed in the following section. But if there are grounds for regarding them as substantially the words of Jesus (as already noted in the Introduction, p. 71), their importance for Christology cannot be dismissed.

---

[333] For a comparison of Luke's approach to the *logos* and also John's, *cf.* A. Feuillet's article, ' "Témoins oculaires et serviteurs de la parole" (Lc 1:2b)', *NovT* 15, 1973, pp. 241–259. He considers that Luke's approach is a step towards the Johannine. It demonstrates that John's doctrine did not fall from heaven. It had a preparation.

[334] In a summary on the NT Logos doctrine, Cullmann, *The Christology of the New Testament*, pp. 268f. makes the following main points regarding its meaning. 1. It is primarily the understanding of the life of Jesus as the centre of all divine revelation. 2. It is the utilization of contemporary speculations about a divine hypostatis to express not a syncretistic, but a genuine Christian universalism.

[335] *Cf.* A. Feuillet, 'Les Ego Eimi christologiques du quatrième Évangile *RScR*, 1966, pp. 5–22, who studies the passages 8:24b; 8:28; 13:19; 4:26; 6:20; 18:5–6. He sees the first three as absolute uses and the others as more qualified. He claims a similarity with prophetic formulae.

We note first the considerably greater frequency with which personal pronouns appear in John's gospel compared with the synoptics. The use of 'I' adds particular dignity to the statements of Jesus.[336] It is remarkable that this use does not sound audacious on the lips of Jesus. What would be presumptuous in others is natural to him. But the very frequency of the 'I' draws attention to his own person in a striking way, which prepares the reader for the more specific 'I am' (*egō eimi*) sayings.[337]

The reason for the special significance of the 'I am' sayings is that the phrase is used in the OT as a description of God. In Exodus 3:14, God names himself to Moses as 'I am that I am', which invests the 'I am' with a specific divine significance. If Jesus in any way had this usage in mind, it would throw important light on the 'I am' sayings recorded in John.[338]

There are seven sayings in John's gospel in which Jesus uses the 'I am' form to describe himself. They cover a wide range of metaphors – bread (6:35); light (8:12); door (10:7); shepherd (10:11); resurrection and life (11:25); way, truth, life (14:6); vine (15:1). In each case the 'I am' illustrates some function of Jesus – to sustain, to illuminate, to admit, to care for, to give life, to guide and to make productive. These are staggering claims if isolated from John's total presentation of Jesus. A statement like 'I am the light of the world' makes no sense except on the lips of one who was agent in the creation of the world. John's prologue makes such a saying not only acceptable, but expected. The light that shone in darkness (Jn. 1:5) is the Logos who made all things, including light for the created order. Through these 'I am' sayings Jesus makes personal what in the prologue is still abstract. This is the case with life and truth as well as light. In John's presentation Jesus claims to be the embodiment of all the higher concepts that people have sought after. Whereas these occurrences must be given full weight, they fall short of establishing the identification of Jesus with the name of Yahweh in the OT. They are certainly evidences of Jesus as

---

[336] J. H. Bernard, *John* (*ICC*, 1928), p. cxvii, cites *egō* as being found 134 times in John compared with Matthew (29 times), Mark (17 times) and Luke (23 times).

[337] There has been some recent discussion on the intellectual milieu of the 'I am' sayings. Some scholars look to the OT to supply the basis for the use, *e.g.*, R. E. Brown, *John*, pp. 533f., who discusses these sayings in an appendix. He finds the OT and Palestinian Judaism to be the most likely background. *Cf.* also P. B. Harner, *The 'I am' of the Fourth Gospel* (1970), who considers that the later part of Isaiah particularly furnishes John with his expression, together with rabbinic thought. On the other hand, it has been suggested by G. W. MacRae that gnostic parallels may be the main factor ('The Ego-Proclamation in Gnostic Sources', in *The Trial of Jesus*, ed. E. Bammel, 1970, pp. 122–134). It is not so much in wording as in religious outlook that MacRae finds parallels. He suggests that the evangelist deliberately makes use of 'a complex and syncretistic religious background'. R. Schnackenburg, *Das Johannesevangelium 2* (*HTKNT*, 1971), who includes in his commentary an excursus on the subject (pp. 59ff.), although admitting the strong OT background, nevertheless thinks that Hellenistic-gnostic thought must be taken into account. The evangelist is open to his syncretistic environment.

[338] It should be noted here that E. Stauffer, *Jesus and His Story* (Eng. trans. 1960), pp. 150ff., maintains that the *egō eimi* of Jesus before Caiaphas (Mk. 14:62) is equivalent to the divine name. But see D. Catchpole's critique of Stauffer's view, *The Trial of Jesus* (1971), pp. 132ff.

revealer of God and the giver of God's gifts.[339] Important as the 'I am' sayings are, however, it could be supposed that the 'I am' form is no more than emphatic self-identification,[340] were it not for a more remarkable use of the formula found in John's gospel in 8:58.

In discussion with the Jews, Jesus was asked the question, 'You are not yet fifty years old, and have you seen Abraham?' The answer given was emphatic in form (*amēn amēn*): 'Before Abraham was (*ēn*), I am (*egō eimi*).' The force of the absolute use of 'I am' here must be gauged against the absolute use of the phrase in John 8:24 and 13:19. This usage cannot be explained by parallels in the synoptic gospels (*e.g.* Mk. 6:50; Mt. 14:27) where the phrase represents a simple affirmative. John 6:20 seems to be a parallel Johannine example of this. Another occurrence which is probably of the same type is John 18:5, although some have seen it as evidence of a divine claim because of the dramatic action of those who had come to arrest Jesus. Yet the contrast between the *ēn* (was) applied to Abraham and the *egō eimi* applied to Christ was undoubtedly intentional in John 8:58. The *egō eimi* here must be seen as linked with the name for Yahweh revealed in Exodus 3 and with the absolute use of 'I am' (*'a'nî hû'*) in Isaiah 46:4. It must be noted that when the form of words used in this latter passage occurs elsewhere in the OT (Dt. 32:39; Is. 43:10), it is attributed to God as speaker, followed by words which express his uniqueness. There seems little doubt, therefore, that the statement of 8:58 is intended to convey in an extraordinary way such exclusively divine qualities as changelessness and pre-existence. The divine implication of the words would alone account for the extraordinary anger and opposition which the claim immediately aroused.[341]

Revelation

Linked with these sayings in John's gospel are those in the book of Revelation. There are no cases of the absolute use, but some significant assertions which are self-descriptions. The 'I am' in the Alpha and the Omega saying in Revelation 1:8 and 21:6 is spoken by God, but an identical saying

---

[339] Cf. H. Zimmermann, 'Das absolute *Egō eimi* als die neutestamentliche Offensbarungsformel', *BZ*, 4, 1960, pp. 54ff, 266ff, who regards the formula in the mouth of Jesus as a revelation formula which conveys the idea of Jesus as revealer of God. A. Feuillet, *RScR* 54, 1966, pp. 213–240, finds the meaning to be 'It is I who', showing that the gifts in the passages mentioned are inseparable from the person.

[340] There is some discussion over the force of the *egō eimi* in these sayings. R. E. Brown, *John*, pp. 534f., comments on Bultmann's view that five of the seven sayings (all except 11:25 and 14:6) are *Rekognitionsformel* (*i.e.* in the form which separates the subject from all others and emphasizes the 'I'). But Brown pays more attention to the predicate. In fact he agrees that there is much to be said for the view that there is a parallelism between these 'I am' sayings and the synoptic parables beginning, 'The Kingdom of God is like . . .'

[341] Whatever the precise meaning of *egō eimi* in Jn. 8:58 and Jn. 18:5, the evangelist shows that a special significance was attached to the saying, in that in the former case the Jews attempt to stone Jesus and in the latter the hearers fall to the ground.

occurring in Revelation 22:13 is attributed to Christ himself, which implies an ascription of deity to him. The Alpha and Omega is explained as the one 'who is and who was and who is to come, the Almighty' in 1:8, as 'the beginning and the end' in 21:6, and the same in 22:13, with the addition of 'the first and the last'. The meaning is clear. The claim is to all-inclusiveness, not in a pantheistic sense, but as embracing all human history. It is highly probable that some indebtedness to such passages as Isaiah 41:4; 48:12 may be traced here. In another claim made in this book the risen Christ declares, 'I am he who searches mind and heart' (Rev. 2:23), where the *egō eimi* is descriptive. There is a striking parallel in John 2:25 where the historical Jesus is said to have known what was in man, a reflective comment by the evangelist. Also after the profound saying of Revelation 22:16, Jesus is recorded as saying, 'I am the root and offspring of David, the bright morning star', which may be indebted to Isaiah 11:1, 10; 53:2, although the offspring idea is different. This statement tells us less about the person of Jesus than about his mission. He was to inaugurate the perfect day.

THE LAST ADAM

Paul

We come now to consider an aspect of Christology which is peculiarly Pauline.[342] While we may not regard the Adam theme to be central to Paul's theology, it nevertheless plays a sufficiently important role in his Christology to necessitate a careful marshalling of the evidence. Our first concern will be to consider the background to the 'Last Adam' motif as a description of Jesus Christ.

Background to the idea. Clearly our understanding of the Adam passages in Paul's letters will be affected by the extent to which it is believed that he was influenced by Hellenistic or Jewish thought. In the case of Paul it may not be easy always to differentiate between the two, but there is a natural inclination to assume a stronger Jewish than Hellenistic background in view of his Jewish upbringing.

From the Hellenistic side and propounded mainly by advocates of the *religionsgeschichte* school of interpreters[343] is the view that Paul was influenced by the gnostic *Urmensch* idea. This idea was that a mythical glorious

---

[342] O. Cullmann, *The Christology of the New Testament*, pp. 144ff., discusses the oriental divine man idea and the Jewish Adam speculation as background to the Son of man concept. Paul's 'Last Adam' exposition is not entirely unrelated to other concepts of Christ already considered. Note that some have seen traces of an Adam-Christ typology in the synoptic gospels, *e.g.*, M. Byskov, 'Verus Deus – verus homo, Lk. 3:23–38', *StTh* 26, 1972, pp. 25ff.

[343] *Cf.* R. Reitzenstein, *Die hellenistischen Mysterienreligionen nach Ihren Grundgedanken und Wirkungen* (³1927, rp.p. 1956). *Cf.* also R. Bultmann, *TNT* 1, pp. 164–183.

creature was believed to be a saviour figure and was to be found in many religions. It was then supposed that this widespread belief was one of the foundations of Pauline Christology. But the evidence was based on so wide a survey of diverse material without regard to dating, that any theory based upon it must be regarded as methodologically suspect. The glorious *Urmensch* was supposed to contain all souls within himself, a kind of ideal Adam. Some see these ideas behind Jewish Adam teaching.[344] Because saving functions are attributed to him, he is said to foreshadow the saving Messiah who is to come. The evidence, however, does not support the linking of Adam with Messiah.[345] Messiah is said in one passage (Num. R XIII. 12) to be the Second Adam who would restore the glory that man had lost, but the passage does not identify Messiah as Saviour, nor does it say anything about Messiah's contribution to mankind as a whole. Scroggs dispenses with the view that Jewish theology shows any indebtedness to the *Urmensch* myth.

We may next briefly summarize the Jewish view in the following ways, bearing in mind that there was no fundamental difference in the interpretation of the Adam theology between Palestinian Jews and Philo of Alexandria. (i) Adam's sin is said to be disobedience to the Torah. (ii) As a result of sin Adam lost his glory, immortality, height, the fruit of the earth, the fruit of trees, the luminaries. What is important here is that Adam's original state was seen to be physically glorious compared with man's present condition. (iii) Adam's sin brought death on the whole of mankind as a result of a divine decree. (iv) The earth was punished because of Adam's sin. (v) The sin resulted in a breach in Adam's relationship with God. Jewish exegetes[346] were pre-occupied with descriptions of Adam's state to show the depth to which he had fallen. Adam is variously seen as the first patriarch, as king of the world, and as wisdom. Adam's important place in rabbinic theology is, in fact, indisputable. The most significant feature in the Jewish teaching about Adam is the preoccupation with his status before his sin rather than after. Jewish hopes were pinned on the belief that there would be for men a restoration to the former glory. It will be seen below that Paul's approach was wholly different, in that he sees Adam only as a type of fallen humanity and includes no speculation about his former glory. The conviction that Adam was the means of sin entering the world, Paul shared with his Jewish contemporaries, but his view of man's restitution was unique.

---

[344] *Cf.* B. Murmelstein, 'Adam, ein Beitrag zur Messiaslehre', *Wiener Zeitschrift für die Kunde des Morgenlandes* 35, 1928, pp. 242ff. 36, 1929, pp. 51–86.

[345] *Cf.* R. Scroggs, *The Last Adam* (1966), pp. x ff., for a strong criticism of Murmelstein's theory.

[346] *Cf.* Scroggs, *ibid.*, pp. 32ff., for details of rabbinic views. He sets out the evidence under such headings as, 'The results of Adam's sin', 'Adam as the exalted father of Israel', 'Adam as the first patriarch', 'The exalted nature of Adam', 'Adam and Sinai', 'Adam and Eschaton'.

Paul's view of Christ as the last Adam. There are two main passages where Paul introduces an Adam theme: Romans 5:12ff. and 1 Corinthians 15. A few other passages indirectly contributed to what has come to be known as Paul's Adam Christology. We shall first survey the evidence and then discuss its significance within the total Pauline theology.

(i) Romans 5:12ff. This section does not set out to expound the nature of Christ by means of the Adam theme. The theme is incidental to the main purpose of explaining man's salvation and how it comes to him. Romans 5:12 is a well-known crux for interpreters, but certain features are clear. Adam's sin is acknowledged without debate, while the universality of sin and of death are also accepted and then brought together. The sequence of sin entering through Adam and through him to all men, followed by death to all men, is in conformity with Jewish beliefs. Since Christ is compared with Adam, we shall need to make an examination of the areas of comparison and contrast. (See also pp. 211ff.).[347]

Whatever view is taken of the doctrine of original sin, the connection of the sin of humanity with Adam's sin is beyond dispute. There is a sense of solidarity between Adam and the race which is also seen between Christ and his people.[348] It is this solidarity which makes it possible for Paul to maintain, 'If many died through one man's trespass, much more have the grace of God and the free gift in the grace of that one man Jesus Christ abounded for many' (Rom. 5:15). The one man Jesus Christ is set over against Adam.[349] One man's (Adam's) trespass and disobedience is contrasted with one man's (Christ's) righteousness and obedience. The conclusion is inescapable: what Adam lost, Christ regained. Through him a new beginning was made for humanity – indeed a new kind of humanity. Christ becomes, therefore, the head of a new type of man, as Adam was the head of the old.[350] But new and old are not necessarily to be regarded as in sequence, for Christ shows humanity in its perfection, whereas Adam's humanity was fallen.[351]

---

[347] For an exposition of the theory that Paul in this passage has been influenced by gnostic ideas, see E. Brandenburger, *Adam und Christus: Exegetisch-religionsgeschichtliche Untersuchung zu Römer 5:12–21* (1962), whose views are summarized and criticized by Scroggs, *op. cit.*, pp. xx ff. M. Byskov, *StTH* 26, 1972, pp. 25ff., opposes Brandenburger's view that Rom. 5:12ff. is concerned with the primitive state rather than the fall. He considers that the emphasis is on neither, but on the importance of Christ for man.

[348] *Cf.* E. Best, *One Body in Christ* (1955), pp. 34ff.; C. K. Barrett, *From First Adam to Last* (1962), pp. 72f.; 92ff. The latter makes a distinction between the anthropological and cosmic effects. In Adam's case both are universal. In Christ's case the cosmic effects are universal (*e.g.* in the overthrow of demonic powers), but the anthropological need not be so.

[349] Adam and Christ are always strongly contrasted in Paul. C. E. B. Cranfield, *Romans 1* (*ICC*, 1975), p. 270, speaks of the vast dissimilarity between them.

[350] In Rom. 5:14 Adam is described as a type of the One to come. J. A. T. Robinson, *The Body* (1952), p. 35 n.1., thinks this refers to Moses. But the issue is between Adam and Christ, not Adam and Moses.

[351] *Cf.* Scroggs, *op cit.*, p. 101. K. Barth, *Christ and Adam. Man and Humanity in Romans 5* (Eng. trans. 1956), maintained that for Paul the anthropology of Christ was prior to that of Adam. This idea is criticized

(ii) 1 Corinthians 15. In this passage Paul is primarily concerned with resurrection, and only incidentally brings in his last Adam theme. Nevertheless, what he says throws further light on the Romans passage. In both passages Adam and Christ are viewed as agents through which others receive the consequences of their actions. 1 Corinthians 15:22 brings out the contrast: 'For as in Adam all die, so also in Christ shall all be made alive.' The diametrically opposing results show vividly the superiority of Christ to Adam. Adam is a man of death, but Christ is a man with power to give life. This contrast is brought out in rather different terms in 1 Corinthians 15:45 where Christ is specifically named as the 'last Adam'.[352] Here the distinction is between the first man Adam as 'a living being' (*psychikon*) and the last Adam as 'a life-giving spirit' (*pneumatikon*). Again the superiority of Christ is indisputable. What is significant for an understanding of the person of Christ is the contrast between the first and the last Adam. What the original Adam should have been, the last Adam is.[353] But more than that, the last Adam, as the perfect man, is 'the mediator of true humanity'. It is in this sense that he can be described as the 'first-fruits' (1 Cor. 15:20). This theme of identity with Christ will later be discussed under the '*en Christō*' theme (see pp. 647ff.). The Adam-nature of Christ here being discussed is of vital importance to a right understanding of that formula.

Another illuminating contrast between Adam and Christ is that between 'a man of dust' (*choïkos*) and 'a man from heaven' (*epouranios*) (1 Cor. 15:47). This description of Christ at once sets the last Adam in true perspective. He shares a different kind of humanity from Adam's, and yet he is nonetheless true man.[354] He is, in fact, 'resurrected man'. But for all his

---

from such diverse points of view as J. Murray, *Romans* 1, Appendix D, pp. 384ff. and R. Bultmann, 'Adam and Christ according to Romans 5', in *Current Issues in New Testament Interpretation* (ed. W. Klassen and G. F. Schneider, 1962), pp. 143–165. Both point out that Barth has departed from what Paul actually says.

[352] M. Black, 'The Pauline Doctrine of the Second Adam', *SJT* 7, 1954, pp. 170ff., comments that Paul uses the terms 'the second man' or 'the last Adam' only in 1 Cor. 15:45ff., and shows marked restraint in the use of such language. Nevertheless Black thinks that the second Adam underlies Paul's thought in other contexts. He discusses passages like Rom. 5; 1 Cor. 11:7; 2 Cor. 6:4; Col. 1:15; Phil. 2 and the old man/ new man passages in Col. 3: 10, Eph. 2:15; 4:22. In Black's opinion 'the second Adam doctrine and the "Son of Man" eschatology have been brought together in Paul's eschatalogy' (p. 179). He further suggests that 'the second Adam doctrine lies behind Pauline Christology of the "image and the glory", and the conception of the church as the Body of Christ'. Note that O. Cullmann, *The Christology of the New Testament*, pp. 144f., similarly links the second Adam with Son of man as two aspects of the same Christological idea.

[353] *Cf.* Scroggs, *The Last Man*, p. 102. There is a distinction here between Paul's view and the messianic ideas in Jewish theology. The concept of Messiah restoring man occurs very little (but see *T. Levi.* 18).

[354] *Cf.* Scroggs, *op. cit.*, p. 101, who follows Barth in suggesting that it is not Adam's humanity which is natural but Christ's. 'The humanity of Christ is prior to that of Adam in the sense that God's intent for man is prior to Adam's rebellion'. He says further, 'Seen from the vantage point of the new creation, Adam's humanity is indeed a derived, distorted humanity'.

perfect humanity, the last Adam is 'from heaven', and Paul never forgets this. It would be incorrect to maintain that Paul thinks of the last Adam as the inaugurator of a new race as the first Adam was of fallen humanity; for this would blur the essential connection between fallen humanity and redeemed humanity. Rather we should think of the last Adam as the perfect representative of humanity, as that humanity should have been and still can be 'in Christ'. Moreover, because Christ is the last Adam there cannot be another. The possibilities are exhausted in the first and the last. There are no shades of existence in the spiritual sense between life and death.

There is some debate about whether Paul thinks that Christ's humanity as the last Adam commences with the resurrection.[355] Scroggs maintains that he does, and considers that the apostle, in referring to the earthly life of Jesus, identifies his nature with that of other men.[356] According to this view the two human natures of which Paul speaks differ radically, but are nevertheless essentially human natures. This discussion, however, concerns more particularly the resurrected body of Christ which is the focus of attention in 1 Corinthians 15. It is important, however, for a true understanding of Paul's Christology to recognize that he nowhere supports any lack of continuity between the earthly Jesus and the risen Lord. He believed that the risen Lord was still essentially Man.[357]

Some comment is needed on the view that an Adam Christology lies behind Philippians 2:6–11. Several scholars have noted a strong parallelism between the text of Genesis referring to Adam and the text of this Philippians passage. The classic expression of this view is given by J. Héring,[358] who maintained that Paul was thinking of the two Adams especially in the terminology of Philippians 2:6, understood as meaning that equality with God was for Jesus a prize which could be attained. It was possible to maintain, therefore, that what Adam grasped at (to be like God), Jesus refused. What Jesus chose, according to this Christological hymn, is the antithesis of what Adam aspired to attain.[359] The parallels are undoubtedly striking, but there is strong difference of opinion over the interpretation of

---

[355] Cf. Scroggs, *op. cit.*, pp. 92ff. Scroggs says, 'Christ has become the model and the means of the resurrection of the Christian. In his body of glory Christ is true humanity, the realization of that existence the Christian will himself have one day.' Scroggs calls this 'eschatological humanity'.

[356] Scroggs, *op. cit.*, pp. 93f., claims that by virtue of his resurrection Christ is 'not changed from being a man; he is rather changed *into* the true man'. He goes on to say that the very fact that Christ is 'first-born of many brethren' is an indication of his continuing humanity.

[357] M. E. Thrall, in an article, 'Christ crucified or Second Adam?', in *Christ and Spirit in the New Testament* (ed. B. Lindars and S. S. Smalley, 1973), pp. 143–156, suggests that the Corinthians may have made wrong deductions from Paul's preaching of Christ as the glorious Last Adam. This, she thinks, might have led them to conclude they shared Christ's character and wisdom. But Paul has to remind them that Christ was crucified – the negation of human wisdom. He does not deny his view of Christ as the glorious Last Adam, but rejects the Corinthians' misunderstanding of it.

[358] J. Héring, 'Kyrios Anthrōpos', *RHPR* 6, 1936, pp. 196–209.

[359] Cf. also O. Cullmann, *The Christology of the New Testament*, pp. 175ff., who thinks the Adam background is essential to make Phil. 2:6 intelligible.

the Philippians passage. If Philippians 2:6 is interpreted from the point of view that Christ already possessed equality with God, the parallels are far less striking.[360] Again it depends on whether the passage Philippians 2:6–11 is regarded as a Pauline production or as a Pauline adaptation of an earlier Christological hymn. If the former, it may be argued that Paul's use elsewhere of the Adam theme would dispose us to see traces of it here. If the latter, it could be claimed as earlier evidence of a comparison between Adam and Christ.[361] It must, however, be noted that the Philippians passage is quite intelligible without the Adam motif, and in the absence of any specific reference to Adam it seems best not to include it in this section of Paul's Christology. The Christological importance of this passage will be brought out more fully in a later section.

GOD

Throughout our discussions of the titles we have been confronted with a wide variety of aspects of the nature of Jesus Christ. We must conclude with the most significant ascription – Jesus described as God. We have already seen strong grounds for affirming that the NT view of Jesus finds an important place for his divine sonship. But when Jesus is called God this is even more remarkable. It is all the more so in view of the strong monotheism of the Jews.

John's gospel

Our first consideration is the contribution of John's gospel. There are two main passages which need examination, the Johannine prologue and John 20:28. We have already discussed in some detail the contribution of the Logos concept towards an understanding of the person of Christ (pp. 327ff.). We noted then the words of John 1:1, which affirm of the Logos that he was not only with God but was God (*Theos ēn ho logos*). There is no denying the force of the predicate which shows that John meant to say that God was the Word, with the emphasis falling on the word for God and not simply that the Word was divine. The absence of the article shows unquestionably that *Theos* is a predicate and not an adjective.[362] The statement therefore is an important evidence in the presentation of Jesus as God. This is further supported by the comment in John 1:18, which we have also previously discussed (p. 313) and found reason to support the reading *monogenēs Theos* (only-begotten God; or, better, only God). This is certainly the more difficult reading, but for that reason alone is more likely to be authentic. It is striking testimony to the firm

---

[360] *Cf.* also L. Bouyer, *RScR* 39, 1951, pp. 281ff.
[361] *Cf.* R. P. Martin, *Carmen Christi*, pp. 161ff., for a fuller description of this view. *Cf.* also J. T. Sanders, *The New Testament Christological Hymns*, pp.64ff.
[362] See the reference to Colwell's article in note 322 above.

conviction of the evangelist that the man Jesus about whom he writes his gospel is none other than God. It is to be noted further that in both these statements in the prologue John also draws a distinction between Jesus and God.

It is not without some significance that this gospel which begins with so strong an affirmation that Jesus is God should end with one of the disciples of Jesus confessing the same truth. The words of Thomas, 'My Lord and my God!' (Jn. 20:28) were almost certainly addressed to Christ. There is no reason for denying the possibility that Thomas uttered these words, but even if, as some suppose, the confession is the evangelist's own composition, it is still a strong testimony to John's belief that Jesus is God.[363] There are insufficient grounds for alleging that 'Jesus is Lord' must have preceded 'Jesus is God' by such an interval that both could not have formed one confession. Indeed both were truths expressed in familiar OT terminology for God.[364]

Paul

There are two lines of evidence here, Romans 9:5 and Titus 2:13. In the former case there has been much debate over whether or not the text is stating that Jesus is God. RSV reads 'and of their race, according to the flesh, is the Christ. God who is over all be blessed for ever. Amen'. The margin has 'Christ, who is God over all, blessed for ever'. It will be seen that the difference between these two renderings, which makes a significant difference for our present discussion, results from a change of punctuation.[365] But since the ancient Greek MSS did not carry any punctuation marks, it is clear that the problem of the choice of readings cannot be resolved on such grounds. Several considerations favour the RSV margin (which NIV has printed in the text). A concluding doxology would normally have placed the word 'blessed' (*eulogētos*) at the beginning and not at the end, and this weighs against the first rendering. The second point is that Paul's normal practice in a doxology is to relate it to the person named immediately before (*cf.* Rom. 1:25), but in this case God is not mentioned in the preceding context. The third reason is that the participle (*ōn*) would

[363] C. K. Barrett, *John*, p. 477, reckons that the present form of this confession took its shape from liturgical usage.

[364] B. Lindars, *John*, p. 616, considers that Thomas' confession is a summary of the gospel as a whole.

[365] *Cf.* Sanday and Headlam's excurses in *Romans* (ICC, [5]1901), pp.233ff. *Cf.* also O. Cullmann, *The Christology of the New Testament*, pp. 312f, who holds that Paul's doxology applies to Jesus. The opposite view is held by Dodd, *Romans* (MNT, 1932), *ad loc.*, and Barrett, *Romans, ad loc.* Cullmann bases his opinion on three considerations: (i) Independent doxologies are differently constructed, *i.e.* they do not begin with *Theos*; (ii) *kata sarka* requires something to be said beyond it; (iii) *epi panta* is more intelligible if applied to Christ. Otherwise the phrase is merely rhetorical. For a thorough discussion of this verse, *cf.* B. M. Metzger, 'The Punctuation of Rom. 9:5', in *Christ and Spirit in the New Testament* (ed. B. Lindars and S. S. Smalley), pp. 95–112. *Cf.* also A. W. Wainwright's caution against using the psychological argument about what Paul could or could not have written: *The Trinity in the New Testament* (1962), p. 57.

be superfluous if the concluding words are a doxology to God, but not if they refer to the antecedent Christ. Certainly these grammatical reasons strongly favour the ascription of Godhead to Christ. It is unacceptable to argue against these evidences that Paul cannot have made such an assertion, either because he does not do so elsewhere, or because of his strong Jewish monotheism.

The other passage mentioned above, Titus 2:13, links God and Jesus together, but again different translations are possible. The most likely refers to 'our great God and Saviour Jesus Christ', but the words might be rendered 'of the great God and our Saviour Jesus Christ'. Again the grammatical evidence favours the rendering which speaks of Jesus as God, for had there been any intention of differentiating between 'God' and 'Jesus', a second article would have been used.[366] Moreover, since within the same epistle the expression 'God our Saviour' is used (Tit. 1:4), it would seem unconvincing to contend for a separating of the concepts in Titus 2:13. There are insufficient reasons to deny that in this context Jesus Christ is being described as God.

Far less convincing is the attempt to render 2 Thessalonians 1:12 as 'the grace of our God and Lord Jesus Christ', instead of 'our God and the Lord Jesus Christ', on the grounds that only one article is used.[367] In this case the expression 'Lord Jesus Christ' is almost a technical term and could therefore exist without an article. Another unlikely statement in support of our present theme is Colossians 2:2.[368]

Hebrews

The quotation from Psalm 45:6 in Hebrews 1:8 has been translated in two ways – either 'Thy throne, O God, is for ever and ever', or 'God is thy throne for ever and ever'.[369] Since these words are applied in Hebrews to the Son, if the first rendering is correct it would mean that the Son was being addressed as God. There is no doubt that the most natural understanding of the Greek favours this reading of the text, although it involves taking the nominative as vocative, which can nevertheless be paralleled elsewhere.[370] The language is of sovereignty, which in the OT sometimes

---

[366] J. N. D. Kelly, *The Pastorals*, pp. 246f., examines the pros and cons and decides in favour of separating God and our Saviour. He is not persuaded by the absence of the article because he points out that Saviour is anarthrous in 1 Tim. 1:1;

[367] *Cf.* L. Morris, *1 and 2 Thessalonians* (NICNT, 1959), p. 212, for a discussion of this.

[368] O. Cullmann, *op. cit.*, pp. 312f., includes Col. 2:2 in his discussion of Paul's designation of Jesus as God. Although some textual uncertainty remains about this statement, Col. 2:3 shows that what is otherwise said to be true of God is here ascribed to Christ. But A. W. Wainwright rejects this as a definite statement that Jesus is God (*op. cit.*, p. 70). Nevertheless in the same context Paul says of Christ that the fulness of God dwells in him (Col. 2:9), which is certainly equivalent to calling Jesus God.

[369] F. F. Bruce, *Hebrews* (NICNT, 1964), *ad loc.*, considers the second reading to be unconvincing. N. Turner, *Grammatical Insights into the New Testament* (1965), p. 15, describes it as grotesque.

[370] A. W. Wainwright, *op cit.*, p. 59, cites Jn. 20:28 as an example.

links the king to God.[371] But the writer here implies that to address the Son as God is perfectly natural, whatever the original meaning of the words of the Psalm are understood to be. Nevertheless it must be admitted that the point is incidental to the main argument of the epistle.

2 Peter

In the opening salutation of this epistle the expression occurs 'the righteousness of our God and Saviour Jesus Christ' (2 Pet. 1:1). The alternative translation which inserts the definite article before Saviour avoids the implication that Jesus is being described as God, but is not as true to the text. It seems unquestionable that the former is the only correct rendering.[372]

Summary

The passages considered above are strong enough to show that Christians in the early church were not averse to ascribing Godhead to Jesus Christ. This impression can be supported by other considerations, especially by the fact that worship normally given to God is sometimes given to Christ. The Romans 9:5 doxology discussed above can be linked with two others, 2 Peter 3:18 and Revelation 1:5, 6. There is some dispute whether 2 Timothy 4:18 is ascribed to God or to Christ, because of the uncertainty over the meaning of Lord. There is at least the possibility, however, that this may be another instance in which a doxology is ascribed to Christ. To these we must add two of the hymnic passages in Revelation (5:13; 7:10), in both of which worship is offered to God and the Lamb without any differentiation between them. Moreover, in the same book the Alpha-Omega ascription which is applied to God (1:8) is also attributed to Christ (22:13).

We may note further the remarkable fact that one or two NT prayers are specifically addressed to Jesus (Acts 7:59–60; 1 Cor. 16:22 and possibly 2 Cor. 12:8).[373] According to John 14:14 Jesus invited prayer in his name. In some of the benedictions his name is linked closely with the name of God (1 Thes. 3:11, 12; 2 Thes. 3:5, 16).

The title 'God' is nowhere directly ascribed to Jesus in the synoptic gospels. We need not, however, infer that the synoptists considered him less than God. Their ascription of deity is indirect and implicit, leaving the reader to draw an inevitable conclusion. When Jesus forgave a man's sins (Mt. 9:2–6 = Mk. 2:5–11 = Lk. 5:20–24), and when he claimed to be lord of the sabbath (Mt. 12:8 = Mk. 2:28 = Lk. 6:5), he was speaking either as a blasphemer or as God. When he stilled the storm on the Sea of Galilee

---

[371] Cf. P. E. Hughes' careful discussion on this verse, *Hebrews, ad loc.*
[372] For a discussion of this statement, cf. E. M. B. Green, *2 Peter and Jude* (*TNTC*, 1968), pp. 60f.
[373] Cf. the section in Wainwright's book on 'The Worship of Jesus Christ', *op. cit.*, pp. 93–104.

(Mt. 8:26 = Mk. 4:39 = Lk. 8:24) the disciples were filled with awe, for in the OT it was God who 'made the storm be still' (Ps. 107:29; cf. Ps. 65:7; 89:9). The demoniac healed by Jesus was instructed to 'declare how much God has done for you'; Mark and Luke record without comment that he proclaimed 'how much Jesus had done for him' (Lk. 8:39; cf. Mk. 5:19–20). Luke closes his gospel with Jesus' declaration that he would 'send the promise of my Father upon you' and his return to heaven (Lk. 24:49,51); Matthew closes with the disciples bowing before Jesus in worship (Mt. 28:9), and Jesus' promise of his perpetual presence during their spiritual conquest of the world (Mt. 28:20; cf. Jos. 1:9). The synoptic presentation agrees perfectly with those NT writers who unhesitatingly ascribe to Jesus the title of God.

The evidence cited is confirmed further by the fact that some of the activities of God are transferred to Christ without any apparent difficulty. Both can be described as creating, saving and judging. It is impossible to avoid the impression that the NT writers thought of Jesus as God, whatever the problem this raises for the modern mind and has indeed raised throughout the history of the Christian church.

It has been suggested that the shift from Son of God to God as a title for Jesus was in general a late development.[374] But the evidence adduced above would not support such a view, particularly in the light of the most probable interpretation of Romans 9:5. It is understandable that difficulties would arise in the milieu of Jewish monotheism, but it is all the more remarkable that a converted Jew such as Paul could set God the Father alongside the Godhead of the Son without being theologically embarrassed by doing so.[375]

SUMMARY OF THE CHRISTOLOGICAL TITLES

The selection of titles which has been examined is by no means exhaustive, but those titles chosen are the most significant and provide an ample basis for a study of NT Christology. It is striking that for most of these titles the evidence is widely spread across all the main grouping of sources. The exceptions are Son of man (confined almost exclusively to the gospels), Logos and 'I am' (confined to the Johannine literature), and the last Adam (a Pauline theme). It is to be expected that different writers would focus on different ideas, but it is remarkable that a large degree of unanimity can be seen in the belief in the exalted character of Jesus.

---

[374] See Longenecker's discussion, *The Christology of Early Jewish Christianity*, pp. 139ff.

[375] *Cf.* R. E. Brown, *Jesus, God and Man* (1967). This book contains an essay entitled 'Does the New Testament call Jesus God', which appeared in *Theological Studies* 26, 1956, pp. 545–573. Brown accepts the use of the title 'God' for Jesus in the NT, but does not consider that it belongs to the earliest layer of tradition.

Some of the titles, such as Servant and Son of David, found most favour in the earliest strata. Son of man is never used as a title in any of the epistles and occurs only once (on the lips of Stephen) in Acts. It is significant as being the title most widely used by Jesus himself, but was superseded by other titles which more explicitly expressed the Christian estimation of the risen Lord. Both Messiah and *Kyrios* quickly became proper names for Jesus, as well as retaining much of their original meaning. Jesus was acknowledged as Lord throughout the Christian church and as the fulfiller of the messianic hopes. There is no strength in the contention that confession of Jesus as Christ was superseded by the confession of Jesus as Lord. Both are well supported in the primitive kerygma.

The Hellenistic world may have contributed other concepts like Logos, but it is not necessary to suppose that such a concept cannot be accounted for by OT and Jewish sources. In any case it is applied to Jesus in the NT in a unique way. The title Son of God points at once to the relationship between Jesus and God, but also reveals vital information about the nature of Jesus. Although the title Son of God does not necessarily imply deity, the supporting NT evidence corroborates such an understanding of it. Especially is this so of the evidence which specially affirms Jesus as God.

There are no grounds for supposing that the early Christians were conscious of any tensions resulting from their high view of Jesus. Unquestionably the Christological titles assume that Jesus was a unique person. The total impression from a careful study of them leaves no doubt that the Jesus who lived and ministered on earth rapidly became recognized in his risen status as God as well as man. His manhood might have been eclipsed in the exaltation which followed from his resurrection, but the NT provides sufficient evidence for it (see pp. 221ff.). This raises at once the problem of Jesus as God and man, which will form the theme of our concluding section (see pp. 401f.).

THE CHRISTOLOGICAL 'HYMNS'

Many scholars have considered that Philippians 2:6–11 and Colossians 1:15–20 were originally hymns which had been composed and used before being incorporated into the respective epistles. While it cannot be affirmed unreservedly that Paul has in these instances made use of already existing hymns about Christ, he clearly recognizes the profound theological significance of the content. If these passages are hymnic fragments, they would contain valuable information about the view of Christ enshrined in the earliest worship forms of the Christian communities, as well as demonstrating the essential unity of the apostle Paul with his contemporaries regarding the essential features of the Christian faith. It is because of the significance of these passages in this respect that they warrant separate consideration. We shall examine to what extent they throw light on the Christological titles already surveyed. In addition to these major passages three minor passages of a similar hymnic kind will be considered, namely 1 Timothy 3:16; Hebrews 1:1–3 and 1 Peter 3:18–22.

Philippians 2:6–11

This is one of the key passages which bear on the person of Christ. Much debate has centred around whether or not it contains a pre-Pauline hymn, and even more discussion has been concerned with its background and interpretation. It will be possible here to give only a brief summary of the problems which have been raised, before giving an analysis of the main contribution it makes to NT Christology.

THE ORIGIN OF THE PASSAGE

Of the possibilities only two concern us here.[376] There is the view that Paul has taken over an already existing hymn to Christ and has adapted it for his own purpose in the Philippian letter, and there is the alternative view that Paul himself composed the section in the course of writing the letter. The style of the passage is certainly more rhythmic than Paul's normal prose, but is not unparalleled in other, though less extensive, Pauline passages.[377] It cannot be argued, therefore, that Paul could not have written it.

The evidence from content is more elusive. It can be argued that certain important Pauline themes are omitted, notably the doctrine of redemption through the cross. If the Philippian passage were taken in isolation it would be possible to maintain that death is seen as no more than the supreme example of Christ's obedience. But no-one could reasonably be expected to pack his whole doctrine into one brief passage of a hymnic nature. This comment may also sufficiently account for the absence of specific reference to the resurrection, although the name Lord applied to Jesus may well imply it. It is noted that there is no reference to the application of the mission of Christ to man's sins. But these omissions tell as much in favour of Paul's authorship of the hymn as against it, for he was concerned in the

---

[376] For a full discussion of the different views about the origin of this passage, cf. R. P. Martin, *Carmen Christi* (1967), and more recently his commentary on *Philippians* (NCB). For a brief summary and critique of Martin's position, cf. I. H. Marshall, 'The Christ-hymn in Philippians 2:5–11', *TB* 19, 1968, pp. 104–127. Note that in his earlier work, *An Early Christian Confession* (1960), Martin adopted a rather different interpretation from that in *Carmen Christi*. Cf. also his earlier commentary on *Philippians* (TNTC, 1959). In his article mentioned above, Marshall mentions the work of R. Deichgräber, *Götteshymnus und Christushymnus* (1967), who regards the Phil. 2 hymn as Hellenistic Jewish Christian, not Palestinian.

[377] As J. Weiss, citing E. Norden, notes (*Earliest Christianity: A History of the Period AD 30–150*, Vol. 2, pp. 406ff). See also E. F. Scott, *Philippians* (IB, 1955), p. 47; R. P. Martin, *Carmen Christi*, pp. 17ff. Martin suggests the probability of hymns within the NT on the grounds that the documents had their setting in the worshipping life of the churches. He finds many traces of hymnic forms within the NT. Cf. his *Worship in the Early Church* (1964), pp. 39ff.

context of the passage to provide an example of humility and would see to it that the doctrinal progression of thought was relevant to that context. Those maintaining a pre-Pauline hymn are faced with more difficulties over omissions, if the hymn is then regarded as a statement of current Christology. For our present purpose it is sufficient to note that even if Paul has used a previous hymn about Christ, he has given his own stamp to it by including it in his epistle. Because of this it may be regarded as part of the total picture of Paul's presentation of the person of Christ.

THE BACKGROUND TO THE PASSAGE

We must consider next a problem which affects our interpretation of the terminology used in this section, that is the background to the ideas expressed. There have been a wide range of suggestions, but many of them spring from the view that the Christological ideas in the passage are developments brought about by the interchange of pre-Christian notions with the proclamations of the church about Christ. Some regard the background as Jewish, and interpret the hymn against the servant passages of Isaiah, or the presentation in the wisdom literature of Wisdom (*Sophia*) or of the idea of the two Adams. Others prefer to see a Hellenistic background, and appeal particularly to the gnostic myth of a primal-Man redeemer. Yet others see a syncretism of the two. Some reference to these various views will be made in the outline of ideas which follows.

THE LEADING IDEAS OF THE PASSAGE

So rich is this hymn in important statements about Christ that it will be most helpful to set them out under three main subdivisions: pre-existence, incarnation and exaltation. The *pre-existence* of Christ is expressed succinctly in the words 'though he was in the form of God' (*hos en morphē Theou hyparchōn*) (Phil. 2:6).[378] It is not, however, without its problems, for the important word *morphē*, has been variously interpreted.

(i) The classical use of the word closely links it with *ousia* (essence), which then suggests that being in the form of God means possessing deity. But since a distinction must be made between *morphē* and *ousia*, we cannot assume that their meaning is identical. Nevertheless, as J. B. Lightfoot[379] maintains, 'the possession of the *morphē* involves participation in the *ousia*

---

[378] The Lutheran 'Dogmatic View' of the nineteenth century (to use R. P. Martin's description, *op. cit.*, p. 63) denies that the hymn referred to the pre-existence of Christ. For a recent advocate of a similar view, *cf.* J. Harvey, 'A New Look at the Christ Hymn in Philippians 2:6–11', *ExT* 76, 1964–5, pp. 337ff. But see D. F. Hudson's criticisms, 'A Further Note on Philippians ii: 6–11', *ExT* 77, 1965–6, pp. 29f. *Cf.* also C. H. Talbert, 'The Problem of Pre-existence in Phil. 2:6–11', *JBL* 86, 1967, pp. 141–153, whose position has, however, been criticized (*cf.* J. A. Sanders, *JBL* 88, 1969, p. 281 n. 12, and I. H. Marshall *TB* 19, 1968, pp. 115ff.).

[379] *Cf.* J. B. Lightfoot, *Philippians* (⁴1878), p. 110. Lightfoot includes a valuable note on the synonyms *morphē* and *schēma*, pp. 127ff.

also'. When the *morphē* phrase is interpreted by means of the 'equality with God'[380] statement which follows, the conclusion is inescapable that *morphē* means existence equal to that of God.[381]

(ii) It is claimed, however, that this idea of essence, although it can be paralleled in Hellenistic literature, is not supported by OT usage. The LXX use of the word is claimed to relate to the visible form of any object under consideration. Hence 'the form of a slave' indicates what is readily recognizable as a slave. What is recognizable as God is more difficult to define, but is often described as his 'glory'.[382] In this case *morphē* must mean something like 'condition'. Another suggestion links *morphē* with 'image' (*eikōn*) and understands Christ's pre-existent state as 'the image and glory of God'. It is claimed that this is supported by OT usage and by Greek usage.[383] It is also paralleled elsewhere in Paul's epistles (*cf.* 2 Cor. 4:4; Col. 1:15, where 'image' and 'glory' are both ascribed to Jesus Christ). More will be said on 'image' when discussing the Colossians passage, but the idea is more than a representation of God: it involves the actual presence of God.[384] In this case *morphē* also cannot be restricted to a merely representative function. If *morphē* = *eikōn* = *doxa* there would here be an allusion to Christ as the last Adam[385] and the expression could be understood from its LXX antecedents.

(iii) A third explanation is based on a mythological understanding of the entire hymn, drawing especially from Hellenistic and gnostic literature.[386] This was the view advocated by the 'history of religions' school, which saw in *morphē* the 'essence' of God, not in the sense of full deity, but in the sense of the gnostic heavenly redeemer.[387]

---

[380] *Cf.* R. H. Fuller, *The Foundations of New Testament Christology*, p. 208.

[381] *Cf.* C. Spicq, 'Notes sur MORPHĒ dans les papyrus et quelques inscriptions', *RB* 80, 1973, pp. 37ff. In this article Spicq shows the wide variety of meanings which *morphē* had in the sources he examines, but prefers the sense of 'condition' because it expresses a person's 'manière d'être' (p. 45).

[382] Several writers conect *morphē* with *doxa* – for details, *cf.* R. P. Martin, *Carmen Christi*, pp. 104ff.; P. Bonnard, *L'épître de S. Paul aux Philippiens* (CNT, 1950), pp. 42f.

[383] As in the Corpus Hermeticum. *Cf.* F. W. Eltester, *EIKŌN im Neuen Testament* (ZNW Bh.23, 1958), pp. 80ff.; J. Jervell, *Imago Dei: Gen. 1. 26f im Spätjudentum, in der Gnosis und in den paulinischen Briefen* (FRLANT 76, 1960), pp. 228f.

[384] *Cf.* R. P. Martin, *Carmen Christi*, pp. 112f.

[385] *Cf.* A. M. Hunter, *Paul and His Predecessors* (²1961), p. 40, who maintains that Jesus as second Adam chose the role of the suffering servant.

[386] For instance, this view is supported by R. Reitzenstein, *Die hellenistischen Mysterienreligionen*, who maintained that Paul used an already existing divine-man idea, although he admitted marked differences in Paul's use of it. *Cf.* also C. H. Kraeling, *Anthropos and Son of Man. A Study in the religious syncretism of the Hellenistic Orient* (1927); R. Bultmann, *TNT* 1, p. 175; G. Bornkamm, 'On Understanding the Christ-hymn, Phil. 2:6–11', in his collected essays *Early Christian Experience* (Eng. trans. 1969), pp. 112f. E. Käsemann, 'Kritische Analyse von Phil. 2:5–11', *ZTK* 47, 1950, pp. 314f. (Eng. trans. in *Journal for Theology and Church* 5, 1968, pp. 45–88).

[387] J. A. Sanders, 'Dissenting Deities and Philippians 2:1–11', *JBL* 88, 1969, pp. 279–290, finds the background of this passage in first century Palestine, in a mixture of OT and Semitic as well as Hellenistic features. Bo Reicke, 'Unité chrétienne et diaconie, Phil. 2:1–11', in *Neotestamentica et Patristica* (ed. W. C.

The decision between the first and second interpretations mentioned above is difficult. The third may be seriously questioned on the grounds that evidence for the gnostic heavenly redeemer idea is lacking for the period under consideration.[388] Whereas the first interpretation would explicitly claim for Christ equality with God, the second would imply it, and both are therefore important witnesses to his deity. Pre-existence is a necessary complement of this.

But the Philippian hymn makes a further statement about the pre-existent state of Christ which has far-reaching consequences for any understanding of the incarnation. The crucial words are those that state that he 'did not count equality with God a thing to be grasped' (*ouch harpagmon*). The Greek word *harpagmos* may be taken in various ways which bear on the Christology of the passage.[389]

The main crux is whether the statement means that Christ did not hold on to what he already possessed (*i.e.* equality with God) but gave it up (*res rapta*)[390], or whether it means that Christ declined the temptation to grasp at what he did not as yet possess (*res rapienda*), but was content to wait for it to be given to him.[391] In the latter case what he did not possess was not 'equality' in the sense of essence, but the dignity of kingship over the universe, which, however, was given him at his exaltation. If equality with God is understood in the further sense of independence of God, the meaning would then be that Christ did not grasp at sovereignty as an act of self-assertion although he possessed the 'form of God'. The hymn certainly suggests some way in which the exaltation went beyond the pre-existent

---

van Unnik *et al.*, 1962, pp. 203ff.), not only maintains the unity of the hymn, but also its relevance to its local (Philippian) context. It was designed to meet a specific ethical need. R. P. Martin (*Carmen Christi*, pp. 88 ff.), does not support an ethical purpose for the hymn, but *cf.* I. H. Marshall's criticisms of his arguments, *TB* 19, 1968, pp. 117ff.

[388] *Cf.* E. Percy in *Untersuchungen über den Ursprung der johanneischen Theologie* (1939), pp. 287–299. *Cf.* also R. M. Wilson, *The Gnostic Problem* (1958).

[389] *Cf.* J. Jeremias, *ThB*, 1940, p. 277. For a recent careful discussion of the various Greek terms used in this Christological section, *cf.* the three articles by P. Grelot in *Biblica* 'Deux expressions difficiles de Philippiens 2:6–7', Vol. 53, 1972, pp. 495–507; 'La valeur de *ouk . . . alla* dans Philippiens 2:5–7', Vol. 54, 1973, pp. 25–42; 'Deux notes critiques sur Philippiens 2:6–11', *idem*, pp. 169–186. In the last article Grelot discusses the structure and possible Aramaic background of the Greek text of the whole passage. On the Aramaic background, *cf.* also I. H. Marshall, 'The Development of Christology in the early Church', *TB* 18, 1967, pp. 90ff.

[390] *Cf.* J. B. Lightfoot, *Philippians* (⁴1878), p. 111. Lightfoot takes the noun and verb together and maintains that the phrase means 'to prize highly'. This view has found a staunch advocate in T. F. Glasson, 'Two notes on the Philippian Hymn (II. 6–11)', *NTS* 21, 1975, pp. 133ff.

[391] Taking the subject of Phil. 2:6 as the human Jesus rather than the pre-existent Son, D. W. B. Robinson ('Harpagmos: The Deliverance Jesus Refused', *ExT* 80, 1969, pp. 253f.) favours a passive rendering of *harpagmos* in the sense of a rapture. According to this view, although Jesus was the Son of God he did not consider being caught up out of the hour of trial, but waited for God to exalt him. He cites L. L. Hammerich (whose booklet *An Ancient Misunderstanding* is discussed in an editorial in *ExT* 78, 1967, p. 193), in support, although he does not follow his idea of mystical rapture.

state[392] and the suggestion therefore that sees this in the universal acknowledgment of his sovereignty seems a reasonable interpretation.

Yet another possibility is to interpret the *ouch harpagmon* as a complete phrase meaning a 'no-snatching' and to regard 'equality with God' as being expressed in giving rather than gaining.[393] This interpretation is based on the position of the negative.[394] There is much to be said for it, for it would fit the context better if Christ's action could more readily serve as a pattern for man's action. The main problem is whether the emptying (*ekenōsen*) in the next statement can bear the meaning this puts on it.

Next we come to the *incarnation* theme, which centres around two important aspects – the act of incarnation (*ekenōsen*, emptying) and the incarnate life. The self-emptying has created problems, for debate has raged over what was emptied. If equality with God is laid aside, the human Jesus was not God and his incarnate life cannot be approached on the assumption that he was. But the difficulty of conceiving any real sense in which a pre-existent divine being could empty himself of his deity is at once apparent. This theory (the kenotic theory) was popular among the advocates of the 'historical Jesus' movement for it effectively removed the divine characteristics from the life of Jesus.[395] Another view is that the emptying relates only to his status of equality with God[396] which was temporarily suspended by the earthly life of Jesus. A third possibility is that the emptying is to be understood as self-effacement, the antithesis of the self-aggrandizement which would follow if Jesus had snatched at the glory which was later to be bestowed on him.[397]

It is evident that only those interpretations of the emptying which are in line with the pre-existent nature of Christ are acceptable in this context.

---

[392] *Cf.* O. Cullmann, *Christology*, p. 180. *Cf.* also R. P. Martin's survey *Carmen Christi*, pp. 143ff. P. Bonnard, *Philippiens*, p. 43, takes *harpagmos* in the sense of exploitation.

[393] *Cf.* C. F. D. Moule, 'Further Reflexions on Philippians 2:5–11', in *Apostolic History and the Gospel* (ed. W. W. Gasque and R. P. Martin, 1970), pp. 264–276. *Cf.* also J. Carmignac, 'L'importance de la place d'une négation: OUCH HARPAGMON HEGESATO (Philippiens 2:6)', *NTS* 18, 1971–2, pp. 131–166, who makes a careful study of the use of the negative in Paul's letters and concludes that in Phil. 2:6 it should not be attached to the verb but to the noun.

[394] For the view that the negative suggests a contrast with someone else who had snatched at equality with God (*i.e.* Satan or Adam), *cf.* R. P. Martin's discussion, *Carmen Christi*, pp. 154–164. M. R. Vincent, *Philippians and Philemon* (*ICC*, 1897), p. 86, firmly rejected all idea of an antithesis between the two Adams in this passage. *Cf.* T. F. Glasson's comments, *art. cit.*, pp. 137f.

[395] For a recent advocate for some kind of kenotic theory, *cf.* D. G. Dawe 'A Fresh Look at the Kenotic Christologies', *SJT* 15, 1962, pp. 341ff. For an exposure of the weakness of such theories, *cf.* E. R. Fairweather, in an 'Appended Note: Kenotic Christology', in F. W. Beare, *The Epistle to the Philippians* (*BC*, 1969), pp. 159–174.

[396] *Cf.* J. B. Lightfoot, *op. cit.*, *ad loc.*, who suggests that Christ divested himself, 'not of His divine nature, for this was impossible, but of the glories, the prerogatives, of Deity. This He did by taking upon Him the form of a servant.'

[397] J. Carmignac, *art. cit.*, p. 142, argues from the position of the negative for the meaning 'usurpation'. But his view of the force of the negative is critized by P. Grelot, 'La valeur de ouk . . . alla . . . dans Philippiens 2, 6–7', *Bib* 54, 1973, pp. 25–42.

For this reason it is impossible to maintain an emptying of Godhead and also to maintain any real continuity between the pre-existent state and the incarnate state.[398] The passage cannot sustain a straight exchange of 'form of a servant' for 'form of God.[399] The emptying is co-incident with the taking the form of a servant (note that the aorist participle is used), and there can be no question that the words mean 'having emptied himself, he took the form of a servant'. It is difficult to decide between the second and third possibilities, but the third has in its favour that it would rather more easily fit the context.

Various suggestions have been made regarding the 'form' of the incarnate life. Some see here an unmistakable allusion to the servant of God in Isaiah,[400] not simply because of the use of the word 'servant', but because the whole passage is thought to be based on Isaiah. On the other hand the words in Philippians refer primarily to the human nature of Jesus. Certainly if the Isaiah passage contributes to the allusion here,[401] it would imply the complete identification of Christ with men. Another view is that the 'form' is a poetic expression for poverty and is to be linked with the idea of humiliation.[402] The idea of 'servant' rests in Christ's perfect submission to the will of another, *i.e.* to God himself. A wholly different view is adopted by those who trace the whole hymn to the gnostic redeemer myth and who maintain that Christ placed himself under the demonic powers of this world.[403] This line of approach stresses the voluntary character of Christ's actions and denies that the theme of the hymn is about relationships within the Godhead. Although the emptying of himself (*heauton*) must be given weight, the subservience of Christ to demonic powers is unthinkable and is contrary to the evidence of the synoptic gospels. Still further it has been argued that 'the form of a servant' relates to the obedient righteous man idea widespread in current Jewish thought.[404] Obedience played a dominant part in Jewish religion and Jesus would be recognized by Christians as having fulfilled this condition *par excellence*.

[398] *Cf.* G. Bornkamm, *Early Christian Experiences* (Eng. trans. 1969), p. 114, who recognizes that in Phil. 2:6, 7, the phrases 'he was in the form of God'; 'to be equal with God'; 'he emptied himself', 'show that the Pre-existent One *was* equal with God and gave up this divine mode of existence'.

[399] This is not, of course, to deny that a connection is clearly intended between the form of God and the form of a servant. *Cf.* J. C. Gibbs, 'The Relation between Creation and Redemption according to Phil. II, 5–11', *NovT* 12–13, 1970–1, pp. 270–283. He deduces that the history of reconciliation 'begins with the pre-incarnate Christ (2:6, *cf.* Eph. 1:4) and shows the identity in one Person of the "form of God" and the "form of a servant" ' (p. 277).

[400] So L. Cerfaux, 'L'Hymne au Christ-Serviteur de Dieu', in *Miscellanea historica in honorem Alberti de Meyer* (1946), pp. 117–130, reproduced in *Recueil Lucien Cerfaux²* (1954), pp. 425–437.

[401] J. Jeremias, *The Servant of God* (W. Zimmerli and J. Jeremias), p. 97, supports this view.

[402] *Cf.* M. Dibelius, *Der Brief des Paulus an die Philipper* (LHB, 1937), p. 37.

[403] So E. Käsemann, 'Kritische Analyse von Phil. 2. 5–11', *ZTK* 47, 1950, pp. 313–360. See note 387 above.

[404] *Cf.* E. Schweizer, *Lordship and Discipleship* (Eng. trans. 1960), pp. 61ff.; idem, *NTS* 2, 1955, p. 88. R. P. Martin, *Carmen Christi*, pp. 195f., combines Schweizer's view with the servant idea.

That the incarnate life of Christ was intended to be seen as perfectly human is further stressed by the phrase 'being born in the likeness of men', which furnishes a key to the reality of the servant form. Indeed the human form, the self-humiliation, the obedience to death, the ignominy of the cross, suddenly focus in few words on the utter antithesis to the pre-existent state. Yet in spite of the stress on humanity there is no suggestion that Christ was no more than a man. Here the problem of the divine nature and the human nature becomes sharpened, but nowhere is there an attempt to resolve the problem. The Philippians passage would not in fact give the impression that the early Christians were acutely aware of the problem. It was not until later when the Christian church sought to express its faith in Greek categories of thought that the problem became acute. This passage gives no exposition of the rationale of the incarnation.

The last major idea of the passage is that of *exaltation*, which consists of a divine act (highly exalted), the bestowal of a unique name, the homage of all people and the universal acknowledgment of the sovereignty of Jesus Christ. The first question is whether the exaltation is equivalent to or is an extension of the resurrection. It would seem reasonable to suppose that exaltation is intended to involve both resurrection and ascension. The vital question is whether the exaltation was to a status higher than the pre-existent status or whether it refers to a restoration to the original status. In other words, is the compound word ('highly exalted') to be understood superlatively (as RSV) or comparatively (*i.e.* more highly exalted than before)? The general consensus of opinion supports the former, although some notable scholars favour the latter.[405] Since the name is said to be 'above' (*hyper*) every name, the same preposition as in the verb 'highly exalted' (*hyperypsōsin*),[406] it is reasonable to suppose that the exaltation is connected with that name.[407]

The identity of the name is not given in this passage. This has led to a variety of different opinions. It is hardly likely that such suggestions as Jesus Christ or God are correct. It is more probable that the name is 'Lord', descriptive of the office which the risen Christ exercises. This would have particular significance since 'Lord' is the LXX equivalent of the Hebrew Yahweh (see discussion on pp. 291ff.). This virtually means that what Jesus did not or could not gain by snatching, he gained by the direct gift of God himself, *i.e.* the dignity of equality with God. Another interpretation sees the name in terms of revelation as if God's character is now made fully

---

[405] F. W. Beare (*Philippians*, p. 85), E. Käsemann (*ZTK* 47, 1950, p. 347), and G. Bornkamm (*Early Christian Experience*, p. 117), all regard it as comparative.

[406] *Cf.* O. Cullmann, *The Christology of the New Testament*, pp. 180f., understands the 'more' in the sense that God conferred on Jesus his name, which represented his lordship. In line with his interpretation of verses 6ff., Cullmann considers that Christ received 'equality' with God.

[407] G. Delling, 'Zum steigernden Gebrauch von Komposita mit *hyper* bei Paulus', *NovT* 11, 1969, pp. 127–153, shows that Paul's *hyper*-compounded verbs are usually elative.

known through Christ's exaltation as Lord of the universe.[408] No longer can there be any uncertainty about the true nature of God in relation to the world. What is indisputable about the statement concerning the name is that it involves a reversal of the fortunes of Christ. There is no need, however, to regard this as a reward for his obedience.[409] Indeed there is no suggestion of the idea of a reward. What Christ receives he receives as of intrinsic right, and this is demonstrated by his obedience.

The exalted position of Christ is further enhanced by the prediction of universal homage to be given to him. This in itself is an admission of deity (*cf.* Is. 45:23), for the same homage is offered to Christ as is offered to God.[410] There has been some discussion over who offers the homage. Some consider that the church is in mind, but others that it is the cosmic powers, in which case the lordship is over the world rather than over the church.[411] Since 'every knee' and 'every tongue' are here involved, it seems more natural to apply these phrases to humans rather than to cosmic forces but the expressions may be no more than symbolic. It is attractive to hold that demonic spirits who have rebelled against God will be obliged to acknowledge the lordship of Christ, not in the sense of a confession of faith, but in the sense of acknowledging his conquest over them. When demonic spirits acknowledge such sovereignty, it will be evident to all creatures that Jesus is exalted to the position of God. The hymn makes clear that he is no usurper of deity. There is no suggestion that there are two Gods. Yet there is no doubt that Jesus Christ is no less deity than God himself. Without embarking on difficult discussions about the trinity (see pp. 111ff.), we may note in this passage evidence that Jesus is treated as God, and this becomes part of the data on which that doctrine is based. The fact that homage to Christ is stated to be 'to the glory of God the Father' further safeguards a right approach to the monotheism of the early Christian church.[412]

For a full appreciation of the Christological significance of this passage, some comment must be made on the time of the homage. Is it now operative or is it still wholly future, or is it both? The verb 'confess' (*exomologēsetai*) is future, although an alternative reading has an aorist subjunctive. Whichever reading is original it does not resolve the problem of the tension between the present actuality of Christ's lordship and the future universal acknowledgment of it. There is ample evidence in the NT

---

[408] *Cf.* E. Käsemann, *ZTK* 47 (1950), pp. 347ff.; and J. Jervell, *Imago Dei, Gen. 1:26 im Spätjudentum, in der Gnosis und in den paulinischen Briefen* (1960), p. 212.

[409] R. P. Martin, *Philippians* (*NCB*), p. 100, comments that the verb used for bestowing (*charizesthai*) suggests a gift of grace and excludes any notion of merit.

[410] *Cf.* M. Meinertz, *Theologie des Neuen Testaments 2* (1950), pp. 62ff.

[411] So E. Lohmeyer, *Der Brief an die Philipper* (*KEK*, Ed. W. Schmauch, ⁹1953), p. 97. Note that Käsemann, *art. cit.*, who sees evidence of a gnostic myth, regards the 'name' here as a distinctive Christian feature added to the myth.

[412] *Cf.* P. Bonnard, *Philippiens*, p. 47, and G. Heinzelmann, *Philipper* (*NTD*, ⁷1955), *ad loc.*

that Christians believed that Christ has already triumphed over his enemies (Rev. 3:21; Col. 2:15). And yet the conflict still rages in the experience of the church. For the present church, it is an act of faith to accept Christ's conquest over his enemies as a *fait accompli*; but at his coming again this will become a universally acknowledged fact. What is important for our present purpose is that the lordship is even now an essential fact.

Colossians 1:15–20

This is another Pauline passage which is widely claimed to have been originally an independent hymn. Since the significance of the hymn depends to some extent on its provenance it will be necessary, before discussing its contribution, to note briefly the different views which have been expressed concerning it.

THE ORIGIN OF THE PASSAGE

Was the passage composed by Paul, or was it already in use as an early liturgical Christian hymn which was then adapted by Paul, or was it in fact a pre-Christian hymn either adapted by Paul or interpolated into his epistle? Because of its rhythmic form, unusual vocabulary and elevated style many exegetes are satisfied that this passage is a hymn.[413] But there is difference of opinion over whether Paul himself wrote it or adapted it from some other source. C. F. D. Moule[414] considers the evidence insufficient to conclude that this is a pre-Pauline passage and inclines towards a Pauline origin for it. Nevertheless, many feel more strongly that rhythmic qualities favour the idea of an independent hymn. It is possible that Paul may be echoing in his language ideas which formed part of a separate hymn, but there are no means of determining whether this is so.[415] Account will be taken of the different possibilities in the discussion in the following section on the background of the passage.[416]

THE BACKGROUND

It would be sensible to look first to a Jewish background as an explanation of the concepts of this passage.[417] Certain terms used in it suggest im-

---

[413] *Cf.* R. P. Martin, *Colossians: The Church's Lord and the Christian's Liberty* (1972), pp. 39f. *Cf.* also J. C. Gibbs, *Creation and Redemption* (1971), pp. 94–114. Gibbs adopts the view that the author of Colossians did not write this hymn, on four grounds: (i) The formal style which differs from its context; (ii) The many relative clauses in the hymn; (iii) The hapax legomena; (iv) The advanced Christology.

[414] C. F. D. Moule, *Colossians and Philemon* (*CGTC*, 1957), pp. 58ff. *Cf.* also A. Feuillet, *Le Christ Sagesse de Dieu d'après les épîtres pauliniennes* (*EB* 1966), pp. 166–273.

[415] P. Ellingworth, 'Colossians 1:15–20 and its Context', *ExT* 83, 1962, pp. 252f., maintains that even if Paul uses a pre-Pauline hymn he has been responsible for its present context. This is clearly the most important factor for understanding its contribution to NT theology.

[416] Many scholars have sought to reconstruct what they consider to be the original form of the hymn and have then concentrated on the ways in which the final redactor has modified it.

[417] *Cf.* C. Masson, *L'Épître de Saint Paul aux Colossiens* (*CNT*, 1950), pp. 97–107, for the view that Jewish tradition sufficiently accounts for the Colossian hymn.

mediate parallels with the OT and other Jewish sources. The idea of Christ as 'first-born of all creation' has been linked with Proverbs 8:22 ('The Lord created me at the beginning of his work', or perhaps 'begat me') and Genesis 1:1 ('In the beginning God created'). Since the subject of Proverbs 8 is 'Wisdom', it is reasonable to suppose that this idea sheds light on the Colossians passage. Indeed C. F. Burney[418] suggested that the combination of Proverbs 8 and Genesis 1 was perhaps a rabbinic-style meditation, in which Paul claims for Christ what the rabbis drew out of these two passages. In this case he may be combating the exaggerated claims of Jewish teachers for the exalted status of the Torah, which was considered to be pre-existent and the agent of creation (see details in the section on the Logos, pp. 325ff.). Such a view would be tantamount to providing a rival for Christ, and this would naturally lead Paul to stress the pre-eminence of Christ (Col. 1:18). The hymn would thus find close parallels with John's prologue, although here Paul brings out more specifically that Christ is subject to no other agency, not even the Torah.

This idea of a Jewish background has been criticized, mainly because of the difficulty of supposing that Judaizers were the sole source of opposition to Paul's doctrine at Colossae. There are some elements which suggest a Gentile infiltration of ideas (*e.g.* vain philosophy, elemental spirits of the universe, 'fulness', *etc.*). The false teaching is so clearly eclectic, however, that there was undoubtedly a strong stream of Judaizing within it, *cf.* Col. 2:8 (tradition); 2:11; 3:11 (circumcision); 2:16 (festivals); and 2:21 (taboos). It seems highly likely, therefore, that ideas absorbed from the wisdom literature were at least a contributory factor in the expression of concepts found in Colossians 1:15ff. Certain parallels with Hebrews 1 would support this view.

Many scholars, however, have looked for a gnostic origin for the ideas,[419] especially appealing to the redeemed redeemer as in the case of Philippians 2:6ff. Several ideas in the present passage are said to have a gnostic flavour, such as 'image of God', 'first-born', the head/body analogy, 'fullness', 'reconciliation'.[420] Undoubtedly parallels can be found which sustain a

[418] *Cf.* C. F. Burney, 'Christ as the APXH of Creation', *JTS* 27, 1925–6, pp. 160ff. *Cf.* also W. D. Davies, *Paul and Rabbinic Judaism* (1948), pp. 150ff., who is a more recent exponent of the same view. T. F. Glasson, 'Colossians 1:18, 15 and Sirach XXIV', *NovT* 11, 1969, pp. 154ff., who stresses the close connection between the Colossian passage and the Wisdom literature, suggests that the Greek text of Sirach 24 known to Paul may have contained expressions corresponding to 'pre-eminence' and 'first-born'. The linking of the two ideas occurs in the Old Latin text and is supported from Ps-Cyprian's *Testimonies* II.i. A. van Roon, 'The Relation between Christ and the Wisdom of God according to Paul', *NovT* 16, 1974, pp. 207–239, argues that Paul's Christology is not based on an identification of Christ with the Wisdom of God described in the Wisdom literature, but is concerned only with the traditional connection between the Messiah and the Wisdom of God (*cf.* esp. p. 238).

[419] *Cf.* E. Käsemann, 'A Primitive Christian Baptismal Liturgy', *Essays on New Testament Themes* (Eng. trans. 1960), pp. 149–168. He considers that the original hymn was a pagan gnostic myth, which became christianized. He sees it as forming part of a baptismal liturgy.

[420] *Cf.* R. P. Martin's summary, *Colossians: the Church's Lord and the Christian's Liberty*, pp. 40ff.

superficial resemblance, but it will be seen that those notions are differently treated. In gnostic thought the 'image' related to a heavenly man, who bore the divine likeness, subjected himself to the powers of fate and has been exalted. Similarly the 'first-born' was the 'original man', who shared the throne of God, who also was to the world as the head to the body. But the idea of a redeemed redeemer is alien to the Colossians passage, as is also the gnostic idea of reconciliation. For gnostics, reconciliation was cosmic, not personal or moral; and although it is possible to put such a construction on the 'all things' in Colossians 1:20, the additional words 'by the blood of his cross' at once introduce a concept totally alien to gnostic ideas. The absence of the redemption concept is claimed by some to be offset to some extent by the recently discovered coptic gnostic Apocalypse of Adam;[421] but even this has been challenged because the Colossians hymn is too indebted to OT concepts and can more readily be understood from such a starting point. It must be remembered also that extant gnostic literature is considerably later than the NT period, which makes it a precarious quarry for finding clues to the background of the Colossians passage.

Another view is that which appeals more generally to a Hellenistic background rather than to gnosticism.[422] Parallels are suggested with Stoicism,[423] Philo and the Hermetic literature. But the parallels depend on some affinity between the Colossians passage and speculations over the cosmos. Philo is perhaps the nearest, for he speaks of the word as being the Son of God, the organ of creation and the 'image' of the heavenly wisdom.[424] It has been maintained[425] that the word 'image' (*eikōn*) is the real key for the understanding of the passage, not only from Philo, but also from the Hermetic tracts.[426] Another view concentrates more on the

---

[421] *Cf.* J. T. Sanders, *The New Testament Christological Hymns*, pp. 130ff., on the Apocalypse of Adam. *Cf.* also R. M. Wilson, *Gnosis and the New Testament* (1968), pp. 138ff.; G. W. MacRae, *Heythrop Journal* 6, 1965, pp. 27ff.

[422] *Cf.* M. Dibelius, *An die Kolosser, Epheser, an Philemon* (LHB, ³1953, ed. H. Greeven), pp. 14ff. J. T. Sanders, *op. cit.*, p. 75, gives a brief summary of Dibelius' position. *Cf.* also E. Norden, *Agnostos Theos* (1913), pp. 250ff., who traces the ideas of the hymn to Stoicism, via Hellenistic Judaism.

[423] J. M. Robinson, 'A formal Analysis of Col. 1:15–20', *JBL* 76, 1957, pp. 270–287, allows only the possibility of Stoic influence in Col. 1:16c.

[424] *Cf. de Migratione Abrahami* 6; *Quod Deus immutabilis*, p. 138. *Cf.* also *Legum Allegoria* 1:43; *Confusione Linguarum* 97, for Philo's use of *eikōn* of heavenly Wisdom and Logos. *Cf.* Sanders, *op. cit.*, pp. 84f., for a useful table of comparisons in Colossians, Philo and the Hermetica.

[425] F. W. Eltester, *Eikon im Neuen Testament* (BZNW, 23, 1958).

[426] *Cf.* the parallels in the Hermetic literature, *Corpus Hermeticum* xi, xii. See W. Manson's comments in *Jesus the Messiah* (1943), pp. 185ff. Although not unsympathetic towards possible Iranian influence on the Apostle Paul, Manson points out five pronounced differences between Paul's view and the heavenly man redemption myth. (i) Christ pre-exists creation as Son of God, not man; (ii) he is the source, not merely the instrument, of creation; (iii) Christ did not possess the rank of triumphant Redeemer before the creation; (iv) he is Man from heaven by virtue of incarnation, not because he pre-existed as man; (v) we are a new creation in him, not by the awakening of an original divine principle in us. Manson's conclusion is worth quoting: 'Hence, while it is possible and indeed likely that traditional or received ideas helped the apostle

wisdom concept, especially as it developed within the Jewish dispersion.[427] Valuable as these background studies are for enabling us to set the passage against the religious atmosphere of the first century, they cannot entirely account for the origin of Paul's ideas, which were more strongly based on the historical revelation which he had received, although no doubt they were expressed in ways which would be intelligible and highly suggestive to people in the contemporary world.[428] We proceed to consider next the leading ideas in the Colossians passage with this in mind.

LEADING IDEAS

For convenience we may examine this passage under three themes.

The superiority of Christ in creation. This is set out in various ways and may be seen in two key concepts ('image' and 'first-born') and in a comprehensive statement about Christ's part in creation. The idea, 'image of the invisible God', is an astonishing thought when applied to Christ, for whatever the nuances in the word 'image' (*eikōn*) it is clear that Paul is claiming that Christ is a perfect revelation of God.[429] Both Judaism and Christianity affirmed the invisibility of God and consequently rejected idolatry, but Christian faith is unique in considering the visibility of the invisible through his perfect likeness in Christ. The same use of 'image' is found elsewhere in Paul (2 Cor. 4:4) in relation to the glory of Christ in the gospel. A

---

here, as at other points, to self-expression, the matter of his gospel must be pronounced independent of extraneous influences, based as it is on Christian historical revelation and on the Christian experience of God' (p. 190).

[427] E. Schweizer, *The Church as the Body of Christ* (Eng. trans. 1964), pp. 64ff. In an article 'The Church as the Missionary Body of Christ', *NTS* 8, 1961–2, pp. 6ff., Schweizer proposes his own outline for the original hymn which is incorporated, according to him, in an edited form in Col. 1:15ff. He sees the original as presenting a Hellenistic conception of a cosmic Christ which by-passed reconciliation as a personal reality. The amendments made to this alleged hymn were to correct this Hellenistic misconception. But Schweizer's comments depend wholly on the probability of his reconstruction of the original hymn being correct, which is seriously open to question. But *cf.* W. Pöhlmann, 'Die hymnischen All-Prädikationen in Kol. 1:15–20', *ZNW* 64, 1973, pp. 53–74. Although he also considers that an existing hymn has been used, he nevertheless maintains that the all-statements belonged to that hymn.

[428] B. Vawter, 'The Colossians Hymn and the Principle of Redaction', *CBQ* 33, 1971, pp. 62–81, has maintained that the final redactor of the hymn has modified the theology of the original. He does not treat the hymn in its present form as a Pauline redaction. He thinks this passage has incorporated diverse theological viewpoints. He nevertheless regards the redactional changes as slight. An example of such a change is that the original hymn is alleged to have referred to an event of cosmic dimensions which in the redaction has been shrunk to the dimensions of the church. There is, however, a high degree of subjectivity in Vawter's method of detecting the original. In any case we are concerned with the hymn in its final form in Colossians, not in any proposed original form. Vawter acknowledges this, but considers that his redaction method brings to light the intention of the author. For other attempts at reconstructing the original text of this hymn, *cf.* J. M. Robinson, *JBL* 76, 1957, pp. 270–287; E. Bammel, 'Versuch zu Col. 1:15–20', *ZNW*, 52, 1961, pp. 88ff.

[429] R. P. Martin, *Colossians: The Church's Lord and the Christian's Liberty*, p. 45, speaks of 'a coming into visible expression of the invisible God'. It is more, therefore, than just likeness.

similar use is found in Hebrews 1:3 (see below). If we enquire in what way the use of the term in Colossians differs from Philo's (see previous section), the answer is found in its combination with the phrase 'first-born (*prōtotokos*) of all creation', which has no precise parallel in Philo.[430]

The word 'first-born' occasions some difficulty, because the statement taken on its own would seem to imply that Christ was a creature. But in view of the context this is impossible. The creator of all things [431] (see below) cannot himself be a creature. In what sense, therefore, is 'first-born' used? Some (including the Arians) maintained that this word must be understood in terms of Proverbs 8:22, which they understood to mean that Wisdom was created. But this is possible only by ignoring the context. The word *prōtotokos* must be understood either (i) in the sense of priority to creation, thus drawing attention to the pre-existence of Christ, which is in line with his creative work;[432] or (ii) in the sense of supremacy over creation (*cf.* verses 17–18). The latter idea fits in well with the main drift of the whole passage, *i.e.* the pre-existence of Christ. He is not the greatest among the multitude of other creatures. There is no suggestion that Paul had this in mind. He was clearly placing Christ above all creatures in the statements that follow. In a particularly full manner, he shows this in Colossians 1:16, where God is said to have created all things 'in him' (*en autō*), 'through him' (*di' auton*) and 'for him' (*eis auton*). In no clearer way could he have set Christ at the very centre of creation, and in no more explicit terms could he have asserted his superiority.

The continuing activity of Christ in the created order. In the next section (verses 17–18a), the creation is still in view, but a new thought is introduced, *i.e.* that all things 'hold together' (*synestēken*) in Christ. This idea of Christ as the principle of coherence in the universe, striking as it is, is found also in Hebrews 1:3, where all things are upheld by his power. This certainly disposes of any idea of Christ being an absentee creator or as being uninterested in the creation. It is diametrically opposed to any suggestion that demonic forces were in control,[433] as the false teachers at Colosse may well have been suggesting. It is evident that Paul does not hesitate to affirm the lordship of Christ over creation, as consisting not merely in a past completed act, but in a present sovereign activity. In this dramatic way he identifies the creative activities of Christ with those of God.

A special aspect of Christ's activity in the created order concerns his

---

[430] Note that Philo does use the word *prōtogonos* in conjunction with *eikōn* (*De Fuga et inv.* 101).

[431] A. Feuillet, 'La création de l'univers "dans le Christ" d'après l'épître aux Colossiens 1.16a', *NTS* 12, 1965–6, pp. 1ff., discusses particularly the meaning of the phrase *prōtotokos pasēs ktiseōs*.

[432] C. F. D. Moule, *Colossians and Philemon*, pp. 66f., discusses the phrase *pro pantōn* in Col. 1:17 and favours the interpretation, 'he exists before all things'.

[433] This triumph of Christ over demonic forces is vividly stated in Col. 2:15 to be a direct result of the work of Christ.

relationship to his own community (*i.e.* the body), for Paul makes the statement that 'he is the head of the body, the church'. In other words, he explains quite specifically what he means by the body. Some, who consider that Paul has used an existing hymn,[434] regard the words 'the church' as an interpretive addition by him; in the supposed original form of the hymn, 'body' was understood as 'the universe'. Even if this were so, it could be said that Paul modified the words to show the special interest which the sovereign Creator has in his church. Those who appeal to a gnostic background see here a reference to the gnostic idea of mankind as an earthly 'body' which has a heavenly head, *i.e.* the gnostic saviour.[435] The parallel is interesting but is no sure guide to origins, for the body-head idea could be a natural development from Paul's use of the body metaphor of the church in both 1 Corinthians and Romans (see a further discussion of this in the section on the church, pp. 744ff.). There is no justification for maintaining that Paul must always use his metaphors in the same way. Here he is more concerned to describe the relationship which Christ at present sustains with his church than to debate the nature of the church (*cf.* also Col. 2:9–10).

Christ as the fullness of God. In this latter part of the passage Paul reaches a climax in his assertions about Christ. He first reiterates the supremacy of Christ by using the word 'beginning' (*archē*), linking it with the formerly used 'first-born' (*prōtotokos*), but qualifying this with the words 'from the dead'. In what sense is he using the word *archē*?[436] Is it equivalent to superiority of rank or priority in time? Or does it refer to creative supremacy, either in the universe or the church? Since 'beginning' is linked so closely with 'first-born' from the dead, it is most natural to suppose that the Christian church is in mind. The clear allusion to the resurrection of Christ is significant in view of Paul's stress on Christ's exalted position. It is through the resurrection that the church is called into being. The theme here is, therefore, re-creation.[437]

It is however the combination of pre-eminence with fullness that is most striking. The pre-eminence stresses the uniqueness of Christ over everything (or in every respect), but what is the meaning of fullness (*plērōma*)?[438] The main clue to its meaning is found in Colossians 2:9 where it means the total essence of God. All that God is, is in Christ. This is a high peak of

---

[434] *CF.* R. P. Martin, *Colossians: The Church's Lord and the Christian's Liberty*, p. 47.

[435] For details, *cf.* H. Schlier, *kephalē*, *TDNT* 3, pp. 673ff.

[436] *Cf.* Moule, *op. cit.*, *ad loc.*, on this word.

[437] R. H. Fuller, *The Foundations of New Testament Christology*, p. 215, sees an Adam Christology here, appealing to the idea in 1 Cor. 15:45 of Christ as a life-giving Spirit. He sees the resurrection of Christ as 'constitutive'.

[438] For a discussion of *plērōma* in Eph. 1:23, *cf.* R. Yates, 'A Re-examination of Ephesians 1:23', *ExT* 83, 1972, pp. 146ff.

Paul's statements about Christ. It sweeps beyond the remarkable statement of 1:15, for the indwelling fullness is more comprehensive than the 'image'. It is even more difficult to grasp. Yet in the light of it no lesser view than the deity of Christ is tenable. It should be noted that '*plērōma*' was a word used by the gnostics of the sum total of intermediary aeons, and it may be that a similar use was current in Paul's day among the false teachers. If so he seizes the word and uses it of the supremacy of Christ in such a way as to place him on a level with God. It is a startling thought, but Paul introduces it without betraying any awareness that it might be inappropriate.[439] It arose, not out of any speculation, but out of his own experience of Jesus Christ.

There is one feature in this passage which affects our understanding of its background, but which belongs to a consideration of the work of Christ rather than his person, *i.e.* the theme of reconciliation (see pp. 486ff.). Its importance for our present purpose is that it excludes a gnostic influence, for nowhere in gnostic mythology does the saviour bring about a personal reconciliation between man and God. What is most significant is that the dwelling of the fullness of God in Christ has a functional purpose, not merely for man alone, but for all things. Indeed, Paul's interest in *plērōma* is practical rather than theoretical. Having experienced reconciliation he does not question the divine sovereignty of Christ which had brought it about.

1 Timothy 3:16

Since this is sometimes regarded as a Christological hymn, it will be included here, although it is not primarily concerned with the person of Christ.[440] A textual problem arises from a variation in the beginning. Some texts have the relative pronoun (*hos*) in which case the hymn opens with an assertion, 'Who was manifested in the flesh', which must refer to Christ, although he is not specifically mentioned. Since the whole statement is regarded as a confession of the Christian church, there can be little doubt that the readers would understand it in this way. The alternative reading 'God was manifested in the flesh' is probably a scribal attempt to provide a suitable subject and was influenced by the fact that God is the nearest antecedent in the text. In any case the hymn affirms the incarnation although in a somewhat indirect way. The words 'in the flesh' focus unmistakably on the human life of Jesus. In a similar way the pre-existence of Jesus is presupposed rather than explicitly stated.

---

[439] Fuller, *op. cit.*, p. 216, compares this use of 'fullness' with the name *Kyrios* in Phil. 2:10, which he understands as the fulness of Christ's divine Lordship.

[440] For a discussion of this passage as a hymn, *cf.* R. H. Gundry, 'The Form, Meaning and Background of the Hymn quoted in 1 Tim. 3:16', in *Apostolic History and the Gospel* (ed. W. W. Gasque and R. P. Martin, 1970), pp. 203–222.

The words 'vindicated in the Spirit' could be understood in one of two ways, either as referring to the human spirit of Christ or as referring to the Holy Spirit. In the former case vindication would come in the spiritual realm; in the latter through the agency of the Spirit (in this case *en* would be instrumental). The difference would not be great, but if the latter interpretation is correct it would celebrate the close connection between the Son and the Spirit in the incarnate life,[441] for which some support may be seen elsewhere in the NT.

The third line in the hymn, 'seen by angels', is the most obscure, but could refer to the principalities and powers, who are mentioned in other NT contexts as adverse agencies in the world (*cf.* Col. 2:15). The phrase would then be a succinct declaration of the triumph of the exalted Saviour, who was displayed to his defeated spiritual enemies.[442] If on the other hand the angels are generally ministers of God, as for instance in Hebrews 1, the phrase may mean the same as the statement in Hebrews 1:4 that Christ became much superior to angels. The idea of good angels desiring to see the triumph of Christ seems to be paralleled in 1 Peter 1:12. This may well have been a variant way of expressing the superiority of Christ.

Some regard the view of Christ in this hymn as being quite different from that of Philippians 2:6ff., because of the absence here of any mention of the 'hidden' nature of Christ, his incarnate life of obedience and the cross.[443] Instead is seen a reference to the Hellenistic divine man. The passage is then claimed to be an epiphany interpretation of the incarnate life, which is seen to be incompatible with 'Paul's cross-centred Christology'. But this does not allow sufficient scope for the compressed statements in 1 Timothy 3:16. It assumes too readily that Paul regarded the incarnation as an obscuring of divine glory, whereas 1 Timothy 3:16 sees it as a manifestation. But Paul would have agreed that Jesus Christ 'manifested' God in his human life, and the 1 Timothy 3:16 hymn does not exclude the view that at the incarnation the eternal Son 'emptied' himself.

Another view of this hymn is to see it as a hymn of ascent to the throne, based on the scheme: exaltation, presentation, enthronement.[444] This does not, of course, deny the reference to the incarnation in the first line. Certainly the conclusion of the hymn 'taken up in glory' may suggest the enthronement theme. There is a marked similarity between the accent on glory here and Philippians 2:11 and Hebrews 1:3. The celebration of the

---

[441] Fuller, *op. cit.*, p. 218, regards 'Spirit' here as indicating the upper or heavenly sphere.

[442] J. T. Sanders, *The New Testament Christological Hymns*, p. 95, links the 'angels' with the 'spirits' in prison' in 1 Pet. 3:19.

[443] *Cf.* Fuller, *op. cit.*, pp. 216ff.

[444] So J. Jeremias, *Die Briefe an Timotheus und Titus* (*NTD*, 1947), p. 21; *cf.* also M. Dibelius, *Die Pastoralbriefe* (*LHB*, ³1955), pp. 50f.

glory of Christ was a theme much favoured among the early Christians (*cf.* also the Johannine prologue).

Hebrews 1:3 and its setting

This is a much briefer, but nonetheless important, statement because it sets out a similar high view of Christ to that seen in Philippians 2 and Colossians 1. In it the writer combines two considerations – the relation of Christ (introduced as Son) to the creation, and his relation to God.

Under the first heading two significant factors are mentioned. First Christ is said to be 'appointed heir of all things'.[445] This plainly asserts that the created order belongs to Christ, and is in line with the Colossians statement that all things were created 'for him' (Col. 1:16). The idea is strengthened by the fact that his part in creation is also brought out as clearly here as in the Pauline passages, although one difference is worth noting. Hebrews uses the term 'ages' (*aiōnes*) instead of 'world' (*kosmos*).[446] The former is more all-embracing than the latter. Moreover, Christ is described in this epistle as upholding all things by his word of power, thus showing his continued activity in creation.

It is the second consideration, the relation of Christ to God, which is most significant for our present purpose, however, because of the combination of two descriptive words – *apaugasma* and *charaktēr*. The first is rendered in RSV as 'He reflects the glory of God', which does not fully capture the sense.[447] The idea is of the radiance which streams from a brilliant light; although a striking metaphor, it is clearly limited because it is essentially impersonal. Nevertheless, the word occurs in the book of Wisdom in describing Wisdom (7:26), which is regarded as a personification, although not as a personal being. It is also used by Philo to describe the *logos* (*The Making of the World*, 146), but here again the *logos* was never personal. The use of the same term of Christ in Hebrews is to be understood in the sense that the glory of God could be perfectly seen in Jesus Christ, an idea exactly parallel to the image idea in Colossians 1:15. We might also link it to John 1:14 where the glory of God has become visible in the Son. All these passages suggest that Jesus Christ was the perfect revelation of God.[448]

---

[445] F. F. Bruce, *Hebrews*, pp. 3f., sees an echo of Ps. 2:8 behind this expression. J. Héring, *Hebrews* (1970), p. 3 n. 12, objects to the rendering 'all things' and suggests that *panta* or *ta panta* is the normal expression for the 'universe' in the NT. It would not appear, however, to make much material difference to the thought.

[446] According to F. F. Bruce, *op. cit.*, p. 4, the expression here embraces 'the whole created universe of space and time'.

[447] Héring, *op. cit.*, p. 5, prefers the idea of 'reflection' as a rendering for *apaugasma*, and dispenses with the objection that the idea implies a mirror. He thinks the author is concerned to make clear that the Son participates in the Father's glory in a wholly special way.

[448] A few scholars have denied that Heb. 1:3 attributes to the Son the divine nature, *cf. e.g.* E. F. Scott, *Hebrews* (1922), pp. 157ff.). But for the contrary, *cf.* H. Strathmann, *Der Brief an die Hebräer* ([6]1953),

The second word, *charaktēr*, expresses the idea of a stamp upon a seal, which is used here to show that there is an exact correspondence between the Son and the Father. The correspondence is moreover related to the nature (*hypostasis*) of the person.[449]. The stamp reproduces in its impress every line of its own form. There cannot exist in the impression what is not in the stamp. But again the use of the metaphor is limited, because it is essentially impersonal, and because it cannot be inferred that the Son is as distinct from the Father as the impression is from the stamp.[450] It is reasonable to suppose that these two metaphors may owe something to the Genesis 1:26 description of Adam made in the 'image' of God, and to the idea which occurs in Paul (in Romans and 1 Corinthians) of Christ as the last Adam. In view of Adam's failure it is heartening to know that Christ perfectly fulfilled the function of a reflection of God.

Yet another assertion is made in this passage which demands mention – that the Son sat down 'at the right hand of the Majesty on high'.[451] This reverential name for God is also used in Hebrews 8:1 and underlines the awe with which the author clearly regards him (*cf.* 12:28, 29). The positioning of the Son at the right hand of God is stressed to serve as a preparation for the high-priest theme (*cf.* 8:1). But some comparison is clear between this view and that of the exaltation of Jesus in Philippians 2:10, 11. What is clearer in Hebrews 1:3, however, is that the exaltation follows from an act of purification of sins, implicit in the Philippians reference to Jesus' obedience to death on the cross. The act of purification will require further discussion under the high-priestly work of Christ (see pp. 471ff.), but for our present purpose it is highly significant that the writer to the Hebrews began his work by introducing the high priest in his exalted state. This is all the more remarkable in view of the complementary presentation in this epistle of the perfect manhood of our high priest (see below and also in the section on the humanity of Jesus, pp. 226f.). Hebrews approaches Jesus as man from the standpoint of Jesus as the exalted Son of God.

Some comment must be made on the interpretation of this passage in line with the gnostic Anthropos myth as advocated by Käsemann.[452] According to this view the Son is not the Son of God as understood in a

---

pp. 73ff.; O. Michel, *Der Brief an die Hebräer* ([11]1960), p. 38; C. Spicq, *L'Epître aux Hébreux* 1 (EB, [2]1952), 287ff.

[449] The word *Hypostasis* played an important part in later Christological controversies. Philo uses the word both in the sense of a copy of the original (*De Plantatione* 12.50) and in the sense of essence (*De Somniis* I, 32. 188).

[450] Bruce, *op. cit.*, p. 6, here remarks that 'just as the glory is really in the effulgence, so the substance (Gk. *hypostasis*) of God is really in Christ, who is its impress, its exact manifestation and embodiment'.

[451] The influence of Ps. 110:1 here should be noted, since there is no doubt that this Psalm exerted a powerful influence on the writer to the Hebrews. Bruce, *op. cit.*, p. 7, suggests that this goes back to our Lord's own use of the Psalm (*cf.* Lk. 22:69). For a discussion of the idea of a heavenly session of Christ in the NT, *cf.* J. Daniélou, 'La Session à la droite du Père', in *The Gospels Reconsidered* (1960), pp. 68ff.

[452] E. Käsemann, *Das wandernde Gottesvolk* (1957), p. 63.

Christian sense, but the gnostic Anthropos. Käsemann regards the background to be what he calls 'Hellenistic aeon theology' (particularly the *pherōn* in Heb. 1:3, 'upholding' the universe). He sees the same religious scheme in Hebrews as in Philippians, with the distinction that the latter relates the effects of Christ's obedience cosmically, whereas the former relates them to the community.[453] But Käsemann gives insufficient attention to the basically Jewish background to Hebrews and to the view that the statements of the epistle can be intelligently understood without appeal to gnostic ideas. There is no suggestion in the text that the 'Son' in the Hebrews passage comes from a Hellenistic background. The allusion to the OT prophets in Hebrews 1:1 would strongly suggest a Jewish background, while allowing for some Hellenistic influence.

So closely linked to the opening statement is the use of the series of OT quotations in Hebrews 1, that the importance of these for an understanding of the person of Christ cannot be minimized.[454] Psalm 2:7 is cited in a way which conveys the idea of the eternal generation of Christ.[455] The idea of pre-existence is followed up later in the epistle in the Melchizedek passage.[456] 2 Samuel 7:14 implies his eternal sonship, distinguishing him at once from the angels. Deuteronomy 32:43 (LXX) is introduced by a statement referring to the 'first-born' (*prōtotokos*), who is clearly to be identified as the 'Son' of the previous verses. It is the same term which occurs in Colossians 1:15, 18 and Romans 8:29, in each case used of the superiority of Christ. Whereas this Pauline emphasis is absent from the Hebrews 1:6 statement, it is nonetheless implied in the whole presentation of Christ in this epistle.

[453] Cf. J. T. Sanders, *The New Testament Christological Hymns*, pp. 92ff., for comments on Käsemann's position.

[454] Cf. R. G. Hamerton-Kelly, *Pre-existence, Wisdom and the Son of Man*, pp. 243ff., who brings out the Christological significance of these OT quotations. Cf. also S. Kistemaker, *The Psalm Citations in the Epistle to the Hebrews* (1961), pp. 88ff., who tends to overstress the parallels between the exegesis of Qumran and Hebrews.

[455] Cf. H. Montefiore, *Hebrews* (BC, 1968), p. 44. He draws attention to the fact that in Jewish tradition Ps. 2 had a messianic interpretation. He cites 1 Q Sa 2:11. He claims, however, that Hebrews does not cite the Psalm messianically. He finds stages in the development in the interpretation of the verse (Ps. 2:7), from its reference to resurrection (Rom. 1:4) to its reference to the generation of the Son as here. A link between the two is found in the voice at the baptism (combined with Is. 42:1) and a further link in the transfiguration account. It is possible, however, that co-lateral rather than straight-line development may have taken place, in which case it would be a mistake to read into the Hebrews' account an advanced Christology. Hamerton-Kelly, *op. cit.*, p. 245, considers that the trajectory traced by this text is paradigmatic of the way in which the doctrine of pre-existence developed – from resurrection, through earthly life to pre-existence.

[456] For further comments on the pre-existence of Christ in Hebrews, see the section on Melchizedek (pp. 483ff.). It is noticeable that nowhere in this epistle is Christ called Melchizedek. O. Cullmann, *The Christology of the New Testament*, p. 84, suggests that Jewish exegetes came to devalue Melchizedek because of their anti-Christian polemic. But F. L. Horton, *The Melchizedek Tradition* (1976), shows that rabbinic tradition considered that the priesthood of Melchizedek was transferred to Abraham and through him to the Levitical priesthood. But this is very different from the exposition in Hebrews, where Melchizedek is seen to be superior to Aaron.

It is noticeable further that for Hebrews the adoration of the angels at the birth of Jesus is seen to be significant and might be compared with the Lukan birth narratives. The quotation from Deuteronomy 32:43 (with parallel in Ps. 97:7) is striking, because it applies to Christ what originally referred to God.[457] By combining the LXX versions of Psalm 104:4 and Psalm 45:7–8, Hebrews contrasts the origin of the angels (they were 'made') with the eternal existence of the Son. Even more striking is the address to the Son as 'O God', which is a direct ascription of deity. In this case, the original application of the psalm to the king might favour the rendering 'God is thy throne', but Hebrews sees it in a different light when applied to Jesus. The concluding citation uses Psalm 102:26–28 of Jesus, although again the original context applies it to God. He is seen as creator (as in Heb. 1:3), but also as judge. Moreover, by implication the citation points to the changelessness of the Son as contrasted with the destructibility of his creation.

One of the most remarkable features about the presentation of Christ in Hebrews is the combination of the undeniably divine nature in chapter 1 with the equally clear emphasis on the perfection of Jesus as man in chapter 2. In no other passage in the NT are the two aspects brought together so clearly. To gain a true appreciation of the former, the main features of the latter must be considered. First we note the temporary inferiority to angels which is asserted and backed up with a quotation from Psalm 8:4–6 (Heb. 2:6–9).[458] To the writer the significant factor is the temporary character of this ('for a little while', *brachy ti*). It is admittedly a contrast with chapter 1, but even the suffering and death which resulted from incarnation are seen as a crowning with glory and honour (2:9). The nature of the incarnation is clearly stated in Hebrews 2:17 – 'Therefore he had to be made like his brethren in every respect' – a claim to real humanity. This is said to qualify Jesus to become a merciful and faithful high priest. Moreover, since those whom Jesus had come to assist were 'flesh and blood' (2:14), so he had to share the same nature. The entire argument of the epistle depends, in fact, on the identity of Jesus with man, and his perfect humanity is therefore as crucial as his deity.

This perfect humanity is not, however, exempt from temptation (2:18), an idea to which Hebrews returns in 4:14f. It is a daring juxtaposition of ideas to maintain that the one who in chapter 1 is identified closely with God in majesty and power, is later seen to be subject to temptation, since God himself cannot be tempted. The author of Hebrews can mention the matter almost incidentally, without raising the theological issues which are

---

[457] Héring, *Hebrews*, p. 9 n. 28, thinks there are grounds for supposing that Judaism may have known an interpretation of Dt. 32:43 similar to that in Hebrews. He cites the *Life of Adam and Eve*, pp. 12ff., which maintains that God commanded the angels to worship Adam.

[458] Hamerton-Kelly, *op. cit.*, p. 247, sees here a comparison with Paul's Adam doctrine.

clearly involved. Neither does he discuss how the eternal Son could be made like his brethren, nor how, being incarnate, he could be tempted. He is concerned only about the qualifications of Jesus for the office of eternal high priest and he has no doubt that both aspects are needed. It is in 5:7ff. that he gives the clearest allusion to the human life of Jesus, which he had previously maintained in chapter 2 to be indispensable. He brings into focus the Gethsemane experience of Jesus to show in a striking way the perfect obedience of the Son to the Father.[459] This obedience theme is reiterated further in Hebrews 10:9, where the words of Psalm 40:6–8 are made to apply to Christ and to set out succinctly the whole mission of Jesus as 'obedience' to the Father's will; this is seen to be the key to the understanding of the self-offering of Jesus.

In this remarkable way this epistle presents the double aspect of the person of Christ. Moreover, the writer sees it as essential to establish that Jesus is both Son of God and yet truly man, as a prerequisite for an exposition of his mission and achievement. It is obvious that he is not approaching the person of Christ in a speculative way. He does not anticipate the historic Christological debates. He certainly does not drive a wedge between the exalted risen Christ and the historical Jesus. To him the one who offered loud cries and tears during his passion was the same one who has now taken his seat at the right hand of the majesty on high (cf. Heb. 12:2). Although expressing his thoughts in a different way, the apostle Paul is in close agreement with the view of Christ here expressed. The obedience unto death, even the death of the cross, in Philippians 2:8, shares the same approach as this epistle to the meaning of the passion. In both the cross is seen as an act of humiliation.

One feature about Jesus as perfect man which has already been separately discussed (cf. pp. 228ff.), is the sinlessness of Jesus. It is specifically mentioned in Hebrews 4:15 and has a vital importance in the whole theology of the epistle.[460] Jesus as man is seen, therefore, as the type of true manhood, i.e. manhood as it ought to be, free from sinful rebellion against God. There is some kinship here with Paul's 'last Adam' presentation, where Christ's perfect obedience is set over against Adam's sin of disobedience (Rom. 5:12ff., especially 5:19).[461]

1 Peter 3:18–20

Some regard 1 Peter 3:18–20 as a Christological hymn.[462] The only state-

[459] Although there is no reason to restrict the reference to Gethsemane here, that experience is the most poignant expression of it that we know from the gospels (cf. Bruce, Hebrews, p. 98). It seems highly probable that the author has Gethsemane in mind.

[460] Cf. also the exposition of Ps. 8 in Heb. 2:6ff.

[461] For a comparison between Paul's Christology and that of Hebrews, cf. H. R. Mackintosh, The Doctrine of the Person of Christ (³1914), pp. 86f. He finds many similarities and some differences (e.g. the high-priest theme, the glory of Jesus' life on earth, Jesus as a pattern, the absence of a mystical element).

[462] Cf. J. T. Sanders, The New Testament Christological Hymns, pp. 95ff.

ment which bears on our present concern is the reference to the resurrection and its sequel in verse 22. The return to heaven is linked to the enthronement idea (at the right hand of God) and the homage of angels, authorities and powers.[463] The parallel with Philippians 2:9, 10 is close in its reference to the exaltation, but the humiliation theme concentrates more on Christ's death in the flesh. His being 'made alive in the Spirit' (verse 18) might be compared with 1 Timothy 3:16 (vindicated in the Spirit). The close link between Christ and the Spirit is also seen in 1 Peter 1:1; 1:11.

Summary of the Christological hymns

These passages are of special value because they bring out more specifically several of the ideas implied in the titles. They too present a high Christology which leaves in no doubt that Jesus was both man and God. It is significant that linked with his exalted character, there is emphasis also on the humiliation of Jesus. Such concepts as the 'no-snatching' of Philippians 2, the 'image' and the 'fullness' of Colossians 1, and the divine radiance of Hebrews 1, make it impossible to view Jesus as no more than a man. Whatever the explanation of the mystery of the incarnation, no view which does not do justice to his exalted nature and status is true to the NT. It was here that the attempts of the liberal 'Jesus of history' school failed.

THE CHRISTOLOGICAL EVENTS:
INTRODUCTORY COMMENTS

Our final section will deal with the virgin birth, the resurrection and the ascension, which the NT presents as historical events, although some of its interpreters have regarded them as 'myths'. We shall consider these alternative approaches, but our main aim will be to establish the importance of these happenings for the Christology of the NT church.

THE VIRGIN BIRTH

The synoptic gospels

No consideration of synoptic Christology is possible without giving due weight to the birth narratives of Matthew and Luke.[465] The evidence from

---

[463] For an exhaustive examination of the problems relating to 1 Pet. 3:18, *cf.* Bo Reicke, *The Disobedient Spirits and Christian Baptism* (1946). He appeals to some parallels with the *Odes of Solomon* 24.

[464] I. T. Beckwith, *The Apocalypse of John* (1919, r.p. 1967), p. 314.

[465] For some basic monographs on the virgin birth, *cf.* J. Orr, *The Virgin Birth of Christ* (1907); G. H. Box, *The Virgin Birth of Christ* (1916); V. Taylor, *The Historical Evidence for the Virgin Birth* (1920); J. G. Machen, *The Virgin Birth of Christ* (1930); D. Edwards, *The Virgin Birth in History and Faith* (1943); T. Boslooper, *The Virgin Birth* (1962); R. E. Brown, *The Virginal Conception and Bodily Resurrection of Jesus* (1973); *idem, The Birth of the Messiah* (1977); M. Miguens, *The Virgin Birth* (1975).

these sources has been widely discounted on various grounds, which will be considered when the evidence itself has first been outlined. Since there is no denying that both gospel writers describe a birth of a totally unusual kind, and since Luke especially devotes so much space in his book to the nativity stories, the virgin birth of Jesus must form an integral part in any account of early Christian theology, whatever modern interpretations of the evidence are advocated.

We shall note first the salient features of Luke's presentation.[466] In the annunciation by the angel to Mary, whom Luke describes as a virgin (Lk. 1:27), the prediction is specifically made that she would conceive and bear a Son whose name should be Jesus and who would also be called 'the Son of the Most High' (Lk. 1:30ff.).[467] Moreover he was to be king in Israel permanently. These features contain a remarkable combination of both the manward side (the name Jesus and the human birth) and the Godward side (the Son of the Most High). This annunciation is given before any intimation of the mode of conception, as if the latter in itself is not the major feature. Indeed, it has been pointed out that the sonship of Jesus is not based by Luke on the virgin birth.[468] Nevertheless it is not out of keeping with it. The mode of conception through the direct intervention of the Holy Spirit is mentioned only in reply to Mary's bewildered enquiry as to the means (Lk. 1:35f.). Without giving details, the angelic announcement makes clear that the birth will not come about by the ordinary method of human generation, but by a totally unparalleled action of the Holy Spirit.[469]

It is noteworthy that Luke in the prologue to his gospel is at pains to show his intention of writing what he has carefully investigated, and since this opening statement is followed immediately by the birth narrative there can be no other conclusion but that he believed the virgin birth to be a fact. Moreover, he claimed that his testimony was based on apostolic witness. Not only is the bare statement about the conception through the Holy Spirit regarded by Luke as authentic, but many details are given which are in line with this, particularly the artless way in which the story

---

[466] The references in Luke to the virgin birth of Jesus occur only in Lk. 1 and 2 and it has been suggested that this section was not an original part of the gospel. In that case its testimony to the virgin birth is then considered to be lessened. The Proto-Luke hypothesis lends some support to this position (cf. V. Taylor, *Behind the Third Gospel* (1926), pp. 164ff, who did not consider Lk. 1 and 2 to be an integral part of the gospel). Nevertheless the Proto-Luke theory is by no means universally accepted (cf. the discussion of it in my *New Testament Introduction*, pp. 175ff.).

[467] As E. E. Ellis, *Luke* (NCB, 1966), p. 69, points out in reference to the title 'Son of the Most High', 'As the virgin's child this title will signify something more, a unique and mysterious unity with Jehovah, God.'

[468] Cf. W. Grundmann, *Das Evangelium nach Lukas* (THNT, ²1961), p. 61.

[469] G. B. Caird, *Luke* (1968), p. 53, regards the Spirit's activity here as the effecting of a new creation. 'The miraculous character of the event is not at all affected by the question whether Jesus had one human parent or not'. But this looks like an attempt to make something of Luke's account, having first concluded that the virgin birth doctrine arose out of a misunderstanding when the story was told in the Greek world (cf. p. 31).

is told. Luke himself does not theorize about how conception independent of a human could have taken place.[470] There is no indication, in fact, that any explanation was needed. It is significant that in the same passage in which the supernatural birth of Jesus is so strongly indicated, a statement is included about the human growth of Jesus (Lk. 2:40), about his obedience to his earthly 'parents' (note the plural, Lk. 2:51) and about his increase in wisdom (Lk. 2:52). Clearly the relating of the virgin birth was not intended to deny the true humanity of Jesus. Luke understood, as the early church generally came to accept, that there was something both natural and supernatural about Jesus.[471] We shall discuss below the theological implications of this.

Matthew's birth narrative is wholly independent of Luke's, but nevertheless supports with equal firmness the fact of the virgin birth. At the end of the genealogy Matthew includes the statement, 'Joseph the husband of Mary, of whom Jesus was born, who is called Christ' (Mt. 1:16).[472] This presupposes the virgin birth and prepares the reader for the further statement that Mary 'was found to be with child of the Holy Spirit' (Mt. 1:18). This is then further reinforced by the angel's explanation to Joseph of Mary's condition: 'Joseph, son of David, do not fear to take Mary your wife, for that which is conceived in her is of the Holy Spirit' (Mt. 1:20). Matthew follows this up with the specific statement that Joseph did not 'know' his wife until she had borne a son (Mt. 1:25), so excluding all possibility of his readers thinking that Jesus was born as a result of natural conception.[473] As if to make the matter doubly clear, he also quotes Isaiah's prophecy of a virgin conceiving and bearing a Son, Emmanuel (Mt. 1:23 = Is. 7:14).

Whatever view is taken regarding the origin of these reports about the virgin birth, it must be accepted that both Matthew and Luke intend to present it as an accepted fact.[474] The differences in their narratives serve

[470] In his book, *The Human Face of God* (1973), J. A. T. Robinson discusses the question of the virginal conception (pp. 56ff.). He thinks the tradition in Lk. 2 arises out of a different tradition from Lk. 1, since he claims that Lk. 2 knows nothing of the virgin birth. Robinson denies the virgin birth.

[471] For an extended study of the structure and theology of Luke's birth narratives, *cf.* R. Laurentin, *Structure et Théologie de Luc I–II* (*EB*, 1964). He particularly draws attention to the evidence for the divinity of Christ in this section (*cf.* pp. 120ff.).

[472] For a discussion of other readings, *cf.* D. Hill, *Matthew, ad loc.* The Syr. sin. has 'Joseph begat Jesus', but the best Greek readings support the virgin birth.

[473] J. A. T. Robinson, *op. cit.*, 59ff., advances the view that Matthew was not worried by the difficulties involved if Joseph was not genetically the father of Jesus. Matthew's attributing the birth to the agency of the Spirit is then interpreted as meaning that God was in it, even if the birth was the result of an irregular union. If, however, the virgin birth is maintained, it would at once exclude the possibility that Jesus was illegitimate, particularly under Jewish law. Matthew, in recording the naming by Joseph of the child, implies that Joseph accepted legal responsibility for Jesus.

[474] It is supposed by some scholars that Matthew's genealogy does not agree with his presentation of the virgin birth. *Cf.* H. von Campenhausen, *The Virgin Birth in the Theology of the Ancient Church* (Eng. trans. 1964), pp. 10ff; F. Hahn, *The Titles of Jesus in Christology*, pp. 258ff. G. D. Kilpatrick, *The Origins of the*

only to heighten their remarkable concurrence in asserting that Jesus was born of a virgin without human father. The word for 'virgin' (*parthenos*), which is quoted by Matthew from the Greek text of Isaiah 7:14, represents a word in the Hebrew Massoretic text meaning a young woman. Yet Matthew clearly has in mind a pure unmarried woman. Indeed neither Matthew's nor Luke's narrative conveys any suggestion that Mary the mother of Jesus was not a virgin.[475]

But many scholars find a difficulty in the silence of Mark and of the rest of the NT on the subject of the virgin birth. To take Mark's silence first, we need to assess two factors. Is Mark as silent as many suppose? And, if he is, what interpretation is to be affixed to that silence?[476] It is worth observing that whereas Matthew refers to popular comment on Jesus as 'the carpenter's son' in spite of his birth narrative, Mark has 'the carpenter' as if he intends to avoid any reference to Jesus as Joseph's son (Mt. 13:55 = Mk. 6:3). Add to this the fact that Mark relates that the people of Nazareth referred to Jesus as Mary's son, contrary to normal Jewish procedure.[477] Any argument from silence is precarious, for it certainly cannot be claimed that silence indicates ignorance. We may not be able to determine precisely why Mark makes no specific reference to the virgin birth, but neither may we with any confidence conclude that it was an alien idea to him.

Those scholars who base their approach to the virgin birth on the silence of Mark and other NT writers[478] are using a type of argument which is open to serious methodological objection. It is, in fact, equally reasonable to suppose that where a facet of Christian truth was not mentioned in a document, the writer knew it to be common knowledge.[479] Indeed, the omission of the virgin birth would be much more significant had Mark included a birth narrative. Since he has not written about Jesus' origins, it is impossible to attach much importance to his silence on the virgin birth.

Gospel according to St Matthew (1946), pp. 52f., regards the genealogy as the work of an editor. He considers the use of the LXX quotation in 1:23 is not due to the evangelist's activity.

[475] James Orr, *The Virgin Birth of Christ* (1907), p. 67, thinks that Matthew's and Luke's narratives were the earliest form of publicizing the virgin birth.

[476] *Cf.* D. Edwards, *The Virgin Birth in History and Faith*, pp. 58ff. Edwards is particularly critical of the emphasis on silence which Vincent Taylor used in his assessment of Mark's evidence for the virgin birth.

[477] H. K. McArthur, 'Son of Mary', *NovT* 15, 1973, pp. 38–59, cites some evidence to show that, although Jewish custom normally used the father's name, there are cases where the mother's name was used. McArthur discusses the textual problem in Mk. 6:3 and regards the reading 'son of the carpenter and of Mary' as slightly more probable. He also examines whether 'son of Mary' was a record of the villagers' use, an invention by the evangelist or of someone else who passed on the tradition, or the work of a copyist. He concludes for the first suggestion, but does not regard it as evidence of the virgin birth. He thinks it was not a formal genealogical identification.

[478] *Cf.* V. Taylor, *The Historical Evidence for the Virgin Birth*, p. 12.

[479] H. von Campenhausen, *The Virgin Birth in the Theology of the Ancient Church*, pp. 12ff., strongly denies that Mark had any knowledge of the virgin birth and considers that the assertion that he was aware of it and silently takes it into account is a *petitio principii*.

If Mark wrote before Matthew and Luke some explanation is needed why the latter include birth stories which Mark omits.[480] But since they include a mass of other material which Mark omits, it seems reasonable to suppose that the inclusion or exclusion of a birth narrative or a specific reference to the virgin birth was dictated entirely by the different purpose of the respective evangelists. Moreover, if the argument from silence is carried to its logical conclusion, it would be necessary to suppose that several of the NT writers were ignorant of various aspects of Christian truth (*e.g.* the Lord's Supper), because they do not happen to mention them.

Before discussing the theological implications of the virgin birth, it is necessary to examine the approach of the Johannine and Pauline literature to the subject.[481]

The Johannine literature

At first sight it might be claimed that John's gospel contains no reference to the virgin birth. There is no birth narrative and no specific statement about the manner of the birth of Jesus. In place of a birth narrative he includes a prologue which focuses on the incarnation of the Logos, who existed before the world and was an agent in its creation. The bare statement, 'The Word became flesh and dwelt among us' (Jn. 1:14), gives no clue to the mode of his becoming flesh, but nevertheless requires a mode in which it is possible for a pre-existent divine being to become man.

Moreover, the presentation in John's gospel of Jesus as God's Son requires some understanding of his origin which is capable of explaining how God's Son could become man. But does this require birth by a virgin? It could be maintained that acceptance of the filial consciousness of Jesus could exist independently of the virgin birth and that this gave rise in popular thought to the latter idea.[482] In this view the manner of birth was immaterial. What mattered was what Jesus thought himself to be. Nevertheless, this is unsatisfactory because it assumes John's ignorance of the virgin birth and supposes that he regarded Jesus' origin in purely human terms. Yet it is impossible to square this human view of Jesus' origin with the strong indications of his pre-existence. The matter is also affected by the exegete's approach to the literary question of John's use of the synoptic gospels. Even if John did not use them in a literary way, it is almost certain that he wrote after them, which raises a high probability that he was fully acquainted with the belief in the virgin birth. If he includes no mention of

---

[480] If, of course, it could be maintained that both Matthew and Luke added the virgin birth idea to an earlier presentation of the Christian faith which knew nothing of this doctrine, it would be possible to maintain that it could be dispensed with. But it is difficult to maintain this position when two lines of evidence, which are clearly not dependent on each other, agree on the basic inclusion of the virgin birth.

[481] Most scholars confine the evidence for the virgin birth in the NT to the infancy narratives of Matthew and Luke. *Cf.* O. Cullmann, *The Christology of New Testament*, p. 297.

[482] *Cf.* J. Moffatt, *The Theology of the Gospels* (1948), p. 135.

it, it does not necessarily mean that he had no knowledge of it. What he writes gives no indication that he rejected the idea, and some reason to suppose that he assumed it. In this he seems to be in line with Paul who assumes rather than enlarges upon it.

Some have seen a significance in the statement in John 1:12–13 that all who receive Christ become children of God by being born of the will of God.[483] Since this immediately precedes the Logos saying about the incarnation, there may well be a connection in thought between the manner of Jesus' birth and the manner of the new birth of believers. But the connection is not explicit and must be treated with some reserve.[484] Nevertheless the Nicodemus discourse in John 3 shows Nicodemus as a man who misunderstood rebirth in terms of natural birth. In both passages the same verb *gennaō* is used, which in NT usage generally refers to physical birth.[485] It is more significant that in John 3 being born by the Spirit is emphasized.

One statement in John 6:42 has been regarded by some as a direct refutation of the virgin birth, where the Jews ask the question, 'Is not this Jesus, the son of Joseph, whose father and mother we know?' But since this statement is made by criticizing Jews, it cannot be regarded as an indication of John's own belief. Indeed the context is against this since the words of Jesus about the Father-Son relationship directly offset his critics' emphasis on his human parentage. It is possible that John 8:41 contains a sly allusion to rumours that Jesus' birth was irregular.

In the Johannine epistles the idea is dominant that Christians have been 'born of God' (1 Jn. 2:29; 3:9; 4:7; 5:4; 5:18).[486] Although spiritual rebirth is clearly in mind, it is noticeable that the same verb *gennaō* as used in John 3 recurs here. If this expression is interpreted against the background of the virgin birth of Christ an interesting light would be thrown upon it, but the expression cannot be said to demand it. All that can be said is that a striking parallel exists between the incarnate Christ and the Christ who dwells in those born of the Spirit.

Paul

It is common among scholars[487] to maintain that Paul's epistles do not

---

[483] Cf. D. Edwards, *The Virgin Birth in History and Faith*, pp. 62ff. Edwards translates the words 'who not of sexual intercourse nor of fleshly impulse nor of a husband's will, but of God was (or were) born', and on the strength of this discusses the significance. But not all would accept his rendering of the words.

[484] Campenhausen, *op. cit.*, p. 16, discusses Jn. 1:12ff., and considers that this statement sets out 'in a quite general way the miraculous, "supernatural" origin of the Christian nature'. He regards both John and Mark as standing over against Matthew's and Luke's infancy stories. It will be noted that Campenhausen's conclusions are based on an *argumentum e silentio*.

[485] So Edwards, *op. cit.*, p. 120. He maintains that *gennaō* is used metaphorically only in contexts where confusion with physical birth would be impossible.

[486] Cf. Edwards, *ibid.*, pp. 128ff., who points out that whenever the expression 'born of God' is used by John of Christians the perfect tense is used, but when it is used of Christ the tense is past. He distinguishes by this means between a state (for Christians) and a specific event (in relation to Christ).

[487] E.g. V. Taylor, *The Historical Evidence for the Virgin Birth*, pp. 6ff.

support belief in the virgin birth on two grounds: (i) because he says nothing about it, and (ii) because, had he known it, there are passages where some statement about it would have enhanced his argument.

In considering the first point, it must be granted that no explicit references occur, but there are certain passages which have a bearing on the subject.[488] We begin with Romans 1:3 where the Son is said to be 'descended from David according to the flesh'. We have noted before that this passage may be a primitive statement of doctrine which Paul has incorporated,[489] or it may equally be Paul's own wording to give the gist of his gospel in summary form in the introduction to his letter.[490] What is important is that Paul uses the verb *genomenos* not *gennaō* in this passage, the precise point of which is not brought out in the English rendering 'descended from'. It is more than a genealogy from David which is in view. It is the existence of the Son, an idea which is in harmony with, although it does not specifically state, the virgin birth.[491] At the same time Paul must have received the tradition of the Davidic descent of Jesus from some reliable source, [492] and this is indirect support for the genealogies in Matthew and Luke which both trace the Davidic descent of Jesus.

The parallel expressions in Galatians 4:4 ('born of woman') and Philippians 2:7 ('born in the likeness of men') use the same verb as in Romans 1:3 and again appear to differentiate the birth of Jesus from normal human birth. In the former passage it is God who sends the Son and his birth of a woman is merely the mode.[493] It may be argued that Paul's concern here is more on the subject of the humiliation of the Son of God than on the virgin birth, but the statement is not out of keeping with the latter doctrine. In the Philippians passage it is again the humiliation which is in mind as a striking contrast to the subsequent exaltation. Again while no specific reference to the virgin birth is made,[494] the statements would accord with this belief.

[488] *Cf.* G. A. Danell, 'Did St Paul know the Tradition about the Virgin Birth?', *St Th* 4, 1950, pp. 94ff., for a discussion of this subject.

[489] So C. H. Dodd, *The Apostolic Preaching and its Developments* (²1963), p. 14.

[490] *Cf.* C. K. Barrett, *Romans, ad loc.*

[491] *Cf.* H. E. W. Turner, 'The Virgin Birth', *ExT* 68, 1956–7, pp. 12ff. He examines the main objections to the truth of the narratives in Matthew and Luke and concludes for the substantial historicity of the traditions. He nevertheless considers it fair to conclude that the tradition of the virgin birth found no place in the primitive *kerygma*. Although he mentions Rom. 1:3 in passing, he does not appear to regard the reference to Davidic descent to imply the virgin birth. He does, however, caution against overlooking the occasional character of Paul's epistles.

[492] *Cf.* C. E. B. Cranfield, *Romans 1*, p. 59, is cautious over whether there is a reference to the virgin birth here. He thinks it is possible that Paul's choice of *ginesthai* here and in Gal. 4:4 and Phil. 2:7 may indicate that he knew of the tradition of Jesus' birth without natural human fatherhood. *Cf.* H. E. W. Turner, *art. cit.*, p. 12.

[493] So H. N. Ridderbos, *Galatians* (*NICNT*, ²1954), p. 155, who considers it to be highly doubtful that Paul is here reflecting on the virgin birth.

[494] R. P. Martin, *Carmen Christi*, pp. 202f., finds Edwards' appeal to the virgin birth here as 'not altogether convincing'.

Conclusions

Although much of the NT makes no specific reference to the virgin birth, the fact that it occurs in both Matthew's and Luke's birth narratives means that an explanation must be forthcoming of its presence there.[495] Some indication of the different approaches to the evidence will be given in order to show how the conclusion reached invariably depends on the starting point.

(i) Many have begun with the assumption that virgin birth is impossible, and for this reason Matthew's and Luke's record of it in reference to Jesus must be historically discounted. The earlier rationalists maintained that the narratives were naïve fabrications[496] and this view left traces on many later theories.[497] But the rationalists did not do justice to the plain statements of the text. Their whole approach was based on the assumption that philosophical considerations justified the critic in making the most violent modifications to the narrative.

(ii) Another school of thought explained the birth narratives in terms of myth. This enables that which is contrary to natural law to be rejected while at the same time retaining some meaning in the record. David Strauss,[498] the main advocate of this kind of theory, thus regarded the genealogies as historical because they traced the origin of Jesus from both Mary and Joseph, whereas he treated the virgin birth story as a later mythical development. This development came about through Christian belief that Messiah must be born of a virgin on the basis of Isaiah 7:14, and that he would be Son of God on the basis of Psalm 2:7. Although Strauss's mythical reconstructions were judged unsatisfactory as exegesis of the text, his appeal to myth to explain the development of the virgin birth idea has left some mark on later interpreters.

(iii) The 'history of religions' school explained away the virgin birth as a Christian adaptation of pagan stories of virgin births. Buddhist traditions, Krishna, Assyrio-Babylonian, Zoroastrian and Mithraic sources were appealed to as parallels, but no true parallel has been proposed.[499] A truly human birth to a virgin by supernatural intervention occurs nowhere in this mass of literature. The only value of the mass of pagan analogies which has been collected lies in the background material it provides. In announc-

---

[495] B. Vawter, *This Man Jesus. An Essay toward a New Testament Christology* (1973), p. 192, rightly points out that 'those New Testament sources that make nothing of a virgin birth of Jesus also say nothing to rule one out, even in a most literal and unavoidable sense'. Vawter devotes his final chapter (pp. 179–194) to discussing the Christology implicit in the tradition of the virginal conception.

[496] Note especially one of the early rationalistic critics, H. E. G. Paulus, *Das Leben Jesus* (1828).

[497] E.g. cf. J. Moffatt, *Introduction to the Literature of the NT* (²1912), pp. 49ff.

[498] D. Strauss, *Das Leben Jesus* (1835, Eng. trans., r.p., *The Life of Jesus Critically Examined*, 1973). Cf. pp. 108ff. in the translation for a discussion of the birth narratives.

[499] Cf. Boslooper, *The Virgin Birth*, pp. 135ff., for details. His conclusion is that although there are analogies to extraordinary birth, there are none parallel to the content of the gospel accounts of the virgin birth of Jesus.

ing the virgin birth of Jesus, the Christian church would find an audience well accustomed to stories of supernatural birth, but it must have been obvious that Jesus' origin was unique. The 'history of religions' school could not explain this uniqueness.[500]

(iv) A line of thinking closer to the text of the nativity narratives is the literary-critical approach, which traces these narratives to sources like Isaiah 7:14 and Psalm 2:7 and sees their present form as due to editorial activity.[501] This view generally inclines against the historicity of the texts. If the editors are creating a new tradition to express in popular modes the conviction (either their own or others') that the Messiah was Son of God, there is a disposition against regarding the narratives as authentic history. This literary method also gave rise to a tendency to regard Matthew and Luke as independently setting out their own particular presentation of the virgin origin of Jesus. Since the rise of redaction criticism, these presentations have been regarded as part of the total picture of each evangelist's theologizing.[502]

(v) The last view might be regarded as midrashic haggadah on OT passages, but there is another view which regards the stories as 'Christian midrashic haggadah', understood in the sense of Christian comment on several themes, such as the relationship between God and Christ, the sanctity of sex and the universality of the gospel.[503] In this case their character as midrash is more important than their character as history.[504] The form-critical school, according to its more sceptical advocates, traces the development of the traditions to Christian imagination, in which case they have no value for the history of Jesus, but great value as evidence of

[500] R. Bultmann, *The History of the Synoptic Tradition*, pp. 291f., maintains that the story of the virgin birth could not have arisen in a Jewish milieu, but arose in a Hellenistic setting. But W. D. Davies, *The Setting of the Sermon on the Mount* (1964), pp. 63f., disputes this on the grounds of the extreme Jewishness of the narrative. G. D. Kilpatrick, *The Origins of the Gospel According to Matthew*, p. 53, who sees an apologetic motive in Matthew's birth narratives, also maintains a Jewish background. His opinion is that Matthew aims to answer the controversy over why Joseph did not divorce Mary. H. Conzelmann, *TNT*, p. 78, traces the origin of the idea of virgin birth to polytheism. He appeals to incarnation and epiphany pagan parallels, but none of the examples he cites are at all close. L. W. Grensted, *The Person of Christ* (1933), p. 64, thinks that it would not have puzzled Christians to hear of other cases of parthenogenesis, because it would not have meant the same to them as it meant in the case of Jesus.

[501] Cf. V. Taylor, *The Formation of the Gospel Tradition* (1957), pp. 152ff. A. H. McNeile, 'Additional Note on the Virgin Birth', *Matthew* (1915), pp. 10ff.

[502] Cf. E. L. Abel, 'The Genealogies of Jesus HO CHRISTOS', *NTS* 20, 1974, pp. 203ff., who does not regard either Matthew's or Luke's genealogies as historical, but suggests that the former was composed to support the view of Jesus as royal-Messiah and the latter as prophet-Messiah. Cf. also the discussion in M. D. Johnson, *The Purpose of the Biblical Genealogies with special reference to the setting of the Genealogies of Jesus* (1969), pp. 103f.

[503] See Boslooper, *op. cit.*, 235f. He does not regard the birth narratives as simply midrashic haggadah on OT passages and concepts, but midrashic haggadah on Christian ethical teachings.

[504] W. D. Davies, *op. cit.*, pp. 61–83, finds similarities between Matthew's birth narratives and Gn. 1—2. He also finds traces of the new exodus and new Moses, although he admits that this is not made explicit in Matthew.

what early Christians believed.[505] If the historical Jesus is displaced by the Christ of faith, the virgin birth becomes dispensable.

(vi) If the narratives are taken at their face value and the virgin birth is regarded as a historical fact, certain consequences follow. First, it must be assumed that miracles are possible and that this particular miracle is unique. In some senses this miracle is linked with the other great Christological miracle, the resurrection.[506] If the latter is possible no objection can be raised against the former. Secondly, it cannot be argued that the virgin birth was intended to maintain the sinlessness of Jesus, although it does not exclude it.[507] The sinlessness is testified elsewhere (e.g. 2 Cor. 5:21; Heb. 7:26; 1 Pet. 1:19, see earlier discussion on pp. 231ff.). It is not so much birth by a virgin which guarantees sinlessness, as the direct action of the Holy Spirit in that birth. It is centred, in fact, in the divine nature of Jesus. Thirdly, it must be noted how completely a literal understanding of the birth narratives is in accord with the general NT presentation of Christ as Son of God, who is also perfect man. It cannot be said that the incarnation demands the virgin birth, for God could have accomplished it in another way. But it can and must be said that the virgin birth of Jesus is entirely appropriate to the nature of the one who became flesh although he was equal with God (Phil. 2:6).

There will always be a mystery about the incarnation.[508] Its uniqueness promotes mystery. No-one other than Jesus has ever had experience of it. That mystery extends to the virgin birth. Whatever theological motifs it may contain, it stands for that unique event in history when God became man. In the nativity narratives we are faced with records of that historic event. To empty it of its historical validity is to detract from a realization of its theological importance. It was so deeply impressed on the consciousness of Christians that it became unnecessary to mention it repeatedly.[509] Without it our total understanding of NT theology would be defective.

---

[505] Cf. M. Dibelius, *Jungfrauensohn und Krippenkind* (1932).

[506] This is not to suggest that the resurrection and the virgin birth necessarily have the same Christological significance, for the former affects Christology more fundamentally than the latter. Yet it is a fact that they both have a part to play in a full appreciation of NT Christology. Cf. the conjunction of the two themes in R. E. Brown's *The Virginal Conception and Bodily Resurrection of Jesus*. In a review of this book P. S. Minear, *Int* 28, 1974, pp. 465ff., thinks the conjunction is caused by dogmatic considerations – they both pose difficulties for inherited dogmas. But there is an inseparable connection between incarnation and resurrection in the NT, and it is not unreasonable to consider them together. If one involves supernatural intervention (as the resurrection clearly does, see below, pp. 390ff.), there is no valid reason for excluding the possibility in the other.

[507] B. Vawter, *This Man Jesus: An Essay toward a New Testament Christology*, p. 190, draws attention to the fact that Jewish minds would never have connected virginal conception with sinlessness and would never have equated sexual union with sinfulness.

[508] Cf. K. Barth, *The Faith of the Church* (Eng. trans. 1958), pp. 68ff. In his discussion of the two statements in the creed affecting the incarnation – *i.e.* 'conceived by the Holy Ghost' and 'Born of the Virgin Mary' – he focuses on the mystery of the incarnation. He distinguishes between the miracle and the mystery, the sign and the thing signified.

[509] In commenting on the lack of specific mention of the virgin birth in both Mark and Paul, W. F.

THE RESURRECTION

The astonishing development of an exalted view of Christ in the thought of the early disciples demands an adequate explanation. That explanation can be found only in the resurrection. No approach to NT Christology is possible without coming to terms with the resurrection. But the quest for understanding has been confused by the debate about the historicity of the event. Some interpreters have ignored its relevance altogether (as the nineteenth-century liberal school); others have denied it as an event, but maintained it as an experience (as Bultmann); and yet others, accepting the supernatural, have regarded it as an event, although even within this group there have been differences in explaining it. The particular view adopted has had a profound effect on the Christological thought of its advocates, and for this reason a brief survey of the main opinions will be necessary. First, however, we shall indicate the pre-Christian background to the idea of resurrection. Then we shall examine the evidence from Acts and the gospels, followed by the evidence from the rest of the NT. This will require the stating of various viewpoints. Our concluding section will discuss the significance of the resurrection for NT theology.

The background

It is natural first of all to look at the OT idea of resurrection, but there is surprisingly little data on which to base any general doctrine among the Jews.[510] The idea of Sheol is shadowy enough, but sums up the general expectancy of the life to come among the Israelites. Jacob expresses the conviction that he would see Joseph in Sheol and seems to regard this destination as final (Gn. 37:35). In the whole of the Pentateuch there is an absence of any specific hope of life beyond the grave. Certainly such hope played little part in pre-exilic Israel. There is perhaps a suggestion of future hope in Job 19:25–26, but it is not developed. A clearer expression of resurrection hope is found in Daniel 12:2: 'And many of those who sleep in the dust of the earth shall awake, some to everlasting life, and some to shame and everlasting contempt.' In the NT the words of Psalm 16:10, which breathe a confidence that the psalmist's soul would not be left in Sheol, are applied directly to the Messiah (Acts 2:27), significantly in relation to the resurrection of Christ.[511]

Arndt, *Luke* (1956), p. 56, suggests that Mark had no occasion to speak of it because he begins with John the Baptist's mission, neither had Paul because his opponents did not deny this particular teaching.

[510] For a discussion of resurrection and the afterlife in Israel, *cf.* S. H. Hooke, *The Resurrection of Christ as History and Experience* (1967), pp. 5–22. See the later discussion on the future life (pp. 818ff.).

[511] Some see the promise of vindication for the suffering servant of Is. 53:11–12, as implying his resurrection. *Cf.* C. R. Noth, *The Suffering Servant in Deutero-Isaiah* (1948), pp. 210f.; S. Mowinckel, *He that Cometh* (Eng. trans. 1954), p. 205.

There is not much more specific evidence of resurrection hope in the intertestamental period, although there does seem to be some advance to greater clarity. For instance 2 Maccabees 7:13ff. and 12:43f. look forward to individual bodily resurrection. But in this period there is no indication that Messiah was expected to rise from the dead. A distinction between the death of the body and the continued existence of the soul is found in Wisdom 15:8; Jubilees 2:24; 4 Maccabees 13:16; 15:2; 17:5,8 – an idea more Hellenistic than Jewish with its emphasis on the immortality of the soul.

The book of Ecclesiasticus contains some confusion over immortality, since 17:31 denies it, while 19:19 promises it. This kind of conflict was present in the marked differences of opinion among the Jews in NT times, the Sadducees denying and the Pharisees maintaining resurrection. Acts 23:8 reflects this conflict (cf. also Mt. 22:23ff.).

The idea of general resurrection may be more clearly seen in certain Jewish apocalyptic books, although here again there is no specific mention of a resurrected Messiah. The nearest reference is 4 Ezra 4:27–30 which states that the Messiah will die after a 400-year reign, but this is followed by a general resurrection and judgment in which Messiah is presumably included. Two passages in 2 Baruch refer to a coming resurrection (30:2–5; 49–52).[512] It is somewhat uncertain what importance should be attached to these evidences since both books are late first-century AD productions. Indeed it may be said that although Jewish apocalyptic was vaguely interested in the idea of resurrection, the idea existed in many and often contradictory forms.[513]

There is considerable dispute whether the Qumran covenanters held to any kind of resurrection. Some maintain that the scrolls bear witness only to the idea of immortality, but not to bodily resurrection. Others find some traces, but do not regard the idea of resurrection as a main doctrine.[514] Others maintain that the covenanters' views are not clear, although some passages express belief in a future existence, yet not linked with a belief in the resurrection of the body.[515] It is possible that the predominant view may still have been the old Jewish view of Sheol.[516]

From the evidence surveyed it becomes increasingly clear that the central

---

[512] Cf. J. van der Ploeg, 'L'Immortalité de l'homme d'après les textes de la Mer Morte', VT 2, 1952, pp. 171ff. On the other hand, M. Black, The Scrolls and Christian Origins (1961), pp. 135ff., denies that the Qumran Essenes held to the immortality of the soul apart from bodily resurrection. Cf. D. S. Russell, The Method and Message of Jewish Apocalyptic (1964), pp. 353–390.

[513] Cf. also the passages from the earlier 1 Enoch 61 and 62, which point to the preservation of the righteous, which are more relevant to the background for the resurrection ideas current in the time of Jesus.

[514] Cf. G. Vermes, The Dead Sea Scrolls in English (²1975), p. 51. Although he can find no specific statements, Vermes finds it difficult to believe that the members of the community would have denied to their dead brethren a share in the messianic kingdom.

[515] Cf. G. R. Driver, The Judaean Scrolls (1965), pp. 74f.

[516] Cf. M. Black, op. cit.

doctrine of the NT – that Christ is risen from the dead – introduces a unique idea, which had been only imperfectly prepared for in the pre-Christian era. This makes it imperative to explain in an adequate way the rapidity of the spread of the belief in the resurrection of Christ.

Some mention must be made of the Greek view of the immortality of the soul, if only because some have interpreted the resurrection of Christ in such terms. If the NT evidence could be understood in this way, it would be easier to rationalize the resurrection. But since there is no evidence that the concept of the immortality of the soul, as distinct from the resurrection of the body, is specifically mentioned in the NT, it cannot command confidence as a means of explaining the evidence for the resurrection of Jesus.[517] This is especially clear because no contemporary Greek ideas of life and immortality are parallels to the concept implied in the resurrection of Christ (see later discussion on the resurrection body, pp. 832ff.).

The key to early Christian experience in Acts

Whatever the assessment of the resurrection, whether it be considered an event or an experience, all would agree that something happened which transformed the band of shattered disciples into people who were convinced that Jesus was alive and that they had a message which would transform the world. Their fearlessness in proclaiming the gospel demands an adequate explanation and no approach to the resurrection is tenable which does not account for this transformation.[518]

Immediately, the early Christian preachers fearlessly announced that the one whom the Jews had crucified had been raised from the dead (Acts 2:24) and that God had made him both Lord and Christ (2:36). In spite of the disciples' earlier lack of understanding, Peter appeals to OT scripture in support of his declaration, even in support of the Messiah's resurrection. The Christians certainly did not borrow this notion from the Jews and the reason for the confident assertion must be sought elsewhere. Something clearly happened to produce such a firm conviction. The NT writers are unanimous that what happened was the resurrection of Jesus Christ. In other words the early preachers were proclaiming an actual event, as unexpected as it was supernatural. Neither the accounts in Acts, nor the epistles, suggest any hesitation on the part of the apostles over the possi-

---

[517] *Cf.* the comments of W. Künneth, *The Theology of the Resurrection* (Eng. trans. 1965), pp. 33ff., for the philosophical approach through Greek thought and its inadequacy for an understanding of the early Christian proclamation. 'The concern of the primitive Christian preaching was not with the continued existence of Jesus after death in a bodiless abstraction of soul, but with witnessing to the resurrection as a new reality embracing also bodily existence' (p. 40).

[518] The prologue of the book of Acts asserts that after his passion Jesus showed himself alive to his disciples during a period of forty days. The readers of the book are thus prepared for the importance of the resurrection theme. What comes out clearly in this passage is a strong sense of continuity between what Jesus began to do and teach, and what the disciples were instructed to do and teach by the risen Lord.

bility of a supernatural event of this nature.[519] We shall discuss below the various approaches which deny the event, mainly because the supernatural is considered to be unacceptable. Yet if the supernatural is rejected *a priori*, those who reject it are obliged to find some other explanation for the extraordinary transformation of the disciples.[520]

The importance of the resurrection is moreover supported by the fact that one of the major qualifications for the office of an apostle, laid down by Peter when the church needed a successor for Judas, was that the person must be a witness to the resurrection of Jesus (Acts 1:22). The reason is obvious from the subsequent story in Acts, where references to the death of Jesus were followed by proclamations of the resurrection.[521] The connecting link between the events in the gospels and the teaching of the rest of the NT is the resurrection (*cf.* Acts 3:15, 26; 4:2, 10, 33; 5:30; 10:40; 13:37; 17:31; 25:19; as instances where the resurrection is stressed in Acts. Note also the three-fold account of the appearance of the risen Lord to Saul at Damascus, chapters 9, 22, 26). In none of these recorded occurrences is there the least suspicion of discontinuity between the risen Christ and the historical Jesus. It is this unshakeable conviction which is the key consideration in evaluating the resurrection accounts. To those who accept the supernatural, the accounts establish the event which led to resurrection faith. But to those who discount the supernatural, the subsequent faith becomes the explanation for the rise of the resurrection accounts. To decide which of these alternatives is the more probable, we must look at the evidence for the event itself and then consider its interpretation.

The predictions in the synoptic gospels

The place of prediction in assessing the importance of the resurrection of Jesus is two-fold. We shall first note his own specific predictions that he would rise from the dead, and then consider his reassessment of the OT regarding his mission. In each of the three predictions of the passion in the

---

[519] M. C. Tenney, *The Reality of the Resurrection* (1963), p. 49, points out that in the book of Acts 'the meaning of the resurrection was explained in terms of the immediate circumstances or topic of discussion'. He proceeds to illustrate his point from the various speeches in Acts.

[520] T. Peters, 'The Use of Analogy in Historical Method', *CBQ* 35, 1973, pp. 475ff., shows the limitation of the use of the principle of analogy when applied to the resurrection of Jesus. Since no historian has knowledge of a resurrection of a dead man, he could only conclude that Jesus could not have risen from the dead. W. Pannenberg (*Jesus, God and Man*), p. 109, claims that as long as historiography does not begin with a narrow concept of reality which asserts that dead men do not rise, there is no reason why it should not be possible to speak of the resurrection of Jesus as the best explanation of the disciples' experiences of the appearances and the discovery of the empty tomb.

[521] G. Delling, in his essay, 'The significance of the resurrection of Jesus for faith in Jesus Christ', in *The Significance of the Message of the Resurrection for Faith in Jesus Christ* (Eng. trans. ed. C. F. D. Moule, 1968), pp. 77–104, considers that in Acts the raising of Jesus is above all Christologically significant. He links salvation with faith in the risen Jesus, although he admits that Acts does not explain how salvation is linked with the resurrection. But Delling does not give sufficient weight to the link in Acts between the death and resurrection of Jesus.

synoptic gospels, it is linked with the assurance of the resurrection to follow (Mt. 16:21 = Mk. 8:31 = Lk. 9:22; Mt. 17:22–23 = Mk. 9:31; Mt. 20:19 = Mk. 10:34 = Lk. 18:33).[522] In all these cases Mark has 'after three days', whereas Matthew and Luke have 'on the third day', but all agree in making quite clear that the resurrection would follow quickly after the passion. The fact that the prediction was made three times suggest that Jesus foresaw that the idea would not sink into the disciples' minds without difficulty. This certainly proved to be true.

In attempting to understand the reason for their inability to grasp the assurance that Jesus would rise from the dead, an important consideration must be noted. They had a wrong idea of the real aim of the mission of Jesus. Their hopes were fixed on a materialistic kingdom (Lk. 24:21). These hopes had been completely shattered by the crucifixion. All the disciples deserted Jesus, with the exception of John, who seems to have been the only one present at the cross (Jn. 19:26f.). Basically they had no faith in the spiritual purpose of the mission which Jesus came to fulfil. They had not even enough faith to penetrate the disaster of the passion. The fact that Jesus had predicted it completely escaped their minds. This unfavourable background is important for assessing the historical circumstances, for the disciples were clearly not in a conducive frame of mind to 'invent' the resurrection. Peter's rebuke to Jesus about his 'suffering' task was no doubt indicative of the attitude of all.

Among the resurrection narratives which have been preserved, a significant feature is found especially in Luke 24:45. Here the risen Lord is said to have expounded from the Scriptures, not only that he should suffer, but that he should rise from the dead on the third day. It is noticeable that Luke records at the third prediction of the passion that none of the disciples understood – 'this saying was hid from them' (18:34), although Jesus had said that 'everything that is written of the Son of man by the prophets will be accomplished' (verse 31). In view of the absence of specific statements in the OT about the Messiah's rising from the dead,[523] it must be assumed that a definite reinterpretation of Scripture was initiated by the risen Lord.

The event

It is not our purpose here to discuss at length the historical problems which arise from the resurrection accounts.[524] Our aim will be to set out the facts

---

[522] For a summary of the objections which have been raised over these passion predictions, *cf.* I. H. Marshall, *Luke*, pp. 367–379, who concludes that it is certainly not impossible that Jesus looked beyond suffering to vindication.

[523] M. Tenney, *The Reality of the Resurrection*, pp. 44f., explores the possible OT references which might have formed the basis of the exposition. *Cf.* also R. T. France, *Jesus and the Old Testament*, pp. 53ff.

[524] For recent studies of the historical and literary problems surrounding the resurrection narratives, *cf.* S. H. Hooke, *The Resurrection of Christ as History and Experience* (1967); C. F. Evans, *The Resurrection and the New Testament* (1970); I. H. Marshall, 'The Resurrection of Jesus in Luke', *TB* 24, 1973, pp. 55ff.; D.

to enable us to arrive at an evaluation of the event and its theological importance.[525]

(i) The fact of the death of Jesus would be accepted by all scholars, even by those who, like Bultmann, deny the possibility of knowledge about the historical Jesus. Moreover, the form of death, *i.e.* crucifixion, cannot be denied as a historical fact.

(ii) The idea of a suffering Messiah was unacceptable not only to the Jews, but also to the closest disciples of Jesus. Peter's abrupt rebuke to Jesus on the mention of the passion reveals a deep unacceptability about the whole idea. It is not surprising therefore that the disciples are said to have fled when Jesus was crucified.

(iii) All the gospels witness to the empty tomb. This is not in itself a proof of the resurrection, but it is a necessary part of it. It demands some explanation.[526] There would have been no possibility of belief in the resurrection if the body had been found. The assertion in 1 Corinthians 15:4 that Christ was buried and raised on the third day presupposes the empty tomb.

(iv) Numerous instances of Jesus appearing to his disciples are also recorded as events which happened. He showed himself to individuals and to groups, on one occasion to as many as over 500 (1 Cor. 15:6). The introduction to Acts sums up the appearances to the apostles in the following way: 'To them he presented himself alive after his passion by many proofs, appearing to them during forty days, and speaking of the kingdom of God' (Acts 1:3). These appearances were seen as having a two-fold aspect, first as offering confirmation of the event and secondly as providing a specific historical occasion (or series of occasions) on which Jesus could

---

Wenham, 'The Resurrection Narratives in Matthew's Gospel', *TB* 24, 1973, pp. 21–54; R. H. Fuller, *The Formation of the Resurrection Narratives* (1972); N. Walter, 'Eine vormatthäische Schilderung der Auferstehung Jesu', *NTS* 19, 1973, pp. 415–429; E. L. Bode, *The First Easter Morning* (1970); G. E. Ladd, *I Believe in the Resurrection of Jesus* (1975).

[525] C. F. Evans, *op. cit.*, p. 116, distinguishes between the synoptic evidence and the Johannine. 'Strictly speaking, there is no place in the Fourth Gospel for resurrection stories, since the ascent or exaltation has already taken place.' He comes to this conclusion because he thinks of the spiritual ascent as having taken place on the cross. His explanation of the fact that the fourth gospel actually contains resurrection stories is that the evangelist has included them in deference to Christian tradition. But why he should have done this if his purpose was to equate resurrection with spiritual ascension is inconceivable. C. F. D. Moule, in his review of Evans' book (*Theology* 73, 1970, pp. 457ff.) criticizes the view that John presents any different view from Luke.

[526] D. Whitaker, 'What happened to the Body of Jesus?', *ExT* 81, 1970, pp. 307ff., who follows G. W. H. Lampe (*The Resurrection*, ed. G. W. H. Lampe and D. M. Mackinnon 1966) in rejecting a physical resurrection, nevertheless criticizes him for dispensing with the empty tomb. Whitaker comes up with the unlikely suggestion that the body of Jesus was stolen by thieves. But how the disciples could have arrived at a spiritual understanding of the resurrection of Jesus if this had happened is not explained. Both Lampe and Whitaker are influenced by the theological consideration that our resurrection cannot be dissimilar from Christ's. But see discussion on the resurrection of believers on pp. 818ff. A recent strong supporter of the historicity of the empty tomb is H. von Campenhausen, *Tradition and Life in the Church* (Eng. trans. 1968), pp. 42–89. *Cf.* also G. Vermes, *Jesus the Jew* (1973), p. 41.

instruct his disciples about the kingdom in the light of his resurrection. In view of the mass appearances, it is difficult however to suppose that Jesus necessarily used all the occasions in the same way.

These facts would on the surface point to an objective event which resulted in the resurrection faith of the early Christians.[527] But we must examine the various approaches which deny the actuality of the resurrection and transfer it to the sphere of experience. The background to the modern movement reaches back to the nineteenth century. Holtzmann[528] may be taken as typical of the approach of liberalism in the latter half of that century. He regarded the resurrection not as an event, but as a hallucination in the mind of Peter, which led to similar hallucinations in the minds of the other disciples. The resurrection happened, therefore, only in the minds of those who believed it.

Early in this century Johannes Weiss[529] and Wilhelm Wrede[530] both made modifications to the nineteenth-century approach. The former considered that the messianic consciousness of Jesus was after the manner of Jewish apocalyptic and that the liberal Jesus of history had become irrelevant for modern man. Wrede conjured up a theory that after the death of Jesus his disciples thought of him as redeemer who would reappear, necessitating a belief in the resurrection, which in turn led to his being thought of as Messiah. For Wrede, therefore, the resurrection was not an event at all, but the result of the church's imagination. Since, according to him, Mark's record was an attempt to explain the life of Jesus from the point of view of this belief in the resurrection, the so-called evidences for the fact of the resurrection were automatically regarded as non-historical accounts. Wrede's views made a profound impression on Bultmann and were a contributory factor in his own sceptical view of history.

Two others about the same time had quite different views of the resurrection. M. Kähler,[531] maintained that the NT message must be approached from the risen Christ as against the liberal human Jesus; and A. Schweitzer,[532] having come to the conclusion that Jesus was deluded, could interpret the resurrection only as Jesus having arisen within men, *i.e.* a completely non-supernatural view.

Further discussion on the significance of the resurrection followed with the emergence of Barth and Bultmann. The former[533] regarded the resur-

[527] *Cf.* D. P. Fuller, *Easter Faith and History* (1968), pp. 52ff.
[528] H. J. Holtzmann, *Lehrbuch der neutestamentlichen Theologie*, 2 vols. (1897).
[529] *Cf.* J. Weiss, *Earliest Christianity. A History of the Period 30—150* 1 (Eng. trans. r.p. 1970), 14ff.
[530] W. Wrede, *Das Messiasgeheimnis in den Evangelien* (1901, Eng. trans. *The Messianic Secret*, 1971).
[531] M. Kähler, *The So-Called Historical Jesus and the Historic, Biblical Christ* (²1896, Eng. trans. 1964).
[532] A. Schweitzer, *The Mystery of the Kingdom of God* (1901, Eng. trans. 1914).
[533] K. Barth, *Romans* (Eng. trans. 1933), p. 204. For a fuller discussion including a criticism of Bultmann, *cf.* Barth's *Church Dogmatics* III, 2 (Eng. trans. 1960), pp. 441ff. Barth seems to have shifted his position, for in the former work (p. 30) he declared that the resurrection was not an event in history (he uses the

rection as a supra-historical event *par excellence*, while the latter totally rejected the resurrection of Christ as an event, because it could not be demonstrated by scientific historical method. The views of the two men were irreconcilable,[534] for Barth was approaching the question from the standpoint of revelation, whereas Bultmann confined himself to man as he is, man pursuing his quest for authentic existence.

Bultmann pressed his point relentlessly to the extent of demanding a complete reinterpretation of the biblical evidence. In the sweeping process of demythologization which began by assuming that the gospels especially were couched in mythical forms, it is not surprising that the resurrection of Jesus was at once pronounced a myth which needed to be stripped. [535] How then is the resurrection to be understood? Bultmann[536] explains, 'The resurrection itself is not an event of past history. All that historical criticism can establish is the fact that the first disciples came to believe in the resurrection . . . The historical event of the rise of the Easter faith means for us what it meant for the first disciples – namely, the self-manifestation of the risen Lord, the act of God in which the redemptive event of the cross is completed.'

It will be seen from this quotation that Bultmann is not referring to the event of the resurrection (which the NT affirms), but to the event of the rise of the Easter faith; by this switch faith is isolated from the resurrection of Christ, and becomes no more than an existential experience.[537] Clearly if Bultmann is right, there is no further need to investigate the historical

---

illustration of a tangent which touches but does not become a part of a circle). In the *Dogmatics*, however, he speaks of the Easter event in terms of Easter event and Easter time. He concedes that for the NT the resurrection is the central event.

[534] H. G. Geyer, in an article, 'The resurrection of Jesus Christ: A Survey of the debate in Present Day Theology', in *The Significance of the Message of the Resurrection for Faith in Jesus Christ* (Eng. trans. ed. C. F. D. Moule) sums up succinctly the difference between Barth and Bultmann in their estimate of the resurrection as follows: 'Bultmann speaks of the events of Easter only as the rise of faith in the saving efficacy of the cross of Jesus Christ, while Barth understands and expounds the resurrection of Jesus Christ as providing the basis of faith, distinct from the act of faith' (p. 119). *Cf.* also the discussion by R. G. Crawford, 'The Resurrection of Christ', *Theology* 75, 1972, pp. 170ff. For a general comparison of the two men, *cf.* J. D. Smart, *The Divided Mind of Modern Theology* (1967).

[535] *Cf.* Bultmann's *Jesus Christ and Mythology* (Eng. trans. 1960). Bultmann's position is based on the assumption that it was easier for first-century men than for twentieth-century men to accept the resurrection, because it was more in harmony with their mythical world. But, as Barth has pointed out, the first-century disciples found it no more easy to believe in the resurrection than we do. *Cf.* Crawford's discussion on this (*op. cit.*, p. 171). D. P. Fuller, *Easter Faith and History*, pp. 87–111, gives details of the Barth-Bultmann debate over the resurrection.

[536] R. Bultmann, 'New Testament and Mythology', *Kerygma and Myth* 1 (ed. H. W. Bartsch, Eng. trans. 1953), p. 42.

[537] H. Conzelmann, *TNT*, p. 68, when discussing the resurrection of Christ, takes a line similar to Bultmann's. He writes, 'The element of event in the resurrection is rather to be characterized thus: faith understands the resurrection objectively as the prior element of the action of God, by understanding that it is founded precisely on this resurrection by God.' But this can hardly be said to throw light on the resurrection of Christ. Conzelmann prefers to speak of the event of proclamation.

basis of the resurrection. It becomes wholly irrelevant. But the more pressing need at once arises for an explanation of the 'event of the rise of the Easter faith'. The fact is that the scepticism of Bultmann over the relevance of historical enquiry into the basis of the Christian faith excludes the possibility of a satisfactory explanation of any event, whether it be the actual resurrection or the rise of Easter faith. The one is in no different position from the other. The rise of faith demands a supernatural activity as much as the resurrection itself, especially since it arose in the most adverse conditions.[538]

It is not surprising that Bultmann's scepticism has given rise to a reaction in the form of a New Quest for the historical Jesus, but how has this affected the approach to the resurrection? Is it still regarded as a non-event? E. Käsemann[539] sees some historical basis in the authority of Jesus, because neither Judaism nor Hellenism nor even Easter faith can account for it. He admits, however, that faith must first exist before history can have any relevance for the historian. But this provides no basis for establishing the historicity of the resurrection. Another of Bultmann's pupils, E. Fuchs,[540] talks of the possibility of believing in the resurrection of Jesus only 'when one dared to imitate Jesus and accept God's grace as God's *true* will and persevere in this even to death'. Although Fuchs' position is nearer to history than Bultmann's, he is still concerned with belief in the resurrection rather than with its event.

In his book on Jesus, G. Bornkamm[541] goes considerably further in reaction against Bultmann's scepticism. Although he stresses the importance of the Easter message rather than the Easter stories, he does not maintain that that message is only the product of the believing community. He admits that God himself had intervened and wrested Jesus of Nazareth from the power of sin and death. He therefore does not hesitate to speak of the resurrection as an event in time and in this world. Nevertheless Bornkamm does not regard the resurrection stories as equally reliable, and treats many details as later accretions. Yet his view represents a decided swing away from the idea of the resurrection as a non-event. Another who concedes that God raised Jesus from the dead is H. Diem,[542] who adopts

---

[538] H. G. Geyer, *art. cit.*, p. 113, points out that it is the difference between providing a basis for faith and the coming into being of faith which is ignored and unexamined in Bultmann's view of the Easter event. W. Künneth, *The Theology of the Resurrection*, p. 47, sums up Bultmann's theology as bearing the stamp of a gnostic myth, which is contradicted by the reality of the history-bound perfect tense of the resurrection of Jesus.

[539] E. Käsemann, 'Das Problem des historischen Jesus', *ZTK* 51, 1954, pp. 125–153. For an English translation, see *idem*, *Essays on New Testament Themes* (Eng. trans. 1960), pp. 15–47.

[540] E. Fuchs 'Die Frage nach dem historischen Jesus' (*ZTK* 53, 1956, pp. 210–229; 57, 1960, pp. 296ff.).

[541] G. Bornkamm, *Jesus of Nazareth*, p. 182f.

[542] H. Diem, 'The Earthly Jesus and the Christ of Faith', *Kerygma and History* (ed. C. Braaten and R. A. Harrisville, 1962), pp. 197–211.

a Barthian position, but he does not concede that the resurrection can be verified historically.

A somewhat different line is adopted by W. Marxsen,[543] who begins his interpretation of the event from the primitive kerygma. But he speaks of the Easter experience as a vision that happened. For him all that can be said is that the disciples, after the death of Jesus, 'saw' him, and this led on to the interpretation that he was raised from the dead. The basis for the Christian community was not the fact of the resurrection but the fact of the 'appearances' (*i.e.* the visions).[544] Marxsen claims on the basis of John 20:21 that the function brought into being by the vision is the continuation of the purpose of Jesus, which means that in their function the disciples now take the place of Jesus. By this means, he distinguishes the function of the first witnesses from the retrospective interpretation of the event (that is, a statement about a person), which he then regards as secondary. Marxsen, therefore, regards the resurrection, not as an event, but as a sign that the purpose of Jesus did not come to an end with his death. He regards the resurrection of Jesus as having a substantiating significance,[545] which he explains in the sense of providing a reason why it is still possible to commit ourselves to the 'purpose of Jesus'. But Marxsen departs from exegesis in distinguishing between 'the risen One' and 'the living One', and he does less than justice to the event of the resurrection.[546]

In view of the wide variety of ideas on the actuality of the resurrection, many fear that the historical fact of the resurrection cannot form a strong basis for a theological interpretation of the NT. Undoubtedly a NT theology which begins by assuming that the resurrection accounts are a myth, will present a very different account of early Christian thought, from that which regards a supernatural event as the real centre and key to Christian thought.[547] It will affect not only the Christological assessment, but also the understanding of the whole mission of Jesus. It is on this point that a fundamental cleavage occurs between different schools of thought. Some regard it as wholly unacceptable that Christian faith should depend on a

[543] W. Marxsen, 'The Resurrection of Jesus as a historical and theological Problem', in *The Significance of the Message of the Resurrection for Faith in Jesus Christ* (Eng. trans. ed. C. F. D. Moule), pp. 15–50.

[544] A. J. B. Higgins, *SJT* 24, 1971, pp. 111–113, comments on Marxsen's view that the resurrection of Jesus is an interpretation, an inference based on awakening faith. He asks the relevant question, 'Is individual faith stressed so much that the Easter event becomes little more than an idea?' For Marxsen the statement 'Jesus is risen' cannot be made apart from our own faith, otherwise we should have an unverifiable event instead of a confession of faith.

[545] *Op. cit.*, p. 40.

[546] K. L. McKay, 'Some Linguistic Points in Marxsen's Resurrection Theory', *ExT* 84, 1973, pp. 330ff., draws attention to instances where Marxsen ignores the force of the aorist tense which is almost invariably used in the NT in reference to the resurrection. A case in point is Marxsen's claim that *ōphthē* in 1 Cor. 15:4 does not imply physical sight, *cf.* his *The Resurrection of Jesus of Nazareth*, (Eng. trans. 1970), p. 98. McKay challenges Marxsen to produce evidence that the aorist passive form of this verb is ever used in a non-physical sense.

[547] *Cf.* A. M. Ramsey, *The Resurrection of Christ* ([2]1946), pp. 7f.

single unverifiable event. Others maintain that belief in the resurrection, even though unverifiable, provides a sufficient explanation for the rise of an otherwise totally inexplicable Christian faith.[548]

We may turn from the event itself to its interpretation in the NT writings. We have already seen the significance of the resurrection in the early Christian preaching from the book of Acts. It is against this background of the kerygma that the testimony of the rest of the NT must now be examined.

Paul

Among those passages in Paul which are considered to be traditional material and therefore pre-Pauline, the most notable centres on the resurrection (1 Cor. 15:3ff.). Because this passage is specifically said by Paul to have been 'received', it is of particular importance in showing his own dependence on earlier tradition for evidence of the basic facts of the gospel – *i.e.* the fact of Christ's death, the interpretation of that fact (for our sins), the burial[549] and resurrection, with a list of appearances, and the value of scriptural attestation.[550] The apostle recognizes that the list of appearances authenticates the fact of the resurrection, and he includes it as a preface to the mention of his own Damascus road experience. Some suppose[551] that because Paul's account is earlier than the gospels, the latter must therefore reflect later accretions to the tradition. But the theory of accretions is not the only possibility. None of the accounts is exhaustive. The variations between them witness to their independence of each other and rule out the

---

[548] H. von Campenhausen, *Tradition and Life in the Church*, pp. 86f., makes the point that the acceptance of a bodily resurrection means the abandonment of an analogical understanding, but shows that this is no difficulty for those who accept it in view of the uniqueness of the event. It is difficult on the other hand, for those who want to take the resurrection faith seriously, but yet hold the bodily resurrection to be superfluous or unacceptable.

[549] J. A. T. Robinson, *The Human Face of God*, pp. 133ff., thinks it to be significant that although in 1 Cor. 15:3f. Paul refers to the burial of Jesus (*etaphē*) he makes no use of the empty tomb. He connects this up with Paul's omission, later in 1 Cor. 15, to refer to the resurrection body of Christ, which suggests to Robinson that his body was like ours, sown in corruption. It must be noted, however, that the sequence – death, burial, resurrection – taken as a whole does not support the theory, for 'resurrection' must be understood in terms of 'burial'. If a bodily resurrection is not in mind it is difficult to see why the ideas are linked. L. Goppelt, *Theologie des Neuen Testaments* 1 (1975), pp. 295f., also attaches importance to the omission of reference to the empty tomb in 1 Cor. 15:3ff. and therefore its omission from the *kerygma* and from Acts. He notes, but attaches no importance to the fact, that it is not omitted from Luke's gospel. But Goppelt considers that the empty grave in Mark simply points to the coming appearances (Mk. 16:7), while Matthew's account is treated as a secondary apologetic and John's account is viewed as representing the meaning of the empty grave to the true, but not the historical, disciple.

[550] There has been a difficulty over the phrase 'according to the Scriptures' in 1 Cor. 15:4, since nowhere in the OT is there any reference to Christ's resurrection on the third day. B. M. Metzger, 'A suggestion concerning the meaning of 1 Cor. 15:4b', *JTS* 8, 1957, pp. 118ff., gets over the difficulty by maintaining that 'according to the Scriptures' relates only to the resurrection, not to the phrase 'on the third day'. He then thinks that Ps. 16:8–11 is in mind since this is cited by Peter on the day of Pentecost (Acts 2:25–32) in support of the resurrection of Jesus.

[551] *Cf. e.g.* G. Bornkamm, *Jesus of Nazareth*, pp. 180ff.

suggestion of collusion. For our present purpose, it is sufficient to note that Paul considers the historical appearances of the risen Christ to be essential as an introduction to his general discussion of the resurrection theme in 1 Corinthians 15.[552] In this discussion Paul goes as far as to say that faith would be futile if Christ were not risen (15:17). The whole idea of salvation from sin would be nullified. The resurrection stands, therefore, at the centre of Paul's theology as well as at the centre of his experience.

Although in no other epistle Paul expounds the resurrection theme so fully as in 1 Corinthians, yet the idea permeates his writings. We may illustrate this from Romans. In Romans 1:4, the resurrection of Christ testifies to his sonship, in a passage which as previously noted some see as a traditional passage.[553] In Romans 4:24–25, the resurrection is linked with our justification. That justification is further linked with the reconciling death of Christ in 5:10, and his life with our salvation. The figure of baptism is used in 6:3ff. to illustrate the entry into new life, and again the death and resurrection of Christ are the basis for the comparison (cf. also Rom. 6:10, 11). In illustrating the new life in the Spirit which follows from justification, Paul refers to the Spirit as 'the Spirit of him who raised Jesus from the dead' (8:11). The transformation from death to life for the believer follows the pattern of the death/resurrection experience of Jesus. Moreover, the resurrection of Christ is the guarantee of his intercession on behalf of his people (Rom. 8:34).

This basic character of Christ's resurrection in Paul's thinking is seen in other epistles. He begins his letter to the Galatians, in which he is at pains to affirm that he received both his apostleship and his gospel from God, with an affirmation of the resurrection (Gal. 1:1). Similarly in Ephesians 1:20 the power which brought about the resurrection of Jesus is seen as the mainspring of the power of God in believers.[554]. Indeed, the idea of the exaltation of Christ to the right hand of God is the immediate sequel to the resurrection. Not only so, but believers are also made alive with Christ (Eph. 2:5) and share in his exaltation. In no more striking way could Paul show the continuing effectiveness of the resurrection of Christ in every part of the believer's experience in Christ.

In the two great Christological passages in Philippians 2 and Colossians 1 there is no specific reference to the resurrection, but the exaltation theme

---

[552] H. von Campenhausen, *Tradition and Life in the Church*, pp. 43ff., maintains that the 1 Cor. 15 account is not only the oldest, but also the most reliable. He therefore contends that an examination of the evidence must begin with Paul.

[553] *Cf.* C. H. Dodd, *The Apostolic Preaching and its Developments*, p. 14.

[554] Another facet of Pauline theology which is based on the resurrection of Christ is the believer's new life in Christ. It is through the power of his resurrection that believers are raised with him. This theme is expounded in the section on the new life (see below pp. 644ff.). But it is clear that the foundation of Paul's argument is the close connection between the resurrection of Christ and the 'new' experience of believers. This is what C. F. Evans calls Paul's 'empirical and experiential' thought on resurrection (*The Resurrection and the New Testament*, p. 159).

in Philippians 2:9 implies it. The lordship which all will confess clearly does not refer to a dead Christ. Although even exaltation is missing in the Colossians passage, the Christology is of such a character as to be meaningless apart from a belief in the risen Christ. The resurrection is, however, specifically mentioned in Colossians 2:12; 3:1, together with the believers' identification with him. Other references occur in Philippians 3:10 and 1 Thessalonians 1:10. There can be no disputing that for Paul the resurrection was central to his whole approach to Jesus Christ. He provides a full exposition of the Easter faith, which is nevertheless expounded in such a way as to leave no doubt that for him the resurrection was a fact of history.[555] This central position of the resurrection is in full accord with the Acts narrative about the apostle's experience and preaching.

Hebrews

Although there are few direct references to the resurrection in this epistle, the whole presentation of Christ as high priest assumes it. There is no need for the author to declare it. He concentrates rather on its results. This is evident from the introductory passage where he sets out the present exalted position of the Son at the right hand of the majesty on high (1:3). It must not be supposed that the writer is not interested in the physical event and has spiritualized it in the exaltation, for this would fly in the face of his obvious interest in the historical Jesus in other parts of the epistle (*e.g.* Heb. 2:10ff.; 5:7ff.). It is impossible to take the leap from the historical Jesus to the exalted Son except via the resurrection.[556] The writer has no doubt that the readers will at once do this. It must be remembered, moreover, that his main concern is the present activity of Jesus as our high priest in heaven, for which the exaltation theme is clearly of utmost importance (*cf.* also 8:1). The resurrection, therefore, is an indispensable assumption in the present intercessory ministry of Jesus (*cf.* 4:14; 7:23ff.). The statement in 4:14, 'passed through the heavens', extends the resurrection theme to include the ascension, and again concentrates on the resultant constant access of our high priest to God, in contrast to the very restricted approach of the Aaronic high priests.

When describing the elementary doctrines of Christ[557] in Hebrews 6:1ff.,

[555] H. Conzelmann, *TNT*, p. 204, considers that any discussion of the historicity of the resurrection of Jesus in Paul is theologically inapposite. 'The question of the historicity of the resurrection must be excluded from theology as being a misleading one.' To Conzelmann the resurrection has point only as Jesus shows himself to us today. Yet to maintain his position Conzelmann is obliged to reinterpret Paul's statements in a radical way.

[556] C. F. Evans, *op. cit.*, pp. 135f., however, claims that Heb. 1:3; 8:1, as well as possibly Phil. 2, virtually ignore the resurrection and pass straight on to exaltation. He considers, therefore, that resurrection is secondary to exaltation in these passages. But the fact that the emphasis falls on exaltation does not exclude the path through which the exaltation came, *i.e.* the event of the resurrection.

[557] It is reasonable to assume that these elementary doctrines of Christ may go back to basic ideas taken over and developed from Judaism, in which case the concept of resurrection may be among them.

the writer includes 'the resurrection of the dead', which must contain an allusion to the resurrection of Christ even if its primary reference is to the resurrection of believers. When he urges the readers to 'leave' these elementary doctrines, he is not turning his back on them, but regarding them as so established that the most urgent need is to press on to a fuller application of them.

The fact that Christ through death destroyed him that had the power of death, the devil, and brought deliverance to those in bondage to the fear of death (Heb. 2:14f.) is rooted in the resurrection. A dead Christ could never deliver from the fear of death, because he had not himself been delivered. But a risen Christ could do so, because in him was the power of life.[558] If this epistle does not expound on the theme as Paul does, it nevertheless assumes it. The possibility of resurrection from the dead is seen in Hebrews 11:35, although it is only incidentally mentioned as one of the effects of faith.

The epistle closes with a benediction which almost has the form of an affirmation. It centres on the one who raised Jesus from the dead to be the great shepherd of his people (13:20f.). This complements the interceding high-priest imagery, for there is a tender aspect to the shepherd figure which is not as vivid in the high priest. The resurrection has made effective the claim of Jesus to be the good shepherd, who not only has power to lay down his life, but also has power to take it up again. (Jn. 10:14ff.). Such a caring figure would bring strong consolation to early Christians exposed to persecution.[559]

The rest of the New Testament

If the apostle *Peter* had anything to do with the first epistle that bears his name (and there are strong reasons for maintaining that he did), his testimony to the resurrection of Christ would be invaluable, not simply because of his apostolic office, but especially because as a former disciple of the historical Jesus he had come to accept what he had once declared unthinkable – a suffering and resurrected Messiah. He had grasped the truth that the new birth which all the believers have experienced is 'through the resurrection of Jesus Christ from the dead' (1 Pet. 1:3).[560] After introducing

[558] F. F. Bruce, *Hebrews*, p. 49, comments that the remarkable change from disillusionment to triumph of the early Christians can be explained only by the conviction that their Master rose from the dead and imparted to them the power of his risen life.

[559] M. C. Tenney, *The Reality of the Resurrection*, p. 85, considers that Hebrews marks a new stage in the development of the doctrine in that the resurrection of Christ is the 'foundation of His present intercession, the source of freedom from fear of death, and the assurance of His continued guardianship through persecution'.

[560] E. G. Selwyn, *1 Peter*, p. 69, comments that in his opening words Peter, 'gathers up all that the resurrection of Christ has come to mean for him and for the Christian Church, through the manifestation of God's power and mercy on the one hand and the widening of men's horizons and the exaltation of their hopes on the other'.

the idea of redemption through the death of Christ, Peter at once notes that the readers' confidence is in God, 'who raised him from the dead and gave him glory' (1 Pet. 1:21). The importance of the resurrection is here linked with Christ's being predestined before the foundation of the world. It was unthinkable that such a one should be overcome by death.

The resurrection is also spoken of as a prelude to the entry of Jesus into heaven to be seated at God's right hand (1 Pet. 3:21–22). This latter concept is closely akin to that in Hebrews, and seems to have been a settled conviction among the early Christians. The enthronement metaphor adds greater dignity to the event of the resurrection. It shows beyond doubt that the resurrection was thought of not as a subjective experience, but as a happening which provides a firm basis for confidence.

The main idea in 1 Peter is that suffering will give place to glory, and the glory is that of the risen Christ (1 Peter 4:11ff.; 5:10ff.). The reality of the resurrection is, therefore, an indispensable basis for Christian hope in the future.[561]

In *the Johannine epistles* there are no direct references to the resurrection, but the underlying assumption is certainly there. John writes about the word of life which has been seen and handled (1 Jn. 1:1), *i.e.* in a human sense. And yet the epistle presents an exalted view of Christ as Son of God. It would make no sense of this epistle if it be maintained that John is interested in the death of Christ, but not in his resurrection. The recurrent emphasis on life (1 Jn. 1:2; 2:25; 3:14; 5:11–13, 16, 20) is the antithesis of death, as the resurrection of Christ is the antithesis of his death. Christ can bring eternal life to people only if he has first overcome death by his resurrection. John takes this for granted to such an extent that he sees no need to mention it.

Revelation is clearly a book centring on the risen Christ. It is the book of the slain Lamb who is nevertheless still active throughout, a fact explicable only in terms of the risen Christ. In the opening chapter, Jesus is described as 'the first-born of the dead' (Rev. 1:5). When John prostrated himself before the shining vision of Christ he is reassured with the words 'I am . . . the living one; I died, and behold I am alive for evermore, and I have the keys of Death and Hades' (1:17–18). The worship scene in Revelation 5 throbs with life, but the anthem of praise is directed to one who had been slain (5:9). The final triumph of the Lamb in this book shows the ultimate achievement of the resurrected Christ, *i.e.* the final judgment of him who had the power of death (the Devil, 20:2, 10) and the conclusive destruction of Death and Hades (20:14). Moreover, the consummation of what the resurrection of Christ achieved is seen in the first and second resurrection of men.

---

[561] Note that although James contains no reference to the resurrection, the use of the title 'Lord of Glory' may be claimed to presuppose it.

Its Christological importance

The major significance of the resurrection is the contribution it makes to our understanding of the person and work of Christ.[562] For the pre-existent Christ to become man is conceivable only if the resurrection were a real event. Otherwise a choice would have to be made between a divine person who never really became man and who did not die (the docetic view), and a human person who was not divine, who died, but never rose. In both cases, parts of the NT evidence would have to be explained away. Only a belief in the event of the resurrection can assure the continuity which is necessary if the conception of Jesus as both God and man is to be maintained; no other view of him is possible if the NT evidence is to be taken seriously.

One of the most significant factors in early Christian understanding of the resurrection is the light it throws on the doctrine of God. The act of resurrection is always an act of God. Although Jesus claimed the power to take up his life again after laying it down (Jn. 10:18), the NT does not suggest that the resurrection was an independent act of Christ. The power behind it was the power of God. Indeed, the resurrection of Christ is viewed as the supreme display of divine power. It is the act by which the ceaseless round of death and corruption in human life has been checked. God has provided a way out of death into life, by raising his own Son from death to life.[563] The resurrection is essentially part of God's plan for the redemption of mankind.

Another important aspect of the resurrection is the way in which it links the person and work of Christ.[564] The resurrection expresses God's satisfaction with what Christ has done. The exaltation of the person is the vindication of his mission.[565] If Christ had not been raised there would have been no certainty that his death had effected anything. Man would,

---

[562] For a discussion of the theology of the resurrection, cf. A. M. Ramsey, *The Resurrection of Christ* (²1946); M. C. Tenney, *The Reality of the Resurrection* (1968); D. P. Fuller, *Easter Faith and History* (1968); W. Marxsen, *The Resurrection of Jesus of Nazareth* (Eng. trans. 1970); W. Pannenberg, *Jesus – God and Man* (Eng. trans. 1968), pp. 54–144; G. Delling, 'The Significance of the Resurrection of Jesus for Faith in Jesus Christ', in *The Significance of the Message of the Resurrection* (Eng. trans. ed. C. F. D. Moule, 1968); W. Künneth, *The Theology of the Resurrection* (Eng. trans. 1965); B. Rigaux, *Dieu l'a ressuscité. Exégèse et théologie biblique* (1973); G. Friedrich, 'Die Bedeutung der Auferwerkung Jesu nach Aussagen des Neuen Testaments', *ThZ* 27, 1971, pp. 305–324.

[563] Cf. M. Tenney, *The Reality of the Resurrection*, pp. 146ff.

[564] On the Christological importance of the resurrection, cf. U. Wilckens, 'The Tradition-History of the Resurrection of Jesus', in *The Significance of the Message of the Resurrection for Faith in Jesus Christ* (ed. C. F. D. Moule), pp. 51–76. In Wilckens' view, however, 'the essential significance of the raising of Jesus was that it was the eschatological confirmation of the authority or truth of the preaching of Jesus' (p. 66). By this means he explains that the earliest preaching was not that Jesus who had died had come to life, but that he had had his preaching eschatologically authenticated. But this does less than justice to the text of Acts.

[565] For a discussion of this theme in Paul, cf. D. M. Stanley, *Christ's Resurrection in Pauline Soteriology* (1961).

390

as Paul says, still be in his sins.[566] The resurrection is seen, therefore, to be indispensable to man's salvation. Further, the conviction that Christ has a continued interest in the welfare of his people and intercedes for them depends on the resurrection. His exalted position, reflected both in the titles assigned to him and the specific statements about his session at God's right hand, has a direct bearing on his present activity. His capacity for effectively acting on behalf of his people in his continued ministry is as unlimited as his sovereignty.

THE ASCENSION

The NT has much to say about the ascension of Christ which is linked with, but separate from, the resurrection theme. Indeed the resurrection without the ascension would be incomplete.[567] It would demonstrate the conquest of death, but would not necessarily imply the exaltation of Christ. It is important, therefore, to note the evidence for the event and to assess its theological significance. Naturally most of the information comes from the Acts and epistles, but certain features from the gospels, which have been thought by some to allude to the ascension, must be considered first.

The synoptic gospels

Among the synoptics Luke alone specifically mentions the departure of Jesus after certain resurrection appearances. His account in the gospel is brief (Lk. 24:50–51). It does not speak, however, of an ascension, although it implies it. Luke's record of Jesus' earthly ministry is the most complete, in that it begins with his coming (the birth of Jesus) and closes with his going (the ascension). The ascension account in the gospel is considerably filled out by Luke in Acts 1, which is the major source for details of the event. Certain problems arise from a comparison of the two accounts, however, and these are discussed below.

Some have seen a parallel between Luke's transfiguration narrative and the ascension and have suggested that he has adapted Mark's narrative to

---

[566] C. F. Evans, *The Resurrection and the New Testament*, p. 166 n. 35, considers that it is a stubborn fact that modern man cannot share the idea of the close relation between sin and death which the NT affirms. But he does not say why modern man cannot accept the NT view. *Cf.* N. Clarke, *Interpreting the Resurrection* (1967), pp. 52ff., for a discussion of the relation of sin to resurrection.

[567] It is not surprising that Bultmann, who does not regard the resurrection of Jesus as a historical event, treats the ascension as legendary (*TNT* 1, p. 45). He considers it to be derived from a gnostic myth (*cf. ibid.*, pp. 176f.). But this takes insufficient account of the OT prefigurement, *cf.* J. G. Davies, *He ascended into Heaven* (1958), pp. 15–26. B. M. Metzger, *Historical and Literary Studies* (1968), p. 84, argues that the ascension of Jesus follows necessarily as part of the logic of his bodily resurrection. But C. F. Evans, *op. cit.*, p. 141 n. 11, disagrees. For a study of the ascension from a Roman Catholic point of view, *cf.* P. Benoit, *Jesus and the Gospel* (Eng. trans. 1973), pp. 209–253 (originally pub. in *RB*, 1949, pp. 161–203).

make the parallel closer (Lk. 9:28ff.).[568] The evidence from the modifications is not convincing, for they consist of verbal changes which give no indication that Luke is intentionally making them in order to suggest an ascension theme. The most significant feature of his account is the use of the word 'departure' (*exodos*) in the description of the theme of conversation between Jesus and Moses and Elijah. No more convincing is the view that the transfiguration is a resurrection appearance read back into the narrative of the ministry.[569] But there is a marked distinction between the transfiguration and the resurrection appearances. The appearances were clearly recognized as appearances of the risen Lord, not a glorification of the earthly Jesus. The transfiguration must be seen rather as a means of preparing the disciples for the coming permanent glorification. In the light of the subsequent ascension at which Jesus entered into his glory, there are some noteworthy parallels – for instance, the cloud as symbolic of the divine presence, and the fact that both events happened on a mountain.[570]

Mark's gospel contains a brief mention of the ascension, but only in the ending (Mk. 16:19), which is generally regarded as non-Markan. Indeed it seems to be based mainly on Luke's gospel. Whatever the origin of Mark 16:9–20, it is an early well-attested witness to a firm belief that Jesus ascended into heaven. In fact, Mark 16:19 is much more specific than Luke's gospel,[571] for it mentions also the session of Jesus at the right hand of God.[572]

We may not attach much importance to two other references in Mark which have been supposed to connect with the ascension theme, *i.e.* the narrative of Jesus' baptism, and the statement of Jesus before the high priest about his coming. In Mark 1:10 Jesus comes up out of the water, *i.e.* in a

[568] *Cf.* J. G. Davies, *op. cit.*, p. 40. Davies suggests that Luke has used the transfiguration narrative as a prefigurement of the ascension (*cf.* also his article, 'The Prefiguration of the Ascension in the Third Gospel', *JTS* 6, 1955, pp. 229ff.). This theory is based on four main points: (i) a comparison of Lk. 9:1–34 with Acts 1:1–12 reveals identity; (ii) in Lk. 9:51 there is a reference to the *analēpsis* of Christ; (iii) Luke's additions to Mark's transfiguration narrative; (iv) the view that the three synoptics understand the transfiguration to foreshadow the parousia and therefore it must also prefigure the ascension.

[569] *Cf.* C. E. Carlston, 'Transfiguration and Resurrection', *JBL* 80, 1961, pp. 233ff., who maintains that the chronological transposition was made for theological reasons. He adopts this position mainly on the grounds that any other explanation encounters more difficulties. He admits that the identification of the transfiguration as a resurrection account lacks proof.

[570] H. Riesenfeld, *Jésus Transfiguré* (1947), p. 275, suggests that the transfiguration is a partial prefiguration of the messianic enthronement. G. H. Boobyer, *St Mark and the Transfiguration Story* (1942), considers that for Mark the transfiguration prophesies the parousia.

[571] H. B. Swete, *Mark* (³1913), p. 407, regards the statement of Mk. 16:19 as credal and as passing beyond the field of history to theology. Nevertheless as H. Anderson, *Mark* (*NCB*, 1976), p. 361, points out, Mark here shares with Acts the conception that the ascension initiated the missionary preaching of the disciples.

[572] *Cf.* Künneth, *The Theology of the Resurrection*, p. 90 n., 'The "ascension" is to be understood only when it is given a place within the revelation of the appearances as a whole and in subordination to it, and is not to be assessed as a saving event parallel to the resurrection. It is the last, specially significant appearance of the Risen One.'

kind of ascent, after which he immediately spends forty days in the wilderness. J. G. Davies[573] sees the influence of an Elijah typology here, because he thinks that Mark thought of John the Baptist as Elijah and Jesus as a second Elijah. But those not given to typology will be less convinced by this style of argument. Rather more may be said for the view that Mark 14:62 presupposes the ascension.[574] Here Jesus speaks of the Son of man sitting at the right hand of Power. Clearly this session is possible only after an ascension. Jesus himself may have had Psalm 110:1 in mind, linked with the passage in Daniel 7. The statement supports the view that Jesus was looking beyond the ascension. Indeed, he was looking far beyond to his future glorious coming.

The most notable feature about Matthew's gospel is the conclusion in which the risen Christ promises his authority to his disciples. Matthew is more interested in the final commission than in the subsequent ascension. The words of authority contain some close verbal parallels with Daniel 7:13, where the Son of man comes to the Ancient of Days. The assurance of Christ's continued authority for the church during the period of making disciples of all nations presupposes, although it does not affirm, the ascension.

John

Although this account does not end with an event of ascension, there are significant hints of it within the body of the gospel.[575] In 3:13, Jesus says, 'No one has ascended into heaven but he who descended from heaven, the Son of man.' The tense is strange since Jesus had not ascended, but it is obviously a forward reference to an event he was anticipating. In 6:62 a question of Jesus to some of his disciples is recorded, 'Then what if you were to see the Son of man ascending where he was before?' This question presupposes the probability of the coming ascension. Among the resurrection occurrences included by John, the appearance to Mary Magdalene is particularly significant because Jesus forbade her to hold him (20:17), 'for I have not yet ascended to the Father; but go to my brethren and say to them, I am ascending to my Father and your Father, to my God and your

---

[573] J. G. Davies, *op. cit.*, p. 35, writes, 'When Christ ascended out of the water He was baptized with Spirit, so the disciples' baptism waits upon His ascension into heaven.'

[574] *Cf.* J. A. T. Robinson, 'The Second Coming – Mark 14:62', *ExT* 67, 1956, p. 337. Davies, *op. cit.*, p. 38, goes as far as to say that this logion contains a direct reference to the ascension.

[575] W. J. P. Boyd, 'Ascension according to John', *Theology* 70, 1967, pp. 207ff., regards Jn. 14–17 as mostly post-resurrection, and particularly the prayer of Jn. 17. His contention is that it makes better sense if it belongs to the post-passion period and is regarded as preparatory to the ascension. If, however, Jesus is anticipating in his prayer the post-passion situation both of himself and his disciples, much of the force of Boyd's contention would be lessened. To explain the dislocation, Boyd proposes the theory that a redactor removed most of Jn. 14–17 from the resurrection sayings to its present context as an anti-gnostic move. J. Daniélou, *The Theology of Jewish Christianity* (Eng. trans. 1964), p. 27, mentions the similar view of V. Bréton.

God.' We need not suppose that Jesus was intending to ascend at once, but his concern was to prepare the disciples for that important event. Neither need we deduce that the giving of the Spirit in 20:22 is an evidence that the ascension had now happened in the light of Jesus' statement in 7:39, since the full outpouring of the Spirit did not occur until Pentecost and John (or the writer) could not have been unaware of this. Nor, in fact, can it be claimed that the invitation to Thomas to 'handle me' (20:20, 27) must be post-ascension in the light of 20:17, since different words for touch are used. It was not Mary's 'touch' but her 'hold' which Jesus forbade.

Acts

In setting out his sketch of early Christian developments, Luke commences with an account of the ascension. But it is as a result of a comparison between the end of the gospel and the beginning of Acts that certain problems arise. He states in 1:3 that Jesus presented himself to the apostles 'alive after his passion by many proofs, appearing to them during forty days, and speaking of the kingdom of God.' This looks like a brief résumé of what Luke has reported about the risen Lord opening the minds of the disciples to understand the scriptures (Lk. 24:44ff.). But there is no mention of the forty days in Luke's earlier account, nor for that matter in any other account (but *cf.* Acts 13:31). Moreover, if it is maintained that Luke 24:44ff. presupposes that the ascension took place on Easter day, this would be in plain contradiction to the Acts account.[576] If Luke was the author of both books, it is inconceivable that he was unaware of the contradiction, which leads to the question whether the theory of an Easter Day ascension is a correct understanding of Luke's words in the gospel.[577] Admittedly on the surface there is nothing in Luke 24 to suggest that an interval separated

[576] The words 'and was carried up into heaven' in some texts of Lk. 24:51 are generally regarded as a later editorial addition. Their omission certainly lessens the difficulties arising from a comparison of Luke's account and Acts 1. Without these words there is no specific mention of the ascension although it might be implied in the words 'he parted (*dieste*) from them'. It must be noted, however, that the disputed words have strong MS support and may be the original text. H. Conzelmann, *The Theology of Saint Luke* (1960), p. 203 n. 4., gets over the difficulty by treating Lk. 24:50–53 as secondary. For supporters of the inclusion of the words relating to the ascension, *cf.* C. S. C. Williams, *Alterations to the Text of the Synoptic Gospels and Acts* (1951), pp. 51ff.; J. Jeremias, *The Eucharistic Words of Jesus* (Eng. trans. 1955), p. 99; V. Larrânaga, *L'Ascension de Notre-Seigneur dans le Nouveau Testament* (1938), pp. 145–167. More recently I. H. Marshall, *Luke*, p. 909, has defended the retention of the words.

[577] Many scholars have resolved the difficulty by supposing that the ending of Lk (24:50–53) was added to the original text when the gospel and Acts were separated. At the same time Acts 1:1–5 was added. *Cf.* P. H. Menoud, 'Remarques sur les textes de l'ascension dans Luc-Actes', in *Neutestamentliche Studien für Rudolf Bultmann* (ed. W. Eltester, ²1957), pp. 148ff. By this means the reference to the forty days of resurrection appearances is regarded as secondary material. In a recent book, G. Lohfink, *Die Himmelfahrt Jesu* (1971), has argued that the ascension narrative in Luke and Acts is basically Luke's invention. His idea is that Luke has historicized Christ's exaltation into a visible act. For brief assessments of Lohfink's theory, *cf.* F. O. Francis, *JBL* 91, 1972, pp. 424f.; I. H. Marshall, *TB* 24, 1973, pp. 94ff.; F. Hahn, *Bib* 55, 1974, pp. 418ff. The theory attributes a high degree of inventiveness to Luke which is not borne out by a study of his use of sources (*cf.* Marshall, *op. cit.*, p. 95 n. 157).

Easter day from the ascension at Bethany, but on the other hand nothing excludes it. Luke's way of connecting incidents in his gospel is not strongly chronological, and to maintain that he presents an unbroken sequence of events in Luke 24 rests on too shaky a support to be conclusive. In view of Acts 1:3 it is reasonable to suppose that the forty days of appearances is based on historical knowledge[578] and does not arise from a use of the Elijah saga as has been suggested.[579]

The significant details of the ascension which are given in Acts 1:1ff. are as follows. The risen Christ commands his disciples to stay in Jerusalem until they are baptized in the Holy Spirit 'before many days' (1:5). This would fix the ascension just prior to Pentecost and would accord with Luke's forty days. The statement also closely echoes Luke 24:49. It is further expanded in answer to the disciples' question, 'Lord, will you at this time restore the kingdom to Israel?' (Acts 1:6; *cf.* Lk. 24:21). The actual event itself is described in Acts 1:9, 'as they were looking on, he was lifted up, and a cloud took him out of their sight.' Objections have been raised because this description presupposes a three-tier universe, but this is not necessarily the case. The upward movement is almost the only possible method of pictorially representing complete removal. The OT instances of Enoch and Elijah present certain parallels. Inevitably a spatial notion is introduced, but this is not the main thrust of the Acts description. The focus falls on the screening cloud, precisely as it does in the transfiguration account.[580] There may be some support for the view that the cloud is symbolic of the divine glory. The reality of the ascension is not seen in an up-there movement, so much as in the fact that it marked the cessation of the period of confirmatory appearances. This is supported by the further question put to the witnesses: 'Why do you stand looking into heaven?' (1:11). Their attention is directed forward to the second coming.

In his account of Peter's first sermon, Luke shows how the ascension was at once interpreted by the first Christians. God had exalted Jesus at the right hand of God (2:33), as a result of which the outpouring of the Holy Spirit had been given. Psalm 110:1 is cited in support. Unlike David, Jesus had ascended into heaven (2:34). In Acts 3:21 Peter describes Jesus as the one 'whom heaven must receive until the time for establishing all that God spoke by the mouth of his holy prophets from of old'. Before his Jewish accusers, Peter affirmed of Jesus that 'God had exalted him at his right

---

[578] C. F. D. Moule, 'The Ascension – Acts 1:9', *ExT* 68, 1957, pp. 205ff., accepts the forty days and considers that the other appearances and movements of the disciples fit such a scheme.

[579] *Cf.* Davies, *He ascended into Heaven*, p. 53. He sees the linking of a forty-day period to the ascension story as support for his view. He sees no reason to suppose that the readers would press the details literally. Such a view, however, assumes that the early Christians were well versed in the symbolical interpretation of narratives which were presented as historical facts. This seems less than convincing.

[580] *Cf.* Davies, *ibid.*, p. 57. He speaks of the 'cloud of the divine presence', as at the transfiguration and at the tent of meeting.

hand as Leader and Saviour' (5:31). Stephen, according to Acts 7:55, saw 'Jesus standing at the right hand of God'. Paul sees a vision of the risen Lord in Acts 9. In his address at Pisidian Antioch, Paul refers to the resurrection appearances as being 'for many days', but implying a limitation (13:31).[581] The importance of the ascension is thus seen to be widely recognized among the early Christian preachers.

Paul

There are several passages where the apostle either directly affirms or indirectly implies the acceptance of the fact of the ascension. In Romans 10:6–7 he introduces an ascent-descent theme based on an exposition of Deuteronomy 30:12–13, which would have little point if it had not been generally accepted that the ascension was a historical fact. A similar passage occurs in Ephesians 4:9, 10 where Psalm 68:18 is cited and where the conclusion is reached, 'He who descended is he who also ascended far above all the heavens.' In the same epistle the result of the resurrection is that God 'made him sit at his right hand in the heavenly places' (1:20).

In the important passage about Christ in Philippians 2:6ff., there is no mention of the resurrection but the climax is reached with the exaltation. We have noted that because of the lack of reference to the resurrection some see this as pre-Pauline. However, the exaltation implies the ascension which presupposes the resurrection. This exaltation theme is also seen in those Pauline passages where the focus is on the session of Christ as in Colossians 3:1 (Christ seated at the right hand of God) or on his return from heaven (1 Thes. 1:10; 2 Thes. 1:7; cf. Phil. 3:20). Some (e.g. Bultmann)[582] would not admit that this evidence presupposes ascension, and would argue that resurrection means simultaneous exaltation. Although some other passages (e.g. Rom. 8:34) may seem to support this, the idea of raising from the dead is separate from the exaltation to the throne. 'Raising from' cannot be stretched to include 'raising to' in the sense of glorification, although it leads to this.[583]

In the pastoral epistles, a statement occurs at the end of the Christological passage in 1 Timothy 3:16 which presupposes the ascension ('taken up in glory'). This is of interest because it follows on the vindication in the Spirit, which implies the resurrection. It was clearly of importance that the

---

[581] It is not unreasonable to suppose that the 'many' days of Acts 13:31 are an allusion to the 40 days of Acts 1:3. It is not convincing to maintain that if Luke had known the tradition of 40 days he would have included it in Acts 13:31 (as Menoud, op. cit., p. 150, claims). It seems clear that a sequence of appearances was common knowledge in the early church (cf. 1 Cor. 15:3ff., where no particular weight can be placed on the absence of mention of 40 days).

[582] R. Bultmann, TNT 1, p. 45.

[583] J. G. Davies, op. cit., pp. 30f., shows that egeirō and anistēmi are never used of exaltation beyond raising from the dead.

present glorification of Jesus should be stressed.[584]

Hebrews

In no part of the NT is the ascension so basic as in the epistle to the Hebrews. The presentation of Christ in the epistle at once sees him seated at the right hand of the Majesty on high (1:3).[585] This is presented as a sequel to the purging of sins, but with no specific reference to the resurrection or ascension. But it is inescapable that these intervening events are assumed. This epistle concentrates on Christ's present ministry, which makes his present status of supreme importance.[586]

Our great high priest is said to have 'passed through the heavens' (Heb. 4:14),[587] to be 'exalted above the heavens' (Heb. 7:26) and to have entered, not an earthly, but a heavenly sanctuary (9:24). Such statements make clear the heavenly status of Jesus, as high priest. The idea is further developed in those passages which echo the opening theme of the session at God's right hand (8:1; 10:12; 12:2). In the last two of these references the heavenly session follows on from the passion.

It is, however, particularly in the Melchizedek theme that the importance of the ascension comes to the fore because of the strong influence of Psalm 110, where the enthronement idea is linked with the order of Melchizedek (*cf.* Heb. 5:6; 6:20; 7:15–17, 21). In none of the references to Melchizedek, however, is there mention of the enthronement theme, which is nevertheless implicit through the citation of this Psalm in other parts of the epistle (*cf.* 1:13). Without assuming the ascension and exaltation of Jesus, the writer would not have been so ready to apply Psalm 110 to him.[588]

The Petrine epistles

There is only one passage in these epistles which specifically refers to the ascension, *i.e.* 1 Peter 3:18–22, especially verses 21 and 22: 'through the resurrection of Jesus Christ, who has gone into heaven and is at the right hand of God, with angels, authorities, and powers subject to him'.[589]

---

[584] *Cf.* J. A. Schep, *The Nature of the Resurrection Body* (1964), pp. 147ff., for a discussion on the ascension in Paul.

[585] In the OT, the expression 'The Right Hand of God' is a metaphor expressing Honour, Bliss, Authority and Power (*cf.* A. J. Tait, *The Heavenly Session of our Lord* (1912), p. 9 n. 2., for detailed references).

[586] The climax in the series of quotations in Heb. 1 is reached in the quotation in 1:13 from Ps. 110 which centres on the exaltation theme. D. M. Hay, *Glory at the Right Hand*, p. 86, thinks that behind this passage there lies 'a cosmic enthronement scheme'.

[587] As P. E. Hughes, *Hebrews*, p. 170, points out, these words refer to something far more than a spatial journey, for they are the language of transcendence.

[588] For a detailed discussion of the use of Ps. 110 in Hebrews, *cf.* D. M. Hay, *op. cit.*, pp. 85–91; and for its Christological significance, *idem*, pp. 143–153.

[589] A. J. Tait, *op. cit.*, p. 21, finds a three-fold significance in the theme in 1 Peter 3:22. It is a declaration (i) of the unending life and power of Christ, (ii) of the permanent withdrawal of his presence, and (iii) of his sovereignty.

Although the context raises difficulties in relation to Jesus preaching to the spirits in prison, his final status is not in doubt.[590] Whatever the interpretation of this verse, it is clearly a witness to the belief in the ascension of Jesus.

Revelation

The whole book centres on the ascended Lord and there can be no doubt from the frequent scenes set in heaven that the present activity of Christ plays an important part in John's thought. Moreover, in addition to the exaltation of the Lamb, the witnesses ascend (Rev. 11:12) and the manchild is caught up (Rev. 12:5).[591] The whole book alternates between earth and heaven, but it is the heavenly scene which is dominant. The final coming of Christ as Word of God in judgment is described as a coming from the opened heaven (19:11). In the worship passage in Revelation 4 and 5, the Lamb stands before the throne (5:6) and shares with God in receiving the homage of all creatures (*cf.* 7:9). This idea is fully in harmony with the other NT references to Christ being at the right hand of God. It is significant, however, that in 5:6 he stands (as in Acts 7:56).

Its theological meaning

From the NT evidence surveyed, it becomes clear that the ascension was an important facet of early Christian belief, which is testified in a wide range of writings.[592] It remains to enquire whether there is general agreement regarding its significance. Some of the points brought out here relate more to the work of Christ than to his person, but are included here for the sake of completeness.

(i) The completion of the resurrection. Although from some NT statements it may be deduced that exaltation is simultaneous with resurrection, the consistent concept behind resurrection relates to the overcoming of death. Ascension and exaltation form a separate concept which sets out the

---

[590] Bultmann, *TNT* 1, p. 176 n., following a gnostic myth, locates the imprisoned spirits in the region of the air and links the preaching with the ascension. On this verse, *cf.* R. T. France's article, in *New Testament Interpretation* (ed. I. H. Marshall, 1977), pp. 264–276.

[591] G. R. Beasley-Murray, *The Book of Revelation* (NCB, 1974), p. 200, considers that the birth and ascension of the Redeemer is here representing the entire Christ-event. The ascension would therefore be seen as the climax involving all the preceding events.

[592] It is important to note that some do not consider that the NT evidence for the ascension demands any kind of physical elevation, *cf.* H. B. Swete, *The Ascended Christ* (1910), p. 8. B. Ramm, *Them He Glorified* (1963), p. 48 n. 54., considers that it may well be that 'theological space' and astronomical space represent an instance of two incoordinables and not a contradiction. According to this argument the spatial objections to the ascension as an event may be entirely misplaced. But this method of expressing the event comes near to questioning whether the ascension was an actual or visible event, and this tendency must be resisted. *Cf.* W. Künneth, *The Theology of the Resurrection*, pp. 68ff., who, in discussing the early Christian world view, regards spatial designations as technical terms of biblical religion, and therefore maintains the validity of using such concepts as 'resurrection', 'ascension' and 'session at the right hand of God', without confusing them with the 'substance' of the contemporary world view.

heavenly status of Jesus.[593] As conqueror of death he became the first fruits among his people. But as the ascended Christ he carries forward that resurrection triumph to an exalted ministry on the part of his people. Resurrection without ascension would leave many essential aspects of Christian truth unaccounted for. The more important of them will now be briefly enumerated.

(ii) The beginning of exaltation and enthronement. The view in Philippians 2 that Jesus was highly exalted and given the name of Lord highlights a significant and immediate result of the ascension.[594] The enthronement idea is intended as a public demonstration of sovereignty, as a result of which universal homage is finally secured. The present position of Christ as sharing the throne of God is of utmost importance for believers as a basis for encouragement. Christ is seen not only as creator of the world, but during the present era as its upholder.

(iii) The inauguration of the ministry of intercession. The work of mediation between God and man depended on the entrance into heaven of the mediator, as the intercessory nature of the Jewish high priest depended on his gaining access to the holy of holies. The session at the right hand of God, secured through the ascension, gives Christ as our heavenly high priest an inestimable advantage over the Aaronic priests. The question naturally arises how Christ could have performed his mediatorial functions only after the ascension, while at the same time offering himself at the passion. Either the high-priestly office must be considered as designate before the ascension and actual after it,[595] or the appointment to the high-

---

[593] H. Sasse, 'Jesus Christ the Lord', in *Mysterium Christi* (ed. G. K. A. Bell and D. A. Deissmann (1930), p. 105, sees great significance in the NT distinction between the resurrection and exaltation of Christ. It is the latter which endorses his sovereignty. On the other hand, H. Conzelmann, *TNT* p. 67, reckons that originally resurrection and exaltation were identical and that their separation is secondary. F. Hahn, *The Titles of Jesus in Christology*, p. 129, maintains that 'exaltation' does not merely imply the motif of an ascent into heaven, 'but denotes principally the special dignity bestowed by virtue of an act of enthronement and the installation in a position of power'. For Hahn the ascension is considered to be a temporary absence, on the grounds that in the OT pattern ascent into heaven meant withdrawal. But it is difficult to see what is gained by this attempt to separate ascension and exaltation. A. M. Ramsey, *The Resurrection of Christ*, pp. 121ff., in a note on the ascension, maintains that although many NT passages do not make a clear distinction between the resurrection and exaltation of Jesus, Luke certainly presents the ascension as a distinct event. He admits that the apostles thought in terms of a three-storeyed universe, but does not hold that the abandonment of their astronomy involves the modification of their doctrine. J. G. Davies, *op. cit.*, p. 57, explains the three-storeyed concept in terms of Hebrew ways of thought and suggests that it was natural for the ascension to be described in pictorial language. In another book, *The Glory of God and the Transfiguration of Christ* (1949), p. 184, A. M. Ramsey speaks of the ascension as the counterpart to the downward movement of the incarnation.

[594] Those who do not regard the ascension as an event nevertheless recognize its Christological importance. J. A. T. Robinson, *The Human Face of God*, p. 234, regards the ascension as 'the assertion of Christ's ascendancy in all the processes, personal and impersonal, conscious and unconscious, that shape the lives of groups and individuals'. This reduces it, however, to a rather nebulous concept.

[595] J. G. Davies, *He Ascended into Heaven*, pp. 65ff., discusses whether at the ascension Christ entered into his priesthood, according to Hebrews, but he concludes that the answer may lie in the view that Jesus was Messiah designate and also high priest designate during his earthly ministry. W. Milligan, *The Ascension*

priestly office must be considered to be effective at the passion–resurrection–ascension conceived as a group of related events.

(iv) The fulfilment of the divine mission. The mission of Jesus on earth which began with the incarnation ended with the ascension. The main thrust of that mission was atonement (see the full discussion of this doctrine, pp. 431ff.). The ascension, therefore, marks its completion. The incarnation is God becoming man. The ascension is the divine man returning to God. Not only did Jesus through his death effect atonement for mankind, but at his ascension he took into the Father's presence the evidence of it, *i.e.* his own perfect obedience to the Father's will, in his sacrifice unto death. Since the ascension is God's initiative, it is God's seal on the whole mission of the Son.[596]

(v) The filling by Christ of all things. Although it is only in Ephesians 4:8–10 where this is given as the reason for the ascension, it connects with other Pauline statements about fullness (*plērōma*). Since all the fullness of deity dwells in Christ (Col. 2:9), the idea of fullness is connected with the totality of God's perfection. Moreover, the church as the body of Christ is his fullness (Eph. 1:23). The filling of all things by Christ is therefore the gathering up of all things into his own perfection, a kind of mystical cosmic process which could be achieved only by the exalted Christ.

(vi) The bestowing of the gift of the Spirit. Jesus himself stated (Jn. 7:39) that only when he was glorified would the Spirit be given and this accords with Ephesians 4:8 where the giving of gifts follows ascension (on the basis of Ps. 68:18). Pentecost could not come, therefore, until after the ascension. Whereas John 20:22 suggests a breathing out of the Spirit between the resurrection and ascension (unless both happened on Easter Day and the Acts record is wrong, which is unlikely), it is necessary to understand this as a foretaste of Pentecost to come. At all events the Spirit's coming is claimed to be the sequel to the ascension in Acts 2:33.[597]

(vii) The opening up of access for believers. As a result of the resurrection, Christ is declared to be the first fruits of those who are asleep (1 Cor. 15:20). As such he implicates all believers in his own resurrection and ascension. As he gained access to the Father so he gained that right for all united to him.[598] Hence the confidence that comes as a result of his work,

---

and Heavenly Priesthood of our Lord (1898), pp. 72–83, treats the crucifixion, resurrection and ascension as three stages of the glorification process of Christ, and finds this in John's gospel as well as in Hebrews.

[596] J. G. Davies, *op. cit.*, p. 61, remarks that Paul 'sees in the Ascension one of the four closely-knit elements in Christ's atoning act, which comprises not only His death, but also His descent into Sheol, His Resurrection and His exaltation viewed as one single process'.

[597] E. Franklin, 'The Ascension and the Eschatology of Luke-Acts', *SJT* 23, 1970, pp. 191ff., points out that Luke views the ascension as the eschatological event and this, he thinks, moulds his treatment of both the bestowal of the Spirit and of the universal mission of Christianity.

[598] H. B. Swete, *The Ascended Christ*, p. 8, suggests that the momentary lifting up of the risen Christ was symbolic of the lifting up of our humanity to a higher spiritual order.

a new and living way, made possible and assured through the atonement.

(viii) The start of the new age. The present age is bounded by two events – the beginning by the ascension and the conclusion by the parousia. The key to this present age is found in the angelic announcement in Acts 1:11, where the ascension is linked with the return. This age is the age of the risen and enthroned Lord, his people's intercessor. The NT philosophy of history is that it must be seen in the light of these two Christological events. The present is inextricably linked with the future.

CONCLUSION: JESUS, GOD AND MAN

Since as we have seen there is evidence in the NT which sees Jesus as both a transcendent pre-existent being (Son of God) who comes to save mankind, and also a perfect human being, it is not surprising that the problem of relating both presentations to the same person has exercised the minds of theologians in all eras of church history.[599] Especially in the early centuries the attempts of orthodox Christians to exclude errors in the doctrine of the person of Christ led to the formulation of the historic creeds. But the NT theologian is not concerned with these credal formulations, for the NT itself shows no awareness of the tension of the two natures. It is striking that the first Christian generation did not ask the questions which later troubled the Greek-speaking church and consequently did not provide an answer to them. Nevertheless the NT theologian cannot present evidence as valid, if it can be shown that the evidence is contradictory or logically impossible. He is bound therefore to pay some attention to the possible objections in so far as they impinge on a right understanding of what the NT actually presents.

The first problem is one of methodology. Do we approach the person of Jesus from God's side or man's? Do we begin with the pre-existent Son and discuss the possibilities of a real incarnation, a coming in real flesh, with all its attendant limitations? If we do, we shall clearly be concerned to see that nothing is attributed to the human nature which is inconsistent with the divine. We shall, in fact, expect to find a sinless person who reflects what true humanity should be. Our major problem will then be to decide in what sense such a person could intelligibly be said to be made like us.

On the other hand we could begin with man's side and proceed to reconcile the extraordinary claims that Jesus made, and that others made about him, with the fact of his humanity. We shall then tend to restrict ourselves to the categories which, as people, we can imagine are true of all

---

[599] On the problems raised in this section, cf. L. Morris, *The Lord from Heaven* (1958); W. Marxsen, *The Beginnings of Christology. A Study of its Problems* (1969); H. Conzelmann, *TNT*, pp. 72–86; 127–137; W. G. Kümmel, *TNT*, pp. 105–125; I. H. Marshall, *The Origins of NT Christology* (1976); C. F. D. Moule, *The Origin of Christology* (1977); J. Knox, *The Humanity and Divinity of Christ* (1967).

people, and our major problem will be to understand in what sense these are reconcilable with the pre-existent Lord. Most modern approaches to Christology begin from the human on the grounds that we must begin with what we know. But too many inadequate Christologies have been built on this process, as if the belief in the divine side of the nature of Jesus was the result of a long process of development. Yet to begin with the divine pre-existent Son makes better sense of the NT approach, especially of Paul and John. If we begin from 'above' we shall take account of revelation, whereas if we begin from 'below' we shall be concerned with concepts within our own experience and develop them in accordance with our existent knowledge of humanity, which leaves little room for revelation.[600] The former viewpoint leads to what has been called an 'incarnational' type of Christology whereas the second approach results in 'reductionist' Christology. It may be wondered whether there is any other way which avoids polarization. But our main concern has been to discover the NT approach and we must be on guard against imposing upon it a methodology which is alien to it.

The next problem we need to consider is whether or not there is a united presentation of the doctrine of Christ in the NT or whether we should conclude that it contains a variety of Christologies. If we follow some scholars (e.g. R. H. Fuller)[601] we shall conclude that in the early stages there were a number of distinctive strata which Fuller calls 'earliest Palestinian', 'Hellenistic Jewish', and 'Gentile mission'.

Under the first, he sees two foci – the historical word and work of Jesus and his parousia. Some attention, he thinks, was given to the soteriological significance of his death as Messiah. In the second stratum Fuller sees what he calls 'exaltation Christology', which he maintains resulted from the delay in the parousia. The Messiah is now enthroned. Nevertheless the earthly life of Jesus comes into prominence as preliminary to his messiahship. Consequently the messianic titles 'are pushed back into the earthly life, though without losing the sense that there was a "plus" conveyed by the exaltation'.[602] In the third stratum the death was related to redemption because of its relevance to the Gentile world.[603] This, according to Fuller,

---

[600] J. A. T. Robinson, *The Human Face of God*, p. 239, maintains that our thinking must begin 'from below' and move 'from immanence to transcendence, from relationships to revelation, from the Son of Man to the Son of God, rather than the other way round'. But he does not enlarge on the kind of revelation he has in mind if it is approached in this way. Surely, the essence of revelation is that it begins with God.

[601] *Cf.* R. H. Fuller, *The Foundations of New Testament Christology*, pp. 243ff., where the three strata are summarized.

[602] Fuller, *op. cit.* p. 245.

[603] In considering the effect of the Gentile mission on the development of doctrine, it should not be forgotten that that mission began not more than five years after the crucifixion. Formative influences were therefore concentrated into a brief period. *Cf.* M. Hengel, 'Christologie und neutestamentliche Chronologie' in *Neue Testament und Geschichte: historisches Geschehen und Deutung im Neuen Testament* (ed. H. Baltensweiler and B. Reicke, 1972), pp. 43–67.

accounts for the introduction by missionaries of the idea of pre-existence and incarnation, together with the idea of a new order of humanity. He maintains moreover that at first incarnation was viewed as kenotic, but later became an epiphany.

It is clear from this brief summary that Fuller not only argues for different Christologies, but maintains that developments arose out of the different cultural backgrounds into which Christianity moved. What advances there were, were occasioned by the cultural needs of the church. In this sense Christology began by being merely functional, with confessions affirming what Christ has done, is doing or will do. Later developments go beyond statements of activity to statements of being (*e.g.* Phil. 2:6; Jn. 1:1, 14).

Are these attempts to establish a sequence of Christologies successful?[604] Are they in fact demanded by the NT evidence or can the evidence be equally or even better interpreted some other way? It is a crucial matter to decide this. Fuller's development sequence may seem reasonable if his separate strata are correct. But can it be argued that the full messianic concept was not attributed to Jesus until the Hellenistic Jewish movement, or that the idea of incarnation and exaltation did not arise until the Gentile mission? The Acts speeches would not support such a contention. Moreover, Fuller is assuming a straight line development instead of coexistent differences of emphasis. It cannot be supposed that there was an immediate and full comprehension of all aspects of the person of Christ. But the various expressions of the way Christians thought of Christ were growing realizations of what was all along implicitly understood. The lordship of Christ is a case in point. It is tampering with the evidence to suggest that this was not grasped by the Palestinian church (*cf.* Acts 2:36).

Another way of attempting to explain the different understandings of the relationship between the human and divine in the NT view of Jesus is that which sees a development from adoptionism through kenoticism to docetism.[605] Here the basic idea is that the earliest Christology began with the remembrance of the human Jesus whom God had raised and exalted to a position of lordship. The development which began with the unquestioned humanity of Jesus and combined with it lordship and messiahship is generally known as adoptionism and is reckoned to be the earliest Christology of all.[606] But this view does not take account of all the evidence in

---

[604] On the idea of stages in Christology, *cf.* G. M. Styler, 'Stages in Christology in the Synoptic Gospels', *NTS* 1963-64, pp. 398–409; G.B. Caird, 'The Development of the Doctrine of Christ in the New Testament', in *Christ for Us Today* (ed. W. N. Pittenger, 1968). See also C. E. B. Cranfield, 'The Witness of the New Testament to Christ', in *Essays in Christology for Karl Barth* (ed. T. H. L. Parker, 1956).

[605] For a straightforward brief account of this theory of development, *cf.* J. Knox, *The Humanity and Divinity of Christ* (1967); idem, *Jesus, Lord and Christ* (1958).

[606] *Cf.* J. A. T. Robinson, 'The Most Primitive Christology of All', *JTS* 7, 1956, pp. 177–189, who finds an even earlier Christology in Acts - that Jesus would not become Christ until his return. But this view has found little support. The article is reprinted in his *Twelve New Testament Studies* (1962), pp. 139–

Acts.[607] It is too simplistic. It does not reckon with the reality of Jesus' divine sonship. It is not supposed anywhere in the evidence of the kerygma in Acts that the human Jesus was adopted to become Son of God.[608] Acts 2:36 does not require the interpretation that God made the human Jesus both Lord and Christ at the resurrection. It certainly affirms that in contrast to men who treated Jesus as a criminal, God exalted him to a position of lordship.

The type of theory under consideration sees the next stage emerging as a result of a belief in the pre-existence of Christ. If Jesus was declared to be the Messiah, it would be a short step to recognize that he must have been known as such to the mind of God, and from this real pre-existence was postulated. It should be noted, however, that the NT writers take for granted the pre-existence of Christ (especially Paul and John).[609] It is never suggested that this is in any sense an alien development. This development, however, gave rise to the problem, according to this theory, of how a pre-existent divine being could have become the human Jesus. The kenotic explanation,[610] based mainly on Philippians 2, seeks to explain it by some emptying of the divine nature in order to safeguard the perfect humanity. But this idea does not sufficiently guard the true humanity of Jesus, neither does it do justice to his divinity. It is not supposed in any case that this stage lasted long. It is suggested that it would have been superseded by a more complicated Christology.

There would soon have been the tendency towards emphasizing the divinity at the expense of the humanity, a tendency which finally led to docetism. There are no parts of the NT evidence which ignore the importance of the humanity of Christ, either explicitly or implicitly. It may be true that Johannine Christology lays greater emphasis on the heavenly origin of Jesus, but this is well balanced by the evidences of true humanity.[611] The NT carefully safeguards both the real human nature and the real pre-existence.

---

153. *Cf.* the criticism of Robinson's position in J. Knox, 'The "Prophet" in New Testament Christology', in *Lux in Lumine* (ed. R. Norris, 1966).

[607] *Cf.* S. S. Smalley's criticisms, 'The Christology of Acts', *ExT* 73, 1962, pp. 358ff.

[608] *Cf.* G. W. MacRae, ' "Whom heaven must receive until the time". Reflections on the Christology of Acts', *Int* 27, 1973, pp. 151–165, who considers that the Christology of Acts is complex and comprehensive, not simply adoptionist.

[609] In reference to Paul, J. Knox says, 'The pre-existence is taken for granted, needing no emphasis, elaboration or proof' (*Jesus, Lord and Christ*, p. 150). He deduces from this that not only Paul himself, but the Christian churches generally accepted the pre-existence without question.

[610] J. Knox, in using the word 'kenotic' in this sense, sharply distinguishes its use from the modern theological use of the word in the writings of people like H. R. Mackintosh and C. Gore (*cf. The Humanity and Divinity of Christ*, p. 12 n. 1). It would have been less confusing to have used a different word. Knox seems to be thinking of interpretations which begin entirely from the point of view of pre-existence.

[611] Such features in John's gospel as the Logos becoming flesh (1:14), the weariness and thirst of Jesus at Sychar (4:6ff.), the tears of Jesus at the touch of Lazarus (11:33-38), the cry of thirst from the cross (19:28), would not have fitted into a docetic view of Christ.

Another attempt to explain the evidence is to suppose that the NT writers were concerned with only a functional and not with an ontological Christology.[612] Certainly the various expressions of Christology give great importance to the functions of both the human and the divine aspects, but a functional explanation cannot be entirely divorced from the reality implied by the function. Although sonship for instance may illuminate relationships, it loses something essential if a real son is not in mind. Although it must be conceded that the NT writers were not concerned to offer philosophical answers to such questions as 'What was the nature of Christ?' there is sufficient evidence to show that their view of Christ did not stop with the simpler question, 'What did he do?'

One aspect of NT Christology to which insufficient attention is generally given is the relation between Christ and the Holy Spirit. This will be discussed more fully in the section on the Holy Spirit (see pp. 570ff.), but some reference here is in place in view of two considerations. The first is the presence of the Holy Spirit in the human life of Jesus, which must affect an adequate assessment of the nature of his humanity. The second is the presence of the Holy Spirit in the Christian community after Pentecost, which must be taken into account in assessing the apostolic reflections on Christology.

If the Holy Spirit was active in a special way in the life of Jesus, the humanity of Jesus was activated in a manner that was not true of other people, until the Spirit applied the work of Christ in an act of renewal. This in itself would throw suspicion on the concept that to be truly human Jesus must have shared fallen human nature. No fallen human nature had previously been so totally dominated by the Holy Spirit. In the NT the Spirit of God is spoken of as a gift. He is never confused with the human spirit in man generally. The Holy Spirit's activity is therefore an important factor in any consideration of the human nature of Jesus.

Similarly the activity of the Spirit cannot be left out of account in considering the place of revelation in Christology. The NT evidence shows that the believers would be led into the truth by the Spirit (see pp. 530ff.), and unless we suppose that they made this claim to justify their own conclusions, they must have been led into their exalted view of Christ through the Spirit. John records the saying of Jesus that the Spirit's work was to glorify Christ. He was to do this by bringing to mind what Jesus had said, which would include his testimony to himself. This testimony would take root in the minds of believers and through them be passed on to others. It would not aim to bolster up man's deductions about Christ. The Spirit's testimony brings in a dimension which would go against the

---

[612] Cf. O. Cullmann, *The Christology of the New Testament*.

idea that the church worked out its Christology independent of Jesus' testimony to himself.

It is more reasonable to suggest that what Christians came to believe about Jesus in NT times was not just an expression of the needs of the church in its various stages of development, but arose from what Jesus actually was. In other words Jesus did not become in the faith of the church what he was not before.[613] It is important to recognize this, if an adequate understanding of the historical Jesus is to be reached. The gospels presuppose that the man Jesus was also the pre-existent Son in a way that cannot reasonably be attributed to the creation of the church. Such a conviction came as a result of the resurrection, which demanded of men that they believe in a paradoxical Person, who went beyond what might reasonably be expected of a representative of mankind.

If we take the NT as our starting point, we are undoubtedly faced with a paradox – a real man who claimed to be and was firmly believed to be God. No attempt is made to discuss or answer such questions as, 'How could Christ be God and yet distinguishable from God?' or, 'How could God become man without the humanity being modified to such an extent that it ceased to be really human?' or, 'How did the two aspects of the nature of Jesus come to co-exist in him?' It was not until the Christian church attempted to express its Christology in Greek terms that it proposed answers to these problems in the form of the Nicene creed and the Chalcedonian formula. In the light of this, can it be said that what is needed is a return to NT theology, where such metaphysical discussions are left severely alone? Such a claim has often been made and would cut the knot of the interminable intricacies of trying to reduce the person of Christ to a credal statement, which makes our understanding of him more stereotyped than in the NT itself.

Yet is it possible to stop at the NT paradoxical presentation of the divine and human natures of Christ? The NT theologian has no alternative but to state the dual nature and leave it there.[614] But he would not suggest that further questions should not be asked. It would, however, be his duty to urge that those further questions may have to remain unanswered, because the NT provides no data for the purpose. Naturally, those who regard early Christologies as developments through the impact on Christian thought of

---

[613] H. Boers, 'Where Christology is Real. A Survey of Recent Research on New Testament Christology', *Int* 26, 1972, pp. 300–327, discusses the dilemma – to retain a true Christology and at the same time to admit the early Christian communities as its true authors. He gets over it by claiming that in developing the Christological titles primitive Christianity was trying 'to express who Jesus was as a response to the claim which was already implicit in his message and activity' (p. 320).

[614] L. Morris, *The Lord from Heaven*, p. 108, concludes his discussion with the statement, 'How these two, the deity and the humanity, are related, or even how they could come to co-exist in the one Person, we do not know.' But he rightly warns against the idea of Jesus as partly God and partly man. H. E. W. Turner, *Jesus, Master and Lord*, p. 185, has the vivid statement, 'His Personality is a seamless robe.'

various cultures, will maintain that the NT will need to be constantly reinterpreted in terms of contemporary cultures, hence a restatement in terms of modern existentialism would be regarded as perfectly legitimate. No objection could be raised against relating the NT presentation of Christ to contemporary culture provided the resultant conception of Christ is recognizable as the same as the NT Christ. Any extraneous features which distort the basic convictions of the NT church must be considered to be illegitimate as a representation of the Christian faith.

Some comment must be made on the supernatural element in the NT view of Jesus Christ. Alongside the assertions of true humanity occur accounts of a virgin birth, of heavenly voices attesting the sonship of Jesus, of miracles of healing and nature miracles which he performed, of a remarkable transfiguration and a resurrection. Rationalism, in its nineteenth-century form and its twentieth-century equivalents, regards these aspects as unacceptable within a scientific view of the world. A stripping process in which all these 'myths' are removed is seen as the only credible way in which the person of Christ can be regarded as relevant today. Yet there is less inclination in modern science to regard the world as a closed system and more possibility of a breaking-in to be maintained. Indeed, if the NT is to be taken seriously the supernatural in Jesus must be regarded as normal rather than abnormal. If the resurrection of Jesus is a *fact* of history, it provides the key for the other supernatural activities mentioned alongside it.

Chapter 4

The mission of Christ

There are two major considerations which arise from a study of the mission of Jesus. The first is the kingdom teaching which formed a major part of the message of Jesus. There is no doubt that he considered his work to involve in some way the inauguration of the kingdom of God. Our first study will therefore examine the evidence to determine what he meant by this and how he conceived his own part in it.

Our second main concern will be the explanation of the death of Jesus. It will be necessary to enquire whether there are any indications that Jesus himself expected his own death and if so how he interpreted it. Moreover, the early church had to come to terms with the cross, which proved not only to be a stumbling block to Jews and foolishness to Greeks, but something of a mystery to Christians. It will be seen that a wide variety of terminology was used in the course of explaining the mystery, but there was never any doubt that the cross of Christ was regarded as a pivotal point for Christian theology.

These two important foci of attention may at first sight seem totally unconnected. The question at once springs to mind why the inaugurator of the Kingdom had to die? The answer must lie at once in the nature of the membership of the kingdom. Since it is spiritual, spiritual qualifications are indispensable. But this at once raises the problem of man's alienation from God. The answer which the NT gives centres in the atoning work of Christ. It is in the light of that atoning work that the kingdom teaching becomes viable.

In this section the emphasis will fall on what Jesus came to do, but the application of his work to the new life will be reserved for a later chapter. It is unavoidable that a division of the subject in this way will lead to some overlap, but our intention here will be to regard the mission of Christ, especially in relation to his death, from God's side, before considering in more detail man's response.

THE KINGDOM

The synoptic gospels

One of the most prominent features of the teaching of Jesus in the synoptics was his emphasis on the kingdom of God. This teaching must be considered as a major contribution to our understanding of the mission of Jesus.

THE MEANING OF THE TERM IN THE NT

We note first that the kingdom is called generally the kingdom of God,[1] but sometimes the kingdom of heaven (literally the kingdom of the heavens). The latter form is confined to Matthew's gospel, while elsewhere and a few times in Matthew the other form is used. Whereas there must have been a reason for Matthew's variation, there is no ground for supposing that he meant to denote anything different. In all probability 'heaven' was chosen as a periphrasis for God out of typical Jewish reverence for the divine name.[2] It is just possible that Jesus himself varied his usage but this is less likely in view of the fact that Matthew alone preserves the form 'kingdom of heaven'. It seems reasonable to conclude that Matthew made no distinction between the kingdom of heaven and the kingdom of God.

We next turn to the meaning of the word kingdom (*basileia*). It is now generally agreed that it means not so much a domain, as a reign; not so much an area over which the king reigns, as the activity of reigning.[3] It is, therefore, a dynamic concept, a view which is in complete agreement with Hebrew usage (*cf.* Ps. 145:11, 13; 103:19). This was also the usual understanding of it in Judaistic thought.[4] The clearest evidence for this in the NT is the linking of the kingdom with the doing of God's will, in the Lord's prayer. When both John the Baptist and Jesus began their ministries with the announcement of the kingdom they must have meant the manifestation of God's sovereign activity among men. We should not, therefore, entirely exclude the notion of the kingdom as the sphere in which God bestows his blessings.[5] Some kind of dynamic understanding of the kingdom would be flexible enough to allow for a present aspect of the kingdom to be linked

---

[1] Many different approaches have been adopted towards an understanding of the kingdom in the teaching of Jesus. For a useful survey of these approaches, *cf.* G. Lundström, *The Kingdom of God in the Teaching of Jesus* (Eng. trans. 1963); N. Perrin, *The Kingdom of God in the Teaching of Jesus* (1963). In a more recent book, *Jesus and the Language of the Kingdom* (1976), Perrin distinguishes between concept and symbol.

[2] *Cf.* J. Jeremias, *NTT* 1, p. 97.

[3] *Cf.* S. Aalen, ' "Reign" and "House" in the Kingdom of God in the Gospels', *NTS* 8, 1962, pp. 215–240. Aalen makes a distinction between God's 'appearing' and his 'coming' (p. 221), but it is questionable whether this distinction is valid.

[4] *Cf.* G. E. Ladd, 'The Kingdom of God: Reign or Realm', *JBL* 31, 1962, pp. 230ff.; *cf.* also *idem*, *The Presence of the Future* (1974), pp. 122–148. Ladd emphatically concludes for the meaning 'reign' or 'rule'.

[5] But note H. Ridderbos' caution, *The Coming of the Kingdom* (1962), pp. 26f. He suggests that a dominion to be effective must create or maintain a territory where it can operate. He thinks the absence of any idea of a spatial kingdom would be very strange.

with a future manifestation. Evidence for this double aspect will be considered below, but since it has given rise to a variety of different interpretations, it is advisable before considering the evidence to bear in mind that the term does not refer to the establishment of a messianic political kingdom on earth. Its present activity must be found in a spiritual and not a material sense.

ITS JEWISH BACKGROUND

Before considering John the Baptist's announcement and the teaching of Jesus, it is necessary to enquire what 'the kingdom' would have conveyed to the average Jew. It must first be observed that the concept is found several times in the OT (cf. Ps. 103:19; 145:11–13; cf. also 1 Ch. 29:11; Ps. 22:28; Dn. 4:3; Ob. 21). Moreover, the general tenor of prophetic teaching is in line with the notion of a divine kingdom since God is portrayed as king, either of Israel (e.g. Ex. 15:18; Dt. 33:5; Is. 43:15) or of all men (cf. Je. 46:18, where the king is described as the Lord of Hosts). There is a sense in which God's kingdom is both present and future in the OT. As sovereign, God is king in his own right,[6] but the prophets looked forward to a time when it would become evident to all that God reigned among his people (cf. Is. 24:23).

If the idea of the kingdom is, therefore, present in the OT, the precise nature of the idea is not as easy to define. There is much support for a restoration of the Davidic kingdom seen as the agency through which God would demonstrate himself as king in Israel. But the apocalyptic idea of some kind of heavenly kingdom is not wholly lacking (cf. Dn. 7).[7] The existence of these two aspects shows that there was no clear distinction between them. The intertestamental period merely extended the dual conception. The earthly aspect is still present (as in Enoch 1–36 and Psalms of Solomon 17—18), but it is also mixed with the transcendental (cf. Enoch 37ff.). During this period the conviction that the kingdom of God would be established on earth was linked with a pessimism regarding the restoration of the Davidic line.[8] There was a tendency to think more of the kingdom as belonging to the coming age. Yet for the average Jew there was probably only the idea that the hoped-for kingdom would soon be

---

[6] Ladd, *TNT*, p. 61, says that God *is* and must *become* King, *i.e.* in the sense of manifesting his kingship in the world of men.

[7] There is a dispute over whether Dn. 7 relates to the kingdom of God. According to K. Koch, *The Rediscovery of Apocalyptic* (Eng. trans. 1972), p. 31, it does. M. Noth, *The Laws in the Pentateuch and other Studies* (Eng. trans. 1966), pp. 215ff., discusses the interpretation of Dn. 7 and sees it basically as a proclamation of the imminent 'heavenly kingdom' (p. 218), as distinguished from the kingdom of God idea in Dn. 2.

[8] In the apocalyptic literature, few references to the kingdom of God occur. Dn. 2:44, Sibylline Oracles III:767 and the Ascension of Moses 10:1ff. may be cited. G. Klein, 'The Biblical Understanding of the kingdom of God', *Int* 26, 1972, p. 397, finds this surprising since the apocalyptists were most concerned with the end time.

present. It was against this kind of background that John the Baptist's announcement must be considered.

In view of the hypothesis that John the Baptist had contacts with the Qumran community, it is worth noting that this eschatological community pinned its hopes on the belief that God would intervene on their behalf and overthrow their enemies. The War Scroll suggests that they had in mind an earthly kingdom in which the Sons of Light would be victorious over the Sons of Darkness (those outside the Qumran community). If the scope of the kingdom was restricted, the Qumran covenanters had at least staunchly grasped that there were conditions attached to it. There was no question, however, of any of the covenanters doing as John the Baptist did in going out to the people and announcing its imminent approach. Their view was one of withdrawal and exclusiveness.

A more activist approach to the kingdom was adopted by the zealots, who regarded political action to be essential as a prelude to the dawning of the kingdom and did not hesitate to use the sword as a means to that end. During the first century many insurrections are known to have taken place connected with this movement. Their battle cry against the occupying power of the Romans was very different from John the Baptist's call for repentance. Although Jesus chose a man who may have been a member of the zealots as one of his disciples,[9] his concept of the kingdom was so essentially different from their ideas that it is impossible to maintain any parallels between the two movements, and certainly impossible to suppose that Jesus was a revolutionary.[10] Nevertheless, it would be wrong to suggest that the zealots were wholly politically motivated, since they opposed the ruling powers on the grounds that they owned only God as king.[11] The movement, therefore, claimed a religious basis.[12]

Enough has been said to demonstrate the strong expectation of the kingdom among many groups, even if the character of the expectation varied from group to group.[13] It is clear that John's announcement of the imminence of the kingdom of God would not have fallen on unprepared ears.

---

[9] It is, of course, possible that Simon the Zealot had acquired a nickname because of his enthusiasm. In any case there is no evidence that the political movement of that name was known by it as early as the time of Jesus. Cf. R. T. France, *The Man they Crucified* (1975), pp. 23f., 108 n.2.

[10] For a contrary opinion, cf. S. G. F. Brandon, *Jesus and the Zealots* (1967). But cf. M. Hengel, *Was Jesus a Revolutionist?* (Eng. trans. 1971), for a careful sifting of the evidence.

[11] Cf. S. Mowinckel, *He that Cometh* (1956), pp. 280–345, for an examination of Jewish expectations of a national messiah.

[12] G. Klein, *op. cit.* p. 399, aptly remarks concerning the zealot's view of the kingdom – 'what kind of God's rule is it whose coming depends on the activity of *man*?' The zealots achieved only the destruction of Jerusalem and the paralysis of the social structures of Judaism.

[13] G. Klein, *op. cit.*, p. 398, mentions that in rabbinic literature the idea of kingship had become an abstraction. Attention was focused on the coming Messiah, not on the coming kingdom.

THE MISSION OF CHRIST

ITS ANNOUNCEMENT

It is necessary briefly to examine the contribution of John the Baptist because of his significance in all the gospels as a herald of the kingdom and of the Coming One.[14] As such he is the link between the old order and the new. He was not typical of Judaism. He was set apart from the scribes and Pharisees whom he criticized. His message was one of repentance in view of the coming kingdom. His whole tone was stern with judgment – the religious leaders are a brood of vipers, the axe is at the root of the trees and the destroying fires are ready (Mt. 3:7–10). When the kingdom came, it would bring with it a moral challenge which could not be ignored. Nevertheless the Coming One, who would be superior to John the Baptist, would also carry out a superior baptism. In place of John's water-baptism of repentance, the Coming One would baptize with the Spirit and with fire (Mt. 3:11; Lk. 3:16; but Mk. 1:8 omits the fire).

The precise nature of the baptism which would accompany the dawning of the kingdom is the subject of debate. Some see the 'fire' as original and 'the Spirit' as a later interpretation, influenced by the experience at Pentecost. This is because baptism with the Spirit was not a current messianic expectation.[15] If 'fire' was the exclusive reference, it would centre on the Coming One's mission as judgment. The same emphasis would be present if 'Spirit' were understood either as the 'breath' of the Messiah in judgment[16] or as the 'wind' which separates the chaff from the wheat.[17] On the other hand the 'Spirit' might refer to the Coming One's impact on believers and the 'fire' to his impact on his enemies.[18] What is important for our purpose is to note that the kingdom was connected with a specific act of God among men, especially connected with the activity of the Messiah.

THE EVIDENCE FOR A PRESENT KINGDOM

Jesus began his ministry with the announcement that the time had come and the kingdom of God was at hand (Mk. 1:14f.). This certainly supposes that with the coming of Jesus some event of great importance was about to take place. Indeed, as Mark includes this announcement at the beginning of the ministry, he clearly implied that the activity of Jesus was a manifestation of the kingdom. Although Judaism expected an eschatological kingdom there was no conception that this kingdom would break into the present except to bring the present to an end. The fact that Jesus taught men to expect a kingdom in the present while the existing situation con-

---

[14] For a fuller account of John the Baptist's work in preparation for the kingdom, cf. G. E. Ladd, *TNT*, pp. 34ff.; C. H. H. Scobie, *John the Baptist* (1964); C. H. Kraeling, *John the Baptist* (1951).

[15] Cf. V. Taylor, *Mark, ad loc.*

[16] Cf. Kraeling, *op. cit.*, pp. 61ff.

[17] Cf. C. K. Barrett, *The Holy Spirit and the Gospel Tradition* (1947), p. 126.

[18] Cf. J. D. G. Dunn, *Baptism in the Holy Spirit* (1970), pp. 8ff.

tinued introduced a new element into current expectations. By doing so Jesus sharply distinguished his teaching from that of Judaism. It is particularly important, therefore, to consider the evidence for this point of view.

In some senses the dawning of the Messianic age presupposed an innovation for the present. The OT prophets had prepared for this. The widespread conviction that Messiah's coming would be associated with signs presupposed a state of considerable activity in the present after Messiah had arrived. Jesus himself made claims akin to this at the commencement of the ministry when he spoke in the synagogue at Nazareth (*cf.* Lk. 4:16ff.).[19]

The most striking kingdom saying which stresses its present reality is found in Luke 17:20–21, 'The kingdom of God is in the midst of you' (*entos*).[20] Since this statement is Jesus' answer to a direct question put to him by the Pharisees regarding the coming of the kingdom, it must be taken as a specific reference to its present reality compared with the current emphasis on a future kingdom. It also brings out its non-political character. Jesus virtually says you cannot see this kingdom so as to point to it ('Lo, it is here' or 'there').[21]

Another passage which directly relates the coming of the kingdom to the present ministry of Jesus is Matthew 12:28 (=Luke 11:20). It concerns the controversy over Beelzebub casting out demons and follows the comment of Jesus that Satan cannot cast out Satan. The statement then reads, 'But if it is by the Spirit of God that I cast out demons, then the kingdom of God has come upon you' (Mt. 12:28). Luke has 'the finger of God' in place of 'the Spirit of God'. Both forms of the saying connect the dawning of the kingdom with exorcism, and regard the evidence of authority over evil spirits as evidence that the kingdom has arrived. There is here a strong contrast implied between the kingdom of God and the kingdom of Satan. This is in line with the spiritual conflict which is seen throughout the ministry of Jesus and reached its climax in the passion. While it is clear that Jesus must have meant a present arrival of the kingdom, it is equally clear that the exorcism of evil agencies is not a once for all event, but a continuing necessity. At last, the kingdom of darkness was being effectually challenged in the ministry of Jesus. It is no wonder the people marvelled at the authority of Jesus (*cf.* Mk. 1:27).

---

[19] Nevertheless, it should be noted, as E. E. Ellis, *Luke* (NCB 1966), p. 97, points out in this context, signs were not for the sceptic, but for the believer. This would explain why Jesus declined to respond to requests for signs from his enemies.

[20] For a detailed discussion on the meaning of *entos* here, *cf.* B. Noack, *Das Gottesreich bei Lukas. Eine Studie zu Luk 17:20-24* (Symbolae Biblicae Upsalienses 10, 1948). *Cf.* also C. H. Roberts, 'The Kingdom of Heaven', *HTR* 41, 1948, pp. 1ff., who makes *entos* mean 'at the disposal of'. W. G. Kümmel, *Promise and Fulfilment*, pp. 32ff., interprets the word to mean 'amongst'.

[21] H. Conzelmann, *The Theology of Saint Luke* (Eng. trans. 1960), pp. 120ff., discusses this passage but concludes that the precise meaning of *entos* is less important than is generally supposed. He rejects, however, the view that the kingdom is an immanent, spiritual entity. In a footnote on p. 107 Conzelmann suggests a parallel between *entos* here and *epi* in Lk. 11:20.

A third passage which must be noted is Matthew 11:11f. (=Lk. 7:28 and Lk. 16:16). After mentioning Jesus' saying about the relative position of John the Baptist in the kingdom, Matthew records the following, 'From the days of John the Baptist until now the kingdom of heaven has suffered violence, and men of violence take it by force.' Luke has the saying in a different context. A problem arises over the meaning of the words, but there can be no doubt about the present reality of what is being described. What, however, is meant by the kingdom suffering violence? An alternative understanding of the verb as middle instead of passive would lead to a different interpretation (*i.e.* 'has been coming violently').[22]

Whichever is right, the problem still remains over the interpretation of the violence. Certainly the kingdom was not being established by physical or political force.[23] John the Baptist had suffered at the violent hands of Herod and since he was the herald of the kingdom, the kingdom could in that sense be said to have suffered violence. But the statement means more than that, since the activity has continued. It seems most likely that the verb must be understood in a bad sense[24] as this would be its normal meaning, in which case it is hostility towards the kingdom which is being stressed.

Some, however, take the verb in the sense of determination, and regard the men of violence as men displaying energetic endeavour to enter the kingdom.[25] A variant of this is the idea that those wanting to enter the kingdom must be as much in earnest as the violent men of Palestine.[26] Yet another view is that which sees Luke's saying as implying a lowering of the standard of entry to the kingdom from the Pharisaic point of view, irrespective of conditions and therefore amounting to forcing entry.[27] It is significant that none of these interpreters has attempted to explain the saying from an eschatological point of view,[28] and we may accept it as

---

[22] For a careful analysis of possible explanation of this 'violence' passage, *cf.* G. E. Ladd, *The Presence of the Future*, pp. 158ff., who considers that an interpretation which regards the verb as middle rather than passive is to be preferred. He understands the saying to mean, 'The Kingdom of heaven acts powerfully and requires a powerful reaction' (p. 163). For others supporting a similar view, *cf.* R. Schnackenburg, *God's Rule and Kingdom* (Eng. trans., 1963), p. 129f.; R. Otto, *The Kingdom of God and the Son of Man* (Eng. trans., 1938), pp. 108ff.

[23] E. E. Ellis, *Luke, ad loc.*, mentions the possibility that Jesus is refuting zealot methods.

[24] *Cf.* F. V. Filson, *Matthew (BC*, 1960) *ad loc.*, and D. Hill, *Matthew (NCB* 1972), *ad loc.* Hill argues on the strength of the parallelism in the two clauses.

[25] So W. Hendriksen, *Matthew* (1973), *ad loc. Cf.* also G. B. Caird, *Luke (1963), ad loc.*

[26] *Cf.* L. Morris, *Luke (TNTC*, 1974), *ad loc.*

[27] So F. W. Danker, *Jesus and the New Age* (1974), p. 175; *idem*, 'An Opposition Logion', *JBL* 77, 1958, p. 235. Danker takes it that the *biastoi* were Jesus' followers as seen through the eyes of their opponents. H. Conzelmann, *The Theology of St Luke*, p. 112, thinks the saying refers to those who wanted to bring in the kingdom by force. *Cf.* I. H. Marshall's discussion of the meaning in Lk. 16:16, *Luke: Historian and Theologian* (1970), p. 130. He makes some incisive criticisms of Conzelmann's position.

[28] Yet *cf.* A. Schweitzer, *The Quest of the Historical Jesus* (Eng. trans. ³1954), who built his eschatological theory upon it.

generally agreed that Jesus saw his present ministry in terms of the present arrival of the kingdom of God.

A saying of Jesus in Matthew 21:31 is relevant here: 'the tax collectors and the harlots go into the kingdom of God before you', addressed to the religious leaders. The present tense shows the present reality of the kingdom and the whole statement vividly contrasts the conception of the kingdom held by Jesus with that of the religious leaders. Those whom the latter despised as social outcasts were already becoming members of the kingdom. Since the saying must be related to the ministry of Jesus, it is a further indication that he was maintaining that the kingdom had already begun.

THE EVIDENCE FOR A FUTURE KINGDOM

Over against the passages just quoted must be set the teaching of Jesus that the kingdom is not yet. There are many indications in the words of Jesus that he was thinking ahead to a time when the end time would be reached. This idea finds its climax in the so-called eschatological discourse (Mt. 24—25; Mk. 13; Lk. 21). In this block of teaching[29] there is much emphasis on events to come, culminating in the coming of the Son of man in glory (*cf.* Mk. 13:24ff.), but there is a conspicuous absence of any mention of the kingdom. Indeed the only specific reference to 'a kingdom prepared for you from the foundation of the world' occurs in Matthew 25:34 as part of the passage about the sheep and the goats. It follows after the coming of the Son of man and is clearly concerned with the end time. We also note the expression 'the gospel of the kingdom' in the same discourse (Mt. 24:14). If the whole of the eschatological discourse relates to the future kingdom, it will be seen that Jesus attaches considerable importance to the idea.

For supporting evidence for a future view of the kingdom, we may turn our attention to the Beatitudes where many references to kingdom benefits are introduced with verbs in the future tense. The kingdom is said to belong to the 'poor in spirit' (Mt. 5:3), *i.e.* in the present, but other Beatitudes look ahead to future fulfilment – the promise of comfort, of inheriting the earth, of obtaining mercy, of seeing God. Although the 'blessed' people are already in possession of the kingdom, there is a fuller consummation yet to come. There is no question of the kingdom being easily established, for the eighth Beatitude predicts persecution, which is

[29] Since Mk. 13 is considered to be the basis for the eschatological discourse material, it is of prime importance to establish its authenticity if the evidence is to be cited as the teaching of Jesus. G. R. Beasley-Murray, *Jesus and the Future* (1954), argues cogently for its basis in the authentic words of Jesus. N. Perrin, *The Kingdom of God in the Teaching of Jesus* (1963), pp. 130ff., finds Beasley-Murray's position unconvincing. *Cf.* also D. Wenham's articles 'Recent Study of Mark 13: Parts 1 and 2', *TSF Bulletin* 71, 1975, pp. 6ff.; 72, 1975, pp. 1ff.

then said to be in line with what the prophets had already endured (*cf.* Mt. 5:12).

The prayer, 'Thy kingdom come, thy will be done' has both a present and a future application. If the kingdom were wholly present, the request for its coming in the Lord's Prayer would lose much of its force.[30] In Matthew 7:21f. Jesus refers to 'that day' (*i.e.* a reckoning day in the future), when commenting on entry to the kingdom, and this points to a future event. Similarly the coming banquet, at which the patriarchs, Abraham, Isaac and Jacob, will be among the guests, will be attended by many from various parts of the world, but the 'sons' (*i.e.* Jews) will be excluded (Mt. 8:11; Lk. 13:28, 29).

As compared with evildoers whose fate is 'the furnace of fire', the righteous will 'shine like the sun in the kingdom of their Father' (*cf.* Mt. 13:42, 43). When the Son of man comes in his kingdom, it will be with glory (Mt. 16:27–28). The similar saying in Mark speaks of the kingdom coming with power (Mk. 9:1). A future aspect may have been in mind, but there are various alternative interpretations of this passage, so that some reserve must be exercised. Nevertheless the occasion when the sons of Zebedee and their mother sought places of privilege in the kingdom must be interpreted of a future kingdom, although in this case a totally wrong conception of the kingdom was in their minds (Mt. 20:21; *cf.* Mk. 10:37 which speaks of glory rather than the kingdom).

There is another reference to 'that day' in Matthew 26:29 (*cf.* Mk. 14:25; Lk. 22:18) when Jesus speaks of refraining from drinking the fruit of the vine until he drinks it with his disciples in his Father's kingdom. Enough has been said to demonstrate that future aspects of the kingdom were constantly present in the mind of Jesus. But we must now note the various ways in which scholars have attempted to resolve the two aspects of the kingdom, present and future.

THE PROBLEM OF THE DUAL ASPECT OF THE KINGDOM

If the two aspects are considered to be mutually exclusive, there are clearly two main interpretations which can be proposed: either the future concept is right and the present aspects must be reinterpreted or in some way excised from the text; or the present is dominant and the future references must be explained away.

The most influential advocates of the 'present kingdom' idea were the nineteenth-century liberal school and their successors. Since this school of thought was concerned to present a portrait of Jesus in history,[31] all ref-

---

[30] *Cf.* E. Lohmeyer, *The Lord's Prayer* (Eng. trans. 1965), pp. 88–110, who speaks of the coming in terms of an imminent 'tomorrow' (p. 99). He points out, however, that 'coming' in both OT and NT often refers to divine things and events, and suggests that the coming of earthly things and events is only derivative (p. 94).

[31] *Cf.* A. Harnack, *What is Christianity?* (Eng. trans. ⁵1958).

erences to a kingdom in the future became irrelevant. The social gospel[32] sought to establish the kingdom here and now. There was no place for a coming Son of man and his kingdom at the end of the age. It was excised in the same way as all references to the supernatural. It was this complete suppression of all teaching on the future which precipitated the reaction of the thoroughgoing eschatological school (see below).

Two British scholars who belong to the rearguard of this kind of approach are T. W. Manson and C. H. Dodd. The former considered that the kingdom was present and consisted of doing the will of God on earth here and now.[33] This was not only the mission of Jesus, but was the commission of the church. If all could be persuaded to obey God's will, the consummation of the kingdom would have happened and any eschatological concepts fade into the background.[34]

C. H. Dodd's solution was rather different, for he contended that Jesus preached only a present kingdom and the supposed references to a future kingdom must be understood in an already realized sense (hence realized eschatology).[35] By means of this device and by denying the genuineness to Jesus of some of the future sayings, or regarding them as symbolic, Dodd considered that he had established his point. What future he admitted related to the day of the Son of man, not to the kingdom. But the unsatisfactory character of Dodd's method of handling the futurist evidence has been criticized.[36] Dodd certainly made an important point, however, in establishing that the 'present' texts show that God was inaugurating his rule through the ministry of Jesus.

We turn next to the view that the kingdom was wholly eschatological and has no present application. The classic examples of this kind of approach are J. Weiss[37] and A. Schweitzer,[38] both of whom reacted violently against the exclusion of eschatological considerations in the liberal 'lives of Jesus'. Their school of thought is often known as 'consistent eschatology'. Schweitzer is the most thorough-going in his contention that Jesus expected the future kingdom to be set up in his lifetime and that he was utterly disillusioned when instead he was placed on trial and then crucified. Every-

---

[32] For an exposition of the social gospel, *cf.* F. C. Grant, *The Gospel of the Kingdom* (1946). *Cf.* also J. W. Bowman, *Prophetic Realism and the Gospel* (1955), who emphasizes relationships.

[33] T. W. Manson, *The Teaching of Jesus* (³1945). *Cf.* also W. Manson, *Jesus the Messiah* (1943).

[34] Even more radically non-eschatological was the theory of A. T. Cadoux, *The Theology of Jesus* (1940), whose one theme was that people must seize the opportunity to follow Jesus in serving him. But by cutting off the kingdom idea from future explanations, Cadoux divorced it from its Jewish apocalyptic antecedents. *Cf.* Lündstrom's comments, *The Kingdom of God in the Teaching of Jesus*, pp. 105ff.

[35] C. H. Dodd, *The Parables of the Kingdom*, (1941); *idem*, *The Apostolic Preaching and its Developments* (1936).

[36] *Cf.* W. G. Kümmel, *Promise and Fulfilment* (1957), and H. Ridderbos, *The Coming of the Kingdom* (Eng. trans. 1962), pp. 38ff.

[37] J. Weiss, *Jesus' Proclamation of the Kingdom of God* (1892, Eng. trans. 1971).

[38] See n. 28 above.

thing was bent to fit in with this theory. The ethical teaching, for instance, came to be regarded as an *Interimsethik*,[39] a temporary code of rules until the establishment of the kingdom. Schweitzer's theory gained little support because of its one-sided character,[40] but the importance of the eschatological aspect had some effect on R. Bultmann,[41] who regarded Jesus as an apocalyptic prophet who expected the imminent arrival of the kingdom. This opinion has been followed by others, such as M. Werner[42] and R. H. Fuller,[43] both of whom maintain that Jesus taught an eschatological and not a present kingdom.

In view of the diametrically opposite positions taken up by the two schools of thought outlined above, and because each in turn is obliged to explain away the evidence on which the other is based, it is reasonable to seek for an interpretation which will not necessitate the excision of any of the evidence. Such a solution would clearly need to offer a satisfactory explanation of the dual aspects. It is admittedly a difficult problem, but there is no insuperable reason why what is now present might not reach its full culmination only in the future.

As Ladd expresses it, God is both *now* king and must *become* king, in a way paralleled in the OT and rabbinic Judaism.[44] He has no hesitation in maintaining that both present and future aspects are integral to a right understanding of Jesus' teaching about the kingdom. 'Jesus' message is that in his own person and mission God has invaded human history and has triumphed over evil, even though the final deliverance will occur only at the end of the age.'[45] Stauffer sees the present and future combined through a new approach to time which he finds in the Christian approach.[46] To him the ministry of Christ consists of an attack on the earthly kingdom of evil, which must find some expression in the present, even if the final overthrow is not yet. Cullmann's approach[47] is somewhat similar for he sees in Jesus the tension between the present and the future, the latter being

---

[39] *Cf.* A. Schweitzer, *The Mystery of the Kingdom of God* (1956), p. 55, where he uses this term to describe the teaching of the Sermon on the Mount. *Cf.* also *The Quest of the Historical Jesus* (Eng. trans. ³1954), p. 352.

[40] Among German scholars Schweitzer gained practically no support, although his views received rather more favourable notice among English scholars (*e.g.* W. Sanday, *The Life of Christ in Recent Research*, 1907, and F. C. Burkitt, *The Gospel History and its Transmission* ³1911).

[41] R. Bultmann, *TNT* 1, p. 22.

[42] M. Werner, *The Formation of Christian Dogma* (Eng. trans. 1957).

[43] R. H. Fuller, *The Mission and Achievement of Jesus* (1954). R. G. Hiers, *The Historical Jesus and the Kingdom of God* (1973), expounds the theory that Jesus believed that the present world was about to end. The coming of the Son of man, the judgment and the kingdom would all soon take place.

[44] G. E. Ladd, *TNT*, pp. 61ff. *Cf.* also his *Crucial Questions about the Kingdom of God* (1952), pp. 63ff.

[45] *Idem*, *TNT*, pp. 67f. Jeremias, *NTT*, 1, pp. 96–108, adopts a view very similar. He speaks of Jesus' proclamation of the dawn of salvation.

[46] E. Stauffer, *NTT* (Eng. trans. 1955), pp. 123ff.

[47] O. Cullmann, *Christ and Time* (Eng. trans. 1951), pp. 144–174.

418

both already fulfilled and yet still expected. For Kümmel[48] the presence of the kingdom exists only in the person and activity of Christ, in whom what is essentially future becomes apparent in the present. Ridderbos[49] declines to speak of two separate kingdoms, one present and one future, but speaks rather of one great coming kingdom of the future which penetrates the present.[50] There seems every reason to suppose that some such view is correct and that the mission of Jesus is in some way bound up with the coming of the kingdom.

ASPECTS OF THE KINGDOM

It is important to attempt some definition of the limits of the kingdom. Although it forms a major part of the teaching of Jesus in the synoptic gospels, the kingdom concept is only part of his total explanation of his mission. It brings out certain aspects which throw light of what he came to accomplish, which explains why the teaching is being considered in the section on the work of Christ.

(i) It may seem unnecessary, because too obvious, to point out the *theocentric* character of the kingdom. Yet this is of fundamental importance in understanding the mission of Jesus. It is essentially the kingdom of God, which means that God is its prime mover and instigator. There is no question of man inventing the kingdom or promoting it. It is infinitely more than an invitation to humanitarian action. However much it may stimulate human response, it is essentially the sovereign activity of God. There is nothing democratic about it. Man is not even invited to comment on it. It is simply announced as a *fait accompli*. God has acted in history. It cannot be over-emphasized that the theocentric interpretation of the kingdom acts as a corrective to much of the man-centred interpretations of the mission and relevance of Jesus. The social gospel as expounded by its liberal advocates took insufficient account of the God-centred character of the kingdom and hence presented an unacceptable picture.[51] The kingdom as expounded by Jesus makes great demands on men (utmost self-denial), which are not flattering to man's ego. He would prefer a type of teaching which required him to apply himself to the construction of a wholly Christian society. But not only is this opposed to the plain teaching of Jesus on the kingdom; it is contrary to man's experience. The kingdom,

---

[48] W. G. Kümmel, *Promise and Fulfilment*, pp. 141–154.

[49] H. Ridderbos, *The Coming of the Kingdom*, p. 55.

[50] G. Klein, *Int* 26, 1972, p. 404, deduces from the chronological tension that the kingdom is 'a power which bursts history asunder: though wholly future, in its effects it is already fully present'.

[51] G. Lundström, *The Kingdom of God in the Teaching of Jesus*, pp. 17ff., discusses the social interpretation of the kingdom. He shows that although statements were made implying that the kingdom is God's, the emphasis falls on the necessity for man's co-operation with God in establishing the kingdom on earth.

as Ridderbos remarked, is 'absolutely transcendent in its origin, it is the revelation of God's glory.'[52]

(ii) Another factor is its *dynamic* quality. This arises out of its theocentric character. What God originates cannot suffer from weakness or ineffectiveness. The kingdom is in no sense an experiment. It is no less than the coming of the king. When commenting on the casting out of demons by the finger of God (Lk. 11:20–22), Jesus describes the present existence of the kingdom in the form of a parable in which a stronger than the armed strong man overcomes, a dynamic conception of Jesus' ministry. It is only when the work of Jesus is seen in terms of a powerful overthrowing of demonic forms that the true spiritual dimensions of his mission can be grasped. The remarkable statement of Jesus following the return of the seventy sums up this dynamic aspect: 'I saw Satan fall like lightning from heaven' (Lk. 10:18). There is something intensely active about the coming of the kingdom in the ministry of Jesus. It involves his total activity – but especially the exorcisms.

(iii) It is important to discuss the *messianic* character of the kingdom, for the messianic role of Jesus must in some ways be linked to the announcement of the kingdom. This messianic emphasis comes out clearly in Luke's birth narratives in the angelic announcement about Jesus which calls him the Son of the Most High, who will occupy the throne of David and whose kingdom will never end (Lk. 1:32–33). In the song of Zechariah, Messiah is referred to as 'a horn of salvation for us in the house of his servant David' (Lk. 1:69). But in both these cases it is the motif of the Davidic kingdom which is in mind. It is basically national. It is in the announcement of John the Baptist that a more specific link is seen between the Messiah and the kingdom of God, although the Messiah is not so called, but merely described as 'him who is coming after me' (Mt. 3:11; Mk. 1:7). What is clear is the supra-national character of the Coming One who will act in judgment, with axe and winnowing fan in his hand.

To demonstrate the connection between the Messiah and the kingdom, it is necessary merely to draw attention to the inseparable connection between the kingdom and the Son of man in many of the sayings, taking Son of man in the sense already discussed as a substitute for Messiah (see pp. 281f.). This is especially true of those Son of man sayings which relate to the future. The most striking evidence for this is seen in a comparison of Matthew 16:28 and Mark 9:1, where Matthew has the idea of 'Son of man coming in his kingdom' and Mark has 'the kingdom of God coming with power.' The Son of man operates only within the kingdom.

If the dual aspect of the kingdom, as suggested above, is valid, it will also go some way to explain why the Son of man sayings are also partially

---

[52] Ridderbos, *op. cit.*, p. 24.

present and partially future. What comes out most clearly from these considerations is that the concept of the kingdom is strongly dominated by the person of Jesus. This means that his awareness of the kingdom can be understood only through his messianic consciousness. In referring to the kingdom itself as messianic, we mean to suggest that Jesus the Messiah as God's agent is acting on his behalf. It is for this reason that both the person and work of Christ are of vital importance in defining the limits of the kingdom.

(iv) Another important aspect of the kingdom is its connection with *salvation*.[53] With the coming of the kingdom, God shows his kingly activity in reaching out to save and bless his people. The miracles of healing, which are seen as motivated by the compassion of Jesus, are an evidence of his desire to bless. Similarly the exorcisms were demonstrations of God's kingly power through the ministry of Jesus (*cf.* Lk. 11:20). But it is the blessing of forgiveness of sins which is most prominent in the proclamation of the kingdom (*cf.* Lk 5:20, 21). This was granted by Jesus, although it was recognized to be the prerogative of God. There is no denying that it shows the activity of God in a powerful way in the ministry of Jesus. Later, in the proclamation of early Christians recorded in Acts, the forgiveness theme was of major importance, but God's offer of forgiveness was already taking place in Jesus' lifetime.

Other aspects which might reasonably be dealt with under this general heading, such as Jesus' concern for the poor and needy or his love for outcasts, will be dealt with later under the section on social ethics (pp. 940ff.). But it should here be noted that for Jesus the kingdom idea was far from abstract. It embraced many aspects of human need.

MEMBERSHIP OF THE KINGDOM

A distinction must at once be made between those who will respond to the challenge of the kingdom and those who will not. There is no evidence to suppose that all would respond to its claims. Such parables as the Sower, and the Tares, for instance, show this kind of distinction. Jesus clearly did not suppose that the kingdom would be identified with all mankind. Some selective procedure is, therefore, operative, but what is it? The Beatitudes are restricted to those who display qualities like meekness, mercifulness and purity, which are certainly not natural to all men. Indeed, if they stood isolated from the rest of Jesus' teaching, there would be some excuse for imagining that the kingdom was out of reach of most and was reserved for a spiritual élite. They occur in a context in which those addressed are declared to be the light of the world.

[53] For a discussion of the salvation theme in relation to the kingdom in Luke's gospel, *cf.* I. H. Marshall, *Luke: Historian and Theologian* (1970), pp. 128–141.

Some commitment to Jesus himself is demanded in such sayings as Matthew 16:24 (cf. 10:38), where the followers must also be cross-bearers. Such must develop entirely new values in which world-gaining becomes of no importance compared with losing life for the sake of Jesus. The commitment is to be so complete that allegiance to Jesus and his kingdom takes precedence even over family ties (Mt. 10:37). Moreover, Jesus did not permit any compromise. Those who were ashamed of him now, the Son of man would be ashamed of in the coming kingdom (Mk. 8:38). From the rich young man Jesus demanded the surrender of his worldly wealth, although in his case it was undoubtedly because he attached too much importance to it (Mk. 10:17ff.). Jesus demanded a responsiveness to the kingdom as a prerequisite for entry, as is clear from his statement that the kingdom of God belongs to children and entry requires a child-like spirit (Mk. 10:13–16). Such a condition entirely rules out any political concept. An attitude of willingness to listen and to obey is essential.

In the passage about the sheep and the goats another feature is introduced, for the kingdom is prepared for those who have accepted some social responsibility and showed compassion on the hungry, ill-clad, imprisoned and homeless (Mt. 25:31ff.). Does this imply that works of compassion are a passport to the kingdom and that no personal commitment to the king is needed? If this passage stood in isolation that might be a fair deduction, but it seems to be a corrective for those who imagined that social compassion was no part of the kingdom.[54] It is not entry qualifications which are in view, but the essential character of the members of the kingdom – a community of those who care for others as well as for themselves.

THE MYSTERY OF THE KINGDOM

There is in the teaching of Jesus about the kingdom an air of mystery which is particularly evident in the parables of the kingdom.[55] One of the reasons why Jesus spoke in parables was to convey that sense of mystery. The passage in which he gives his reason for his use of parables (Mt. 13:10–

[54] G. E. Ladd, *The Presence of the Future*, pp. 316f., sees the meaning of this passage as confined to showing that the final destiny of all men will depend on the way they respond to Jesus' representatives. Ladd spells out his argument in greater detail in his article, 'The Parable of the Sheep and the Goats in Recent Interpretation', in *New Dimensions in NT Study* (ed. R. N. Longenecker and M. C. Tenney, 1974), pp. 191ff. Cf. also J. Mánek, 'Mit wem identifiziert sich Jesus (Matt 25:31-46)? in *Christ and Spirit in the New Testament* (ed. B. Lindars and S. S. Smalley, 1973), pp. 15-25.

[55] A. Jülicher, *Die Gleichnisreden Jesu* (²1910), did not see the parables as illuminating the kingdom theme. They were interpreted rather as moralizing stories. C. H. Dodd, *The Parables of the Kingdom* (1935, ⁴1948), strongly maintained the eschatological importance of the parables, although the eschatology was in his view already realized. The setting is the present ministry of Jesus. J. Jeremias, *The Parables of Jesus* (Eng. trans. ²1963), modifies Dodd's position by insisting that the parables have both a present and a future reference. For a survey of approaches to the interpretation of the parables, including more recent German and American schools of interpretation, cf. N. Perrin, *Jesus and the Language of the Kingdom*, pp. 89–193.

17; *cf.* Mk. 4:10–12; Lk. 8:9–10) is notoriously difficult, because it seems to suggest that parables were intended to obscure the truth from the common people. But such a view does not rightly understand the meaning. The fact that some do not understand the secrets of the kingdom is in line with what has just been said about the membership of the kingdom. It requires a responsive attitude of mind, a desire to unravel the real meaning of the parables, a determination to come to terms with them. Without such an attitude the parables fall on deaf ears.

This principle of interpretation of the mystery of the kingdom is important for an understanding of each individual parable. The meanings may not be immediately clear, but the mystery is now known to the disciples of Jesus. Our purpose here is to summarize the main features of the kingdom as seen in those parables which concentrate on the kingdom teaching.

We may first note the development of the kingdom. The growth idea occurs in several parables, those of the sower, the tares, the mustard seed. In the first of these the different soils represent different responses to the same seed (= the Word of God). By means of this parable Jesus illustrates his own conception of the success of his public ministry, only one type of soil out of four being productive. That part which is productive is remarkably so, for some seed yielded an unprecedented return of a hundredfold. Here is combined both the success and limitation of the mission of Jesus. The parable of the tares is also assuming the certain growth of the kingdom, but it focuses on the difficulties of defining the limits of membership of the kingdom in the present. In the interpretation of this parable recorded by Matthew (13:36ff.),[56] there is a definite emphasis on the future kingdom when the righteous will shine like the sun.[57]

By means of the parable of the mustard seed (Mt. 13:31f.; Mk. 4:30–32; Lk. 13:18–19), Jesus turned his disciples away from its inconspicuous beginnings and pointed out the amazing growth which would follow. In this way the present, represented by a very small seed, is related directly to the future, represented by a very large tree. This speaks eloquently of Jesus' remarkable assurance of the ultimate success of his mission.

Some difficulty surrounds the interpretation of the parable of the leaven

---

[56] It is widely supposed that the interpretation of the parable of the tares is not authentic. *Cf.* J. Jeremias, *op. cit.*, pp. 81ff.; W. G. Kümmel, *Promise and Fulfilment*, pp. 132ff. Both these scholars attribute the interpretation to Matthew himself. D. Hill, *Matthew*, p. 235, is much more cautious and suggests that while the elaboration may be Matthew's work, it is carried out on an authentic kernel. He sees Zph. 1:3 as the starting point of both parable and interpretation.

[57] Many scholars consider that in the interpretation of the parable of the tares, Matthew defines the church as the earthly kingdom – *cf.* G. Bornkamm, in *Tradition and Interpretation in Matthew* (ed. G. Bornkamm, G. Barth and H. J. Held, Eng. trans. 1963), pp. 43f.; J. Jeremias, 'Das Gleichnis vom Unkraut unter dem Weizen', *Neotestamentica et Patristica*: Freundesgabe für O. Cullmann (ed. W. C. van Unnik *et al.* 1962), pp. 59–63. But the setting in this passage is definitely at the end time and it therefore has a distinctly eschatological context.

(Mt. 13:33 = Lk. 13:20), since leaven normally has a bad connotation when used metaphorically (as in the 'leaven of the Pharisees'), but it serves as an apt illustration of the imperceptible character of the coming of the kingdom. It was present in dynamic activity,[58] but few realized that it was there. Some have taken the parable to mean that the kingdom will work imperceptibly until it permeates the whole of society, in which case the world will become identical with the kingdom.[59] This, however, presses a detail of the parable in a way which was not intended. The main lesson is that complete results may be obtained by inconspicuous methods,[60] a very different approach from the contemporary revolutionary tactics of the zealots.

Jesus was at pains to stress the incomparable value of the kingdom. It was so much a prize to be sought after that a man will sell everything to possess it (the parables of the treasure and pearl, Mt. 13:44–46). These parables suggest that its value is not appreciated by all. A rather different aspect is given in the parable of the net, where those who are unrighteous are mixed up with the righteous until the end time (Mt. 13:47–50), a state of affairs akin to that of the wheat and tares.

One parable suggests that the membership of the kingdom is not conceived of in nationalistic terms. The parable of the vineyard implies that the other tenants to whom the vineyard is given are not Jews but Gentiles, if this is the correct understanding of the saying 'The kingdom of God will be taken away from you and given to a nation producing the fruits of it' (Mt. 21:43).[61] The parable of the two sons shows the need for repentance and obedience (Mt. 21:28–32). Even tax-collectors and harlots will enter before the religious leaders if the former fulfil the conditions and the latter do not (verse 31). The point of the parable of the virgins seems to be a strong warning against ignoring or treating lightly the summons of the kingdom (Mt. 25:1–13). It is essentially future in its setting, but immediate in its challenge ('watch therefore'). A similar warning is contained in the parable of the marriage feast (Mt. 22:1–14).

These indications from the parables of the way in which Jesus himself thought about the kingdom show how strongly it formed the background

---

[58] The parable of the leaven as interpreted by Dodd is taken to mean that the ministry of Jesus mightily permeated the dead lump of Judaism, *The Parables of the Kingdom*, pp. 192f.

[59] So A Jülicher, *Die Gleichnisreden Jesu* 2, p. 578; R. Otto, *The Kingdom of God and the Son of Man*, p. 125.

[60] *Cf.* Kümmel, *Promise and Fulfilment*, p. 132.

[61] There is dispute over the authenticity of the parable of the vineyard. W. G. Kümmel, *op. cit.*, p. 83, argues that the parable could not have originated with Jesus because (i) Judaism did not know the messianic name (Son of God) and (ii) the transference of the promise to a new people is described as punishment for the murder of the son, whereas elsewhere Jesus links the punishment with rejection of his person without mention of his death. These reasons, however, are particularly unconvincing, since Jesus was not tied to contemporary Jewish ideas and rejection is certainly involved in the parable. For a defence of the parable, *cf.* A. M. Hunter, *Interpreting the Parables* (1960), pp. 116ff.

to his mission, even although it carried such an air of mystery for the hearers.[62] No approach to an interpretation of the death of Jesus can be considered adequate which does not set it against this background. The conviction that the kingdom was not only present, but would successfully progress to a climax, did not prevent Jesus from steadfastly setting his face towards the passion. There is no indication that there was anything incongruous in the two concepts. It must be considered certain that in some way his death was an integral part of his mission to inaugurate the kingdom. Any exposition of the kingdom theme, on the other hand, which by-passes the redemptive significance of the death of Jesus, is guilty of ignoring major evidence on the nature of the messianic task.

Some features which might reasonably have been dealt with under the theme of the kingdom, such as ethics, will be included in other sections.

The Johannine literature

In comparison with the synoptic gospels, the fourth gospel is astonishingly sparse in references to the kingdom. In fact there are only two passages where the idea occurs. In view of the dominance of such teaching in the synoptic gospels, some explanation is needed of the omission in John's gospel. If we suppose that John wrote to supplement the synoptic records, he could not have been ignorant of the frequency with which the kingdom teaching occurs in them. He appears to have avoided such sayings (except in the two passages) quite deliberately. He may have thought that enough had been said. On the other hand, he has specifically set out teaching which stresses eternal life in a manner parallel to the synoptic kingdom teaching. Nevertheless, we note that the two passages included are highly significant contributions to the total view of the kingdom.

The first passage comes in the dialogue between Jesus and Nicodemus (Jn. 3). The words of Jesus, 'Truly, truly, I say to you, unless one is born anew (or from above), he cannot see the kingdom of God' (Jn. 3:3), proved totally enigmatic to Nicodemus. The whole idea of rebirth was taken literally and therefore regarded with incredulity. But the idea of the kingdom did not perplex. There is no way of knowing what Nicodemus thought about it, but some notion of it must have been familiar.[63] As in the synoptics, the idea is introduced without explanation. But the statement

---

[62] In a sense the kingdom has continued to perplex and modern man has sought to find a way of adapting it. O. Cullmann, *Jesus and the Revolutionaries* (Eng. trans. 1970), suggests that Jesus' teaching must be adapted, because modern man does not think in terms of an imminent end of the world (p. 52). His idea of what that adaptation must involve is that reform of social structures must go hand in hand with individual conversions. But the question arises whether this adaptation remains true to the radical character of Jesus' teaching.

[63] R. Bultmann, *John* (Eng. trans. 1971), p. 134, remarks that Jesus replies to Nicodemus 'on the self-evident assumption that for the Jews the question of salvation is identical with the question of participation in the rule of God.'

here goes beyond the synoptics in linking regeneration with participation in the kingdom.

The second saying in the same passage is even more specific – 'Truly, truly, I say to you, unless one is born of water and the Spirit, he cannot enter the kingdom of God' (Jn. 3:5). In this saying it is more than a matter of 'seeing'. There can be no doubt about the entry qualifications. Moreover, the agency of the Spirit in regeneration shows clearly that a divine work is in mind (see the section on regeneration). This statement rules out of account any idea of the kingdom being the work of man. Every member must have submitted to a radical change that makes him a new creature. We need not discuss at this junction the problems associated with the interpretation of 'water' in the context, although some discussion of it will be included in a later section on baptism (see pp. 728f.). Spiritual regeneration, therefore, is seen to be indispensable as a condition of entry, or more precisely it forms the actual point of entry itself.

The other passage is the dialogue between Jesus and Pilate in John 18. Pilate asks, 'Are you the King of the Jews?' (verse 33), which leads Jesus to speak of his kingdom (RSV here has 'kingship') as not being of this world (Jn. 18:36). He is distinguishing between the political and spiritual interpretations of kingship, an idea fully in harmony with the synoptic evidence. Jesus goes on to admit being a king[64] and then adds, 'For this I was born, and for this I have come into the world, to bear witness to the truth' (18:37). This is a totally sublimated view of kingship. It was intended not to overwhelm but to testify. It is also wholly personal: '*My* kingdom'.

In addition to these two specific passages there are a few other allusions which must be included. Nathanael links the title 'King of Israel' with 'Son of God' in addressing Jesus (Jn. 1:49), and both titles were accepted by Jesus without protest. Whatever Nathanael may have conjured up in his own mind, Jesus knew himself to be a spiritual king and would interpret the title in this way.[65] The same title is again attributed to Jesus in John 12:13 ('Hosanna! Blessed is he who comes in the name of the Lord, even the King of Israel'[66]) on his entry into Jerusalem. None of the synoptic writers records the use of the title, but all present the entry as a royal event. Subsequent to Pilate's dialogue with Jesus over kingship, he insists on describing Jesus to the Jews as 'your king', and did not hesitate to include

---

[64] R. E. Brown, *John* (AB, 1966), pp. 853f., discusses Jesus' answer ('You say that I am a king'), and prefers to regard it not as an affirmative, but as a qualified answer (='It is you who say it, not I'). He cites the support of O. Merlier, *Revue des Études Grecques* 46, 1933, pp. 204ff. B. Lindars, *John* (NCB, 1972), p. 559, considers that John means to give the words a double sense - a denial of kingship in a political sense, and an avowal in the sense of his calling.

[65] Brown, *op. cit.*, p. 87, regards Nathanael as the 'genuine Israelite' and therefore representative of those who like him believe. The title King of Israel is therefore understood in this sense.

[66] The phrase 'even to the King of Israel' alludes to Zc. 9:9. Cf. B. Lindars, *op. cit.*, p. 423, who regards the insertion of the words as important for John's account of the trial.

'King of the Jews' in the inscription on the cross.[67] Unwittingly Pilate had drawn attention to a paradox. He who had taught much about the kingdom died a criminal's death, yet with a royal inscription. It is only John who mentions Pilate's obstinate refusal to amend the inscription.

Paul

The kingdom of God is not a major theme in Paul's letters, but there are in fact thirteen passages where the idea occurs. It is not as dominant for Paul as it is for Jesus. It is rather assumed than specifically stated. There are no definitions of it, although there are conditions which are laid down. Whereas Jesus frequently used parables to explain the kingdom, this is no longer necessary for Paul. Everyone is presumed to know what the kingdom is.

We note first those passages which express clearly what the kingdom is not, in contrast to what it is. It is not food and drink, but is righteousness and peace and joy in the Holy Spirit (Rom. 14:17). This is evidently a corrective for those who wrongly imagined that the kingdom was a matter for food taboos. In 1 Corinthians 4:20, it is denied that it is a matter of talk, in contrast to the opinion of those who relied on arrogant speech.[68] Members of the kingdom are expected to live lives worthy of God (1 Thes. 2:12).[69] All these passages seem to imply a present aspect of the kingdom. They also make clear its ethical demands.

There are several passages, however, which imply a future inheritance of the kingdom.[70] In 1 Corinthians 6:9–10 the idea of the kingdom-inheritance is used as a basis for a moral appeal. Paul sees the kingdom as designed for the morally pure ('you were washed, you were sanctified'), which excludes those who behave in an immoral or criminal manner. The same idea is found in Galatians 5:21, where the 'works of the flesh' exclude a person from the kingdom, and in Ephesians 5:5 where again immorality, impurity, covetousness exclude from the inheritance.[71] This latter passage

---

[67] Matthew and Mark both record the mockers using the title at the cross (Mt. 27:42 = Mk. 15:32).

[68] This contrast becomes meaningful against the Corinthians' claim to be already possessors of the kingdom and Paul's ironical denunciation of their claim.

[69] Some regard 1 Thes. 2:12 as fully eschatological; *cf.* H. Lietzmann – W. G. Kümmel, *An die Korinther 1-2* (*LHB* [5]1969), p. 22: E. Best, *1 and 2 Thessalonians* (*BC*, 1972), pp. 108f. Best suggests that the linking of 'kingdom' and 'glory' under one article implies the meaning 'glorious kingdom'. But it is better to see both a present reality *and* a future hope in this passage, *cf.* A. L. Moore, *1 and 2 Thessalonians* (*NCB*, 1969), p. 42.

[70] E. Lohse, *Colossians and Philemon* (Eng. trans. *Hermeneia*, 1971, from *KEK*, 1968), pp. 37f., maintains that when Paul mentions the kingdom of God he presupposes a future meeting. But such passages as 1 Cor. 4:20 and Rom. 14:17 would be against such a view.

[71] There is a close connection between Paul's expression about inheriting the kingdom and Jesus' words about entering the kingdom. R. Schnackenburg, *God's Rule and Kingdom*, p. 285, suggests that Paul may have been influenced in his choice of expression by the LXX ('inherit' occurs more than 50 times in Deuteronomy).

is significant because the kingdom is described as 'of Christ and of God'.[72] Inheritance of the kingdom is not available for flesh and blood (1 Cor. 15:50),[73] which presumably means it is not entered through human effort, but Paul does not enlarge on the thought.

He can talk about his 'fellow workers for the kingdom of God', assuming that the kingdom is the goal of his missionary work (Col. 4:11). In this case the kingdom seems to stand as a comprehensive term for God's activity on man's behalf. It must, however, be understood against the background of the reference in Colossians 1:13–14, where God is said to have 'transferred us to the kingdom of his beloved Son, in whom we have redemption, the forgiveness of sins'.[74] The transfer has been from the dominion of darkness. For the apostle, therefore, believers at once belong to a different kind of dominion, the antithesis of their previous state. Here we meet with the same kind of dynamic overthrow of the powers of evil as is found in the synoptic exorcisms. Paul has a different way of expressing it, but the basic concept is the same.

There are three other references in Paul's epistles to the kingdom, in all of which the idea appears to be future (2 Thes. 1:5; 2 Tim. 4:1, 18). There are clearly a wide variety of ways in which he uses the term.

In one passage (1 Cor. 15:24–28), which deserves special mention, Paul writes of Christ handing back the kingdom to the Father.[75] Although it will be considered later in the section dealing with the future (see pp. 809ff.), it is necessary to note here that the main thrust of the passage is that Christ is already reigning. No starting point of the reign is stated, but since the passage occurs in the midst of a discussion on the resurrection, it is reasonable to suppose that at his resurrection Christ began his reign.[76] This passage, therefore, emphasizes a present activity, while at the same time pointing to a future climax.

Another aspect of Paul's teaching about the kingdom of God, which is not as extensive as we might expect, is his strong emphasis on the lordship

---

[72] The linking of Christ with God in Eph. 5:5 shows the influence of Christology on Paul's view of the kingdom. M. Barth, *Ephesians 4-6* (*AB*, 1974), pp. 564f., admits the possibility that Eph. 5:5 could be translated 'the kingship of the Messiah, that is of God', in which case the passage would assert the deity of Christ. *Cf.* also F. Foulkes, *Ephesians* (*TNTC*, 1963), *ad loc.*

[73] For a discussion of this verse, *cf.* J. Jeremias, ' "Flesh and blood cannot inherit the kingdom of God" (1 Cor. 15:50)', *NTS* 2, 1955-6, pp. 151ff.

[74] C. K. Barrett, *From First Adam to Last* (1962), pp. 99ff., maintains that Paul distinguished between the kingdom of God (which was eschatological) and the kingdom of Christ (which refers to the reign between the resurrection and the parousia). R. Schnackenburg, *God's Rule and Kingdom*, p. 297, strongly denies any distinction between the two expressions.

[75] G. Klein, *Int* 26, 1972, pp. 406f., considers that in 1 Cor. 15:24 Paul is employing a previously existing Jewish idea of an interim messianic kingdom. He cites R. Bultmann, *TNT* 1 p. 306, and H. Conzelmann, *Der erste Brief an die Korinther* (*KEK* 1969), p. 319, in support. Yet Klein admits that Paul has made a transformation. The process of subduing enemies is already going on.

[76] Schnackenburg, *op. cit.*, p. 295, points out that this view is confirmed by Paul's use of Ps. 109(110):1 in 1 Cor. 15:25. A similar use is found in Acts 2: 34; Eph. 1:20; Col. 3:1.

of Christ (see pp. 295ff.). The exercise of lordship implies the exercise of a dominion which is closely akin to the idea of dynamic rule seen in the teaching of Jesus. Many similar ideas to that teaching are involved in the exposition of the lordship theme in the apostle's letters. This is another pointer to the close connection between the person and mission of Christ in NT teaching.

The rest of the New Testament

In the book of *Acts* the kingdom is several times mentioned as the subject of preaching and testimony (19:8; 20:25; 28:23). In the case of 19:8, this is followed in 19:10 by the expression 'the word of the Lord' which is more usual in Acts. The two expressions seem to be synonymous. Similarly in Acts 20:24–25, the kingdom is paralleled to the 'gospel of the grace of God', in Paul's address to the Ephesian elders. When he was a captive at Rome he was able to preach the kingdom of God and teach about the Lord Jesus Christ to all who came (Acts 28:31). He did the same when invited to address the Jews (Acts 28:23).

In the epistle to the *Hebrews* a case is made for the readers to be thankful that they have received an unshakeable kingdom, which suggests both a present experience and a future hope (Heb. 12:28). It is especially contrasted with the lack of stability in everything else. Moreover the epistle is permeated with the idea of inheritance.[77]

James mentions those who are 'rich in faith and heirs of the kingdom which he has promised to those who love him' (Jas. 2:5).[78] This occurs in a passage in which distinctions on the grounds of worldly wealth are condemned. Although James does not explain the kingdom,[79] it is reasonable to suppose that the expression was sufficiently well understood not to require elucidation.[80] It is, of course, possible to understand this in a purely Jewish sense, but the statement in James 2:1 giving the Lord Jesus Christ as the object of faith shows that it is intended in a Christian sense.

There is in *2 Peter* a reference to the provision for an entry into 'the eternal kingdom of our Lord and Saviour Jesus Christ' (2 Pet. 1:11),[81]

---

[77] For a fuller discussion of the kingdom idea in Hebrews, *cf.* R. Schnackenburg, *op. cit.*, pp. 322ff. He sees in this epistle a combination of the 'heavenly' and the 'eschatological' kingdom.

[78] The specific reference to those who love God in Jas. 2:5 is sufficient reason for rejecting the view that the kingdom is equated with the materially poor. James seems to imply, however, that the poor are more likely to be candidates for an inheritance in the kingdom. *Cf.* M. Dibelius and H. Greeven (Eng. trans. *Hermeneia*, 1976, from *KEK*, 1964), p. 137.

[79] C. L. Mitton, *James* (1966), p. 86, rightly sees the reference to the kingdom here as an evidence of James' faithfulness to the teaching of Jesus. Certainly the idea of inheriting the kingdom is paralleled in the synoptic records of Jesus' sayings (*cf.* Mt. 25:34).

[80] R. J. Knowling, *James* (*WC*, 1904), p. 46, reckoned that the expression 'heirs of the kingdom' would have been quite natural on the lips of a Jew. *Cf.* Mt. 8:12 for a similar phrase addressed to Jews.

[81] Schnackenburg, *op. cit.*, p. 325, sees the phrasing of 2 Pet. 1:11 as recalling the 'entry' passages in the synoptic gospels. He finds in 2 Peter the idea of the kingdom becoming 'the imperishable glory of heaven'.

where the allusion is wholly eschatological. Although *1 Peter* does not use the expression, there is nonetheless a reference to 'an inheritance which is imperishable' (1 Pet. 1:4).

There are more references to the kingdom in the book of *Revelation*. In Revelation 1:6 John states that Jesus Christ has made us a kingdom, which focuses on the members, *i.e.* those freed from sins through his blood.[82] And then in Revelation 1:9 he speaks of sharing with his readers who are 'in Jesus' the tribulation, the kingdom and the patient endurance. The present reality of the kingdom of God must here be in mind. It is subject to considerable pressure from the enemies of God, which is the characteristic theme of the whole book. The blowing of the seventh trumpet marks the point at which the kingdom of the world becomes the kingdom of our Lord and of his Christ (Rev. 11:15), an interesting instance of God and Christ being linked in the kingdom, an idea implicit in the synoptic teaching.[83] The dawning of the kingdom is the central theme of the liturgical passage which follows the seventh trumpet. A similar announcement of the kingdom is found in 12:10, again a heavenly voice. A pseudo-kingdom is set up by the Beast as a counterfeit to the kingdom of God, but its existence is strictly limited (chapter 17). The Apocalypse shows the triumph of the personalized Word of God, who has inscribed on his side the name King of kings and Lord of lords (19:16). In the New Jerusalem the throne of God and of the Lamb is central (22:1). In this vision is therefore fulfilled all the eschatological promises of the synoptic kingdom teaching (see the section on the future, pp. 868ff.).

In these various uses there will again be seen present and future ideas, and within these a rich variety. It is perplexing to discover considerably less references numerically to the kingdom outside the synoptic gospels than within them, but the incidental references which occur elsewhere show that the kingdom concept was continued in the ongoing church. In this respect the statement of Luke in Acts 1:3 is highly significant.[84] He makes clear that in the period of forty days between the resurrection and ascension of Jesus, Jesus appeared to them and spoke to them about the kingdom of God. He presumably gave them instructions about what to preach. And yet Luke in his record of the earliest Christian preaching

---

[82] In this statement it is probable that 'kingdom' is not intended in the sense of a kingdom consisting of priests, but kings and priests who made up the holy nation. *Cf.* G. R. Beasley-Murray, *Revelation* (NCB. 1974), pp. 57f.

[83] R. H. Mounce, *Revelation* (*NICNT*, 1977), p. 230, considers that the expression 'Our Lord and . . . his Christ' would not be appropriate for the church since their Lord is the Christ. But E. Lohmeyer, *Die Offenbarung des Johannes* (³1933), p. 95, points to the singular *basileusei* as showing the unity between Lord and Christ.

[84] F. F. Bruce, *The Acts of the Apostles* (²1952), pp. 67f., suggests that the teaching about the kingdom mentioned in Acts 1:3 was intended to make clear the bearing of the crucifixion and resurrection on Jesus' message of the kingdom.

makes no reference to it. It must be assumed that there were many other concepts into which the main kingdom teaching of Jesus was translated. The absence of the name is no indication of the absence of the fundamental idea. Preaching about Jesus was preaching about the kingdom, because Jesus himself was proclaimed as king. This is the explanation of the Jewish charge against the Christians at Thessalonica (Acts 17:7), when they asserted that Christians held to another king, Jesus.

Concluding comment

In view of the variety of ideas concerning the kingdom which have been thrown up in the course of our examination of the evidence, it would not be surprising if no clear conception of its meaning has emerged. Much of the difficulty which has dogged the debate over the kingdom in the teaching of Jesus has arisen from the assumption that it should be possible to tie it down to a specific meaning. The use of such phrases as the concept of the kingdom or the idea of the kingdom have contributed to this assumption. It has been suggested, however, that kingdom should be regarded as a symbol rather than a single concept,[85] in which case its meaning will never be constant. There is much to be said for this suggestion, for it would facilitate an understanding of the kingdom wide enough to embrace all that is central to the teaching of the NT. It is then possible to see that not only the life of Jesus, but also his death is a part of the total significance of the kingdom. It is impossible, in short, to exhaust the meaning of the symbol. This explanation will lead into our next section which is a specific examination of the meaning of the passion of Jesus.

THE SAVING WORK OF CHRIST: PRELIMINARY CONSIDERATIONS

From our survey of the various aspects of the person of Christ in the NT it became evident that the early Christians were not merely interested in who Jesus was, but also in his activity. Indeed there is a close connection between these two ideas. Our present purpose will be to consider the categories under which either Jesus spoke of his work or his disciples expounded it. To do this we shall obviously need to bear in mind the connection between the teaching of Jesus and the developments seen later by the apostles. One event, the death-resurrection-ascension of Jesus, separated them. It will not be surprising that in the period before his death, Jesus did not give any extended explanations of how that event fitted into his mission. Nevertheless we find sufficient evidence to justify the contention that the apostles expounded the mission of Jesus in terms which

---

[85] *Cf.* N. Perrin, *Jesus and the Language of the Kingdom* (1976), pp. 29ff.

naturally follow from his own awareness of the purpose of his coming.

It must at once be recognized that the NT concepts used to express the mission of Jesus owe much to the cultural background of Jesus and his apostles. For this reason it is impossible to proceed intelligently without some attention to background studies. These will be included as a preface to each section where they are appropriate.

The method of arranging the evidence calls for some comment. Whilst a systematic presentation is indispensable to a full understanding of Christian thought, no such presentation is found in the NT; care must therefore be taken to avoid imposing on the scattered material categories which are alien to it. Such a process would almost certainly distort. Our procedure will be to begin with the idea of sacrifice which has its roots in Jewish thought; then to move on to those concepts where Greek ideas come into prominence, but where Jewish ideas are by no means absent, as for instance in reconciliation and redemption; and also to consider any which seem more specifically Greek, such as perfection and illumination. We shall find many aspects which belong more to a kaleidoscopic presentation than to a neat theory. Indeed, the NT shows as many facets of the work of Christ as of his person. All too often the classic statements of the atonement in the later church have attempted to squeeze the variegated material into a single too restricting mould; the NT does not do this.

Old Testament ideas associated with sacrifice

On no theme in NT theology is the Jewish background more important for a right understanding of Christian thought than the theme of sacrifice. It was an integral factor in man's approach to God under the Jewish system. It forms the core of the OT levitical cultus and colours many of the NT terms applied to the work of Christ in the NT. What is particularly significant is the meaning that the various sacrificial terms had in NT times, and also what meaning would at that time have been attached to the whole idea of sacrifice among the Jews.

There are certain *general features* which are clear. Sacrifice in the OT was a means by which man was enabled to approach God. The levitical priestly system contained five different kinds of offerings: the burnt offering, cereal offering, guilt offering, sin offering and peace offering. Each had its particular purpose and was intended to facilitate man in his relationship with God. Sacrifice was essentially viewed as a condition of the covenant. It was moreover instituted by God (*cf.* Lv. 17:11). It was, therefore, a provision of mercy. It was intended to enable man to draw near to God, not to keep him away. Many theories have been proposed to explain its function. Some see it as a gift, others as communion and yet others as the releasing of life.[86]

---

[86] For studies on the background to sacrifices, *cf.* G. B. Gray, *Sacrifice in the Old Testament* (1925); J. G. Frazer, *The Golden Bough* (⁹1949), ii. 3; V. Taylor, *Jesus and His Sacrifice* (1937), pp. 49ff.

Although no decision need be reached between these possibilities for our purpose, some consideration must be given to certain inadequate theories regarding OT sacrifice which have been used in the attempt to reach an understanding of the work of Christ.

It is maintained that sacrifices were not intended to be *propitiatory* in the sense of appeasing an angry deity. Certainly if this is the definition of propitiation, it must be agreed that it is absent from the OT and NT conceptions.[87] The OT certainly presents a God of judgment, who by his very nature can do nothing other than condemn sin. There is at once a barrier between man and God. The appeasement idea is mistakenly brought in from pagan practice, and it will not do to jettison the whole idea of propitiation simply because it was wrongly understood in pagan quarters. It cannot be dispensed with by interpreting the Greek word (*hilastērion*) as expiation. When the point mentioned above, that the sacrificial system is a provision of God's grace, is borne in mind, the idea of propitiation as appeasement will at once be seen to make nonsense. It must then be given another meaning and must involve some means that guarantees a gracious attitude from a holy God towards an approaching sinner (see the section on propitiation, pp. 468ff.). At the same time, the sacrificial system demanded man's cooperation, and some place for God's displeasure must be allowed if any Israelite showed his disobedience by failing to offer the appropriate sacrifice.[88]

A second contention is that the fundamental idea of the OT sacrifices was that the *blood* of sacrifice is the life and not the death of the victim. This is claimed to be supported by such passages as Leviticus 17:11, Genesis 9:4ff., Deuteronomy 12:23; Psalm 72:14. Undoubtedly these statements establish that blood was identified with life, but what precise meaning does this have in connection with sacrifice? Leviticus 17:11 states that 'I (*i.e.* God) have given it for you upon the altar to make atonement for your souls; for it is the blood that makes atonement, by reason of the life.' But for blood to be placed on the altar involves death, understood as the giving up of life. Moreover, on the majority of occasions when 'blood' is used in the OT, it involves some kind of violent death.[89] Whatever the meaning of the blood-life equation, it is impossible to deny that death is involved, and this is certainly a major factor in the meaning of 'blood' when applied to the work of Christ.

A third point is the significance of the *laying on of hands* in the scapegoat

---

[87] *Cf.* R. H. Culpepper, *Interpreting the Atonement* (1966), pp. 23ff.

[88] *Cf.* W. Eichrodt, *The Theology of the Old Testament* 1 (Eng. trans. 1961), pp. 165f., sees the laying on of hands in the OT sacrificial system as showing the willingness of the offerer to surrender what belongs to him. It was certainly an act of cooperation on the offerer's part.

[89] *Cf.* L. Morris's *The Apostolic Preaching of the Cross* (1955), pp. 108ff.; *cf.* also A. M. Stibbs, *The Meaning of the word 'Blood' in Scripture* (1947).

ritual. It is argued that this performance transferred guilt, but did not involve a sacrifice for the sins of the people, for the reason that the scapegoat was not killed, but only driven into the desert. Nevertheless, the goat was certainly identified with the sins of the people and in some sense carried those sins away. Some care must be taken when applying the ritual to the NT teaching about the work of Christ. Even if the scapegoat was not killed, its banishment was certainly sacrificial. The ritual of laying on of hands was required for the other main sacrifices also and was an act of identification of the offerer's sins with the offering.

Another important consideration is the idea of *covering of sins*, as this lies behind the idea of the sprinkling of the blood on the mercy seat by the high priest in the Leviticus ritual. The Hebrew word (*kipper*) which describes this covering has been much discussed.[90] In most cases some notion of covering-over is in view,[91] which naturally led to the idea of removing defilement. There is a close link, however, between this covering and the idea of propitiation (both coming from the same root in the LXX).

Even the briefest survey of the OT background to sacrificial concepts in the NT cannot ignore the *criticisms of the prophets*. Many times they call in question the way the people were observing the sacrifices, in terms which look at first sight like a complete repudiation of them (*cf.* Am. 5:21ff.; Is. 1:11; Mi. 6:7, 8; Je. 7:22). But these prophets were protesting about the abuse of the sacrifices as a mere ritual observance. If the attitude of the worshipper was not affected, the sacrifices themselves could be a hollow sham. There were moral requirements like justice and mercy which were being neglected, and it was this inconsistency which led to the prophets' criticisms.

This leads to some consideration of the main *weaknesses* of the sacrificial system, which are, in fact, echoed in the epistle to the Hebrews.

(i) The fact that sacrifices could be a mere ritual without any corresponding moral commitment of the worshipper was obviously a weakness. Yet it should be remembered that this was never the intention of the system.

(ii) Sacrifices were effective only for inadvertent sins and not for deliberate sins (sins with a high hand), and this clearly imposed a serious limitation upon them. Nevertheless the distinction goes some way to explaining the first weakness, since those who came with a rebellious spirit at once placed themselves outside the means of grace. The limitation was in this case in the mind of the would-be worshipper.

(iii) The victims of the sacrifices were passive and not active participants in the ritual. The moral element was lacking.

(iv) The inadequacy of the system is also seen in the fact that they had

---

90 *Cf.* C. H. Dodd, *The Bible and the Greeks* (²1954), pp. 82–95.
91 *Cf.* V. Taylor, *Jesus and His Sacrifice*, pp. 52f.

to be constantly repeated. They could, in fact, be effective only for sins already committed.

When we come to the NT, we are aware of this general background of sacrifice, of the use of concepts which were familiar in a Jewish setting and which must at an early stage have permeated into Gentile Christian thinking through the adoption of the LXX as Scripture. No doubt the ceremonial levitical ritual was a perplexity to newly converted Gentiles, but it may have been an equal perplexity to Jewish Christians, who wondered where it fitted into their new-found faith in Christ. In all probability the epistle to the Hebrews was intended to provide a satisfactory answer to such perplexity. The NT interpreter cannot without distortion appreciate the doctrine of the work of Christ, unless he gives pride of place to these essentially Jewish sacrificial ideas. He must beware of any appeal to pagan parallels unless he can satisfy himself that the NT writers were directly affected by such parallels. It cannot be too strongly stressed that the Jewish sacrificial system, with all its limitations, was nevertheless superior to pagan notions which had no moral or spiritual content.

Our next consideration must be the importance of the *covenant* since this is brought into the NT in the form of a new covenant. The basis of Yahweh's redemptive act for his people Israel was the old covenant. The root idea of a covenant is of an agreement between two equals, but this has to be modified when applied to God's dealings with Israel. Indeed the very fact that it was established on the basis of a redemptive act shows it to be an act of grace on God's part and not of merit on man's part. The old covenant was sealed with the blood of sacrifice (Ex. 24:3–11). It must be noted, however, that this covenant was no mere ritual enactment, for it carried with it moral demands, expressed in essence in the Ten Commandments. Throughout the OT God's redemptive act on behalf of his people is the inspiration of the pious. It forms the pivot for prophetic exhortations (*cf.* Ho. 11:1; 13:4; Is. 43:14–19; Ezk. 20:5; *cf.* also Pss. 68, 77, 114, 135, 136). It is the key to God's love for his people, his covenant love.[92]

Although the old covenant was a wonderful provision of God for his people, even within the OT a better covenant was predicted. The significant passage to this effect is Jeremiah 31:31, in which a covenant of an inner nature, written on people's hearts, is foreseen. This passage played an important part in NT thought (*cf.* especially Heb. 8). It undoubtedly lay behind the reference to the new covenant in the institution of the Lord's Supper. This inner nature of the covenant points to the ethical obligation of those under it. Those under the old covenant tended to disregard their responsibilities and it was a main task of the prophets to counteract this tendency. The new covenant was able to supply what the old lacked, *i.e.*

---

[92] *Cf.* N. Snaith, *The Distinctive Ideas of the Old Testament* (1944), pp. 94–130.

the power to enable people to live in a manner worthy of the salvation which God had provided.

THE SAVING WORK OF CHRIST: JESUS AND THE GOSPELS

The synoptic gospels

The mission of Jesus was inaugurated at his baptism. We have already discussed the significance of this in relation to the person of Christ (pp. 308f.). But it is relevant here to note the many important aspects of the mission which are in evidence in the account of the baptism and which illuminate that mission. The various messianic allusions like servant, Son of God and Spirit of God and the identification of Jesus with his people are all relevant to his public ministry. The fact that the mission was inaugurated in this way gives particular significance to the apparently disproportionate space that all the evangelists devote to the passion narratives.

In all the accounts of the mission of Jesus the cross stands out as the most important feature, and its significance is carried over into the rest of the NT. No understanding of the work of Jesus can be reached without coming to terms with his death. We have already seen that many of the Son of man sayings are connected with the theme of his suffering. The coming passion formed a basic ingredient in the consciousness of Jesus, and, this aspect must now be considered in more detail, first from the synoptic gospels and then from John's gospel.

INDICATIONS OF THE COMING DEATH

General indications. At the baptism of Jesus there was a clear awareness of a special mission, but no indication is given at that stage regarding its nature. In all the synoptic gospels, the unfolding of the passion is gradual. There is in Mark's gospel early indication of the intention of the religious leaders to kill him (Mk. 3:6). The plot against him was not something hatched up at the last minute. It was something that had been simmering throughout the ministry. Because he challenged some of the accepted religious practices of his day, he was at once in conflict with the custodians of the *status quo.* Seeing that Mark explains the opposition at an early stage in his gospel, it is not surprising that he devotes so much space to the passion narratives. Indeed, from a biographical point of view Mark's gospel is remarkably lopsided. It is as if the rest of the gospel is preparatory to the climax of the passion.[93] It must be supposed that for him the whole gospel

---

[93] M. Kahler, *Der sogenannte historische Jesus und der geschichtliche biblische Christus* ([2]1896), p. 80 n. 1, refers to passion narratives with extended introductions. *Cf.* G. Bornkamm, *Jesus of Nazareth,* p. 17, who approves of Kahler's description.

is a gospel of salvation, expressed more in historic act than in teaching.[94] The other synoptic gospels, although devoting less space proportionately to the passion, nevertheless show it unmistakably to be the climax towards which the preceding narrative inevitably moves.

Our major task is to discover what Jesus himself thought about his own death. Did he think of it as inevitable, because he conceived of himself as a prophet, and expected no better fate?[95] Or was he aware that death on the cross was an integral part of his mission without which the mission could not be effective? Or was he utterly disillusioned at the end? It is vital to give careful consideration to the evidence if adequate answers to these questions are to be found.

A saying of Jesus, which is placed early in all the synoptic gospels and is an answer to the Pharisees' question about his attitude to fasting, has some relevance to our quest. Jesus pointed out that wedding guests do not fast while the bridegroom is present, but when the bridegroom is taken away (Mk. 2:18–20; Mt. 9:14–17; Lk. 5:33–38). There have been various views as to the meaning of the bridegroom's removal. Some deny that there is any suggestion of violent removal, but the verb used (*aparthē*) would certainly support such a view. There can be no doubt that Jesus was thinking of himself as the bridegroom, and it is not improbable that his words contain a hint that some kind of violent death awaits him. There is no suggestion that relationships between the disciples and Jesus could continue as they were. A catastrophe which would separate them is plainly in view.

Another indirect allusion to the coming passion is the saying of Jesus that the Son of man would be three days and three nights in the heart of the earth, after the pattern of Jonah's three days and nights in the fish's belly (Mt. 12:40).[96] Luke's account omits the details and speaks only of the 'sign' to this generation, giving no indication of the content of the sign (Lk. 11:29–32). Matthew's more explicit account recognizes the nature of the parallel and can be understood only as an indirect reference to the death and resurrection of Jesus. It is highly unlikely that the scribes and Pharisees would have understood the allusion, but the saying is important because of the light it throws on Jesus' own consciousness of his approaching death.

---

[94] *Cf.* J. A. Allan, 'The Gospel of the Son of God crucified: Recent Study in the Gospel according to Mark', *Int* 9, 1955, pp. 131–143. *Cf.* R. H. Lightfoot *The Gospel Message of St Mark* (1950), p. 31.

[95] *Cf.* J. Jeremias, *NTT*, p. 280. But O. Cullmann, *The Christology of the New Testament*, p. 45, in his discussion of Jesus as a prophet, comments that 'conscious, vicarious suffering and dying is not a characteristic function of the eschatological prophet'. Clearly more is needed to explain the work of Christ than a prophet's exposure to martyrdom.

[96] D. Hill, *Matthew*, p. 220, suggests that this Jonah saying is concerned with judgment and death, not with deliverance and resurrection. It is to be noted that Luke's omission of any reference to Jonah's experience in the fish's belly places the emphasis on his preaching of judgment. But there is no denying that in Matthew's account, Jesus is drawing attention to his coming suffering. Hill thinks that the Jonah sign might be connected with the role of the servant of God to be a 'light to the Gentiles'.

The specific predictions of the passion. The first prediction was not made until after Peter's confession at Caesarea Philippi, which is significant since it follows from a right appreciation of the messianic office. Matthew specifically says that it was from that time that Jesus began to show his disciples that he must (*dei*) suffer and be killed and on the third day rise again (Mt. 16:21; *cf.* Mk. 8:31; Lk. 9:22).[97] The main difference between Matthew's account and the others is that whereas Mark and Luke record it as a Son of man saying, Matthew uses the direct personal pronoun. All the accounts, however, stress the necessity for the death. The Greek *dei* must not, however, be regarded in a fatalistic sense, but rather in the sense of being indispensable to the whole mission of Jesus.[98] This is the first indication that he regarded the passion as part of a divine plan. It is not reading too much into the expression here to recognize that the 'killing' is regarded as a prelude to the rising. In other words, the forecast was not made in a gloomy manner, but in the confident assurance that violent death would not be the end. There is a positive emphasis on the triumphant rising. It is not surprising, however, that the disciples failed to appreciate this aspect, and that Peter had to be rebuked for his attempt to correct what he detected mistakenly to be a defeatist attitude on the part of Jesus. To him there was a sense of unavoidable tragedy about death. But clearly Jesus thought differently.

The prediction was repeated soon after the transfiguration (Mt. 17:22, 23 = Mk. 9:30–32 = Lk. 9:43–45). All the synoptic writers make a point of noting the disciples' reactions. Matthew says they were greatly distressed, while Mark and Luke both say they did not understand and were afraid to ask. Luke actually adds that the understanding of it was concealed from them. The third prediction goes into more detail (Mt. 20:17–19 = Mk. 10:32–34 = Lk. 18:31–34; Luke has another prediction between the second and third, *ie.* Lk. 17:25), mentioning the mocking and the scourging. Matthew's account even specifies crucifixion as the method of death.

These predictions are generally regarded as a reading back after the event,[99] but in view of the evidence already examined for Jesus being Son of God as well as Son of man (see p. 301), the truly predictive element cannot be regarded as impossible. Indeed, the main problem is not so much whether or not Jesus could have foreseen the details, but why he chose at this stage to state the details as explicitly as he does. He clearly wanted to warn the disciples before his entry into Jerusalem in case they should form

---

[97] H. Conzelmann, *The Theology of St Luke*, p. 153, in dealing with Luke's presentation of redemptive history, acknowledges that his use of *dei* is the most important indication about the whole complex of ideas. He rightly states that in Luke the necessity of the Passion is fully brought out. G. Caird, *Luke* (²1968), p. 129, maintains that meditation on the Scriptures had brought Jesus himself to the conclusion that the Messiah must suffer. *Dei* ties up with the fulfilment motif.

[98] W. Lane, *Mark* (NICNT, 1974), p. 301, explains it of the over-ruling purpose of God.

[99] So J. Jeremias, *NTT*, pp. 276ff.

a totally wrong impression of that event. As he approached the city his awareness of the imminent cruelty became more acute. If the theory of a reading back is followed, it would imply that either the writer or the tradition had intentionally adapted the third saying more fully than the other two. It seems more reasonable to suppose that Jesus' own awareness of the details came into sharper focus the nearer he came to the event, than to suppose that the community imagined that this should have happened and ingeniously modified the series of predictions accordingly.

There are various other sayings in line, in a general way, with these passion predictions which contribute to the over-all impression that Jesus was under no illusions regarding the fate which awaited him. When criticizing the scribes and Pharisees (in Mt. 23), Jesus announces the sending of prophets and wise men to them and predicts that some of them would be killed and crucified, scourged and persecuted (Mt. 23:34). He is, in fact, predicting for his followers a fate similar to that which he had predicted for himself. He is acutely aware of the kind of fate which constantly threatens the messengers of God (*cf.* Mt. 23:30). Yet again it must not be maintained that this amounts to no more than the inevitability of martyrdom. It is clear that Jesus recognized that all too often suffering accompanies the divine mission. The same idea comes out in Jesus' lament over Jerusalem (Mt. 23:37; Lk. 13:34). He did not suppose that his own disciples would fare any better, for he predicted tribulation and death in the days ahead (Mt. 24:9), akin to the prediction in the mission charge to the twelve (Mt. 10:16–18).

THE EVIDENCE FOR THE INTERPRETATION OF THE PASSION

So far we have been concerned with Jesus' awareness of his approaching death. We turn next to the interpretation of that death. Had there been no evidence of the significance that Jesus placed on his death, there would be some excuse for supposing that he had no other view than that of martyrdom.[100] Although the synoptic evidence is sparse, it is nevertheless highly important because it includes the words at the institution of the Last Supper. Before examining this there are other considerations which should precede it.

First we should consider Luke's narrative of the transfiguration, for he includes one comment that the others omit (Lk. 9:31). He gives the theme of the discussion between Moses, Elijah and Jesus as 'his departure (*exodus*) which he was to accomplish at Jerusalem'.[101] The word *exodus* is inter-

---

[100] This is not to maintain that a theology of martyrdom has no contribution to make, but rather that it falls short of an adequate account of the passion, by failing to explain its uniqueness.

[101] It is remarkable that the transfiguration becomes for Luke an occasion when the death of Christ is foreshadowed. H. Conzelmann, *op. cit.*, p. 57, sees this as the main purpose in the heavenly manifestation. The passage certainly links suffering with glory. G. Florovsky, 'The Lamb of God', *SJT* 4, 1951, p. 20, points out that it was at Golgotha, not Tabor, that salvation was completed. But the cross was foretold on Tabor.

esting because it seems to lack any suggestion of a violent end, a feature which has contributed to the theory that Luke's approach to the passion is less tragic than that of his fellow synoptists. There may be such a suggestion in the term used, but it must be remembered that the exodus theme was inextricably tied up with the passover lamb; if Luke intends such a connection in his choice of words, there could be overtones which at least imply a sacrificial motif. Such a suggestion is admittedly far from conclusive. There may be on the other hand an implied contrast between the 'departures' of Moses and Elijah, which were both mysterious, and that of Jesus, but such a connection must be regarded as somewhat speculative.

This statement in Luke should also be linked with another which shows how acutely Jesus anticipated a violent time ahead (Lk. 12:49, 50), when he referred to his coming 'baptism'. About this anticipated experience he remarked with intensity, 'how am I straightened until it is accomplished'. This baptism theme, which is linked with the sending of fire in Luke, occurs in a different context in Matthew and Mark, and this feature will be considered below. It is Luke alone who records the saying of Jesus which was to be told to 'that fox' (Herod), 'I cast out demons and perform cures today and tomorrow, and the third day I finish my course' (Lk. 13:32). Here the approaching radical change (which must refer to his death) is described in terms of 'perfecting', as if death itself was regarded as the necessary finishing touch.

The most important interpretation of the passion before the Last Supper is the statement about the *ransom* of the Son of man (Mk. 10:45; Mt. 20:28). After saying that the Son of man did not come to be served but to serve, Jesus added 'and to give his life a ransom (*lytron*) for many'. The precise meaning of the Greek word is not in doubt. It represents the purchase money for manumitting slaves. The idea is of an exact equivalent exchange. The root notion in the saying is therefore one of deliverance.[102] It is closely tied up with the idea of redemption, which occurs elsewhere in the NT and was a familiar notion in both Hebrew and Greek thought.[103]

In considering the meaning of this saying, two factors are of great significance. The emphasis in the first part on serving connects up with the Isaianic suffering servant. Many exegetes see here an allusion to Isaiah 53, although some have disputed it.[104] Jeremias links *lytron* with the Hebrew

---

[102] *Cf.* V. Taylor, *Jesus and his Sacrifice*, p. 103. Taylor is critical of the view of H. Rashdall, *The Idea of Atonement in Christian Theology* (1919), pp. 29ff., who considered that Mk. 10:45 was a doctrinally coloured insertion. Rashdall virtually empties the ransom concept of its real meaning, by making it no more than a description of self-service. I. H. Marshall in *Reconciliation and Hope* (ed. R. Banks, 1974) p. 168, takes Mk. 10:45 as speaking of the martyr death of the servant and thinks that Rom. 3:24 interprets the death of Jesus as having the atoning power of a martyr's death. According to him this led on to the use of Jewish sacrificial terms.

[103] See F. Büchsel, *lutron, TDNT* 4, p. 341.

[104] *Cf.* R. H. Fuller, *The Mission and Achievement of Jesus*, p. 57; R. T. France *Jesus and the Old Testament* (1971), pp. 110–132. *Contra, cf.* M. D. Hooker, *Jesus and the Servant* (1959). In his later book *The Foundations*

(*'āšām*) of Isaiah.[105] In this case there can be no doubt that it implies a sacrificial offering. The second factor is the meaning of the Greek preposition *anti* which is used here. Some dispute that *anti* has any different meaning from *hyper, i.e.* 'on behalf of'. But even the force of *hyper* must be determined by its context and this is certainly true of *anti*.[106] In the present context it must have the stronger meaning 'in the place of ' (*i.e.* a substitutionary force), for this properly belongs to the sense of ransom.[107] It is significant that the word *lytron*, in the only other place that it occurs in the NT, is compounded with *anti* (1 Tim. 2:6). The force of the preposition shows clearly that this *lytron* passage supports an interpretation of the death of Christ which sees his death as an act undertaken by Jesus in the place of others (*i.e.* many).

Because the ransom in the manumission of slaves is always paid to the owner, certain speculative suggestions were made in the later church to explain the recipient of the ransom. Origen, for instance, suggested it was the devil. But the idea of Jesus Christ offering his life (*psychē*) to the devil in exchange for the liberation of men is totally alien to the sense of the NT passage. There is no suggestion anywhere that Christ bargained with the devil. In fact, the reverse is implied. He aimed at and achieved all-out victory over the devil. The statement of Jesus, moreover, gives no indication to whom the ransom was paid. The basic concern was to show deliverance through substitutionary means, without pressing the metaphor too far. If it be argued that the vagueness of the ransom metaphor militates against the idea of substitution, it should be noted that the freeing of slaves through payment was so well known that some kind of equivalence would have been recognized. It is the force of *anti* rather than *lytron* which supports the notion of substitution.

We must next consider the only other synoptic passage which specifically

---

of New Testament Christology (1965), pp. 118, 153f. R. H. Fuller not only denies the Is. 53 allusion in Mk. 10:45, but maintains with Miss Hooker and H. E. Tödt, *Der Menschensohn in der synoptischen Überlieferung*, pp. 143–161, that Mk. 10:45b was liturgical in origin. But the basis for this claim is by no means clear. He admits the sceptical nature of Tödt's conclusions, but nevertheless is strongly influenced by them. J. Roloff, 'Anfänge der soteriologischen Deutung des Todes Jesu (Mk. 10:45 und Lk. 22:27)', *NTS* 19, 1972, pp. 38–64, thinks that the earliest and most fundamental meaning of the ransom is Jesus' act of service. In fact he interprets Mk. 10:45 in the light of Lk. 22:27. He denies that it has any connection with Is. 53 and rejects all substitutionary ideas.

[105] *Cf.* Jeremias, *NTT*, pp. 292f. O. Cullman, *The Christology of the New Testament*, p. 65, sees in Mk. 10:45 a clear reference to Is. 52–53 and opposes Bultmann's view that Mk. 10:45 has formed its conception of Jesus from the redemption theories of Hellenistic Christianity (*The History of the Synoptic Tradition*, p. 144). C. K. Barrett, 'The Background of Mk. 10:45', in *New Testament Essays* (ed. A. J. B. Higgins, 1959), pp. 1ff., thinks that the connection between Mk. 10:45 and Is. 53 'is much less definite and more tenuous than is often supposed' (p. 15). He denies that *lytron* ever renders Hebrew *'āšām* (pp. 5 and 16 n. 21).

[106] For a discussion of the meaning of *hyper* and *anti* in the NT, *cf.* R. E. Davies' article, 'Christ in our Place – the Contribution of the Prepositions', *TB* 21, 1970, pp. 71–91.

[107] *Cf.* L. Morris, *The Apostolic Preaching of the Cross*, pp. 29f., for an excellent discussion of this passage.

focuses on the significance of the passion, *i.e.* the account of the institution of the Last Supper.[108] The words of institution, because of their central place in the continuous observance of the supper in the Christian church, are of great importance for the light they throw on Jesus' attitude to his own death. They have added force because they were uttered on the eve of the crucifixion when the mind of Jesus must have been particularly concentrated on the imminent passion.

The first problem arises over the various forms of the words of institution when the synoptics are compared with the account in 1 Corinthians 11:23–25. The relevant passages are Matthew 26:26–29 = Mark 14:22–25 = Luke 22:15–20. Our present purpose is to bring out the essential features common to all the synoptic accounts, to single out any distinctive features in the individual gospels, and to point out the continuity in the Pauline tradition. Matthew and Mark's accounts are closely parallel, with one significant variation. In the words accompanying the cup, Matthew adds to Mark's 'This is my blood of the covenant, which is poured out for many', the words 'for the remission of sins'. Many scholars regard the additional words as unauthentic because editorial, but without sufficient justification. The addition certainly gives a theological interpretation of the coming sacrifice, and is in line with other evidence which connects forgiveness of sins with the whole mission of Jesus. If it is claimed that the church deduced from Jewish usage a connection between the blood of the covenant and forgiveness, it must be recognized that Mark's and Luke's omission to mention forgiveness may be accounted for on similar grounds, *i.e.* that the blood of the covenant already implies forgiveness. A problem arises in Luke's account because of a variant in the text, a longer reading referring to two cups and a shorter one placing the cup before the bread. In both readings the words of institution differ in form from Matthew's and Mark's.

The words, 'Take, eat; this is my body' (Mt., *cf.* Mk, Lk.), leave the precise significance unexpressed. In Paul's version the explanation 'broken for you' is added,[109] but in the synoptic gospels the breaking of the bread

---

[108] Because the institution of the last supper occurs in the passion narratives, it is necessary to point out that many form critics do not regard these accounts as recording fact. For instance, M. Conzelmann, 'History and Theology in the Passion Narratives of the Synoptic Gospels', *Int* 24, 1970, pp. 178–197, considers that what can be established as fact from these narratives is minimal – *i.e.*, the crucifixion and a Roman court procedure. All the rest is shaped by intensive theological interpretation. He is committed to the messianic secret idea for Mark's setting for the passion narrative. He gives what he calls 'a contemporary approach' to the passion narrative. There are various different opinions as to the creative power of Scripture, for instance, in Mark's passion narrative. Contrary to many scholars. A. Suhl, *Die Funktion der alttestamentlichen Zitate und Anspielungen im Markusevangelium* (1965), maintains that Mark did not create events out of the OT, but related history with the help of it. H. Conzelmann, *op, cit.*, p. 182 n. 9, criticizes Suhl for ignoring form criticism.

[109] For the view that Paul's addition does not refer to Christ's sacrificial death, *cf.* E. P. Sanders, *Paul and Palestinian Judaism*, p. 466 n. 49.

is mentioned but not applied. There can be no doubt, however, that the breaking of the bread was intended to indicate what would happen to the body of Jesus.[110] It may further be claimed that a sacrificial element is most likely implied. To the question of the probable background to this idea, the most likely answer is that an echo is found from Isaiah 53 where the servant is said to make his soul an offering for sin (Is. 53:10) in a clearly sacrificial sense.[111] It is beyond our present scope to discuss the later view that the words involve transubstantiation. We are concerned, however, to note that it is highly improbable that identification of the bread with the body is in mind.[112] The copula (*estin*) has the force of 'signifies', which removes any idea of identification.[113] As in the Jewish passover, which must have been in the mind of Jesus at this time, the procedure was intended to be symbolical.

This symbolical aspect is brought out even more clearly in the words accompanying the cup. 'This is the blood of the covenant, which is poured out for many (Mk.) for the forgiveness of sins (Mt.).' The statement comes in the longer text of Luke, but in the shorter there is no reference to either the blood or the covenant. There are several significant features here. The 'blood' (*haima*) is used in a sacrificial sense implying death.[114] It means more than 'life poured out', although it includes that.[115] Its effectiveness must be determined by its close connection with the covenant, which recalls the sealing of the old covenant with sacrificial blood (Ex. 24). Some texts which insert 'new' before covenant may be less original, but may nevertheless have captured the implied contrast between the old covenant and that being instituted by Jesus. The idea of a new covenant directly links with Jeremiah 31:31ff., which not only stresses the inward and spiritual character of the new covenant, but also contains the promise of forgiveness for the iniquity of the people.[116]

---

[110] N. A. Beck, 'The Last Supper as an efficacious Symbolic Act', *JBL* 89, 1970, pp. 192ff., compares the act of Jesus at the supper with the symbolic teaching methods of the prophets. He is doubtful whether Jesus commended his act to be repeated, although he thinks that he may have expected a continuation of table fellowship. It is clearly of some importance to decide whether continuance of the act was envisaged, for the decision affects the meaning of the act. Note that A. M. Hunter, *The Work and Words of Jesus* (1950), p. 48, erroneously supposes that the disciples rose from the table redeemed.

[111] *Cf.* R. T. France, 'The Servant of the Lord in the Teaching of Jesus', *TB* 19, 1968, pp. 26–52, who classifies both Mk. 10:45 and Mk. 14:24 as 'clear allusions' to the servant passages. He finds three points in the words of institution which support an allusion to Is. 53 – the reference to the covenant, the verb *enchynnomenon* and the phrase *anti pollōn*.

[112] *Cf.* V. Taylor, *Jesus and His Sacrifice*, pp. 122f. He prefers the rendering, 'This *means* my body'.

[113] For a detailed discussion of this expression, *cf.* J. Jeremias, 'This is my Body', *ExT* 83, 1972, pp. 196ff. There are parallels to this use of *estin* (*cf.* Mt. 13:37–39), which show that literal identification is not intended.

[114] *Cf.* A. M. Stibbs, *The meaning of the word 'Blood' in Scripture* and L. Morris, *The Apostolic Preaching of the Cross*, pp. 108–124, who both maintain that 'blood' represents life yielded up in death.

[115] *Cf.* B. F. Westcott, *The Epistle to the Hebrews* (1892), pp. 293f., who sees in the blood 'the energy of present human life made available to others'.

[116] It should be noted that Paul in his account speaks of the *new* covenant (1 Cor. 11:25).

This latter point is in full accord with Matthew's addition, 'for the forgiveness of sins'. Although many have treated this addition as an interpretative gloss, the question arises whether Jesus would have avoided all mention of the application of the shed blood. It is not apparent why Matthew's account could not have preserved the original form and that Mark's and Luke's were shorter versions. But even if the addition is Matthew's own interpretation, it is fully in line with the conviction of the early church that forgiveness followed directly as a result of the death of Jesus.[117]

What is clear from a survey of this evidence is that the Lord's Supper was intended to be a reminder of the central importance of the death of Jesus as a sacrifice for his people. It is worth noting that in the words 'for many', the Greek preposition *hyper* is used rather than *anti*, but although the substitutionary emphasis is not as explicit as in the ransom passage, it cannot be altogether avoided in view of the nature of the sacrifice. There is no suggestion that Jesus was acting as no more than a representative on behalf of his followers. The shedding of his blood was in a special way an act which no other man could do. This death was not to be an ordinary death, but a substitutionary sacrifice which would bring spiritual benefits to his people.

Some comment must be made on another aspect which comes to the fore in the focus on the future. Both Matthew and Mark record the saying, 'I tell you I shall not drink again of this (Mk. 'the') fruit of the vine until that day when I drink it new (with you, Mt.) in my Father's kingdom (Mk. in the kingdom of God).' (Mt. 26:29; Mk. 14:25). Luke has words similar to Mark's, but it is significant that he omits the word 'again' (Lk. 22:18). There is some question whether his account intends us to understand that Jesus did not himself participate in the cup.[118] What is most important, however, is the reference to the coming kingdom.[119] Not until this kingdom is established will the new fellowship based on the new covenant be fully realized. This future view is in line with the formula used by Paul in 1 Corinthians 11:26 – 'you proclaim the Lord's death until he comes.' The supper is essentially a proclamation of the significance of the death of Jesus during the whole period culminating in the parousia.

Luke's account of the Supper contains the least indication of its theological meaning, if the shorter text is correct, for there would then, in fact, be no word of interpretation apart from the statement 'This is my body'.[120]

---

[117] *Cf.* L. Morris, *The Cross in the New Testament* (1965), p. 51, points out that the additional words are a faithful representation of Jesus' thought.

[118] Note that Lk. 22:15 implies that Jesus did eat the supper.

[119] It is, of course, possible to regard the expression as relating to the resurrection/exaltation of Jesus, but a reference to the coming messianic feast is more probable (*cf.* E. E. Ellis, *Luke*, p. 253).

[120] *Cf.* M. Rese, 'Zur Problematik von Kurz und Langtext in Lk. 22:17ff', *NTS* 22, 1976, pp. 15–31. For other comments, *cf.* H. Chadwick, 'The "Shorter Text" of St Luke xxli. 18–20', *HTR*, 1957, pp. 257f.;

It seems strange that an ordinance should be devised which did not contain within it some explanation of its purpose. The close connection between the Last Supper and the Jewish passover, which Luke specifically mentions ('I have earnestly desired to eat this passover with you before I suffer', 22:15), is sufficient guarantee that he fully recognized the symbolic significance of the act. Also, if the shorter text of Luke is taken there is a reversal of order of the bread and cup, but if the longer text is accepted there were two cups instead of one. One explanation may be found in the normal procedures of the Jewish passover. Indeed, if the form of the passover service is here in mind with its several cups,[121] it is to be expected that the Jewish practice of interpreting the symbolic meaning of the procedure would have left its mark on the words of institution. Luke has apparently compressed his account. Another possible explanation of the confusion may be Luke's use of different sources. If there is support for the longer reading, which seems likely, it could not then be supposed that Luke attached no sacrificial significance to the death of Christ.

Since we have had cause to see behind the narratives of the Lord's Supper some reference to Isaiah 53, as also in the ransom passage, it is instructive to note a few other sayings where an allusion to Isaiah 53 is either explicit or implicit.[122]

(i) There is, for instance, the Elijah saying in Mark 9:12f., where the suffering of the Son of man is linked with that of Elijah (John the Baptist) and where a reference is made to what is written, presumably a reference to the Isaianic servant. This prediction of contempt for the Son of man shows a strong probability that Isaiah 53 was constantly in the mind of Jesus as he faced death.

(ii) In three passages (Mk. 9:31; 14:41; Lk. 24:7) the idea of Jesus being delivered up into the hands of men (*paradidonai*) occurs, and the use of this verb may be compared with its use in Isaiah 53:12 (LXX). Both in the OT passages and in the NT the verb occurs in the passive. It seems to be used as a 'divine passive'.[123]

(iii) Yet another reference to Isaiah 53, in this case specific, is Luke 22:35–38. After advising his disciples to buy a sword, Jesus says, 'For I tell you that this scripture must be fulfilled in me, "And he was reckoned with transgressors"; for what is written about me has its fulfilment.' This is an unmistakable appropriation of Isaiah 53:12 by Jesus and suggests that it is

R. Bultmann, *History of the Synoptic Tradition*, p. 286 n., who support the shorter reading. For the longer reading, *cf.* H. Schürmann, 'Lk. 22:19b, 20 – als ursprüngliche Textüberlieferung', *Bib.* 32, 1951, pp.364–392, 522ff. E. Schweizer, *The Lord's Supper according to the New Testament* (Eng. trans. 1967), pp. 18ff. For a classic discussion of the whole question, *cf.* J. Jeremias, *The Eucharistic Words of Jesus*, pp. 87–106.

[121] For the passover ritual, *cf.* A. J. B. Higgins, *The Lord's Supper in the New Testament* (1952), pp. 13ff.; J. Jeremias, *op. cit.*, 14–60; N. Hook, *The Eucharist in the New Testament* (1964), pp. 35–47.

[122] *Cf.* the article by R. T. France, *TB* 19, pp. 26–52, for a fuller discussion of these further allusions.

[123] See J. Jeremias, *NTT*, p. 296, on the significance of the use of the verb *paradidonai* here.

reasonable to suppose that he considered the whole concept of the suffering servant to be fulfilled in himself.

It was in the garden of Gethsemane that his awareness that he had reached the critical point in the passion experience comes clearly into view.[124] The intense sorrow and even perspiration of blood[125] (according to the most probable reading in Luke's gospel) give particularly poignancy to the words of Jesus' prayer, 'My Father, if it be possible, let this cup pass from me; nevertheless, not as I will, but as thou wilt' (Mt. 26:39). Mark (14:36) has 'all things are possible' and Luke (22:42) has 'if thou art willing'. The variations in the first part are incidental and do not affect the striking character of the concluding words. Jesus is seen as perfectly obedient to the Father's will. He was aware of the cost of the passion and voluntarily accepted it because it was part of a predetermined divine plan. The necessity for the passion is once again stressed in this incident.[126] It should be noted that the use in this context of 'cup' for 'destiny' is paralleled in the OT.[127] It stands for a man's lot, in this case the lot of a shameful death by crucifixion.

The only other important saying bearing on the atonement is the cry of dereliction from the cross. The words themselves made so notable an impression on the hearers that both Matthew and Mark, who alone record it, preserve it in its Aramaic form, as well as its Greek translation: 'My God, my God, why hast thou forsaken me?' (Mt. 27:46 = Mk. 15:34). It is a quotation from Psalm 22, but clearly much more than this. Was the sense of separation caused by the bearing of man's sin? There is no specific reference to this in the passage, which has led to its rejection by some. Nevertheless, the consciousness of Jesus that his mission would end in death and would involve an act of substitution would be a sufficient explanation of the sense of separation.[128] Such separation from God was not possible for a perfect man whose mind was wholly committed to the fulfilment of God's will. In this case it must have been an acute consciousness of the extent and meaning of his vicarious suffering[129] that caused the intense distress of dereliction.

[124] R. S. Barbour, 'Gethsemane in the Tradition of the Passion', *NTS* 16, 1969–70, pp. 231–251, discusses the problems behind the Gethsemane accounts and considers that these accounts are attempting a description which they cannot compass. He considers, in fact, that there is a historical realism behind the narratives which conveys a universal meaning. He sees a confrontation between Jesus and the powers of evil and darkness.

[125] *Cf.* R. V. G. Tasker's note against the authenticity of the 'bloody sweat' text, *The Nature and Purpose of the Gospels* (1944), p. 60.

[126] R. Bultmann, *The History of the Synoptic Tradition*, pp. 267ff, regards the whole incident as legendary.

[127] M. Dibelius, *From Tradition to Gospel* (Eng. trans. 1934), p. 213, considers the Gethsemane incident to be built up from OT material.

[128] *Cf.* V. Taylor, *Jesus and his Sacrifice*, pp. 157ff. for a discussion of various explanations of the cry of abandonment. He concludes that the cry must imply a sense of utter desolation.

[129] V. Taylor, *op. cit.*, p. 161, admits that the fellowship was broken, but contends that Jesus himself broke it. He thinks the sense of abandonment was due to Jesus' preoccupation with the fact and burden of

Other explanations have been proposed. Schweitzer considered this cry to be the moment of disillusionment.[130] But his interpretation was tied up with his whole eschatological theory for the ministry of Jesus, and since this has proved untenable, his explanation of the cry is equally unconvincing. Neither the gospel narratives nor the Acts and epistles suggest that the death of Jesus was ever regarded as a mark of failure.[131] There is no doubt that the sense of separation is a fact, but it did not detract from, and indeed was integral to, the messianic mission of salvation.[132]

In view of the clear evidence outlined above, a problem arises over the nature of God's love. Since he has power to forgive without sacrifice, why did he require the sacrifice of his own Son? The parable of the prodigal son is appealed to in support of the view that God's nature is to forgive. Nevertheless no doctrine can be fully constructed on the sole basis of a parable. In any case no human father can provide an adequate analogy to the forgiving love of God. Nowhere in the NT is God's love set over against his justice. The sacrifice of Christ has to do with both. It shows God's love for man as the motive for the death and his justice as its reason. Jesus himself did not expound on this theme, but there is nothing in his teaching which leads to the view that his death could have been avoided in the carrying out of the plan of redemption.[133]

SUMMARY

In summarizing the evidence from the synoptic gospels on the work of Christ we may make the following points:–

(i) Jesus approached death as a *voluntary* act. In fact he considered it to be a necessity in accordance with the divine will, but nevertheless when he undertook it he was fully conscious of the cost.

(ii) The death of Christ was seen to be directly related to the *remission* of sins. No understanding of the passion is adequate which does not take full account of this and does not seek to explain it.

---

sin. R. Bultmann, *The History of the Synoptic Tradition*, p. 313, sees the use of the Psalm 22 as secondary and therefore not original to Jesus. But surely nothing could be more in keeping than the citing of this psalm at the climax of the passion. If this was an editorial process, why did the editor introduce such an enigmatic saying?

[130] As for instance was expounded by A. Schweitzer in *The Quest of the Historical Jesus.*

[131] C. Ryder Smith, *The Bible Doctrine of Salvation* (1941), pp. 199ff., sees a paradox here. He thinks logic is never adequate to explain experience.

[132] L. Morris, *The Cross in the New Testament*, pp. 47f., warns against watering down the cry of dereliction. He contends, rightly, that no satisfactory understanding of the atonement can be reached without taking full account of this cry. *Cf.* J. P. Hickinbotham, *The Churchman* 58, 1944, p. 56, who cites it in support of the view that Mark presents a view of penal substitution (quoted approvingly by Morris). It is less satisfactory to see in this cry the experience of loneliness, anxiety, desolation and sense of defeat 'which make up the cross for the mind of man' (D. L. Edwards, *God's Cross in our World* (1963), p. 86).

[133] O. Cullmann, *Immortality of the Soul or Resurrection of the Dead?* (1958), pp. 21f., maintains that Jesus faced death with horror and sees in this an evidence of his true humanity. (*Cf.* further comment on p. 825f.).

(iii) There is evidence to show that Jesus recognized that his death would be *vicarious* in the sense that he was doing something in the place of others.

(iv) Moreover, the death was conceived as a *sacrifice* with special links with the new covenant. In some respects it ratified the new covenant in the same way that sacrificial blood ratified the old covenant.

(v) There is no doubt that Jesus regarded himself as a *substitute* in a sense which was reminiscent of, and in fulfilment of, the suffering servant of Isaiah.

(vi) Since these emphases on death are found within the context of the kingdom teaching, it must also be noted that the passion has an *eschatological* aspect. The death was regarded as a necessary prelude to the full realization of the kingdom. The kingdom must be regarded as a community which has been redeemed through the blood of Christ.

NOTE ON LUKE'S PRESENTATION OF THE PASSION

In setting out the above evidence, only incidental differentiation has been made between the three synoptic writers.[134] In view of recent tendencies to regard each writer as a theologian in his own right, it is necessary to enquire whether any distinctive features can be observed. Whereas little difference can be detected between Matthew's[135] and Mark's passion sayings, there are aspects in Luke's gospel which have led some scholars to maintain that his approach to the passion is less tragic than the others.[136]

There are a number of points which have been quoted in support of this. A possible prefiguring of it is found in the transfiguration narrative where, as we have already noted, Luke says that the subject of conversation between Jesus, Moses and Elijah was the 'exodus' of Jesus (Lk. 9:31). But it is Luke's passion narrative[137] which has been strongly appealed to as non-tragic. The main issues may be summarized as follows:

(i) Luke omits the anointing at Bethany, which is seen as specifically for the burial of Jesus.

(ii) Judas in Luke's account leaves the upper room before the institution of the supper, having been possessed by Satan (Lk. 22:3ff.). In the other synoptics he was present at the supper and received the special sop. Moreover Jesus said it would have been better if he had never been born.

(iii) Luke does not mention that all the disciples forsook Jesus as the others do (Mk. 14:50; Mt. 26:56).

(iv) The denial by Peter is somewhat mitigated in Luke by the inclusion

---

[134] R. Leivestad, *Christ the Conqueror* (1954), pp. 65–76, summarizes and compares each passion account and considers the theological approach of each.

[135] For a discussion of Matthew's special emphasis, *cf.* B. Gerhardsson's essay 'Sacrificial Service and Atonement in the Gospel of Matthew', in *Reconciliation and Hope* (ed. R. J. Banks), pp. 25–35.

[136] *Cf.* R. V. G. Tasker, *The Nature and Purpose of the Gospels*, pp. 54ff.

[137] *Cf.* M. Kiddle, 'The Passion Narrative of Luke', *JTS*, 36, 1935, pp. 267–280.

of Jesus' prayer for his restoration (Lk. 22:32).

(v) Luke alone records the prayer of Jesus for his persecutors (Lk. 23:34) and his request to the Jerusalem women not to weep for him, but for themselves and their children (Lk. 23:28).

(vi) The account of the crucifixion ends with Jesus committing his spirit into the Father's hands (Lk. 23:46). The cry of abandonment is omitted.

(vii) Luke's account is the only synoptic record which tells of Jesus ministering to the needs of others even on the cross (Lk. 23:39–43).

Opinions will differ on the interpretation of this evidence. Some see Luke's narrative as presenting a heroic martyr,[138] who triumphs over his adverse circumstances in a way calculated to inspire the readers. But this interpretation overlooks some important features. The Gethsemane passage in Luke, if the reference to the perspiration of blood is authentic, is even more poignant than the record of the other synoptics. It is not easy to see why such a passage would be inserted if it were not original. The intensity of conflict must offset the alleged 'martyr' image.[139] Moreover, in Luke's account of Jesus leaving Galilee for Jerusalem (Lk. 9:51), he makes it clear that Jesus set his face to go to Jerusalem, which shows a deliberate and voluntary act on his part.

Since Luke's gospel is a prelude to the Acts account, his passion narrative cannot be divorced from the approach adopted by the early preachers. In the speeches there is no question of interpreting the passion as a martyrdom. Rather it happened by God's determination (Acts 2:23). It is only if a divorce is made between Luke and Acts that the non-tragic aspect of the gospel can be maintained. Further, Luke's portrait must be regarded as complementary to that of the other synoptics. It is drawn with somewhat softer lines, but he has no doubt about the necessity of the sufferings of Christ.[140] It is in Luke's birth stories that a prediction is given to Mary of a 'sword piercing her soul' (Lk. 2:35). In addition, it must be noted that Luke includes in his resurrection narratives the references to the expositions of Jesus from the OT about his own sufferings (Lk. 24:26f., 44ff.).

John's gospel

As John's presentation of the person of Jesus contains distinctive features, so also his approach to the meaning of the work of Christ is different.[141]

---

[138] *Cf.* M. Dibelius, *Gospel Criticism and Christology* (Eng. trans. 1935) p. 62.

[139] A George, 'Le Sens de la mort de Jésus pour Luc', *RB* 80, 1973, pp. 186–217, gives a detailed examination of Luke's particular approach. He concludes that Luke prefers the image of martyrdom to that of sacrifice and expiation (p. 217). *Cf. idem.*, *Études sur l'Oeuvre de Luc* (1978), pp. 204f.

[140] I. H. Marshall, *Luke: Historian and Theologian* (1970), pp. 209ff. discusses the view that Luke had no doctrine of the atonement, but considers that this opinion is false.

[141] For studies on the Johannine witness to the work of Christ, *cf.* V. Taylor, *Jesus and His Sacrifice*, pp. 218–249; L. Morris, *The Cross in the New Testament*, pp. 144–179; W. H. Rigg, 'The Atonement in the Johannine Writings', in *The Atonement in History and in Life* (ed. L. W. Grensted, 1929), pp. 154–176.

Some scholars account for this by supposing that John has brought his own theological reflection to bear on the significance of the mission of Jesus. Many claim Hellenistic influences, although more recently greater acknowledgement has been made of Hebraic ideas. Undoubtedly some of the comments are John's own, but several are specifically attributed to Jesus. It is not unreasonable to suppose that John has presented the teaching of Jesus in a way which reflects the mind of Jesus regarding his own work.

SAYINGS WHICH IMPLY THAT JESUS' DEATH WAS ACCORDING TO PLAN

First we note those sayings in which Jesus shows an awareness that his life and death are proceeding according to a definite pre-arranged pattern. In the first narrative of a miracle, at Cana in Galilee, Jesus announces to his mother, 'My hour has not yet come' (Jn. 2:4). He makes a similar statement to his brothers in John 7:6, 8. John notes this theme of the 'hour' because in 7:30 he comments that Jesus was not arrested, for his hour had not yet come. A similar comment explains why no-one seized Jesus in the treasury (Jn. 8:20). In reply to the Greeks who had come to seek him, Jesus announced 'The hour has come for the Son of man to be glorified' (Jn. 12:23). What this announcement meant to the Greeks, John does not say. But he himself had no doubt about the significance of the statement, for he comments in John 13:1 that it was Jesus' knowledge that his hour had come that prompted him to wash his disciples' feet. In both cases the hour is directly linked with the passion – in John 12:23ff. with the corn of wheat and in John 13:1 with his departure. Moreover in John 12:27f. Jesus prays to be saved from that hour,[142] which shows that he was not impervious to extreme tension as the climax drew nearer, while at the same time knowing that the 'hour' had been moving on throughout the ministry.

This was the hour for which he came. The tension is less apparent in the prayer in John 17:1 where Jesus says, 'Father, the hour has come; glorify thy Son that the Son may glorify thee.' It was his own conviction that his destiny was in the hand of God. His death was no accident, but the occasion for the Father to glorify him. John has himself sensed the inevitability of the cross and has skilfully traced the undeviating movement of Jesus towards that goal. That the hour was the hour of Jesus' death is supported by other sayings which show his awareness of coming suffering. This will be amply demonstrated as each is discussed.

SAYINGS WHICH VIEW THE PASSION AS A SACRIFICE

(i) Even before the start of the ministry, John the Baptist twice declared that Jesus was the Lamb of God (Jn. 1:29, 35). In the first case a significant statement is made: 'Behold the Lamb of God, who takes away the sin of

---

[142] Some take the prayer here as hypothetical because it is immediately negated, and this seems better than to suppose an actual request. *Cf.* L. Morris, *John* (*NICNT*, 1971), p. 595.

the world!' Here the language is drawn from sacrificial imagery. The Lamb taking away sin is reminiscent of OT ceremonial sacrifices. But the problem of the precise origin of this idea has been widely discussed. Is 'Lamb of God' a messianic title? Dodd thinks it is[143] and for that reason considers that John the Baptist may have used it. But in all probability there is an echo here from Isaiah 53:7, which says of the servant that he did not open his mouth, 'like a lamb that is led to the slaughter'.[144] It has been claimed that this identification cannot be maintained since at his trial Jesus was not silent.[145] But there is more to be said for this interpretation than that which considers the gentle qualities of a lamb to be in mind (as in Je. 11:19),[146] since the bearing away of sins clearly involves sacrificial language.

It is possible that Isaiah 53:12 (he bore the sins of many) may be linked with Isaiah 53:7 in a composite idea of the suffering servant.[147] The evidence that Jesus probably considered himself to be the suffering servant has already been outlined in dealing with his messianic consciousness (see pp. 258ff.). It is not impossible that John the Baptist may have had some flash of insight into this identification in his announcement of Jesus. The early Christians certainly used the servant idea to explain the mission of Jesus (see Acts, 1 Peter). A difficulty is raised because the verb used in Isaiah 53:12 (*pherein*) is different from that used by John (*airōn*). Since John the Baptist's statement requires the idea of 'bearing away' rather than simply 'bearing', it has closer links with the scapegoat ceremonial of the day of atonement. Indeed the lamb may point to the paschal lamb, although this is sometimes erroneously objected to on the grounds that in Judaism the paschal lamb was not sacrificed as a sin-atonement.[148]

Another reason why Dodd rejects a sacrificial notion here is that he maintains, surely erroneously, that John does not elsewhere introduce an expiatory element (but *cf.* Jn. 11:50f.).[149] Even so, evidence cannot be dispensed with on the grounds that it is not repeated elsewhere. This

[143] C. H. Dodd, *The Interpretation of the Fourth Gospel* (1953), pp. 233ff.

[144] For the connection between 'Lamb of God' and 'Servant of God' behind Jn. 1:29, *cf.* C. F. Burney, *The Aramaic Origin of the Fourth Gospel* (1922), pp. 107f., who traces both ideas back to the same Aramaic form. *Cf.* also J. Jeremias, '*Amnos tou Theou – pais Theou*', *ZNW* 34, 1935, pp. 117ff. On the Lamb of God, *cf.* C. K. Barrett, 'The Lamb of God', *NTS* 1, 1954–5, pp. 210ff.

[145] So Dodd, *op. cit.*, p. 235, who points out that in Jn. 18:34–7; 19:11, Jesus makes a spirited defence.

[146] V. Taylor, *Jesus and His Sacrifice*, p. 226, considers that this view is unlikely.

[147] J. Jeremias, art. *amnos, TDNT* 1, p. 339, thinks that the basic Aramaic behind Jn. 1:29 would contain a reference to the servant of God, and in this case the most serious objections to its historicity would be dispelled.

[148] L. Morris, *The Cross in the New Testament*, p. 174 n. 71, thinks that the expression 'Lamb of God' is purposely vague so as to sum up all that the various sacrifices suggest. *Cf.* C. K. Barrett, *John*, p. 147. Barrett's contention may be refuted by reference to Pesahim 10:6, which shows that in Judaism the paschal lamb was thought to take away sin.

[149] A recent Roman Catholic writer, J. T. Forestell, *The Word of the Cross* (1974), p. 60, has pointed out that the language of redemption and expiation is completely absent from this gospel. But see the further comments on Forestall's position below, n. 173.

statement of John the Baptist's recorded at the commencement of the ministry is significant because it marks the goal of that ministry: a sacrifice related to sins. In all probability it should be regarded as an amalgam of various OT ideas. Whatever its origin, it is indisputable that Jesus is here seen in a vicarious and sacrificial capacity. Its outworking was to be seen in the subsequent narrative of the passion.

It should be noted in passing that various views have been held regarding John the Baptist's statement. It is seen as a dramatic representation,[150] or as an echo of an early Christian liturgical formula,[151] or as the evangelist's own idea because he is dominated by the idea of Jesus as the paschal lamb (as seen, for instance, in his dating of the Last Supper and his 'no bones broken' saying in 19:33ff.). But it seems reasonable to suppose that it was a brilliant insight on John the Baptist's part, which nevertheless at a later time became clouded.[152]

(ii) Another passage which brings out the sacrificial character of the mission of Jesus is his own saying in John 6:51f. about the heavenly bread: 'The bread which I shall give for the life of the world is my flesh,' and 'Truly, truly, I say to you, unless you eat the flesh of the Son of man and drink his blood, you have no life in you.' Many see this as a reference to the Christian sacrament, but this is certainly not its primary meaning.[153] Where flesh and blood are separated, death is implied. The imagery[154] suggests a sacrificial meaning, for 'flesh and blood' are seen to be essential for the life of the world. This brings out both the vicarious nature of Christ's death and its universal relevance. It is further evidence that Jesus was conscious of moving on towards an event which would result in the separation of flesh and blood, *i.e.* in death. Another significant feature at once differentiates the coming sacrifice of Christ from all Jewish sacrificial offerings: it is a self-giving. What is even more important is that the giving up of life by Jesus is seen as the basis of life for the world.

Those who see in John 6:51ff. a direct reference to the Last Supper naturally interpret it in a different way.[155] It would then support the view

---

[150] *Cf.* V. Taylor, *op. cit.*, p. 226.

[151] Cf. R. H. Strachan, *The Fourth Gospel* (³1941), p. 114.

[152] E. K. Lee, *The Religious Thought of St John*, p. 184, sees this statement, set as it is at the beginning of the gospel, as a decisive expression of the evangelist's conception of Jesus and his work. But C. F. Burney, *op. cit.*, pp. 104ff., defends it as an opinion of John the Baptist.

[153] *Cf.* L. Morris, *John*, pp. 377ff. A recent refutation of the sacramental view of Jn. 6 is the article by J. D. G. Dunn, 'John vi – A Eucharistic Discourse' *NTS* 17, 1970–71, pp. 328–338. Dunn maintains that John omitted the account of the institution of the last supper to combat too much attention being given to the ritual act.

[154] C. H. Dodd, *The Interpretation of the Fourth Gospel*, pp. 338f., recognizes that the terminology here could not fail to suggest the idea of death, indeed violent death. Dodd, however, thinks that John is thinking in sacramental terms. *Cf.* also R. Schnackenburg, *Das Johannesevangelium 2* (*HTKNT* 1971), pp. 82ff.

[155] *Cf.* J. H. Bernard, *John* (*ICC* 1928), pp. clxviiff.; W. F. Howard, *Christianity according to St John* (1943), pp. 211.

that participation in the Christian eucharist enables the believer to obtain eternal life and mystical fellowship with Christ.[156] Yet the word 'flesh' is never used in the NT in connection with the sacrament. The words of institution in all the accounts use 'body'.[157] Moreover, the verbs 'eating' and 'drinking' are both aorists and denote not an often-repeated action, but a once-for-all action. It is not convincing to apply these words to participation in the Lord's Supper, which by its very nature must be continually observed. It is further out of line with general NT teaching and with Johannine teaching elsewhere to interpose a bodily act between man and his salvation. Nevertheless, if there is no primary reference to the sacrament, there may well be a secondary one.[158] The idea behind the present saying would prepare the minds of the disciples for a spiritual approach to the imagery of eating and drinking which would later safeguard them against an over-literal interpretation of the words of institution, 'This is my body.'[159]

The saying in John 12:24, on the necessity of a corn of wheat to die if it is to become fruitful, carries unmistakable sacrificial implications.[160] There can be no doubt that Jesus was referring to himself under the figure of a seed. He recognized the need for his own approaching death, but he also saw death as a means of multiplication. It introduces a paradox – that death produces life.

PASSAGES WHICH BRING OUT THE VOLUNTARY CHARACTER OF JESUS' DEATH

In John's gospel there are several passages which show Jesus not merely moving inescapably towards death, but doing so in a fully voluntary manner. There is no question here of blind fate. Jesus is seen in control of his own destiny, in line with his Father's will. In the good-shepherd discourse, there are three statements which make this clear – John 10:11, 15f., 17f. This is reinforced by the saying, 'No one takes it (*i.e.* life) from

---

[156] *Cf.* V. Taylor, *op. cit.*, p. 236.

[157] Bultmann, *TNT* 2, p. 48, regards this passage as an ecclesiastical redaction and therefore dismisses it from consideration.

[158] R. E. Brown, *John*, pp. 287ff., propounds the theory that Jn. 6:51–58 was made up of material which originally stood in the last supper scene, but which has been adapted for the bread discourse. But this theory makes the passage an editorial construction, which may solve some difficulties, but creates others. It is not conclusive that such a break is necessary after verse 50. Further, it is open to the objection that the eucharist is not specifically mentioned, *cf.* L. Morris' view, *John*, p. 376. G. Richter, 'Zur Formgeschichte und literarischen Einheit von Jn. 6:31–58', *ZNW* 60, 1969, pp. 21–55, maintains that from a form-critical point of view verses 51b–58 are not in harmony with the stated purpose of the gospel (Jn. 20:31).

[159] R. E. Brown, *John*, p. 285, argues from the fact that no Aramaic (or Hebrew) word exists for 'body', that what Jesus actually said is 'This is my flesh'. But it is difficult to understand why the consistent NT testimony preserved the form, 'This is my body', if Brown is correct.

[160] C. H. Dodd, *Historical Tradition in the Fourth Gospel* (1963), pp. 366ff., classes this saying as a parabolic form and finds some parallels in structure to the synoptic parables. He considers it represents a primitive and authentic tradition. Brown, *op. cit.*, p. 471, agrees that it is meant to refer to Jesus' own death.

me, but I lay it down of my own accord' (Jn. 10:18).[161] Moreover, the laying down of life is linked with power to take it again. This voluntary character is also brought out in the saying in John 15:13,[162] that as the greatest demonstration of love a man will lay down his life for his friends, a clear allusion to what Jesus intended to do for his disciples, whom he calls his friends (15:14).

The theme of love as the motive for the self-giving of the Son comes out in John 13:1ff. – 'Jesus . . . having loved his own who were in the world, he loved them to the end . . . knowing that the Father had given all things into his hands, and that he had come from God and was going to God.' The voluntary act was not in the interests of personal heroism, but because of the dynamic of love. He knew that it was for this purpose he had come into the world. John 3:16 states clearly that the sending of his Son into the world was prompted by the Father's love for those in the world who would otherwise perish.[163] This theme of love is expounded further in the Johannine epistles (cf. especially 1 Jn. 3:16; 4:10).

PASSAGES WHICH SPEAK OF DEATH IN TERMS OF UPLIFTING

The use of the concept of lifting up is significant,[164] because it refers both to the manner of death (i.e. crucifixion) and to the interpretation of it (i.e. as a triumph). The idea is supported by four passages.[165]

The first occurs in John 3:14f., in the words of Jesus, 'As Moses lifted up the serpent in the wilderness, so must the Son of man be lifted up, that whoever believes in him may have eternal life.' The OT allusion to the serpent may not immediately illuminate the coming passion of Jesus, but the parallel is seen in the verb. The lifting up of the Son of man is further elucidated by the other passages, in the light of which it clearly alludes to the crucifixion. What is important in the present statement is the sense of

---

[161] L. Morris, John, p. 510, cogently draws out the contrast between a shepherd who accidentally dies for his sheep (a disaster for them) and the good shepherd who voluntarily gives his life (which brings life to them).

[162] L. Morris, The Cross in the New Testament, p. 174, when discussing this passage which does not use unambiguous substitutionary language, maintains that it nevertheless preserves such a thought.

[163] Care must be taken not to place so much emphasis on the love motive that vicarious sacrifice is interpreted entirely in terms of it (as in the writing of H. Bushnell, The Vicarious Sacrifice (1891)). Undoubtedly love is an important factor, but it is the kind of love that cannot act in an unjust way. John's gospel and first epistle especially focus on love, but both also stress the need for the cross in terms of an objective vicarious sacrifice.

[164] C. K. Barrett, John, p. 356, points out that in John one word (hypsoun) expresses both suffering and glorification, whereas in Mark the two ideas are distinguished. It was a difficult, although necessary step, for the disciples to grasp that suffering for Jesus was a path to triumph and glory, the exact opposite to the contemporary views. Cf. R. Schnackenburg, John 1 (Eng. trans. 1968 from HTKNT, 1965), pp. 535f. The Johannine 'lifting up' is a reference to both the cross and exaltation, but behind it stands the tradition of the suffering Son of man.

[165] On the lifting up passages, cf. L. Morris, The Cross in the New Testament, pp. 165ff. He links these passages with the theme of 'glory' which is characteristic of John.

necessity which it conveys. (In the Greek the *dei* construction with accusative and infinitive is used to express this idea.)

The second passage (Jn. 8:28) gives Jesus' words to his Pharisaic hearers, 'When you have lifted up the Son of man, then you will know that I am he', which are again an indirect allusion to the cross. What might appear to most as a tragedy is seen by Jesus to have a *revelatory* value relating to his own person. It is worth noting that the lifting up here is directly attributed to the Jews.

In the third passage the immediate *effects* of the uplifting are brought out (Jn. 12:31f.). It coincides with the judgment of this world when the ruler of the world is cast out. This again focuses on the triumphant aspect of the cross and its connection with the overthrow of evil forces. Moreover, the uplifting is seen as a means by which Jesus would attract men to himself. It views the cross as possessing a magnetic power. In this context the uplifting is specifically identified with the death (Jn. 12:33), so as to leave no doubt in the reader's minds.

The evangelist puts in a comment in John 18:32 with relation to the dialogue between Pilate and the Jews as to the method of Jesus' execution. The *fulfilment* of the word which Jesus had spoken must refer to the 'uplifting' passages which would require crucifixion rather than, for instance, stoning. The stress is on fulfilment here: John recognized that Jesus clearly knew his destiny.[166]

In line with this approach to death is the cry from the cross which John records in 19:30, 'It is finished.' This is certainly not a cry of despair, but of accomplishment.[167] It marked the completion of the mission which Jesus came to do. That mission included the uplifting on the cross.

PASSAGES WHICH STRESS THE EXPEDIENCY OF THE DEATH OF JESUS
There is one notable passage which focuses on expediency. It is all the more notable because it is attributed to Caiaphas, and John makes a special point of this (Jn. 11:49f.). The occasion was a scare among the chief priests and Pharisees because many were believing in Jesus. When Caiaphas pronounced, 'it is expedient for you that one man should die for the people

---

[166] R. Bultmann, *John*, p. 653, attributes this to the ecclesiastical redactor. But *contra, cf.* B. Lindars, *John*, p. 557.

[167] Some see this cry from the cross as the key to the understanding of John's gospel. *Cf.* A. Corell, *Consummatum Est* (1968), pp. 106f. Corell thinks that throughout his gospel, John is pointing beyond the death and resurrection of Jesus to the new situation created through them. R. Bultmann, *John*, p. 675, attempts to find some gnostic parallels and thinks that *tetelestai* may be derived from gnostic tradition. But he admits that the gnostic sought perfection for himself, not simply for his work as Jesus here does. E. Haenchen, 'History and Interpretation in the Johannine Passion Narrative', *Int* 24, 1970, pp. 98–219, denies any eyewitnesses behind the passion accounts. All the details are seen as theological. The evangelist is portrayed as incredibly ingenious in inventing events to illustrate his point. This goes also for this last cry of Jesus (p. 219).

and not that the whole nation should perish' (11:50), he was clearly thinking of political expediency.[168] The hierarchy was concerned that a popular following of Jesus would undermine its own status and cause the Roman occupying powers to step in. Caiaphas' kind of expediency was very different from John's understanding of the death of Jesus. John twice emphasizes the fact that Caiaphas was high priest that year, as if he saw particular significance in his representative position. 'That' year is clearly the fateful year in which Jesus died.[169] John is convinced that Caiaphas, without knowing it, expressed a truth which was highly important for understanding the meaning of the death of Christ. He adds the words, 'He did not say this of his own accord, but being high priest that year he prophesied that Jesus should die for the nation' (11:51). Indeed, John goes further by explaining that the death was 'to gather into one the children of God who are scattered abroad'; in other words the 'nation', which might have been defined in nationalistic terms, is further defined in spiritual terms.

Two aspects are brought out in this passage. The first is the 'fittingness' of the passion of Jesus. It is astonishing that the Christians so soon after the crucifixion came to recognize the basic truth of Caiaphas' remark. They came to do so only after the resurrection of Jesus. John's comment reflects that reassessment of the event. The other important principle which is here seen is that of substitution. One man was dying to save the whole nation.[170]

Another statement in which the idea of expediency occurs in a rather different sense is in John 16:7 where Jesus shows the expediency of his own departure, because then the Spirit (the Counsellor) will come. In this context it is clear that Jesus saw this as a definite advantage which would follow from his death. Again there is a complete absence of any idea that the death of Jesus would be catastrophic to the fulfilment of his mission; indeed quite the reverse.

ADDITIONAL PREDICTIONS

Included in John's account of the cleansing of the temple is a statement of Jesus, 'Destroy this temple, and in three days I will raise it up' (Jn. 2:19), which the Jews misunderstood, but which John interprets as referring to

---

[168] B. Lindars, *John*, p. 406, discusses the variant reading in Jn. 11:50 and concludes that the phrase 'for the people' should probably be omitted. He suggests the original was, 'It is expedient that one should die, and that the whole nation should not perish.' Although this would make excellent sense, the grounds for omitting the words 'for the people' are not strong in the MS evidence, neither is the evidence for the omission of 'for you' (*hymin*).

[169] The significance of the prophecy being made by the high priest is that John sees it as a declaration of God. This conviction accounts for the repetition of the phrase 'that year'. Lindars, *op. cit.*, p. 407, gives some weight to the view that the high priest may have been thought to have prophetic powers. He cites Josephus' comment about John Hyrcanus.

[170] L. Morris, *John*, p. 567, sees John's inclusion of this saying of Caiaphas as an example of his irony. The course of action which the high priest advised did not in fact save the nation in a political sense.

his body.[171] This must refer to some kind of violent death and it would not have been difficult for the disciples after the passion to see the force of the saying. They recognized it as a fulfilment of scripture as well as of the prediction of Jesus. It is important to note that, as in the synoptic prediction of the passion, the death is linked immediately with the resurrection.

In John 12:7 there is a prediction of the burial, in connection with the anointing of Jesus at Bethany. In response to Judas' complaint about the waste, Jesus said, 'Let her alone, let her keep it for the day of my burial,' showing his own consciousness of that approaching day and linking up with the 'hour' sayings. Moreover, in John 13:21 Jesus predicts the betrayal, as he does in the synoptic records.

SAYINGS WHICH SUGGEST THE REVELATIONAL CHARACTER OF THE MISSION OF JESUS

A particular emphasis in John's gospel is the stress on the revelational aspect of Jesus' work.[172] Indeed this has led some scholars to believe that John presents redemption as being attained by revelation. It will be discussed below whether this is a departure from the synoptics, but first the evidence must be presented.[173]

In the prologue this idea comes out in the presentation of Christ as the Logos (Word) and as light (Jn. 1:1ff.). The two ideas are not unconnected with each other. Each is part of the process of communicating. The Word or Reason represents God's message to man, but for John that message is not abstract but personal. Moreover, the light is also personal, for Jesus himself claimed to be the light of the world (Jn. 8:12). Since John at once introduces Jesus in this dual way, there can be no doubt that he saw him as God's means of revelation. Did he then see him in an educative way as if his task was to show people what God was like and what was his plan for man? There are some statements which may seem to suppose this view especially where Jesus claims that those who have seen him have seen the Father (14:7, 9). Moreover, 'No man has ever seen God: the only Son, who is in the bosom of the Father, he has made him known' (Jn. 1:18). A

---

[171] This saying was clearly intended to have a double meaning. John's comment suggests that before the passion and resurrection of Jesus the disciples as well as the Jews generally misunderstood. E. C. Hoskyns and F. N. Davey, *The Fourth Gospel* (1940), p. 195, see in this a sign to the Jews of resurrection analagous to the Jonah saying in the synoptics.

[172] E. F. Scott, *The Fourth Gospel* (²1908), p. 225, reached the conclusion that the fourth gospel finds no place for the death of Christ as an atonement. But this cannot be sustained in the light of the evidence cited above. It will not do to maintain, as Scott does (p. 208), that the sacrifice of Christ is connected with the incarnation instead of the death of Christ.

[173] Bultmann, *TNT* 2, pp. 11ff., interprets John from the background of gnosticism and lays some stress on the revelatory character of this gospel. A more recent interpreter of the mission of Christ through the concept of revelation is J. T. Forestell, *The Word of the Cross*. This writer gives insufficient attention to other aspects of Johannine theology, especially relating to the death of Christ. He dismisses too readily a statement like Jn. 1:29 which does not easily fit into his scheme.

true understanding of the mission of Jesus must make room for the revelation which he alone could make.

Another aspect of the same idea is the emphasis in John's gospel on truth. The incarnate Word is said to be full of grace and truth (Jn. 1:14). Truth came through Jesus Christ (1:17). Jesus claimed to be the truth (14:6). He promised that the other Counsellor would be the Spirit of truth (14:16–17). Truth is of the essence of his revelation.

Nevertheless, it would not be correct to say that John's main interest is to portray Jesus as coming simply to reveal. He has as much interest in his death as in his incarnation. Revelation there certainly was, but it was a revelation which included the passion, seen as a means of drawing people to Jesus Christ. In the stated purpose of the gospel in John 20:31, it is believing in Jesus, not knowing him, which is the target (compared with 1 Jn. 5:13).

THE VIEW THAT JESUS' MISSION INVOLVED A SANCTIFYING PROCESS

It is important to recognize that in John's gospel Jesus conceived of his mission as involving other people. This is succinctly brought out in John 17:19 where Jesus says in his prayer, 'For their sakes I consecrate (*hagiazō*) myself, that they also may be consecrated in truth.'[174] He is not only doing something vicariously (for their sake), but he is doing something which involves them. The right response to his work is faith (Jn. 3:16; 20:31). In other words the mission of Jesus has a subjective as well as an objective side to it.

SUMMARY OF JOHN'S PASSION SAYINGS AND COMPARISON WITH THE SYNOPTICS

We may list the following features which have been demonstrated by the preceding evidence.

(i) There is undoubtedly a strong emphasis on the *sacrificial* character of Jesus' death. As Lamb of God, bread from heaven and corn of wheat, Jesus must die a sacrificial death.[175]

(ii) The *necessity* for that death is also strongly seen, especially in the 'hour' of destiny.

(iii) There is moreover a definite *vicarious* element in the Lamb and shepherd passages and in the 'greater love' saying.

[174] R. Bultmann, *John*, p. 510 n. 10, points out that when the verb *hagiazō* is used with *hyper auton* it means to consecrate for the sacrifice. C. K. Barrett, *John*, p. 427, suggests that the meaning of this statement may be that the Son is asking that he may re-enter the divine life. Appeal is made to the *Corpus Hermeticum*.

[175] R. T. Fortna, 'From Christology to Soteriology', *Int* 27, 1973, pp. 31–47, provides a redaction-critical study of salvation in the fourth gospel. By positing a signs gospel, Fortna maintains that the author did not consider Jesus' death as itself effective, accomplishing in any way man's salvation. To do this he is obliged to declare that Jn. 1:29 was not in the signs gospel and Jn. 11:48–50 was not intended to provide a theology of atonement (p. 37). But this method of dealing with evidence is not convincing.

(iv) Behind the Lamb and shepherd passages there is also the concept of the *suffering servant*.

(v) A decided note of *exaltation and triumph* is present in the lifting up passages and in the assurance of the resurrection.

(vi) The motive for the death of Christ is seen to be the *love of God*.

(vii) The passion is applied in a *universal* manner. The bread is for the life of the world, the shepherd seeks sheep not of this fold (*i.e.* the Jewish), and the dying of one man for the nation is extended to God's children scattered abroad.

(viii) The death of Christ is specifically related to *sin* in the Lamb passage.

(ix) It is also related to the *overthrow of the devil* (Jn. 12:31).

(x) The application of the mission of Jesus to man is mediated through *faith*, although no explicit statement connects faith with his death.

John's presentation is, therefore, seen to be rich and varied. But we need next to compare his teaching with the synoptics, to discover what is common and what is distinctive.

So many of the points summarized above occur also in our summary of the synoptic gospels, that we cannot fail to see a common basis which had its origin in the sayings of Jesus and in some cases in early Christian reflection on his death. Some, however, see a difference in approach in the emphasis on revelation in John, which is absent from the synoptics. But this would be serious only if it excluded the sacrificial and vicarious elements, which it does not. Another issue is the different emphasis on the sacrament of the Lord's Supper (which assumes that chapter 6 deals with this), since John's account is said to stress communion with Christ rather than a sharing of Christ's self-offering.[176] But this difficulty arises from a wrong identification of chapter 6 as an exclusive reference to the Last Supper.

Again it is said that the emphasis on the sufferings of Christ is less evident in the Johannine passion narratives than in the synoptic gospels (especially Matthew and Mark). John's parallel to the Gethsemane incident is thought to be toned down because Jesus at once dismisses the hypothetical possibility of being saved from that hour of his passion (Jn. 12:27), whereas it is a real prayer in the synoptics. There is no saying from the cross comparable to the cry of abandonment in Matthew and Mark. There is, further, no glorification theme associated with the passion in Matthew and Mark, as there is in John. The application of the death of Christ is universalistic in John, but not in the others, and there is more emphasis in John on the motive behind the passion. Differences of emphasis must surely be admitted, but does this amount to a totally different evaluation? The variations of emphasis serve rather to throw into sharper relief the richness

---

[176] *Cf.* V. Taylor, *Jesus and His Sacrifice*, p. 242.

of the approach of both Jesus and the evangelists to the all-important meaning of his death. These basic reflections provide a jumping-off ground for the further expositions of the early church in Acts and the epistles, reflecting as they do both early proclamation and developed teaching. The brief references in the Johannine epistles may be found under the section on sacrifice (pp. 474f.) and justification (pp. 506f.).

THE SAVING WORK OF CHRIST: DEVELOPING UNDERSTANDING

In the foregoing study we have been confronted with two lines of evidence. Our main concern has been to discover from the gospel records what Jesus himself thought about his mission and particularly about his death. He did not present a doctrine of atonement, for he met with lack of understanding and opposition to the whole idea of a suffering Messiah. Nevertheless he gave sufficient indication of the significance of his death to provide a basis for the apostolic reflection upon it. Indeed, it is necessary to suppose that the apostles were fortified by their subsequent understanding of what Jesus had to say about his death.

Those who maintain that most of what is attributed to Jesus in the gospels is really the theological reflection of the early church, with little or no basis in his teaching, will naturally seek a different explanation of the atonement expounded in the Acts and especially in the epistles. According to this view, it arose out of the need for the Christian church to come to terms with the stern realities of the crucifixion. It is impossible to explain how Christians came to understand the death of Jesus in the way they did, unless some real basis for an explanation was found in his own teaching. It is significant that Luke, the only one of the evangelists to continue the story into the period of Christian proclamation, is at pains to include the incidents which record Jesus' expositions to the disciples about the necessity for the Messiah to suffer (Lk. 24:26f., 44ff.), although he does not give any explanation in terms of atonement. It makes greater sense to regard the resurrection narratives as providing the link between the historical events of the passion and the apostolic proclamation of the meaning of Christ's death, than to suppose that the interpretation was entirely the church's own construction. At the same time Paul and other NT writers, on the basis of the primitive interpretation, went on to supply further interpretations about the death of Christ.

In considering the evidence we shall first look at Acts and then group the rest under the following categories: (i) sacrifice and substitution, (ii) redemption (iii) the mediator and high priest, (iv) reconciliation, and (v) justification. Inevitably there will be some overlapping within these categories and care must be taken to avoid a splintering approach. But no view of the atonement in the NT will be complete without taking into account all these factors.

Acts

As a preliminary consideration we note that the death of Christ was seen to be part of the *divine purpose*. This comes clearly to the fore in Peter's first sermon in Acts 2:23, where near the beginning the preacher declared that Jesus was 'delivered up according to the definite plan and foreknowledge of God', although immediately afterwards he added, 'crucified and killed by the hands of lawless men.' This extraordinary juxtaposition of divine purpose and human responsibility is introduced without any attempt to explain the tension, or indeed any apparent awareness that such a tension existed. It was born of a strong conviction about the sovereign purposes of God, even in face of the crucifixion. It is astonishing, moreover, that the first proclamation of the Christian gospel should contain such a reference to God's foreknowledge. It was clearly important for the apostles to establish at once that what had happened to Jesus had not happened by accident, nor merely through cunning intrigues.

This line of thinking was closely linked with the conviction that Jesus' death was a *fulfilment of Scripture*. In Peter's second address he drew attention to the fact that 'what God foretold by the mouth of all the prophets, that his Christ should suffer, he thus fulfilled' (3:18). In this case, he is less harsh on the hearers and their rulers, since what they did to Jesus they did in ignorance (3:17). He spoke also of 'the time for establishing all that God spoke by the mouth of his holy prophets from of old' (3:21). In his speech in Cornelius' house Peter speaks of Jesus as 'the one ordained of God to be judge of the living and the dead' (Acts 10:42). This all-pervading sense that the crucifixion and resurrection of Jesus were predicted before his birth, and were therefore the fulfilment of God's purpose, is an important factor in the interpretation of his death. No explanation which does not take sufficient account of this is valid. We shall note the recurrence of this idea in other parts of the NT.

Our next line of evidence from Acts concerns '*the servant*' as a description of Jesus and his work. There are four statements where the title occurs (Acts 3:13, 26; 4:27, 30). It is generally agreed that these passages support identification of Jesus with the suffering servant of Isaiah (see earlier discussion, pp. 260ff.), although there are dissentient voices.[177] We have already noted that it seems reasonable to suppose that the apostles, after the resurrection, saw the relevance of the Isaiah servant passages (especially Is. 53) to Jesus. These Acts references speak of the raising up or glorifying of Jesus, of his turning people away from sin, of his being the agent through

---

[177] Notably M. D. Hooker, *Jesus and the Servant*, pp. 107–116.

whom signs and wonders are performed, and of his being anointed of God and yet opposed by men. In other parts of the NT the servant, in his vicarious and sacrificial function, is more clearly stressed than here, but the fact that the idea occurs in the earliest strand of the *kerygma* is of great importance.[178] What is seen here in embryonic form was later to be more fully appreciated.

Another feature to note is the conception of Jesus as *saviour*, with all that this involved. The title occurs twice in Acts, the first linked with the title 'Leader' in Peter's statement before the Sanhedrin (Acts 5:31), and the second in Paul's Antioch sermon (13:23). Salvation is seen to be directly related to sins, an aspect of the work of Christ which is prominent in Acts (*cf.* 2:38; 3:19; 5:31; 10:43; 13:38). The idea is that a blotting out of sin has taken place, a forgiveness has been granted. Moreover, Acts shows that salvation is obtainable only through Christ (Acts 4:12).

One other reference in Acts throw light on our present theme, *i.e.* Acts 20:28, 'Take heed to yourselves . . . to feed the church of the Lord which he obtained with his own blood.'[179] An alternative and strongly supported text has 'God' instead of 'Lord', but this introduces a more difficult idea. It might, however, for that reason be more original. What is significant for our present discussion is that both readings carry a sacrificial implication. The idea of the death of Christ being a purchase price is a distinctive emphasis in Paul's epistles. This gives Acts 20:28[180] an authentic ring on the lips of the apostle. That the people of God were not a self-sufficient people, but a people totally dependent on an act of grace and indeed totally belonging to God, is a profound aspect of NT theology, giving rise to radical reappraisals of contemporary lifestyles.

It is important to recognize that Acts does not present a complete picture of what the primitive church thought about the work of Christ. The evidence collected above is only incidental. It would be illegitimate to construct from it a theology of Acts, as some have attempted to do. This is not to deny that there are theological trends in Acts, as there are in the gospels. But Acts does not present a concerted picture of early Christian theology. It needs the testimony of the epistles to supplement it, and this is never more evident than in the doctrine of Christ's work. It may be wondered why the Acts account of early Christian preaching provides so little information about the atoning significance of Christ's death. It must

---

[178] C. H. Dodd, in *The Apostolic Preaching and its Developments*, p. 25, includes Acts 3:26 in the primitive kerygma, with its reference to Jesus as servant.

[179] So RSV first edition. The verb (*peripoieōmai*) which is here rendered 'obtained' means 'to keep for oneself' and then 'to gain possession of'. *Cf.* K. Lake and H. J. Cadbury, *The Beginnings of Christianity* 4 (1933), p. 261.

[180] I. H. Marshall, *Luke : Historian and Theologian*, p. 173, maintains that Acts 20:28 contains a traditional phrase. He considers that Luke has several times taken over traditions about the meaning of Jesus' death without developing them.

be supposed that the proclamation of the cross and resurrection was regarded as a sufficient basis for the message of forgiveness, without the necessity, on the initial preaching of the gospel, to give the rationale.

The epistles and Revelation

We shall set out the evidence from the epistles in a slightly different way as already indicated, but the different views of Paul, Hebrews, Peter and the Johannine epistles will be considered separately under each theme, where relevant.

Before coming to Paul's distinctive contribution[181] we must first note the indications of his indebtedness to earlier teaching on the work of Christ. His statement in 1 Corinthians 15:3 is specific, in which he clearly says that he had received, as the essence of his gospel, 'that Christ died for our sins in accordance with the scriptures, that he was buried, that he was raised. . .' For our present purpose there are two important considerations, (i) that the death of Christ was directly related to man's sins, and (ii) that it was seen as a fulfilment of scripture. Since these are part of the primitive tradition that Paul had received, they were both of essential importance for the earliest reflection on the passion.[182] The death was not presented as bare fact without any theological interpretation, even though at times the interpretation was limited. It remained for Paul and others to explore means of explaining the relationship between Christ's death and man's sin.[183]

We note that Paul acknowledges his indebtedness 'to the Lord' for the information about the institution of the Last Supper (1 Cor. 11:23ff.). It is not immediately clear what he meant by this, but it seems reasonable to suppose that he wished to emphasize the divine origin of the words of institution, although his words do not necessarily exclude the transmission of the tradition through other means. It is important to note that what Paul 'delivered' to the Corinthians he had himself first 'received'. The significance of this becomes clear in the section below which deals with the Lord's Supper. The importance of the work of Christ in the thought of Paul is evident from the central place he gave it in the proclamation of the gospel

---

[181] For detailed studies on Paul's doctrine of the work of Christ, *cf.* V. Taylor, *The Atonement in New Testament Teaching*, pp. 55ff.; L. Morris, *The Cross in the New Testament*, pp. 180ff.; G. E. Ladd, *TNT*, pp. 423ff.; H. Ridderbos, *Paul*, 159ff.; D. E. H. Whiteley, *The Theology of St Paul*, pp. 155ff.; *idem*, 'St Paul's Thought on the Atonement', *JTS* n.s. 8, 1957, pp. 240–255; E. Käsemann, 'The Pauline Theology of the Cross', *Int* 24, 1970, pp. 151–177.

[182] On the question whether 1 Cor. 15:3-5 reflects a Semitic background, *cf.* I. H. Marshall, *The Origins of New Testament Christology* (1976), p. 93, who regards it as beyond doubt. W. Kramer, *Christ, Lord and Son of God* (Eng. trans. 1966), pp. 38ff., considers that 'Christ' has been introduced into this kind of statement from Greek-speaking Jewish Christianity. *Cf.* also B. Klappert's brief note on the question, 'Zur Frage des semitischen oder griechischen Urtextes von 1 Kor. xv. 3–5', *NTS* 13, 1966-7, pp. 168ff.

[183] H. Ridderbos, 'The Earliest Confession of Atonement in Paul', in *Reconciliation and Hope* (ed. R. J. Banks, 1974), pp. 76–89, considers that 1 Cor. 15:3 constitutes the point of departure for Paul's doctrine of the atonement.

(*cf.* 1 Cor. 2:2). He recognized that many would regard this as foolishness, but for him it was nothing less than the power of God.[184]

SACRIFICE AND SUBSTITUTION

Paul. There is no doubt that sacrificial ideas played a major part in Paul's approach to the passion of Jesus. This is not surprising in view of his Jewish background. In his Corinthian correspondence he makes the claim that Christ is our paschal lamb who has been sacrificed (1 Cor. 5:7). This statement comes in a non-theological passage. Paul is dealing with the case of incest and is urging the Corinthians to purge out the old leaven. The use of this metaphor may well have given rise to this paschal lamb idea. But it comes so naturally that Paul must have reflected many times on the connection between Christ and the lambs sacrificed for the passover feast. His words may echo the belief that Jesus died at the precise time that the paschal lambs were being slain, but this is not essential to Paul's thought. He certainly saw Jesus as fulfilling the same function as a sacrifice. Since it was only a passing reference, he does not enlarge on the theme.

The words of institution, 'This cup is the new covenant in my blood' (1 Cor. 11:25),[185] carry the idea of a sacrifice which seals the new covenant, as the blood of sacrifice had sealed the old (Ex. 24). This use of the term 'blood' is frequent in Paul's epistles. In fact, he speaks of the blood of Christ more often than he speaks of his death (note such passages as Rom. 3:25; 5:9; Eph. 2:13). The idea of 'blood'[186] is more meaningful than 'death' since it draws attention to life as well as death. But it cannot be supposed that the primary significance is life given, for 'blood' is generally used with the implication of sacrifice (see also pp. 443ff.), especially in Paul's writings, where it is linked with propitiation (Rom. 3:25) and justification (Rom. 5:9).

The most specific identification of Christ's self-giving as a sacrifice is in Ephesians 5:2, which again occurs incidentally in a practical passage. The train of thought may be expressed as follows, 'Walk in love, because Christ loved us, and the best expression of that love is that "he gave himself up for us, a fragrant offering and a sacrifice to God".' The incidental nature of this reference shows the profound effect that Christian doctrine had on Christian practice. It also brings out the fact that the sacrificial idea was

---

[184] *Cf.* E. E. Ellis, 'Christ Crucified', in *Reconciliation and Hope*, pp. 69ff.

[185] In connection with the words of institution, it must be noted that the words, 'This do in remembrance of me' cannot be constructed to mean, 'Do this to remind God of me' *cf.* J. Jeremias, *The Eucharistic Words of Jesus* (Eng. trans. 1955), pp. 162ff. *Cf.* also D. Jones, '*anamnēsis* in the LXX and the interpretation of 1 Cor. xi.25', *JTS* n.s. 6, 1955, pp.183ff. This would detract attention from the once and for all divine self-offering of Jesus, and would involve the church in becoming a sort of mediator between God and Christ.

[186] J. Behm, in his article in *TDNT* 1, pp. 172ff., on *haima*, regards it as symbolic of self-giving and denies any cultic background. But *cf.* A. M. Stibbs, *The Meaning of the word 'Blood' in Scripture*.

rooted in love. There is certainly no thought of the sacrifice being the means by which man placates an angry deity, an idea quite alien to the whole teaching of the NT. Christ's self-giving is seen, in fact, as an acceptable offering, as the metaphor of fragrance shows.

The sacrificial imagery may lie behind Paul's statement in Romans 8:3 about God sending his Son 'in the likeness of sinful flesh and for sin (*peri hamartias*)'. This latter expression in Greek is in the LXX used at times for 'sin-offering', and this may well have been in Paul's mind. The subsequent statement that God condemned sin in the flesh shows the close connection in Paul's mind between judgment on sin and the sending of the Son. A similar idea is found in Galatians 1:4, where it is said of Christ that he 'gave himself for our sins.'

The idea of substitution is closely linked with that of sacrifice, but warrants separate consideration. As a Jew Paul would be familiar with the cultus in which sacrifices were offered by worshippers as an offering to God. He would know of the symbolism of the scapegoat on the day of atonement. He would know that hands[187] were placed on the goat to symbolize the laying of sins upon the animal, which was then driven into the wilderness. The notion of substitution associated with sacrifice would not be alien to Paul's mind. Indeed, it would be strange if some evidence of it were not found in his letters. Admittedly, questions of interpretation arise over this issue since some deny substitution and prefer to speak of Christ's death as representative. We shall discuss this distinction after stating the evidence for Paul's usage.

We begin with passages in which Paul uses the preposition 'for' (*hyper*) in a substitutionary sense. The classic expression of Paul's doctrine of substitution is seen in 2 Corinthians 5:21. What precisely Paul meant when he said that 'for our sake (*hyper*) he (God) made him to be sin who knew no sin' has been much debated.[188] It is none too easy to conceive how the sinless Messiah could possibly be made sin. It must imply that Christ became something which he was not before. In being made sin, moreover, he could not sully his own absolute purity and excellence of moral character. It must mean that in some sense Jesus did something of an objective nature in taking the place of those who would themselves otherwise suffer death. Paul's words seem to imply a definite identification of Jesus with sin in a way which is profound and unfathomable.[189] He clearly did not want to say that Jesus became a sinner, but he gets as near as possible to

---

[187] See comment on the laying on of hands on p. 433f.

[188] H. Lietzmann and W. G. Kümmel *An die Korinther I/II* (LHB,⁵1969), p. 127, links the expression, *hamartia epoiēsen*, with Gal. 3:13 in the sense that Christ was bearer of the sin as he was bearer of the cross.

[189] H. E. Guillebaud, *Why the Cross?* (1937), p. 79 n., rightly rejects the view that Paul was thinking of a subjective self-identification of Christ with human sin, since if he had meant that he would have written, 'He made himself to be sin for us'.

it. Perhaps the best way to express it is to say he was regarded as a sinner.[190] In Romans 8:32, 'He (God) gave him (his own Son) up for us all,' Paul is clearly thinking of an action by God and his Son on man's behalf and in all probability also in man's place. The substitutionary element is more clearly expressed in 2 Corinthians 5:15, in which the statement 'He died for all'[191] is immediately followed by a statement of the consequence that those who live might live 'for him who for their sake died and was raised'. There is an identification of the believer with Christ in his death and resurrection.

The profoundness of 2 Corinthians 5:21 is matched in some measure by the statement in Galatians 3:13, 'Christ redeemed us from the curse of the law, having become a curse for us.' The allusion is based on a citation from Deuteronomy 27:26 (LXX), which pronounces a curse on those who do not abide by everything written in the law. A second citation from Deuteronomy 21:23 pronounces a curse on everyone who hangs on a tree. In the first case there can be no application to Christ except vicariously. In the second case the circumstances surrounding the death of Christ connect that death with a curse, but still do not explain how Christ could become a curse for us. Paul is in no doubt that in order to redeem us from the curse Christ had to become identified in some way with the condition of those he was sent to redeem.[192] God could never curse his Son, but since he has already pronounced a curse on sin, his Son could not avoid the implications of this if he identified himself with man's sin. At this point we are undoubtedly faced with a mystery, but we nevertheless cannot fail to see the substitutionary implications of statements like 2 Corinthians 5:21 and Galatians 3:13.[193]

Some importance must be attached to the form of wording used in Paul's account of the institution of the Lord's Supper in 1 Corinthians 11:24.[194]

[190] In commenting on this verse, E. L. Kendall, *A Living Sacrifice* (1960), p. 88, remarks that it is 'part of the horror of sin that in order to repair its ravages it was "necessary" for Jesus, himself completely sinless, to identify himself even to the point of death with the full condemnation which sin entails.'

[191] Some have deduced from this statement that Paul saw Christ's work as having universal significance. *Cf.* D. M. Lake, 'He died for all: The Universal Dimensions of the Atonement', in *Grace Unlimited* (ed. C. H. Pinnock, 1975), pp. 31–50. But he acknowledges that only by faith does it apply to individuals.

[192] J. W. C. Wand, *The Atonement*, p. 51, explains Paul's words by maintaining that Christ accepted the condition of a person 'accursed'. The act of substitution involved him in identifying himself with the lot of those he was seeking to save. As L. Morris points out, the statement that Christ became a curse must mean that he bore the curse (*The Cross in the New Testament*, pp. 222f.).

[193] V. Taylor, *The Atonement in New Testament Teaching*, p. 88, agrees that Gal. 3:13 must mean that Christ participated in the reprobation which rests on sin. Some aspect of substitution in Paul's words cannot be denied. *Cf.* D. Dawson-Walker, 'The Pauline view of Atonement' in *The Atonement in History and Life* (ed. L. W. Grensted, 1936), pp. 133–153, esp. pp. 145f. R. H. Culpepper, *Interpreting the Atonement*, pp. 71f., criticizes V. Taylor's arguments.

[194] Some do not take this statement as referring to Christ's sacrificial death (*cf.* E. P. Sanders, *Paul and Palestinian Judaism*, p. 466 n. 49). But for the contrary opinion, *cf.* R. Bultmann, *TNT*, 1, p. 296. Sanders cites D. Daube, *Wine in the Bible* (1974), pp. 15f., in support of his view.

The preposition *hyper* occurs in the phrase 'broken for you', and since this refers to Christ's body a sacrificial and also substitutionary significance seems clear. The bread symbolizes an act of Jesus on behalf of others.

Yet another statement that uses the preposition *hyper* and links the death of Christ with the life of his people is 1 Thessalonians 5:10. Christ 'died for us so that whether we wake or sleep we might live with him'. This suggests again that Christ's death achieved something on our behalf which enables us to live in an entirely new way. There is no question here of an objective action which absolves the believer of any moral or spiritual responsibility. Since the statement occurs in a mainly practical epistle, it is not surprising that Paul does not give an explanation of how Christ's death can secure the believer's life. He takes it for granted that his readers will recognize the force of his statement, for no doubt he had expounded this theme when he was among them. As in Paul's epistles as a whole, there is a connection between doctrine and practice.

We cannot leave this section without further comment on the distinction which is often drawn between a substitute and a representative. A man may act on another's behalf, as for instance when a lawyer pleads the cause of his client. He is acting as his client's representative, but not as his substitute. Yet if another were to identify himself so closely with a man's cause that he were prepared to accept for himself the consequence of that man's action, it would be substitution. Clearly the latter case involves a more radical identification than the former. It makes a considerable difference to our understanding of Paul's meaning which concept we consider to be the more appropriate.

V. Taylor[195] has strongly argued for the representative character of Christ's work on the grounds that Paul does not use distinctive substitutionary vocabulary, such as the preposition *anti* (in place of), or a concept such as 'ransom' (*lytron*) and its related nouns. The use of the latter word in its strengthened form in 1 Timothy 2:6 is dismissed by Taylor because he does not regard 1 Timothy as Pauline. But those who accept the Pastorals as reflecting Paul's thought will see less force in the representative argument. Admittedly *hyper* (for, on behalf of) is frequently used in a representative sense; but, where the context requires it, the preposition sometimes assumes the force of *anti*, as in the case cited above. Taylor

[195] V. Taylor, *op. cit.*, pp. 85ff. *Cf.* F. W. Camfield, 'The Idea of Substitution in the Doctrine of the Atonement', *SJT* 1, 1948, pp. 282–293. He strongly maintains that substitution is part of the background of everything that is said about Christ and his meaning. He criticizes V. Taylor for restricting himself to specific statements about Atonement and not giving sufficient attention to the background. In his article 'Paul's Understanding of the Death of Jesus', in *Reconciliation and Hope* (ed. R. J. Banks, 1974), J. D. G. Dunn makes the attempt to justify a preference for 'representative' by suggesting that Jesus died as the representative man. At the same time he does not want to lose sight of the substitutionary idea altogether. The problem with this is that the word 'representative' need not, although it might, involve a substitutionary act.

admits that Romans 3:25 may have a substitutionary force because of the use of *hilastērion* (propitiation), although he takes the word to mean expiation (see discussion below).

There is no doubt that the idea of representation would weaken the force of the passages which have been considered above. Indeed when Christ was made 'sin' and became a 'curse' for us, it is difficult to see what is meant if Jesus merely acted on our behalf rather than in our stead. Even Taylor[196] admits that these statements must mean that Jesus participated in the reprobation which rests on sin. He goes as far as to say that 2 Corinthians 5:21 is the nearest Paul gets to the idea of sin-bearing. In the face of this it is enigmatic that he so strongly rejects the idea of substitution.

We must now consider the classic passage which introduces the idea of propitiation (Rom. 3:25).[197] This is closely linked with sacrifice, but it has a distinctive contribution of its own which needs comment. The statement about Christ says, 'whom God put forward as an expiation by his blood, to be received by faith.' Here the RSV has translated the word *hilastērion* as 'expiation', which literally should be rendered 'propitiation'. The difference is important. Expiation relates to sins, and propitiation to God. Expiation is an act which allows for the removal of the consequences of sin, and propitiation is an act which enables God to receive the sinner.

But what is Paul's meaning here? We may at once reject the idea of man

---

[196] V. Taylor, *op. cit.*, p. 88.

[197] For recent studies on Rom. 3:22b-25, *cf.* W. D. Davies, *Paul and Rabbinic Judaism*, pp. 237ff.; J. Reumann, 'The Gospel of the Righteousness of God', *Int* 20, 1966, pp. 432–452; C. H. Talbert, 'A non-Pauline Fragment at Rom 3:24–26?' *JBL* 85, 1966, pp. 287ff.; G. Howard, 'Romans 3:21-31 and the inclusion of the Gentiles', *HTR* 63, 1970, pp. 223–233; E. Lohse, *Märtyrer und Gottesknecht* (*FRLANT* 64 NF 46, Göttingen ²1963), pp. 147ff. *Cf.* also E. Käsemann, 'Zum Verständnis von Rom. 3:24-26', *ZNW* 43, 1950-1, pp. 150ff.; W. G. Kümmel *ZTK* 49, 1952, pp. 154–167. L. Morris, 'The meaning of *hilastērion* in Romans 3:25', *NTS* 2, 1955-6, pp. 33–43. C. H. Dodd, *The Bible and the Greeks* (1935), p. 94, argues for the meaning 'expiation'. E. P. Sanders, *Paul and Palestinian Judaism*, p. 465, declines to distinguish between expiation, propitiation and substitution, on the grounds that there is no evidence that such distinctions were made in the first century AD, or that they are relevant to Paul. He takes this passage to mean 'the atonement for the past transgressions of all by Christ's death' (p. 464 n. 43). W. D. Davies, *Paul and Rabbinic Judaism*, p. 242, maintains that although Paul uses sacrificial terms he leaves them inchoate. *Cf.* also D. E. H. Whiteley *The Theology of St Paul*, pp. 130–151, who rejects the idea of substitution and speaks rather of 'salvation through participation'. It has been suggested that the leading idea behind Rom. 3:25 is Jewish martyr theology, *cf.* D. Hill's discussion of various possibilities, *Greek words and Hebrew meanings*, (1967), pp. 41ff. But the fact that it is God himself who provides the propitiation shows that more is involved than would be possible under martyr theology alone.

H. Conzelmann, *TNT*, p. 71, claims that in Rom 3:24f., we have an accumulation of non-Pauline concepts and ideas. He bases this on the different use of words (*e.g. dikaiosynē*) and on the idea of forgiveness depending on an atoning sacrifice. He thinks that Paul does not regard the concept of forgiveness of sins to be adequate. If by this Conzelmann means adequate in itself, we would agree. But he has not given sufficient grounds for disputing that Paul wrote of Christ's death as an atoning sacrifice. He certainly has other ideas, but that is no justification for supposing that sacrificial ideas are alien. Nor is it evident (as Conzelmann maintains) that forgiveness can deal only with past sins.

For a survey of recent views on this passage, *cf.* P. Stuhlmacher, 'Zur neueren Exegese von Röm. 3, 24-25, in *Jesus and Paulus* (ed. E. E. Ellis and E. Grässer, 1975), pp. 315–333.

placating an angry deity, since in this case God himself provides the pro-pitiation.[198] The word[199] itself is connected with the mercy-seat and may convey the idea of a covering. Alternatively it may be regarded as a 'means of propitiation' (*i.e.* propitiatory) or as 'expiation'.[200] In all probability Paul intended his wording to convey both the thought that God was in some way propitiated and also that sin was expiated by a sacrificial offering. James Denney explained his understanding of Paul's words as follows: 'Something is done which enables God to justify the ungodly who believe in Jesus, and at the same time to appear signally and conspicuously a righteous God'.[201] This is considerably more powerful than Taylor's par-aphrase that God 'had confronted men with a means of expiation or atone-ment, operative in Christ and His sacrificial death.'[202]

We cannot properly appreciate the idea of propitiation in Paul's thought without setting it alongside his teaching on the wrath of God (*orgē*). It is significant, for instance, that Dodd evaporates from the idea of wrath all thought of anger.[203] For him the wrath of God describes 'an inevitable process of cause and effect in a moral universe'. He admits that this deper-sonalizes it, but justifies this as a development away from the more pri-mitive concept of a God who strikes terror into men. This, however, weakens Paul's strong comparison between the revelation of the righteous-ness and wrath of God (*cf.* Rom. 1:17, 18).[204] If righteousness is personal in the sense of belonging to God, it is difficult to deny the same to wrath. Moreover, there is no distinction in meaning between wrath and anger (*thymos*).[205] These are sometimes used synonymously. Nevertheless the latter is more suited to passionate anger or strong emotion, whereas the former is more settled.

In view of this it cannot be denied that wrath when applied to God must indicate more than passively watching the effects of natural causes. It must denote an active revulsion of holiness against unholiness. The anger is not directed against men as such, as if God were hostile to his own creation.

---

[198] So L. Morris, *The Apostolic Preaching of the Cross*, pp. 144ff.

[199] *Cf.* F. Büchsel, *TDNT* 3, pp. 320ff. He maintains that, since God is the subject not the object in this passage, the reference must be to expiation not propitiation. This would certainly be true if propitiation were understood in its pagan sense. But Büchsel admits that the word serves the revelation of God. It must in some way relate to God and cannot be wholly devoid of a subjective meaning.

[200] *Cf.* W. Sanday and A. C. Headlam, *Romans*, (*ICC*, ⁵1902)) *ad loc. Cf.* the comments of M. Black, *Romans* (*NCB*, 1973) *ad loc.* and C. E. B. Cranfield, *Romans* (*ICC*, 1975), *ad loc.*

[201] J. Denney, *The Death of Christ* (1911), p. 119.

[202] V. Taylor, *op. cit.*, p. 91. *Cf. idem*, 'Great Texts Reconsidered (Rom. 3:25f)', *ExT*, 50, 1939, pp. 295ff.

[203] C. H. Dodd, *Romans* (*MNT*, 1932), p. 23.

[204] F. F. Bruce, *Romans* (*TNTC*, 1963), p. 106, contends that the context of Rom. 3:25 demands that the *hilastērion* removed the wrath of God, in view of what Paul says in Rom. 1:18. *Cf.* G. Bornkamm, 'The Revelation of God's wrath (Romans 1—3)', in *Early Christian Experience* (Eng. trans. 1969), who declares that Rom. 1:18 belongs inseparably with Rom. 1:17, '. . . the "righteousness" given to believers preserves them before the "wrath" of God, a wrath now already revealed to the lost world' (pp. 63f.).

[205] *Cf.* L. Morris, *The Apostolic Preaching of the Cross*, p. 180.

But he cannot abide sin.[206] In this case wrath plays as active a part in God's approach to men as righteousness. Indeed the two concepts are inseparable. When Paul speaks of propitiation, he must have had in mind God's righteous wrath against sin. It must therefore relate in some way to the removal of God's hostility.[207] For Paul this is involved in his whole concept of salvation. What Christ did was a substitutionary act by which God shows that his anger is turned away, so that men are now freed to come into a new relationship with him. This is very different from the appeasement idea, in which the worshipper was obliged to adhere to certain rituals to persuade the god to change his attitude. In Christian thought it is God himself who takes the initiative.

It need not be supposed that there was any thought in Paul's mind that this sterner side of the divine nature contradicts God's love. For him the sacrificial work of Christ was a provision of God's love (Rom. 5:8). It is because of the limitations of human analogies that many problems arise for the theologian when he is grappling with the concept of wrath. Because it is difficult for man to conceive of the co-existence of perfect love and hate, it is therefore imagined to be impossible with God. But it is as impossible to think of a pure love existing in God, which made no move against evil. Paul makes no attempt to do so. It may be that both wrath and propitiation are now considered to be unsatisfactory terms to be used in relation to God because they are anthropomorphisms, but there are no more adequate terms. In using them Paul recognizes that they have unique meaning when applied to God's action in Christ.[208] We shall note below the recurrence of the propitiation theme in the Johannine epistles.

It is mainly on the grounds of Paul's statements about substitution, especially Romans 3:24ff.; Galatians 3:13 and 2 Corinthians 5:21, that a penal theory of atonement has been advocated. Whereas there is strong modern objection to this theory, it cannot be denied that Paul's language gives some support to the view that Christ suffered what in some sense sinful man should have suffered.[209] Even if we avoid the term 'penal', which Paul himself does not use, there is no way of avoiding the conclusion that in his thought Christ had died the sinner's death.

---

[206] Cf. the severe sayings of Jesus. R. V. G. Tasker, *The Biblical Doctrine of the Wrath of God* (1951), p. 36, comments on these passages.

[207] Cf. L. Morris, *op. cit.*, p. 198.

[208] Some modern scholars have attempted to shift the emphasis in Paul's theology away from the sacrificial idea. E. P. Sanders, *Paul and Palestinian Judaism*, p. 466, for instance, claims that in reference to Christ's death, Paul was thinking more in terms of a change of lordship than in terms of the expiation of past sins. He agrees with D. E. H. Whiteley, *The Theology of St Paul*, pp. 130–151, in not supporting a substitutionary view and preferring a participationist explanation. Nevertheless, Pauline substitutionary language is notoriously stubborn in face of such opinions. It is more central than these views allow.

[209] Cf. A. M. Hunter, *Interpreting Paul's Gospel* (1954), pp. 91f.; R. G. Crawford, 'Is the Penal Theory of the Atonement Scriptural?' *SJT* 23, 1970, pp. 257–272.

In view of his definite use of sacrificial language,[210] it is noteworthy that the apostle Paul nowhere sees Christ as high priest, as Hebrews does. The nearest he gets is to comment on the mediatorial work of Christ (see section below). Yet it cannot be said that he would have found the idea uncongenial. He is concerned rather to explore the meaning of the death of Christ as a sacrificial offering for sin.

Hebrews. It would not be an exaggeration to call the epistle to the Hebrews the NT textbook on the sacrifice of Christ.[211] The theme permeates the whole argument because it is so inextricably linked with the high-priesthood of Christ. Since the function of a priest was essentially related to the fellowship of God and man, the priesthood was concerned about the means by which an approach to God could be made.[212] It is this aspect of priesthood which will be considered here (but see the section on the mediator for other aspects).

We shall aim to bring out the most significant features in the teaching on sacrifice in this epistle. We note first that it is *related to sin*. This comes out as early as Hebrews 1:3, where purging of sins is mentioned as the prelude to the Son's enthronement.[213] No specific mention is made of the mode of purging, but since the action precedes the exaltation the reference must be to the crucifixion, especially in view of the many references to the death of Christ or the blood of Christ in the epistle. The purging refers to the removal of sins and to the cleansing of the sinner. The writer mentions in Hebrews 2:17, on the first introduction of the high priest theme, that our high priest had to become like his brethren in order to make 'expiation for the sins of the people' (*hilaskomai*),[214] which may be compared with Paul's statement in Romans 3:25. The verb in this case is related specifically

---

[210] While E. Käsemann, 'The Pauline Theology of the Cross', *Int* 24, 1970, pp. 151–177, admits that Paul speaks unmistakably in terms of sacrifice, he claims that Paul never unambiguously designates the death of Christ as a sacrifice (*cf.* p. 161). But several Pauline passages come sufficiently near to doing this to make it clear that sacrificial terms were of great importance to the apostle in his theology of the cross. *Cf.* also Käsemann, *Perspectives on Paul* (Eng. trans. 1971), pp. 42ff. For a criticism of Käsemann's position, *cf.* J. D. G. Dunn, 'Paul's Understanding of the Death of Christ', in *Reconciliation and Hope* (ed. R. J. Banks), p. 131. M. Barth, *Was Christ's Death a Sacrifice?* (1961), p. 48, concludes his study with the assertion that Christ's death was sacrificial in the sense that it was *the* sacrifice.

[211] For a detailed discussion of the work of Christ in Hebrews, *cf.* L. Morris's section on this epistle in *The Cross in the New Testament*, pp. 270–308.

[212] *Cf.* S. Lyonnet, 'Expiation and Intercession', *Bib* 40, 1959, pp. 900f., for a discussion of the link between these two ideas.

[213] It is important to note that the verb in Heb. 1:3 is an aorist participle, which totally excludes any thought that Christ continued to offer his sacrifice in heaven. *Cf.* P. E. Hughes' comment on this, *Hebrews*, 1977, p. 47 n. 24.

[214] This statement in Heb. 2:17 must not be isolated from its context, which stresses the true humanity of Jesus. It is an essential qualification for the one who was to make expiation for the sins of the people that he should share the same nature. L. Morris, *op. cit.*, p. 288 n. 35, criticizes G. Aulén for failing to give significance to Christ's manhood in his exposition of the atonement.

to sin, whereas in Romans 3:25 the noun is not so specific. The idea of expiation involves some kind of substitutionary action by which sins can be removed.

There are incidental references to the relation of the levitical cultus to sins. For instance, the Aaronic priest was 'bound to offer sacrifice for his own sins as well as for those of the people' (5:3). This statement is a sequel to the statement in 4:15 to the effect that our high priest was without sin. But it is not until 7:26f. that the comparison is fully drawn out in the statement that Christ 'has no need, like those high priests, to offer sacrifices daily. . .; he did this once for all when he offered up himself'. Christ's self-offering distinguishes it from the sacrifices offered by the priests; nevertheless, like theirs, his was related to sins, while being infinitely more effective because of its once-for-all character. The statement in Hebrews 9:22 that 'without the shedding of blood there is no forgiveness of sins' sums up the central character of sacrifice in the OT system (cf. also 13:11). Yet immediately afterwards, in 10:5ff., the author cites Psalm 40:6–8, which shows that God does not delight in burnt offerings and sin offerings. The emphasis falls rather on the fulfilling of God's will, which is seen supremely in the 'offering of the body of Jesus Christ once for all'.

The 'once for all' character of Christ's sacrifice is particularly connected in this epistle with the putting away of sins.[215] In addition to 7:26f. and 9:22, mentioned above, we can add 9:26 and 10:12; in both references the conclusive nature of Christ's offering is set against the endless repetition of the Aaronic ritual (cf. also Heb. 8:3). It is because of this that the priesthood of Christ must be placed in a different category from the Aaronic priesthood (i.e. the order of Melchizedek). There is also a different location for the presentation of the offerings, for the Aaronic high priest presented an annual blood offering in the earthly holy of holies (Heb. 9:7ff.), whereas Christ presented his offering in a heavenly and perfect sanctuary (Heb. 9:12).[216] The totally different character of the offering of Christ is seen

---

[215] Some have tended to play down this once-for-all character of Christ's act by appealing to Heb. 10:5-10 as evidence that his obedience rather than his sacrificial act provided a satisfaction to God. Cf. T. H. Hughes, The Atonement (1949), p. 35. But this does not do justice to the thought of this epistle, and ignores the finality of an offering which certainly consisted in more than an obedient attitude of mind. As C. F. D. Moule, The Sacrifice of Christ (1956), p. 25, comments, 'The obedient self-offering of a personality was not a unique event'. He finds the uniqueness in Christology.

[216] C. Gore, The Body of Christ (1901), pp. 253f., claims that atonement was accomplished at Christ's entrance into heaven, not on the cross. But he identifies the propitiation with the intercession of Christ. This view, however, contravenes the once-for-all character of Christ's sacrifice. Cf. A. Vanhoye, 'De "aspectu" oblationis Christi secundum Epistolam ad Hebraeos', Verbum Domini 37, 1959, pp. 32ff., who points out that in Hebrews the aorist tense is always used in references to the sacrifice of Christ. W. E. Brooks, 'The Perpetuity of Christ's sacrifice in the Epistle to the Hebrews', JBL 89, 1970, pp. 205ff., discusses the point at which Jesus offered his sacrifice, and claims that it must have been subsequent to the resurrection. He disagrees with L. Morris that blood refers to violent death and maintains that the killing of the sacrifice was not the central feature of the atonement ritual (p. 209 n. 16). But it is difficult to see how the manipulation of the blood can be central without implying a violent death of the victim.

most clearly in Hebrews 9:14 where the writer says of Christ, 'who through the eternal Spirit offered himself without blemish to God.' Such an offering is distinguished from animal sacrifices by being the sacrifice of a man. The absolute perfection of the offering and its completely voluntary nature contrast strikingly with the helpless victims of the Jewish sacrificial system. Another feature is the cooperation between the Son and the Spirit in this completely adequate offering.

The climax of the exposition of the theme in Hebrews is reached in 10:19, 'Therefore, brethren, since we have confidence to enter the sanctuary by the blood of Christ', where 'blood' stands for all that is implied in the sacrifice of Christ. This provides a 'new and living way' for God's people. We now have a different kind of altar (Heb. 13:10) from the old Jewish altar. It is situated outside the 'camp' of Judaism altogether.

Some comment must be made on the significance of the word '*blood*' in Hebrews, since this has been claimed to denote not death but life.[217] Yet this cannot be maintained in this epistle. We have already noted that it is highly questionable whether such a construction can be put on the OT conception of sacrificial blood (p. 433). Certain passages in Hebrews, moreover, definitely exclude this view. In Hebrews 9:14f. 'the blood of Christ' is linked to the clause 'a death having taken place' (verse 15), which would make no sense if the meaning of 'blood' was a life given. Similarly in Hebrews 12:24 the allusion to the blood of Abel, which is contrasted with the blood of Christ, must refer to Abel's death, and by inference the same must be said of Christ. It should be noted that in this latter context the expression 'the sprinkled blood' in all probability refers to the sin offering. Hebrews 13:11f. is another passage which places emphasis on the dead bodies of the levitical sacrifices and not on the blood as representing life.

It is significant that in the concluding prayer in 13:20–21, there is reference to the 'blood of the eternal covenant', for this shows the centrality of the idea and also demonstrates it to be the mainspring for practical action (*i.e.* for equipment and inner activity).

1 Peter. In this brief letter with its strongly practical purpose, it is striking that several passages refer directly to the sacrificial nature of the work of Christ. The theme was clearly not regarded as of purely academic interest. The first allusion is in 1 Peter 1:2, where the elect are said to be 'sanctified by the Spirit for obedience to Jesus Christ and for sprinkling with his blood'. Since this statement comes after an introductory address to the exiles of the dispersion, it is reasonable to suppose that an 'exodus' imagery is in mind, especially as in other parts of the letter this is clear (as, for instance, in 2:1–10). The sprinkling would then be an allusion to the blood

---

[217] So B. F. Westcott, *Hebrews*, pp. 293f. See above, n. 114 for other views.

which ratified the old covenant (Ex. 24).[218] The sacrificial nature of the blood is here indisputable.

In the ransom passage in 1 Peter 1:18ff. (see further comment in the section on redemption, p. 480), it is 'the precious blood of Christ like that of a lamb without blemish or spot'. Again no doubt can exist that the blood is sacrificial blood.[219] The third main passage is 1 Peter 2:22–24, which uses language which is strongly influenced by the servant passage in Isaiah 53, where the sacrificial significance is expressed in substitutionary form: 'He himself bore our sins in his body on the tree, that we might die to sin and live to righteousness.' The 'bearing of sins' may be related to Leviticus 5:17. That the sins were not Christ's own must mean that he was substituting for those who had sins, since he had none of his own. When the further statement is made, 'By his wounds you have been healed,' the vicarious quality of his work on the cross comes immediately into focus.

In the fourth passage the substitutionary character becomes even more explicit. 'For Christ also died for sins once for all, the righteous for (*hyper*) the unrighteous, that he might bring us to God, being put to death in the flesh but made alive in the Spirit' (1 Pet. 3:18). Although the preposition used does not in itself demand a substitutionary meaning, the context shows this to be Peter's intention. It would weaken the force of the argument if a representative and not a substitutionary interpretation is in mind. The meaning is unmistakable – the righteous took the place of the unrighteous. There is also a noticeable parallel here with the passages in Hebrews which emphasize the once-for-all character of the sacrifice of Christ.[220]

These four passages in 1 Peter support a sacrificial and substitutionary interpretation of the atonement. A further important observation is that this truth is used to support an appeal to the exemplary nature of Christ's sufferings in 1 Peter 2:13ff. The example of Christ is not regarded as an interpretation of his death, *i.e.* that people should see how he suffered and died and should regard this as a pattern for themselves. It is the reverse: Christ in his suffering becomes an example because he has first become a substitute. The linking of the ideas, moreover, shows that for Peter as for Paul, Christian ethics were firmly rooted in Christian doctrine.

The Johannine epistles. There are two statements in 1 John which introduce the idea of expiation. In 1 John 2:1–2, 'Jesus Christ the Righteous' is said to be 'the expiation (*hilasmos*) for our sins, and not for ours only but also for the sins of the whole world'. As in the case of Romans 3:25, the word

---

[218] *Cf.* E. G. Selwyn, *1 Peter*, 1946, pp. 120f., on this exodus allusion to the covenant.

[219] As L. Morris, *The Cross in the New Testament*, p. 322, states, 'Peter is sure that something with far-reaching implications was effected by Christ's death, and something completely objective'.

[220] *Cf.* R. T. France's article in *New Testament Interpretation* (ed. I. H. Marshall, 1977), p. 267, for comments on the sacrificial echoes in the wording of 1 Pet. 3:18.

translated in RSV as 'expiation' should more properly be understood in the sense of 'propitiation'. We have already seen (p. 468f.) that propitiation would involve more than the cancelling of guilt and the purification of the sinner. The fact that in this context Christ is described as an advocate, who is needed only if the wrath of God against sin is a present reality, supports the view that in some way he was a propitiation, and not just an expiation.[221] The same goes for the statement in 1 John 4:10, 'In this is love, not that we loved God but that he loved us and sent his Son to be the expiation for our sins.' This is a remarkable case of God providing the propitiation, a reinterpretation of the idea which totally transforms it. Moreover, the motivating force is love, the very antithesis of anger.[222]

In neither of these passages is the action connected specifically with the death of Christ, but in 1 John 1:7 it is 'the blood of Jesus Christ his (*i.e.* God's) Son' which 'cleanses us from all sin'. Again the 'blood' must mean the 'death' in common with other NT usage. In all these three passages the focus falls on the relation between what Christ has done and man's sins. 1 John 3:5, also relates Christ's mission to the removal of man's sins, and gives as the basis of such an achievement the fact that in Christ was no sin. The bearing (*arei*) of sins finds a close parallel in the 1 Peter 2:24 passage discussed above. The word has sacrificial and vicarious implications. In 1 John 3:16, John says, 'By this we know love, that he laid down his life for (*hyper*) us', which again may suggest a substitutionary act. If it be understood in a representative way, it would weaken the statement to mean no more than an example, but admittedly the following words, 'and we ought to lay down our lives for the brethren', would support this contention. Taken in conjunction with the other passages in 1 John, it is not unreasonable to suggest that a substitutionary idea may also be in the writer's mind, but that he does not specifically state this because he wishes to use the work of Christ as the basis for an exhortation.

Revelation. In this book the sacrificial idea is strongly represented by the Lamb, a name for Jesus Christ which occurs 29 times. He is described in Revelation 5:6 as 'a Lamb standing, as though it had been slain'. The Lamb is undoubtedly a sacrificial Lamb, although he is now triumphant. There is here, therefore, a combination of the sacrificial Lamb, seen in Isaiah's servant passage (Is. 53) and in John the Baptist's announcement (Jn. 1:29), and the symbolic leader lamb of the Jewish apocalypses.[223] A striking feature of the Lamb of John's Apocalypse is the statement that he was slain before the foundation of the world (if this is the correct understanding of

---

[221] *Cf.* C. H. Dodd, *The Johannine Epistles* (1964), *ad loc.*

[222] B. F. Westcott, *The Epistles of St John* (³1892), p. 44, points out the significance of Christ being called 'our propitiation' and not our 'propitiator'. The former can include the latter, but not vice versa.

[223] *Cf.* L. Morris, *The Apostolic Preaching of the Cross*, pp. 136f.

Rev. 13:8; but RSV translates differently, presumably on the basis of 17:8, where the phrase refers to the writing in the book of life).

One passage which connects Christ's work with man's sins is Revelation 1:5, 'To him who loves us and has freed us from our sins by his blood'. The second verb (*lyō*) contains the idea of deliverance (see below on redemption), but the fact that the loosing is directly linked with Christ's blood supports a sacrificial interpretation. This is even more pronounced if the alternative reading (*lousanti*, 'washed') is the original.

In view of the fact that the emphasis of this whole book is on the work of the heavenly Christ, it is not surprising that the death of Christ is not much stressed. Nevertheless the risen Christ is still the Christ who has been sacrificed.

REDEMPTION

We have already noted the use of the word 'ransom' (*lytron*) by Jesus and have seen reason to regard this as being connected with Isaiah 53 in his mind. It was argued that the idea of substitution is inescapable in the form of the saying in Mark 10:45 (= Mt. 20:28). We come now to consider the conception of redemption in Paul's theology.

Paul. Although Paul does not use the word that Jesus used (*lytron*), he did use an important derivative (*apolytrōsis*), which conveys the idea of *redemption*.[224] The root meaning of this word is the process of obtaining release by payment of a ransom, and this seems to be true of the NT uses. Certainly Paul seems to have chosen this word because it expresses an idea of ransom which he wants to associate with the work of Christ.[225]

The word 'redemption' (*apolytrōsis*) occurs only ten times in the NT, seven times in Paul, twice in Hebrews and once in Luke. It is therefore particularly characteristic of Paul. A brief survey of the occurrences will show in what sense he intended it.

The passage in Romans (3:24ff.), already discussed in reference to propitiation, is relevant here. Indeed the mention of 'redemption' immediately precedes the mention of 'propitiation'. The statement runs, 'They are justified by his grace as a gift, through the redemption which is in Christ Jesus, whom God put forward as an expiation (propitiation) by his blood.' There is here an indirect, but nonetheless certain, allusion to the cost of deliverance (*i.e.* blood), which shows that the root idea of ransom is in mind.[226] Although the blood here is more closely linked to propitiation,

[224] *Ibid.*, p. 41.

[225] H. Conzelmann, *TNT*, p. 158, sees three types of redemption in Paul: eschatological, juridical and mystical (the latter he regards as authentically Pauline). Justification, Conzelmann thinks, is merely a 'subsidiary crater'. A. Schweitzer, *The Mysticism of Paul The Apostle* (1930, Eng. trans., ²1953), p. 100, considers that Paul's mysticism is an 'objective mysticism of facts'.

[226] *Cf.* Sanday and Headlam, *Romans*, p. 86.

the idea of cost involved in it may legitimately be read back into redemption. Another Romans passage (8:23) which uses the word 'redemption' has a somewhat different meaning, since it is applied in a future sense. The adopted sons wait for the redemption of their bodies. Here the deliverance takes on an almost cosmic significance as the whole creation joins with the adopted sons in groaning for complete deliverance.

The idea is even more specific in Ephesians 1:7f., where Paul says, 'In him (*i.e.* Christ, the Beloved) we have redemption through his blood, the forgiveness of our trespasses, according to the riches of his grace which he lavished upon us.' Since the method of redemption is here connected with the shedding of blood in the sense of the cost involved, the idea of a ransom payment seems undeniable. It has been suggested that the word means 'to hold to ransom'[227] rather than the payment of a ransom price. But this is not the general meaning of the Greek word and is less suitable to the present context.[228] An important feature of this passage is the use of the present tense ('we have'), which shows the effects of the redemption to be immediate. Another feature is that the act of redemption is seen to be an act of God's grace. The ransom was provided by the divine initiative. This aspect is also present in the Romans 3:24 passage.

Ephesians uses the same term twice more, in 1:14 and 4:30. In the former statement RSV has 'which is the guarantee of our inheritance until we acquire possession of it (*eis apolytrōsin tēs peripoiēseōs*)', spoken of the gift of the Spirit. But since this follows closely on Ephesians 1:7, it may be argued that in both occurrences the word means the same, in which case the idea of redemption must be retained. But there is no exegetical certainty that Paul must have used the word in the same way in both cases. In Ephesians 4:30 he speaks of the sealing of believers 'for the day of redemption'. This certainly has a future look. It should be noted that the Jews looked forward to an experience of redemption in the future; there are many interesting points of contact between this and the Christian idea, as for instance the hope of messianic deliverance associated with it. Paul's idea of ransoming was not present in current Jewish thought. Moreover, since for Paul the redemption is linked with the cross, the most striking distinction between Jewish and Christian redemption comes sharply into focus. While Paul constantly links redemption to a past event (the cross), this does not mean that it is exclusively past. Ephesians 4:30 is a significant reminder that the concept spans past, present and future.

A parallel to the Ephesians 1:7 passage is found in Colossians 1:14, where Paul says of Christ, 'in whom we have redemption, the forgiveness of sins.' The difference between the two passages is that the Colossians state-

---

[227] *Cf.* T. K. Abbott, *Ephesians and Colossians* (ICC, 1899), *ad loc.*
[228] L. Morris, *op. cit.*, p. 42.

ment does not mention the means of redemption, but the context definitely shows the redemption to be a deliverance from the captivating powers of darkness. A superior kingdom has displaced the existing kingdom. The people are set free by a redemptive act.

The remaining Pauline statement is found in 1 Corinthians 1:30, where God is said to have made Christ Jesus 'our redemption', linked with wisdom, righteousness and sanctification. There is no indication here of the sense in which redemption is meant, but it is reasonable to suppose that it bears the same meaning here as elsewhere in Paul's epistles. Since people are to glory in the Lord, this suggests an act of redemption which is effected by the Lord.

In addition to those passages where the word 'redemption' is used we must add two others from the pastoral epistles where the idea occurs, in different derivations from the same root. One is Titus 2:14 which says of Christ, 'who gave himself for us to redeem us from all iniquity'. This is closely parallel to the ransom passage of Mark 10:45. It is important because it makes clear that Christ's self-giving is the ransom price. The statement, moreover, makes clear the condition from which men have been ransomed (*i.e.* an evil state of iniquity). The second passage is 1 Timothy 2:6 where it is said of Christ that he 'gave himself as a ransom for all', another reminiscence of the ransom passage in Mark. In this case an unusual form (*antilytron*) is used, which occurs nowhere else in the NT. It is a strengthened form of Mark's *lytron*, drawing special attention to its substitutionary character. Once again the ransom price is mentioned (Christ giving himself). It is not possible to erase from Paul's letters this strong sense of redemption, and it is equally impossible to deny that Paul was building on a foundation which Jesus had already laid for the interpretation of his death.

In support of the cost element implied in the ransom idea, we should note other terms which Paul uses with a similar meaning, such as commercial words applied to the work of Christ. 1 Corinthians 6:19–20 is the most explicit example: 'You are not your own; you were bought (*agorazō*) with a price. So glorify God in your body.' It is, however, paralleled in another passage in 1 Corinthians 7:22–23 – 'For he who was called in the Lord as a slave is a freedman of the Lord. Likewise he who was free when called is a slave of Christ. You were bought with a price; do not become slaves of men.' The imagery of the purchase price in both passages is drawn from the redemption money for the freeing of slaves, and Paul is clearly applying this in a spiritual sense without specifying in either case what he means by 'a price'. In any case he is here more concerned with the result of being bought – *i.e.* slavery to Christ.[229] If the former passages point to

---

[229] In commenting on the use of *agorazō* in 1 Cor. 6:20, 7:23, I. H. Marshall, 'The Development of the Concept of Redemption in the New Testament', in *Reconciliation and Hope* (ed. R. J. Banks, 1974), p. 157, points out that the emphasis in this term falls not on deliverance but on purchase leading to slavery.

Christ's death as the means of deliverance from the bondage of sin, these focus on the believer's commitment to a different kind of service which results from the payment of the redemption cost.

Another passage where a similar verb (*exagorazō*) is used is Galatians 3:13, where the word is rightly understood in the sense of 'redeem'. This passage has already been mentioned in the section on substitution (see pp. 466f.). All we need remark here is that Christ is said to have redeemed us from the curse of the law, which must mean that in some sense he released us from the curse which would otherwise have fallen on all who have not fulfilled the law. The release comes through substitution. Paul has no doubt about the means used in the redeeming activity: Christ became a curse by hanging on a tree (Gal. 3:13). There has been some debate about the originator of the curse. Some deny that it can be thought that God instituted the curse which fell on his Son.[230] But the curse which Paul describes as the curse of the law must indirectly be traced to God, since he was the instigator of the law. It is important to note therefore that he who instigated that law was also he who redeemed from the curse. The other passage in Galatians where the same verb occurs is Galatians 4:4f. where Paul says of Christ that he was 'born under the law, to redeem those who were under the law'. The redemptive process required that Jesus himself should be under the law. Others placed themselves under a curse; Jesus not only escaped the consequences of the law, but freed those who had succumbed to its curse, by himself becoming a curse. Redemption for Paul, therefore, contains within it the same implication of substitution as sacrifice.

Hebrews. Our first consideration is the mention of eternal redemption (*lytrōsis*) in Hebrews 9:12. It occurs in the description of Christ our high priest entering into the Holy Place and taking, not animal blood, but his own, thus securing final redemption. Since in Hebrews 9:14 the blood of Christ purifies the conscience from dead works, the redemptive activity is clearly linked with release in the same way as the ransom passages in the other writings. The sacrificial blood shows the cost of the redemption. Indeed, Hebrews has much to say about the cost of the work of Christ in terms of suffering (*c.f.* Heb. 2:10, 18; 5:7f.; 12:2–3). In the same context (in 9:15), a death is said to have secured redemption (*apolytrōsis*) (RSV has 'which redeems them') 'from the transgressions under the first covenant'. This implies, but does not explicitly state, that no less than the death of Christ redeems or looses from sin under the new covenant.

The idea of deliverance from the bondage of fear of death, in which the devil holds men, is seen as a specific result of the death of Christ in Hebrews 2:14, although no explanation is given how the incarnate Jesus

---

[230] *Cf.* S. Cave, *The Doctrine of the Work of Christ* (1937), p. 45.

could, through death, destroy him who had the power of death. But the ransom idea must underlie the thought in view of the redemptive language mentioned above.

In one other mention of 'redemption' in Hebrews, the word is also used in the sense of deliverance. Indeed RSV renders Hebrews 11:35 as 'refusing to accept release', words which may be an allusion to Maccabaean martyrs who accepted death rather than gain release by apostatizing. This draws attention to the cost of deliverance, but is used in this context of something other than the redemptive work of Christ. It is valuable, however, for the light it throws on the meaning of the word 'redemption' (*apolytrōsis*).

The Petrine epistles. There is only one passage in which ransom is expressed in these epistles and that is 1 Peter 1:18, 19, already mentioned in the section on sacrifice. What concerns us here is the idea that Christians are redeemed not with corruptible things, but with the precious blood of Christ. Although linked with sacrifice the main thrust of the passage is the cost. The 'silver and gold' comparison alludes to the money paid for the redeeming of slaves. The imagery is also coloured by the redemption of the people of Israel out of Egypt. The passage is therefore a vivid expression of the effective deliverance wrought by Christ, even at the cost of his own blood. It is for this reason that the blood is here described as 'precious'.

The same idea is probably in the statement in 2 Peter 2:1, which speaks of false prophets who were denying the Lord who bought them. The denial is seen at its worst when considered against the cost of their redemption. They were turning their backs against all that Jesus had come to do on their behalf.

Revelation. The redemption theme clearly appears in this book. It comes in the worship section in Revelation 5, where the song of the elders before the Lamb centres on his worthiness: 'for thou wast slain and by thy blood didst ransom men for God from every tribe and tongue and people and nation, and hast made them a kingdom and priests to our God' (Rev. 5:9–10). The ransoming here is directly connected with the death of Christ as its price. Moreover the result is a far-reaching transformation. Redemption is presented here as leading to a new concept of royal and priestly service, but no mention is made of the original state from which the deliverance has been made. The whole book with its focus on the conflict between God and Satan supplies the background. A similar idea of redemption occurs in Revelation 14:4–5 where the 144,000 are said to be redeemed 'as first fruits for God and the Lamb, and in their mouth no lie was found, for they are spotless'. Again redemption results in a new allegiance and a deliverance from all that is false. What is clear from both these passages is that those redeemed now belong to God.

480

Summary. It will be seen that the redemption idea must be regarded as an important aspect in NT theology, although it is only one aspect of the NT explanation of the work of Christ. We may note three facts which are involved in redemption.

(i) The existence of a state requiring redemption. This is understood under the metaphor of slavery which would in NT times have been a widely familiar phenomenon. Slaves were regularly being freed from physical bondage by means of the payment of an equivalent exchange price. The concept of slavery to sin in a spiritual sense, which the NT assumes, would not have been an alien idea.[231] Most men sensed that they needed deliverance from sin.

(ii) Next came the act of redemption. Nowhere does NT thought speculate on the question, To whom was the ransom price paid? But it does relate the cost of redemption to the death of Christ. Moreover, as L. Morris rightly says, 'To the extent that the price paid must be adequate for the purchase in question this indicates an equivalence, a substitution.'[232]

(iii) Finally, comes the resultant state of the believer. Those redeemed are delivered from sin but now belong to God, which brings with it new moral obligations.[233] In many of the NT passages this concept of 'deliverance to' is linked with the twin idea of 'deliverance from'.

Redemption cannot explain wholly the NT idea of atonement. The writers use a wealth of ideas to do this. But lack of balance will result if the idea of redemption is watered down because it is less amenable to modern concepts. It contains within it a strong reminder that Christians are no longer their own. Freedom from sin involves bondage to Christ, a vital NT doctrinal and ethical concept. Moreover, there is a sense in which in NT thought redemption is part of the creative intention of God.[234] It is an indispensable idea in NT theology.

THE MEDIATOR AND HIGH PRIEST

Closely linked with both the preceding aspects is the NT view of Jesus Christ as mediator between God and man. It will be considered under two

---

[231] W. Elert, 'Redemptio ab Hostibus', *ThLZ* 72, 1947, pp. 265ff., advocates the idea that Christ has delivered Christians from bondage to an enemy. For the idea of sacral manumission to explain the NT idea of redemption, *cf.* A. Deissmann, *Light from the Ancient East* (Eng. trans. [2]1927), pp. 322–334.

[232] L. Morris, *The Apostolic Preaching of the Cross*, ([3]1965), p. 61.

[233] We have already noted the passage in Acts 20:28 (see above, p. 462) which speaks of the church being purchased with blood, and this clearly has some bearing on the redemption theme, particularly in focusing on the cost of God's saving work for man and the fact that the believer is no longer his own. This passage is an agreement with the Pauline evidence.

[234] In considering the theme of redemption, J. C. Gibbs, *Creation and Redemption* (1971), discusses its relation to God's creative act and comes to the conclusion that redemption must not be thought of as 'the reflex of God' as if he were caught by surprise. He sees a redemptive purpose in the very act of creation (pp. 139ff.).

aspects. There are a few passages where the word or a parallel concept occurs and these will first be mentioned. This general use will then be linked with the specific high priestly office of Christ.

Paul. One passage in Paul's epistles where the word mediator (*mesitēs*) occurs is in Galatians 3:19–20, although it must be admitted that this is among Paul's obscurer statements. Speaking of the law, he mentions that it was given by angels 'through an intermediary' (*i.e.* Moses) and then goes on to say, 'Now an intermediary implies more than one; but God is one.'[235] There have been a vast number of interpretations of this statement, but it is at least clear that the 'mediator' performs the function of a go-between where there is a dispute between two other parties. He is in this case the people's representative to God and God's representative to the people. In the Galatians passage the mediator idea is introduced to demonstrate the superiority of promise to law, since no mediator was necessary between God and Abraham. Although Paul does not go on to develop his mediator theme and does not apply it here to Christ, his usage well illustrates the meaning of the word.

It is directly applied to Christ, however, in 1 Timothy 2:3f., where the unity of God is also brought out, as it is in the Galatians passage. It refers to 'God our Saviour, who desires all men to be saved and to come to the knowledge of the truth. For there is one God, and there is one mediator between God and men, the man Christ Jesus.' This occurs in the same passage as the ransom statement and in fact immediately precedes it. The function of the mediator is to take action on behalf of the people he represents. What is most significant about this present statement is that the mediator is a man, for only a man could properly represent men before God. Another essential point is the uniqueness of Christ as mediator. There can be no other. This unique quality is specially brought out in the exposition of the high priest theme in Hebrews.

Hebrews. Before discussing the priestly function of Christ in this epistle, we must note the three occasions in Hebrews where the term 'mediator' (*mesitēs*) is used and the one occurrence of 'surety' (*enguos*). Jesus is called 'the mediator of a new (or better) covenant' in Hebrews 8:6; 9:15; 12:24. The background to the expression is the superiority of the new covenant to the old covenant.[236] This new covenant is particularly explained in

---

[235] See the discussion in my *Galatians* (NCB, 1969), pp. 109ff.

[236] R. A. Harrisville, *The Concept of Newness in the New Testament* (1960), pp. 48ff, points out that the supersession of the old covenant was not due to the people's unfaithfulness to it, but took place because a new unfolding of the divine was being made. Thus the mediator is one who unites the earthly and provisional with the heavenly and final. Harrisville maintains that God intended the first covenant to be provisional (p. 53). He regards the Heb. 12:21-24 passage as eschatological.

Hebrews 8 where, after a long citation from Jeremiah 31:31–34, the conclusion is reached that the old covenant is obsolete. A new covenant requires a new mediator, who is identified as Christ. But what was the function of a mediator? A. Oepke[237] gives three possible meanings: (i) an arbitrator between two parties, (ii) a mediator in a spatial sense, and (iii) a negotiator to restore relationships. It is the first that is thought to be the meaning in Hebrews, and the third the meaning in Paul's use of the term. These two meanings are closely allied. In two of the three Hebrews passages (9:15 and 12:24), the covenant is related to the death of Christ. His mediatorial work, in fact, consists of dying in order to bring about a reconciliation between man and God.

A somewhat different emphasis is seen in the word 'surety' which is applied to Christ in Hebrews 7:22, and describes him as the guarantee of the new covenant. Since he has established it, he is himself the proof of its validity. This concept is, therefore, the complement of the other.

We next turn our attention to the high priest theme in Hebrews since this sets out Christ's present work which is carried on by virtue of his own sacrifice. We have already considered the uniqueness of his offering up himself, but we need also to think of the work of the priest. It is paradoxical that Christ could be both offering and priest at the same time. But the writer does not attempt to resolve the difficulty. He would probably have been surprised if others were bothered by it. He was working within a two-fold framework: that Jesus was our high priest, and that he offered himself.

The first feature of his high-priesthood is that it is not according to the order of Aaron. The writer goes to some pains to show the inadequacy of that order in Hebrews 5:1–4 and then immediately announces that Jesus is of a different order, that of Melchizedek (Heb. 5:6, 10), which he then develops in Hebrews 6:20–7:28.[238] His exposition is based on Psalm 110,[239] which itself goes back to the Genesis account (Gn. 14:18ff.). There are difficulties in the manner in which the writer handles his theme for he comes near to allegorizing it in a way which at first appears to be forced.[240]

---

[237] A. Oepke, *TDNT* 4, pp. 610ff.

[238] The Melchizedek theme has aroused widespread interest. The following are a selection of recent studies on it. F. L. Horton, *The Melchizedek Tradition* (1976); M. de Jonge and A. S. van der Woude, '11 Q Melchizedek and the New Testament', *NTS*, 1965, pp. 301–326; B. Demarest, *A History of Interpretation of Heb. 7:1-10 from the Reformation to the Present* (1976), esp. pp. 129ff.; M. Simon, 'Melchizédech, dans la polémique entre juifs et chrétiens et dans la légende', *RHPR* 17, 1937, pp. 58ff.; E. Käsemann, *Das wandernde Gottesvolk; Eine Untersuchung zum Hebräerbrief* (²1957), pp. 5-58. *Cf.* also J. Fitzmyer, *CBQ* 25, 1963, pp. 305–321; idem, *JBL* 86, 1967, pp. 25–41; J. Carmignac, *Revue de Qumran* 7, 1970, pp. 343–378.

[239] On the use of Ps. 110 in relation to Christ's priestly work, *cf.* the discussion of D. M. Hay, *Glory at the Right Hand* (1973), pp. 143–153. For an investigation of the use of Ps. 110 in the general structure of Hebrews, *cf.* G. Schille, 'Erwägungen zur Hohenpriesterlehre des Hebräerbriefes', *ZNW* 46, 1955, pp. 97f., esp. 108.

[240] On the method of argument employed in Hebrews, regarding the origin and destiny of Melchizdek,

But the following features are significant for an understanding of Christ's priestly work.

(i) The order of Melchizedek is continuous. It does not need a line of succession. It is, moreover, eternal. In this feature, it is clearly immeasurably superior to Aaron's line. Because of the mystery surrounding Melchizedek's origin and end in Scripture, he serves as a better pattern for our high priest than Aaron, since our high priest as seen earlier in this epistle is the pre-existent Son of God.

(ii) The qualifications of Jesus to be the true successor of Melchizedek are not based on tribal alignment as Aaron's successors were. In any case, Jesus belonged to Judah, not Levi, and would not have qualified as an Aaronic priest. But the qualification for the order of Melchizedek is different – it is 'the power of an indestructable life' (Heb. 7:16), a qualification possessed by Christ alone.

(iii) Another feature that distinguishes Melchizedek's order from Aaron's is that it is a royal priesthood.[241] The royal aspect of Christ's priesthood is particularly seen in the several references to his enthronement (cf. Heb. 1:3; 8:1; 10:12). This factor adds considerable dignity to the high-priestly office of Christ. The Genesis account of Melchizedek, though mysterious, is nonetheless impressive. Even so he is but a shadow of his great antitype.

We may wonder why the author thought of using Melchizedek in his discussion. Several explanations are possible. One is that Psalm 110 was a great favourite with him. He cites it many times. Another is that he was drawn towards it by his interest in Abraham (Heb. 2:16; 6:13f.; 7:4f.; 11:8f.). A further possibility is that he was aware of contemporary Jewish speculation on Melchizedek as the 11 Q Melchizedek document at Qumran reflects, although this speculation was applied in a different way.[242] Perhaps some of the Jewish Christians were having difficulty in fitting a Messiah from the tribe of Judah into the familiar levitical ritual for coming to God. We may, at least, note that Christ is performing a high-priestly work,

---

we should note the rabbinic principle 'what is not in the Torah is not in the world' (cf. Strack-Billerbeck 3, pp. 694f.).

[241] L. Morris, *The Cross in the New Testament*, p. 286, draws attention to the fact that Hebrews does not compare Christ with Melchizedek, but vice versa. He regards Melchizedek simply as an illustration, with Christ as a standard.

[242] For studies on 11 Q Melchizedek in relation to Hebrews, cf. J. Carmignac, op. cit., pp. 371ff.; A. J. B. Higgins, 'The Priestly Messiah', NTS 13, 1967, pp. 211–239; Y. Yadin, 'A Note on Melchizedek and Qumran', *Israel Exploration Journal* 15, 1965, pp. 152ff.; F. L. Horton, op. cit.; M. de Jonge and A. S. van der Woude, op. cit. Although there are some similarities between 11 Q Melchizedek and Hebrews, there are more major differences. In 11 Q, Melchizedek is a warrior saviour, not a priest. He is moreover a heavenly creature, whereas in Hebrews he is a human person. The 11 Q Melchizedek is related to levitical laws, unlike the presentation of a non-levitical high priest in Hebrews. Moreover, 11 Q does not allude, as Hebrews does, to either Gn. 14 or Ps. 110. Cf. also M. Delcor, 'Melchizedek from Genesis to the Qumran Texts and the Epistle to the Hebrews', *JJS* 2, 1971, pp. 115–135.

whatever the reason for the Melchizedek theme.[243]

As representative of the people in their approach to God, it was the high priest's task to intercede. This aspect of the high-priesthood of Christ is prominent in Hebrews (*cf.* 2:17, 18; 4:15–16; 7:25f.; 10:19ff.). His present intercessory ministry is seen to be a direct result of his sacrificial work.[244] This idea is closely paralleled in the advocacy of Christ mentioned in 1 John 2:1. It is characteristic of Hebrews that the work of the earthly priests is regarded as an illustration of the work of our high priest whose sphere of activity is nonetheless transferred to heaven. Indeed, since Christ's work is so much superior to Aaron's priestly activities it may be said that the Aaronic line was but a shadow of the true high priesthood. The intercessory work of Christ is not merely a perfect fulfilment of the work of the Aaronic priests. It was rather the perfect ministry of which Aaron's intercessory work was a vague premonition. Our high priest has perfect understanding, is merciful and faithful, is ever ready to help, knows our weaknesses and is constant in his readiness and ability to save. No-one of Aaron's line ever came near to the fulfilment of so comprehensive a ministry.

The particular work of Christ in the sanctification of his people is specially seen in this epistle. It may be summed up in the use of the word 'sanctify' (*hagiazō*),[245] which is used in Hebrews 2:11; 10:10; 10:14;13:12. We note first that the word means, according to its OT usage, 'to set apart for a holy purpose'. In the occurrences mentioned above all of them connect the sanctifying process with the death of Christ. It is because of the action of Christ in suffering outside the 'camp' (having been rejected by official Judaism) that he expects others to join him (Heb. 13:12–13). His present high-priestly office is concerned to enable his people to enter into the fruits of his sanctifying work.

Linked closely with this process is that of 'perfecting' (*teleioō*),[246] especially as Hebrews 10:14 brings them together: 'For by a single offering he has perfected for all time those who are sanctified.' This cannot mean that all who come to God through Christ are immediately perfected. The statement sets out the potential. The writer is concerned to demonstrate the perfections of our high priest, because only a perfect high priest could

---

[243] O. Cullmann, *The Christology of the New Testament*, p. 84, points out that Jewish exegetes came to play down the Melchizedek theme, perhaps because of an anti-Christian polemic.

[244] Hay, *op. cit.*, considers that Heb. 7:25, which views the work of Jesus as a priestly work of intercession and presents a fundamentally different view from the rest of the epistle, is best viewed as a foreign element. Hay does not give sufficient weight, however, to the idea that Jesus in heaven pleads on the basis of his sacrificial death.

[245] *Cf.* the discussion on the meaning of this term by O. Procksch, *TDNT* 1, pp. 111ff. Of its use in Hebrews he speaks of a clear connection between atonement and sanctification.

[246] *Cf.* G. Delling, '*teleioō*' *TDNT* 8, pp. 82f. Delling thinks that *dikaioō* and *teleioō* in Hebrews are parallel, but the difference is due to the difference between legal and cultic thinking (p. 83 n. 28).

make his people perfect. It is significant that perfection is not even ascribed to the law (cf. Heb. 7:19). More will be said on this theme in the section on the Christian life (pp. 697ff.). Our present purpose has been to see the work of sanctifying to be a present activity of our high priest. This aspect is important in considering the work of Christ because of the bearing it has on the moral effects of Christ's death. Our high priest did not merely make an offering once and for all on the basis of which men may now come to God. He began a sanctifying work in his people which needs his present work on their behalf to be continually appropriated. So a distinction must be made between a religious and ethical influence. The ethical influence follows and is dependent upon a religious change.

RECONCILIATION

This is one of the most fundamental concepts of the Christian message, which assumes man's alienation from God (see section on Man, pp. 187ff.) and proceeds to show how reconciliation can be effected.[247] Taking reconciliation in this broad sense, it could be said that the whole of the work of Christ has to do with reconciliation.[248] But our present intention is to concentrate on the narrower sense of the actual process of reconciliation, based on the occurrence of the words used in the NT to express the idea, and on those expressions which speak of the establishment of peace with God. It is remarkable that in the former group the occurrences are confined wholly to the Pauline epistles, although the latter group is more evenly spread. Because the idea of reconciliation is so characteristic of Paul, we shall begin with an examination of his statements. In his epistles they are few in number, but they are highly significant and well repay careful attention.

The background. There is surprisingly little use in the LXX of the word group which in the NT expresses 'reconciliation' (*katalassō* and its cognates). The root word occurs only once (Je. 31:39, LXX), where it does not mean 'reconciliation' but 'change'. Other passages where cognates occur are Isaiah 9:5, LXX, and 1 Samuel 29:4, LXX, but only in the latter case does it refer to reconciliation between two people and that of the offended party rather than the offender. In view of the paucity of LXX support, the NT statements must be considered within their own contexts, which must determine their precise meaning.

We should note in passing that the idea of reconciliation is found in early Judaism. There was an awareness of the need for people to be reconciled

---

[247] For studies on the NT teaching on the reconciliation, *cf.* V. Taylor, *Forgiveness and Reconciliation* (1946); L. Morris, *The Apostolic Preaching of the Cross*, pp. 186–223; H. Ridderbos, *Paul*, pp. 183–204; J. Denney, *The Christian Doctrine of Reconciliation* (1917).

[248] *Cf.* T. H. Hughes, *The Atonement* (1949), p. 312.

to each other as a necessary prelude to being reconciled to God. Moreover, the sense of estrangement from God was present in the form of a belief that the people of Israel had made God angry, as for instance in their wilderness wanderings. But there was the conviction that the provision of the tabernacle was the means of reconciliation. Linked with this idea of God's anger was a strong belief that he was merciful. He is a God who makes peace in his creation and among his creatures.

What is most significant for our examination of the NT evidence is that the Jews did not hesitate to speak of God being reconciled in the sense that his anger against the sinner was abated. Although the use of *katalassesthai* is infrequent in Greek-speaking Judaism, there are references in 2 Maccabees (1:5; 7:33) which speak of God being reconciled. The rabbis similarly often used words to express God being well-disposed towards them.[249]

Paul. We begin with the two most important passages in which both the verb 'to reconcile' (*katalassō*)[250] and the noun 'reconciliation' (*katallagē*) are used. In Romans 5:8–11, Paul discusses the death of Christ and comments that 'God shows his love for us in that while we were yet sinners Christ died for us'. In other words enmity was present and God through the motive of love sent his Son to do something about it. Paul continues to explain the consequence of this. 'Since, therefore, we are now justified by his blood, much more shall we be saved by him from the wrath of God. For if while we were enemies (*echthroi*) we were reconciled to God by the death of his Son, much more, now that we are reconciled, shall we be saved by his life.'

In this passage, we note first that reconciliation is set over against enmity, which cannot be confined to man's hostility to God,[251] but must include God's hostility to man's sin. This is borne out by the earlier statements about God's wrath in this epistle (Rom. 1:18; 2:5, 8; 3:5; 4:15). This build-up of the idea of wrath furnishes an important clue to the understanding of enmity in the present passage. Moreover there are later references to the same idea (Rom. 9:22; 12:19; 13:4–5). Since there are more allusions to God's wrath in this epistle than in any other NT book, the reconciling work of Christ is seen as a work of fundamental importance. No-one can face such wrath except by the intervention of God himself. This aspect of God's dealings with man, however, does not, for Paul, centre in his wrath so much as in his love; but the quality of the love is seen more intensely against the background of the coexistent hostility. Love is seen in the process of overcoming a formidable obstacle to fellowship between God and man.

---

[249] *Cf.* F. Büchsel, '*Katallasso*', *TDNT* 1, p. 254, for details.
[250] *Ibid.*, pp. 255ff.
[251] *Cf.* V. Taylor, *op. cit.*, p. 75.

The second feature in this passage is that reconciliation is spoken of as an objective reality which has been brought about by the death of Christ. It is not simply a matter of a change of approach on the part of the sinner, for if reconciliation meant no more than that, there would have been no need for the death of Christ. There is no support, in this context, for the view that the death of Christ produced such a radical impression on those who were hostile that they were persuaded to drop their hostility. The reconciliation is expressed in a passive form, which shows that what was effected was outside of man's reaction. It cannot mean less than that God himself became reconciled to man through the death of Christ. Moreover, the act of reconciliation is expressed as a completed act (aorist tense). The finished character of Christ's part in the process of reconciliation is brought out most strongly in Romans 5:11: 'Not only so, but we also rejoice in God through our Lord Jesus Christ, through whom we have now received our reconciliation.' Denney says, 'The work of reconciliation, in the sense of the New Testament, is a work which is *finished*, and which we must conceive to be finished, *before the gospel is preached*.'[252]

Reconciliation in this context has both a Godward and a manward aspect. Its primary concern is to effect a change in God's attitude towards us, in that the death of Christ has made a new relationship possible. Only through the response of faith to what God has already done, an acceptance of an already finished reconciliation, can a moral change be effected in man to enable him to be reconciled to God. In effect God brings about reconciliation by removing the cause of alienation, *i.e.* our sins.

It may be thought that Paul's exposition of reconciliation in this Romans passage is one-sided, whereas the normal understanding of reconciliation between two parties is that both parties must have a hand in it. But Paul suggests that a reconciliation can exist in God before it has been appropriated by man through faith. In this case reconciliation has a slightly different meaning from its normal sense. Leon Morris[253] maintains that it is important to recognize the difference between the Greek and English usages, if the NT concept is to be properly understood.

The second important Pauline passage is 2 Corinthians 5:18ff. 'All this is from God, who through Christ reconciled us to himself and gave us the ministry of reconciliation; that is, God was in Christ reconciling the world to himself, not counting their trespasses against them, and entrusting to us the message of reconciliation. So we are ambassadors for Christ, God making his appeal through us. We beseech you on behalf of Christ, be reconciled to God.' It is first to be noted that there is no hint in this passage of the wrath of God, although the following words (verse 21) focus on sin

---

[252] J. Denney, *The Death of Christ*, p. 103.
[253] *Cf.* L. Morris, *op. cit.*, p. 228.

in such a way as to show that sin was the main obstacle to right relationship. Indeed the words 'not counting their trespasses against them' bear this out. There is no possibility of true reconciliation until sin has been removed.

Another important feature, paralleled in the Romans passage, is that the initiative is with God, as the opening words in the above statement show. Indeed it was God in Christ who was doing the reconciling. There is no suggestion here that reconciliation can be summed up as a change of attitude on man's part involving a cessation of hostility towards God.[254] While this occurs as a result of the reconciling work of God, it is not the cause of it. Paul assumes that man cannot reconcile himself to God. But if God is doing the reconciling, there must be some sense in which he can be said to be reconciled, apart from man's response.

While no mention is made in the passage above of the death of Christ, this must be assumed, especially in the statement that God made Christ to be sin who knew no sin. We cannot escape the conclusion that reconciliation involved a sacrificial act on the part of Christ. In this sense we cannot divorce reconciliation from substitution, although it brings out a different emphasis. The apostle mentions both the ministry and the message of reconciliation and the latter involves some understanding of its content. Certainly the exhortation 'be reconciled to God' expects some moral response on man's part, which shows that Paul did not view reconciliation as one-sided. The appeal to man to respond must not be separated from God's action in Christ. Apart from the objective reconciling work of Christ there would have been no basis on which to urge people to be reconciled. The message is good news because God has already provided a means by which he does not account people's trespasses against them.

It is important to note that the use of the passive 'Be reconciled' is not to be regarded as a passive approach. Some comparison may be made with Matthew 5:23–24 where the worshipper who comes to the altar and remembers that his brother has a grievance against him has to leave his gift and first be reconciled. It is noticeable that it is the worshipper who is expected to take the first step in seeking reconciliation, and this has some bearing on what Paul says about reconciliation between man and God. A similar usage is found in 1 Corinthians 7:11 where the reconciliation concerns a husband and wife.

An extension of the idea of reconciliation occurs in Ephesians 2:11f. and Colossians 1:19ff.,[255] where a cognate word (*apokatallassō*) is used. We

---

[254] *Cf.* C. Ryder Smith, *The Bible Doctrine of Salvation*, p. 218.

[255] R. P. Martin, in discussing this Colossians passage in relation to the theme of reconilication, regards the statement about the blood of Christ as a Pauline addition to an original hymn which conceived of reconciliation in terms of cosmic theology: 'Reconciliation and Forgiveness in Colossians' in *Reconciliation and Hope* (ed. R. J. Banks), pp. 104–124. *Cf.* E. Schweizer, 'Versöhnung des Alls, Kol 1, 20', in *Jesus Christus in Historie und Theologie* (ed. G. Strecker, 1975), pp. 487–501. *Cf.* also P. Stuhlmacher, 'Jesus als Versöhner. Überlegungen zum Problem der Darstellung Jesu im Rahmen einer Biblischen Theologie des

begin with the Colossians passage which states of Christ, 'For in him all the fullness of God was pleased to dwell, and through him to reconcile to himself all things, whether on earth or in heaven, making peace by the blood of his cross.' Here is the same conception of reconciliation based on the death of Christ, but with a significant extension to include 'all things'. This cosmic view[256] may perhaps tie up with Paul's thoughts in Romans 8:19ff. about the whole creation groaning together in travail and waiting for its redemption. But whereas in Romans 8 the main thought is deliverance from bondage to decay, here it is the reconciliation of an estranged creation with its creator. This extension of the peacemaking mission of Jesus to include inanimate creation demonstrates the comprehensive effects of the death of Christ.

In the Colossians passage Paul continues, 'And you, who once were estranged and hostile in mind, doing evil deeds, he has now reconciled in his body of flesh by his death, in order to present you holy and blameless and irreproachable before him' (Col. 1:21–22), which reiterates the close connection between reconciliation and the death of Christ. It also clearly shows both the activity of God in initiating the reconciliation and the resultant moral change effected in believers. Paul's statement in fact is qualified by Colossians 1:23, 'provided that you continue in the faith'. The manward side is seen to be as important as the Godward side. Nevertheless the removal of hostility is not man's work but God's.

The Ephesians passage (2:11f.) occurs in the context of a discussion of the hostility existing between Jews and Gentiles,[257] but in the course of it some important statements are made about reconciliation. The state of affairs which made reconciliation necessary is that people were 'separated from Christ, alienated from the commonwealth of Israel, and strangers to the covenants of promise, having no hope and without God in the world' (Eph. 2:12). This description of the Gentile world is reinforced by the expression 'far off' (2:13, 17). But they are said to be 'brought near in the blood of Christ' (2:13). Moreover, Jew and Gentile have both been reconciled to God 'in one body through the cross, thereby bringing the hostility to an end' (2:16). Although there is no indication how this results from the cross, the statement requires for its understanding the view that the death of Christ achieved on the Godward side an effective reconciliation by the removal of hostility. It is summed up in the words 'so making

---

Neuen Testaments', *idem*, pp. 87–104. For a special study linking the creation with the redemptive work of Christ in Paul's epistles, see J. C. Gibbs, *Creation and Redemption* (1971). He gives careful consideration to this theme in Col. 1:15–20 (pp. 94–114).

[256] On the cosmic aspect of reconciliation, cf. D. von Allmen, 'Réconciliation du monde et christologie cosmique', *RHPR* 48, 1968, pp. 32–45.

[257] T. F. Torrance, 'Atonement and the Oneness of the Church', *SJT* 7, 1954, pp. 245–269, in discussing church unity concludes that the path to unity lies through atonement. This was certainly the case in Jewish-Gentile reconciliation according to Paul's exposition of it.

peace' (Eph. 2:15). Reconciliation has as its aim the establishment and maintenance of peace. When it is a question of reconciliation between God and man, so essential is the part of Christ in it that he is here called 'our peace' (2:14).

It should be noted that the former state of the Ephesians is described as 'children of wrath' (Eph. 2:3), which links up with the mention of wrath in the Romans passage. God's wrath must express itself against man's sin.

We must consider the concept of establishing peace which arises out of this passage, on the basis of other NT passages. In the OT peace (*šālôm*) is used in the general sense of well-being, which includes such notions as the cessation of hostility as well as more positive spiritual blessings.[258] Leon Morris points out that in a majority of the occurrences of peace in the NT it is seen as the gift of God.[259] It is essentially a quality possessed by Jesus himself and promised by him to his disciples (*cf.* Jn. 14:27; 16:33). Paul has much to say about peace and calls God the God of peace (Rom. 16:20). This does not indicate a state of passive peacefulness. It has an active, not simply a negative, force. It speaks of the perfect poise and well being of God even when he is engaged in resisting evil. This is an important aspect of the NT doctrine of reconciliation. Enmity and hostility are alien to God except where wrath has to be exercised against all that is unrighteous.

Summary. Although reconciliation is almost an exclusively Pauline theme in the NT, there is general agreement over man's alienation from God. Man's position before God is one of hostility (see section on the doctrine of man in the New Testament). But the state of hostility which exists affects God as well as man, because it has been occasioned by man's sin.[260] If by his nature God cannot fail to have hostility towards all unholiness, it is inescapable that the alienation arising from man's sin has created a barrier which must be removed before reconciliation is possible.

The NT idea of reconciliation is, therefore, concerned with overcoming the rift caused by the enmity which exists between man and God. But the question arises whether in order to rectify this alienation all that is needed is a change of approach on man's part.[261] Since it cannot be supposed that God wills or is pleased with a state of hostility between himself and his people, it has been maintained that reconciliation is possible if man drops his hostility to God. According to this view there is no need for God to be reconciled to man. The death of Christ is then seen as an exhibition of love

---

[258] See L. Morris, *The Apostolic Preaching of the Cross*, pp. 237ff.

[259] *Ibid.*, p. 240.

[260] *Cf.* L. Morris, *ibid.*, pp. 222f.; D. W. Simon, *The Redemption of Man* (1906), pp. 271f. H. M. Hughes, *What is the Atonement?* p. 20, points out that 'Reconciliation is necessarily two-fold, even though one side may be more ready for it than the other.' But F. Büchsel, *TDNT* 1, p. 255, denies that there could have been any change of mind on the part of God since his will had already been revealed in the OT.

[261] *Cf.* J. Oman, *Grace and Personality* (²1919), pp. 118f.

which prompts man to change his attitude and become reconciled to God. But there are several objections to this view.

(i) It concerns itself almost wholly with man's response in a psychological way.[262] It approaches the concept of reconciliation from man's side and gives insufficient attention to God's side. It is, therefore, entirely subjective.

(ii) A more serious objection is that it fails to do justice to the death of Christ in the process of reconciliation. From the evidence considered above, it is abundantly clear that Paul regards the significance of the death of Christ as far greater than a mere exhibition. It achieved an objective result which was independent of man's response, although it formed the basis of that response.

(iii) A difficulty must be faced in any view which considers the reconciliation of God in the same terms as the reconciliation of men. The moral influence view disposes of the difficulty by denying the former. But this arises from a failure to distinguish the difference in meaning of the word 'reconciliation' when applied to God and when applied to man. On God's side there is no basic unwillingness, as there is on man's side, to effect a reconciliation.[263] In man's case his nature, which was created to be in harmony with God, is corrupt, and it is this that has led to the hostility. But in God's case no such corruption has given rise to hostility towards sinful men – only a burning holiness, which remains the same whether man is reconciled or not. Paul's view is clear. He insists that the process of reconciliation does not begin with man, but with God. The close connection between reconciliation and redemption bears this out. The removal of sin means that perfect holiness no longer remains hostile to sinful man, and makes possible the idea of an objective act of reconciliation as a finished act. The summons to man to be reconciled to God is a challenge to put aside his hostility to God and to enter into the blessings of peace.

In this section we have been restricting ourselves to the work of Christ on the cross as it affects reconciliation. We reserve the complementary concept of forgiveness until our discussion on salvation (see later section, pp. 577). It naturally affects the manward side of reconciliation, for no reconciliation is possible until man is assured of forgiveness of his sins.

JUSTIFICATION

It certainly cannot be said that the NT teaching on justification and its related themes is slight. It is especially dominant in the Pauline epistles. It is, moreover, the aspect of the work of Christ which has been most often distorted by lack of a true understanding of the background of the termi-

---

[262] *Cf.* V. Taylor, *Forgiveness and Reconciliation*, pp. 107f., for a critique of this view.

[263] G. Aulén, *The Faith of the Christian Church* (Eng. trans. 1954), p. 229, says 'To Christian faith the matter appears thus, that God is reconciled in and through his reconciliation of the world to himself'.

nology and concepts used. We shall need to survey this background material before coming to the NT evidence.

The OT background. There are a great many occurrences in the OT of words expressing judgment, justification and law and, since the NT is heavily dependent on the OT for its concepts, it is important to note the way in which these concepts dominate OT thought.[264] We shall group our observations under the following points.

(i) God is portrayed as a universal judge. Judgment and justice are seen as being essential characteristics of God. But more important still, his judgments are considered to be right (*cf.* Gn. 18:25). There is no suggestion in the OT that God ever acts capriciously. In this, he is in stark contrast with pagan deities. His judgments are according to a predictable pattern of moral law. Indeed it may not be wrong to say, not only that God is judge, but also that God is law.[265] Whatever else the OT says about law proceeds from the conviction that law represents the normal standard of God's judgments. This is of great importance in understanding the NT, for it cannot be maintained that God is acting in accordance with a law outside himself. It leads to serious misconceptions if law is considered to be above God. The real genesis of all moral law is seen to be in God himself.

(ii) The concept of law in the OT is generally associated with God. The characteristic word *torah* is very frequently described as the law of Yahweh. Even where it occurs as the law of Moses it is recognized as having come from God. Other words denoting 'statute' or 'commandment' or 'judgment' are all linked to the character of God. This is important because law is seen not only as an expression of the essential nature of God, but also as something not arbitrarily imposed on his people. What he demands of us is conformity to his own way of acting. The codified law is a tangible expression of the dynamic rightness of the activity of God. So deeply ingrained in the OT is the idea that law finds its validity in God, that it must affect our understanding of the NT approach to legal concepts, especially in the sphere of justification.

(iii) It is assumed without question that when God judges, his judgments are right, and when he rewards the recompense is deserved. There is no question of God using his power in an unjust way. Indeed it is because of the conviction of the absolute rightness of God's judgments that people could delight in them. Consequently the men of the OT did not regard God as harsh because he made legal demands upon them. Legal imagery was seen as a proper medium to express divine righteousness in action.

---

[264] On the OT and Jewish background, *cf.* L. Morris, *The Apostolic Preaching of the Cross*, pp. 224–243. *Cf.* also A. Marmorstein, *The Doctrine of Merits in Old Rabbinical Literature* (1920); M. Barth, *Justification* (Eng. trans., 1971), pp. 14ff.; N. H. Snaith, *The Distinctive Ideas of the Old Testament* (1944), pp. 51–78.

[265] *Cf.* H. G. G. Herklots, *A Fresh Approach to the New Testament* (1950), p. 18.

(iv) The idea of the covenant as a basis for an on-going relationship between God and his people is essentially a legal conception. Such covenants were widespread in the ancient world and generally involved an undertaking between two parties that both would honour the pact. In the case of God's covenant with Israel, it was the latter who did not keep the agreement, for they rebelled against God. The whole levitical system of sacrifice was a provision of God to maintain the possibility of fellowship in spite of Israel's breaking the covenant.

(v) It should be remembered that in the OT, judgment is frequently tempered with mercy. Even the codified law was seen as a provision of grace. Indeed the whole concept of justification must be examined against the background of divine mercy.

(vi) The words used in the OT for justification, righteousness and cognate ideas are of vital importance in the study of the NT doctrine of justification and their precise meaning must be noted. In the LXX the Greek word *dikaioō*, 'to justify', does not mean 'to make righteous', but 'to deem righteous'. The word for 'justify' and the word for 'righteousness' (*dikaiosynē*) came from the same root. Righteousness was regarded as conformity to an acknowledged pattern. The pattern was based on the nature of God,[266] and thus the righteous man was the man who conformed to the law, which in itself was an expression of that nature. In the OT, therefore, righteousness has to do with relationships.[267] Justification must be seen in this context. A man was justified when he was declared among men to be in a right relationship with God. And yet in Psalm 143:2, the statement that no man living can be justified in the sight of God shows the ultimate confession of failure under the OT order.

(vii) In considering the OT idea of 'righteousness' in men, we note that there is a preponderance of the forensic element. When the judge pronounces a man 'righteous', it means that he is free from guilt (Dt. 25:1; 1 Ki. 8:32). Thus the unrighteous man is the man who is condemned.[268] Whereas this may be a frequent OT usage, it is not the only use. Nevertheless it is the use which has most significance for the NT and we need not investigate the matter further. It will become evident, when Paul's doctrine is examined, how important it is to recognize that 'righteousness' is a religious rather than an ethical concept.

The intertestamental background. There was a continuation of the OT concept of justification in the forensic sense among the Jews of this period. The judgment of God was considered to be a present and continuous reality, and the recurrent days of atonement were constant reminders to those who

---

[266] *Cf.* N. H. Snaith, *op.cit.*, p. 77.
[267] *Cf.* also L. Morris, *op. cit.*, pp. 260f.
[268] *Cf.* G. E. Ladd, *TNT*, p. 440.

did not repent that the judgment of God was upon them. But there was also belief in a future judgment (*cf.* 1 Enoch 1–5; Wisdom 3:2–10; 4:20).

During this period it was supposed that man could by his own efforts earn merit before God.[269] It was not supposed that complete fulfilment of the law was possible and indeed it was not imagined that God required this. As already noted on pp. 119f., the view was held that man had an impulse towards evil (*yēṣer hārāʿ*) as well as an impulse towards good (*yēṣer haṭôḇ*). To be considered righteous a man must develop the good impulse and resist the evil. God's opinion of him would depend on how well he succeeded in doing this. It was this concept which led to the emphasis on good works as the only method of maintaining favour with God. There were two special ways of earning merit: the diligent study of the Torah and the giving of alms. The intertestamental period witnessed the growth of an astonishing reverence for the Torah, which largely contributed to the legalistic approach of the Pharisees in the time of Jesus. As a direct consequence of the emphasis on good works there followed a marked absence of any personal assurance, since no-one could ever be sure that he was acceptable to God. The main aim of the good works was to ensure that one stayed 'in' the covenant. Those who achieve this are the righteous.[270]

Another aspect was the tendency to lessen the emphasis on the mercy of God, for the system of merit left little room for mercy. Some lip service was paid to it, but the idea of a righteous God pardoning the guilty was a genuine difficulty to the Jews. A judge who did that would at once be considered unjust. How then could a righteous God overlook either the debit or credit side of a man's account? To the Jew, with his strong sense of the justice of God, the only fair way was to balance both sides of the account. He definitely believed that salvation was by works. Where then did faith come into the picture? For Judaism there was no concept of faith as a full committal of oneself to another, as it is in Paul's dynamic understanding of faith. Those Jews who believed in merit-earning would have considered justification by faith an unintelligible concept viewed in the light of a just and holy God. It should be noted in this connection that Jews, when they became Christians, would continue to have some problems over the means of a man's justification before God.

Some reference needs to be made to the idea of justification in the Qumran scrolls, especially because many scholars have found a close link with Paul's doctrine. There are certainly passages which support the view that righteousness does not belong to man but to God (*cf.* 1 QS 11:12; 11:14), which comes close to Paul's idea of justification by the righteousness

---

[269] E. P. Sanders, *Paul and Palestinian Judaism*, pp. 183–205, challenges the widely held view that among the Jews there was a doctrine of merit, in which merit could offset demerit and could be stored and transferred. He admits, however, that there was a strong doctrine of rewards.

[270] *Cf. ibid.*, p. 518.

of God.[271] It has been affirmed that both in Paul and in Qumran justification is *sola gratia*.[272] On the other hand there are passages which link the judgment of God with mercy, although these tend to regard mercy as an equivalent for righteousness. But this is not Paul's view, for although he mentions both the righteousness and the mercy of God, he does not confuse them.[273]

Paul.

(i) *Introduction*. It is Paul of all the NT writers who majors on an exposition of justification (especially in Romans and Galatians).[274] But lest it should be thought that Paul has inaugurated an entirely new concept, his teaching must be seen against the background of the teaching of Jesus on righteousness. He was critical of those of his contemporaries who claimed a false righteousness (Lk. 18:9). He was devastating in his portrait of the self-satisfied Pharisee who was clearly not 'justified', in contrast with the tax-collector, who humbly acknowledged his shortcoming. The justification in this case was due to confession and repentance. In other words it depended on the attitude of the worshipper. On the other hand, Jesus denied that people could justify themselves, although the Pharisees were attempting to do this (Lk. 16:15).

In the Sermon on the Mount, Jesus urged his hearers to seek the kingdom of God and his righteousness (Mt. 6:33), which shows that pursuit of the righteousness of God is not identical with the pursuit of the kingdom, although it is closely linked with it.[275] Righteousness is seen to be a desirable and realizable aim. In the same sermon, Jesus makes it clear that those who want to enter the kingdom should possess a righteousness which exceeds that of the scribes and Pharisees (Mt. 5:20). In what sense did he mean that their righteousness can be exceeded? Since their idea of righteousness was based on merit which outweighed the adverse balance of sin, the implication is that a wholly different conception of righteousness is needed. Jesus does not enlarge on how this can be achieved.

---

[271] *Cf.* M. Burrows, *The Dead Sea Scrolls* (1955), p. 334; *cf.* also M. Black, *The Scrolls and Christian Origins* (1961), p. 128.

[272] S. Schulz, 'Zur Rechtfertigung aus Gnade in Qumran und bei Paulus', *ZTK* 56, 1959, pp. 155–185, contends that Paul derived this doctrine from Qumran. For another comparison between Paul and Qumran on justification, *cf.* P. Benoit 'Qumran et le Nouveau Testament', *NTS* 7, 1960–1, pp. 292ff.

[273] *Cf.* E. P. Sanders, *op. cit.*, pp. 306ff.

[274] On the general theme of justification in the New Testament, *cf.* G. E. Ladd, *TNT*, pp. 437–450; L. Morris, *The Cross in the NT*, pp. 240ff.; J. Jeremias, *The Central Message of the NT*, pp. 51–70; R. Bultmann, *TNT* 1, pp. 270–284; E. Käsemann 'Justification and Salvation' in his *Perspectives on Paul* (Eng. trans. 1971), pp. 60–78; E. J. Goodspeed, 'Some Greek Notes: III. Justification', *JBL* 73, 1954, pp. 86ff.; M. Barth, *Justification* (1971); J. A. Ziesler, *The Meaning of Righteousness in Paul* (1972); H. Ridderbos, *Paul*, pp. 159–181; D. E. H. Whiteley, *The Theology of St Paul*, pp. 156ff.

[275] D. Hill, *Matthew*, p. 145, considers that 'righteousness' here means 'righteousness of life in agreement with the will of God'.

The parable of the prodigal son is sometimes regarded as a non-forensic approach to justification and therefore particularly distinctive. The main element in the story is the father's generous forgiveness of the wayward son on no other grounds than his own love for the son and the son's decision to repent (Lk. 15:11ff.). If this is regarded as an illustration of the heavenly Father's love for his wayward children, are we to suppose that Jesus is teaching here that divine love could forgive without the intervention of an intermediary? This would be tantamount to maintaining that Jesus, according to Luke's gospel, could see no need for any atoning work. But this would build too much on a parable, which was intended not to present a doctrine, but to answer the murmuring of the scribes and Pharisees against Jesus' mixing with sinners. It is precarious to base a doctrine about God on this one parable, although it could be deduced from it that God loves to restore those who have wandered from him.[276]

Another passage which may illustrate a further truth is that of the great assize in Matthew 25:31f. Here the basis of judgment appears to be good works. The righteous are those who have done deeds of social compassion in the name of Christ. Nothing is said about repentance or about the problem of sin. The passage is intended to impress on the hearers their personal accountability to God. This teaching is important because it draws attention to social responsibility. It is part of the total picture of the implications of the gospel for those who embrace it. But it does not set out to deal with the problem of man's relationship to God. The inheritance of the kingdom is for those who act in harmony with their profession and do what the king would have done. It cannot be maintained that this parable teaches justification by works, although if it stood on its own it might seem to point in that direction. Jesus never taught that man could save himself by his own good works.

In Matthew's gospel there are several different uses of the term 'righteous' (*dikaios*). In many instances it is applied to people who strive to live in conformity to the will of God (Mt. 1:19; 13:17; 23:35). In Matthew 25:37, 46, the *dikaioi* are those who have practised love in unconscious acts of kindness towards the Son of God. In Matthew 3:15; 5:6; 6:33, the term relates to those who continue in the will of God, yet there is no suggestion that righteousness is merited. It is a pure gift of God.[277]

To sum up these introductory remarks, we may say that Jesus was concerned that people should seek righteousness. He also taught that righteousness could not be attained through man's own efforts. The way of justification lay along the path of humble repentance. Although justification is seen mainly in a forensic sense, other aspects of God's mercy and

---

[276] James Denney, *The Death of Christ*, p. 251, comments that the parable of the prodigal son illustrates the freeness of forgiveness, but it does not deal, as atonement does, with the cost of forgiveness.

[277] *Cf.* G. Schrenk, *TDNT* 2, pp. 187ff.

his forgiveness are not treated rigidly in legal terms. Furthermore, although the concept of justification by faith does not specifically occur in the teaching of Jesus, the widespread requirement of both faith and righteousness in his followers prepares the way for the classic exposition of the doctrine in Paul.

(ii) *The use of the term 'righteous' and 'righteousness' in Paul.* The classic passage in Habakkuk 2:4, which affirms that the righteous man will live by faith, forms the key to Paul's theological discussion in both Romans and Galatians (Rom. 1:17; Gal. 3:11). In what sense has he understood this Habakkuk passage? There is undoubtedly a strong influence of the Hebraic idea that the 'righteous man' is one who is accepted by God, but Paul extends his own understanding of it to see its fullest expression in personal faith in Jesus Christ.[278] When someone exercises such faith he becomes 'righteous' in God's sight. The sense in which the word 'righteous' must be understood in the NT depends on two considerations: its forensic background, and the distinction between its application to man and to God. It is essentially a word derived from the language of the lawcourts. 'Righteous' (*dikaios*), 'righteousness' (*dikaiosynē*), 'judgment' (*dikaiōma*), 'justly' (*dikaiōs*), and 'to justify' (*dikaioō*), all come from the same forensic root. It is impossible, therefore, to examine Paul's doctrine of justification without recognizing this legal background. At the same time since both 'righteous' and 'righteousness' are applied to God, this must modify our understanding of the terms when they are applied to man.[279]

At the beginning of his Romans letter, Paul asserts that in the gospel a righteousness of God has been revealed (Rom. 1:17) and this is further expounded in Romans 3:21ff., where God's work in Christ for sinners is in mind. The righteousness of God must be understood in the sense of the righteous character of God (as in Rom. 3:26 and 2 Tim. 4:8).[280] It is because he is righteous that he justifies those who believe in Jesus (Rom. 3:26). In spite of the forensic flavour of the word, 'righteousness' is based on a

---

[278] E. Käsemann, *Perspectives on Paul*, pp. 60f., 73f., considers righteousness by faith to be central to Paul's theology, but thinks that it did not take its bearings from the individual. In this he is not supported by Bultmann, 'DIKAIOSYNĒ THEOU', *JBL* 83, 1964, pp. 12ff.; Bornkamm, *Paul*, pp. 146f.; and Conzelmann, *TNT*, p. 172. Käsemann's view is criticized by G. Klein, *Int* 26, 1972, p. 409, who suggests that the individual has great importance for Paul's theology. He claims that such an emphasis was necessary to snatch people away from the disintegrating forces of mass society. Klein points out that Paul does not support individualism as an end in itself, since groups of believers formed a new kind of society, *i.e.* a church.

[279] E. P. Sanders, *Paul and Palestinian Judaism*, p. 518 n.5, points out that in rabbinic Judaism the term 'righteous' is used for those who behave correctly, and stay 'in' the covenant. This is clearly different from Paul's terminology.

[280] H. Ridderbos, *Paul*, p. 163, considers it to be established that the expression 'the righteousness of God' means the quality of righteousness which can stand before God. *Cf.* his *Romans*, pp. 35ff. On this phrase, *cf.* also C. H. Dodd, *The Bible and the Greeks*, pp. 57ff.; E. Käsemann, 'The righteousness of God in Paul', in his *New Testament Questions of Today* (Eng. trans. 1969), pp. 168ff.; R. Bultmann, *op. cit.*, pp. 12ff.

personal understanding of the just character of God. But if this is understood against its OT background, it will not be surprising that God's action is always seen as indisputably righteous.

The righteousness of God becomes for Paul the standard by which people's actions are judged. He maintains that the Jewish people did not submit to God's righteousness, but sought a righteousness of their own (Rom. 10:3). Righteousness is not conceived as an abstract quality, but as a personal status. When in Romans 9:30–32, Paul shows that Gentiles attained a righteousness which they did not seek, whereas the Jews failed in their quest for righteousness, he is speaking in forensic terms, because he centres his thought on 'a law of righteousness'. What is in mind is a status which the Gentiles secured by faith, and which the Jews failed to secure by works. Is there, then, any difference between the concept of righteousness in God and the righteousness attained by man? Certainly a difference must be maintained, for in God there is a perfect correspondence between his righteous status and his righteous nature. Indeed, in God 'status' has no meaning apart from character. In man it is different. What he may obtain by faith is a new status (justification, acquittal from guilt), which does not at once tie up with his nature. There are several important questions which therefore arise. What is the precise nature of justification? What are its grounds? What is the relationship between justification and the justified man's ethical life? We shall proceed to consider these questions.

(iii) *The nature of justification.* The frequent use of the verb 'to justify' (*dikaioō*) leads us to believe that for Paul it is generally used in a forensic sense.[281] As we have seen, this would be in line with OT usage. In other words it has to do with acquittal from the just condemnation on sin. As in a court of law a man may be declared acquitted, which means he cannot be touched by law, so Paul conceives that a man may be declared righteous and his sins no longer held against him.

This forensic view of justification has, however, been objected to by some scholars on the grounds that it distorts Paul's meaning. We first note the view that Paul was thinking of justification as a fiction: that is to say, that the justified man is treated as if he were righteous, although he still remains unrighteous. The concept of justification is therefore a kind of device which has no basis in reality. 'God is regarded as dealing with men rather by the ideal standard of what they may be than by the actual standard of what they are' (Sanday and Headlam).[282] This really means in practical terms that justification is identical with forgiveness. But it is an unsatis-

---

[281] John Murray, *Redemption Accomplished and Applied* (1955), pp. 119ff., in discussing the meaning of the word 'justify' in Scripture, maintains that it never means 'to make righteous or upright'. He notes that in Romans it conclusively means 'to declare righteous'.

Cf. D. Hill's discussion of the term in *Greek Words and Hebrew Meanings*, pp. 155ff.

[282] W. Sanday and A. C. Headlam, *Romans*, p. 36.

factory interpretation of the important Pauline doctrine of justification to reduce it to a fiction. Unquestionably forgiveness is implied, but Paul has a more far-reaching view than this interpretation suggests.

It was the strangeness of treating justification as fictitious that led to the development of the idea of 'imparted' righteousness.[283] This is an attempt to relate the righteousness of the justified man to the actual righteousness which he possesses. The problem is to conceive how a sinful man can be regarded as righteous without possessing any righteousness. Because this is difficult, it is proposed that some righteousness of the mind may be real without as yet the accompanying achievement in the life.[284] Justification, according to this view, is equivalent to the possession of a righteous mind. But this interpretation of justification is confusing, because it omits the forensic aspect of Paul's terminology and then merges justification into sanctification, which Paul keeps separate (more will be said on sanctification in the section on the Christian life, pp. 667ff.).

An even more inadequate view of justification is that which divorces it altogether from the requirement of righteousness.[285] It is supposed that the forensic view requires righteousness as a condition for salvation and therefore exalts righteousness as a requirement which even God must meet. By this line of argument righteousness would be exalted above God. But this view must at once be challenged on the grounds that it is based on a wrong conception both of God and of righteousness. If righteousness is, as indicated above, the way a righteous God acts, there can be no clash between them. Indeed, it is Paul's unquestionable conviction that God could do no other than act in righteousness. He has no problems about a clash between righteousness and love, since he considers God to be holy love. If justification were not concerned with righteousness, moreover, it could be defined only in terms of faith. But Paul does not confuse justification and faith; he regards faith as the means by which man identifies himself with God's act on his behalf. When he says, for instance, in Romans 3:24, that men 'are justified by his (i.e. God's) grace as a gift, through the redemption which is in Christ Jesus', it is difficult to see how justification here can be equated with faith.

If Paul's statements are to be taken seriously a forensic understanding of justification is inescapable.[286] But this is not to be regarded as fictional. If

---

[283] In contrast to imparted righteousness, it is generally claimed that Paul holds to the idea of imputed righteousness. L. Morris, *The Cross in the New Testament*, p. 246, says, 'Imputation is a way of saying that God accords believers that standing that they could never reach of themselves'. A. Marmorstein, *The Doctrine of Merits in Old Rabbinical Literature* (1920), p. 29, maintains that the idea of imputed righteousness was not thought of until Judaism proclaimed it. It would not have been an entirely new conception of Paul's.

[284] *Cf.* V. Taylor, *Forgiveness and Reconciliation*, p. 57.

[285] N. H. Snaith, *The Distinctive Ideas of the Old Testament*, p. 165.

[286] M. Barth, *Justification* (1971), bases his exposition of Paul's view on a juridical interpretation. Paul's

righteousness concerns man's relationship with God, justification cannot be considered to be fictitious. It must be maintained that Paul regarded justification as real, since he speaks of it in the past tense and links it directly with an objective historic event, *i.e.* the death of Christ. God does not look on man *as though* he were righteous on the strength of the atoning work of Christ.[287] He treats the believing man as actually righteous as far as his relationship to God is concerned. Justification in this sense must, of course, be distinguished from ethical righteousness, which is the pattern for a man's Christian life and not the basis of a man's standing before God. The forensic view of justification is intensely humbling to man, because it rejects as of no value man's own righteousness. Paul does not embrace the view that a man may clock up merit to offset his sins. He faces man with the devastating prospect that he can do nothing to earn his own justification. For him justification is the work of God.

(iv) *The grounds of justification.* For the apostle the means of justification had a particular importance in view of certain Jewish conceptions of merit which led to an emphasis on works. This may account for Paul's negative approach to justification by works of the law. The negative aspect sets off the superiority of the positive Christian view of justification. For those Jews, who held that merit could be stored up by meticulous observance of the law, 'works of the law' became the life-line for salvation. In common with other Jews, he had held that faith itself was a kind of work which could count as merit. He had known nothing of faith as personal committal until his conversion to Jesus Christ. Consequently his first concern was to reject all thought of justification by works of the law (Rom. 3:20; Gal. 2:16; 3:11).

In his positive exposition of justification, Paul at once links it with the death of Christ (Rom. 3:21ff.), seen as a propitiation. His reasoning is that, since man cannot attain righteousness himself, it is God who has provided it. But the problem with which he deals is, 'How can God forgive man's sin and still remain righteous himself?' Paul has no doubt that the cross is the explanation. The fact that he sees it as a propitiatory offering, stressing its substitutionary character, suggests that the process of justification is possible because of the transfer of sin to Christ (*cf.* 2 Cor. 5:21).[288] On the

---

statements are set against a dramatic judgment scene. R. Y. Fung, 'The forensic Character of Justification', *Themelios* 3, 1977, pp. 16ff., examines various modern views of justification which deny a forensic interpretation, but concludes that the correct view is that which sees it primarily in legal terms. Nevertheless, Fung cites approvingly G. Shrenk's comment (*TDNT* 2, pp. 204ff.), that in justification 'an act of grace replaces customary legal procedure'.

[287] J. Jeremias, *The Central Message of the New Testament*, p. 64, maintains that although it is certain that justification must be taken as a forensic action, yet the forensic image is shattered. It is not just 'as if', for God's word is always effective.

[288] For comments on this passage see p. 513f.

strength of this, God acquits sinners without violating his own righteousness.

But we may ask why this was really necessary? Paul himself does not supply the answer. We may further ask whether it is just to punish the guiltless in order to acquit the guilty? Paul again does not discuss this matter, but he does make clear that it is God himself who provides the necessary offering in the person of his Son. There is no sense of reluctance on his part.[289] He was in fact giving himself. However much the penal view of the atonement may be disliked, there is no doubt that Paul thought in these terms, although it must be stressed that this was only one of a number of different insights that he had about the meaning of Christ's death. The idea of transference of guilt was familiar in a Jewish setting, again by the provision of God in the cultus. This sacrificial basis for justification is therefore a provision of grace. It explains Paul's statement in Romans 3:24 that we are justified by grace.

A major objection to this interpretation of justification is that it appears to take place irrespective of the attitude of the person justified, *i.e.* that it is an act done for him rather than in him. But justification, while it is not based on a man's achievements, is nevertheless not irrespective of his attitude. It is appropriated only by faith (see next paragraph). Paul takes pains to show that justification brings a moral responsibility to those who are justified, but is convinced that Christ died for the ungodly while they were still at enmity with God (*cf.* Rom. 5:6–8). The Christian proclamation of forgiveness of sins through Christ rests on an already accomplished work which Christ has done. On the strength of that work a believer finds acceptance with God and begins the process of sanctification by which righteousness becomes increasingly actualized.[290]

The appropriation of the justifying work of God by the individual is mediated by faith.[291] Paul sets faith over against works of law as the means of appropriation. It is essential, as he sees it, for all merit to be removed from the basis of the relationship between man and God, since the best

[289] It is important to bear in mind that Paul does not present the atonement as in any sense an afterthought of God. Side by side with God's redeeming activity he places God's creating activity. *Cf.* J. C. Gibbs, 'Interpretations of the relation between Creation and Redemption', *SJT* 21, 1968, pp. 1–12; *idem, Creation and Redemption* (1971). *Cf.* also F. H. Maycock, 'Justification by Faith and the Means of Salvation', in *The Doctrine of Justification by Faith* (ed. G. W. H. Lampe, 1954), pp. 69–80; B. F. Westcott, 'The Gospel of Creation', *The Epistles of St John*, pp. 285–328.

[290] L. Morris, *The Apostolic Preaching of the Cross*, p. 291, maintains that justification is essentially concerned with the legal status of the believer, and we must leave the descriptions of the new life to other categories.

[291] In an article on 'The Sacraments and Justification' in *The Doctrine of Justification by Faith* (ed. G. W. H. Lampe, 1954), pp. 50–68, G. W. H. Lampe defines faith as 'the personal response to grace which grace creates in the soul of man' (p. 62). In the same volume, H. E. Symonds, speaks of baptism as 'the instrument of justification' (p. 72), an idea which finds no support from Paul's letters. Jeremias, *The Central Message of the New Testament*, p. 59, adopts a similar view when he asserts that it is in baptism that God saves the believer.

that man could do would be totally inadequate. Faith involves a personal committal of oneself to God's way, without which justification is not possible (see later discussion on faith, pp. 591ff.). Faith's part in justification is to admit the rightness of God's act.[292] An act of faith is an act of praise for the justifier, an open confession that God's saving work has not detracted from, but has enhanced his holy character.[293]

(v) *Justification, present and future.* Because Paul on several occasions uses the past tense when speaking of justification (Rom. 5:1, 9; 1 Cor. 6:11), it is clear that he thinks of it as an already completed act. But the fact is, on other occasions he views it as still future. G. E. Ladd,[294] for instance, maintains that justification in Paul is eschatological. The idea of a final judgment is taken over from Jewish thought, but since it also comes in the teaching of Jesus (Mt. 12:36–37), it is integral to the Christian view of the future. A day of reckoning will come (see section on judgment, pp. 848ff.) and on that day those who believe will not meet with condemnation – they will be justified. Paul expresses this conviction in Romans 8:33–34: 'It is God who justifies; who is to condemn?' Again in Romans 2:13 he uses the future tense ('it is . . . the doers of the law who will be justified'), and this may well point ahead to the final judgment, although it is not specifically stated.[295] A similar use of the future tense is seen in Romans 5:19.

In Jewish thought judgment lies in the future and, being based on works, is fraught with uncertainty, since no-one can be sure whether or not he will be accepted; it is radically different in Paul's thinking.[296] For him believers are already justified as a result of the work of Christ. Yet in that case, to what extent has justification still a future significance? Ladd[297] explains that justification really relates to the final judgment, but it has already taken place in the present. This merging of the future with the present is of vital importance for the believer's Christian experience. There is no question about the final issue. The verdict has already been announced. There is no reason why the believer need fear the Judge's decision (Rom. 8:1). He is already justified and will be saved from the coming wrath (Rom. 5:9). A verdict of 'guilty, but pardoned', rather than 'guilty and condemned', has already been declared. It is this conviction of pardon that forms the basis of Christian assurance. The believer knows that the future can hold nothing for him which cannot be entered into as a present reality.

A further consideration arises from Paul's use of the past tense of an

---

[292] *Cf.* M. Barth, *Justification*, p. 64.

[293] It seems clear that Paul does not regard faith as a work. Such a view is challenged by F. Prat, *The Theology of St Paul* (Eng. trans. 1933), p. 175. He considers that the Protestant view of faith deprives faith of all ethical value. But this argument arises from a confusion between justification and sanctification.

[294] G. E. Ladd, *TNT*, pp. 441f.

[295] Bultmann *TNT* 1, p. 273, remarks that the eschatological meaning is here as clear as day.

[296] *Cf.* Ridderbos, *Paul*, p. 164.

[297] *Op. cit.*, p. 442.

accomplished act of justification. If at the point of faith a believer's past sins are dealt with, does this cover his further sins? The question itself presupposes that justification has a numerical basis instead of being an active principle of righteousness. But apart from this, if justification relates to the final judgment, a man's liabilities are dealt with *in toto*. Paul recognizes that this might lead some to take an irresponsible attitude towards sin (*cf.* Rom. 6:1). But he rejects as unthinkable that those who believe should continue in sin. Justification, with its assurance of acquittal, is no goad to sin, but the reverse. The present consciousness of being declared righteous by God is surely a powerful deterrent to abusing the grace of God. In the mercy of God no part of a man's life is outside Christ's act of justification.

(vi) *Justification and the resurrection of Christ.* The importance of the resurrection of Christ for Paul's doctrine of justification cannot be exaggerated. If the death of Christ was to be the basis for the acquittal, evidence would be needed that this basis was acceptable to God. Since the resurrection of Christ was itself an act of God, a demonstration of his power, it is also a demonstration of his justifying activity. This seems to be the significance of Paul's statement in Romans 4:25 that Jesus 'was raised for our justification'. It is as if the judge accepts the substitute's death and then at once raises him from the dead to plead the cause of those on whose behalf he has died. Markus Barth [298] maintains that, 'By raising Jesus Christ from the dead, God reveals his own nature: he proves that he is faithful.' In this sense the resurrection attests the nature of the justifier. It could be regarded as God's response of love to his Son in raising him to his own right hand to plead our cause. Yet while it is true that the resurrection is a demonstration of love, it is also an essential feature of the forensic nature of justification.

The rest of the NT. Whereas almost all the evidence for the concept of justification in relation to the death of Christ is found in Paul's epistles, there are a few other statements which have a bearing on it. Certainly the concept of righteousness is found elsewhere. In *Acts* Peter declares that the man who does righteousness is acceptable to God (Acts 10:35), an acceptance of the close connection between right action and status before God. The statement is introduced almost incidentally to demonstrate the impartiality of God. At Antioch in Pisidia, Paul announces forgiveness of sins through Christ and then adds, 'and by him every one that believes is freed from everything from which you could not be freed by the law of Moses' (Acts 13:39). [299] In both cases the verb 'freed' is the normal Greek word for

---

[298] M. Barth, *Justification*, p. 53.

[299] E. Haenchen, *Acts* (Eng. trans., 1971), p. 412, thinks that the author is here intending to reproduce Pauline theology. This is at least an admission that there is some kinship between the theme in this Antioch

'justified'. This amounts to a declaration of acquittal, but it does not explain how it is done. Righteousness and future judgment were among the themes expounded by Paul before Felix (Acts 24:25), which again shows their close relationship.

In the epistle to the *Hebrews*, the Son is said to have loved righteousness and hated lawlessness (on the basis of Ps. 45:7; *cf.* Heb. 1:9). 'The word of righteousness' becomes the standard of maturity (Heb. 5:13).[300] Melchizedek is described as king of righteousness (Heb. 7:2). Noah by faith became an heir of righteousness (Heb. 11:7). And discipline is said to produce the fruit of righteousness (Heb. 12:11).[301] But none of these usages has much bearing on the specific doctrine of justification.

It is in the epistle of *James* that the major discussion outside the Pauline epistles takes place. This concerns the means by which it can be attained, rather than the objective basis of it. Much debate has surrounded James 2:14–26, because it has been alleged that James with his emphasis on works contradicts the Pauline doctrine. James is concerned about the man who claims to have faith, but shows no evidence of it in any expressions of compassion. He is, therefore, exposing the inconsistency of pious words which are not backed by appropriate action. He concludes that faith without works is dead (Jas. 2:17). When he develops his theme he brings in the same passage from Genesis which Paul cites in support of the view that Abraham was justified by faith.[302] He poses the question, 'Was not Abraham our father justified by works?' (Jas. 2:21). He does, however, cite the Genesis passage with its emphasis on faith.[303] It would seem on the surface that James is saying the opposite from Paul, since he puts so much stress on works.

The contradiction between the two is, however, more apparent than real. There is an essential difference in the way the two writers use their terms. James is not thinking of works in the sense of legal works, but works in the sense of benevolence or almsgiving, a recognition of the social

---

speech and in Paul's epistles. There is no reason to deny that Luke is reporting genuine Pauline theology. R. P. C. Hanson, *The Acts* (1967), p. 145, simply says that 'Luke evidently had some acquaintance with Pauline vocabulary'.

[300] P. E. Hughes, *Hebrews*, p. 191, thinks this expression indicates 'the teaching about righteousness which is fundamental to the Christian faith, namely, the insistence on Christ as our righteousness'.

[301] F. F. Bruce, *Hebrews*, p. 361, describes this as 'the cultivation of a righteous life, responsive to the will of God'. It therefore has more to do with sanctification than with justification.

[302] On Paul's appeal to Abraham's justification, *cf.* A. T. Hanson, 'Abraham the Justified Sinner', in his *Studies in Paul's Technique and Theology* (1974), pp. 52–66. Hanson explains that for Paul 'Abraham was justified in the pre-existent Christ' (p. 66).

[303] J. B. Adamson, *James (NICNT*, 1976), p. 131, thinks that James is more traditional than Paul in his treatment of Gn. 15:6. He maintains that that James has combined it with Gn. 22:1ff. in typically Jewish fashion. On the other hand Paul keeps them separate. Adamson cites M. Dibelius and H. Greeven *Der Brief des Jakobus* (*KEK*, 1964), p. 168 n.1, to the effect that the major differences between Judaism, Paul and James on the faith of Abraham were that Judaism stressed that his faith was work, Paul that it was faith instead of works, and James that it was both faith and works which counted for righteousness.

implications of the gospel. These are works which are prompted by a man's love for his fellows, especially fellow believers. At least on this matter there would have been no disagreement between Paul and James.[304] Paul is not slow in exhorting his converts to foster brotherly love. Another difference is the concept of faith. Whereas James uses it in the sense of 'confession' or 'acknowledgment', almost an intellectual assent, Paul in his discussion of justification uses it in the sense of personal committal. A man is justified by faith when he identifies himself with Christ, which in itself is an admission that apart from Christ he has no standing. James' idea of faith is nearer to the Jewish model, although James is not maintaining, as the Jews did, that faith is meritorious, *i.e.* equivalent to a work. Since he can speak of devils believing (Jas. 2:19), this must clearly be a different kind of faith from that which Paul supposes. The key to James' position is found in James 2:24: 'You see that a man is justified by works and not by faith alone.' He considers the means of justification to be faith which results in works. Another point is that James seems to use the word 'justification' in a different way from Paul. For Paul it has a definitely forensic sense, but this is less clear in James. It is rather that a man is justified in his claim to have faith if his works demonstrate the reality of his claim. 'Faith was completed by works' is his comment on Abraham's act in offering Isaac (Jas. 2:22).

It is possible that either Paul or James is attempting to correct a misunderstanding of the other. But the different use of terms seems to be a more satisfactory understanding of the relationship between them.

In *1 Peter* a statement is made giving the result of believers dying to sin (*i.e.* in Christ who bore our sins) as initiation into a life of righteousness (1 Pet. 2:24). Righteousness becomes the pattern for the new life, the very antithesis of sin. But righteousness in this sense properly belongs to the NT teaching on sanctification. In this epistle the believers suffer for righteousness' sake (1 Pet. 3:14). In *2 Peter* righteousness is linked with faith (2 Pet. 1:1). Moreover, a distinctly future concept is presented in 2 Peter 3:13, where the prospect is presented of a new earth where righteousness dominates. Although these are little more than passing references, they show the importance of the theme in the writer's mind. It is worth noting also that, as in Hebrews 11:7, Noah is presented as an example of righteousness (2 Pet. 2:5).

In the *Johannine epistles*, God is declared to be just to forgive and to cleanse from unrighteousness (1 Jn. 1:9). It is the conviction that the Son is righteous which brings certainty to those who believe in him. Their 'righteousness' is evidence of their new birth (1 Jn. 2:29). In this latter case

---

[304] F. Mussner, *Der Jacobusbrief* (*HTKNT*, ³1975), pp. 152ff., has an excursus in which he compares Paul and James over their use of the term 'work'.

it is best understood in connection with the process of sanctification. The same may be said of 1 John 3:7, 10.

In the book of *Revelation* the final judgment, executed by the triumphant Lamb, is based on the concept of righteousness (Rev. 19:11). The whole book in fact works towards this climax. The writer visualizes a time when everything will be assessed in accordance with the righteousness of God (*cf.* Rev. 22:11). The apocalypse gives no more specific basis for the final judgment, but agrees with the consistent NT pattern that God will demand righteousness. Those already justified by faith, in Paul's mind, will be deemed to have met that demand in Christ.

The relevance of the NT doctrine of justification. To many moderns the relevance will not be at first apparent. Indeed, it is meaningless to those who do not admit man's guilt, or else explain it in psychological terms in a way which does not fit into Paul's forensic framework. Nevertheless there is enough evidence to show that modern man is no different from his first century counterpart in being conscious of failure. He is still preeminently a slave to self. Justification offers a path to freedom. Man has no longer to justify his own existence. His right to new life is a gift from God.

It is on the basis of man's acquittal that the whole NT teaching on salvation is expounded. Whereas justification is but one of the expressions of the work of Christ, it is a key concept and no appreciation of the magnitude of what he did for man is possible without giving full weight to it.

Although for our present purposes we have considered justification as a separate facet of the mission of Jesus, it is necessary for a true appreciation of this truth to link it closely with the NT teaching on sanctification, especially in Paul's exposition of it (see pp. 667ff.). Indeed justification and sanctification cannot be divorced. If one is stressed at the expense of the other a distortion of NT teaching will result. We may regard our discussion of justification, therefore, as an indispensable basis for our understanding of the new life in Christ to which we turn our attention in a later chapter.

SUMMARY

The preceding survey has shown many different aspects of the meaning of the death of Christ. Some attempt must now be made to show how these various aspects fit together as facets of the one basic truth that Christ died for our sins.

Although the evidence from the gospels is fragmentary, it lays the foundation for the subsequent Christian exposition of the doctrine of the atonement. Especially is this true of the institution of the Last Supper and its theological implications. Since this ordinance became the central observance of the early church, it serves as a valuable key to the interpretations of the death of Christ in the epistles. It is particularly a link between Jesus' own understanding of his death and Paul's exposition of that death. The NT lends no support to the view that the various explanations arose because of the need to explain away the embarrassing death of the long-awaited Messiah. The death of Jesus did not come as a surprise to him. He expected it and prepared for it. No understanding of the atonement is adequate which does not recognize that it was an essential part of his mission.

It must further be noted that no real understanding of the teaching of Jesus about the kingdom can be gained apart from some understanding of his death. Since this had redemptive significance, the kingdom can only be properly understood in terms of a redeemed community. The one idea is inextricably linked with the other. Although the rest of the NT outside the gospels concentrates less on the kingdom, there is no suggestion that this teaching is superseded. The developing understanding of the death of Christ focused attention more on the important matter of the conditions of membership.

The various ways in which Paul and others explained the death of Christ throw light on the different problems which man experienced as a result of sin. One interpretation or figure of speech was not enough to embrace a total understanding. Sacrifical language was needed to show the fulfilment in Christ of all the levitical ritual which God had provided to facilitate man's approach to him; it was also needed to demonstrate the end of all sacrifices. Moreover the imagery of sacrifice is closely linked to the idea of substitution, which when applied to the work of Christ expresses the essentially objective nature of his work. It is impossible, in the light of the total NT evidence, to consider the death of Christ exclusively in terms of moral influence, as if it were no more than an example to be followed, *i.e.* as a purely subjective experience.

The more specific concept of redemption is mainly concerned with deliverance from bondage to sin and the establishment of new spiritual commitments. Redemption, in the various NT expositions of it, has the double aspect of freedom from the shackles of the past and the nobler bondage of a spiritual kind, an awareness that being redeemed involves present and future responsibilities.

The intercessory work of Christ is highly significant in view of the weakness felt by the redeemed community in approaching God. The high priestly function of intercession is an essential feature of the total present-ation of Christ's work, especially because it shows that work to have continuing importance. It is a great encouragement to Christian believers to know that Jesus still lives to plead for them on the grounds of his own death.

In the realm of relationships reconciliation is of vital importance. Where fellowship has been broken between man and God, there can be no peace until reconciliation has been made. No full understanding of the death of Christ can dispense with this strongly expounded NT truth that God was in Christ reconciling man to himself. It is an even more profound realization that in his death he brings about the reconciliation of the created order.

Our last consideration is to see where justification fits into the total picture. A man's standing before God in the light of God's judgment against sin has been radically changed by the death of Christ, on the strength of which the believer is justified. Although this interpretation makes use of legal terminology, it must not for that reason be dismissed as a fiction. Although the imagery must not be pressed, justification deals essentially with the problem of guilt, the removal of which is one of the most fundamental aspects of a true understanding of the death of Christ.

These many facets show God's way of dealing with sin and form the basis for our study of the Christian life. When considering the various aspects of the new man in Christ, it must never be forgotten that the death of Christ was necessary before even the possibility of the new spiritual life could be envisaged. Atonement is the foundation on which Christian experience is based.

Chapter 5

The Holy Spirit

The references to the Holy Spirit in the NT are widespread. Before examining them, we shall enquire into the background in order to discover whether the NT experience of the Spirit is something entirely new or whether it is a continuation of earlier manifestations. Our background studies will be almost entirely confined to the OT.[1]

The background

The part played by the Spirit in the created order is focused particularly in the creation narrative where the moving of the Spirit of God brought order out of chaos (Gn. 1:2).[2] Since the same word (*rûaḥ*) is used for both 'Spirit' and 'wind', the idea conveys the powerful, almost violent, movement of the Spirit.[3]

The continuing part played by the Spirit as the source of man's life is echoed in Genesis 6:3 ('my spirit shall not abide in man for ever'), and a similar thought is expressed in Job 27:3 ('as long as the Spirit of God is in my nostrils'). In two other passages in Job, the claim is made that the breath of the Almighty is in man (Jb. 32:8; 33:4). There is a clear connection between man's spirit and the Spirit of God, but the dominant idea is that man's very life is attributed to God.

---

[1] G. S. Hendry, *The Holy Spirit in Christian Theology* (1957), p. 16, prefers to begin with the NT rather than the OT on the grounds that the NT witness is soteriological and eschatological in character. He considers OT categories to be cosmological and anthropological. But a summary of OT teaching provides a valuable background to the NT position. G. T. Montague, *The Holy Spirit: Growth of a Biblical Tradition* (1976), devotes a third of the book to discussing the OT evidence. He recognizes that the biblical teaching is progressive.

[2] The comments here are on the assumption that Gn. 1:2 refers to the Holy Spirit. Many versions (*e.g.* NEB) have eliminated 'the Spirit' from the text, and substituted 'wind'. But *cf.* F. Baumgärtel, *TDNT* 6, p. 366, who concludes that in this context the *rûaḥ* of God is the personal creative power of God.

[3] F. Baumgärtel, *ibid.*, pp. 362ff., discusses *rûaḥ* in relation to God under four points: (i) effective divine power, (ii) specifically God's creative power, (iii) the inner nature of God, (iv) as a personal being. In these usages of the word it is closely linked with God's activity.

Not only so, but the continued activity of the Spirit in God's providential dealings with people is also reflected in Psalm 104:29–30 and in relation to creation in Isaiah 40:7. In other words, there are strong grounds for maintaining that in the OT, God's activity in the world of things and of men is often mediated through the Spirit of God. This dynamic aspect of the Spirit is inescapable in our approach to the biblical evidence and must colour our understanding of the NT evidence. The Spirit of God acts with considerable disturbing effect. It is part of his nature to do so.

It must be recognized that the activity of the Spirit in the created order does not imply any clash with the OT view of the transcendence of God. God is not only active in his world through his Spirit, but is also apart from his world.

Another aspect of the Spirit's work on a more human level is his endowment of men with intellectual and artistic powers, as in the case of Bezalel (Ex. 35:30f.). This may have significance for a consideration of the gifts of the Spirit in the NT church.

The concern of God for his people and his activity on their behalf, which forms a dominant thread through the OT, is at times closely linked with the Spirit. In the period of the judges, both Othniel and Gideon are named as being possessed by the Spirit (Jdg. 3:10; 6:34). It was, moreover, the activity of the Spirit in them that equipped them for their task. There is no indication that either of them had any special natural endowments. The Spirit of God made them leaders. The office of judge was a charismatic office.

When Saul became king, he was possessed by the Spirit (1 Sa. 11:6). The measure of his failure was signified by the withdrawal of the Holy Spirit from him, as a result of which he could no longer adequately fulfil his kingly function (1 Sa. 16:14; *cf.* 15:26). The activity of the Spirit is therefore as much concerned with the royal function, as it is with the judges. Moreover, in 1 Samuel 18:10 the antithesis of this possession of the Spirit of God is said to be 'an evil spirit from God'. The Spirit of the Lord came mightily on Saul's successor, David, when Samuel anointed him (1 Sa. 16:13). Again the activity of the Spirit is closely linked with charismatic leadership. The subsequent history of kingship in Israel was not marked by a succession of Spirit-filled men. In 2 Samuel 23:2 David claims that the Spirit speaks through his words, which foreshadowed the later prophetic ministry.

It is particularly in the prophetic office that the Spirit's work is important. Ezekiel was conscious of being possessed by the Spirit at the outset of his prophetical work (Ezk. 2:2).[4] Micah was aware of being filled with power

---

[4] L. Dewar, *The Holy Spirit and Modern Thought* (1959), pp. 12f., notes that in Ezekiel the word *rûaḥ* is without the article and is used in the sense of *rûaḥ*-substance entering into Ezekiel and controlling his utterances. But this way of putting it tends to depersonalize the prophetic activity of the Spirit.

and with the Spirit of the Lord (Mi. 3:8). Zechariah claims that the words of the Lord of hosts were sent by the Spirit through the former prophets (Zc. 7:12). This implies that those prophets who do not specifically link their work with the Spirit nevertheless were recognized as giving the Word of the Lord through the Spirit. There is, in fact, a close connection between the Word and the Spirit in OT thought.[5] Hosea's idea of a prophet is 'a man of the Spirit' (Ho. 9:7). Thus the pronouncements of God regarding the destiny of his people may be regarded as the messages of the Spirit.

There is one conception of the redemptive activity of the Spirit which is of special importance as a prelude to the NT testimony, and that relates to the promised Messiah. There are three passages in Isaiah to be noted in this respect. In Isaiah 11 it is said of the 'stump of Jesse' that 'the Spirit of the Lord shall rest upon him, the spirit of wisdom and understanding, the spirit of counsel and might, the spirit of knowledge and the fear of the Lord' (Is. 11:1–2). Since Jesus was the fulfilment of this prediction, it furnishes a direct link between the OT preparation and the Spirit's activity in the incarnate life of the Messiah. The second passage is Isaiah 42:1–4, spoken of the servant: 'I have put my Spirit upon him, he will bring forth justice to the nations. He will not cry or lift up his voice or make it heard in the street; a bruised reed he will not break, and a dimly burning wick he will not quench. . .' The whole passage was recognized by Matthew as prophetic of the healing ministry of Jesus (Mt. 12:18ff.). It is significant, moreover, that he quotes it immediately before inserting the Beelzebub controversy in which the truth of the Isaiah passage was deliberately called into question. The third passage is Isaiah 61:1, 'The Spirit of the Lord GOD is upon me, because the LORD has anointed me.' Luke records how Jesus read this passage and publicly claimed to fulfil the prediction himself (Lk. 4:18–21). Since Luke records this as the commencement of the ministry it provides a key to the understanding of the preaching and healing work of Jesus.

There are two further considerations: one is the Spirit's work in individuals and the other is his corporate operation. Some indication has already been given of the way in which the Spirit endowed individuals for specific tasks. In Saul's case the coming of the Spirit made a different man of him (1 Sa. 10:6), but this kind of phenomenon is rare until the later prophetical books. Another early remarkable instance of a sudden coming of the Spirit on an individual is the narrative of Samson (Jdg. 14:6). Having come upon him with considerable power, the Spirit is presumed to be present with him until the point of his specific withdrawal.

It is more particularly in the prophets, as shown in the preceding section,

---

[5] For the close connection between Spirit and Word in the OT, *cf.* E. M. B. Green, *I believe in the Holy Spirit* (1975), p. 22.

that the individual activity of the Spirit took place, not so much in feats of power as in the realm of communication. But the prophets themselves also visualized the outpouring of the Spirit in a corporate way. There are three significant passages.[6] The first is Ezekiel 37 in which the valley of dry bones comes alive through the activity of the Spirit of God, with the result that an exceedingly large multitude appeared, representing in fact the whole house of Israel. In this case the Spirit's activity is described in terms of the breath (*rûaḥ*) of God. Its massive extent prepares us for the corporate outpouring of the Spirit at Pentecost. Another passage is Isaiah 44:3, where the imagery of water on parched ground describes a similar refreshing and reviving ministry. Here the outpouring is wider, since it is not confined to the house of Israel. The third passage is Joel 2:28, which declares, 'I will pour out my spirit on all flesh,' which Peter claimed to be fulfilled on the day of Pentecost. This is of particular significance because it shows that the mass descent of the Spirit was not without prior preparation. Indeed Peter makes particularly clear that Pentecost was the precise fulfilment of what Joel had predicted.

In view of the wide variety of ways in which the Spirit operated in the OT, it is not surprising that a similar breadth of activity is found in the NT. The question arises, however, whether the NT conception of the Spirit is an entirely new phenomenon, or whether it may be regarded as a continuation and development of the OT conception. We have already seen that the NT writers saw the fulfilment of certain OT passages in the ministry of Jesus and the experience of the early church. Nevertheless the special activity of the Spirit in the church is definitely subsequent to the glorification of Jesus, which means that a new dimension enters into the activity of the Spirit in the new age. The outpouring of the Spirit was corporate and powerful, but it was nevertheless communicated through faith. The key is the dynamic event of the resurrection of Jesus. This becomes abundantly clear in our survey of the evidence from the NT.

The intertestamental period was not strong on the doctrine of the Spirit, but there are certain significant references in the Qumran literature which are worth noting.[7] The Holy Spirit is a cleansing, purifying power and this certainly foreshadows some aspects of the Spirit's work which come to clearer expression in the NT. The holiness of God's Spirit is frequently emphasized and in one passage (*CD* 2:12) a prediction is made that God will grant the Messiah a spirit of holiness. This idea focuses attention on

---

[6] L. Dewar, *op. cit.*, p. 9, considers that these passages predicting a corporate reception of the Spirit led to a revolution in the whole doctrine of the Spirit of God. He sees the corporate idea as the only means by which the nation could be preserved against false prophecy.

[7] *Cf.* A. R. C. Leaney, *The Rule of Qumran and its Meaning* (1966), pp. 34ff. The main relevant passages are: 1 QS 3:7–9; 4:21; 1 QH 16:12; 17:26, frag. 2:9ff. *Cf.* also A. A. Anderson, 'The use of "*Rûaḥ*" in 1 QS, 1 QH and 1 QM', *JSS* 7, 1962, pp. 293–301. J. A. T. Robinson, *HTR* 50, 1957, pp. 175–191, discusses the purifying of the Spirit in Qumran literature.

an essential difference between the Qumran approach and the NT teaching. The Qumran view falls far short of that teaching in that it has no doctrine of a personal Holy Spirit. Nevertheless the close link between *pneuma* and personal holiness went some way along the road to fuller revelation of the Spirit in Christ. It is significant that cleansing in Qumran was both moral and ceremonial and this again falls short of the NT view of the purity of the indwelling Spirit, *i.e.* in an exclusively moral act of cleansing. Moreover, in the NT the cleansing is linked with the work of Christ, not with a continuing ceremonial.

In addition much discussion has ranged around the fact that the expression 'Spirit of truth' occurs in Qumran literature.[8] This has been seen as a source for John's identification of the term with the Paraclete. Further comments will be made on this term in the appropriate section, but it is significant that nowhere in the Qumran literature is there any equivalent to the expression 'Paraclete' and it is certain that any connection between John and Qumran on this issue must be regarded as highly tenuous. We must draw a distinction between the parallel use of the phrase 'the Spirit in truth' in Qumran and John, and the various theories that in Qumran the Spirit was regarded either as a heavenly spokesman or as identified with Michael. The latter two theories are matters of considerable dispute and can hardly provide a firm basis for an understanding of the Johannine teaching about the Spirit. Nevertheless it may be said that the Qumran evidence shows that the idea of a Spirit of truth as opposed to a spirit of error would not have been unfamiliar in the time of Jesus.

The synoptic gospels

One of the features which marks out these gospels from John's gospel is that they contain less teaching about the Holy Spirit. Luke contains more than Matthew and Mark, but the references in none of the four gospels can be said to be prolific. Indeed, in view of the multiplicity of references in the Acts and epistles, it is surprising that the gospels contain so few references.[9] We shall consider the evidence in two main sections: The Holy Spirit in the mission of Jesus, and The Holy Spirit in the teaching of Jesus.

THE HOLY SPIRIT IN THE MISSION OF JESUS

There are seven aspects of the part played by the Spirit in the life and work

---

[8] For discussion of the Qumran teaching on the Spirit as a background to John's Paraclete passages, *cf.* G. Johnston, *The Spirit-Paraclete in the Gospel of John* (1970), esp. 102ff., where he summarizes and criticizes the view of O. Betz, *Der Paraklet* (1963), that the Spirit has replaced the archangel Michael as legal spokesman for the people of God. Both Betz and Johnston draw heavily on the Qumran evidence.

[9] J. E. Fison, *The Blessing of the Holy Spirit* (1950), pp. 81–109, attempts to explain the silence of the synoptics on the Spirit compared with the much fuller teaching in John's gospel by appealing to the development in the OT from ecstatic outbursts to prophetic mysticism. But neither of these categories is a precise parallel to the references to the Spirit in the gospels, as a survey of the evidence shows.

of Jesus, most of which are recorded by Luke with some parallels in the other gospels.

The promise of the Spirit through the words of John the Baptist. Since in so many features John the Baptist belongs to the order of OT prophets, it is fitting that he should introduce in his preparatory ministry the relation of Jesus to the Spirit. According to Luke, it was in answer to questions put to him that John made his specific declaration that Jesus would baptize with the Holy Spirit and with fire (Lk. 3:15ff.; *cf.* Mt. 3:11–12; Mk. 1:7–8). It will be noticed that Mark omits the words 'with fire', which has led to various theories about the original form of the words.[10]

One theory is that the original reference was not to the Holy Spirit at all, but either to fire or to fire and wind.[11] Both are then taken in the sense of judgment. The references to the Spirit in the present texts must then be treated as Christian commentary read back into the event. But this is untenable for the following reasons. The first is that John's message of repentance is against it. The coming of the kingdom is good news, not bad.[12] John was predicting not only an imminent catastrophe, but also a Coming One whose own righteousness would inaugurate a kingdom of righteousness. The winnowing process which would result would be aimed mainly to separate and preserve the wheat, although it necessarily involved an act of rejection of the chaff. If there is no reference to the Spirit here, there is certainly enough reference to the provision of God's mercy to make it highly improbable that judgment was exclusively intended. The existing texts, with the prominence they all give to the Spirit, would be in complete harmony with the aspect of mercy which is implied. Moreover, if John the Baptist had had contact with Qumran he would have been familiar with the idea of the purifying activity of the Spirit.

There seems to be no good reason to maintain that the reference to the Holy Spirit is a later addition in the light of the Pentcost experience, where 'fire' is linked with the Holy Spirit. Admittedly the context in which the saying comes mentions 'the wrath to come' (Mt. 3:7; Lk. 3:7), which sets the background of judgment; but this does not make improbable a simultaneous reference to the Holy Spirit, unless it be maintained that John the Baptist saw the coming Messiah wholly in terms of a Messiah of judgment.[13] But this is unthinkable.

---

[10] R. Bultmann, *The History of the Synoptic Tradition* (Eng. trans. 1963), p. 246, regards Mark's omission as 'Christianizing editing'. *Cf.* J. M. Creed, *Luke* (1930), p. 54, who inclines to the view that the introduction of the Spirit into the context is a Christian gloss. G. B. Caird, *Luke* (²1968), p. 74, favours a similar view.

[11] *Cf.* C. K. Barrett *The Holy Spirit and the Gospel Tradition* (1947), p. 126. Also C. H. Kraeling, *John the Baptist* (1951), pp. 59ff.; E. Best, 'Spirit-Baptism' *NovT* 4, 1960, pp. 236ff.

[12] Mk. 1:4 uses the verb *euangelizesthai* which involves good news.

[13] *Cf.* D. Hill, *Matthew* (NCB, 1972), pp. 94f., who maintains that both 'spirit' and 'fire' may refer to *redemptive* rather than destroying judgment.

If we establish the possibility that the combination of Spirit and fire is original to John the Baptist, we need then to discuss what was meant by the words 'baptize with the Holy Spirit and with fire.' We note first that the Greek text makes clear that one action[14] is involved (the *en*, 'with', governing both). The expression could then mean that both repentant and unrepentant people would be involved, the former would experience blessing and the latter judgment. But another view is that only the repentant are addressed, in which case the 'fire' would be symbolic of the purging function of the Spirit. There is a parallel to this in the reference to the refiner's fire in Malachi 3:2,3. Fire, however, is more often used of judgment.[15] It is difficult to be sure what John the Baptist had in mind, but at least the importance of the Spirit's role is indisputable. On any interpretation the role of the Spirit is seen as uncomfortable, even disturbing. His purpose is to combat all that would hinder the fulfilment of the kingdom.

We need also to enquire when John the Baptist's prediction of Spirit-baptism was actually fulfilled. Some relate it to the minsitry of Jesus by equating it with the water-baptism practised by Jesus and his disciples. But the baptism of the Spirit is clearly distinguished from the water-baptism which John himself was using.[16] It must refer, therefore, to the spiritual experience of those who would come to believe in Jesus, and must have a primary reference to Pentecost.

The Spirit's part in the virgin birth. The debates surrounding the virgin birth have already been mentioned (see pp. 365ff.), but our present purpose is to focus on the function of the Spirit in the birth of Jesus. Both Matthew and Luke specifically attribute the conception of Jesus to the Spirit. Matthew 1:18 says of Mary that 'she was found to be with child of the Holy Spirit' (a statement confirmed by the angel, 1:20). Luke 1:35 records the angel's address to Mary, 'The Holy Spirit will come upon you . . .; therefore the child to be born will be called holy.' Luke draws a distinction between the birth of John the Baptist and the birth of Jesus. Of the former Zechariah is told that his coming son will be filled with the Holy Spirit from his mother's womb (Lk. 1:15); but this is very different from conception through the Spirit.

---

[14] J. D. G. Dunn, *Baptism in the Holy Spirit* (1970), p. 11, makes the point that only one baptism is in mind, *i.e.* in Spirit-and-fire. *Cf. idem*, 'Spirit-and-Fire Baptism', *NovT* 14, 1972, pp. 81–92.

[15] *Cf.* E. E. Ellis, *Luke* (*NCB*, 1966), pp. 89f., who considers that 'fire' is a Christian *pesher*-ing to the Pentecostal fulfilment, and by this means avoids the need to account for John the Baptist's use of it.

[16] It has often been supposed that the difference between John's baptism and Christian baptism is that the latter was the occasion for the gift of the Spirit (so O. Cullmann, *Baptism in the New Testament* (Eng. trans. 1950, p. 9). But see the careful weighing of the evidence by J. K. Parratt, 'The Holy Spirit and Baptism', *ExT* 82, 1971, pp. 233f. He takes the view that the Holy Spirit comes in addition to water baptism, not through it. *Cf.* also C. F. D. Moule, 'Baptism in Water and in the Holy Ghost', *Theology* 48, 1945, p. 246.

In view of the strong OT background of the birth narratives, it is probable that some parallel exists between the act of the Spirit in creation and his part in the birth of Jesus. But there is a distinction between creation and conception which must be maintained. There are no indications in the birth narratives regarding the manner in which the conception took place.[17] It remains a mystery. The rationalist view that the birth was normal and came only later to be thought of as birth through a virgin has already been rejected as unsatisfactory (see pp. 372f.).

What is most significant in the assertion that Jesus was conceived through the Holy Spirit is the implication that the whole mission including the incarnation was directed by the Spirit. This fact comes out in the other major events in the life of Jesus.

The Spirit and Simeon's prediction. In his birth narratives Luke brings out strongly the part played by the Spirit in guiding the words which Simeon pronounced over Jesus. The Holy Spirit was upon him (Lk. 2:25), the Spirit had revealed to him that he should see the Lord's anointed (Lk. 2:26), and he is said to have been 'inspired by the Spirit' on his meeting with Jesus and his parents (Lk. 2:27). He was led to make the prediction that Jesus would be a light to the Gentiles and a glory to Israel (Lk. 2:32). The function of the Spirit, therefore, is highly significant in the revelation he gives of the universal extent of the mission of Jesus, and in the prediction of the sword which would pierce the soul of Mary. Here then is the Holy Spirit in his prophetic role.

The Spirit at the baptism of Jesus. Since the baptism of Jesus may be regarded as the inauguration of his ministry, it is not surprising that all the synoptic writers draw attention to it. Moreover, all mention the dove-like descent of the Spirit upon him as a prelude to the heavenly voice calling on men to heed his words (Mt. 3:16 = Mk. 1:10 = Lk. 3:22). This description leads us to consider why Jesus requested John's baptism and why the Spirit put a special seal upon it.

Although John's baptism was a baptism of repentance, Jesus submitted to it. Since he had no cause to repent, the act must be regarded as representative. Moreover, the baptism was a communal act in which all who had really repented were bound together into a whole. The identification of Jesus with this group is part of the significance of his baptism. The descent of the Spirit marked the dawning of a new age, an age of righteousness (*cf.* Jesus' answer to John's hesitation over baptizing him, Mt. 3:15). We have already seen that John the Baptist distinguished between his own

---

[17] *Cf.* C. K. Barrett, *op. cit.*, pp. 5ff., who examines the various aspects of the relation of the Holy Spirit to the virgin birth. He suggests that the transition from creation to begetting was effected by the migration of the gospel from Palestinian to Hellenistic Judaism (p. 24).

ministry and that of Jesus, which shows that he considered the advent of the Coming One would mark a definite transition. The new element was the announcement of the messianic office through the anointing of Jesus by the Spirit.[18] This role of the Spirit in the public inauguration of the Messiah is important because it set a divine seal on his mission. Although he was Messiah before this event, yet it was only then that his messianic office became public.[19]

A further point that needs comment is the dove-like form of the Spirit's descent. The dove is clearly symbolic, but why was it introduced and what does it mean? There are Jewish parallels which contain allusions to the Spirit in terms of a dove, brooding over the face of the waters.[20] This close connection between the Spirit and dove, although not specifically symbolic language, suggests the same kind of connection as at the baptism of Jesus. Although all the synoptics liken the descent of the Spirit to a dove, they do not equate the Spirit and the dove. Luke says most clearly that the descent was in 'bodily form'.[21]

It is evidently the intention in all the accounts to emphasize the objective reality of the event. Whether the dove symbolizes gentleness or peace or whether it is merely symbolic of descent is difficult to say.[22] It makes little difference to the fact of the Spirit's anointing of Jesus for his public mission. There is truth in the view that the main reason for the descent of the Spirit on Jesus was that he should baptize others with the Spirit as John the Baptist had predicted.[23] In other words the mission of Jesus was not only Spirit-initiated, but also Spirit-orientated. It should also be noted that the heavenly voice attesting the sonship of Jesus follows immediately after the descent of the Spirit and must be closely connected with it. It is particularly

[18] In the view of A. Schweitzer, *The Mysticism of Paul the Apostle* (²1953), p. 233, John's baptism arose as an eschatological sacrament.

[19] Note that C. K. Barrett, *op. cit.*, pp. 41ff., considers that Jesus assumed the messianic office at the baptism. *Cf.* D. E. Nineham, *Mark* (1963), pp. 62f. But against this *cf.* V. Taylor, *Mark* (²1966), p. 162. G. B. Caird, *Luke* (²1968), p. 77, comments that the words from heaven 'were the divine approval of the course to which Jesus had committed himself in accepting Baptism'. J. D. G. Dunn, *Jesus and the Spirit* (1977), p. 29, speaks of Jesus' new role as a result of the anointing of the Spirit as a 'fuller messiahship'.

[20] *Cf.* Strack-Billerbeck 1, p. 124.

[21] L. E. Keck, 'The Spirit and the Dove', *NTS* 17, 1970, pp. 41–67, maintains that the baptism account did not originate in Hellenistic circles, as Bultmann claimed (*cf. History of the Synoptic Tradition*, pp. 249ff.), but in Palestinian, Aramaic-using Christianity. His theory is that Mark's words were ambiguous and what was intended to be understood adverbially came to be taken adjectivally. In his view the Spirit came in a dove-like way, not in a dove-like form. This theory implies that Luke misunderstood Mark.

[22] It is to be noted that the main idea in the use of the term Spirit is that found in both OT and Jewish usage, *i.e.* the idea of power, *cf.* J. M. Robinson, *The Problem of History in Mark* (⁴1971), p. 29. But this does not rule out the gentler aspect as illustrated by the dove imagery. It is more probable that the dove was symbolic of Jesus as the true Israelite, in accordance with Jewish ideas of the dove as symbolic of the community of Israel, *cf.* W. L. Lane, *The Gospel of Mark* (*NICNT*, 1974), p. 57.

[23] *Cf.* G. R. Beasley-Murray, *Baptism in the New Testament* (1962), p. 61. J. D. G. Dunn, *Baptism in the Holy Spirit* (1970), p. 32, maintains that the most important purpose of the descent of the Spirit was to equip Jesus for the messianic task of baptizing in the Spirit.

significant that Father, Son and Spirit here combine in a common witness.

When in Acts 10:38 Peter says that God anointed Jesus with the Spirit, it is an interpretation of the baptism narrative. The idea of being anointed with the Spirit is foreshadowed in Isaiah 61:1, and is supported in various Jewish writings which connect the Spirit with the messianic office.[24]

The Spirit at the temptation of Jesus. If the baptism was marked by the Spirit's activity, this is equally true of the temptation of Jesus. The two are strikingly juxtaposed at the close of Mark's account of the baptism: 'The Spirit immediately drove him out into the wilderness' (Mk. 1:12). The temptation was as much a *must* as the baptism experience. The parallel account in Matthew, while not so stark, is nevertheless as decisive in connecting the temptation narrative with the baptism (Mt. 4:1). Luke's account of the two events is bisected by the genealogy (Lk. 3:21–4:1), but the positive part played by the Spirit is reinforced by the statement that Jesus was full of the Holy Spirit when he returned from Jordan and was led by the Spirit in the wilderness. It is generally agreed that the temptations were messianic, in which case they have a direct relationship to the messianic reference in the baptism. The Spirit who descended on Jesus led to the testing of his mission.[25] The Spirit is seen as the organizer of the main stages of the mission.

The Spirit and exorcism in the ministry of Jesus. There are several allusions to the exorcism of demons in the synoptic gospels and on one occasion Jesus implies that the casting out was 'by the Spirit of God' (Mt. 12:28). In this case Luke has 'finger of God' (11:20), but Matthew's wording avoids the anthropomorphism.[26] Since this whole operation is centred in the world of spirits, it is natural to find the Holy Spirit as the agent for casting out evil spirits.[27] The many exorcisms in the gospels, as earlier noted (p. 127ff.), remind us of the spiritual conflict into which Jesus was

---

[24] *E.g.* 1 Enoch 49:3; *cf.* 52:4; Pss. Sol. 17:42; Test. Lev. 18:2–14.

[25] W. F. Arndt, *Luke* (1956), p. 126, notes that immediately after Jesus was anointed with the Spirit, the Spirit imposed on him one of his main tasks, the struggle with Satan. L. Morris, *Luke* (*TNTC*, 1974), p. 102, sees in Luke's statement that Jesus was led *en tō pneumati* the fact that it was in God's plan that Jesus should face the question what kind of Messiah he should be. I. H. Marshall, *Luke* (*NIGTC*, 1978), p. 169, suggests that Luke's form of words may give a clearer allusion to Dt. 8:2, where Israel was led in the wilderness by God in order to be tested.

[26] J. E. Yates, 'Luke's Pneumatology and Lk. 11:20', *Studia Evangelica* 2, (ed. F. L. Cross, 1964), pp. 295ff., favours the originality of Matthew's 'Spirit' on the grounds of his general usage. J. D. G. Dunn, *Jesus and the Spirit*, pp. 45f., comes to the same conclusion, but on the ground that Luke avoided 'Spirit' because he believed that Jesus, although he was uniquely anointed, was not yet Lord of the Spirit.

[27] C. K. Barrett, *The Holy Spirit and the Gospel Tradition*, pp. 62f., favours Luke's wording, but admits that Luke intended as much as Matthew to portray Jesus as a 'pneumatic' – a spiritual person potent against evil spirits.

plunged. Although exorcisms were widely practised in the contemporary world and there are several instances of parallels from Jewish sources, yet in two respects the exorcisms of Jesus were unique – they were regarded as messianic signs and they were performed through the Holy Spirit (not by magic). If Jesus was to establish his own kingdom, he must first over-throw the kingdom of evil. The exorcisms were powerful manifestations of the Spirit which demonstrated that a stronger person had come.

The ministry of exorcisms which Jesus himself practised was intended to be passed on as the seventy experienced on their mission. It was the subjection of the demons that most impressed them when they returned to report to Jesus (Lk. 10:17ff.), but he cooled their enthusiasm, no doubt to ensure that spiritual power did not go to their heads. Yet at the same time he himself is said to have rejoiced in the Holy Spirit (Lk. 10:21) because of the discovery that his disciples had made.

The Spirit and the public ministry of Jesus. According to Luke's gospel Jesus began his public ministry in the synagogue at Nazareth, having returned to Galilee from the temptation experience 'in the power of the Spirit', and at once publicly claimed that the promise of the Spirit in Isaiah 61:1,2 was fulfilled in himself (*cf.* Lk. 4:16ff.).[28] Moreover, the Isaiah passage describes the kind of ministry on which he had embarked in terms of preaching, healing and deliverance. Again the messianic emphasis is present in the 'anointing' of the Spirit-possessed person predicted in the OT passage. A similar deduction may be made on the basis of Matthew's inclusion of a quotation from a servant song (Is. 42: 1–4), which again links the healing ministry with the possession of the Spirit (Mt. 12:15ff.). Even if his con-temporaries, the Pharisees, placed a wrong construction on the healing ministry of Jesus (see the discussion of the Beelzebub controversy below), Matthew later rightly understood that that ministry was the direct work of the Spirit, based on the clear implication of the words of Jesus (*cf.* Mt. 12:28).

Enough has been said to show that the ministry of Jesus was conceived by the evangelists as being the work of a man of the Spirit. This is important in any consideration of the teaching of Jesus on the ministry of the Spirit. What he predicted for others was true *par excellence* of himself. This does not mean to say that Jesus' own experience is a prototype of Christian experience, since this would obscure his uniqueness.[29] Neverthe-

[28] J. D. G. Dunn, *op. cit.*, p. 54, considers it probable that Luke himself put the words on the lips of Jesus. But why should it not be attributable to Jesus?

[29] J. D. G. Dunn, *Baptism in the Holy Spirit*, pp. 23–37, strongly maintains that the experience of Jesus at his baptism was his entry into the new age of the Spirit. He regards this as the bridge between Jesus' religion and Paul's. For a critique of this, *cf.* M. M. B. Turner's Tyndale Lecture, 'Jesus and the Spirit in Lukan Perspective' (forthcoming *TB*).

less, the Spirit who is active in the Christian community is the same Spirit who was active in the ministry of Jesus.

THE HOLY SPIRIT IN THE TEACHING OF JESUS

Although there are relatively few passages in the synoptic gospels which record statements of Jesus about the Holy Spirit, those that occur are particularly significant. They present his thought about various aspects of the Spirit's activity in the coming community.

The blasphemy saying. All the synoptics record the occasion when Jesus was accused of casting out demons by the prince of demons (Mk. 3:22–30; Mt. 12:22–32; Lk. 11:14–23).[30] The charge led to a statement by Jesus (recorded only by Mark and Matthew in this context and by Luke elsewhere, Lk. 12:10) that blasphemy against the Holy Spirit was unforgivable, a statement which has led to misunderstanding and must therefore be carefully weighed.[31]

To begin with, blasphemy against the Holy Spirit is contrasted with blasphemy against the Son. It is difficult, therefore, to see how the distinction can be upheld if the reference is to the Holy Spirit's activity in Jesus. At the same time the charge was brought (according to Matthew and Luke) after a specific case in which Jesus exorcized a demon. In Mark the charge was made after a general reference to exorcisms (*cf.* Mk. 3:29). There was a definite connection, therefore, between Jesus' ministry of exorcism and the charge. The accusers were, in fact, maintaining that Jesus was possessed by Beelzebub which amounted to a direct affront against the Holy Spirit. But what are we to understand about the distinction between such an affront and blasphemy against the Son? Would not the latter be equally an affront against the Spirit? Evidently Jesus makes a distinction between general opposition to himself in his teaching ministry and a deliberate distortion of the Holy Spirit's ministry within him. Mark brings out the distinction by contrasting the approach of his friends who called him mad and the scribes who implied that he was demon-possessed. The latter approach was tantamount to calling the Holy Spirit the devil, and it is not

---

[30] Luke places the Beelzebub discussion after recording Jesus' promise of the gift of the Holy Spirit (Lk. 11:13), and as arising immediately out of the healing of the man with a dumb demon. The setting of the warning directly after the promise in Luke's account shows the responsibility that rests on those who receive the gift. The critics of Jesus were deliberately perverting his teaching.

[31] Some trace the original of this saying to the Palestinian community. *Cf.* A. Fridrichsen, 'Le péché contre le St. Esprit', *RHPR* 3, 1923, pp. 367ff.; E. Schweizer, *Mark* (Eng. trans., 1971, from *NTD*, 1967), pp. 82ff.; R. Scroggs, 'The Exaltation of the Spirit by some Early Christians', *JBL* 84, 1965, pp. 360ff.

Some scholars consider that blasphemy against the Spirit was possible only after Pentecost: D. Procksch, *TDNT* I, p. 104; C. K. Barrett, *The Holy Spirit and the Gospel Tradition* (1974), pp. 106f.; M. E. Boring, 'How may we identify oracles of Christian prophets in the Synoptic Tradition? Mk 3:28–29 as a Test Case', *JBL* 91, 1972, pp. 501–522, argues that this is a *pesher* on Is. 63:3–11 (see pp. 517f.). But the words become unintelligible unless considered to be a saying of Jesus.

surprising that Jesus describes this attitude as unforgivable. It revealed such a moral deterioration that good had become evil, and true values no longer had meaning.

But an alternative explanation of the saying has been proposed. If the contrast between the Spirit and the Son of man is taken to indicate different spheres of operation, the Spirit's sphere referred to in the blasphemy saying would have to refer to man's conscience generally.[32] In this case the calling of good evil and evil good would be such a blurring of the Spirit in man's conscience, that it would virtually extinguish the light of conscience altogether. While this would explain the seriousness of the sin as described in the words of Mark 3:29, 'guilty of an eternal sin (literally, 'liable to eternal judgment'), it tends to confuse the Holy Spirit with conscience. Mark's comment, 'for they had said, "He has an unclean Spirit" ', is more in favour of the interpretation given above, which centres on the consciousness in Jesus of the special endowment of the Holy Spirit for his messianic mission. At the same time, this is not to deny the activity of the Spirit within man's conscience, but rather to question whether this can be regarded as the interpretation of the present passage.

In the same context, the statement of Jesus in Matthew 12:28 must be noted: 'If it is by the Spirit of God that I cast out demons, then the kingdom of God has come upon you.' It has already been noted that Luke's 'finger of God' clearly means the same thing.[33] But the significance of the statement cannot be by-passed by regarding this as no more than 'current Jewish terminology'.[34] It shows how intimately the establishment of the kingdom is linked with the activity of the Spirit in the ministry of Jesus. Its contribution to the doctrine of the Spirit lies in the assurance that the Holy Spirit would overcome the spirits of evil through the mission of Jesus.

The Spirit's guidance in times of persecution. Jesus left his disciples in no doubt that they could expect opposition. He prepared them for possible defence of their cause before political councils by assuring them that the Spirit would speak through them (Mk. 13:11=Mt. 10:19–20=Lk. 12:12). Mark includes the saying in his eschatological discourse, Matthew in the mission charge of Jesus to the twelve, and Luke in a general group of sayings, closely linked with the blasphemy saying (*cf.* also the similar saying in Luke's eschatological discourse, 21:14–15). The fact that the contexts are different suggests that this assurance may have been repeated, and if so was

---

[32] *Cf.* L. Dewar, *The Holy Spirit and Modern Thought* (1959), p. 19, maintains that Jesus 'teaches that the Holy Spirit is at work at the natural level in every man'.

[33] G. W. H. Lampe, 'The Holy Spirit in the Writings of St Luke', in *Studies in the Gospels*' (ed. D. E. Nineham, 1955), pp. 159–200, points out that in biblical usage finger of God and hand of God are practically identical and that this is especially true of Luke's writings (*cf.* Acts 4:28, 30; 7:35; 11:21; 13:11) (p. 172).

[34] *Cf.* Dewar, *op. cit.*, p. 21. He claims that this statement throws no light on the Christian doctrine of the Spirit. But he makes too fine a distinction between 'the power of God' and the 'Spirit of God'.

regarded by Jesus as particularly important. It was in any case of general relevance and the context remains unimportant. Jesus did not envisage that his followers would be expected to make their own *apologia* for the gospel. His prediction of the Spirit's aid is stated in language which is akin to the Paraclete sayings in John (see below), especially in Matthew where the title 'Spirit of your Father' is used. Matthew and Mark both make clear that it would not be the disciples speaking, but the Holy Spirit speaking within them. In no clearer way could Jesus have brought out the superintendency of the Spirit over the ongoing work of the church. The disciples were to be channels for the Spirit's ministry.

The Spirit's part in the inspiration of Scripture. Another saying about the Spirit is in Mark 12:36 (= Mt. 22:43), where Psalm 110 is introduced by the words, 'David himself, inspired by the Holy Spirit, said . . .' (Matthew omits 'holy' here). This reflects contemporary Jewish belief in the inspiration of the OT. It is a reminder that Jesus shared the approach of his contemporaries towards the inspiration of Scripture, an approach which served as a pattern for the early Christian evaluation of Scripture (see section on Scripture, pp. 951ff.). The fact that there is no distinction between the Jewish and Christian viewpoints is not insignificant for the Christian doctrine of the Spirit,[35] since it corroborates the connection between the old and new order. The Spirit who indwells the believers is the same Spirit who inspired Scripture.[36] This ties in with the view on inspiration expressed in the epistles (2 Tim. 3:16; 2 Pet. 1:21). It is clearly an important part of the understanding of the Spirit's activities among Christians and accounts for the strong appeal to OT *testimonia*.

The question has been raised why the synoptic gospels contain only one statement about the Spirit's inspiration of the OT.[37] The matter must not, however, be judged quantatively, as if the absence of other cases suggests a failure to appreciate its importance. In fact, the very opposite may well be true. If it was universally assumed, it would be necessary to draw attention to it only on occasions when its truth affected the point of the discussion, as in the case of the question posed over Psalm 110:1. The crux was not that anyone would dispute the inspiration of the Psalm, but that it was specifically by the Spirit that David called the Messiah 'Lord'.

The promise of the Spirit in response to prayer. In the course of his teaching on prayer Jesus affirms that the Father will give the Holy Spirit to those

---

[35] Here Dewar, *ibid.*, p. 22, argues that because Jesus uses the formula of a pious Jew of his time, the passage tells us nothing fresh about the Christian doctrine of the Spirit. But this continuity between the Jewish and Christian view of inspiration is of great significance for NT theology.
[36] C. K. Barrett, *op. cit.*, pp. 108ff., gives a brief summary of Jewish and Greek views of inspiration.
[37] *Cf.* Barrett, *ibid.*, p. 108.

who ask him (Lk. 11:13). Matthew, who gives the saying in a different context (Mt. 7:11) has 'good things' instead of 'Holy Spirit'. This may be an instance of a saying repeated in a modified form. In any case it may be assumed that 'the Holy Spirit' is the best possible fulfilment of the 'good things'. What concerns us here is its assurance of the availability of the Holy Spirit. It throws some light on the post-Pentecost experience of the Spirit, when all believers, although possessors of the Spirit, might request a greater fullness of the Spirit.

The place of the Spirit in the baptismal formula. The concluding commission of Jesus to the disciples (Mt. 28:19) has been the subject of much debate. Its authenticity has been questioned both on textual and on historical grounds. The only external support for a form of the commission to the disciples which omits the baptismal formula is found in Eusebius, who frequently cites a shorter version. But since all the Greek MSS contain the formula its authenticity cannot be challenged on the slender ground of Eusebius' shortened citation. Nevertheless, many scholars, who would admit the textual evidence in support of it, challenge its historicity on other grounds. It is noted that baptism in the name of the trinity is not found in Acts, but only baptism in the name of Jesus. It is supposed that the latter formula fits into the believer's relationship to Christ, but that it cannot be transferred to the other persons of the trinity.[38] Matthew's baptismal formula is then declared to be a later development designed to safeguard the doctrine of the trinity.[39] In this case the mention of the Spirit in the formula tells us nothing about our Lord's teaching about the Spirit. But is this a right conclusion?

It was crucial for the disciples, if they were to baptize at all, to know what terms to use to describe the baptism. But is there any essential difference between the shorter and longer formulae? Has the Spirit now become an object of faith as well as an object of experience?[40] Certainly the earliest believers had experience of the Spirit at the time of baptism (Acts 2:38; 8:16–17; 9:17–18; 10:44ff.). Unless we regard the wording of the baptismal formula as a stereotyped rather than a living expression, we cannot categorically rule out the possibility that Matthew has recorded a

---

[38] Barrett, *ibid.*, p. 108, expresses the opinion that the present saying belongs, not to the period of theological origin and growth, but to a period of theological consolidation and fixation. D. Hill, *Matthew*, p. 362, points out that trinitarian formulations are found in Paul's epistles, although he thinks the formula in Matthew belongs to a time when the church has already experienced the universality of the Christian message.

[39] E. Schweizer, *Matthew*, pp. 531f., regards Matthew's formula as a later addition and his view would represent the majority opinion. W. F. Albright and C. S. Mann, *Matthew* (AB, 1971), p. 363, warn against treating this saying as a liturgical formula and suggest the words may describe what baptism accomplished. In this case the supposed difference from the practice in Acts would be less acute.

[40] *Cf.* Barrett, *op. cit.*, p. 103.

genuine statement of Jesus. There is moreover some parallel between Matthew's commission account ('teaching them to observe all that I have commanded you') and the promise to the disciples of the Spirit's aid to enable them to recall the words of Jesus (Jn. 14:26). It is more reasonable to hold that Jesus instructed his disciples to pass on his teaching than to maintain that this commission originated with Matthew.

The Spirit and the promise of power. Although in Luke's account of Jesus' farewell words (Lk. 24:49) no mention is made of the Spirit, the words 'stay in the city until you are clothed with power from on high', taken in conjunction with Luke's second volume, clearly refers to the descent of the Spirit of Pentecost. There is, moreover, similarity between the words 'I send the promise of my Father upon you' in Luke, and the expression 'the Spirit of your Father' in Matthew 10:20. Undoubtedly the expectation that the coming of the Spirit would be an endowment with power was amply fulfilled at Pentecost and in the subsequent events recorded by Luke in Acts.

SUMMARY OF SYNOPTIC EVIDENCE FOR THE DOCTRINE OF THE SPIRIT

We may make the following four observations from the evidence surveyed:

(i) Many major events of the life of Jesus are specifically connected with the activity of the Spirit. These include the incarnation, the baptism, the temptation, the exorcisms, the healing and preaching ministry. Whereas Jesus was unique and cannot, therefore, be held as an example for believers, yet it is true to say that his dependence on the Spirit prepares the way for his disciples' own dependence.

(ii) In his teaching Jesus prepared his disciples for the age of the Spirit which would follow his death and resurrection. Although more fully expounded in John's gospel, there is some indication in the synoptics of exciting possibilities: provision is made for guidance in apologetic, for a right approach to the OT, for ability to overcome adverse spiritual forces, for power in witness.

(iii) It must be accepted that the major background for the synoptic presentation of the Spirit's work is the OT. There is no reason to deny that Jesus himself continued to act and teach in harmony with the OT revelation, while at the same time exemplifying in his own person the fulfilment *par excellence* of the OT foreshadowings.

(iv) In answer to the question why these gospels say so little about the work of the Spirit,[41] it seems most natural to suppose that Jesus said little

---

[41] V. Taylor, 'The Spirit in the NT' in *The Doctrine of the Holy Spirit* (ed. N. Snaith, 1937), pp. 53ff., discusses this problem and suggests that 'the sayings about the Spirit are few in the recorded words of Jesus just because the doctrine was dominant'. C. K. Barrett, *op. cit.*, pp. 141f., is sceptical of this explanation because it assumes that controversy was the most important formulating factor in the early handling of the tradition. Nevertheless Taylor's suggestion deserves more weight than Barrett gives it.

because it required the experience of Pentecost to make the teaching intel-ligible.[42] This would precisely parallel the paucity of references to the meaning of the passion in the synoptics. Both are completely intelligible if there was no reading back from early Christian experience, but well nigh unintelligible if there was. Indeed, it may be claimed that the paucity of references is an indication of the authenticity of those which have been preserved, and gives added signficance to the flood of references to the Spirit in the post-Pentecost period.

The Johannine literature

Whereas there are more references to the Spirit in John and more specific information about his coming activities, it is remarkable that most of the material is contained in the more intimate teaching given exclusively to the apostles on the eve of the passion.[43] It is best to consider the evidence under two divisions – statements about the Spirit before the passion narratives and statements within those narratives.

THE SPIRIT IN THE EARLIER PART OF THE GOSPEL

In this section there is one narrative passage and five teaching passages. The former has parallels in the synoptic gospels, but there are no parallels to the latter.

The Spirit at the baptism. The main difference between John's account of the baptism of Jesus and the synoptic accounts is that John gives insight into the reactions of the baptizer (Jn. 1:29–34). According to the fourth gospel, he declared that he saw the Spirit descending as a dove on Jesus. He does not actually mention the baptism of Jesus, but this is clearly assumed. The dove is precisely parallel to the synoptics. The verb for seeing used by John (*theasthai*) cannot be construed as a visionary experi-ence, but demands a literal object (*cf.* Lk. 3:22 – in bodily form). Moreover, the descent of the Spirit identified for John the Baptist the Coming One who would himself baptize with the Spirit. Indeed, John the Baptist claims to have had a divine revelation which enabled him to identify the Coming

[42] R. N. Flew, *Jesus and His Church* (1938), pp. 70f., argues that the OT conception of the Spirit had first to be baptized into the death of Christ before the disciples could grasp the fuller meaning.

[43] For studies on the Spirit in John's gospel, *cf.* H. Schlier, 'Zum Begriff des Geistes nach dem Johannesevangelium', *Neutestamentliche Aufsätze: Festschrift für J. Schmid* (ed. J. Blinzler, O. Kuss, F. Mussner, 1963), p. 233; G. Bornkamm, 'Der Paraklet im Johannes-evangelium', *Geschichte und Glaube* 1 (1968), p. 69; R. E. Brown, 'The Paraclete in the Fourth Gospel', *NTS* 13, 1966–7, pp. 126f.; G. Johnston, *The Spirit-Paraklete in the Gospel of John* (1970); F. Mussner, *The Historical Jesus in the Gospel of St John* (1967), ch. 5; *idem BZ* 5, 1961, pp. 59ff.; E. Bammel, 'Jesus und der Paraklet in Johannes 16', *Christ and Spirit in the NT* (ed. B. Lindars and S. S. Smalley, 1973) pp. 199–216 (hereafter cited as *Christ and Spirit*); C. K. Barrett, 'The Holy Spirit in the Fourth Gospel', *JTS* 1, 1950, pp. 12–15; J. M. Boice, *Witness and Revelation in the Gospel of John* (1970), pp. 151ff.; E. Käsemann, *The Testament of Jesus* (Eng. trans. 1968), pp. 45f.; S. S. Smalley, *John: Evangelist and Interpreter* (1978), pp. 228ff.; H. Sasse, 'Der Paraklet im Johannesevangelium', *ZNW* 24, 1925, pp. 260ff.; H. Windisch, *The Spirit-Paraclete in the Fourth Gospel* (Eng. trans. 1968). For a very detailed recent study, *cf.* F. Porsch, *Pneuma und Wort* (1974).

One as one who would baptize with the Spirit. By the same means he was able to identify him as Son of God.

There are, therefore, both substantial agreements and significant variations between John and the synoptics. They may be said to corroborate each other. John omits the heavenly voice, but gives valuable insight into the meaning of the descending Spirit.[44] The close connection between the mission of Jesus and the activity of the Spirit is basic to all the records.

The function of the Spirit in Christian regeneration. We turn now from Jesus' experience to his teaching. The well-known saying to Nicodemus has great importance for the doctrine of the Spirit: 'Unless one is born of water and the Spirit, he cannot enter the kingdom of God' (Jn. 3:5). We need not here discuss the meaning of water, whether it refers to baptism or to physical birth, because our present concern is with birth by the Spirit. The focus is undoubtedly on the renewing or re-creative power of the Spirit in believers. This is the germ of regeneration (see the fuller discussion of this later, pp. 585f.). The idea is reinforced by the use of an analogy: 'That which is born of the flesh is flesh, and that which is born of the Spirit is spirit' (Jn. 3:6). In other words, like begets like. It cannot be argued from these words that there is any moral connotation of 'flesh', in the sense in which Paul sometimes uses 'flesh' in antithesis to 'spirit'. But the main thrust is in the fact that new birth cannot be achieved through 'flesh', only through 'Spirit', in this case the Holy Spirit. This idea is a considerable advance on the promise of the Spirit as a guide or a power for life. It means in short that the believer's whole spiritual existence depends on the activity of the Holy Spirit. It involves a totally new mode of existence. It is not surprising that Nicodemus misconstrued this radical teaching. Spiritual renewal of this kind is bound to affect every part of a man's life, but Jesus does not enlarge on this. It was left especially to the apostle Paul to give a fuller exposition of its implications.

Another factor is the impossibility of tracking down with precision the movements of the Spirit. Jesus used the analogy of wind, which is not only a play on words (*pneuma*), but is a fitting symbol for what is itself invisible, but nonetheless has visible effects. It is also suggestive of considerable power, sometimes boisterous, sometimes gentle.

The unlimited nature of the gift of the Spirit. In all probability the concluding section of John 3 is the evangelist's own comment. If this is so, he makes a significant assessment which is demonstrated fully in the case of Jesus.

[44] On Jn. 1:33, *cf.* C. H. Dodd, *The Interpretation of the Fourth Gospel*, p. 311; R. E. Brown, *John* (AB, 1966), pp. 158f.; R. Schnackenburg, *John*, 1 (Eng. trans., 1968 from *HTKNT*, 1965), pp. 399f. C. K. Barrett, *John*, p. 148, argues from the *kai* that Jesus was empowered to be both Lamb of God and Giver of the Spirit.

527

'For he whom God has sent utters the words of God, for it is not by measure that he gives the Spirit' (Jn. 3:34). It should be noted that an alternative rendering is possible, in which the Spirit is the subject rather than the object of the giving; but the context suggests that the translation quoted is to be preferred. The statement implies that the words of God need the Spirit of God to interpret them and that there would be no stinting of such assistance. The context shows that the sent one is the Son (Jn. 3:35), and thus draws attention to the close connection between the Spirit and the ministry of the Son.

The function of the Spirit in true worship. In the dialogue between Jesus and the Samaritan woman, a statement is made about the spiritual nature of God (Jn. 4:24). The fact that God is Spirit would not be a new revelation to the Jews, nor in all probability to the Samaritans. It is the principle deduced from this that is distinctive. Worship must be in spirit and in truth, and this can hardly be intelligible if it is not an indirect allusion to the Spirit of truth, who would lead the believers in Christ into true worship. It is important to note that it occurs in the context of a discussion of living water, a well known symbol of the Holy Spirit (see comment below on Jn. 7:38–39).

The link between the Spirit and life. It is possible that the word *pneuma* in John 6:63 may refer to the human spirit (as RSV supposes), but it makes good sense to see in it a reference to the Holy Spirit. In this case it would be aligned to the teaching on regeneration in John 3:5. Two other features are important: another antithesis between flesh and spirit, and a reference to the spiritual character of the words of Jesus. Believers are again viewed as belonging to a different order from the natural man (flesh). Faith is linked with Spirit, not with flesh.

The promise of the Spirit. Following the statement of Jesus about the rivers of living waters which would flow out of believers, John adds the comment, 'Now this he said about the Spirit, which those who believed in him were to receive; for as yet the Spirit had not been given, because Jesus was not yet glorified' (Jn. 7:38–39). John interpreted the living waters as symbolic of the Spirit. Jesus had made allusion to the water ceremonial at the feast of tabernacles.

Yet a problem arises over the quotation from Scripture, for there is no scripture which speaks of living waters flowing out of believers. There are some passages like Ezekiel 47:1–12; Joel 3:18 and Zechariah 14:8 which bear some resemblance. It has been suggested that the reference is to what Jesus himself had said in John 4:14, and that the present report is at fault.[45]

---

[45] *Cf.* Dewar, *The Holy Spirit and Modern Thought*, p. 31.

Another suggestion is that the word for belly (*koilias*) may in Aramaic have been confused with the word for fountain, in which case the difficulty would be avoided.[46] A further possibility is to refer the words of the quotation to Christ himself, (*i.e.* to living waters flowing out of Christ) and to punctuate with a comma at the end of verse 37 so as to attach the words 'he who believes in me' to the previous verse. This would agree with the view that Christ, not the believer, is the source of spiritual life. But 'faith' seems to belong better to the following words than to the preceding, and there is no preparation in the passage for a shift of subject from the believer to Christ.[47] It is better to regard the OT quotation as an allusion to OT promises relating to the coming of the Spirit, which according to the prediction of Jesus were about to be fulfilled.

The most important aspects of this passage are the direct relation between the Spirit's coming and the glorification of Jesus,[48] and the view that the purpose of the Spirit in believers is to promote a sharing ministry. The two themes are not unconnected, for when the Spirit is given, he also gives. Since the glorification theme is prominent in John's portrayal of the ministry and passion of Jesus, its connection with the gift of the Spirit is significant. It was at the resurrection that Jesus was glorified and subsequent to the resurrection that the Spirit was outpoured in full measure. The words 'the Spirit was not yet (= had not yet been) given' (Jn. 7:39b) mark a clear line of distinction between the Spirit's activity in the ministry of Jesus and his subsequent work in the church.[49]

THE SPIRIT IN THE PASSION NARRATIVE

Because of the remarkable detail about the Holy Spirit in the farewell discourses given by Jesus to the disciples on the eve of the passion, many scholars have regarded this whole section of John's gospel as a reading back.[50] In view of the activity of the Spirit reflected in the Acts and epistles

---

[46] *Cf.* C. F. Burney, *The Aramaic Origin of the Fourth Gospel* (1922), p. 109.

[47] *Cf.* L. Morris, *John* (*NICNT*, 1971), p. 423.

[48] D. E. Holwerda, *The Holy Spirit and Eschatology in the Gospel of John* (1959), p. 1, claims that in John's gospel the Holy Spirit is presented primarily as a post-ascension figure. Holwerda (pp. 20ff.) discusses the view that the Spirit was bestowed at Easter because that was the day of Jesus' glorification. H. Strathmann, *Das Evangelium nach Johannes* (*NTD*, 1954), *ad. loc.*, considers that in John, Easter and Pentecost coincide. But this view assumes that John is concerned with chronological considerations, whereas it is better to suppose that his concern is to demonstrate that it would be the glorified Lord who would bestow the Spirit.

[49] H. R. Boer, *Pentecost and Missions* (1961), pp. 76f., discusses the relation between the operation of the Spirit in the OT age and the NT church. He contends that it is the same Spirit who was active: the Spirit of Christ. The Spirit who worked in the OT saints could do so 'only because He was to come as the life-giving Spirit indwelling the New Testament church' (p. 87). Boer supports his view from Acts 7:51, 52a; 1 Cor. 10:1–4, 9a; Gal. 4:28, 29; 1 Pet. 1:10,11. He cites F. Büchsel, *Der Geist Gottes im Neuen Testament* (1926), p. 469, for the view that the 'not yet' was intended to mean not in the glorious present manifestation in the church age.

[50] For a careful examination of the relation of the Paraclete sayings to the rest of the gospel, *cf.* G. Johnston, *The Spirit-Paraclete in the Gospel of John* (1970). He is critical of the view of H. Windisch (*The*

it is supposed that the evangelist, in the light of his own experience of the Spirit and that of others, has attributed the teaching to Jesus. But this would leave the extraordinary activity of the Spirit at Pentecost and after without sufficient explanation, if Jesus had not prepared the disciples in the manner that John's narrative supposes. It may not unjustly be claimed that the Paraclete sayings in John provide the key for the right understanding of the Spirit's activity in Acts. The sayings are contained in the following passages: John 14:15–17; 14:25–26; 15:26–27; 16:5–11; 16:12–15. We shall consider what information these passages give about the character of the Spirit, about his various functions and about the manner in which the Spirit is given.

The character of the Spirit. Apart from the title "Holy Spirit' used once in John 14:26, there are two distinctive titles used in these passages which both convey some aspect of his character. The first is the word Paraclete (Jn. 14:16; 14:26; 15:26; 16:7) which is notoriously difficult to translate into English. It is variously rendered Comforter, Advocate, Counsellor, or simply Helper.[51] Since its root meaning in Greek is 'one called alongside', there is no doubt an element of truth in all these suggestions. It should be noted that the word also occurs in 1 John 2:1, where Advocate would be the most appropriate translation. The main characteristics conveyed by the name Paraclete are more precisely seen in the functions attributed to the Spirit.[52]

The other title, the Spirit of truth, speaks for itself. Truth is a recurrent theme in the gospel of John and it is not surprising, therefore, that the Spirit is described as the embodiment of truth (Jn. 14:17; 15:26; 16:13).[53] In the prologue, grace and truth are seen to come through Jesus Christ (1:17). The whole message of the gospel exalts truth above error. The Spirit is therefore seen as the custodian of truth. In these passages there is a close connection between the Spirit and the Word, which may be regarded

---

Spirit-Paraclete in the Fourth Gospel, Eng. trans. 1968) that the sayings are interpolated into John's text. *Cf.* also R. E. Brown, 'The Paraclete in the Fourth Gospel', *NTS* 13, 1966–7, pp. 113–132.

[51] See pp. 513f. for comments on the view that Paraclete should be understood against the background of the Qumran evidence.

[52] I. de la Potterie, in a brief report of a SNTS seminar on the Holy Spirit in John's gospel, notes the view expressed by H. Riesenfeld that the origin of the Paraclete title is to be found in the wisdom literature, the verb *parakaleō* being often applied to wisdom (*NTS* 18, 1971–2, p. 490).

[53] Mention has already been made on p. 514 above of the occurrence of the term 'Spirit of truth' in Qumran literature. A. R. C. Leaney, *The Rule of Qumran and its Meaning* (1966), p. 53, maintains that this expression is an already existing concept which the author of the fourth gospel has taken over and deliberately identified with the Holy Spirit. Yet there is a wide difference between the concept of the Spirit in Qumran and in the NT. In view of the strong emphasis on truth in John's gospel in relation to the ministry of Jesus, it seems quite unnecessary to trace the origin of this description of the Spirit to Qumran. It should be noted that in Qumran 'spirit of truth' like 'spirit of holiness' does not occur in a personal sense.

as an important characteristic of the gospel. Not only does the Spirit share the nature of truth, but he also communicates truth. Moreover this function of testimony and also that of guidance demand a quality of absolute dependability.

There is one statement which asserts that the Spirit 'proceeds from the Father' (Jn. 15:26). Whatever this means, it suggests that the Spirit shares the same nature as the Father. This is in line with the character of the Spirit as seen elsewhere in this gospel. Not only does the Spirit come from God, but he is sent by both Father and Son (*cf.* 16:7; 14:26). The Paraclete is seen to be both one with God and 'at one' with man.[54]

One other feature is the personal character of the Spirit.[55] This comes out clearly in the variety of functions he performs, many of which would be unintelligible if not regarded as personal. In addition to this, the fact that Jesus spoke of *another* Paraclete shows that the Paraclete must be as personal as Jesus himself. These considerations completely override the neuter gender of the noun *pneuma* in Greek. Moreover, they are in full agreement with the striking use of the masculine pronoun (*ekeinos*) of the Spirit in John 16:13 (placed immediately before *pneuma*) which underlines the personal characteristic of the Spirit. By no stretch of imagination can the teaching in these Paraclete sayings be made to refer to impersonal force.

Another characteristic of the Spirit is his indwelling presence in believers (Jn. 14:17). The presence of the Paraclete is said to be for ever (14:16), which suggests that once the Spirit has taken possession, he remains in residence. The indwelling of the Spirit becomes more dominant in Paul's epistles. But it is important to recognize that the idea did not originate with Paul. It was an essential part of Jesus' promise of the Spirit.

The functions of the Spirit. It is under this consideration that a wider spectrum of information is given. Taken together these sayings supply an amazingly varied selection of the Spirit's activities.

(i) We may sum up the major function as glorifying Christ (Jn. 16:14). The Spirit is essentially self-effacing, never speaking on his own authority (16:13). He does not seek his own glory; only that of Christ. This was to prove a valuable test; for any movement claiming the possession of the Spirit, and yet which glorifies the Spirit instead of Christ, would be seen to be alien to the teaching of Jesus about the Spirit.

(ii) Closely allied to this is the Spirit's function in enabling believers to witness to Christ (Jn. 15:26). The Spirit bears witness to Christ, and

[54] *Cf.* S. S. Smalley, *John: Evangelist and Interpreter*, p. 230.

[55] There is a tendency among many scholars to see the Paraclete only in terms of power, not in terms of a person. *Cf.* G. Johnston, *The Spirit-Paraclete in the Gospel of John*. E. Malatesta criticizes Johnston on this account in his article, 'The Spirit-Paracelete in the Fourth Gospel', *Bib* 54, 1973, pp. 539–550.

believers through the same Spirit bear witness to the same Christ.[56] Since it was only through witnessing to others that the church developed its missionary movement, there is a direct link between this statement and the experiences in the book of Acts. Without the Spirit the witness to Christ would never have spread.

(iii) Because of the necessity of communicating the gospel, the promise of the Spirit would be indispensable, not only for the task for bearing witness to Christ, but also for recalling and understanding his teaching. John 14:26 is of special importance in this respect: 'He (the Spirit) will teach you all things, and bring to your remembrance all that I have said to you'. There seems to be here a direct link between the 'all things' and 'all that I have said'. If so the authentic tradition of the teaching of Jesus must be in mind. The preservation of this priceless tradition was not to be left to chance. The Spirit would be the custodian of truth.[57] This promise is significant for the subsequent history of the canon, at least as far as the gospels are concerned. The traditions did not develop in an uncontrolled way, as some scholars suggest, but under the guidance of the Spirit (see the section on Scripture). It is worth noting that there is some parallel here with the final commission in Matthew's gospel, where those addressed were to teach disciples to observe all that Christ had commanded them (Mt. 28:20). They could not have done that without the special facility of recall given by the Holy Spirit. Whereas this promise has a continued relevance, in the special sense mentioned above it could apply only to the apostles.

(iv) Another activity of the Spirit is to guide, especially into all the truth (Jn. 16:13). This is akin to, but an extension of, the last promise. 'All the truth' embraces the developing understanding of the meaning of the mission of Jesus, the significance of his death and resurrection, and the application of the newly established faith to life. Indeed, the promise of guidance into all truth accounts for the authority of the epistles. Again the Spirit would prevent haphazard development and ensure the preservation of truth.

(v) There is yet one more aspect of the activity of the Spirit in revelation and that is in the sphere of the future (Jn. 16:13).[58] The very general 'things that are to come' which the Spirit was to declare is sufficiently comprehensive to include all the eschatological teaching of the epistles and the Apocalypse. It is therefore significant that in his Apocalypse John was in

---

[56] J. M. Boice, *Witness and Revelation in the Gospel of John*, pp. 151ff., brings out this function of the Spirit in the witness of believers.

[57] F. Mussner, *The Historical Jesus in the Gospel of St John* (1967), p. 60, rightly warns against the view that the Spirit is here no more than a prop to the memory.

[58] *Cf.* the discussion of this passage by E. Bammel, 'Jesus und der Paraklet in Johannes 16', in *Christ and Spirit*, pp. 199–217. Bammel treats the whole passage as a Johannine construction.

the Spirit when he was commanded to write down in a book what he saw.

(vi) All the previous functions of the Spirit have related to believers, but one of the Paraclete sayings is concerned with the world (Jn. 16:8–11). Nevertheless even this would appear to be mediated through believers. This passage predicts the convincing (or convicting) work of the Spirit. The world would be convicted of sin, righteousness and judgment. Some explanations are added to ensure that the three aspects are rightly understood. Sin is defined here as unbelief in Jesus. The Spirit's ministry is both to glorify Christ, and to focus on men's refusal to glorify him through their unbelief. Righteousness is also defined in relation to Christ. His passion would bring a new dimension to the understanding of righteousness, and would show the world its ignorance of what true righteousness means. Judgment is related to the prince of this world. It is the Spirit's task to show how the forces of darkness have been effectively overthrown. This passage suggests that apart from the activity of the Spirit the world would never come to recognize its true condition. This shows the sterner aspect of the Spirit's work.

The reception of the Spirit. It remains to note in these passages any indications of the manner in which the Spirit comes into human experience. Several passages show the Spirit to be a gift from the Father (Jn. 14:16, 26) or from the Son (15:26; 16:7). The initiative is not with man. The Spirit's presence cannot be earned. Moreover, as in John 7:39, so in 16:7, the coming of the Spirit depends on the departure of Jesus. There is a clear cleavage between the world, which cannot receive the Spirit, and the believers who know him (14:17). This would eliminate any suggestion that the Spirit overrules and guides the minds of non-Christians,[59] at least in the sense in which these Paraclete sayings portray the Spirit's activity. Indeed, as indicated above, the only function at all related to non-Christians is that of bringing conviction in a specifically Christologically orientated way.

The foreshadowing of Pentecost. In his account of the Easter appearances of Jesus John includes an incident in which Jesus breathed on the disciples and said 'Receive the Holy Spirit' (Jn. 20:22). He then continued, 'If you forgive the sins of any, they are forgiven; if you retain the sins of any, they are retained' (Jn. 20:23). The two statements are clearly intended to relate closely to each other.

The first problem is the relation this inbreathing of the Spirit has to the outpouring at Pentecost. Three different answers have been proposed.

(i) A distinction is suggested between the form 'Holy Spirit' without the

---

[59] L. Dewar, *The Holy Spirit and Modern Thought*, p. 204, sees the Spirit working at two levels, guiding the supernatural community and overruling at the natural level.

article (as here and in Jn. 7:39) and the form with the article, as at Pentecost.[60] But it is difficult to attach any meaningful significance to this distinction. It can hardly be maintained that the anarthrous form refers to the gift and the other form to the person. In any case in John 7 both forms are used side by side.

(ii) Another suggestion is that John's account is irreconcilable with Luke's, and the latter must therefore be regarded as an invention. But John's account cannot supplant the historic outpouring at Pentecost. It has even been suggested that Luke has been influenced by rabbinical patterns in his Pentecost narrative.[61] But this is wholly unsupportable in view of the lack of evidence that Luke was susceptible to rabbinical influences. Moreover, such a suggestion would be contradictory to Luke's statement of purpose in his prologue. It is equally unsatisfactory to regard John's account as unhistorical, particularly in view of John 16:7 where Jesus' departure was seen as a prelude to the coming of the Spirit (cf. also Jn. 7:39). It is difficult to suppose that John regarded these conditions as having been fulfilled by the time of the resurrection appearance in John 20, since Jesus was not yet glorified (in the sense of being exalted).

(iii) This leads to the third explanation, which is the view that the breathing of the Spirit upon the disciples in John 20 must be regarded as proleptic, a foreshadowing of Pentecost.[62] No statement is actually made that the Spirit was immediately received, although this in itself would not exclude the possibility. The account of the first sermon on the day of Pentecost contains a promise of the Spirit but no precise statement of the Spirit's descent on the converts. Nevertheless it may reasonably be supposed that it happened. If John 20 also presupposes that it happened, it would suggest that the disciples experienced a double coming of the Spirit. Yet the emphasis falls on the result that will follow in the bestowing of authority to forgive or to retain sins. In other words the action of Jesus was a reminder of the Spirit's function in the disciples' all important task of proclaiming and applying the gospel.[63] Peter's sermon at Pentecost was a specific fulfilment of this promise (Acts 2:38).

In 1 John there are four passages which present various aspects of the

---

[60] Cf. B. F. Westcott, John (1887), ad loc. Cf. J. H. Bernard, John (ICC 1942), p. 284, for a criticism of Westcott's views.

[61] So A. Richardson, TNT, pp. 118f.

[62] Cf. H. B. Swete, The Holy Spirit in the New Testament (1931), p. 167.

[63] For a full discussion of Jn. 20:22, cf. J. D. G. Dunn, Baptism in the Holy Spirit, pp. 173ff. Some scholars contend that John believed the ascension in some way took place between 20:17 and 20:19; cf. R. H. Strachan, The Fourth Gospel (³1941), p. 328; C. H. Dodd, The Interpretation of the Fourth Gospel, pp. 442f.; F.-M. Braun, Jean le Théologien 3 (EB, 1966), pp. 225–258; J. Marsh, John (²1968), pp. 639f. Certainly Jn. 7:39 supports the view that the gift of the Spirit is connected with the ascension. Dunn, op.cit., p. 178, considers the proleptic explanation to be an unsupported speculation. He draws a distinction between Jn. 14:16, 26; 15:26; 16:7 (Paraclete promises), which point to the Pentecost coming in Acts, and the coming in Jn. 20:22.

Spirit. Christ abides in believers by the Spirit (1 Jn. 3:24). We know that we abide in him 'because he (*i.e.* God) has given us of his own Spirit' (1 Jn. 4:13). This connection between abiding and the work of the Spirit strongly echoes the language of John's gospel. Abiding in this sense is not a natural pursuit and clearly demands the activity of the supernatural Spirit to make it possible.

As in John's gospel, the Spirit's part in witness is clearly expressed. 'The Spirit is the witness, because the Spirit is the truth' (1 Jn. 5:7). There are different ways in which the Spirit may be said to witness to the truth. He may do so by witnessing through the life and ministry of Jesus (seen in the gospels). He may further be witnessing in the contribution he makes through the OT to our understanding of Christ. John seems to be alluding to a Spirit-directed testimony from the past which is still a present reality.[64] Moreover, the Spirit is linked with water and blood as witness bearers (1 Jn. 5:8). In spite of the debate over the meaning of this passage, the Spirit's witnessing function is not in dispute.[65] Where the Spirit abides truth must reign. The Holy Spirit and falsehood do not go together. This is vividly brought out by the strong contrast between the Holy Spirit and the spirit of antichrist (1 Jn. 4:1–6). The sign of the Holy Spirit is his witness to the real incarnation of Jesus Christ. Antichrist denies this. There can be no confusion over this. The distinction is unmistakable.

Acts

In turning from the gospels to the Acts, we at once find ourselves in a different era. Whereas in the ministry of Jesus the activity of the Spirit in believers was only foreshadowed, in Acts we move into the age of the Spirit. The activity of the Spirit is in fact in continuity with the mission of Jesus. What the church does is seen to be the work of the Spirit. The whole development of ideas in the early history of the Christian movement is dominated by the Spirit. This makes a study of Acts with a view to establishing the NT doctrine of the Spirit of paramount importance. As compared with the epistles there is less reflection on the role of the Spirit, but more on actions of the Spirit.[66] For this reason the Acts evidence is more historical than didactic, but is nonetheless as important for the special contribution it makes.[67]

---

[64] For a valuable discussion of this point, *cf.* I. H. Marshall, *The Epistles of John* (*NICNT*, 1978), p. 235.

[65] F. F. Bruce, *The Epistles of John* (1970), pp. 120f., sees the witness of the Spirit in the baptism of Jesus (water) and in the passion (blood). He mentions, but does not accept, the view of W. Nauck, *Die Tradition und der Charakter des ersten Johannesbriefes* (1957), pp. 147ff., that three stages of Christian initiation are here being referred to. Even in this latter view the predominant witness of the Spirit is not in dispute.

[66] J. E. Fison, *The Blessing of the Holy Spirit* (1950), pp. 116f., regards as a gross exaggeration the attempt to drive a wedge between the ecstatic Spirit of Acts and the ethical Spirit of the epistles.

[67] For a recent discussion of the importance of the Acts account of the coming of the Spirit, *cf.* I. H. Marshall, 'The Significance of Pentecost', *SJT* 30, 1977, pp. 347–369.

THE PRELUDE TO PENTECOST

Even before the account of the outpouring of the Spirit at Pentecost, there are four references to the Holy Spirit in Acts 1 which set the scene and enable a true assessment of that event to be made. First of all Luke clearly shows that he sees his book as the outcome of revelations of the Spirit from the risen Lord to the apostles (Acts 1:2). In other words the key to the understanding possessed by the apostles was their communication with the risen Lord to which Luke had already drawn attention in Luke 24:27, 44ff. Moreover, the recognition that this continued the work of Jesus 'through the Holy Spirit'[68] is in line with the promise in John 14:26. This explains the authority for the apostolic proclamation. Pentecost was not something that burst on the waiting church unprepared. The disciples were reminded to wait for the coming baptism with the Spirit (Acts 1:5).[69]

Of equal importance is the promise of Christ before his ascension in Acts 1:8: 'You shall receive power when the Holy Spirit has come upon you; and you shall be my witnesses in Jerusalem and in all Judea and Samaria and to the end of the earth.' This dynamic aspect of the Spirit has previously been met in Luke 24:49, and in the promise of aid for witnessing in John 15:26,27. Since this statement may be regarded as a foreshadowing of the expanding ministry of the church, the activity of the Holy Spirit in this ministry has key importance.

In passing it should be noted that Peter shows himself to be in line with the view of both the Jews and Jesus himself on the inspiration of Scripture. He cites Psalms 69:25; 109:8 under the formula, 'The Holy Spirit spoke beforehand by the mouth of David' (Acts 1:16). As the disciples faced the world with the gospel, they did so with the full conviction that the same Spirit who had spoken through the Scriptures had taken possession of them.

THE OUTPOURING AT PENTECOST

The origin of the Christian church must be traced back to Pentecost. It was that event which began the church age, which may also be regarded as the age of the Spirit.[70] This new age was distinct from, although a

---

[68] E. Haenchen, *Acts* (Eng. trans. 1971), p. 139, links the words 'through the Holy Spirit' in Acts 1:2 with the following words referring to the choice of the apostles, and thinks this is Luke's way of making plain to the readers the authority of the apostles. But it is more probable that the Spirit is to be seen as the agency through whom the commandments of Jesus were recalled.

[69] F. D. Bruner, *A Theology of the Holy Spirit* (1970), p. 156, writes, 'Luke's first sentence makes clear an intention of his entire book: the Spirit is not to be dissociated from Jesus. The Spirit *is* Jesus at work in continuation of his ministry'.

On Acts 1:5, Bruner points out that the announcement of the baptism of the Spirit is here set out as the 'promise of the Father', not the responsibility of the believers. Another point is that all disciples were assured of the baptism of the Spirit without conditions (*cf. idem*, p. 157).

[70] G. W. H. Lampe, *God as Spirit* (1977), p. 70, considers that Luke does not share Paul's profound understanding of life in Christ. He sees a parallel between the birth and baptism of Jesus, and the beginning

continuation of, the age of the ministry of Jesus. Whereas the Jews thought of an age to come which would immediately follow the present age, the NT portrays the ministry of Jesus as a unique event separating the OT age from the age of the church.[71] It is only when it is recognized that the Spirit's activities were concentrated in a different way in the ministry of Jesus and the ministry of the church that the full significance of the Pentecost experience can be seen. Jesus was the perfect example of a man of the Spirit, but not until Pentecost were others empowered to become men of the Spirit in a dynamic way.

We may sum up the main features of the Pentecost experience in the following way.

(i) Pentecost was the concluding act of the ascension. It was not only subsequent to it chronologically, but was dependent upon it. This had been foreshadowed by Jesus in John's gospel (Jn. 7:39; 16:7). It implies that Pentecost introduced a new age.

(ii) The accompaniments of the outpouring of the Spirit were symbolic. The wind and fire represented the power of the Spirit, one unseen, the other seen. These extraordinary signs must be regarded as singular to this initial experience, since they are not repeated elsewhere. The uniqueness of Pentecost adequately explains these features. Although the Spirit would continue to be outpoured, the outpouring would never again signify the inauguration of a new era.[72] Once launched, the Christian church would have no further need for these objective signs. This may also apply to the distinctive manifestation of the Spirit when the apostles began witnessing in tongues (see below). The symbolic use of wind for Spirit has already been met in John 3:8 and the connection between fire and Spirit ties up with John the Baptist's prediction in Matthew 3:11.

(iii) The infilling of the Spirit extended to *all* believers. Not only does Luke say that 'they were all filled with the Holy Spirit' (Acts 2:4), but that the tongues of fire distributed and rested on 'each one of them' (2:3). The Spirit's coming is, therefore, seen as both corporate and individual. There is certainly no room for the idea that any believers were excluded from this initial experience. In fact, the wording in Luke's account is wholly in keeping with Paul's assertion that anyone who does not have the Spirit of

---

of the Acts account. His view is that the Pentecost story is a theological reconstruction modelled on the giving of the law at Sinai. But this suggestion is not convincing since the Acts record gives no indication of any connection between the Spirit and the law. It must be conceded that Paul's doctrine of the Spirit goes further than Luke's, but this is no justification for regarding Luke's as a reconstruction.

[71] H. Conzelmann, in his *The Theology of St Luke* (1960), has drawn attention to this three-age scheme, although he attributes it to Luke.

[72] It is significant that in the Qumran community the coming of the 'holy spirit' was associated with the inauguration of the new age (*cf.* 1 QS lv. 20f.). F. F. Bruce, 'The Holy Spirit in the Acts of the Apostles', *Int* 27, 1973, p. 172, considers that the Qumran passage may be a rewording of Ezk. 36:25ff. Both in this passage and in Acts 2 dependence on the OT can be seen, but a vital difference is that in the former case the 'holy spirit' cannot be considered to be personal.

Christ does not belong to him (Rom. 8:9). The whole company of believers were, therefore, in one act sealed by the same Spirit.

The expression, 'filled with the Holy Spirit' in Acts 2:4 is highly significant. It does not occur in any of the OT references to the Spirit. There is one use of it in relation to Jesus at his baptism (Lk. 4:1). But it became the hallmark of Christians (*cf.* Acts 6:3ff.). Evidently the phenomenon of being filled with the Spirit was easily detectable. At least at Pentecost the distinction was clear: those filled with the Spirit were believers; those outside the circle of believers were not possessed by the Spirit. There is no suggestion in this passage that anyone who believed was either not filled or only partially filled. 'Being filled' is equivalent to receiving the Spirit as a believer in Jesus. It is equally equivalent to being baptized with the Spirit (*cf.* Acts 1:5).

(iv) The gift of tongues is specifically said to be 'in other (*heterais*) tongues' (Acts 2:4). Moreover, the various racial groups present in Jerusalem heard the apostles speak in their own language (Acts 2:6). What amazed the people was not the sudden phenomenon of men speaking in unintelligible tongues, but that they heard simple Galileans speaking in their own language. It is not clear whether Luke thinks of the miracle as a miracle of speaking or of hearing, but he has no doubt that the Spirit was responsible.[73] There is no suggestion in the rest of his book that the gift of tongues was repeated as linguistic aid to the missionary endeavours of the church. In other words the gift of tongues did not facilitate the subsequent preaching of the gospel by providing a medium of communication.[74] There was no need for this since all the areas with which Luke deals in Acts would have been familiar with koinē Greek.

It does not seem unreasonable to regard this particular manifestation of the gift of tongues as exceptional,[75] and to draw some distinction, at least in purpose, between the Pentecost experience and the later *charismata* of which Paul speaks in 1 Corinthians (see later discussion, pp. 764ff.).[76] In

---

[73] It has been pointed out that the Pentecost experience was a reversal of the Babel story in Gn. 11. G. T. Montague, *The Holy Spirit: Growth of a Biblical Tradition*, p. 282, notes that the Genesis passage was one of the prescribed readings in the triennial lectionary for the Jewish feast of Pentecost.

[74] Rabbinic tradition maintained that although the law on Sinai was given with a single sound, the voice went forth into seventy tongues and every people heard in their own language (Midrash *Tanchuma* p. 26). This provides an interesting parallel to Luke's account of Pentecost. The giving of law, like the inauguration of gospel preaching, was regarded as a unique event.

[75] R. J. Banks and G. Moon, 'Speaking in Tongues: A Survey of the NT Evidence', *Churchman* 80, 1966, pp. 278–294, points out that in Acts 10:44-46 and Acts 19:5,6, there is no hint of foreign languages being spoken when *glossolalia* was manifested (see pp. 282f.). These writers favour the view that *glossolalia* is the ability to speak in a spiritual language which might be a language of men or of angels.

[76] D. M. Smith, 'Glossolalia and Other Spiritual Gifts in a NT Perspective', *Int* 28, 1974, pp. 307–320, draws a distinction between Luke's reference to *glossolalia* as foreign languages and Paul's. He thinks Luke was unfamiliar with 'tongues'. But without agreeing with Smith that Luke has given his own interpretation, we may still recognize a major difference between the function of tongues at Pentecost and in subsequent Christian experience, due to different circumstances.

only two other places in Acts is speaking in tongues mentioned, in both cases as an accompaniment of the outpouring of the Spirit (Acts 10:46; 19:6). In neither case is any mention made, as in Acts 2, of the hearers being able to understand, and these occurrences may perhaps be closer to the 1 Corinthians experience than to Pentecost.[77] It should be noted, however, that in Acts 10 the manifestation accompanied the initial outpouring of the Spirit on Gentiles and there may be significance in that. Moreover, the Acts 19 occasion could be regarded as another Pentecost-type experience for the benefit of former disciples of John the Baptist, but this is debatable.

(v) The Spirit's activity at Pentecost is claimed to be a direct fulfilment of OT prophecy. The quotation from Joel 2:28–32 in Acts 2:17–21 refers to 'the last days' and to the inauguration of 'the great and manifest day of the Lord'. The way in which Peter grasps the significance of the fulfilment of this prophecy, and indeed his bold manner in proclaiming it, are evidence of the Spirit's activity. He was, in fact, exemplifying what he was proclaiming.

(vi) In his exposition Peter declared, not only that the gift of the Spirit came direct from the throne of God, but also that it followed the exaltation of Jesus (Acts 2:32–33). There is a similar understanding here as in the statement of Jesus in John 7:39. Peter's remarkable insight regarding the session of Jesus at the right hand of God, only a few weeks after the crucifixion, must have been through the revelation of the Holy Spirit. Indeed, the pouring out of the Holy Spirit was for the apostles an evidence that Jesus had been exalted.[78]

(vii) The promise of the Holy Spirit was made to those who repent, are baptized and receive forgiveness (Acts 2:38). This meant in effect that all who truly repented and believed and identified themselves with the existing group of believers would receive the gift of the Spirit. It must be assumed therefore that all the 3,000 who were baptized also received the Spirit. The Spirit was available to all believers.[79] There is no suggestion in Acts 2 that the outpouring of the Holy Spirit was primarily to give power to existing

---

[77] A. A. Hoekema, *Holy Spirit Baptism* (1972), pp. 48f., points out four differences between the experience of tongues in Acts compared with the mention in 1 Corinthians. (i) Tongues in 1 Cor. needed interpretation; (ii) In 1 Cor. the purpose of tongues was edification, in Acts confirmation. (iii) In Acts tongues irresistible, in 1 Cor. a continuing gift under the Spirit's control. (iv) In Acts all in the group spoke in tongues, in 1 Cor. only some (*cf.* 1 Cor. 12:30).

[78] On the possible influence of Ps. 68:19 on Acts 2:33, *cf.* J. Dupont, 'Ascension du Christ et don de l'Ésprit d'aprés Actes 2:33', *Christ and Spirit* pp. 219ff.

J. D. G. Dunn, *Baptism in the Holy Spirit*, p. 44, draws a distinction between the ascension and Pentecost by relating the former to the climax of Jesus' ministry for himself and the latter to the climax of Jesus' ministry for the disciples.

[79] E. Schweizer, *TDNT, pneuma,* 6, p. 412, maintains that the obedience must precede the reception of the Spirit. But the giving of the Spirit is past tense and the obeying is present (*cf.* Acts 5:32). *Cf.* E. Haenchen, *Acts* (Eng. trans. 1971), *ad loc.*, who takes 'those who obey him' to be all believers.

believers as some have maintained. On the contrary it relates to the experience of conversion.

THE SPIRIT IN JERUSALEM AND SAMARIA

From the initial outpouring we turn to the continuing work of the Spirit through the early church leaders. Luke selects various samples to demonstrate how fundamental the Spirit's activity was in all aspects of the developing work of the church.

(i) The Spirit gives *courage* for witness before rulers. In view of the predictions of Jesus that his disciples would have to answer for their faith before rulers (Lk. 12:12 and parallels), it is not surprising that at an early stage in Christian history Peter and John were put to the test. There can be no doubt that Luke saw a connection between the promise that the Holy Spirit would teach the disciples what to say, and the extraordinary boldness of Peter and John which mystified the rulers (Acts 4:13; *cf.* also 4:31). Luke notes that Peter was filled with the Spirit as he addressed the council (Acts 4:8), and regarded this as a sufficient explanation of the transformation which had taken place in Peter.

(ii) The Spirit supports the *prayer and praise* of the believers. In the passage Acts 4:23–31, there are two mentions of the Spirit, one in connection with Scripture (a citation from Ps. 2 in verse 25) and one in connection with another dramatic demonstration of spiritual power in the course of worship (verse 31). The former is exactly parallel with Acts 1:16 and the latter with Acts 2:4. Moreover, this second affirmation of fullness of the Spirit is accompanied, as the former, with exceptional boldness in proclaiming the word of God.

The Spirit's power was clearly not given simply to strengthen the circle of believers. This is an instance in which the Spirit's activity is outgoing in witness.

(iii) A somewhat different aspect of the Spirit's work is seen in the promotion of *corporate awareness* among the believers. It began on the day of Pentecost (Acts 2:41ff.) and it became strengthened in Acts 4:32ff. While in neither case is the communal consciousness of Christians attributed to the Spirit, yet in both cases it follows a reference to the infilling with the Spirit. It is important to recognize this communal aspect of the Spirit, for its explains the seriousness of the defection of Ananias and Sapphira. Indeed in keeping back part of his possessions while purporting to give the whole to the community, Ananias is charged with having lied against the Spirit (Acts 5:34). The subsequent judgment upon him and his wife, although at first sight seeming to be out of proportion to the offence, nevertheless impressed on the community the extreme seriousness of lying to the Spirit. In no more awe-inspiring way could they have learnt that the Spirit was presiding over the affairs of the church. Moreover, Peter equated lying to

540

the Spirit with lying to God (5:34). Ananias' and Sapphira's great mistake was to treat the church as an organization of man instead of a community of the Spirit.

(iv) At an early stage the *administrative* activity of the Spirit in the community is seen in the method adopted to resolve the internal problem of the dispute between the Hellenistic and Hebrew believers. All the men appointed to assist the apostles by distributing food were to be men 'full of the Spirit and of wisdom' (Acts 6:3). Stephen is specially marked out as such a man. Although the task was essentially practical, it needed to be done by men under the direction of the Spirit. There could be no dichotomy between the sacred and the secular while the Spirit presided over the church's affairs. In Stephen especially the two aspects merged, for he powerfully disputed with men of the Hellenistic synagogue who 'could not withstand the wisdom and the Spirit with which he spoke' (Acts 6:10). The Spirit's sovereign transference of Stephen from a table-server to an effective apologist demonstrates again that he, not the apostles, was in charge. At the conclusion of his defence before the council Stephen still shows evidence of his fullness of the Spirit (Acts 7:55). Moreover, what caused the uproar among his hearers was the charge that they were resisting the Holy Spirit as their fathers had done (7:51). This is an interesting instance of continuity between the old and the new as far as the Spirit is concerned. Stephen accepted that the same Spirit who was dwelling in him had been active in Jewish history.

(v) The first outpouring of the Spirit on *non-Jews* happened at Samaria. Philip, like his fellow administrator Stephen, was led to preach. The change of location was due to circumstances outside his control (Saul's persecution), but there is no mention of the activity of the Spirit until the arrival of Peter and John from Jerusalem. The Samaritan situation (Acts 8:4ff.) raises an interesting question, for many had believed Philip and had been baptized, and yet had not received the Spirit.[80] Luke gives no indication of why the Spirit had not confirmed the preaching as he confirmed Peter's preaching at Pentecost. It has been suggested that Philip had no authority to lay hands on these Christians since he was not an apostle.[81] But the case of Paul in Acts 9:12, 17, who received the Spirit through the laying on of

---

[80] *Cf.* J. D. G. Dunn's full discussion of the Acts 8 problem, *op. cit.*, pp. 55–72. He takes the view that the Samaritans were not true believers until they received the Spirit.

Some regard the reception of the Spirit through the laying on of the apostles' hands as the visible manifestation of what had already happened (*eg.* J. H. E. Hull, *The Holy Spirit in the Acts of the Apostles* (1967), pp. 106ff. *Cf.* also G. R. Beasley-Murray's discussion, *Baptism in the NT* (1963), pp. 118f. For a Pentecostalist view, which regards it as a second reception of the Spirit, *cf.* H. M. Ervin, *These are not Drunken, as ye Suppose* (1968), pp. 92ff.

[81] For further comment on this passage, *cf.* L. Dewar, *The Holy Spirit and Modern Thought*, pp. 54ff.; W. F. Flemington, *The NT Doctrine of Baptism* (1948), p. 41; J. Munck, *Acts*, p. 75; R. B. Rackham, *Acts* (*WC*, 1901), p. 116.

hands of Ananias, sufficiently refutes this view. It will hardly do to attribute apostolic status to Ananias for this exceptional task,[82] since this would weaken the whole concept of 'apostle' for which Paul so staunchly contended. It cannot therefore be argued that Luke held the theory that only the Jerusalem apostles could confer the Spirit.

How then is the distinction between the Samaritans' believing and being baptized, and their receiving of the Spirit, to be explained? Can it be maintained that the Spirit's coming was some kind of later experience distinct from the earlier experience of faith? It has been suggested that the separation was intentional because of the need for some special sign to show that the despised Samaritans had really been received.[83] Another view is to maintain that there was something defective about the Samaritans' belief. Luke uses an unexpected construction when he says that the Samaritans gave heed to what Philip said, *i.e.* in the sense of intellectual assent rather than in the sense of personal commitment to Christ.[84] If this is a valid interpretation it would be reasonable to conclude that the Samaritans entered into true faith only when the Spirit came upon them. This would be supported by the fact that Simon the magician also 'believed', but did not receive the Spirit. In fact Peter gave judgment that he was 'in the gall of bitterness and in the bond of iniquity' (Act 8:23).

There was clearly something defective about both his belief and baptism. It seems reasonable to suppose, in view of their high regard for magic, that the Samaritans were particularly superstitious and needed some remarkable demonstration of spiritual power to overcome this characteristic. The transformation effected was sufficiently electrifying to be noted by Simon and sufficiently impressive for him to desire to work such transformation in others. The whole incident again vividly draws attention to the sovereign character of the Spirit. Peter at once rejects as unthinkable any idea of the manipulation of the Spirit by man, especially by bribery which marks the worst antithesis to real spiritual power.

A further note is needed on the fact that only in Acts 8:17 and in two other places in Acts is reception of the Spirit linked with the laying on of

---

[82] *Cf.* G. W. H. Lampe, *The Seal of the Spirit* (1951), p. 68, who maintains that Ananias was commissioned as an apostle for this particular task. His reason for this view is that Ananias had seen the Lord and had been 'sent'. But this suggests a 'temporary' apostleship, for which there is no other NT support.

[83] F. F. Bruce, *Int* 27, 1973, p. 174, suggests that the Samaritans, who had so long been the objects of Jewish disapproval, needed a special gesture from the Jerusalem apostles to assure them of incorporation into the fellowship of believers. Hence the delay in the reception of the Spirit. F. D. Bruner, *A Theology of the Holy Spirit*, pp. 175f., inclines to the view that the delayed reception was due to the design of God that the apostles should see for themselves the descent of the Spirit on the racially despised Samaritans. He takes the 'not yet' of this passage to point to an exceptional separation between baptism and the receiving of the Spirit.

[84] *Cf.* Dunn's discussion of the whole section, *Baptism in the Holy Spirit*, pp. 55f., in a chapter he calls, 'The Riddle of Samaria'. He points out that *episteusan* in Acts 8:12 is followed by the dative and does not have the same meaning as with *eis* or *epi*.

hands (Acts 9:17; 19:6). It cannot, therefore, be claimed to be an essential means. Again the Spirit is sovereign and sometimes dispenses with such means, as in the case of Cornelius and his household (Acts 10:44). Moreover, laying on of hands is also used for special commissioning, as in the case of the Antioch church sending out Saul and Barnabas (Acts 13:3).

(vi) The activity of the Spirit is also seen in *individual guidance* in the narrative of the encounter between Philip and the Ethiopian. While Luke says that an angel of the Lord directed Philip away from Samaria towards Gaza (Acts 8:26), it is the Spirit who superintends the approach of Philip to the Ethiopian (8:29) and who transfers Philip from the scene after Philip had baptized the eunuch (8:39). In this instance no mention is made of the descent of the Spirit on the Ethiopian. It is noticeable that one textual variant attempted to remedy this omission by adding that the Spirit fell on the eunuch. The focus falls rather on the guidance of the evangelist. This constant presentation of the varied activities of the Spirit is particularly characteristic of Luke's narrative. It leaves the reader with the vivid impression that those activities cannot be reduced to a stereotyped pattern. The idea of the Spirit transporting a person to a different place is familiar in the OT (1 Ki. 18:12; 2 Ki. 2:16; Ezk. 3:14; 8:3). It is a striking acknowledgment of the direction of the Spirit in individual movements. In view of the importance of the conversion of the Ethiopian for the on-going mission of the church, the Spirit's control in the event is particularly significant.

THE SPIRIT'S WORK IN TWO NOTABLE CONVERSIONS
The key to the whole experience of the conversion of Saul of Tarsus is his infilling with the Holy Spirit. The prior questionings in his mind, the cataclysmic experience on the Damascus road, the challenge of the heavenly voice, the temporary blindings, and the sending to him of Ananias as the result of a vision were all steps in the way leading to the climax of his receiving the Spirit. Ananias announced to Saul that the scales would fall from his eyes and he would be filled with the Spirit (Acts 9:17).[85] Luke relates the falling of the scales but says nothing about the actual infilling. This, however, may be assumed. It is noticeable that in Saul's case the Spirit's infilling seems to be prior to Saul's baptism, which in Luke's narrative followed immediately after, unless, of course, the infilling was co-incident with the baptism. The main feature of importance in Luke's account is the indispensable activity of the Spirit in the conversion of Saul.

When later the apostle relates his own conversion experience before non-Christian hearers (Acts 22, 26), he understandably says nothing about the

---

[85] G. Stählin, *Die Apostelgeschichte* (*NTD* 10, 1962), pp. 137f., maintains that the construction in Acts 9:17 and 18 indicates that the infilling is connected with baptism. *Cf.* also W. Heitmüller, *Im Namen Jesu: Eine sprach- und religionsgeschichtliche Untersuchung zum Neuen Testament, speziell zur altchristlichen Taufe* (1903), p. 302 n. 3, who regards being filled with the Spirit as a paraphrase of baptism.

Holy Spirit. But his epistles confirm the central place of the Spirit in his Christian experience and form an exposition of the outworking of the initial experience to which Luke refers. Until then he had identified himself among those who, in Stephen's words, had resisted the Spirit (Acts 7:51), but at the point when that resistance was finally overcome he was filled with the Spirit.

The other notable conversion was that of Cornelius, particularly because he is the first Gentile to embrace the Christian faith. The events leading up to Peter's visit to his home in Caesarea are related in detail by Luke because of the significance of the event in the development of the Christian church. After the vision, the Spirit directed Peter to go with Cornelius' men (Acts 10:19). In the course of his address Peter describes Jesus as being anointed by God 'with the Holy Spirit and power' (Acts 10:38), an interesting tie-up with the historical Jesus. But the climax came when the Spirit fell on the hearers while Peter was still speaking (10:44). Luke notes that Peter's Christian companions (clearly Jews) were amazed that the Gentiles received the Spirit. Again, on the strength of the Spirit's infilling, baptism followed, because the former had demonstrated that the people concerned were true Christians. It was the Spirit who had confirmed for Cornelius and his household the forgiveness of sins through Christ's name (Acts 10:43). As at Pentecost, the gift of tongues was seen to be a sign of the giving of the Spirit.[86]

When later Peter reported the events leading to Cornelius' conversion he mentioned the Spirit's leading (Acts 11:12) and the descent of the Spirit while he was speaking (11:15), but further reflection had jogged his memory about the Lord's promise that his disciples would be baptized with the Holy Spirit (11:16). Peter represents the growing awareness of the Christians that what was happening was no accident, but the planned operation of the Spirit.[87] This is reflected in the statement in Acts 9:31 that the church in Judea, Galilee and Samaria had peace and multiplied as it walked in the fear of the Lord and the comfort of the Holy Spirit.

THE SPIRIT IN PROPHECY

One of the gifts of the Spirit which figures in Paul's discussions is the gift

---

[86] Bruner, *op. cit.*, p. 192, drawing support from O. Dibelius, *Die werdende Kirche: Eine Einführung in die Apostelgeschichte* (Hamburg, Im Furche-Verlag, ⁵1951, claims that tongue-speaking in Acts is 'a corporate, church-founding, group-conversion phenomenon, and never the subsequent Spirit-experience of an individual'.

[87] H. R. Boer, *Pentecost and Missions*, pp. 32f., considers that Luke's main interest is to demonstrate how Gentiles were included, *i.e.* by recording the gift of the Spirit to them. He questions whether the great commission had anything to do with Peter's preaching to the Gentile Cornelius. The form of words used in Acts 11:16 – 'Be baptized with the Spirit' – is not Luke's normal phraseology. He uses 'receive'. The form in Acts 11:16 probably echoes the pre-Pentecostal promise of Jesus.

of prophecy and this is twice manifested in Acts in the person of Agabus.[88] In Acts 11:28 he foretold by the Spirit a world-wide famine, as a result of which the Antioch Christians at once sent contributions to their Judean brethren. To them prophecy through the Spirit carried with it a responsibility to act. The spontaneous nature of the response reveals the sensitivity of the Antioch church to the Spirit's leading. The second exercise of Agabus' prophetic gift is recorded in Acts 21:10ff. and is again directly attributed to the Holy Spirit. It concerned the destiny of Paul at Jerusalem. Luke notes how he and the other people tried to dissuade Paul from going, but the apostle puts a totally different construction on the prediction, recognizing its truth.[89] For him the only suitable response was 'The will of the Lord be done' (Acts 21:14). It is also possible that prophecy was the means through which the Spirit directed the Antioch church to send out Barnabas and Paul and also restrained the missionaries from entering Asia and Bithynia.[90]

THE SPIRIT'S ACTIVITY IN RESOLVING CONTROVERSY

When the question of Gentile circumcision was referred to the Jerusalem church, Peter's contribution centred on the fact that the Holy Spirit had been given to Gentiles as well as Jews (Acts 15:8). His key argument is that the Holy Spirit had made no distinction between Jew and Gentile. In James' letter sent to Gentile churches he gives his conclusion in the words, 'It has seemed good to the Holy Spirit and to us to lay upon you no greater burden than these necessary things. . .' (Acts 15:28f.). In no clearer way could the Jerusalem Christians indicate that they accepted the dictates of the Spirit on this issue, the result of which vitally affected the future of the Gentile mission. On so crucial an issue it was the Spirit who did not permit a decision to be made which would have caused Christianity to remain a sect of Judaism. This event brings out clearly the way in which the leaders of the early Church were themselves Spirit-led.

Since the prohibitions suggested in Acts 15:29 do not appear to have been regarded as absolute demands, they must be treated as matters of

[88] J. D. G. Dunn, *Jesus and the Spirit*, pp. 174f., points out that Luke links prophecy and *glossalalia* and describes these in ecstatic terms. He says nothing, however, about false prophecy and how this is to be distinguished from Spirit-directed prophecy. Nor does Luke comment on the fact that Paul disregarded the Spirit-prompted advice of the people of Tyre not to go to Jerusalem (Acts 21:4).

[89] It is significant that even before Agabus' Spirit-directed prophecy, Paul had declared that the Spirit had in every city testified that imprisonment and afflictions awaited him (Acts 20:23). The Acts record certainly gives the impression that Paul was prepared for the opposition facing him at Jerusalem. Commenting on the phrase 'bound by the Spirit' in Acts 20:22, F. F. Bruce, *Int* 27, 1973, p. 182, says that it probably refers more to the driving power of the Spirit, than to inward spiritual constraint. On the subject of Christian prophecy in Acts, *cf.* E. E. Ellis, 'The Role of the Christian prophet in Acts', *Apostolic History and the Gospel* (ed. W. Gasque and R. P. Martin, 1970), pp. 55–67.

[90] This is suggested by G. T. Montague, *The Holy Spirit: Growth of a Biblical Tradition*, p. 296. As far as Luke is concerned the detailed means are unimportant. His purpose is to show the Spirit's initiative.

temporary expediency which later became modified. James refers to them again in discussion with Paul in Acts 21:25, but they are not mentioned elsewhere in the NT (unless some allusion to them is seen in Rev. 2:14. 20).[91] What is more important for NT theology is the way in which Paul argues for the basic unity of Jew and Gentile (*cf.* his Galatian letter and in Eph. 2:16–22), in the course of which discussion he has much to say about the part played by the Spirit.

THE SPIRIT IN THE GENTILE MISSION

It was unquestionably a highly significant policy move on the part of the Antioch church to contemplate the Gentile mission, for it was a break-through which launched a movement of rapid expansion.[92] Luke describes the move explicitly in terms of the Holy Spirit, who issued the charge to set Barnabas and Saul apart for other work (Acts 13:2). Not only was the selecting, but also the sending, seen to be the work of the Holy Spirit (13:4). The whole of the subsequent first missionary itinerary is, therefore, seen as an operation of the Spirit. Indeed in his encounter with the magician Elymas in Cyprus, Paul is said to be filled with the Holy Spirit (13:9). This is seen as the explanation of his clear perception of the true state of Elymas' heart and mind. It was Elymas' sudden blindness that convinced the pro-consul of the truth of Christianity. He must have seen it as an evidence of the authoritative word of Paul, which was in fact the voice of the Spirit.

Luke comments that the Christians, whom Paul and Barnabas left behind at Antioch in Pisidia, were filled with joy and with the Holy Spirit (Acts 13:52). Since this was in face of considerable opposition from Jews and others whom they had incited, it is a strong testimony to the continual reality of the fullness of the Spirit in believers.

Another feature of the Spirit's work in the Gentile mission is his guid-ance, an aspect which comes out clearly in Acts 16:6. Luke states that Paul and his party were forbidden by the Holy Spirit to speak the word in Asia and equally forbidden to enter Bithynia (16:7).[93] Luke does not tell how the missionaries knew they were forbidden, but his narrative leaves no doubt that he himself was convinced that the assessment that it was the work of the Spirit was right. Since Luke joined Paul's party immediately after this (*cf.* the use of the first person in Acts 16:10), it is reasonable to

---

[91] *Cf.* G. R. Beasley-Murray's discussion, *Revelation*, pp. 86f.

[92] See E. M. B. Green, *I Believe in the Holy Spirit* (1975), pp. 58ff., for a succinct discussion on the Spirit and mission.

[93] It is noticeable that whereas in Acts 16:6 Luke refers to the Holy Spirit, in 16:7 he uses the expression Spirit of Jesus. This throws some light on Luke's theology of the Spirit, for it is inseparably linked with the person and work of Christ. G. Stählin discusses the implication of this in an article in *Christ and Spirit*, pp. 229–252. He concludes that the Spirit of Jesus is the Spirit who belongs to Jesus. In this sense the Spirit is God's representative. At the same time 'he is the personal spiritual power whereby the Lord Jesus is present and active in the church.'

suppose that he learned firsthand that Paul himself was equally convinced. Moreover, the prohibitions led immediately to the vision of a European mission, and it is not unreasonable to suppose that this represents the positive side of the Spirit's leading. One highly significant feature is that in Acts 16:7 the Spirit is named as 'the Spirit of Jesus', indicative of the continued work of the risen Christ through the Spirit. The Spirit is the representative of Jesus.

THE SPIRIT AND THE 'DISCIPLES' AT EPHESUS

Luke's account of Paul's meeting with the twelve men at Ephesus merits careful comment because it has been variously understood. Paul's immediate question to them was, 'Did you receive the Holy Spirit when you believed?' (Acts 19:2). He clearly detected a lack. Their response that they have not heard of the Holy Spirit prompts Paul to ask, 'Into what then were you baptized?' Since their baptism was John the Baptist's, it is clear that these people had not yet reached the stage of Christian belief. Although they are called 'disciples', the term must be understood here in a different sense from elsewhere in Acts.[94] In Luke's normal usage 'disciples' means Christians, but he generally uses the word with the article to denote a specific group. In the present case the reference is vague and some distinction seems to be implied. They probably considered themselves to be Christians, but if they knew only the baptism of John their knowledge of Christianity was clearly defective. Moreover, even their knowledge of John's baptism was not precise, since he had predicted a baptism of the Spirit by Jesus. We must conclude that these 'disciples' were not in the main stream of Christianity.[95] It is no surprise, therefore, that as yet they had not received the Spirit.

Does Paul's question imply the possibility of faith without the possession of the Holy Spirit? In his epistles Paul emphatically denies such a possibility (cf. Rom. 8:9). Could it be that Luke is portraying a different approach? But there is no support in Acts for such a view. It is more reasonable to suppose that Paul detected the lack of the Spirit (otherwise why the question?), and inferred from this that these 'disciples' were not as yet Christians.

---

[94] Cf. Dunn's discussion of this passage, *Baptism in the Holy Spirit*, pp. 83ff.

[95] L. Goppelt, *Apostolic and Post-Apostolic Times* (Eng. trans., 1970), p. 90 n. 36, regards the disciples as not yet real disciples, but adherents of John the Baptist. Cf. H. Conzelmann, *Apostelgeschichte* (*LHB* 1963), p. 110. G. Stählin, *Apostelgeschichte*, pp. 252f., disagrees. It seems clear that baptism and the receiving of the Spirit are closely linked for Paul's question to be intelligible. Cf. W. F. Flemington, *The New Testament Doctrine of Baptism*, p. 47. F. D. Bruner, *A Theology of the Holy Spirit*, pp. 207–244, strongly combats the use of this passage in support of a 'second' experience. R. Bultmann, *History of the Synoptic Tradition* (Eng. trans. 1963), p. 247 n. 1, maintained that for Acts baptism and the reception of the Spirit belong together. The contrast of John's baptism with Christian baptism in Acts 19:1-7 shows that for Christian baptism it is the gift of the Spirit that is characteristic. Cf. also his *TNT* 1, p. 139.

Another problem which arises from this passage concerns the interval which separated the baptism of these twelve believers and their receiving the Spirit when Paul laid his hands on them. Some see this as evidence of the fact that the receiving of the Spirit is subsequent to the initial act of conversion. But the passage before us hardly supports such a view. Luke records the baptism and the laying on of hands as if they were parts of one act, not two. Although it is a possibility, it is not the most natural understanding of these words to claim that they support a baptism of the Spirit subsequent to conversion.[96] The exercise of gifts of the Spirit (speaking in tongues and prophecy) was a tangible evidence in this case of the reality of the infilling (see later section under Paul's doctrine).

Some comparison might be made between these Ephesians and Apollos, who also knew only of John's baptism (Acts 18:25). Nevertheless, he is said to be 'fervent in spirit', which may legitimately be taken to refer to the Holy Spirit.[97] He still needed further instruction, but was nevertheless already a Christian.

There is one other reference to the Holy Spirit in Acts, also related to the Ephesian church. In Paul's address to the elders, he asserts of them that the Holy Spirit has made them guardians of the flock, to feed it (Acts 20:28). This suggests that Paul accepts as a matter of course that elders were appointed by the Holy Spirit.[98] This is is line with the earlier allusions to the table administrators in Acts 6 and the mission delegates in Acts 13. It is the Spirit who not only sets men aside for the work of the ministry, but also directs them into the kind of ministry to which they are to be appointed. The work of oversight and the work of shepherding was the direct concern of the Holy Spirit.

SUMMARY OF THE HOLY SPIRIT IN ACTS

We may observe at once that this evidence from the book of Acts does not provide us with any reflection on the theology of the Spirit. It is wholly concerned with his activity. In this there is a close parallel with his activity in the ministry of Jesus, although much more detailed. The theological exposition of the doctrine of the Spirit did not fit into Luke's purpose in Acts, but comes to fuller expression in the epistles.

---

[96] It must be noted that the book of Acts does not present an entirely consistent procedure. Cornelius received the Spirit before baptism and the 120 in Acts 2 independently of baptism. This shows that some caution must be exercised before concluding that there was a fixed order.

[97] G. W. H. Lampe, *The Seal of the Spirit*, p. 66, suggests that the fact that Apollos is so described, although he knew only the baptism of John, may be because Luke regarded as normal that the Spirit was imparted through baptism. But he admits that Luke may have thought that a direct commission of the Lord conferred the Spirit in view of his high ranking among the apostles (as for instance at Corinth).

[98] Since Luke gives no indication of the manner in which the Spirit appointed elders, there is much to be said for F. F. Bruce's view that the men were appointed and recognized because they were those on whom the Spirit had bestowed the necessary qualifications (*The Book of Acts*, 1954, p. 416).

There is no question in Luke's mind that the emergence of the Christian church is due to the work of the Spirit. Moreover, the Spirit is clearly the same Spirit who worked in the ministry of Jesus, which justifies the occasional use of the title 'the Spirit of Jesus'.[99]

Another feature of the Acts narratives is that the Spirit's activities are a fulfilment of the promises given by Jesus himself. Luke illustrates the Spirit's guidance, his power to convict, his abiding with the people of God, the overflowing of the message through Christians like rivers of living water and the abundant power seen in witnessing. There is therefore a direct link between what Jesus said about the Spirit and what the early church experienced.

It is worth noting that each new stage in Christian development is seen as a work of the Spirit. The beginnings at Pentecost are the most obvious illustration of this, but not the only case. The Spirit's activity is seen in the early defence of the gospel, in the extension of the church to the Gentiles, in the launching of world-wide mission, in the resolution of the terms for Gentile admittance, and in the specific control of mission activities. The emphasis falls more on the corporate than on the individual aspects, which again are more to the fore in the epistles. This may also account for the fact that Acts says virtually nothing about the ethical aspects of the Spirit's work. The writer's main interest is the narration of the church's activities rather than the attitudes of individuals or groups. This need not imply that ethical issues were of no interest to him, but simply that space did not permit him to include such issues in his writing.

Paul

Moving into the epistles of Paul, we are met with a profusion of references to the Holy Spirit. So widely did the Spirit's activities permeate Paul's thinking that there is hardly any aspect of Christian life and experience outside the sphere of his activities. Our purpose here will be to summarize the main facets of the Spirit's work. We shall do this by first considering his work in proclamation, then in the response of the individual and his place in initiation, followed by an examination of the Spirit's part in the Christian life and in the community. We shall need to give special attention to such themes as baptism in the Spirit, the fullness of the Spirit and the gifts of the Spirit. These studies will be basic for our further investigation of what Paul says about the new life in Christ. Some overlap is unavoidable, but in the present section the aim will be to illuminate the person and character of the Spirit.

---

[99] H. Flender, *St Luke, Theologian of Redemptive History* (Eng. trans. 1967), p. 139, notes that in Acts there is a clear distinction between Christ and the Spirit. 'The Spirit-endowed church remains the counterpart of its Lord, nor merely the extension of his personality'.

THE WORK OF PROCLAMATION

There are a few statements in these letters which confirm the indispensable work of the Spirit in the preaching ministry of the apostle Paul. The clearest autobiographical statement in this respect is 1 Corinthians 2:1–4. The apostle first disclaims using lofty words of wisdom in his ministry among the Corinthians. He then gives his main message (Jesus Christ and him crucified), and concludes that his speech and message was 'in demonstration of the Spirit and power' (1 Cor. 2:4).[100] In this expression the Spirit is the source of the power. Paul is concerned that faith should not rest in man's wisdom. Proclamation which is dependent on the Spirit is seen to be independent of human wisdom. This does not mean that Spirit-endowed preaching is opposed to human wisdom, but that human wisdom is not the source of the message. The fact that the Spirit plays so important a part at once places the proclamation of the gospel on a higher plane than man's reason.

A similar conviction about the Spirit's part in preaching is seen in 1 Thessalonians 1:5, where 'power', 'the Holy Spirit' and 'full conviction' are linked together. In Ephesians 3:5 the revelation which had been given to apostles and prophets is said to be by the Spirit. The particular subject of the revelation in this case is the inclusion of the Gentiles (*cf.* also Eph. 2:18).

If we may regard Romans 1:1–4 as part of a pre-Pauline statement which Paul incorporates in his letter, the statement in verse 4, referring to Jesus as 'designated Son of God in power according to the Spirit of holiness by his resurrection from the dead',[101] is of added significance as representing both primitive and Pauline theology. It is not that the Spirit designates what was not previously a reality, but that he performs the function of confirming by a demonstration of power and majesty that Jesus had been appointed Son of God. The Spirit's part in the resurrection of Jesus was a most powerful demonstration of this.[102]

Perhaps something of the same idea is seen in the formula which forms part of the Christological hymn in 1 Timothy 3:16, 'vindicated in the Spirit'. There is dispute, however, over this interpretation of *pneuma* as the Holy Spirit, for some understand it to relate to Christ's spiritual nature, in

---

[100] The word *apodeixis* (demonstration) is a technical term in rhetoric, *cf.* H. Conzelmann, *1 Corinthians* (Eng. trans. *Hermeneia*, 1975, from *KEK*, 1969), pp. 55 n. 26. The whole phrase would therefore reject the idea that the gospel was presented with pure rhetoric. Conzelmann understands the genitives as possessive.

[101] John Murray, *Romans 1* (*NICNT*, 1959), p. 11, understands the statement in Rom. 1:4 in the sense of the stage of pneumatic endowment upon which Jesus entered through the resurrection. The post-resurrection stage is thus distinguished from the pre-resurrection stage by the investiture of power. F. J. Leenhardt, *Romans* (Eng. trans. 1961 from *CNT*, 1957), p. 37, understands the expression to mean the Holy Spirit which is also the Spirit of Christ.

[102] Some have seen this as a reference to the human spirit of Jesus, *cf.* W. Sanday and A. C. Headlam, *Romans* (*ICC*, 1895), p. 9. But this is less meaningful in the context.

parallel with 'flesh' referring to his human nature. But if the reference is to the Spirit, it would relate to the Spirit's part in the resurrection of Christ through which he was vindicated.[103] According to this interpretation it is the Spirit who acts on behalf of the Son, and this would be in line with his Christ-glorifying function. In all probability no clear distinction was intended between Christ's spiritual nature and the Holy Spirit.

THE WORK OF INITIATION

According to Paul the Spirit's task is not simply to draw attention to the glories of the risen Christ, but also to take an essential part in the process of regeneration. Paul's approach is here closely akin to the teaching in John 3:5. Indeed it is a fundamental assumption of Paul's theological position that all believers are possessors of the Spirit. In other words no-one can respond to the claims of Christ without being activated and indwelt by the Holy Spirit. So important is this aspect of the Spirit that the evidence for this statement must be carefully weighed.

Paul takes it for granted that God has given the Spirit to believers (1 Thes. 4:8). There is no distinction here between those of the Thessalonians who have and those who have not received the Spirit. Paul simply says that God 'gives his Holy Spirit to you'. Since the present participle is used, a present reality must be in mind – and the 'you' is inclusive of all believers. This comes out strongly in several different ways in the Corinthian letters. All believers are said to be baptized into one body 'by one Spirit' (1 Cor. 12:13). The unity brought about by the same Spirit exists across such diverse groups as Jews and Gentiles, slaves and freemen, two of the most strongly marked divides in the ancient world. As if to reinforce his point Paul adds 'all were made to drink of one Spirit.' We note a similar parallel in Ephesians 4:4 where 'one body', 'one Spirit' and 'one baptism' are all linked. Both these statements are significant in the discussion on the baptism of the Spirit (see below).

The clearest statement in the Corinthian letters is found in 1 Corinthians 12:3 where Paul says that 'no one can say "Jesus is Lord" except by the Holy Spirit'.[104] The force of this statement is conditioned by the fact that

---

[103] *Cf.* J. N. D. Kelly, *The Pastoral Epistles* (BC, 1963), pp. 90f.; *cf.* also my *The Pastoral Epistles*, pp. 89f.

[104] C. K. Barrett, *1 Corinthians* (BC ²1971), pp. 279ff., discusses the various possible ways of understanding this confession, linked as it is with its antithesis 'Jesus is accursed'. He maintains that Paul's purpose here is not to affirm that to confess Jesus as Lord is the Spirit's work, but to provide a test for judging ecstatic utterance. T. Holtz, 'Das Kennzeichen des Geistes (1 Kor. 12:1-3)', *NTS* 18, 1971-2, pp. 365–376, considers that the cursing of Christ refers to those whose lives show, whatever their profession, that they are in fact rejecting Christ. A. Bittlinger, *Gifts and Graces* (Eng. trans. 1967), pp. 15ff., thinks that the two statements were being uttered by the same people and that these were separating the historic Jesus from the pneumatic Christ. R. Bultmann, *TNT* 1, pp. 159f., takes 1 Cor. 12:3b to refer to a temporary seizure by the Spirit. But F. D. Bruner, *A Theology of the Holy Spirit*, p. 287 n. 3, disputes this on the grounds that *eipen*, not *lalein*, is used, the latter being taken as a technical term for charismatic speech (*cf.* J. Dupont, *Gnosis* (²1960), pp. 222ff., for a discussion of Paul's use of *lalein*). R. Scroggs, 'The Exaltation of the Spirit

it occurs within a discussion of *glossolalia*. It does not, therefore, relate to the ordinary confession of the believer. Nevertheless it shows clearly that the test for the genuine experience of ecstatic utterance is whether the content of the utterance is Christ centred.[105] A more general affirmation is found in Romans 8:9, 'Any one who does not have the Spirit of Christ does not belong to him.' It is noticeable that in this context the Spirit is also called 'the Spirit of God' and this interchange of titles is valuable in showing the close connection between the persons of the trinity in believers (see further the comment on this on pp. 111f.).[106] It is clearly the Spirit's work to ensure that a Christian knows that he belongs to Christ. What distinguishes a believer from an unbeliever is that the former possesses the Spirit, whereas the latter does not. The Spirit is therefore intimately concerned with the whole process of initiation into Christian experience.

Paul uses several figures of speech which show the corporate character of the work of the Spirit. The body metaphor has already been mentioned. Another is the temple metaphor. In 1 Corinthians 3:16, Paul speaks of the Corinthians as 'God's temple' and points out that because of this God's Spirit dwells in them.[107] In 1 Corinthians 6:19 he uses the expression 'a temple of the Holy Spirit' of the physical body of believers, a surprising idea, especially in a Greek environment in which the body would be regarded as evil because composed of matter. Again the only distinction is between those in whom the Spirit dwells whose very body becomes sanctified, and those who are not temples in this sense. Compare also Paul's statement 'He who is united to the Lord becomes one spirit with him' (1 Cor. 6:17).[108]

---

by some Early Christians', *JBL* 84, 1965, pp. 359–373, compares the blasphemy against Jesus passage in 1 Cor. 12:2f. with the blasphemy against the Holy Spirit passage (Mk. 3:28f. = Mt. 12:32f. = Lk. 12:10). He attributes the former to a group of strong pneumatics who consider themselves to be free even to blaspheme against Christ when in a state of ecstasy. It is difficult to imagine, however, a situation in which people would believe that such action was acceptable.

[105] *Cf.* F. F. Bruce, *1 and 2 Corinthians* (NCB), *ad loc.*; F. W. Grosheide, *1 Corinthians* (NICNT), *ad loc.*

[106] C. K. Barrett, *Romans*, p. 158, dismisses as 'idle' the attempt to make a distinction between 'Spirit of God' and 'Spirit of Christ' in this context. M. Black, *Romans*, p. 116, regards them as almost synonymous for the spiritual frame of mind of the Christian, and then links the two expressions with a third 'Christ in you'. F. Leenhardt, *Romans*, p. 207, rightly considers that Paul uses a variety of terms of this kind to complement each other. *Cf.* also the comments of E. E. Ellis, 'Christ and Spirit in 1 Corinthians', *Christ and Spirit*, pp. 272f., who links 1 Cor. 12:4-6 with 1 Cor. 15:45 and 1 Cor. 6:17, and agrees with E. Schweizer (*TDNT* 6, p. 433) that these passages identify the Spirit with the exalted Lord. But see comments on pp. 570f.

[107] F. F. Bruce, *1 and 2 Corinthians* (NCB, 1971), p. 45, notes that in Qumran teaching 'the institution of the "holy house" is associated with the laying of the "foundation of holy spirit for eternal truth" (1 QS 9:3f.). But there the parallel ends for the Qumran conception of the Spirit lacks the personal element so prominent in Paul.'

[108] Although in this context 'spirit' is introduced after a reference to 'flesh', Paul's meaning is that to be one with the Lord is possible only through the Holy Spirit. As Barrett, *1 Corinthians*, p. 149, comments, 'The *Lord* (Christ) provides the means by which man may achieve the God-centred existence which means life in the Spirit'. That the Holy Spirit is in mind is also clear from 1 Cor. 6:19.

Another figure is that of the 'seal', the badge of authenticity which the Spirit gives to believers. Paul includes the Corinthians with himself when he claimed that God 'has put his seal upon us and given us his Spirit in our hearts as a guarantee' (2 Cor. 1:22). The *arrabōn*, here translated 'guarantee', is used literally in the sense of a first instalment of what was to follow. Here it certainly indicates commitment. It is a vivid metaphor to show that possession of the Spirit sets a man apart as belonging to God. Paul repeats the same idea in 2 Corinthians 5:5. In Ephesians 1: 13–14, the same metaphor is used of those who have believed, who are said to be 'sealed with the promised Holy Spirit, which is the guarantee (*arrabōn*) of our inheritance until we acquire possession of it.'[109] It will be noted that the guarantee is somewhat shifted from the believer to his destiny, but the root idea is the same.[110] It is important to note that present and future become closely linked in the Spirit. There is, in short, a continually repeated idea of the eschatological aspect of the Spirit. What he does now is initiatory, a foretaste of greater things to come.

The remarkable transformation of the Corinthians from unrighteous people to those who are now washed, sanctified and justified is said to have been effected 'in the name of the Lord Jesus Christ and in the Spirit of our God' (1 Cor. 6:11). Since in this case Paul gives a list of unrighteous types (1 Cor. 6:9, 10), this serves to heighten the contrast between the then and the now and to focus attention on the powerful operation of the Spirit.

If any further evidence were needed to demonstrate that all believers in Paul's view were possessed by the Spirit, reference could be made to 2 Corinthians 3:3 where he speaks of the Corinthians as a letter written 'with the Spirit of the living God' in contrast to anything written with ink. The conclusion is overwhelming that Paul assumes that all believers are indwelt by the Spirit, who manifests his presence in them at the time of their conversion. This latter point is confirmed by the statement in Titus 3:5 that God saved us 'by the washing of regeneration and renewal in the Holy Spirit'. A person is regenerate only through the action of the Spirit.[111] We shall next consider the immediate effects of such a regenerating activity in the believer.

THE SPIRIT IN THE LIFE OF THE BELIEVER

Our purpose in this section will not be to discuss in full the believer's new

---

[109] *Cf.* G. W. H. Lampe, *The Seal of the Spirit*, pp. 3ff., who connects the sealing with baptism and confirmation. But against this, *cf.* M. Barth, *Ephesians* (*AB*, 1974), pp. 135ff. He considers that all the later chapters in Ephesians unfold the meaning of the spiritual seal.

[110] In reference to this guarantee in 2 Cor 1:22 and Eph. 1:13,14, H. R. Boer, *Pentecost and Missions*, pp. 91f., takes the genitive as epexegetic (*i.e.* the guarantee consists of the Spirit).

[111] See the discussion on this verse in the writer's *The Pastoral Epistles*, pp. 205f. J. N. D. Kelly, *The Pastoral Epistles*, p. 253, supports the rendering 'through the Holy Spirit' rather than 'in', on the grounds that the genitive is causative.

life, for this is considered in a later section (see pp. 573ff.). We are concerned rather to note the various functions attributed to the Spirit in his continued activity in the regenerate life.

Sanctification. We use this term comprehensively of the over-all process by which the new believer moves towards a life of holiness. In one sense it is so comprehensive that it includes everything that the NT says about Christian living. More reference will be made to sanctification later (see pp. 641ff.), but our present remarks will concentrate on those passages which bring out the work of the Spirit in sanctification.

In 2 Thessalonians 2:13, Paul reminds his readers that God chose them to be saved 'through sanctification (*hagiasmos*) of the Spirit'. The words could refer to the human spirit, but there is nothing to prepare us for such a use, although admittedly there is no other reference to the Holy Spirit in this epistle. To sanctify is in any case one of the main functions of the Spirit as 1 Corinthians 6:11, already cited above, shows. There is no question of believers being able to sanctify themselves. The verbal form is passive with the Spirit as the agent. Moreover, the act of sanctification is stated as a completed act (aorist tense) although this must be understood in a proleptic sense. When thinking of the Gentiles in his letter to the Romans, Paul speaks of the 'offering of the Gentiles' as being 'acceptable, sanctified by the Holy Spirit' (Rom. 15:16). The meaning of 'sanctified' is governed by its close association with the word 'acceptable'. The standard of sanctification is a holiness acceptable to God, that is, a holiness in line with the Spirit's own character. The process of making holy is, therefore, peculiarly characteristic of the Spirit's activities.

Adoption. The idea that Spirit-filled believers are now children of God leads Paul to use the metaphor of adoption in connection with the Spirit's activities. There are two important passages to be considered. In Romans 8:14ff., Paul states that all who are led by the Spirit of God are sons of God, and that 'when we cry, "Abba, Father"', it is the Spirit himself bearing witness with our spirit that we are children of God'. Here it is specifically claimed that the believers' filial consciousness is directly induced by the Holy Spirit. In other words, no-one would learn to approach God as Father in the familiar way indicated by the word 'Abba' except through the Spirit. It is his constant work to remind us of the new family into which we have been adopted.

The other passage is Galatians 4:6 where Paul says that 'God has sent the Spirit of his Son into our hearts, crying, "Abba, Father!" ' The retaining of the Aramaic form alongside the Greek in a second passage shows the importance attached to the words, especially in view of their use by Jesus in Gethsemane, according to Mark 14:36. This is all the more remarkable in view of Paul's description of the Spirit as 'the Spirit of his Son'.[112] It is the same Spirit who enabled Jesus at the hour of his agony to cry 'Abba', who now enables all the adopted children of God to approach the Father in the same way. It is one thing to know we are children of God, it is another to act like children of God, with full awareness of utter dependence on and love for God as Father. This could never have happened without the aid of the Spirit.

In both these passages the word 'adoption' (*huiothesia*) is used of the new relationship into which believers have entered.[113] The same word is used on three other occasions by Paul. In Romans 8:23 he follows on from the passage discussed above and points out that those who have the first fruits of the Spirit 'wait for adoption as sons, the redemption of our bodies'. If this at first sight suggests that adoption is not as yet a reality, this would make Paul contradict himself and must, therefore, be rejected. What he must mean is that believers anticipate through the Spirit a time when the full benefits of the adoptive status will be realized. The use of the same term in Romans 9:4 applies to Israel and has no relevance for our present purpose. The other use, in Ephesians 1:5, although referring to the believers' sonship through Christ Jesus, comes in the same passage which later mentions the sealing of the Spirit already discussed (Eph. 1:13), but does not specifically describe adoption as the work of the Spirit. This interchangeability of the roles of Christ and the Spirit is significant for a right appreciation of the work of the Spirit. What he does is inextricably bound up with Jesus Christ.

Illumination. Because the Spirit of God is essentially the revealer of the gospel, as already noted, it is not surprising that he is also active in bringing further understanding to believers. The expression 'taught by the Spirit' in 1 Corinthians 2:13 sums up Paul's whole approach to spiritual understanding. He makes no attempt to intellectualize the things of God, for he never supposes such matters can be subjects for man's unaided quest for knowledge. He moves in a different realm, the realm of the Spirit.

Paul goes into considerable detail in 1 Corinthians 2:10–16 in establishing the distinction between man's wisdom and the Spirit's understanding. It was clearly of great importance for this distinction to be drawn to the attention of the Corinthians who had evidently misunderstood the nature of the gospel. Paul first establishes the fact that the revelation that they had

---

[112] J. Jeremias, *The Central Message of the NT* (1965), p. 18, has no doubt that Rom. 8:15 and Gal. 4:6 reflect the usage of the Christian communities and echo the prayer of Jesus. Paul is convinced that this usage is prompted only by the Spirit. *Cf.* N. Q. Hamilton, *The Holy Spirit and Eschatology in Paul* (1957), p. 11, who sees this cry as evidence that the Spirit performs the same function in the believer as in Christ. Both share the same attitude to the Father.

[113] On Paul's use of this term, *cf.* E. Schweizer, *TDNT* 8, p. 399.

received had come through the agency of the Spirit (1 Cor. 2:10). Indeed, it could be regarded as Paul's basic presupposition that the Spirit's aid was indispensable if man was to know anything about God. He talks about the 'depths of God', of which all men are ignorant. Only the Spirit understands and only he, therefore, is in a position to reveal (1 Cor. 2:11).[114] This is a corollary of the teaching of Jesus that the Spirit's task was to glorify him. The Spirit is the channel through whom both Father and Son are communicated to men. What revelations of God there had been in the past had been through the agency of the same Spirit. But now in Christ more of the depths of God had been revealed.

The Spirit undertakes the task of interpreter (1 Cor. 2:12). Those who have received the Spirit have a capacity for understanding, which was previously denied them. There is no support here for the view that man initiates a search for God. Paul is convinced that revelation must come through the Spirit. Not only is this the essence of his proclamation of the gospel; it is also the key to his approach to the teaching ministry. If the somewhat ambiguous statement in 1 Corinthians 2:13 means that Christians who are taught by the Spirit are able to interpret spiritual truth to those who possess the Spirit (as in RSV), it demonstrates the Spirit's teaching ministry. Even if the meaning is 'interpreting spiritual truths in spiritual language', it shows the indispensable function of the Spirit in communication of spiritual truths.[115] Moreover, Paul was not baffled by the fact that his gospel was derided as foolish by some of his contemporaries, because he recognised that what the Spirit gives needs to be spiritually discerned (1 Cor. 2:14; cf. 1 Cor. 1:21,22).

But we must go back to Romans 8 for a classic statement on this theme, 'Those who live according to the Spirit set their minds on the things of the Spirit' (Rom. 8:5). In this context Paul is maintaining the need for an entirely new way of thinking.[116] The non-believer has 'the mind of the flesh', which Paul declares to be hostile to God. The mind of the Spirit is the precise opposite: what the Spirit thinks can never be hostile to God. This throws light on Paul's exhortation in Romans 12:2, 'be transformed by the renewal of your mind'. He would never have supposed that this could be achieved in any other way than through the Holy Spirit. It is

---

[114] Although Paul speaks of the Spirit searching the depths of God, he cannot mean that the Spirit seeks to gain fresh knowledge of God, but that the Spirit penetrates to the deepest understanding of God, cf. L. Morris, *1 Corinthians* (*TNTC*, 1968), p. 57. The 'depths' are also linked in this context with 'mystery' which is not some esoteric knowledge as in gnostic usage, but is derived from a Jewish background. The Spirit makes known the mystery of God in Christ.

[115] Cf. J. D. G. Dunn's discussion of the alternatives (*Jesus and the Spirit*, p. 235). He thinks that some evaluation of *pneumatica* is in mind, and that the Spirit's purpose is that believers might come to know better the things of God.

[116] This involves more than simply intellectual activity. As J. Murray, *Romans* 1, p. 285, rightly says of the mind of the Spirit, it 'is the dispositional complex, including the exercises of reason, feeling and will, patterned after and controlled by the Holy Spirit'.

essential to recognize that the Spirit is concerned for the transformation of the whole man.

Liberation. Against the background of Paul's inner struggles in Judaism in his pre-Christian days, the theme of liberty becomes important. He had known the frustrating experience of seeking for salvation through works of the law and recognizes that liberation had come through the Spirit, not through his own efforts. He asks the Galatians the pointed question, 'Did you receive the Spirit by works of the law, or by hearing with faith?' (Gal. 3:2).[117] He had experienced the futility of works as a means of possessing the Spirit. He knows that none of the Galatians could retort that they had in fact received the Spirit through human effort. The sense of release from bondage is reflected in Galatians 5:1 ('for freedom, Christ has set us free'). This liberation is seen in the possibility of escaping from the desires of the flesh (Gal. 5:16). Those led by the Spirit are no longer under the law. Nevertheless this freedom does not come instantaneously in a full sense, otherwise Paul would not have exhorted the Galatians to refrain from gratifying the desires of the flesh (Gal. 5:16). It is an important function of the Spirit to break shackles which have been carried over from pre-conversion days.

This is expressed even more tellingly in Romans 8:13, 'For if you live according to the flesh you will die, but if by the Spirit you put to death the deeds of the body you will live' (*cf.* also Rom. 8:4).[118] This contrast and indeed conflict between flesh and spirit is a constant factor in Christian experience. It is because the Spirit is more powerful than the flesh that the believer's sense of liberty can be real. Otherwise life would continue to be a yoke of bondage (*cf.* Gal 5:1). It is in Romans 8, which may justly be considered the chapter of the Spirit, that Paul writes about the glorious liberty of the children of God (Rom. 8:21).[119]

This theme of spiritual liberty is a direct fulfilment of the Isaiah passage cited by Jesus at Nazareth (Lk. 4:18). It is one of the most characteristic functions of the Spirit. It is summed up in 2 Corinthians 3:17 where Paul says, 'Where the Spirit of the Lord is, there is freedom.' This is in contrast to the position of the Jews whose minds were closed when they read

[117] The chiastic arrangement of the wording in Gal. 3:3 serves to bring into juxtaposition the strong contrast between the Spirit and the flesh, *cf.* W. Hendriksen, *Galatians* (1969), pp. 113f. Paul is concerned that the Galatians are losing their freedom by devoting themselves to fleshly means. He has no doubt that freedom comes only through spiritual means.

[118] W. Lüthi, *The Letter to the Romans* (Eng. trans. 1961), p. 105, commenting on Rom. 8:4 says, 'The justified man can become free in the Spirit not only for the defensive and offensive battle against evil, but he is also given the freedom to do good.' Lüthi applies this in the sense of a son's freedom to obey his Father ungrudgingly.

[119] C. K. Barrett, *Romans*, p. 166, does not take the genitive 'of glory' adjectivally as RSV, but renders the whole phrase 'the freedom which springs from the glory of the children of God'. In this case the Christian's glory is contrasted with the corruption which is allied to bondage.

Moses. Liberation by the Spirit is essentially the liberation of the mind. In this latter context Paul talks about believers 'being changed into his (*i.e.* the Lord's) likeness from one degree of glory to another; for this comes from the Lord who is the Spirit' (2 Cor. 3:18). Not only does the Spirit bring deliverance from the old slavery as a continuous process, but he brings continuous enhancement in the new found freedom. In fact the whole passage in 2 Corinthians 3 sets out the greater splendour of the new dispensation, while not denying that the old had some splendour. But the new splendour is directly attributed to the Spirit (2 Cor. 3:8).

Guidance. Because Christian experience introduces an entirely new world of values, Paul recognizes that the guidance of the Spirit is indispensable. In this he was developing a theme already promised by Jesus (*cf.* Jn. 16:13). There are several aspects of this guidance which Paul picks out. He maintains that all who are children of God are led by the Spirit of God (Rom. 8:14). This refers not simply to the initial conversion experience, but to a constant awareness of the Spirit's guidance. The Spirit, in short, breathes in the true spirit of sonship so that the children are responsive to the direction of the Father. It is important to notice that the Spirit's guidance is never independent of the will of the Father. Such an idea would have been unthinkable for the apostle.

It is particularly in the prayer life of the believer that the Spirit's aid is needed. Paul sets this out in a penetrating way in Romans 8:26f. First the Spirit recognizes our weakness and comes to our assistance, particularly in prompting our minds in the direction of dependence upon him during prayer.[120] But his assistance goes much further than that, since he intercedes on our behalf. There is nothing mechanical about this, as if the Spirit's work in prayer proceeds wholly independently of the individual's own mind. It is rather that the Spirit in some way impresses his own mind on the believer so that what he asks is in accordance with the will of God. This intercessory ministry of the Spirit has close affinity with the intercessory work of Christ, but bears more directly on the mental and spiritual aspects of prayer rather than on the grounds of approach to God. The help of the Spirit is also specifically connected with prayer in Philippians 1:19, while Ephesians 6:18 urges prayer at all times 'in the Spirit'. The more general idea of access comes out in the discussion on Jewish-Gentile relationships in Ephesians 2:18: 'For through him (*i.e.* Christ) we both have access in one Spirit to the Father'.

In describing the Christian life, Paul frequently uses the metaphor of

---

[120] For a discussion of the Spirit's unutterable sighs, *cf.* A. J. M. Wedderburn, 'Romans 8:26 – Towards a Theology of Glossolalia?', *SJT* 28, 1975, pp. 369ff., who criticizes the view that the Spirit's sigh is a reference to *glossolalia*. He particularly confronts Käsemann's exposition of this view in his article, 'The Cry for Liberty in the Worship of the Church', in his *Perspectives on Paul* (1971), pp. 122–137.

walking. Christians are to walk in newness of life (Rom. 6:4), in love (Rom. 14:15; Eph. 5:2), according to the way assigned by God (1 Cor. 7:17; Eph. 2:10; 4:1), by faith (2 Cor. 5:7), as children of light (Eph. 5:8), as wise men (Eph. 5:15; Col. 4:5), in Christ (Col. 2:6), as pleasing God (1 Thes. 4:1). Moreover, there are some passages in which warnings are given against walking in wrong paths, *e.g.* in Ephesians 2:2; Colossians 3:7, where the Christian's pre-conversion walk is referred to as incurring God's wrath. In Philippians 3:18 he speaks of those whose 'walk' qualifies them to be described as 'enemies of the cross of Christ.' These devious routes are specifically non-Christian, but in 2 Thessalonians 3:6, Paul speaks of Christians who walk in idleness.

It is against this background of Paul's use of the metaphor that the statements in which he urges his readers to 'walk in the Spirit' gain particular significance. In Galatians 5:16 he sets walking in the Spirit in opposition to gratifying the desires of the flesh. The fundamental clash between the 'Spirit' and the 'flesh' in this context highlights a vital function of the Spirit, *i.e.* to direct the Christian's behaviour patterns in a way totally different from the normal dictates of the flesh. A similar idea is expressed in Romans 8:4 where Christians are described as those 'who walk not according to the flesh but according to the Spirit'. This comes in a context in which Christ is said to have condemned sin in the flesh. Walking in the Spirit is, therefore, contingent on the effectiveness of the work of Christ.

One other aspect of the guiding ministry of the Spirit relates to the future. In 1 Timothy 4:1 the Spirit expressly says that some will depart from the faith in later times. Since no previous passage to this effect may be cited, the reference must be to the general tenor of apocalyptic predictions, especially to the teaching of Jesus (*cf.* Mk. 13:22).[121] If so this is a case of the Spirit's work in recalling and applying that teaching (Jn. 14:26). What is most significant here is that what the Spirit says is clearly regarded as authoritative. This connection of Spirit with apocalyptic prediction finds some parallels in the ecstatic state associated with general apocalyptic, but in 1 Timothy the statement is more specific and personal, entirely in line with John 16:13 which promises that the Spirit will declare things to come (*cf.* also 2 Tim. 1:14, where Timothy is urged to guard the truth entrusted to him 'by the Spirit'). It is not, of course, necessary to restrict the references here to past predictions, for the prophetic element was prominent in the NT church. Paul prophesied the rise of false teachers on more than one occasion and he presumably did this through the Spirit (*cf.* 2 Thes. 2:1–12; Acts 20:29).

[121] *Cf.* my *The Pastoral Epistles*, p. 91. In this context the Spirit of truth is contrasted with the spirits of error. J. N. D. Kelly, *The Pastoral Epistles*, p. 94, cites Acts 11:27f.; 13:1f.; 1 Cor. 14 as illustrating the way in which the Spirit warned the Christian community.

Power. It is usual to think of power as the major characteristic of the Spirit, but it is as well to see it against the background of the many other functions. One of Paul's classic statements puts it as follows: 'that . . . he may grant you to be strengthened with might through his Spirit in the inner man' (Eph. 3:16ff.). The inner man has no resources other than the resources of the Spirit.[122] The concept of the total dependence of the Christian on the empowering of the Spirit shows how utterly indispensable the Spirit is for Christian living, and demonstrates the impossibility of any Christian not possessing the Spirit.[123]

The idea of spiritual power for personal advancement was as alien to Paul as it was to Peter (*cf.* Acts 8:18ff.). If there was special power to perform signs and wonders by the power of the Spirit, it was only for the advancement of the gospel (*cf.* Rom. 15:18ff.). Extraordinary manifestations of divine powers, which played an important part in the Acts story, are not unknown in Paul's epistles; however, he makes little of them, except in apologetic as in 2 Corinthians 12:12. To Paul spiritual power, which enabled him to preach the gospel, was of greater consequence.

When he speaks of the Word of God in terms of 'the sword of the Spirit' in Ephesians 6:17ff., it is worth noting that this is the only attacking weapon in the Christian's armour. The close connection between the Word and the Spirit has already been noted in discussing the proclamation. In what sense the 'Word' is here meant, either as a reference to the OT or more generally to the totality of God's message to man, is not clear, but the powerful activity of the Spirit in applying it is indisputable. Paul does not enlarge on the sword metaphor, as Hebrews does in Hebrews 4:12.

In view of the indispensable character of the Spirit's power, it is not surprising that Paul urges his readers in Ephesians 4:30 not to grieve the Spirit. To do so would be tantamount to opposing the dynamic life-source. It was a timely reminder that there are moral responsibilities resting on all who possess the Spirit; he is capable of being 'grieved', a highly personal aspect. If the following words (Eph. 4:31–32) are any indication of the way in which the Spirit can be grieved, the focus falls on antagonistic attitudes like bitterness, wrath, anger, malice, while what proves acceptable is kindness, tenderheartedness, forgiveness. The Spirit is not portrayed as sheer power, but as sensitive to human relationships in the execution of his power.

Growth. The classic passage in Paul's epistles which bears on the Spirit's

[122] H. Conzelmann, *TNT*, pp. 37f., always writes of the 'spirit' (with a small 's') and regards 'it' as a power manifested in worship and as filling the new man. But there is no concept of the personality of the Spirit in his presentation.

[123] To Bultmann (*TNT* 1, pp. 153f.) the *pneuma* can be identified with miraculous divine power. In other words it represents what is extraordinary and seemingly inexplicable. It is strange, however, that Bultmann wants to demythologize the miraculous in other manifestations of it, as for instance in the gospels.

direct participation in the development of Christian character is Galatians 5:22. Paul speaks of the 'fruit of the Spirit' and adds a list of nine virtues which constitute the 'fruit'. Our purpose here is simply to draw attention to the contrast between the 'fruit' of the Spirit and the 'works' of the flesh. The contrast in terminology is not accidental. The metaphor of fruit implies an organic relationship which is absent from 'works'. Indeed whereas 'works' are essentially associated with self-effort, fruit is not. The growth metaphor is admirably suitable to express complete dependence on the Spirit. The type of quality of which Paul speaks cannot be engendered from self-effort. Each needs the fertilizing activity of the Spirit to bring out its full development.

It is not to be supposed that such qualities as love, joy, peace, for instance, are qualities which are superimposed upon a Christian's character independent of his natural characteristics. Love can exist apart from the Spirit, but a Spirit-prompted love is of a type which goes beyond natural bounds so as to include, for instance, love towards enemies. Similarly 'gentleness' may be found in some people more than others, according to temperament, but as a fruit of the Spirit it is an expression of a regard for others which can transform those who are not naturally of a gentle disposition and can enhance those whose nature is conducive to it. Of even greater significance is the fact that some of these qualities were then (and are still in some quarters) actively despised. Patience, kindness and goodness were not qualities sought after in contemporary society and Paul recognizes the need for more than a natural impetus for their development. What is clear is that he makes no distinction here, either between the qualities or between different recipients. Moreover, he uses the singular 'fruit' to show that all the qualities mentioned form a corporate whole. They all go to make up a Spirit-filled character.

One or two other statements might be included here. God's love is said to be poured into our hearts through the Holy Spirit (Rom. 5:5), which emphasizes the Spirit's agency in communicating God's love. In Colossians 1:8, Epaphras is said to have made known to Paul the Colossians' 'love in the Spirit' (the only specific reference to the Spirit in this epistle).[124] When the apostle speaks of the meaning of the kingdom he describes it as 'righteousness and peace and joy in the Holy Spirit' (Rom. 14:17), which not only shows the same kind of Spirit-produced qualities as in Galatians 5:22, but also shows that the present manifestation of the kingdom of God

---

[124] E. Schweizer, 'Christus und Geist im Kolosserbrief', *Christ and Spirit*, pp. 297–313, discusses the rarity of the mention of the Spirit in this epistle. He sees 2:5; 3:16 and 1:9 as references to the Spirit, in addition to 1:18, but explains that the emphasis has shifted from pneumatology to Christology and suggests that this may be because of an over-emphasis on the activity of the Spirit among the Colossians. Schweizer does not regard Paul as author and therefore sets the epistle in the post-Pauline era as an attempt to maintain orthodoxy through Christology. But he is assuming too sharp a distinction between 'in Christ' and 'in the Spirit'.

consists in inner spiritual qualities and not in political activity. The Spirit, in short, dictates what attitudes are desirable in the kingdom in its present form. If this age is the age of the Spirit, Paul's statement is understandable. His words complement some of the teaching of Jesus on the present aspect of the kingdom. It is noteworthy that linked with this present view is the Spirit's activity in promoting hope for the future (Gal. 5:5; Rom. 15:13).

Using agricultural imagery in describing service, Paul makes the statement in Galatians 6:8 that 'he who sows to the Spirit will from the Spirit reap eternal life'. Here again 'the Spirit' is contrasted with 'flesh'. For Paul service for God must proceed on a higher level than that associated with the 'flesh'. Certainly the rewards are of a totally different kind, *i.e.* spiritual. This does not mean that material considerations do not enter into the service of God, but that they do not constitute its motive power.

THE SPIRIT IN THE CORPORATE LIFE

The basis for unity. Some comments on the corporate activity of the Spirit have already been made in the section on initiation but more needs to be said about the unifying aspect. Two passages are important in this respect. Philippians 2:1–4 enlarges on this unity theme, but the key to it is seen in the common 'participation in the Spirit'. This expression occurs twice in Paul's epistles and has some bearing on the corporate oneness of the church through the Spirit (2 Cor. 13.14; Phil. 2:1). Whether the phrase means 'participation in the Spirit' or 'fellowship created by the Spirit' is not certain, but either way it suggests a linking of believers through a common bond in the Spirit.[125] It is the Spirit who binds Christians together and enables them to be of the same mind. The 'pattern' mind which the Spirit sets before them is nothing less than the mind of Christ (assuming this to be the correct understanding of Phil. 2:5).

The other passage is Ephesiahs 4:3, 4, where Paul declares that the responsibility of all believers is to maintain 'the unity of the Spirit in the bond of peace'.[126] This serves as the basis for the list of unifying facts which follows (verses 4–5), including the statement that there is one Spirit. This indivisible quality is of utmost importance in the consideration of the gifts of the Spirit and of the so-called baptism of the Spirit, to which we now turn.

The baptism in the Spirit. Much discussion has surrounded this subject, because of difference of opinion whether it refers to an experience identical

---

[125] *Cf.* L. S. Thornton, *The Common Life in the Body of Christ* (1941), p. 74.

[126] The importance of this theme of unity in Ephesians is not lessened in the view of those who do not regard Paul as the author of this epistle, although a different historical situation is naturally envisaged. R. Schnackenburg, 'Christus, Geist und Gemeinde', *Christ and Spirit*, pp. 279–296, for instance, regards the author as presenting a theology of the ministry as Christ's gift to the church, an extension of Paul's own teaching. But the theme of unity was undoubtedly an important consideration for the apostle himself. For an exposition of this passage which maintains Pauline authorship, *cf.* M. Barth, *Ephesians, ad loc.*

with or subsequent to the conversion experience. If the former, it becomes no more than another way of expressing the Spirit-dominated character of the Christian life. But if the latter, it marks a superior stage in Christian experience. We have already seen that the evidence from Acts in support of the latter is questionable. It is even more so in the Pauline epistles. Indeed, if Acts is approached *via* the Pauline epistles, the idea of a second once-for-all experience is difficult to support from the NT. But not all would agree to this principle of interpretation. The following observations should be noted.

(i) Nowhere in the Pauline epistles are Christians exhorted to be baptized in the Spirit.[127] The nearest is in Ephesians 5:18 ('Be filled with the Spirit'), but this is not baptism (see separate discussion below).

(ii) Paul specifically says that for Christians there is 'one baptism' (Eph. 4:5), which cannot be subdivided into water-baptism and Spirit-baptism. The only natural understanding of this passage is to suppose that it refers to initiation.

(iii) The only passage in Paul where Spirit and baptism are definitely linked is 1 Corinthians 12:13,[128] which reads, 'For by (*en*) one Spirit we were all baptized into (*eis*) one body . . . and all were made to drink of one Spirit.' But although the preposition (*en*) could here be instrumental, making the act of baptism to be the work of the Spirit, this would not agree with the other NT instances of the verb 'baptize' used with *en*. In all these instances the preposition refers to the sphere in which the baptizing takes place, *i.e.* either in water or in the Spirit. Moreover, the baptism has as its aim incorporation into the body, which implies that no-one can be in the body without the operation of the Spirit. If baptism in the Spirit here meant a post-conversion experience, it would lead to the impossible conclusion that there were those converted who were not part of the body.[129] In any case the concluding statement that 'all' were made to drink of one Spirit shows the basic solidarity of all Christians in the Spirit.[130] The idea

[127] J. D. G. Dunn, *Jesus and the Spirit*, p. 261, comes down firmly for this. He cites in support J. Y. Campbell, 'KOINONIA' and its cognates in the NT', *JBL* 51, 1932, pp. 352ff.; F. Hauck, *TDNT* 2, p. 807; Barrett, *2 Corinthians*, (BC, 1973), pp. 344ff.

[128] *Cf.* J. D. G. Dunn, *Baptism in the Holy Spirit*, pp. 127f. for the various interpretations which have been given to this verse.

[129] G.W.H. Lampe, *The Seal of the Spirit*, p. 56, does not relate this to the believer's experience of conversion, but to baptism. *Cf.* also H. A. A. Kennedy, *St Paul and the Mystery Religions* (1913), p. 239. R. Bultmann, *TNT* 1, pp. 136f., who also relates the Spirit to baptism, sees this as a third stage in the development of the initiatory rite (the earlier stages being purification and the naming of the name). J. R. Williams, *The Era of the Spirit* (1971), in his critique of Bultmann, suggests that Bultmann has created a problem for himself by saying that all Christians at baptism are endowed with the Spirit.

[130] A. A. Hoekema, *Holy Spirit Baptism* (1972), p. 21, argues that the *all* here is against the view that Spirit-baptism is a post-conversion experience. *Cf.* also J. D. G. Dunn, *Baptism in the Holy Spirit*, pp. 127ff. H. M. Ervin, *These are not Drunken as ye Suppose'* (1968), pp. 46f., draws a distinction between the second part of the verse – 'all were made to drink of one Spirit' – and the first part. The drinking of the Spirit is then interpreted as Spirit-baptism. But the context does not suggest any distinction between the two mentions of the Spirit.

seems to be of the pouring out of the Spirit on a thirsty land, an OT metaphor (*cf.* Is. 32:15; 44:3; Ezk. 39:29; Joel 2:28). It is clearly intended to remind the Corinthians of the remarkable transformation made by the Spirit's coming.

It must be concluded that Paul gives no support for the view that baptism in the Spirit is a concept distinct from conversion experience. We need, however, to consider a closely related, but nevertheless different, concept.

The fullness of the Spirit. As mentioned above, Ephesians 5:18 exhorts believers to be filled with the Spirit and some consideration of this is needed if the interpretation given above is correct.[131] Since this exhortation is addressed to Christians, it can mean only that they are expected to seek a fuller manifestation of the Spirit than they have already experienced.[132] Two points need noting. The first is that Paul uses the present continuous tense (keep on being filled), which excludes all thought of a once-for-all experience. The second is that the idea of 'fullness' implies degrees of spiritual experience, according to the extent to which the believer is yielded to the direction of the Spirit. The context in Ephesians 5 makes quite clear that fullness of the Spirit is contrasted with fullness of wine (*i.e.* drunkenness), and the exhortation is therefore a positive antidote to over-indulgence. The contrast is dramatic and effective. No-one can have a surfeit of the Spirit as he can of wine. Moreover, this fullness of the Spirit finds immediate expression in corporate praise and worship (Eph. 5:19–20). Fullness is not, therefore, to be regarded as an individual endowment of some specific gift, but an experience which can and should be common to all Christians.[133]

The Spirit as the giver of gifts. Paul has a great deal to say about spiritual gifts, especially when writing to the Corinthian church. It seems probable that an over-emphasis on the gifts had caused a situation in which it was necessary for Paul to give a more balanced view. He mentions a number of gifts which had been exercised among them, although he devotes more attention to the gifts of utterance (tongues, interpretation, prophecy) than to others, presumably again because these were being the most abused at

---

[131] A. A. Hoekema, *op. cit.*, p. 27, contends from Col. 2:9f., that to be full in Christ must also mean to be full in the Spirit. Paul in this passage is combating the adding of something more to the Colossians' life in Christ. Hoekema also points out that in Acts there are nine instances where being filled or being full of the Spirit is mentioned without reference to tongues, and twenty-one instances where people come to salvation without mention of this gift (p. 44).

[132] R. Bultmann, *TNT* 1, p. 59, speaks of possession of the Spirit in varying quantity or intensity. But 'quantity' is not the right word to use in relation to the Spirit.

[133] J. R. W. Stott, *Baptism and Fullness*, (²1975), pp. 48ff., maintains that baptism resulted in fullness. The former is a unique initiatory experience which cannot be repeated. The latter needs continual repetition. He finds three senses of fullness in the NT: (i) as a normal characteristic of the Christian; (ii) as an endowment for special ministry; (iii) as an endowment for an immediate task.

Corinth. When he introduces the matter in 1 Corinthians 12:4–11, his chief concern is to show that whatever the gifts, the giver is the same Spirit. Indeed he contrasts the variety of gifts with the word 'same', applied to God, to the Lord and to the Spirit (verses 4, 5, 6). His concern is clearly to combat the divisiveness which had occurred at Corinth. He is at pains to point out that when the Spirit gives gifts he gives them 'for the common good' (verse 7). The gifts are related to the community and must contribute to the welfare of the whole. This is borne out by the fact that in the context of his discussion on spiritual gifts, Paul points out the unity of the church under the metaphor of a body. The Spirit as giver of gifts will see to it that concord and not division results.

Moreover, the actual bestowing of the gifts is seen to be the sovereign decision of the Spirit. Paul puts the matter succinctly, 'All these (*i.e.* gifts) are inspired by one and the same Spirit, who apportions to each one individually as he wills' (1 Cor. 12:11). This establishes the important principle that no-one is expected to seek for any specific gift, since the Spirit of God exercises sovereign control. This means, moreover, that no-one can claim superiority over another on the grounds of possessing particular gifts.[134] In 1 Corinthians 12:31ff., he considers the best gifts to be love, hope and faith, of which the greatest is love. But this kind of gift is expected to manifest itself in all Christians.[135]

It is essential to approach the subject of the NT teaching on the gifts of the Spirit from the standpoint of the giver and not of the recipients. We have already adduced ample evidence to show that the Spirit's main task is to guide and empower the people of God, and when he bestows gifts on men he does not abdicate his sovereign control. The gifts are still his, whoever happens to be the channel through whom they are exercised. Paul insists that the only valid outcome of the exercise of these gifts is the building up of the church.[136] In a significant exhortation to the Corinthians

[134] This has frequently been done over the gift of tongues. S. Tugwell, 'The Gift of Tongues in the NT', *ExT* 84, 1973, pp. 137ff., maintains that there is value in speaking in tongues, but he warns against the assumption that one speaking in tongues must necessarily be doing so by the Spirit. He thinks that Paul's main concern in 1 Cor. is to provide adequate tests. The gift of tongues is less important than the Spirit who gives the gift. Cf. also J. C. Hurd, *The Origin of 1 Cor.* (1965), p. 193. See later section on the *charismata*, pp. 764ff.

[135] It has been argued that *zēloute* in 1 Cor. 12:31 should be taken as an indicative rather than as an imperative, in which case Paul would be correcting what the Corinthians were imagining to be a better way (*cf.* G. Iber, 'Zum Verständnis von 1 Kor. 12:31', *ZNW* 54, 1963, pp. 43ff.). But *cf.* D. L. Baker, 'The Interpretation of 1 Corinthians 12–14', *EQ* 46, 1974, p. 227 n. 10, who considers that the imperative makes better sense and a better parallel to 1 Cor. 14:1.

[136] D. L. Baker, *ibid.*, pp. 224–234, distinguishes between *pneumatika* and *charismata*, which leads him to the conclusion that speaking with tongues is not to be confused with ecstasy. If ecstasy is involved, the element of control is clearly diminished. For the view that Paul himself was essentially ecstatic, *cf.* H. Saake, 'Paulus als Ekstatiker', *NovT* 15, 1973, pp. 153ff. (= *Bib* 53, 1972, pp. 404ff.). R. H. Gundry, ' "Ecstatic utterance" (NEB)', *JTS* n.s. 17, 1966, pp. 299ff. criticizes the NEB rendering on the grounds that tongues was non-ecstatic.

he says, 'since you are eager for manifestations of the Spirit, strive to excel in building up the church' (1 Cor. 14:12). He is clearly implying that the Corinthians were not doing this, but were valuing the gifts of the Spirit for their own sake (*cf.* 1 Cor. 14:4–5, 17ff. for other references to edification).

Other gifts mentioned by Paul concentrate on specific functions, and these must never be separated from those gifts enumerated in 1 Corinthians 12:8–10. The functional aspect appears in the list in 1 Corinthians 12:28, where gifts which are not specifically called gifts of the Spirit are named as being appointed by God: apostles, prophets, teachers, miracle-workers, healers, helpers, administrators, speakers in tongues. The fact that some of these have already been included under the list of gifts in 1 Corinthians 12:8–10, but are repeated in conjunction with offices, shows the close link between them. It is particularly significant that the most clearly ecstatic function in this list, speaking in tongues, is placed last. Another list occurs in Romans 12:6–8, where again the Spirit is not mentioned, but where some of the gifts elsewhere attributed to the Spirit are included (prophecy, helps). Yet another occurs in Ephesians 4:11 where the gifts are given by the ascended Christ and where the list wholly concentrates on functions: apostles, prophets, evangelists, pastors, teachers. In this case the purpose is again stated to be the building up of the body of Christ (Eph. 4:12).

From these evidences we may note that Paul never conceives of the Spirit as the giver of a certain number of circumscribed gifts. His manner of mentioning them, with variations of order and content, supports the view that he not only regarded the Spirit as sovereign, but as acting in a completely non-stereotyped way. Moreover, the mixing of gifts and functions shows conclusively that nothing designed for the edification of the church can take place apart from the operation of the Spirit. The fact that the Spirit is not always mentioned as giver is immaterial, since in Paul's mind there does not appear to be any distinction between God, Christ and the Spirit as bestower of spiritual benefits. There is a close connection here between the evidence from Acts and the Pauline epistles.

Our purpose in this section has been to concentrate on the Spirit rather than the gifts, but the latter must be considered in more detail in the discussion of the ministry of the church (see pp. 764ff.).

Hebrews

Although in comparison with the Pauline epistles, Hebrews supplies little information about the Holy Spirit, it contains some significant statements.

(i) We note first that it is assumed, in line with all the evidence so far adduced, that believers are partakers of the Holy Spirit (6:4). Although this comes in one of the much debated apostasy passages, it seems clear that enlightenment and the experiencing of the heavenly gift is the direct work of the Spirit. There is no support for the view that anyone can have a real experience of Christ without being a partaker of the Spirit.

(ii) We observe further that those who spurn the Son are said to outrage the Spirit of grace (10:29), which brings to the fore the close connection between the function of the Spirit and the glorification of the Son. In this there is a link with Jesus' own prediction in John's gospel. The author of Hebrews clearly feels that to outrage the Spirit invites just retribution.

(iii) There is a passing reference to the gifts of the Holy Spirit in 2:4 with no details of their characteristics, but linked with signs, wonders and miracles. What is most significant is the statement that the gifts of the Spirit are 'distributed according to his own will', which is in direct line with Paul's statement in 1 Corinthians 12:11. The sovereignty of the Spirit was evidently a firm conviction for the early Christians.

(iv) Three passages in this epistle assert the part played by the Spirit in revelation. When quoting from Psalm 95, Hebrews introduces the citation with the formula 'as the Holy Spirit says' (3:7), which assumes the Spirit's inspiration of the OT Scriptures. A more general statement along the same line is found in 9:8, where some details of the OT cultic procedure are cited as the means by which 'the Holy Spirit indicates'. In 10:15 the reference is again more direct, introducing a citation from Jeremiah 31 with the words, 'The Holy Spirit also bears witness to us'. This function of the Spirit in the interpretation of Scripture is obviously of particular significance in an epistle which contains so much exposition of the OT.[137]

(v) The remaining occurrence is perhaps the most significant in that it relates to the atoning work of Christ. As a direct contrast to the continual offering of animal sacrifices, Christ is said to have offered himself without blemish to God, 'through the eternal Spirit' (9:14).[138] If this is a reference to the Holy Spirit no greater contrast could be conceived, for here at last was a self-offering of an entirely moral kind. No animal victim could offer itself and none was prompted by the Spirit. The Spirit's part in the atoning work of Christ is nowhere brought out more clearly than here. This

---

[137] P. E. Hughes, *Hebrews* (1977), p. 141, points out that for this author the message of Scripture is not only the voice of the Spirit but is also fully existential in its significance 'so that what was spoken or written in the wilderness situation centuries before continues to have a dynamic applicability to the people of God in his own day'.

[138] It should be noted that not all interpreters take the *dia pneumatos* in this verse as a reference to the Holy Spirit. B. F. Westcott, *Hebrews* (1892), *ad loc.*, relates it to Christ's divine nature (*cf.* also Spicq, *Hebrews* (EB ²1952), *ad loc.*). But F. F. Bruce, *Hebrews* (1964), *ad loc*, interprets it in the light of the Spirit-empowered Isaianic Servant. P. E. Hughes, *op. cit., ad loc.*, n. 17, prefers to render the phrase 'through his eternal spirit'. He thinks the theological context is against referring it to the Holy Spirit. Whereas the primary reference is to the spirit of Jesus as compared with his flesh, it cannot be doubted that there is here a secondary reference to the Holy Spirit. It is highly unlikely that the early Christians sharply differentiated between Christ's *pneuma* and the activity of the Holy Spirit within him. It is legitimate in the context of Heb. 9:14 to see the agency of the Holy Spirit, although care must be taken not to confuse the Holy Spirit with the *pneuma* of Christ.

presentation of his part in the sacrifice of Jesus is in line with the evidences from the gospels in which the Spirit's work is seen in the initiatory aspects of the ministry, although nothing is said about the Spirit's specific co-operation in the passion. The statement in Hebrews is a logical deduction from the gospel portrait of Jesus. If, of course, 9:14 contains no reference to the Holy Spirit, this would not alter the uniqueness of the offering of Jesus, but would add nothing of value for our present investigation.

The rest of the New Testament

The interpretive ministry of the Spirit seen in Hebrews also comes into focus in *1 Peter*. The prophetic predictions of the sufferings of Christ are attributed to the Spirit (1:11ff.).[139] His activity, therefore, draws together promise and fulfilment. There is indeed a close link between this statement and one in 2 Peter which attributes prophecy to the Spirit moving men to speak from God (2 Pet. 1:21; see section on Scripture for a fuller exposition of this passage, pp. 977ff.). An interesting feature about the 1 Peter 1:11 statement is that the Spirit is called 'the Spirit of Christ', an expression used elsewhere only by Paul (*cf.* Rom 8:9; Phil. 1:19; also Gal. 4:6). It is another striking combination of the Spirit with the Son, which is inescapable in the NT.

In common with the other streams within the NT, Peter thinks of believers as possessing the Spirit. In fact he talks about their being 'sanctified by the Spirit' (1:1). This statement is noteworthy because it links sanctification by the Spirit with the idea of predestination by God. The Spirit's activity in fact is to carry out the choice of God. If the reference to Spirit in 3:18 (made alive in (*en*) the Spirit) refers to the Holy Spirit rather than to the human spirit, it would show that Peter thinks of Christ in his resurrection as Spirit-activated.[140] Moreover in the context this life-giving activity is contrasted with Christ's death in the flesh. On the other hand the reference here is probably to the spiritual sphere (as contrasted with flesh), in which case it contributes nothing to the doctrine of the Spirit. The Spirit's activity in the resurrection of Christ as seen here is somewhat akin to the thought of 1 Timothy 3:16: 'vindicated in (*en*) the Spirit'.

There is a close connection between the sufferings of believers for the name of Christ and the sufferings of Christ himself, as Peter maintains in 4:12ff. In that case the believers are in a state of blessedness because 'the

---

[139] F. W. Beare, *1 Peter* (²1958), pp. 65f., in discussing this passage sees no need to refer it to the pre-existence of Christ in the sense that he was present in spirit in the OT age, although he does not rule out the possibility. But K. H. Schelkle, *Die Petrusbriefe, Der Judasbrief* (1976), p. 41, is more definite in seeing a reference to Christ's pre-existence.

[140] *Cf.* E. Best, *1 Peter* (*NCB*, 1971), p. 139, who regards the antithesis here between flesh and spirit, as in the NT elsewhere, to refer to the 'opposition of divine Spirit to human existence'.

spirit of glory and of God' rests upon them, which seems a clear reference to the Holy Spirit.[141]

The Petrine epistles are in line with the mainstream NT documents in assuming a high doctrine of the Spirit's activity. It might also be noted that in the epistle of *Jude*, it is a presupposition that believers possess the Spirit, for the scoffers are denoted by their lack of the Spirit (verse 19), and believers are exhorted to pray 'in the Holy Spirit' (verse 20).

In the book of *Revelation* one feature is introduced which is unique to this book, the references to the seven Spirits of God (1:4; 3:1; 4:5; 5:6).[142] It cannot be supposed that John thought of a plurality of spirits, for on other occasions he speaks of the Spirit in the singular. In view of the frequent symbolic use of the number seven in this book, it is reasonable to suppose that the expression draws attention to the perfection of the Spirit. Indeed since the first mention of the number seven occurs in connection with the Spirit, we may go further and suggest that the perfection of the Spirit furnishes the cue for a right understanding of the other symbolic uses of the number. The seven spirits are linked to the seven stars in 3:1, to seven torches of fire in 4:5, and to seven horns with seven eyes in 5:6.[143] The plurality is therefore that of perfection, not of number.

At the conclusion of all the seven letters to the Asiatic churches, the readers are urged to listen to what the Spirit says.[144] This ties in with the function of the Spirit in revelation. Moreover, since the messages are from the resurrected and glorified Lord, the close link between the proclamation of Christ and that of the Spirit is again unmistakable. What Christ speaks, the Spirit speaks. It is not surprising therefore that early in his book John speaks of being 'in the Spirit' (1:10; 4:2), and that at the conclusion he is carried away 'in the Spirit' (21:10). It is the Spirit who joins with the Bride in urging people to respond (22:17). In one of the visions John is actually carried by the Spirit into the wilderness in an ecstatic experience (17:3). Furthermore, in another the Spirit is identified with the heavenly voice (14:13). John ensures that his readers are in no doubt that his extraordinary visions were under the direct control of the Spirit of God. The Spirit in this book is essentially the Spirit of prophecy.[145]

---

[141] *Cf.* E. G. Selwyn's detailed discussion of this phrase in its context, *1 Peter* (1946) *ad loc.* He translates as 'The Presence of the Glory, yea, the Spirit of God rests upon you', which brings out most clearly the reference to the Holy Spirit.

[142] *Cf.* F. F. Bruce's discussion, 'The Spirit in the Apocalypse', *Christ and Spirit*, pp. 333–344, a concise survey of the evidence in this book. He sees a connection between the seven spirits and Is. 11:2.

[143] H. B. Swete, *The Holy Spirit in the NT* (1909), p. 274, considers that the spirit is sevenfold simply because the churches number seven.

[144] It is significant that each message is said to be a word from the exalted Lord and yet the hearers must pay attention to what the Spirit says. As Bruce, *op. cit.*, p. 340, says, 'it is not that the Spirit is identical with the exalted Lord, but that the exalted Lord speaks to the churches by the Spirit'. He is here combating the view of E. Schweizer, *TDNT* 6, p. 440, who supposes an identity.

[145] *Cf.* D. Hill, 'Prophecy and Prophets in the Revelation of St John', *NTS* 18, 1971–1, pp. 401–418.

Concluding comments

The preceding survey has shown the importance given to the Holy Spirit in all sections of the NT. Moreover, in spite of the widely differing character of the writings, there is a remarkable unity in the importance attached to the Spirit and in the kind of functions attributed to him. It remains to discuss the relationship between the NT teaching on the Spirit and the teaching on Christology and eschatology, since both these themes have an important bearing on NT theology. They are in fact closely interrelated.

Our comments will concentrate mainly on Paul since the major considerations arise from his epistles. In the field of Christology the question is whether or not Paul identifies Christ and the Spirit. The main statement which might lead to an affirmative answer is 2 Corinthians 3:17, 'The Lord is the Spirit.' If this were an isolated statement there would be no doubt that it would amount to an explicit identification. Many scholars have regarded it in this light, but they have generally not done full justice to the context.[146] Since 'Lord' is mentioned in the previous verse, it is sound exegesis to interpret one in terms of the other.[147] There are grounds to support the view that 2 Corinthians 3:16 is a reference to Yahweh rather than to Christ, since the whole passage contains an allusion to Exodus 34:29–35. In this case the identification with the Spirit would mean that the Lord of Exodus 34 is in our present experience the Spirit. In any case even those who interpret 'Lord' in 2 Corinthians 3:17 as Christ maintain only a functional and not an ontological identity. The Spirit performs a similar function in this era to that performed by the law under the old covenant. Paul's words are then understood in the sense that the Spirit brings the risen Lord to earth again by making the benefits of the risen Lord so real to believers that a practical identity arises.[148] Nevertheless the fact that Paul can use the expression 'the Spirit of the Lord' in the same context is proof that he maintained a distinction between the Spirit and the Lord.

Other passages[149] which have been claimed to support a functional identification are 1 Corinthians 12:3 ('no one can say "Jesus is Lord" except by the Holy Spirit'), Romans 8:9b ('Anyone who does not have the Spirit of Christ does not belong to him'), Galatians 4:6 ('The Spirit of his Son'), Philippians 1:19 ('The Spirit of Jesus Christ'), together with passages which

---

[146] *Cf.* N. Q. Hamilton, *The Holy Spirit and Eschatology in Paul* (1957), pp. 4ff. I. Hermann, *Kyrios und Pneuma* (1961), devotes his monograph to this passage and concludes for a functional identification of Lord and Spirit.

[147] *Cf.* J. D. G. Dunn, '2 Corinthians iii.17 – the Lord is the Spirit', *JTS* 21, 1970, pp. 309–320. who strongly criticizes Hermann's view. C. F. D. Moule, 'II Cor. 3:18b: *kathaper apo kyriou pneumatos, Neues Testament und Geschichte: historische Geschehen und Deutung im Neuen Testament* (ed. H. Baltensweiler and B. Reike, 1972), pp. 231ff., adopts a view similar to Dunn.

[148] So Hamilton, *op. cit.*, p. 6.

[149] A brief survey of the implications of these passages is given in Hamilton, *ibid.*, pp. 8ff.

link the Spirit with the resurrection, as in Romans 1:4 (*cf.* also 1 Corinthians 15:45).[150] From these passages it is clear that a close connection exists between Christ and the Spirit, but it cannot be established that they are to be identified. There is no doubt that the Spirit is the link between Christ and the believer. It is not surprising, therefore, that some functions are fulfilled by both Christ and the Spirit (*cf.* for instance the parallel concepts 'in Christ' and 'in the Spirit'). The fact that the Spirit specifically represents Christ, a view not only supported by Paul but also by John 16:14, would lead to a close identity of function. But it is important to recognize that some activities are exclusively attributed by Paul to the Spirit and others to Christ.

The NT as a whole supplies little data about the *nature* of the relationship between Christ and the Spirit. It is more interested in the practical relation of the Spirit to the believer.[151] But it would be true to say that the doctrine of the Spirit is Christ orientated. The relation reaches to more than a functional similarity. The scattered references noted above were never intended to give a structured exposition of the doctrine of the trinity, but it was the close connection between Christ and the Spirit and at the same time the clear distinction between them that led to the later convictions about the doctrine.

Some consideration must be given to the relation between the Spirit and the future, in view of the proposition that the Spirit's work belongs essentially to the future and that his present activity is preliminary.[152] This view is based on the future emphasis which is implied in such descriptions as 'first fruits', 'beginning' and 'first-born' (1 Cor. 15:20, 23; Col. 1:18), together with the fact that the Spirit is described as a guarantee (*arrabōn*) (2 Cor. 1:22; 5:5; Eph. 1:14) and is connected with the kingdom (Rom. 14:17; *cf.* 1 Cor. 4:20). Granted that these descriptions imply a fuller experience which will not happen until the consummation, would it lead to greater clarity to speak of 'the eschatological Spirit'?[153] If by this expression is meant that the Spirit who is now active in believers is the same Spirit who will bring to fruition in them the work already begun, there can be

---

[150] On 1 Cor. 15:45, J. D. G. Dunn, '1 Corinthians 15:45 – Last Adam, Life-giving Spirit', in *Christ and Spirit*, pp. 127–142, supports an identity between Christ and the Spirit. But *cf.* M. M. B. Turner's criticism of this position, 'The significance of Spirit endowment for Paul', *Vox Ev* 9, 1975, pp. 61ff.

[151] As L. Morris says on 2 Cor. 3:17, Paul is not giving a theoretical description of the nature of the Lord (or of the Spirit), but is affirming the source of spiritual life, *Spirit of the Living God* (1960), p. 42.

[152] *Cf.* J. D. G. Dunn, *Jesus and the Spirit*, p. 67, who speaks of Jesus as being anointed by the eschatological Spirit, and *ibid.*, pp. 308ff., where he discusses Paul's views on eschatology and the Spirit. R. Bultmann, *TNT* 1, p. 37, who equates the Spirit with power, approaches the NT evidence from the point of view of the 'eschatological congregation'. His idea is that the congregation is the vestibule of God's reign. For a brief critique of Bultmann's approach to the Pauline evidence, *cf.* N. Q. Hamilton, *op. cit.*, pp. 71–82; for a fuller critique of his approach to the eschatology of the fourth gospel, *cf.* D. E. Holwerda, *The Holy Spirit and Eschatology in the Gospel of John* (1959).

[153] *Cf.* especially N. Q. Hamilton's exposition of this view, *op. cit.*, pp. 17ff.

no objection. But the description 'eschatological Spirit' suggests that the Spirit's main activity is postponed until the end, and this does not lead to a clear understanding of the Spirit's work. There are certainly far more references to the Spirit's present activity, and it would seem to be more logical to view the future references in the light of these rather than *vice versa*.

There can be no doubt that Paul recognized that what the Spirit had begun he would certainly complete. Moreover, the present activity of the Spirit cannot be properly assessed except in the light of the consummation.[154] The importance of the future hope for an understanding of the NT doctrine of the Spirit is the assurance it gives that the Spirit's present work will not be thwarted by the present evil environment of the people of God. There is a strong sense in which the future hope has begun to be realized in the new life of the Christian community. Our consideration of the Spirit here will, therefore, have a bearing on our later consideration of the NT teaching about the future, and will help to tie together the Spirit, the new life and the consummation. There will also be a strong link between the person and work of the Spirit in relation to the church.[155]

[154] There is no denying that there is in the NT a tension between the 'now' and the 'not yet'. Any lessening of this tension would distort the NT position. And yet it is the essential unity between the present and the future which the Spirit of God exemplifies.

[155] On the relation between the Spirit and both Christology and ecclesiology, cf. J. D. G. Dunn, 'Rediscovering the Spirit', *ExT* 84, 1972, pp. 7–12; 40–44.

Chapter 6

The Christian life

We might have named this whole section salvation, for our concern is to discuss the application of what Christ has done to the present life. We have already considered aspects of salvation in discussing the work of Christ and the term at its widest would also need to include man's future destiny, which is dealt with in the section on the future. The object of our immediate enquiry is to consider man's response to God's provision. This naturally falls into two sections, one dealing with man as an individual and one with man in community. This chapter will discuss the first, and the next, on the church, will deal with the second. There will be many points on which the two interact and overlap, but this is unavoidable. The Christian life will be subdivided into the following five sections: The beginnings (repentance, faith, forgiveness), grace (its means, election, predestination, perseverance), the new life in Christ (the concept of a new humanity), sanctification, and law.

THE BEGINNINGS

We shall be mainly concerned in this section with the initiation of the individual into Christian experience. It involves conversion, although it goes beyond this. We shall need to consider the nature of repentance, the relationship between repentance and faith, regeneration and forgiveness. We are, therefore, approaching the study of Christian initiation on a broad front. We shall discover that different parts of the NT emphasize different aspects, and in order to gain a complete understanding we must aim for an over-all view. The fact that John's gospel, for instance, says more about regeneration than Paul's epistles needs to be balanced against the latter's greater stress on incorporation into Christ.

The synoptic gospels

REPENTANCE

The ministry of Jesus is presented in all the synoptics as a continuation of the mission of John the Baptist. In his announcement of the mission of Jesus, John called on people to 'repent' and this call was reiterated by Jesus at the commencement of his ministry (Mk. 1:14ff.; Mt. 4:17).[1] The question arises in what sense both John and Jesus were calling on people to repent. God acts first in calling people to repentance, and 'repentance' therefore takes on the nature of response. One essential difference between the Jewish view and that of Jesus[2] is that the former related repentance to the law and made it out to be a change of approach to the law, breaking off disobedience and embracing obedience,[3] whereas the approach of Jesus is entirely different. It involves a radical change of direction, not only in behaviour but also in thought.

John the Baptist connected his act of baptism with repentance (Mt. 3:1ff.; Mk. 1:4; Lk. 3:3).[4] He challenged people to bear fruit befitting repentance (Mt. 3:8). When Jesus sent out the twelve they sounded the same message of repentance (Mk. 6:12). In Luke's gospel there is most emphasis on this theme. Jesus announces that he has come to call sinners, not righteous people, to repentance (Lk. 5:32). He warns his hearers that unless they repented they would share the fate of the Galileans slaughtered by Pilate and those killed by the collapse of the tower of Siloam (Lk. 13:1ff.). In other words, people are divided into two classes, the repentant and the non-repentant. In the parables in Luke 15 it is over the repentant that there is joy in heaven (Lk. 15:7, 10).[5] In the story of Dives in Hades, the view

---

[1] It is to be noted that whereas Mark describes John's preaching as 'a baptism of repentance for the forgiveness of sins' (Mk. 1:4), Matthew omits the reference to forgiveness. He does, however, use the same phrase in his account of the words of institution at the last supper (Mt. 26:26), thus linking it with the passion. Some scholars dispute that the message of Jesus was initially the same as that of John the Baptist. K. Romaniuk, 'Repentez-vous, car le royaume des cieux est tout proche (Matt. 4:7 par)', *NTS* 12, 1965–6, pp. 259–269, for instance, maintains that Jesus in his preaching made no reference to repentance or to remission of sins. He simply announced the proximity of the kingdom. The repentance then, according to Romaniuk, was introduced through the catechesis of John the Baptist. But this seems unnecessarily restrictive of the message of Jesus. The repentance theme is integral to the forgiveness theme in the ministry of Jesus. Both Matthew and Mark are convinced that the announcement of the kingdom was initially linked with repentance. In Mark's account the repentance is also linked with faith in the good news.

[2] *Cf.* G. E. Ladd, *The Presence of the Future* (1974), p. 177.

[3] For a discussion of the rabbinic approach to obedience and disobedience, *cf.* E. P. Sanders, *Paul and Palestinian Judaism* (1977), pp. 107ff. He points out (p. 112) that the cure for non-obedience is repentance, even in reference to cultic regulations.

[4] For a discussion of the significance of repentance in John the Baptist's rite, *cf.* C. H. H. Scobie, *John the Baptist*, pp. 110ff. Scobie thinks that John would have imagined that the forgiveness of sins promised as a sequel to repentance would become effective at the day of judgment.

[5] Some have seen the reference to repentance here as a key word in Luke's theology (*cf.* L. Schottroff, 'Das Gleichnis vom verloren Sohn', *ZTK* 68, 1971, pp. 27–52). I. H. Marshall, *The Gospel of Luke* (*NIGTC*, 1978), p. 602, commenting on Schottroff's view that Lk. 15:7 is a summary of Luke's theology, notes that only the repentance motif is Lukan and does not spring directly from the parabolic situation.

that men would repent if one went to them from the dead is rejected (Lk.
16:30), a comment on the paramount importance of repentance in relation
to the afterlife. It is Luke who records Jesus' demand that his disciples must
be ready to forgive as often as a person repents (Lk. 17:1ff.). In Luke's
version of Jesus' concluding commission to his disciples, he not only urged
them to preach repentance and forgiveness, but also based it on an interpretation of Scripture (Lk. 24:46–47).[6]

From this survey of the evidence there is no doubt that repentance is
regarded as an essential prerequisite for those who are to become followers
of Jesus, precisely because it is a duty for all people. Until people repent
they show no consciousness of their need of salvation. What Jesus came to
do can be applied only by those who show recognition of their own
inability to save themselves and their desire to change their present relationship to God. Repentance is clearly not enough in itself, but is an integral
initial part in the experience of salvation. It has both a negative and a
positive side, a turning away from sin and a turning towards God. It is the
latter aspect which may more properly be described as conversion.

FAITH

In all parts of the NT prominence is given to faith, or to the act of believing.[7]
Sometimes it is merely a question of believing what someone says, that is,
believing it to be true or believing the person to be trustworthy. But the
specifically Christian use of the word 'faith' is in the sense of committing
oneself to Christ. This will become clear in varying degrees as the evidence
is surveyed. Our concern here is with the idea in the teaching of the
synoptic gospels.[8]

In Mark's account of the beginning of the ministry of Jesus, his first
proclamation linked faith and repentance (Mk. 1:15).[9] In view of the dawn

[6] This links up closely with the emphasis on repentance in Acts (see pp. 587f.). H. Conzelmann, *The Theology of St Luke* (Eng. trans. 1960), pp. 99ff.; pp. 228ff., considered that Luke narrowed down the concept of repentance as a reference to conversion to a condition of salvation. But I. H. Marshall, *Luke : Historian and Theologian* (1970), p. 194, rightly criticizes this view. He considers repentance is not synonymous with conversion, but expresses its positive side.

[7] For a full linguistic examination of the term and its associate ideas, together with its OT background, *cf.* R. Bultmann and W. Weiser, *TDNT* 6, pp. 174ff.

[8] J. Jeremias, *NTT*, p. 160, cautions against the view that the 'faith' references in these gospels have been strongly influenced by the early church. He notes the paucity of references to faith, the linguistic evidence and the different objects of faith compared with the rest of the NT.

[9] Mk. 1:15 is the only instance in the NT where *pisteuō* is used with *en.* V. Taylor, *Mark* ([2]1966), p. 167, attributes this to 'translation Greek'. He renders Mark's phrase as 'believe the Good News', and sees no reason to dispute it as an authentic word of Jesus. On the relation between faith and repentance in this passage, E. Schweizer says, ' "Repentance" is nothing less than a wholehearted commitment to the "Good News" ' (*Mark*, Eng. trans. 1971, from *NTD*, 1967, p. 47). This must not be taken to lessen that element in repentance which involves a turning away from an existing manner of life, *i.e.* a connection with past offences against God.

of the kingdom, faith in the gospel must be added to repentance.[10] The sense in which this is meant must be that the hearers were expected to commit themselves to all that Jesus himself stood for – *i.e.* his whole mission. To believe in the gospel meant precisely to believe in Jesus himself. The record of the ministry of Jesus is a record of challenges to faith. After the statement in Mark 1:15, Mark immediately proceeds to illustrate by his account of the demand to the first disciples to leave their fishing and follow Jesus (Mk. 1:17). In the miracle stories of healing the faith aspect is strong, even where no mention is made of it apart from the fact that people came or were brought to be healed. But in many cases the healing is said to be the direct result of faith (*cf.* Mt. 8:10, 13; 9:22, 29; 15:28; Mk. 9:24; 10:52; Lk. 7:50; 17:19). In the stilling of the storm incident, the disciples were rebuked because of their unbelief (Mt. 8:26; Mk. 4:40; Lk. 8:25). Moreover, Jesus promised remarkable achievements to people of faith (*cf.* Mt. 17:20; 21:21–22; Lk. 17:5). The greatness of achievement is not, however, commensurate with the amount of faith, for mountains can be moved by grain-sized faith.

All these instances of the achievements of faith are examples of the necessity of faith in the power of Jesus. But he had more to say about faith than this. Faith was seen as an assertion of possibilities in the face of seeming impossibilities (Mk. 9:23).[11] The mission of Jesus was based on the conviction that what God expected of people was impossible through human effort, but became a viable proposition when faith linked them to God's way of doing things, *i.e.* to his redemptive plan.[12] This 'impossible' aspect becomes intelligible only when it centres in a known person (*i.e.* in Jesus himself). It is in Christ that God does the impossible.

In the Lukan birth narratives, the difference between faith and unbelief is seen in a comparison between Mary (Lk. 1:45) and Zechariah (Lk. 1:20). The kind of faith (or lack of it) here encountered is in line with the OT usage of trust in God, and contributes little to the special NT approach to faith, except to remind us that the demand for faith in God by Jesus was not an entirely new concept. There is some hint of the Christian approach in the interpretation of the parable of the seeds according to Luke's account, in which Jesus refers to the devil taking away the word from hearers 'that

---

[10] L. Hartman, in his discussion on 'Baptism "Into the Name of Jesus" and Early Christology', *StTh* 28, 1974, p. 42, considers that Jesus' preaching meant a challenge to *metanoia*, through which challenge God exercises his reign when it is received in faith. On the interpretation of *euangelion* in Mark's usage *cf.* W. Marxsen, *Mark the Evangelist* (Eng. trans. 1969), pp. 117–150. In his opinion Mark has a different view of the gospel from Matthew and Luke. Mark sees it as centred in Jesus himself, whereas according to Marxsen the others see it as the whole story of Jesus. All are agreed however, that Jesus is central to the gospel.

[11] The seeming paradox of the man's desperate cry in Mk. 9:24 ('I believe . . . help my unbelief') brings out an essential feature of Christian faith – that belief is possible only with the help of one who is himself the object of faith. W. Lane, *Mark*, p. 334, interprets this cry as expressing 'humanity and distress at being asked to manifest radical faith when unbelief is the form of human existence'.

[12] *Cf.* E. Stauffer, *NTT*, pp. 168f.

they may not believe and be saved' (Lk. 8:12). 'Believing' is equated to 'receiving the Word' in a permanent, not simply temporary way (*cf.* Lk. 8:13). If the word stands for the whole message and mission of Jesus, the importance of faith in it and the disastrous consequences of unbelief at once become clear. Since the parable reflects the various responses to Jesus' ministry, the vital function of faith is vividly seen and the good soil hearers show their faith by hearing and holding fast to the word and working it out in practice (Lk. 8:15). Matthew has 'hearing and understanding' rather than believing, but it means the same thing.

For Jesus, faith must have active consequences. It expresses itself in prayer (Mt. 21:22; Mk. 11:24). This sets out a norm of faith for those who wish to communicate with God. There must be a certain simplicity about this approach. Indeed Jesus likens it to the attitude of a child (Mt. 18:1–6). Faith is therefore the negation of self-confidence. It says 'no' to pride in human achievement. It involves throwing oneself unreservedly on the mercy of God. The falseness of the people who challenged the crucified Jesus that if he would come down they would believe (Mt. 27:42; Mk. 15:32) is seen in the absence of any moral content in this offer of faith. Jesus would never gain faith in this way (*cf.* also Lk. 22:67 for a similar evidence of his insight into the true nature of faith). He knew too well the weakness of even his closest followers. He prayed that Peter's faith might not fail (Lk. 22:32), because he knew that faith was essential if the power of Satan was to be overcome.[13] This theme of faith is more fully expounded in the Johannine and Pauline literature, but the indispensability of faith is already established in the synoptics.

FORGIVENESS

It is basic to the NT doctrine of man that sin is the insuperable obstacle to his reconciliation with God (see pp. 187ff.). The initial steps towards restoration of fellowship with God must, therefore, make provision for forgiveness. Only when this has been achieved can there be any radically different approach to human living. It is not surprising, therefore, that the NT writers present a wide spectrum of teaching on this theme.

We have already noted that Mark refers to John the Baptist's baptism of repentance (Mk. 1:4), but it is significant that he adds 'for the forgiveness of sins' (which Luke also echoes, Lk. 3:3). The concluding commission in Luke (24:47) also links repentance with forgiveness. It is this that was to form the basis of appeal in the proclamation of the gospel in the apostolic age. People were to be challenged to repent and were to be offered forgiveness. But we need to consider the other teaching of Jesus in order to

[13] For a concise survey of Luke's use of *pistis-pisteuō*, *cf.* S. Brown, *Apostasy and Perseverance in the Theology of Luke* (1969), pp. 36f. He finds three uses in Luke's gospel: faith in Jesus' miraculous power of healing, charismatic faith, and faith in Jesus as the Christ.

appreciate what was involved in his promise of 'forgiveness'.

Jesus himself, as Son of man, claimed the prerogative to forgive (as Mk. 2:10 shows),[14] although this was regarded by the Jews as the right of God alone. It is not surprising that his claim was immediately challenged.

It has often been supposed that Luke has a doctrine of forgiveness rooted in God's love as seen in the parable of the prodigal son (Lk. 15). If this parable were the sole source for understanding the theme of forgiveness, it might be deduced that all that was necessary was for man to repent and for God to forgive.[15] In that case the sacrificial work of Christ would be totally unnecessary. But Luke 15 cannot be isolated from the rest of the narrative in Luke with its detailed account of the passion. The view that his account of the work of Christ is less tragic than the others has already been discussed (pp. 448f.), but support for it was found to be less convincing than is often supposed. Certainly no doctrine of forgiveness can be based on this parable, alone, although its evidence has value. The major teaching of the parable is that God's forgiveness is completely unearned.[16] The son did nothing to merit it – rather the reverse. The parable illustrates a basic NT truth, i.e. that forgiveness is an act of grace as far as man is concerned. At the same time it shows a link between forgiveness and penitence, which is essential if the moral aspect of forgiveness is to be maintained. In the parable, the son had to be willing to accept forgiveness if the father was to bestow it.

Jesus stressed the connection between God's forgiveness of us and our forgiveness of each other. This comes out clearly in the Lord's prayer (Mt. 6:12; Lk. 11:4). Again we must not isolate the words from the other teaching of Jesus, otherwise we might conclude that God's forgiveness is conditioned only by our attitude to others. We must not lose, however, the main point of the prayer. Those who ask for forgiveness and yet harbour an unforgiving attitude to others are asking the impossible.[17]

There may also be a sense in which our attitude towards forgiveness

---

[14] For a comment on the claim of Jesus to forgive sins, cf. V. Taylor's detached note, *Mark*, p. 200. He rejects the view that this was a reconstruction of the believing community without any basis in fact. Some have attempted to make son of man here = man, which then makes the expression mean no more than that man can forgive sin. But see D. E. Nineham's rejection of this, *Mark* (1963), pp. 93f. V. Taylor, *op. cit.*, maintains that Jesus' act of forgiveness is divine rather than declaratory, but that it does not invade the prerogatives of Almighty God.

[15] Much will obviously depend on whether it is held that this parable is Luke's composition or that it comes from Jesus. For a defence of the latter view, cf. C. E. Carlston, 'Reminiscence and Redaction in Lk. 15:11–32', *JBL* 94, 1975, pp. 368–390.

[16] For a discussion of the legal background to this parable, cf. J. D. M. Derrett, 'Law in the NT: The Parable of the Prodigal Son', *NTS* 14, 1967–8, pp. 56–74. On the father's forgiveness, see pp. 65ff. I. H. Marshall, *Luke*, p. 604, rightly points out that the parable is concerned not so much with the repentance of the son as the communal joy of the reunited family. It is 'ultimately concerned to justify the attitude of God to sinners'.

[17] Cf. I. H. Marshall, *Kept by the Power of God* (1969), p. 65, who discusses Mt. 6:14f., and Mk. 11:25 and says that a person who does not forgive ceases to experience divine forgiveness.

should bear some faint resemblance to God's forgiveness for which we are praying. This is a reminder that a prayer for such is not a request for something of which on the human level we have no experience. We do forgive, and this is a pattern, though inadequate, for God's forgiveness. If we do it, how much more will our heavenly Father do it.[18] The parable of the unforgiving servant (Mt. 18:23–35) shows that one who accepted forgiveness is expected *ipso facto* to forgive.[19] There must be a common bond between the forgiven person and the forgiver. The fact that the servant, in spite of the massive remission of debt which he had received, refused to show mercy himself, demonstrates his lack of sympathy with his forgiving master. Moreover, on one occasion Jesus made clear the limitless character of forgiveness when he demanded that a man must be forgiven seven times a day if he repents seven times (Lk. 17:4). Matthew notes that in answer to Peter's question about how often he should forgive, Jesus says seventy times seven, to avoid any suggestion that a restriction is permissible.

Two other passages may be noted. The city woman, who anointed his feet, was told by Jesus that her sins though many were forgiven (Lk. 7:47). In her case, her loving action witnessed to the fact that she was repentant and was ready to receive forgiveness.[20] In the words from the cross, Jesus prays for forgiveness for his murderers (Lk. 23:34), on the grounds of their ignorance of what they were really doing.

Our final passage is Matthew's account of the institution of the Lord's Supper, in which the words, 'this is my blood of the covenant, which is poured out for many for the remission of sins' (Mt. 26:28), occur. We have previously noted (p. 442) that because the concluding words do not occur in Mark's and Luke's accounts, many do not regard them as original. The addition provides the only instance in the gospels in which forgiveness is directly connected with the death of Jesus.

From this evidence we note that the scope of forgiveness in these gospels is the removal of barriers. The very fact that in two cases it is connected with the cancelling of debts shows that it must be regarded as a prerequisite for the renewal of fellowship, but not itself an equivalent to reconciliation.

[18] It must not be supposed that there is any thought here of a *quid pro quo* approach. Matthew's wording (*hōs kai*) might perhaps imply this, but Luke's (*kai gar*) excludes it. See I. H. Marshall's comment, *Luke*, p. 461.

[19] This passage is regarded by some as Matthew's redaction in which he expands on the earlier passage on forgiveness in the Lord's prayer (Mt. 6:14–15), *cf.* W. G. Thompson, *Matthew's Advice to a Divided Community* (1970), pp. 223ff. If the Lord's prayer is considered to be original to Jesus, however, it would be natural to suppose that he gave precisely the kind of explanation of the forgiveness concept as Matthew records in 18:23–35. J. C. Fenton, *Matthew* ([2]1977), p. 302, thinks the application in verse 35 is probably Matthean.

[20] Many commentators take these words to mean that forgiveness was granted on the basis of the woman's love. But the past tense *ēgapēsen* may not refer to acts prior to the forgiveness, but to acts prior to the words being spoken. She had already shown her love (*cf.* I. H. Marshall, *Luke*, p. 313). In this case, *hoti* means 'as is evidenced by the fact that', not 'because'.

It is this aspect of removal of barriers, particularly in relation to guilt, that links forgiveness so closely with redemption. While the distinction between forgiveness and reconciliation should be noted, it should not be overemphasized. There is nothing to suggest that forgiveness was ever offered without a call to return to God.

There is one further reference to be discussed, *i.e.* the blasphemy sayings, which regard sin against the Holy Spirit to be incapable of forgiveness (Mk. 3:22ff.; Mt. 12:22ff.; Lk. 11:5ff.; *cf.* Lk. 12:10). The sin in this case must mean a hardened state of sin which forms an insuperable barrier. A distinction is made between this attitude and sin against the Son of man. If a man really desires forgiveness and could not bear the prospect of the lack of it, it is evidence that he has not reached a hardened state. For when a man has reached the state of being hardened against the Spirit, forgiveness ceases to have any meaning for him (see pp. 608f. for further discussion of this passage in connection with grace).

One feature which relates to human forgiveness, but which may throw light on divine forgiveness, is the obligation of the offended person to take the initiative in setting the processes of reconciliation in motion. Anyone about to offer an offering to God must first be reconciled with the offender (Mt. 5:23, 24).[21] He must take the initiative, which requires him to adopt a forgiving attitude. It is noticeable that in the story of the prodigal son the father takes no steps to urge the prodigal to repent, but he certainly takes the initiative in the actual reconciliation. His readiness to forgive the prodigal is implicit.

We may sum up the synoptic teaching on the theme of forgiveness under four main statements. (i) God's readiness to forgive is implied, although there is more evidence for the demand for people to forgive one another. (ii) It is assumed that forgiveness can follow only from repentance and must be accompanied by a forgiving spirit. (iii) Some connection exists between the work of Christ and forgiveness, although it is true that the death of Christ is only once said to be for the remission of sins. (iv) Forgiveness seems always to relate to sin or sins or debts, and not to renewal of fellowship, although this follows from it. Those who embark on the Christian life must both have experienced the free pardon of God and possess a willingness to forgive others. There is no place in the kingdom for those who have never accepted forgiveness. It puts everyone at once in God's debt and provides a cause for thanksgiving (as with the prodigal's father) and a motive for love (as with the sinful woman).

---

[21] There is no need to suppose that Mt. 5:23 implies that a person fulfilling his temple duties is at fault, *cf.* D. Hill, *Matthew* (NCB, 1972), p. 122. The saying is concerned with disputes between fellow disciples of Jesus. P. Bonnard, *Matthieu* (CNT 1963), p. 64, notes that in contemporary Judaism reconciliation was enjoined, but in order not to defile the temple or oneself, not as here out of respect for a brother.

The Johannine literature

When we turn to the fourth gospel, we find a great deal about faith (or rather believing), but very little on the other themes. Repentance does not occur at all and forgiveness in only one passage. Our main preoccupation will therefore be the theme of faith.

FAITH

We note first that the noun does not occur in John's gospel, although the verbal form is frequent. The purpose of the whole book is that the readers might 'believe' (Jn. 20:30–31), and it is not surprising that it contains so many statements relating to believing, either in the sayings of Jesus or in John's own comments. There are, in fact, more than 100 occurrences of the verb in this gospel. It is all the more striking because the noun occurs so frequently in other parts of the NT (more than 100 times in Paul). In the synoptic gospels there are more than twenty occurrences. Various reasons have been given for John's avoidance of the noun. It could hardly have been by accident, nor could it have been due to a desire to avoid the terminology of Hellenistic mysticism (as for instance *gnōsis*, knowledge), for the noun *pistis*, faith, is not prevalent in such literature.

There seems little doubt that the preference for the verb was occasioned by the need to stress the act of believing more than the content, because throughout this gospel faith is a matter of relationships and not of creed.[22] This is borne out by the fact that more cases of the verb followed by the preposition *eis* (with the meaning 'trust in') occur in John's gospel than anywhere else in the NT.[23] It has been said that this usage (and the less frequent use of *epi*) probably originated in Christian circles in order to differentiate between mere belief and personal trust. Neither the LXX nor koinē Greek had grammatical constructions to differentiate between the two uses. At the same time John does not always use the prepositions to denote 'trust', but sometimes expresses the same idea with the simple dative. What is most important to notice is that Jesus as teacher is bound up with his teaching as the object of faith.

We note that faith is sometimes seen in terms of the acceptance of the message, *i.e.* the belief that what is said is true. The disciples after the resurrection believed 'the scripture and the word which Jesus had spoken' (Jn. 2:22). Faith is more frequently directed to Jesus himself and involves an element of trust in him (Jn. 4:50; 8:30; 12:11; 14:1). In some instances faith is prompted by the works which Jesus did (*cf.* Jn. 2:11; 10:38). The

---

[22] *Cf.* C. H. Dodd, *The Interpretation of the Fourth Gospel* (1953), pp. 179ff.
[23] *Cf.* J. H. Moulton, *Grammar of NT Greek* 1 (1906), p. 68. *Cf.* also R. Schnackenburg, *John* 1 (*HTKNT*, Eng. trans. 1968), pp. 558ff.

supreme importance of a personal faith in Jesus is seen throughout the gospel.

There is no doubt that salvation comes as a result of faith. John comments in his prologue, 'But to all who received him, who believed in his name, he gave power to become children of God' (Jn. 1:12).[24] Thus faith is the means by which people are inaugurated into the new community, seen as a family. In this opening section of the gospel a clear distinction is made between believers and the world, a distinction which is reflected throughout the gospel. It is faith which secures eternal life (Jn. 3:16) and lack of it that leads to condemnation (Jn. 3:17). If the latter seems harsh it must be remembered that it is the natural consequence of the former. If Jesus' claim to bring life, abundant life (Jn. 10:10, 28), is true, then refusal to accept it on his own terms is tantamount to rejecting his whole mission. Jesus charged his opponents with not believing in him because he told them the truth (Jn. 8:45). Those who really 'hear' God's word in the sense of believing its truth are said to be 'of God'.

To believe in Jesus involves a radical transformation.[25] If John says nothing about repentance, it is certainly not because no repentance is necessary. There is need for a renunciation of the world. The crowds at the feeding miracle see no further than physical bread, but when they recognize that Jesus' view of life is essentially different from their own, they have no part with him (cf. Jn. 6:66). The vivid contrast between their abortive efforts to make him king and his own spiritual teaching about eating his flesh and drinking his blood shows the chasm separating unbelief and faith. But how is a person to bridge the chasm? When Jesus says, 'You do not believe, because you do not belong to my sheep' (Jn. 10:26), he suggests that only 'his sheep' can believe. While there are passages which suggest a predetermined action of God to ordain some for himself (see the section of predestination, pp. 611f.), these must never be permitted to obscure the individual call to decision and faith without which no-one can inherit eternal life. What is most important to note is that faith involves renunciation of oneself.[26] Those who seek glory from men, bolstering each other up in this way, cannot believe (Jn. 5:44).

To appreciate the force of faith in John's gospel, it is necessary to

---

[24] There is some dispute whether this statement relates to the ministry of Jesus or to the activity of the Word in the OT period. R. E. Brown, *John* 1 (*AB*, 1966), pp. 28ff., takes the former view because he thinks most of the phrases in Jn 1:10–12 re-occur in the gospel in relation to the ministry. On the whole this seems preferable to the latter view. In this case the aorist *ēlthen* refers to a unique coming, *i.e.* the incarnation (*cf.* C. K. Barrett, *John* ²1978, p. 163).

[25] Bultmann, *TNT* 2, pp. 75–92, gives a detailed explanation of faith in Johannine theology under the caption 'Faith as Eschatological Existence'. He would agree that a radical transformation is involved, but expresses it in terms of 'desecularization' (p. 78), by which he means transition into eschatological existence. The believer is lifted out of secular existence, although he is still in the world.

[26] *Cf.* R. Bultmann, *TDNT* 6, pp. 223f.

recognize that faith has varying degrees. Though someone may not have attained to fullness of faith, his position is very different from an unbeliever who has no faith at all. When Thomas doubted, Jesus said to him, 'Do not be faithless, but believing' (Jn. 20:27). The faith of the Samaritans (Jn. 4:40) was different from that required from the readers in recognizing Jesus as Messiah and Son of God (Jn. 20:30–31), but was nevertheless faith.[27] Indeed the concept of faith is not a static once-for-all experience, but an on-going exploration.

As compared with the synoptic gospels, this gospel is more specific in showing Jesus requesting faith in himself from his followers. That faith is to be of the same kind as faith in God (Jn. 14:1). When Philip wanted to be shown the Father, Jesus called on him to believe that he was in the Father and that the Father was in him (Jn. 14:10). Moreover, another feature of this gospel is that faith relates to present experience, not merely to the future. Even eternal life has already begun, having been appropriated by the act of faith (Jn. 3:16).

In the Johannine epistles, the importance of faith is still evident. There is one mention of the noun (1 Jn. 5:4), *i.e.* of faith which overcomes the world.[28] But what is the content of this faith? The context implies that it is believing that Jesus is the Son of God (1 Jn. 5:5). It must not be supposed that this overcoming faith consists in no more than acceptance of a creed,[29] for this would put the statement out of line with the general tenor of this epistle and of the other Johannine literature. It is important to note that the noun (in verse 4) gives place to the verb in the affirmation (in verse 5), which therefore calls attention to a dynamic entrusting of oneself to Jesus as Son of God. 1 John is written to those who believe, in order that they may know that they have eternal life (1 Jn. 5:13). The close connection between faith and knowledge is thus brought out. A similar link between faith and love appears in 1 John 3:23.[30] Clearly faith is expected to have moral consequences and the idea of a mere intellectual acceptance is quite foreign to this group of literature. 1 John concentrates on the character of the life of faith. Believing leads to abiding. The initial act leads on to fellowship with God and to the process of sanctification. The close connection between believing in Jesus and confessing him is also found in this

---

[27] *Cf.* E. K. Lee, *The Religious Thought of St John* (1950), p. 232.

[28] J. R. W. Stott, *The Epistles of John* (*TNTC*, 1964), p. 175, commenting on the claim for faith made in 1 Jn. 5:4, notes that confidence in the deity of Jesus is one weapon against which error, evil, or the world cannot prevail.

[29] So E. F. Scott, *The Fourth Gospel* (²1908), p. 267.

[30] In 1 Jn. 3:23 faith appears to be the subject of a commandment, but the meaning seems to be that the keeping of commandments is a part of believing (*cf.* W. G. Kümmel, *TNT*, p. 303). Kümmel, *ibid.*, p. 299, thinks that in John faith is primarily an attitude and not 'intellectual agreement with a content of belief'. But no interpretation of faith which did not take account of the nature of its object could satisfactorily explain the Johannine use.

epistle (*cf.* 1 Jn. 4:15 and 1 Jn. 5:1). This shows that faith in Christ is not secretive but open. Again we are not to restrict 1 John 4:15 to a confessional formula,[31] although it may be present in embryonic form. Faith of this kind arises from experience, not from an intellectual assent to a credal statement.

Before concluding this brief survey of faith, we note that the initiation process is sometimes expressed in other terms. It amounts to receiving him (Jn. 1:12), or hearing his voice (Jn. 5:24; 6:45; 8:43, 47; 12:47; 18:37) in an effective way, *i.e.* obeying it, or seeing him (Jn. 6:40; 12:45), or knowing him in an initial sense (Jn. 14:7, 9; 17:23). This rich variety of terms shows the wide connotation of the act of faith. It is essentially response to an invitation of God. God presents to us his Son and we are bound to make a decision about him.[32] If we receive him, obey him, see him, know him, our response is affirmative. If we do not respond in these ways, we have no faith. We are classed with those who have rejected God's provision.

FORGIVENESS

It is unexpected that there is only one statement in John's gospel on the theme of forgiveness and even that is not without its problem. It is a word of the risen Lord, following his breathing on them with the words, 'Receive the Holy Spirit' (Jn. 20:22). As a result Jesus declared, 'If you forgive the sins of any, they are forgiven; if you retain the sins of any, they are retained' (Jn. 20:23). There is probably a parallel to this saying in Matthew 16:19; 18:18, where in the former Peter and in the latter the body of disciples are given authority to bind and loose. We are not justified in seeing the statement in John as a secondary version of Matthew's saying,[33] since no mention is made of sins in the binding and loosing sayings, and the dependence of one upon the other is less credible than the assumption that they are independent sayings.[34] The link with the special outpouring of the Spirit at once marks a distinction (see the discussion on pp. 533ff.). Yet what does the Johannine saying mean? Does it relate to sins against God or to sins against one's fellows? To whom were the words addressed, to a select group or to a group representative of the whole church? These are questions which must be faced, but our present interest is in the nature of forgiveness. One interpretation which must be rejected is that the words

[31] As I. H. Marshall notes, *The Epistles of John* (*NICNT*, 1978), p. 220, this is not simply a statement about the metaphysical status of the Son of God, but an expression of obedient trust in him.

[32] John does not leave the object of faith undefined, as his statement in 20:31 shows. The kind of faith he is writing about is that which confesses that Jesus Christ is the Son of God. For a concise summary of what faith in this gospel does, *cf.* A. Corell, *Consummatum Est: Eschatology and Church in the Gospel of St John* (1958), pp. 128–139.

[33] *Cf.* V. Taylor, *Forgiveness and Reconciliation* (1956), p. 11.

[34] *Cf.* L. Morris (*NICNT*, 1971), p. 847 n. 58.

invest in an ordained ministry the power of absolution;[35] for even if the words relate exclusively to the ten apostles, there is no hint given that this facility would be passed on to a special group. Moreover, such a view is not supported by any other NT evidence.

The real key to the understanding of this passage is that the verbs (are forgiven, are retained) are both in the perfect tense. This means that they refer to accomplished facts. It suggests that people can forgive or retain only what has already been effected in heaven. Their function is therefore a declaratory function. There is no suggestion, moreover, that the sins are of individuals. It is more probable that the passage relates to classes of sins. What seems therefore to be in mind is that the Spirit will guide his people to know what class of offences may come under the forgiveness of God and what class does not (*cf.* the case of Ananias and Sapphira in Acts 5). If this interpretation is correct, the forgiveness in question is God's forgiveness declared through his people for sins against God. It excludes any possibility that man can forgive independent of God's forgiveness. This is, therefore, in line with the synoptic gospels, although it goes further in attributing the ministry of forgiveness to the Holy Spirit, which is illustrated in the book of Acts.

That divine forgiveness is an ongoing need for believers comes across sharply in 1 John. 'If we confess our sins, he is faithful and just, and will forgive our sins and cleanse us from all unrighteousness' (1 Jn. 1:9). Such a statement shows the need for repentance within the Christian life, rather than before. But this is the sole condition for forgiveness. Since 1 John is concerned with the maintenance of fellowship with God, provision for the removal of any barrier to that fellowship is essential (*cf.* 1 Jn. 3:5; 5:16). It is for this reason that the theme of expiation is so prominent. Sins are said to be forgiven 'for his sake' (1 Jn. 2:12). Whereas forgiveness is final as far as past sins are concerned, the present imperfections of the Christian life need provision for cleansing and we are indebted to 1 John for making this so clear. We shall need to discuss below the question of sinless perfection in this epistle (see pp. 666f.).

SPECIAL NOTE ON REGENERATION IN THE JOHANNINE LITERATURE

It is necessary at this point to note a particular feature of the teaching in John's gospel, which has a bearing on the theme of new life. It concerns the new birth which comes to explicit expression only in John 3. When Jesus told Nicodemus that he must be born anew, *i.e.* in a spiritual sense, his meaning was not at first understood (*cf.* Jn. 3:4). The words of Jesus implied something so radical that it cannot be effected by man's own

---

[35] *Cf.* R. E. Brown, 'The Kerygma of the Gospel according to John', *Int* 21, 1967, pp. 387–400 (esp. 391). In some respects Brown holds that the apostles in John are symbols for all Christians, but he makes an exception for Jn. 20:23.

efforts. The new birth is the work of the Holy Spirit (Jn. 3:5) (see discussion on p. 527). It requires a supernatural activity to transform a man into a new creature.[36] It is for this reason that Jesus called it a birth from above. It is undeniable that Jesus was expecting more than a deepening of understanding in Nicodemus. He was not called upon to initiate moral reforms. Nothing short of a complete renewal would satisfy the meaning of Jesus' words.

Nicodemus' scepticism, based on a literalistic notion of new birth, which in fact reduced it to an absurdity, is strongly answered by Jesus' affirmation of its spiritual character. This means that it cannot be explained in terms of natural phenomena. The new birth involves a person's exchanging his old nature for a new nature, an acceptance of a new kind of origin, an entry into a new relationship with God.[37]

The concept of new birth is first hinted at in John 1:13, where those who believe in Jesus received power to become children of God, and this experience is then defined as being born by the will of God. Since in John 3 the new birth is specifically linked with the kingdom, it is seen to be a vital factor in the initiation process. It has links both with the repentance-faith approach and the 'in Christ' development. It is important to note in fact that it is in this same gospel that Jesus speaks so specifically of the need for the disciples to abide in him. It is a natural outcome of the new birth that the new life must be sustained in spiritual ways.

The concept of new birth is also found in 1 John. Believers are regarded as those who are born of God (cf. 2:29; 3:9; 4:7; 5:4; 5:18).[38] John affirms that certain spiritual consequences follow from the new birth. He asserts that no-one born of God continues to commit sin (3:9; 5:18). The person born of God loves others (4:7). Moreover, new birth leads to knowledge of God (4:7). Regeneration affects the believer in relation to the world, for he overcomes the world through his faith (5:4). This suggests that new birth leads to an entirely new appraisal of the 'world', a deliverance from its normal pull.

Regeneration figures explicitly in three other NT books, in Titus 3:5, which refers to 'the washing of regeneration and renewal in the Holy Spirit;[39] in 1 Peter 1:23, which states 'you have been born anew, not of

---

[36] R. E. Brown, *John* 1, p. 130, draws a distinction between the sense of *gennaō* as 'to be born' (as of a feminine principle) and 'to be begotten' (as of a masculine principle). But this distinction throws little light on the precise meaning of the passage, since the birth in question is spiritual in character and the agent is stated to be the Spirit.

[37] *Cf.* A. Ringwald, *NIDNTT* 1, p. 179.

[38] It is noticeable that although John is contrasting the children of God with the children of the devil, he never uses the expression 'born of the devil'. For a treatment of 'born of God' in 1 Jn., *cf.* R. Schnackenburg, *Die Johannesbriefe* (1975), pp. 175ff. He discusses the relation of the concept to OT and Jewish thought, mystery religions, gnosticism and early Christianity.

[39] For a discussion of the meaning of these words in Titus 3:5, *cf.* my *The Pastoral Epistles*, p. 205. The linking of regeneration and renewal here is significant because the second term refers to the quality of life

perishable seed, but of imperishable, through the living and abiding word of God';[40] and in James 1:18 which says that 'of his own will he brought us forth by the word of truth'.[41] The idea may be said to be assumed and is definitely connected with the concepts of renewal. It is moreover closely linked with Paul's teaching on adoption.

There is certainly no room in NT theology for the view that man can regenerate himself by developing his latent capacities.[42] All the allusions support the view that it results from an activity outside of man. Indeed no-one can effect his own new birth any more than he can bring about his physical birth. A rationalist explanation of Christian conversion is impossible. The new birth, in the NT sense, must be regarded as a miracle.

The processes of renewal which follow from regeneration are progressive and may be summed up as sanctification (see later section). Renewal cannot precede regeneration, but it does accompany it. The new-born person has already experienced the first stage of renewal. A discussion of this leads into the whole concept of new life in Christ.

Acts

It is clearly of great interest to follow through the requirements made by the first Christian preachers on their hearers, and we shall do this by noting what is said about repentance, faith and forgiveness.

REPENTANCE

When at the climax of Peter's speech on the day of Pentecost the hearers 'were cut to the heart', Peter exhorts them to 'repent and be baptized for the forgiveness of sins' (2:38); This sequence of conviction of sins, repentance and forgiveness has strong affinity with the testimony of the synoptic gospels. The same connection between repentance and forgiveness is found in 3:19; in this case the result is expressed in terms of the blotting out of

---

which results from the new birth. The word *palingenesia* (regeneration) is found only here and in Mt. 19:28, where it is applied to the whole creation. *Cf.* also R. A. Harrisville *The Concept of Newness in the New Testament* (1960), pp. 67f., who considers that 'regeneration' denotes the essence of the Jewish eschatological hope.

[40] It is most reasonable to see the 'Word' which brings about the new birth as the preaching about Jesus, rather than Jesus himself in the Johannine sense (Jn. 1:1–18). So E. Best, *1 Peter*, p. 95.

[41] M. Dibelius and H. Greeven, *James* (Eng. trans. *Hermeneia*, 1976 from *KEK*, 1964), pp. 103ff., discuss the possibility that the bringing forth might be understood cosmologically, but they reject this in favour of a soteriological interpretation which means that this is a reference to the new birth. They further prefer to think of rebirth here as a way of referring to conversion, rather than finding any mystical significance in it. J. B. Adamson, *The Epistle of James* (NICNT, 1976), pp. 75ff., also firmly rejects a reference to creation here, because the figure of begetting is never used for creation.

[42] For a review of the idea of regeneration (in its background and NT use), see the article on *gennaō* by F. Büchsel and K. H. Regnstorf, *TDNT* 1, pp. 665ff.

sins.[43] Repentance and forgiveness are declared to be gifts of God (5:31). They are, in fact, directly linked to the exaltation of Christ. In 11:18, Peter declares that God has given repentance to Gentiles 'unto life'. Before the Areopagus Paul declared that God commanded people everywhere to repent (17:30) in view of the coming judgment, and before Agrippa Paul makes clear that he was commissioned to urge the Gentiles to repent and turn to God and perform deeds worthy of repentance (26:20). This latter point is crucial for a true understanding of Paul's idea of repentance. The initial act must be followed through.[44]

In the case of Simon the magician, an opportunity for repentance was given (8:22), so that if possible the intent of his heart might be forgiven. But when Ananias and Sapphira sinned, they had to suffer drastic consequences without an opportunity to repent (5:1ff.). It would seem that their case was intended to be exemplary. In the book of Acts as a whole there can be no doubt that repentance was considered a *sine qua non* for admission into the Christian church. It is worth noting that whereas at first it was closely linked with baptism, this is not specifically stated in the later sections.

FAITH

The exercise of faith as an accompaniment of repentance and as an indispensable possession of Christians is amply testified in Acts. In fact the community are 'those who believe' (*hoi pisteuontes*) (2:44; cf. 4:4; 4:32; 9:42; 11:21; 14:23). The object of faith is sometimes the Lord Jesus Christ, or the Lord, (11:17; 14:23; 16:31; 19:4; 20:21; 24:24) and sometimes the word preached (cf. Acts 4:4; 17:11–12), while sometimes no object is given (4:32; 19:18). This evidence is sufficient to show that a personal faith in Jesus was a hallmark of the early Christians. The message of Jesus had to be received and believed before all that Jesus had done for people could be appropriated. In Acts faith is less than the full Pauline exposition of it, but is nevertheless equally indispensable. Since it is sometimes used of belief in the message and sometimes of belief in Christ himself, no clear cut distinction can be made between them.[45]

In many instances 'the faith' (*pistis*) is used to denote the Christian message (cf. 6:7; 13:8; 14:22). In other cases people are said to be 'full of

[43] In Acts 319, repentance is closely linked with, but is distinct from, conversion. According to Luke's usage, the former may relate to the past sins and the latter more specifically to turning to God, cf. E. Haenchen, *Acts* (Eng. trans. 1971), pp. 208. But the religious aspect of repentance must not be lost sight of. It was more than moral reformation. It was acknowledgment of rebellion in God's sight and sorrow because of it.

[44] I. H. Marshall, *Luke: Historian and Theologian*, p. 193, thinks that for Luke the content of repentance was undoubtedly moral as well as religious.

[45] R. Bultmann, *TDNT* 6, pp. 211f. notes that faith in the kerygma is inseparable from faith in the person mediated. There is no doubt that Luke brings out vividly in Acts the personal character of Christian faith.

faith' (6:5; 11:24). The expression 'door of faith' is used of the admittance of Gentiles into the community (14:27). In all these instances faith is a dynamic reality. There is no suggestion of mere acceptance of a creed, but this does not mean that there was no common basis of faith. The commitment of oneself to Christ involves acceptance of his mission and message.

FORGIVENESS

We have already noted the close connection between repentance and forgiveness in 2:38; 5:31; 8:22. A similar connection between faith and forgiveness is found in 10:43. Forgiveness as a blotting out of sins is seen as a prelude to times of refreshing (3:19). In every case some act or acts of sin are in mind and forgiveness amounts to the removal of an obstacle. Forgiveness certainly comes through Jesus Christ (13:38). Paul asserts in that Antioch sermon that people may be freed from whatever they could not be freed from by the Mosaic law (13:39). This close link between forgiveness and deliverance is expounded more fully in the Pauline epistles.

It is not surprising that Paul says some important things on this theme, since in his commission he was sent to the Gentiles that they might receive remission of sins (26:18). The theme is thus seen in every part of the Acts record. Wherever the gospel was proclaimed it carried with it the message of forgiveness.

Paul

The sequence of repentance, faith and forgiveness is not evenly distributed in Paul's letters, for faith receives much fuller treatment than the other concepts. This is understandable since the epistles were written to those already inaugurated into the Christian community. Nevertheless, it is worth considering certain aspects of each concept.

REPENTANCE

If we assess Paul's approach by the number of times he uses the verb 'repent' or the noun 'repentance', we shall have to conclude that he had little interest in the subject.[46] There is one occurrence of the verb and four of the noun.

In 2 Corinthians 12:21 Paul is concerned that some of the Corinthians have not repented of their sins and he fears he will need to mourn over them because of this when he visits them.[47] In Romans 2:4 he challenges

[46] E. P. Sanders, *Paul and Palestinian Judaism*, points out that Paul makes virtually no use of the strong Jewish emphasis on repentance and forgiveness (p. 499). He explains this by maintaining that they do not respond to the real plight of man. Paul did not come to understand man's plight by analysing his transgressions, but on the basis of God's work in Christ.

[47] In 2 Cor. 12:21 repentance is not related to soteriology but to conditions within the Christian community. As P. E. Hughes, *2 Corinthians, ad loc.*, points out, the lack of repentance on the part of some shows that their heart was not right with God.

the readers to remember that God's kindness is intended to lead to repentance. The opposite of this is a hard and impenitent heart (Rom. 2:5). This comes in a context in which Paul is showing the universality of sin. His clearest statement on repentance comes in 2 Corinthians 7:9, 10, where, after remarking that the grief caused by a former letter had led to his readers' repentance, he maintains that godly grief leads to repentance, which in turn leads to salvation. It is clear, therefore, that he regards repentance as a *sine qua non* for continuance in the full fellowship of the redeemed community.[48] In 2 Timothy 2:24f. the Lord's servant is required to act in such a way towards his opponents that God may perhaps grant them repentance that they might come to a knowledge of the truth. It has sometimes been supposed that Paul regards repentance as taking place after, rather than before, conversion. But this would fail to take into account the fact that his letters were all written to those who were already Christians. Repentance for Paul was an ongoing necessity wherever sin had marred the individual's life and witness.

Although the above evidence is sufficient to show the importance of repentance for the apostle, it needs supplementing by other considerations. Paul has a thorough appreciation of man's condition of sinfulness. His understanding of salvation is that man cannot save himself, but that God has provided a way of saving him. His doctrine of justification has to do with God's provision for the sinner, but he never suggests that man himself has no part in it. God's gift of righteousness needs only one response, *i.e.* to be received. Nevertheless, the response of faith implies a refutation of all that belongs to unrighteousness. Since Paul argues that a man cannot continue in sin in order to experience more grace (Rom. 6:1), he shows that he is making a basic assumption that a justified man cannot be unrepentant. A deliberate refusal to admit any sovereignty of sin over the believer necessarily involves a rejection of former sins. No-one can remove the guilt of his own sin, for Christ alone can do that; but he can and must change his attitude towards sin and accept an entirely different norm. Paul can talk of Christians being ashamed of their former lives (Rom. 6:21; *cf.* also Eph. 2:3; Col. 3:5ff.).[49]

Nevertheless, the comparatively little emphasis on repentance and forgiveness has led some to conclude that Paul gave no adequate answer to the removal of guilt from those who had transgressed.[50] But in view of Paul's doctrine of justification there can be no doubt that he sees Christians

[48] Paul's statement here cannot be made to mean that he regarded repentance as a *ground* for salvation, as Calvin rightly noted. As P. E. Hughes, *op. cit.*, p. 272, comments, Paul's concern is not with the ground of salvation, but with the commendation of repentance.

[49] As C. E. B. Cranfield, *Romans (ICC*, 1975), 1, p. 328, remarks, 'The mention of their being ashamed is by no means otiose for to be ashamed of one's past evil ways is a vital element in sanctification.'

[50] *Cf.* J. Knox, *Chapters in a Life of Paul* (1950), pp. 141ff., who considers that sin has two equally important aspects, as transgression and as power.

as delivered not only from the power of sin, but also from its guilt.[51] It is of course true that the term 'guilt' is even more rare in Paul than repentance. It occurs only in 1 Corinthians 11:27 and it would be reasonable to deduce from this that the guilt aspect is not the most dominant feature in Paul's thought. It is rather implied that specifically expressed.

FAITH

The teaching of Paul on faith is particularly rich and is the most varied in the NT. There is no denying that faith was central both to Paul's experience and to his theology. The appropriation of salvation was, for him, solely effected 'by faith'. As with other NT writers, Paul sometimes uses the word *pistis* to refer to God, in which case it means his faithfulness (Rom. 3:3; 1 Cor. 1:9; 2 Cor. 1:18; 2 Tim. 2:13). He is seen as entirely reliable in keeping his word. That word can therefore be unhesitatingly trusted. 'He who calls you is faithful, and he will do it' (1 Thes. 5:24). It is on the basis of God's faithfulness, that there are sayings in the Pastorals which can be described as 'faithful sayings' (1 Tim. 1:15; 3:1; 4:9; 2 Tim. 2:11; Tit. 3:8).[52]

It is against this background of God's faithfulness, that Paul's use of *pistis* for man's faith in God must be examined. There is no question of man being expected blindly to put faith in one who has not shown on every hand that he is dependable. But we need to consider in what ways, according to Paul, the response of faith is effective. We note first that faith is essentially acceptance of God's message.[53] It is man's response to the preaching of the gospel (1 Cor. 1:21; Eph. 1:13). Indeed, the apostle maintains that 'faith comes from what is heard, and what is heard comes by the preaching of Christ' (Rom. 10:17). The object of faith is Christ, and Christ comes to have meaning only through faith. The evidence of the response of faith is in the confession with the lips that Jesus is Lord (Rom. 10:8ff.). This involves, therefore, a definite decision about Jesus Christ. Faith in this sense of the word is not divorced from the understanding.[54] Although the gospel is the 'power of God for salvation' (Rom. 1:16), *i.e.* it is not a

---

[51] E. P. Sanders, *Paul and Palestinian Judaism*, pp. 500ff., in commenting on Knox's position, admits that Paul is more interested in the conception of sin as power, but considers that his lack of adequate response to sin as transgression is because he sees man's plight mainly as bondage.

[52] According to J. N. D. Kelly, *The Pastoral Epistles* (BC, 1963), p. 54, the formula 'This is a trustworthy saying' has Jewish precedent and some close parallels in Greek literature. In this case it may not distinctively draw attention to God's faithfulness, although a Jewish or Greek formula would be invested with new meaning when employed in a Christian setting.

[53] Bultmann, *TNT* 1, pp. 315f., maintains that for Paul the acceptance of the message in faith takes the form of an act of obedience. Man is expected to surrender his previous understanding of himself. He also says that faith always has reference to its object, *i.e.* it is always faith in . . . Bultmann's interpretation of faith is strongly influenced by his existentialism.

[54] F. Prat, *The Theology of St Paul* [2] (Eng. trans. [2]1933), pp. 241f., considers that Paul's description of Christian faith contains three elements: an intellectual element, confidence, and obedience. But this threefold summary does not give sufficient emphasis to the notion of personal commitment to Christ, although the three elements named are undoubtedly important.

product of man, but a dynamic provision of God, it is nevertheless only powerful to those with faith (*cf.* 1 Cor. 1:18). It is moreover concentrated in the Christ of the cross, *i.e.* in Jesus and his whole mission culminating in the cross.

Closely linked with this view of faith, is Paul's view of faith which is integral to his doctrine of justification (see pp. 502ff. on the justifying work of Christ). To him justification, seen as the establishing of a right relation between God and man, can be achieved only through faith. This is the burden of his discussion in Romans 1–8. His starting point is the quotation from Habakkuk 2:4 in Romans 1:17 ('He who through faith is righteous shall live'). He sees righteousness as a gift. Man can do nothing to earn it. But if it is a gift, it needs to be received and this is an act of faith. The classic statement of this is Romans 3:21ff., which speaks of 'the righteousness of God through faith in Jesus Christ for all who believe' (Rom. 3:22). Paul goes on to say that people are justified by his grace as a gift (Rom. 3:24) and that the propitiation which God has provided has to be received by faith (Rom. 3:25). It is this firm conviction that causes the apostle to refute so strongly any possibility that justification can be by works (Rom. 3:27ff.). He knows from his own experience that faith is the antithesis of self-achievement. To believe in Christ is the cessation of believing in oneself. Boasting is automatically excluded.

Faith for the apostle is not simply the initial act of acceptance of God's free gift, but involves a continuing process.[55] When he says that God's righteousness is revealed 'through faith for faith' (Rom. 1:17), he is expressing this progressive character of faith.[56] It is because faith is not simply the accepting of a justifying act of God, but the establishing as a result of a new relationship with Christ. This focuses on Paul's 'in Christ' and 'Christ in you' expressions which will be considered later (see pp. 647ff.). But it is important to note here that faith develops. It is dynamic, not static (*cf.* 1 Thes. 1:3). Paul said that the life he was now living in the flesh, he was living 'by faith in the Son of God, who loved me and gave himself for me' (Gal. 2:20). The new life was seen as a continual act of faith, a continual appropriation of what Christ had done for him. This does not lessen the once-for-all character of justification, but highlights the constant grip of faith upon it.

Faith is also seen as commitment to the new life, which is manifested in varying degrees. It can be deficient, in which case it provides the motive

---

[55] L. Cerfaux, *The Christian in the Theology of St Paul* (Eng. trans. 1967), p. 146, in discussing the place of faith in the Christian life calls it the chief theological virtue.

[56] This expression (*ek pisteōs eis pistin*) has received many different interpretations. Those which understand the first *pistis* in any sense which differs radically from Habakkuk may be ruled out. See C. E. B. Cranfield's discussion, *Romans*, 1, pp. 99f. It is most likely that the phrase means, as Barrett suggests (*Romans*, BC, 1957, p. 31), faith from start to finish, emphasizing the indispensability of faith.

for the earnest prayer that its deficiency may be met (1 Thes. 3:10). The increase of the Corinthians' faith is seen as opening further opportunities for the preaching of the gospel (2 Cor. 10:15, 16). Abraham's developing faith is cited as an example for others (Rom. 4:20–21). Though faith may begin weakly, it can grow in strength as the new life develops. Not only individuals (Phm. 5), but whole Christian communities may become known by their faith (Rom. 1:8; Eph. 1:15; Col. 1:4; 1 Thes. 1:8). Faith is not so indefinite as to escape detection once a person has it. It amounts not simply to assent to the Christian message, but also to a worthy and manifest commitment to the Christian way of life. It is this quality of faith that was noised abroad.

We should note that within the community of believers, some are said to possess the gift of 'faith', which must mean special faith (1 Cor. 12:9). Faith in this case is a specific gift of the Spirit and probably refers to those called upon to exercise faith of a special intensity (*cf.* 'the prayer of faith' in Jas. 5:15).[57] But Paul insists that even that kind of faith is valueless if it is divorced from love (1 Cor. 13:2). He gives no mandate to a superfaith which regards itself as superior. The gifts are meant for service, and love takes precedence over faith.

We must note in concluding this survey of Paul's teaching on faith that on occasions he used the word with an article, to denote the sum total of what Christians believe. Some scholars cannot accept that Paul would have approached faith in this stereotyped, almost credal way. It has been supposed that the references in the Pastorals to 'the faith' (linked with 'the truth' and 'the deposit') are alien to Paul, the creative theologian (*cf.* 1 Tim. 1:2; 3:13; 2 Tim. 4:7; Tit. 1:13).[58] But there are ideas in other epistles which may be quoted as parallels. Galatians 1:23 is possibly an example, for Paul is reporting that it was said after his conversion that he now preached 'the faith' he previously sought to destroy. In 2 Corinthians 13:5 Paul urges his readers to self-examination to determine whether they were 'in the faith'.[59] This could be interpreted of the act of believing, but is more likely to refer to the object of believing.

The ambiguity may be an indication that for Paul these aspects were not mutually exclusive. For him faith would always be more than a body of doctrine. Yet at the same time we cannot suppose that Paul was not

[57] H. Conzelmann, *1 Corinthians* (Eng. trans. *Hermeneia*, 1975, from *KEK*, 1969), p. 209, considers that faith here is the ability to perform miracles. J. Héring, *1 Corinthians* (Eng. trans. 1962), p. 127, considers faith is a special charisma, especially manifest in miraculous cures.

[58] M. Dibelius and H. Conzelmann, *The Pastoral Epistles* (Eng. trans. *Hermeneia*, 1972, from *LHB*, 1955), p. 13, maintain that the usage of *en pistei* in 1 Tim. 1:2 is not Pauline, but is characteristic of a later time. The only definitely later passages which are cited in support are Polycarp, *Phil.* 92:122. But this evidence in no way shows that it could not belong to Paul's own time.

[59] A. Plummer, *2 Corinthians* (1915), p. 376, understands *pistis* here as a comprehensive term for the principles of the new spiritual life.

concerned with the objective side (*cf.* Phil. 1:27,[60] where the expression 'the faith of the gospel' occurs). It is not unnatural that a community, bound together by faith in the one Lord and committed to the same exalted view of him, could speak of their common salvation as 'the faith'.[61]

FORGIVENESS

There are only two occurrences of the noun 'forgiveness' (*aphesis*) in Paul's epistles and these are parallel expressions. Ephesians 1:7 has 'in whom we have redemption through his blood, the forgiveness of our trespasses', and Colossians 1:14 has 'in whom we have redemption, the forgiveness of sins.' It is significant that in both these statements forgiveness is linked with redemption but in neither case is there any mention of faith.[62] The only time Paul uses the verb (in the passive) is in Rom. 4:7 in a quotation from Psalm 32:1–2 ('Blessed are those whose iniquities are forgiven'). To these references must be added the allusion to God's forbearance in passing over (*dia tēn paresin*) former sins (Rom. 3:25),[63] and the reference to God not counting trespasses against man (2 Cor. 5:19).

Although there are few specific references to Paul's doctrine of forgiveness, the idea is basic to Paul's theology. Justification would be meaningless if the justified man had no assurance that his sins were forgiven. Similarly, reconciliation with God would be equally unintelligible if the burden of guilt were not removed. Indeed Paul's doctrine of death to sin in Romans 6 is but another way of expressing forgiveness, but in a more dynamic form. Not only is sin forgiven, but is also robbed of its power, of its very life. Paul is specific that this has been achieved by the death of Christ. It may be true that he nowhere makes the statement that Christ died that we

---

[60] R. P. Martin, *Philippians* (*NCB*, 1976), p. 83, understands this statement to refer to faithfulness to the apostolic teaching.

[61] In one case the unique expression the faith of Jesus is used (Rom. 3:26). It cannot be construed here as subjective genitive, as the parallel phrase relating to Abraham's faith in Rom. 4:16. Paul must mean the faith of which Jesus is the object, *cf.* J. Murray, *Romans* 1 (*NICNT*, 1959), p. 121.

[62] E. P. Sanders, *Paul and Palestinian Judaism*, pp. 499ff., discusses the virtual absence of repentance and forgiveness from Paul's thought he maintains that his main starting point was not transgressions but faith in the gospel message, leading to participation in the Spirit and the consequent recognition of a new lordship. Sanders notes the contrast between Paul and Judaism in this respect. But he does not accept Colossians or Ephesians or the pastorals as Pauline, and his interpretation is coloured by this. J. Knox, *Chapters in a Life of Paul*, pp. 141ff., thought that Paul's choice of justification rather than forgiveness led to his not offering a solution to guilt. For other discussions of Paul's view of forgiveness, *cf.* P. Schubert, Paul and the NT Ethic in the Thought of John Knox', and C. F. D. Moule, 'Obligation in the Ethic of Paul', in *Christian History and Interpretation* (ed. W. R. Farmer, *et al.*, 1971), pp. 363ff. Some scholars consider that the absence of the forgiveness theme in Paul was because he regarded sin as power, *cf.* R. Bultmann, *TNT* 1, p. 287; G. Bornkamm, *Paul* (1971), p. 151. Mary E. Andrews, 'Paul and Repentance', *JBL* 54, 1934, p. 125, maintained that for Paul repentance was replaced by something better, *i.e.* possession of the Spirit.

[63] Although in his forbearance God 'passed over' sins, yet as Matthew Black, *Romans* (*NCB*, 1973), p. 70, expresses it, 'a righteous God could not "connive at" iniquity'.

might be forgiven,[64] but there is reason to believe on the basis of Ephesians 1:7 and Colossians 1:14 that he could not conceive of forgiveness apart from the death of Christ.

Some have sought to make a distinction between forgiveness and restoration of fellowship, on the grounds that forgiveness relates to sins, not to people.[65] But the distinction is surely academic, since forgiveness is an essential part of the process of reconciliation. The obstacle (sins, trespasses) must first be removed before true fellowship can be restored. When the fellowship is with God, the nature of God demands that those in fellowship with him should be holy and blameless (Eph. 1:4) and this is possible only when sins are wholly forgiven.

Mention must be made of another word (*charizomai*) which is sometimes translated 'to forgive', although it never has this meaning in classical Greek or in the papyri.[66] Its meaning is 'to show favour'. It occurs in the following passages, however, in a different sense: 2 Corinthians 2:7, 10; 12:13; Ephesians 4:32; Colossians 2:13; 3:13. Here there is another dimension added to forgiveness, that of gracious dealing, applied both to God's dealing with us in respect of sin and of our dealing with each other.

Hebrews

In this epistle, all three of our present themes occur and involve some important statements. These must be set against the background of the danger of apostasy which may have faced some of the readers. Some of the statements are therefore dealing with a special case.

REPENTANCE

Of the three occurrences of the idea, one (in 12:17) deals with the rejection of Esau, who, although he sought to repent, found no chance to do so (or, literally, no place of repentance). This seems to mean that he had no opportunity to reverse the circumstances which had been brought about by his own sin.[67] It is cited as a warning for those who might imagine that the consequences of deliberate sin are negligible.

The other uses of the word repentance come in Hebrews 6 and are connected with the apostasy issue. 6:1 exhorts the readers not to lay again 'a foundation of repentance from dead works'. In no other NT literature is deadness applied to works (*cf.* 9:14). Dead works are presumably works which had only the appearance of being works, but lacked the power. The

---

[64] *Cf.* V. Taylor, *Forgiveness and Reconciliation*, pp. 3f.

[65] *Cf. ibid.*, p. 3.

[66] According to H. Conzelmann, *TDNT* 9, p. 396, the verb (*charizomai*) does not have the same meaning as the noun (*charis*), but is to be construed in the sense of 'give'. He finds in 2 Cor. 12:13, 17ff., a special sense of giving, *i.e.* pardoning.

[67] H. Montefiore, *Hebrews* (*BC*, 1964), p. 226, points out that for Roman jurists 'no place of repentance' would mean 'no opportunity for changing a former decision'.

Christians were obliged to regard the Jewish approach to justification by works as dead because the works could not achieve their end (*cf.* Paul's view of justification by works, pp. 501ff.). Jews who had become Christians had already had to repent of their reliance on works for their salvation, a process which could hardly be repeated. Some of the readers appear to have thought that this initial act could happen again, hence the warning against this view.[68]

Hebrews 6:4 is a more difficult statement about repentance. It asserts the impossibility of restoring to repentance anyone who, having tasted the heavenly gift, has committed the apostasy of re-crucifying the Son of God. This could mean only that such a person had identified himself with those who had crucified Christ. No apostasy could be more final than this.[69] It amounted to a complete negation of all that Christianity stood for. The renunciation of the core of the Christian message (the cross of Christ) could not be more total. This statement shows both the supreme importance of repentance for the Christian and the utter indifference of those who have renounced the faith (see further discussion affecting this on pp. 631ff.). Repentance here is a necessary prerequisite for a person to be a sharer of the Holy Spirit, *i.e.* it is a *sine qua non* of the Christian experience of new life.

FAITH

This theme is more dominant in the epistle. It is introduced in various ways, although the most significant is the catalogue of people of faith in chapter 11, and especially the statement about faith which opens the chapter. It is not intended to be a precise definition, but it gives an indication of the writer's approach.

He considers faith to be 'the assurance of things hoped for, the conviction of things not seen' (11:1). It should be noted that 'faith' here is without the article[70] and therefore may be considered in a general sense, although it has some particular bearing on Christian faith. If *hypostasis*, here translated 'assurance', is intended to bear that meaning, the sense would be that faith is certain that what is hoped for will happen. In this sense it is closely linked with the theme of the faithfulness of God, about which this epistle has much to say. But *hypostasis* can also mean 'essence' (as in 1:3), and if this is the sense implied here, it would mean that faith gives reality to

[68] It is significant that in this context 'repentance from' is linked with 'faith to'. Repentance involves a turning away from reliance on works and a turning to reliance upon God.

[69] As P. E. Hughes, *Hebrews*, p. 216, expresses it about the apostate, 'by a deliberate and calculated renunciation of the good he has known he places himself beyond forgiveness and renewal'.

[70] The anarthrous form of the word here does not imply any kind of faith, for the context clearly shows that religious faith is in mind. J. Héring, *The Epistle to the Hebrews*, p. 99, maintains that in this context faith takes the place of a proof of 'things' (*i.e.* invisible realities not rationally demonstrable). For a detailed discussion of faith in Hebrews, *cf.* E. Grässer, *Der Glaube im Hebräerbrief* (1965).

things that are hoped for.[71] Neither of these interpretations gives a meaning for faith in the Pauline sense of commitment to Christ. The further statement, which introduces the word 'conviction' (*elenchos*), may suggest that faith gives reality to what cannot be seen. If the two statements are parallel, this would support the view that faith has a demonstrating function.

The list of exploits of the men of faith that follows illustrates the persistence of faith in face of innumerable difficulties. Certainly hope and vision of the unseen play a major part in the list. When the writer moves to the end of his discussion he admits that these people without us cannot be made perfect (11:40) and then asserts that Jesus is the pioneer and perfecter of our faith (Heb. 12:2). The writer seems to think of Jesus as the inspirer of both the people of old and the people of his own day. In other words he considered that past ages were working towards a faith which was perfectly seen only in Jesus.[72] In this case the article with the word 'faith' implies that the expression is used comprehensively of the whole Christian position, but again there is an absence of that sense of personal commitment so dominant in Paul.

The Hebrews are urged to be 'imitators of those who through faith and patience inherit the promises' (6:12). The theme of imitation of faith recurs in Hebrews 13:7. In both instances faith is seen as steadfast persistence. It is paralleled in this epistle by the exhortation to hold fast (*cf.* 3:6; 10:23). It is because of this that faith and hope are closely linked.

In addition to the examples of faith, there is the striking illustration of the effects of unbelief in chapters 3 and 4. Unbelief barred entry into the promised rest. By implication it was only faith that could secure entry. The message the Israelites heard did not benefit them because it did not meet with faith in the hearers (4:2). This concept of faith in the message is the nearest Hebrews comes to faith as an act of appropriation. In 6:1 it is God, not Christ, who is the object of faith (*epi theon*). It may seem strange that the Pauline sense is lacking, but it must be borne in mind that the writer makes many assumptions about his readers. They already know 'the first principles of God's word' (5:12). They need to go on to greater exploits of faith.

FORGIVENESS

In one sense it may be said that this epistle concentrates on man's approach

---

[71] In addition to the two views mentioned, P. E. Hughes, *Hebrews*, 439ff., gives two further possibilities: 'foundation' (in the sense that faith stands under hope as its basis), and 'guarantee' (in the sense of an attestation of a document).

[72] P. E. Hughes, *Hebrews*, p. 522, considers that Jesus Christ himself is the man of faith *par excellence*, that his whole earthly life was the embodiment of trust in God. F. Rendall, *Hebrews* (1883), p. 121, denies that *tēs pisteōs* in Heb. 12:2 can mean 'our faith' because the context does not support the introduction of the pronoun. Montefiore, *op. cit.*, p. 215, considers that a reference to the faith of Jesus is improbable because the next clause is concerned with the end of his life. But his reasoning is not clear.

to God. Forgiveness is specifically mentioned twice (9:22; 10:18). The first connects forgiveness of sins with shedding of blood, which shows a basic link with the sacrificial system.[73] The same goes for the second mention which maintains that where sins are forgiven (as in the new covenant, *cf.* Je. 31:33–34 which is cited in this context), there is no longer any offering for sin. Forgiveness under the new covenant is still based on sacrifice, but a non-repeatable sacrifice. The writer's view of forgiveness is intimately linked with his doctrine of the atonement. Indeed, in the two chapters mentioned above, the idea of forgiveness is basic to the whole discussion of sacrifice.

The rest of the epistles
The evidence from the epistles of James, Jude and Peter will be grouped, but where relevant the distinctive contributions will be emphasized.

REPENTANCE
This theme occurs only in *2 Peter* 3:9, which stresses the Lord's desire that all should reach repentance. The importance of repentance is seen from the context in which this statement occurs, *i.e.* in the light of the coming day of the Lord. Although repentance is not mentioned by *James*, he commends those who turn back a sinner from the error of his way (Jas. 5:20), which implies a measure of repentance.

FAITH
All the letters mention faith and each has a distinctive contribution to make. *James* acknowledges that his readers 'hold the faith of our Lord Jesus Christ, the Lord of glory' (Jas. 2:1). He recognizes that faith, once it is initiated, needs testing (Jas. 1:3). It cannot be taken for granted. When someone prays he must do so in faith without doubting (Jas. 1:6). The prayer of faith can achieve healing (Jas. 5:15), but this kind of faith is parallel to the kind which is a gift of the Spirit (*cf.* 1 Cor. 12:9). In these passages faith amounts to trust in God, but in James 2:14ff. there is a different idea.

The concept of faith in James 2:14–26 is important, for it highlights a distinction between James' idea of faith and Paul's.[74] On this issue many have seen a contradiction, since James has been alleged to maintain salvation by works rather than by faith. But this would be a superficial understanding

---

[73] On the unusual occurrence of *aphesis* without qualification in Heb. 9: 22, *cf.* B. F. Westcott, *Hebrews*, p. 269. He considers that this focuses on the broad sense of 'deliverance, release'.

[74] J. B. Mayor, *James* ([3]1913, r.p. 1954), pp. 216ff., points out the different ideas of faith in James, and gives a clear exposition of the use in Jas. 2:14ff. He justifies the different usage on the grounds that James attaches different meanings to *peirasmos* and *peirazomai* (1:2, 13) and *sophia* (3:15, 17). James shifts from faith itself to profession of faith (*cf. legei* in 2:14).

of James. He is not discussing, as Paul does, the view that a man may be justified by works of the law. The kind of works that James is concerned about is the kind that results from genuine faith. In fact, the key statement in this passage is James 2:24 ('You see that a man is justified by works and not by faith alone'), which shows conclusively that justification by faith is not being combatted.[75] James is insisting that a faith which shows no results in practical ways is no real faith. It is dead (Jas. 2:17), and is clearly wholly different in kind from the faith which Paul presents as a person's commitment to Christ. Paul would have been as opposed as James is to mere intellectual assent. Even demons have that kind of belief (Jas. 2:19).

The kind of faith James is interested in is the kind exercised by Abraham. But Paul was also interested in that kind of faith. They both quote the same statement from Genesis 15:6; where James says that Abraham was justified by works, Paul says that he was justified by faith (Jas. 2:21–23; Rom. 4:2ff.; *cf.* Gal. 3:6). James cites Abraham's offering up of Isaac as an example of Abraham's works; from this it is clear that it is not the kind of 'works' in which Abraham could boast, the kind which Paul deplores. This very example demonstrates that James is looking on the active side and Paul on the passive side of the same thing, *i.e.* response to the word of God. It may well be that James is correcting a misunderstanding of Paul or vice versa, but it cannot be said that James and Paul are contradicting each other.[76] James lends no support to the view that man can do anything to earn his salvation.[77] But he gives a salutary reminder that initial faith must have a practical outcome. He is concerned about the social implications of a man's belief (*cf.* Jas. 2:15–16). It is worth noting that there is strong affinity between James' approach to faith and that of Hebrews. In the reference to Abraham's offering up of Isaac in Hebrews 11:17ff., it is specifically Abraham's faith in God's power to raise Isaac which is emphasized. The 'work' was essentially faith.

In *1 Peter*, salvation is firmly linked with faith. 'As the outcome of your faith you obtain the salvation of your souls' (1 Pet. 1:9). This aspect of faith as appropriation is also associated with the consummation of salvation

---

[75] If, of course, James' words about works *and* faith in Jas. 2:24 are taken to mean that salvation depends partly on works and partly on faith, this would at once place him at variance with Paul. For a discussion of this and a rejection of contradiction between James and Paul on this score, see the section on 'Faith and Works' in J. G. Machen, *What is Faith?* (1925), pp. 199ff. A. Schlatter, *Der Glaube im Neuen Testament* (⁴1927, r.p. 1963), discusses the approach of both Paul and James and compares them (pp. 323–466). While concluding that Paul's view is the richer, he acknowledges the value of James' presentation.

[76] R. V. G. Tasker, *James* (*TNTC*, 1956), p. 66, wonders whether the objector with whom James is debating might be appealing to some such idea as the diversity of gifts mentioned in 1 Cor. 12:10 and from it were deducing that faith and works were separable gifts. As Tasker points out, James strongly condemns such a dichotomy.

[77] R. J. Knowling, *James* (*WC*, 1904), p. xlii, suggests that 'faith' in this passage is faith in God, the kind of faith which would be shared by Jew and Christian alike. He compares the wrong sort of faith which James attacks with the picture of a Jew in Rom. 2:17.

(1 Pet. 1:5). Faith operates throughout until the full inheritance is secured. It is not surprising to find faith and hope spoken of in the same context (1 Pet. 1:21). Moreover, Peter recognizes the necessity for faith to be tested (1 Pet. 1:7). Its great value is said to exceed that of gold (*cf.* 1 Pet. 2:7). There is definite concern that faith should be genuine. Persecuted Christians are called on to entrust their souls to a faithful Creator (1 Pet. 4:19). When faced with the adversary (the devil) they are expected to stand firm in faith (1 Peter 5:9). This epistle is therefore particularly rich in references to faith. The people of God are essentially a believing people.

If *2 Peter* was sent to the same group of Christians as 1 Peter, it is not surprising that they are described as 'those who have obtained a faith of equal standing' (2 Pet. 1:1).[78] Even if they are different people, this epistle is an added witness to the importance of faith. It occurs as the bottom rung of the ladder of virtues expounded in 2 Peter 1:5–7,[79] which suggests that faith is the starting point which makes way for further developments (such as virtue, knowledge, self-control, love). These other virtues are unattainable until the step of faith has been taken. In the kindred epistle of *Jude*, the readers are to build themselves up on their faith which is described as 'most holy' (Jude 20). Moreover, they are to contend for 'the faith' (Jude 3), which shows a use of the term for the body of Christian truth, with which we have discovered some parallels elsewhere, especially in the Pastorals.

FORGIVENESS

There is only one specific reference to forgiveness in these epistles and that is in *James* 5:15, where the prayer of faith has power to save a sick man and to lead him into an experience of God's forgiveness of his sins. Although nothing is said about prior repentance, there is mention of confession of sins. The man himself must face the challenge to new moral demands when healing has been achieved.

In *1 Peter*, although the theme of forgiveness is absent, the idea of mercy is present. The readers are those who have now received mercy (1 Pet. 2:10). 'To receive mercy' is another way of saying 'to be forgiven', although it more precisely draws attention to the quality of the one who forgives (*cf.* Rom. 9:15–18; 2 Cor. 4:1; 1 Tim. 1:13, 16). Neither *2 Peter* nor *Jude* mentions forgiveness or mercy, but Jude speaks of God's ability to present his people 'without blemish before his presence' (verse 24). This looks

---

[78] E. Käsemann, 'An Apologia for Primitive Christian Eschatology', in his *Essays on NT Themes* (Eng. trans. 1960), pp. 169–195. (first published in *ZTK*, 49, 1952, pp. 272–296), maintains that 'faith' in 2 Peter 1:1 is 'the saved state of the citizens of heaven'. He links it with the apostles of Jesus who are specially elect. Faith certainly involves more than an act of committal here, but there is nothing to suggest that the more common usage is excluded.

[79] J. N. D. Kelly, *Peter and Jude* (BC, 1969), p. 306, draws a distinction between the meaning of faith here and in 2 Pet. 1:1. Here it is 'loyal adhesion to Christian teaching', but there it stands for the teaching itself.

ahead to the final consummation, but Jude expresses it in the form of a prayer which embraces the present ('keep you from falling').

Revelation
REPENTANCE

There are no fewer than ten occurrences of the idea of repentance in this book, and six of them are in the messages to the churches (2:5, 16, 21, 22; 3:3, 19). Only two of the churches escape the exhortation to repent (Smyrna and Philadelphia). It is evident that the repentance required is not an initial act, but a challenge to reform their Christian way of life. They must repent of what has been displeasing to God. The statement in 9:20–21, that in spite of the plagues men did not repent (*i.e.* of their evil ways), presupposes that even the judgments were intended to have a beneficial effect in re-pentance.[80] The same may be said of people's reactions to the bowls of wrath (16:9, 11). It is highly significant that, in a book which says so much about coming judgment, repentance, as a demand from God to men, should have so prominent a place.[81]

FAITH

Mostly in this book *pistis* occurs in the sense of 'faithfulness'. Christ himself is 'the faithful witness' (1:4; 3:14). When appearing as the final victor, he is called 'Faithful and True' (19:11). His words are thoroughly trustworthy (21:5; 22:6). It is not surprising therefore that those in the churches are exhorted to be faithful (Rev. 2:10) or are described as faithful (2:13; *cf.* 17:14). On a few occasions 'faith' is used in a more comprehensive way. It is linked with love (Rev. 2:19) and with endurance (13:10; 14:12). It is also described as 'my faith' (2:13) and 'the faith of Jesus' (14:12), in which case Jesus is clearly the object and not the possessor of faith. The sense of personal committal to Christ is not evident, but there is reason to think that it may be assumed. The purpose of this book was not concerned so much with the terms of admittance into Christian fellowship as with the challenges and destiny facing those who have already made such a commitment.

FORGIVENESS

This concept does not occur, but it may perhaps be implied in the idea of the saints' robes being washed in the blood of the Lamb (*cf.* 7:14). The people of God are certainly those who have been freed from their sins

---

[80] Yet, as R. H. Mounce, *The Book of Revelation* (*NICNT*, 1977), p. 204, points out, 'once the heart is set in its hostility towards God not even the scourge of death will lead men to repentance'.

[81] G. R. Beasley-Murray, *Revelation*, p. 248, rightly remarks that 'it is basic to the Revelation that the judgments of God should quicken the consciences of man as to the gravity of their rebellion against the God of creation'. This should lead them to repentance.

(1:5). It may be said to be assumed rather than stated as far as the 'saints' are concerned; the whole tenor of this book, however, reflects more on the theme of judgment on evil than on God's plan for sinful man.

GRACE

In the previous section we discussed the process of initiation into the Christian community. We noted the consistent emphasis on repentance and faith from man's side and the assurance of forgiveness from God's. That forgiveness related both to past and continuing sin. But our enquiries must now be pressed further. Forgiveness is itself an act of grace, but what part does grace play in repentance and faith? Arising out of the debate on this issue come the problems of predestination, election, perseverance and apostasy. We need to discover whether the NT presents any consistent account of these themes. It certainly does not present a systematic discussion, and it is clear that the systematic resolution of the problems never crossed the mind of any of the NT writers. It is perhaps in this area that NT teaching seems most paradoxical. As would be expected the problems come into clearer perspective in the epistles than elsewhere, but there is need to sift the considerable evidences in the other books, especially John's gospel.

Before coming to the variety of evidences we must first define the meaning of 'grace' and show why it has been used as an umbrella-title for the problems discussed in this section. Although there is a variety of ways in which the word *charis* (grace) is used in the NT, its most characteristic sense is the undeserved favour of God to those who deserved condemnation. In this sense it speaks of God's provision for man's salvation, especially in the mission of Jesus. Grace is therefore what God shows, as contrasted with what man does. Grace also involves God's provision for the Christian life, but this will be more specifically discussed in the sections dealing with the new life (pp. 641f.) and sanctification (pp. 661ff.).

The synoptic gospels
THE CONCEPT OF GRACE

The word *charis* (and its cognates) does not occur in either Matthew or Mark. In Luke's gospel it has a few uses which may be summarized as follows. In Luke 1:30 it is said to Mary that she has found favour with God, in a sense which makes clear that it is a continuous state (note the use of the perfect in the parallel description in Luke 1:28). The general sense of favour is in mind in Luke 2:40, 52 where the word *charis* is applied to Jesus. When Jesus began his ministry, his hearers were struck by his 'words of grace' (*i.e.* in the sense of being attractive, or appealing, Lk. 4:22). The expression here could be understood to refer to God's free favour proclaimed by Jesus (*i.e.* words filled with divine grace) or it could refer to pleasing speech or it could imply both.[82] In the other occurrences the cognate verb means the granting of a boon (*cf.* Lk. 7:21, 42–43), while *charis* itself is elsewhere used in the sense of thanks (*cf.* Lk. 6:32–34; 17:9).

The frugal evidence for the word and its associates is however of little relevance, since the concept of grace may not only be found in a number of incidental allusions which supply sufficient information to provide some kind of pattern, but is also basic to God's dealings with people in salvation. What we shall be concerned to discover is the relationship, in the teaching of Jesus, between God's gracious favour towards people and man's responsibility, and the place of both in the process of initiation into and continuance in the Christian life. The synoptic gospels are full of ethical exhortations which make considerable demands on the members of the kingdom, as for instance in the Sermon on the Mount. It must, however, be noted that these requirements are not conditions for entry, but rather norms within the kingdom. They depend on the prior acceptance of the gospel. The ethic of Jesus is an ethic of grace. None of the demands is expected to be carried out in human strength without the enabling of the power of God. But do these gospels give any indication of exclusion of members from the kingdom on the grounds of lack of fulfilment of the conditions? We shall consider first certain of the parables and then turn to other evidences.

INDICATIONS FROM THE PARABLES

Those parables we shall note are described as parables of the kingdom, and may therefore be taken to set out in the form of analogy the conditions of initial and continuing membership of the kingdom.[83] The application of the parables for this purpose will obviously depend on our understanding of the kingdom. If we think mainly of a future kingdom which has not yet begun, the point of entry will also be future. If, however, we think of a present aspect of the kingdom, a bringing forward of the future hope, membership now must somehow be tied up with future entry. The latter proposition is more in harmony with the NT teaching (see the section on the kingdom, pp. 409ff.), but it raises the problem whether present members can, in fact, lose their inheritance at the end.

The parable of the sower (Mt. 13:1–9, 18–23; Mk. 4:3–9; 14–20; Lk. 8:4–8, 11–15) shows that all increase depends on two factors: the seed and the soil. The seed, according to the interpretation given in Matthew, is the 'word of the kingdom' (Mt. 13:19), which contains within it the germ of life. No-one but God could fuse life into it. The sowing of the seed is the pronouncement of God's provision of grace. But the soils focus on the

---

[82] *Cf.* I. H. Marshall, *Luke*, p. 186.

[83] *Cf.* I. H. Marshall, *Kept by the Power of God*, pp. 44ff., who briefly considers the contribution of a number of parables to our present theme.

human response, which is clearly varied (some begin well and then for various reasons fall off, while only one class of soil out of the four produces fruit). What is most noticeable is the suggestion that some may believe for a time and then fall away (cf. Lk. 8:13). The crucial question is whether the believing represents true faith.[84] Since Matthew and Mark have 'endure' instead of 'believe' it seems evident that Luke's 'believe' may not mean full Christian commitment. On the other hand Luke uses the same word in 8:12, where it clearly relates to saving faith. In 8:12 however the verb is in the past tense and in 8:13 in the present continuous.

In the case of the interpretation of the parable of the weeds (Mt. 13:36–43), the field is said to be the world, not the kingdom. It cannot therefore be claimed that the kingdom will be a mixture of good and bad, and that finally some in the kingdom will be cast out. The main message of the parable is the clear-cut distinction between those who belong to the kingdom and those who do not in spite of present appearances. There is no suggestion that the weeds have any right to continued existence. It is only for the sake of the good seed that the destruction of the weeds is delayed. The parable, however, supports the view that in the world the distinction between true and false members of the community may be blurred.

A parable which focuses on the invisible yet certain operation of grace is that of the leaven (Mt. 13:33)[85] But this must not be taken to mean that the church will gain the whole world, for in that case it would conflict with the parable of the sower. The meaning must simply be that the effects of the kingdom cannot be judged by external appearances. It tells us nothing about the composition of the kingdom. The parable of the drag-net suggests that a mixture of people will be found in the kingdom, some good and some bad. The immediate discarding of the bad would not suggest that some had responded to divine grace, only to fall away later; rather the parable shows the clear-cut difference between those who respond (the good) and those who do not (the bad). The distinction is not in the nature of the proclamation (one net), but in the nature of those who come under the proclamation.

A parable which brings out clearly the operation of grace is the parable of the labourers in the vineyard, where the vineyard owner reserves the right to do what he wants with his own (Mt. 20:1–16). It is not a question of merit (i.e. amount of work done), but of promise.[86] The marriage feast

---

[84] E. E. Ellis, *Luke* (NCB, 1966), p. 126, regards the word 'believe' in Lk. 8:13 as 'probably an adaptation to the terminology of the post-resurrection mission'.

[85] J. Jeremias, *The Parables of Jesus* (Eng. trans. ²1963), pp. 146ff., sees the main point of both the leaven and the mustard seed parables to be a message of assurance. What seems so small will nevertheless achieve results.

[86] As Jeremias points out, in this parable none of the labourers received more than a subsistence wage (J. Jeremias, *Rediscovering the Parables* (Eng. trans. 1966), p. 28. The complaint about injustice is therefore an attempt to censure the kindness and compassion of the employer.

(Lk. 14:16–24) illustrates certain cases of invitations given but not accepted, with the consequence that those who declined excluded themselves from the kingdom banquet. If grace is seen in the invitations given, the qualification for entry into the kingdom is not unconditional. It requires the response of acceptance. Again divine initiative and human responsibility run parallel.

Similarly, the parable of the wedding garment in Matthew's account (Mt. 22:1–14) shows that more is required than simply attendance at the feast, for the man who arrived without adequate preparation showed contempt for the invitation and consequently excluded himself. It cannot be maintained from this parable that the kingdom is a mixed community,[87] for its real point is that those originally invited were not worthy, but that others, some of whom men considered unworthy ('good and bad', Mt. 22:10), would attend. There is no indication whether the man without the garment was from the good or the bad section.[88] If the garment is symbolic of God's provision of salvation, the message is clear: those who stand in their own strength have no part in salvation.[89]

Another parable which may contribute to the discussion is that of the virgins in Matthew 25:1–13, which, while it does not illustrate grace, has been thought by some to suggest that among the disciples will be those who do not ultimately gain admittance. The question is whether the foolish virgins represent real or only professing disciples. Since these were told by the bridegroom that he did not know them, it seems reasonable to suppose that they could not represent true disciples.[90] It would be precarious to base any concept of a possible forfeiting of membership of the kingdom on a parable of this kind. We may wonder whether the parable of the talents gives any indication of the idea of forfeiture (Mt. 25:14–30). But since the man who did not use his talent is assigned to Gehenna, this cannot apply to a true disciple. The implication is that a man who shows no recognition of having received anything is no true disciple.

In the parable of the prodigal son (Lk. 15:11–32), the readiness of the father to receive back the erring son is an illustration of grace, for the son had done nothing to deserve it, as the elder son noted. The father's gracious attitude was experienced by the son only when he showed a repentant approach. The elder son missed out because of his wrong attitude. The parable was an answer to the murmuring of the Pharisees, who found it

---

[87] So Marshall, *op. cit.*, p. 47.

[88] So Jeremias, *op. cit.*, p. 227 n. 90.

[89] Jeremias, *op. cit.*, pp. 149f., interprets the garment as God's provision of salvation after OT analogies. He mentions Jewish parallels in which repentance appears as a garment, but prefers the OT as a key.

[90] Marshall, *op. cit.*, p. 47, takes the view that the foolish virgins were meant to portray the professing disciples of Jesus as distinct from the true. He quotes approvingly R. V. G. Tasker, *Matthew* (*TNTC* 1961), p. 233, to the effect that the church contains both prepared and unprepared, though not necessarily in equal proportions.

inconceivable that God would bestow grace apart from any merit on man's part. The merit-conscious elder son was in fact incapable of even recognizing his father's grace towards his brother.[91]

OTHER INCIDENTAL INDICATIONS OF GRACE

The gracious character of God in wanting to give is illustrated in such passages as Matthew 7:7–12; Luke 11:9–13. All that disciples need to do is to ask, seek, knock. Even human fathers love to give. It is infinitely more so with God. His grace can be received for the asking. This shows clearly that although grace is an unmerited gift of God, there is human responsibility to appropriate it. Jesus does not discuss the question of those who refuse to ask. He does not, in fact, envisage a situation in which people will fall from grace after receiving it simply through their failure to ask.

There are several exhortations which demand effort on the part of disciples and imply disastrous consequences if that effort is not exerted. For instance, in Matthew 3:7ff., the need for fruit-bearing is stressed by John the Baptist, together with a warning that an unproductive tree is cut down and cast into the fire (cf. the similar ideas of Jesus in Mt. 7:15–20). There is, however, a close connection between character and fruit, which means it is incongruous to suppose that a bad character can produce good fruit, any more than a good character can produce bad fruit. There is no support here for the view that a believer would unpredictably bring forth bad fruit.

Faith itself is regarded as a gift of God, otherwise the disciples would not have asked for their faith to be increased (Lk. 17:5). Nevertheless, the answer Jesus gave suggests that faith, however small, is increased with exercise.

Certain other considerations are important. Do the repeated predictions of coming temptations and deceptions suggest that trials lay ahead which Christians would not be able to overcome? If so, then even some who now belong to the community by faith may not endure to the end. In what sense are such sayings as 'Lead us not into temptation' (Mt. 6:13; Lk. 11:4) and 'Pray that you may not enter into temptation' (Mk. 14:38; Mt. 26:41; Lk. 22:40, 46) to be understood? Do they imply that temptation is avoidable? It should be noted that the root meaning of 'temptation' is test, but that the meaning in these passages implies a test that could result in a fall.[92]

---

[91] Jeremias, op. cit., p. 104, regards this parable as essentially apologetic, which sets out against the view of the critics of Jesus God's unbounded love for repentant sinners. The murmurers were in effect limiting the grace of God.

[92] This sense of the word does not suppose that an escape route will be provided. It is therefore something to be positively avoided. Cf. S. Brown, Apostasy and Perseverance in the Theology of St Luke, pp. 15ff. A different concept of peirasmos is found in other NT passages, e.g. 1 Cor. 10:13 where an ekbasis (escape route) is provided. Brown contests Conzelmann's understanding of Lk. 22:28 of temptation which can have a positive outcome (i.e. of the disciples remaining with Jesus). But peirasmos here has a different meaning, i.e. danger (cf. I. H. Marshall, Luke, ad loc.).

It is clear that prayer can provide a buffer against such temptation. Divine grace does not leave the Christian without support in face of such tests. Nevertheless, nothing is said about the fate of those who fall.

At the conclusion of the parable about the unjust judge (Lk. 18:1–8), we meet the question, 'Nevertheless, when the Son of man comes, will he find faith on earth?' This follows the assurance that God will vindicate his elect. The question has been taken to imply the possibility that there will be no elect because they have apostatized through times of persecution,[93] but this is not the most reasonable explanation. The position of the elect is not in question since God's action on their behalf is assured. Luke's purpose in including this question of Jesus is to warn God's people to persist in faith and prayer, and the passage says nothing about those who do not persist.

We must note, moreover, that there are other references to the 'elect' in the synoptic gospels which may enable us to determine the meaning. There are three references in Mark 13:20, 22, 27. The 'elect' are here introduced without any definite information about them.[94] Yet it is clear that they are special objects of God's care (note the shortening of tribulation for their sake) and are to be gathered from all parts at the coming of the Son of man in glory. Matthew's one mention of the word occurs in the statement that many are called but few are chosen or elected (Mt. 22:14), which draws a specific distinction between invitation and choice, while at the same time implying that the chosen are those who, in fact, accept the invitation. Since this saying concludes the parable of the marriage garment, the 'chosen' ones are clearly those who are found acceptable at the feast, *i.e.* those who have accepted the terms of the invitation.

It is a moot point whether the idea of the 'chosen' in the synoptic gospels conveys any sense of predestination.[95] In so far as those who actually share the wedding feast are described as 'elect', these must be regarded from God's side as being predestined to share the kingdom. But these gospels give no indication of whether the elect could apostatize. The question does not seem to have arisen. It would be going beyond the synoptic evidence to suppose that either Jesus or the evangelists considered the 'elect' to be specially protected against the possibility of disobedience to God's call. As

---

[93] *Cf.* G. Schrenk, *TDNT* 4, p. 188.

[94] The ideas of Mk. 13:20f. are essentially Jewish. The shortening of an allotted span and the concept of the elect are found in Jewish writings (*cf.* V. Taylor, *Mark*, pp. 514f.). W. Lane, *Mark*, p. 472, thinks that Dn. 12:1 may have suggested the use of 'elect' here. In the OT sense the 'elect' are the 'remnant'. On the background to the shortening of days, *cf.* G. R. Beasley-Murray, *A Commentary on Mark Thirteen* (1957), pp. 80f. He considers that it is typical of our Lord's eschatological teaching that there is no unalterably fixed time-table of events. God's decision is therefore an act of grace.

[95] W. Hendriksen, *Matthew* (1973), *ad. loc.*, considers that this statement shows that salvation is the gift of God's sovereign grace. He takes the few as chosen from eternity and therefore supports predestination here. A totally different interpretation is put on this saying by E. Schweizer, *Matthew* (*NTD*, 1973, Eng. trans. 1976), p. 421, who considers that 'called' means taking up the initial invitation and 'chosen' means persevering to the end. But this is not a typical understanding of the word 'chosen'.

in the OT, so in these gospels, the elect are a special group, the people of God, who are aware of God's grace towards them. It is as erroneous to maintain that these gospels show the elect to be unable to resist God's grace as to say that the elect are capable of apostatizing. They show neither, only that the elect have found God's grace and it is assumed rather than stated that they will continue to do so.

We have earlier mentioned the unforgivable sin (see p. 580), but we need to consider whether this passage contributes anything to our understanding of the doctrine of grace. It will certainly have a bearing on the doctrine if it be maintained that a true disciple of Jesus could commit the unforgivable sin, and by that act place himself outside the realm of grace. There is some problem about the context of the saying since Luke does not place it in the Beelzebub controversy (Lk. 12:10), as both Mark (3:20–30) and Matthew (12:22–32) do. When seen against the background of the charge that Jesus was casting out demons by the prince of demons, the nature of blasphemy against the Spirit becomes clear. It amounts to calling good evil, a complete reversal of values which shows a man to be totally out of sympathy with the Spirit, without whose mediation no repentance or forgiveness is possible. It is difficult to see how a true disciple, who has been possessed by the Spirit, could reach a state of mind to declare that Spirit to be evil, thus reflecting a hardened state. Luke's context puts a somewhat different complexion on the saying by setting it in the midst of statements about confession of faith before men.

Some see, therefore, the distinction between blasphemy against the Son of man and the Spirit to be the difference between pre- and post-baptismal sin.[96] But this interpretation bears little relation to the context. It is better to suppose that although Luke's context differs, the saying probably means the same as in Matthew and Mark.[97] In both contexts, the emphasis falls on the warning against blaspheming the Spirit. Moreover Luke includes the Beelzebub controversy in his previous chapter. It could be argued that Luke's context for the blasphemy saying applies it to the disciples, whereas Matthew and Mark apply it to the enemies of Jesus. Nevertheless, even in Luke multitudes were present and it is not conclusive that the blasphemy saying was meant to apply to the committed disciples.[98] Indeed since they

---

[96] Cf. C. K. Barrett, The Holy Spirit and the Gospel Tradition (1947), pp. 105ff. Barrett thinks that Matthew and Luke must have thought that the Holy Spirit was a characteristically Christian possession. To blaspheme the Spirit was tantamount to apostasy. But to blaspheme the Son of man was the attitude of an outsider, who if he repented and believed would be forgiven.

[97] I. H. Marshall, Luke, pp. 518f., favours the view that the difference between Mark's form of the saying (with the sons of men's sins being forgiven) and Luke's 'Son of man' is due to different interpretations of an Aramaic original.

[98] I. H. Marshall, ibid., p. 511, considers that the presence of the crowds does not mean that the words are addressed to them. He compares this context with the sermon on the plain where crowds hear the teaching of Jesus to the disciples. Yet it cannot be said to be certain from Luke's context that the words are primarily addressed to those who have already become disciples.

were promised the aid of the Spirit in confession before the authorities, what relevance has the blasphemy saying to them? It seems precarious on the strength of this evidence to maintain that believers could become apostates.

Two other sayings in Matthew must be included for the sake of completeness. When Jesus commented that it would have been better for anyone who caused a 'little one' to stumble to have a millstone round his neck and be thrown into the sea (Mt. 18:6), did he imply that this could happen to a true believer? The context gives no indication of this and merely contrasts the attitude of receiving with the attitude of abusing. The extended passage Matthew 18:15–20 has been seen as probably making provision for excommunication (represented as being like a 'Gentile and tax collector', who were excluded from the community of Israel).[99] But this interpretation is not certain. The offender, by his own refusal to listen to the church, puts himself out of sympathy with the community. The question as to whether by that action he shows himself to be no true believer is simply not raised.

One problem which affects our understanding of grace is the position of Judas. Although one of the chosen apostles, Judas became the betrayer of Jesus. Jesus, in fact, foretold the betrayal (Mk. 14:17–21). Can Judas be held to be fully responsible for it? As compared with Peter, who denied Jesus and was yet prayed for by him, Judas appears to have gone his way without restraint. Was more grace extended to one than to the other? We are undoubtedly here faced with a mystery, but the gospels make clear how totally out of sympathy Judas was with the work and ministry of Jesus, and in this he contrasts radically with Peter and the other disciples. The case of Judas shows how classification among the people of God is not sufficient, unless there is identity of purpose with the plan of God.[100] In short, the divine choice and human response go hand in hand.

The Johannine literature

It is particularly to the gospel of John that we must turn for statements relating to predestination, both in the teaching of Jesus and in the comments of the evangelist. The evidence from this source is as strong as the exposition of the theme in Paul's letters.

---

[99] *Cf.* I. H. Marshall, *Kept by the Power of God*, pp. 66f., who inclines to the view that an authentic saying of Jesus has been recast in the course of transmission.

[100] S. Brown, *Apostasy and Perseverance in the Theology of Luke*, pp. 82–97, discusses at length the apostasy of Judas, and insists that Luke's account makes clear that the apostasy was the result of a deliberate choice on Judas' part. He goes as far as to say, 'In pledging himself to the mammon of iniquity Judas has in fact concluded a pact with Satan himself' (p. 85). He gets over the problem of Judas being one of the twelve by maintaining that the appointment or choice of Jesus related to the number and not specifically to the individuals. But this view tends to impersonalize the choice of Jesus.

THE GRACIOUS ACTS OF GOD

The prologue, which sets the scene for the whole gospel, has much to say about grace. The statement that it is the true Light (= the Word) which enlightens every man (Jn. 1:9) shows the importance attached to God's activity in the world. It was the Word in whom life dwelt and who became light to men (Jn. 1:5). In other words the dispelling of darkness was an act of grace. The central feature of God's plan of redemption (the incarnation) was entirely brought about by the divine initiative (Jn. 1:14). Indeed, the coming of the 'light' into the world met with resistance: 'his own people received him not'. Yet those who 'believed' in his name were given power (authority) to become sons of God (1:12), which is brought about, not by man's will, but by the will of God (1:13). In this introductory section, therefore, John is expressing strongly his conviction that believing in Jesus and becoming a member of God's family is the result of an operation of grace.

John follows up his point with the statement 'from his fullness have we all received, grace upon (*anti*) grace' (1:16).[101] The source of spiritual life for believers is seen to be the fullness of the Word, again an act of sheer grace. The expression 'grace upon grace' literally means 'grace over against grace'. The idea seems to be that the more man experiences of grace, the more grace multiplies, or so it appears to the believer. The kind of grace that John is thinking of is that which has come through Jesus Christ (Jn. 1:17). He compares 'law' through Moses with 'grace and truth' through Jesus Christ. In this context therefore grace is seen as the antithesis to law. Law depended for its effectiveness on human effort in keeping it, whereas grace depended on the effectiveness of the source through which it came (*i.e.* Jesus Christ).

The word of Jesus to Nicodemus about the need to be born of the Spirit, as well as of the flesh (Jn. 3:4,5), is parallel to John 1:13.[102] Indeed the whole concept of regeneration is expressed in terms which assume the action of God (see pp. 585ff). In a physical sense no-one decides on his own birth, and the use of the analogy in a spiritual sense presupposes an act of grace. Jesus talks to the Samaritan woman about 'the gift (*dōrea*) of God' (Jn. 4:10), which is parallel to the grace of God. Whenever God gives, it is an act of grace.

---

[101] There have been various interpretations of this expression, but that which sees it as referring to the developing experience of grace seems best suited to the context. J. Moffatt, *Grace in the New Testament* (1931), p. 368, notes an interesting parallel from Philo, but the difference is that Philo speaks of graces in the plural.

[102] There is no real discrepancy between Jn. 1:12,13, where faith seems to be primary, and Jn. 3:3ff. where the new birth seems to be primary. As A. Corell, *Consummatum Est: Eschatology and Church in the Gospel of St John*, p. 195, rightly notes, John thinks theologically and not chronologically when describing this experience. Both the new birth and faith are equally gifts of God and no end is served in attempting to press a time-sequence on them.

Through the gospel the teaching of Jesus presupposes that God is at work in his mission. What Jesus does is what God sent him to do. The strong Father-Son relationship supports the view that the whole operation involved in the incarnation proceeded from the divine initiative and therefore is an expression of grace. There is no suggestion that God was responding to any merit in man.

THE GRACIOUS CHOICE OF GOD

The strong emphasis on God's initiative in grace predisposes us to expect indications in this gospel that God did not leave man's appropriation of salvation to chance. There are several passages which demand attention. We begin with the bread discourse (Jn. 6). 'All that the Father gives me will come to me; and him who comes to me I will not cast out' (Jn. 6:37).[103] 'No-one can come to me unless the Father who sent me draws him' (Jn. 6:44).[104] 'No-one can come to me unless it is granted him by the Father' (Jn. 6:65). These three statements leave no doubt that 'coming' to God, which means coming in a meaningful way (*i.e.* a way of faith), is not accomplished without a prior action on the part of God. He exerts a drawing power upon those who come.[105]

In John 8:47 Jesus says, 'He who is of God hears the words of God', which suggests that grace is needed before a man can rightly tune in to God. The Jews were flatly told that the reason they were not hearing those words was because they were 'not of God'. The passage gives no indication of the way in which anyone could be 'of God'. Jesus had just affirmed that these Jews were of their father the devil (Jn. 8:44), which presumably means they were under his influence. Those who were 'of the devil' were obviously not 'of God'.

A more crucial passage for our purpose is John 10:26–30, where Jesus makes five assertions: first, his critics did not believe because they did not belong to his sheep; second, he gives his sheep eternal life, which means

---

[103] Some exegetes consider that the second clause in Jn. 6:37 should be taken to mean that Jesus will welcome any who come, thus putting an emphasis on human responsibility. *Cf.* C. H. Dodd, *The Interpretation of the Fourth Gospel* (1953), p. 432; B. Lindars, *John*, p. 261; L. Morris, *John*, pp. 367f. However, the verb used (*ekballō*) is against this. C. K. Barrett, *John*, p. 294, says, 'The verse sums up the universalism, the individualism, and the predestinarianism of the gospel. Jesus rejects no-one who comes to him, but in coming to him, God's decision always precedes man's.' W. Hendriksen, *John* 1, pp. 234f., points out that Jn. 6:39 stresses human responsibility, whereas the previous statement is viewed from the point of view of divine predestination.

[104] On the force of the verb used here (*helkō*, draw), *cf.* A. Oepke, *TDNT* 2, p. 503, who concludes that 'the choice of grace and the universality of grace are both of a gravity and significance to shake the conscience'. For a discussion of the doctrinal implications of this word, *cf.* G. C. Berkouwer, *Divine Election* (1960), pp. 47ff.

[105] The believing community in John's gospel is seen as the Father's possession. As E. K. Lee, *The Religious Thought of St John* (1950), p. 169, points out, 'But no people can by its own choice become God's possession: it is only by God's grace that men are called into his fellowship.'

they will never perish; third, his Father had given them to him; fourth, no-one would be able to snatch them from the Father's hand; and fifth, Father and Son had perfect unity.

The unmistakable message of this passage is the certainty of God's protection of his own people. It is more a matter of preservation than of choice, but the latter implies the former. To maintain that God chose a flock to shepherd and then left it to its own devices removes all intelligible meaning from the idea of God's act of choosing. The emphasis throughout the sheep allegory falls on the security of the sheep. The divine care for the believing community is contrasted with the careless attitude of strange shepherds.

It will not do to claim that Jesus meant to imply that a man might pluck himself out of the Father's hand, *i.e.* by ceasing to follow the Shepherd.[106] This would detract from the force of the promise and the effectiveness of grace. It is highly questionable whether Jesus intended this in the present context. Those looking for assurance need a strong conviction in the divine power to protect.[107] Such a conviction finds other support in John. Jesus declares it to be God's will that he should lose nothing of all that God had given him (Jn. 6:39). In his prayer in John 17, Jesus states that he has kept those whom the Father has given him (verses 6, 11, 12).[108] This prayer cannot be restricted simply to those who had been with Jesus on earth, for he continues to pray for all who are to believe in him (17:20).

There is no reasonable doubt that a strong conviction about the sovereign operation of God among his people pervades John's presentation of Christ.[109] It is not possible to water it down. Attempts are made to make the 'drawing of God' (Jn. 6:44) coincide with the believer's own coming, in the form of the surrender of his own self-assertion. Faith then becomes an understanding that God is working in him. Although surrender of self is undoubtedly involved in the act of faith, this view empties the divine influence of its supernatural content. There is no doubt that a true under-

---

[106] *Cf.* E. Jauncey, *The Doctrine of Grace* (1925), p. 42, for this view.

[107] Bultmann, *TNT* 2, p. 77, has a different view of assurance when he says, 'As faith that hears, it is to itself the proof of its own assurance'. In his opinion the expression, 'I know my own' (Jn. 10:14) must not be confused with any sort of guarantee, a view which considerably waters down the meaning of the words.

[108] B. Lindars, *John*, p. 521, maintains that there is no rigid doctrine of predestination in Jn. 17:6, and appeals to Semitic thought, which saw the whole contained in the beginning, to explain the impression of such a doctrine. Yet it cannot be explained away in this manner, for some notion of predestination is undoubtedly present.

[109] Bultmann, *TNT* 2, pp. 21ff., has a section on Johannine determinism, but this is really a misnomer in his approach since his interpretation is anthropocentric. On the Father's drawing in Jn. 6, for instance, he comments that everyone has the possibility of letting himself be drawn by the Father (p. 23). Yet this is not what John says. It virtually gives the power of choice to men and not to God. Bultmann explicitly says that the Father's drawing does not precede the believer's 'coming' to Jesus. The decision of faith takes place first. For a criticism of Bultmann on this point, *cf.* I. H. Marshall, *Kept by the Power of God*, p. 176.

standing of the text of John 6:44 requires us to take the drawing of God as previous to the act of faith.

One passage which focuses on election is John 15:16, 'You did not choose me, but I chose you.'[110] The purpose of the election is that 'you should go and bear fruit'. Can these words mean that God chose those who came to believe on him? The more natural meaning is that man's choice does not influence the choice made by Jesus. At the same time the believer has the responsibility of producing the fruit. The clear indication of God's sovereign purpose does not exclude the need for response on man's part. It is significant that the idea that Jesus had made a choice is repeated in John 15:19,[111] as if it were doubly important for the disciples at this stage to know this.

It is all the more significant that both these sayings occur in a passage in which believers are likened to the branches of a vine. The task of the branches is to produce fruit, but it is affirmed that this is not possible apart from Jesus the true vine (Jn. 15:5). This signifies a total dependence of the branches on the vine. The idea of abiding in the vine is akin to Paul's doctrine of 'in Christ' (see pp. 647ff.), but brings out even more vividly the sole source of life and fruitfulness for the believer.[112] Nevertheless, against this strong background of the dependence of the human on the divine, the statement that the fruitless branch must be cut out and burned (Jn. 15:6) presents a stark contrast. The statement is admittedly introduced by a conditional clause, but this must be regarded as a real possibility. The crux in this case is whether the fruitless branch was ever a real part of the vine. Since, however, in John 15:2, Jesus says that the Father will take away every branch in him (*en emoi*) which does not bear fruit, it is difficult to think that he had in mind those who were never disciples.[113] On the other hand those who abide in Christ are assured of bearing much fruit (Jn. 15:5), which shows that those bearing no fruit were not abiding in Christ.

Does Jesus mean to suggest that abiding in him is a human responsibility and that his own abiding in believers in a fruitful way is dependent upon

---

[110] It has been suggested that this passage, together with Jn. 6:70 and 13:18, should be restricted to the twelve. But against this view, *cf.* A. Corell, *Consummatum Est: Eschatology and Church in the Gospel of St John*, pp. 188ff. R. E. Brown, *John* 2, p. 683, considers that in Jn. 15:16, the Johannine Christ is addressing himself to all Christians, the elect and chosen of God. He suggests that in Johannine thought the twelve were models of all Christians.

[111] In this reference it is noticeable that the election is 'out of the world', which at once places the elect at variance with the world and open to persecution. As L. Morris notes, it is inevitable that the world reacts against Christians (*John*, p. 679).

[112] C. K. Barrett, *John* (²1978), p. 474, notes that Christian life apart from Christ is unthinkable, butnevertheless considers that it is not a static condition that John has in mind.

[113] I. H. Marshall, *Kept by the Power of God*, p. 184, maintains that since the burnt branches were once in the vine, they must represent believers, although he grants the possibility that these might be people who never passed the stage of intellectual belief. He nevertheless treats it as a warning to believers in general.

the believer's continued abiding in him? If the passage means that the continuance of the branches in the vine totally depends on human responsibility, there would be no basis for preservation, which would contradict the other statements in John. It seems best, therefore, to recognize the limitations of the vine analogy and to regard it as illustrating, not the final destiny of believers, but the appalling futility of fruitlessness.[114] Jesus was most concerned about glorifying the Father (Jn. 15:8). It is precarious to base a theological doctrine on a detail of an analogy, but its main point, abiding in Christ, is indisputable.

Another consideration which comes to the fore in John's gospel is the idea of eternal life as a present possession. Such statements as John 3:16, in which the believer is said to have eternal life, and John 17:2,[115] where the Son claims to have been given power to grant eternal life to all who have been given to him, and John 6:54, where Jesus says that those who eat his flesh and drink his blood have eternal life, show the present character of the life which is described as 'eternal'. The question arises whether 'eternal life' can be conditional. If it could, possession of it now would depend on perseverance in faith, and its quality as 'eternal' would not apply until after the end of this life when the possibility of losing it would be excluded. But such a view seems to be alien to the general tenor of the passages. While this point should not be pressed, it certainly supports the predestination passages already discussed. Nevertheless, the Johannine account is not without some insistence on human responsibility and this must next be considered.

HUMAN RESPONSIBILITY AND THE POSSIBILITY OF APOSTASY

In John 5:40 Jesus charged the Jews with refusing to come to him that they might have life. The refusal points to man's responsibility, but in no way bears on the possibility of falling away.[116] These Jews had never come near to accepting. Jesus set store on human freedom (Jn. 8:32–36), but the kind of freedom which he advocated was different from that normally meant by free will. It was a freedom linked to faith in Christ involving a commitment to the word of Jesus. There was certainly a measure of responsibility to continue in that word, which would be the sign of true

---

[114] L. Morris, *John*, p. 609, declines to see the cutting off of the branches as evidence that true believers may fall away. The emphasis, he maintains, is on fruit bearing.

[115] *Cf.* Barrett, *op. cit.*, p. 502, who regards this statement and others in Jn. 17 as showing that the idea of predestination is given prominence. He points out two differences between this idea and the gnostic view of a small circle of people foreordained to knowledge. These are that the believer's status rests on God's act and gift, and on the historical work and call of Jesus.

[116] The frequently repeated language in this gospel which lays on people the obligation to come (*e.g.* 6:35), or to hear (as 5:24), or to follow (as 8:12), or similar expressions of invitation have led Bultmann to approach the whole gospel from the point of view of human responsibility (*TNT* 2, pp. 21ff.). This is undoubtedly an aspect of John's theology, but it is not the controlling factor. There is a tension between the divine and human sides which is never formally resolved.

discipleship. But no suggestion is made in this passage that anyone really free would ever again come into bondage.

Another passage which speaks of the hardening of the heart in unbelief is John 12:36ff., where the hardening is seen as a fulfilment of Isaiah 6:10. Paradoxically, although this was true of the people as a whole, some believed, including some holding official positions. But again there is no suggestion that such hardness would come on any who had once believed.

The case of Judas needs some comment. In John 6:70 Jesus says to the disciples, 'Did I not choose you, the twelve, and one of you is a devil?' In referring to this saying John adds the comment that he was referring to Judas Iscariot, one of the twelve, who was to betray him. Not until John 13:27 does John say that Satan entered into Judas. There is the problem of Jesus choosing one who was a 'devil' among the twelve, but nothing in John's account suggests that Judas was a real disciple of Jesus in the sense in which he speaks of a faith-commitment. In any case Judas is clearly a special case and can hardly be regarded as evidence for a general possibility of falling away. In the strictest sense of the word Judas did not commit apostasy since he was out of sympathy with the real mission of Jesus. The mystery is not so much his betraying of Jesus as his being numbered by Jesus among the twelve. It is a mystery of the divine choice. It shows that God's choice need not necessarily result in true faith, although in all other cases it seems to have done so.[117] When addressing the disciples in the farewell discourses, Jesus reminds them that his teaching is to prevent them from falling away (Jn. 16:1). This appears to envisage a real danger if the warning is to have any relevance.

SIMILAR CONCEPTS IN THE JOHANNINE EPISTLES

In these epistles the word 'grace' occurs only once, in the familiar form of greeting in 2 John 3. Nevertheless the idea of grace is fully assumed in 1 John. It is asserted that God has made provision for those who sin, provided there is a right approach of confession (1 Jn. 1:6–10). There is an obligation to walk in the light, which draws attention to human responsibility. But the cleansing blood of Christ is provided as a continual means of grace. Moreover, this grace is not restricted, but is available 'for the sins of the whole world' (1 Jn. 2:2). The aim of the Christian life is to avoid lawlessness (*i.e.* disobedience, *cf.* 1 Jn. 3:4).

The believer is not expected to live in his own strength. He is born of God (1 Jn. 3:9; 4:17).[118] He is assisted by the Spirit of God (1 Jn. 3:24). Although he is expected to be without sin (1 Jn . 3:6; 5:18), he can achieve

---

[117] I. H. Marshall, *op. cit.*, p. 179, rightly notes that we are not entitled to conclude from Judas' case that in general divine choice does not lead to lasting faith.

[118] B. F. Westcott, *The Epistles of St. John* (³1892, r.p. 1966), p. 107, considers the *sperma* in 1 Jn. 3:9 is the ruling principle of the believer's growth, which God gives.

this only on the grounds that God's nature abides in him (1 Jn. 3:9). In no clearer way could John emphasize the gracious provision of God to enable people to live the new life.

There is a strong emphasis in this epistle, as in the gospel, on the preserving power of God. Those who are 'of God' are distinguished from those 'of the world' (1 Jn. 4:5,6). The distinction is so clear-cut that John assumes that all Christians are 'of God' (1 Jn. 4:4), or 'born of God', or 'children of God' (1 Jn. 3:10). Moreover, they can know God (1 Jn. 2:3) and love him (1 Jn. 2:5; 4:7) and obey him (1 Jn. 2:5; 5:3). The man 'born of God' has the assurance that God will keep him (1 Jn. 5:18). Moreover, the power of the evil one cannot touch him. The believer, therefore, has a considerable hedge against the possibility of falling away. Although John exhorts his readers to abide in Jesus Christ (1 Jn. 2:28)[119] and to keep his commandments, he does not suggest that they may not be able to do this. As in the gospel, so here, the powerful operation of God in the believer's life is sufficient to enable each one to overcome the world.

There is, of course, need for discernment, since counterfeit spirits attempt to lure away the people of God (1 Jn. 4:1ff.). But even here the issue is not left in doubt, for believers have someone greater with them, *i.e.* Christ (1 Jn 4:4), than is in the world.[120] Because believers are of God they are certain of gaining victory over these opposing forces (the antichrist, the world). It must be recognized, therefore, that 1 John breathes an atmosphere of quiet confidence, without denying the responsibility of man.

One passage which has drawn out much discussion is that which deals with the difference between mortal and non-mortal sins (1 Jn. 5:16–17). Does the passage mean that Christians can commit mortal sin? If the answer is affirmative, it must involve a fall from grace. But John does not say this. He is reminding his readers of the deadly effects of sin, but wants to assure them of the possibility of repentance for non-mortal sin. Is the distinction he is drawing between the sin committed by unbelievers (as mortal) and the sin of believers (as non-mortal)? It would make good sense to take it that way, but if so there would be no case for apostasy. John wants his readers to refrain from supposing that all sin is mortal.[121] If it be maintained

---

[119] The words 'abide in him' in 1 Jn. 2:28 are clearly imperative, although they echo the expression in the previous verse which may be either indicative or imperative. *Cf.* I. H. Marshall, *The Epistles of John* (NICNT 1978), p. 162, who takes 1 Jn. 2:27 in an indicative sense. Bultmann, *The Johannine Epistles* (Eng. trans. *Hermeneia*, 1973, from *KEK*, 1967), p. 41, maintains that the indicative includes the imperative. This indicative-imperative motive is of great importance in considering the tension between divine election and human responsibility.

[120] As J. R. W. Stott, *The Epistles of John*, p. 157, remarks, 'We may thank God that, although (it is implied) the evil spirit is indeed "great", the Holy Spirit is greater'. This means protection against error and victory over it.

[121] It should be noted that the distinction between mortal and non-mortal sins in 1 Jn. differs from the Roman Catholic distinction between mortal and venial sins. John gives no kind of classification, neither does he give a definition of mortal sin.

that the 'sin unto death' warning is specifically addressed to believers, it would have to be conceded that apostasy was in view. But it must be noted that the focus of attention in this passage is on those who sin 'not unto death' *i.e.* the passage is meant as an encouragement.[122] There is much to be said for the view that the mortal sin must be connected up with the blasphemy against the Holy Spirit or else deliberate apostasy from Christ (as in Heb. 6:4–6). The sin would in this case be a state of hardened impenitence.

Acts

The idea of grace is more prevalent in the book of Acts than in the gospels. Not only is this true of the word, but of the whole concept of the divine initiative in salvation. We have already noted the call to repentance in this book (*cf.* pp. 587ff.) and this is plainly seen against God's own provision (*cf.* 3:19). Grace is seen as a special endowment which could be recognized in those who possess it (as in 4:33;[123] 11:23). Grace is therefore more than God's favour towards sinners; it includes the state of grace of the recipient. Christians are people of grace. Sympathetic Jews and converts to Judaism at Pisidian Antioch were urged to continue 'in the grace of God' (13:43). The expression 'grace of God' cannot here represent the full state of salvation, but it is moving in that direction.[124]

In 14:3, the 'word of his grace' is synonymous with the gospel which the Christian preachers preached (*cf.* also 20:32).[125] In fact, Paul refers specifically to the 'gospel of the grace of God' when addressing the Ephesian elders (20:24). Luke says on two occasions that the Christian missionaries were commended to the grace of God (14:26; 15:40), by which is presumably meant that they were committed to God's gracious favour and protection. At the council in Jerusalem, Peter concludes his statement by saying, 'But we believe that we shall be saved through the grace of the Lord Jesus, just as they will' (15:11). This could mean that salvation was through his favour, or it could mean that salvation was secured through Jesus Christ and was recognized equally as an objective gift of grace both to Jew and Gentile. The latter fits the context better. It should be noted that in this passage, as in Paul's epistles, there is a close tie-up between grace and faith.

---

[122] *Cf.* R. Law, *The Tests of Life* (1909), pp. 135ff., for a discussion of this passage.

[123] It is not satisfactory to take grace in 4:33 in the sense of favour which Christians enjoyed as a consequence of their liberality. *Cf.* H. B. Hackett's comment on this (*Acts*, 1877, p. 75). F. F. Bruce, *The Book of Acts*, p. 109, sees a combined reference to the grace of God and the favour of the Jerusalem populace.

[124] It may be claimed that this use of grace approximates more closely to the characteristic Pauline sense of God's special gift in redemption and justification. *Cf.* R. B. Rackham, *Acts* (*WC*, 1901), p. 220.

[125] J. Moffatt, *Grace in the New Testament*, p. 362, sees this collocation of gospel and grace as peculiar to Luke. He considers that grace here denotes 'the extra-national extent of the gospel'.

Having surveyed these various uses of the idea of grace, we next turn our attention to evidences of predestination in Acts. The idea of God's choice is strong in this book. It begins with a recollection of Jesus' choice of his apostles (1:2). The prayer before the casting of lots was that through it God would reveal his choice (1:24). In his Pisidian Antioch address Paul reminds his hearers of God's choice in the history of Israel (13:17). It was God's choice that Peter was used to be the first to preach to Gentiles (15:7).

It is not surprising in view of this strong emphasis on the divine choice that certain statements in Acts focus on predestination. We may note in passing the conviction that the passion of Jesus was 'according to the definite plan and foreknowledge of God' (2:23). This is all the more remarkable since responsibility is squarely placed on the lawless men who crucified and killed him. There is no sense of incongruity between the two aspects. Peter declares that God had foretold by the prophets that Christ should suffer (3:18). In the Christians' prayer in 4:24f., the sovereign purpose of God is clearly affirmed and predestination is specifically mentioned (verse 28). This is the only place in the NT where the verb translated 'predestined' (proōrizō) occurs outside the Pauline epistles. Its root meaning is to choose beforehand, or to foreordain. In this context it implies that God has made previous plans for his people.[126] Through all the Acts speeches the same theme of God's overruling in the plan of salvation occurs. It is against this background of the sovereign operation of God's grace that certain statements about the predestination of believers must be considered.

We first note 13:48, where Luke comments that when the Gentiles heard the word of God 'as many as were ordained to eternal life believed'. This implies that the ordaining was prior to the believing, in which case an act of predestination is clearly being recognized. It has been maintained that since 13:43 refers to those already 'in the grace of God',[127] the ordaining refers to these and says nothing about other Gentiles who might have believed. But this goes beyond what Luke says. He seems to suggest that all who believed were those who had been ordained to eternal life. Luke is not interested in, because not conscious of, the alleged antithesis between divine choice and human freedom of will. What concerns him is that eternal life is not only received by faith, but is essentially the plan of God.

Two other passages confirm Luke's strong conviction that God is the initiator of salvation. He says the Lord opened Lydia's heart to heed what Paul said (16:14). In the account of Apollos' work, Luke says he 'greatly

---

[126] For a discussion of the meaning of this word, cf. I. H. Marshall, 'Predestination in the New Testament', *Grace Unlimited* (ed. C. H. Pinnock, 1975), pp. 127–143.

[127] Cf. I. H. Marshall, *Kept by the Power of God*, p. 84, in discussing Acts 13:43, suggests that if the people concerned were already 'in the grace of God' and were now led to believe the good news of Jesus, there is no question of there being other Gentiles who were not predestined to eternal life having no chance of believing. What is clear, as Marshall notes, is that the initiative in salvation remains with God.

helped those who through grace had believed' (18:27). In both cases an act of grace preceded the act of faith. 18:27 has been alternatively translated 'to help through grace those who had believed', but this is not the most natural understanding of the passage; the order of the words is against it.

When God assures Paul in a vision that he has many people in the city of Corinth (18:10), the question arises whether this is to be interpreted as relating to Paul's opportunity for evangelism or to those whom God was about to save. The former, while a possibility, is without parallel. When God is said to have or possess people, a special sense is involved, and the second alternative is more natural. It would have conveyed to Paul that God intended doing a work of grace among the Corinthians and would have provided strong encouragement to the apostle in face of opposition.

The three accounts of Paul's conversion in Acts all stress the overruling hand of God. He is a 'chosen instrument' (9:15; *cf.* 22:10; 26:16). When before Agrippa he says he was not disobedient to the heavenly vision (26:19), the question does not arise in Luke's account whether he could have disobeyed. Neither Luke nor Paul was interested in this speculative point. Both knew that it was impossible to decline a command which had so clearly come from God. There is complete agreement between Luke's account and Paul's epistles on the divine initiative in the calling and commissioning of the apostle.

Our survey of the Acts evidence would not be complete without some reference to the cases of Ananias and Sapphira and of Simon Magus. For our present purpose we are concerned only to enquire whether either of these accounts contributes anything to the discussion of the possibility of apostasy. Ananias and Sapphira are both convicted of an offence against the Holy Spirit (5:3,9).[128] The Christian church saw their immediate deaths as a judgment upon them. It could be supposed that in some way these people had committed the unpardonable sin. But Luke gives no information which makes it safe to draw this conclusion. We cannot with certainty say whether physical death involved exclusion from salvation. The passage is not intended to answer such a question.

According to 8:13 Simon believed and was baptized,[129] and yet Peter sternly tells him later when he wanted to possess the same powers and authority as the apostles that he had no part or lot in the matter (8:21) and that he was in the gall of bitterness and the bond of iniquity (verse 23). Nevertheless, Simon is offered the opportunity to repent and his request for the apostles' prayer on his behalf suggests that he was willing to do so.

---

[128] For a study of the Ananias and Sapphira incident, *cf.* S. Brown, *Apostasy and Perseverance in the Theology of Luke*, pp. 98ff. He interprets the sin as a failure to renounce property for the benefit of the poor, which he thinks was expected of all disciples. But Acts 5:4 seems to be against that interpretation.

[129] S. Brown, *ibid.*, pp. 110ff., also considers the case of Simon. He points out the differences between this incident and the Acts 5 passage.

We may, of course, wonder whether Simon was ever a true believer; but if he was not it is difficult to explain 8:13, unless it refers simply to a profession of faith. The Acts record may be said to leave open the possibility of a baptized believer apostatizing, but it does not specifically describe Simon as an apostate. Peter's words are a potent reminder of the seriousness of imagining that the Holy Spirit could be manipulated. On the whole it is better to regard Simon as a man who had never believed in the fullest sense, in which case the concept of apostasy does not apply.

Paul

PAUL'S EXPOSITION OF GRACE

Without doubt the doctrine of grace comes into clearer focus in these epistles than anywhere else in the NT. Yet because Paul makes statements on the subject of grace, predestination and free will which are both profound and enigmatic, his teaching has been the centre of controversy. We should note at once that since Paul had been brought up a Pharisee, he would not have been unfamiliar with discussions on predestination and human responsibility. He would have shared the conviction about God's sovereignty in the affairs of men, while at the same time considering man accountable for his actions.

We begin with a survey of Paul's conception of the grace of God.[130] It is not without significance that in all his letters, he includes 'grace' in his greeting at the beginning and in his salutation at the end. Grace is an extension of the normal Greek greeting (*chairein*), but filled out with the idea of God's favour. There is no denying that the grace of God was a dominant feature in Paul's theology.[131]

It looms large particularly in his doctrine of salvation in Romans. He declares that sinners are 'justified by his (*i.e.* God's) grace as a gift' (Rom. 3:24), although this is appropriated through faith. What grace provides, faith accepts (*cf.* Rom. 4:16). Hence, Paul can sum up salvation as 'by grace . . . through faith' (Eph. 2:8). When comparing Adam and Christ, he says that 'much more have the grace of God and the free gift in the grace of that one man Jesus Christ abounded for many' (Rom. 5:15). In this the free gift is contrasted with the 'trespass' brought in by Adam. 'Where sin increased, grace abounded all the more' (Rom. 5:20), but Paul hastens to

---

[130] J. D. G. Dunn, *Jesus and the Spirit*, pp. 203ff., suggests the following five usages of the term 'grace' in Paul's epistles: (i) of the historical event of Christ, (ii) of the grace of conversion, (iii) of the continuing experience of God, (iv) of individual endowments, such as 'grace given to me', and (v) of ministry resulting from grace. Dunn finds no essential difference between these varied usages. Grace is always God's action and the whole of life for believers is an expression of grace.

[131] D. J. Doughty, 'The Priority of *Charis*. An Investigation of the Theological Language of Paul', *NTS* 19, 1973, pp. 163–180, maintains that grace is prior to faith in Paul's theology. His article pays particular attention to the semantic function of the word *charis* in Paul's theological thinking. He seeks to correct Bultmann's approach by asking from what standpoint 'faith' is interpreted by Paul.

refute the suggestion that this gives licence for continuing in sin (Rom. 6:1–2). His purpose rather is to assert the effectiveness and extensiveness of grace (cf. Rom. 5:17). Paul does not hesitate to set grace over against law (Rom. 6:14), although he would not have denied that the law itself was an expression of grace (cf. Rom. 7:12). The distinction is that what the law could not do grace accomplished.

When Paul discusses the position of Israel in Romans 9–11, he speaks of the remanant as 'chosen by grace' (Rom. 11:5), and therefore not based on works. In this whole section Paul is conscious that both Jew and Gentile are equally indebted to God's grace.[132]

This strong conviction regarding the operation of God's grace is not confined to Romans. It occurs in the Corinthian epistles. In 1 Corinthians 1:4 the grace of God given in Christ is said to enrich the speech and knowledge of the Corinthians. Paul is deeply conscious that his own experience is due to the grace of God (1 Cor. 15:10)[133] which is operative in his work. Indeed, he contrasts the grace of God with earthly wisdom (2 Cor. 1:12) as the basis of his behaviour. He sees the extending of grace to more and more people in his ministry as contributing to the glory of God (2 Cor. 4:15). For the perfect exhibition of grace, he turns to Jesus Christ whose becoming poor for our sakes is seen as an act of grace (2 Cor. 8:9). The abundance of God's grace for human needs is strongly attested (2 Cor. 9:14;[134] 12:9). In only one place in the Corinthian letters is anything said about the acceptance of God's grace, for in 2 Corinthians 6:1 Paul entreats his readers 'not to accept the grace of God in vain'. The 'grace' must be defined in the light of the preceding statement, *i.e.* that Christ was made sin for us that we might become the righteousness of God in him (2 Cor. 5:21). It would certainly appear from this that Paul means us to understand that God's grace is not mechanical: it requires acceptance.

In the rest of the epistles the same pattern of dependence on the grace of God emerges. The calling of God to the believer is through grace (cf. Gal. 1:6, 15). That grace is freely bestowed on us (Eph. 1:6–7). Paul's circumstances as well as his work for God are seen as 'grace', which others can share (Phil. 1:7). The Colossians' experience of the gospel is said to have resulted from their hearing and understanding the grace of God in truth

---

[132] In this context the emphasis falls on God's power rather than on his grace. Yet as J. Murray, *Romans* 2, p. 89, comments, 'underlying the exercise of power is the recognition that the grafting in again is consonant with his counsel and the order he has established'. God's power is never arbitrarily exercised.

[133] O. Glombitza, 'Gnade – das entscheidende Wort. Erwägungen zu 1. Kor. xv. 1–11, eine exegetische Studie', *NTS* 2, 1958, pp. 281ff., understands Paul to mean in 1 Cor. 15:10 that when he does not live from grace, he is not what he is. This he bases on Ex. 3:14. This does not, however, illuminate the context. *Cf.* H. Conzelmann's dismissal of it, *1 Corinthians*, p. 260.

[134] In 2 Cor. 9:14, Paul significantly linked the superabundant grace of God with its production of a liberal spirit of giving in believers, *cf.* C. Hodge, *2 Corinthians*, p. 227. In no clearer way could Paul express the practical outcome of the effective operation of divine grace.

(Col. 1:6), a passage where 'grace' is equivalent to 'the word of the truth' (Col. 1:5). The giving of grace to Christians is likened to 'the measure of Christ's gift' (Eph. 4:7), which vividly expresses its inexhaustible quality (*cf.* also 2 Thes. 1:12; 2:16).

Although some scholars deny the Pauline origin of the pastoral epistles on doctrinal grounds, the view of grace found in these epistles is certainly Pauline. Justification is by grace (Titus 3:7). The whole plan of salvation is viewed as an appearance of grace (Titus 2:11). Here as in other epistles, Paul is aware of his personal indebtedness to the grace of God (1 Tim. 1:14). In 2 Timothy 1:9 the focus on the sovereign character of grace is unmistakable. Grace is given in Christ Jesus. Moreover, it is given 'ages ago', long before the historic appearance of Jesus Christ.[135] This grace, therefore, reaches back to the giving of grace in the mind of God.[136] Paul can nevertheless urge Timothy to 'be strong in the grace that is in Christ Jesus' (2 Tim. 2:1), so stressing the side of man's appropriation of God's grace.

There are three statements in Paul's letter to the Galatians which give the impression that it is possible to fall from grace. He is astonished that his readers have so quickly deserted 'him who called you in the grace of Christ' (Gal. 1:6). In doing so they had turned to a different gospel. 'Grace' here stands for the gospel which Paul had preached. Paul declares of his own position that he does not nullify the grace of God (Gal. 2:21). Moreover he says of those who are insisting on circumcision that they 'are severed from Christ' and 'have fallen away from grace' (Gal. 5:4). The question arises whether Paul regards them as having been true believers or whether he is maintaining that they had shown themselves not to be true believers by their preference for circumcision rather than grace. The apostle does not discuss here the problem of man's rejection of grace. His concern was to set grace against law as a means of salvation.

THE GRACIOUS CHOICE OF GOD

A consideration of those passages where Paul is specifically dealing with election and predestination must proceed from the strong emphasis on the grace of God as the effective agent in salvation. In writing to the Romans, Paul spells out his predestination theme in some detail.

We shall consider first the classic statement in Romans 8:28–30, which succinctly sums up the apostle's view of predestination. We note the fol-

---

[135] *Cf.* my *The Pastoral Epistles*, p. 129. J. N. D. Kelly, *The Pastoral Epistles*, p. 163, compares the statement here with Eph. 1:4. It is characteristically Pauline. Dibelius and Conzelmann, *The Pastoral Epistles*, p. 99, who do not accept the Pauline authorship of these epistles, nevertheless recognize here 'traditional Pauline teachings'.

[136] H. N. Ridderbos, *Paul: an Outline of His Theology* (Eng. trans. 1975), p. 348 n. 50, takes up the words *pro chronōn aiōniōn* in the sense of 'before inconceivably long periods of time'. He considers this statement sets 'antecedent divine grace over against human merit' (p. 349).

lowing four features: (i) Paul is convinced of *God's providential care* of those who love him and who have been called by him (Rom. 8:28). This suggests that for believers God is 'in everything' in control.[137] There is therefore a strong sense of God's sovereignty in Paul's words. (ii) *Foreknowledge by God* accompanies predestination (whom he foreknew he also predestinated, verse 29). (iii) The predestination relates specifically to *conformity to the image of God*. It does not relate primarily to initial salvation, although it cannot be referred exclusively to final salvation independent of the initial calling. It cannot, in short, be argued that God predestined those who had already shown their love for him, for this would not do justice to God's foreknowledge.[138] God's foreknowledge is knowledge of events prior to their occurrence.[139] (iv) *The sequence* – predestined, called, justified, glorified – bears this out. It would seem that Paul is here guarding against the assumption that man determines the predestination of God.

Yet when all this has been said, it must be admitted that the apostle is not dealing with predestination to faith. Indeed he is writing to those who already believe.[140] He enters into no speculation on whether a man can lose his justification. He rather takes it for granted that God's actions move in a straight line from predestination to glorification. So impressed is he with God's designs for man that he does not stop to ask the question over what happens when people reject those designs. He certainly does not speak of God predestinating unbelievers.

It has been maintained, in an effort to preserve man's freedom of action, that Paul does not say that *all* who are justified are also glorified.[141] This objection, however, cannot be sustained in view of the most reasonable interpretation of Paul's words in Romans 8:30, although a difficulty arises

[137] There has been much difference of opinion over both the text and interpretation of Rom. 8:28. It is preferable to accept the shorter text, which leaves the subject of the verb undefined, but which nevertheless implies that the subject is God; *cf.* the careful weighing of the evidence by C. E. B. Cranfield, *Romans* 1, pp. 424ff. He criticizes C. H. Dodd's view, which takes 'all things' (*panta*) in the sense 'in everything', and the verb *synergō* in the sense 'to co-operate with'. Cranfield considers that these ways of taking the words are not the most natural, *cf.* Dodd, *Romans* (*MNT*, 1932), pp. 137f. M. Black, 'The Interpretation of Romans viii. 28', in *Neotestamentica et Patristica*, Cullmann Freundesgabe (ed. W. C. van Unnik, 1962), pp. 166ff., takes the Spirit as the subject, but since the subsequent verbs cannot have the Spirit as subject, this is an unlikely suggestion.

[138] K. Grayston, 'Election in Romans 8:28–30', in *Studia Evangelica* 2 (ed. F. L. Cross), pp. 574ff., considers that the goal for mankind is predetermined, but the answer to the question whether we reach the destination or not is not predetermined. Yet this interpretation weakens the full force of God's foreknowledge and does not conform closely to Paul's stress on divine sovereignty, especially in chs. 9–11.

[139] F. J. Leenhardt, *Romans* (Eng. trans., 1961, from *CNT*, 1957), p. 233, interprets the force of the prefix in *proegnō* in the sense that God's regard rests on people before they are aware of it.

[140] H. Ridderbos, *op. cit.*, p. 350, rightly points out that this statement was intended as a pastoral encouragement for the persecuted and embattled church. The encouragement was based on the unassailable character of the divine work of redemption.

[141] I. H. Marshall, *Kept by the Power of God*, p. 93, thinks it is doubtful whether justification is inevitably followed by glorification. He bases this on the assumption that the aorists in this passage may be regarded as gnomic. But it must be admitted that it is more natural to regard the aorists as affirming the certainty of the process.

over the meaning of Romans 11:22 (God's kindness to you, provided you continue in his kindness; otherwise you too will be cut off). It must first be recognized that the words in Romans 11:22 were addressed to Gentiles, who are being warned that it is through no merit of theirs that they have been grafted on to the olive tree. It was through faith (11:20). Therefore they should stand in awe. The strong warning that Paul gives would have less force if it was impossible for the Gentiles to be cut off. There is therefore an element of human responsibility which must be set over against the predestination passage.

Further on in Romans 8 are two other statements which warrant attention. Paul asks the question, 'Who shall bring any charge against God's elect?' (Rom. 8:33), but he gives no further explanation of the elect. He must have had in mind those mentioned as predestined in Romans 8:29. He, in fact, uses the word 'elect' (*eklektos*) only six times, two of which do not refer to God's election of man. The precise expression 'elect of God' occurs in Colossians 3:12 (where it is linked with 'holy and beloved') and in Titus 1:1 ('to further the faith of God's elect'). The more general expression 'the elect' is used in 2 Timothy 2:10, where Paul says that he endures everything for their sake, 'that they also may obtain the salvation which in Christ Jesus goes with eternal glory'. This seems to mean that the elect are not those who have already obtained salvation, but are on the way to obtain it. It is final salvation which is here in mind, but the possibility that any of the elect will not obtain it is not discussed. We may conclude therefore that in view of Paul's usage elsewhere the 'elect' in Romans 8:33 are those who believe, who are an object of God's choice.

The second passage is that which states that nothing can separate Christians from the love of God in Christ (Rom. 8:35–39). This contains a firm assurance which Paul not only possesses himself, but assumes that all believers in Christ can also share. The assurance, moreover, does not rest on human response, but on the intercession of Christ (Rom. 8:34).

In the central section of the epistle (Rom. 9–11),[142] the sovereignty of God (chapter 9) is set side by side with the responsibility of man (chapter 10). The illustration of the potter and the clay shows God's sovereignty in an unmistakable form, although the analogy cannot be pressed, since man is more than a lump of clay. What Paul is guarding against is any assumption that man can dictate to God or question his plans. The OT speaks of the election of a nation, Israel, as in a special sense the people of God; but it also testifies to the way that nation, except for a remnant, rejected God's plan. Paul sees clearly that God cannot be held responsible for Israel's rejection, but at the same time his plans had not been thwarted by Israel's hardness of heart. The need for faith and human response is dealt with in

---

[142] For a discussion of the importance of Rom. 9-11 in Paul's theology of grace, cf. J. Moffat, *Grace in the New Testament*, pp. 254–273.

chapter 10. All with faith may be justified (Rom. 10:4). All who call on the name of the Lord will be saved (10:13).

Some reconciliation of God's plan and man's response is suggested in chapter 11. The key thought is that all Israel will be saved (11:26); but does this mean that every individual Israelite will be saved? Since this would not fit in with the general tenor of Paul's argument, it is best to regard the restoration of Israel as representative.[143] Paul never conceives of salvation apart from faith. His words are intended to be an encouragement to Jewish Christians, rather than a contribution to the philosophical discussion of predestination.

We turn next to Paul's statements in Ephesians 1:3–14, which provide another succinct summary of his position. He addresses himself to 'saints who are also faithful' (pistoi, Eph. 1:1), and declares that God has blessed us 'even as he chose us in him (i.e. Christ) before the foundation of the world' (verse 4). Paul goes on to explain his understanding of the divine choice. It is directed to ensure that Christians are 'holy and blameless before him'. It is further defined as predestination 'in love' of sons in accordance with his purpose, unless the words 'in love' should be joined to the preceding phrase 'before him'. It is moreover shown to have come from what Paul calls 'the glory of his grace' (or his glorious grace). This grace, in fact, is made part of us (charitoō) 'in the Beloved'.

There is no doubt in this whole passage that Paul is viewing salvation from the point of view of God's initiative and his intention that that salvation shall be brought to a successful conclusion. The process of redemption and the consequent forgiveness of sins is portrayed as an act of grace ('according to the riches of his grace which he lavished upon us', (Eph. 1:7, 8). God's purpose and plan are reiterated several times in the passage (verses 4, 9, 10, 11, 12). This is undoubtedly the focal point of Paul's thinking. When he says of the readers, 'In him also you who have heard . . . and have believed . . . were sealed with the Holy Spirit, which is the guarantee of our inheritance until we acquire possession of it' (1:13–14), it is difficult to see how his words can mean anything other than a definite assurance of the final inheritance for those who now believe.[144]

Nothing is said here about human responsibility and the passage does not therefore contribute to an understanding of the problem whether the eternally conceived plan of God can be frustrated. It must be admitted, however, that the general tenor of this Ephesians passage would not allow much scope for man to hinder the fulfilment of the divine will. As far as Paul is concerned in this passage, it is a great encouragement to him that

---

[143] This follows rabbinic practice. Cf. W. Sanday and A. C. Headlam, Romans (ICC, 1895), p. 336.

[144] Contra I. H. Marshall, op. cit., p. 97. Cf. also J. Farrelly, Predestination, Grace and Free Will (1964), p. 61, who considers predestination in this passage is to heaven, not to a state of grace. C. Spicq, Les épîtres pastorales (²1947), p. 58, considers that boulomai is used of the absolute decrees of God.

God will bring to pass what he has promised. Whatever the possibilities that some may not inherit the promises, there is no question here of Paul suggesting that either himself or his readers were to depend on their own persevering efforts to achieve their final inheritance.

There are certain passages in the Thessalonian correspondance which have a bearing on God's choice. In 1 Thessalonians 1:4 Paul says, 'For we know, brethren beloved by God, that he has chosen you'. He enlarges on this by claiming that the gospel came to them 'in word . . . in power . . . in the Holy Spirit . . . with full conviction'. (1:5). As a result they had 'received the word' (1:6). Again Paul wishes to emphasize the divine initiative, but he does not ignore the need for a human response (cf. also 1 Thes. 2:13). In a prayer in 1 Thessalonians 3:11ff., Paul asks that the Lord may make them increase in love and establish their hearts unblamable in holiness. A more specific reference to predestination is found in 1 Thessalonians 5:9: 'For God has not destined us for wrath, but to obtain salvation through our Lord Jesus Christ'. The divine election is again seen to be specifically concerned with salvation.

There is one passage in 2 Thessalonians which must be considered, i.e. 2 Thessalonians 2:13ff. Paul rejoices because God chose the Thessalonians 'from the beginning' (ap' archēs).[145] It has been suggested that these words could refer to the beginning of the preaching of the gospel at Thessalonica. But it is more natural to suppose that Paul is referring to a choosing before the call which came through the gospel (verse 14), a choice which must surely belong to the eternal counsels of God.[146] Nevertheless it must be noted that after mentioning the divine choice Paul exhorts the believers 'to stand firm' and to hold the traditions the apostles had taught (verse 15). Believers have received 'eternal comfort and good hope through grace'. There is, therefore, a nice balance between divine sovereignty and human responsibility, but the emphasis falls on the strong basis for Christian assurance.

In his Philippian letter, Paul says nothing about God's choice, but he asserts that he who has begun a good work in them will complete it (Phil. 1:6), which reflects not only the divine initiative, but the divine determination to see his people through. In the same epistle Paul maintains that God is willing and working in believers for his good pleasure (Phil. 2:13), although he urges them to work out their own salvation (Phil. 2:12).[147] He

---

[145] If the alternative reading is preferred, i.e. aparchēn, the comments made in the text would not apply. In this case the meaning would be that God had chosen the readers 'as the first converts' in Thessalonica. The textual evidence is nicely balanced, but ap' archēs is probably to be preferred.

[146] I. H. Marshall, Kept by the Power of God, p. 92, concedes the possibility that the act of choice preceded the historical call, although he favours the view that the call through preaching is in mind. He rejects the idea that 'arbitrary predestination' is implied, whichever interpretation is followed.

[147] Cf. R. P. Martin, Philippians (TNTC, 1959), ad loc., considers that the verb means 'effective working'. J. H. Michael, Philippians (1928), pp. 98ff., argues that salvation in this context is communal, not individual.

does not raise the question whether anyone would be unable to work out their salvation and would therefore lose it.

Throughout his epistles Paul expounds on God's care for his people. He is confident that the Lord will sustain his people to the end on the ground that God is faithful (1 Cor. 1:8,9; *cf.* 1 Thes. 5:24). For the same reason he will keep his people from evil (2 Thes. 3:3), and will not permit more testing than they can bear (1 Cor. 10:13). The faithfulness of God is, therefore, a guarantee that he will not fail his people. But does it equally guarantee that believers may not prove to be unfaithful? In the contexts so far considered the question has not been raised by Paul. We need, however, to consider what evidence he may give elsewhere for the possibility of apostasy among believers.

THE POSSIBILITY OF FALLING AWAY

One of the real problems in appreciating to the full Paul's teaching on predestination concerns the significance of his exhortations to perseverance in the Christian life. Throughout his epistles he makes much of the need to avoid sinful practices (*cf.* his 'put off' teaching, discussed later, pp. 657ff.). But since his doctrine of election does not presuppose a doctrine of perfection in this life (see pp. 670f.), the believer's continual conflict with sin is assumed. Moral challenges, however, do not in themselves justify the view that moral lapses will exclude a Christian from final salvation. We need to consider whether Paul makes any specific statements which might support the view that believers might finally fail to inherit the kingdom. He certainly makes clear that those who do 'the works of the flesh' shall not inherit the kingdom (Gal. 5:21), and consequently issues a strong warning to his readers. But this can hardly be taken as evidence of Paul's belief that any true believers might fail to inherit the kingdom, in view of his further statement that all who belong to Christ Jesus have crucified the flesh with its passions and desires (Gal. 5:24). Those still committed to the flesh would know that they had no part in the kingdom.

Can it be maintained that Paul regarded it as a possibility that he might be disqualified from salvation if he did not run well? Some have suggested this on the strength of 1 Corinthians 9:24–27.[148] But the context supports the view that Paul is thinking here of reward for service and not salvation, since the latter concept is not mentioned. It is precarious to deduce the idea from the mention of preaching. It must be considered highly doubtful that Paul thought of the possibility of losing his eternal salvation.[149] But when

---

[148] *Cf.* I. H. Marshall, *op. cit.*, pp. 110f.

[149] C. K. Barrett, *1 Corinthians* (BC ²1971), p. 217, takes the athletic metaphor to mean that those who have entered the Christian life through baptism have no guarantee of final perseverance. This view cannot be pressed, since Paul would hardly have used an illustration from running where only one can win, if he was thinking of salvation. The main burden of the passage assumes that those who enter a race will want

627

he exhorts the Corinthians, 'Examine yourselves, to see whether you are holding to your faith' (2 Cor. 13:5), is he implying that they may fail to meet this test? The answer must be sought in the following words, 'Do you not realize that Jesus Christ is in you? – unless indeed you fail to meet the test!'[150] Paul seems to mean that failure is defined more in terms of the indwelling Christ, than in terms of holding to the faith. In other words, those conscious of the indwelling Christ will certainly pass the test. Nevertheless the challenge to self-examination draws attention to human responsibility.

Another passage which could be taken to imply doubt about Paul's attaining the resurrection of the dead is Philippians 3:11.[151] But no-one can suppose that Paul thought of failure to attain the resurrection as a serious possibility, in view of his firm assurance expressed in Philippians 1:23 of being with Christ, and in view of his conviction elsewhere that believers would be raised with Christ (Rom. 6:5; 2 Cor. 4:14). Was he then thinking of a special resurrection reserved for martyrs?[152] The passage does not specifically refer to martyrdom, although it does refer to 'becoming like him in his death' (Phil. 3:10). It may be the manner of death rather than the fact of resurrection that concerns the apostle. He is certainly convinced that he is 'in Christ'.

Some discussion has centred on the 'delivery to Satan' passages in 1 Corinthians 5:5 and 1 Timothy 1:20. In the former passage Paul urges the Corinthians to do the 'delivering', while in the latter he does it himself. It is general to regard these as acts of excommunication, but there is no suggestion in either case that the judgment places the persons concerned outside final salvation. In fact the first act is definitely taken with a view that the man's spirit 'may be saved in the day of the Lord Jesus'. In the second case it is in order that the two men 'may learn not to blaspheme'.[153] In neither case is it stated that the misdemeanours place the offenders outside the kingdom, although the immediate judgment on them is drastic.

---

to finish the course. Conzelmann *op. cit.*, p. 162, gets over the difficulty that one only receives the prize by calling this no more than 'an auxiliary notion'.

[150] Again Barrett, *2 Corinthians* (*BC*, 1973), p. 337, favours the view that these words imply that a believer may cease to be a Christian. He cites W. G. Kümmel in Lietzmann-Kümmel, *An die Korinther* (*LHB*, ⁵1969), *ad loc.*

[151] *Cf.* J. J. Muller, *Philippians and Philemon* (1955), pp. 117f., denies that the phrase 'if by any means I may attain' expresses any uncertainty. R. P. Martin, *Philippians* (*NCB*, 1976), pp. 135f., maintains that the uncertainty implied by the words relates only to the way in which Paul would attain the resurrection either by martyrdom or at a more distant time. To W. Hendriksen, *Philippians* (1962), p. 170, the words imply that Paul distrusts himself, but not God.

[152] So E. Lohmeyer, *Die Briefe an die Philipper, Kolosser, und Philemon* (*KEK*, ⁹1953), *ad loc.*

[153] M. Dibelius – H. Conzelmann, *The Pastoral Epistles*, p. 34, describe the purpose of the delivery to Satan as 'education through punishment'. J. N. D. Kelly, *The Pastoral Epistles*, pp. 58f., claims that the verb used (*paideuthōsin*) conveys the idea of stern punishment and suggests that some physical disability was in Paul's mind.

Paul does not enlarge on what the situation would be if the people concerned did not respond to the corrective discipline. He seems to take it for granted that they would.

Throughout his letters Paul shows strong convictions about the preserving power of God to effect what he had himself determined. He has no doubt about either election or predestination. He recognizes that the outworking and application of the work of Christ is not left to chance. The Spirit sets his seal on those who believe. God provides salvation and nothing can prevent men from enjoying its benefits. This unshakeable conviction gives tremendous stability to the apostle's own faith and communicates itself through his letters.

Nevertheless, a paradox is present in the evident need for man to respond to God's provision, in order to appropriate it. Paul does not set out salvation as if God decreed that so many people, irrespective of human responsibility, should be saved and the rest condemned. That would make men into robots, mere tools in the hand of God. The remarkable balance between God's sovereignty and man's responsibility does not remove the tension, but illustrates the greatness of the mind of Paul. His conviction about God's sovereignty springs from his own experience of God's grace. But he never views himself as pressed into a mould that he, as a responsible individual, did not want. At one time he had kicked against the pricks (Acts 26:14),[154] but he knew that Christ had given him the victory (*cf.* Rom. 7:24–25). For Paul, therefore, predestination was not a result of speculation, but of inner conviction. The possibility of apostasy among the elect did not engage his attention as a speculative problem, but he was sufficiently down to earth to see the need for constant appeals to Christians to persevere in faith.

Hebrews

GENERAL OBSERVATIONS

It is at once evident that this writer first of all approaches the theme of man's salvation from the point of view of God's initiative. It is God who has spoken in these last days through a Son (1:2). That salvation is of grace is seen from the statement in Hebrews 2:9 about Jesus that 'by the grace of God he might taste death for every one'. (*Theou* here has no article and may therefore draw attention to grace as part of the nature of God.) The calling of the Christian is named as 'heavenly' (3:1),[155] which is a way of

---

[154] According to E. Haenchen, *Acts*, p. 685, this statement is a common Greek proverb, meaning 'opposition to me is senseless and impossible' (he is citing Bauernfeind). Haenchen considers that Greek hearers would understand that Paul was completely in the power of Jesus.

[155] H. W. Montefiore, *Hebrews* (*BC*, 1964), p. 71, takes 'heavenly calling' in the sense of a calling to heaven rather than a calling from heaven. F. F. Bruce *Hebrews* (*NICNT*, 1964), p. 55, understands the words in the sense of those set apart by God for himself. The words draw attention to the divine initiative.

saying it has a divine origin, and is therefore a provision of grace. The exposition of the high-priest theme includes within it several statements about the finality of God's provision. What he has done is once for all and needs no repetition. This saving aspect has been achieved independently of man. Yet man needs not only to appropriate it, but to hold on to it (3:6; 10:23). The readers are exhorted to strive to enter the spiritual rest, lest they fall (4:11). But that God is essentially a God of grace is seen clearly from the expression 'throne of grace' (4:16).

Although the theme of foreknowledge and election is not as prominent in Hebrews as in Paul, there are a few indications of it. God has a specific plan for his people in history (11:40). The heroes of faith in the pre-Christian era would not have been 'perfected' apart from the Christians. It has been maintained that this statement is an assurance that God will fulfil his promises and has no bearing on the salvation of individuals.[156] But since the list of people of faith (11) concentrates on individuals, it is difficult to see how the complementing of this list can be anything other than individualized. This is supported by 12:23 which refers to 'the assembly of the first-born who are enrolled in heaven'. The first-born are Christians,[157] after the analogy of the Israelites (Ex. 4:22), or perhaps are 'all the redeemed'. It is the idea of enrolment which suggests some elective process. The same thought comes in Revelation (see the section below, pp. 638ff.).

The heavenly Jerusalem is peopled by those whom God has 'made perfect'. There is no suggestion in this epistle that people can make themselves perfect. It is even said of Christ that God made him perfect through suffering (2:10). But neither is there any suggestion that man need do nothing, as the warning passages show. It may be wondered whether the mention of Esau's loss of birthright (12:16) is intended to warn the readers that their enrolment in heaven could be forfeited in the same way. But the writer does not draw out such a parallel.

Before considering the warning passages, we should note that there are several strong assurances given to Christians to assist them to persevere in the faith. There is the faithfulness of God to his promises (6:13ff.), the changelessness of Jesus Christ (13:8), the intercessory work of Christ (1:3; 2:18; 4:15; 7:25), the example of others (12:1ff.), especially Christ himself as the pioneer and perfecter of our faith. This latter point is particularly focused on his conquest of temptation. With such aids the Christian has every incentive to persevere.

THE WARNING PASSAGES

These passages, which draw out the serious consequences of failing to

---

[156] Cf. I. H. Marshall, *Kept by the Power of God*, p. 147.

[157] P. E. Hughes, *Hebrews*, pp. 552ff., favours the view that the 'first-born' in Heb. 12:23 signify the totality of redeemed mankind from every age.

appropriate the message, are interspersed throughout the epistle. In one sense they are interludes which temporarily delay the development of the main theme, but they are not entirely divorced from that theme. If, as seems likely, the epistle was originally a homily, these direct exhortations become more intelligible.

The first is 2:1–4, where the danger of drifting away from what has been heard is first introduced. The very fact that the writer uses the metaphor of drifting shows that he is not speaking of a deliberate refusal, but of an almost helpless slipping away. Nevertheless it is recognized that a responsibility rests with Christians since the question is asked, 'How shall we escape if we neglect such a great salvation?' (verse 3).[158] The salvation is that declared by Christ and supported by divine signs and sovereignly distributed gifts of the Spirit. Is the author implying the possibility of apostasy here? Unless we take his question as purely rhetorical we should have to admit that he regarded the danger as real. Nevertheless, he is not specific about what he means by neglect. We must consider this passage alongside the others for a true understanding of it.

The second passage is 3:7ff. with the key warning, 'Take care, brethren lest there be in any of you an evil, unbelieving heart, leading you to fall away from the living God' (3:12). The writer cites a passage from Psalm 95:7–11, which focuses on 'today' and urges the Israelites not to harden their hearts. Clearly the falling away is therefore equivalent to a hardened heart, which is impervious to the influences of the Holy Spirit. It was unbelief which prevented the Israelites from entering, but the writer sees that no different conditions of entry apply to Christians. There is here no definite affirmation that any of the readers had fallen away, only a strong warning to them to take care.[159]

The third passage is perhaps the most important, 6:4–8.[160] It deals with the impossibility of restoring to repentance those who, after being enlightened, 'crucify the Son of God on their own account and hold him up to contempt' (verse 6). This is a deliberate rejection of the Christian position. It is first to be noted that the supposition is expressed in its most extreme form. The writer envisages a person who has (i) tasted the goodness of the Word of God, (ii) tasted the heavenly gift, (iii) been enlightened and (iv) become partaker of the Holy Spirit. It may be argued that these

---

[158] Hughes, *ibid.*, p. 76 n. 48, points out that the verb translated 'neglect' means 'to be unconcerned' and is the opposite of the careful consideration enjoined in Heb. 2:1.

[159] I.H. Marshall, *op. cit.*, p. 135, while regarding this passage as evidence of the possibility of backsliding, nevertheless recognizes that Heb. 4:11-13 shows 'that apparent outward conformity to the faith is useless if it is not accompanied by heart belief'.

[160] For a full discussion of Heb. 6:1-6, *cf.* Hughes, *Hebrews*, pp. 193–222. He thinks that those in view in verses 4-6 are those who have been baptized and have then renounced their Christian faith. He goes on to conclude that those who are genuinely Christ's cannot fall away. *Cf. idem*, 'Hebrews 6:4-6 and the Peril of Apostasy', *WTJ*, 35, 1973, pp. 137–155.

terms can apply only to a believer. If such a person commits apostasy, restoration would be impossible.[161]

Much debate has surrounded the interpretation of the 'if' clause. That the writer is thinking of a hypothetical case is hardly to be disputed. He cannot be referring to an actual case, as Hebrews 6:9 shows ('in your case, beloved, we feel sure of better things'). But why does he introduce the subject at all? The most probable answer is that some may have talked about a return to Judaism, with the intention of combining their Christian position with the trappings of Judaism. But a turning away from the Christian position with its central message of the cross would be tantamount to re-crucifying the Son of God. Such an action would involve a deliberate rejection of the Christian gospel, and would automatically remove any basis for repentance. It was imperative for these Christian readers to recognize at once the serious consequence of undermining the Christian gospel. It seems better to regard this as a warning stated in categorical terms, than to suppose that the people envisaged were deluded into thinking they were Christians (so Calvin), or to maintain that they were unbelievers who had been granted a mere taste of Christian enlightenment but had turned their back upon it (Owen).

At the same time there are difficulties in the view which interprets the passage to mean that a Christian may be saved and then lost, for it involves the contention that a person who shares the Spirit can treat Christ with contempt. At what point does the apostasy occur? Is it after the withdrawal of the Spirit? If it is, how can the person himself be held responsible for his apostasy? It almost looks as if the writer is intentionally setting out an impossible paradox.[162] It is worth noting that he does not specify who does the restoring, or rather who cannot do it under the circumstances specified. Is it the writer, the Christian community or God?[163] The writer may have wished it to remain general so that it could meet several situations.

It seems that the only fair conclusion in this case is that apostasy is being seriously considered, but no specific instance of such apostasy is actually reported. We may consider this to be a variant form of the unforgivable sin, since it is definitely apostasy against the Holy Spirit. It should further be noted that this warning passage could not be intended to lessen the assurance of believers, since the writer asserts in 6:11 the possibility of

---

[161] R. A. Harrisville, *The Concept of Newness in the New Testament*, pp. 15ff., interprets the passage eschatologically. A second renewal is impossible because people reject the eschatological situation. 'The renewal by faith is final; it cannot be repeated because the believer has been placed within that last and final period of God's redemptive activity which hastens on towards its goal'.

[162] Some understand the word 'impossible' to refer only to man, but not to God (*cf.* C. Spicq, *L'Épître aux Hébreux* (EB ²1952), *ad loc.*). If this were the correct understanding, the way would be left open for God to give a second opportunity. But this is not the real message of the passage.

[163] I. H. Marshall, *Kept by the Power of God*, p. 136, rejects the view that restoration by God is intended, because of the lack of *autō* and the use of God's word in verse 5.

realizing the full assurance of hope (*cf.* 10:19ff.).

The fourth warning passage, which is closely akin to this passage, is 10:26–31. Since this section immediately follows the conclusion of the doctrinal exposition with its emphasis on the Christian's confidence, the warning passage must be set against this background. The writer reflects on the position of the person who has deliberately sinned after believing in Christ. But the sin is specified as spurning the Son of God, profaning the blood of Christ and outraging the Spirit of grace (10:29). Again the example given is an extreme type involving a complete *volte-face*. Furthermore, the sin is again mentioned in a hypothetical way and no information is given whether anyone had committed it.

It has been suggested that non-Christians are here in mind who have some knowledge of the truth, but who have not committed themselves in repentance to Christ. It must be acknowledged that a somewhat different situation seems to be envisaged here from that in chapter 6, although a similar hardened and contemptuous attitude towards Christ is found in this passage. What the writer has in mind is a contortion of the truth about the sacrifice of Christ. Anyone who spoke disparagingly of the sacrifice of Christ placed themselves outside the terms of repentance (hence the statement in 10:26). Since the blood is referred to as 'the blood of the covenant', some allusion to the profaning of the Lord's Supper may be in mind. The outraging of the Spirit once again seems to run parallel to the words of Jesus about the unforgivable sin.[164] Nothing short of an absolute rejection of the Christian faith satisfies the terms in which the offence is described in this passage, perhaps under the stress of persecution.[165]

The final warning passage is 12:12ff., where the readers are urged, 'See to it that no one fail to obtain the grace of God' (verse 15). Since the verb 'obtain' (*hysterōn*) is in the present tense, it must refer to the continuous appropriation of grace, not to the initial reception of grace.[166] This may be no more than an exhortation to let the grace be seen in moral living, since the root of bitterness referred to is defined as 'immoral' and 'irreligious'. Esau is cited as an example. Moreover, there is a solemn warning against refusing him who is speaking (*i.e.* God, 12:25ff.), with a further statement 'how much less shall we escape' (*i.e.* less than the Israelites). This latter statement is an echo of 2:3.

These warning passages express more strongly than elsewhere in the NT

---

[164] F. F. Bruce, *Hebrews*, p. 259, sees a direct connection between the apostasy here and that mentioned in Mk. 3:29.

[165] J. Héring, *Hebrews* (Eng. trans. 1970), p. 94, in discussing the apostates, says, 'Such people are not condemned by an arbitrary decree of God; by excluding themselves from the Christian community they lose *ipso facto* the benefit of the sacrifice of Christ.'

[166] B. F. Westcott, *Hebrews*, p. 406, understands the passage to refer to those who were not keeping pace with the movement of divine grace.

the consequences of falling away and lay greater emphasis on human responsibility. A delicate balance is maintained, however, so as not to give the impression that believers have to keep themselves in the grace of God. There are ample aids provided by God, but these are not available to the person who treats them contemptuously.[167]

The rest of the New Testament

Although *James* is essentially a practical epistle, it is not without some theological basis for its many exhortations. The approach to grace is on a simpler level than in Paul's epistles, but grace is equally indispensable. Every good endowment and perfect gift comes from God (1:17).[168] His word of truth brought us forth (1:18).[169] It was the result 'of his own will'. His intention was that we should be 'a kind of first fruits of his creatures'. Believers are confronted with what James calls 'the perfect law, the law of liberty, (1:25), which is not intended to suggest an external law, but rather an inner principle. James does not define this law any further, but urges the need to persevere in it. It is the 'implanted word' which is able to save the soul (1:21). Although the faith and works passage in 2:14–26 might suggest an emphasis on human effort, this would be a wrong deduction (see the discussion on p. 598f.). The need for showing faith by means of works does not lessen the need for faith. A specific reference to grace is found in James 4:6 ('But he gives more grace; therefore it says, "God opposes the proud, but gives grace to the humble" ').[170] Since humility is itself a sign of grace, James must be thinking of an increasing experience of grace. There is no room for pride in human achievement; it is all of grace.

Over against this emphasis on God's provision are several passages which stress man's responsibility. The person who wants wisdom must ask for it (1:5f.). Those passing through trials and temptations are expected to endure (1:12ff.). It is assumed to be normal to do the word as well as to hear it (1.22). In the mass of practical exhortations in this epistle, it is

[167] E. Jauncey, *The Doctrine of Grace*, pp. 77f., after examining the evidence from Hebrews, concludes that the teaching is not essentially different from Paul's teaching, though differently expressed. There is the same insistence that all ability to work comes from God, and there is the same emphasis on human free-will and effort.

[168] There is some debate whether these words mean that all God's gifts are good or that all good gifts come from God. C. L. Mitton, *James*, p. 74, prefers the latter, but the former would be in line with Jewish theology (*cf.* R. J. Knowling, *James*, p. 23). Whichever is correct, the statement underlines the gracious generosity of God.

[169] L. E. Elliott-Binns, 'James 1:18 : Creation or Redemption?' *NTS* 3, 1956-7, pp. 148–161, sees no reference here to the new birth. He understands the first fruits as a reference to mankind, not as a reference to Christians. It is more likely, as noted by R. V. G. Tasker (*James*, p. 49), that the first fruits are Christians, perhaps implying the many others who would become Christians through the Christian mission.

[170] *Cf.* J. Moffatt, *Grace in the New Testament*, p. 317, for a discussion of 'more grace' in this context. He points out that James' use of grace here differs from Paul's use in that there is no special mention of forgiveness of sins.

assumed that the readers are able to respond.[171] But there are no passages which suggest the consequences of failing to persevere. One passage, 5:13ff., raises problems. Prayer over a sick man can be effective to heal and, if the man confesses, to secure forgiveness. But does this imply a connection between the sickness and the sin? It certainly seems to be assumed that physical healing without spiritual healing would be incomplete, but nothing is said about the position which would obtain if the sick man had not called the elders and solicited the prayer of faith. It cannot be assumed that without it the man would have died in his sins.

It is clear from the opening words of *1 Peter* that believers are regarded as 'chosen and destined by God the Father' (1:2).[172] This concept of election is followed up by a statement about what the mercy of God has achieved: believers born again, 'who by God's power are guarded through faith for a salvation ready to be revealed in the last time' (1:5). The sovereign purposes of God are clearly seen to work out in his people. The ultimate inheritance is secured to them only by virtue of God's power. The genuineness of their faith, which like gold could be tested,[173] would redound to God's praise (1:7). No doubt is cast on that genuineness. As a result of it salvation would be secured.

The electing grace of God is also seen in 2:9–10, where the Christians are called 'a chosen race . . . God's own people' (or a people for God's possession). Peter recognizes the possessiveness of God towards his people; they are of infinite value in his sight, as Christ is in theirs (*cf.* 2:7). The statement in 2:8 may suggest that some are appointed to disobey the word, but since the reference is to stumbling over the stone (*i.e.* Christ), the element of human responsibility cannot be omitted.[174] The focus is on the preciousness of Christ which only those who obey the word can appreciate. There is a sharp cleavage between the destinies of those who stumble over Christ, and of those to whom he is a precious cornerstone. Peter makes no attempt to resolve the tension which arises between God's sovereignty and man's freedom.

In view of existing or impending persecution, there are many exhorta-

---

[171] I. H. Marshall, *Kept by the Power of God*, p. 155, decides that James' view of the Christian life is optimistic. Temptation is present, but is a pathway to perfection of character.

[172] The use of the words *eklektois* and *prognōsin* is in full agreement with Paul's usage. God's foreknowledge implies his power to bring to pass what he knows. There is no denying that the stress falls on the divine initiative. See E. G. Selwyn, *1 Peter*, *ad loc.*, for the background of these terms. They are both firmly based in OT concepts.

[173] The word *dokimon* refers to faith which has been tested, hence is seen to be genuine. *Cf.* A. M. Stibbs, *1 Peter* (*TNTC*, 1959), p. 78. Genuine faith is distinguished from superficial profession. J. W. C. Wand, *The Epistles of Peter & Jude* (*WC* 1934), p. 47, speaks of 'the genuine residuum'. On *dokimon* in the NT, see W. Grundmann, *TDNT*, 2, pp. 255ff.

[174] The wording of 1 Pet. 2:8 ('as they were destined to do') certainly seems to suggest that the disobedience was divinely ordained. E. Best, *1 Peter*, p. 106, speaks of God predestinating men to stumble. *Cf.* also C. Spicq, *Les Épîtres de Saint Pierre* (1966), p. 90.

tions to believers to endure (*e.g.* 2:21; 4:1). Christians are not promised exemption from persecution, but there are aids provided to enable them to persevere. There is the example of Christ (2:21; 4:1), the example and testimony of others (5:1), the promise of God's restoration (5:10), the assurance of God's protection (1:5; 4:19), and God's gifts of grace (4:10ff.). There is surprisingly no concentration on failure or falling away. Peter is confident that his readers will obtain 'the unfading crown of glory' when the chief Shepherd appears (5:4). They are to fix their hope firmly on the 'grace' that is coming at Christ's revelation (1:13). The interim is regarded (as in Hebrews) as a period of exile (1:17), which demands right conduct particularly in an attitude of reverence before God. Special stress falls on love, which is said to cover a multitude of sins (4:8),[175] a statement which seems to mean that the quality of love makes up for many offences (*cf.* the similar idea in Jas. 5:20).

In *2 Peter*, it is at once apparent that the same emphasis falls on the divine initiative as in 1 Peter. It is God's power which has granted to us everything relating to life and godliness (1:3). He called us to 'his own glory and excellence (1:3). He has given us great promises. He has enabled us to share his nature (1:4). This latter idea has been considered to be of Greek origin.[176] But whatever the source of the expression, it cannot be denied that its truth could be effected only by divine action. It certainly does not mean, as in Greek thought, an absorption into the deity.[177] It is, in fact, a variation of other NT concepts like being 'in Christ' or 'abiding in Christ' (see section below, pp. 647ff.). The Christian has to make some effort to increase in virtue (1:5–7) in order to confirm his call and election (1:10). In no clearer way could Peter bring out the human responsibility side of his doctrine of election.[178]

But does this suggest that if the effort is unsuccessful, the election will be annulled? If that were so no assurance would be possible, for no-one would know whether his virtues matched the divine requirements, even if the virtues are the working out of divine grace and not merely 'human works'. It is difficult to see what meaning can be attached to divine election in these circumstances. It seems better to take the various warnings in this letter as reminders that those who are 'elect' are called on to face up to

---

[175] There is some question here whether the sins covered are of those who love or of those loved. See the discussion in E. Best, *1 Peter*, p. 159. The question does not, however, affect our present purpose which is to focus attention on aids to perseverance.

[176] *Cf.* the excursus on deification in J. W. C. Wand, *op. cit.*, pp. 150ff.

[177] In a recent book, T. Fornberg, *An Early Church in a Pluralistic Society* (1977), p. 88, has strongly contended that the divine nature is immortality. He finds parallels here with the mystery religions.

[178] K. H. Schelkle, *Die Petrusbriefe, der Judasbrief* (1976), p. 192, questions whether the emphasis on human effort in 2 Pet. 1:10 does not show that the letter is a later NT writing. I. H. Marshall, *Kept by the Power of God*, p. 167, however, sees these words as showing that election is not automatic. According to him it 'does not offer absolute assurance of salvation'.

moral responsibilities, and that by this means they will not fall. Peter reinforces his moral challenge by an appeal to coming events, which in his view should make men ask what kind of persons they should be (3:11).[179] The readers are warned to avoid the error of lawless men, so as not to lose their stability (3:17). There is, nevertheless, confidence that the Lord knows how to rescue the godly from trial (2:9). Further, God does not will that any should perish (3:9).

A question arises from 2:18 as to whether the people enticed by the false teachers are lapsed believers ('men who have barely escaped from those who live in error'). 2:20 would seem to suggest that they had once been believers[180] ('For if, after they have escaped the defilements of the world through knowledge of our Lord and Saviour Jesus Christ, they are again entangled in them and overpowered, the last state has become worse than the first'). Peter goes on to say that it would have been better for them never 'to have known the way of righteousness' than to turn back from the holy commandment (2:21). It is noticeable that in none of these statements is there any mention of faith, nor anything to show that these people were any more than acquainted with God's moral demands. Moreover, since the third person is used, some distinction from the readers themselves is evidently intended. For the false teachers themselves there is nothing but the judgment of God.

The brief epistle of *Jude*, which is closely akin to 2 Peter in its condemnation of false teaching, is addressed to those 'who are called, beloved in God the Father and kept for Jesus Christ' (verse 1). Certainly the false teachers are in marked contrast to these, for they are seen as 'devoid of the Spirit' (verse 19). God has a special care for his people, but condemnation for those whose immoral lives deserve it.

It has been argued that the OT allusions in verses 5–7 are intended to warn those who had lapsed from the faith,[181] as many others had lapsed in OT times (Israelites, fallen angels, Balaam, Korah). But it is precarious to suppose on these grounds that lapsed Christians are being addressed. The false teachers are those 'who pervert the grace of our God into licentiousness and deny our only Master and Lord, Jesus Christ' (verse 4). In stark contrast to these, the readers are to build themselves up on their most holy faith (verse 20). The main question is whether any but lapsed Christians could pervert the grace of God. There seems no good reason for supposing that an experience of God's grace is necessary before it can be perverted. If

---

[179] J. N. D. Kelly, *Peter and Jude*, pp. 366f., paraphrases the word *potapos* (= what sort of) used here as 'how outstandingly excellent', thus bringing out the strongly positive aspect of the whole question.

[180] If, of course, the people in 2 Pet. 2:20 are not the same as those in 2:18, the interpretation given would need modification. E. M. B. Green, *2 Peter and Jude* (*TNTC*, 1968), p. 118, thinks that the false teachers are in view in 2:20.

[181] *Cf.* I. H. Marshall, *Kept by the Power of God*, p. 160, considers the false teachers were lapsed believers.

these false teachers were proposing that licentiousness was an evidence of God's grace, they can hardly have had a true experience of it. What is in mind is more than a misunderstanding. It is nothing short of a deliberate distortion.

There is in this epistle a balance between God's action and man's. The Christians are to keep themselves in the love of God (verse 21), but are assured that God is able to keep them from falling (verse 24).[182] They are to contend for the faith (verse 3), but are assured it is God who will present them without blemish before his presence (verse 24). The exhortation to build up in the faith is linked with prayer 'in the Holy Spirit' (verse 20). Christians have every encouragement to press on until they possess eternal life.

Some have supposed that Jude 22–23 refers to believers who have fallen prey to the false teaching, but who may still be rescued.[183] The words, 'on some have mercy with fear, hating even the garment spotted by the flesh', have received various interpretations, but at least it may be assumed that hope is not completely at an end even for them. Although Jude is harsh on the false teachers, he does not give the impression that they will have much impact on the true believers, because of the provisions of grace mentioned above.

In a special sense *Revelation* is directed to Christians under trial. It is concerned to encourage them to persevere and we need to examine in what ways the book suggests that this can be accomplished. In the seven letters there are several assessments of the state of the churches. The Ephesian church lost its first love and was exhorted to repent, otherwise its lampstand would be removed (Rev. 2:5). Does this suggest that those who have once believed can finish up by being excluded from the true church? Since a church is being addressed it is difficult to be sure whether this could be applied to individuals. Nonetheless the possibility of removal seems to be implied. Paradise is for those who 'conquer' (2:7).[184] Since this theme of conquering occurs at the end of each letter, with differing rewards promised, it would not be unreasonable to suppose that some possibility of not conquering is being envisaged. At the same time nothing is said about the fate of any who do not conquer, and it is evident that the message is positively to those who do.

In one case, the letter to Sardis, the overcomer is promised that his name will not be blotted out of the book of life (3:5); this raises the question

---

[182] J. N. D. Kelly, *op. cit.*, p. 290, comments that Jude emphasized the ability of God to keep because the readers left to themselves would too easily lapse.

[183] E. M. B. Green, *op. cit.*, pp. 187f., finds three groups of people which have reacted in different ways to the false teachers. But in none of these cases is the position portrayed as hopeless. I. H. Marshall, *op. cit.*, p. 161, considers that verses 22f. described the treatment of those who lapse from the faith, but this is not demanded by the text. Certainly, however, those in view are in danger of lapsing.

[184] G. R. Beasley-Murray, *Revelation*, p. 77, rejects the view that the conquerors are the martyrs.

whether the book of life is a comprehensive record of believers.[185] If it is, the possibility of a person being erased from the book of life must be granted. Yet the statement in this context cannot be decided apart from other references to the 'book of life'. It is a favourite theme in this book (*cf.* 13:8; 17:8; 20:15 and 21:27).

The first two of these references imply that the writing was done 'before the foundation of the world'. Some have suggested that in 13:8 the qualifying phrase could refer to the slaying of the lamb, but this could not be so in 17:8 where the lamb is not mentioned. If the writing was done before the foundation of the world, the concept of predestination is plain. Are we then to suppose that some whose names were written before the foundation of the world can, as a result of their own actions, be deleted? Final judgment is based on the omissions from the book of life (20:15) and entry into the New Jerusalem depends on inclusions in the book of life (21:27).[186] The latter passage specifies that nothing unclean, nor a doer of abomination or falsehood can be included. There is, therefore, a moral qualification. We are not to think of a pre-creation 'entry' which becomes automatically effected irrespective of the moral response of the individual.

The letters to the churches contain challenges for Christians to be faithful (2:10), or to hold fast (2:25; 3:11), or to keep what has been received and heard (3:3), or to be zealous (3:19). The constant calls for repentance furthermore show that grace is still available to deal with past deficiencies. These letters were clearly not intended to rob the Christians of assurance, but were aimed to keep them on their toes.

The whole book is designed to promote encouragement towards patient endurance (*cf.* 1:9; 2:2, 3, 19; 3:10; 13:10; 14:12). Christians are assured that they will be kept by God (3:10). It may seem that only those who keep God's Word will be assured of being kept, but that would empty the keeping power of God of much meaning. It is better to suppose that a reciprocal action is implied in which God's keeping power is an essential factor in the Christian's keeping of God's word (*cf.* Rev. 12:17; 14:12). Indeed it is assumed that Christians are those who keep the commandments. We may surmise that some were associating with the Christians who needed to be reminded about what was involved if they were really to be numbered among true believers.

The other feature of this apocalypse is its reference to the sealing of the saints. In 7:1–8 is recorded the sealing of the servants of God upon their foreheads (verse 3). The mention of a specific number of people (*i.e.*

---

[185] G. B. Gaird, *Revelation* (BC, 1966), p. 49, speaks of conditional predestination here: 'A man cannot earn the right to have his name on the citizen roll, but he can forfeit it'. He claims that the decrees of God are not irreversible.

[186] G. E. Ladd, *Revelation* (1972), p. 274, points out that entry in the book of life points to the fact that salvation is only through the Lamb of God. No-one is saved by his works.

144,000) has given rise to the view that the sealing is for martyrdom, not for membership of the whole Christian community. It is more likely, however, that the number is symbolic, in line with the use of numerals elsewhere in this book. In that case the 144,000 stand for all the people of God. If this interpretation is correct, it raises the question of the significance of the sealing.[187] Does it preserve those sealed from falling away? This book never raises such a question. It seems to be assumed that the judgments will not be able to touch those who are sealed (*cf.* 9:4).[188] Indeed since the rest of mankind is sealed with the number of the beast (13:16ff.), it is evident that the seal of God sets his people apart from the rest. There is a powerful assurance given that the people of God are a victorious people, not through their own efforts, but through the grace of God. It is the Lamb who conquers and those who accompany him are 'the called and chosen and faithful' (17:14).

Conclusion

We have seen that throughout the NT there is a consistent presentation of God's initiative in man's salvation. At the same time there is equally clear evidence that man is called upon to respond. There is, however, no formal discussion of the problem of reconciling God's sovereignty with man's freewill. The teaching of predestination has to be balanced against the warning passages. The NT, nevertheless, does not leave the issue in doubt. God will certainly win for himself a people who will be presented faultless before his throne. There is no impression that man will have the last word. One of the deeper truths of NT theology is that God is as gracious as he is sovereign. This gives strong grounds for assurance that he will work out his purpose for men.

An attempt to come to grips with the NT concept of grace is an essential stepping stone for the study of sanctification and perfection. Indeed it may reasonably be maintained that the processes of sanctifying and perfecting properly belong to the doctrine of grace. The next two sections in this chapter will show the extent to which the constant exhortations in the NT, which set before the reader some goal or standard to which they should strive, can be achieved only through the means that God himself provides. We shall first examine the spiritual dimensions of the new life, and then pass on to the more specific teaching about sanctification and perfection.

---

[187] R. H. Mounce, *Revelation*, p. 167, suggests on the basis of the usage in Ezekiel 9 that the sealing symbolizes God's protection over his people.

[188] R. H. Charles, *Revelation* (*ICC*, 1920), p. 200, considered that the sealing must be co-extensive with the peril and must relate to the whole Christian community.

NEW LIFE IN CHRIST

The synoptic gospels

When considering the concept of new life in the teaching of Jesus in these gospels, we must first concentrate our attention on the nature of the kingdom. We have already considered the kingdom teaching in relation to the mission of Jesus (pp. 408ff.), but our present concern is the practical outworking of the kingdom teaching in the lives of its members. Did Jesus give any indication of the inner resources which would be at the disposal of his followers to enable them to follow out his instructions? Or did he expect them to work out their own salvation? We have already considered the synoptic teaching on grace (see pp. 602ff.), which drew attention to the divine initiative as being essential if man is ever to live as God wants him to live. But the synoptic gospels do not record any specific teaching which corresponds to the Johannine and Pauline ideas of being in Christ.

The only comment which needs to be made on indirect material in these gospels which has any bearing on this theme are those passages which show the close association the disciples of Jesus would have with Jesus himself. These sayings have been used as evidence for the view that Paul's mysticism was grounded in the teaching of Jesus.[189] Persecution (*cf.* Mt. 5:11) and martyrdom (Mk. 8:35) would come to the disciples for Christ's sake, *i.e.* because of their identification with him. In the commissioning of the twelve, Jesus said, 'He who receives you receives me' (Mt. 10:40). His 'true' relatives are those who do his will (Mk. 3:35). Those who receive a child in his name receive him (Mt. 18:5). In the parable of the sheep and the goats, those receiving needy people are said to have received him (Mt. 25:35). In all these passages there is a sense of solidarity, and these considerations at least lay some foundation in the teaching of Jesus for the more explicitly expressed 'in Christ' and 'with Christ' teaching, particularly in the Johannine literature and in the Pauline epistles.

The Johannine literature

The gospel of John records several sayings of Jesus which speak of a mystical association between believers and himself or believers and God. The ideas are then continued in 1 John. The most characteristic is the notion of 'abiding in' or simply 'being in' Jesus.[190] This will provide valuable parallels with the 'in Christ' idea in Paul's epistles and will furnish some light on its meaning.

In the bread discourse the person who eats Christ's flesh and drinks his

---

[189] So A. Schweitzer, *The Mysticism of Paul the Apostle* (Eng. trans., ²1953), pp. 105ff.
[190] *Cf.* C. H. Dodd, *The Interpretation of the Fourth Gospel*, pp. 187–200.

blood is said to abide in Christ ('abides in me, and I in him', Jn. 6:56).[191] The idea of abiding is especially frequent in the farewell discourses. In John 14:10 Jesus asks, 'Do you not believe that I am in the Father and the Father in me?' He promises that his disciples would know that he was in the Father and the Father in him (Jn. 14:20).[192] He prays for his disciples 'that they may all be one; even as thou, Father, art in me, and I in thee, that they also may be in us, so that the world may believe that thou hast sent me' (Jn. 17:21). In these passages the union between the Father and the Son is seen to be the pattern for the believer's life in God. In the vine allegory in John 15 the idea of abiding is expressed in the double form 'Abide in me and I in you' (Jn. 15:4; cf. 15:5).[193] Moreover, the branches become useless unless they abide in the vine. Fruit is impossible and the branches must be stripped off and burnt (15:5–6).[194] In no more vivid way could Jesus have expressed the centrality of his own life in the on-going life of his people. He even went so far as to say that those abiding in him would be able to ask whatever they willed and it would be done (15:7). Only as a result of the infusion of the mind of Christ into the believer would this be intelligible.

This type of mysticism must be strongly differentiated from Hellenistic mysticism by its accompanying ethical note. This is particularly brought out in 1 John. The man who abides in Christ has an obligation to walk as Christ walked (1 Jn. 2:6).[195] He must, moreover, keep his commandments (1 Jn. 3:24). Abiding in Christ issues in love of the highest kind, for it is nothing less than God's own love in us (1 Jn. 4:12). Even more exacting is the statement that whoever abides in him does not sin (1 Jn. 3:6), a statement which presents the negative aspect of the Christian ideal of perfection (i.e. sinlessness). So closely linked is the idea of the indwelling God with its ethical effect that John can say 'he who abides in love abides in God and God abides in him' (1 Jn. 4:16). The great frequency of the

---

[191] B. Lindars, John, p. 269, comments on Jn. 6:56, 'John's thought never moves in ontological or quasi-magical categories'. He contends that the effect of receiving Jesus must be expressed in terms of personal, ethical relationship. The present tense here stresses a continuous relationship and not a merely fleeting experience (cf. L. Morris, John, p. 380).

[192] W. Hendriksen, John (²1961), ad loc., makes a distinction between the 'unity of essence' existing between Father and Son and the 'ethical' and 'spiritual' unity existing between the Son and believers. He thinks the former is incapable of growth, but this is not so of the latter. This may be a valuable distinction from the point of view of a systematic understanding, but it cannot be said to arise from the context.

[193] R. E. Brown, John, p. 678, rightly points out that this is more than a simple comparison. Both parts of the statement are parts of a whole.

[194] The idea of stripping off here cannot be understood simply in terms of excommunication. The basic idea is a total lack of union with the only source of life, i.e. Christ himself. R. Bultmann, John (Eng. trans. 1971), p. 538, denies a reference to ecclesiastical excommunication, but thinks the destruction is already a reality for the man who belongs to the community only outwardly.

[195] As R. Law, The Tests of Life, p. 213, puts it, 'From the union of nature there springs an ethical union of will; and of this the test is that we "walk even as Christ walked." ' Or as J. R. W. Stott, Epistles of John, p. 92, expresses it, 'We cannot claim to abide in Him unless we behave like Him.'

idea of 'abiding' in 1 John (*cf.* 1 Jn. 2:6, 24, 27, 28; 3:6, 24; 4:12–13, 15–16), shows that John sees a special need to stress the source of power for the new life. There is a corporate sense in the believer's identification with Christ. Moreover, John does not hesitate to say that we can know we are 'in him' (1 Jn. 2:5; 5:20).[196]

The parallels which exist between the type of teaching in John's gospel and in 1 John compared with Paul's 'in Christ' and 'Christ in you' teaching are close. The Johannine passages are neither as numerous nor as developed as the Pauline passages (see pp. 647ff.), but are highly significant because they fix the 'incorporation' ideas of Paul firmly in the teaching of Jesus, unless the Johannine statements are regarded as later developments and therefore as not original to Jesus. Yet so revolutionary would be the Pauline idea if it stood alone that some explanation of its origin would be needed, and none seems more appropriate than to suppose that Jesus himself spoke of men abiding in him.

Some reference must here be made to the particular Johannine teaching on eternal life (*zōē aiōnios*) as a present reality.[197] The believer in Christ now possesses eternal life (Jn. 3:15, 16; 6:40, 47). This new quality of life is received as a result of faith. It is noteworthy that in the first occurrence of the expression in John's gospel it occurs after a reference to the kingdom (Jn. 3:5, 15), for it seems certain that in John's gospel 'eternal life' stands in place of the synoptic teaching on the kingdom (*cf.* Mk. 9:43–47, where 'life' and 'kingdom' appear as equivalent terms).

There is no awareness of a tension between 'eternal' life and present life. The references to eternal life in John's gospel correspond to the present emphasis on the kingdom in the synoptic gospels. As in the latter case we may say that what is future is also present, so what is essentially 'eternal' has also became a present reality. The 'life' theme is of paramount importance in John's gospel, as John 20:31 shows. It points to a new manner of existence, which provides a framework for what has already been said above about abiding in Christ. We might approach this theme of present/ eternal life from the standpoint of Johannine dualism, which includes the comparison between what is above and what is below. The quality of life which the believer now shares is that which is characteristic of life above. It belongs essentially to God. The idea of 'eternal life' occurs also in 1 John (*cf.* 1:2; 2:25; 5:20), where the thought of fellowship with God is closely linked with it.

Acts

It is significant that this book, which says so much about the activity of

---

[196] B. F. Westcott, *The Epistles of St John*, p. 50, sees a progressive closeness of relation in this section (1 Jn. 2:1–6): to know him, to be in him, to abide in him. He cites Bengel's *cognitio, communio, constantia*.

[197] For a concise discussion of *zōē* and *zōē aiōnios* in John's gospel, *cf.* D. Hill, *Greek Words and Hebrew Meanings* (1967), pp. 192ff.

the early Christians, says very little about the new quality of life which they now lived. Beyond calling for repentance and faith, there is no indication of what instructions new converts were given about the new life. Nevertheless, the activity of the Spirit is so frequently stressed that his part in the new life is indisputable. Indeed a reading of Acts would lead to the impression that nothing else was required but dependence on the Spirit for guidance and for living. In this aspect Acts is closely aligned with the Johannine and Pauline literature. Although the expression 'in Christ' does not occur and 'in the Spirit' occurs only once, there are frequent references to being filled with the Spirit, which resulted in the Spirit dwelling within them. The one occurrence of 'in the Spirit' is in Acts 19:21 (Paul resolved in the Spirit), where it is not used in the characteristic sense found in Paul's epistles. In Acts the early history of the church was one of Spirit-filled people and it is not difficult to see some connection between this and the more mystic idea of incorporation in the Spirit.

Paul

The apostle Paul, more than any NT writer, expounds at length on the implications of the plan of God for the salvation of his people. He expresses the theological consequences in a variety of different ways, some of which find parallels elsewhere, while others are peculiar to him.

It should first be noted that the apostle, although using the expression 'eternal life', does not stress (as the Johannine literature does) its present reality. It stands mainly for a future inheritance (*cf.* Rom. 2:7; 5:21; 6:22; Gal. 6:8). Nevertheless, Paul's emphasis on life in Christ shows strongly a present aspect of life. Our examination of Paul's approach to the new life must not be divorced from the new quality of life which is so emphasized in the Johannine literature.

UNION WITH CHRIST

In his exposition of union with Christ the apostle introduces two complementary aspects, one backwards, the other forwards. In view of his strong conviction about man's need (see pp. 200ff.), he is naturally concerned about God's way of dealing with the effects of sin on the life of the believer.

In this context we may note first his use of the metaphor of *baptism*. We shall discuss elsewhere the significance of the rite in the doctrine of the church (see pp. 754ff.), but here our concern will be the theological meaning of identification with Christ in his death and resurrection as symbolized in the act of baptism. The classic exposition of this is found in Romans 6, but the basic ideas are reiterated in several epistles. It is clear that when Paul asks the question, 'Do you not know that all of us who have been baptized into Christ Jesus were baptized into his death?' (Rom. 6:3), he is drawing attention to a corporate aspect of the death of Christ. As that death was an historical event, so the incorporation of believers in that death was also historical. In other words when Christ died on the cross, all who were to be incorporated in him also died. This implies that when a person puts his faith in Christ, he is at once identified with a death that has already happened. The identification with death is necessary before there can be a participation in the risen life of Christ.[198]

It is important to note that Paul does not visualize a company of people, who have each individually been identified with Christ's death, discovering that that fact provided a common basis for the formation of a community. His concept is that the community is itself identified with Christ in his death in a corporate sense, and that each individual believer becomes identified with that community. They are baptized into one body (1 Cor. 12:13;[199] *cf.* also Gal. 3:27). One important distinction is necessary here. Although there is identification of the body of believers with Christ in his death, there were aspects of that death that were unique to Christ himself. It is for this reason that Paul speaks of Christ condemning sin in the flesh by sharing in the *likeness* of sinful flesh (Rom. 8:3).

This latter statement seems to mean that 'sinful flesh', *i.e.* life lived under the dominion of sin, has been put to death when Christ died on the cross. Christians, according to this view, are people who become identified with a new kind of life in which sinful flesh has no longer the authority it had before. It is already crucified, although this does not mean that it no longer presents obstacles. This fact at once leads to the need for the process of sanctification (see below, pp. 667ff.), which is a process of applying what is already an accomplished fact to every part of a believer's experience. In Romans 6:11 at the conclusion of his section on baptism into Christ's death, Paul finds it necessary to urge his readers to consider themselves 'dead to sin and alive to God'. They need to develop an attitude of mind which is nevertheless based on an established event in the history of redemption. By dying to sin is meant robbing sin of its authority.

In view of what has already been said about repentance and faith as a prerequisite for belonging to the body of Christ (see pp. 573ff.), we need to enquire what part baptism has to play as a public avowal of being 'in Christ'. Is the reality of Christ's death and resurrection appropriated by the

---

[198] R. A. Harrisville, *The Concept of Newness in the New Testament*, pp. 62ff., in discussing Rom. 6, argues that Paul does not construe the transference of the effects of Christ's resurrection in terms of present sinlessness. He interprets it in a dynamic way. Participation in Christ's resurrection is seen in terms of a gradual approximation to a final goal.

[199] Many scholars see a further reference in 1 Cor. 12:13 to confirmation or to the Lord's supper as an explanation of 'drinking of the Spirit'. *Cf.* R. Schnackenburg, *Baptism in the Thought of Paul* (Eng. trans., 1964), pp. 83f., for details. C. K. Barrett, *1 Corinthians*, p. 289, takes the second part of the verse as the necessary supplement to baptism, *i.e.* we were baptized in the Spirit. But he cautions against pressing Paul in all the details of the analogy. F. F. Bruce, *1 and 2 Corinthians* (*NCB*, 1971), p. 121, prefers the rendering 'we were all watered with one Spirit', *i.e.* in the sense of refreshment.

believer at the moment of faith or at the moment of baptism? Paul certainly connects up 'union with Christ' with baptism, but does he imply that only through the baptismal act is identification with Christ possible? In other words does he regard baptism as a sacramental incorporation into Christ? While it is true that he does not drive a wedge between faith and baptism, and would undoubtedly have rejected the validity of any baptism which was divorced from faith, he is not maintaining that the external rite of baptism is in itself a means of grace.[200] It is rather a confirmation of what is already accomplished at the moment of faith, *i.e.* a crucifixion of the sinful self. This is made clear in the passage in Galatians 3:23–27, where Paul affirms that through faith people become sons of God and that those baptized have 'put on Christ'.[201] For the apostle the adoption into sonship and the putting on of Christ are therefore inseparable.

Paul makes much of the dying process effected by Christ, for not only has it spelt death to sin, but also to the law (Rom. 7:4ff.), which he describes in terms of a conqueror holding people captive. Dying to the law is linked with living to God (Gal. 2:19).[202] We must not jump to the conclusion that Paul saw no helpful aspects of the law (*cf.* Rom. 7:12), but its effect was to make men feel like captives, because they had no power to carry out its demands (see later discussion, pp. 691ff.). The company of believers who were crucified with Christ had become free from the bondage of the law. They were now free to live a mode of existence which was no longer dominated by law.

The same could be said of the world, for Paul also speaks of Christians having died to the 'elemental spirits (*stoicheia*) of the world' (Col. 2:20), or to the first principles of the world (as *stoicheia* could mean). Whichever is the correct rendering, the dying to the 'world' as the controlling system of life seems to be uppermost in Paul's mind. In Galatians 4:9 he defines the same concept (*stoicheia*) as 'weak and beggarly', where he may be referring to the law, but more probably is thinking of the Galatians' former pagan lifestyle. Dying with Christ means nothing short of a complete break with sin, the law and the world as forces which dominate the life of man. The dying metaphor may be said to be an integral part of Paul's theology, for it shows the imperative nature of the new life which comes through the

---

[200] G. R. Beasley-Murray, *Baptism in the New Testament* (1962), p. 265, writes, 'Baptism saves, not because water washes dirt from the body, but as the occasion when a man is met by the Risen Christ.' He further speaks of the grace offered in baptism as being 'the gracious act of God Himself'.

[201] W. F. Flemington, *The New Testament Doctrine of Baptism* (1948), p. 80, maintains that this and other passages imply that for Paul in baptism 'something is not merely expressed but actually accomplished'. He considers it to be untenable to maintain that baptism was a bare symbol.

[202] *Cf.* R. Schnackenburg, *op. cit.*, p. 62, commenting on Gal. 2:19, writes, 'That Paul has died to the hapless Jewish *nomos* precisely through this same *nomos*, gives the sentence its terseness and sharpness'. He further notes that Paul has been drawn into an event (I have been crucified with Christ), in which *nomos* has been dethroned.

risen Christ. It also vividly highlights the contrast between the old and the new life.

The baptism symbolism, in fact, focuses most attention on the risen life of the believer. As with the dying, so with the rising, the process is both corporate and individual. The church as a whole has already entered into a new experience of life at the resurrection of Christ, although this has to be realized in the lives of each individual believer. The resurrection experience understood in a corporate sense comes over clearly in Colossians 3:1ff. In this passage the dying results in life being hidden with Christ in God, that is to say that life gains a new centre, which although less manifest than the old is nevertheless more real. It means seeking higher things and thinking in higher modes of thought.[203] The resurrection involves a complete transformation of the way of life. The old life has to be resolutely put to death, a fate which it deserves, and conversely the new life has to be embraced.

Paul uses the metaphor of stripping off old garments and putting on new ones to describe the process of transformation (Col. 3:9ff.; Eph. 4:22–24) (see the fuller discussion on this on pp. 657ff.). This idea leads into the whole process of sanctification which will be discussed later (see pp. 667ff.). What is most important to note at this point is the combination of a definite act with a continuous process. Because of the historic event of the resurrection of Christ, the church is controlled by the risen Christ (*i.e.* in heaven), but the process by which the risen life of Christ manifests itself is on earth, through a progressive sanctifying of the body of believers.

IN CHRIST – IN THE SPIRIT

The idea of identification which has just been considered naturally leads to an examination of another characteristic emphasis found in Paul, that of indwelling. Sometimes he speaks of the believer in Christ or in the Spirit, and sometimes of Christ or the Spirit indwelling the believer. These are complementary, not contradictory, concepts.

We note first Paul's idea of the *new creation*, which takes place for the believer when he is 'in Christ' (2 Cor. 5:17). By using the present tense ('he is a new creation') Paul is pointing to a present reality which obtains for all who are 'in Christ'. The phrase here must refer to a radical change which occurs coincident with a man becoming a Christian. But 'in Christ' is infinitely more than an alternative phrase for 'Christian'. It vividly expresses the thought that what happened to Christ affects every believer

---

[203] The form of exhortation in Col. 3:1, *i.e.* imperative *zēteite*, shows the obligation which the new life entails. R. P. Martin, *Colossians and Philemon* (NCB, 1974), p. 100, understands this of the orientation of the will.

in him. The new creation happens to the believer because of what happened to Christ. But some important questions arise. What does Paul mean by the new creation? And what precisely does he mean by 'in Christ'?

Since by the new creation he is referring to a present and not simply to a future reality, it is important to ascertain in what sense the believer can be said to be a 'new creation'. Paul undoubtedly connects this new creation with a past event, *i.e.* the historical death and resurrection of Jesus (*cf.* 2 Cor. 5:15). And yet he is not doing so according to men's usual approach to the historical ('though we once regarded Christ from a human point of view, we regard him thus no longer', 2 Cor. 5:16). He sees in the death of Christ more than the death of the human Jesus. He sees also the death of the old creation dominated by adverse spiritual forces, and the emergence of a new creation in which everything is Christ-centred.

Some identify the new creation with the church which forms a proto-type of the recreated world. But in this case the church must not be considered as an ecclesiastical body, but as a group of believers who share a common Christocentric life. The new creation involves new principles of living, new moral ideas, new methods of thought. It affects individuals, but it involves also a corporate idea. Paul talks about God in Christ reconciling the world to himself, by which he seems to mean the world order.[204] He regards the old order as dead in actual fact, as far as the Christian is concerned. But this does not mean that any visible change has come over the existing order. In Paul's thought each succeeding group of Christians could look at the cross and know that the old order, alien to God, has been effectively destroyed.

It is against this background of an already existing new creation in Christ, that the fuller implications of the 'in Christ' phrase must be examined, for the realization of the new creation happens only to those who are 'in Christ'. In view of the obvious contrast between the actual and the potential in the present historical situation, there is bound to be tension, and this tension must be set alongside the 'in Christ' concept if the meaning of that concept is to be understood.

The attempt to arrive at a precise understanding of Paul's 'in Christ' formula has given rise to various interpretations. Some consider it to be evidence of the influence of mysticism on the apostle.[205] One theory claims

---

[204] P. E. Hughes, *2 Corinthians*, p. 201, describes the new creation as 'a reborn microcosm belonging to the eschatological macrocosm of the new heavens and the new earth'. He goes on to show the rich variety of meaning to be attached here to the phrase 'in Christ'.

[205] On mysticism in Paul, *cf.* A. Wikenhauser, *Pauline Mysticism* (Eng. trans. 1960), who presents full discussions of the forms 'In Christ', 'Of Christ' and 'Christ in us', and proceeds to bring out the specifically Christian character of Pauline mysticism. To avoid confusion it would be better perhaps to avoid the use of the word 'mysticism' in relation to Paul. R. C. Tannehill, *Dying and Rising with Christ. A Study in Pauline Theology* (1967), p. 3 n. 7, points out the variety of ways in which the word 'mysticism' is used and chooses to speak of Paul as a mystic, but denies that Paul has a mystical theology.

that the preposition (*en*) must be regarded as pointing to locality,[206] but this is possible only if Christ is seen as the all-pervasive Spirit, as a kind of spiritual atmosphere in which the believer lives. It is not necessary to suppose that Paul was a pure mystic in the same sense as contemporary oriental mystics,[207] for he was clearly concerned with the moral outcome of his doctrine. A believer in Christ is not a person who waits to be ecstatically transported to a spiritual level which has no relationship to his historical situation. He experiences a moral change through being 'in Christ'. The strength of this interpretation lies in its achievement in translating into moral action now what Jesus Christ did in past history, but its weakness lies in its effusion of the personality of Christ into Spirit.[208] It achieves its end through an inadequate Christology.

No interpretation of Paul's 'in Christ' doctrine which does not explain how the historical Christ can be linked with present experience will stand examination; but the moral mysticism mentioned above is not the only kind of mystical interpretation.[209] Another view is that 'in Christ' and 'in the church' are to be identified and that the new life, therefore, is mediated through the church. The believer who belongs to the church belongs to the body of Christ.[210] Thus the 'in Christ' formula is interpreted ecclesiastically and each believer actually shares in the divine life through being incorporated in the church. This view is generally tied up with a sacramental approach to the function of the church. The new life is life lived at a new level, not as individuals, but as a community. The 'in Christ' formula takes on a social aspect, but affects only the society of Christians, *i.e.* the church.[211] This view has in its favour that it takes seriously the continuity between the historical Jesus and the community of believers by maintaining that the church is an extension of the incarnation. But it is open to dispute since it rests on the assumption of a strong mystical element in Paul's approach.

---

[206] *Cf.* A. Deissman, who published his monograph, *Die neutestamentliche Formel 'In Christo Jesu'* in Marburg, 1892. If Deissmann represented an almost totally subjective approach to the meaning of the formula, E. Lohmeyer, *Grundlagen paulinischer Theologie* (1929), and W. Schmauch, *In Christus* (1935), are representatives of an objective (metaphysical) view. For a brief summary of their views, *cf.* M. Bouttier, *En Christ* (1962), pp. 10ff.

[207] For a penetrating critique of the Hellenistic Mystery religious background of Paul's approach, *cf.* A. Schweitzer, *The Mysticism of Paul the Apostle*, pp. 26ff.

[208] For an appraisal of Deissmann's view, *cf.* Schweitzer, *ibid.*, pp. 33ff.; M. Bouttier, *op. cit.*, pp. 5ff.

[209] *Cf.* E. L. Mascall, *Christ, the Christian, and the Church* (1946), pp. 109ff.

[210] *Cf.* Schweitzer, *op. cit.*, pp. 116ff., who deduces the collective sense of 'in Christ' (= the body) in reaction against the purely subjective view of Deissmann. He was against the mystical understanding of the phrase. *Cf.* also R. Bultmann, *TNT* 1, p. 311; G. Bornkamm, *Paul*, H. Conzelmann, *TNT*, p. 184. E. P. Sanders, *Paul and Palestinian Judaism*, pp. 458f., discusses the matter and prefers the 'participationist' sense.

[211] R. Bultmann, *TNT* 1, p. 311, maintains that the 'In Christ' formula, 'far from being a formula for mystical union is primarily an ecclesiological formula'. His view is that the believer is taken up into the body of Christ through the sacrament of baptism.

Other exponents of Paul's thought have preferred to put the emphasis on positive action. 'In Christ' is to be regarded more from the point of view of joint action by Christ and the believer than from the point of view of ontological unity.[212] When someone is 'in Christ', he is brought into the service of Christ, hence the experience is inseparable from a sense of vocation. But this does not involve the present actuality of the new creation. It only sets out the goal towards which those 'in Christ' are moving. Its full manifestation will not take place until the future.[213]

Another position is that which maintains that a new situation has arisen within history in that the principalities and powers which had previously enslaved the world have now been defeated. To be 'in Christ' therefore means being in a new situation.[214] This differs from being infused with new life, for it focuses attention on a new set of circumstances in which the believer can face the world having been liberated from bondage to hostile forces. The new situation means that the believer is now under the control of the Spirit of God and not the spirit of evil.[215] 'In Christ', he finds himself still in a hostile world, but not enslaved by the hostility, after the example of Christ himself. This interpretation has the advantage of maintaining the present relevance of the 'in Christ' concept, without supposing that the new situation obtains for creation at large. The Christian has a freedom which he did not previously possess (cf. Rom. 7:25).

So far we have discussed the different meanings proposed for Paul's characteristic expression, but we need to look closer at the ways in which he uses it.[216] Sometimes the *en* (in) may be used in the sense of instrument, *e.g.* sanctified by Christ Jesus (1 Cor. 1:2); justified by Christ (Gal. 2:17); entreating in or by the Lord Jesus (1 Thes. 4:1); although it is disputable whether this exhausts the meaning. At other times the expression is used in a general sense; *e.g.* Paul sends greetings 'in Christ' (Rom. 16:3), which almost stands for 'Christian' greetings although expressed more tellingly. There are many instances such as these, but they would undoubtedly be

---

[212] *Cf.* K. Barth, *Church Dogmatics* IV, 3, pp. 540ff.

[213] There is a close connection in thought between Paul's 'in Christ' formula and the idea of communion with Christ. A. R. George, *Communion with God in the New Testament* (1953), pp. 150ff., attempts to show the relationship by suggesting that 'in Christ' relates to the 'now', and 'with Christ' to the future. Yet he admits that in most instances where the 'with Christ' concept occurs the past tense is used. He cites W. T. Hahn, *Das Mitsterben und Mitauferstehen mit Christus bei Paulus* (1937), pp. 31–45, for the view that Paul is presenting two sides of a unity: new life is given as a whole, but not until the *parousia* will it be a final and undisputed possession.

[214] F. Neugebauer, 'Das paulinische "en Christo" ', *NTS* 4, 1957-8, pp. 124–138. approaches the phrase from the point of view of salvation history. This article was published before his book *In Christus* (1961), but is based on the examination of the evidence in the latter.

[215] *Cf.* L. B. Smedes, *All Things Made New* (1970), pp. 90ff.

[216] For a concise survey of Paul's usage, *cf.* C. F. D. Moule, 'The Corporate Christ' in his *The Phenomenon of the New Testament* (1967), pp. 21–42. Moule points out that while Paul does occasionally speak of Christ in the believer, this is rare compared with its converse, the believer in Christ. He thinks that when Paul uses the former idea, he tends to think of Christ as 'at work' or 'living his life' in believers (p. 25).

enriched if some notion of incorporation into Christ is assumed.[217]

In attempting some kind of classification of Paul's 'in Christ' passages we may note that he uses the expression in two main ways, first as applied to persons, and second as applied to abstract qualities. Under the first we may note that 'God in Christ' furnishes the key to the meaning of this 'in Christ' relationship. This means for Paul that what happened in history when Christ fulfilled his mission was an act of God (*cf.* Rom. 3:23, redemption in Christ Jesus; Col. 2:15, triumph over principalities and powers; Rom. 8:39, the exercise of divine love). The application of the formula to believers is a modification of the same idea, but with a completely different emphasis. The fact that the believer is in Christ, which is so strongly characteristic of Paul's thought (*cf.* Rom. 8:1; 1 Cor. 3:1; 1 Cor. 15:22; 2 Cor. 5:17), has one aspect in common with 'God in Christ' and that is the sense of incorporation, which leads to identity of action.

A particular example of this is the apostle's own view of his apostolic work. His ministry among his converts (1 Cor. 4:15); his manner of addressing them (2 Cor. 2:17; Phil. 2:1); his labours among them (Rom. 16:3, 9, 12); his circumstances as a prisoner (Phil. 1:13); his weakness (2 Cor. 13:4) and strength (Phil. 4:13), are all viewed as 'in Christ'. The same personal emphasis is found when Paul speaks of whole communities being 'in Christ' (*cf.* 1 Thes. 1:1; Phil. 1:1; 1 Thes. 2:14).[218] What is true of the individual is also true of the community. Indeed it is questionable whether Paul separated the two concepts in his own mind.

Examples of the second application of the 'in Christ' formula, to abstract qualities, are as follows. A Christian's wisdom is known by its 'in Christ' quality (1 Cor. 4:10). Paul claims that his own ways are 'in Christ', by which he apparently means that his whole pattern of life is controlled by his dwelling in Christ (1 Cor. 4:17). Spiritual wealth is described as being 'in him' (1 Cor. 1:5). The kind of life which believers now live is said to be 'in Christ' to distinguish it from the life lived by the non-Christians. Whereas the latter are immersed in the principles of a world alien to God, the Christian is controlled by principles of a totally different kind. Paul's doctrine here is quite clear. Nothing for the Christian in the present world can be approached except 'in Christ'. As the old humanity was 'in Adam', so the new creation is 'in Christ'. Until Christ came, all were adversely affected by Adam's transgression and only a new creation made possible an escape from those crippling effects (*cf.* Rom. 5:12ff. and see the section on Adam theology, pp. 333ff.).

---

[217] M. Bouttier, *En Christ*, pp. 132f., summarizes the uses of the *en Christō* formula as instrumental (or historical), inclusive and communal, and eschatological. He has moved away from the polarization seen in the earlier work of Deissmann, Schweitzer and others.

[218] Paul certainly means more by 'in Christ' than that the readers are Christians. They live in him every day, *cf.* L. Morris, *The First Epistle of Paul to the Corinthians* (*TNTC* 1958), pp. 49f.

In the above discussion no mention has been made of the kindred phrase 'in the Spirit'. Paul's use of such an expression throws light on his understanding of the Christian's new position.[219] Some have equated Christ and the Spirit, claiming a kind of spiritualized presence as replacing the personality of Christ for this age. Others, recognizing the inadequacy of this Christology, have nevertheless approximated to an equating of Christ with the Spirit, mainly on the grounds of 2 Corinthians 3:17 ('the Lord is the Spirit'). This statement has already been touched on in the section on the Holy Spirit (see pp. 570f.), but our present concern is to discuss its relevance to the 'in Christ' theme. It has been shown that Paul regards the Christian life as dominated by the Spirit. Christians are 'not in the flesh' but 'in the Spirit' (Rom. 8:9). Since Paul in the same context speaks of the Spirit as the Spirit of Christ, the conclusion is inescapable that 'in the Spirit' and 'in Christ' must mean the same thing. All that has been said above about the radical change which has been effected in Christ could come about only through the activity of the Spirit.

In view of this we may enquire in what sense Paul related the believer's position 'in Christ' to the present activity of the Spirit.[220] Did he view the Spirit as Christ in action pursuing his redemptive plan on earth? Was the Spirit regarded as Christ being experienced in and by the community? There is undoubtedly some truth in the view that Paul drew no distinction between Christ and the Spirit as far as the on-going work in the believer is concerned.[221] Since Christ was exalted in heaven he could dwell in believers only through the Spirit (hence 'Christ in you' and 'the Spirit in you' are used interchangeably; see the discussion in the next section). But if Paul did not distinguish their functions, he also did not confuse their natures. It may perhaps be helpful to think of 'in Christ' as static, providing the basis for the new creation, while 'in the Spirit' is dynamic giving the powerful motivation in the working out of that new creation. The latter makes clear that the power behind the new creation is not an impersonal natural energy, but a personal divine Spirit.

In this double way Paul means his readers to realize that through the Spirit they may be linked with Jesus Christ who lived in history, but who

---

[219] In discussing the relation between *en Christō* and *en Pneumati* in Paul's letters, M. Bouttier, *op. cit.*, pp. 61ff., mentions the following passages where *en Pneumati* occurs – Rom. 2:29; 8:9; 9:1; 14:17; 15:16; 1 Cor. 6:11; 12:3, 9a, 9b, 13; 2 Cor. 6:6; Gal. 6:1; Eph. 2:18, 22; 3:5; 4:30; 5:18; Phil. 1:27; Col. 1:8; 1 Thes. 1:5. He then discusses Deissman's comparisons with *en Christō*. He cites E. Percy, *Der Leib Christi* (1942), p. 36, for the opinion that it is necessary to be *in Christ* in order to have any share *in the Spirit*.

[220] See the discussion of Smedes, *op. cit.*, pp. 54ff.

[221] For the view that communion with Christ is interchangeable with communion with the Spirit, *cf.* L. S. Thornton, *The Common Life in the Body of Christ* (³1942), pp. 137, 142. Thornton's general approach, however, does not seem to bear out these isolated statements. A. B. Come, *Human Spirit and Holy Spirit* (1959), pp. 158f., criticizes Thornton for confusing the issue, especially when he equates 'communion with Christ' with 'the grace of Christ'. It should be noted that Thornton generally regards the Spirit as impersonal.

is now exalted. So real is the link that he can speak of believers as being 'in Christ' without any fear that his readers will misunderstand his language.[222] This is not because there were contemporary parallels to this kind of language, but because they had experienced, as Paul had done, the reality of being incorporated 'in Christ'. It was this that made Christian experience unique.

THE INDWELLING CHRIST AND INDWELLING SPIRIT

So rich is Paul's idea of the relationship between Christ and the believer that he complements his 'in Christ' concept with a 'Christ in us' concept. In the same way 'in the Spirit' finds its counterpart in the indwelling of the Spirit. In both of these ideas the initiative is outside the believer's control. Another presence takes over. It is more active and positive than the other forms. It presents a somewhat different, though kindred, approach to the new life.

The apostle is conscious of the indwelling Christ as Galatians 2:20 shows: 'It is no longer I who live, but Christ who lives in me'. The indwelling Christ displaces the already crucified self.[223] But this is not some unique experience of Paul. It is meant to be the norm. Paul prays that his converts may know the same experience (Eph. 3:17): 'that Christ may dwell in your hearts through faith'. He speaks of the mystery, which God has chosen to make known, as being 'Christ in you, the hope of glory' (Col. 1:27).[224] He recognizes the difficulty of the concept, as the use of the word 'mystery' shows, but he has no doubt about its truth. This passage is significant because of its corporate character; it applies to the body of believers. When writing to the Corinthians Paul challenges them with the question, 'Do you not realize that Jesus Christ is in you?' (2 Cor. 13:5). Moreover the indwelling of the Spirit of Christ is declared to be the possession of all believers (Rom. 8:9).

Closely allied and almost indistinguishable from this is the concept of the indwelling Spirit. There are in fact more references to the indwelling Spirit than to the indwelling Christ. The classic passage is Romans 8, but the activity of the Spirit within the believer runs consistently through Paul's

---

[222] *Cf.* C. F. D. Moule *The Phenomenon of the New Testament*, pp. 39f.

[223] A. Schweitzer, *The Mysticism of Paul the Apostle*, p. 125, considers that Gal. 2:19, 20 shows that for Paul the Christian 'is only a form of manifestation of the personality of Jesus Christ'. He speaks of the 'corporeity of Christ'. This brings out a positive contribution of the passage, but Schweitzer's purpose is to contrast Paul's mysticism with Hellenistic mysticism.

[224] E. Lohse, *Colossians and Philemon* (Eng. trans. *Hermeneia*, 1971, from *KEK*, 1968), p. 76, takes this in the sense 'Christ among you' (as preached in the midst of the community). R. P. Martin, *Colossians: The Church's Lord and the Christian's Liberty*, p. 65, interprets it of Christ's presence among the Gentiles. See also Martin's *Colossians and Philemon* (*NCB*, 1974), p. 72, where he suggests a trace of Paul's second Adam teaching. W. Hendriksen, *Colossians and Philemon* (1971), p. 89, thinks the phrase points to the equality of Gentiles and Jews in that Christ was in them both. C. F. D. Moule, *Colossians and Philemon*, p. 85, is content to see 'among you' as at least a very plausible alternative to 'within you'.

epistles. He says to the Romans, 'You are not in the flesh, you are in the Spirit, if the Spirit of God really dwells in you' (Rom. 8:9). This antithesis between 'in the flesh' and 'in the Spirit', which is characteristic of Paul, is important for a right understanding of the indwelling Spirit. It implies an altogether different principle of living.[225] In some sense the Spirit of God takes possession of the believer, who becomes a temple of the Spirit (1 Cor. 3:16; 6:19). The presence of the Spirit within us is regarded as a guarantee of our position (2 Cor. 1:22, 5:5). It is the Spirit also who convinces the believer of his sonship (Rom. 8:16). Paul even connects up the indwelling Spirit with the conviction that he makes right judgments (1 Cor. 7:40).[226]

The apostle never makes any significant distinction between the function of Christ and of the Spirit within the believer. The indwelling Christ is possible only through the indwelling Spirit. It must be noted also that when Paul speaks of the indwelling Christ, he means no-one other than the risen Jesus. No explanation of the 'Christ in you' idea which sidetracks the essential continuity between the historical Jesus and the indwelling Christ does justice to Paul's theological thinking. At the same time no-one supposes that it is easy to attach precise meaning to Paul's 'indwelling' terminology.

Some explain the concept from a mystical point of view, supposing that in some way Christ's indwelling in man means that man is taken up to a higher level of existence. Man's life, in short, becomes infused with God's life. Pushed to its limits this amounts to the deification of man. So long as we are content to believe that Paul meant his readers to conclude that when he spoke of Christ within us, he was thinking of the infusion of an impersonal, although divine, principle of life which takes possession of us, this mystical point of view is tenable.[227] It takes seriously the 'indwelling' concept. But does it do justice to Paul? Its fundamental weakness is in its depersonalizing of the indwelling Christ, who becomes no more than a deifying infusion.[228] So many of the references in Paul's letters lose much of their force if the personal emphasis is denied. He never says that an effusion of divine life dwells in us, but only that Jesus Christ, or the Holy Spirit dwells in us. Another weakness of this mystical interpretation is its basic assumption that man already possesses the same kind of nature as

---

[225] F. J. Leenhardt, *Romans*, p. 207, takes *en* here as instrumental and not locative, and declares that the phrase here indicates 'a way of life'.

[226] Paul is speaking about a personal opinion here. But as J. Héring, *1 Corinthians*, p. 65, notes he does not claim to speak in Christ's name, nor by virtue of his apostleship, but because he has the Spirit.

[227] E. L. Mascall, *Christ, the Christian and the Church*, pp. 77ff., thinks of the Christian as a person who has been reborn by a real incorporation of his or her human nature into the human nature of the incarnate Word. But his exposition is theological rather than exegetical.

[228] A similar view was earlier expressed by the Catholic writer, M. J. Scheeben, Eng. trans. *Nature and Grace* (1954), from the German *Natur und Gnade* (1861, ⁴1949).

God, *i.e.* it assumes a doctrine of man which is inadequate.

It is not surprising that other Pauline interpreters have understood the 'indwelling' passages in a different way, regarding Paul as less a mystic and more a man of action. Instead of supposing a fundamental change in man's nature to something akin to deification, an alternate view insists that Paul was thinking of an objective Christ: outside ourselves, he accomplished a complete and sacrificial act for us on the cross, which has now become meaningful to us through faith. There is almost, in this view, an identification of the indwelling Christ with faith.[229] As God accepts Christ, so he accepts the believer. According to this interpretation Christ is always expressing his presence in the believer through action, rather than through some mystical diffusion. Whenever the believer actively obeys, this is considered to be tantamount to Christ indwelling him. Christian life is then seen as co-action with Christ.[230] It may be objected that this view does not do justice to Paul's concept of 'Christ in us', and the criticism deserves to be taken seriously. It is to be commended in retaining to the full the actual presence within of a personal Christ, but it does not explain what Paul meant by 'Christ in us'.

Another view which mediates between the two ideas expressed above is that which sees the indwelling Christ expressed in terms of spiritual power.[231] In other words, the indwelling Christ is seen as the indwelling Spirit who always acts dynamically in power. Paul's view of the gospel certainly concentrated on its power (Rom. 1:16).[232] The Christian's motive power comes directly from God (Eph. 3:20). This suggests that the indwelling Christ results in powerful living. God's power in Christ becomes at once available. Wherever the Spirit of God is manifesting his activity in powerful lives, it is an evidence that Christ dwells within. This becomes intelligible if the Spirit is identified with Christ, but the problem here is to retain the real person of Christ without his becoming spiritized as in mysticism.

In the final analysis it must be admitted that there is no way of being sure what Paul meant by the indwelling Christ, but he shows no consciousness of any difficulties his readers might find in grappling with the idea. He assumes that they would at once instinctively grasp the significance of the 'Christ in you' concept for the new life. It would convey the idea that all life should henceforth be Christ-centred, and Paul's readers would recognize that this was possible only through the powerful operation of

---

[229] *Cf.* the discussion of faith by E. Brunner, *The Christian Doctrine of the Church, Faith, and the Consummation* (1962), pp. 174f.

[230] *Cf.* also K. Barth, *Church Dogmatics*, IV 3, pp. 543ff.

[231] So Smedes, *All Things Made New*, pp. 176ff.

[232] W. Lüthi, *The Letter to the Romans*, (Eng. trans. 1961), p. 11, points out that gospel as power does not try to compete with the powers of this world. It is superior to all others.

the Spirit. Far from being deified, the believer has been placed in a position of continual dependence on a source of power totally beyond his own resources.

INTO CHRIST

It is not surprising to find in Paul's writings the idea of 'into (*eis*) Christ' appearing alongside 'in (*en*) Christ.' It occurs in Romans 6:3 in the expression 'baptized into Christ', which seems to mean that baptism inaugurated us into a condition in which we now become 'in Christ'. In this case there is no essential distinction between the two expressions with regard to new life in Christ.[233] There is also in this passage a close relationship between 'in Christ' and 'with Christ'. If these latter expressions both contain within them a corporate concept, then 'into Christ' means more than admittance into the Christian body, and must include some sense of identification with the personality of Christ himself. This comes out more clearly in Galatians 3:27, where baptism into Christ is linked with the annulment of social, racial and sexual discrimination. Again in this passage 'into Christ' appears alongside 'in Christ' and there is no clear distinction between them. The emphasis on all in Christ Jesus being 'one man' underlies the corporate nature of the 'into Christ' formula.

The idea of baptism into Christ also occurs in 1 Corinthians 12:13, although 'into Christ' is represented by the 'into one body' formula. In this case it is explicit that Spirit-baptism is the point of entry into the body. The body, moreover, represents the church of Christ as a corporate whole, and the local force of 'into' (*eis*) must be given full weight. The enigmatic statement in 1 Corinthians 10:2 about 'our fathers' being all 'baptized into Moses' has been variously understood. Since 'into Moses' is intended as a comparison with 'into Christ' some regard it as meaning no more than becoming a follower of Moses. The parallel Christian formula would therefore be equivalent to 'in the name of Christ'.[234] On the other hand, some exegetes regard the 'into Moses' formula as being abnormal and modelled on the Christian side of incorporation into Christ.[235]

It must be noted that the connection of the 'into Christ' idea with baptism gives no warrant for attaching any magical significance to baptism divorced from faith, for there is no evidence that Paul thought in such terms. Indeed, his insistence on the Spirit's part in this initiation is sufficient to show that faith is necessary, for faith and the operation of the Spirit in the individual are inseparably connected.

---

[233] For a careful assessment of the evidence on this formula, *cf.* E. Best, *One Body in Christ* (1965), pp. 65ff.

[234] *Cf.* G. R. Beasley-Murray, *Baptism in the New Testament*, pp. 128f.

[235] *Cf.* E. Best, *op. cit.*, pp. 71ff. *Cf.* also C. F. D. Moule, *Colossians and Philemon*, pp. 38f.; C. K. Barrett, *From First Adam to Last* (1962), pp. 49f.

PUTTING OFF AND PUTTING ON

In one sense the process of discarding the old life and embracing the new life comes under the subject of sanctification, which is examined in the next section, but certain aspects of it belong properly to the subject of the new life. This is especially true of the idea of putting on Christ which occurs twice in Paul's epistles (Rom. 13:14; Gal. 3:27). We need to consider in what ways 'putting on Christ' relates to being 'in Christ' and Christ being in us.

In Romans 13:14 it is clear that putting on Christ is the antithesis to being dominated by the flesh and its desires. It amounts to putting on a whole new way of life, conducting oneself in a manner consonant with Christ.[236] In this case 'putting on Christ' has no mystic connotation and may be regarded as a metaphorical way of speaking of the adoption of Christian principles of living. The Galatians 3:27 passage, however, has further implications, since it is connected with Christian baptism ('For as many of you as were baptized into Christ have put on Christ'). The symbolism is of the newly baptized wrapping themselves with a new robe, Christ. Again, however, the idea of the new life is meant to be in marked contrast to the old life. There is a clear connection between this idea and that of being baptized 'into Christ' (*cf.* Rom. 6:3).[237] It is almost as if the baptized person enters into a new sphere, which may symbolically be likened to being clothed with Christ.

The apostle uses the 'putting-on' metaphor in other ways. He speaks of the Christian putting on armour (Rom. 13:12; Eph. 6:10), or immortality or incorruption (1 Cor. 15:53–54), all of which suggest a new approach or condition. In the light of this, we note the classic passage in which Paul speaks of putting on the new nature, or new man (Eph. 4:24). This idea did not involve for Paul the superimposing of the new man upon the old, but a radical transformation.[238] It is linked with a renewal of the mind. Its pattern is nothing short of 'the likeness of God' and is expressed in terms of righteousness and holiness, terms which are wholly inapplicable to the old nature. In Colossians 3:12 the putting on process involves the addition of virtues like compassion, kindness, meekness, patience and above all love.

The question arises whether Paul is here thinking of the enhancement of natural qualities or the endowment of the believer with specifically Chris-

[236] For a survey of possible parallels to Paul's 'putting on' and 'putting off' language, *cf.* P. W. van der Horst, 'Observations on a Pauline expression', *NTS* 19, 1973, pp. 181ff. He suggests Paul may have derived it from a current philosophical usage to denote transition from an unenlightened to an enlightened state.

[237] W. F. Flemington, *The New Testament Doctrine of Baptism*, pp. 57f., discusses the parallels with the initiation procedures in the mystery religions.

[238] E. Best, *op. cit.*, pp. 67f., mentions, but does not favour, the view that the new man = Christ.

tian qualities previously not experienced, which need to be accepted as a new norm for Christian living. The latter is more likely, since it better fits the 'putting on' metaphor. In Christ, the believer is called on to embrace virtues which must now be regarded as normal. Before a person is in Christ he may certainly perform acts of compassion, but in Christ compassion (and the other virtues) become a permanent attitude of mind.

Paul cannot conceive of 'putting on' a new nature without stressing the need to 'put off' the old. There is a negative side as well as a positive.[239] The one is as important as the other. The negative side in fact highlights the radical aspect of the new nature. There are three main passages of this kind. In Romans 13:12 the readers are exhorted to cast off the works of darkness and to put on the armour of light, which suggests that the casting off and putting on are simultaneous, the one being the obverse side of the other. Light and darkness are mutually exclusive. The Christian life involves turning one's back on works which before had seemed perfectly natural.[240]

In Colossians 3:5ff. Paul gives a list of vices which the Christians are exhorted to put to death. The list includes sins of the mind like impurity, evil desire and covetousness. To put these to death means again a radical approach to one's mental state. It involves no less than a moral revolution. The old nature with its practices must be resolutely put away. But is Paul suggesting that each person must put off the old nature before he can hope to put on the new? This would impose an intolerable burden on the individual and would smack too much of works to be a plausible understanding of Paul's thought. The only reasonable interpretation is to suppose that 'putting off' and 'putting on' are opposing sides of one action. It is only when the new nature is embraced that the old nature can be put to death.[241] The apostle gives no indication that this putting off is a once-for-all operation except in an ideal sense[242] (cf. Col. 3:9f. where the putting off appears as a *past* act, and possibly Eph. 4:22f,. where the putting off could refer to a past event rather than a command). It is rather a process, in short, the process of sanctification.

[239] W. Hendriksen, *Ephesians*, p. 215, in order to stress the necessity for both positive and negative aspects uses the interesting illustration of the uselessness of one scissorblade. Paul does not suggest that the putting off must be complete before the putting on is possible. As in so many NT passages there is an inescapable tension.

[240] According to R. A. Harrisville, *The Concept of Newness in the New Testament*, p. 75, the 'old' man is non-eschatological man, 'man as he lives in relation to a seemingly unchanging world'. Harrisville sees the new element in Paul's approach, as compared with contemporary Greek and Jewish views, to be the goal towards which man moves. The new man is the eschatological man.

[241] J. B. Lightfoot, *Colossians and Philemon* (⁹1890) speaks of each person having a two-fold moral personality.

[242] It could, of course, be argued that a decisive act is being envisaged in which the old man is 'put off' as the principle of life. Harrisville, *op. cit.*, pp. 83f., is strongly critical of the view that the new man and the old man exist side by side, on the grounds that Paul commands the readers to put off the old man absolutely.

The parallel passage in Ephesians 4:22ff. similarly urges a putting away of the old nature and the former manner of life. Samples are given like falsehood, anger, theft, idleness, wrong speaking; an interesting mixture of attitudes and actions. This implies that such things do not belong to the new nature, but are alien to it. One interesting feature is the warning against grieving the Spirit of God (Eph. 4:30), which implies that those who possess the new nature, and yet continue to manifest the vices mentioned, would be grieving the Spirit. It is only through the indwelling Spirit that the new nature is possible. Consequently those who possess the new nature must be sensitive to the dictates of the Spirit in their approach to the old.

Hebrews

In Hebrews there is surprisingly little evidence of any idea of union with or in Christ. Instead the approach is almost wholly objective, concerned with what Christ has done and is still doing 'for us' rather than 'in us'. Indeed, in this area of thought there is a marked distinction between this author and Paul. In Hebrews 3:14 he speaks of Christians (*i.e.* those who hold their first confidence to the end) as sharing in or being 'partakers' (*metachoi*) with Christ (or of Christ). There is debate over whether this expression is to be understood in the same sense as Paul's 'in Christ'. The context shows a close relationship between Christ and his people.[243] Hebrews 3:6 states: 'we are his house', *i.e.* in a possessive sense. It fits the context best, therefore, if we understand 3:14 in the sense of our being 'confederate with' Christ (as *metachoi* with the genitive bears this meaning in both LXX and koinē Greek).[244]

While we draw a distinction, therefore, between Paul and Hebrews, this does not mean that there is any antithesis between them. It is sufficient to suppose that each writer is concerning himself with a different problem. In concentrating on man's approach to God, Hebrews sees the main importance in the worshipper having an advocate with God with whom he can be closely identified. The same term, *metachoi*, occurs again in Hebrews 6:4, where those who have tasted the heavenly gift are said to be 'partakers of the Holy Spirit' (again with the genitive). It is a remarkable expression and bears some resemblance to Paul's 'in the Spirit', but again without mystical connotation. It is almost as if it stands for those who possess the Spirit and are possessed by the Spirit. The only other statement which approximates to Paul's indwelling idea is the concluding prayer that God would equip the readers, working in them what is well pleasing to him

---

[243] H. W. Montefiore, *Hebrews*, p. 78, considers that the use of *metachoi* in Heb. 3:14 is not in the Pauline sense of sharing in Christ, but as the Son among his brothers. He is giving the word a different sense from its occurrences in Heb. 3:1 and 6:4.

[244] *Cf.* Moulton and Milligan, *VGT* (1930), p. 405. *Cf.* also F. F. Bruce, *Hebrews*, p. 68, who thinks that sharing of the heavenly kingdom is in mind.

through Jesus Christ (Heb. 13:21).[245] But the emphasis in this case is on the activity rather than on the indwelling.

The rest of the New Testament

In the *Petrine epistles*, the 'in Christ' formula in the Pauline sense is lacking, although the concluding greeting refers to 'all of you that are in Christ' (1 Pet. 5:14). The only other occurrences of the form of words are in 1 Peter 5:10, where Peter speaks of the eternal glory to which we are called 'in Christ' (where the formula is instrumental), and in 1 Peter 3:16, which refers to those 'who revile your good behaviour in Christ' (where it virtually means 'Christian' but with added dimension).[246]

There is no expression in 2 Peter which suggests an indwelling in Christ or Christ dwelling in us. We have already noted (p. 636) that some have seen 2 Peter 1:4 as being derived from the Greek idea of absorption into the deity. But the idea of the deification of man is not supported anywhere else in 2 Peter, nor is it found in the NT elsewhere. It is very different from Paul's concept of 'Christ in us' where there is no suggestion of deification through identification. In the 2 Peter passage, sharing the divine nature stands in antithesis to the corruption in the world. This seems, therefore, to be a way of saying that the believer no longer shares the world's corruption, but shares a new nature derived from God. It is more reasonable to suppose that 2 Peter uses a pagan catch-word and then transforms it into a meaningful concept within the Christian framework. *Jude* 1 has the expression 'beloved in God . . . and kept for Jesus Christ', but this does not refer to mystical union. In *Revelation* also this concept finds no explicit mention, although throughout the book Christ is closely identified with his people. Nevertheless the idea of incorporation of believers in Christ is absent.

It will be seen from this survey that abiding in Christ or being in him is almost exclusively confined to the Johannine and Pauline literature. Since these contain the most profound theological reflection, it is not surprising that the idea of union with Christ figures so prominently. It provides the key to the understanding of the early Christian approach to sanctification, which is next to be considered.

In these epistles there are traces of the Pauline idea of putting off. Hebrews sets out things to avoid, although it does not spell them out in specific moral details. The quest for perfection (see the next section) implies

---

[245] This statement in Heb. 13:21 could be compared with Paul's ideas in Phil. 2:12f. and Eph. 2:10. *Cf.* P. E. Hughes, *Hebrews* p. 591.

[246] H. Balz and W. Schrage, *Die 'Katholischen' Briefe*, (1973), p. 100, note that the Christian way of life is grounded 'in Christ', which introduces more content than the adjective 'Christian' would do. J. N. D. Kelly, *Peter and Jude*, p. 145, goes as far as to claim that the expression in 1 Pet. 3:16 betrays the impact of Pauline theology. *Cf.* also E. Best, *1 Peter*, p. 134.

an existing imperfection. The spiritual athlete must 'lay aside every weight and the sin which clings so closely' (Heb. 12:1). The same idea of 'putting off' also occurs in *James* 1:21: 'Therefore put away all filthiness and rank growth of wickedness'. Peter gives a warning that Christians should no longer live 'by human passions, but by the will of God' (1 Pet. 4:2), and then follows a list of vices which are no longer permissible.

We may also note that the 'putting on' idea is found in Revelation 6:11 where the saints crying for vengeance are given a white robe; the same applies to the Bride in 19:8. In these cases the 'putting on' has no corresponding 'putting off', but this is implied rather than stated.

SANCTIFICATION AND PERFECTION

We have so far considered initiation into the Christian life, the nature of grace and the principles of the new life in their personal and corporate aspects. We need next to discuss the Christian ideal and its practical effects. We shall concern ourselves with the NT view of perfection to discover whether the fullest expression of the ideal is possible in this life. It would be valuable at first to explain the terminology. The NT is more concerned with the process of sanctifying or of becoming sanctified than with debating the nature of sanctification. When we use the latter word for the sake of convenience, it must not be supposed that the dynamic side of the idea is being neglected. We shall arrive at a true understanding of NT teaching only if we refuse to fossilize the concept. We shall find good reason to suppose that the NT evidence supports a process rather than a once-for-all happening. The same applies to the concept of perfection. We shall have to consider, in view of this, whether the NT teaches the possibility of achieving sinless perfection. The word *hagiazō* (to sanctify) means 'to set apart for a holy purpose' and is used in biblical Greek of both things and persons. The word *teleioō* (to perfect) has two main meanings, 'to bring to completion, or maturity', and 'to finish, accomplish'. It will be necessary to give careful consideration to the precise meaning in those passages which will be cited, in order to ensure that exegesis determines doctrine and not vice versa.

The synoptic gospels

It is clear from even a cursory reading of these gospels that Jesus frequently dealt with moral questions and attached considerable importance to them. At the same time there was no systematic discussion of ethical principles, no definition of the 'good'. Indeed, Jesus reflects no interest in ethics as an end in itself. It is seen wholly as an aspect of the religious life. It has been said that the ethical teaching presented in the synoptic gospels is not unique, since most of the injunctions can be paralleled among rabbinical writers.[247] But although the form of wording may be comparable, it is the power inherent in the teaching which distinguishes Jesus from all his contemporaries. It will be our purpose here to examine in what sense Jesus may be said to have expected people to reach the ideal he set before them.

Certain qualities are expected from the followers of Jesus like meekness, humility, compassion, purity (Mt. 5:5–8), a forgiving spirit, love for enemies (Mt. 18:21ff.; 5:44). These qualities are not natural to man and require a radical change. Humility, for instance, was not regarded as a virtue either among Jews or Greeks.[248] Indeed, among the Greeks it was regarded as a sign of weakness, and was treated with contempt. Jesus gives no indication that he expected such virtues to be in evidence immediately, but he did not hesitate to set out the ideal. Over against the positive side, he set a list of vices to be renounced, such as hypocrisy, retaliation and censoriousness (Mt. 6:5ff.; 23:2ff.; Lk. 6:29ff.; Mt. 7:1ff.). He made much of the fact that what defiles a man is what comes from within, not what comes from without (Mk. 7:15).[249] In other words, the sanctifying process is concerned primarily with attitudes of mind rather than actions. This is supplemented by the view that right action will follow from right thought. Some of the demands of Jesus are so far-reaching as to appear impossible, like bearing a cross (Mk. 8:34), or accepting a cup of suffering (Mk. 10:38). The radical nature of the challenges issued by Jesus shows the revolutionary character of the process of sanctification.

One of the most far-reaching statements on the Christian ideal made by Jesus is in Matthew 5:48, 'You, therefore, must be perfect, as your heavenly Father is perfect'.[250] This concept of perfection has the highest possible pattern, nothing less than the perfection of God himself.[251] Such an ideal required the authority of Jesus himself to sound authentic. Some, however, shy away from regarding the Matthew statement as authentic to Jesus and prefer the Lucan parallel which has 'be merciful' instead of 'be perfect' (Lk.

---

[247] Cf. C. G. Montefiore, *The Synoptic Gospels* (1909); *idem, Rabbinic Literature and Gospel Teachings* (1930).

[248] Cf. W. Grundmann, *tapeinos, TNDT* 7, pp. 1f., who gives examples of the word being used disparagingly. Cf. R. Leivestad, "*Tapeinos-Tapeinophrōn, NovT* 8, 1966, pp. 36–47, disagrees with Grundmann's view that the profane usage differed from Jewish and Christian usage.

[249] This statement is not to be understood as suggesting that the inward spiritual life of man is superior to his bodily life, but rather as drawing attention to the source of the greatest danger. Cf. H. Anderson, *Mark, (NCB, 1976), pp. 186f.

[250] G. Barth in *Tradition and Interpretation in Matthew* (G. Bornkamm, G. Barth, H. J. Held, Eng. trans. 1960), p. 96, regards the *teleios* in this verse as a Matthean insertion. He refers to the theory that a superior group of *teleioi* accepted complete poverty, as distinct from those who were not *teleioi*. But Barth, rightly rejects such a notion, because it involves a two-level morality.

[251] Some restrict the application of the perfection principle to the injunctions occurring immediately before, *i.e.* especially in love towards enemies. H. Windisch, *The Meaning of the Sermon on the Mount* (Eng. trans. 1937), p. 84, however, considers it to be a regulative principle which allows for other applications.

6:36).[252] There are no good reasons why both should not have had some basis in Jesus' thought, but even if we must choose between them, it is by no means certain that Matthew's form must be rejected. No-one would deny that perfection is a more difficult ideal than showing mercy. It is unconvincing to suppose that either Matthew or some community created so hard a saying. If we accept its authentic character, we are bound to see in it an aim to bring the purpose of God for man to its final fulfilment.

The word used (*teleios*) strictly means complete.[253] Moreover, this saying appears in a context which speaks about love, and it is possible that the perfection in mind is primarily the perfection of love.[254] Perfection is the characteristic of the nature of God. It should be noted that the only other occasion when Jesus spoke of perfection was to the young ruler when he told him that to be perfect he needed to sell his possessions and give to the poor (Mt. 19:21), where the meaning of 'perfect' seems to be 'complete'.

There are ample indications in the synoptic gospels that the ideal set before people was unattainable, consisting rather of a goal to be fulfilled in the future. The beatitudes, according to many interpreters, but not all, focus on eschatological rewards (*cf.* Mt. 5:3–10). The great commandment is all-embracing in its demand for love to God and to one's neighbour (Mk. 12:29–31). The pursuit of the ideal will never be understood unless some element of the impossible is recognized in Jesus' demands. No man who considers himself to have attained perfection already has a right understanding of perfection (see the note on sinless perfection pp. 670f.). Neither is anyone who claims to have arrived at a state of complete love likely to have done so.

The Johannine literature

There is more evidence on our present theme in John's gospel than in the synoptic gospels and this is supplemented especially by 1 John. Jesus expects his disciples to obey his commandments (Jn. 14:15). This is a condition of being his friends (*philoi*, Jn. 15:14). Life with him involves conformity to

---

[252] *Cf.* T. W. Manson (with C. J. Wright, H. D. A. Major), *The Mission and Message of Jesus* (1940), p. 347; R. N. Flew, *The Idea of Perfection in Christian Theology* (1934), p. 4.

[253] R. V. G. Tasker, *Matthew*, p. 70, thinks that because perfection is impossible for man the word *teleios* cannot here mean perfection. He follows C. C. Torrey in deriving a meaning 'all-including' from a possible aramaic original. But this is not the usual meaning of *teleios* in the NT. Moreover, perfection is no more out-of-reach than a God-like holiness which is enjoined in both the OT and the NT. E. Schweizer, *Matthew*, p. 135, suggests that the words here refer to devotion to God, but this imports an idea into *teleios* which is not immediately apparent. D. Hill, *Matthew*, p. 131, considers that 'the emphasis is not on flawless moral character, but on whole-hearted devotion to the imitation of God'. *Cf.* B. Rigaux, 'Révélation des Mystères et Perfection à Qumran et dans le Nouveau Testament', *NTS* 4, 1958, pp. 237–262, especially on the Qumran background.

[254] W. Hendriksen, *Matthew*, pp. 317f., sees 'perfection' in this context specifically in the love which the Father shows to all. The word for 'perfect' here properly means 'full-grown, complete' and points to that moral and spiritual maturity which is seen *par excellence* in God the Father.

his thought, not as an optional extra, but as an obligation. Moreover, Jesus sums up his demands on his disciples in one commandment, 'a new commandment', which requires them to love others as he has loved them (Jn. 13:34; 15:12). As in the synoptics, Jesus sets out his own and his Father's example as the pattern for his disciples. The radical nature of this demand is seen in the comment that the greatest love is the love of a man who gives everything, including life itself, for his friend (Jn. 15:13), which is not only a commentary on the love of Jesus in his passion, but also on the Christian ideal.

The theme of love is particularly characteristic of the Johannine literature. As a desirable Christian virtue it has its roots in God's love for his Son. All things are delivered into the hands of the Son because of the Father's love (Jn. 3:35).[255] What the Father designs is revealed to the Son on account of his love (Jn. 5:20). The Father's love is bound up in the self-giving of the Son (Jn. 10:17; *cf.* 3:16; 1 Jn. 4:10). Moreover, the Father's love for the Son is the pattern for the Son's love for his people (Jn. 15:9). This love of the Father for the Son is timeless ('before the foundation of the world', Jn. 17:24). Not only is God's love mentioned, but the love of Christ for his people is often stressed (Jn. 13:1; 15:9, 12). In John 21:15ff., Jesus challenges Peter three times about his love for himself. On many occasions he pointed out that love for himself was to be a motive for ethical behaviour (*cf.* Jn. 8:42; 14:21f.; 14:28; 16:27). There can be no doubt that the new life as Jesus conceived it centred on love.

So far we have drawn attention mainly to the personal element. But the community aspect is also strong. Love for God and for Jesus Christ must spread to love for others. The enshrinement of this idea in the 'new commandment' has already been mentioned above, but the idea is strongly stressed in John 15:17 which states, 'This I command you, to love one another'. It is probable that the commandment to love is to be taken in the sense that love sums up all the other instruction which Jesus had just given.[256]

John's gospel not only sets out love as an ideal in the process of sanctification, but presents Jesus as sanctifying himself (Jn. 17:19). The same word (*hagiazō*) is used for Jesus as is used for his disciples (Jn. 17:17), but it must clearly bear a different, although kindred, meaning. When Jesus said, 'for their sake I consecrate myself (*hagiazō*), that they also may be consecrated in truth' (Jn. 17:19), he could not have meant 'to become holy', but 'to set himself apart for a holy task'; hence 'consecrate' is a better rendering than 'sanctify'. Nevertheless there is clearly intended to be a link

---

[255] C. H. Dodd, *Interpretation of the Fourth Gospel*, p. 195, sees a connection between the Father's love for the Son, and the idea of the Son in the Father and the Father in the Son in establishing 'a community of life between Father and Son'.

[256] *Cf.* L. Morris, *John*, pp. 677f.

between the consecration of Christ to the task of fulfilling his mission, and that involved in the work of his disciples.[257] The latter are expected to be as devoted to the task of fulfilment as Christ himself.

Another expression of the ideal in John is purification (Jn. 15:2). The quest for purity shows the marked distinction between the new life and the old. In fact, in the allegory of the vine, the purging out of the old promotes greater growth. As elsewhere in the NT the negative is linked with the positive; the purifying of the life from impurities is linked to the development of a holier life.

Especially noteworthy is the emphasis in John's gospel on the work of the Holy Spirit in the life of the believer. This evidence has already been surveyed in considering the person and work of the Spirit (see pp. 526ff.). All that is needed here is to draw attention to those passages which emphasize the indispensability of the Spirit in achieving the ideal. The work of the Spirit in the giving of new life is basic in John's account of Jesus' teaching. Nicodemus was told of the need for rebirth through the Spirit (Jn. 3:3, 5, see section on regeneration pp. 585f.). The germ of new life does not come from the flesh, but from the Spirit (Jn. 6:63). Moreover man cannot control it, for God gives his Spirit unstintingly (Jn. 3:34). In the farewell discourses, Jesus promises the Spirit as teacher (Jn. 14:26), guide (Jn. 16:13), witness (Jn. 15:26) and convicter of the world (Jn. 16:7ff.). The assumption throughout is that the new life is to be life in the Spirit. It is not a matter of self-effort, but of complete reliance on the Spirit. This aspect of sanctification receives fuller treatment in the Pauline epistles.

Many of the themes mentioned above recur in the Johannine epistles. The love motive is succinctly summed up in the statement that God is love (1 Jn. 4:8, 16).[258] Moreover, man's love for God comes more to the fore in the epistles than in the gospel as a motive for the Christian life. The keeping of God's word leads to people being 'perfected' in love for God (1 Jn. 2:5). The proof that God's love is not dwelling in a person is that he loves the world (1 Jn. 2:5).[259] Love for one another is as imperative as love for God (*cf.* 1 Jn. 4:7, 11, 18f.). It is not only a binding force in linking people together; it is also a banishing force in disposing of fear. The ideas

[257] O. Procksh, in his article on *hagiazō* in *TDNT* 1, pp. 111f., states that the sanctification of Christ by the Father is achieved prior to the incarnation. On the other hand the sanctification of the disciples 'is accomplished in the atonement'.

[258] There is truth in Bultmann's comment (*The Johannine Epistles*, p. 66), that this statement is not intended to define the nature of love. He considers that the statement 'indicates the basis of the demand to love'. He concedes that the nature of God may also be depicted, but declines to see the statement as a definition. Yet John is surely thinking of God as love in his inmost being. The saying may not be a precise definition, but its truth affirms that God cannot be other than love. See the section on this verse in Robert Law's *The Tests of Life* (1909), pp. 70ff.

[259] There is a significant switch from 1 Jn. 2:4 (knowledge) to 1 Jn. 2:5 (love). G. G. Findlay, *Fellowship in the Life Eternal* (1909), p. 141, points out 'that while commandment-keeping is the test of a genuine knowledge of God, *love is its characteristic mode*'.

expressed in 1 John may seem idealistic, concentrating as they do on the power of perfect love (1 Jn. 4:8), but they point in the direction in which Christians must move. They set a high target, but are not expected for that reason to defer people from reaching towards it. Indeed, for Christians, loving is not an option but an obligation.

An issue which is raised in 1 John, but not in the gospel, is that of sinless perfection. 'No-one who abides in him sins; no-one who sins has either seen him or known him' (1 Jn. 3:6). 'No-one born of God commits sin; for God's nature abides in him, and he cannot sin because he is born of God' (1 Jn. 3:9). 'We know that anyone born of God does not sin, but he who was born of God keeps him, and the evil one does not touch him' (1 Jn. 5:18).

These three passages certainly seem to demand sinless perfection in the believer. Nevertheless, it is significant that in all these passages the verb is put in the present time, presumably to denote an approach to continual sinning. This distinguishes the habitual acts of sinning from specific completed acts (*cf.* the aorist in 1 Jn. 2:1). In any case the passages must not be taken in isolation. The epistle clearly recognizes two types of sin, mortal and non-mortal. The latter is possible for a Christian brother (1 Jn. 5:17), but provision is made for this. Indeed 1 John 1:8f. makes clear that a man who says he has no sin deceives himself, and Jesus Christ is described as an advocate with the Father for those who sin.[260] We cannot imagine that in a brief epistle like this a writer would so blatantly contradict himself and we are therefore obliged to consider carefully what possibilities there are for reconciling the statements.[261]

The issue can be decided only by a correct understanding of sin. The very fact that John differentiates between mortal and non-mortal shows that he uses the word 'sin' in different ways. The most probable meaning is that those who abide in God are no longer living in habitual sin, for the regenerate person cannot accept such a state within his new norm. At the same time isolated sins, as against fixed sinful habits, can still happen, and yet provision is made for them. There is here a mixture of idealism (the banishment of sin from the believer)[262] and realism (the realization that sin

---

[260] When discussing 1 Jn. 3:6, Bultmann, *The Johannine Epistles*, p. 51, denies that there is a real contradiction with 1 Jn. 1:8, because he notes the different contexts. In 1 Jn. 3:6 there is a statement of a basic truth – abiding is the condition of not sinning – whereas 1 Jn. 1:8 faces the pressing question, 'Who can assert of himself that he always fulfills this condition?'

[261] J. R. W. Stott, *The Epistles of John*, pp. 130ff., provides a valuable extended note on this passage. He examines seven different proposed solutions. He favours the interpretation which sees the 'does not sin' and 'cannot sin' related to persistent sin. He comments that while a Christian may sin, he is overwhelmed with grief at the realization and could never accept a persistent attitude to sin. I. H. Marshall, *The Epistles of John*, pp. 178ff., in his discussion of these passages points out the subtlety of any view based on such an interpretation of the tenses and favours some kind of idealistic or eschatological explanation.

[262] R. N. Flew, *op. cit.*, p. 112, maintains that the early Christians experienced an astounding moral transformation and would not have regarded sinlessness as incredible.

still lingers on, but is no longer master of the situation). Like the perfection ideal in Matthew 5:48, the 'sinlessness' of 1 John cannot actually be achieved in the present, but nevertheless provides an indispensable pattern.

Paul

It might be assumed that a man who had such interest in justification would not have given much attention to sanctification, but Paul does not allow his exposition of justification to blind him to the need to reflect on man's quest for perfection. He did not see the doctrines as mutually exclusive, since one concerned man's relationship to God and the other the practical working out of what was already a *fait accompli* in Christ. One statement of Paul succinctly sums up his approach. 'Work out your own salvation with fear and trembling; for God is at work in you, both to will and to work for his good pleasure' (Phil. 2:12–13). For Paul sanctification was working out what God was working within, a combination of human effort and divine activity. This linking of man's work with God's power runs through Paul's account of the Christian pursuit of the ideal.

We note first Paul's appeal to the example of Christ,[263] all the more remarkable in view of the paucity of references to the life of Christ in his epistles. Christians are not to please themselves because Christ did not please himself (Rom. 15:1–3). They are to welcome one another as Christ has welcomed them (Rom. 15:7). They are to be generous in giving because Christ, though rich, became poor for the sake of others (2 Cor. 8:9). They are even to mould their ways of thinking according to the pattern of Christ's mind (Phil. 2:5).[264] Paul claimed to be an imitator of Christ and on this account did not hesitate to urge others to imitate him (1 Cor. 11:1; 1 Thes. 1:6). He himself sometimes echoes the ethical teaching of Jesus when giving his own exhortations (*cf.* Rom. 12).[265] It is undeniable that the person and work of Jesus was a dominant factor in Paul's approach to the Christian life, as was the activity of the Spirit (see below).

If we seek for more specific ideas as to what ideal for Christian living Paul considered his target, we may suggest several dominant qualities, but none is so characteristic as love. His classic exposition of the theme is in 1 Corinthians 13, which is all the more remarkable because it is sandwiched between two parts of his discussion on spiritual gifts. For Christians who had been dazzled by ecstatic experiences, the intensely practical implications

---

[263] For a discussion of the imitation motive behind Paul's ethical teaching, *cf.* V. P. Furnish, *Theology and Ethics in Paul* (1968), 218ff. *Cf.* also E. J. Tinsley, *The Imitation of God in Christ* (1960), p. 150.

[264] Much discussion has surrounded the interpretation of Phil. 2:5. *Cf.* R. P. Martin, *Philippians* (*NCB*), pp. 91ff., who gives five different interpretations, only one of which treats the mind of Christ as exemplary. Martin himself prefers Käsemann's view that takes Phil. 2:5 in the sense of a salvation-event. Although the imitation interpretation may not exhaust the meaning, it cannot be disposed of on grounds that 'Paul does not habitually point to the earthly life of Jesus as an ethical example'.

[265] *Cf.* C. A. A. Scott, *Christianity according to St Paul* (1932), p. 215.

of Paul's hymn of love would no doubt come as a shock when they discovered that their most prized 'gifts' were way down the list behind love. The apostle has much to say about God's love for man and it is in the light of this that the Christian's love for his fellows must be seen. No-one would suppose that Paul's appeal is easy to fulfil, but nevertheless he gives love the priority, involving as it does not a once-for-all achievement, but a continuous, persistent process.

The apostle gives various lists of virtues which are desirable, of which the most significant are the qualities which go to make up the fruit of the Spirit; love, joy, peace, patience, kindness, goodness, faithfulness, gentleness, self-control (Gal. 5:22). In one sense these may all be said to be different expressions of the first virtue, love. Paul lays special emphasis on the quality of Christian thinking, for in addition to the Philippians 2:5 reference mentioned above, he advocates the noblest kind of content for thought in Philippians 4:8. Christians are given an exhortation which would raise their manner of thinking to a higher plane. It should be noted, of course, that the virtues mentioned in this passage would not have been unfamiliar to Greek readers,[266] but when they are regarded as part of the total Pauline picture of the ideal Christian person they take on new meaning. It is not the qualities themselves which are specifically Christian, but the power with which they are exercised, which marks them out as notable aspects of the follower of Christ.

Some scholars have discovered evidence in Paul's epistles and other NT epistles of moral codes which set out behaviour patterns for various social groups, such as husbands, wives and children and slaves and masters.[267] These were known to have existed in the Gentile world and it is possible that Paul adapted them for his own Christian use. Combining these and Paul's general list of virtues we can piece together some kind of picture of what he considered the new life in Christ to be. It is not a static picture. It does not present a kind of life which can be instantaneously attained. It rather presents an ideal which should be pursued. Paul's picture of the new life may be thought to be incomplete because there are many issues which are not discussed, such as slavery and military service; others are incidentally touched on, such as attitudes to marriage and the state. But it must be constantly borne in mind that Paul does not set out to give a systematic structure for the new life. His teaching is in response to practical issues and his comments must be regarded as supplying guiding principles.

We must next note the references in Paul's letters to 'sanctification'

---

[266] F. W. Beare, *Philippians* (BC ²1969), p. 148, reckons that no single word in this list is specifically Christian. He goes as far as to suggest that these are no more than copybook maxims. J. Gnilka, *Der Philipperbrief* (HTKNT ²1976), p. 221, claims that the list must be understood against a Stoic background.

[267] *Cf.* E. G. Selwyn, *1 Peter* (1946), pp. 363f., for a discussion of the relation between these social codes and the NT ethical teaching. *Cf.* also J. W. C. Wand, *The Epistles of Peter and Jude* (1934), pp. 3ff.

(*hagiasmos*) or to the verb 'sanctify' (*hagiazō*).[268] The noun is used several times, although not always with the same meaning. The most significant is in 1 Corinthians 1:30 where Paul says that God made Christ 'our sanctification', so clearly emphasizing the divine initiative. Since the context refers to the 'presence of God' (verse 29), sanctification (like righteousness) must be viewed from the Godward side.[269] It must convey the sense of 'holiness'. God looks at the 'holiness' of Christ rather than the lack of it in the believer. This is a use of sanctification which closely approximates to justification and does not indicate a complete moral condition in the believer. What Paul probably means is that Christ could be described as 'our sanctification' because he was the only perfectly sanctified person.

Although it is a *fait accompli* in the sight of God it still needs to be worked out in the lives of believers. This interpretation is supported by Romans 6:19 ('Yield your members to righteousness for sanctification') and 1 Thessalonians 4:3 ('this is the will of God, your sanctification: that you abstain from immorality. . . . ') These statements show the human side of sanctification, the need for continued commitment to the pursuit of holiness. In other cases the word stands for 'holiness' as contrasted with uncleanness (1 Thes. 4:4, 7). In Romans 6:22 the stress falls on the future rather than the present, for sanctification is spoken of in terms of reward and is linked to its end, eternal life. In Paul's use of the verb, the same general pattern is discernible. Some statements suggest an accomplished fact, while others suggest a process. Examples of the former are 1 Corinthians 1:2 ('those sanctified in Christ Jesus, called to be saints') and 1 Corinthians 6:11 ('But you were washed, you were sanctified'). Examples of the latter are Ephesians 5:26 ('that he (Christ) might sanctify her (the church), having cleansed her') and 1 Thessalonians 5:23 ('May the God of peace sanctify you wholly').

There are three instances in which sanctification is specifically linked with the work of the Spirit (Rom. 15:16; 1 Thes. 4:7–8; 2 Thes. 2:13). Nevertheless, Paul's repeated references to the activity of the Holy Spirit in the believer must be considered an essential part of his doctrine of sanctification (*cf.* pp. 554ff.). The Christian's walk is not 'by flesh' but 'by Spirit' (Rom. 8:4; Gal. 5:25). The Spirit aids prayer (Rom. 8:26). He dwells in believers as in a temple (1 Cor. 3:16). More especially the virtues desirable for cultivation are described as the 'fruit' of the Spirit (Gal. 5:22). The Spirit gives to believers the guarantee of greater fulfilment to come (2 Cor. 1:22). The Spirit also brings strength (Eph. 3:16) and unity (Eph. 4:3). Paul leaves us in no doubt that whatever demands are made on Christians in this life, they are not left to their own devices. If justification

---

[268] O. Procksh, *hagiazō, TDNT* I, p. 113, maintains a distinction between the use of the noun and the use of the verb in Paul's epistles, the former having more emphasis on the moral element.

[269] *Cf.* C. K. Barrett, *1 Corinthians, ad loc.*

cannot be achieved by human effort, neither can sanctification. Paul maintains a delicate balance between God's provision and man's responsibility.

This leads on to a consideration of Paul's approach to sinless perfection.[270] Does he suggest that it is possible? The most relevant passage for discussion is Romans 6. There are several statements in this passage which give the impression that Paul is maintaining the possibility of sinless perfection. 'How can we who died to sin still live in it?' (6:2);[271] 'We know that our old self was crucified with him so that the sinful body might be destroyed, and we might no longer be enslaved to sin. For he who has died is freed from sin' (6:6–7); 'so you also must consider yourselves dead to sin' (6:11); 'For sin will have no dominion over you' (6:14); 'but now you have been set free from sin' (6:22).

There can be no denying that in these passages Paul is asserting triumph over sin; but is he saying that it is possible for the Christian to reach a state of perfection in which sin is effectively destroyed? It is unnecessary to suppose that the answer must be in the affirmative, for the key to the understanding of these statements is that sin is no longer master. It has met its match. Paul can exhort his readers, 'Let not sin therefore *reign* in your mortal bodies, to make you obey their passions' (6:12). Man is no longer vassal to sin, but has become a slave to God. Yet he still needs urging to avoid obedience to sin.

Admittedly, at first sight, it seems that Paul is saying two contradictory things. A correct understanding of the passages quoted above can be obtained only when they are set in their context, which is certainly not a discussion on sinless perfection. The burden of the passage is whether grace is increased in proportion to the sin, as if abundance of sin would be an advantage. Paul rejects the suggestion by pointing out that the believer shares Christ's conquest over sin. What he wants them to know is that deliberate sinning would be a denial of that conquest. The enemy (sin) is still active, but is a defeated foe as far as the believer is concerned.

Some note should here be taken of the passage which immediately follows. The problems surrounding the interpretation of Romans 7 have already been mentioned in an earlier section (see pp. 173ff.), but if Paul is in any way describing his own experiences as a Christian the passage would also have relevance here. There is clearly a tension between the ideal and the real, together with a deep consciousness of failure. Paul's concluding

---

[270] On the theme of perfection in Paul, cf. H. Ridderbos, *Paul: an Outline of His Theology*, pp. 265ff. Ridderbos draws a distinction between the concept of perfection and that of ethical perfectionism. He maintains that Paul supports the idea of growth towards perfection. Using dogmatic categories, he declares that Paul speaks of a *posse non peccare*, not of a *non peccare*, nor of a *non posse peccare*.

[271] C. E. B. Cranfield, *Romans* 1 pp. 299f., suggests four senses in which Christians have died to sin: (i) In God's sight, when Christ died for them (*juridical* sense). (ii) In baptism. Cranfield sees this as a ratification of their acceptance of God's decision on their behalf and as a seal and a pledge (*baptismal* sense). (iii) A daily dying to sin and a daily rising (*moral* sense). (iv) At their actual death (*eschatological* sense).

remark that deliverance comes through Christ (Rom. 7:25) points the way towards the solution to this kind of tension. If this is the right interpretation of Romans 7, it would warn against supposing that all absence of conflict in the process of sanctification was realizable in the present life.

Again, we might ask whether Paul gives any indication of the possibility of attaining holiness. One of his most characteristic descriptions of believers is 'holy ones' (*hagioi*), by which he is clearly not wishing to imply that they were actually holy. In several instances he uses the adjective 'holy' to describe the believers' goal. They are to be presented before God as holy, provided they continue in the faith (Col. 1:22; *cf.* Eph. 1:4; 5:27). Yet it is also a present reality. Believers are now a holy temple of God (1 Cor. 3:17). At the same time, Paul can speak of the Christian community growing into a holy temple (Eph. 2:21). In the moral life, Christians are to regard their bodies as living sacrifices, holy to God (Rom. 12:1). Christian salvation is linked with a calling which is described as holy (2 Tim. 1:9). It is evident that Paul regards holiness as a process which reaches its climax only when believers are presented blameless before God. It has, therefore, both a present and future reference. Paul's own testimony in Philippians 3:12–16, where he affirms that he is not yet perfect, is relevant here; for he nevertheless has his eye on the final prize, thus again combining present and future aspects.

There is one idea in Paul's first letter to the Corinthians which needs mention, because it has given rise to some confusion. He claims that an unbelieving partner in a marriage may be sanctified by a believing partner (1 Cor. 7:14). He cannot mean that the unbeliever is sanctified in the same way as the believer; but he seems to be claiming that while the believing partner is in process of being sanctified, something of the influence of that process must brush off on the unbeliever. But he is citing this as an argument against divorce, not as a sample of sanctification by proxy.

The rest of the New Testament

The epistle to the *Hebrews* is especially noteworthy for its emphasis on the theme of perfection.[272] The model of this perfection is Christ himself, who is said to be made perfect through suffering (2:10). Indeed, the perfection of Christ qualified him to become the source of eternal salvation to those who obey him (5:9). Not only is Christ himself said to be perfect, but perfection is held up as the goal for the worshippers of God. The writer points out the inability of the law to bring perfection (7:11, 19). Its sacrificial system could do no more than point forward to a better way, but could not enable anyone to reach perfection (10:1). The real inadequacy of the

---

[272] G. Delling, *TDNT* 8, p. 82, considers that in Hebrews the use of the verb *teleioō* follows the LXX usage. He thinks it means 'to put someone in the position in which he can come, or stand before God'. However, he detects a somewhat different usage in Heb. 11:1f.

law was in its inability to 'perfect', *i.e.* cleanse the conscience (9:9). Yet for the Christian perfection is seen as the goal. The past heroes of faith had perfection as their goal, although they could not attain it 'without us' (11:40). By his single sacrifice Christ is said to have perfected 'for all time those who are sanctified' (10:14), which shows that 'perfection', as Hebrews understand it, is not a matter of human effort. We are to look to him who is the perfecter of our faith (Heb. 12:1).[273]

Against this background of the perfect ideal, we must note some passages in the epistle, which support the view that sanctification is a process. The exhortation in 12:14, 'Strive for . . . the holiness without which no one will see the Lord,' shows that this author did not regard holiness as instantaneous. It had to be worked at and yet it is considered indispensable for the ultimate destiny of the believer. The author is acutely conscious of the majesty of God (*cf.* 12:29, 'our God is a consuming fire'). He sees holiness as a necessary requisite for coming into the presence of God. When he refers to the heavenly Jerusalem, he mentions, 'the spirits of just men made perfect' (12:23), which suggests that the perfection theme relates to the future rather than to the present.[274] The statement in 13:12 that Jesus suffered 'to sanctify the people through his own blood', shows the method by which the process of sanctification is inaugurated. But the epistle is full of exhortations to the readers which demand the application of the principles of holiness in their lives.

As in Paul's letters, so here in Hebrews, the ideal is said to be both *already* effected and *not yet* attained. Even more clearly than Paul, this author sees nothing short of perfection as the Christian's goal. Nevertheless there is no suggestion of a belief in sinless perfection in this life. The concluding benediction in 13:20f. contains the prayer that the readers might be made perfect (*katartizein*) in everything good that they might do his will (RSV has 'equip you with everything good'). The work is clearly not yet complete, for otherwise the prayer would be unnecessary. Indeed in one of his most powerful hortatory passages, the writer urges his readers to press on to perfection (6:1; RSV has 'maturity').[275] Moreover, the present lack of perfection is heightened in this epistle by the strong warnings against neglecting salvation (2:3) and against apostasy (chapters 6 and 10).

The essentially practical epistle of *James* is full of moral exhortations. They assume a standard which must be regarded as a target, although little is said about sanctification or perfection. A statement like 'Whoever knows

---

[273] For a discussion of the perfection concept in Hebrews, *cf.* A. Wikgren, 'Patterns of Perfection in the Epistle to the Hebrews', *NTS* 6, 1959–60, pp. 159ff.

[274] J. Héring, *Hebrews*, p. 117, thinks this expression could relate to Christian martyrs (*cf.* Rev. 6:9). But it is more probable that the whole Christian community in its perfected state is in mind (*cf.* F. F. Bruce, *Hebrews*, pp. 376f.).

[275] P. E. Hughes, *Hebrews*, p. 590, relates this perfection to the restoration of harmony between God's will and ours, but he is careful to point out that this does not involve the eclipse of the human will.

what is right to do and fails to do it, for him it is sin' (4:17) shows the crucial nature of the demand for right action. The Christian is to seek wisdom from above which manifests itself in purity, peaceableness, gentleness, reasonableness, mercy (3:17). The list of virtues is closely parallel to those in Paul's epistles. The Christian is to be transformed in his attitudes and not simply in his practical actions (as stressed, for instance, in 2:15, 16). The burden of the controversial passage in 2:14ff. is that faith must find expression in 'works', which for James is linked with essentially benevolent acts. It would not be true, however, to classify James' idea of sanctification in purely activist terms, as 3:17 shows.

The concept of sanctification is met with at the beginning of 1 *Peter* where the readers are described as 'sanctified by the Spirit', in addition to being 'chosen and destined by God the Father' (1:2).[276] We have already seen the close link between sanctification and the Spirit, and this was evidently widely accepted. The theme is stated, but not elaborated on, in 1 Peter; but the several exhortations to holy living must be regarded as a commentary on 1:2. The most telling is 1:15, 'as he who called you is holy, be holy yourselves in all your conduct'. The ideal is therefore nothing short of God's holiness. This may be regarded as Peter's pattern of perfection for Christian living.

A significant feature in this epistle is that another pattern is set before the readers in the form of Christ's example of suffering (2:21).[277] The direct connection between ethical obligation and the work of Christ is brought out more clearly here than in any other passage in the NT. As in Paul's letters, we meet in this epistle with lists of instructions for guiding Christians in the art of living (*e.g.* 3:1ff.; 2:18ff., which are parallel to contemporary moral codes). There is to be a constant quest to inculcate qualities like love, tenderness and humility, especially towards others (3:8ff.). There is need for spiritual growth (2:2). There is, moreover, acknowledgment of an opposing force (the devil), who nevertheless can and should be resisted (5:8).

A similar list of desirable qualities is found in 2 *Peter* 1:5–11, again containing both individual and social virtues.[278] Some have seen this passage as influenced by Hellenistic thought, because of the statement that believers 'may escape from the corruption that is in the world because of passion,

---

[276] J. N. D. Kelly, *Peter and Jude*, p. 43, notes that Paul uses almost identical language in 2 Thes. 2:13 and suggests that the formula was a cliché. It is worth noting however that Silvanus is mentioned in both epistles.

[277] As E. Best, *1 Peter*, p. 119, well points out the statement in 1 Pet. 2: 21 involves more than simply an example. To follow a person's steps is easier than to pioneer. 'In creating the way Christ is saviour as well as example'. The connecting of the ethical example with the redemptive nature of Christ's sufferings is therefore natural.

[278] J. N. D. Kelly, *op. cit.*, p. 305, sees in this passage a cultivated Hellenistic atmosphere. He notes that many of the words in the list are paralleled in Greek ethics.

and become partakers of the divine nature' (verse 4). We have noted the possible meaning of this in the last section (see pp. 636), but whatever the interpretation, it is undeniable that it is here applied in terms of high morality. Anyone failing to measure up to it is said to be blind and to have forgotten that he has been cleansed from his sins (verse 9). The urgent need is to confirm 'your call and election' (verse 10). There is no suggestion that believers become deified so as to be beyond the need for constant watchfulness and effort in the moral realm.

In the concluding chapter of 2 Peter the final dissolution of all things is held out as a motive for the present pursuit of a life of holiness (3:11). Believers are to be zealous to be found 'without spot or blemish' (3:14). They are to grow in grace and knowledge of our Lord and Saviour Jesus Christ (3:18). There can be no doubt that this epistle presents the same view of progressive sanctification as found elsewhere in the NT. The same may be said of the epistle of *Jude* (*cf.* verses 20–21). The conclusion of this brief letter contains the prayer that believers might be kept from falling and might be presented to God without blemish (verse 24). The present merges into the future.

Considering the nature of the book of *Revelation*, we would not expect to find much on sanctification, but a few considerations are worth noting. The survey of churches in chapters 2 and 3 contains a promise at the conclusion of each message to those who 'conquer'. Moreover, the commendation or criticism of works is sufficient to show that moral attitudes and actions are involved in the process of conquering. Such qualities as endurance (2:2, 19), love (2:19), and faithfulness (3:8) are commended. The would-be conqueror is given the example of Christ as his pattern (3:21). As the apocalypse unfolds, the overcomers are seen as those clothed in white robes, a symbol of their purity in God's sight (*cf.* 7:14). The focus is too much on the future to supply information about the demands of the present. We are confronted with culmination rather than process, but there is no essential difference from the rest of the NT view of sanctification and perfection.

Conclusion

We may summarize the NT teaching on sanctification in the following way. Various ideals are set before believers to serve as goals, of which the most dominant are the example of Christ and the ideal of love to one another after the pattern of Christ's love towards believers. The goals are impossibly high, but great stress is laid on the powerful assistance of the Holy Spirit. Whereas perfection is set out as the target, there is no clear support for sinless perfection. Provision is made for lapses, and the many exhortations to holy living suggest that the attainment of a holy life would never be easy.

To give some guidance on the pursuit of such holy living, various lists of desirable virtues are included in some of the NT writings. While these show some resemblance to the contemporary moral codes, the powerful motives which prompt Christian living at once set them apart from their pagan counterparts.

Since a parallel to these lists is found in the OT law, it is necessary to discuss what relevance this law still had for the developing Christian church. This issue was important for all Christians, but particularly so for Christian Jews. This subject will occupy our attention in the next section.

THE LAW IN THE CHRISTIAN LIFE

In considering the place of the law for the Christian, we must at once recognize the importance of a right answer to this problem as far as the NT is concerned. It would have been a vital matter for those who in their pre-conversion days had lived under the law, to know what their Christian approach should be. It would have been equally essential for Gentiles, who were presented at their conversion with scriptures (LXX) whose central theme was the law of God. In many parts of the NT we find an interest in the subject of the relation of the law to Christ. We shall be concerned to discover Jesus' own attitude towards the law as seen both in his practices and in his teaching. It will naturally be necessary to discover whether any indications were given to the disciples regarding the future status of the law, in order to establish the connection between the law in the epistles and the law in the gospels.

The synoptic gospels

We are concerned here with more than the use of the word 'law' (*nomos*), but it will be valuable to note its various usages.[279] It is never used in Mark, but occurs eight times in Matthew and nine times in Luke. Its main use is to describe the Pentateuch, more particularly in respect of its legal demands. It announces what should be done and what should not be done. Its use as 'commandment' is sometimes closely linked with its use as 'scripture' (*cf.* Mt. 5:17f.). In Luke's gospel, the word occurs five times in the infancy narratives (Lk. 2:22, 23, 24, 27, 39) and only four times elsewhere (Lk. 10:26; 16:16, 17; 24:44). In Matthew's gospel, three occurrences are found in the Sermon on the Mount (Mt. 5:17, 18; 7:12) and five elsewhere. The word itself is not, therefore, of wide use, but the idea of law and of commandment is much more frequent.

It would be clearest if we consider the evidence for Jesus' approach to

[279] For a detailed survey of *nomos* in the synoptic gospels, *cf.* W. Gutbrod, *TDNT* 4, pp. 1059ff., who compares Jesus' negation of the law with his affirmation of the law.

law in these gospels under two main divisions: (i) evidence which shows Jesus' high regard for the law, and (ii) evidence which shows him as a critic of the law.

JESUS' REGARD FOR THE LAW

We observe first of all the way in which Jesus observed the law as far as its customs were concerned. He frequented the synagogue, although it cannot be claimed that he did so for any formal reason but rather to seek for opportunities to further his mission (*cf.* Lk. 4:15–16, 31f., 44 and parallels).[280] Jesus did not exempt himself from the payment of the temple tax (Mt. 17:24ff.), although there was no agreement among the Jews generally as to how far this was binding. It is clear that Jesus did not pay it out of a legal obligation as Matthew 17:26 shows; rather, he did not wish to give offence. Many scholars do not accept this whole passage as authentic as it stands, mainly on account of the miraculous method of paying the tax from money found in a fish's mouth. The passage in any case does not give any clear indication of Jesus' attitude to the law itself.[281]

Of more importance is the fact that frequently in the teaching of Jesus a positive acceptance of the tenets of the law is implied. He upholds the sanctity of the law in a classic passage in Matthew 5:17–18. 'Think not that I have come to abolish the law and the prophets; I have come not to abolish them but to fulfil them. For truly I say to you, till heaven and earth pass away, not an iota, not a dot, will pass from the law until all is accomplished.' A saying similar to the latter sentence occurs also in Luke 16:17. Although the first sentence has often been regarded as a creation of Matthew,[282] this is unjustified and there is no reason for not regarding it as a genuine expression of Jesus' approach to the law. In this case it is of great importance to establish the meaning of the word 'fulfil' (*plēroō*) as used in this context.

Various suggestions have been made. (i) It has been suggested that Jesus claimed to bring out the true meaning of the law so as to 'complete' it.[283] But there is nothing to support the division of the inner and outer meaning which this supposes. (ii) Another suggestion is that *plēroō* means to

---

[280] *Cf.* R. Banks. *Jesus and the Law in the Synoptic Tradition* (1975), p. 91.

[281] *Cf.* W. G. Thompson's discussion of this saying in his book, *Matthew's Advice to a divided community: Mt 17:22–18:35* (1970), pp. 51–68. He finds many redactional elements. He sees the passage as supplying guidance about what Jewish Christians were to do about the Jewish contribution to the newly established council at Jamnia. Such a view presupposes a late date for the gospel of Matthew, which is nevertheless open to dispute.

[282] *Cf.* R. Banks, *op. cit.*, pp. 204f., for views against its authenticity. He himself supports it. *Cf.* also C. F. D. Moule, 'Fulfilment-words in the New Testament: Use and Abuse', *NTS* 14, 1967–8, pp. 317f.; A. Feuillet, 'Morale ancienne et Morale Chrétienne d'après Mt. v. 17–20; comparaison avec la doctrine de l'épître aux Romains', *NTS* 17, 1970–1, p. 124.

[283] So F. V. Filson, *Matthew* (BC, 1960), p. 83, who interprets it in the sense that Jesus 'gives the fullest expression to the divine intent in the ancient utterances'.

'establish',[284] but this is not supported by LXX usage. (iii) The word could mean 'fulfilment' in the sense of completion, *i.e.* full realization,[285] and there is something to be said for this. The main difficulty is that the verb used is not the most usual word for expressing the sense of realization. (iv) Since the fulfilling is related to both law and prophets, a meaning must be sought which does service for both.[286] The word is used in a specifically Christian sense in which Christ is the perfect realization or perfection of what both law and prophets foreshadowed. Jesus most probably meant that he fulfilled the law in the sense of transcending it, *i.e.* going beyond it, while at the same time showing what the law (and the prophets) pointed forward to.

The second sentence in Matthew's statement is slightly more impressive than Luke's version in that it is introduced by the words 'Truly I say to you', which emphasize the importance of the inviolability of the law, but which focus attention on the concluding clause 'Until (*heōs*) all is accomplished (*genētai*)'. This clause has been referred (i) to Christ's death,[287] (ii) to the eschatological events of the last days,[288] (iii) to the accomplishment of the law by the gathering of it up into a new love-commandment,[289] (iv) to the fulfilment of the OT scriptures by Jesus Christ.[290] If we suppose that the 'accomplishment' in verse 18 is to be identified with the 'fulfilling' in verse 17, this would support the meaning suggested in (iv). The statement becomes, then, an indication that Jesus regarded the law as pointing forward to himself.

For a complete understanding of the force of Matthew 5:17–18, attention must be paid to Matthew 5:19 which warns against relaxing any of the commandments and advocates their observance.[291] Does this refer to the Mosaic law or to the commandments which Jesus himself will give (*cf.* Mt. 28:20)? Some think that the latter seems most probable, since even those who 'relax' them are still regarded as members of the kingdom, whereas condemnation is later pronounced on those scribes and Pharisees who keep

---

[284] B. H. Branscomb, *Jesus and the Law of Moses* (1930), pp. 227ff., prefers this interpretation because (i) the preceding words lead up to an affirmation of the law, (ii) the succeeding verses support it, (iii) Aboth 4:11 parallels it, (iv) it is consistent with Jesus' other teaching about the law.

[285] This view is adopted by G. Barth, 'Matthew's Understanding of the Law', in *Tradition and Interpretation in Matthew* (G. Bornkamm, G. Barth, J. J. Held, Eng. trans. 1960), pp. 68f. He speaks of 'actualization'.

[286] Banks, *op. cit.*, p. 210, sees both discontinuity and continuity implied in this statement of Mt. 5:17.

[287] *Cf.* J. Jeremias, *The Sermon on the Mount* (Eng. trans. 1961), p. 24; W. D. Davies, *Christian Origins and Judaism* (1962), pp. 60ff.

[288] *Cf.* F. V. Filson, *Matthew*, p. 84.

[289] *Cf.* E. Schweizer, *Matthew* (1976), pp. 107f.

[290] *Cf.* W. Hendriksen, *Matthew*, pp. 288ff.

[291] Many scholars regard this as a non-authentic saying, *cf.* Branscomb, *Jesus and the Law of Moses*, p. 231, who thinks that to regard verse 19 as an authentic utterance is frankly out of the question. E. Schweizer, *Matthew*, pp. 108f., thinks the saying belongs to a different context and relates 'these things' to the commandments of Jesus, not to the law.

the lesser but neglect the weightier matters of the law (Mt. 23:23).[292] Matthew 5:20 seems to support this interpretation, suggesting that Jesus expects from his disciples more than the scribes and Pharisees were achieving in their adherence to the law. Jesus was expecting more, not less, regard for the true nature of the commandments. Nevertheless, such an interpretation rests on a disjunction between Matthew 5:18 and Matthew 5:19 which does not seem warranted in the text. It is more natural to suppose that the commandments of verse 19 are the same as the law in verse 18.

When the rich man wanted to know how to inherit eternal life (Mk. 10:17f.), Jesus answered by quoting the commandments (specifying six parts of the Decalogue). He implied that these commandments are a revelation of goodness,[293] because they are indications of God's standards. There is no sense, therefore, in which Jesus considered the moral demands of the law as no longer valid. Nevertheless he recognized that more was needed than a mere verbal claim to have fulfilled the law. The rich man was called upon to surrender himself. In line with this is Jesus' summing up of the commandments as love for God and love for one's neighbour (Mk. 12:28ff.). When the scribe recognized that love was superior to the ritual requirements, Jesus pronounced him not far from the kingdom (Mk. 12:34).

Jesus' respect for the law is also seen in Matthew 23:2–3 where he acknowledges that the scribes and Pharisees sit on Moses' seat.[294] His advice to his followers to do what the Pharisees say, but not what they do has raised difficulties. In view of Jesus' strong criticisms of the Pharisees, this has been seen as an inconsistency. But the real point of Jesus' statement was to show that the Pharisees' claim to keep the law was in fact not true. His major criticism was against some of the additions placed on the law through the oral tradition. The motive for observing the law in order to be seen of men was specifically condemned (Mt. 23:5). So was the view that to keep the lesser matters exempted a person from keeping the weightier (Mt. 23:23).

JESUS' RECOGNITION OF THE INCOMPLETENESS OF THE LAW

There is a contrast between the 'law and the prophets' (which were until John the Baptist) and the kingdom of God (which is being preached by

---

[292] E. P. Blair, *Jesus in the Gospel of Matthew* (1960), p. 124, concludes that in Matthew Jesus' attitude towards the written law 'is one of respect and obedience towards its true requirements'.

[293] *Cf.* W. Gutbrod, *TDNT* 4, p. 1062, who says of Jesus that he 'does not accept as good any other will than the will of God revealed in the Law'.

[294] Many scholars see an inconsistency between Mt. 23:2–3 and Mt. 16:12, where Jesus warns the disciples against the 'leaven' of the Pharisees. *Cf.* Blair, *op. cit.*, pp. 112f. Branscomb, *op. cit.*, pp. 231f., denies the authenticity of the Mt. 23:2, 3 saying. On the other hand, D. Hill, *Matthew*, p. 310, thinks it doubtful that the meaning intended in Mt. 23:2–3 included the rabbinic traditions. If 23:2–3 refers mainly to the written law and Mt. 16:12 to some aspects of the oral law, the inconsistency would be lessened.

Jesus, Lk. 16:16; *cf.* Mt. 11:12–13). From this it is evident that the kingdom goes beyond the 'law and the prophets'. This presumably means that the OT revelation has given place to the revelation in Jesus Christ. The one prepared the way for the other. Some indication of this may be seen in the wineskin illustration that Jesus used (Mt. 9:17), in answer to a question about fasting put by John's disciples. The suggestion is that new teaching needs new forms.

Jesus summarized the law and the prophets in what has come to be known as the golden rule ('Whatever you wish that men would do to you, do so to them', Mt. 7:12).[295] This interpretation of the essence of the law robs it of its legalism without denigrating it. Luke 6:31 records the same precept, but does not mention the law and prophets.

In the well-known antithesis in the Sermon on the Mount, the teaching of Jesus goes beyond the law in such matters as murder, marriage, perjury, the *lex talionis* (Mt. 5:21ff.). The authoritative nature of Jesus' interpretation of the law is seen in his words, 'But I say to you' contrasted with the statement 'You have heard that it was said'.[296] In what sense is Jesus modifying the law? In some cases he puts an entirely new complexion on it as in the *lex talionis* which is replaced by the other-cheek principle (Mt. 5:38ff.). The law was designed to restrict unrestrained vengeance, but Jesus acts to free people from the urge for revenge altogether. This modification is radical in the extent to which it far outstrips the demands of the law. The classing of anger with murder is another example of the same radical unveiling of the real intentions of the law. These antitheses are not an annulling of the law, but a bringing out of more radical principles which went beyond the demands of the law. Jesus exercises an authority of his own in the way he interpreted it.[297]

On the question of divorce Jesus explains that the Mosaic provision was because of 'your hardness of heart' (Mt. 19:8; Mk. 10:5); he goes behind the law to the creation ordinances and on the strength of these ordinances counsels against divorce except for adultery (see further comment on this on pp. 949ff.). It must not be supposed that Jesus is lessening the standard set by the law by declaring the law to be no longer applicable, since his own teaching makes even more stringent demands.[298] Another matter about which Jesus modified the law was the sabbath. In affirming that the

[295] Banks, *Jesus and the Law in the Synoptic Tradition*, p. 216 n. 4, criticizes E. Schweizer, 'Matthäus 5:17–20 – Anmerkungen zum Gesetzesverständnis des Matthäus', in his *Neotestamentica* (1963), pp. 399ff., for understanding Mt. 5:18 to relate to Mt. 7:12 linked with Mt. 22:40, on the grounds that it is extremely doubtful whether the 'love-commandment' can be considered the focal point of Jesus' new teaching. Banks makes a distinction between the real significance of the law and prophets (seen in the love-command) and Jesus' own more radical demands (p. 219).

[296] For a full discussion of these antitheses, *cf.* Banks, *op. cit.*, pp. 182ff.

[297] There is no support for the view that Jesus set forth his own law in antithesis to the Mosaic law. *Cf.* Branscomb, *op. cit.*, p. 249.

[298] Banks, *op. cit.*, p. 152, comments that 'Matthew's rearrangement and alteration of Mark places in

Son of man is Lord even of the sabbath (Mk. 2:28), Jesus set himself above the Mosaic law. What he was criticizing was the interpretation of that law which had transformed it from a blessing into a burden.

In respect of the ritual law, Jesus seems to have treated it with indifference. He did not hesitate to touch a leper, although he advised conformity to the legal practices for lepers who had been cleansed (Lk. 5:13–14; 17:11ff.). He opposed the 'tradition of the elders' on the matter of hand washing (Mk. 7:1ff.) and the Pharisaic practice of Corban (Mk. 7:9ff.) and he repudiated the idea of unclean food (Mk. 7:19). He claimed that the Pharisees were nullifying the word of God through tradition. There is no support for the view that Jesus advocated observance of the oral law.

In summing up the approach of Jesus to the law in the synoptics we may note the following points. (i) Jesus regarded the law as a divine institution, possessing religious authority. (ii) He recognized the need to penetrate its inner meaning, which effectively transcended it as a legal requirement. (iii) He never supposed that man's relationship to God could now be based on observance of the law. This is replaced by God's willingness to forgive men on the basis of the mission of Jesus. (iv) The old covenant was replaced by a new covenant (Mt. 26:26) which nevertheless fulfilled the old.[299] The teaching of Jesus, in requiring more than obedience to the law by man's own efforts, which could only lead to pride, prepares the way, not only for Paul's exposition of the true place of law, but also for an understanding of the relevance of law for Christian life.[300]

The Johannine literature

The usage of the word *nomos* in John is roughly similar to that in the synoptics, although the issues raised over the law are rather different. We note first that the word 'law' is used of the Pentateuch (Jn. 1:45). In this sense Moses is distinguished from the prophets. Yet in other instances citations from books outside the Pentateuch are said to be the law (Jn. 10:34; 12:34; 15:25), hence law must represent the whole OT. In some cases it refers to legal principles (Jn. 7:51; 8:17; 18:31; 19:7). In one case (Jn. 1:17) law seems to stand for the whole basis of Israelite religious life under the old covenant. In spite of the different uses of the precise term, the general idea of law behind this gospel is most comprehensive and it is in this sense that it is compared with grace which comes through Christ (Jn. 1:17).

---

bolder relief both the error of the Pharisees and the authority of Jesus'. It is the latter point which is most relevant for our present purpose.

[299] Gutbrod's conclusion from the synoptic evidence is that Jesus' teaching must be approached from two standpoints. First it calls for full repentance and secondly it exhibits true obedience. 'Only when he renounces his own achievement and receives forgiveness is man truly able to set himself under the judgment of the law and to offer the obedience of love' (*TDNT* 4, p. 1065).

[300] C. L. Mitton, 'The Law and the Gospel' *ExT* 68, 1957, pp. 312ff., finds three areas in which the law was fulfilled: in the teaching of Jesus, in the character and life of Jesus, and in the obedience of believers.

Basic issues concerning the law are raised constantly in the confrontation between Jesus and his Jewish opponents in the gospel. We must examine these controversies to discover what information they yield about Jesus' approach to the Jewish law. There can be no doubt that the Johannine account of Jesus' ministry found many parallels with the later conflicts between the Jewish church and the synagogue.

As in the synoptic accounts, so in the Johannine, the controversies over the sabbath form a focal point in discussions over the law.[301] It comes to expression in John 5:1–18 and in John 9. Some scholars do not regard the reference to the sabbath as an original part of the healing narrative, but the reasons are not sufficiently cogent to affect our use of this passage to demonstrate the attitude of Jesus towards the sabbath. Certainly as John records it, the sabbath controversy is crucial. Jesus plainly condemned the casuistry of the Jews in their interpretation of the law. It must be recognized that Jewish conviction that a person who broke one part of the law had broken the whole law accentuates the Jews' concern over Jesus' apparent sabbath breaking. To them it was defiance of the whole law. This is further heightened by Jesus' claim that he and the Father were working (5:17), which for him explained why he could do what he did on the sabbath (since God's activity does not cease on the sabbath); but for the Jews this amounted to blasphemy (because he made himself equal with God, *cf.* 5:18). Unless the Jews were prepared to accept in faith the validity of the claims of Jesus, a fundamental clash over the law was inevitable.

In John 9 the man born blind was healed on the sabbath (Jn. 9:14), which immediately raised the comment from some of the Pharisees that Jesus could not be of God, because he did not keep the sabbath (Jn. 9:16).[302] No humanitarian considerations could be allowed to modify this deduction. On their own tenets the Pharisees were logical, but what needed modification was their method of deciding whether or not Jesus was from God. Yet other Pharisees were more direct in their condemnation of Jesus as a 'sinner' (*hamartōlos*), *i.e.* because of his attitude towards the law. The bitterness of the Pharisaic opposition to the cured man, on the grounds of his association with Jesus, foreshadowed the strength of the coming clash between the church and synagogue over the law.[303]

In this gospel the law issue is inextricably bound up with the Christo-

---

[301] *Cf.* S. Pancaro, *The Law in the Fourth Gospel* (1975), pp. 9ff.

[302] As Pancaro, *op. cit.*, p. 20, points out, Jn. 9:16 is important in two respects – the *sēmeia* are considered either as violations of the law or as works of God. Consequently according to the first view Jesus is a 'sinner', and according to the second he is 'of God'.

[303] This theme is worked out in a particular way by J. L. Martyn, *History and Theology in the Fourth Gospel* (1968), who sees the actors in the drama in Jn. 9 as portrayed on two levels: one in the life situation of Jesus, and the other in the ongoing clash between church and synagogue in the early church. Without subscribing to Martyn's dramatic theory, we may nevertheless note the relevance of the conflict in Jn. 9 to the later scene.

logical issue. It is what Jesus claims himself to be which affects his attitude to the law and his opponents' attitude towards him.[304] Before Pilate the Jews claim, 'We have a law, and by that law he ought to die, because he has made himself the Son of God' (Jn. 19:7). Jewish opposition was roused on the score of Jesus' alleged blasphemy (Jn. 5:18; 8:58–59; 10:22–39). In each case the Jews concluded that Jesus was worthy of death. It was because Jesus, being a man, made himself God (Jn. 10:33). In answer to that charge Jesus appealed to the very law that they were using to condemn him.

Arising out of the claims and teaching of Jesus his opponents feared he would undermine the authority of the law on which the stability of the Jewish nation depended (Jn. 7:45ff.). This comes out specifically in the fear expressed by Caiaphas in John 11:47–53, when he considered the removal of Jesus from the scene to be preferable to the destruction of the whole nation. He saw Jesus as a threat to the temple (the centre of religious worship based on the law). The Johannine account, with its frequent references to the enmity of the Jews against Jesus, makes more intelligible the blasphemy charge before Caiaphas (which the synoptic gospels record as the charge on which the condemnation of Jesus was sought).

So far we have concerned ourselves only with the opposition aroused by Jesus' approach to the law. We need next to note how he uses the law to show that the traditional Jewish interpretation was wrong. In fact, he demonstrates that they were going against the true spirit of the law. When the Jews criticized Jesus at the feast of tabernacles he asserted, 'Yet none of you keeps the law. Why do you seek to kill me?' (Jn. 7:19). He further pointed out that they permitted circumcision on the sabbath (Jn. 7:22f.) in order to fulfil the Mosaic law, but were unconcerned about the man with the paralysed body. Jesus is suggesting that his sabbath work was not inconsistent with a true understanding of the law. Similarly in John 10:34 he appeals to what the law says, in support of his contention that he is the Son of God. He further affirms that it is not he who will accuse the Jews before the Father, but Moses ('If you believed Moses, you would believe me', Jn. 5:45, 46). This suggests that for Jesus the law witnesses to him rather than condemns him, as the Jews were maintaining.[305] Hence even his death is a true fulfilment of the law (because it is God's will) and is not a penalty for breaking it.

---

[304] It was not so much a conflict over the law between Jesus and the Jewish authorities as a conflict over Jesus' claims to possess authority over the law. Cf. Pancaro, op. cit., pp. 492f.

[305] Martyn, op. cit., pp. 91f., lists six points in John's presentation of the Jewish approach to law, which he considers to represent 'the very life nerve of Judaism'. These are: (i) We know that God spoke to Moses (9:29). (ii) We are Moses' disciples (9:28). (iii) Moses gave the law (7:19). (iv) The law must not be broken (7:23). (v) The Am-ha-Aretz, who do not know the law, are cursed (7:49). (vi) True Jews diligently search the scriptures (5:39).

It should be noted that points (iii), (iv) and (vi) occur in passages where Jesus is the speaker. Yet John's gospel shows Jesus giving a reappraisal of the law against this Jewish approach.

The Johannine account shows very clearly that the law condemns those who condemn Jesus, a view which would have been entirely unintelligible to the Jews of Jesus' time. Jesus shows them to be those who were in fact refusing to do God's work, for otherwise they would have believed in him (Jn. 6:28ff.). They were judging by appearances (Jn. 7:24). They judged, moreover, 'according to the flesh' (Jn. 8:15).

We must next enquire what significance is to be attached to the frequent representation in the gospel of the law as the law of the Jews (*cf.* Jn. 8:17; 10:34; 15:25). Nicodemus speaks of 'our law' (Jn. 7:51). The accusers at the trial of Jesus say 'We have a law' (Jn. 19:7). The question arises whether Jesus wished to dissociate himself from the Jewish law. If he did, it was presumably because he set himself above the Jewish law in the sense that the law was not binding on him because he was Son of God.[306] If this is the true interpretation, it has a direct bearing on the relevance of the law for the followers of Jesus. But some interpret the expression, 'your law' as meaning simply 'the law on which you are relying',[307] which would remove the suggestion of distance between Jesus and the Jews in relation to the law, and would not contradict or make inconsistent Jesus' own appeal to the law.

It has been suggested that the dissociation meaning (the first interpretation) reflects the milieu of the later conflict between the church and the synagogue,[308] but this dissociation of Jesus from the law would hardly have been suggested had it had no basis in fact. Since the whole mission of Jesus depended on people's personal relationship to him and not on their fulfilment of the law, the law had effectively ceased to mean the same thing for Jesus as for his Jewish contemporaries. There is a sense, therefore, in which Jesus was preparing his followers for the conflict that he knew would be continued after his death. One aspect of this conflict which is taken up by the apostle Paul concerns the relation of the Gentile Christians to the law. But John's gospel would have been most helpful in connection with the Jewish Christians. These had come from the same background as those who were opposing Jesus on the grounds of the law, and the approach taken by Jesus would be an invaluable pattern for them.

It would seem right to conclude from the evidence so far presented that Jesus' conception of law differed from that of his opponents, who reflect the typical Jewish approach of the intertestamental period. Undoubtedly John regards the approach of Jesus as the true pattern for Christians. This is borne out by the important saying in the prologue where he gives a clear

---

[306] R. H. Lightfoot, *John* (1956) p. 196 maintains that there was a wide gulf between Jesus and his hearers in respect to his attitude to the Law.

[307] *Cf.* Gutbrod, *op. cit.*, 133, *Cf.* also B. F. Westcott, *John* (1887), on Jn. 8:17; J. P. Charlier, 'L'exégèse johannique d'un précepte légal: Jean viii. 17', *RB* 67, 1960, pp. 503–515.

[308] *Cf.* Pancaro, *op. cit.*, pp. 519f.

indication of the relation of Jesus (the Logos) to the law (Jn. 1:17).

It is generally supposed that in his prologue John made use of an existing hymn. Whether or not this is a correct view, it is not our present purpose to discuss.[309] We need only note that if John did use an existing hymn he has made it his own in a very real way, and 1:17 may be regarded as a statement of his understanding of the relationship between Moses and Jesus. John sets out his view in the statement, 'For the law was given through Moses; grace and truth came through Jesus Christ'. Several important deductions may be made from this. (i) The law is recognized as being of divine origin as the passive 'was given' (*edothē*) implies; (ii) The law is compared with 'grace and truth' linked together; and (iii) The comparison is made between the respective agencies through which the different results were achieved (*i.e.*, Moses is compared with Jesus Christ).[310]

We note that what comes through Jesus Christ is particularly described as 'truth' which is a concept which points to revelation. It is a frequent word in John's gospel, whereas 'grace' (*charis*) is used only here in the prologue. A revelatory word is particularly apt to describe the function of the Logos, who is also identified as light. The statement does not, however, imply that no 'grace and truth' came through Moses, but that *par excellence* they came through Jesus Christ.[311] There is a sense in which the provisions of the law were provisions of God's grace, but John is obviously using the word 'grace' in a way which is contrasted with the law. It seems best to see here an affirmation of Christian values which would contrast with Jewish beliefs that 'truth' was to be found in the law. Now that the Logos had become flesh (with all that that involved), there was a better, more adequate source of truth. As compared with Moses who mediated the law, the superiority of Jesus Christ is seen from the fact that his fullness can be imparted in the form of grace on all believers. There is an essentially personal aspect which is lacking from the law. Moses never shared himself in the way that Jesus has done.

This passage is of considerable value in demonstrating the way in which Christians reinterpreted the function of the law. There is no suggestion that Moses and his law are in any way belittled. Rather the focus falls on the inadequacy of the law as a full revelation of God.[312] The whole gospel bears out the view that an entirely new approach to law has been inaugurated by Jesus.[313] Without in any sense abrogating the law, John helps his

---

[309] H. Ridderbos, 'The Structure and Scope of the Prologue to the Gospel of John', *NovT* 8, 1966, pp. 180–201, denies the composite character of the prologue.

[310] *Cf.* Pancaro's extensive discussion of this verse, *op. cit.*, pp. 534–546.

[311] *Cf.* G. A. F. Knight, *Law and Grace* (1962), pp. 61ff.

[312] C. H. Dodd, *The Interpretation of the Fourth Gospel*, p. 86, holds the view that the law stands over against the revelation.

[313] Bultmann, *EvT* 4, 1937, p. 128, entirely underestimates the importance of law in this gospel.

readers to see the greater clarity of truth which has come through Jesus Christ. It is worth observing that in this gospel the law is not regarded as a norm for Christian behaviour. The emphasis falls rather on commitment to Jesus Christ. Nevertheless there is also no evidence of antagonism between the right understanding of the law and the gospel. That right understanding establishes a continuity by showing how the law leads towards, not away from, Christ. There are many points of contact between the Johannine approach to law and that of Paul, as will be seen later. It should further be noted that the other Johannine literature contributes nothing to our understanding of the Christian approach to the law.

Acts

In the earlier stages of the Christian mission the law does not seem to have been a problem. Since the Christians were all Jewish, they would continue to have respect for the law. They frequented the temple just as Jesus had done. It is true that they ran up against strong Jewish opposition, but it was not on the grounds of opposition to the law. The first concern was over the messianic claims the disciples were making about Jesus and particularly about the resurrection (*cf.* 4:1, 2).

It was not until the ministry of Stephen that the Christian approach to the law became a problem. The Jews set up false witnesses to declare that he was continually speaking against 'this holy place and the law' (6:13). There was also the allegation of blasphemy against Moses and God (6:11).[314] What ostensibly bothered them was their fear that the customs of Moses were being undermined (6:14). Assuming that there was a modicum of truth in the charge, it must be an indication that there was a clear distinction between the way Christians and Jews were approaching the law. This is all the more striking since the opposition in Stephen's case came from a Hellenistic Jewish source.

Stephen's speech in Acts 7 is cut short when he reaches his defence of the Christian approach to the temple ('Yet the most High does not dwell in houses made with hands', 7:48). He does not explicitly expound or defend his attitude towards the law, but his review of Israelite history gives pride of place to Moses. Moreover, it was Stephen's concluding charge, that those 'who received the law as delivered by angels and did not keep it' (7:53)[315] had murdered the Righteous One, that enraged his hearers. They would have claimed that it was because they kept the law that they

---

[314] F. F. Bruce, *The Book of the Acts* (*NICNT*, 1954), p. 134, maintains that the charge of blasphemy against Moses was brought because Stephen was assumed to be challenging the abiding validity of the law. 'Moses' here stands for the 'law'.

[315] It is noticeable that the mention of angels in the giving of the law is evidently intended to make more acute the blameworthiness of the hearers for not keeping it. It serves a different purpose in Gal. 3:19. But here the contrast is between the Righteous One, who alone had perfectly fulfilled the law, and those who in spite of their privileges had not done so.

killed Jesus, the same fundamental misunderstanding of the law on the part of the opponents of Jesus which is reflected in the synoptic records. The breach was already deep-seated.

The Jerusalem church, in discussing the case of Cornelius and his household, accepted Peter's evidence on the grounds that the Spirit had descended on Gentiles and had shown that God had granted them 'repentance unto life' (11:18). This was regarded as a sufficient proof that the Christian faith depended on the activity of the Spirit and not on legal observances. This was an important step, but it required a full debate on the circumcision issue before the law problem was generally agreed. Peter's own problem was at first on the grounds of fellowship (10:28). He needed a divine vision to convince him that what was unlawful for him as a Jew was no longer unlawful as a Christian. But the incident shows the tension which the early Christians faced. On neither the fellowship issue nor the circumcision issue did the example of Jesus' attitude to the law provide any direct guidance, although the universality of his message made the problem inevitable.

The circumcision issue finds its sharpest focus in chapter 15 and in Paul's letter to the Galatians. We shall comment here only on Acts 15, although some account must be taken of the light Galatians throws upon it. Whereas Cornelius and his household might be treated as an exception, the problem of a complete Gentile community raised the issue in a more acute form. Disquiet over Gentiles, who were claiming to be Christians and yet were not committing themselves to the observance of the law by circumcision, came from a particular group of Jews at Jerusalem (15:1). These were acting on an essentially Jewish rather than Christian understanding of the law. They had not recognized that there was a distinction. Jewish Christians had seen the law (OT) as pointing to the messianic claims of Christ. The testimony of the law had been an important part in their Christian experience. It was difficult for them to reconcile this with any Christian groups who were not carrying out the precepts of the law. Moreover, any evangelistic mission to Jews would be weakened if it became known that Christians did not observe the law. Nevertheless, this perfectly understandable Jewish approach would have throttled the Gentile mission and would have confined Christians to a Jewish understanding of the law. The discussion in Acts 15 is of crucial importance.

The key question at the Jerusalem assembly was not so much whether circumcision should be insisted on, but whether all Christians should be required to keep the law of Moses (15:5). James' summing up in 15:19–21 recommended that the Gentiles should not be troubled, except to abstain from certain things (generally known as the Council decrees). It was a compromise that offered a means of reconciliation by giving some recognition to Jewish scruples without committing Gentiles to Jewish legal requirements. Acts 15 tells us nothing, however, about the way in which the early Christians interpreted the law. It is conclusive that membership of the Christian church did not depend on legal observance, but it does not imply that the law had no longer any relevance to Christians.

The Acts record of Paul's attitude towards the requirements of the law is worth noting because of the allegation that it conflicts with Paul's approach in the epistles.[316] It concerns three matters: his acceptance of the Council decrees, his action in circumcizing Timothy (Acts 16:3) and his undergoing a Jewish vow (Acts 21:17–26).[317] Although Paul passed on the decrees to the Galatian churches (Acts 16:4), there is no evidence that he did this elsewhere. It looks as if he regarded it as a temporary measure. His circumcision of Timothy was not in conflict with his non-circumcision policy for Gentiles, since Timothy's mother was Jewish. It was purely in the interests of his mission. The vow is rather more difficult, since James regarded it as evidence that Paul lived 'in observance of the law' (21:24). But even here Paul consented in order to alleviate misunderstanding. The opposition did not, however, see it this way (21:28).[318]

Paul

For a right understanding of Paul's theological position it is essential to grasp his attitude to the law both before and after his conversion.[319] His own experience greatly coloured the way of expressing his convictions, but his teaching nevertheless forms an important basis for a normative Christian approach to law and liberty. We shall first consider the meaning of the word 'law' in Paul, then the background to his Christian approach, followed by an examination of his teaching on the place of law in the Christian life.

---

[316] Some have found puzzling the silence of Acts on the controversies over the law which are reflected in Paul's epistles. *Cf.* K. Lake's note on 'Paul's Controversies', in *The Beginnings of Christianity* 5 (ed. K. Lake and H. J. Cadbury) (1933), pp. 212ff. Lake's conclusion is that Luke wanted to represent the apostolic church as harassed from without, but not from within. But there are sufficient hints of internal problems to support the more detailed information given in the epistles.

[317] *Cf.* R. N. Longenecker's excellent discussion of these Pauline practices in *Paul, Apostle of Liberty* (1964), pp. 246ff.

[318] It has been alleged on other grounds that Luke has a different approach to the law compared with other NT testimonies. J. Jervell, 'The Law in Luke-Acts', *HTR* 64, 1971, pp. 21–86, attempts to show that Luke's approach is the most conservative in the NT. His contention is that Luke was intending to show that Jewish Christians' observance of the law and the salvation of Gentiles as Gentiles, as an associate people, are the distinguishing marks of that Israel, which Moses and the prophets predicted as the people of the promises and of salvation'.

[319] There have been widely different interpretations of Paul's approach to the law. H. J. Schoeps, *Paul. The Theology of the Apostle in the Light of the History of Jewish Religion* (Eng. trans. 1961), p. 13, maintains that Paul misunderstood the law, since in Jewish circles the law was the sign of election for Israel. But in Hellenistic Judaism it had become legalistic and it was this that Paul combats. H. Conzelmann, *TNT*, p. 160, on the other hand, argues that Schoeps has misunderstood the radical nature of Paul's approach to the law. For a well-argued case, *cf.* E. P. Sanders, *Paul and Palestinian Judaism.*

THE MEANING OF LAW IN PAUL'S EPISTLES

The apostle uses the word *nomos* in a variety of ways and it is essential to note this before examining his statements. Most of the time he means the Mosaic law. He normally sees no reason to define this usage and expects his readers to understand. On one occasion he refers to the 'law of Moses' (1 Cor. 9:9) and a few times to 'the law of God' (Rom. 7:22, 25; 8:7). In Jewish usage the law would refer primarily to the Pentateuch, although it came to be used of the whole of the Scriptures. Both usages are found in Paul. In Romans 3:21 he links the law and the prophets, thus differentiating between them, whereas in Romans 3:19 the term 'law' relates to the preceding quotations which are culled from various parts of the OT, but none are from the Pentateuch.

In a general way Paul sometimes uses *nomos* of a principle of action, as when he speaks of the 'law of sin' or the 'law of the mind (Rom. 7:23). But even when he speaks of the law in this general way, his usage is coloured by the Mosaic law. Law is, in fact, seen *par excellence* through the Mosaic law. It cannot be maintained that in cases where the word *nomos* is used without the article it is to distinguish it from 'the law' referring specifically to the law of Moses,[320] for on occasions the form without the article is used in the same sense, as in Romans 2:14 where Gentiles are described as 'not having law'.[321] It is noticeable also that Paul does not use the word in the plural and never compares the laws of other nations with the Jewish law.

On occasions the law is spoken of as if it were personal (*e.g.* Rom. 3:19; 4:15; 1 Cor. 9:8). This personal quality is derived from the divine origin of the law. What the law says, God says. It has an authoritative and binding quality about it (*cf.* Rom. 7:1). It is this aspect of the law which makes so important the whole Pauline discussion of it. For the apostle the law is holy (Rom. 7:12), whatever else he says about its inadequacy as a means of salvation.

Moreover, as will become clear in the following discussion, the law is considered from several points of view; as the standard of God's judgment, as a legislative provision,[322] and as a prophetic voice. There are no cases, however, where Paul draws a distinction between the ceremonial and moral law. It is a unity.

PAUL'S PRE-CHRISTIAN EXPERIENCE UNDER THE LAW

No real appreciation of the radical nature of Paul's approach to the law is possible without a recognition of what the law meant to him as a Jew. We

---

[320] *Cf.* R. N. Longenecker, *op. cit.*, p. 118, who cites the study of E. Grafe, *Die paulinische Lehre vom Gesetz* (1893), pp. 2ff.

[321] *Cf.* Gutbrod, art. *nomos* in *TDNT* 4, p. 1070.

[322] Longenecker, *op. cit.*, pp. 125f., speaks of the contractual obligations of the law.

shall consider this from the evidence which he provides, somewhat incidentally, in the course of his epistles. It would be as well to point out
before doing this that contemporary Judaism contained two different approaches.[323] One was a strictly legalistic approach, which considered man's
religious obligation to consist of faithful adherence to the tenets of the law,
the emphasis falling on what man could do. The result was a religion of
merit. The other approach concentrated more on trust in God and began
from God's doings rather than man's. Whereas this second view was
preferable to the first, both regarded law as the main means by which man
could approach God.

Many scholars have considered Romans 7 as an evidence of Paul's preconversion experience under the law. But it is by no means certain that
this interpretation is right.[324] The use of the first personal singular could
possibly be understood in a gnomic sense, in which case he is expressing
a truth which is applicable to people in general (*cf.* Rom. 3:7; 1 Cor. 13:
1–3 for a similar gnomic use). But the relevance of Romans 7 to the
pre-conversion experience of Paul does not depend entirely on the use of
the first person, for certain temporal references in the passage must also
be considered.

We note first Romans 7:9, where Paul declares: 'I was once alive apart
from the law.' Does he mean by this that he did not consider the law
binding upon him in his childhood? This was highly unlikely in view of
his Jewish upbringing.[325] Does he then mean that he was unaware of the
law making demands upon him? This too is difficult to believe in view of
the early age at which Jewish boys were instructed in the law. There is
much to be said for a corporate understanding of the 'I', in which case
Paul's statement is raised above the purely biographical and becomes an
allusion to past history, to the time before the giving of the law. This is
supported by several parallels between Romans 7 and Genesis 3 and is in
line with Paul's Adam theology[326] (see pp. 333ff.). This transforms Romans
7 from a biographical to a theological statement.[327] Such an interpretation
not only throws light on the statement in Romans 7:9, quoted above, but
also on its continuation: 'When the commandment came, sin revived and
I died'.

Paul points out further that sin in the commandment deceived, and this
deception is best understood to be an allusion to the deception of Adam
and Eve. In that case, the words 'I died' refers to Adam's death and alludes

---

[323] *Cf.* Longenecker's discussion, *ibid.*, pp. 65ff.

[324] *Cf.* W. G. Kümmel, *Römer 7 und die Bekehrung des Paulus* (1929), pp. 121ff.

[325] For the Jewish concept of the pre-existent Torah, built up on the conviction that man could not at
any time be without specific instruction from God, *cf.* G. F. Moore, *Judaism* 1, 262–277.

[326] *Cf.* Longenecker, *op. cit.*, pp. 92f.

[327] *Cf.* W. Manson, 'Notes on the Argument of Romans', *New Testament Essays* (ed. A. J. B. Higgins,
1959), p. 161.

to the death of all men in him (as in Rom. 5:12f.).[328] But if Romans 7 is best understood theologically in the sense of solidarity with Adam, it does not remove altogether the relevance of the passage for a right understanding of Paul, for he considers himself to have experienced the common lot of mankind. What seems positive is that Paul is not describing his own pre-Christian position as a Pharisaic legalist.

Nevertheless there are other passages in Paul's letters which give some indication of his assessment of his former life with Judaism. There was certainly a strong element of self-righteousness about it. He claimed to be extra zealous for the traditions of his fathers (Gal. 1:14) and 'blameless' under the law (Phil. 3:6). There is no doubt an element of religious pride in these claims, which Paul must have strongly felt in his pre-Christian days to recall them here. But his claims are not necessarily legalistic, as demonstrated by parallels from Qumran (cf. 1 QS 1:9; 3:9, 10; CDC 2:15f.; 3:2), which do not imply a merely external approach to the law.

The book of Acts reports similar statements made by Paul (Acts 22:3; 26:5) and, in addition, records the words of the risen Christ to Paul about kicking against the goads (Acts 26:14). Do these words about the goads imply that Paul had become increasingly dissatisfied with Judaism prior to his conversion? It is difficult to see what other evidence can be adduced in support of this view, since Paul's own persecuting zeal sprang from the conviction that he was doing God service. If the goads cannot be related to Paul's inner conflict, what meaning can be attached to them? It seems best to suppose that the idiom of the goads is intended in the sense in which it is found in certain Greek writers, i.e. to act in opposition to the deity.[329] In this case the words would not imply any awareness on Paul's part that when he persecuted Christians he was opposing God's will. He had regarded it as a duty to maintain the law, although it is highly probable that he found it 'hard' to pursue his persecuting policy. His radical change of attitude towards the law did not take effect until his conversion, and even then only as a result of a direct revelation from God.

It should further be noted that Paul shows a real appreciation of the glory of the old covenant. This is particularly evident in 2 Corinthians 3:7–18. Although he calls it a ministration of death, he nevertheless speaks of the splendour of it. Although it is surpassed in splendour by Christ, its

---

[328] R. Bultmann, *TNT*, 1, p. 252, regards Rom. 5:13 ('sin is not counted where there is no law'), which is parallel to Rom. 7:8,9 as unintelligible. But if account is taken of the Jewish concept that at no time is man without law, it becomes clear that Paul is agreeing with and not contradicting this. This interpretation admittedly requires the view that Paul is using 'commandment' to refer to the pre-Mosaic law in Rom. 7:8ff., whereas he usually means the Mosaic law, and this must be reckoned a difficulty. Nonetheless, Paul uses the word 'law' in a variety of ways.

[329] *Cf.* R. N. Longenecker's discussion of this in *Paul, Apostle of Liberty*, pp. 98ff. He thinks that a well-informed Jew like Agrippa would understand by the expression an opposition to God. J. Munck, *Paul and the Salvation of Mankind* (Eng. trans. 1959), p. 21 n. 9, considers the meaning to be 'cease rebelling against what is inevitable'.

own splendour is not to be despised. We may suppose, therefore, that Paul was proud of the law and saw an immense value in it. The next question to which we must address ourselves is, What modifications did Paul the Christian need to make in his appraisals of the law?

PAUL'S TEACHING ABOUT THE LAW

Although Paul himself does not give any systematic teaching about the place of the law in the Christian life, there are some basic concepts around which his evidence can be grouped. We shall discover first of all that there are two apparently contradictory approaches, which can only stand side by side if their paradoxical relationship is recognized. Otherwise the Pauline evidence will tend to be polarized into passages which suggest an affirmation of the law and passages which imply a negation of it. We cannot avoid considering the evidence under these categories, but our intention is to see in what ways Paul considered a *via media* to be possible.

It is the major key to the argument in Galatians that the promise is historically prior to the law and consequently must be superior to it. Indeed Paul states that the law was introduced 430 years after the promise was given to Abraham (Gal. 3:17). He saw clearly the implications of this. He was convinced that once a promise was made, nothing could change it. Since the promise required the response of faith he considered that the law could not annul it and could not require any different approach to righteousness from God's promise to Abraham. For Paul there was no choice but to see the law as subordinate to the promise.

This did not mean, however, that law and promise were antagonistic to each other (Gal. 3:21). Paul recognized in the law an expression of God's grace. Indeed, the law itself was based on promise. If the whole law had been kept, salvation would have been assured. But Paul knew full well that no-one ever had kept the whole law (except Jesus Christ). The main weakness of the law was that it could only show that people had transgressed. It could not make alive (Gal. 3:21). In these ways Paul brings out clearly the essentially negative aspect of the law. But if law is so inadequate, what was its purpose? If it did not conflict with the promise, it must have had some positive aspect. This is to be seen in its function, which differed from that of the promise. Both run side by side. The promise was never superseded by the law. It was always there, and found its fulfilment in Christ.

The function of the law. In explaining the present function of the law, Paul makes several assertions about the nature of law in respect to the individual.

(i) It brings the knowledge of sin (Rom. 3:20; 4:15; 7:7). The law is conceived as a standard for the pronouncements of the judgment of God (*i.e.* as a revelation of what God expects man to be), which explains why

Paul can say that apart from the law he would not have known sin. He was not implying that before the establishment of the Mosaic law sin was unknown. In Romans 5:13, he concedes that sin was in the world, but was not 'counted' before the law was given. It seems clear, therefore, that Paul sees the function of law in this sense as didactic. What it teaches man is that sin is a direct affront to God. But does it have the same function for Christians? Since Paul maintains that the commandment is 'holy and just and good' (Rom. 7:12), it cannot be wholly set aside. If it revealed God's demands in the past, the standard is still the same. But the Christian approach inevitably differs from the OT approach in that the promise supersedes the law. Knowledge of sin is still needed, but the promise brings immediate assurance of cleansing.

(ii) The law stimulates sin. This is a more difficult aspect of Paul's teaching.[330] He makes statements like 'Law came in, to increase the trespass' (Rom. 5:20), and 'that sin might be shown to be sin, and through the commandment might become sinful beyond measure' (Rom. 7:13). It looks as if Paul is portraying law as the villain of the piece, but his purpose is otherwise. He would never have admitted that what was good could promote evil. Indeed in the Romans 7:13 passage he attributes the result not to the law, but to sin making use of the law for its own purposes. Paul's underlying thought seems to be that prohibition provokes resistance.[331] Man has to be convinced that his sin was of such a character that he has no hope of attaining righteousness through his own efforts. It is because the law does this that Paul can assert that the strength of sin is the law (1 Cor. 15:56). In all these passages he is using the word 'law' in the sense of legal statutes which must be observed.

(iii) Yet the law is spiritual. Lest anyone should think, however, that we should have been better off without the law, Paul at once brings out its 'spiritual' purpose. In fact, he contrasts this characteristic with the 'carnal' nature of man, sold under sin (Rom. 7:14). In other words, if the law makes sin more sinful it is not the law's fault. The fault lies with man. Sin would not be stimulated if man was not carnal. The real function of the law is spiritual, *i.e.* to achieve spiritual results. If it had the right material to work with it could do it, but its failure lies in the inability of man to respond to it. Naturally in the Christian approach to law a different situation arises, and it is in the spiritual nature of the law that some carry over into the Christian life is possible (see below).

---

[330] Some exegetes in an attempt to avoid the idea that the law stimulates sin suggest that the law leads man to seek a righteousness of his own, *i.e.* self-justification. So Bultmann, *TNT* 1, p. 267. But he does not regard sin as transgression of the law. Against this view, *cf.* H. N. Ridderbos, *Paul : an Outline of His Theology*, p. 145f.

[331] Longenecker, *op. cit.*, p. 124, explains the law's effect in making sin exceeding sinful on the principle that forbidden fruits are always sweetest.

(iv) The law is burdensome. Paul, as a Jew, would have accepted without question that one committed to the law was committed to the whole law (*cf.* Gal. 5:3).[332] The breaking of one commandment was tantamount to breaking the whole (Gal. 3:10). It was this that tended to make life under the law so burdensome.[333] In an attempt to safeguard against unwitting breaches the Pharisees had hedged round the law with a mass of traditions, which however good their purpose only added to the burdens. The Christian gospel offered release from the minute regulations. There was never any suggestion that the 'traditions' should be taken over by Christianity (*cf.* Col. 2:8, 16).

(v) The law pronounces a curse. Not only does law reveal and promote sin, it actively condemns it. It is this fact that leads Paul to show the impossibility of anyone attaining righteousness through the law (Gal. 3:11). It is also because of this that he sees Christ becoming a curse for us to redeem us from the curse of the law (Gal. 3:13).[334] The curse-pronouncing function of law can no longer apply to those for whom Christ has become a curse.

(vi) Works of the law cannot earn righteousness. It is the apostle's dominant message in both Romans and Galatians that righteousness is by faith, not by works of the law (*i.e.* human acts done in conformity to the demands of the law).[335] Paul sees evidence from the OT that faith is the key to righteousness (Rom. 1:17; Hab. 2:4). For a fuller discussion on this see the section on righteousness (pp. 498f.), but our present purpose is to show the inability of the law to provide for the basic need of man. It should be noted that the importance of the law is confined to this question of righteousness. Paul never suggests that there is anything intrinsically weak about the law. But the vital function of providing a means of attaining righteousness was reserved for faith. It is for this reason that Paul is so

---

[332] According to E. P. Sanders, *Paul and Palestinian Judaism*, p. 137, the Hebrew word used in Dt. 27:26 means 'confirm', which is the sense in which the rabbis understood the verse. It is not so much that people were expected to keep the law without error. It is in this sense of confirming the law that we may understand the Jewish commitment to the law. W. Schmithals, *Paul and the Gnostics* (Eng. trans. 1972), pp. 13–64, argues from Gal. 5:3 that the opposition consisted of Gnostics who had not required adherence to the whole law and treated circumcision as symbolic. But Schmithals' interpretation is vitiated by the lack of sufficient evidence of gnostic groups as early as this.

[333] E. P. Sanders, *op. cit.*, pp. 110f., maintains that the rabbis never regarded the multitude of commandments as burdensome. In fact, he cites evidence to show that some at least considered obedience to the law as a blessing which should bring joy. Yet whereas this may have been the rabbinic interpretation, it says nothing about the position of ordinary Jews. Sanders, however, compares the rabbinic regulations with the mass of laws which affect all who live in modern societies. He admits that the Jewish regulations had a special function through being divine commandments.

[334] See the discussion on this verse in my *Galatians* (NCB, 1969), pp. 102f. The sense of Gal. 3:13 seems to be that Christ was implicated in the law's condemnation of those with whom he was identified.

[335] J. B. Tyson, ' "Works of the Law" in Galatians', *JBL* 92, 1973, pp. 423ff., argues that the phrase 'works of the law' does not mean works in obedience to the law, but what he calls 'nomistic service', *i.e.* a system of service to God's revealed will: life under law.

adamant that justification is by faith and not by works of the law.

(vii) *The law is a tutor until Christ.* An important positive function of the law was to act as a tutor (*paidagōgos*) until Christ came (Gal. 3:24).[336] The word Paul uses denotes the person who had charge of the moral education of a child until the child reached maturity and independence. His task included the idea of guardianship.[337] Looking back before the era of faith Paul acknowledges that law had a protective function, but he is clear that the man of faith is no longer under a custodian (Gal. 3:25). This function of law has no further relevance for the Christian. Paul certainly did not mean that the law leads people to Christ, for his language makes clear that Christ changed this pedagogic function of law.

(viii) *The law finds its end in Christ.* Paul writes, 'For Christ is the end (*telos*) of the law, that everyone who has faith may be justified' (Rom. 10:4). It is important to determine in what sense Paul uses the word *telos*. The word here would normally mean 'termination', and the question immediately arises in what sense Paul conceived of the abrogation of the law in Christ.[338] The key is found in the words *eis dikaiosynēn*, which are paraphrased in the RSV by 'may be justified', but which literally mean 'unto righteousness' or 'in connection with righteousness'. This shows again that the law is abrogated in respect of contractual obligations, but not in respect of its function as the standard of God's judgments.[339] In the passage in which the statement comes, it is not the function and status of law which is under discussion, but the Israelites' attempts to seek a righteousness of their own. It was important in Paul's exposition to show that since Christ's coming the law had ceased to have any function in this quest. It should be noted nevertheless that the word *telos* can also convey the idea of completion, and in this case Paul's statement includes the thought that what was preparatory in the law finds its fulfilment in Christ.[340] Since Christ has met all the demands of the law and has redeemed men from its curse, it has for this further reason ceased to have any contractual function.

In close connection with this statement is another from Romans (*i.e.* 7: 1–6). In this passage Paul suggests that Christians are 'dead to the law'. The illustration he uses is of a married woman who is freed from the law of the

---

[336] *Cf.* G. Bertram's article on this word in *TDNT* 5, pp. 619ff. See also my *Galatians*, p. 114, and A. Oepke, *Der Brief des Paulus an die Galater* (*THNT*, 1937), pp. 66ff.

[337] It is important to recognize that a son under a *paidagōgos* was in no better position than a slave. Ridderbos, *op. cit.*, p. 148, points out that Paul's thought centres on the lack of liberty and not on the educative functions.

[338] G. E. Howard, 'Christ the End of the Law : The Meaning of Romans 10:4ff.', *JBL* 88, 1969, pp. 331ff., takes *telos* to mean goal. He interprets it in this way in view of its context, *i.e.* the inclusion of the Gentiles. He declares that Christ was the goal of the law to everyone who believes.

[339] C. A. A. Scott, *Christianity according to St Paul*, p. 41, makes a distinction between the contents of the law and law as a system. It is the latter which is terminated in Christ.

[340] *Cf.* Longenecker, *Paul, Apostle of Liberty*, p. 145.

husband when her husband dies.[341] The analogy is not precise for it may be questioned whether the law can be said to die. Yet there are two thoughts here which seem to be combined in one idea, *i.e.* the Christian dies to the law and the law dies to him, as far as attaining righteousness is concerned.

The continuing value of the law. The preceding discussion has highlighted many features of the law which no longer apply in Christ. But it would be wrong to suppose that Paul advocates the total abrogation of the law. He is in no sense an antinomian, in spite of all he has said about the end of the law. It is important to note his positive approach on this theme, because of its value in assessing the nature of Christian liberty.

(i) The law is still regarded as holy. Paul's statement about the holiness of the law in Romans 7:12 is clear, whether we regard the passage as autobiographical or not. For the apostle the law is still holy, because it is God's law.[342] In this he shared the same approach as Jesus. Now that he has become a Christian, he no longer recognizes law as a means of salvation, but it still represents for him the authoritative standard of God. It is, therefore, of crucial significance to discuss in what sense the law is still valid for the believer.

(ii) Nevertheless the law has a different meaning for believers. No longer is the law approached as a written code which kills (2 Cor. 3:6). It is approached through the Spirit. When a man turns to the Lord the veil is removed from his mind when he reads the Mosaic law (2 Cor. 3:16). The result is freedom through the Spirit. But does this mean that the law no longer applies and that the believer has freedom to act contrary to the law? Paul would never have agreed to that, for he was highly critical of antinomian tendencies, as Romans 6:1 shows. For him freedom was not disregard of the law, but a release from being entangled by it (*cf.* Gal. 5:1). Yet he does not precisely define what part the law plays in his new found freedom in Christ. He seems to hold that although he is no longer in bondage to the law, he cannot dispense with it. In Christ he approaches it from a new point of view. He is controlled by the law of Christ rather than by the law of Moses. The commandments of Christ have now become authoritative for him (*cf.* 1 Cor. 7:19), but these are developments from the law of Moses and are not in opposition to it.

(iii) Keeping the commandments is now dominated by love. In the

---

[341] *Cf.* W. Manson, in *New Testament Essays : Studies in Memory of T. W. Manson* (ed. A. J. B. Higgins, 1969), pp. 160f.

[342] Although there is here a specific reference to law, the Scriptures which contain the books of the law are equally holy. This idea of the holiness of the law is characteristic of rabbinic understanding. *Cf.* W. Gutbrod, *TDNT* 4, pp. 1054f. Especially is this seen in the principle that the Scriptures pollute the hands, making ritual cleansing necessary before turning to secular activity.

practical section of his Roman letter Paul cites several commandments, but sums them up, as Jesus had done, in the commandment about love (Rom. 13:9). He considers that love to one's neighbour fulfils the law, which shows a totally different approach from legalism. Love of this kind is possible only through Christ. It brings a whole new dimension to the understanding of the law.[343]

Although Paul appeals to the Mosaic law, he nevertheless argues that all things are lawful (1 Cor. 6:12). Yet by stressing that the law of love is dominant he does not allow such a principle to land him in antinomianism.[344] It means that he judges what is expedient, not by whether it is permissible by law, but by whether it is helpful to others (cf. his argument about foods offered to idols, 1 Cor. 10:23ff.).[345] Legalism is replaced by love, which may, in fact, be more limiting than a legal contract, but is motivated by a more powerful urge.

This change of approach to the law furnishes the real key to an understanding of Paul's view of the moral law. He does not distinguish between the ceremonial and moral law and then discard the former and retain the latter. If he had done that, it would have suggested that the moral law was something apart from Christ. But his whole approach to Christian ethics shows that he recognizes that Christ changes a man's view of his obligations and this must inevitably modify his estimate of the place of law in the Christian life.

(iv) It is the Christian's obligation to uphold the law. Paul makes this quite clear in Romans 3:31, where he rejects the view that faith overthrows the law. In what sense did he mean that we uphold the law?[346] Since Christ, in meeting the sacrificial demands of the law on people's behalf, fulfilled the law, in that sense the law was upheld. In a similar way, the believer 'in Christ' upholds the law by his identification with Christ. In a sense, therefore, the law becomes inward. It no longer consists merely of external demands, but requires an inward conformity to the one who has perfectly fulfilled its moral and ceremonial demands. The believer has become subject to the law of Christ (cf. 1 Cor. 9:21 – ennomos Christou).[347] He keeps the

[343] As M. Black, *Romans*, p. 162, comments, '*agapē* produces the results aimed at by the Law'.

[344] It is generally supposed that Paul is quoting a claim of his opponents, but in doing so is modifying the principle to avoid the antinomianism which he had detected in them. C. K. Barrett, *1 Corinthians*, pp. 144f., favours the view that this was a watchword of the gnostic party.

[345] 1 Cor. 10:24 makes quite specific that each must put his neighbour's goal before his own. As G. Carey, *I Believe in Man*, p. 98, says, 'Here is the heart of true Christian freedom – it is never egocentric but centred on the good of others'.

[346] Note that the idea of upholding the law does not conflict in Paul's mind with not being under the law (cf. 1 Cor. 9:20).

[347] On the meaning of *ennomos Christou*, cf. C. K. Barrett, *1 Corinthians*, pp. 212ff. He considers Paul here intentionally avoided saying that he was under the law of Christ (as he does in Gal. 6:2), because he wants to bring out that he is 'Christ's law abiding one'. It is thus the opposite of *anomos* (lawless). *Cf.* C. H. Dodd, 'Ennomos Christou', in *Studia Paulina in honorem J. de Zwaan*, ed. J. N. Sevenster and W. C. van Unnik (1953), pp. 96–110.

commandments, not through fear of the consequences if he breaks them, but through a passionate desire to conform to the mind of Christ (hence the love-principle mentioned above). But this does not mean a legalistic approach to the requirements of the law. Paul's view of the sabbath is a modification of the Mosaic law, since the first day of the week was apparently observed (1 Cor. 16:2). There is nothing in Paul's epistles to suggest that he differed from Jesus in his view of the binding character of the law. Indeed, the whole inspiration of his liberated view of the law must be attributed to Jesus.

It is not surprising that many of the problems raised by false teachers in Paul's churches involved a legalistic approach to Christian life (*cf.* Galatians and Colossians. Note also Tit. 3:9; 1 Tim. 1:7; 4:3). It is no more surprising that Paul saw the need to affirm the liberty of the believer in Christ, because he is no longer under law but under grace.

Hebrews

Generally in this epistle *nomos* is used of the OT law. It is just possible that 7:16 might be understood in the sense of a legal ordinance, but even here a reference to the Mosaic requirements makes good sense. This epistle makes no distinction between the word used with or without the article. It is twice used in the plural, but only in quotations (8:10; 10:16). Sometimes the word is used in a restricted way of regulations relating to the cultus, but the writer does not distinguish between the moral and ceremonial law, although he is mainly concerned with the latter.

We note first of all a different approach to the law from that found in Jesus and Paul. The shift of emphasis is entirely dictated by the subject matter.[348] In Paul the law is seen as a standard for man's actions and the apostle shows only a passing interest in its ceremonial aspects. The levitical regulations concerning the priesthood are in Hebrews approached from the conviction that Christ our high priest is superior in every way to the priesthood provided by the Mosaic law. The burden of this letter is to show how Christians may now look back to the law and reinterpret it. There is no suggestion that the law itself has lessened in value. The references to the phrase 'according to the law' (*kata nomon*)[349] testify to the respect for the law (*cf.* 8:4; 10:8), but both, however, in relation to the old order. There are certain factors which may be seen to govern the view of the law which Hebrews expounds.

---

[348] F. F. Bruce, *Hebrews*, p. 145, suggests that whereas Paul has mainly the moral law in mind, Hebrews has the ceremonial law in mind. But he cautions about the appeal to a distinction which neither OT nor NT use. He finds a common principle shared by both Paul and Hebrews, *i.e.* that both regard law as a temporary provision of God.

[349] Gutbrod, *op. cit.*, p. 1078 n. 257, suggests that *kata* here = 'in the strength of', or almost 'through'.

THE LAW HAS PROVIDED A HIGH-PRIESTLY SYSTEM

The system was designed to enable men to approach to God. The priests were 'appointed' (5:1), *i.e.* the whole institution was a provision of God. The epistle shows in many particulars the limitation of the system, particularly because death overtook all the appointed high priests and because their sacrifices had a limited effectiveness and could never take away sin, even their own (7:27). This epistle expounds the high-priestly theme, based as it was on the law, with the intention of showing its inadequacy.

THE LAW, CONNECTED WITH THE OLD COVENANT, IS NOW SEEN TO BE OBSOLETE

In Hebrews 8, the long quotation from Jeremiah 31, which emphasizes the inward character of the new covenant, leads the writer to conclude that the old is obsolete (*cf.* 8:13). In this case it is the superiority of laws written on hearts rather than on stones which is mainly in mind, but there are similar statements about the inadequacy of the cultic system. It could not make perfect (7:19; 9:9; 10:1). It could not purify the conscience (9:14), and therefore could not remove guilt. It could not save, for that is exclusively the function of Christ (7:25; 9:28; 10:19ff.).

It is the inability of the law to bring men to perfection which causes the writer to speak of its 'weakness' and 'uselessness' (7:18). In this, it is contrasted with the ability of Christ (*cf.* Heb. 10:14). The weakness inheres, not in the law or its purpose, but in the people on whom its operation depends. By way of comparison, Paul's emphasis is on the fact that men are incapable of fulfilling the demands of the law. Another difference between Hebrews and Paul is that whereas for the former the law is finished as a mode of worship (13:10ff.),[350] for the latter it is finished as a way of righteousness. Although expressing their ideas in different ways, they are in substantial agreement about the inadequacy of the law in the Christian life. The main distinction between them is that for Hebrews the question of using law as a means of attaining favour with God (so prominent in Paul's arguments) is no longer an issue.

James

The controversial passage on faith and works (Jas 2:14ff.) has already been discussed in the section on faith (pp. 598f.), where it was noted that James never speaks of works of the law as Paul does. For him the problem whether the law can be a means of salvation does not arise, for he is interested in the genuineness of a Christian's profession of faith. But he does refer to the law on a few occasions. He speaks of 'the perfect law, the

---

[350] The Mosaic 'altar' is totally reinterpreted. For the Christian the death of Christ becomes the new altar. There is no support in the NT for the view that this altar is connected with the Christian eucharist. *Cf.* P. E. Hughes, *Hebrews*, pp. 577f.

law of liberty' (1:25; 2:12), and of the royal law (2:8).[351] He seems to qualify the law in this way in order to distinguish it from the more common meaning of law. It suggests a new way of looking at law, especially in view of the connection between law and liberty. The old approach to the law was certainly not one of freedom.

It is significant that the law is summed up in the law of love (*i.e.* love to one's neighbour), precisely as Jesus and Paul had summed it up (2:8). The motive power behind the keeping of the law is more important than the commandment itself. This is equally true of the reference in 1:25, which is immediately followed by a definition of religion that centres on loving concern for others. The perfect law, which leads to a practical religious faith, is very different from the old law.[352] James shows that the law still convicts transgressors and this includes a condemnation of partiality (2:9). In this case the law, whether it be the Mosaic law or the law of love, serves as a standard for judgment. In view of James 1:25 it seems best to understand the law here as the law of love (the perfect, royal law), in spite of the fact that in 2:11, two of the Mosaic commandments are cited. James recognizes that one sin is enough to make a man a transgressor and that anyone who sins in one point is guilty of the whole (2:10).[353]

One other reference to law in James deserves comment. In James 4:11ff., it is maintained that a man who speaks evil of his brother speaks evil of the law and judges it. Such an action is clearly against the law of love and James may be thinking of this.[354] But in view of the reference to judging the law, it may be taken more widely of the purpose of God in the law, in which case a misconstruing of God's plan is in mind. James gives no credence to the view that the law has still an obligatory function, for Christian freedom has replaced legalism with love.

Conclusion

There is clearly a tension in the NT evidence regarding the Christian ap-

---

[351] According to J. H. Ropes, *James* (1916), pp. 198f., the adjective *basilikon* (royal) has the sense of 'supreme'. He calls the adjective decorative and suggestive only. He admits, however, that *nomos* here means God's law as known through the Christian understanding of the OT. G. H. Rendall, *The Epistle of James and Judaic Christianity* (1927), p. 67, considers that the epithet 'royal' is associated with Jesus' preaching of the kingdom and points to the many echoes of the Sermon on the Mount in James' epistle in support of this view.

[352] M. Dibelius and H. Greeven, *James*, pp. 116ff., see the reference to the perfect law of liberty against the Stoic idea of the freedom of the wise man. Consequently they consider James' words to belong to a time when Judaizers no longer constituted a danger. But it makes better sense to approach Jas. 1:25 from its OT antecedents, especially Je. 31:31-34. So C. L. Mitton, *James*, p. 72. The liberty then follows from the 'inner' character of the law.

[353] There is some evidence of rabbinic support for such a contention. *Cf.* J. B. Mayor, *James* (³1913, r.p. 1954), p. 92f.

[354] C. L. Mitton, *op. cit.*, p. 166, suggests that 'speaking against the law' is a way of saying that the person sets himself above the law by slighting and ignoring the law. To disregard the law of love is to undermine its validity.

proach to the law. On the one hand there is general agreement regarding the abiding validity of the commandments. On the other hand, there is recognition that observance of the law as a means of salvation is not viable because of the impossibility of such observance.

Jesus himself penetrated to the inner meaning of the law, but in no way abolished it. Paul, although struggling with the problems which the law had posed for his life, nevertheless still regarded it as holy. The law as God's standard still remains valid, but the coming of Christ has affected the function of the law in the Christian life.

We may now sum up the whole of this chapter by pointing out that there is a progression in the subjects we have studied. The natural man, who is under the condemnation of the law, is nevertheless presented with a new possibility if he repents and believes in Christ. He then finds forgiveness and through regeneration becomes a spiritual man. As a spiritual man, he is 'in Christ' or 'in the Spirit', or to put it another way, Christ is dwelling in him. This makes possible a new ideal towards which he must strive. The consequence is that he has a new approach to the law.

The considerations in this chapter have concentrated on the new man in Christ as an individual, but since man is also a social being we must next turn our attention to the new man in community, *i.e.* the Christian in the context of the church.

Chapter 7

The Church

Although for some considerable time interest in the doctrine of the church had been slight, particularly because of an over-emphasis on the social gospel, the ecumenical movement has stirred up renewed questioning about the nature of the church. Our task will be to survey the NT evidence with a view to providing a biblical basis for a consistent doctrine. Admittedly it is difficult, when considering this theme, to approach it without some prejudice regarding church order and organization. But it is the task of the NT theologian to discover the NT doctrine, although he must clearly bear in mind that first-century conditions differed greatly from twentieth-century situations and the NT concepts will accordingly need modification in their modern application. Nevertheless, in surveying the evidence the greatest care must be taken not to read back a twentieth-century background into the first century.

The NT theologian is faced with many problems when dealing with the church, because of the wide variety of views on what is the basic question, *i.e.* whether the idea of the Christian church originated with Jesus, or whether it was a later development. Many subsidiary problems derive from consideration of this central problem, *e.g.* whether the church is to be identified with the kingdom; whether eschatology plays any major part in a true presentation of the church; whether there are evidences of the development of church order in the NT. To deal with these issues in the clearest way, it will be necessary to regard the evidence in two main parts: the testimony of Jesus to the idea of a community, and the testimony of the apostles. Some think there was no clear connecting link between these two lines of evidence and the objections raised will be borne in mind. But if a clear link can be established it will obviously have a strong effect on our whole approach to the NT doctrine.

701

THE EARLY COMMUNITY

The synoptic gospels

A cursory survey of these gospels might lead an investigator to conclude that Jesus was not interested in the church. Indeed, if the evidence was restricted to occasions when the word 'church' (*ekklēsia*) is used, it would be surprisingly sparse and even then restricted to one gospel (Mt. 16:18ff.; 18:17f.). Those who deny both of these sayings to Jesus and who do not consider that he ever taught anything about the church imagine that this exhausts the evidence.[1] What else occurs in the synoptic gospels which appears to foreshadow the church is regarded as testimony of the early church to itself. It is impossible to account satisfactorily for the rise of the concept of the church, if Jesus himself did not originate it; this raises serious objections against questioning the validity of the *ekklēsia* sayings. It will be shown that no sufficient grounds exist for denying these sayings. Nevertheless, in order to demonstrate that the approach of Jesus does not simply hang on two Matthean sayings, we shall consider the supporting evidence for a community idea first and then examine in detail the particular significance of Matthew 16:18. Our first quest must be to discuss the relationship of the kingdom of God to the church.

THE KINGDOM AND THE CHURCH

We have already discussed the kingdom teaching of Jesus in the context of his mission (pp. 409ff.).[2] We noted then that according to the teaching of Jesus the kingdom was both present and future. The view that the kingdom was either wholly present or wholly future did not square with the evidence. If, however, it is present it must clearly have a direct bearing on our understanding of the church, for we must then decide what relation it bears to the present Christian community.

The relation of the church to the kingdom. We must first note that not all statements concerning the kingdom apply to the church. When Jesus sent his disciples to preach, they preached the kingdom not the church, *i.e.* the rule of God (Mt. 10:7). It was not identified with them. Jesus never regarded his disciples as constituting the kingdom; in fact it is Jesus himself who represents on earth the kingly rule of God[3] (*e.g.* Lk. 11:20, where Jesus claims to cast out demons by the finger of God and so demonstrates the presence of the kingdom). The kingdom centres, therefore, on Christ

---

[1] *Cf.* E. Schweizer, *Church Order in the New Testament* (Eng. trans. 1961), pp. 20ff.

[2] For a detailed discussion of the relation between the kingdom and the church, *cf.* G. E. Ladd, *The Presence of the Future* (1974), pp. 239–273; H. Küng, *The Church* (Eng. trans. 1968), pp. 88ff.

[3] *Cf.* K. E. Skydsgaard, 'Kingdom and Church', *SJT* 4, 1951, pp. 383–397. 'In Jesus the eschatological Kingdom of God was a perfect and ever present reality' (p. 390).

and not on the disciples. This is fully in line with the fact that *basileia* does not, in the teaching of Jesus, nor indeed anywhere in the NT, primarily indicate the sphere over which the king rules.[4] The main idea is that the disciples are people in whom the rule of God can be manifested. It naturally follows that since the rule of God does not operate in a vacuum, there is a sense of community among all those prepared to allow the rule of God to dominate their lives. Hence the kingdom in this respect presupposes some sphere in which God's sovereignty is exercised; this suggests a future community, but does not require that the two concepts be identified.[5]

In this context it should be noted that various scholars have denied that Jesus intended to form a community[6] and these automatically exclude all possibility of the kingdom being identified with the church. Indeed, if the kingdom teaching can be worked out only by individuals, there would be no problem about the church and kingdom in the mind of Jesus. Individualism of this kind, however, is not only unsupported by the general tenor of the teaching of Jesus, it is also contrary to Hebrew thinking. This leads us to our second consideration.

The church finds its basis in the kingdom. Several of the sayings of Jesus about the kingdom have the notion in them of 'entering' (Mk. 9:47; Mt.7:21; Lk. 16:16). The Pharisees were charged with preventing people from entering the kingdom (Mt. 23:13; *cf.* Lk. 11:52). Moreover, Jesus speaks of 'the keys of the kingdom of heaven' (Mt. 16:19). It is clear from these references that the language is metaphorical and must be understood in the sense that man now has the opportunity to 'enter' a new way of life in which God's will becomes the norm. But in what sense does this lead to a community idea?

We may note that some of the parables of the kingdom denote a community idea. The mustard seed was used to show what remarkable results could follow from small beginnings (Mk. 4:30-32).[7] Indeed, the parable implies that the kingdom, which has already begun, would have far-reaching effects.[8] The imagery of birds to represent people finds parallels in Ezekiel 31:3b and Daniel 4:12. Another relevant parable is the drag-net (Mt. 13:47f.) which shows the kingdom to be all-embracing in its scope, affecting both good and bad, but requiring a process of selection at the

---

[4] R. N. Flew, *Jesus and his Church* (1938), p. 22, points out that during the first four centuries of the Christian era, the kingdom was never identified with the church.

[5] It should be noted that in Mt. 16:18f., the ideas of the church and the kingdom are mentioned together and their meanings are seen to be closely related.

[6] Conzelmann, *TNT*, p. 33, is emphatic that Jesus did not found a church. He claims that Jesus' eschatological awareness of himself excludes the idea of a present church.

[7] *Cf.* Flew, *op. cit.*, pp. 26ff., on this parable.

[8] But see H. N. Ridderbos' criticism of Flew's suggestion in *The Coming of the Kingdom* (1962), pp. 346f. He considers that the thought is too general to point to the *ekklēsia*.

close of the age for the ejection of the bad. The present state of the kingdom cannot, therefore, be identified with the pure church, but the latter clearly rises out of the former. It is best to suppose that all who belong to the kingdom belong to the ideal church, but that all who belong to the visible church do not necessarily belong to the kingdom.[9]

The church is a partial manifestation of the kingdom. Since the disciples were commissioned to proclaim the coming of the kingdom, we must enquire in what sense that message was related to the total teaching of Jesus about the kingdom, particularly in view of the fact that the kingdom theme largely drops out of the epistles. It seems clear that the announcement of the kingdom both by John the Baptist and by Jesus was intended to be continued by the followers of Jesus, as is seen in the commission to the twelve (Mt. 10:7; Lk. 9:2) and to the seventy (Lk. 10:9). The announcement was therefore closely linked with group activity. It has been suggested that the twelve represented the true Israel and the seventy the nations of the world, in which case the commissioning of the disciples shows the wide application of the kingdom teaching. Since the twelve, among other followers of Jesus, were closely associated with the subsequent establishment of the church, it is inescapable that the church is conceived of as a present manifestation of the kingdom in so far as those who proclaim it are committed to it. As future developments show, it was not without problems that the Christians settled down to accept Gentiles on an equal footing with Jews, but there can be no doubt that this was implicit in the concept of the kingdom taught by Jesus.

There is no suggestion that the disciples, after the death and resurrection of Jesus, conceived the idea of constituting a church contrary to the intention of Jesus. Of course, if it be maintained that Jesus envisaged the presence of the kingdom only in his own ministry,[10] there would be no alternative but to maintain that the apostles had themselves conceived the idea of a church. This, however, restricts too much the concept of the kingdom, although it would explain the reduced emphasis on the word 'kingdom' in the apostolic testimony. Another suggestion which is also unacceptable is that Jesus did not want to constitute a community because this would deflect people from meeting God in the life and work of Jesus.[11] But this would leave entirely unexplained any connection between the subsequent church and the message and mission of Jesus. We must conclude that the kingdom concept was neither fully established in the earthly ministry of Jesus, nor was it wholly remote, relating to the end time. The present

[9] *Cf.* R. Schnackenburg, *God's Rule and Kingdom* (Eng. trans. 1963), p. 231. *Cf.* also G. E. Ladd, *TNT*, p. 113.

[10] So W. G. Kümmel, *Promise and Fulfilment* (Eng. trans. 1957), pp. 105ff.

[11] *Cf.* E. Schweizer, *Church Order in the New Testament*, p. 24.

church has the task of witnessing to it, but its full realization does not belong to this age.

The bearing of eschatological theories on the interpretation of the kingdom-church relationships. Enough has already been said to show the far-reaching consequences of various eschatological theories concerning the kingdom for an understanding of the origin of the church (see also the section on the future, pp. 868f.). It is necessary at this point to classify the different possibilities with a view to establishing the significance of any conclusion drawn from them. They may conveniently be grouped under the following headings.[12]

(i) The view of the kingdom as consisting of the rule of God in the individual, which excludes from the teaching of Jesus all idea of a community.

(ii) The view that the kingdom was intended to inaugurate a new social order and the church was merged into society as a whole, providing the catalyst for its reformation.

(iii) The view that the kingdom is future and is wholly the work of God, which is therefore nothing to do with the church and is present only in the consciousness of Jesus.

(iv) The view that the kingdom is wholly future and was not even present in the experience of Jesus, in which case the church finds no basis in his experience or teachings.

(v) The view that the kingdom really belongs to the future, but has over-spilled into the present in the experience of the Christian community.

(vi) The view that the kingdom is already realized in the present (or is in the process of being realized), which virtually identifies the kingdom with the church, but at the expense of ignoring or explaining away the future aspects.

(vii) The view that a distinction must be made between the kingdom of Christ, which relates to the present, and the kingdom of God which relates to the future.[13]

If we are to take seriously all the evidence from the synoptic gospels regarding the kingdom, some link between the present and the future, which adequately explains the origin and function of the church, must be maintained. It seems reasonable to suppose that the greater emphasis on the future in the teaching of Jesus was intended as a spur to urge men to

---

[12] For a full survey of views on the kingdom, *cf.* G. Lundström, *The Kingdom of God in the Teaching of Jesus* (Eng. trans. 1963).

[13] In his essay on 'The Kingship of Christ and the Church in the New Testament', in *The Early Church* (Eng. trans. 1956), pp. 105–137, O. Cullmann introduces a distinction between the *Regnum Christi* and the kingdom of God. This *Regnum Christi* is closely allied to the church, but is not identical with it. Cullmann sees the *Regnum Christi* as stretching from the ascension to the second coming. He sees the kingdom of God as extending beyond it. J. Héring, *Le Royaume de Dieu et sa Venue* (²1959), p. 176, also distinguishes between the kingdom of God and the kingdom of the Son, because the former is in the future.

reach towards a fulfilment which could be fully realized only in the future kingdom, but was already represented in the present community. It is impossible to excise from the teaching of Jesus all consciousness of such a community, without postulating a Messiah without a messianic community, which is itself unthinkable.[14] We conclude therefore that a right understanding of the kingdom teaching of Jesus does not exclude the possibility that he envisaged a community of his people between his resurrection and his parousia.

THE COMMUNITY IDEA IN THE TEACHING OF JESUS

Since the mission of Jesus was conducted against the background of OT thought, there are important considerations which arise out of the continuity between the mission and the dealings of God with his people Israel. Other considerations arise from the nature of the teaching of Jesus. These will provide no more than pointers, but will supply a valuable introduction to a study of the specific *ekklēsia* passages in Matthew.

The Christian community as the true Israel. The OT has as one of its predominant ideas the covenant dealings of God with his people Israel. The Israelites are portrayed in a special sense as the people of God. He made promises to them, but also made demands upon them. Their failure to meet the demands was countered by God's provision of a means of redemption, revealing himself to be the redeeming God. Although the majority rejected God's provision, there was always a faithful remnant, an idea which is taken up in the NT. What is most significant for a right understanding of Jesus' view of the church is that God dealt with a community rather than with isolated individuals.

Although Jesus confined his activities to the Jewish people and especially to those whom he calls 'the lost sheep of the house of Israel' (Mt. 15:24), he did not incorporate into his message or mission any idea of nationalism. He was essentially concerned with the 'people of God' in a new and vital way. Opposition, hatred and ultimately violent action came from the official representatives of Israel. Yet until the ultimate rejection of the Messiah by Israel, Jesus still concentrated on his compatriots. The 'lost sheep' were his concern, an idea which involves a community.

The 'lost sheep' saying in Matthew may be compared with the reference to the disciples as sheep (*cf.* Lk. 12:32), not as individuals, but as 'a little flock'.[15] Moreover, Jesus cites a passage from Zechariah 13:7 in predicting that his sheep (*i.e.* disciples) would be scattered (Mk. 14:27). These references follow the OT imagery, in which Israel is seen as a flock of sheep.

The parable of the wicked husbandmen illustrates Jesus' expectation that

---

[14] *Cf.* Ridderbos, *op. cit.*, p. 348.

[15] E. Schweizer, *op. cit.*, pp. 22f., disputes that either of these sayings implies a community.

the Jewish nation would reject the Son and that the vineyard would be let out to other tenants (*i.e.* a nation producing the fruits of the kingdom of God, Mt. 21:40ff.). Since the kingdom here is linked not only to the rejection of the old Israel, but to the establishment of a new people of God, it is an important witness to the thinking of Jesus about the future community. The linking of this in Matthew's account with the 'rejected stone' prophecy from Psalm 118 also contains within it the community idea of a building in which Christ himself was to be the chief stone. This imagery would make little sense if some envisaged community of the rejected Messiah were not in mind.

Admittedly Jesus' lament over Jersusalem might at first sight suggest that he expected Israel to respond (Mt. 23:37-39 = Lk. 13:34-35). But this cannot be the right interpretation, since he also forecast the destruction of the city (Lk. 19:41ff.). It was not through disillusionment that Jesus wept over it, but because through its rejection of God's way it had sealed its own inevitable fate. He pinned no hopes on the liberation of Jerusalem from the yoke of Rome, but predicted a new community, a spiritual Israel.

That spiritual Israel was closely identified with his own followers. It would no longer be a merit to be a descendant of Abraham (Mt. 3:9 = Lk. 3:8), as John the Baptist predicted. The new community was not to be based on national descent. But the disciples, as the embryo of that new community, were intended to be significantly linked with the old Israel. The number *twelve* was surely not accidental, but symbolic of the groups into which the whole nation of Israel was divided.[16] Some have seen the Sermon on the Mount as the new law for the new Israel, but this adds nothing to our present contention that since the old Israel was a corporate concept, so was the true Israel as adumbrated by Jesus. He never actually called his disciples 'Israel', but since he proclaimed to them the messianic salvation and commissioned them to proclaim it to others, it is reasonable to suppose that he saw them as the true successors of the faithful remnant of Israel.

The disciples as a nucleus of the new community. It is undeniable that Jesus gathered around him a group of men who were in a special sense his disciples. The word used (*mathētēs*) is applied to many of the followers of Jesus in addition to the twelve, and the question naturally arises whether the twelve were intended to occupy a special place in the future com-munity.[17] The synoptic gospels single out and name these men and assign

---

[16] L. Goppelt, *Apostolic and Post-Apostolic Times* (Eng. trans. 1970), pp. 27f., suggests that Jesus' disciples did not, as the Essenes and Pharisees, consider themselves to be the *true* Israel, but the *new* Israel. The calling of the twelve by Jesus is seen as an expression of Jesus' claim to Israel as a whole.

[17] T. W. Manson, *The Church's Ministry* (1948), pp. 50f., strongly maintains the uniqueness of the twelve. Indeed, he suggests that their special status could not be passed on. Even Paul, while claiming parity with the twelve, never claims to be one of them.

to them the office of apostle (Mt. 10:2 = Lk. 6:13; cf. Mk. 6:30). No indication is given of their precise function. It is in fact, only Luke who tells us that Jesus named these men 'apostles' (Lk. 6:13) and it is worth noting that this evangelist uses the term *apostolos* more frequently than the others in describing them (cf. Lk. 9:10; 17:15; 22:14; 24:10).[18] We may conclude, therefore, that although Jesus regarded all who followed him as 'disciples', not in the Jewish sense of those bound to the Torah, but in the sense of those committed to himself, he nevertheless separated from them a smaller group for the purpose of instruction.[19]

It is, of course, true that Jesus never said to these men that they were to be office bearers in the new community, nor that they should establish an *ekklēsia*. But it cannot be claimed that there was never a thought of this.[20] In Matthew 19:28 (Lk. 22:30) there is a direct indication from Jesus that he expected the apostles to have some authority in that they would share with him in his future judgment over the tribes of Israel. Moreover all the synoptic writers construct their gospels on the plan that after Caesarea Philippi Jesus devoted more attention to teaching the disciples (cf. Mt. 16:21 = Mk. 8:31 = Lk. 9:43), especially to prepare them for his coming passion. It was natural that these men who had been with Jesus in a special way during his ministry should form the 'core' of the coming community. At the same time it should be noted that his appointment of witnesses to testify to what the risen Lord had expounded to them before his ascension is not specifically restricted to the apostles (Lk. 24:45ff.).[21] The notion of 'apostle' in the early church will need further examination later (see pp. 739ff. 768f.), but our concern here is to demonstrate that the selection of a special group of men as well as the wider group of disciples presupposes in the intention of Jesus an ongoing community.

The character of the ethical teaching of Jesus excludes the notion of hierarchy among the disciples. In fact, Jesus expressly criticized those who sought positions of superiority and he inculcated humility as a more desirable quality (Mt. 18:1ff.; Mk. 9:33f.; Lk. 9:46f.). He also criticized the use of status titles like 'Rabbi', since he maintained that his disciples were all

---

[18] H. Conzelmann, *TNT* p. 29, denies that the twelve were 'twelve apostles', although he admits the existence of a group (the twelve) distinct from apostles. He considers the term 'apostle' to extend over the whole church. The apostles are the proclaimers and therefore became bearers of the tradition (p. 46). Only later were they restricted to the twelve. Cf. also H. von Campenhausen, *Ecclesiastical Authority and Spiritual Power in the Church of the First Three Centuries* (Eng. trans. 1969).

[19] Cf. Ladd, *TNT*, p. 107.

[20] As Schweizer, *Church Order in the New Testament*, p. 28, maintains. Cf. also T. W. Manson, *Ministry and Priesthood* (1958), pp. 18f.

[21] Schweizer, *op. cit., ad loc.*, accepts the probable historicity of the twelve, but states, without citing any evidence, that they were not 'apostles'. Nevertheless, it is most probable from the evidence that the term 'apostle' was wider than the twelve, since some outside the twelve are named apostles. It would be truer to say that the twelve were apostles but were not the only apostles. Cf. E. E. Ellis' remark, 'In Luke-Acts the twelve are qualified by apostleship, but apostleship is in no way qualified by or limited to the twelve' (*Int* 28, 1974, p. 96).

brethren who had the same teacher, *i.e.* himself (Mt. 23:8). He linked with 'Rabbi', the title of 'father' and 'master'. The greatest among his group of followers were those willing to be servants (*douloi*) utterly obedient to their master's wishes. The only privilege that could be claimed by any of the disciples was the privilege of service and sacrifice (such as taking up a cross).[22] We must clearly approach the passage in Matthew 16 against this background and exclude any interpretation of that passage which exalts one man above the rest of the disciples.

The view that the community idea was implicit in the Son of man concept. We noted when discussing the Son of man concept that there is a strong possibility that Daniel 7 contributed to the background of the term. If we suppose that the Son of man was not only an individual, but a corporate individual representing the saints of the Most High,[23] we have at once a symbol of a community. If this interpretation is correct, or even if as seems most likely it is only partially an explanation of the title,[24] it could be inferred that Jesus' own use of the title reflects something of his awareness of the community which would follow from his mission. But this view has not gone unchallenged.[25] It implies that the Son of man title was used ambiguously, sometimes in a collective sense, and sometimes in an individual sense. It would have been confusing for Jesus' contemporaries and cannot be said to be required by the gospel statements. It would therefore be a somewhat precarious peg on which to hang any community idea. If, on the other hand, the Son of man is considered to be an individual, this would not necessarily exclude the idea of community, if he were thought of as leader of a group, which Daniel 7 makes possible.

The special ethical demands made on the disciples presuppose a community. A problem arises over the relevance of the ethical teaching of Jesus. If it is regarded as applicable to everyone in society,[26] it would not point to a group of people who would be marked out from the rest by reason of a higher ethical ideal. Similarly if the ethical teaching was no more than an interim measure (*Interimsethik*), it would have no bearing on a future community.[27] But if the teaching was meant for the followers of Jesus, the

[22] This idea of service rather than office is strongly brought out by H. Küng in his book *Why Priests?* (Eng. trans. 1972), pp. 25ff.

[23] *Cf.* T. W. Manson, *The Teaching of Jesus*, pp. 227ff.; K. L. Schmidt, 'Die Kirche des Urchristentums', in *Festgabe für A. Deissmann* (ed. K. L. Schmidt, 1927), pp. 258–319; *idem*, *TDNT* 3, pp. 501ff.

[24] *Cf.* Ridderbos' comments on this interpretation, *op. cit.* pp. 339f.

[25] *Cf.* R. N. Flew, *Jesus and His Church*, p. 54, who points out the unnaturalness of this interpretation in the Son of man sayings.

[26] As, for instance, advocates of the social gospel would maintain. *Cf.* H. J. Cadbury, *The Peril of Modernizing Jesus* (1937), pp. 86ff., discusses the limitations of Jesus' social teaching.

[27] *Cf.* A. Schweitzer, *The Quest of the Historical Jesus* (1906, Eng. trans. ³1954) and *The Mystery of the Kingdom of God* (1901, Eng. trans. 1914).

practice of the moral teaching of Jesus would at once mark people out as different from those whose ethics conformed to contemporary practice. This is particularly true because of the seemingly impossible character of some of the demands of Jesus in the Sermon on the Mount and the obviously pressing need for more than human power. We have already discussed the teaching on the Holy Spirit in the synoptic gospels (pp. 514ff.), and it is relevant here to remark that the promise of the Spirit to the disciples not only carried with it a source of power for the ethical demands, but implied a community of people who were to be directed by the Spirit.

It must be admitted that the community ideas which have been discussed above are shadowy and cannot with any confidence be held to point precisely to the kind of *ekklēsia* which evolved in the post-resurrection period. But they are sufficient to dispose of any notion that Jesus was not at all interested in developing a community. This must have a bearing on our assessment of the Matthew 16 and 18 passages in which the word *ekklēsia* occurs.

THE EKKLĒSIA SAYINGS IN MATTHEW

Since there are only two statements in the gospels which use the word *ekklēsia* and both are in Matthew's account (16:18; 18:17), it is not surprising that much debate has surrounded them.[28] If they are authentic, why are Luke and Mark lacking in similar statements? Many scholars have responded by concluding for their non-authenticity. Clearly it is essential to decide this issue before the full force of the statements can be assessed. If Jesus did speak in advance of his church, what he said is obviously of great importance in considerations of the origin and nature of the church.[29]

Before examining the statements themselves, we will note the following points about their authenticity. (i) Authenticity has mainly been disputed by those who have emphasized a particular interpretation of the kingdom. Naturally those who locate the kingdom in the life of Jesus alone[30] or at the end of the age can maintain that Jesus showed no interest in founding a church.[31] But we have seen these approaches to be unacceptable. (ii) The supporting evidence for the community idea cited above provides no reason to doubt that Jesus could have spoken about the church and strong reason

---

[28] On Jesus' expectation of the church and the authenticity of Mt. 16:18f, *cf.* W. G. Kümmel's discussion and bibliography, *Promise and Fulfilment*, pp. 138f.

[29] It should not be supposed that these *ekklēsia* sayings can be interpreted in isolation from Matthew's other teaching about the church. *Cf.* D. O. Via, 'The Church in the Gospel of Matthew', *SJT* 11, 1958, pp. 271–286, who bases his exposition on the body metaphor. *Cf.* also E. Schweizer's note on 'The "Matthean" Church', *NTS* 20, 1974, p. 215.

[30] *Cf.* W. G. Kümmel, *Promise and Fulfilment*, pp. 141–155.

[31] Bultmann rejects the view that Jesus thought of founding a church because he considers that Jesus spoke only of a coming kingdom (*ThB* 20, 1941, 265ff.).

for supposing that he did. (iii) The absence of any satisfactory explanation of the origin of the sayings predisposes in favour of their authenticity. Can it seriously be maintained that the Christian community universally decided to call itself the *ekklēsia* and then created two sayings of Jesus, to make out that he, rather than the church, created the idea? (iv) Some scholars, while not necessarily denying authenticity, consider that some dislocation has occurred[32] and that Matthew 16:17-19 does not belong to its present context; but this is without textual evidence.

If we adopt the view that there are no conclusive reasons for denying that the *ekklēsia* sayings are authentic, we have not thereby resolved all the problems, for there remains the important question of interpretation. This affects several issues, particularly in reference to Matthew 16. What is the meaning of *ekklēsia*? What is the identification of the Rock? What part was Peter to play in the future community? What is the significance of the keys? What is intended by the gates of Hades? In some sense the answer to the first question will inevitably affect the other questions since it impinges on the more far reaching problem of the relationship of Jesus to the church.

What did Jesus mean by ekklēsia? In view of the widespread use of the word in the LXX for the congregation of Israel,[33] it should be noted that *ekklēsia* represents a Hebrew word, *qāhāl*, but never *'ēdâ*. Both of these are used of the community of God's people. If the word used by Jesus is used in the LXX sense of *qāhāl*, *ekklēsia* refers to God's people conceived as a new community specially related to the Messiah (hence the expression 'my church' used by Jesus).[34]

An alternative suggestion is that *ekklēsia* represents the Aramaic *kenishta*, and that it refers to a separate messianic synagogue.[35] In Judaism each synagogue, although regarding itself as an entity, nevertheless looked on itself as a microcosm of Judaism as a whole. But it is difficult to uphold this as the explanation of Jesus' use of *ekklēsia* for several reasons. The

---

[32] So O. Cullmann, *Peter: Disciple, Apostle, Martyr* (Eng. trans. ²1962), pp. 176ff. Cullmann gives a concise summary of leading interpretations of this passage, pp. 164–176.

[33] W. Schrage, ' "Ekklesia" und "Synagogue"', *ZTK* 60, 1963, pp. 178ff., denies that the church took this word over from the LXX (as Conzelmann, *TNT*, p. 35, claims). He argues that the word was taken over from secular Greek by the Hellenists, who used it to express rejection of the law; hence they did not use the word 'synagogue'. Conzelmann calls this a desperate expedient in relation to Matthew's use of the term. He does not mention the possibility of Jesus' use of the term.

[34] J. Y. Campbell, 'The Christian Use of the Word Ekklesia' in *Three New Testament Studies* (1965), pp. 41–54 (from *JTS* 49, 1948), denies that the word *ekklēsia* was borrowed from the LXX to express the view that the church was the true people of God. He thinks the Christians first used the word to describe simple meetings, and later to describe local congregations. He pays no attention to its possible origin in the teaching of Jesus. For a thorough discussion of the NT meaning of the term in relation to its original meaning in the LXX, with special attention to its probable Hebrew and Aramaic equivalents, *cf.* I. H. Marshall, 'The Biblical Use of the word 'Ekklēsia', *ExT* 84 (1973), pp. 359ff. He concludes that in the NT the doctrine of the *ekklēsia* owes little to the theological use of corresponding terms in the OT.

[35] *Cf.* K. L. Schmidt, *ekklēsia*, *TDNT* 3, pp. 524ff.

message and mission of Jesus was too extensive to be confined by the idea of a Jewish synagogue. The connection of the community with Israel, although of some importance, is not the only consideration,[36] for Israel's rejection of its Messiah puts it at once not only in a different camp from the Christian community, but in positive variance to it. Moreover, the attack of the 'gates of Hades' suggests a more fundamental clash than appears credible if a synagogue within Judaism is in mind. Although it is true that this derivation would in the context fit the metaphor of a building, the building metaphor is equally applicable to the idea of a people of God, after the manner of OT usage (cf. Je. 12:16; 18:9; 24:6; 31:4; 42:10; Am. 9:11).[37]

We conclude, therefore, that by *ekklēsia* Jesus is not referring to an organization, but to a group of people whom he considered to belong to him and of whom the disciples were in some way representatives.[38] This naturally means a much looser concept than that which later developed in early Christian history. There is no reason to suppose that the *ekklēsia* of Jesus did not form the embryo of the church in the Acts and NT epistles. It should further be noted that the word *ekklēsia* could represent a particular assembly as well as be used as a generalized form for the people of God,[39] and as such would be easily recognized as a suitable term for the initial community in Acts which formed the basis of the NT church.

What is the meaning of the rock? When Jesus says 'You are Peter (*Petros*) and on this rock (*petra*) I will build my church' (Mt. 16:18), it is vital for a correct understanding of the church to decide the meaning of 'rock'.[40] Some have argued on the strength of the word-play in Greek that 'Peter' and 'rock' are intended to be identified, but that the change of gender shifts the emphasis from person to content. But there is no need to appeal to word-play since in Aramaic both words would be rendered by *kēphas*.[41] In view of the clear Semitic background to the saying (Bar-jona, 'flesh and blood'), it is most reasonable to suppose that an Aramaic interpretation will lead to a right understanding of the saying. This would seem at once to exclude Luther's view that the rock was Christ himself. Calvin's adaptation of this to Peter's faith in Christ is more acceptable, although it would be better to

---

[36] Cf. Ridderbos' criticisms, *The Coming of the Kingdom*, pp. 356ff.

[37] J. Jeremias, *NTT* 1, pp. 167ff., makes much of the fact that Jesus frequently spoke in terms of a gathering of the people of God, and points out that *ekklēsia* must be understood in this sense. Such an interpretation is supported by the Qumran evidence for the use of the word, as Jeremias points out.

[38] P. G. S. Hopwood, *The Religious Experience of the Primitive Church* (1936), pp. 233ff., interprets the *ekklēsia* in Matthew's statements to refer to Israel. According to him when Jesus said 'My church', he meant 'My Israel'.

[39] Cf. J. Barr's discussion on *ekklēsia* in *Semantics of Biblical Language* (1961), pp. 119ff.

[40] Cullmann, *Peter: Disciple, Apostle, Martyr*, pp. 158ff., gives a survey of the different interpretations which have been given to this passage.

[41] Cf. O. Cullmann, *ibid.*, pp. 19f., for details of the linguistic question (cf. also pp. 192ff.).

maintain, as Cullmann does,[42] that the rock was Peter the confessor (*i.e.* representative of those confessing Jesus to be Messiah and Son of God).[43]

If the rock and Peter are in this way identified, is there any justification for the Roman Catholic view that Jesus was not only addressing Peter, but also his successors?[44] There is certainly no suggestion of this in the passage. It must be regarded as an extension of the meaning. If it be regarded as a legitimate extension because of the representative character of Peter, it must be noted that Peter as representative of all those who make a similar confession is considerably wider than the view that it applies only to Peter's successors in the see of Rome. It is certain that the apostles would never have understood it in this way. It is equally certain that the disciples would never have supposed that Jesus intended building a church on the person of Peter.

If some special importance is being given to Peter, it is better to view his primacy chronologically, for not only was he the first confessor of faith in Jesus as Messiah and Son of God, but was also the first to declare the resurrection faith to the Jews (Acts 2) and to the Gentiles (Acts 10). But beyond this the evidence does not stretch. Jesus cannot be said, on the basis of these words, to be establishing a hierarchy.

What is the significance of the 'gates of Hades'? Jesus clearly had in mind a community which would meet with opposition, but would prevail against that hostility. But what is meant? Who is the attacker? Two interpretations are possible: either the *ekklēsia* attacks the view that the 'powers of death' (as RSV renders it) are all-powerful; or the realm of the dead is the attacker, but will not be able to overcome the *ekklēsia*.[45] As the Messiah has gained victory over death, so the community will itself demonstrate that victory. It is practically certain that the expression 'gates of Hades' is a synonym for Hades, which here stands for 'death' (*cf.* Rev. 1:18; 6:8; 20:13f. for the close connection between death and Hades).[46] In this case there may be an indirect allusion to the resurrection of Christ, since death had no power over him.[47]

The meaning of 'the keys of the kingdom of heaven'. Since the imagery so far points to a building metaphor, the introduction of 'keys' is not surprising.

---

[42] Cullmann, *ibid.*, pp. 206f.

[43] T. Zahn, *Matthäus* (⁴1922) *ad loc.*, considers that Peter has a special place as the first confessor (cited by Cullmann, *op. cit.*, p. 169).

[44] *Cf.* M. Meinertz, *Theologie des Neuen Testaments* I (1950), p. 74.

[45] So R. Eppel, 'L'interprétation de Matthieu 16:18b' in *Aux sources de la tradition chrétienne* (Mélanges offerts à M. Goguel, 1950), pp. 71ff.

[46] W. C. Allen, *Matthew* (ICC, ³1912) *ad loc.*, sees Hades as an allusion to the abode of evil spirits, but this idea finds no parallel in the NT.

[47] *Cf.* A. H. McNeile, *Matthew* (1915) *ad loc.*

But much depends on the interpretation of these 'keys'. Do they convey authority or do they merely relate to entrance into the kingdom? To some extent it depends on how closely the 'keys' statement is linked with the 'binding and loosing' saying which follows. If it is a case of the exercise of discipline, the authority idea would be dominant. But if the 'entry' idea is foremost, the keys refer to the fact that chronologically Peter, acting as the representative of Jesus, was the first to announce the message both to Jews (Acts 2) and to Gentiles (Acts 10). It should further be noted that the keys are said to be 'of the kingdom' and not 'of the church' which removes them from the idea of an ecclesiastical office. It is moreover possible to interpret the 'keys' in the light of Luke 11:52 (*cf.* Mt. 23:13), where Jesus charges the lawyers with taking away 'the key of knowledge', which effectively prevented others from entering. If the 'keys' of Matthew 16:19 are understood in the same sense, Peter would be seen as the special medium through whom the proclamation of the kingdom would be made.

The binding and loosing metaphor. The final consideration in the Matthew 16 passage is the 'binding and loosing' metaphor. For a right interpretation of this the parallel passage in Matthew 18:17ff. must also be taken into account.[48] The metaphorical language seems to be of rabbinical origin. It can mean either 'prohibit or permit', or 'ban or acquit'. If the former alternatives are accepted the saying would refer to the establishment of rules, and it might, therefore, have some bearing on future church discipline. If, however, the latter alternative is accepted, it would relate to the forgiveness of sins. It is somewhat unlikely that Jesus would have given directions about organization, and the reference to the forgiveness of sins must, therefore, be preferred, especially as this finds a parallel in John 20:23. But in what sense can power to forgive sins be conferred on another, since this is the prerogative of God? Jesus himself exercised the right (Mt. 9:4ff. = Mk. 2:5ff.) and it would be necessary to suppose that anyone else could do so only under his delegated authority. Did Jesus intend to invest this authority exclusively in Peter? The answer must be negative in view of Matthew 18:18, which is addressed to the disciples as a group. This must mean that Matthew 16:19 was addressed in the singular to Peter as the representative of all the disciples. It is again significant that historically Peter was the first to proclaim a loosing from sins (Acts 2:38) and a binding (Acts 5:3). The theme of forgiveness was a cardinal one in the early Christian proclamation.

The reference to church discipline in Matthew 18. In the Matthew 18 passage there appears to be a direct reference to church discipline (verses 15-17). It has been maintained that this saying could not possibly be authentic, since

---

[48] *Cf.* Strack-Billerbeck, *ad loc.*

it reflects the life situation of the early church.[49] But this is not a sufficient objection. It was well known that in Jewish circles cases of dispute were frequently referred to the synagogue (*i.e.* the community centre), and the reference to the *ekklēsia* here may be understood in a similar community sense. This is not to suggest that Jesus regarded his disciples as a synagogue, but the synagogue pattern may not have been entirely lacking. It does not require the concept of a fully organized ecclesiastical community for the idea of disputes being settled in an assembly to be intelligible. It seems most natural to suppose that the saying in Matthew 18 should be understood to imply that Jesus envisaged the need for corporate decisions over disciplinary issues. Some refer the passage wholly to disciplinary decisions,[50] others to the definition of what is sinful,[51] yet others to the principles of discipline.[52] The wording seems general enough to include any issue which called for corporate action and it seems unnecessary to define it further.

THE COMMISSION TO THE DISCIPLES

We have seen that Jesus conceived of his disciples as forming a community, although with few indications of structure. What is clear, however, is the message which he committed to them. This is to be seen from the commission both to the twelve and to the seventy. The message concerned the coming of the kingdom (*cf.* Lk. 9:2; 10:9). To these commissions, which related to the time of the ministry of Jesus, must now be added the post-resurrection commission to the disciples recorded by Matthew (28:19f.; *cf.* also Lk. 24:46–48). This passage[53] makes a valuable contribution to our present purpose.

We may note the following features. (i) Authority is vested in Christ himself, not in the disciples. There is no suggestion here of an authoritative ecclesiastical body. (ii) The commission is universal in that disciples are to be sought from all nations. Again the description of the future community is expressed in the most general terms. The same word (*mathētēs*), which had been used of the followers of the earthly Jesus, is now used of the community of the risen Lord. It carries with it the simple connotation of those ready to learn. (iii) Baptism is to be used as a sign of discipleship. (iv) The group of disciples is to be taught the content of what Jesus had himself taught. This is the basic core of the apostolic teaching. It rested wholly on the authoritative teaching of Jesus ('all that I have *commanded*

---

[49] *Cf.* E. Schweizer, *Church Order in the New Testament*, p. 21, who follows Bultmann.

[50] *Cf.* P. Bonnard, *Matthieu* (CNT, 1963), *ad loc.*, F. V. Filson, *Matthew* (BC, 1960), *ad loc.*

[51] *Cf.* E. Schweizer, *Matthew* (NTD, Eng. trans. 1976), *ad loc.*

[52] *Cf.* W. Hendriksen, *Matthew, ad loc.*

[53] *Cf.* E. Schweizer, *Church Order in the New Testament*, p. 40 n. 119. *Cf.* G. Barth, in *Tradition and Interpretation in Matthew* (G. Bornkamm, G. Barth and M. J. Held), pp. 131f. *Cf.* D. Hill, *Matthew* (NCB, 1972), p. 362.

you'). (v) The presence of Jesus is assured throughout the present age. The one theme which stands out is the centrality of Christ in the coming community.

The Luke passage is set in a slightly different, but nevertheless highly significant, context. The risen Lord expounds from the Scriptures everything written about himself (Lk. 24:44f.) and then declares, on the basis of the fulfilment of what has been written, 'that repentance and forgiveness of sins should be preached in his (*i.e.* Christ's) name to all nations, beginning from Jerusalem'. Here the content of the message is made more specific, but is clearly a continuation of the ministry of Jesus, although now backed by his death and resurrection. Whether any distinction should be made between the 'teaching' in Matthew's passage and the 'preaching' in Luke's is a matter of debate,[54] but a combination of keygma and didachē undoubtedly reflects the procedure which was actually adopted in the developing church. That procedure finds its basis in the commands of the risen Lord.

Although Mark does not include anything in the nature of a final commission,[55] he does record the statement of Jesus that the gospel must be preached to all nations (Mk. 13:10). The ministry of preaching which Jesus himself had exercised (Mk. 1:14f.) was to be continued after his death.

In view of the evidence outlined above it would seem reasonable to suppose that Jesus had in mind a community of his people who would be taught his commands, who would be bound together by a common allegiance to Christ signified by baptism, and who would regard it as their responsibility to reach out beyond their own immediate circle to add others to their number irrespective of nationality. It was a remarkable vision for a group of Jewish disciples of Jesus to accept as a possible concept, let alone a desirable one. The early church did not work itself up into an evangelistic community. It inherited a command from the risen Christ which it could not ignore. He did not give much indication on church organization, but he left in no doubt what the main aims of the community of his followers was to be. The idea of a closed, inward-looking community finds no support from his teaching. The message entrusted to his disciples was intended for all the world.

THE ORDINANCES

It is important to enquire whether the synoptic gospels give any indications that Jesus intended the community of his followers to follow any pattern

---

[54] I. H. Marshall, *Luke* (*NIGTC*, 1978), pp. 903f., suggests that some common traditions underlie the account in Lk. 24:44–49; Mt. 28:16–20 and Jn. 20:21–23.

[55] This is assuming that Mk. 16:9–20 was not an original part of Mark's gospel. A final commission is mentioned in verse 15, but if this is later than the gospel, as the textual evidence suggests that it is, it at least represents an early witness to the Christian conviction that the commission to preach went back to the words of the risen Lord.

of religious observances, either in regard to baptism or the Lord's Supper.[56] These observances are called sometimes ordinances and sometimes sacraments. The former has been preferred, but no distinction in meaning has been intended. What is basic to these observances is the fact that they are prescribed rites within the Christian church. The word 'ordinance' clearly brings out this sense.

Baptism. In the time of Jesus, there are three aspects of baptism to be considered: the baptism of John the Baptist and its relevance to Jesus himself; the baptism which Jesus himself practised through his disciples; and the command of Jesus to his disciples to baptize. It will be valuable to examine these aspects separately to build up a true picture of the importance that Jesus attached to the rite.

(i) The baptism of John. We must first enquire about the significance of John's baptism against the background of contemporary practices. Judaism probably practised proselyte baptism for the admission of Gentiles who wished to embrace Judaism,[57] but the evidence for this in NT times is uncertain. According to the Mishnah this type of baptism was discussed among the Rabbis in the schools of Shammai and Hillel. In the Qumran community, daily lustrations appear to have been performed, but it is not clear if initiatory baptism was observed. Not only among the Jews was some form of baptism familiar, but also among the pagans, for it is known to have been practised in Egypt.

John's baptism would not, therefore, have been a complete innovation.[58] In what sense then did it introduce a new element? There were several parallels between John's baptism and Jewish proselyte baptism. They both had an application beyond Judaism. Indeed, Jewish people were called on by John to place themselves in a similar position to Gentiles. Both John's baptism and proselyte baptism involved a voluntary step on the part of the candidates. Both also involved immersion. But John's was unlike Jewish baptism in that it was designed for Jews, not to make them Jews, but to make them aware of the need for repentance. The new element was not in the rite itself, but in its connection with the announcement of the kingdom and the requirement of repentance. It has been suggested that John's baptism may go back to OT requirements for the ritual cleansing of priests or to the prophets' use of water imagery for moral cleansing (*cf.* Is. 1:16ff.; Je. 4:14; Ezk. 36:25; Zc. 13:1). An interesting combination of 'water' and 'Spirit' occurs in Isaiah 44:3, which may link up with John the Baptist's

---

[56] For an essay on baptism in the synoptic gospels, *cf.* R. E. O. White, in *Christian Baptism* (ed. A. Gilmour, 1959), pp. 84–115.

[57] *Cf.* H. H. Rowley, 'Jewish Proselyte Baptism, *Hebrew Union College Annual* 15, 1940, p. 316 (reprinted in Rowley's *From Moses to Qumran* (1963), pp. 211–235.

[58] For discussions on the baptism of John, *cf.* C. H. H. Scobie, *John the Baptist* (1964), pp. 90–116; H. G. Marsh, *The Origin and Significance of the New Testament Baptism* (1941), pp. 15–100.

prediction about the baptism of Jesus (*cf.* Mt. 3:11).

When John baptized, it is described as 'a baptism of repentance for (*eis*) the forgiveness of sins' (Mk. 1:4 = Lk. 3:3), which follows on his call for repentance in view of the approach of the kingdom. It has been suggested that John's baptism implies that forgiveness is the result of the outward rite of baptism.[59] But another interpretation is possible. It could be said that baptism is an expression of the repentance which leads to forgiveness of sins.[60] In this case the forgiveness is not the result of the outward rite. The act of baptism is a public demonstration that it has happened. The former interpretation, if true, would be the only NT example of forgiveness resulting from a rite, and it is almost certain that this impression was not intended. The alternative suggestion is to be preferred. A further implication of John's baptism is that it carried with it specific moral obligations according to Luke 3:10ff.: the sharing of coats and food, the application of justice in the collection of taxes, the recommendation to soldiers not to rob.[61] It is evidence that John's baptism was no mere ritual act. John was particularly critical of the Pharisees and Sadducees (according to Matthew's account, Mt. 3:7), who were exhorted to bring forth fruits worthy of the repentance they were professing.

We need now to consider the relevance of John's baptism to Jesus. Why did he come if he needed no repentance-baptism? Matthew records hesitation on the part of John to baptize Jesus (Mt. 3:14). Because the other evangelists do not record the hesitation, its authenticity in Matthew is called into question. It is maintained that it reflects a later enhanced view of Jesus which found difficulty in his requesting repentance-baptism and which therefore led to the introduction of the hesitation episode to provide an explanation ('it is fitting for us to fulfil all righteousness').[62] However, even without this Matthean addition there would still be the problem as to why Jesus was baptized. There is only one satisfactory answer, *i.e.* that Jesus was identifying himself with those who were repenting and being baptized. He was acting, therefore, in a representative capacity.[63] His sub-

---

[59] *Cf.* J. Behm, *baptō, baptizō*, *TDNT* 1, pp. 529ff. Behm considers that the thought of a sacramental purification for the coming aeon is at least suggested in relation to John's baptism.

[60] *Cf.* J. D. G. Dunn, *Baptism in the Holy Spirit*, p. 15, who considers that Luke 3:3 refers not to a repentance baptism which leads to forgiveness, but to the repentance which results in the forgiveness of sins.

[61] R. Bultmann, *The History of the Synoptic Tradition* (Eng. trans. 1963), p. 145, treats Lk. 3:10–14 as a catechism-like section naïvely put into the Baptist's mouth. But his only reason is that soldiers would not have gone on a pilgrimage to John. This is an inadequate basis for disputing it as a saying of John the Baptist.

[62] *Cf.* E. Schweizer, *Matthew*, p. 53, for the view that this addition is Matthew's own comment.

[63] *Cf.* O. Cullmann, *Baptism in the New Testament*, p. 18. Cullmann is right when he maintains Christ's identification with the sins of his people, but when he maintains that the reference to *dikaiosynē* also relates to his people's righteousness, he appears to be interpreting *dikaiosynē* in a Pauline sense. D. Hill, *Matthew*, p. 96, prefers to understand 'righteousness' as righteousness of life. It is reasonable to suppose that the baptism of Jesus has some relevance to a right understanding of his whole mission.

mission to baptism formed the link between John's baptism and that which he himself practised through his disciples.

(ii) The baptism of Jesus. It is against the background of John's baptism that we must now note the salient features about Jesus' own adoption of the rite. He began his ministry with the same basic demand for repentance, thus recognizing the essential rightness of John's preparatory approach. Yet there was one important modification. Jesus was to baptize with fire and Spirit (Mt. 3:11 = Lk. 3:16), an extension of John's exclusively water ritual.[64] This connection between water-baptism and Spirit-baptism came to have more significance in the Acts and epistles, but its importance here is that it conclusively shows that Jesus never thought of baptism as a merely mechanical act.

(iii) The commission to the disciples to baptize. This brings us to consider the command given to the disciples to baptize (Mt. 28:19ff.). Since those to be baptized are described as 'disciples' it is reasonable to suppose that conditions of repentance and faith would be required, although these are not specified. The dispute over the authenticity of the triune formula revolves around the comparison with the simpler formula used in Acts (cf. 2:38; 8:16; 10:48; 19:5). The question arises whether the triune formula requires a late date.[65] The objection on this score presupposes that the Christians would have been conscious of any distinction between baptism in the name of Jesus and baptism in the triune name.[66] But this places more emphasis on the formula than is justified by the evidence. There is no support for the view that the use of the triune name would be regarded as any more or less effective than the simple name of Jesus, especially in view of the fact that trinitarian formulas do occur elsewhere in the NT (see pp. 112f.). What was important was not the precise structure of a formula, but the fact that the baptism was Christian baptism, and not Jewish or pagan or John's baptism. Moreover, it was certainly believed to be a command of Jesus.[67]

The Lord's supper. Our concern here is not to discuss the theological contribution of the words of institution, for this has already been done in discussing the work of Christ (see pp. 442ff.). What we need to consider

[64] I. H. Marshall, *Luke*, p. 147, points out that the way for John to connect baptism with the Holy Spirit and fire had already been laid in Judaism, and consequently there is no ground for supposing that John referred only to baptism with fire, as some have affirmed.

[65] W. F. Flemington, *The New Testament Doctrine of Baptism* (1948), pp. 105ff., discusses fully the authenticity of the passage and concludes against the words being the *ipsissima verba* of Jesus, mainly on the grounds of historical probability. Flemington nonetheless admits that the early church believed that the practice of baptism rested on the authority of Jesus himself.

[66] R. P. Martin, *Worship in the Early Church* (1964), p. 96, explains the Triune formula in Mt. 28 on the grounds that the Gentile mission was in mind, whereas in Acts those baptized were Jews or God-fearers.

[67] For an exposition of the view that baptism was a command of the risen Lord and for the supporting New Testament evidence, *cf.* P. W. Evans, *Sacraments in the New Testament* (1946).

here are the indications that Jesus intended the supper to become an integral part of the procedure of the coming community. In Matthew's account there is no statement regarding the perpetuation of the ceremony (cf. 26:26ff.). The only suggestion is that there will come a day when Jesus will drink of the fruit of the vine new with his disciples in his Father's kingdom (verse 29). A similar emphasis is found in both Mark's and Luke's accounts (cf. Mk. 14:25ff.; Lk. 22:14ff.).[68] Luke adds a further saying which identifies the kingdom as the messianic feast at the time of the judging of the twelve tribes of Israel (Lk. 22 :29-30),[69] which Matthew records in an earlier context (Mt. 19:28).[70] This, however, relates to the end of the present church age.[71]

It is striking that none of the synoptic gospels gives any indication that the Lord gave a specific command that the supper was to be observed in the future. It is only in Paul's record of the institution that the words are recorded, 'Do this, as often as you drink it, in remembrance of me' (1 Cor. 11:25). It is natural to suppose that the disciples after Pentecost recognized the theological importance of the words of institution, and not only preserved the words, but also repeated the act because of the particular authority with which the words were given. One other consideration must not be overlooked. According to Luke 24:30, the risen Christ broke bread, gave thanks and gave it to the two who had walked with him to Emmaus, and this may well have prompted the disciples to perpetuate the act.[72] It is not, of course, certain that this act of the risen Christ is here definitely connected with the Lord's supper,[73] but in view of Luke's use of the expression 'breaking bread' in Acts (2:42, 46; 20:7) it is at least probable that the ordinance was in mind, especially because in the Emmaus story it was the means of fellowship and recognition of the presence of Jesus.

John's gospel
Since there is no direct reference to the church in John's gospel[74] and since

[68] W. L. Lane, *Mark* (*NICNT*, 1974), p. 506, considers that the word of Jesus concerning the bread anticipates the resurrection and the real presence of the Lord in the celebration of the eucharist. In this case, the breaking of bread was anticipatory of future fellowship with his people.

[69] Although this is primarily eschatological, there may be an allusion to fellowship with Christ in the Lord's supper, cf. I. H. Marshall, *Luke*, p. 817.

[70] W. G. Kümmel, *Promise and Fulfilment*, p. 47, accepts Matthew's version as the more original form.

[71] T. F. Glasson, *The Second Advent* (³1963), pp. 144ff., prefers Luke's version to Matthew's, but removes the eschatological reference by relating Lk. 22:30 to the new Israel.

[72] Cf. J. Wanke, *Beobachtungen zum Eucharistieverständnis des Lukas auf Grund der Lukanischen Mahlberichte* (1973), who regards all Luke's references to meals as indications that he thought that the dominant idea of the eucharist was the presence of Christ in a fellowship meal.

[73] I. H. Marshall, *Luke*, p. 898, refutes Bultmann's suggestion that the early church associated the resurrection appearances of Jesus with meals because they expected Jesus to 'appear' at the Lord's supper. He remarks that it was because Jesus had appeared at meal times that the church expected his presence at the Lord's supper.

[74] For a discussion on the church in John's gospel, cf. W. F. Howard, *Christianity according to St John*

most scholars consider that this gospel reflects later developments, an apparent difficulty at once arises.[75] It is, in fact, in the sphere of church doctrine that the development theory for John's gospel becomes most vulnerable. For if it represents church theology rather than the teaching of Jesus, it is surprising that nothing was included about the very institution which is supposed to have created the ideas. It is more reasonable to suppose that the traditions preserved in John's gospel had their roots in the teaching of Jesus before the emergence of the church. Indeed John's gospel is in many respects in line with the synoptics in what it suggests with regard to the coming community.[76] Lack of specific reference to an *ekklēsia* is counterbalanced by many allusions which become significant in the light of the early Christian experience.

THE COMMUNITY IDEA IN JOHN

We have noted earlier (pp. 425f.) that John relates only two sayings of Jesus about the kingdom. This idea, therefore, made very little contribution to the understanding of the community in this gospel. For the community idea in John's gospel we must look elsewhere. Jesus, according to John, anticipated a time following his passion when his death and resurrection would be a challenge to all people to follow him. It is an uplifting of himself that draws people (12:32). The result of the death would not be for the nation of Israel only, but 'to gather into one the children of God who are scattered abroad' (11:52), as John comments on the saying of Caiaphas about the expediency of Jesus' death. The fulfilment of both these statements requires the emergence of a Christian community based on the redemptive work of Christ (*i.e.* a redeemed community). The way that the evangelist adds his comment in 11:52 throws light on the way he understood the prediction of Jesus in 12:32. The idea of oneness is highly significant in view of 17:22 ('that they may be one even as we are one'), which cannot fail to support the idea of a prospective community. It is important, however, to observe that there is no suggestion here of an organizational unity, but only of an organic one.[77] Since the oneness is paralleled to the oneness between Father and Son and is communicated to the believing group, which nevertheless needed to be perfected into one, the spiritual

---

(1943), pp. 129ff.; E. Schweizer, *Church Order in the New Testament* (1959), pp. 117ff.; R. N. Flew, *Jesus and his Church*, pp. 172ff.; E. F. Scott, *The Fourth Gospel. Its Purpose and Theology* (^{2}1908), pp. 104–144; A. Corell, *Consummatum Est* (1958).

[75] E. F. Scott, *op. cit.*, p. 105, recognizes that although the evangelist does not mention the church, his mind is penetrated with the thought of it. He considers, however, that the writer represented the church and is writing from that perspective.

[76] For a discussion of the historical problem in this gospel, *cf.* L. Morris, *Studies in the Fourth Gospel* (1969), pp. 65–138.

[77] For a discussion of the idea of unity in John 17:20–23, *cf.* R. E. Brown's comments, *John* (AB, 1966), pp. 774ff. He maintains that the unity must be more than spiritual. It must be sufficiently visible to challenge the world to believe in Jesus.

conception of unity must obviously be in mind.[78] It may be said, therefore, that Jesus prayed for a group of people who would be united into a corporate whole, and would be moulded after the same principles of one-ness which exist in God. This is clearly a more profound community idea than that seen in the teaching of Jesus recorded in the synoptics.

What indication does John give about the conditions of being identified with the prospective community? In attempting to answer this question, we note first of all the frequent emphasis in this gospel on 'believing' (the word 'faith' (*pistis*), however, does not occur). A fuller discussion of faith in John's gospel has been given in the section on faith (see pp. 581f.), where it was noted that Jesus clearly expected people to believe in him as a basis for community. The promise of eternal life was only in response to faith (3:15; 6:47). Those who did not believe were already under condem-nation (3:18). In the farewell discourses there are frequent references to faith in Jesus either for his own sake or on account of his words (*cf.* 14:10-11). There is no doubt that Jesus foresaw a community of believing people, knit together by a common faith in him. This is borne out further by the evangelist's own specified purpose in 20:31. Statements which suggest a community which embraces all people (such as 12:32) must be interpreted in the light of this clear call for faith. The 'all' must be modified in terms of faith. The same must be said of a statement like 17:21 ('so that the world may believe that thou hast sent me'). It would be wrong exegesis to suppose that Jesus in this prayer was prophesying that the coming com-munity would be identified with the world, for in this context 'world' is a generalizing term for those who are not as yet committed and does not represent the inhabitants of the world in their totality.

Moreover, this faith-community is no more an accident of circumstances than the Messiah himself. Those who form the community have been given to the Son 'before the foundation of the world' (17:24). A fuller discussion will be found under predestination (see pp. 611ff.). Whatever problems arise over the mystery of God's choice cannot obscure the clear conviction that the potential community was part of the mission committed to the Son. This Johannine statement of Jesus implies that if no community had been established as a result of the ministry of Jesus, he would have failed in his mission, but that since it was predetermined this could not have happened.

The community idea is further supported by means of two allegories which occur in John's gospel. The *shepherd* allegory[79] in John 10 rests on

---

[78] E. Käsemann, *The Testament of Jesus* (Eng. trans. 1968), p. 59, warns against reducing unity to what we call love. His point is that love can often be a vague term. 'If love should turn out to be the concrete expression of unity, unity still remains love's origin and basis.' It is quite clear that a close connection exists between unity and love, but the main emphasis in Jn. 17 is certainly on unity.

[79] A. Corell, *op. cit.*, pp. 25ff., in commenting on both the shepherd and vine passages, notes the significant fact that in each occurs an allusion to the death of Jesus. It is important to note that the

a well-known image used of God's people Israel in the OT (*cf.* Je. 23:1; Ezk. 34:11; Is. 40:11; Ps. 23). Most of the passage deals with the work of the shepherd, but the one significant statement for our purpose is 10:16 which focuses on the flock. The shepherd is concerned not only about 'this fold'[80] (the Jewish Christians) but with the 'other sheep' (Gentiles), which together will constitute one 'flock'. Many of the Jews did not believe in Jesus and therefore did not belong to his sheep (10:26).[81] The centrality of Jesus in this allegory is unmistakable. The flock is a group for whom Jesus, the shepherd, has laid down his life (10:17). The sheep are not only bound into a corporate unity, but are each known individually by the shepherd (10:3-4).

The *vine* allegory is even more suggestive regarding the corporate character of the coming community. This also recalls OT imagery (*cf.* Is. 5 where it is used of Israel).[82] The idea of many branches being knit together by being joined by one stem or stock is a vivid illustration of corporateness.[83] Not only can no branch exist without being in living contact with the vine, but the branches could have no relation to each other except through the vine.[84] The illustration presents the concept of a community viewed not as an organization but as an organism. Since membership depends on a definite spiritual relationship to Christ as the vine, this controls the nature of the community.

THE MISSION OF THE PROSPECTIVE COMMUNITY

The prayer of Jesus in John 17 is particularly important for the light it

---

community idea cannot be divorced from the work of Christ for his people. R. E. Brown, *John*, p. 398, recognizes that the unique feature in John's picture of the shepherd is the willingness to die, although he thinks the idea of a deliberate laying down of his life may have been a reinterpretation in the light of the death of Christ. There is no reason, however, why Jesus could not have seen the necessity for his own death.

[80] N. A. Dahl, 'The Johannine Church and History', in *Current Issues in New Testament Study* (ed. W. Klassen and G. F. Snyder, 1962), pp. 124–142, finds some connection between the reference to this fold and the addressing of Nathanael as a true Israelite (*i.e.* this fold is the Jewish 'fold' as it should be, *cf.* p. 137). T. W. Manson, 'The New Testament Basis of the Doctrine of the Church', *JEH* 1, 1950, pp. 1ff., also sees the idea of the new Israel as a basic idea.

[81] S. Pancaro, 'The Church and Israel in St John's Gospel', *NTS* 21, 1975, pp. 396ff., considers that this Johannine passage suggests that the Christian Jews were considered to be Israelites who were taken away from the Jewish fold. For a criticism of Pancaro's view, *cf.* J. Painter, 'Christ and the Church in John 1:45–51, in *L'Évangile de Jean* (ed. M. de Jonge, 1977), pp. 359ff.

[82] E. Schweizer, 'The Concept of the Church in the Gospel and Epistles of St John', in *New Testament Essays: Studies in Memory of T. W. Manson* (ed. A. J. B. Higgins, 1959), pp. 230–245, thinks that Israel is replaced by Christ, the true vine (*cf.* p. 234). He views Christ as a corporate personality in whom all believers are incorporated.

[83] *Cf.* D. O. Via, 'Darkness, Christ and Church in the Fourth Gospel', *SJT* 14, 1961, pp. 172–193, notes that in John's Gospel there is a combination of individuality and community. He says, 'It is not just that Church members form an organism, but they with Christ do. He is the Vine in which they have life' (p. 188).

[84] R. N. Flew, *Jesus and His Church*, p. 173, points out that the vine imagery is used in the *Didachē* ix. 2 applied to the sacramental cup.

throws on the intention of Jesus for his group of disciples.[85] There is strong evidence to show that Jesus looked forward to the continuation of his own mission through his disciples. The words of 17:18 specifically compare the mission of the Son with that of the disciples ('as thou didst send me into the world, so I have sent them into the world'). The disciples were commissioned as a group to continue the mission task. They could not achieve this end as individuals. The whole emphasis on unity in John 17 shows how indispensable a corporate community is for the continuation of the mission of Jesus.[86] The common purpose of the disciples is a vital factor contributing to the sense of oneness.

The disciples have received the words of God (17:7, 8). They are described as having kept the Word (17:6). And what they have received they are to make known (17:20,21). Their mission is directed to the world (17:21). Through them Christ is to be glorified (17:10). They are to share the same consecration to their task as Christ did to his (17:19). They are to be a group of people marked out as not belonging to the world (17:14), although they are 'in the world' (17:11,15). An unmistakable sense of solidarity runs through this chapter which is inexplicable if a prospective community were not in mind.[87]

The mission idea is also implied in 11:52, since the gathering of the scattered people of God requires some agency through which it could be accomplished. Indeed, the gathering 'into one' points to a community.

THE PROMISE OF THE SPIRIT AND THE COMMUNITY

A full discussion of the Johannine passages about the Spirit has been included in the section on the Holy Spirit (pp. 526ff.). The weighty evidence points unmistakably to a distinction between the world and the men of the Spirit. Possession of the Spirit marks out the disciples as not belonging to the world, which cannot receive the Spirit because it does not see or know him (Jn. 14:17). There is a clear-cut division between them. The indwelling Spirit, promised to all the disciples on equal terms, guarantees a body of people committed to a common purpose: to witness to Christ (15:27). Although this does not require an organization to be effective, it does

---

[85] E. Käsemann, in his treatment of John 17 in *The Testament of Jesus* treats the passage as a farewell discourse. He does not regard it as a prayer in the sense of petition, but only as a thanksgiving. Nevertheless, the prayer itself is fully in accord with what might be expected from Jesus himself and there is no solid reason for regarding it as a composition of the evangelist without basis in historical event.

[86] A. Corell, *Consummatus Est*, pp. 98f., sees three fundamental facts in John's view of the church: unity, universality and exclusiveness. The last point is derived from the emphasis on believing.

[87] B. Lindars, *John* (NCB, 1972), pp. 515f., who regards the prayer of Jn. 17 as an afterthought, composed and inserted by the evangelist, recognizes the overriding need to maintain the unity of the Christian community as a prime motive for the prayer. It is not self-evident, however, why the evangelist should have been more conscious of this need than Jesus himself. It is consonant with his view of his mission that his followers should be united in him.

presuppose a strongly united purpose which depends, not on human ingenuity, but on the Spirit's power.[88]

HINTS OF THE CHRISTIAN MINISTRY

We have noted from the synoptic gospels the part played by the disciples, particularly the twelve, in the preparation for the coming community. In John's gospel the significance of the twelve is more assumed than explicitly stated. There is some priority given to Peter (*cf.* 1:42, the allusion to the Rock, and 6:68-69 the confession of Peter), but it is not expressed in the explicit terms of Matthew 16. The great importance attached to Jesus' final teaching of the twelve is sufficient evidence of the key place that they would occupy in the coming community. This is further emphasized in the appearances of the risen Lord to the apostles as recorded in John 20-21 and especially in the restoration of Peter and the commission given to him. There are, in fact, four passages of some importance in giving adumbrations of functions within the coming community.

We note first the least explicit, the door and shepherd allegories in John 10. Since in both cases Jesus identifies himself as the fulfilment of the symbol, it is not easy to see how it can apply to those who were to exercise ministry in the future community. Nevertheless, in view of the strong condemnation of the hireling shepherds, it is a warning against a wrong approach to the shepherding of the flock. The imagery used here finds a close parallel in Ezekiel 34.

Another passage in John which appeals to similar imagery is John 21 where the pastoral commission is given to Peter. Its threefold nature is intended to emphasize its importance. There is little significance to be attached to the different terms used; *i.e.* 'sheep' (*probata*) and 'lambs' (*arnia*), 'feed' (*boskō*) and 'tend' (*poimainō*). A distinction has been maintained by some between the two words for 'love' (*phileō, agapaō*),[89] but it does not affect the terms of the commission, which involves shepherding and is specifically addressed to Peter. The whole passage suggests the need to maintain a sharing attitude towards the flock.

The third passage which may throw light on the ministry is that which describes the risen Lord breathing on the disciples with the words, 'Receive the Holy Spirit' (20:22). This was linked with the commission 'As the Father has sent me, even so I send you' (20:21) and the saying about forgiving and retaining of sins (20:23).[90] A crucial question is whether these words were intended to be restricted to the apostles. In view of the close

---

[88] R. E. Brown, *John*, p. 700, rightly points out that the witness of the Spirit and the witness of the disciples are not separate witnesses; the Spirit speaks through the disciples.

[89] *Cf.* W. F. Howard, *Christianity according to St John*, pp. 137f., who sees no need to distinguish between these words. To him, the main point is that Peter is to be a faithful pastor of the flock.

[90] For a discussion of the forgiving and retaining of sins, see pp. 584f.

parallel with the sayings in Matthew 16:19; 18:18, it is best to regard the apostles as representatives of the coming community.[91] The saying certainly enjoins responsibility for moral instruction, which would be involved in the task of all those whom Jesus, the risen Lord, sends. The Spirit's coming clearly foreshadows Pentecost.

Finally, the incident of the foot-washing must be considered in view of the specific injunction of John 13:15 ('For I have given you an example, that you also should do as I have done to you'). Does this imply that Jesus expected his disciples to perpetuate this as an observance to be followed in his future community, or is his meaning that the disciples should emulate his example of humility? In view of the fact that Jesus does not elsewhere in this gospel institute a ritual act, it seems improbable that such an act is meant here. The second explanation is to be preferred. Its significance for the Christian ministry is obvious. Categories of relative importance are wholly excluded; 'a servant is not greater than this master' (13:16). Any hierarchical system which exalted one above another would seem to be wholly alien to the intention of Jesus.[92]

THE ORDINANCES

It is at first perplexing to find that John's gospel contains no specific references to the institution either of baptism or of the Lord's supper as a prospective ordinance of the Christian community.[93] It has been suggested that he wished to play down what had become an over-emphasis on the ordinances and had therefore deliberately omitted the account of the institution of the Lord's supper from the passion narrative.[94] The suggestion is not impossible, particularly in view of the inclusion of teaching in John 6 which bears on the spiritual ideas behind the ordinance. Since John's gospel clearly complements the synoptic gospels and assumes details from them, it cannot be maintained that he was ignorant of the ordinance. Indeed, it must have been a well-established church practice when this gospel was produced. We must particularly note the reflective material which John

[91] *Cf.* A. Corell, 'The Church and the Ministry in the Gospel of John', ch. 2 of *Consummatum Est*, pp. 12–43. From the words in Jn. 20:21–23, Corell concludes that (i) the apostolate came into existence simultaneously with the church, (ii) the apostolate functions through the power of the Spirit, and (iii) the apostolate is the means by which the church is to spread.

[92] As Corell, *op. cit.*, p. 43, puts it, John's conception of the ministry is wholly religious and Christocentric. Its authority lies in the institution and commission of Christ himself. This means that the human holder of the office is not the most important, but the real minister is Christ.

[93] Corell, *op. cit.*, 44ff., has a chapter on 'The Liturgy in the Fourth Gospel', in which he draws on a number of other passages in addition to John 3 and 6. He accounts for the omission of specific reference to baptism and the eucharist by maintaining that both were bound up with the risen life of Jesus and that both would be impossible before the death of Jesus. They both belong therefore to the new age.

[94] Bultmann, *TNT* 2, pp. 58f., recognizes that John plays down the sacraments of baptism and the Lord's supper, but he refrains from alleging a direct polemic. John's attitude towards them 'is nevertheless critical or at least reserved.'

includes on this ordinance.[95] We will begin, however, with baptism.

Baptism. We have already discussed the baptism of John in the synoptic gospels and our purpose here must be to show how far John's gospel is in agreement and to what extent it brings out its own special emphases. First, the relation between John the Baptist and Jesus has already been set out in the prologue. It is no surprise therefore to find them baptizing at the same time and place in the early ministry (Jn. 3:22-24). The dispute which ensued (Jn. 3:25ff.) is evidently included because the evangelist wanted to report on John's answer to the question of purificatory rites. This led the Baptist to make his famous bride-bridegroom saying which concluded with the conviction that he (John the Baptist) would decrease, while the Christ would increase. It is important to note that John the Baptist's testimony to Jesus is more extensive and personal in John's gospel than in the synoptic gospels. If any were over-exalting John the Baptist's position, the evangelist shows that the Baptist himself would have opposed it.

In this gospel there is no account of Jesus being baptized by John, and neither is there any mention of a heavenly voice; there is instead a specific human testimony to Jesus, reinforced by the attesting of the Holy Spirit, who identified him as the one who was to come after John (1:30ff.). But the most significant aspect is the linking of baptism with the identifying of Jesus as the Lamb of God (1:29). This shows in the clearest possible way that in the case of Jesus baptism was to be understood in the light of the passion.[96] The fact that John describes the baptism of Jesus only indirectly (*cf.* 1:32, especially the mention of the descending dove), shows that he is more interested in its significance than in the event itself. As in the synoptic accounts, baptism for Jesus possessed a representative character. Yet what concerns us most here is the extent to which the submission by Jesus to baptism had any bearing on the later practice of baptism in the early church.[97]

John makes clear in 3:22ff. that Jesus and his disciples baptized. In 4:2 he mentions that the disciples alone performed the baptismal act.[98] He does

---

[95] R. E. Brown. *John*, p. cxiv, suggests that since both the explicit and symbolic references are scattered throughout the ministry, this fits in with the evangelist's intention to show that the institutions of Christian life are rooted in the words and life of Jesus.

[96] O. Cullmann, *Baptism in the New Testament*, p. 21, maintains that the Baptist regarded the call (echoed from Is. 42:1) as a demand upon Jesus to fulfil the *Ebed-Jahweh* mission.

[97] O. Cullmann, *Early Christian Worship* (Eng. trans. 1953), who detects the baptism theme in many places through John's gospel, sees in the account of the baptism of Jesus a reference to the institution of Christian baptism (p. 65). W. F. Flemington, *The New Testament Doctrine of Baptism*, p. 121, regards Christian baptism as a counterpart in the life of the believer of the baptism of Jesus.

[98] G. R. Beasley-Murray, *Baptism in the New Testament* (1962), pp. 67ff., is of the opinion, on the basis of the Johannine evidence, that Jesus authorized baptism during his ministry. He rejects the view, based on John 4:2, that Jesus prohibited baptism. *Cf.* also H. G. Marsh, *The Origin and Significance of New Testament Baptism*, pp. 122f.

not, as the synoptics, connect the practice of baptism with the call to repentance and the announcement of the kingdom. Nevertheless the mission of Jesus was closely linked with baptism, and it is no surprise that subsequent to his death and resurrection the early believers continued the practice. John's gospel alone gives no clear indication that there was any connection between the baptism of Jesus and early Christian baptism. But the practice of Christian baptism would not unreasonably be connected with Jesus' baptism in the minds of the readers.

One passage in John which may have a bearing on baptism is John 3:5 ('born of water and the Spirit'), for some interpret the water as referring to the baptismal rite.[99] A problem which arises is to decide what Nicodemus would have understood by the allusion to water. If he had understood baptism it would presumably have referred to the baptism of John the Baptist. Yet there is no hint that the Baptist ever linked his baptismal rite with regeneration, nor is there reason to suppose that Nicodemus would have done so.[100] Since Nicodemus regarded the allusion to new birth in a literal sense and referred it to a mother's womb, it would be reasonable to suppose that being born of water was a reference to physical birth, which was therefore being linked with spiritual birth. It was as if Jesus had said, 'You must be born spiritually as well as physically.' Indeed, even if Nicodemus had not understood the reference to 'water' in the sense of baptism, it is perhaps more likely that John's readers would have done so.

There is no way of being certain which of these alternative interpretations is correct, and at most it can be said only that there is a possible reference to baptism.[101] If so there would be not only a linking of water-baptism with spiritual regeneration, but also a clear distinction between them.[102]

---

[99] Cf. Cullmann, op. cit., pp. 12f. He sees the possibility that one effect of baptism (forgiveness of sins) might have been regarded as a vestige from the past with no connection with the new gift of the Spirit. This would account for the linking of water-baptism (like John's baptism of repentance) with Spirit-baptism. R. Bultmann, John (Eng. trans. 1971), ad loc., treats this as an interpolation.

[100] Cf. H. Odeberg, The Fourth Gospel (1929, r.p. 1974), pp. 48–71, for a discussion of Jn. 3:5 from the viewpoint of Jewish mysticism. He denies a reference to baptism, but interprets the water as a 'divine efflux' (see p. 67). This view, however, has not received much support.

[101] G. R. Beasley-Murray, Baptism in the New Testament, p. 228, considers that it is difficult to take seriously any other view than that ex hydatos in Jn. 3:5 refers to baptism. He takes the statement to refer to both water-baptism and Spirit-baptism. Beasley-Murray rejects the view advanced by A. Schweitzer, The Mysticism of Paul the Apostle (1930, Eng. trans. ²1953), p. 15, that divorces Paul's doctrine of new creation from John's doctrine of new birth (p. 232). B. Lindars, John (NCB, 1972), p. 152, while admitting the connection between baptism and the giving of the Spirit, does not regard it as 'absolutely necessary' to assume a reference here to Christian baptism. Cf. also R. Schackenburg, John 1 (HTKNT, Eng. trans. 1968), p. 370, who does not see Jn. 3:5 as directly concerned with baptism, but with the new creation by the Spirit.

[102] W. F. Flemington, The New Testament Doctrine of Baptism, pp. 86f., takes the view that Jn. 3:5 refers to baptism, but finds it difficult to believe that it formed part of the teaching of Jesus. He therefore sees it as a conception of Jesus restated by the evangelist in the light of the church's faith and practice. Cf. J. H. Bernard, John 1 (ICC, 1928), p. cixv, p. 105, for a similar view. Also H. Strathmann, Johannes (1959), p. 69.

They cannot be made to support the view that regeneration takes place in the act of baptism. Indeed, the fact that Jesus speaks of the impossibility of detecting the precise movements of the wind, and then uses it as an illustration of spiritual rebirth, suggests that spiritual renewal cannot be identified in time with any external event like baptism. Some have attempted to avoid this conclusion by differentiating the baptismal act from the subsequent affirmation of faith,[103] but the John passage gives no indication of this. The most important contribution of this passage, if it refers to baptism at all, is its emphasis on the spiritual life.

The Lord's supper. With the absence of any account of the institution of the Lord's supper, our sole source of information about John's approach to it is his inclusion of the bread discourse of Jesus in John 6. The crucial statement for our purpose is 6:53, 'Truly, truly, I say to you, unless you eat the flesh of the Son of man and drink his blood, you have no life in you.' There is difference of opinion over whether these words refer in a prophetic sense to the Lord's supper, or whether they originally belonged to the passion story and have been misplaced.[104] There are certainly difficulties in treating the words as an allusion to the Lord's supper and yet retaining them in their present context, in view of the fact that the 'Jews', not the disciples, are being addressed. Since there is no evidence for historical displacement, it is reasonable to suppose that the words would not have been understood in any sacramental sense. Indeed 6:52 specifically mentions the Jews' failure to understand. The words must have posed a riddle to all who heard them, until the twelve sat with Jesus in the upper room. It would have been strange indeed if Jesus had provided no previous preparation for the meaning of the words of institution.

A different question is whether John's readers would have connected this passage with the Lord's supper. It is certainly probable that they would have done so if they had already participated in the observance of the rite. It is possible that John's inclusion of these words of Jesus was intended to counteract an over-emphasis on the rite itself rather than its spiritual significance.

If we regard the words as an indication of the spiritual significance of the symbolism for the mind of Jesus and his intention for his people, we may note the following points. (i) The word *sarx* (flesh) is used instead of *sōma* (body), and this must be regarded as a significant difference. There

---

[103] *Cf.* Cullmann, *op. cit.*, pp. 48f.

[104] It is unlikely that Jn. 19:34 throws any light on the interpretation of Jn. 6, although those who favour a sacramental interpretation of John are disposed to this view. *Cf.* J. Swetnam's review of H. Klos, *Die Sakramente im Johannesevangelium* (1970) in *Bib* 53, 1972, pp. 590ff. Klos denies the connection, but Swetnam criticizes him for not taking into account the literary unity of John. In addition to Jn. 6 and 19:34 Klos deals with Jn. 3:1-21; 20:22,23 and 13:1-20.

is no mention of the eating of Jesus's flesh in the synoptic accounts of institution (or in Paul's). The words must bear a symbolic meaning, since they are connected with heavenly bread (6:58). The difference in wording between *sarx* and *sōma* should introduce a caution against too readily assuming that John is simply giving his own version of the words of institution.[105]

(ii) The act of eating flesh and drinking blood is not connected in John 6 with the covenant as in the synoptics. Instead it is linked with the promise of eternal life. The emphasis is on food for life and not on the significance of the death of Jesus, which does not come into focus at all in John 6. It is rather the provision of more effective sustenance than the Israelites found through the manna in the wilderness (*cf.* Jn. 6:58).

(iii) The spiritual 'meal' to which Jesus refers in John 6 leads those who partake to abide in him (6:56). This is a characteristic concept in John's gospel (especially in the farewell discourses). It also occurs in 1 John. The words cannot mean that the partakers only enter into an 'abiding' relationship with Christ at a eucharistic meal, but must mean that an essential dependence on Christ himself is an indispensable prerequisite for abiding in him.

(iv) There is a forward look in Jesus' reference to the last day (6:54), which finds parallels in the synoptic references to the day when Jesus would drink the wine new in the kingdom of God (Mk. 14:25 = Mt. 25:29 = Lk. 22:18; *cf.* 1 Cor. 11:26).

We may summarize our discussion of the ordinances in John by noting the occurrence of several ideas which contribute to a better understanding of their spiritual significance, but there is no information about the part they were to play in the future life and worship of the church.

The Johannine epistles

It is surprising that there is virtually no reference to the church, from the point of view of either its nature or its government, in *1 John*. The letter has all the appearance of being addressed to any individual Christian who might be interested, rather than to a community of Christians. And yet, although it contains no specific address and mentions no names or officials, the writer clearly has in mind a group of people that might be affected by docetism (1 Jn. 2:2ff.). John also says that there are those, whom he calls antichrists, who have gone out from us (1 Jn. 2:19; 4:1). This must mean some kind of community from which the false teachers had withdrawn.[106]

---

[105] L. Morris, *John* (NICNT, 1971), p. 374, refutes the view that 'flesh' here refers to holy communion. *Cf.* A. Plummer, *John* (1899), p. 154, who although admitting an allusion to the eucharist, recognized that this was not exclusively or directly the case.

[106] There is no need to suppose that these people truly belonged to the community. *Cf.* I. H. Marshall's discussion of this, *The Epistles of John* (NICNT, 1978), pp. 151f.

Nevertheless John is more concerned to warn the readers about the erroneous nature of the teaching and to build up a positive antidote, than about the nature of the community (which is assumed rather than stated).

It may certainly be said that 1 John breathes a strong spirit of community in its basic doctrine. The inculcation of love for each other among believers and the repeated exhortation to abide in Christ are both themes which contribute to a strong sense of unity. This is supported by the frequent use of the term 'brother(s)' in this epistle.

Some scholars see a reference to the practice of baptism in the mention of the 'anointing' in 1 John 2:20, 27, and deduce from this that the Spirit is imparted at baptism. But this allusion can tell us nothing more specific about the rite itself.[107]

2 John, if it is addressed to a church, may provide some indication of the attitude that Christian communities should adopt towards those who are known to teach false doctrine. They are to be refused admittance. If the epistle is regarded as being sent to an individual lady, this would mean keeping them out of the house. In both 1 John and 2 John the concern to maintain purity of teaching within the church is uppermost.

In *3 John* we are presented with what appears to be a personality clash within a church or a pair of churches. One man was attempting to exalt himself above others and was adopting a contemptuous attitude towards John and towards 'the brethren' (verses 9-10). As far as church organization is concerned it was a question of authority. The action of Diotrophes in usurping the apostle's authority is strongly condemned. Again it is strange that no church offices are mentioned, and in view of this it is not permissible to charge Diotrophes with seizing a particular office. In any group the possibility exists of one person wanting the pre-eminence. But within the Christian church this is not regarded with favour by John.

Acts

In any consideration of the doctrine of the church in the NT the book of Acts provides a vital link between the gospels and the epistles. In the latter there are various evidences of the way in which the early Christians came to interpret the community which had come into existence, especially by the use of suggestive images. In surveying the evidence from Acts we shall consider the following three aspects: the emergence of the church, its mission, and its ministry. In these early stages we shall discover little more than trends, which reach fuller expression particularly in Paul's epistles.

---

[107] *Cf.* G. R. Beasley-Murray, *Baptism in the New Testament*, pp. 233ff., for a discussion of this passage. He suggests that the gospel is the true *chrism* into which the Christian is initiated at baptism. The same writer (pp. 236f.) does not see any certain reference to the Christian ordinances in 1 Jn. 5:5-8.

Our purpose here is to look for the dominating principles which guided the first group of believers to regard themselves as a church. If our conclusions drawn from the synoptic evidence are correct (see pp. 702ff.), the first disciples were conscious that the community they formed was foreseen and to some extent prepared for by Jesus. We have seen reason to suppose that he himself spoke of the coming *ekklēsia*, although the term did not mean an ecclesiastical organization in the sense which it later acquired. The emphasis was on community rather than organization.

(i) The key event which preceded the establishment of the church was the resurrection of Jesus. This event at once transformed the death of Jesus by banishing its finality. But even more important was its implication that all that Jesus had come to do was acceptable to God (see pp. 390f.). It had both a practical and a theological significance of unparalleled importance to the disciples. This was the event that bound them together in a way which marked them out from other men. They accepted as fact that Jesus was risen, and this faith meant that they were at once conscious of a continuity with the historical Jews. This is a more reasonable assumption than to suppose that the disciples had an inner conviction that Jesus was risen which was not based on fact. The unanimity with which the disciples believed and proclaimed the resurrection as an objective fact is amply attested in the book of Acts. Indeed, the early Christians could not mention the death of Christ without at once linking it with resurrection. No true understanding of the emergence of the church is possible without grasping the significance of the resurrection as an historical event (see pp. 379ff.).

Those who interpret the resurrection in existential terms see it as the great dividing line between the historical life of Jesus and the community of believers with their convictions about the Christ of faith. But those who are convinced of the resurrection as historical fact see it as the dynamic link between the historical Jesus and the Christ of faith. Clearly whatever approach to this question is adopted will profoundly affect one's view of the church. If a link is established, the Jesus of history and his teaching is seen to be the basis for the community.

(ii) It was not only the resurrection as a fact, but also the resurrection appearances which made a deep impression on the disciples. In line with the synoptic narratives, Acts mentions 'the commandment' which Jesus had given to his chosen apostles before his ascension (1:2).[108] Luke also refers to 'many proofs' and to Jesus 'speaking of the kingdom of God'

---

[108] E. Haenchen, *Acts* (Eng. trans. 1971), pp. 139ff., makes a distinction between the ending of Luke's gospel, which gives the impression that Jesus' final departure from his disciples was on Easter Day, and the beginning of Acts which speaks of appearances over forty days. Haenchen treats forty as a sacred number. But the distinction is more apparent than real, for Luke's gospel does not depend on the interpretation which Haenchen assigns to it, and it is inconceivable that Luke should change his view of the ascension between writing his gospel and Acts.

(1:3). In his gospel he has mentioned that Jesus opened the Scriptures to his disciples (Lk. 24:45), but he does not repeat this in Acts. His narrative, however, assumes a solid basis of teaching from Jesus, as is clear from the demand that Judas' successor must be a man who had been a companion of Jesus throughout his ministry. This certainly stresses the continuity between the historical Jesus and the resurrection faith, and gives some explanation for the careful preservation of the traditions about Jesus. The community was in a real sense a Jesus community. What it did was a continuation of what he had done (*cf.* 2:23; 2:32; 2:36; 3:6, 16; 4:2, where the name 'Jesus' is prominent).

(iii) The first group of believers, which waited for the descent of the Holy Spirit, consisted of the apostles (who are named, *cf.* 1:13) and many others including women and the relatives of Jesus.[109] It was clearly a representative gathering of those who were bound together by their common bond of allegiance to Jesus and a belief in his resurrection. In the pre-Pentecost period Peter alone is singled out as taking any active leadership in the group. It was his suggestion that led to the whole group choosing a successor to Judas, which nonetheless shows that there was a general acknowledgement of a special significance attaching to the 'twelve'. What is important here is that the order established for the community was of the loosest kind; what existed was based essentially on the realization that Jesus himself had specially appointed twelve men (see further the discussion below, pp. 768f., on the apostolate).

(iv) The critical event in the launching of the Christian community was undoubtedly Pentecost.[110] Not until the descent of the Spirit was the community activated (Acts 2:1ff.). The power of the Spirit was promised for witnessing to Jesus throughout the world (1:8). But the disciples are not said to have discussed any mission plans. When they started their witnessing it happened spontaneously. Acts leaves us in no doubt that the church was essentially a community of the Spirit. It was controlled and directed by the Spirit and this has an important bearing on the function of the ministry (see the section below). We shall need to consider to what extent offices are related to the gifts of the Spirit. It is significant that immediately the

---

[109] There is significance in the special mention of women in the company of believers. This at once shows the Christian company to be distinct from their environment, since few in the ancient world assigned value to women for their own sake. The Christians at once recognized that male and female are on an equal footing through the gospel. It is also not without some importance that the only woman specifically mentioned in this context was Mary the mother of Jesus. The disciples carried on the same attitude towards women that Jesus had displayed.

[110] S. M. Gilmour, 'Easter and Pentecost', *JBL* 81, 1962, pp. 62ff., developed E. von Dobschütz's view (*Ostern und Pfingsten*, 1903, pp. 33f.) that the appearance of the risen Christ to the 500 mentioned by Paul in 1 Cor. 15:3ff. refers to the event at Pentecost. Gilmour claims that it is Luke who has interpreted the event as the beginning of the church's world-wide mission. For a criticism of this view, *cf.* J. D. G. Dunn, *Jesus and the Spirit*, pp. 144ff. See also the article by I. H. Marshall, 'The Significance of Pentecost', *SJT* 30 (1977), pp. 347–369.

Spirit descends on the community, it is at once enlarged in an astonishing manner, wholly on the grounds of repentance and faith (2:41). Moreover, this growth continued after the day of Pentecost (4:4). This expansive characteristic of the church is reflected in the epistles (see later section).

(v) Another important consideration is that the Christian community continued its Jewish connections. At first the believers, who were all Jewish, saw no reason to dissociate from Judaism. They still worshipped in the temple (3:1ff.). They regarded themselves as a true part of Israel. Indeed, since the official representatives of Israel had rejected the Messiah, the Christians regarded themselves as the 'true' Israel.[111] This is further borne out by the fact that the apostles, although Galileans, remained in Jerusalem and preached their message in the very centre which had rejected the Messiah. It was clearly important to the early church to be located in Jerusalem. It was as important as it was for Jesus to die there (as Luke demonstrates). Had the early church begun and developed in Galilee, it might have been regarded as no more than a provincial sect. But the command of the risen Lord to his followers to remain in Jerusalem until the Spirit came (Lk. 24:49) and to begin their witness there (Acts 1:8), gives some indication of the importance of location for the early community. Even when later the centre of activity for Gentile evangelism shifted from Jerusalem to Antioch, the key place of Jerusalem was still apparent (Acts 21:17ff.). This notion of the church as the true Israel finds further expression in the epistles.[112] It seems to have been an integral part of the early Christian understanding of the *ekklēsia*.

(vi) The rapid shift from an exclusively Jewish community to a mixed Jewish-Gentile community did not come without difficulties.[113] It took a vision to convince Peter that Gentiles had as much right to hear the message as Jews (chapter 10). There were further problems over the circumcision issue (chapter 15). But the early Christian church was in marked contrast to the Qumran community which found no place for Gentiles within it. The development of a universal *ekklēsia* is a direct fulfilment of what Jesus had himself commanded (Mt. 28:19). The Christians soon learned to banish all racial discrimination.

(vii) As an indication of the type of community which sprang into being,

---

[111] F. Hahn, *The Worship of the Early Church* (Eng. trans. 1973), pp. 42f., who takes a traditio-critical view of Acts, makes out that it was not until James took sole charge of the Jerusalem church that a Jewish Christianity developed which was based on strict observance of the Jewish law and fidelity to the cult. Hahn, however, contends that for the earlier Christians the temple cult had lost its meaning, although the temple was still respected (as in Acts 3:1ff. in the context of prayer).

[112] H. Küng, *The Church*, p. 115, warns against simply transferring the term Israel to the NT *ekklēsia*, although he concedes a close link between the two ideas.

[113] L. Goppelt, *Apostolic and Post-Apostolic Times*, pp. 68ff., speaks of an ascending order in the relating of the development of Gentile Christianity in the book of Acts, *i.e.* Samaria, the Ethiopian eunuch, Cornelius and Antioch. This growth, he maintains, came about without the assistance of the Jerusalem church.

we should also note certain spontaneous patterns of behaviour. The most outstanding was the community living of the believers. This is specifically mentioned twice (2:44; 4:32), with an emphasis on the fact that the believers had all things in common. Does this mean that there was a spontaneous exercise in communism as far as common ownership of property was concerned? The answer seems to be that a common fund was established from which the needs of each were supplied. Some disposed of their possessions to contribute to the fund, but the act seems to have been voluntary. Peter told Ananias that it was his own decision whether he conformed to this pattern or not (5:4). It was clearly not regarded as obligatory for the members of the community to act in this way. What was more important than community of property was the strong social concern which Christians felt towards each other. Special provision was made for widows (6:1), which caused some dispute between the Hebrews and Hellenists and led to the appointment of seven special administrators. The whole emphasis within the community seems to have been prompted by a sense of responsibility towards those who were socially deprived. It must be remembered that in all probability a high proportion of the members of the community were drawn from the lower levels of society, which would have imposed on the Christians a common need to take some kind of concerted action. Later the Antioch church expressed the same kind of practical concern for the more needy Jerusalem church (Acts 11:27ff.), an action which no doubt prompted the apostle Paul in the organization of his collection scheme (*cf.* 1 Cor. 16:1f.), as a means of demonstrating the Gentiles' concern for their Jewish brethren.[114]

Other behaviour patterns which spontaneously developed were common worship in the temple and common meals in the Christians' homes. The sharing of material things was not the only expression of fellowship. What is significant is the combination of common worship with a common concern for the physical needs of each. The worship aspect included times for corporate prayer and for breaking of bread (Acts 2:42-47). These were activities which helped to bind the believers into a fellowship and made them recognize their essential oneness in Jesus Christ. Acts gives no indication of how the Lord's supper was observed, but there is no doubt that the earliest Christians saw at once the need to observe it. At first it seems to have been on a daily basis (2:46), but it was also linked with continuance of worship in the temple. The record gives the impression of spontaneous sessions of praise to God which had a unifying effect on the group of disciples. The emphasis on the value of corporate prayer in the early part

---

[114] For an extensive examination of Paul's collection theme, *cf.* K. F. Nickle, *The Collection* (1966). He sees great significance in the collection in three directions: as an act of charity, as an act of solidarity and as an act of eschatological pilgrimage. The third point is interpreted as a means of moving the Jews through jealousy to accept the gospel.

of Acts is impressive (cf. 1:14f.; 2:42; 3:1; 4:24ff.; 6:6; 12:12; 13:1f.).

THE MISSION OF THE CHURCH

It is clearly stated in the risen Christ's commandment to his disciples in Acts 1:8 that the task of the new community is to witness. Our concern here is to discover the nature of this witness. Since the witness consisted of proclamation, it has become common to use the Greek word *kerygma* (which means 'preaching') to denote the content of what was preached. This usage has become familiar since the time of C. H. Dodd, but it should be noted that a different meaning is attached to the word by Bultmann, who uses it to emphasize the act of proclaiming rather than the content of what is proclaimed.[115] It must not be supposed, of course, that it would exhaust the concept of the church's mission to catalogue the details of what was preached. But it is a highly questionable procedure to leave undefined the witness of the community. There is no question at this stage of a fixed creed, but it is not unreasonable to expect that there was general agreement among the believers regarding the tenets of their faith. We shall note particularly the suggestions advanced by Dodd regarding the content of the primitive kerygma.[116]

It is the speeches in Acts which provide the material for the reconstruction of the kerygma, which means that our assessment of the speeches will necessarily affect our assessment of the church's witness contained in them. If we regard the speeches as substantially accurate accounts of what the early church proclaimed, they provide invaluable insight into the church's awareness of its mission at an early stage in its development. Those who regard the speeches as entirely the compositions of the author could still use them as evidence of Luke's estimate of the early kerygma, but they become less dependable as evidence of the content of the first preaching. It seems reasonable to suppose that as a result of his historical researches Luke was not uninformed about the gist of what the early preachers said.[117] From the Petrine speeches, Dodd deduces the following points:[118]

(i) There was a strong conviction that the age of the newly formed community was the age of the fulfilment of prophecy (cf. 2:16; 3:18, 24).

---

[115] Cf. C. H. Dodd, *The Apostolic Preaching and its Developments* (1936); R. Bultmann, *TNT* 1, pp. 33ff. Cf. J. P. M. Sweet's discussion of the difference between these writers' use of the term kerygma, 'The Kerygma', *ExT* 76, 1965, pp. 143ff. Cf. also C. F. Evans, 'The Kerygma', *JTS* 7, 1956, pp. 25–41, for a consideration of the subject from the point of view of the Lukan composition of the Acts speeches.

[116] There is some discussion whether it is correct to speak of a kerygma in view of the various emphases which are found in the records. Cf. J. D. G. Dunn, who has a chapter entitled 'Kerygma or Kerygmata?' in his book *Unity and Diversity in the New Testament*, pp. 11–32. He contends that any attempt to find a single, once-for-all kerygma is bound to fail. But he goes too far in claiming that different situations call forth different gospels, for this makes the 'gospel' entirely relative. Dunn tends to arrive at incompatibilities by heightening differences and playing down agreements.

[117] For a discussion on the historicity of these speeches, cf. my *New Testament Introduction*, pp. 359ff.

[118] C.H. Dodd, *op. cit.*, pp. 21ff.

This accounts for the strong appeal to OT testimonies. So basic is this in the formation of the church that the NT generally witnesses to the continuity of the Christian message with OT predictions of the coming age.

(ii) The core of the message was the death and resurrection of Jesus, mentioned in all the speeches.[119] Reference was made to Messiah's Davidic descent, and to his human life and works. Both the death and resurrection of Jesus were the result of the divine initiative (*cf.* the reference to the definite plan of God, 2:23), although human responsibility for the death was also recognized.

(iii) It is the exalted Christ which constituted the major focus in the kerygma. We should not expect, and in fact do not find, a fully developed Christology, but the early believers all knew that Jesus was Lord and Christ (2:33–36), that he was the servant (3:13), that he was the rejected stone (4:11), and that he was prince and saviour (5:31).

(iv) The witnesses were bound together in the common conviction that the Holy Spirit was witnessing through them (2:33; 5:32). The presence and power of the Spirit is an indispensable facet of the church's sense of mission.

(v) There was also the conviction that the present age would be consummated by the return of Christ (3:21; *cf.* 10:42).

(vi) The aim of the proclamation is seen in the exhortation to people to repent and believe and therefore to receive salvation (*cf.* 2:38, 39; 3:19, 25–26; 4:12; 5:31; 10:43). The basis of the new community was the work of Christ, but the qualification for membership was repentance and faith. The community consisted only of those who sought a new relationship with God through faith in Christ.

It is noticeable that there were no specific appeals in the Petrine speeches (or indeed in the Pauline) for the hearers to join the community. They were, however, exhorted to be baptized, which would imply incorporation into the Christian 'body'. It was perfectly natural that those who had come through repentance and faith to a new understanding of God's purposes for them would be bound together in a common bond and united in a mission to proclaim to others the way of repentance and faith.

In considering the mission of the church mention must be made of the practice of baptism.[120] Those who believed were baptized (2:38, 41, 8:12;

[119] For a discussion of the place of an outline of the life of Jesus in the kerygma, *cf.* C. H. Dodd's article, 'The Framework of the Gospel Narrative', in his collected essays, *New Testament Studies* (1953), pp. 1–11. This view was criticized by J. M. Robinson, *A New Quest of the Historical Jesus* (1959), p. 57. *Cf.* also D. E. Nineham's critique 'The Order of Events in St Mark's Gospel – an Examination of Dr Dodd's Hypothesis', in *Studies in the Gospels* (ed. D. E. Nineham, 1957), pp. 223–239.

[120] For a detailed study of baptism in Acts, *cf.* Flemington, *The New Testament Doctrine of Baptism*, pp. 37–51; Beasley-Murray, *Baptism in the New Testament*, pp. 93–125; Marsh, *The Origin and Significance of the New Testament Baptism*, pp. 153–166; S. I. Buse, in *Christian Baptism* (ed. A. Gilmour, 1959), pp. 115ff.

8:36; 16:15, 33; 19:5; 22:16), and this seems to have been regarded as a rite of initiation.[121] It was an act which demonstrated the unity of all those who had responded to the word. We shall need to consider in the section on Paul's teaching the significance of this ordinance within the organization of the church. But the introduction of baptism in the mission proclamation (as in Acts 2:38) maintained a continuity with the final commission of Jesus as recorded in Matthew 28:19. It is noticeable that in Acts baptism is carried out in the name of Jesus rather than in the triune name as in Matthew 28:19. This may suggest that for Luke no great importance was attached to the precise formula used, except to make clear that it was Christian baptism as distinguished from any other. It would seem probable, however, that some comprehensive theological content was also intended.[122]

In Acts there are two instances of household baptisms (Acts 16:15, 33) and the question arises over how these are to be interpreted. Some have supposed that the baptism of the whole households of Lydia and of the gaoler was on the strength of the faith and baptism of the head. Although there is no mention of the faith of the 'household', there is no particular reason for supposing that faith was exercised by only one person. The matter must remain open, but in view of the fact that in other cases it is the individual's own faith which is linked with baptism, it is difficult to see the basis for baptism of 'households' who do not themselves exercise faith.[123]

THE MINISTRY OF THE CHURCH

In the previous sections it has become abundantly clear that the primitive church did not exist as an organized community. In fact, it existed at first as a group within Judaism, which nevertheless possessed a marked identity of its own. It must be assumed therefore that the general religious practices of Judaism were continued as far as attendance at the temple worship. It must be taken into account, therefore, when considering the organization

---

[121] Some have seen three different accounts of Christian baptism in Acts: (i) baptism entirely in the Holy Spirit; (ii) baptism with water which conferred the Holy Spirit; and (iii) baptism in the name of Jesus. These three ideas are then traced to different sources, cf. F. Foakes-Jackson and K. Lake, *The Beginnings of Christianity* 1, pp. 337ff. But see Marsh, *op. cit.*, pp. 159f., for comments on the supposed differences in the Acts account.

[122] Cf. L. Hartman, 'Baptism "Into the Name of Jesus" and early Christology. Some Tentative Considerations', *StTh* 28, 1974, pp. 21–48, who reckons that baptism into the name of Jesus had both the function of suggesting a comprehensive content and of distinguishing Christian baptism from the baptism of John. He sees the content as being specifically Christological.

[123] Many explain the references to household baptism by an appeal to the place of the household in the covenant of grace (Gn. 17:27; Ex. 12:48), and the command that all males should be circumcised, cf. P. Dale, 'Church and Sacraments in the New Testament', in *Evangelical Essays on Church and Sacraments* (ed. C. Buchanan, 1972, p. 13). For a critique of opinions over household baptisms, cf. P. K. Jewett, *Infant Baptism and the Covenant of Grace* (1978), pp. 47ff. He concludes that the NT evidence does not show that infants were baptized in the early church. G. Delling has an article on the same subject in his *Studien zum Neuen Testament und zum hellenistischen Judentum* (1970), pp. 288–310.

of the primitive church which might be expected to have been influenced by Jewish procedures.

The office of apostle in the community was of great importance. Indeed, the Jerusalem church was spontaneously led by the *apostles*. Because of the defection and death of Judas, it was regarded as natural that another should be appointed in his place. In fact, this was supported from Scripture. There was no doubt about the authority of those whom Jesus had appointed to be apostles. Peter naturally took the leadership. Moreover, there was no dispute over the terms on which candidates for the vacancy were to be selected. Acts 1:21f. is significant for the light it throws on the primitive Christian approach to organization. The field was at first extremely limited, for aspirants for apostleship had to be companions of Jesus during the time of his ministry and a witness of his resurrection. It is not surprising that only two were found who fulfilled the conditions. It was assumed without dispute that the leaders of the new community must possess firsthand knowledge of the historical Jesus as well as knowledge of the risen Christ. The office of apostle was therefore regarded as a guarantee of the connection between the historical Jesus and the ongoing community.

Some have supposed that the role of apostle in the early church can be paralleled by an appeal to Jewish procedures.[124] But it seems more likely that the special importance of the apostolic office was derived from the fact that Jesus had himself appointed the twelve.[125] It is curious in view of this that the replacement for Judas, selected by means of the casting of lots (Acts 1:26), was ranked on the same level as those personally appointed by Jesus. Moreover, although Matthias was appointed, nothing more is heard of him. In fact, Acts refers to the exploits of only three of the twelve apostles, Peter, James and John, the trio whom Jesus himself had treated as an inner group, although all the rest are named in Acts 1:13ff. Twice Paul and Barnabas are referred to as apostles (14:4, 14), but Luke seems generally to draw a distinction between them and the Jerusalem apostles (*cf.* 15:2).[126]

Another group of administrators was inaugurated when trouble arose

---

[124] *Cf.* K. H. Rengstorf, on *apostolos* in *TDNT* 1, pp. 407ff. T. W. Manson has based his discussion of the apostolate mainly on Rengstorf's appeal to the Jewish šālîaḥ (*The Church's Ministry*, pp. 35ff.), an official who was commissioned for specific tasks. But this opinion has been called in question. *Cf.* W. Schmithals, *The Office of the Apostle in the Early Church* (1969), pp. 98–110; J. H. Schütz, *Paul and the Anatomy of Apostolic Authority* (1975), pp. 25ff.

[125] J. A. Kirk, 'Apostleship since Rengstorf: Towards a Synthesis', *NTS* 21, 1975, pp. 249–264. Kirk argues that the NT evidence shows that the twelve held a special place in the early church. He sees no reason to dispute that the concept of apostles goes back to Jesus. The twelve were therefore apostles, but this does not exhaust the term. Kirk sees the NT idea of apostle as a person who is sent by Jesus to proclaim the gospel and to plant churches. He finds no distinction between Paul's and Luke's idea of apostleship. There is no discontinuity in the call and task, but there is in the historical circumstances.

[126] *Cf.* also Gal. 1:19 (James) and Rom. 16:7 (Andronicus and Junias) where others are also classed as apostles. *Cf.* also 2 Cor. 8:23.

over the daily distribution to widows (6:1). The seven men chosen for this task were to be men of good repute and full of the Spirit and of wisdom, although their task was essentially practical. Two of the men chosen, Stephen and Philip, proved to be capable of the preaching ministry. They are not described in Acts as 'deacons' (although the cognate verb *diakonein* is used in 6:2), but their functions appear to be similar to the later order of deacons. As yet, however, there had not been established any such office. The seven were appointed to serve a particular need which was mundane, but nevertheless important.[127]

Soon after this event mention is made of *elders* (Acts 11:30), who are evidently distinct from the apostles, since they came to be linked with the latter as separate groups (*cf.* 15:2, 22; 16:4).[128] Both groups appear to have shared in making decisions of policy, as for example over the circumcision issue. Later the office of elder was to become secondary to that of bishop, but in its origin no such distinction was made. Indeed it is certain that in the period covered by the NT literature, no hierarchy of ecclesiastical officials had developed (see pp. 763f. for the evidence from the pastoral epistles). Paul and Barnabas, on the first mission tour, appointed elders in each of the churches established (14:23). No explanation is given of the function of these elders, but as they were the only officials appointed they must have performed what functions of government were necessary.[129] Later when Paul addressed the elders at Ephesus (20:28) he gave rather more specific instructions to them to feed the church of which the Holy Spirit had made them overseers (Gk. *episkopos*, bishop). The combination of 'elder' and 'bishop' in this context shows clearly that the latter is no more than a function of the former (*cf.* Tit. 1:5ff.).

Another group of men were named as *prophets*, of which the main example in Acts is Agabus, who is mentioned twice (11:28; 21:10). In his case the prophetic gift definitely took the form of predictions of the future, and in each case the prediction was treated as authoritative. More is said in Paul's writings on the gift of prophecy (see pp. 770ff.). The prophet certainly played no administrative part in the community. Agabus' function was entirely ecstatic, prompted by the Holy Spirit. Philip's daughters are also said to have prophesied, but no further details are given.[130]

The term *evangelist* is applied in Acts only to Philip (21:8) and even there

---

[127] E. Schweizer, *Church Order in the New Testament*, pp. 70f., considers that it is Luke who has made the seven into servants subordinated to the apostles. But there is no reason to believe that historically they were not subordinate to the apostles.

[128] It has generally been supposed that the Christian church borrowed the elder system from the Jews. But A. E. Harvey, 'Elders', *JTS* 25, 1974, pp. 318–332, disputes this. He considers seniority to be the more likely origin.

[129] Schweizer, *op. cit.*, p. 71, considers that in Acts the term 'elder' relates to function and is not an official title. His suggestion is that it goes back to Jewish models. But it is not easy to see why 'elder' could not have been a title. The word itself gives no indication of function.

[130] On the subject of the Christian prophet, see here E. E. Ellis, 'The Role of the Christian Prophet in

only for purposes of identification. The reference is probably an allusion to his evangelizing work in Samaria (chapter 8). He had forsaken table-management for the work of proclamation. Whether there was a separate class of evangelists is not known from Acts, although it is mentioned by Paul (*cf.* Eph. 4:11; 2 Tim. 4:5).

As far as church organization is concerned, it is evident that this was very loose in the primitive church. In fact, Acts presents us with a group of house communities scattered about in various cities rather than with a unified church. Each group came to be known as an *ekklēsia* in a local area. Acts does not present a universal church. And yet since each local *ekklēsia* stood for the same basic beliefs, all the ingredients existed for the concept of one church. In fact, each local church was a microcosm of the whole church. Each group of believers was united in Christ and found a strong affinity with other groups who were similarly united, for all were under the authority of the same Lord. The idea of church organization was therefore dynamic, not static. These early communities displayed a remarkable virility, which was a particular characteristic of that age. The churches were living organisms rather than organizations. The promptings of the Spirit were more important than ecclesiastical edicts or episcopal pronouncements. When decisions were made, they were made by the whole company of believers, not simply by the officials (15:22).

It would be a mistake, nevertheless, to suppose because of this that the church was run on democratic lines. The Acts record makes unmistakably clear that the dominating factor was the guidance of the Holy Spirit. It must, of course, be borne in mind that the record gives few indications of policy decisions and practically no information (apart from Acts 6 and 15) about the internal organization and problems of the separate communities. Much more information comes from the epistles, and it is to these that we must mainly look for insights which will enable us to evaluate the NT doctrine of the church.

The other feature which needs considering is the evidence in Acts for the *charismata*, particularly because of the importance of these in the Corinthian church and Paul's advice concerning them. The phenomenon at Pentecost, when the disciples who had been filled with the Spirit spoke in tongues, is explicitly stated to be in languages which could be understood without the aid of an interpreter (2:6, 11). It seems clear enough that Luke intended his readers to understand that the tongues were known languages. This puts the situation in Acts 2 on a different footing from that at Corinth. When the phenomenon was repeated in the house of Cornelius (Acts 10:46), no details are given as to the manner in which this took place. Yet in both

---

Acts', in *Apostolic History and the Gospel* (ed. W. W. Gasque and R. P. Martin, 1970), pp. 55–67.

cases the utterances are said to praise God. The third Acts reference is when the disciples of John at Ephesus received the Spirit (Acts 19:6) and in this instance the tongues were specifically linked with prophesying. There is no suggestion that in any of these occurrences the gifts gave any special status to the recipients. Nor is there any suggestion that tension existed between the *charismata* and the official leaders, for in Acts there is no indication whether or not the elders spoke in tongues or prophesied.

The debate over the charismatic gifts in Acts is important because of the development of two schools of thought in interpreting the relationship between the Acts evidence and the Pauline epistles. Some regard the Acts phenomena as the starting point and approach the epistles in the light of Acts. Others adopt the reverse procedure. The main difference arises over the nature of the tongues. If the Acts phenomena are regarded as exceptional and especially adapted for the initiation of the Christian church, a distinction would need to be maintained between these and the Corinthians' phenomena. But if the Corinthian situation is regarded as a norm, speaking in tongues in Acts would then be regarded as initial instances of a continuing phenomenon. This subject will be more fully discussed on pp. 764ff.

The Acts narrative contributes little on the subject of the role of women in the NT church, but one or two significant considerations need mentioning. Women were certainly among those who received the outpouring of the Spirit at Pentecost. Part of the quotation from Joel which Peter gave in his first address refers to daughters as well as sons who would prophesy (2:17). Luke mentions also that Philip the evangelist had four daughters who prophesied (21:9). This prophetic ministry of women is reflected in the Corinthian situation (1 Cor. 11:5). Moreover, the part played by Lydia in the origins of the Philippian church (16:14) is specially mentioned by Luke. The church in that place, the first in Europe, seems to have been based on her house. Another important woman was Priscilla, who together with her husband Aquila instructed Apollos in the right understanding of Christian truth (18:26). It may not be without significance that in this case Luke mentions Priscilla first and Aquila second (in contrast to 18:2).

THE DEVELOPING CHURCH

Paul

We shall deal with the evidence on the church in the Pauline epistles by consideration of the following aspects: its scope, its worship (including the ordinances), and its government.

THE SCOPE OF THE CHURCH

Our aim will be to discuss what light is thrown on the nature of the church, particularly through the various images used to describe it. It is customary to consider Paul's images of the body, the bride and the building as a key to his understanding of the church, but there are many minor images which must also be taken into account. Before coming to these, some preliminary comments are necessary on the use of the word *ekklēsia* in Paul's epistles.

There are two main ways in which Paul refers to the church. In most of his epistles it is the community of believers in a specified locality. The Corinthian correspondence is addressed 'to the church of God which is at Corinth (1 Cor. 1:2; 2 Cor. 1:1). A similar formula is found in the Thessalonian letters, which are addressed to 'the church of the Thessalonians in God the Father and the Lord Jesus Christ' (1 Thes. 1:1; *cf.* 2 Thes. 1:1). When writing to Galatia, Paul simply addresses 'the churches of Galatia' (Gal. 1:2), without further description. In other cases he addresses the saints in Rome, Philippi, Colossae. It is clear that the word 'church' was, therefore, used in the sense of a group of believers in a stated locality. There is no suggestion of an organization. In fact, only in the case of Philippians 1:1 is there mention of any officials, who are in any case referred to only after the mention of the 'saints'.

The second sense in which Paul uses the term is of the universal church. Although this sense is implied in some of the imagery that he employs, it becomes explicit only in Ephesians and Colossians, where the headship of Christ over his church is expounded (Eph. 1:22; Col. 1:18). It is a natural progression from local groups to think of the sum total of those groups as a unified concept. Yet it would not be correct to say that the universal church was simply a conglomerate of many local communities, for each local community was in essence *the* church of God. Nor can it be maintained, as some have done,[131] that this universal concept is too developed for the time of Paul and that consequently both Ephesians and Colossians should be considered to be non-Pauline, which would mean that evidence from them in support of Paul's view of the church could be discounted.[132] There is no reason to think that the apostle himself could not or would not have moved from the idea of local churches being in Christ to the idea of the whole fellowship of believers being one in him. For any adequate understanding of Paul's view of the nature of the church, both local and universal aspects must be given full weight.

[131] *Cf.* C. L. Mitton, The *Epistle to the Ephesians* (1951), p. 18. *Cf.* my *New Testament Introduction* p. 495, for a discussion of the evidence. D. E. Nineham, 'The Case against the Pauline Authorship', in *Studies in Ephesians* (ed. F. L. Cross, 1956), p. 32, draws a distinction between the idea of church in Colossians and in Ephesians. In the former the universal idea occurs as an occasional innovation, whereas in Ephesians it is assumed throughout. But F. F. Bruce, *BJRL* 49, 1967, pp. 312f, while admitting some elements of *Frühkatholizismus* in Ephesians, disputes that this means that its Pauline character must be denied.

[132] E. Schweizer, *Church Order in the New Testament*, pp. 105ff., considers that there is a development here from the Pauline view. He claims that the apostle is no longer the father of a particular church, but the foundations of a worldwide entity.

Within the Pauline epistles there are certain indications of the nature of the local communities. The expression 'in church' (*en ekklēsia*) is used several times in 1 Corinthians (11:18; 14:19, 28, 35), where it refers to an assembly of believers. There is no suggestion of a special building. Indeed, the idea of a church as representing a building is totally alien to the NT. There is some evidence of churches meeting in houses. Indeed, some churches consisted of a number of such house-groups (*cf.* Rom. 16:5, 10, 11). It seems highly likely that when the word *ekklēsia* is used of the total number of believers in a given place (in addition to those mentioned above, *cf.* Rom. 16:1, Cenchrea; Col. 4:16, Laodicea; Gal. 1:22, the churches in Judea), the groups often consisted of a number of associated house-fellowships. The Pauline pattern for the church seems to be that each local group was in its own right a church of God, but none could be isolated from the rest. This characteristic is strongly borne out by the images that Paul uses, which will be our next concern.

The church as a body. Of all the images of Paul, that of the body is the most vivid and expressive.[133] There appear to be stages of development in Paul's thought about the Christian community as a body. In Romans he uses the metaphor to show how different gifts can exist within the one church (12:4–8). There is a clear distinction, therefore, between unity and uniformity. The body is the symbol of the church's unity. In 1 Corinthians the body is identified with the church, since the human body serves as an illustration of the relationship between Christ and believers (*cf.* 1 Cor. 12:12ff.). This concept of the body of Christ is again highly suggestive of the closeness of the bond which links all believers. The body in this context is, of course, the local church, but this is significant in view of the diversity of spiritual gifts which were being manifested. The various parts of the body are necessary to each other if the whole is to function efficiently. The exercise of special charismatic gifts must be within these limits. There is here a distinctly corporate view of the church[134] which excludes individualism, but leaves room for the use of individual abilities[135] (see the later

---

[133] *Cf.* E. Best, *One Body in Christ* (1955), pp. 83ff., for a review of the various theories of the origin of the body metaphor. *Cf.* also the detailed discussion of this theme by P. S. Minear, *Images of the Church in the New Testament* (1961), pp. 173ff. *Cf.* also E. Käsemann, *Leib und die Leib Christi* (1933), who traced Paul's views of the matter to gnosticism. Note also F. W. Dillistone, 'How is the Church Christ's Body?', *Theology Today* 2, 1945, pp. 56–68; M. Barth, 'A Chapter on the Church – the Body of Christ', *Int* 12, 1958, pp. 131–156; P. Bonnard, 'L'Èglise corps du Christ dans le Paulinisme', *RThPH* 8, 1958, pp. 281ff.; A. Wikenhauser, *Die Kirche als der mystische Leib Christi nach dem Apostel Paulus* (1937).

[134] D. O. Via, 'The Church in the Gospel of Matthew', *SJT* 11, 1958, pp. 271–286, takes the view that the background to the body metaphor is the idea of corporate personality, *i.e.* the attempt to deal with the concept of the one and the many. He sees this idea not only in Paul but in the church ideas in Matthew.

[135] R. H. Gundry, *Sōma in Biblical Theology* (1976), p. 223ff., takes a different view from J. A. T. Robinson, *The Body* (1952), pp. 26ff., in which he argues for a solidarity concept. Gundry understands the references to the church as the body of Christ as a metaphor.

section on charismatic gifts, pp. 764ff.). Another strong emphasis on the unity of the church in 1 Corinthians comes in the account of the Lord's supper in 1 Corinthians 10:17: 'Because there is one bread, we who are many are one body, for we all partake of the one bread'. The idea of the common sharing of the Lord's supper establishes the principle of the essential oneness of the members of the community.[136]

A more developed use of the metaphor is seen in Ephesians and Colossians. Now the *ekklēsia* is identified with the body of Christ (Eph. 1:22, 23; 4:12, 15–16; 5:23; Col. 1:18, 24). A more specifically Christological concept is introduced. Christ as head is clearly the controlling factor.[137] He is seen as the source of the church's life and fullness. He has the pre-eminence (Col. 1:18). The headship of Christ is specially emphasized as a unifying factor (Eph. 1:22–23; 4:15).[138] The process of unification into one body is, moreover, said to be accomplished through the cross (Eph. 2:16), which overcame the enmity between the Jewish and Gentile elements, breaking down the dividing wall of hostility (Eph. 2:14).[139] The body metaphor would have been inappropriate if hostility had existed between Jewish and Gentile Christians. The body would cease to function if one part of it was hostile to another. This development of the body metaphor applied to the church emphasizes particularly its universal aspect.

There is some question over Paul's precise meaning when he connects the body with 'fullness' (as in Eph. 1:23). Some suppose that the church 'fills up' Christ, in the sense that his mission would be incomplete without the mission of the church.[140] An alternative and more probable understanding of the statement is that the fullness of Christ flows through the church, his body, and provides it with its vital life and power. This would be in line with the use of *plērōma* (fullness) expressly of Christ (Eph. 1:23; Col. 1:19). It is essentially God who does the filling, not the church, and it is for this reason, that the second interpretation is to be preferred.

There is no support in the epistles for the view that Paul regarded the

---

[136] L. Cerfaux, *The Church in the Theology of St Paul* (Eng. trans. 1959), p. 263, considers that it was in the celebration of the supper that the formula 'the body of Christ' received its stamp.

[137] *Cf.* G. Howard, 'The Head/Body Metaphors of Ephesians', *NTS* 20, 1974, pp. 350ff., who maintains that in Ephesians 'head' is connected with 'body' only in a secondary sense. The primary connection, he thinks, is with the 'feet'. For a discussion of the problems arising from Eph. 1:23, *cf.* R. Bates, 'A Re-Examination of Ephesians 1:23', *ExT* 83, 1972, pp. 146ff.

[138] S. Bedale, 'The meaning of Kephalē in the Pauline epistles'. *JTS* 5, 1954, pp. 211ff., considers that the word 'head' has a primary meaning equivalent to *archē*. He thinks nonetheless that Paul may also have been invoking the anatomical image. On the specific use of the body and head metaphor in the captivity epistles, *cf.* P. Benoit, 'Corps, tête et pleroma dans les epîtres de la captivité', *RB* 63, 1956, pp. 5–44.

[139] For a discussion of the wall imagery in relation to the church, *cf.* M. Barth's extensive note in *Ephesians* (*AB*, 1974) pp. 282ff.

[140] *Cf.* Barth, *op. cit.*, pp. 200f., for a survey of various suggestions over the meaning of the statement. He concludes that there is no sense in which the church fills Christ or the world. It is always God or Christ who fills.

church as an extension of the incarnation.[141] The suggestion is that in the same way that God was incarnate in Christ, so is Christ incarnate in his church. But the body metaphor makes clear that a distinction is maintained between the head and the body, between Christ and his church, which would exclude the view that Christ could be incarnate in the church. Since each member of the church is separately in Christ, the totality of members are therefore indwelt; but this is a different concept from incarnation.[142] The head is exalted and occupies a heavenly position, which is both a contrast to and yet at the same time an encouragement for that section of the body whose present sphere is earthly.

To sum up, we may say that the body metaphor is a significant contribution to our understanding of Paul's doctrine of the church, and shows that it was inseparable from his doctrine of the person of Christ. He never considered the church unrelated to its head. The totality of believers constituted the body of Christ. In one place Paul speaks of the bodies of Christians as members of Christ (1 Cor. 6:15), but his more normal expression is that Christians are members of the body of Christ. We shall note that this strong corporate concept recurs in several of the other images used by the apostle.

The church as a bride. The use of wedding imagery has support from the teaching of Jesus. In the parable of the virgins it is found, but the meaning of the parable does not depend on the identification of the bride (Mt. 25:1–13). Similarly the imagery used in the parable of the wedding feast to illustrate the characteristics of the kingdom makes use of the general idea, but makes no references to the bride (Mt. 22:1–14). John the Baptist uses the illustration of bride and bridegroom in order to distinguish himself from both. He claims to be the friend of the bridegroom, but he does not identify the bride (Jn. 3:29–30).[143]

It is not until Paul reflects on the church that the imagery is applied to the Christian community (*cf.* Eph. 5:25). But even here the church is not specifically identified as the bride. It is rather that the relationship between husband and wife is viewed as analogous to that between Christ and his church. Clearly in the Ephesians passage the whole church is meant by *ekklēsia*, as elsewhere in the epistle. Thus the whole community is seen to

---

[141] This is essentially the Roman Catholic view.

[142] Closely allied with this view are those which see the body as an extension of Christ's personality (as C. H. Dodd, *The Apostolic Preaching and its Developments*, p. 62) or as his *alter ego* (V. Taylor, *The Names of Jesus*, 1953, p. 101). Yet another interpretation sees in the body the continuing revelation of Christ (E. F. Scott, *The Epistles of Paul to the Colossians, to Philemon and to the Ephesians*, MNT, 1930, pp. 24, 205). But these views all suffer from the same defect, *i.e.* they adduce an ontological identity from metaphorical language. See E. Best's criticism of such a process (*One Body in Christ*, pp. 81ff.).

[143] M. Barth, *Ephesians*, pp. 668–699, has an extensive excursus on the bridegroom and bride imagery as used in Eph. 5:25-32. *Cf.* also J. P. Sampley, *'And the Two shall become one Flesh'* (1971), for a full examination of the whole passage, Eph. 5:21-33.

746

sustain a special relationship with Christ. In the NT interpretation of marriage the bride is urged to adopt an attitude of subjection and obedience to her husband because this is regarded as the pattern in the church's relationship with Christ. The bride imagery is here linked with Christ's redemptive purpose (*cf.* Eph. 5:25). The bridegroom is not only the head of the church, but also its saviour. But bride and bridegroom become one flesh and it is this that the apostle designates as a mystery.[144]

This use of the bride imagery in Ephesians is paralleled in two passages in the Corinthian letters. In 1 Corinthians 6:15ff. the bride metaphor is linked with the body metaphor. Paul asks, 'Shall I therefore take the members of Christ and make them members of a prostitute?' which contrasts the true bride with a prostitute. In the context this passage is a plea against immoral behaviour, but it hints at the idea that individual Christians were the bride of Christ. The other passage is 2 Corinthians 11:2, 'I betrothed you to Christ to present you as a pure bride to her one husband'; there the bride is representative of the local Corinthian community,[145] which Paul fears may have acted wrongly by espousing itself to another Jesus than the true Christ (2 Cor. 11:4). This passage comes in the section of 2 Corinthians which deals with those who are still rebellious against the apostle. Paul fears that the Corinthians might be deceived in the same way that Eve was deceived.[146] What is most to the fore is the requirement that the church, as the bride of Christ, must remain pure and loyal to its one husband, Christ.[147] This bride figure is a particularly intimate illustration of the relationship between Christ and his church, for it presupposes a strong bond of love between them. This is the only feminine analogy which Paul uses of the church.[148]

The church as a building. There are two epistles where this imagery occurs in Paul's teaching, and although this illustration is inanimate as compared with the other two, it is no less suggestive. The imagery has a strong

---

[144] R. Batey, 'The *mia sarx* Union of Christ and the Church', *NTS* 13, 1966-7, pp. 270–281, discusses the background of the idea of male and female becoming one flesh and sees significant implications in this for understanding the NT doctrine of the church. *Cf.* also B. M. Metzger, 'Paul's Vision of the Church', *Theology Today* (1949), p. 60, who traces to this idea Paul's speaking of the church in the same breath as both the body and the bride of Christ.

[145] E. Best, *One Body in Christ*, p. 171, suggests that since Paul does not consider himself here to be part of the bride, he may have thought of himself as the father of the bride who arranges the marriage.

[146] C. K. Barrett, *2 Corinthians* (BC, 1973), p. 272, points out that Paul is not setting out to give a new interpretation of the marriage figure or of the Adam and Eve story. He thinks these are purely incidental. E. E. Ellis, *Paul's Use of the Old Testament* (1957), p. 129, thinks that there may be an extension of Paul's Adam-Christ parallel in 2 Cor. 11:2ff. E. Best, *op. cit.*, rejects the view that Paul was thinking of the church as the second Eve.

[147] Sampley, *op. cit.*, p. 156, accepts that although only an idealized picture of the church is here presented, it involves an hortatory function: the church must aim to live up to this picture.

[148] It should be noted that Paul's use of the bride imagery here militates against the view that he despised marriage. *Cf.* E.-B. Allo, *Seconde Épître aux Corinthiens* (EB, 1956), p. 276.

parallel in Matthew 16:18: 'On this rock will I build my church'. This idea is developed by Paul in 1 Corinthians. He declares that the Corinthians are God's building (1 Cor. 3:9), and then likens himself to a master builder (1 Cor. 3:10), drawing attention to the sole permissible foundation, *i.e.* Christ himself.

This leads him to reflect on the idea of God's temple (1 Cor. 3:16). The totality of local believers are regarded as God's dwelling place, but this assumes that each Christian is the temple of God. As God dwelt in the holy of holies, so the Spirit dwells in the *ekklēsia*. The same figure of speech occurs in 1 Corinthians 6:19, where the bodies of individual believers are regarded as temples of God. The idea is carried over from the OT picture of God's dwelling-place being the inner sanctuary of the temple. As God dwelt among his ancient people in a position of remoteness because of his holiness, Paul does not want his readers to have any less reverence for his temple, even though it is now transferred from a sacred building to human hearts. This not only shows an advance in thought, in replacing an external by an internal reality, but also demonstrates the negation of the idea of a special temple. If the believer himself (and consequently the whole body of believers) is the dwelling place of God, location ceases to have importance. Whatever value attached to the central sanctuary for Israel, the Christian church had no need for one. The notion of a building became wholly metaphorical and therefore spiritual.

In the Ephesians passage the whole church is regarded as God's temple (Eph. 2:19–22). Paul talks of 'the whole structure' being joined together and growing 'into a holy temple in the Lord; in whom you also are built into it for a dwelling place of God in the Spirit'.

Several important features emerge from this passage. Since the temple is now the whole community, each part of the structure represents separate churches or individuals. Importance is attached to the parts in so far as they are an integral part of the whole. There is an understandable mixing of metaphors here, since the structures do not *grow* into temples.[149] But the meaning is unmistakably clear. The function of all the separate Christian communities was to form an observable part of the whole church. It is important to note that the 'building' is neither an edifice nor an organization, but the dwelling place of God.

A further significant feature of the Ephesian passage is that the temple is said to be built on 'the foundation of the apostles and prophets', with Jesus Christ as cornerstone. Does this represent a shift from the position in 1 Corinthians 3:11, where Christ alone is the foundation? Some who see a contradiction here appeal to this as one reason to dispute the Pauline

---

[149] The transference from the idea of household to house has already been made in this passage and prepares the readers for various other adaptations of the metaphor. This involves, as M. Barth, *Ephesians*, p. 270, notes, an important theological transition. The inhabitants have become the building materials.

748

authorship of Ephesians.[150] But it is possible to understand the words without concluding that they point to a contradiction. Paul would well know, as a matter of historical experience, that the Christian church had grown as a result of apostolic testimony and that the keystone in the whole structure was Jesus Christ. It is true that this interpretation understands the 'foundation of the apostles and prophets' as the foundation which the apostles laid, in the sense of their proclamation, but this is neither an impossible nor an improbable meaning (*cf.* 1 Cor. 3:10 where Paul says, 'I laid a foundation'). The words occur in a context which has just referred to the proclamation of peace (Eph. 2:17). Since the apostles preach and prophets prophesy, the linking of the foundation with witness is readily intelligible,[151] especially if Christ is the centre of the message.

But this does not explain why Christ is now the cornerstone rather than the foundation. Paul's main thought is that it is Christ who unites the separate parts into a whole. It is this rather than the precise definition of the foundation which is in mind. This would in fact fit in with the understanding of the 'cornerstone' in the sense of the keystone of the arch, if this is the correct interpretation.[152]

Another significant feature is that the church is here seen as a dwelling place of God 'in the Spirit'. The work of the Spirit is prominent, as it is in the 1 Corinthians 3 and 6 passages. The separate parts of the edifice would never become a united whole without the ministry of the Spirit. There is no suggestion in Paul's use of the building metaphor that human organization has much to do with his conception of the church. There are striking parallels between this metaphor and that of the body, both of which bring out the unity of the church, while preserving the individual characteristics of its constituent parts. A kindred idea which appears in the Ephesians passage is contained in the expression 'members of the household of God', used as a description of the community of Christians (Eph. 2:19). The focus clearly falls on the fact that Christians belong together as members of a spiritual household or family circle.

The church as the true people of God. The idea of *the* people of God becomes familiar to us by its frequent application in the OT to the nation of Israel.[153]

---

[150] *Cf.* C. L. Mitton, *The Epistle to the Ephesians*, p. 18, who considers that what Ephesians says about the church is far in advance of what Paul wrote elsewhere.

[151] *Cf.* M. Barth, *Ephesians*, pp. 314ff., for a discussion of the expression 'the foundation of the apostles and prophets'. He strongly rejects the view that this belongs to the post-apostolic age.

[152] *Cf.* J. Jeremias, 'Kephalē gōnias - Akrogōniaios', *ZNW* 29, 1930, pp. 264–280. But against, *cf.* R. J. McKelvey, 'Christ the Cornerstone', *NTS* 8, 1962, pp. 352ff.; *idem*, *The New Temple* (1969), pp. 114f., 195ff.

[153] P. S. Minear, *Images of the Church in the New Testament*, pp. 66–104, groups his evidence on the people of God theme under three headings: political and national analogies, metaphors drawn from the pastoral economy, and metaphors drawn from cultic traditions. This gives him very wide scope and results in a strong emphasis on this theme within his study of the NT view of the church.

Yet it has its own distinctive characteristic which at once distinguishes it from a purely political or racial concept. Israel was regarded from a theocratic point of view. It was a people chosen by God and watched over by him. It retained its identity only on the strength of its God-centred origins, never by its own efforts. It was natural that Paul, with his strong Israelite background should think of the church in terms of *the* people of God. The OT relates the story of Israel's failure to fulfil the divine plan for it, but holds out the strong promise of the coming Messiah. The disciples of Jesus, the Messiah, were naturally regarded as the true Israel, as the fulfilment of those promises which the old Israel failed to inherit.[154]

Paul uses a number of images to express the idea of the church as the collective people of God. It is important to notice that the NT use of the word 'people' differs from modern usage, where 'people' generally denotes an aggregate of a number of individuals. It tends to lack identity. But the idea of an exclusive 'people' as a well-defined community of those who believe in the risen Lord is a basic notion of the NT. 'The people of God' is not ill-defined. What were a no-people have become God's people (Rom. 9:25–26; cf. 1. Pet. 2:9, 10).

The fact that Paul can refer to Christians as sons of Abraham, when writing to Gentiles (Rom. 4:16; Gal. 3:29), shows the radical new way in which he is regarding descent from Abraham. It is no longer a matter of race or circumcision. It is a matter of common faith. The whole concept of God's people has therefore shifted from the theocratic nation to a community of faith, and has thereby become both enlarged in its scope (universal) and more defined in its membership (faith in Christ).

The analogy between the people of God in the NT and the experience of Israel in the OT is frequent. Paul expounds on the wilderness experience in 1 Corinthians 10:1ff. and sees a direct spiritual connection between Christ and the rock which Moses struck. Again in his detailed discussion of the relation between Jews and Gentiles in Romans 9–11, Paul makes use of the OT concept of the remnant, and applies it in a spiritual way. Admittedly in this case it is not certain that Paul is equating the remnant with the whole church, since he may have had in mind only a Jewish group; but it is certainly clear that he is thinking of a community who are believers in God. Perhaps in this connection we might note the way in which the apostle applies the concept of election to those who belong to God's people (Rom. 11:5; 8:33; Eph. 1:4ff.). The people of God are those chosen by him

---

[154] W. D. Davies, *The Gospel and the Land* (1974), p. 182, recognizes that the logic of Paul's Christology and missionary practice 'seems to demand that the people of Israel living in the land had been replaced as the people of God by a community which had no special territorial attachment.' But Davies notes that Paul never actually calls the church the new Israel, nor does he call the Jewish people the old Israel. *Cf.* also his *Paul and Rabbinic Judaism* (1948), pp. 101ff. Another who interprets the church in terms of Israel as far as Luke-Acts is concerned is J. Jervell, *Luke and the People of God* (1972), although he claims that Luke thinks of two peoples of God. *Cf.* E. E. Ellis' review in *Int* 28, 1974, pp. 94ff.

to fulfil his purpose, and this sense of being called and chosen brings a strong sense of solidarity to them.

Apart from those passages in which Paul speaks either of individual believers or of communities as 'temples', he makes little use of cultic imagery in his conception of the church (as compared for example with Hebrews). He does, however, see his own work as a 'priestly service' (*leitourgos*) (Phil. 2:17) and the believing Gentiles as an acceptable 'offering' (*prosphora*) (Rom. 15:16). Moreover, the imagery of aroma which is applied to Christians (2 Cor. 2:15; Eph. 5:2) is derived from the use of incense in Jewish worship.[155] These passing allusions show how completely the whole concept of the sacrificial system was adapted to a spiritual form when applied to Christians. The fact that Paul does not expound the priesthood theme does not mean that he saw no significance in the sacrificial system as applied to the community. For him the people of God are a community of those who have been redeemed and for whom there is no further obstacle in their relationship to God. They are in fact a reconciled community. They have become the true Israel.

THE WORSHIP OF THE CHURCH

General procedures. We turn next to the subject of worship.[156] We shall first note what evidence there is of worship procedure, including hymns, ministry of the word, creeds and prayers, and then we shall consider the evidence about the ordinances. The study of early Christian hymns raises problems because there is no general agreement about what fragments of Christians hymns are to be found in Paul's epistles. It is widely supposed that he used a previous hymn in Philippians 2:6–11, Colossians 1:15–20 and in 1 Timothy 3:16.[157] All of these are Christological and may reflect the practice of composing hymns in rhythmic forms ascribing honour to Jesus Christ (see pp. 343ff. for detailed comment on them).

In Ephesians 5:19 Christians are exhorted to address one another in 'psalms and hymns and spiritual songs'. If the 'psalms' are OT psalms, there is no clue as to the character of the other two categories, nor of the distinction between them. Some regular singing in Christian assemblies is not only admitted by the evidence (*cf.* 1 Cor. 14:26), but would be paralleled in contemporary Jewish synagogue practice. In Ephesians 5:14 there is

---

[155] The word *osmē* (odour) is used only by Paul in the NT, except for Jn. 12:3. Paul always links it with *euōdia* (fragrance). It is essentially an OT usage. The phrase occurs about forty times in the Pentateuch.

[156] *Cf.* C. F. D. Moule, *Worship in the* (1961); R. P. Martin, *Worship in the Early Church* (1964); F. Hahn, *The Worship of the Early Church* (1973), for discussions of various aspects of Christian worship in the NT. *Cf.* also A. B. Macdonald, *Christian Worship in the Primitive Church* (1934); G. Delling, *Worship in the New Testament* (1962).

[157] According to J. T. Sanders, *The New Testament Christological Hymns* (1971), pp. 1ff., a distinction should be made between hymns and confessions, but he admits that the distinction is at times blurred (as in the case of 1 Tim. 3:16, *cf.* p. 16).

what appears to be a brief extract of a hymnic form, which consists of an invocation to Christians to stir for action. Some have seen this as associated with Christian baptism, which is not improbable.[158] The words had become so familiar that it seemed natural to Paul to cite them in a different context and with a wider connotation.

In 1 Corinthians 14, Paul discusses certain problems which had arisen in the worship service of the Corinthian community. He mentions the custom of having a hymn, a lesson, a revelation, a tongue or an interpretation (1 Cor. 14:26). He gives no further detail, and it is impossible to know whether his list implies a regular sequence. He is more concerned with the purpose and manner of the exercise. All must be done for edification, the controlling factor in Paul's approach to the worship service. To achieve this he advises that attention must be paid to orderliness (1 Cor. 14:30ff.).

As far as the ministry of the word is concerned it need only be noted that Paul's frequent allusions to Scripture in his various epistles presuppose that his Gentile readers were acquainted with the LXX. It is reasonable to suppose therefore that regular public reading of Scripture formed an essential feature of Christian worship meetings.[159] The only direct reference to this is 1 Timothy 4:13, where Timothy is exhorted to attend to the public reading of Scripture, to preaching and to teaching.

How early in the development of Christian worship other specifically Christian material was included in this public reading it is impossible to say. Paul himself urged the public reading of his own letters in those churches he was addressing (1 Thes. 5:27). Moreover, he urged the exchange of his letters between churches (Col. 4:16). He expected Christians to hold to the traditions they had been taught by the apostles, whether orally or by letter (2 Thes. 2:15). He gives no indication of the inclusion of traditions about the life and teaching of Jesus, although in one statement in the pastoral epistles he appears to class a saying of Jesus recorded by Luke as Scripture (1 Tim. 5:18). It would seem therefore that in addition to worship the function of the community included the task of supplying an intelligent grasp of the faith, by means of public reading and teaching.

It is important to consider how far credal statements were used in early Christian communities, for this would affect the constitution of those communities.[160] It has sometimes been argued that the apostle Paul was

---

[158] Cf. J. Ysebaert, *Greek Baptismal Terminology. Its Origin and Early Development* (1962) cited by R. P. Martin, *Worship in the Early Church*, p. 48.

[159] On the use of the Word in early Christian assemblies, cf. R. P. Martin, *op. cit.*, 66ff. G. Delling, *op. cit.*, pp. 92ff., considers there is no evidence that Jewish Christians had public readings from the Old Testament.

[160] For a treatment of early confessions, cf. V. H. Neufeld, *The Earliest Christian Confessions* (1963), especially pp. 42ff. in respect of the Pauline literature. Cf. also R. P. Martin, *An Early Christian Confession* (1960) on Phil. 2. J. D. G. Dunn has a section entitled 'Primitive Confessional Formulae' in his *Unity and Diversity in the New Testament*, pp. 33-59.

too much of a creative theologian to have supported the use of credal statements of doctrine, and this has then been used to relegate any literature (such as the pastoral epistles) which seem to support this to the post-apostolic period.[161] But this puts a wrong construction on the evidence, for it supposes that he found no place at all in his thinking for concise statements of doctrine.

Paul certainly acknowledged brief confessions like 'Jesus is Lord' (Rom. 10:9; Phil. 2:11). But he also recognized a core of Christian traditions. He claims to have received such confessional information himself (1 Cor. 15:1ff.), and mentions that the Roman Christians had received a 'standard of teaching' to which they were committed (Rom. 6:17). He urges the Philippians to hold fast to the 'word of life' (Phil. 2:16).[162] These varied expressions must refer to a certain acknowledged body of Christian doctrine. It is not altogether unexpected, therefore, when we meet terms like 'the faith', 'the pattern of sound words', or 'the deposit' in the Pastorals. In fact, there are many instances where Paul uses the expression 'the faith' where the reference must be to more than the act of faith (Phil. 1: 27; Eph. 4:5; Col. 2:6, 7). The same may be said of 'the truth' (Col. 1:5; 2 Thes. 2:12).[163]

Paul is clearly concerned that Christian communities should not only know, but also steadfastly maintain, the basis of their Christian commitment. There is an understood entity which he calls 'my gospel', by comparison with which all others are false (*cf.* Gal. 1:8).[164] It has been suggested that the statement of tradition set out in 1 Corinthians 15:3ff. is a basic primitive Christian creed which served as a hallmark of what was Christian and what was not. If this is correct, it is important to note that the emphasis falls on the death and resurrection of Christ and on the interpretation of the death 'according to the Scriptures'. We may conclude therefore that some kind of primitive statement of belief was accepted by Paul as being the authentic basis of membership of the developing communities.[165]

---

[161] *Cf.* the discussion in my *New Testament Introduction*, pp. 594ff., pp. 604ff.; *idem, The Pastoral Epistles* (*TNTC*, 1957), pp. 38ff.

[162] Even if the alternative 'hold forth' is preferred, it makes no difference to the content of the 'word of life', which seems to be used here in the sense of 'gospel'. *Cf.* R. P. Martin, *Philippians* (*TNTC*, 1959), p. 117.

[163] E. Lohse, *Colossians and Philemon* (Eng. trans. *Hermeneia*, 1971, from *KEK* 1968), p. 18, considers that the word of truth in Col. 1:8 is the gospel which consisted of fixed traditional formulae. It must be remembered that the idea of truth in this epistle should be seen against the background of the false teaching being combated (*cf.* E. Schweizer, *Der Brief an die Kolosser* (*EKK*, 1976), p. 37).

[164] J. D. G. Dunn, *Unity and Diversity in the New Testament*, pp. 23ff., suggests that there are reflected in Paul's epistles several gospels which were equally valid. But the statement of Paul in Gal. 1:5ff. militates against this view. Paul's reference to 'my' gospel was not intended to distinguish what he preached from other valid gospels, but from perversions of the gospel. *Cf.* my *Galatians*, pp. 62f.

[165] It may be that the statements in 1 Cor. 15:3ff. provide a clue rather to the basic content of the apostolic proclamation than to the basis of church membership. C. K. Barrett, *1 Corinthians* (*BC*, ²1971), p. 340, views it as an outline of Christian preaching which Paul considers to be normative.

The place and importance of prayers in the communities must be noted.[166] Paul himself includes many prayers in his epistles and this in itself shows the importance he attached to prayer for his converts. He also reflects the importance of prayer as far as his own needs are concerned (cf. 2. Cor. 12:8). But more than this he acknowledges the value of corporate prayer. Christians may be described as 'those who in every place call on the name of our Lord Jesus Christ, both their Lord and ours' (1 Cor. 1:2). As to the content of the prayers of the early Christians, Paul's own prayerful reflections in Ephesians 1: 3–14 may be cited as an example, and indeed it is not impossible that he is echoing language which he has known through actual experience of the church's worship. In his adoration of God he introduces some profound theological concepts, reminding us that Christian prayer is inseparable from Christian tenets of faith. The Colossians are exhorted to continue in prayer and to include special prayer for the apostle and his assistants (Col. 4:2; cf. also 1 Thes. 5:25).

One feature in Paul's references to prayer is the importance he attaches to 'thanksgiving'. He sets an example in his own prayers and urges the same on his readers (Col. 4:2; Phil. 4:6; cf. also 1 Cor. 14:16). Prayer in both individual and corporate worship was intended to be a joyful occasion when the amazing goodness of God in Christ was recognized. Another feature was the use of brief set forms like *Amēn* (2 Cor. 1:20) and *maranatha* (1 Cor. 16:22); both are significant because they are non-Greek forms which have become used in a Greek setting.[167] Neither must be regarded simply as a liturgical catchword, for the first affirms the reliability of God's promises and the second affirms belief in the Lord's return. Both therefore have theological overtones. Another Aramaic word which seems to have been preserved in its original form together with its Greek translation is *Abba* (Father), and this is a form used by Christians, prompted by the Spirit (Rom. 8:15; Gal. 4:6).

THE ORDINANCES

It is against this general background of worship that the Pauline approach to the ordinances must be considered. We shall deal first with baptism and then consider the Lord's Supper.

Baptism. There is ample evidence to show that Paul followed up the practices which had been 'delivered' to him. This was certainly true in regard to the Lord's Supper (1 Cor. 11:23) and there seems no reason to suppose it was any different in the case of baptism. That converts were baptized is clear from 1 Corinthians 1:13f. (cf. also 1 Cor. 6:11). Paul disclaims having performed the ceremony himself in the case of the Corinthians, but he does

---

[166] Cf. G. Delling, *Worship in the New Testament*, pp. 104–127. for a section on prayer.

[167] Cf. C. F. D. Moule's note on the language of worship, *Worship in the New Testament*, pp. 67ff.

not deny its importance.[168] When he says that Christ did not send him to baptize but to preach (1 Cor. 1:17), he is counteracting a superstitious importance attached to the ceremony itself by certain groups, which were regarding the act as of superior significance to the understanding of the content of the gospel, centred in the cross of Christ.

Paul's own expositions of the ordinances give the lie to any who were charging him with attaching magical significance to the rites. In 1 Corinthians 12: 13, he regards baptism as the means of initiation into one body, *i.e.* the Christian community. He gives this a specifically spiritual meaning by insisting that it was effected by the Spirit. The act of baptism was not restricted to any class of people (Gal. 3:27f.). There are no distinctions of race (Jew or Greek), sex (male or female) or social status (slave or freeman). All are regarded as having been 'baptized into Christ' as a result of which they had 'put on Christ',[169] a favourite Pauline idea, as Romans 13:14; Ephesians 4:24 and Colossians 3:10 show. In one passage Paul uses the phrase 'one baptism' (Eph. 4:5), which not only draws attention to a basic acceptance of a unified concept, but to the fact that the unity is centred in the one Lord.[170]

It is in the passage in Romans 6:1–4[171] that the apostle sets out most fully his thoughts about baptism. It is essentially connected with death and resurrection, and not with cleansing.[172] Baptism signifies burial with Christ in his death (Rom. 6:4). But baptism also means new life: a sharing of Christ's risen life. It exhibits the transition which has occurred from death to life.

Paul goes on to expound the significance of the change, particularly in relation to the death of the old self. He clearly saw the theological meaning in the baptismal act. But the crucial question arises over the time when the radical change occurred. Did it happen at baptism? Or did it happen before baptism, in which case the ordinance has the function of a public demonstration of what had already happened? The issue has been hotly debated.

---

[168] G. R. Beasley-Murray, *Baptism in the New Testament*, pp. 178f., considers that Paul sees the fact that he had baptized so few as a fortunate overruling of Providence. He denies that Paul is intending to minimize the importance of baptism.

[169] O. Cullmann, *Baptism in the New Testament*, p. 31, in rejecting Barth's view that there is a cognitive aspect to the act of baptism, decisively appeals to 1 Cor. 12:13 and Gal. 3:27f. 'God sets a man within, not merely informs him that he sets him within, the Body of Christ.' *Cf.* G. R. Beasley-Murray's discussion of these passages, *Baptism in the New Testament*, pp. 146ff., 167ff.

[170] *Cf.* W. E. Moore, 'One Baptism', *NTS* 10, 1963–4, pp. 504–516, who discusses the significance of this statement. He gives a critique of J. A. T. Robinson's approach in his *Twelve New Testament Studies* (1962), pp. 158–175.

[171] For a full discussion of this passage in relation to the mystery religions, *cf.* G. Wagner, *Pauline Baptism and the Pagan Mysteries* (Eng. trans. 1967), who denies that Paul derived his ideas from the cults, but nevertheless notes some parallels.

[172] *Cf.* C. F. D. Moule, *Worship in the New Testament*, p. 57, who points out that cleansing is not the most prominent idea in baptism in the NT. He sees it connected with washing only in 1 Cor. 6:11; Eph. 5:26; Tit. 3:5; and 1 Pet. 3:21.

Most Pauline scholars would agree that Paul would not have countenanced the view that baptism could have any validity without faith.

The issue is of some importance for assessing Paul's view of baptism and indeed for his view of the constitution of the church. Although a purely mechanical view of baptism must be rejected as being alien to Paul's thought, this does not mean that he did not see in it a means to an end.[173] It dramatically presented the death and rising of Jesus, and each candidate was required to identify himself with this experience. The act itself therefore set a seal on the act of faith[174] which had led the candidate to submit to it. It must, of course, be recognized that for Paul, as for the other early Christians, conversion and baptism were regarded as one event. There is no suggestion in Paul's writings that any others than those already converted had any claim to baptism.

The necessity of faith in the baptismal act is brought out in Colossians 2:12: 'You were buried with him in baptism, in which you were also raised with him through faith in the working of God, who raised him from the dead.' Without the exercise of faith, then, there would be no validity in the baptismal act.[175]

There are two other passages which need mentioning. In Titus 3:5 the expression 'the washing of regeneration' occurs, and this might be a reference to baptism. Nevertheless since the word 'baptism' is not used, it would be precarious to argue for a connection between the act of baptism and the actual experience of regeneration,[176] in view of the fact, noted above, that in Romans 6:1–4 baptism is not thought of as a cleansing operation. Similarly Ephesians 5:26[177] cannot be claimed to support the

---

[173] G. R. Beasley-Murray, *Baptism in the New Testament*, pp. 131ff., thinks that Paul has a three-fold connection in mind between baptism and Christ's death and resurrection. First, it involves the believer in the actual dying and rising of Christ in a kind of re-enactment. Second, a death takes place in the life of the believer and a new life begins. Third, it demands a 'crucifixion' of the flesh, and a new life in the Spirit. The second and third are clearly closely related.

[174] On the relation between faith and baptism, *cf.* O. Cullmann, *Baptism in the New Testament* (Eng. trans. 1950) and G. R. Beasley-Murray, *op. cit.*, pp. 266ff.

[175] Many exegetes, by linking the reference to baptism in Col. 2:12 to the reference to circumcision 'which belongs to Christ' in Col. 2:11, interpret the latter as a periphrasis for baptism. *Cf.* J. B. Lightfoot, *Colossians and Philemon* (⁹1890), pp. 181ff; O. Cullmann, *Baptism in the New Testament*, p. 59; P. C. Marcel, *The Biblical Doctrine of Infant Baptism* (Eng. trans. 1953), p. 157.

[176] J. N. D. Kelly, *The Pastoral Epistles* (BC, 1963), p. 252, does not hesitate to connect baptism and regeneration here. But he understands it from the point of view of the use of the word *palingenesia* among the Stoics and the mystery religions (*i.e.* as rebirth).

[177] Beasley-Murray, *op. cit.*, p. 203, finds two important elements of baptismal teaching in this passage: that baptism is rooted in the redemptive death of Christ, and that cleansing in baptism is *en rhēmati*. This author takes the latter phrase in its widest meaning of the Word heard, confessed and submitted to. Some scholars link the whole of Ephesians with baptism. N. A. Dahl, for instance, sees the letter as addressed to newly established churches to remind them of the blessings of their baptism: 'Addresse und Pröomium des Epheserbriefes', *TZ*, 1951, pp. 241–264. *Cf.* also J. C. Kirby, *Ephesians, Baptism and Pentecost* (1968), whose theory has been criticized by G. B. Caird, *SJT* 22, 1969, pp. 225f. and J. C. O'Neill, *JTS* 20, 1969, pp. 615f.

same doctrine since the cleansing is directly linked to the self-giving of Christ for his church, not to a ritual cleansing (*cf.* also 1 Cor. 6:11)[178]

One of the accompaniments of baptism in the teaching of the apostle is the challenge to embrace a new way of life.[179] The metaphor of putting off and putting on is especially stressed in Colossians in a baptismal context (*cf.* 2:12 with 3:5, 8, 10, 12). It is clear from the kind of language used here that the baptismal act was intended to call forth the beginning of a definite moral transformation; this involved a process which made both negative and positive demands on each believer. The putting-off/putting-on imagery may well be drawn from the action of baptismal candidates divesting themselves before and reclothing themselves after the baptismal act. But the new life requires a whole new set of values.[180] It may well be that the act of baptism was a valuable teaching medium, as candidates were led to appreciate its symbolic meaning.

The Lord's supper. It is a fact that apart from the discussion of the Lord's supper[181] in 1 Corinthians, which was introduced into the epistle because of aberrations from a true observance of it, we should know little of Paul's doctrine about it[182]. This highlights the almost accidental way in which important positive doctrine is introduced in the NT. Much of it is expounded against a background of erroneous doctrine or practice. Nevertheless, because the other Pauline letters are silent about the Lord's supper, this in no way reflects on the importance of it. We may be thankful that the apostle has preserved for us a clear exposition of his own thinking.

We note first that Paul did not innovate with regard to the Lord's supper. What he 'delivered' to the Corinthians, he had himself 'received' (1 Cor. 11:23).[183] When he says he 'received from the Lord', he is surely not suggesting that it was a supernatural revelation; rather, he had received the traditions through others, but had recognized them as authentic accounts

---

[178] Many commentators regard 1 Cor. 6:11 as a definite allusion to baptism as a cleansing. But it is by no means certain that baptism is in mind. Paul does not use the verb *baptizō*, but *apolouō*, which he nowhere else uses of baptism in his epistles. The only other NT use is in Acts 22:16, where it is linked with baptism. It is more likely that a spiritual cleansing is in mind as in Rev. 1:5 (*cf.* L. Morris, *1 Corinthians* (*TNTC*, 1958) *ad loc.*), since this links up better with the references to justification and sanctification which follow.

[179] For a discussion of the ethical implication of baptism, *cf.* G. R. Beasley-Murray, *op. cit.*, pp. 284ff.

[180] As Beasley-Murray, *op. cit.*, p. 290, has rightly said, we have to do with something more than ethic; this is grace for grace.

[181] For a discussion of Paul's view of the Lord's supper, *cf.* D. E. H. Whiteley, *The Theology of St Paul* (1964), pp. 178ff.; H. Ridderbos, *Paul*, pp. 414ff.

[182] *Cf.* C. F. D. Moule on 'The Fellowship Meal and its Developments' in his *Worship in the New Testament* (1961), pp. 18ff.; A. B. Macdonald, *Christian Worship in the Primitive Church* pp. 140ff.; G. Delling, *Worship in the New Testament*, pp. 140ff.

[183] For a form-critical approach to this passage and other NT passages relating to the Lord's supper, *cf.* W. Marxsen, *The Lord's Supper as a Christological Problem* (Eng. trans. 1970), pp. 1ff. He considers that both 1 Cor. 10:16 and 11:23f. show that Paul has added his own interpretation to pre-Pauline formulations.

of what the Lord had himself instituted.[184] This is of utmost importance for a correct understanding of his doctrine. It at once excludes any theory that Paul added to the original idea of the supper and that he was indebted to models drawn from the Greek mystery religions.[185] In 1 Corinthians he takes particular trouble to set out the tradition in detail, so that it can be seen to accord with the forms which were generally observed in the church. While there are some differences between Paul's record and the synoptic gospels, the substantial agreement between them shows both the consistency of the tradition, and also the fact that Paul was continuing what had become the established ordinance.

It is in Paul's additions and further comments that his own distinctive teaching shines through.[186] We may note the following considerations. First of all Paul sets the Lord's supper in the context of the fellowship meal. At this stage they were not separate events, but in the Corinthian church this had led to abuses. It is important to note that the fellowship idea (koinōnia) played an essential part in early Christian experience. It is for this reason that Paul interprets the Lord's supper in terms of sharing. He implies that the broken bread is a participation (koinōnia) in the body of Christ, and the cup of blessing in the blood of Christ (1 Cor. 10:16).[187]

The Lord's supper is, therefore, in some way a sharing in the sacrifice of Christ. As in the passover the Jews relived the experiences of the exodus, so the Christians participate in the sacrifice of Christ by symbolically identifying themselves with it. This is not to be understood as if it were divorced from reality, for it has meaning only as Christ himself gives the sign or symbol in the act of participation.[188] The participation in the blood and body of Christ are not a sharing in corporeal elements, but in an experience of Christ in terms of his sacrifice. This koinōnia has, therefore, a deep theological significance. The participants in the Lord's supper are also committing themselves to an identification with the mission of Christ.

---

[184] C. F. D. Moule, op. cit., p. 24, considers that the words 'from the Lord' is a reference to apostolic traditions going back to the Lord himself, and that therefore Paul is claiming to be in line with tradition.

[185] Cf. A. Schweitzer's discussion on 'Mysticism and the Sacraments in Paul' in his The Mysticism of Paul the Apostle, pp. 227ff. H. A. A. Kennedy, St Paul and the Mystery Religions (1913), p. 279, agrees with Von Dobschütz's opinion that the unique sacramental conception of the early church has no analogy in the history of religion and has its origins wholly in Christian faith and experience. E. Käsemann, Essays on New Testament Themes (Eng. trans. 1960), p. 108, is a more recent writer who recognizes that the attempt to trace Paul's teaching to Hellenistic cult-meals has broken down. On the other hand, he finds indebtedness to the gnostic myth of an Archetypal Man in Paul's interpretation of eucharistic tradition.

[186] Cf. R. P. Martin, Worship in the Early Church, pp. 122ff.

[187] For a discussion of koinōnia in the NT, cf. F. Hauck, art. in TDNT 3, pp. 797–809. Also for a fuller examination, cf. H. Seesemann, Der Begriff KOINŌNIA im Neuen Testament (1933), especially pp. 34ff. on the occurrence of the idea in Paul's epistles. By comparing 1 Cor. 10:16 with the reference to sōma in Col. 1, Seesemann sees a double meaning: the body of the earthly historical Lord and of the church (p. 36). But the former is undoubtedly primary in 1 Cor. 10:16. Seesemann's conclusion is that in Paul the word has a religious sense which is peculiar to him. He claims it to be a technical expression for the Lord's supper.

[188] For the definition of symbol and reality in this context, cf. G. C. Berkouwer, The Sacraments (1969), pp. 202–218.

It is for this reason that Paul points out the impossibility of people partaking of the Lord's table and also of the table of demons as in idol worship (1 Cor. 10:21). The former is no mere formality, but involves the whole person. The Lord's supper becomes the test by which a person's real allegiance is seen. There is no room for compromise. Partakers in Christ's death are by that fact excluded from any fellowship which compromises their position 'in Christ'.

It is clear that Christian fellowship included all who participated in Christ and were therefore united into one body. This is the implication of Paul's one-loaf/one-body contention in 1 Corinthians 10:17.[189] The Lord's supper has an in-built theological basis for unity, according to Paul. It is a tragic reflection on the modern church's inability to grasp Paul's teaching, that the Lord's supper has so often been a major cause for division. Paul would not have accepted any definition of 'body' which was not based on a Christian profession supported by worthy actions.[190] Those who eat and drink 'without discerning the body' (1 Cor. 11:29) are condemned, which presumably refers to those who do not maintain the purity of the body. In this epistle there are strong warnings against having fellowship with immoral people. It may be said that Paul has a dynamic approach to the Lord's supper. Participation has definite practical implications.

The fellowship aspect of the observance is further seen to be affected by the Corinthian's wrong approach to the accompanying meal. If some eat well and others go hungry, the integrity of the 'body' is again violated. The Lord's supper was never intended to focus on different styles of living, and Paul unhesitatingly maintains that if anyone is hungry he should eat at home. In this way the religious significance of the ordinance could be preserved (*cf.* 1 Cor. 11:17ff.).[191] The fact that Paul gave such instructions shows what store he placed on maintaining the dignity of the Lord's supper.

Another aspect of Paul's doctrine is based on the wording which he especially preserves, which shows the Lord's supper as a memorial. Both eating and drinking are said to be 'in remembrance of me' (1 Cor. 11:24–25). In the Jewish passover liturgy the head of each household recounts the history of past national events to remind each participant that he has some

---

[189] It is important to note that this statement of Paul comes in a passage dealing with idolatrous practices. *Cf.* C. K. Barrett, *1 Corinthians*, p. 234, who points out three ways in which the Lord's supper is relevant to such a discussion: a guarantee against falling into sin, a means of uniting them to Christ, a sharing with others in love. This brings out the powerful practical effect of the Lord's supper.

[190] H. Conzelmann, *1 Corinthians* (Eng. trans. *Hermeneia*, 1975, from *KEK*, 1969), p. 202, takes the self-examination as relating to the sacrament, 'that is to the propriety of the participation'. But C. K. Barrett, *1 Corinthians*, p. 273, relates it to moral scrutiny and this seems the most probable interpretation.

[191] C. F. D. Moule, *Worship in the New Testament*, p. 33, states that the separation of common fellowship from sacramental rite is utterly alien to Paul's mind. 1 Cor. 11:33 makes clear that orderliness is essential in the fellowship meal. Those who were too hungry to wait for their brethren should first have eaten at home.

continuity with those events. Something similar may be in mind in the Christian ordinance, obliging those sharing in it to call to mind the death of Christ, not only as a past fact, but as a present reality. This is not to suggest the real presence of Jesus Christ in the bread and wine, as one line of eucharistic doctrine later asserted, but to maintain that in a real sense the participant is confronted again with the death of Christ,[192] both in its cost and in its achievements.

The memorial aspect involves a proclamation (1 Cor. 11:26). It is not a re-enactment. It declares the historic event which lies at the very centre of the Christian faith. The memorial is not of merely antiquarian interest to keep alive what is long since dead, for it is not the life of Christ which is commemorated,[193] but his death: a death of unique significance for its saving value. There was to be no opportunity for that death to sink out of sight.

It should also be noted that there was a future aspect in Paul's record of the Lord's supper, for the words 'until he comes' show that the ordinance has relevance only to the present age. When Christ returns there will be no further need for it. His presence will render 'memorials' unnecessary.[194]

The value of Paul's contribution to an understanding of the Lord's supper cannot be overestimated. He was not an innovator, but he possessed a profound insight into the theological meaning of what others had preserved of the ordinance instituted by Jesus himself.

THE LEADERS OF THE CHURCH.

Any examination of Paul's view of the leadership within the Christian community must begin from his basic idea that the church is a body of which Christ is the head. No authority structure is possible without the supreme authority being vested in Christ himself. Moreover, even here the authority must be understood as organic and not organizational. The head essentially belongs to the body as the body belongs to the head. It is the most intimate kind of authority, since the body functions efficiently only when it responds at once to the dictates of the head. Any officials who are mentioned must be regarded as exercising their various functions under the direction of the head.

Before discussing the various categories of leaders, we should note that Paul has much to say about service (*diakonia*) which is given out of love without having any official status. The important feature of such service

---

[192] C. H. Dodd, *History and the Gospel* (1938), p. 83, suggested that some form of passion narrative may have accompanied the Lord's supper.

[193] It is not without significance that the memorial is to 'the Lord's death' (1 Cor. 11:26), which points beyond the death to the glorified Lord in heaven. *Cf.* F. W. Grosheide, *I Corinthians* (²1954), p. 273, who maintains that this is further borne out by the reference to the Lord's return.

[194] Some interpret the future aspect rather differently, suggesting that the Lord's supper is an anticipation of the eschatological meal of the Messiah (*cf.* H. Küng, *The Church*, p. 217).

is that it must be for the edification of the church (*cf.* 1 Cor. 16:15; Eph. 4:11f.). While practical acts of loving and caring may have been mainly in mind (as happened in Acts 6:1), it is likely that the function of proclamation was included (as 2 Cor. 5:18f. presupposes). Moreover, *diakonia* is placed between 'prophecy' and 'teaching' in the list in Romans 12:6, 7. Our investigation of the various church offices should not lose sight of this background of loving service which all Christians were expected to give.

Church officials. There is surprisingly little information about the organization of church life in the Pauline letters except in the Pastorals. In the Thessalonian correspondence the reference to the officials is expressed in the vaguest way as 'those who are over you in the Lord' (*proïstamenoi*, 1 Thes. 5:12).[195] Paul gives them no title, but they were probably elders (*presbyteroi*), since according to Acts Paul and his companions were in the habit of appointing elders in every church which they established (Acts 14:23).[196] Clearly in addressing the Thessalonians Paul is more concerned about the function than the office,[197] and it would be true to say that this is generally evident in what we might call his theology of church government.

Philippians is the only church epistle in which the apostle mentions definite officials. The letter is addressed to the saints, with the bishops and deacons (Phil. 1:1). It is noticeable that no special priority is given to the officers over the members generally. Since the former are referred to in the plural, it is evident that the bishops are to be identified with those who are elsewhere called elders.[198] It is probable that the reason why both sets of officials are mentioned here is that special reference is made in this epistle to gifts sent by the church to Paul, for which the officials would presumably have been responsible. Clearly Paul had no desire to give the impression that he was addressing the leaders to the exclusion of those led.

The Corinthian church shows a rather different pattern since Paul con-

---

[195] E. Best, *1 and 2 Thessalonians* (BC, 1972), p. 226, thinks that Paul describes them by their activities rather than by their office. He suggests that we cannot be sure that Luke has not read back the reference to elders in Acts 14:23. His interpretation of *proïstamenous* is those who 'care for', which does not bring out so clearly the idea of rule. It still, however, implies a special group apart from the rest.

[196] Many scholars do not regard Acts 14:23, with its reference to 'elders', to be historical. E. Haenchen, *Acts*, p. 436, simply assumes that Luke has taken for granted that the ecclesiastical constitution of his own day existed in Paul's time. But not only does he provide no supporting evidence, his theory is highly improbable, since it would be most natural for the earliest Christian churches to adopt an elder system after the pattern of the Jewish synagogues, *cf.* W. Neil, *Acts* (NCB, 1973), p. 166.

[197] In 1 Thes. 5:12, a single article governs three functions, which points to one group which exercises all the functions. L. Morris, *1 and 2 Thessalonians* (NICNT, 1959), p. 165, rightly asks what group other than elders would perform such a triple function.

[198] R. P. Martin, *Philippians* (NCB, 1976), p. 62, draws a distinction between the mention of bishops and deacons here and in the Pastorals. He thinks that here the words are probably functional rather than references to an ecclesiastical office. But there is no need to draw such a sharp distinction between the two uses.

cerns himself with a discussion of the *charismata* (see further comments below), among which he names 'helpers, administrators' (1 Cor. 12:28).[199] What is most significant is his emphasis that these, among other gifts, are the appointments of God. It is noticeable also that these helpers and administrators are in addition to apostles, prophets and teachers. This latter triad of functions was obviously not intended to be encumbered with administrative duties; in this Paul parallels the opinion which the apostles conveyed to the whole Jerusalem church in Acts 6. We must enquire, nonetheless, what governing powers were vested in the apostles, prophets and teachers. There is no evidence to suggest that either prophets or teachers exercised any rule within the churches, but the apostles are another matter in view of Paul's own concern to establish his claim to apostolic office.

As far as his own position is concerned, Paul unquestionably regarded his apostleship as investing him with particular authority. This is specially evident in the case of the incestuous person at Corinth (1 Cor. 5:5). He makes his pronouncement and expects the assembled church to accept his decision. He does not even suggest that the matter should be discussed. The Christian approach, in his view, is clear-cut. It was not so on all matters affecting the Corithian church, but even on these he expresses a fairly definite opinion (*cf.* 1 Cor. 7:12, 40). We may further say that in all his letters, whether to churches he has founded or to those where his personal presence is unknown, he assumes that his readers will accept his authority. We may deduce therefore that when he separates apostles from administrators, he is not dealing with matters of authority, but rather with practical organization. The task of apostles was authoritative for proclaiming and teaching (see the section below, pp. 768f.), but the administrators were presumably called to deal with the practical outworking of the principles laid down by the apostles.

Another list occurs in Ephesians 4:11, where once again the functions are described as 'gifts'. This list embraces apostles, prophets and teachers as in 1 Corinthians 12:28, but adds evangelists[200] and pastors. Again the functional aspect is uppermost. It is not to be supposed that these gifts did not sometimes overlap. What is again significant is that for Paul the work of the ministry is of much greater importance than any hierarchy of officials.

But the question arises whether in the pastoral epistles a totally different approach to church organization is encountered, and whether in view of this the Pauline origin of the epistles can be maintained. We need first to

---

[199] C. K. Barrett, *1 Corinthians*, pp. 295f. takes the word *antilēmpseis* (gifts of support) as possibly a foreshadowing of the work of deacons and *kybernēseis* (gifts of direction) of that of bishops.

[200] M. Barth, *Ephesians 1*, p. 438, notes that the evangelist's work was narrower than that of apostles, but nevertheless resembled and continued that of the apostles.

examine the approach in the Pastorals before a convincing answer can be given and we note the following facts.

First of all, only two groups of officials are mentioned, bishop-elders and deacons. There may have been a third group, an order of deaconesses, but this is a matter of debate. Two passages deal specifically with bishops (1 Tim. 3:1–7[201] and Titus 1:7–9). The second passage furnishes the key to the first, because Titus 1:5–7 speaks of elders, which are then linked to the office of bishop. The *episkopos* was therefore an elder who performed the special function of oversight.[202] There is no need to suppose that we are at any different stage from the Philippian situation, only here we have lists of desirable qualities to be sought in those aspiring to the office.

The qualities are so basic that it reflects on the general lack of suitable people. The chief concern is that the holders of the office should set a worthy example to others. They were to be apt to teach, because their function was to pass on what they themselves had been taught (*cf.* also 2 Tim. 2:2).[203] These references to bishops are far removed from the monarchical episcopacy (one church, one bishop) which developed later. It should be noted that both Timothy and Titus were instructed to make appointments. They were not, however, adopting an archiepiscopal role, as some have suggested, but were performing the function of delegates of the apostle Paul. Care must be taken not to read back into the pastoral epistles the processes of a later age.

The function of deacons is not defined (1 Tim. 3:8ff.), but the qualities required for eligibility for the office run parallel to those for bishops in that most emphasis is placed on the example of their lives.[204] Those chosen to run the church must be known by their capacity for running their own households. No machinery is suggested for choosing the right men. These epistles give no more support than the rest of the NT for the view that the Christian community should be democratically run. We have not moved far, in fact, from the position in Acts 6:3, where it was left to the discernment of the church to pick men full of the Spirit who were suitable for the job in hand.

Although it is not clear whether an official order of deaconesses existed,[205] since the remarks in 1 Timothy 3:11 could refer to deacons' wives,

---

[201] A recent Catholic writer has attempted to make a distinction between the use of *presbyteros* in 1 Timothy and Titus, and would not, therefore, agree that the Titus passage must be used to interpret the passage in 1 Tim. 3:1–7. *Cf.* J. P. Meier, '*Presbyteros* in the Pastoral Epistles', *CBQ* 35, 1973, pp. 323–345.

[202] Dibelius-Conzelmann, *The Pastoral Epistles* (Eng. trans. *Hermeneia*, 1972, from *LHB*, [3]1955), p. 132, comment that the abrupt introduction of 'bishop' in 1:7 supports the hypothesis that this is an interpolation. J. N. D. Kelly, *The Pastoral Epistles*, p. 230, is nearer the point when he recognizes that the bishop was chosen from among the elders, which lessens if it does not remove the abruptness. He considers the two titles 'not virtually, though not strictly interchangeable'.

[203] For comments on this process of authorized teaching, *cf.* my *The Pastoral Epistles*, pp. 138f.

[204] *Cf. ibid.*, pp. 83ff.

[205] J. N. D. Kelly, *op. cit.*, p. 83, thinks that an order of women deacons is a more likely interpretation

there was certainly an authorized list of widows who were eligible for church support (1 Tim. 5:9). These widows, who were to be over sixty years of ago, were regarded as still useful for practical duties within the community. Again it may be noted that the organizational side was loose, dictated by practical considerations rather than by a rigid system.

There is no reason to suppose that the approach to church order reflected in the Pastorals must be later than Paul's time.[206] A dominant factor in his approach is order, and it is not difficult to see how he would have taken steps to instruct his closest associates, Timothy and Titus, in the best way to ensure this. The situation in the Pastorals is no more advanced than that in the Philippian church.It would have been short-sighted if Paul had left no instructions about the government of the church. This point about 'order' is also supported by Paul's advice to the Corinthian church that 'all things should be done decently and in order' (1 Cor. 14:40). In spite of this, Paul does not impose any system of church government upon the local communities to achieve this end. We shall consider next his approach to charismatic gifts, to discover what part these played in his conception of the church.

Charismatic gifts. There is a full discussion of spiritual gifts in 1 Corinthians, and brief lists in addition in Romans 12:6–8 and Ephesians 4:11. In the 1 Corinthians passages there are in fact three separate lists (12:28, 29–30, 8–10). From this evidence Ladd compiles a composite list of eighteen items.[207] An analysis of these items shows a wide variety, including offices (like apostle, teacher, prophet, evangelist), personal qualities (like discernment of spirits, faith, mercy, generosity) and other gifts (like knowledge, tongues, interpretation, administration). Some of the gifts are parallel to natural qualities, while others are more extraordinary phenomena. It would seem therefore that the *charismata* embraced the comprehensive spread of activity which made up the experience of the community. In view of this the 'gifts' must have played an important part in Paul's view of the church, and with this in mind require careful consideration, particularly because there have been many misunderstandings over this issue.

Mention has already been made of the *charismata* in the section on the doctrine of the Spirit (see pp. 564ff.). But here it will be the ecclesiastical importance of the gifts which are mainly in mind. We shall deal with the nature of the *charismata*, their relation to the baptism of the Spirit, and their

---

of 1 Tim. 3:11 than a reference to the wives of deacons. He is particularly influenced by the absence of the article before the word 'women', whereas the article would be expected if deacons' wives are in mind. Kelly suggests that the form of words means 'deacons who are women'. Kelly also thinks that the lack of any technical word for deaconesses in the NT is a significant pointer to the primitiveness of the Pastorals.

[206] *Cf.* the careful weighing of the evidence by J. N. D. Kelly, *op. cit.*, pp. 14ff.

[207] *Cf.* G. E. Ladd, *TNT*, pp. 534f.

relation to the official leadership of the churches.

(i) The nature of the charismatic gifts. The word *charisma* is found only once outside the Pauline epistles in the NT (in 1 Pet. 4:10), and may, therefore, justly be said to be particularly characteristic of the apostle.[208] It is clearly intended to show a close connection between the gifts and grace (*charis*). It is a reminder at once that spiritual gifts have meaning and relevance only within the covenant of grace. The gifts would never have been given if God's grace had not first paved the way through the processes of redemption. The gifts do not side-step the central redemptive activity of God, but are the consequence of it.

A question which needs settling is whether the *charismata* are specific possessions or whether they relate to the activity of exercising them. Take, for instance, the gift of faith; is this to be regarded as a possession in the sense of a gift of a special kind of faith, or is it an intensification of already existing faith? The problem is that Paul gives no definitions in his list of gifts. But since he includes a mixture of gifts, some of which may be regarded as activities and others of which may be understood as possessions, it is likely that he did not make a clear distinction between them.

Some have confidently asserted that *charisma* is not a possession or office, but a particular manifestation of grace.[209] But others as confidently assert that possession of an office can itself be a *charisma*.[210] There is no doubt an element of truth in both points of view, and neither should be stressed to the total exclusion of the other. If a person, for instance, manifests the gift of leadership, he may exercise that activity independent of any specific office in the church. On the other hand, if a person possesses an office, he will only effectively fill it if he also possesses the *charisma* for it. It is highly questionable whether in Paul's mind the two things were ever separated. The right understanding of the character of the gifts affects our interpretation of his view of the relationship between the *charismata* and the institutions within the church, which is discussed below.

Another issue is the relation of *charismata* to natural gifts. Because of the nature of the former as essentially an activity of the Spirit of God in which God himself takes the initiative, some distinction must be made between them and natural gifts. This is not to say that in Paul's view God did not make use of natural gifts.[211] Indeed, we cannot exclude the intensification

---

[208] J. D. G. Dunn, *Jesus and the Spirit*, pp. 205f., maintains that the concept is almost entirely of Pauline origin.

[209] *Cf.* Dunn, *ibid.*, p. 254.

[210] *Cf.* H. Ridderbos, *Paul*, p. 446.

[211] F. C. Baur, *Paul* 2 (Eng. trans. 1875), p. 172, regarded the *charismata* as exaltations of natural gifts. J. R. W. Stott, *Baptism and Fullness* (²1975), pp. 90ff., takes a similar line when he affirms that *charisma* does not give gifts which are not naturally present. He maintains that the Spirit's work 'intensifies' or 'Christianizes' natural endowments. He cites John Owen's *Pneumatology or A Discourse concerning the Holy Spirit* (⁴1835), p. 310, to the effect that two kinds of spiritual gifts exist: those exceeding men's faculties, and those consisting of extraordinary improvements in men's faculties.

of natural gifts through the operation of the Spirit. Paul's view of the running of the community was nevertheless God-centred, not man-centred. Man, whether individually or in community, must be dependent on the Spirit of God, and all Paul's teaching on the *charismata* is directed to that end. We may say that the wide-ranging variety of the gifts testifies to Paul's conviction that nothing worthwhile could be accomplished apart from the activity of God. He never supposed that knowledge, or wisdom, or utterance in the service of God could come by natural intellectual capacities.

(ii) The reception of the charismatic gifts. As there has been debate over their precise nature, so there has been difference of opinion over when the gifts are bestowed. The two main views are either that the gifts are received with the coming of the Spirit at conversion, or that they are bestowed at a subsequent baptism of the Spirit which is distinct from the conversion experience. As far as the evidence of Paul is concerned there seems little support for the second view, which is almost always argued from certain passages in Acts. Paul is certainly explicit that no-one can call Jesus Lord except by the Spirit (Rom. 8:16ff.; 1 Cor. 12:3). He nowhere speaks in terms of a subsequent baptism of the Spirit, and it must be assumed, therefore, that the *charismata* were not given as a special endowment.

It cannot be denied that he writes as if all the Corinthians share in the gifts of the Spirit (*cf.* 1 Cor. 12:4f.). Admittedly he urges the readers to desire the higher gifts (1 Cor. 12:31) as if some strong urge is needed if the best gifts are to be obtained.[212] But since in the same passage, he has just categorically stated that the Spirit distributes to each one according to his own will (1 Cor. 12:11), he cannot mean that any particular gift can be had for the asking. What he is combatting is an over-emphasis on the ecstatic manifestations to the neglect of those less spectacular, but nevertheless more significant, gifts. It is not without considerable importance that in the passages in this chapter in which lists of gifts are given, an ecstatic gift such as speaking in tongues takes a lowly place, while the less spectacular gifts are given priority.

The key to Paul's approach lies in his conviction that the gifts of the Spirit are intended 'for the common good' (1 Cor. 12:7) and for the building up of the church (1 Cor. 14:12). Where the Corinthians were clearly going wrong was in regarding the gifts as means of personal display; the community aspect of the gifts was being forgotten. Paul's approach comes over unmistakably when he insists that all public manifestations of speaking in tongues should be accompanied by interpretation, because only so could the church be edified (*cf.* 1 Cor. 14:13ff.). It is this aspect of the edification

---

[212] A. Bittlinger, *Gifts and Graces*, (1967), p. 73, interprets 1 Cor. 12:31 rather differently, by considering it to mean, 'You are striving after the greatest gifts'. He then takes this to mean that the Corinthians were striving after being apostles, preachers, teachers.

of the community which is basic in understanding Paul's view of the place of *charismata* in his doctrine of the church. This leads to a consideration of the effect of the gifts on the organization of the church.

(iii) The place of the charismata in the government of the church. We have already summarized Paul's references to certain offices within the Pauline churches, which carried with them a degree of authoritative leadership. We have also considered some of the *charismata* which touched on qualities of leadership. We need now to discuss the specific relation between the two aspects, the institutional and the charismatic.

One theory holds that Paul's basic view was that the church was charismatically controlled, that is to say that God makes his will known by those led by the Spirit and endowed with the gift of leadership. The church needed no organization, since individuals responded to the dictates of the Spirit. If this theory were correct, it would mean that the need for institutional offices did not arise until the charismatic ministry failed through a failure on the part of the church to respond to the dictates of the Spirit. It must, of course, be noted that in the Corinthian church there is no mention of church officials, only of charismatic gifts. It may seem reasonable to suppose that in this case church order was charismatically controlled and that this sets out the ideal state of affairs. Moreover, Paul views the church as a body in which each member has some *charisma*, although these vary and no-one is assumed to have *all* the gifts (*cf.* 1 Cor. 12:14ff.).

He certainly regarded the Corinthian church as a charismatic community, but his use of the body metaphor suggests that not all was harmony within this community. But lack of reference to any leadership may have arisen because the Corinthians considered themselves to be too 'spiritual' to require it.[213] There is strong probability that the Corinthian church was the exception rather than the general pattern, in which case it cannot be regarded as a norm. The other Pauline epistles, as well as the book of Acts, require that Paul saw some need for organization, and the theory expounded above makes no adequate allowance for this. It glosses over the fact that, parallel with charismatic ministry, there was also some kind of institutional ministry (especially apostles, elders, bishops, deacons). No account of Paul's doctrine of the ministry which does not include both elements is true to the evidence.

The most reasonable view of the relationship between the *charismata* and other ministries is that the exercise of *charisma* is itself considered to be a ministry.[214] The gifts are considered to be in the service of others with the

---

[213] *Cf.* J. D. G. Dunn, *Unity and Diversity in the New Testament*, pp. 109ff., who regards Paul's view of the ministry from the point of view of the body of Christ as a charismatic community. Certainly the body metaphor implies that every member performs a function, but Paul's letters to Corinth do not suggest that this was actually happening.

[214] *Cf.* Ribberbos, *Paul*, p. 443.

sole purpose of the edification of the church. Whether the church is edified by means of *charismata* or by the regular ministry of church teachers is immaterial. The cleavage supposed between the two is occasioned by the view that the former is superior to the latter, but this grading finds no support in Paul's epistles. Moreover the antithesis between them is false since it assumes, erroneously, that the offices are not appointments of the Spirit.

A more pressing problem is to decide where the basis of authority lay, whether in a *charisma* or in an office.[215] To answer this we must begin by considering Paul's view of apostolic authority since this played an important part in his concept of the church. Moreover, apostles are included in Paul's list of *charismata*, and a proper understanding of his views on this will throw light on the relation between gifts and office.[216]

There is no denying that Paul held a high view of apostolic authority. He further regarded apostleship as a special gift from God (Rom. 1:5; Gal. 1:1). His own calling as apostle placed him on an equal footing with the Jerusalem apostles (*cf.* his argument in Gal. 2). He recognizes that the special qualification of an apostle was that he was a witness to the resurrected Christ and was commissioned by Christ. He claims a revelation which fulfils these conditions (Gal. 1:1, 12). The apostles were entrusted with a missionary task and Paul appeals to his calling as minister to the Gentiles (Rom. 1:5f.; Gal. 2:8). In his list of specific resurrection appearances in 1 Corinthians 15, Paul includes himself as one 'untimely born' (15:8), which suggests that he was the last. For him apostleship was an office restricted to a definite group and was in no sense an ongoing phenomenon.

There appear to be some who were calling themselves apostles at Corinth, whose views Paul found it necessary to combat. In 2 Corinthians 11:13 he calls them 'false apostles' who had disguised themselves as 'apostles of Christ'. They had clearly done this because of the authority it gave them. Since there is a somewhat scornful reference in 2 Corinthians 11:5; 12:11 to 'superlative apostles', they were obviously claiming greater authority than Paul. One possible explanation is that these 'false apostles' were from Jerusalem and were claiming to speak on the authority of the Jerusalem apostles.[217] In this case it could be that Paul is in opposition to the idea of the Jerusalem apostles imposing their authority on a local Gentile church, but it is more probable that the false apostles were usurping an

[215] *Cf.* Dunn, *op. cit.*, pp. 272f.
[216] A. von Harnack, *The Constitution and Law of the Church in the First Two Centuries* (Eng. trans. 1910), tried to distinguish between religious (charismatic) and administrative ministries: Apostles were placed among the former.
[217] *Cf.* C. K. Barrett, 'Paul's Opponents in II Corinthians', *NTS* 17, 1970–1, pp. 233–254. *Cf.* also E. Käsemann, 'Die Legitimatät des Apostels', *ZNW* 41, 1942, pp. 33–71.

authority which is no sense belonged to them.[218] The Corinthian situation highlights the great influence which appeal to apostolic authority could command.

Granted the unique authority invested in the apostles, we note the following consequences. (i) Apostolic ministry was distinguished from all other ministry. (ii) Apostolic authority was not localized but universal. (iii) The apostles were in no sense appointed by the church, but rather were foundations to it (*cf.* Eph. 2:20). (iv) Their task was not only to lay foundations, but also to contribute to the upbuilding of the church. At least this is how Paul views his office, as his letters abundantly demonstrate. As an apostle he also exercised his authority in combating wrong doctrine (as in Galatians and Colossians) and in ensuring the development of an orderly society.

If we enquire further into the manner in which Paul exercised his own authority, we shall gain valuable insights into the whole area of church government. Dunn[219] makes three observations which concisely sum up the matter. (i) Paul rarely uses words of command except where obliged to do so by his opponents. The great majority of his instructions are exhortations rather than commands. (ii) He is careful not to infringe the freedom of his converts. He does not exercise his authority in an authoritarian way. He recognizes that its effectiveness depends on the support of the Spirit-led community (*cf.* 1 Cor. 5:3–5; 2 Cor. 2:6–8). (iii) The exercise of apostolic authority is limited to matters arising out of his commission. Where, for instance, Paul has the backing of a word from the Lord, he commands obedience; but he refrains from this authoritative approach when offering his own opinion, even when he is convinced that he is led by the Spirit (*cf.* 1 Cor. 7:25 and 1 Cor. 7:40).

Although Dunn concludes that outside certain limits Paul was as dependent on the *charisma* of the Spirit as any other, it must be recognized that Paul expected his own example to be powerful, even when he gave no commands. Due weight must be given to his frequent appeals to his own work among them when he writes to those churches which he has founded. We cannot under-rate the unique position that the apostle held, and knew that he held, among the Gentile churches. It is also clear that he never holds up his apostolic office as a pattern for other offices. The apostolic office existed for a specific purpose and for a limited time. Even where no commands are given, we cannot imagine, therefore, that Paul is leaving his readers the option whether or not to follow his advice.

The other ministries within the church are on a different footing, but

---

[218] L. Goppelt, *Apostolic and Post-Apostolic Times*, p. 100, takes the view that these people had a wrong idea of the apostolic office. They were emphasizing their Palestinian roots and thought that was the way to become 'apostles of Christ'. He thinks that they represented a pre-gnostic Judaism.

[219] *Cf.* Dunn, *op. cit.*, pp. 277ff.

the question of their authority still remains important for the purpose of assessing Paul's doctrine of the church. *Prophets* speaking under the inspiration of the Spirit could command some authority while the gift was being exercised,[220] but there is nothing to suggest that they possessed authority in an official capacity at other times. Revelation can come through prophecy (1 Cor. 14:6, 26, 30).[221] Moreover prophets are twice linked with apostles (Eph. 3:5; 2:20), although there may be some doubt here whether Christian prophets are meant. Paul himself makes prophetic pronouncements (*cf.* Rom. 11:25; 1 Cor. 15:51; 1 Thes. 4:13ff.) about future events. He also recognized the function of prophecy in revealing the will of God for the present (*cf.* 1 Tim. 1:18). Naturally those who continually exercised the gift of prophecy would be placed in some kind of leadership,[222] although it would not necessarily be in an official capacity.

Parallel to the prophets were the *teachers*, and the question arises how Paul distinguished between the functions of each. The task of teaching was probably more concerned with passing on the traditions than with such new inspirational insights as prophets would transmit. All that constituted the 'gospel', including the careful passing on of the oral traditions of the life and teaching of Jesus (before the circulation of written accounts), would be the special concern of teachers. They were probably occupied with the catechetical instruction of new converts. Their part in the upbuilding of the church was indispensable for the development of a strong community whose members had a grasp of doctrine.

Two other functional ministries may be considered together: evangelists and pastors. *Evangelists* are mentioned by Paul only rarely, but several of his associates certainly shared with him in the task of evangelism. The main function in mind seems to be the proclamation of the gospel to those outside the church (*cf.* 2 Tim. 4:5). Naturally the function of evangelism was shared by the various members of the communities.[223] The gift might be found as much among the non-office bearers as among office bearers.[224] It is highly improbable that Paul was thinking of a special group whose sole task was evangelism. Evangelists do not appear *per se* to have exercised

---

[220] *Cf.* E. E. Ellis, 'Prophesy in the New Testament Church – and Today', in *Prophetic Vocation in the New Testament and Today* (ed. J. Panagopoulos, 1977), pp. 46–57. *Cf.* also D. Hill, 'Christian Prophets as Teachers or Instructors in the Church', pp. 108–130, in the same volume. The latter sees the role of prophets in the Pauline churches as a ministry of pastoral teaching and instruction. *Cf.* also certain essays in E. E. Ellis, *Prophecy and Hermeneutic in Early Christianity* (1978).

[221] G. Delling, *Worship in the New Testament* (Eng. trans. 1962), pp. 29f., suggests that the high estimation of prophecy in 1 Cor. 14 is probably derived from recollection of OT prophecy and from its value for building up the church.

[222] H. Greeven, 'Propheten, Lehrer, Vorsteher bei Paulus', *ZNW* 44, 1952–3, pp. 1–43.

[223] M. Barth, *Ephesians*, p. 438, suggests that although the work of evangelists was narrower than that of apostles, their work resembled and continued that of the latter.

[224] Philip is specifically called an evangelist in Acts 21:8 and Timothy is urged to do the work of an evangelist in 2 Tim. 4:5. Not many have followed D. Hadidian's view that the 'evangelists' mentioned in the NT were gospel writers, 'tous de evangelistas in Eph. 4:11', *CBQ* 28, 1966, pp. 317ff.

any function in the administration of the church.

Pastors were concerned with the care of the church. This function is drawn from the metaphor of the shepherd watching over his flock.[225] In Paul's epistles the idea has a distinct link with Jesus' own function as shepherd (Jn. 10; *cf.* 1 Pet. 2:25), with Jesus' commission to Peter (Jn. 21), and with the Acts account of Paul's exhortation to the Ephesian elders (Acts 20:28). This 'caring' function was not lost when the overseeing function of the elders (bishops) was expounded by Paul (1 Tim. 3:5). The pastoral function was therefore an activity of leadership rather than an office in its own right. It was essential for the well-being of the church that care should be extended to the members, and it is not surprising that pastoral qualities should be expected in overseers. The *charismata* could not be separated from the office. Indeed, it would seem most reasonable to suppose that the charismatic ministries are not to be placed as antitheses to the non-charismatic offices, as if the latter supplanted the former. In the Pauline churches the two groups had no clear line of distinction between them. Both carried authority in their own way.

To conclude this section we must consider the place of certain gifts within the church which have been the subject of considerable debate, notably speaking with tongues (*glossolalia*) and the ministry of *healing*. They must consequently find some place in a discussion of Paul's idea of the church. He not only admitted the legitimacy of *glossolalia*,[226] but claimed to possess the gift himself (1 Cor. 14:18). The main question which arises is the importance he attached to it.[227] Did he regard it as a gift which should be exercised in public worship or in private? And did he regard it as a gift which all should covet?

In answer to the second question, it must be said that Paul did not imagine that all would possess it (*cf.* 1 Cor. 12:29–30). As far as the first question is concerned, there seems little doubt that Paul preferred to regard it as a private rather than a public manifestation. He is most concerned with the edification of the church, and rates prophecy as preferable to *glossolalia* in this respect (*cf.* 1 Cor. 14:3, 4). The only circumstance in which he will grant the value of a public manifestation of tongues is when an interpretation is also given (1 Cor. 14:27–28). Moreover, the phenomemon even then must be arranged in an orderly manner, so that at most

---

[225] For one view of the function of the bishop which recognizes his caring function while placing greater emphasis on his presiding function, *cf.* C. Spicq's excursus in *Les Épîtres Pastorales* (EB, 1947), pp. 84ff.

[226] On the difficulty of determining the precise meaning of *glōssais lalein* in the NT even against the background of early Christian and non-Christian writings, *cf.* S. D. Currie, 'Speaking in Tongues', *Int* 19, 1965, pp. 274–294.

[227] We cannot discuss here the precise nature of *glossolalia* as understood by Paul. C. K. Barrett, *1 Corinthians*, p. 299, interprets it in the sense of unintelligible speech and considers the possibility that 1 Cor. 13:1 may imply some kind of heavenly speech (tongues of angels). J. Behm. *TDNT* 1, pp. 722ff., understands it of ecstatic utterance. But R. H. Gundry, ' "Ecstatic Utterance" (NEB)?' *JTS* 17, 1966, pp. 299ff., strongly contests this and argues that the tongues must mean foreign languages.

not more than three speak in tongues on one occasion, and then only singly (1 Cor. 14:27). It seems that *glossolalia*, which Paul mentions only in his Corinthian correspondence, had got out of hand at Corinth and was being over-rated to such an extent that confusion had resulted. Unbelievers were calling the Christians mad (1 Cor. 14:23).[228]

While Paul therefore does not forbid *glossolalia* (1 Cor. 14:39) and urges the same approach on the Corinthians, he does not consider that this gift is to be sought after in the same way as prophecy. This cautious approach shows that in the government of the church he places high value on orderliness (1 Cor. 14:40), and would certainly not support the giving of priority to anyone on the grounds of the exercise of *glossolalia* alone.[229] The same may be said of the gift of healing which he recognizes as among the *charismata*. It is linked with 'working of miracles' (1 Cor. 12:10, 28), and with 'faith' as a special gift (1 Cor. 12:9). We note that Paul acknowledged that he himself performed signs (Rom. 15:18–19); 2 Cor. 2:12). But he is careful not to over-rate healings. Healers are not placed in a position of leadership. They are simply regarded as possessing special manifestations of the Spirit's power, and their ministry does not imply that all sickness will be banished by the gospel. Moreover not all are expected to possess the gift of healing (1 Cor. 12:30).

Because the *charismata* are so evidently the work of the Spirit and are distributed according to the sovereign will of God (1 Cor. 12:11), it is impossible to predict when and where they will be manifested. It may be that only Corinth witnessed the phenomenon of the more spectacular gifts, although it cannot be deduced from the lack of reference to them in other letters of Paul that they were necessarily unknown in the other churches. What may confidently be said is that these spectacular gifts did not play a dominant part in the activity of those churches, at least to the extent apparent at Corinth.[230] All the evidence suggests that the *charismata* and the institutional ministries existed side by side and that the edification of the church was dependent on both.

Order and discipline. Although insights are gained from other sources, it is again to the Pauline epistles that we must turn for clearer light on early Christian order and discipline. We have already noted that Paul lays down

[228] J. P. M. Sweet, 'A Sign for Unbelievers: Paul's Attitude to Glossolalia', *NTS* 13, 1967, pp. 240–257. Sweet draws a distinction between Paul's attitude towards *glossolalia* which was not hostile and the Corinthians' estimate of it which he sees as 'childish'. He rejects the view that Paul regarded *glossolalia* as necessary for the Christian life.

[229] J. D. G. Dunn, *Jesus and the Spirit*, p. 248, suggests that Paul was trying to control what he could not forbid without loss of his authority. In 1 Cor. 14:19 he comes near to discouraging the gift of tongues in public worship.

[230] J. D. G. Dunn, *op. cit.*, pp. 266ff., discusses the threat to the community which arose from the *charismata*. Although this is most obvious at Corinth, he finds traces of it also in Rome and Thessalonica.

the need for decency and order (1 Cor. 14:40), which covers the wide spectrum of the church's activities. There must be a certain dignity in the conduct of affairs.[231] In some cases he gives instructions, which come to have the character of guiding principles. This is specially evident in 1 Corinthians, 1 and 2 Thessalonians and the pastoral epistles. Nevertheless, there is an absence of legalism in Paul's approach. In the case of incest Paul expects disciplinary action to be taken (1 Cor. 5:5) and this is to be done by the community in assembly. On the other hand, the same church is warned not to crush an offender through an over-severe discipline (2 Cor. 2:5 ff.).[232] The same concern for order and discipline is found in the pastoral epistles (*cf.* 1 Tim. 1:20; 2:1–7; 4:11f.; Tit. 2:1f.). If the advice has become more formalized, this is because it is given to close associates; but no wedge can be driven between the earlier Pauline epistles and the Pastorals on the question of church discipline.

Some comment must be made on the form of judgment decided by Paul in respect of the case of incest. The man concerned was to be delivered to Satan 'for the destruction of the flesh, that his spirit may be saved in the day of the Lord Jesus' (1 Cor. 5:5). There seems little doubt that some form of expulsion from the church is intended here, at least temporarily. The 'destruction of the flesh' may refer to some physical affliction which might effect a spiritual change of heart (*cf.* also 1 Cor. 11:30).[233] This disciplinary concept of the Christian community is in line with the teaching of Jesus in Matthew 18. Those whose activities or attitudes put them in opposition to the true aims of the community are not to be tolerated (*cf.* 1 Tim. 1:20; Tit.3:10f.). Paul advises strong action where impurity or false doctrine are undermining the church's stand.

Arising out of what has just been said about authority it follows that sufficient sanction existed for the carrying out of discipline. There was constant constraint. The spirits of the prophets were subject to the prophets (1 Cor. 14:29–30).[234] There was no place for individualism. Paul does not permit his converts to forget that all are answerable to Christ. This close-

---

[231] A. Bittlinger, *Gifts and Graces*, pp. 116f., speaks of dynamic orderliness which is sharply distinguished from static orderliness. He sees the guiding principle of the former as the willingness of each member to listen to the one Spirit.

[232] For an examination of Paul's approach to discipline in both Corinthian letters, *cf.* D. R. Hall, 'Pauline Church Discipline', *TB* 20, 1969, pp. 3–26.

[233] C. K. Barrett, *1 Corinthians*, pp. 126f. considers the possibility that the destruction of the flesh may refer to physical death. But this interpretation is not without its difficulties, since it is not clear how physical death can lead to spiritual salvation. Barrett suggests that all that Satan can claim is the flesh. He is severely limited in the scope of his destructive activities. *Cf.* J. N. D. Kelly, *The Pastoral Epistles*, p. 58, for a discussion of the similar statement in 1 Tim. 1:20.

[234] H. Conzelmann, *1 Corinthians* (Eng. trans. *Hermeneia*, 1975, from *KEK*, 1969), p. 245, is of the opinion that 'the others' (*hoi alloi*) who are to test what the prophets said were themselves prophets, not the whole congregation. C. K. Barrett, *op. cit.*, p. 328, however, supports the latter view, on the grounds that the test mentioned in 12:3 could be applied by any Christian, not just a prophet.

knit community 'in Christ' must in his view be mindful that no part can act without affecting the whole. Discipline is therefore necessary to ensure the healthy operation of the whole body.

There is little information in Paul's letters about the process of ordination, except in the pastoral epistles. Timothy is reminded of his own 'ordination', if this is a right interpretation of the 'gift' that was received through the laying on of hands (2 Tim. 1:6). According to 1 Timothy 4:14 the hands were the hands of elders, and the 'gift' was given 'by prophetic utterance'.[235] It is significant that in 1 Timothy 4:14 Paul does not say that he himself had any share in this, although he did in 2 Timothy 1:6. The laying on of hands did not convey the grace of office, as some would maintain who claim an apostolic succession of ministry which perpetuates itself. It indicated that the person concerned was set apart for a specific task in the presence of the members of the community through its representatives (cf. the commissioning of Paul and Barnabas in Acts 13:1–3, which was also accompanied by the laying on of hands).

THE ROLE OF WOMEN IN THE CHURCH

The main teaching on the important subject of the position of women in the NT church is found in Paul's epistles. At the same time Paul's approach to the matter has given rise to considerable debate. It is important to note at the outset that in the contemporary world women were almost universally regarded as inferior to men. This was particularly so in the Jewish world which was entirely male-dominated. A few areas in the Gentile world, like Macedonia, accorded women more rights, but the pagan world as a whole had no conception of the equality of the sexes. Moreover education was denied to Jewish girls and was not widespread among the girls of other nations. It was in such a climate of male orientation that the Christian communities developed.

Paul's firm assertion in Galatians 3:28 that in Christ there is 'neither male nor female' was revolutionary, for it went against the contemporary belief in the superiority of the male. It cannot be reserved simply for the standing of the sexes in relation to salvation, as if the principle of male superiority still applied to every other field except salvation; for it must be understood in a parallel way to the abolition of the other antitheses linked with it in the context. The tension between Jew and Gentile, or slave and freedman, would never have been resolved if the equality was intended only in a spiritual sense. What is true 'in Christ' affects all other human relationships. There is no doubt that Paul saw the crumbling of the most deep-rooted prejudices through the Christian gospel. If all are one in Christ Jesus, as he affirms, this must mean that former prejudices can no longer be carried

---

[235] On this verse, cf. my *The Pastoral Epistles*, p. 98.

over in the Christian church. In order to appreciate the apostle's teaching on the position of women his statement in Galatians 3:28 must be given full weight. Indeed, it must be regarded as the key for understanding his other statements, some of which at first sight appear to be in conflict with the emancipation of women.

In the spiritual communities women had an equal status with men in that all were accepted on the same basis of the work of Christ on their behalf. Men could claim no advantage over women. Such new-found equality on the part of women was in stark contrast with their Jewish[236] or pagan environment, and it is no wonder that problems arose while the process of adjustment was being put into effect. Some of the Christian women were undoubtedly over-reacting and were tending to abuse their liberty. The apostle Paul found it necessary to propose certain restraints to maintain decency and order within the community, especially in worship.

His advice falls into two categories: one in relation to women speaking in the church, and the other in relation to the question of authority. In 1 Corinthians 14:34f. he urges that women should keep silent in the churches,[237] but there has been much debate over what he meant. He urges subordination, but he does not specify to whom. Since this statement is followed by another which urges women to consult their husbands at home, the subordination has been interpreted in relation to the husband. But it could relate to teaching,[238] or to judging men (in view of verse 29b),[239] or to the order of worship.[240] Moreover, the statements in verses 34 and 35 have been regarded as the views of a certain faction within the church[241] rather than of Paul himself. Whatever the solution to the problem, the burden of the whole context within which this saying occurs is the need for orderly worship. Paul would tolerate nothing which reduced Christian worship to disorder, and if the behaviour of certain women was resulting in such disorder it is understandable that he would urge silence. But it is by no means certain that he was enunciating a principle which was applicable in all contexts.

The fact that women were permitted to pray and prophesy on an equal footing with men should be set over against the discussion on 1 Corinthians 14:34–35. 1 Corinthians 11:5 appears to be at variance with the injunction to silence, but it cannot be supposed that in writing to the Corinthians Paul

---

[236] On the position of women in Judaism, *cf.* P. K. Jewett, *Man as Male and Female* (1975), pp. 86ff; J. Jeremias, *Jerusalem in the Time of Jesus* (Eng. trans. 1969), pp. 359–376.

[237] S. Aalen, 'A Rabbinic Formula in 1 Cor. 14:34', in *Studia Evangelica* 2 (ed. F. L. Cross, 1964), discusses the use of 'not permitted' in this verse and shows why it is linked with a reference to the law. Prohibition deriving from the law carried a binding character, according to contemporary Jewish usage.

[238] *Cf.* K. Stendahl, *The Bible and the Role of Women* (1966), p. 30, who relates the 'silence' to the practice of women asking questions publicly in worship.

[239] So J. B. Hurley, 'Did Paul require Veils or the Silence of Women?', *WTJ* 35, 1973, pp. 190–220.

[240] *Cf.* E. Kähler, *Die Frau in den Paulinischen Briefen* (1960), p. 61.

[241] *Cf.* J. A. Anderson, *Women's Warfare and Ministry* (1935), pp. 20ff.

would have so blatantly contradicted himself.[242] It is, of course, possible to maintain that women would pray and prophesy only in private,[243] in which case there would be no contradiction with 1 Corinthians 14:34–35. Nevertheless, the discussion over women's hair and the wearing of veils would have no point if the praying and prophesying were in private.[244] Because of this some have concluded that there is no way of reconciling the two passages. This, however, is a counsel of despair. It is better to suppose that Paul's distinction between the function of the sexes in worship in the Corinthian situation applied only when the women were going beyond the bounds of good order.

In the second relevant passage, 1 Timothy 2:11–15, the issue is different.[245] Paul urges women to learn in silence and to refrain from exercising authority over men. Whereas there is no specific reference to subordination, the OT passage cited in support sets out Adam to be less blameworthy than Eve, which might imply an element of subordination. At the same time a good case can be made for contending that Genesis 1 and 2 do not require the subordination of women since it was to be the man who would leave his family to join his wife, not vice versa. Nevertheless, Paul's own understanding of the teaching of the law certainly included some notion of subordination.

The main problem is to decide what kind of authority was in Paul's mind in 1 Timothy 2:12. It may be understood within the marriage relationship, but the context suggests a more general application. Since it is teaching which is the main focus of attention, it would seem best to relate the authority to the teaching, in which case the meaning would be that a woman was not entitled to instruct a man in an authoritative way.[246]

---

[242] W. O. Walker, '1 Corinthians 11:2–16 and Paul's view regarding women', *JBL* 94, 1975, pp. 94–110, not only regards the passages in the Pastorals and in Eph.–Col. as non-Pauline, but also rejects 1 Cor. 14:33b–36 and 1 Cor. 11:2–16. By this means he removes all the available passages which might be used to show Paul's approach to women.

[243] H. Ridderbos, *Paul*, p. 462, concludes for this view.

[244] On the question of veils and hair as affecting the position of women at Corinth, *cf.* W. J. Martin, '1 Cor. 11:2–16: An Interpretation', *Apostolic History and the Gospel* (ed. W. W. Gasque and R. P. Martin, 1970), pp. 231–241; M. Hooker, Authority on her Head', *NTS* 10, 1963–4, pp. 410ff.; A. Feuillet, 'L'homme "gloire de Dieu" et la femme "gloire de l'homme" ', *RB* 81, 1974, pp. 161–182; J. Fitzmyer, 'A feature of Qumran Angelology and the Angels of 1 Cor. 11:10', *NTS* 4, 1957–8, pp. 48–58; J. C. Greig, 'Women's Hats: 1 Cor. 11:1–16', *ExT* 69, 1958, pp. 156f.; S. Bedale, 'The meaning of *kephalē* in the Pauline Epistles', *JTS* 5, 1954, p. 211; J. B. Hurley, 'Did Paul require Veils?' *WTJ* 35, 1973, pp. 190–220.

[245] It must be noted this passage occurs in a context which deals with public prayer (1 Tim. 2:8–10). Some have seen verse 8 as implying that only the men should pray (*cf.* J. N. D. Kelly, *The Pastoral Epistles*, pp. 65f.; C. K. Barrett, *The Pastoral Epistles*, 1963, pp. 53f.). But this is not the only interpretation (*cf.* my *Pastoral Epistles*, pp. 73ff.). It is highly unlikely that Paul would link the manner in which men pray with the way in which women dress, unless he was also thinking of women praying (*cf.* again 1 Cor. 11:5).

[246] There is some question over the exact meaning of *authentein* in 1 Tim. 2:12. According to Dibelius-Conzelmann, *The Pastoral Epistles* (Eng. trans. Hermeneia, 1972, from LHB, [3]1955), p. 47, there is evidence from the first century BC of the word bearing the meaning 'self-assured, firm conduct'. If this is the sense in which Paul uses it, it would refer to self-confident teaching on the part of women over men, and it is

It is not impossible that this should then be understood against the background of the Adam and Eve story, in which Adam allowed himself to be incorrectly instructed by Eve and therefore deceived. Paul's words cannot be made to mean that it is part of a woman's nature to be deceived,[247] nor do they exempt Adam from responsibility for his own transgression.

Since in the pastoral epistles women are permitted to teach children and other women (2 Tim. 1:5; 3:14f.; Tit. 2:3–4), it is clear that Paul is not suggesting that by nature women are not eligible to teach at all. Moreover, the deception of Eve is used in 2 Corinthians 11:3 as a parallel for any (male as well as female) who may be led astray from pure devotion to Christ. In view of the fact that Paul numbered several women among his fellow-workers, including Priscilla who had had a share in instructing a man (Apollos), it is hardly likely that he intended his words to Timothy to contain an absolute prohibition. It is more probable that he had in mind a particular situation at Ephesus, in which perhaps some of the women were proving gullible in face of the false teaching.[248]

It is a matter of considerable interest to discuss whether Paul permitted any women to have a part in the Christian ministry. We have already noted that 1 Timothy 3:11 could refer to women who were acting as deacons, although some interpret this verse as referring to deacons' wives. If deacons are in mind there is no need to suppose that an office is intended, but rather the thought is that any women who are doing the work of a deacon must possess certain specified qualities. Phoebe, of the church at Cenchrea, is described by Paul as a 'deacon' (Rom. 16:1); it is to be noted that no feminine form of this word occurs in the NT.[249]

Comment has already been made on women prophets and women praying at Corinth. At Philippi there were certainly several capable women, as the references to Lydia in Acts 16 and to Euodia and Syntyche in Philippians 4:2 show. Moreover, the older widows at Ephesus were to be enrolled for service as well as being supported financially (1 Tim. 5:9f.). All this evidence suggests that Paul saw the work of Christian women as indispensable

---

this which Paul deplores. Nevertheless, the stronger meaning 'to lord it over, to domineer' is equally relevant. If the latter is the true meaning, it provides a justification for Paul to urge silence.

[247] A. T. Hanson, *Studies in the Pastoral Epistles* (1968), pp. 65–77, discusses fully the reference to Eve in this context and comes to the conclusion that the author of the Pastorals (not Paul in his view) believed that women were more gullible than men and that they are redeemed through child-bearing and Christian behaviour. It is highly unlikely that Paul would have regarded child-bearing as a means of salvation. There is some justification in Jeremias' view that the reference to child-bearing is to offset the abstinence from marriage which the false teachers were advocating.

[248] *Cf.* my *The Pastoral Epistles*, p. 76.

[249] It is noticeable that various other women are mentioned in Rom. 16. One, Junia, appears to be numbered among the apostles, although not all are agreed that the name must refer to a woman. RSV has interpreted Rom. 16:7 differently in speaking of 'men of note'. Others mentioned are Mary, Tryphaena and Tryphosa, all of whom are noted for their work, and Julia. M. Goguel, *The Primitive Church* (Eng. trans. 1964), p. 553, admits as a bare possibility the idea that Junia was a woman apostle.

in any Christian community. Nevertheless there is no suggestion that he recognized that any woman was in a position of authority.

Another aspect of the radical change which the coming of Christ brought to the status of women relates to the married state. We have already noted that Paul uses the metaphor of the bride to represent the church, which illustrates the high regard in which he held the union between a man and a woman. It must be recognized that this gave the married woman a status within the Christian community which was fundamentally different from her status in the contemporary world.[251] Outside the church she had no rights, but 'in Christ', she was an essential part of her husband and without her the man was incomplete. The two became one flesh as God had intended. Paul gives no specific teaching about the position of the unmarried women, although he clearly regarded the single state as advantageous under certain circumstances.

The above survey has shown that Paul was very far from being the women-hater he is sometimes made out to be. On the contrary he grasped with uncanny clarity the liberating power of the gospel as it related to the inferior status of women. He saw the Christian communities to be in the vanguard of bringing dignity to womanhood.

Hebrews

In this epistle the Christian community is viewed almost entirely in terms of the wandering people of God.[252] The typology of the OT is exploited in the exposition. It comes out clearly in the application of the inheritance theme in Hebrews 3 and 4 and in the more extended high priest theme, both of which are based on the Israelite's experience in the wilderness.[253]

The writer identifies his readers with God's house in 3:6.[254] He is expounding his theme, therefore, not to individuals but to a corporate group. He has already alluded to the high priest's 'brethren' on whose behalf he makes expiation for the sins of the people (*laos*, 2:17). He is not thinking of an undefined group of people, but of those who become related to Christ through his sacrificial death. He uses the expression 'the people of God' to describe those for whom a rest remains (4:9). These are clearly the spiritual successors of the Israelites, who have exchanged faith for unbelief, and have therefore become eligible in the present ('today', 3:7, 13, 15; 4:7–8) for the inheritance of rest which the former Israelites forfeited.

In the exposition of the high-priest theme, the writer everywhere as-

---

[250] *Cf.* W. D. Thomas, 'The Place of Women in the Church at Philippi', *ExT* 83, 1972, pp. 117ff.

[251] *Cf.* P. K. Jewett, *Man as Male and Female*, pp. 139f.

[252] This led E. Käsemann to call his study of this epistle *Das wandernde Gottesvolk* (1957).

[253] F. F. Bruce, *Hebrews* (*NICNT*, 1964), pp. 62f., considers that both writer and readers of this epistle were familiar with the exodus typology in early Christian thinking.

[254] This concept may be paralleled to the words of Jesus in Mt. 16:18. It is also in line with Eph. 2:19 and 1 Pet. 4:17. *Cf.* P. E. Hughes, *Hebrews* (1977), pp. 137ff.

sumes the corporate nature of God's people, although there is little explicit expression of it. The high priest is *our* high priest, *i.e.* of those who draw near to God with full assurance of faith (10:22). He belongs to those who have made confession of their hope (10:23). Although the major exhortations emphasize individual responsibility, the OT background of the whole epistle forbids any individualizing of believers apart from the community. Each is a member of the community on the grounds of individual faith. Both in the OT and in this epistle, those in mind are God's people, for whom the high priest acts as a representative.

Nowhere in this epistle is there the suggestion that the church is the body of Christ. Rather the metaphor of a city finds a mention.[255] Mount Zion, the city of the living God and the heavenly Jerusalem are used in Hebrews 12:22, but they refer to those in heaven, not to those on earth. There is, of course, an implied connection between the earthly and the heavenly, with the heavenly regarded as the reality. The writer also speaks of the enrolment of the first-born in heaven (12:23), which points to a community[256] of a specific kind, recognized in heaven although not necessarily identifiable with any designated group on earth. In keeping with the general approach of this epistle what appears on earth has its true counterpart in heaven, and the heavenly aspect is more important than the earthly. We may say that the writer has no concept of the church as an ecclesiastical organization. He thinks only of a group of people, like nomads with no settled abode in this life, moving on to a city which is to come (13:14).[257]

On the theme of worship within the early community there is again very little in this epistle, surprisingly so in view of the cultic background of the whole. There is a clear exhortation not to forsake assembling together (10:25), which draws attention to the tendency of some to deviate from what was evidently common practice. But no indication is given of what the Christians did when assembled together, beyond mutual encouragement. The main burden of the epistle urges believers to draw near to God (*cf.* 4:16; 10: 24). Worship and adoration are therefore of utmost importance and must have formed the major constituent in the procedure in Christian assemblies. God is portrayed in a way to invite awe of him (12:28–29) as a result of which believers are exhorted to offer him acceptable worship. There is mention of 'confession' but again no indication of any form of liturgical creed. As already noted, the sacrificial ritual has been given a spiritual meaning and no longer consists of a *sine qua non* for worship in view of Christ's once for all and sufficient offering of himself.

---

[255] *Cf.* P. S. Minear, *Images of the Church in the New Testament*, pp. 92f.

[256] The word *ekklēsia*, which was an appropriate term for the assembly of Israel under Moses, is here used of the people of God under the new covenant, *cf.* Hughes, *op. cit.*, p. 548.

[257] *Cf.* R. J. McKelvey's discussion of the theme of the heavenly temple in the epistle to the Hebrews, *The New Temple* (1969), pp. 147ff.

Although the ministry of the Word is not described, there are allusions to the effectiveness of the Word. The many references to the OT not only show the powerful effect of the Word on the author, but also his assumption that the readers will recognize its authority. The description of the Word as living and active, more penetrating than a sword (4:12) also shows the powerful effect of the Word. Indeed, the universe is said to be upheld by the powerful word of the Son (1:3). The writer is intent on attaching special importance to the spoken and written Word of God, but he gives no indication of the public reading or studying of the Word. It should be noted that some scholars regard the whole epistle as being originally a homily; if this theory is correct, it would furnish an admirable example of an early Christian sermon in which expositon is intermixed with frequent exhortations.

With regard to church government we again find little indication. The epistle is not addressed to anyone in particular. No specific officials are named. When in the last chapter the leaders are mentioned (13:7, 17), the word used is *hēgoumenoi*, a Hellenistic Jewish term which conveys authority, but is not used in the sense of office.[258] The only apostle who is mentioned is Jesus Christ himself (Heb. 3:1). Church order seems still to be at a primitive stage.[259] There is as yet nothing approaching an ecclesiastical government. The church is under the supervision of the Spirit.

There are two probable references to baptism in this epistle. In 6:2 the mention of instruction about ablutions is best understood as including a reference to Christian baptism although not exclusively so (otherwise the plural would not have been used).[260] Since the statement occurs in a list of basic elements, this shows the importance of the rite.[261] It is also significant that it is linked with the laying on of hands. The other passage is 10:22–23, where the reference to hearts sprinkled and bodies washed is undoubtedly an allusion to Christian baptism.[262] Since it occurs in the context of a reference to the new way of approach 'by the blood' (10:19), this is yet

---

[258] *Cf.* F. Büchsel, *hēgeomai*, TDNT 2, p.907. He distinguishes the community seen in Heb. 13:7, 17, 24 from the 'pneumatic organism' in Paul, and thinks that we have here a high estimation of office which suggests a transition to catholicism. But respect for leaders is not incompatible with charismatic gifts, although admittedly no reference is made to the activity of the Spirit in the Hebrews references.

[259] It is noteworthy that although the ministry of Christ is described in Hebrews in priestly terms, nowhere is any office in the church so described. *Cf.* H. Küng, *Why priests?* (Eng. trans. 1972), pp. 28ff.

[260] P. E. Hughes, *Hebrews*, pp. 199ff., discusses the various explanations of the plural and concludes for a view which sees the ablutions as 'washings and baptisms, but, quite naturally, with particular respect to Christian baptism, by which all others are surpassed and replaced.'

[261] G. Delling, *Worship in the New Testament*, p. 135, thinks that Heb. 6:2 presupposes some form of baptismal instruction before baptism.

[262] J. D. G. Dunn, *Baptism in the Holy Spirit* (1970), pp. 211ff., relates Heb. 10:22 to conversion-initiation. He claims that no other view would have occurred to the writer, or to any other NT writer. But *cf.* G. R. Beasley-Murray, *Baptism in the New Testament*, p. 249, for the view that heart and body must be considered individually. Dunn regards them as together representing the entire personality, and, therefore, regards baptism as part of the process of conversion.

another instance of NT baptism being linked with the death of Christ.[263]

Some see an allusion to the Lord's supper in 13:10, where the Christian's altar is contrasted with the levitical altar. It must be noted, however, that there is no support for the view that the 'altar' is a description of the Lord's table, for nowhere else is such an identification made in the NT. Its use here is to represent the whole sacrificial work of Christ. The point of the statement is not to present an interpretation of the ordinance, but to demonstrate the superiority of Christianity over the Jewish cultus.[264]

James

The address of this letter ('To the twelve tribes in the dispersion', 1:1) shows at once a Jewish flavour in the author's view of the community. The specification of twelve tribes suggests in fact that Jewish Christians are in mind. In that case the 'dispersion' (*diaspora*) is probably to be understood in a sense similar to the Jewish dispersion, *i.e.* as a composite term for Jewish people living in non-Jewish areas. It must be admitted that this address is particularly vague and gives no indication whether scattered individuals or communities are in mind.

In the body of the letter two concepts are found side by side. In 2:2 'your assembly' (*synagōgē*) is mentioned, and yet in 5:14 there is a reference to the elders of the 'church' (*ekklēsia*). This mixture of the Jewish word for assembly with the term which came to be applied to both Jewish and Gentile communities is significant because it suggests that we are in a very early stage of church development.[265]

There are two main contributions which this epistle makes to our understanding of the doctrine of the church. The first concerns the essentially practical application of the principle of equality among members of the community. The rich cannot claim any privileges over the poor. Partiality in a Christian worship assembly is completely ruled out (2:1–7). The temptation for some to imagine that higher social status gave special facilities in a spiritual community shows how insidious the encroachment of purely economic power could be even in an early Christian assembly. James unequivocally condemns such an approach in Christian meetings.[266]

The second feature is the responsibility of the church over the individual

---

[263] *Cf.* Beasley-Murray, *op. cit.*, pp. 247ff. *Cf.* also Flemington, *The New Testament Doctrine of Baptism*, p. 98.

[264] *Cf.* P. E. Hughes' discussion of this passage, *Hebrews*, pp. 574ff.

[265] It is not likely that the reference to *synagōgē* means that Christians were still meeting in a Jewish synagogue, as if the latter belongs to the period before the break-away from Judaism. For a history of the word, *cf.* M. Dibelius and H. Greeven, *James* (Eng. trans. *Hermeneia*, 1976, from *KEK*, 1964), pp. 132ff. It is probable here that a Christian assembly was in mind, and if this is correct it would support an early period.

[266] According to Bo Reicke, *James, Peter and Jude* (*AB*, 1964), p. 27, the fact that the rich man wears a ring and a splendid garment (a toga) suggests that he was seeking political office and adherents. James is against the use of Christian assemblies for this purpose.

needs of its members, illustrated particularly in the case of spiritual healing (5:13ff.). Each believer has the facility to call on the elders of the church to anoint him if he is sick, and there is a promise that their prayers for him will be effective.[267] This is the only instance in the NT of specific instructions being given for spiritual healing. What is most important for our present purpose is that the community had elders in whom special authority in matters of prayer and faith were vested. This seems to suggest that corporate intercession is more effective than individual. The elders represented the whole community. No details are given regarding other duties, and it is highly probable that 'elders' here is a loose term for those most respected in the community, *i.e.*, the senior men.

One other feature may be noted. James discourages too many of his readers from becoming 'teachers' (3:1).[268] This suggests that there was a recognized teaching function and that some were exercising it in an improper way.

The Petrine epistles

Since the word' church' does not occur in either of these epistles, we are confined to certain allusions. The description of the people addressed in *1 Peter* as 'exiles' at once furnishes a clue. Christians are considered to be a group with no fixed anchorage here. In this there is a close parallel with Hebrews. There is also a marked difference between this view and the later ecclesiastical establishment. The 'exiles' in 1:1–2 are also known as those chosen, destined and sanctified by God.[269] The group in mind has therefore been initiated by God. It is a corporate whole only by virtue of the salvation inaugurated by God in Christ. The idea of exile is calculated to have a salutary effect on conduct (1:17).

The building imagery is also found in 1 Peter in the classic passage 2:4–8. Believers are like living stones built into a spiritual house. Here the individuals are given importance only as parts of a corporate whole, but again there is no question of an organization to which the believers belong. The organic has priority over the organizational. The cornerstone of the whole spiritual edifice is the rejected stone, *i.e.* Christ. (2:6). Although the building is not here described as a temple, as in Paul's epistles, the allusion to

---

[267] J. B. Mayor, *James* (³1913, r.p. 1954), p. 169, considers that *ekklēsia* is preferred to *synagōgē* when referring to elders because the former word is more appropriate to describe the general body of believers. He thinks the reference to elders here is after the Jewish pattern.

[268] R. V. G. Tasker, *James* (*TNTC*, 1956), p. 72, compares the mention of teachers here with the ambition of many Jewish parents to have their sons trained as rabbis. J. B. Adamson, *James* (*NICNT*, 1976), p. 140, mentions that in the Jewish diaspora there was an order of teachers and suggests that James was himself a member of that order. Nothing more is known about this except for the advice James gives to teachers about controlling their words.

[269] The strong OT flavour of the opening of this epistle leads to the conclusion that the 'elect' must be regarded as referring to the corporate people after the manner of Israel. Nevertheless, the selection under the new covenant is individual, as C. Spicq, *Les Épîtres de Saint Pierre* (*SB*, 1966), p. 39, points out.

the holy priesthood shows that that idea is not far from the writer's mind.

Another concept which has prominence is that of the people of God. Those who were once 'no people' have now become God's people (2:10). Moreover they are designated 'a chosen race, a royal priesthood, a holy nation, God's own (or God's special) people' (2:9).[270] Here there is a piling up of national and political images, which are nevertheless applied in an entirely non-political way. The qualifying adjectives in each case make this abundantly clear. Again the idea of an elect people is dominant and the divine initiative unmistakable. Each of the figures used here is essentially corporate. The repetition of the priesthood theme is significant, because it seems that Peter wished explicitly to stress that priesthood no longer was reserved for a select group, but belonged to all believers. The distinction between the Christian church and a community run by priests like Qumran is at once most marked. The whole community has the right of approach to God.

Arising from the images just considered is the implicit understanding of the Christian community as the spiritual Israel. One of the most notable features of 1 Peter is the strong background of exodus typology which is found. The description of the exiles in 1:1–2 (especially the 'sprinkling' with blood), the allusion to the passover (1:18–19), the whole range of imagery in 2:9, are all strongly indebted to the OT exodus theme.[271] This is in line with the other NT evidence which seen the Christian church as a spiritual fulfilment of Israel. It is particularly significant in an epistle written to Gentiles who were previously regarded as no-people. Indeed, the Gentile Christians must now regard themselves as distinct from their Gentile contemporaries (cf. 4:3).

Because both Petrine epistles are concerned with specific issues, it is not surprising that there is nothing in either on the subject of Christian worship. We may simply note that in both epistles there is a high view of God and this must have inculcated a worshipful approach. Moreover there is in 5:6 a specific injunction to humility.

There is rather more on Christian leadership, although even here the allusions are very general. Some system of eldership clearly existed, as 5:1 shows. The elders appear to be the only officials. Some indication is given of their function in pastoral terms. Peter is fond of the shepherd imagery, applying it not only to Christ, but also to the elders (2:25; 5:2). In the former case it is instructive to note that Christ is called 'Bishop' (*episkopos*). but none of the elders is. The church is described as 'the flock of God' (5:2)

---

[270] For a full discussion of the whole passage in which this comes, cf. J. H. Elliott, *The Elect and the Holy* (1966). See especially pp. 38–49 on the epithets for Israel. He sees verses 6–8 and verses 9–10 as conflations of OT passages centering on *lithos* and *laos tou Theou*.

[271] The way in which this exodus theme permeates the NT is well brought out by R. E. Nixon, *The Exodus in the New Testament* (1963). For comments on 1 Peter, cf. pp. 27f.

which needs shepherding. This is to be done in a non-authoritarian manner. The main function of the spiritual shepherds is to serve as examples and to lavish care on the flock.

This essentially tender view of the aim of office in the church is again in marked contrast to the authoritarian approach of the later monarchical bishops. The only kind of hierarchy is that of age, the more junior being subject to the more senior (5:5). It is probable in the light of this that the term 'elder' is used in this epistle in the sense of seniority in age rather than in the sense of ruling elder. Since each is to display humility towards others, there is no question of eldership implying superiority. The fact that Peter calls himself a fellow elder, considered by some to be an indication of non-apostolic origin, is more easily explicable if 'elder' refers to older men rather than to the office of presbyter. In addition to the mention of elder, there is the allusion to gifts in 4:10f. These gifts are specified as gifts of utterance and service.[272]

There is one passage in 1 Peter which mentions baptism (3:20–21), which is nevertheless a notorious crux of NT exegesis. Much debate has ranged around the connection between Christian baptism and the flood.[273] Whatever the answer to this problem there is no denying the importance which Peter places on baptism. It is set here in a confessional context.[274] It is probable that baptism is seen as a pledge in response to God's demand for faith and obedience.[275] It is specifically linked to the resurrection of Christ and the exaltation of Christ. The passage, moreover, denies any importance to the external act. The water itself possesses no magical properties. The moral response is all-important.

It would not be relevant here to discuss the baptismal liturgy theory of the origin of 1 Peter,[276] but if that theory could be substantiated it would give some insight into the form of service conducted at a baptism. If, as some suggest, the baptismal act took place at an interval between 1:21 and

---

[272] E. Best, *1 Peter*, pp. 167, suggests on the basis of 1 Pet. 4:10, that the elders would have received gifts for their office and the charismatic leadership was not set over against the administrative.

[273] J. D. G. Dunn, *Baptism in the Holy Spirit*, pp. 215f., in discussing the phrase 'saved through water' (1 Pet. 3:21), contends that Peter means that the water of baptism saves, but he goes on to relate this to the conscience: 'the prayer or pledge of baptism is efficacious of salvation simply because it is addressed to the risen one, is based on his resurrection, and results in a sharing of that new life from the dead' (p. 218). R. E. Nixon, *Studia Evangelica* 4 (ed. F. L. Cross, 1968), pp. 437ff., argues that *baptisma* here refers to Christian suffering. *Cf.* also R. T. France, in *New Testament Interpretation* (ed. I. H. Marshall), pp. 273ff.

[274] Some have seen this as part of a Christological hymn as, for instance, P. Lundberg, *La Typologie Baptismale dans L'Ancienne Église* (1942), pp. 101f.

[275] *Cf.* G. R. Beasley-Murray, *Baptism in the New Testament*, p. 261.

[276] *Cf.* H. Preisker, in the third edition of H. Windisch's *Die Katholischen Briefe* ([3]1951), pp. 156ff. *Cf.* also the similar theory of F. L. Cross, *1 Peter: A Paschal Liturgy* (1954), who sees a passover liturgy behind 1 Peter. But the weakness of all liturgy theories is the complete absence of any known liturgies before the end of the second century, with which to compare them. G. R. Beasley-Murray, *Baptism in the New Testament*, pp. 251ff., discusses Preisker's theory and other forms of baptismal theory for 1 Peter; he is favourable towards a modified form of this idea, and concludes that 1 Pet. 1:3–4:11 contains baptismal instruction.

22, and the subsequent passage up to 4:11 represents an address to the new baptizands, while the beginning and end of the epistle were addressed to the whole community, it would furnish an example of an early liturgy. But the theory is by no means proved.

2 Peter, dealing as it does with serious matters of doctrinal and moral deviation, is nevertheless addressed in a strikingly general way to those with similar faith (1:1). There is no appeal to any church authorities. The body of believers are expected to respond to the clear exhortations in the letter. It is surprising, if 2 Peter is as late as some claim, that there is a complete absence of allusion to any of the orders of officials which began before the end of the apostolic age and were developed early in sub-apostolic times. One feature that stands out in 2 Peter is the strong desire to keep the community pure, both in teaching and behaviour.

Revelation

Some valuable insights are supplied by this book into church matters, although its main burden relates to the future. The whole book is, in fact, addressed to a group of Asiatic churches. Whereas these are separately addressed in Revelation 2 and 3, they are nevertheless regarded as a corporate group. The right hand of the exalted Christ holds the stars, symbols of the churches, (1:16). He is also said to be in the midst of the seven lampstands, another symbol for the group of churches. Whatever the differences in the condition of the various churches, they are united into one by several features. All are addressed by the risen Lord, who claims complete knowledge of their doings. All are also said to be addressed by the Spirit who speaks to all the churches through the specific message to each (*cf.* 2:7). In the address to each, the 'angel' (*angelos*) is mentioned; there is some dispute whether this refers to angels, or to leading representatives of the churches, or heavenly counterparts of earthly congregations.[277] Although the address is always to *angelos* in the singular, it cannot be maintained that the term refers to an official of the churches in a monarchical sense.

From the seven letters we may gain some knowledge of the function of the Christian church in those areas. The 'works' performed by each church are left undefined. What is more specifically stated is the attitude different churches had towards false teaching (2:2, 13ff., 20; 3:8f.). In other cases there is an assessment of the general attitude within the church (3:15ff.). The burden is, therefore, for the purity of the communities and their commitment to Christ. One interesting feature which bears on the doctrine

---

[277] *Cf.* G. R. Beasley-Murray, *Revelation* (*NCB*, 1974), pp. 68ff., who discusses various interpretations and favours the view that the congregations were viewed as existentially in heaven although living on earth. He thinks it is best to think of the angels as heavenly counterparts of the churches, since in each case it is the community itself which is being addressed, not simply the leader.

of the church is the expression 'who say that they are Jews and are not, but are a synagogue of Satan' (2:9; *cf.* also 3:8), which suggests that John regarded the church as the only true Israel. Hence all Christians whether Jewish or Gentiles are 'true Jews'; but those advancing views contrary to the Christian message are not 'Jews', even those who were Hebrews. In harmony with this would be the interpretation of the woman in Revelation 12 as the ideal Mother Zion,[278] and the mention of the twelve tribes of Israel (7:4–8; *cf.* 21:12). These references are in agreement with the NT passages which imply that the church is the true Israel.

Another metaphor used for the church is the 'bride'. This first occurs in 19:7f., where reference is made to the marriage supper of the Lamb.[279] Since the personification of apostasy, Babylon, is described as a gorgeously dressed woman, the appearance of the true church of God as a woman in pure bridal attire is clearly meant to contrast the false with the true. The bride imagery recurs in 21:9, where it is linked with the heavenly Jerusalem, whose glorious appearance is described in terms of sparkling jewels. This combination of imagery has already occurred elsewhere (in Paul's epistles). In the final invitation in the book, the bride is linked with the Spirit (22:17).[280]

There appear to be in existence a group known as prophets, among whom John would class himself (22:9), but no information is given about them.[281] There are no references within the book to officials, except the apostles, whose names are inscribed on the foundations of the 'city' (21:14), and who are linked with saints and prophets in the dirge against Babylon (18:20). There are also counterfeit apostles (2:2), which suggests that considerable advantage could be gained by claiming the apostolic office. The church, however, was alert to this.

The main contribution which the book of Revelation makes to our understanding of the church is in the sphere of worship. There are many passages of a liturgical kind which relate a form of heavenly worship, which may well have served as a pattern for church worship. Some have in fact seen them as derived from Greek-speaking Jewish Christian liturgical procedure.[282] What is beyond dispute is the over-all impression of the book that the author has a high view of worship. He relates his own reaction of

---

[278] For an assessment of possible interpretations of the woman in Rev. 12, *cf.* G. R. Beasley-Murray, *op. cit.*, pp. 193ff.

[279] Although Rev. 19:7 uses the word *gynē* instead of *nymphē* as we should expect, there is no distinction intended between the two words. In fact, in Rev. 21:9, they are linked together. As L. Morris, *Revelation* (*TNTC*, 1969), p. 227, remarks, 'Nothing seems to turn on the choice of word'.

[280] In this context Beasley-Murray, *op. cit.*, p. 345, considers that the bride is the church viewed in the light of her destiny, but does not necessarily connote the consummation of the future age.

[281] *Cf.* D. Hill in *Prophetic Vocation in the New Testament and Today* (ed. J. Panagopoulos), pp. 119ff., for the prophet idea in Revelation. He cites U. Müller, *Prophetie und Predigt im Neuen Testament* (1975) to the effect that the letters to the churches contain a prophetic message which builds up the church.

[282] *Cf.* R. P. Martin, *Worship in the Early Church*, pp. 45f.

awe at the vision of the exalted Christ (1:17). In the liturgical portions, the emphasis is wholly on the greatness of God and the Lamb. There are strong resemblances between these passages and OT poetic forms which show a natural progression from the OT to the NT method of worship.

In calling the passages 'liturgical', it is not intended to imply that a set liturgy had by this time developed. There is no evidence that it had. We have already seen that the other NT books contain only the most fragmentary indications of a liturgical form of words. It is understandable that at an early stage adoration of Christ would be placed alongside adoration of God as an essential feature of worship, but this is far removed from a definite liturgy. The passages in Revelation would certainly serve as examples which could be repeated in worship services, but the book itself gives no indication that this was done. It is worth noting also that in Revelation 4 and 5 the worshippers sing.

The special blessing pronounced on the person who reads aloud the words of the prophecy (1:3) supplies a clue to the practice of public reading for which some parallels have already been noted in the Pauline epistles.

Summary

The importance of the community idea in the NT cannot be over-stressed. Although salvation is applied individually and the processes of sanctification must be personally pursued, yet there is no sense in which the NT conceives of lone believers. The repeated emphasis on groups of believers shows the basic character of the idea of the church.

We have seen that there are many incidental allusions to a community idea in the teaching of Jesus in the gospels. There is no solid ground for maintaining that Jesus did not expect that a community of his people would come into existence following his departure. It may be said that much of his teaching has relevance only in view of the later formation of groups of disciples into Christian churches. This is particularly so in respect of the kingdom teaching. Moreover, the final commission of Jesus to his disciples gives his authority to the later developments as seen in the Acts record.

Of particular significance is Jesus' prediction in John's gospel promising the Spirit to guide the disciples and to aid them in their witness. The coming community was to be essentially a community of the Spirit and the book of Acts makes abundantly clear that this promise was fulfilled.

We are now in a position to summarize the NT teaching about the church. We begin with its *basis*. There is no doubt that the key events in the development of the Christian community were the resurrection of Christ and the outpouring of the Spirit at Pentecost. It was the resurrection which gave rise to the faith of the early believers. The communities were made up of those who had an unshakeable conviction that Jesus had risen from the dead. They also shared possession of the Spirit. The first spontaneous communities consisted of men and women of faith, guided by the Spirit and with a deep commitment to Jesus Christ, whom God had raised from the dead for their salvation. There was therefore a circumscribed membership of the community, although there was no credal statement to specify this. It was further assumed that all believers would be baptized.

Our next point to summarize is the *scope* of the church. It is not surprising that the initial idea of the church was of local communities of believers meeting together in one place. The extended idea of a universal church which linked these local groups into one entity or body took time to develop, but is well attested in the NT period. It was a logical extension of the local community idea, for if individual members were knit together locally, the same principle would link together communities which were formed on the same basis.

Undoubtedly this general community idea owed much to the strong community spirit in Israel in the OT. Indeed, the notion of individual Israelites linked together as a group in their dealings with God is considerably stronger than the idea of individual piety. If, as many NT passages suggest, the Christian church as a whole was thought to be the true Israel, this further supports the strong OT background to the NT community emphasis.

From a theological point of view Paul's wide use of the 'in Christ' and 'in the Spirit' themes gives backing to the Christian community. Whatever the precise significance of the 'in Christ' formula, it undoubtedly possesses some corporate aspects. The church must itself be 'in Christ' if this is true of every one of its members. This notion is supported by many of the metaphors which are used to describe the group of believers, such as the body/bride/building metaphors used by Paul, all of which have a corporate aspect. There is no doubt that through these metaphors, especially those of the body and the building, the responsibility of each member towards other members of the community is emphasized. One part of the body cannot exist without the other parts of the body, any more than individual parts of a building can be removed without weakening the whole. This sense of social responsibility within the community is particularly strong in the NT teaching on love. The Christian church was intended to be a loving fellowship.

We next note the salient features of *worship* within the community.

Although in some parts of the NT there are more references to the ordinances than in others, the practice of baptism as an initiatory rite and the observance of the Lord's supper seem to be everywhere assumed. There is no reason to believe that either of them was not followed in any church. The baptism formula and the words of institution would serve to remind the churches of the essential basis of their spiritual life. Paul was nearer than the other NT writers to expounding a theology of the ordinances.

The scattered references in the NT to worship procedures are sufficient to suggest that importance was attached to regular assemblies in which the singing of hymns, the public reading of Scripture and public prayer were normal. At the same time there is insufficient information to determine whether any standard procedure was adopted. Some have found evidence of early Christian hymns incorporated into some of the epistles, and others have found liturgical material. But the evidence in neither case is conclusive.

There are some indications of the *practices* of the early communities. In the Jerusalem church the Christians showed a strong desire to share their possessions with each other. But this does not explicitly repeat itself in the later literature. There are, however, indications that aid schemes, like Paul's collection, were regarded as having some importance.

Such a matter as church discipline finds a firm place within NT teaching. This applies to moral matters and to the question of orderliness in church worship. In the Corinthian situation this is particularly connected with the exercize of spiritual gifts, especially those of *glossalalia* and prophecy. That charismatic gifts were exercised is not in doubt, but the view that all Christians were expected to possess all the gifts does not appear to be supported by the evidence. Paul's approach to *glossalalia* illustrates an important principle, in that what is edifying and lawful takes precedence over what is merely lawful. Paul does not condemn the gift (on the contrary), but he places greater emphasis on orderliness in worship. It is moreover assumed that a Spirit-led community will reveal a wide variety of spiritual gifts.

With regard to *organization*, it is clear that on the matter of leadership there was no universal policy. Even within the Pauline churches there was wide variety, from the charismatic type of leadership within the Corinthian church to the more structured approach at Philippi, Ephesus and Crete. There was certainly no hierarchical system. The purpose of the church officers was to ensure orderliness and to teach. The NT does not present any clear indications of one man being in charge of one community. This looseness of structure is in keeping with the view of the church as the body, with Christ himself as the head.

The variety of offices reflected in the NT includes apostles, elders (bishops), deacons, evangelists, pastors and prophets. These offices reflect the many-sided ministry which the Christian community is called on to perform. They range over authoritative teaching, caring concern, evangelistic outreach, orderly administration and prophetic pronouncement. But over them all is the presiding work of the Holy Spirit.

Chapter 8
The future

Having considered the scope of the Christian life in the present, we shall next enquire about the NT teaching concerning the future. This is generally grouped under the caption of eschatology, from the Greek word *eschatos* meaning 'final'. We have preferred, however, to use 'the future' as the heading for this section because of the wide variety of ways in which the word eschatology has been used.[1]

This section will not only deal with the destiny of individuals, but will include within it the destiny of history. It is of such importance for a right understanding of the Christian position that many scholars have attempted to approach all the major theological aspects from the point of view of the end.[2] Thus the life of Jesus became an account of an 'eschatological' prophet, *i.e.* concerned only with the future, not with the present. The ethics of Jesus, according to this view, may not be regarded as guidance in an absolute sense, but must only be seen as an interim measure until the coming kingdom has arrived.

To maintain a view like this, it would be necessary to by-pass much evidence in the gospels which simply cannot be forced into an eschatological mould. We shall discuss the variety of different theories regarding the end in their respective places. But it is of fundamental importance to bear in mind the relationship between the present and future aspects of the kingdom, the 'now' and the 'then' of Christian experience[3] (*cf.* the discussion on pp. 416ff.). If the future hope has any relevance, it is valuable to know whether the present should be understood in the light of it, or whether the reverse is the case.

---

[1] *Cf.* I. H. Marshall's discussion on the variety of uses of the word, *ExT* 89, 1978, pp. 264ff.

[2] *Cf.* J. Weiss, *Jesus' Proclamation of the Kingdom of God* (1892, Eng. trans. 1971); A. Schweitzer, *The Quest of the Historical Jesus*, (1906, Eng. trans. ³1954).

[3] F. V. Filson, *Jesus Christ, the Risen Lord* (1956), pp. 260ff., in discussing eschatology considers that it has already begun and that the decisive battle has already occurred. He sees three reasons for the value of

We shall approach the subject under four main sections: the future coming of Christ, the resurrection of believers, the judgment, and eternal destiny. The manner in which certain themes are classified may appear arbitrary, but these four divisions of the subject have been used for the sake of clarity. These divisions will be supplemented by some extended notes which do not belong to any of them, such as the consummation of the kingdom and the millennium (see pp. 868–874).

THE FUTURE COMING OF CHRIST

The synoptic gospels

The period in which Jesus lived and taught was familiar with the idea of a coming age which would see the establishment of the Messiah's rule. The coming age (*ōlām habā*) was distinguished sharply from the present age, and the point of transition from one to the other was known as the day of the Lord.

When Jesus came as Messiah to his people, the question immediately arose among Christians whether the new age had already come. There was inevitable tension between the realization that a new age had dawned and the firm hope in a second coming of the Messiah. This tension first comes to focus in the kingdom teaching of Jesus, where the present and future aspects occur side by side. The future aspect of the kingdom itself will be dealt with later (see pp. 868ff.). But some of the futurist teaching centres on the appearance of Christ, and this will be our concern here. It should be noted here that the word *parousia* which is often used of the coming of Christ occurs only once in this sense in the gospels (*i.e.* in Mt. 24), and even then there is some dispute whether this applies to the descent of the Son of man. We shall use the term in its technical sense of a future coming of Christ to earth.[4]

We should first note that some scholars understand the future coming as a coming of Christ to the believer in a special sense at his death, or as the coming of the Spirit at Pentecost, in which case no future event is in mind.[5] Yet, although this may sound plausible for the fourth gospel, it cannot

eschatology in NT thought: (i) because it says something essential about God, *i.e.* that he will vindicate his justice; (ii) because it is necessary for a sound faith in human destiny, *i.e.* the idea that believers will have a fair dealing at God's hands; (iii) because it sets the world conflict in perspective, *i.e.* God will be victorious over all forces of evil.

[4] *Cf.* R. T. France, *Jesus and the Old Testament* (1971), pp. 235f., who denies that Mt. 24:26 refers to the parousia, but interprets it of the coming of the Son of man to God to receive power. *Cf.* also Jeremias, *NTT* 1, pp. 273f.

[5] For an interpretation of eschatology which denies that Jesus expected a future *parousia*, *cf.* C. H. Dodd, *The Parables of the Kingdom* (1941); T. F. Glasson, *The Second Advent* (³1963); E. Stauffer, 'Agnostos Christos: Joh. ii.24 und der Eschatologie des vierten Evangeliums' in *The Background of the New Testament and its Eschatology* (ed. W. D. Davies and D. Daube, 1964), pp. 281ff.; J. A. T. Robinson, *Jesus and His Coming* (1957), pp. 36–82.

hold for the synoptic gospels, if the evidence is treated seriously.[6] We shall list the sayings and let them speak for themselves, noting the various problems which have arisen concerning them. These futurist sayings are so explicit that it is incredible that the early church 'read them back' into the teaching of Jesus, if they had no genuine basis in his own words. The strong and widespread belief that Jesus was to make a personal return has only one satisfactory explanation, and that is that Jesus himself predicted it. If the 'coming' had been understood in the sense of 'at death' or 'at Pentecost', this would surely have been made more plain in the narrative.[7]

THE COMING DESCRIBED AS THE COMING OF THE SON OF MAN

The title has already been discussed in the section on Christology (see pp. 270ff.). It was seen that in all probability it possessed messianic significance for Jesus, although not so for his hearers. We see in the sayings strong evidence of the way in which Jesus looked into the future. For him the coming was not just a possibility, but a certainty. In one case the future coming is specifically connected with the kingdom (Mt. 16:28; Mk. 9:1), and this furnishes a clue to the right understanding of the other futurist sayings about the 'coming'. Admittedly in this case problems arise about the understanding of the words (see below), but there can be no reasonable doubt that a future coming of some sort is in mind.

THE COMING EXPRESSED IN APOCALYPTIC IMAGERY

It was common among the Jewish apocalyptic writers to use such symbols as signs in the heavens to describe the coming of the hoped for Messiah.[8] It was also used in a non-eschatological way in the OT of political upheavals. When Jesus echoed this familiar language in communicating with his contemporaries he invested the apocalyptic usage with a deeper meaning, because he was referring to himself as the Coming One. The coming in clouds is mentioned in Mark 13:26 = Matthew 24:30; Mark 14:62[9] = Matthew 26:64 = Luke 21:27. The language in this case is directly paralleled

---

[6] For specific books on the Second Coming, cf. A. L. Moore, *The Parousia in the New Testament* (1966); J. A. T. Robinson, *op. cit.*; T. F. Glasson, *op. cit.* O. Cullmann, *Salvation in History* (Eng. trans. 1967), pp. 32ff., gives a useful survey of recent approaches to eschatology, especially in relation to salvation history.

[7] On the question whether of not Jesus expected a future parousia, cf. in support of an affirmative answer, G. R. Beasley-Murray, *Jesus and the Future* (1954); A. L. Moore, *The Parousia in the New Testament*, pp. 175ff.; O. Cullmann, 'The Return of Christ', in *The Early Church* (Eng. trans. 1956), pp. 141–162.

[8] Apocalypticism has exerted considerable influence on many NT interpreters. Cf. W. A. Beardslee, 'New Testament Apocalyptic in Recent Interpretation', *Int* 25, 1971, pp. 419–435, who considers the apocalypticism of Schweitzer, Buri, Bultmann, Käsemann, Pannenberg and Altizer. He approaches his study from the point of view of the basic principles behind apocalyptic literature.

[9] T. F. Glasson, 'The Reply to Caiaphas (Mk. 14:62)', *NTS* 7, 1960-1, pp. 88ff., rejects the literal interpretation of these words and agrees with C. H. Dodd, in *Companion to the Bible* (ed. T. W. Manson, 1939), p. 375, that the words were symbolic in the mouth of Jesus. Glasson is answering H. K. McArthur, 'Mark xiv.62', *NTS* 4, 1958, pp. 156ff.

in Daniel 7:13, which also connects the coming of the Son of man with the kingdom.[10] The same may be said of the accompanying 'glory' mentioned in Luke 9:26 and Mark 13:26, and paralleled in Daniel 7:14. There can be little doubt that this Daniel passage provides the background for the language that Jesus used when describing his coming, although he applied it in a different way.

THE COMING TO BE PRECEDED BY SIGNS

In all accounts of the eschatological discourse,[11] various events are mentioned which must happen before the coming: wars, earthquakes, famines, persecutions (Mk. 13:7–9; Mt. 24:6–9; Lk. 21:10–12). There is difference of opinion whether these signs should be regarded as literal or metaphorical. In view of strong OT and apocalyptic parallels, it is at least a possibility that the signs were intended to be metaphorical. If the eschatological discourse does not refer to the parousia, as some believe, the cataclysmic signs would not apply to actual future events. There will be false prophets who will lead many astray (Mt. 24:5, 24; Mk. 13:6, 22; Lk. 21:8). All these signs have been fulfilled in many stages of the history of the church, but they will presumably be intensified in the end time.

In all the accounts, however, there is mention of special signs in the heavens, such as the darkening of the sun and moon and cataclysmic happenings in the heavens, which immediately precede the coming (Mt. 24:29–30 = Mk. 13:24–26 = Lk. 21:25–27), and which cannot so easily be paralleled in history. They result in great distress among men and are evidently intended to have an overawing effect as an immediate prelude to the parousia.

Another special sign of a totally different kind is that the gospel was to be preached to all nations (Mk. 13:10 = Mt. 24:14).[12] The parousia will not happen until the work of grace has been accomplished. This sets the parousia at the end of the present age. Both Mark's and Matthew's accounts specifically link this sign to the end. A similar idea is presupposed by the statement in Mark 14:9; Matthew 26:13, which anticipates a worldwide preaching of the gospel.

Since the eschatological discourse[13] contains a curious mixture of allu-

---

[10] N. Perrin, 'Mark xiv.62: The End Product of a Christian Pesher Tradition', *NTS* 12, 1965–6, pp. 150–155, regards verse 62 as an expansion of the narrative and an historicization of the *pesher*. As a result he does not regard the saying as original to Jesus.

[11] *Cf.* G. R. Beasley-Murray, *Jesus and the Future*, for a detailed examination of the eschatological discourse.

[12] Several scholars question the authenticity of this saying in Mk. 13:10 on the grounds that (i) it interrupts the continuity of verses 9 and 11; (ii) the idea of a universal mission is foreign to Jesus. *Cf.* W. G. Kümmel, *Promise and Fulfilment* (1957), pp. 84ff. For a response to these objections, *cf.* A.L. Moore, *The Parousia in the New Testament*, p. 87 n. 1; G. R. Beasley-Murray, *op. cit.*, pp. 194f.

[13] For a full discussion of the theory that Mk. 13 was a separate Jewish apocalypse, *cf.* G. R. Beasley-Murray, *op. cit.*, who effectively refutes the suggestion. Since this book was published, many other works

sions to the more immediate event of the fall of Jerusalem and the more remote parousia, some reference should be made to the former to show what light they throw on the latter. The desolating sacrilege of Daniel's vision is mentioned by both Mark and Matthew (Mk. 13:14 = Mt. 24:15; cf. Dn. 9:27), but Luke gives it as armies surrounding Jerusalem (Lk. 21:20). All we need note for our present purpose is the way in which Daniel's language is used to point to a comment on the religious aspect of the siege of Jerusalem. What took place then may be regarded as a foreshadowing of events at the end of the age.

THE COMING IS REGARDED AS IMMINENT, BUT THE TIME UNKNOWN

The most explicit statement showing that the time of the coming is un-known is Mark 13:32 ('But of that day or that hour no one knows, not even the angels in heaven, nor the Son, but only the Father'; cf. Mt. 24:36).[14] This raises some problem over the limitation of the knowledge of Jesus about his own coming, but the impossibility of precise prediction is clear enough. The statement that this was in the Father's hands confirms the consistent conviction expressed by Jesus that every detail of his mission was in response to divine arrangements.[15]

When other sayings which exhort the disciples to watchfulness are linked to this, the concept of imminence emerges. In Luke 12:35–40 (the marriage-feast passage) Jesus declares that the Son of man is coming at 'an hour you do not expect'. The day will come suddenly (Mk. 13:35, 36; cf. Lk. 21:34; Mt. 24:27). Some illustration of this is given in the advice to Christians to withdraw speedily when the desolating sacrilege appears (cf. Mk. 13:14ff.), but this refers specifically to the siege of Jerusalem. Nevertheless the same alertness is expected from those awaiting the Son of man (cf. Mt. 24:36ff.), who will come when not expected (Mt. 24:44; 25:13).

There is a curious mixture of urgency and delay in the teaching of Jesus.

---

on Mk. 13 have appeared. D. Wenham, 'Recent Study on Mark 13', *TSF Bulletin*, 71, 1975, pp. 6ff.; 72, 1975, pp. 1–13, provides a concise survey of several recent expositions of this chapter. He has shown that there is still some support for the view that Mark has used an apocalyptic source, although he does not align himself with this view. *Cf.* for instance, R. Pesch, *Naherwartungen: Tradition und Redaktion in Markus 13* (1968).

[14] Although some scholars regard this saying as a Jewish apocalyptic creation, *cf.* Bultmann, *The History of the Synoptic Tradition* (Eng. trans. 1963), pp. 123ff. or as a community product, *cf.* E. Grässer, *Das Problem der Parusieverzögerung in den synoptischen Evangelien und in der Apostelgeschichte* (³1977), p. 82, it is impossible to suppose that a saying so Christologically embarrassing should have been invented. There is no strong reason to question its authenticity, *cf.* V. Taylor, *Mark* (²1966), p. 522. I. H. Marshall, *The Origins of New Testament Christology* (1976), p. 116, is more cautious about the authenticity of this saying.

[15] For a survey of theories which have denied the authenticity of Mk. 13:32, *cf.* G. R. Beasley-Murray, *A Commentary on Mark Thirteen* (1957), pp. 105f. Although this may appear to be the easiest solution, it raises as many difficulties as it solves. If Mk. 13:32 is regarded as unauthentic, an adequate explanation must be given for the rise of the saying.

The delay motif is seen in such parables as the virgins (Mt. 25:5) and the talents (Mt. 25:19). Even in the face of the delay, however, there is an emphasis on the need to be ready. It would seem reasonable to suppose that Jesus distinguished between imminence and immediacy. The former implies the notion of a coming 'at any time' without the additional idea of it being 'soon', as the latter would imply. Nevertheless, there are problems in some of the sayings of Jesus which do not seem to support that contention.

Matthew 24:29 is the major difficulty since it seems to imply that the parousia would immediately follow the tribulation accompanying the fall of Jerusalem. Various suggestions have been made to explain this use of the word 'immediately' (*eutheōs*). It is well known that in prophetic language far-off events were often described as if they were just about to happen.[16] This 'telescopic' theory for Matthew 24:29 would mean that the parousia would be regarded as the next major event in the future sweep of world history. This interpretation, however, has been criticized on the grounds that it waters down the meaning of *eutheōs*.

The only alternative, however, is to hold that Jesus thought of his parousia as more immediate than it turned out to be. If this solution is correct, it would involve Jesus in making an error of judgment, which raises other difficulties. If Jesus disclaimed knowledge of the time of the parousia, how could he have meant 'immediately' in a temporal sense?[17] It may be true that the early Christians took his words too literally, but this does not affect what he himself meant by the words.

It is noticeable that Mark 13:24, which is parallel to Matthew's statement, does not include the *eutheōs*, and the question naturally arises whether Matthew's addition is his own wrong interpretation of the original meaning. Yet in this case some explanation of Matthew's addition would certainly be necessary. It is difficult to find an adequate reason if the insertion was made after the fall of Jerusalem, for the 'immediately' would be patently wrong. But if the sayings in the eschatological discourses were written before AD 70, their predictive character must be recognized and the chronological interpretation of *eutheōs* is less conclusive. It seems clear that in both Mark and Matthew the desolating sacrilege passage merges into the parousia idea almost imperceptibly. In this case the 'tribulation' is extended from the fall of Jerusalem to embrace all tribulations between that event and the parousia. This would make some sense of the promise that

---

[16] *Cf.* Beasley-Murray, *Jesus and the Future*, pp. 170, 186f., on the prophetic sense of speedy fulfilment. A. L. Moore, *The Parousia in the New Testament*, p. 101, prefers to appeal to apocalyptic literature, in which 'temporal nearness is subordinated to a theological conviction'.

[17] *Cf.* J. W. Wenham, *Christ and the Bible* (1972), pp. 67f., for a statement of the view that there are really four questions, not simply two. R. T. France, *Jesus and the Old Testament* (1971), pp. 231ff., argues that Mk. 13:2-31 all refers to the destruction of Jerusalem, while the rest of the chapter (together with Mt. 25) refers to the parousia and the final judgment.

the Lord would shorten the days for the sake of his elect (Mk. 13:20 = Mt. 24:22), because of the unprecedented character of the tribulation.

We have still to deal with another saying which raises difficulties about the parousia, i.e. Mark 13:30 = Matthew 24:34 = Luke 21:32, 'This generation will not pass away before all these things take place'.[18] Since this saying is placed after the sayings just discussed, it must be taken into account in arriving at a complete picture of our Lord's teaching.[19] It comes in the passage about the fig tree. Some have attempted to explain 'generation' in the sense of the human race or the Jewish nation, but this is not the normal use of the word in the NT. In the gospels it refers to Jesus' contemporaries. Does this then mean that Jesus expected the end during the life-time of some of his own contemporaries?[20] The fig-tree illustration was chosen because it was a clear indication of coming springtime. In a similar way the disciples were expected to be able to discern the signs before the end. There would be less difficulty if the words 'before all these things take place' were not so comprehensive. The fig-tree parable is intended to be encouraging and this must affect our understanding of 'these things'. Jesus was clearly against any idea of fixing the date of the coming and the question must, therefore, be raised whether he was implying by the words 'this generation' a definite time limitation.

The only reasonable alternative, however, would be to seek some other meaning for 'generation'. Since there is evidence in the papyri for *genea* meaning 'family'[21], it is a possible understanding of the present passage to suppose that *genea* may refer to the Jewish 'family' or race. The statements would then amount to an assurance that in spite of the intensity of tribulation the people of God would not pass away until everything predicted should be fulfilled. This interpretation is difficult because this is clearly not the usual meaning of the word, but it may be preferable to one which implies that Jesus expected the parousia too soon. It may be that he intended to present a tension between imminent and remote, in order to keep his followers alert for any eventuality; for 'this generation', if it means Jesus' contemporaries, passed away without the Christian church losing faith in his future parousia.

If, on the other hand, this passage does not refer to the parousia, the word *genea* with its normal meaning of 'generation' would raise no difficulties. Indeed, if the references in the eschatological discourse are primarily

---

[18] For a survey of different opinions on the interpretation of this verse, *cf.* G. R. Beasley-Murray, *A Commentary on Mark Thirteen* (1957), pp. 99ff.

[19] For a discussion of the differences between the synoptic evidences for this saying, *cf.* A. L. Moore, *The Parousia in the New Testament*, pp. 131ff. He concludes that there is no reason to suppose a parousia-delay crisis behind this passage.

[20] So Beasley-Murray, *A Commentary on Mark Thirteen*, p. 100.

[21] *Cf.* Moulton and Milligan, *VGT*, 1930, pp. 122f.

to the destruction of the temple, they would have no relevance at all for our present theme.[22]

SOME FURTHER DIFFICULT SAYINGS

Matthew has two sayings which have raised special problems and which seem to relate to the parousia. Matthew 10:23 contains a statement which is part of the mission instructions given to the disciples: 'When they persecute you in one town, flee to the next; for truly, I say to you, you will not have gone through all the towns of Israel, before the Son of man comes.' There is no parallel to this in the other synoptics. The crux of the problem is the way in which the coming of the Son of man is to be understood. If this is the parousia, it is difficult to see what the rest of the statement can mean, unless it points to a belief that the end will dawn in that generation. On the other hand, the coming might refer to Pentecost, in which case the words apply only to the commission of the twelve.

There is no easy interpretation. If it be maintained that Jesus was referring to the fall of Jerusalem,[23] it could be argued that not all of the cities of Israel were evangelized before that event, if the verb (*teleō*) is intended in this sense.[24] What is clear is that the mission work of the disciples is directly related to some future coming of Jesus.[25] The statement is not an exposition of the coming, however, but an assurance that there would be plenty of opportunity to flee from one city to another. The whole passage is not explicitly referring to a coming at the end of the age.[26]

The other saying (Mt. 16:28) has a Markan and a Lukan parallel (Mk. 9:1; Lk. 9:27), but it is Matthew's record which creates more problems than the others. Whereas Mark reports a saying of Jesus that some standing there would not taste death 'before they see the kingdom of God come with power', Matthew has 'before they see the Son of man coming in his kingdom'. Luke's is similar to Mark's account, but without the words 'come with power'. Mark's and Luke's wording could readily be interpreted of the commencement of the present activity of the kingdom empowered by the Holy Spirit at Pentecost. But Matthew's account fastens on the coming of the Son of man rather than on the kingdom. This is an

---

[22] So R. T. France *op. cit.*

[23] P. Nepper-Christensen, *Das Matthäusevangelium* (1958), p. 187, considers the view that Mt. 10:23 refers to the destruction of Jerusalem as quite arbitrary. Against this, *cf.* C. F. D. Moule, *The Birth of the New Testament* (1962), p. 90; *cf.* also R. T. France, *op. cit.*, p. 140.

[24] A. H. McNeile, *Matthew*, p. 142, takes the statement in the sense that there will be enough room in the Palestinian cities to afford refuge to the fleeing Christians in view of the expectation of an imminent coming.

[25] W. G. Kümmel, *Promise and Fulfilment*, p. 63, relates it definitely to a parousia, but then restricts it to the lifetime of Jesus' disciples. But see A. L. Moore's criticism of the latter point, *The Parousia in the New Testament*, p. 145.

[26] According to E. Schweizer, *Matthew* (Eng. trans. 1976, from *NTD*, 1973), p. 244, concludes that Mt. 10:23 means that there will be no end to the mission to Israel or to Jewish persecution against Christians.

extension of the idea in Mark's account. Clearly if the parousia is in mind, the saying proved to be inaccurate. But the same principle of interpretation applies here as was mentioned above: if Jesus claimed not to know the time of the parousia, it would be strange for him to have used the remaining lifespan of some of his hearers as a yardstick to indicate the limited interval before that parousia. There seems no alternative but to suppose that Matthew's account does not refer to the parousia, but to some other kind of vindication.

Nevertheless this is not without considerable difficulties in view of verse 27, which clearly must refer to a future coming. If verse 28 refers to a more imminent coming, two comings must be in mind: one at the end of the age and the other a continuous process, beginning with the inauguration of the church at Pentecost. If, however, Matthew had intended the sayings to relate to the parousia, it is surprising that he does not use the word 'parousia' as he does in 24:3, where in the parallels neither Mark nor Luke uses it (cf. also Matthew's use of the word in 24:27, 37, 39, all without parallel usage in the other synoptics).[27] An alternative understanding is to regard the 'coming' as relating to the transfiguration, and to suppose that that event reveals privately what will be manifested publicly at the parousia.[28] This makes the reference to the parousia secondary and removes the difficulty of the limited time span.[29]

Although there are no completely satisfactory solutions to some of these problems, there is no reason to doubt that Jesus himself foresaw and intended his disciples to recognize that some kind of interval would separate the parousia from the resurrection, and that although the timing of the coming is unknown, the event itself is certain.[30] Other NT passages throw further light on the importance of this theme for early Christian life and thought.[31]

The Johannine literature

Before commenting on the passages in *John's gospel* which deal with the

---

[27] E. Schweizer, *op. cit.*, p. 347, suggests that Mt. 16:28 may mean that the disciple of Jesus may now die secure in the knowledge that death has been overcome.

[28] Cf. E. E. Ellis, *Luke*, p. 141, and I. H. Marshall, *Luke*, pp. 377ff., for comments on this view.

[29] A. L. Moore, *The Parousia in the New Testament*, pp. 127f., considers that the transfiguration story contains many overtones suggesting the parousia.

[30] There is no foundation for H. Conzelmann's contention that Luke departs from early eschatology in favour of historicizing, *The Theology of Saint Luke* (Eng. trans. 1960), pp. 95–136. A. L. Moore, *op. cit.*, gives a point by point criticism of this theory (pp. 85ff.).

[31] Some recent studies have concentrated on the eschatology of the separate evangelists. *Cf.*, for instance, C. B. Cousar's redaction study of Mark's passion narratives from this point of view, 'Eschatology and Mark's Theologia Crucis', *Int* 24, 1970, pp. 321–335. For Luke, *cf.* S. G. Wilson, 'Lucan Eschatology', *NTS* 16, 1970, pp. 330–347, who considers that Luke presents two strands – delay and imminence – and approaches them from a pastoral rather than a theological point of view. *Cf.* also E. E. Ellis, 'Die Funktion der Eschatologie im Lukasevangelium', *ZTK* 66, 1970, pp. 387–402.

coming and other eschatological themes, we need to make certain preliminary observations. It has often been argued that a different dualism occurs in this gospel compared with the synoptics, and this has a direct bearing on the teaching about the future. The horizontal view, presented in the synoptics, sees God's acts of salvation in history moving on towards a final climax. The vertical view, more in evidence in John, is that which sees God's saving acts as belonging to a heavenly, but nevertheless 'real', world above the present earthly existence. Yet both views find support in the gospel. The Son of man has come down from heaven (3:13), but the climax of his mission is reached when he is 'lifted up' and draws people to him (12:32). What he offers men is 'eternal life', *i.e.* life which belongs to a heavenly and not an earthly sphere of existence (3:16). This approach is heightened by the view that the truth which lies behind the symbolic language (the water of life, the bread, the vine) is spiritual.

Alongside this view is that which sees the mission of Christ as moving towards a climax at the end of history. The record is dominated by the 'hour' of Jesus, which 'dawns' in the passion and resurrection narratives, and is viewed as the crucial hour of human history.[32] That 'hour' stretches forward into the activity of the church (see pp. 721ff., for John's doctrine of the church). There would be conflict between believers and the world (17:18), but the people of God would be an expanding community (*cf.* 10:16; 11:52; 21:15–17). It is impossible to do justice to the teaching in John unless both the vertical and horizontal aspects are recognized.

Another matter which arises out of the evidence which has just been outlined is the concept of 'realized eschatology' which has been regarded as particularly relevant to this gospel. The theory of C. H. Dodd[33] that the kingdom is to be seen only in the ministry of Jesus and has no relevance for the future, in the apocalyptic sense of the word, has been widely acclaimed, although with modifications. According to this view the apocalyptic type of future expectation was a distortion, and only the more spiritual 'realized' eschatology represents the true position of Jesus. There is certainly evidence in John's gospel that Jesus regarded the present time as definitive. People had seen the glory (1:14). The concept of judgment is not so much of some future event as of a present reality.[34] Those who

---

[32] *Cf.* R. E. Brown, *John* (*AB*, 1966), pp. cxv ff.

[33] *Cf.* C. H. Dodd, *The Apostolic Preaching and its Developments* (³1963), pp. 65ff.; *idem*, *The Interpretation of the Fourth Gospel* (1953). R. Bultmann is another who plays down the primitive eschatology in John by regarding it as demythologized (*TNT* 2, p. 8). But the salvation-history theme in John is far too strong for Bultmann's position to be tenable.

[34] F. J. Moloney, *The Johannine Son of Man* (1976), p. 79, gives two reasons against the elimination of future eschatology from John. (i) John does not revolutionize the synoptic tradition in which both present and future eschatology is found. (ii) John's historical situation (*cf.* J. L. Martyn's *History and Theology in the Fourth Gospel*, 1968) militates against his omission to refer to the future life. *Cf.* also S. S. Smalley, 'Diversity and Development in John', *NTS* 17, 1970-1, pp. 276–292.

do not believe are condemned already (3:18). The judgment of this world is 'now' (12:31).

While these aspects are undeniable, it would not be true to restrict eschatology in John wholly to the 'now'.[35] There are several passages (5:28, 29; 6:39, 40, 44, 54; 12:48) which convey a future emphasis which will not bend to the realized-eschatology theme.[36] In dealing with these two streams some (like Bultmann[37]) have dispensed with the future references by maintaining that they are later editorial additions. This view has been strongly criticized.[38] Others (like Boismard) consider the apocalyptic to be the earliest notion in Johannine thought and the realized to be the maturer concept. But it is possible to unite the present and future elements in John's gospel in the same way as in the synoptic gospels. Indeed, it may be said that the presence of both in John not only adds confirmation to the synoptic accounts, but also requires that the whole Johannine presentation should be regarded as complementary and not contradictory to the synoptic records.

There are undoubtedly differences of emphasis, but they present a basic view of Jesus as one who saw his mission as having both immediate and future implications. It will not do to maintain that John reflects a time when Christians were in perplexity about eschatology, for they did not create their eschatological tensions. These were already present in the mind and teaching of Jesus. One way of looking at the tension which has much to commend it is C. F. D. Moule's view[39] that the present-future tension represents shifts of emphasis between individual and collective sayings. If it is true that Jesus stresses the present when an individual believer is in mind, and the future when the group is in mind, this would provide a satisfactory explanation. The church will be complete only in the future.

The clearest statement in John's gospel in which Jesus foretells his own coming is in 14:3, 'I will come again and will take you to myself'; this certainly appears to demand a future event to complement the statement

[35] D. E. Aune, *The Cultic Setting of Realized Eschatology in Early Christianity* (1972), explores a new approach to realized eschatology in the cultic life of the community. For his discussion of the theme in John's gospel, *cf.* pp. 45–135. Aune explains the 'coming of Jesus' in this gospel in terms of the recurring cultic vision of Jesus (p. 126).

[36] J. A. T. Robinson, *In the End, God* (London, James Clarke, 1950), p. 59, while not accepting Dodd's attempts to refine away these references to the 'last days', maintains that the function of the 'last day' imagery is to indicate the 'finality of the processes of life and death, salvation and judgement, already set in motion by the events of the Incarnation'.

[37] *Cf.* R. Bultmann, *John* (Eng. trans. 1971), p. 261. He has some difficulty in explaining why, if the editor adds verses 28f. to correct the evangelist, he leaves the statements of this passage side by side.

[38] *Cf.* the criticisms of D. M. Smith, Jnr, *The Composition and Order of the Fourth Gospel. Bultmann's Literary Theory* (1965). *Cf.* also L. van Hartingveld, *Die Eschatologie des Johannesevangeliums* (1962), who stresses the future aspects; M. E. Boismard, 'St Luc et la rédaction du quatrième évangile', *RB* 69, 1962, pp. 185–211.

[39] *Cf.* C. F. D. Moule, 'A neglected factor in Johannine Eschatology', *Studies in John presented to Prof. Dr. J. N. Sevenster* (ed. W. C. van Unnik *et al.*, 1970), pp. 155ff. He cites E. Käsemann, *Jesu letzter Wille nach Johannes 17* (1967), pp. 74ff. as supporting individualism (Eng. trans. *The Testament of Jesus*, 1968, pp. 40ff.).

about a going away (*cf.* 14:28). Some have seen here a reference to Christ's coming to his people at death or in the person of the Holy Spirit at Pentecost, thus dispensing with a future coming.[40] This interpretation may claim some support from John 14:18 ('I will not leave you desolate; I will come to you'), where the reference is not specifically to the second coming of Christ. All Jesus' sayings in John about his parousia are capable of another interpretation, but there seem to be insufficient grounds for excluding the possibility that a future coming of an apocalyptic type is intended.[41] Further support for the futurist as well as the present aspect of eschatology in John is found in the repeated 'in the last day' in 6:39, 40, 44, 54, for this certainly contains a forward look.

There are fewer references in the *Johannine epistles* to the parousia than in the gospel. But in 1 John 2:28, John warns his readers to abide in Christ 'so that when he appears we may have confidence and not shrink from him in shame at his coming'. The coming is regarded as a certainty, although no details are given. It is regarded as common knowledge. It clearly marks an important occasion for the Christian, but no indication is given about the 'shame'; presumably it is connected with judgment.

Another statement bearing on this is 1 John 3:2, which looks forward to the parousia and asserts that when Christ appears we shall be like him.[42] As in some other NT passages, the coming is regarded as a motive for moral purity ('every one who thus hopes in him purifies himself as he is pure', 1 Jn. 3:3).

In 1 John 2:18 there is a reference to the 'last hour', which in the context is related to antichrist's coming.[43] The expression which John uses can be understood in two ways. It could mean the same as 'the last days', generally understood of the period linking the ascension with the parousia. Or it could refer to the last stage of the last days. The latter view is the more difficult, since it requires some explanation of the long period of delay which has since elapsed. Admittedly the difficulty is not entirely absent from the former view, but it is less acute.

Acts

The theme of the return of Christ is introduced at the commencement of this book, as a promise given at the ascension by the two heavenly beings

[40] *Cf.* C. H. Dodd, *The Interpretation of the Fourth Gospel*, p. 395.

[41] Aune, *op. cit.*, p. 129, reckons that if the second person plural pronouns are taken seriously, Jn. 14:3 must refer to a future and final coming of Jesus and cannot refer to what he calls 'an individualized Parousia'.

[42] Although the use of *phaneroō* in 3:2 need not refer to a future coming, its link with *parousia* in 2:28 suggests that it is intended to bear a future meaning.

[43] *Cf.* I. H. Marshall's discussion of this passage, *The Epistles of John* (*NICNT*, 1978), pp. 148ff. In reference to antichrist and antichrists in this passage, he considers that John saw the false teachers of his day as antichrists who are possessed by the spirit of the antichrist whose coming still lay in the future.

in 1:11 ('This Jesus, who was taken up from you into heaven, will come in the same way as you saw him go into heaven'). It is noticeable in this statement that the second coming is specified as being in the same manner as the departure, which rules out any suggestion of a spiritual coming as at Pentecost or at the death of the believer. It is clear support for a futurist interpretation of the coming.[44] It is not surprising that Luke should report the prediction of a similar apocalyptic coming in view of his record of a similar view in the teaching of Jesus. One notable feature is that a cloud was associated with the ascension in Acts and with the parousia in the gospel (Lk. 21:27). It is impossible to impose a 'realized eschatology' interpretation on this Acts passage.

But did this early indication of a future coming have any further impact on the developing church? In Peter's first sermon the quotation from Joel not only speaks of the coming of the Spirit, but also of the day of the Lord and the signs which will accompany it (2:17–21). Yet this prediction is seen to have an immediate and not a future reference. Peter and the early Christians regarded the day of the Lord[45] as in a sense already arrived and yet at the same time still future. They were already living in the 'last days' (2:17; 3:24). In their minds there was no contradiction between being in the last days and yet still awaiting a future coming of the Lord. When predicting times of refreshing from the presence of the Lord (3:19ff.), Peter recognizes that heaven must receive Jesus 'until the time for establishing all that God spoke by the mouth of his holy prophets from of old'.[46] While there is no specific mention of a coming, it is implied. It would seem that again both present and future aspects of the coming of Jesus are in mind.

Some have seen in Stephen's vision of the Son of man 'standing' at the right hand of God an indication of Christ's readiness to return (7:55), but this is probably reading too much into the language.[47] In the discourse of Peter to Cornelius, Jesus is declared to be the one whom God has ordained to be judge (10:42), but no details are given about a future coming.

The book of Acts is too taken up with the everyday developments in the church to record much about the future hopes of the early Christians.[48]

---

[44] F. F. Bruce, *The Book of the Acts* (*NICNT*, 1954), p. 41, does not consider that an immediate return is implied. During the interval possession of the Spirit would guarantee the coming consummation.

[45] W. Neil, *Acts* (*NCB*, 1973), p. 75 regards 'the day of the Lord' as a reference to the parousia.

[46] J. A. T. Robinson, *Jesus and his Coming*, pp. 140ff., argues that Acts 3 represents a more primitive position than Acts 2, because he thinks that Acts 3 does not support the view that Jesus became Christ at the resurrection, whereas he thinks that Acts 2 does. Robinson then goes on to suppose that Acts 3 was a factor in the development of the parousia hope, while its theology is the theology of the 'absentee Christ' (p. 153). But this theory involves Luke in setting out in a highly improbable juxtaposition two allegedly contradictory Christologies. It is unlikely that a right perspective can be gained through such atomistic exegesis.

[47] A. L. Moore, *The Parousia in the New Testament*, p. 184, takes the *hestōta* in Acts 7:56f. as expressing the idea of welcoming the martyr.

[48] J. A. T. Robinson, *Jesus and his Coming*, pp. 27ff., denies that the idea of a future coming can be found

Yet there is reason to believe that they at first regarded the parousia as imminent and there is some possibility that the early experience of communistic living may have been prompted to some extent by such a belief. But it would be true to say that the Christians' main preoccupation was the proclamation of the gospel for the present age.

Paul

Many problems arise over Paul's references to a future coming of Jesus, but there can be no doubt that the apostle looked forward to it as an important event. We shall deal with his teaching under the following considerations: the various terms he uses for the coming; imminence and the problem of delay; the intervening signs; the question whether Paul changed his mind.

TERMS USED TO EXPRESS THE COMING

We note first the term *parousia* which has come to be used in a technical sense of the return of the Lord.[49] Paul uses it several times, mostly in the Thessalonian epistles (1 Cor. 15:23; 1 Thes. 2:19; 3:13; 4:15; 5:23; 2 Thes. 2:1, 8), in each case of the parousia of Christ. In NT usage the word denotes the arrival or presence of the person concerned. It does not mean 'return', although that idea is implied, for it certainly denotes a coming of Christ distinct from his coming at the incarnation. The word quite naturally came to stand for that climactic event in the future when Christ would come again in the last days.

Another word, which the apostle uses, is 'revelation' (*apokalypsis*) which occurs in 2 Thessalonians 1:7; 1 Corinthians 1:7; 3:13.[50] This term carries more theological implications than the first, for it involves an unveiling of some heavenly truth which has until then remained hidden. In a real sense the incarnation was such a revelation, but a further revelation is involved in the second coming of Jesus, which has become the focus of the church's future hope. The revelation will be an unveiling of glory to believers and an unveiling of judgment to unbelievers. The same term (in its verbal form) is used of the man of lawlessness in 2 Thessalonians 2:3ff. A kindred term *epiphaneia* (glorious manifestation) is used by Paul in 1 Timothy 6:14, 2 Timothy 4:1 and Titus 2:13 of the appearing of Jesus Christ.

---

in Acts. Admittedly, emphasis on the parousia is nowhere explicit, but it must be remembered that the early speeches were basically evangelistic in character, and lack of mention of the parousia is no evidence that no-one believed it.

[49] For a discussion of parousia in Paul's epistles, *cf.* A. Oepke, *TDNT* 5, p. 868.

[50] On this term and its antecedents to Paul's use, *cf.* the article by A. Oepke, *TDNT* 3, pp. 563ff. He contends that while Paul did not use the term in reference to the earthly life of Jesus, which was considered to be a phase of concealment, nevertheless the disclosure begins with the resurrection of Christ and culminates with the parousia.

The third word is 'the day', familiar from the OT in the expression 'the day of the Lord'. But Paul applies it to 'the day of Christ' as well, and draws no distinction between the usages. Admittedly in some cases there may be doubt, where the former is used, whether or not Jesus is meant (cf. 1 Thes. 5:2; 2 Thes. 2:2).[51] But in most cases there can be no doubt that Christ's coming is meant (cf. 1 Cor. 1:8; 2 Cor. 1:14; Phil. 1:6, 10; 2:16). The 'day' is more than an indication of a cataclysmic event, although it is that. Paul brings out the idea of 'day' in connection with the light (cf. Rom. 13:11–14, where the statement that the day is at hand is in direct contrast with the darkness of night). The coming of the Lord and the coming of dawn are inextricably linked in Paul's thought.[52]

IMMINENCE

The nearness of the coming seems to have been the mainspring of Paul's thought in several of these epistles[53], although never more clearly than in 1 Thessalonians 4:13ff. It is a classic apocalyptic passage with many of the familiar apocalyptic details.[54] What is significant for our present point is that by using the first person plural, Paul implies a distinct possibility that he might be present ('we who are alive, who are left until the coming of the Lord, shall not precede those who have fallen asleep').[55] The most natural understanding of this passage is that Paul expected an imminent parousia.[56]

Yet there are various interpretations of the passage which avoid the implication that Paul was mistaken.[57] Was he identifying himself with the last generation before the end? Even if he did, he gives no indication that a long delay period would first elapse. Nevertheless, because he could not claim any special knowledge of the timing of the parousia, it is highly

---

[51] G. Delling, in his article on *hēmera* in *TDNT* 2, p. 952, considers that the primary concern of these two occurrences is the parousia of Christ.

[52] M. Black, *Romans* (NCB, 1973), pp. 163f., points out that dawn in the East was a period of maximum activity. The imagery served a useful purpose in alluding to the dawn of the era to be introduced by the parousia.

[53] J. A. T. Robinson, *In the End, God*, (1950) pp. 56f., thought that a future parousia had only a minor place in the eschatological message. But in his later book, *The Body* (1952), p. 79, he seems to attach more importance to it at the end of time in his interpretation of Paul's theology.

[54] B. Vawter, 'And He shall come again with Glory', *Studiorum Paulinorum Congressus Internationalis Catholicus* (ed. C. D'Amato, 1963), pp. 143ff., combats the view that Paul's eschatology owes nothing to apocalyptic. He criticizes J. A. T. Robinson in this respect.

[55] The use of *hēmeis* in 1 Cor. 15:32 has been regarded by some as evidence that Paul expected the parousia in his own lifetime. Cf. A. Robertson and A. Plummer, *1 Corinthians* (ICC, 1911), p. 376; H. Lietzmann, *Korinther* (LHB, [4]1933), p. 87; R. Bultmann, *TNT* 1, p. 103. Whereas he lived in the expectation of this, it does not mean that he was convinced that he would not die. The same applies to the 1 Thes. 4:17 statement.

[56] For support for this view, cf. among many others, O. Cullmann, *The Early Church*, p. 152; W. Neil, *1 and 2 Thessalonians* (MNT, 1950), pp. 98f.

[57] So. J. Bonsirven, *L'Évangile de Paul* (Paris, 1948), pp. 338ff.; cf. also L. Morris, *The Epistles to the Thessalonians* (NICNT, 1959), pp. 141f.

unlikely that he thought of it as in the distant future. If the time was unknown, Paul had no alternative but to expect is as imminent, although it is noticeable that in none of his later epistles is there a passage which stresses imminence so clearly (*cf.* 1 Thes. 5:1f.). Even if Paul was later obliged to think that he would not after all be alive at the parousia, this cannot be construed as a blunder which had to be modified or corrected. In any age it is possible to contemplate a coming at any moment without being guilty of a delusion if it does not happen within one's lifetime. The expectation of the event is more important than its timing.[58] This admittedly raises a problem in view of the centuries which have since passed. But the problem is lessened if it is recognized that for the Christian it is always five minutes to midnight.[59]

Other passages also point to an imminent event. The reference in 1 Corinthians 7:26 to the 'impending distress' (*enestōsa anangkē*) seems to envisage a time of severe persecution, although it is not specifically related to the end time. It is something which Paul clearly believed could come in the lifetime of the Christians to whom he is writing. There is point in the additional words in 1 Corinthians 7:29 – 'the appointed time has grown very short' (*ho kairos systalmenos estin*) – which show clearly that some event of great importance is regarded as imminent.[60] In 1 Thessalonians 5:4, the approaching day is said to come as a thief, which brings out the element of surprise in it, and directly echoes Jesus' own words (Mt. 24:43).

Sufficient has been said to make it certain that Paul accepted an imminent view of the parousia.[61] But a problem arises because he also suggests certain events which would precede the parousia (see next section), for this would appear to introduce a contradictory element. In view of this some have maintained that Paul abandoned his belief in an imminent return.[62] Others have considered 2 Thessalonians, the chief witness for the anticipatory signs, to be unauthentic.[63] Others have sought to understand both aspects

---

[58] This is clear from 1 Thes. 5:1–11, where the emphasis falls on the need for preparedness, not on any awareness of imminence. The thief metaphor draws attention to the surprise element, not to the timing.

[59] F. F. Bruce makes a point of this in commenting on the last hour in 1 Jn. 2:18, *The Epistles of John* (1970), pp. 65f.

[60] If *kairos* does not specifically indicate duration (*cf.* G. Delling, *TDNT* 3, pp. 459f.; O. Cullmann, *Christ and Time* (Eng. trans. 1951), p. 39, these words may not necessarily imply a restricted time, although *systalmenos* does suggest some degree of imminence (*cf.* A. L. Moore, *The Parousia in the New Testament*, p. 116).

[61] We have not included 2 Cor. 5:2, 3 as evidence that Paul was longing for the parousia in order to avoid the 'naked' state at death (*cf.* Kennedy, *St Paul's Conception of the Last Things* (1904), p. 256; J. N. Sevenster, 'Some Remarks on the *Gymnos* in II Cor. 5.3', in *Studia Paulina in honorem Johannis de Zwaan* (ed. J. N. Sevenster and W. C. van Unnik, 1953), pp. 202ff.) because no specific mention is made of the parousia in this context. See further discussion of this passage on pp. 831ff.

[62] For the view that Paul abandoned his belief in the imminence of the parousia, *cf.* C. H. Dodd, *New Testament Studies* (1953), pp. 108ff.

[63] For a discussion on the authenticity of this epistle, *cf.* my *New Testament Introduction*, pp. 569ff.

as part of the same mind.[64] The pros and cons of this will be discussed after the intervening signs have been considered.

THE INTERVENING SIGNS

Jewish apocalyptic writers frequently referred to signs which would precede and herald the appearing of the Messiah or the coming of the day of the Lord. It is a similar apocalyptic type of teaching found in Paul, which has led to some confusion since, if he considered the parousia to be imminent, the idea of signs which must first take place appears contradictory. Before concluding that these two features are actually contradictory, however, we must examine the purpose of the signs. In 1 Thessalonians 4:13ff., the signs mentioned accompany the parousia and do not therefore raise difficulties. Even so these accompanying signs have a definitely apocalyptic flavour: the commanding cry, the archangel's call, the trumpet sound and the clouds. Moreover, this passage mentions that believers will be caught up to meet the Lord in the air. No information is given about the sequel to this, whether or not it involves a return to earth of these caught-up believers. What is clear is the permanent character of the meeting with Christ ('so we shall always be with the Lord', 1 Thes. 4:17).

Problems arise when 1 Thessalonians 4:13ff. is compared with 2 Thessalonians 2. This second passage is linked with the first in its opening words which refer to the parousia of the Lord Jesus Christ and to our meeting with him. But here other signs are mentioned which are not accompanying signs. There is a definite repudiation of the view that the day of the Lord had already happened (2 Thes. 2:2). This reflects that some were making a mistaken claim about a spiritual rather than an actual coming. It must have arisen from an attempt to explain the delay of the parousia in the face of a conviction about its imminence. It was a kind of early form of 'realized eschatology'. The apostle reinforces the reality of a future event by the reference to signs which will herald the coming.

In the light of 2 Thessalonians 2:5, it cannot be supposed that the Thessalonians were not already aware of these intervening signs. It must be maintained that 'the man of lawlessness' was an already familiar idea to the readers (*cf.* 1 Thes. 5:1), but that some at least had not appreciated the significance of what they had been told. It is noticeable that the 'lawless one' will have a parousia (2 Thes. 2:9) and will act in a specifically anti-Christian way. He is 'the son of perdition' (*apōleia*) who will inaugurate a

---

[64] A. L. Moore, *The Parousia in the New Testament*, p. 170, draws attention to the well-known tension in NT thought between 'already' and 'not yet', and applies this to the end events, not in the sense of 'fulfilled' and 'unfulfilled', but in the sense of a tension between those fulfilled in a mystery (*i.e.* in Christ) and their open manifestation at the parousia. This is worth bearing in mind in considering Paul's references to the signs.

special rebellion which is singled out as '*the* rebellion' (*hē apostasia*) (2:3).[65] Although the word used could mean 'falling away', it has a much stronger meaning here, for it implies deliberate opposition to God. This opposition reaches its climax when the man of lawlessness demands worship for himself in the temple of God. He will demand to be treated in a manner equivalent to God. He is the complete counterfeit.[66] He corresponds to the antichrist figure in John's Apocalypse (see later section, p. 815).

But linked with this idea of a future parousia of the man of lawlessness is the statement that he is already at work (2:7), in the form of a 'mystery'.[67] The difference between the present activity and the future parousia centres around 'the restrainer' (verses 6–7). In the former verse he is present, in the latter removed. His identity is, however, a problem. Paul clearly has some personal agency in mind since he uses the masculine article (*ho katechōn*).[68]

There can be no doubt that the interpretation of this restrainer will widely affect our understanding of Paul's eschatology.[69] Paul must have been referring to a specific agency which is nonetheless applicable both in his own day and in a future intensified manifestation. There are three main ways in which the 'restrainer' has been understood. (i) He has been identified with the Holy Spirit, whose activities include the counteracting of evil influences.[70] But if this interpretation is correct, it would be the only instance in which the Spirit's withdrawal is mentioned in the NT. Furthermore, it would be strange for Paul to refer to the Spirit in this obscure way, although it must be noted that there is only one specific reference to the Spirit in this epistle (2 Thes. 2:13). (ii) Another suggestion is that the restraint at the present time is the preaching of the gospel.[71] The meaning would then be that the withdrawal of the proclamation would mark the dawning of the close of the present age.[72] But the context gives no indication of this. (iii) The more widely held view is that the restraining effect of the Roman empire on warring factions is in mind, summed up in the

---

[65] For a discussion of this theme from the point of view of the history of religions school, *cf.* W. Bousset and A. H. Keane, *The Antichrist Legend* (1896).

[66] T. F. Glasson, *The Second Advent*, p. 204, suggests that the adoption of the antichrist legend was one of the reasons for the spirit of expectancy.

[67] On the man of sin theme, *cf.* G. Vos, *The Pauline Eschatology* (1953), pp. 94ff.

[68] O. Betz, 'Der Katechon', *NTS* 9, 1963, pp. 276–291, regards the *katechōn* concept as pre-Pauline. This would not, however, affect the authenticity of the letter. Paul would then be expressing himself through an already existing idea (mainly derived from the book of Daniel).

[69] For a full discussion of the 'restrainer' (*katechōn*), *cf.* E. Best, *1 and 2 Thessalonians* (BC, 1972), pp. 295ff.

[70] *Cf.* J. D. Pentecost, *Things to Come* (1958, r.p. 1964), pp. 270f.

[71] *Cf.* O. Cullmann, *Christ and Time*, pp. 164ff, who notes that Theodore of Mopsuestia, Theodoret and Calvin all took a similar view. Cullmann suggests that the neuter form (*to katechon*) which occurs in verse 6 refers to the preaching and the masculine form in verse 7 refers to the apostle.

[72] It has been argued that gospel preaching is mentioned several times in 2 Thes. 1 and 2 (*cf.* 1:8, 10; 2:5, 10, 13), *cf.* A. L. Moore, *The Parousia in the New Testament*, p. 113, but there is no clear connection between the preaching and the 'restrainer', and the masculine participle would be inappropriate.

person of the emperor.[73] It would not be unnatural in an apocalyptic passage for cryptic reference to be made to political power. Nevertheless, in the present context, spiritual issues seem to be more dominant than political issues.

How then are we to resolve the problem and decide on Paul's true meaning? On the whole, in view of the fact that Paul is using his material to correct a wrong tendency among the Thessalonians, it is reasonable to suppose that the third proposal is most likely to be Paul's meaning, since it would be recognized by the readers that the *Pax Romana* had restrained much evil in the contemporary world. It is probable, however, that he looked beyond the state towards those spiritual agencies which were much more powerful in the restraint of evil than the best of the Romans. The fact is, the work of the restrainer is not referred to as an indication of the impending parousia, but rather the reverse, as an evidence that the day of the Lord could not have come already.

One important feature which must be noted in Paul's forward look at these apocalyptic signs is the existence of parallels between this passage and the teaching of Jesus about the future (the apocalyptic imagery, the abomination of desolation). Both Jesus and Paul go back to the earlier passages in Daniel 7:13ff.; 9:27. This continuity, which comes to the fore here, is to be assumed in other cases where it is not so explicitly expressed.

Among the signs some reference must be made to Israel, particularly in Paul's exposition in Romans 11. In one passage (Rom. 11:25ff.), he looks ahead to what he calls the coming in of the full number of the Gentiles as a crucial stepping stone for the salvation of Israel. It would appear that Paul differentiates the salvation of *some* Israelites (Rom. 11:14), as a result of being provoked to jealousy by the conversion of the Gentiles, from the statement that *all* Israel would be saved (Rom. 11:27)[74]. Much debate has ranged over the meaning of Paul's 'all'. Some invest it with a comprehensive meaning, while others regard the word as showing that 'all' does not necessarily mean every individual.[75] Paul is ambiguous in his use of the word, but at least it is clear that he believed that some kind of mass response would be seen in Israel in contrast to the 'few' that had so far responded as a result of his proclamation.

He does not, however, explain the way in which this future happening will take place. Some kind of collective coming to God must be in mind.[76]

[73] G. E. Ladd, *TNT*, p. 530, inclines to this view.

[74] C. K. Barrett, *Romans* (BC, 1957), p. 223, cites an interesting parallel from *Sanhedrin* x.1, which in spite of using the expression 'all Israel' goes on to enumerate a long list of exceptions. Barrett speaks of Paul using representative terms (remnant, Gentiles, Israel as a whole). *Cf.* W. Lüthi, *Romans*, pp. 154f.

[75] J. Murray, *Romans* (1961), II, p. 98, considers that analogy is against the assumption that 'all' must mean the conversion of every Gentile.

[76] F. J. Leenhardt, *Romans* (Eng. trans. 1961, from *CNT*, 1957), p. 293, points out that 'all Israel' and 'the full number of the Gentiles' are to be understood in a collective sense without prejudging the condition of any individual.

In Romans 11:12 Paul refers to the 'full inclusion' of Israel. It should be noted that Paul is here not referring to the political restoration of the Jewish nation, but to the turning of Jewish people to God. Another interpretation equates Israel with the church, in which case 'all Israel' relates to the completion of the church. Whereas this avoids the difficulty of Paul's 'all', it does not fit in so well with the drift of Paul's argument in Romans 11.

In the pastoral epistles, two passages have a bearing on the preparatory signs. In 1 Timothy 4:1 we meet with the statement that the Spirit expressly predicts a falling away 'in later times'.[77] Although there is no specific reference to the parousia, the eschatological understanding of the words is inescapable.[78] A similar prediction is found in 2 Timothy 3:1ff. where a list of the kind of people who would not be lovers of God is given. The list, which shows some similarities with catalogues of sin found elsewhere in Paul's epistles, nevertheless goes beyond them in placing these classes of people in a future setting. At the same time 2 Timothy 3:5 advises turning away from them, which demonstrates a present as well as a future relevance.[79]

Certainly Paul envisaged a time coming when Christ will overcome all opposition (1 Cor. 15:24–25). He will put down all opposing rule, authority and power. All enemies, including death, will be put under his feet. It would seem that in Paul's mind the parousia was the consummation of the reign of Christ (but see the section on the millennium, pp. 869ff.).[80]

THE CONSISTENCY OF PAUL'S TEACHING ABOUT THE PAROUSIA

Some scholars have maintained that Paul changed his views about future happenings. This is largely on the basis of a comparison between the earlier and later epistles. If the theory of development could be established, it would explain satisfactorily the apocalyptic language of the early epistles compared with its absence in the later.

It was Dodd[81] who popularized the 'development' view for Paul's eschatology. He maintained that before the crisis of his dealings with the Corinthians, Paul was puritanical and that his clash with the Corinthians

[77] In 1 Tim. 4:1, the expression *en hysterois kairois* is equivalent to the more usual *eschatai hēmerai* (*cf.* C. Spicq, *Les Épîtres Pastorales* (EB, ⁴1969), p. 494. Those who regard the Pastorals as non-Pauline regard the different expression as evidence of the writer's stylistic choice (*cf.* M. Dibelius-H. Conzelmann, *Pastoralbriefe, ad loc.*).

[78] A. L. Moore, *The Parousia in the New Testament*, pp. 163f., regards the statement as pregnant with overtones of the parousia.

[79] See the discussion of this passage in my *The Pastoral Epistles* (TNTC, 1957), *ad loc.*

[80] Although many scholars take the commencement of the reign to be at the parousia (*cf.* H. Lietzmann, *Korinther, ad loc.*), others prefer to date it from the resurrection (*cf.* Bultmann, *TNT* 1, p. 346; C. K. Barrett, *From First Adam to Last* (1960), pp. 94, 99f.). O. Cullmann, *The Early Church*, p. 112, sees it as beginning at the ascension and overlapping into the future age. But see further discussion on pp. 868ff.

[81] *Cf.* C. H. Dodd, *New Testament Studies*, pp. 67ff.; W. L. Knox, *St Paul and the Church of the Gentiles* (1939, r.p. 1961), pp. 125–145.

THE FUTURE

had been such a humiliating experience that he softened his approach in his later letters. Whereas at first he denied the world, he is said to have sought to claim it for Christ at a later stage. The whole theory is based on an understanding of 2 Corinthians, which places chapters 1–9 among the later epistles and the rest among the earlier. This enables Dodd to maintain that 2 Corinthians 1–9, where Paul is conciliatory, shows the first evidence of his new approach. Dodd then claims that only in the earlier letters does the apostle reflect a belief in the imminence of the parousia. In the later epistles, according to him, no such indication is given.

Yet Romans 13:11–14 refers to the nearness of the day.[82] Moreover, a stronger eschatological explanation must be given to some of the references to the coming in Philippians (classed among the later epistles by Dodd). Philippians 3:20 is the most specific: 'awaiting a Saviour, the Lord Jesus Christ, from heaven'. Also in Philippians 4:5, Paul makes the statement, 'The Lord is at hand.' Philippians 1:6 looks ahead to the completion of the day of Jesus Christ (cf. also 1:10; 2:16). Furthermore, a statement like Colossians 3:4, 'When Christ . . . appears, then you also will appear with him in glory', is reminiscent of some of the statements in 1 and 2 Thessalonians. There is, in fact, no evidence that Paul made any change in his eschatology, although as he grew older he would realize that the possibility of his being alive at the parousia was diminishing. This does not mean that even at the end of his life Paul abandoned his belief in the imminence of Christ's return.[83]

The rest of the epistles

Without doubt, eschatological considerations are strongly in the mind of the writer of *Hebrews* throughout his letter.[84] He and his readers are 'in these last days' (1:2), in which God has communicated with man. The last days have therefore already begun. Moreover, the focus of attention throughout the epistle is on the heavenly realities as superior to their earthly

[82] Some consider that this Romans passage shows a stock theme which Paul has incorporated. Cf. the discussion of D. E. H. Whiteley, *The Theology of St Paul* (1964), pp. 244ff.

[83] Cf. J. A. Schep's discussion of the alleged development in Paul's eschatology, *The Nature of the Resurrection Body* (1964), pp. 206ff. For other studies critical of the 'development' view, cf. G. Vos, *The Pauline Eschatology*, pp. 172ff.; J. Lowe, 'An examination of Attempts to Detect Developments in Paul's Theology', *JTS* 42, 1941, pp. 129-142. Cf. also J. W. Drane, 'Theological Diversity in the Letters of Paul', *TB* 27 (1976), p. 3–26, who offers a corrective to the attempt to divide Paul against himself on the subject of eschatology. J. A. T. Robinson, *Jesus and his Coming*, p. 160 n.1, admits a change (from apocalyptic to non-apocalyptic) but disagrees with Dodd and Knox over a radical break between 1 and 2 Corinthians. Cf. also W. Baird, 'Pauline Eschatology in Hermeneutical Perspective', *NTS* 17, 1971, pp. 314-327, for the view that Paul's language has undergone change, which involves some modification of meaning.

[84] J. A. T. Robinson, *op. cit.*, p. 27, does not think that the parousia hope was an early belief because it is not mentioned in the foundation beliefs in Heb. 6:1f. Yet as A. L. Moore, *The Parousia in the New Testament*, p. 148, points out, the parousia was not an object of faith so much as of hope. In any case, it is open to dispute whether Heb. 6:1ff. was intended to provide a doctrinal basis.

810

counterparts. It may, in fact, be said that the whole letter has about it an air of expectancy. The clearest statement about the parousia is in 9:28: 'Christ . . . will appear a second time, not to deal with sin but to save those who are eagerly waiting for him.' No further details are given about the parousia, but the linking of it with salvation in the sense of its actualization is significant. It shows the parousia to be the key event in the consummation of the process of salvation.

Another important statement mentions the approach of 'the Day' (10:25), which calls attention to the imminence of an important event.[85] Again, the matter is mentioned almost in passing as an incentive for Christians to encourage one another. The 'appearing' of 9:28 and 'the Day' of 10:25 would no doubt have been connected in the readers' minds. Much more is assumed than specifically stated in this respect. The various references to judgment in this epistle (see pp. 863ff.) enhance the importance of the eschatological theme.

In the letter of *James*, a brief reference to the imminence of the coming of the Lord occurs in 5:7–8. Some exegetes have declined to see this as a reference to Jesus, but have professed to see in it an allusion to the coming of Yahweh in an OT sense.[86] Nevertheless, if we regard this epistle as essentially a Christian exposition of practical theology, it is most natural to see in these verses a reference to the parousia of Jesus, introduced into the practical exhortations to provide a basis for the exercise of patience.

Again the readers are reminded that they are living under the shadow of the last days (5:3), although in this passage the last days are a foreboding of doom for the rich who have oppressed others (see the section on judgment, p. 865). This is further borne out by the statement that the judge stands at the doors (5:9). In view of 5:7–8, it is clear that the judge and the Lord are the same person.[87] Some kind of imminent parousia is, therefore, undeniable in this passage. Again no details are given, but the event is certain. It is important to note that an epistle which brings so many practical exhortations to the readers can nevertheless at the same time assert the imminence of the coming.

1 Peter, like Hebrews, is strongly influenced by eschatological thought. Again the idea of imminence is prominent: 'the end of all things is at hand'

---

[85] Some have taken the day here to refer to the destruction of Jerusalem. But P. E. Hughes, *Hebrews* (1977), p. 416, rightly rejects such a view on the grounds that in prophetic usage the Day always pointed to the final day of judgment. In this context the day must be the day of Christ's parousia.

[86] This was maintained by F. Spitta, *Cf.* R. J. Knowling's discussion of this view, *James* (WC, 1904), xv, pp. 127f., *Cf.* also Dibelius-Conzelmann, *James* p. 242, who consider Spitta's theory as possible but not necessary.

[87] A. L. Moore, *op. cit.*, pp. 149f., comments on three statements in the passage James 5:7-9 which relate to the parousia: 'until the coming of the Lord', 'the coming of the Lord is at hand', and 'the Judge is standing at the doors'. Moore denies that any of these expressions delimits the expectation of the parousia. The nearness idea is linked with a coming which is not precise as to timing.

(4:7).[88] Yet God is said to be keeping his people for a salvation ready to be revealed 'in the last time' (1:5), a statement which gives no idea of imminence. The keyword of the whole letter is hope. Suffering will be replaced by glory (cf. 1:11; 4:13; 5:1, 10). The manifestation of this glory is clearly personal, although it is not specifically linked with the parousia. A definite time is envisaged when the glory will be revealed and it is natural to equate this with the coming of Christ.[89]

2 Peter and Jude have more to say about future judgment and destiny than about the parousia. Whatever the relationship of these epistles to each other, their eschatology is similar, and this justifies our classing their evidence together. The 'last days' have been predicted (2 Pet. 3:3; Jude 17f.) and the inference is to be drawn that they have now arrived. Confusion has nevertheless arisen over the parousia, for some had been scoffing as a result of its delay (3:4). Everything, according to the scoffers, had continued unchanged since the beginning of creation. These people had apparently misconstrued the character of the gospel and had eliminated the eschatological hope.[90]

Peter assures his readers that the day of the Lord will come as a thief, and then proceeds to identify that day as the consummation of both heaven and earth (3:10). This is presumably identified with the inauguration of the eternal kingdom of Christ (1:11). Jude speaks of waiting for the mercy of our Lord Jesus Christ unto eternal life (verse 21), which may be a reference to the parousia. It certainly implies some future event which can be anticipated.

Revelation

Whereas in other NT books incidental references to the end times occur, in this book it is the central theme. The viewpoint is futuristic, although not entirely so, as the messages to the churches show. The book is both a word to a specific first-century historical situation and at the same time a vision of the end times. Its presentation of the consummation of human history is valuable, because it is the only treatment of the theme within the NT. It shows the ultimate triumph of the Lamb over all his enemies. We shall

[88] For a comparison of this passage with the evidence from 1 Thes. 5:1ff., *cf.* E. G. Selwyn, *1 Peter* (1946), pp. 375ff. He shows strong links between the two passages, and also between other statements in 1 Peter and 1 Thes. 5.

[89] In 1:20, Peter sets the incarnation at the end of time. C. E. B. Cranfield points out that this implies that all subsequent history is an epilogue in which men have an opportunity to come to terms with the meaning of their lives (*1 and 2 Peter and Jude*, 1960, p. 112). In this case the coming of Christ (parousia) would be the close of the epilogue.

[90] E. Käsemann, 'An Apologia for Primitive Christian Eschatology', in *Essays on New Testament Themes* (Eng. trans. 1964), 169ff., originally published in *ZTK* 49, 1952, pp. 272ff., is a strong supporter of the view that the eschatology of 2 Peter 3 is de-Christologized, de-ethicized, and de-centralized. But *cf.* A. L. Moore's perceptive criticism of this view on the grounds that the main features can be paralleled in Mk. 13 and 2 Thes. 2 (*Parousia*, pp. 152f.).

note the following features: the description of the coming; its imminence; preliminary signs; the place of the coming in the structure of the book.

THE DESCRIPTION OF THE COMING

Although the coming is not actually described until chapter 19, it may be said that the whole book prepares for this event from the first hint of it in 1:7. It must be noted, however, that 19:11ff. does not speak of a coming, but of a manifestation. This appearing of Christ marks the climax of the book and the salient points of this event will therefore be brought out before commenting on the immediately preceding events.

We note first the use of apocalyptic imagery: the white horse, the flaming eyes, the robe and the sharp sword (19:11ff.).[91] Some of these features occur in the description of the exalted Christ in 1:12ff. The manifestation is of the same exalted person. He proceeds out of heaven. He is given various names: Faithful, True, Word of God, King of kings and Lord of lords (19:11, 13, 16), which reflect his nature. Moreover, he appears for the purpose of judgment. A sharp sword for combat and an iron rod for rule show the supremacy of Christ over all opposition. His appearing signals the concluding scene of carnage, after which the prophet's vision focuses on the New Jerusalem (chs. 21, 22).

The relation of this vision to the totality of future events has been the subject of a wide variety of interpretations (see the section below on the place of the parousia). For the present we are concerned to note that the fact of the future manifestation of Christ is undeniable in the Apocalypse, and is in line with the evidence in other NT books.

ITS IMMINENCE

Since the manifestation is located in the end time and must be preceded by numerous preliminary events, it would not be expected that much emphasis would be found on its imminence. Yet in the opening of the book, John speaks of the revelation of what must soon take place and asserts that the time is near (1:1–3).[92] He could not have made clearer that his book was not to be regarded as relating to remote times in the future. Other similar statements about the nearness of the coming are found in 3:11; 22:7, 12, 20. Indeed the book ends as it begins with this theme.

It is admittedly difficult to reconcile this sense of proximity with the long series of intervening events. We may resort to one of two possibilities.

---

[91] As G. R. Beasley-Murray, *Revelation* (NCB, 1974), pp. 277f. notes, this passage describing the coming is one of the most powerful and impressive in the whole book. The author uses hyperbole with little regard for consistency. It is clear that for him the coming is the key event in the consummation of history.

[92] There are two possible interpretations of *kairos* in Rev. 1:3. It can either refer to an immediately impending crisis, such as approaching persecution of the Christians, *cf.* G. B. Caird, *Revelation* (BC, 1966), p. 12. Or it can have a specifically future reference relating to the end, *cf.* M. Rissi, *Time and History* (Eng. trans. 1966), p. 22.

Either the two points of view are irreconcilable and must be attributed to different apocalyptic traditions,[93] or it must be supposed that the intervening signs, though occupying the major part of the book, were not intended to imply an extended period of time. If the view is adopted that the visions are parallel[94] rather than consecutive, the second solution is preferable. Moreover, since the purpose of the book was to give immediate encouragement, it is more reasonable to suppose that no long delay was expected. But this leads us to consider the preliminary events.

THE EVENTS BEFORE THE PAROUSIA

The main section of the book is taken up with the description of events, couched in apocalyptic imagery, which must happen before the parousia. We may consider these under various heads.

The pronouncements of judgments. At the opening of the seals, trumpets and bowls we find a divine visitation. If, as seems probable, these series run concurrently, we are meant to see various aspects of divine judgments. The over-all impact of God's wrath is more important than the separate details. Some of the judgments are natural plagues, though intensified in their impact, while some have supernatural characteristics of fiendish proportions. The intention is to build up an impression of inevitable judgment on those who refuse to serve God, while at the same time leaving room for repentance (*cf.* 9:20; 16:9).[95] It should be noted that, as is usual in apocalyptic literature, the prophet's words cannot always be interpreted in a literal way. He makes widespread use of poetic symbolism to emphasize the eternal truth that final judgment is in the hand of God.

The suffering of God's people. In harmony with the testimony in other parts of the NT, the people of God are not expected to escape unscathed from the malicious opposition of opposing forces. The readers were passing through a time of stress through the policy of the political powers, and many had either already suffered (as Antipas, Rev. 2:13)[96] or were threatened with persecution in the near future. With the rise of a person with the fullest possible antagonism to God (the antichrist), the persecution of God's people

---

[93] *Cf.* I. Beckwith, *The Apocalypse of John* (1919, r.p. 1967), p. 157.

[94] *Cf.* W. Hendriksen, *More than Conquerors* (1962).

[95] M. Kiddle, *Revelation* (MNT, 1940), *ad loc.*, on 9:20 considers this statement to show how God has now exhausted every attempt to bring the world to a better mind. But the recurrence of this idea of repentance in 16:9 would indicate that the possibility of repentance was still present. G. B. Caird, *Revelation*, p. 124, sees the reference here to be an encouragement to the martyrs: what the trumpets of judgment could not bring about, their witness might. That witness was, therefore, indispensable.

[96] Beasley-Murray, *Revelation*, p. 85, suggests that as only Antipas had apparently died, this circumstance would better fit mob violence than official persecution.

would also be intensified (*cf.* 12:1ff.). This intensification of persecution is frequently called 'The great tribulation' (after the expression in 7:14).

There are various opinions regarding the people who will pass through this tribulation. Some hold to the view that Christians will be caught up to be with Christ (the 'rapture'), before the great tribulation (see pp. 845ff.).[97] But Revelation does not in fact describe a pre-tribulation 'rapture', and this view must be regarded as speculative. Moreover, Christians clearly do not escape from persecution in this book. The theory is based on a distinction between a 'coming' of Christ for his people and a 'coming' to execute judgment. In view of the difficulties in this theory, others prefer to hold to one coming and to place that coming after the period of intense tribulation. Clearly the interpretation adopted will affect the question whether the tribulation itself can be considered a sign of the parousia. It is significant that all the signs mentioned by Jesus in the Matthew 24 = Mark 13 discourse recur among the woes of the Apocalypse.[98]

The rise of antichrist. The concept of counterfeit Christs has already been met in other NT books,[99] but in this book there are agencies which are the most intense embodiments of all that is evil. Such personifications of evil are in line with the lawless man in 2 Thessalonians 2. These anti-Christian agencies will make an all-out attempt to crush the true worship of God. Although evil is sometimes portrayed as Satan, the dragon, it is also personified in a beast. Indeed, Satan and the first and second beast form an infamous trinity of evil, whose over-riding passion is to oppose Christ. The antichrist idea has more than one facet and gathers up all those acts of tyranny, oppression and sheer antagonism to God, which have occurred throughout human history.

The significance of this personification of all evil is that it assures the people of God that when the Lamb overcomes evil it is in its intensest form. The worst that Satan can do will prove ineffective against the superior power of God and his Christ.[100] The parousia of antichrist is in reality the announcement of the impending doom of all antichrists. There is a linking up between the kind of activity of the abomination of desolation in Mark 13 and the final act of apostasy instigated by Satan and his agents.

---

[97] So J. Walvoord, *The Millennial Kingdom*, (²1963), pp. 256ff. *Cf.* also A. S. Wood, *Prophecy in the Space Age* 1963), pp. 103ff.

[98] G. R. Beasley-Murray, *Revelation*, p. 130, makes a useful comparison between Mk. 13 and Rev. 6. He suggests that John knew a version of the eschatological discourse which was independent of and prior to the synoptic gospels.

[99] *Cf.* R. Yates, 'The Antichrist', *EQ* 46 (1974), pp. 42ff., who studies the occurrence of the word, plus those passages which highlight opposition in the last days (*e.g.* Dn. 7:7ff., 21f.; 2 Thes. 2 and Rev. 13).

[100] It should be noted that in all parts of the book Satan is seen as strictly limited in his operation. The sovereignty rests firmly with God. *Cf.* M. Rissi's section on 'The time of the Antichrist', *Time and History*, pp. 62-86.

The destruction of the existing world order. The symbol of the political forces
is Babylon the Great, which in the first century would have been recognized
as the imperial power of Rome, but which in any age can be identified
with political powers which are set purely on material aims apart from
God. The vision of Babylon's fall is, therefore, a vision of the fall of all
such political powers.[101] The symbol of Babylon was chosen because it
stood for the oppressors of God's people. The destruction of the symbolic
city is not so much a precursor as an accompaniment of the coming of the
victorious Lamb. The lament over Babylon in chapter 18 brings out mag-
nificently the utter impotence and ultimate futility of material power and
wealth face to face with the righteous anger of God (see pp. 866ff.).

THE PLACE OF THE PAROUSIA IN THE STRUCTURE OF THE BOOK

The importance of the parousia of the victorious Christ is not only seen in
chapter 19, where it marks the real climax of the book, but is prepared for
in many earlier passages (*cf.* 1:7; 14:14–20; 16:15). Some note must therefore
be taken of the various interpretations of the significance of the event.
Those who adopt the view that the whole book is no more than a tract for
its own times dismiss the prophetic element of a future parousia. The same
result could be reached from a purely symbolic interpretation,[102] although
it need not be so. Much of the imagery clearly cannot be explained in a
literal manner, but this does not detract from the fact of a future coming
as an actual event.

A different approach is that which maintains that Revelation is concerned
with a double programme, one for Israel and one for the church.[103] The
key to the interpretation of the whole book, according to this view, is that
the seals, trumpets and bowls, representing the great tribulation, apply
only to Israel and not to the church. The church in fact is removed from
the scene (the rapture) before the visions (chapter 4–19) commence. In the
heavenly vision, the elders represent the church. The major scene of conflict, therefore, is between the beast and Israel, and not the church.[104] In
this view the signs preceding the final parousia are for Israel and not for
the church, which has already experienced a secret parousia of Christ at
the time of the rapture. Some link with this the view that the letters to the
seven churches represent successive stages in the history of the church.

It cannot be claimed, however, that the book itself gives any indication
of this two-fold programme, and the fact that the beginning and ending of

---

[101] As L. Morris, *Revelation* (*TNTC*, 1969), p. 214, comments, John is thinking of the collapse of
civilization, not simply of one city or empire.

[102] J. A. T. Robinson, in *Jesus and his Coming*, does not examine the passage, Rev. 19:1-11, presumably
because he regards the parousia as a myth (*cf.* pp. 181f.).

[103] *Cf.* J. D. Pentecost, *Things to Come*; J. F. Walvoord, *The Millennial Kingdom*.

[104] For a critique of this view, *cf.* J. W. Hodges, *Christ's Kingdom and Coming* (1957).

the book (*cf.* 22:16) refer to the churches suggests that the intervening visions were addressed to, and intended to have relevance to, Christians. This view fails to give adequate weight to the original historical background of the book and to the numerous specifically Christian elements in Revelation 4–19.

A more moderate futurist view sees in the first part of the book (chapters 1–6) an historical application, with the seven churches representing the whole Christian church and the seals referring to various historical forces impinging on the period prior to the end event.[105] In this view chapters 7–22 alone refer to the future winding up of human history.

Whatever the specific interpretation of the details of the book might be, no interpreter can fail to see that the coming of Christ marks the climax to the history of the ages and forms a fitting conclusion to the redemptive purposes of God in human history. Those who deny the fact of the second coming by attaching to it a wholly spiritual significance are left with a view of human history which has no effective conclusion. A NT theology which finds no place for a second coming of Christ must necessarily be incomplete and unsatisfactory.

Summary

There is no doubt from the evidence we have considered that Jesus himself predicted and the early Christians firmly believed in a future coming. Although the fact of the coming is indisputable, it is not possible to be certain of many of the details. The date of the coming is unknown, but some indication of the manner of it may be deduced.

Apocalyptic imagery is in some cases used to describe the coming, as for instance the clouds, trumpets and loud voices, which are employed to indicate a future public manifestation. This imagery is not confined to the synoptic gospels, but is found also in 1 Thessalonians and Revelation.

The note of surprise is introduced several times, for instance by the use of the thief analogy to express the suddenness or unexpectedness of the coming. Indeed, this emphasis gives rise to the belief in the imminence of the coming. Side by side with this feature is the complementary problem of the delay in the coming, heightened by the intervening signs which must first be fulfilled. The NT does not present any clear programme, and a certain tension is evident. The problems raised by the 'rapture' will be discussed in a separate note later (see pp. 845ff.).

It has been seen that there are no strong grounds for supposing that Paul changed his mind about the future coming. There is no reason to suppose that he considered the intervening signs as necessarily requiring an extended period of time. He is not the only NT writer who considers that a constant

---

[105] *Cf.* G. E. Ladd, *Revelation* (1972).

preparedness carries with it a strong moral challenge for everyday living.

It is Revelation which focuses most clearly on the coming of Christ as the climax of the present age. There is never any doubt that the coming will mark a triumph. The Lamb is sovereign throughout and the coming is portrayed as the final manifestation of his victory. This book uses the event of the coming as a key to the Christian philosophy of history.

THE AFTERLIFE

Under this section we shall concern ourselves mainly with the subject of the resurrection of believers and immortality, as well as considering the evidence about the intermediate state. The subject of the resurrection was currently important among the Jews and caused a marked rift between the Pharisees and Sadducees.[106] The former accepted it (as did the Essenes), but the latter rejected it. It is against this background that the specific teaching of Jesus must be considered.[107]

The synoptic gospels

THE RESURRECTION OF THE BODY

In view of the controversy between the Sadducees and Pharisees over this subject, it is reasonable to begin by considering the attempt of the former to trap Jesus with a trick question (Mk. 12:18–27 = Mt. 22:23–33 = Lk. 20:27–40).[108] The question was designed to test Jesus' ideas of a bodily resurrection. If a woman had been married to seven brothers, whose would she be in the resurrection? In reply Jesus pinpoints their wrong view of resurrection. Marriage does not belong to the resurrection state. That state is compared to that of the angels. Jesus' further statement that God is not the God of the dead, but of the living, recorded in all the synoptic gospels, is based on the continued relationship between God and Abraham, Isaac and Jacob.[109]

The method of debate is typically rabbinic. Jesus is pointing out that the very expression, 'The God of Abraham, Isaac and Jacob', with its strong

---

[106] A thorough examination of the Jewish background of this subject may be found in H. C. C. Cavallin, *Life after Death* (1974). This study was designed as a preparation for an investigation of Paul's arguments in 1 Cor. 15.

[107] For an account of resurrection hopes in the intertestamental period, *cf.* G. W. E. Nickelsburg, Jnr, *Resurrection, Immortality, and Eternal Life in Intertestamental Judaism*, 1972). For the Qumran belief, *cf.* K. Schubert, *The Dead Sea Community* (Eng. trans. 1959), pp. 108ff.; *idem*, 'Die Entwicklung der Auferstehungslehre von den Qumrantexten und in der frührabbinischen Zeit', *BZ* 6, 1962, pp. 177–214.

[108] *Cf.* W. Strawson's discussion of this passage in *Jesus and the Future Life* (1959), pp. 203ff.

[109] In a comment on Lk. 20:27-40, E.E. Ellis, *Luke* (*NCB*, 1966), *ad loc.*, considers that this passage does not support Abraham's immortality, that he is now individually in heaven. He agrees with R. Bultmann, *TNT* 1, p. 209 and W. G. Kümmel, *Man*, pp. 43ff., 86, that the NT view of man does not support a body-soul dualism. Ellis considers that the passage teaches resurrection, not survival.

OT attestation (Ex. 3:6), presupposed that the patriarchs were still in existence in some form or another.[110] Although the method of argument may seem strange, there is no denying that Jesus was affirming the existence of a resurrection state in opposition to the Sadducees.[111] In Luke's account, Jesus' words are more explicit about the resurrection state than they are in Mark's or Matthew's. He speaks of those 'worthy to attain to that age and to the resurrection from the dead'. Jesus definitely asserts that the dead are raised. It is also Luke who records a saying of Jesus about the resurrection of the just when rewards for good deeds will be received (Lk. 14:14).

Another saying involving the patriarchs is Matthew 8:11f. = Lk. 13:28f., where it is said that many will come from east and west to sit at table with Abraham, Isaac and Jacob in the kingdom, while 'the sons of the kingdom' will be consigned to outer darkness to weep and gnash their teeth. Again the language used presupposes some kind of bodily resurrection.

When in the Sermon on the Mount (Mt. 5:29f.) Jesus comments on adultery, he speaks of the possibility of the 'whole body' being cast into hell (see the section on hell, pp. 887f.). Moreover, Jesus warns his disciples to fear him who can destroy both soul and body in hell (Mt. 10:28), which shows again the importance of the bodily aspect of the afterlife.

In the synoptic gospels, we find very little information about life after death, but what we possess is positive in affirming it. Jesus gives no data, however, on the nature of the resurrection body, nor on the nature of death, both of which are touched upon in the Pauline epistles. In John's gospel there are a few significant sayings which throw more light on the subject and which help to complement the synoptic presentation.

A further question arises. Did Jesus lend any support to the idea of the immortality of the soul? The idea of an immortality of the soul as distinct from the resurrection of the body is an essentially Greek idea, expressed, for instance, in Plato.[112] This arose partly out of the belief that the body, being matter, was evil and therefore mortal. According to this view, all people are essentially immortal in their souls, but not in their bodies. The NT, however, does not support such a sharp dichotomy. There is, in fact, nothing of relevance on the subject in the synoptics apart from the passages mentioned above, none of which supports it.[113] This theme will require fuller comment when Paul's doctrine of the afterlife is considered (see pp. 832ff.).

[110] R. Otto, *The Kingdom of God and the Son of Man* (1938), p. 239, notes claims that the patriarchs were delivered from death, but not resurrected.

[111] V. Taylor, *Mark* (²1966), p. 483, says that Jesus is thinking only of the righteous here. Strawson, *op. cit.*, p. 209, agrees.

[112] *Cf.* Plato in *Phaedo* in which he describes the death of Socrates and records Socrates' exposition of immortality before his death.

[113] *Cf.* O. Cullmann, *Immortality of the Soul or Resurrection of the Dead?* (1958), for a full discussion of this theme.

We next turn our attention to the ideas about the intermediate state. This is a term used of the state of existence between the believer's death and the resurrection at the last day. Although we find no direct details of this from the synoptic gospels, there are certain relevant passages which warrant our attention. In the OT, Sheol was considered to be the abode of shadowy existence. In the intertestamental period, however, Sheol had come to be regarded as a stage between death and judgment. In the teaching of Jesus, Sheol, now known as Hades, occurs three times in the synoptics (Mt. 11:23; 16:18; Lk. 16:23). In saying that Capernaum would be brought down to Hades, Jesus was indicating its complete destruction, a case in which Hades is used figuratively. In the second saying the church is shown to be impregnable against the gates of Hades, which here appear to stand for human opposition, another metaphorical use.

The third occurrence is in the parable of Dives and Lazarus (Lk. 16:19–31), which supposes a division in the abode of the dead with an impassable gulf between. Some parallel with this is found in the book of Enoch and appears to have been a current Jewish idea at the time.[114] It would be precarious to regard the parable as a sufficient basis for deducing the nature of the afterlife as understood by Jesus, for the intention of the parable was clearly not doctrinal, but moral. The focus falls on the selfish life of the rich man. The parable says nothing about the possibility of the man changing his status; indeed, it implies the opposite. The only certain fact about the afterlife which emerges from the parable is the reality of its existence.[115] The parable would make no sense if the afterlife itself were a myth. The state of the departed, moreover, is directly linked to their behaviour in this life, which raises the question whether the parable is intended to teach that there would be a direct reversal of status in the afterlife. It cannot be maintained that Jesus intended to teach this, irrespective of circumstances.

In the case of the rich man it was not the fact of his riches, but what he did with his riches, which is the point of the parable. He was thoroughly selfish and self-indulgent and completely unconcerned about his social responsibilities. He was, in fact, a typical representative of a Saducean approach to life.[116] He had clearly never considered that his behaviour in his lifetime would affect his after-existence. He probably did not believe

---

[114] J. M. Creed, *Luke* (1930), pp. 209f., refers to current Egyptian and Jewish stories about a rich and a poor man.

[115] K. Hanhart, *The Intermediate State in the New Testament* (1966), pp. 190ff., discusses this passage in detail and concludes, 'The problem of the interim state arises when one attempts to combine the two "ends" in a logical system.' *Cf.* also J. D. M. Derrett, 'Fresh Light on Lk. xvi. I. The Parable of the Unjust Steward', *NTS* 7, 1960-1, pp. 198ff., and II. Dives and Lazarus and the Preceding Sayings', *NTS* 7, pp. 364ff. He connects the two passages together. In his interpretation Lazarus is linked with Eliezer, Abrham's servant. Derrett regards the story as intended to encourage, not to dismay. It focuses on what remains of this life.

[116] *Cf.* T. W. Manson, *The Sayings of Jesus* (1949), p. 299.

in an afterlife, as he knew his brethren did not. He is moreover reminded that they would not believe if one returned from the dead.[117] Here again it is assumed that the testimony of the Scriptures (Moses and the prophets) was sufficient to demonstrate life after death, not because of their explicit teaching on the subject, but because of their revelation of the nature of God (as in the controversy of Jesus with the Sadducees, already noted).

Another passage which has some relevance for our present discussion is Luke 23:42f., in which Jesus assured the dying evildoer that he would be with him that day in Paradise.[118] Since this is in answer to the request that Jesus would remember the man when he comes into his kingdom, it raises the question of the relationship between Paradise and the kingdom. Two possible explanations of the passage have been proposed. One is that Paradise is an interim realm in which both the evildoer and Jesus will await the kingdom. The other is that Paradise is a synonym for heaven and that Jesus would enter into his kingdom that same day. Since Paradise, in the intertestamental period, had come to be regarded as an intermediate resting-place for righteous souls, this would support the first interpretation.[119] Nevertheless in 2 Corinthians 12:3 and Revelation 2:7 Paradise is used as a symbol for heaven, which would lend support for the second view.

Both interpretations raise difficulties over the resurrection of Christ and over his parousia. The most that can be said is that the passage may supply evidence about the intermediate state, but does not necessarily do so. What is more certain is that the wrongdoer, presumably on the grounds that his petition involved repentance, would after death be in the presence of Christ.[120]

THE ATTITUDE TO DEATH

It would be incomplete to discuss the hereafter without discussing death. Undoubtedly one's belief about the afterlife affects one's attitude to death. Although many avoid the subject of death and consider morbid anyone who faces up to the problems it raises, Jesus never adopted an evasive approach. Both his teaching and his example are full of inspiration on this matter. In his day human life was cheap and violent death was a common occurrence. Children even played at funerals (Mt. 11:16f.; Lk. 7:32), so uninhibited was the general approach to the subject. In Luke's nativity narrative, Simeon expresses a willingness to depart in peace after having seen the Christ (Lk. 2:25–35). His approach to death was affected by his

---

[117] By this expression it is just possible that Jesus may have been thinking of his own resurrection.

[118] For a full discussion of this passage, *cf.* K. Hanhart, *op. cit.*, pp. 199ff. He maintains that the passage does not support an intermediate state. He further maintains that Paradise is not in contrast to kingdom, but parallel to it.

[119] On Paradise, *cf.* J. Jeremias, *TDNT* 5, pp. 765ff.

[120] I. H. Marshall, *Luke*, p. 873, compares the criminal's hope to attain life at the parousia with Jesus' assurance that he would have immediate entry into Paradise.

knowledge of the advent of Christ. In Simeon's song the reference to the sword piercing Mary's heart brings the passion of Jesus into close proximity to his coming.

When 'the dead' are referred to in the synoptics, the word is usually plural, pointing to a group idea of death. While death comes to everyone individually, it is corporate in the sense that no-one is excluded. Violent death features in some of the parables (Mt. 21:39; 22:6). Jesus laments over the killing of the prophets (Mt. 23:37) and predicts that some of his disciples would be killed (Mt. 24:9; Lk. 21:16). Our concern, however, is to consider Jesus' attitude to death itself. Here we note that he did not support the view that suffering and death were evidences of special sinfulness (as for instance the examples cited in Lk. 13:1–5). Although in conformity to the Mosaic law, death was regarded as contaminating to the extent that anyone who touched a dead body was defiled (*cf.* whitewashing of tombs, Mt. 23:27), Jesus did not teach such a view. In fact he said nothing about the corrupting effects of death. He maintained a respect for death, without becoming obsessed with it.

We need further to consider the significance of 'sleep' as a figure for death. This was familiar in Hebrew thought.[121] It finds expression in a few cases in the words of Jesus. In the OT the concept of 'sleep' when applied to death always stands in a context which shows it is being used metaphorically. In the intertestamental period it was also used as a synonym for death. But in the account of the raising of Jairus' daughter, Jesus says of the girl that she is 'not dead but sleeping' (Mt. 9:24 = Mk. 5:39 = Lk. 8:52). He was not understood by the mourners to be identifying sleep and death, for they laughed him to scorn. It would, on the other hand, make nonsense of the whole incident if Jesus was merely saying she was in a coma. All the evangelists portray the miracle as a raising from the dead.

How then is the sleep metaphor to be understood? It has been suggested that 'sleep' was a description of death seen from God's point of view.[122] But this would imply a state of 'sleep' between death and resurrection, a view which does not seem to be supported elsewhere in the gospels (*cf.* for instance Jesus' words about Paradise to the dying thief, which presuppose a conscious experience). It seems better to maintain that, from the mourners' point of view, this death would turn out to be a 'sleep', because the girl was about to be roused out of it. It amounts to a new way of looking at death by virtue of the power of Christ, who would not himself be held by it (see next section for a similar approach to the death of Lazarus).

Some comment must be made on Jesus' attitude to his own death. It has already been demonstrated that he predicted it and considered it to be

---

[121] *Cf.* C. Ryder Smith, *The Bible Doctrine of the Hereafter* (1958), pp. 42ff.

[122] So W. Strawson, *Jesus and the Future Life*, pp. 84f.

connected with man's sin (see pp. 438f.). He knew, therefore, that his own death possessed special significance. There is a difference between Jesus' approach to death and that of other people in respect of its significance. But was there a difference in approach to the physical experience of death? Some scholars[123] maintain the 'distress' which Jesus experienced when contemplating his passion (in Gethsemane, Mt. 26:38 = Mk. 14:34 = Lk. 22:44) was occasioned by fear of physical death. Indeed, it is claimed that a horror of death on the part of Jesus would link him with true humanity, for all must die and most fear death.

But this explanation cannot by itself sufficiently account for the nature of the distress. More weight must be given to our Lord's consciousness of the tremendous significance of his own death, an awareness which no other person ever experienced. We must take account of the effect on a sinless person of consciously bearing upon himself the sin of the world. Moreover, the cry of dereliction becomes doubly perplexing if what is involved is simply the natural fear of death (Mk. 15:34 = Mt. 27:46). It is more intelligible to hold that it was the bearing of sin, which by its very nature separates from God, which explains the cry from the cross.

The Johannine literature
THE RESURRECTION OF THE BODY

There are two main passages in John's gospel which have a direct bearing on this theme. The first concerns the account of the raising of Lazarus, the central passage of which for our purpose is John 11:21–26. The Johannine teaching on the resurrection theme is essentially similar to the synoptic teaching. When Jesus declares that Lazarus will rise again, Martha at once concludes that he is speaking of the resurrection at the last day (John 11:23f.). There is no doubt in her mind that some kind of future resurrection will take place, but no details are given of the nature of the resurrection body.

It is impossible to say what Martha's understanding of resurrection was, but Jesus' answer to her comment is distinctive, because it relates resurrection to himself. The words, 'I am the resurrection and the life' (Jn. 11:25) suggest that Jesus was clarifying the whole conception of resurrection, by identifying the resurrection of believers with his own: 'He who believes in me, though he die, yet shall he live.' Admittedly in this statement Jesus does not specifically refer to the resurrection of the body, but he makes clear that believers in him may expect life in place of death. A firm assertion of immortality is undeniable. Since Jesus later raised Lazarus from the dead in a physical form, it is reasonable to suppose that he was not suggesting immortality of the soul apart from the resurrection of the body. Indeed,

[123] *Cf.* O. Cullmann, *Immortality of the Soul or Resurrection of the Dead?* pp. 21f.; W. Strawson, *op. cit.*, pp. 95f.

in stating, 'I am the resurrection', Jesus implies that his own resurrection body may be taken as a pattern for the resurrection of believers.[124]

The other passage is John 5:25–29, where resurrection is closely linked with judgment. Jesus is describing a coming event: 'The hour is coming' (verses 25, 28).[125] That event is further designated as the resurrection of life and the resurrection of judgment (verse 29). The idea that 'life' here is simply a spiritual concept is excluded by the description of the opening of the tombs. Certainly the passage supports the view that the resurrection applies to everyone, although a sharp distinction is made between those who have done good and those who have done evil. In this case the resultant 'life' is contrasted with the resultant 'condemnation'. It is important to note that Jesus does not separate in time the resurrection of the just from that of the unjust, either in John or in the synoptics. They are assumed to happen simultaneously.

THE INTERMEDIATE STATE

We have already seen that the synoptic gospels give little information about the intermediate state. In John's gospel there is even less. Some have seen John 14:2, 'I go to prepare a place for you', as implying some special place which might be identified with the intermediate state.[126] The context lays stress on the expectation that 'where I am you may be also', and presupposes an immediate entrance of the righteous into the Father's presence. A similar theme is expressed in John 17:24, when Jesus prays that those whom the Father had given to him might be with him where he was to be. In that state they would see the glory which the Father had given to the Son. There is no suggestion that any interval of time would elapse before the believer would be with Christ subsequent to death, although it admittedly is not specifically excluded.[127] The focus is definitely on the blessedness of being with Christ, which could hardly refer to a temporary state nor to a state of unconsciousness.

---

[124] Note also Jn. 6:44 which affirms that Christ will raise up at the last day anyone who comes to the Father by him.

[125] R. E. Brown, *John*, p. 220, assigns Jn. 5:25 to the previous verses 19-24 and sees in it realized eschatology. Verses 26-29 are taken as final eschatology. Brown understands the dead in verse 25 as spiritually dead. However, he rejects Bultmann's dichotomy between the two eschatologies. *Cf.* P. Gächter's essay on the form of Jn. 5:19-30 in *Neutestamentliche Aufsätze. Festschrift für J. Schmid* (ed. J. Blinzler, D. Kuss, and F. Mussner, 1963), pp. 65ff.

[126] U. Simon, *Heaven in the Christian Tradition* (1958), p. 216, takes Jn. 14:2 as a specific confirmation by Jesus of an interim state.

[127] E. Käsemann, *The Testament of Jesus* (Eng. trans. 1968), p. 72, rejects the view that Jn. 17:24 is to be understood in the sense that Jesus brings his own to himself in the hour of death. He rejects a similar interpretation of Jn. 14:2ff. His idea is that John has spiritualized old apocalyptic traditions. But see R. E. Brown, *John*, pp. 779f., for a comment on this view. He appeals to Phil 1:23 to show that it may have been a Christian view that Christians would be with Christ at death. Brown is too cautious, for there are strong grounds for maintaining that it *is* the NT view.

THE ATTITUDE TO DEATH

There are a few sayings in John's gospel which relate to the subject of death. Jesus said, 'If any one keeps my word, he will never see death' (Jn. 8:51).[128] It is not surprising that the Jews who were contending that Jesus had a demon felt that this saying confirmed their opinion. They clearly thought that Jesus was propounding a way of escaping from physical death. They point out that even Abraham and the prophets died. In answer Jesus does not elucidate this point, but it is clear from the sequel that he was not thinking of physical death. It is in this context that he says, 'Before Abraham was, I am' (Jn. 8:58).[129] The saying tells us nothing about death, but focuses on the character of Jesus. It is worth noting that whereas Jesus said 'see' death, his critics altered the word to 'taste' (Jn. 8:52), presumably because it bore the same meaning.[130] Jesus must have meant that his followers would have a totally different approach to the experience of death from others, an experience which would remove from it its terrors. An alternative interpretation would be to assume that Jesus was referring to spiritual death, which his own followers would not experience. This is possible, but there is nothing in the preamble to prepare his hearers for such a transference of thought.

Two statements in the Lazarus passage have relevance for our subject. In John 11:4 Jesus says, 'This illness is not unto death; it is for the glory of God.' Here he must be looking beyond the event of physical death to the restoration of Lazarus to life. It contributes little therefore to our understanding of death, beyond the fact that death is no obstacle in the path of God's glory. The second statement is 11:11, 'Our friend Lazarus has fallen asleep, but I go to awake him out of sleep.' John comments that the disciples thought that Jesus literally meant that Lazarus was asleep, although he at once explained to them that Lazarus was dead. We have noted a similar distinction between sleep and death in the synoptics, for Jesus is again using sleep as a synonym for death. It is fundamentally the same idea as in the case of Jairus' daughter. It is not an unconscious state, but a state of death from which a man may be released. Neither Lazarus nor Jairus' daughter has left on the gospel records any impression of the experience of death through which they had passed.

When considering the synoptic material we noted various views about our Lord's attitude to death. In John's account the Gethsemane narrative is missing, but a parallel saying is found in John 12:27: 'Now is my soul troubled. And what shall I say? "Father, save me from this hour"? No, for

---

[128] L. Morris, *John*, p. 469, comments that the word 'death' here is in an emphatic position.

[129] J. Marsh, *John* (²1968), p. 371, reckons that this saying joins terrestrial time and heavenly eternity. It would still, however, tell us nothing about the state of existence in the heavenly realm.

[130] B. Lindars, *John* (*NCB*, 1972), pp. 332f., is of the opinion that this statement is built on Mt. 16:28, the only other passage where the expression 'to taste death' occurs in the Gospels.

this purpose I have come to this hour'. Again, it would not be evident from the context that Jesus is expressing fear of death. It is true that he has his passion in mind (as 12:32 shows), but it is the 'hour' which is uppermost. It is not death itself, but the nature and purpose of the death, which causes the distress. It should be noted that in the previous chapter Jesus was deeply moved and wept when he saw the distress which death had brought to Lazarus' family (Jn. 11:33–35). In neither case does the distress of Jesus directly result from the mere fact of physical death. Another feature in John's gospel is the triumphant cry ('It is finished') from the cross just prior to the moment of death (Jn. 19:30), which transforms the horror into a completed mission.

In the resurrection appearance in John 21:15ff., Jesus predicted what kind of death Peter would die (verses 18–19). The evangelist recognized when he wrote that Jesus regarded Peter's death as a means by which he would glorify God. Death for the disciples was not to be feared if it was a means to achieve such an end. When Jesus said of the beloved disciple, 'If it is my will that he remain until I come, what is that to you?' he implies that only those would escape death who would still be alive at his coming (cf. Mk. 13:27). It is Paul who enlarges on this theme, but the germ of it is found in the teaching of Jesus.

Because in the Johannine epistles the focus falls on the quality of this life, it is not altogether surprising that little is said about the afterlife. But as in John's gospel, so in 1 John, much is said about eternal life, which must imply more than this life. Moreover, when death is mentioned it has a moral connotation, the opposite of life. What is explicit in most other NT books, seems to be assumed here.

Acts

It is perhaps not surprising in view of the nature of this book that its contribution to the subject of the resurrection of believers is slight. Indeed the major statement occurs in Paul's Areopagus address. The Epicureans and Stoics had heard that Paul had been preaching Jesus and the resurrection (17:18). The subsequent address at the Areopagus was cut short at the first mention of the resurrection of the dead.[131] Paul speaks of the resurrection of a 'man' whom God had appointed (17:31). The strong reaction of mockery reflects the scepticism of the hearers over the whole idea of resurrection. In a Greek setting this must be understood as relating to the resurrection of the body in distinction from the immortality of the soul, which the Greeks who followed Plato accepted. Paul's stress on the resurrection of Christ immediately set him in conflict with the prevailing

---

[131] Cf. F. F. Bruce, *The Acts of the Apostles* (²1952), p. 340, who regards the plural ('dead men') as a generalizing plural.

opinion in Athens.[132] But since it formed the core of his Christian gospel, he had no option but to proclaim it even in the face of scepticism.[133]

In the earlier speech of Peter at Pentecost, there are two references to Hades (2:27, 31). The first is in a citation from Psalm 16:8–11: 'For thou wilt not abandon my soul to Hades, nor let thy Holy One see corruption'; the second is a comment upon it that saw its fulfilment in Christ. The psalm itself contains more profound truth than the psalmist himself knew. For him it was a tension between life with God and life without God. The former at least held out some continuance after death. The connection between Hades and corruption is important when applied to Christ since it is impossible to attribute corruption to him, and therefore Hades has no relevance for him. Paul, in his Pisidian Antioch address recorded in Acts 13, makes the same point from the same psalm (13:35–37). He draws out the contrast between David who saw corruption and Christ who did not. Neither Peter nor Paul, however, relates the resurrection of Christ to the resurrection of believers. Both are content to bring out the practical result of the resurrection of Christ, *i.e.* the availability of the forgiveness of sins.

On the theme of death, Acts is no more explicit. It relates the deaths of several people. In some cases death appears to be in the nature of a divine judgment, as with Herod for his arrogance (12:23) and Ananias and Sapphira for their deceit (5:1ff.). In the latter case Luke merely comments that great fear fell on the church. On two occasions people were brought back to life, Dorcas by Peter (9:36ff.) and Eutychus by Paul (20:9). In neither case is any particular surprise expressed, although when Dorcas was raised many more believed in the Lord. Admittedly cases of restoring the dead to life do not in themselves tell us anything about the afterlife.

One other comment on Acts is needed, since Luke describes Stephen's passing in terms of 'falling asleep', which he nevertheless at once identifies as death (Acts 7:60; 8:1). This is in harmony with the usage in the gospels cited above. It is probable that Luke wished to contrast the inner peacefulness of Stephen's passing with the cruelty and violence of the outward circumstances of his death. He certainly wanted to highlight the parallel between Stephen's attitude to his murderers ('Lord, do not hold this sin against them', Acts 7:60) and the prayer of Jesus from the cross, which Luke alone records (Luke 23:34). It seems evident that Jesus' own attitude to death was regarded by his followers as a pattern for their own. There is no sign in the first Christian martyr of fear of man's last enemy. The further prayer, 'Lord Jesus, receive my spirit', is also reminiscent of the attitude of Jesus at the point of death (*cf.* Lk. 23:46).

---

[132] *Cf.* Plato's *Phaedo*. See note 112.

[133] J. A. Schep, *The Nature of the Resurrection Body*, pp. 185f., points out that it was the idea of resurrection of dead men which caused offence to the Athenians, not the idea of immortality. *Cf.* N. B. Stonehouse, *Paul before the Areopagus and other New Testament Studies* (1957), pp. 1–70.

Paul

THE RESURRECTION OF THE BODY

Paul has considerably more to say about the afterlife, but there are many questions which he leaves unanswered, especially about the resurrection body. We shall note, first of all, the evidence for Paul's belief in the resurrection of believers. There are several passages which establish this without doubt.

We consider first Philippians 3:20f.: 'we await a Saviour, the Lord Jesus Christ, who will change our lowly body to be like his glorious body.' There are two important factors emphasized in this statement. A transformation is predicted for believers which will be effected at the parousia, and the final condition is a bodily one, likened to the body of glory of the resurrected Jesus. This close connection between the resurrection body of Jesus and the resurrection body of believers is the key to an understanding of Paul's teaching on this subject. We must note, however, that he does not refer to our Lord's exalted body of flesh. This has led many scholars to argue that he did not believe in it.[134] Instead the heavenly body of Jesus is alleged to consist of 'glory'. But since in the parallel phrase describing our present bodies, the genitival noun (translated 'lowly') cannot be made to express the form of our bodies but their quality,[135] so the word 'glory' must equally be given a qualitative sense. In that case the statement gives no indication of the substance either of the Lord's or of the believers' resurrection body.

In 1 Corinthians 15 Paul gives a full discussion of the resurrection theme and again links the resurrection of Christ with that of believers. The first part of the chapter aims to establish the fact of Christ's resurrection and points to the miserable consequences for Christian faith if Christ had not risen (cf. 1 Cor. 15:17).[136] He deals with a different issue in the latter part, summed up in the question, 'How are the dead raised? With what kind of body do they come?' (verse 35). Paul's answer takes us into two main areas: the seed imagery and the Adam-Christ comparison. Since he uses the Adam analogy in the early part of the chapter, and also makes use of it in Romans 5, we will deal with the second point first.

The Adam-Christ parallel has relevance to both the person and work of Christ (see pp. 333ff.), as well as throwing light on the resurrection-body. In 1 Corinthians 15:22 Paul says, 'For as in Adam all die, so also in Christ shall all be made alive', a statement which some have claimed to support

---

[134] Cf. R. Bultmann, TNT 1, p. 192; O. Cullmann, Immortality of the Soul or Resurrection of the Dead? pp. 46f.

[135] R. P. Martin, Philippians (TNTC, 1959), ad loc., maintains that it means 'the state of humiliation caused through sin'.

[136] In all probability there were those at Corinth who rejected the idea of resurrection because the thought of the reanimation of corpses was repugnant to them. They might well have argued that Paul should drop this notion which he inherited from Judaism. Cf. F. F. Bruce, 'Paul on Immortality' SJT 24, 1971, pp. 464f.

a universal resurrection to life. Further comment will be made on this in the paragraph below dealing with the extent of the resurrection, but our concern at the moment is to note the conviction that there is a definite link between the risen life of Christ and that of believers. In this context the resurrection of Christ is viewed as 'the first fruits' (1 Cor. 15:20, 23). It is a guarantee that others will follow.

When Paul returns to the Adam-Christ parallel in 1 Corinthians 15:45, he makes an important distinction between the first Adam as 'a living being' and the last Adam as 'a life-giving Spirit'.[137] Although it has been supposed that Paul is echoing the idea of Philo's heavenly man in referring to Christ as the last Adam, this may be dismissed on the grounds that Philo's heavenly man was the first, not the last, Adam. It is not impossible that the Corinthians had been mistakenly influenced by Philo and that Paul is correcting their misapprehensions. It seems natural to suppose that he derived his inspiration direct from the OT and that he intended to draw attention to the essential difference between the spiritual potential for mankind of Adam and of Christ. There is a vast difference between receiving life and giving life.

That Christ is described as a life-giving 'Spirit' does not mean that the risen Christ had no bodily form. This observation has importance in our consideration of the believer's resurrection-body, for if Christ has power to give life (*i.e.* to raise to life) he may be expected to give the same kind of life as he himself possesses. As the last Adam, Christ is the representative of all who have a full measure of the Spirit. It is this and not a contrast in bodily substance between Adam and Christ which is in view. Both Adam and Christ are described, in fact, as 'a man'.

The second theme in the 1 Corinthians 15 exposition is the seed analogy in verses 35–44.[138] It is expounded by Paul in an attempt to answer the question of the *kind* of body the dead have. The discussion must be read against the scepticism of the Greeks over the resurrection of the body, and it is probable that Paul's seed analogy was designed to answer such a scepticism which had crept into the church. The force of the seed illustration lies solely in the evidence it gives of God's power to bring life from dead things. It is not an exact analogy. It illustrates that the new life is not just a reproduction of the former life, but something better. No-one would deduce from the dead appearance of the seed, if he had not had previous experience of it, that pent up within it was a potentially new and more glorious form of existence. Paul maintains that although there is continuity between the present body of flesh and the resurrection body, there is also

---

[137] Some see here traces of Philo's distinction between a heavenly and an earthly man. *Cf.* R. Bultmann, *TNT* 1, p. 174; E. Käsemann, *Leib und die Leib Christi* (1933), pp. 166ff. *Cf.* the comments of E. E. Ellis, *Paul's use of the Old Testament* (1957), p. 64.

[138] See Schep's full discussion of this passage, *The Nature of the Resurrection Body*, pp. 189ff.

transformation. There is no escaping the conclusion that Paul is arguing for some kind of glorious body which bears a direct relationship with the present body of flesh.[139] This is further supported by his point that each kind of seed has its own body (verse 38), the significance of which is that a definite continuity exists between the seed and its own plant. A wheat grain will never produce a barley plant. So Paul extends his argument to other aspects of the natural world – to the animal world and to the heavenly bodies – to demonstrate further the power of God in providing suitable forms for his creations.

In applying this, the apostle says that what is dead is raised 'imperishable' (verse 42), 'in glory' and 'in power' (verse 43). It becomes 'a spiritual body' (verse 44).[140] Such a transformation is, moreover, necessary, since 'flesh and blood' cannot inherit the kingdom of God (verse 50). Only the imperishable can inherit the imperishable. There seems little doubt that Paul sees the process as consisting of a change from mortal substance to immortal substance, with a continuity between them. The expression 'spiritual body' mentioned above is remarkable because it is directly connected with the 'physical body' (verse 44). While in both the word 'body' occurs, 'spiritual' (*pneumatikon*) is clearly intended to denote an entirely different kind of substance from 'natural' (*psychikon*).[141] This must be borne in mind in any conception of the resurrection body as 'flesh'. It may, of course, be argued that had Paul wished to exclude the idea of 'flesh' from the conception of the spiritual body, he would have contrasted it with a fleshy (*sarkikon*) body rather than a natural (*psychikon*) body.[142] Even so, the real point of Paul's statement is that our present natural bodies will be resurrected into a spiritual form.[143]

Another passage of some significance for our subject is Romans 8:11: 'He who raised Christ Jesus from the dead will give life to your mortal bodies also through his Spirit which dwells in you.' It is again clear that some transformation of our present bodies is guaranteed. Some deny that this refers to the future state at all, and interpret the words of our present

---

[139] R. Bultmann, *TNT* 1, p. 192, who cannot accept this view, has to maintain that Paul allowed himself to be carried away by his opponents' argumentation. Käsemann, *op. cit.*, pp. 135f., considers that Paul made a mistake.

[140] *Cf.* H. Clavier's 'Brèves Remarques sur la Notion de soma pneumatikon', in *The Background of the New Testament and its Eschatology* (ed. W. D. Davies and D. Daube, 1964), p. 348. He opposes the view that Paul contends for a resurrected body of flesh.

[141] On the use of these two words in 1 Corinthians, *cf.* B. A. Pearson, *The Pneumatikos-Psychikos terminology in 1 Corinthians* (1973). Pearson remarks that although the Christian may be regarded proleptically as *pneumatikos*, his full attainment of *pneumatikos* existence is yet to be realized in the resurrection of the dead (p. 41).

[142] So Schep, *op. cit.*, p. 200.

[143] R. H. Gundry, *Sōma in Biblical Theology* (1976), p. 165, maintains that the *psychikon sōma* is a physical body animated by the *psyche*, and that the *pneumatikon sōma* is a physical body renovated by the Spirit of Christ.

Christian experience.[144] Although there is truth in this, the close connection between the resurrection of Christ and the revitalizing of our mortal bodies must not be clouded, and it is not impossible to detect some principle which applies to the resurrection body, even if resurrection is not the burden of the context. The effect of the indwelling Spirit is most noticeable, for it draws attention to the agency through whom all the quickening processes are achieved. Not only in the present life, but in all the life-giving and transforming processes the work of the Spirit is dominant. In Galatians 6:8 Paul speaks of reaping eternal life 'from the Spirit' in contrast to reaping corruption 'from the flesh',[145] The Spirit is, therefore, an indispensable agency in the whole process of transformation from a state of corruption to incorruption.

For our present purpose the most important as well as the most difficult passage is 2 Corinthians 5:1–10.[146] It is prepared for by the clear conviction expressed in 2 Corinthians 4:14: 'knowing that he who raised the Lord Jesus will raise us also with Jesus and bring us with you into his presence'; this statement closely parallels Romans 8:11. In 2 Corinthians 5, Paul speaks of what happens when our 'earthly tent' is destroyed (*i.e.* on the death of our physical bodies). He asserts that we 'have a building from God, a house not made with hands, eternal in the heavens' (verse 1).

There are two possible interpretations of this statement. It may either be understood in an individual sense or in a corporate sense. It has generally been supposed that the 'building' is the resurrection body of Christians, which will house the soul either at death[147] or at the parousia. This is based on the assumption that Paul is here influenced by Greek ways of thinking, since the concept 'house' was used in this sense in contemporary Greek writings (*cf.* Philo, *de praem.* 120; *de som.* 1.122).

This view, which has played an important part in discussions of the intermediate state in Paul's theology (see the section below), is, however, open to serious challenge. Other occurrences of the idea of a building not

---

[144] Whiteley, *The Theology of St Paul*, p. 254, regards the context as soteriological rather than eschatological.

[145] *Cf.* G. Vos' detailed discussion on the importance of the Spirit in Paul's eschatology, *The Pauline Eschatology*, pp. 159ff.

[146] For discussions of this difficult passage, in addition to the commentaries, *cf.* E. E. Ellis, 'The Structure of Pauline Eschatology (2 Cor. 5:1-10)', in his *Paul and His Recent Interpreters* (1961), pp. 35–48; W.L. Knox, *St Paul and the Church of the Gentiles* (1939, r.p. 1961), pp. 125–145; M. J. Harris, '2 Corinthians 5:1-10: Watershed in Paul's Eschatology', *TB* 22, 1971, pp. 32–57; R. Cassidy, 'Paul's Attitude to Death in 2 Cor. 5:1-10', *EQ*, 43, 1971, pp. 210ff.; O. Cullmann, *Immortality of the Soul or Resurrection of the Dead?* pp. 52ff. For a thorough summary of recent opinion, *cf.* F. G. Lang, *2 Korinther 5:1-10 in der neueren Forschung* (1973).

[147] For the view that this happens at death, *cf.* R. F. Hettlinger, '2 Cor. 5:1-10' *SJT* 10, 1957, pp. 193ff., and C. Masson, 'Immortalité de l'âme ou résurrection des morts?' *RThPh* 8, 1958, pp. 250–267. For the alternative view, *cf.* R. Bultmann, *Exegetische Probleme des zweiten Korintherbriefes* (1947), p. 12; *TNT* 1, pp. 202f. For a criticism of Hettlinger, *cf.* R. Berry, 'Death and Life in Christ', *SJT* 14, 1961, pp. 60-76.

made with hands appear in a quasi-technical sense with a corporate meaning. Mark 14:58 gives a report of those who had heard Jesus say he would build another temple not made with hands. Although his hearers misunderstood, it is reasonably certain that Jesus was thinking of the corporate 'body of Christ' (*i.e.* his church). A similar allusion is probably present in Stephen's reference to the new temple (Acts 7:48f.). If the same idea is in mind in 2 Corinthians 5:1, Paul is affirming that those in Christ already have another 'building'. They have put on Christ at conversion and the putting off of the earthly tent cannot affect the believer's incorporation into the body of Christ.[148] Such an interpretation implies that 'the earthly tent' style of existence must be regarded as corporate, a state which affects all those in Adam. Those who still groan because of the limitations of the earthly tent, but who are nevertheless in Christ, long to put on the 'heavenly dwelling' (2 Cor. 5:2).

Another important consideration arising from the same passage is the meaning of the word 'naked' (*gymnos*) in verse 3. It is usually understood of the disembodied spirit and the statement is then claimed to support the idea of a bodiless existence in the intermediate state (see the discussion below). Our present concern is to decide whether, in fact, the correct understanding of Paul's thought is arrived at by interpreting *gymnos* in this way.[149] Again, too much attention has been given to an alleged Greek background and not sufficient to a Hebrew background. It can be shown that 'naked' in the OT is frequently linked with 'shame' in the presence of God's judgments (*cf.* Ezk. 16:37, 39; 23:26, 29).[150] It must be regarded, therefore, as having an ethical meaning, and there is support for this elsewhere in the NT (*cf.* Rom. 10:11; 1 John 2:28). The idea of 'putting on' (*endyō*) would then refer to the believer's standing within the body of Christ at the judgment (see later section, pp. 859ff.).[151]

The third factor which arises from 2 Corinthians 5 is the clear connection between the work of the Spirit and Paul's eschatological thought here. The Spirit has already been given as a 'guarantee' (*arrabōn*, 2 Cor. 5:5). This ties up with what had already been said about the significance of the Spirit in the resurrection of believers. Since the word *arrabōn* was commonly used of a sample which would guarantee the quality of what was to follow, Paul's statement must mean that the Spirit's presence now is an assurance of the life with which the present mortal will be clothed.

---

[148] So E. E. Ellis, 'The Structure of Pauline Eschatology' in his *Paul and his recent Interpreters*, pp. 35ff., who considers the Greek trail to have been a false detour.

[149] H. N. Ridderbos, *Paul*, p. 503, rejects a Greek understanding of *gymnos* and regards it as meaning not a state of incorporeality, but a state in which the glory of God is lacking.

[150] *Cf.* E. E. Ellis' discussion, *op. cit.*, pp. 44ff. His interpretation is criticized by Whiteley, *The Theology of St Paul*, pp. 256ff.

[151] O. Cullmann, *Immortality of the Soul or Resurrection of the Dead?*, pp. 52ff., connects the *gymnos* with the sleep state in 1 Thes. 4 and 1 Cor. 15.

Our next consideration is whether Paul gives any support to the Greek idea of the immortality of the soul as distinct from the resurrection of the body. Sufficient evidence of the latter has already been given, but some scholars who interpret this evidence in a spiritual way maintain that Paul embraced the Greek view of immortality.[152] When Paul speaks of immortality, however, he never relates it to the soul. He explicitly states in 1 Timothy 6:16 that God alone has immortality. To the Greek, death was a release from the prison house of the soul (*i.e.* the body), but for Paul immortality is considered to be a gift of God. The notion that he held to a Greek view of the afterlife must be rejected in the light of his total teaching.

Some comment must be made about the alleged development in Paul's teaching on the resurrection of the body. Various scholars[153] have claimed a four-state progression. (i) The Jewish form of eschatological belief in which it was assumed that bodies would be resurrected in the same form in which they went to the graves. This is supposed to be reflected in 1 Thessalonians. (ii) The beginnings of pneumatic eschatology, in which it was believed that the Spirit would bring about a change at the moment of resurrection. This is claimed to be seen in 1 Corinthians. (iii) The bringing forward of the moment of dramatic transformation to the moment of death. This is sometimes linked with the view of the believer's body being already prepared in heaven and is based on 2 Corinthians 5:1–8. (iv) The view that the transformation of the body has already begun in this life in the believer, a view said to be reflected in 2 Corinthians 3:18 and 4:17.[154]

Before any support can be given to any theory of development in Paul, it would have to be shown, not only that these alleged differences are based on a valid understanding of the evidence, but also that a sequence of development is the best interpretation of the differences. Only if each new stage involved the supercession of the last would a true development be established. But this is an over-simplification of a complex set of data. Paul's views are expressed only in the most general terms. It is, in fact, more reasonable to suppose that he expresses himself in a variety of ways which are not self-contradictory although they present different emphases. Moreover, it is inconceivable that Paul would have changed his views in

---

[152] For Greek ideas of immortality, *cf.* E. Rohde, *Psyche: The Cult of Souls and Belief in Immortality among the Greeks*, 2 vols. (r.p. 1966); W. Jaeger, 'The Greek Ideas of Immortality', in *Immortality and Resurrection* (ed. K. Stendahl, 1965), pp. 97–114; O. Cullmann, *op. cit.*, pp. 19ff. For other background studies, *cf.* R. B. Laurin, 'The Question of Immortality in the Qumran "Hodayot" ', *JSS* 3, 1958, pp. 344–355; J. van der Ploeg, 'L'Immortalité de l'homme d'après les textes de la Mer Morte', *VT* 2, 1952, pp. 171ff.; F. F. Bruce, 'Paul on Immortality', *SJT* 24, 1971, pp. 457–472.

[153] *Cf.* G. Vos, *The Pauline Eschatology*, pp. 172ff., for a full discussion of these alleged stages of development. *Cf.* R. H. Charles, *A Critical History of the Doctrine of a Future Life* (²1913), pp. 455ff. *Cf.* also the comments by Schep, *The Nature of the Resurrection Body*, pp. 206ff.

[154] *Cf.* Vos, *op. cit.*, pp. 200ff., for a critique of Stage 4.

the incredibly short time between 1 and 2 Corinthians.[155] Another inconceivable feature is that, since the alleged earliest stage in 1 Thessalonians bears marked similarities with the teaching of Jesus, Paul's later thought would then amount to a correction of Jesus. But there is no justification for supposing that Paul was doing this.

A careful comparison between 1 Thessalonians 4:13ff., 1 Corinthians 15 and 2 Corinthians 4 and 5 reveals no fundamental change in Paul's eschatology. The advocates of the development theory confuse the present effect of the resurrection life in the believer with the form of the resurrection body after death. Paul's ideas, however, embrace both the present and the future.

Our concluding consideration is to determine the extent of the resurrection of believers. We must begin with 1 Corinthians 15:22: 'in Christ shall all be made alive'; on the face of it this seems to imply not only a universal resurrection, but also a universal salvation. The 'all' in this verse is paralleled in the statement 'as in Adam all die'. The two statements may, however, be understood to mean that all who are 'in Adam' will die and all who are 'in Christ' shall be made alive. Paul is affirming 'not the universality of the law, but the universality of its *modus operandi* within the compass in which it works'.[156] The emphasis falls not on the 'all' taken by itself, but the 'all' joined with 'in Adam' and 'in Christ'. The statement tells us nothing about the extent of the resurrection of the body beyond its application to believers and cannot be held to teach universal salvation. In the same context (verse 23) the words 'each in his own order' (*tagma*) occur, and these have been held to support a two-stage resurrection.[157] But since Christ is himself one order and the resurrected saint another, there is no support here for a two-stage resurrection subsequent to the resurrection of Christ.

We cannot deal with this present theme without taking into account Paul's teaching in 1 Thessalonians 4:13–18, which involves some who are alive at the parousia being gathered with the resurrected dead to meet the Lord in the air (see pp. 845f.). The question arises whether these survivors will receive a resurrection body in the same sense as those who are raised from the dead. Paul does not appear to be aware of any difficulty over this. In this passage he is not concerned with the nature of the resurrection body. The focus of his interest is on the relation between the survivors and the resurrected dead. The Thessalonians fear that the dead will be at a disadvantage at the parousia, but Paul maintains there would be no distinction between them. It is fair to assume that he would have held that all

---

[155] It was C. H. Dodd who strongly argued for a development between 1 and 2 Corinthians, see n. 81 in this chapter.

[156] So G. Vos, *op. cit.*, 241.

[157] On the resurrection of Christians and non-Christians, *cf.* H. Molitor, *Die Auferstehung der Christen*

would possess the same kind of resurrection-body which would involve an instant transformation of those caught up. Paul is insistent that all would be 'with the Lord' (verse 17), but makes no further comment on their state. There is no more suggestion in this passage than in 1 Corinthians 15:23 of a two-stage resurrection.

Some comment must be made on Philippians 3:10–14, in which Paul expresses his own yearnings about the future. What does he mean when he says of his aspirations, 'that if possible (*ei pōs*) I may attain the resurrection from the dead' (verse 11)?[158] Some have interpreted this of a special resurrection reserved for martyrs. But this clearly cannot be supported in view of Philippians 3:20–21 in which Paul asserts that the body-change, which will happen at the parousia, affects everyone and no distinction is made between martyrs and others.[159] Paul's statement has otherwise been interpreted to mean that he was expressing the hope of surviving until the parousia, but again there is no justification for supposing that he would have confused his terms, especially as in Philippians 1 he is quite ready to depart and be with Christ.

If *ei pōs* means 'with a view to attaining' the resurrection, it would then be possible to suppose that the apostle is expressing his recognition that profession of Christian faith must be matched by corresponding Christian living. This conviction is amply in evidence throughout his epistles, but in no way gives any credence to the view that attaining the resurrection would depend wholly on his own efforts. In the Philippians passage Paul is giving only one side of the picture, but a true appreciation of his meaning must take account of the other (*i.e.* his doctrine of justification by faith alone).

THE INTERMEDIATE STATE

Two closely linked questions have been raised about Paul's teaching which may be subsumed under the general heading of the intermediate state. The first is what information Paul gives about the state of existence subsequent to the believer's death until the resurrection at the parousia; and the second

---

und Nichtchristen nach dem Apostel Paulus (1933), pp. 44ff. *Cf.* R. Schnackenburg, *God's Rule and Kingdom* (Eng. trans. 1963), p. 293. See the excursus in E.-B. Allo, *Première Épître aux Corinthiens* (EB, ²1956), pp. 438–454.

[158] *Cf.* Vos, *op. cit.*, p. 253. J. D. G. Dunn, *Jesus and the Spirit* (1975), p. 334, suggests that what Paul meant is that only those who suffer Christ's death will attain to resurrection, since only Christ's death has resulted in resurrection. *Cf.* J. Gnilka, *Der Philipperbrief* (HTKNT, ²1976), pp. 196ff. E. Lohmeyer, *Philipper, Kolosser und Philemon* (KEK, ⁹1953), pp. 139f., restricts the suffering to martyrdom. *Cf.* also R. C. Tannehill, *Dying and Rising with Christ* (1967).

[159] Certainly Phil. 3:21 firmly supports the view that the resurrection involves a transformation of the body. *Cf.* B. Ramm, *Them He Glorified* (1963), pp. 101–122, who points out that Paul's wording implies a direct link between Christ's body of glory and our bodies. M. E. Dahl, *The Resurrection of the Body* (Eng. trans. 1962), pp. 103f., takes the combination of the word *metaschēmatizō* and *symmorphon* in this verse as suggesting 'that Christ will outwardly change our state of humiliation'.

is whether he supports the idea of 'soul-sleep' during this period. This expression is used to describe a state of existence of the soul, which is comparable to an experience of sleep, that is, of unconsciousness. It must at once be admitted that Paul does not deal with either of these themes head-on. He is much more interested in the resurrection, which he discusses in detail, than in the state of the believer at death. Nevertheless, there are certain passages in which he gives indications of his way of thinking.[160]

We return to 2 Corinthians 5:1f., which has already been discussed under the last section, because this has been the major bastion in exposition of Paul's teaching about the intermediate state.[161] The crucial statement is in verse 3: 'We would rather be away from the body and at home with the Lord.' From earliest times it has been assumed that 'away from the body' relates to the intermediate state,[162] and this is strongly supported by most modern exegetes. It is at once clear that Paul does not intend his readers to suppose that at death they will be separated from Christ. In Romans 8:38f. he makes clear that death has no power to do this. In the present context the words 'at home with the Lord' must carry the force of an experience which immediately follows being 'away from the body'. No conception of the intermediate state is therefore valid which does not make provision for an awareness of the presence of the Lord.

Yet it has been questioned whether 2 Corinthians 5:1ff. should be cited in reference to the intermediate state at all. 'Away from the body' need mean no more than separation 'from the solidarities of mortal body'.[163] In this case 'at home with the Lord' points to the state of the spiritual life, but gives no indication about the 'bodily' form of such a condition.

Another statement of Paul has some bearing on his view of the intermediate state. In Philippians 1:23 he expresses a dilemma which exists in his own mind: 'My desire is to depart and be with Christ, for that is far better'.[164] Again, it is undeniable that Paul is not suggesting any gap between departing (*i.e.* dying) and being with Christ. His concept of the

---

[160] *Cf.* J. N. Sevenster, 'Einige Bemerkungen über den "Zwischenzustand" bei Paulus', *NTS* 1, 1954-5, pp. 291ff., who considers that it is essential to presuppose that Paul held to an intermediate state even if he had not specifically mentioned it.

[161] K. Hanhart, *The Intermediate State in the New Testament*, p. 73, who relates both the 'house' and the 'clothing' to heavenly realities, to the heavenly temple and to life lived with Christ in the heavens, does not regard this as pointing to an intermediate state. *Cf.* also his full discussion of the whole passage, pp. 149-179. On whether Paul is thinking of a judgment at death or at the final judgment is not clear. Hanhart maintains that the emphasis falls on the *fact* rather than on the *moment* (p. 178). He denies that by a building in heaven Paul was thinking of the anthropological question of body or soul (p. 167).

[162] *Cf.* Clement of Alexandria, *Stromata* iv, xxvi; Tertullian, *De resurrectione carnis*, xliii.

[163] E. E. Ellis, *Paul and his recent Interpreters*, p. 46. He considers that it is probably a misconception to speak of the intermediate state in relation to 2 Cor. 5:8. *Cf.* Schep, *op. cit.*, p. 210 n. 69; H. A. A. Kennedy, *St Paul's Conceptions of the Last Things*, p. 269.

[164] On Phil. 1:21-23, *cf.* J.-F. Collange, *Philippiens* (1973), pp. 62-65; R. P. Martin, *Philippians* (NCB, 1976), pp. 76ff. A. Schweitzer, *The Mysticism of Paul the Apostle* (1930, Eng. trans. ²1953), p. 137, suggested that Paul expected special treatment of himself as a martyr.

intermediate state was of a state of existence in which he was fully conscious of the presence of the Lord.[165]

There are various opinions, however, about Paul's view of the state of believers between their death and the parousia. The following possibilities are open. (i) Believers are existing as disembodied spirits and are awaiting the resurrection when they will be given glorious and eternal bodies. (ii) Believers receive a 'temporary' body at death which will be replaced by the glorious resurrection body at the parousia. This view involves a kind of two-stage process for the resurrection of the body. (iii) A modification of the last view is that the full resurrection of believers takes place at death and the resurrection of unbelievers at the parousia. (iv) Yet another view is that the dead enter into a state of unconsciousness until the resurrection, when they will be roused and given a glorious body.

It is not easy to determine what Paul would have imagined if he was suggesting that Christian dead exist as disembodied spirits.[166] There is, in fact, no specific evidence in the Pauline epistles for such an idea as disembodied spirits, if 2 Corinthians 5 is excluded. Nevertheless, there is equally nothing specifically to exclude this idea, provided some state of existence is in mind which allows for full consciousness of the presence of Christ.

The second proposal of a two-stage clothing of the spirit is difficult to imagine because the full resurrection body at the parousia becomes diminished in meaning. There is no explanation for the latter if the temporary body is adequate.[167] Some forms of the theory suppose a kind of heavenly storehouse of bodies prepared for believers at death, but this seems removed from Paul's manner of thinking. Nevertheless, this view does attempt to explain how existence between death and the parousia can be considered, without resorting to a two-stage resurrection. But the theory leaves the main problem unanswered.

The problem with the third view, that the believer's resurrection takes place at death, is that it would appear to involve a whole series of resurrections rather than one single event, which seems to be required by Paul's various references. The only way to avoid this is to hold that a different time-consciousness operates, as explained below.

The fourth view mentioned above – the sleep of the soul – requires more specific examination, because of the strong support which it has recently

[165] Bultmann, *TNT* 1, p. 346, regards Phil. 1:23 as in contradiction with the resurrection doctrine when Paul expresses the idea that being with the Lord immediately follows death. But as H. Ridderbos, *Paul*, p. 499 n. 29, points out, such contradictory ideas within the same epistle on so basic a matter are difficult to accept.

[166] *Cf.* P. E. Hughes, *2 Corinthians* (NICNT, 1962), pp. 160ff. *Cf.* also J. N. Sevenster, 'Some remarks on the *Gymnos* of 2 Cor. v.3', in *Studia Paulina in honorem Johannis de Zwaan* (ed. J. N. Sevenster and W. C. van Unnik, 1953), pp. 212ff.

[167] *Cf.* J. Lowe, 'An examination of attempts to detect developments in Paul's Theology', *JTS* 42 (1941), pp. 129ff.

gained (especially in the work of Cullmann). Our first concern is to note those passages where Paul refers to the dead as those asleep. The verb Paul uses is the word *koimaomai* which basically means sleep, but was used of the dead in the intertestamental period.[168] It does not necessarily imply unconsciousness.[169] The apostle uses it in 1 Corinthians 7:39; 11:30; 15:6, 18, 20, 51; 1 Thessalonians 4:13, 14, 15. More often he uses another word (*apothnēskō*) for dying, which gives some special point to his choice of the sleep metaphor in the cases cited.

It will be noted that, except for the first two, they occur in eschatological contexts. In 1 Corinthians 15:18, Paul is specifically thinking of those who have fallen asleep in Christ. In two cases (1 Cor. 11:30 and 1 Thes. 4:13)[170], he uses the present tense, and this has been claimed to support the idea of a continuous condition of sleep, as distinguished from a single act. But in both cases he is probably thinking of a continuing number of deaths, in which case his words do not support the idea of continuous soul-sleep. In 1 Thessalonians 4:14–15, when Paul speaks of those who have died in comparison with those who remain at the parousia, he chooses the expression 'those who have fallen asleep'.[171] He does the same when referring to Christ as 'the first fruits' in 1 Corinthians 15:20 ('the first fruits of those who have fallen asleep'). He declares in 1 Corinthians 15:51 that not all will 'sleep' but all will be changed.

What then is the significance of Paul's sleep imagery for death? Is he implying a state of soul-sleep prior to the resurrection? It is not surprising that he employed the sleep metaphor for death, but such use would not carry with it in contemporary usage the idea of unconsciousness. There seems to be no reason to suppose that Paul believed that the believer at death lapsed into a state of unconsciousness from which he would be aroused only at the resurrection. It would contradict the plain meaning of both Philippians 1:23 (to be with Christ) and 2 Corinthians 5:8 (at home with the Lord). These statements demand an awareness of being with the Lord, which must affect any exposition of the soul-sleep theory.[172] In this, Paul's teaching is in line with the words of Jesus to the penitent thief in

---

[168] *Cf.* Whiteley, *The Theology of St Paul*, pp. 264f.

[169] B. F. C. Atkinson, *Life and Immortality* (n.d.), p. 51, concludes that men lie asleep in death and that the grave 'is a place of darkness and silence where there is no activity, no remembrance of God and no praise of Him'. It is noticeable that most of the reasoning deduced in support of this is based on the Old Testament.

[170] *Cf.* Grosheide, *1 Corinthians* (NICNT, 1953), *ad loc.*, and Barrett *1 Corinthians* (BC, ²1971) *ad loc.*, on 1 Cor. 11:30. *Cf.* also L. Morris, *The Epistles to the Thessalonians* (TCNT, 1956), *ad loc.*, on 1 Thes. 4:13.

[171] For a discussion of the 1 Thes. 4 passage in relation to the idea of soul-sleep, *cf.* K. Hanhart, *The Intermediate State in the New Testament*, pp. 111ff.

[172] Atkinson, *op. cit.*, p. 64, explains these references as evidence that the dying believers' subjective experience is that he passes instantly from this world to resurrection glory. So profound is the soul's unconsciousness, according to Atkinson, that for the believer the next instant is the resurrection morning. But this would not appear to be the most natural understanding of Paul's words in Phil. 1:23 and 2 Cor. 5:8.

Luke 23:43 (note also the story of Dives and Lazarus, Lk. 16:22f., and the cry of the martyrs under the altar in Rev. 6:11).

Part of the problem of the NT teaching on the afterlife arises from the time-interval between death and the parousia.[173] Cullmann claims a different time-consciousness in the afterlife, and if he is right, we must not apply our present time-consciousness to the interval. It is in fact possible that viewed from God's point of view there will be no interval, that the resurrection at the parousia will be immediately after the believer's death. But we are here in an area of thought in which, in the nature of the case, we have had no experience. Our conclusion must be that we cannot get any closer to Paul's idea of the state immediately following death than to say that it will consist of fellowship with Christ. When we go beyond this we enter the sphere of speculation.

It is remarkable that Paul says practically nothing about the resurrection of the unrighteous, but it is not possible to deduce from this that he excluded the idea. It might be inferred from his conviction that all would be judged (see next section, pp. 859f.), but the possibility must be allowed of judgment of incorporeal beings. The fact is, Paul gives no specific indication about the state of the wicked. In 2 Timothy 4:1 he speaks of Christ Jesus 'who is to judge the living and the dead', which might presuppose a resurrection of both, although he makes no mention of it. We may say that his preoccupation is not with final destinies, but with concern over what the afterlife holds for the believer.

THE ATTITUDE TO DEATH

We shall confine ourselves here to physical death. What has been said above shows that the apostle has an optimistic approach to death. He considers that through Christ death has lost its sting, which he identifies with sin (1 Cor. 15:55–56). This optimistic approach to death is based on the view that the entry of death into the world was caused by sin (Rom. 5:12ff.), and that Christ has effectively dealt with the cause.[174] Paul no longer sees death as an enemy to be feared, but rather as a point of transition to a fuller life. His own experience bears this out. He lived under constant threats of death (1 Cor. 15:31; 2 Cor. 1:8; 11:23ff.). He can coolly debate whether life or death in Christ is preferable (Phil. 1:19ff.). He exemplifies a man who has conquered all fear of death.[175]

Some reference must be made to death conceived as judgment. In

---

[173] Cullmann, *Immortality of the Soul or Resurrection of the Dead?* p. 57.

[174] A. J. M. Wedderburn, 'The Theological Structure of Romans v. 12', *NTS* 19, 1973, pp. 339–354, argues that the background is apocalyptic determinism, which claimed that Adam was responsible for death.

[175] K. Hanhart, 'Paul's Hope in the Face of Death', *JBL* 88, 1969, pp. 445ff., argues that Paul had no specific future expectation, but a radiant hope of eternal life.

1 Corinthians 11:30 Paul, in commenting on those who participate in the Lord's supper in an unworthy manner, states, 'That is why many of you are weak and ill, and some have died (fallen asleep).' It appears that he is acknowledging that the illnesses and deaths could have been avoided by more worthy living. But the reference to death in this context is perplexing. There is a possibility that some kind of disciplinary assessment of death is in mind parallel to that which befell Ananias and Sapphira (Acts 5). There are, of course, many instances where Paul uses 'death' in a spiritual sense as a judgment of God upon sin (Eph. 2:1; Col. 2:13).

The rest of the New Testament

On the subject of the afterlife, *Hebrews* has little explicitly to say, although there are certain valuable insights which might act as signposts. Belief in the resurrection of the dead is treated as one of 'the elementary doctrines of Christ' (6:1–2). It is a basic doctrine without which no one could be a Christian. It is moreover linked with 'eternal judgment'. But no further explanation of resurrection is given. The writer does not concern himself with the resurrection body in this context.[176] When he speaks of Christ in heaven, he refers to him seated on the right hand of God (1:3; 8:1; 10:12), but give no indication of what kind of body he had.

When the second coming of Christ is referred to in 9:28, mention is made of those who are eagerly waiting for him, but no distinction is made between the living and the dead in Christ (as in 1 Thes. 4). It was evidently not a problem in the communities for which this letter was intended. Perhaps the most illuminating passage for our purpose is Hebrews 12:22, which although it is a description of a heavenly scene, nevertheless embraces the present worshippers (note the verb 'you have come'). The whole passage suggests a present combination of angelic worshippers with the assembly of the first-born, and the spirits of just men made perfect, all in assembly in the heavenly Jerusalem.[177] There is no suggestion here of an unconscious or shadowy existence for the just men, although the use of the word 'spirits' (*pneumata*) might give the impression of disembodied existence. Since in Hebrews the same word is used in 1:14 of the angels (ministering spirits) no conclusions can be drawn from the word itself about bodily form. It would be safe to conclude that the writer shows no interest in the subject of the resurrection body, and does not say anything on the subject of the intermediate state.

As far as the future state of believers is concerned, the writer contents himself with the idea of 'glory' (2:10; *cf.* also 2:9; 3:3), but this tells us nothing about the substance with which the believer will be clothed. In-

---

[176] The ability of God to resurrect the dead is echoed in Heb. 11:19, 35.

[177] In Heb. 12:1 the witnesses are said to surround Christians, but this cannot be taken as evidence that the spirits of the dead are present in this life. 12:1 must be interpreted in the light of 12:22.

deed, although the epistle concentrates on the heavenly realities behind the old cultus and thus has an essentially forward view, yet its aim is to outline the right approach to God in the present. There is a basic conviction that although there is a future rest reserved for the people of God, the most urgent matter is the challenge of 'today' (chapters 3 and 4). The rest, moreover, is not to be conceived as promising inactivity, since the pattern of the believer's rest is nothing other than the sabbath rest of God. The epistle is a superb example of the merging of both present and future aspects, with the accent falling on the challenge of the present.[178]

As far as the attitude to death is concerned, Hebrews reflects the radical nature of the change of approach which comes to those who are the children of God. Whereas fear of death is natural to those in bondage to the devil, Christ has brought deliverance (2:14–15). His people need no longer approach death with fear, because he who has the power of death (*i.e.* the devil) is destroyed. If Christians fear death it is only because they have failed to appreciate that they are no longer in bondage to it. The writer has no doubt that deliverance has already come.

In an epistle as essentially practical as *James* , it is not surprising that little is said about the afterlife. A 'crown of life' is offered to the one who endures temptation (1:12), and this will presumably be attainable in the coming life. Similarly the humble will be exalted (4:10). But James is too down-to-earth to indulge in speculation about the resurrection body.

It may be said of Peter and Jude that interest in eschatology, where it occurs, is practical rather than speculative. *1 Peter* begins by mentioning the inheritance reserved in heaven (1:4), but says nothing about the heirs in their resurrection state. Although he says that the end of all things is at hand (4:7), Peter adds nothing about the parousia, or the resurrection of the dead, or the relation between these and the survivors at the end. He seems mainly interested about the moral challenge which the approaching end should bring for present living. The approaching climax is also called the 'day of visitation' (2:12), where again it is used in moral exhortation (*cf.* also 1:13).

There is one distinctive passage in this epistle which has been thought to have specific reference to the afterlife, *i.e.* 3:19, a notoriously difficult passage which refers to Christ preaching to the 'spirits in prison'.[179] The context mentions their former disobedience and connects them with the flood. Some see here a proclamation to the dead, but there is no statement to this effect in the passage. It is highly improbable that the passage refers

---

[178] *Cf.* G. E. Ladd's discussion on dualism in Hebrews, *TNT*, pp. 572ff.

[179] Bo Reicke, *The Disobedient Spirits and Christian Baptism* (1946), has a detailed analysis of this passage. Most scholars agree that the spirits are demons, and proclamation is one of victory. This is based on the assumption that the book of Enoch is behind this passage. *Cf.* also W. J. Dalton's fine exegesis, *Christ's Proclamation to the Spirits* (1965).

to the preaching of the gospel to give the unbelieving dead a second chance. No other NT passage would support this suggestion. Even if this interpretation is right, the passage would tell us nothing about the state of believers after death or the resurrection body. Nevertheless, the word 'preaching' certainly favours a preaching of the gospel rather than a proclamation of judgment. No interpretation, however, which does not relate it in some ways to Noah's time and that does not have some relevance to Peter's readers is satisfactory.

No final answer can be given. It would, however, seem most reasonable to suppose that the preacher was Christ (not specifying the form in which he preached), but that the preaching was done in Noah's generation.[180] In this case the 'spirits in prison' are those condemned for disobedience in the time of the flood, and the ark, a divine instrument of salvation, was the means through which Christ preached to them in time past. The whole passage would be a part of Peter's appeal to the example of Christ. This interpretation is not without its difficulties; but if it is accepted it means that the passage gives no clue about the state of affairs in the afterlife, apart from the expression 'spirits in prison' describing those who had been disobedient in this life. The 'spirits' (*pneumata*) are not more closely defined. The description of Christ as being 'put to death in the flesh but made alive in the spirit' simply points to his being in a spiritual form, but is not to be related to his preaching in antiquity. It is noteworthy, moreover, that no mention is here made of Hades.

A second, equally difficult, statement is made in 1 Peter 4:6 ('For this is why the gospel was preached even to the dead'). As with the previous passage, there have been various attempts to explain this enigmatic statement. What concerns us here is the view that the gospel is preached to those already dead, *i.e.* to the departed, whether just or unjust. If this view were correct, it would mean that in the afterlife there would be opportunities for responding to the gospel, even among those who had not responded in this life. This interpretation, whatever attractions it might have, does not accord with the precise wording of the statement, for a past occasion of preaching is referred to (aorist tense).

A more likely explanation is that Christians who are now dead and have had the gospel preached to them need not fear the judgment[181]; for although they are judged as far as the flesh is concerned (*i.e.* they died), they may, nevertheless, be assured of renewed life in a spiritual state (see the next section on judgment, p. 865). This explanation assumes that the 'dead' are those who have been abused (verse 5) and that the words are intended as an encouragement for their brethren, perplexed because Christians were

---

[180] *Cf.* S. D. F. Salmon, *The Christian Doctrine of Immortality* (³1897), pp. 471f.

[181] *Cf.* E. G. Selwyn's extensive essay on 1 Peter 3:18–4:6 in his commentary on *1 Peter*, pp. 314–369.

not escaping physical death.[182] In this case the 'dead' here are different from the 'spirits in prison' in 3:19.[183] We may conclude from this passage, as from the other, that the most likely interpretations do not favour an extension of the ministry of grace to Hades.

The epistle of *Jude* contains no reference to the resurrection. Although there is an allusion to the fallen angels being kept in darkness until the judgment day (Jude 6), there are no specific references to the ungodly dead. More will be said later on Jude's theme of judgment, but Jude offers no help on the afterlife. The same may be said of *2 Peter*, which goes into greater detail about the day of the Lord (*cf.* especially 2 Pet. 3). There are, however, two statements in 2 Peter which warrant attention. In 1:14, Peter speaks of 'the putting off of my body' and of his 'departure' (verse 15). Nothing is said of the state after death. In 3:4 death is referred to under the metaphor of sleep, but again nothing more can be deduced about what happened to the fathers after death.

In *Revelation,* a book which focuses upon the future, it is not surprising to find references to the resurrection of the dead. But these references raise certain problems. We note first the martyrs seen 'under the altar' (6:9). It has been maintained that their presence under the altar shows that they were not yet in the immediate presence of God, which would not happen until the first resurrection.[184] But this is probably a wrong deduction, for parallels with the expression 'under the altar' in Jewish literature suggest that it might mean under the throne of God and therefore in the presence of God.[185] Nothing is said in the passage about the resurrection body. The martyrs are clothed with a 'white robe', which some have thought to be a glorified body; but this can hardly be regarded as special 'clothing' for martyrs, and is more likely to refer to the robe of righteousness which Christ provides (*cf.* 7:13f.; *cf.* also 19:8).[186] The fact that they are described as 'souls' (*psychai*) does not mean that they are specifically regarded as incorporeal.[187] But the statement would seem to point to some kind of pre-resurrection state, though clearly not a state of unconsciousness.

A problem arises from the reference in 20:4, 5, 13 to the first resurrection which seems to be restricted to martyrs. According to this passage the first

[182] K. Hanhart, *The Intermediate State in the New Testament*, pp. 218f., considers Selwyn's explanation to be forced and prefers to conclude from the use of the aorist tense that the reference is to an accomplished act (*i.e.* the act of Christ preaching in Hades). It is not therefore a repeatable event.

[183] K. Hanhart, *op. cit.*, p. 218, does not agree that the 'spirits' of 3:19 are to be identified with the 'dead' of 4:6, but he supports some connection between the two passages.

[184] *Cf.* I. T. Beckwith, *The Apocalypse of John*, ad loc.

[185] *Cf.* G. R. Beasley-Murray, *Revelation*, ad loc.

[186] K. Hanhart, *op. cit.*, pp. 229f., concedes that if Christian martyrs are in mind, the expression 'a little longer' does refer to an interim period. But he suggests that martyrs might be saints who died for their faith under the old covenant, in which case the expression would refer to the period immediately prior to the incarnation.

[187] *Cf.* E. Schweizer, *TDNT* 9, p. 654.

resurrection is before the millennium, and the second is after it. The second is for the wicked and unbelievers. Naturally our interpretation of the stages of resurrection will depend on our interpretation of the millennium (see pp. 869f.). If we treat the latter as a literal period of 1,000 years during which Christ will reign on earth, there is no doubt that the 'rest of the dead' who do not come to life until after the period is finished must be identified with the unbelieving dead. But if a distinction is made between the martyrs and other believers, this necessitates a two-stage view of the first resurrection.[188]

There is certainly no specific statement to this effect, in which case the reconstruction must be regarded as speculative. It may be argued, of course, that it is the most probable hypothesis to account for all the facts, but it cannot be claimed to be the only possible interpretation. If the 1,000 years is not regarded as literal but as symbolic, the above reconstruction would not apply. Indeed, the view that the two-stage resurrection theory is the most probable must be challenged. It involves a position which finds support nowhere else in the NT. All the references to the resurrection of the body assume only one resurrection. In Revelation 20 alone there is a mention of a first and second resurrection.

The question arises whether Revelation 20 can be understood in any way which does not imply two physical resurrections? The problem does not arise from the fact that Revelation 20 is the only reference to a double resurrection, for a single witness cannot be condemned simply because it stands alone. The problem springs from the reconstruction which the two-resurrection theory makes necessary, including the assumption that physically resurrected bodies will mix with non-resurrected people during the millennium.[189]

If, however, the millennium is symbolic of the present kingdom of Christ on earth, the first resurrection could be considered as a spiritual and the second as a physical act. This is supported by the fact that the first resurrection is distinguished from the second death, which must clearly be spiritual death (20:6).[190] It is noticeable that no mention is made of bodies in connection with the millennium, only souls (20:4). Moreover, the statement that these 'came to life' (ezēsan) includes a verb not usually used of physical resurrection (although it is so used in Rom. 14:9). What is uppermost in John's mind is the position of those threatened with Christian martyrdom whom he is encouraging in face of the coming threat. They

---

[188] Cf. R. Pache, *The Future Life* (1962), pp. 190ff., distinguishes between a resurrection before and after the three and a half years of tribulation.

[189] Cf. J. W. Hodges, *Christ's Kingdom and Coming*, pp. 229f.

[190] There is force in H. Alford's contention that to make *ezēsan* mean one thing in verse 4 and another in verse 5 empties language of its significance (*The Greek Testament*, 4, revised by E. F. Harrison, 1958, p. 732).

are assured of reigning with Christ. Revelation 20:4 could be understood to include others beside martyrs, since John speaks also of those who had not worshipped the beast nor borne his mark. These two groups together could then account for all the Christian dead.[191]

In the various letters to the churches in Revelation 2–3, promises are given to conquerors (2:7, 11, 17, 26; 3:5, 12, 21) and it is relevant to ask whether these promises throw any light on the afterlife.[192] Certainly the conquerors are Christian believers and would not appear to denote a specific group within the body of the redeemed. They may look forward to eternal life, deliverance from the second death (a reference to judgment), a unique relationship with God, a white robe (*i.e.* through Christ), an important place in the city of God and a share in the conquest of Christ. But nothing is said about the state of believers after death.[193]

NOTE ON THE 'RAPTURE'

As a result of Paul's clear teaching about the parousia and the resurrection of believers, it is not surprising that some of his converts were perplexed about the comparative position of believers who had died before the parousia and those who are still alive at the coming. This gave rise to his teaching about the 'rapture'. The expression 'rapture' comes from the Latin *rapio* which means 'catch up' or 'snatch', and renders the Greek *harpazō* in 1 Thessalonians 4:17.[194] In this passage Paul affirms that those who remain at the coming will be caught up together with those Christians who are resurrected to be with the Lord in the air. The function of the 'rapture' is two-fold: (i) to unite survivors with the coming Lord, and (ii) to transform them into the same resurrected state as the rest. The 'rapture' is, therefore, a necessary part of the coming. There is no indication of the state of the raptured believer, neither is there any indication of timing. These observations are important in view of the theory that the rapture takes place before the great tribulation (see discussion on this p. 814). Some comments must be made on the evidence brought in support of this.

The only other passages in which a sudden transformation is mentioned in connection with the coming of the Lord are 1 Corinthians 15:51–52 and

---

[191] N. Shepherd, 'The Resurrections of Revelation 20', *WTJ* 37, 1974, pp. 34ff., proposes a different interpretation of the two resurrections. He understands the first as individual in the sense of baptism and identification with the resurrection of Christ, and the second as cosmic involving not only the unbelievers, but also the whole cosmos. In this case *ezēsan* could not be understood in the sense of coming to life.

[192] *Cf.* G. R. Beasley-Murray, 'The Contribution of the Book of Revelation to the Christian Belief in Immortality', *SJT* 27 (1974), pp. 85ff., for an examination of these promises in the context of the teaching on immortality.

[193] *Cf.* K. Hanhart, *Intermediate State in the New Testament*, pp. 225f., for a comment on this.

[194] E. Best, *1 and 2 Thessalonians*, p. 198, interprets the verb here in a sense somewhat between what it means in 2 Cor. 12:2, 3, where it denotes a temporary spiritual experience, and in Acts 8:39, where it is used of a material irreversible event. At the 'rapture' it has both a spiritual and material aspect, but Paul does not enlarge on the latter.

Philippians 3:20–21. In the former passage Paul speaks of a 'mystery', but it cannot be maintained, as some allege, that this mystery is the timing of the mystery (*i.e.* pre-tribulation) for no reference is made in the context to such a tribulation. Indeed the only time reference is 'the last trumpet', which whenever it happens must clearly refer to a public event. The idea of a secret 'rapture' is entirely ruled out. Nor is there support for the view that the saints must first have been caught up in order to descend with Christ from heaven; for the text does not say that the raptured saints will come from heaven, only that they will be changed. The mystery is therefore the instantaneous transformation of living believers. The same idea comes out in Philippians 3:20–21, where the believers are promised glorious bodies like Christ's own body (see pp. 828ff.).[195]

Two passages in 2 Thessalonians, which point to the future coming and at the same time refer to believers, do not any more clearly require the theory of a secret pre-tribulation rapture.[196] 2 Thessalonians 1:6–10 refers to the appearing of the Lord Jesus from heaven with his mighty angels in flaming fire, and this cannot apply to a coming other than a public demonstration. This passage does not describe the event as a *parousia*[197] and this has led some to draw a distinction between a coming for the saints (at the rapture) and a manifestation to all people (at the final day of reckoning).[198] But Paul does not make such a distinction, for it is at the 'appearance' that all will be judged (believers and unbelievers alike). This would not support the theory of a double judgment scene (see the later section pp. 859f.), which is integral to the pre-tribulation rapture view.

In the second passage, 2 Thessalonians 2:1–8, the coming is linked with judgment, which takes place after the restrainer is removed and the Wicked One is made known. Some who interpret the restrainer as the Holy Spirit maintain that his removal will coincide with the rapture (see pp. 807ff.).[199] But this passage makes no mention of the rapture, which seems strange if it forms the focal point for the release of a greater intensity of wickedness.

There is one passage in the teaching of Jesus which might have some bearing on the subject of the 'rapture'. It occurs in Matthew 24:40–41 = Lk. 17:34–35, in relation to the coming of the Son of man. Of two men

---

[195] In all probability Paul is combating the view that the state of the redeemed is already effective and there is therefore no point in the parousia hope (*cf.* R. P. Martin, *Philippians* (NCB, 1976), p. 149.

[196] *Cf.* R. H. Gundry, *The Church and the Tribulation* (1973), who argues for a post-tribulation rapture against the pre-tribulation theories.

[197] In 1 Thes. 3:13 the word parousia is used, but there is no reason to suppose that the *apokalypsis* mentioned in 2 Thes. 1:7 refers to any different event. *Cf.* L. Morris, *1 and 2 Thessalonians* (TNTC, 1959), p. 118.

[198] J. D. Pentecost, *Things to Come*, pp. 206f., strongly maintains a distinction between the rapture and the second coming, based on the assumptions of dispensationalism.

[199] Dispensationalists who maintain that the Holy Spirit is removed at the rapture, are obliged to maintain also that the evangelization of the world after this will be performed by Jews without the aid of the Spirit (see section on the millennium, pp. 869ff.).

in the field, one shall be taken, the other left; similarly, with two women grinding at the mill (Luke refers to two in bed at night). Some kind of sudden removal happens simultaneously with the coming, in precisely the same way as Paul describes the rapture.[200] But Jesus gave no indication of when it would happen. Indeed, he used the 'thief in the night' illustration to indicate its unpredictable nature. The passage could refer to a secret rapture, but does not require such an interpretation, for there is no reason why the words could not refer to the final manifestation of Jesus, at which only those who believe in him will be caught up to meet him in the air.

In addition to the above passage, there are a few others which use the thief illustration in relation to the coming: Luke 12:39–40; 1 Thessalonians 5:1–4; 2 Peter 3:10–12; Revelation 3:3; 16:15. In all these passages the coming of the thief illustrates suddenness and unexpectedness, but in none of them secrecy. Further in 1 Timothy 6:14 and 2 Timothy 4:1, Paul used the word 'appearance' (*epiphaneia*), which describes a glorious manifestation. Indeed, in the latter passage Paul is expecting to receive a crown of righteousness. In none of these passages is there any support for a secret rapture.[201]

Summary

Although there is a dearth of explicit statements about the afterlife in the gospels, there are sufficient indications to establish the existence of life after death. Jesus takes it for granted, as is evident in the account of Dives and Lazarus, although it is not possible to fill in many details. He foresees his own position as in Paradise, instead of the shadowy Sheol.

Jesus speaks of a resurrection of life and a resurrection of judgment. The resurrection of people is an assured event in the future. On some occasions Jesus spoke of death as sleep, but there is no indication that this was any more than a metaphorical expression. Certainly Jesus faced his own death with fortitude and expected his followers to do the same.

It is mainly in Paul's epistles that the subject of the afterlife is more fully dealt with, but there are still many details which are obscure. Paul has no doubt that believers will receive a resurrection body. Moreover, he links their resurrection to that of Christ who is regarded as the first fruits. He has a resistance to the idea of being naked. His whole approach is radically different from the Greek idea of the immortality of the soul released from the body regarded as a prison house. On the question of what happens to believers at death, Paul implies that they are with the Lord, but he gives little data about when the resurrection body is received. He sometimes uses the sleep imagery to describe death, but he does not seem to mean uncon-

---

[200] Some have referred this to the fall of Jerusalem, in which Jews were 'carried away', cf. P. Benoit, *Matthieu*, (1961), p. 151. But against this view, cf. P. Bonnard, *Matthieu (CNT*, 1963), p. 355.

[201] For a summary of different theories concerning the rapture, see J. D. Pentecost, *Things to Come*,

scious existence. All that can be definitely affirmed is that the believer will be clothed with a spiritual body.

There are difficulties about the two resurrections mentioned in Revelation 20. There is no disagreement, however, about the fact that a general resurrection will take place at the consummation of the present age.

JUDGMENT

In the OT the idea of judgment is prominent, but it is judgment on earth in the present life of the nations. There is little awareness of judgment after death and where it occurs it is restricted to Israel.[202] In the interestamental period, there are evidences of a development towards a more individual approach, although the collective approach is still dominant as in the OT. In the book of Enoch there are frequent references to judgment and the judgment day.[203] Many of the features which are found in the NT allusions to judgment are found here (*e.g.* the throne, sealed books, names written, judgments pronounced). Yet neither in the OT nor in the intertestamental literature is there any specific reference to the Messiah in the office of judge, unless the passage in Daniel 7:13ff. be understood in this way. It is both in the strong teaching about individual accountability and in the presentation of Jesus himself as judge, that the gospels make a distinctive contribution to the theme of judgment.

The synoptic gospels

There are several passages which refer in a general way to a future reckoning. One of the Son of man passages predicts that when he comes 'he will repay every man for what he has done' (Mt. 16:27). This makes no mention of good or bad and must include both.[204] The idea of recompense is as frequent as the idea of condemnation, and both must be considered for a true appraisal of the theme of judgment. We will concentrate first on the aspect of condemnation and then note the references to recompense.

It is noticeable that our present theme comes more frequently in Matthew's gospel than the other synoptics. Certainly Jesus, in some of his parables, made clear that distinctions would be made between different

---

p. 156ff. He summarizes the partial, mid- and pre-tribulation rapture theories, all from a dispensationalist point of view.

[202] S. G. F. Brandon, *The Judgment of the Dead* (1967), pp. 56–75, discusses the Hebrew approach to judgment and then claims that the NT approach is heavily indebted to the Jewish. In his view the main idea is one of divine vindication. For a careful survey of the OT evidence on judgment, *cf.* L. Morris, *The Biblical Doctrine of Judgment* (1960).

[203] For the theme of judgment in Enoch, *cf.* S. G. F. Brandon, *The Judgment of the Dead*, pp. 68ff.

[204] E. Schweizer, *Matthew*, p. 347, considers that Matthew has here used Ps. 62:12, and since the Psalm refers to the righteous he thinks that Matthew may be thinking of the same thing. The reference is to 'deeds' instead of works.

classes of people. In the account of the marriage supper (Mt. 22:1ff.), differences are made between those who refused the invitation and those who ultimately came in. In a sense it may be said that the former group had judged themselves and could not complain of the judgment that fell on them. Similarly the parable of the weeds and the parable of the drag-net both include judgment on what is pronounced to be bad. A sharp distinction is made between the righteous and the unrighteous (*cf.* Mt. 13:36–43; 45–50). This comes out most vividly in the passage about the sheep and the goats (Mt. 25:31ff.), which is discussed below.

It is Matthew alone who records the use of the term 'day of judgment' (Mt. 10:15; 11:22, 24; 12:36). In the first three cases reference is made to the condemnation of Sodom. Because Luke in 10:14 and 11:31, 32 records similar sayings containing the words 'the judgment', some have concluded that Jesus probably did not speak of a future day of judgment.[205] But it should be noted that Matthew also records the shorter form in Matthew 12:41–42, which is parallel to Luke 11:31–32. Admittedly Matthew 10:15 has the fuller form in a parallel to Luke's shorter form (*i.e.* in Lk. 10:14), but the evidence is not sufficient to show that Matthew's expression could not have been used by Jesus. It is surely pedantic to attach any significance to the difference in the two forms. Both refer to a particular judgment which relates to all, whether to the patriarchal world, the world of Solomon and the Queen of Sheba, or to the world of Jesus' contemporaries. It cannot be maintained that there is no thought of a great assize in these passages, for that seems the most natural meaning of the words.[206]

A few other passages of a general kind draw attention to the theme of judgment. In the Sermon on the Mount Jesus warns against a judging spirit, 'for with the judgment you pronounce you will be judged' (Mt. 7:2); while this may not necessarily refer to the final divine judgment, it could conceivably do so. In 5:21–22 Jesus declares that not only murder, but anger against a brother, makes one liable to judgment. One stage of condemnation is even described as 'gehenna of fire' (another expression found only in Matthew, *cf.* also 23:33), which must have reference to a final condemnation. It should be noted that Matthew includes a saying of Jesus that men must give an account of every careless word (Mt. 12:36).[207] When could this take place if not on the day of judgment?

It is not quite so clear that a future judgment is in mind in Mark 12:40 (= Lk. 20:47) in Jesus' criticism of those who 'devour widows' houses': 'They will receive the greater condemnation'. It would be more effective

---

[205] *Cf.* T. F. Glasson, *The Second Advent* (³1963), p. 130.

[206] Glasson argues otherwise. He thinks Sodom has already been judged and that Chorazin and Capernaum are urged to take note. He denies any reference to a final judgment. (*op. cit.*, pp. 130f.).

[207] D. Hill, *Matthew* (NCB, 1972), p. 219, draws attention to a rabbinic belief that a man's record in heaven included his words as well as his deeds. He concedes that Mt. 12:36 has an eschatological reference.

to relate this to a future judgment, since in this life it is all too familiar for the oppressors to get away with it. But the words of Jesus make clear that judgment will catch up with them.[208] The pursuit of justice is enjoined on the followers of Jesus (*cf.* Mt. 23:23; Lk. 11:42). Indeed, they are even assured that when the Son of man comes, they will sit with him on the thrones judging the twelve tribes of Israel (Mt. 19:28; Lk. 22:30). There is a clear linking of judgment with the parousia in Matthew, although Luke's saying speaks instead of a kingdom. In both accounts, however, the act of judging is clearly futuristic.

Before commenting on the sheep and goats passage, we note some of the sayings of Jesus which mention rewards, which cannot be understood in terms of this life. At the close of Luke's beatitudes, Jesus says, 'Rejoice in that day . . . for behold, your reward is great in heaven' (Lk. 6:23; *cf.* also Mt. 5:12).[209] Similarly in the same passage, he says to those who love their enemies (*cf.* Mt. 5:45), 'your reward will be great, and you will be sons of the Most High' (Lk. 6:35).[210] Jesus assured his disciples that the Father who sees in secret will reward them (Mt. 6:4, 6, 18). This is in contrast to the hypocrites who already have their reward (*i.e.* in this life). Although nothing is said about the timing of the reward, its fullest expression is probably intended to refer to a future time.

It is against the background of these numerous references to judgments and to the giving of rewards, that the passage in Matthew 25:14–46 must be considered.[211] In the parable of the talents, faithfulness was rewarded with greater responsibility. Yet it is not specifically linked with a final day of reckoning. It is different in the passage about the sheep and goats, which is explicitly linked to the occasion of the Son of man's coming in glory and the establishment of a great assize. Some scholars attach little importance to this section on the grounds that it is Matthew's own construction,[212] although most would agree that some genuine words of Jesus are pre-

---

[208] Many theologians reject the concept of everlasting punishment, not on exegetical, but on theological grounds. W. N. Pittenger, *The Christian Understanding of Human Nature* (1964), p. 124, for instance, claims that it is beneath the level of Christian faith to speak of commending Christianity to others on the grounds that unless they accept the faith they are doomed to perish eternally. But Jesus never uses the theme of judgment to inculcate faith. Its purpose is warning with a view to leading to repentance.

[209] E. E. Ellis, *Luke*, pp. 113f., deduces from this statement that the reward already exists in heaven, but is to be received in the coming age. He rightly points out that fulfilment in this age is its own reward.

[210] I. H. Marshall, *Luke*, p. 264, although accepting that this saying is primarily implying that disciples will show themselves to be God's children by imitating his character, nevertheless thinks that the idea of the promise of divine sonship as a reward for service cannot be ruled out.

[211] G. de Ru, 'The Conception of Reward in the Teaching of Jesus', *NovT* 8, 1966, pp. 202–220, brings the parable of the vineyard (Mt. 20:1-16) into the discussion on rewards. He claims that in the NT man never earns anything. His 'reward' is communion with God. Man needs this and cannot be self-sufficient so as not to need a reward. *Cf.* also P. C. Böttger, *art.* on Recompence *NIDNTT* 3, pp. 141f.; H. Preisker, *TDNT* 4, pp. 714ff., for a discussion of reward in the teaching of Jesus.

[212] *Cf.* T. F. Glasson, *The Second Advent*, pp. 129ff., who reaches the conclusion that Jesus did not regard himself as judge at a final great assize.

served.[213] There is no valid reason to dispute the authenticity of the section, even if the imagery used is familiar in apocalyptic sources. If there is to be a reckoning of any sort, it is not unreasonable to suppose that it would be expressed in terms of an assize. Even so there are differences of opinion over the interpretation of this passage.

The real key to the understanding is the identification of the 'brethren' of whom Jesus speaks ('as you did it to one of the least of these my brethren, you did it to me', Mt. 25:40). One interpretation is to assume that the King's 'brethren' are his own people, and since Jesus is identifying himself with the King (as verse 31 clearly suggests that he is), then the 'brethren' would be Christians generally.[214] If this interpretation is correct, the section can be applied either nationally or individually.

Since it is stated that all the nations will be gathered before the Son of man, it would be reasonable to see the separation between the sheep and goats as being carried out on the basis of the treatment of the followers of Jesus by national groups. Certainly the action portrayed, which involved the alleviation of purely physical needs, could apply to the conditions facing those whom Jesus would send out. The mission charge in Matthew 10:5ff. is instructive in this connection since it warns the disciples of two possible attitudes which would face them – acceptance or rejection – and relates these to the day of judgment (verse 15). Moreover, some would persecute the followers of Jesus. In both passages judgment is concerned with groups – households, towns, councils, governors, kings (in Mt. 10) and nations (in Mt. 25). Nevertheless, a judgment on groups is in the end a judgment on the individuals who form the groups.

A variant of this view sees the 'brethren' as more particularly apostles engaged in their mission work, in which case others will be judged according to the attitudes they had adopted towards God's servants. There is no need, however, to draw a sharp distinction between the apostles and Christians in general.

While there is much to be said for this view, some prefer to see Matthew 25 as judgment decided on the basis of general social concern, in which case 'brethren' is taken to refer to all in need.[215] Under this view there is

---

[213] T. W. Manson, *The Teaching of Jesus* ([2]1935), pp. 34ff., traces the construction to Matthew's special source which separates people into two classes.

[214] This interpretation is followed by G. E. Ladd, 'The Parable of the Sheep and the Goats in Recent Interpretation', *New Dimensions in New Testament Study* (eds. R. N. Longenecker and M. C. Tenney, 1974), pp. 191ff. *Cf.* also J. Mánek, 'Mit wem identifiziert sich Jesus (Matt.25:31–46)?', *Christ and Spirit*, pp. 15–25, who regards *elachistoi* as a title of high honour. G. Gay, 'The Judgment of the Gentiles in Matthew's Theology', *Scripture, Tradition and Interpretation* (ed. W. W. Gasque and W. S. LaSor, 1978), pp. 199–215, does not consider that 'brethren' in this passage relates to all Christians, but to a special group of downtrodden believers. *Cf.* also W. G. Kümmel's article, 'Gottes geringste Brüder – zu Mt. 25.31-46', *Jesus und Paulus* (ed. E. E. Ellis and E. Grässer, 1975), pp. 363–383.

[215] J. Jeremias, *The Parables of Jesus* (Eng. trans. [2]1963), p. 207, identifies the brethren as the poor and needy generally, but admits that in that case *touton* (verses 40, 45) is a superfluous demonstrative. Jeremias

condemnation of any society which neglects the underprivileged, with whom Jesus identifies himself. This interpretation would be in line with the OT condemnation of nations which dealt harshly with Israel.[216] It has also been argued, in line with this interpretation, that this passage provides a basis for understanding how those who have never heard the gospel will be judged. If general acts of love and concern are the standard, this would apply equally to Christians and non-Christians. While there is much to attract in this view, the major objection is that nowhere else does Jesus use the term 'brethren' in this general sense to denote all men in need.

Yet another view is that which identifies the 'brethren' as a Jewish remnant who will proclaim the gospel among the nations during the great tribulation.[217] This interpretation is favoured by those who hold to a pre-tribulation rapture of the church. According to the way in which the nations respond to the converted Jewish remnant, so they would be classified in the final judgment. But there is no indication in the context that the 'brethren' are specifically Jewish. Moreover, the invitation to the 'sheep' to inherit 'the kingdom prepared for you from the foundation of the world' (Mt. 25:34), and the condemnation of the 'goats' to eternal punishment (verse 46), seems a more radical separation than can be accounted for by the brief tribulation period which this theory supposes.

We need to investigate yet one other possibility and that is that the passage does not refer to collective action, but to individual. The separation is then not between nations, but between individuals at the final judgment. 'All the nations' is then equivalent to 'all men'. In this case, the same problem arises over the word 'brethren'; but if this means Christians, it would set out the basis of judgment as being social action rather than the gracious work of Christ on man's behalf.[218] It is difficult to believe in the light of the NT teaching on justification before God that Jesus could here have meant that people could obtain an eternal inheritance simply on the grounds of good works. This moreover is not supported by verse 37, which calls the sheep 'the righteous'.

It may be wondered what relation the final judgment has to any intervening acts of judgment. Some hold that judgment takes place at the moment of death and consequently do not favour those interpretations

---

is persuaded that in essence this parable is authentic to Jesus, although he admits some editorial work in it.

[216] L. Cope, 'Matthew xxv 31-45, "The Sheep and the Goats" Reinterpreted', *NovT*, 1969, pp. 32–44, regards the passage as a poetic picture of the last judgment constructed by the evangelist. In Cope's mind the passage cannot provide a legitimate basis for Christian concern for the poor. The brethren are the disciples and the ethic is 'a churchly, sectarian one', no significant advance over Jewish ethics of its day.

[217] Cf. J. D. Pentecost, *Things to Come*, p. 420.

[218] G. E. Ladd, *TNT*, p. 206, says, 'This is not a program of eschatology but a practical parable of human destiny'.

which propose a final assize.[219] The Dives and Lazarus passage is cited in support (Lk. 16:19ff.). But there is no reason to suppose from any of the synoptic gospels that Jesus taught that judgment takes place at death (see the discussion on the judgment seat of Christ, pp. 860ff.). No more acceptable is the view that judgment is a continuous process in this life, for it does not do justice to the significance of the parousia for judgment. There is a sense in which present and future judgment are linked, because a condemnation which can be pronounced on the ground of present rejection will certainly be upheld and made absolute at the final assize. The latter cannot be dispensed with simply by saying that it is unnecessary. The idea of a judgment linked to the parousia is undeniably in the teaching of Jesus in the synoptics, whatever we make of it.

The Johannine literature

There is no doubt that Jesus looked forward to a future judgment according to John's account. John 12:48 is the clearest statement to this effect: 'He who rejects me and does not receive my sayings has a judge; the word I have spoken will be his judge on the last day.' It is impossible to excise from John's gospel the references to the last (*eschatē*) day, however much it may be maintained that this is apocalyptic language.[220] The linking here of judgment with the last day must point to a final judgment, although the basis of it is the present reactions of people to Christ.

It is noticeable that Christ himself is the touchstone as in Matthew's account, although here there is emphasis on the words of Christ rather than works for the sake of Christ (although *cf*. Mt. 7:22). This difference of emphasis, however, does not imply a totally different basis for judgment. In the same context Jesus declares that he himself did not judge (12:47), for this was not the purpose of his mission. This passage does not mean that Jesus would not be judge at the last day, but that he is not judge now. His present purpose was not to judge, but to save (verse 47). This is in agreement with John 5:22, 27 in which Jesus states that the Father has given to the Son authority to execute judgment, a statement which is immediately followed by references to the resurrection of life (for those who have done good) and the resurrection of judgment (for those who have done evil).[221] Clearly Jesus set himself out as judge, even more specifically in John's record than in the synoptics (*cf*. also Jn. 9:39). Moreover the basis of the distinction between the two classes is a moral one, linked however with works (as in Mt. 25).

---

[219] *Cf.* Glasson, *op. cit.*, pp. 129ff.

[220] G. Kittel, in his article on *eschatos* in *TDNT* 2, pp. 697f., has no hesitation in grouping Jn. 6:39f., 44, 54; 11:24; 12:48 with other NT evidences for the coming last day.

[221] R. E. Brown, *John.*, p. 219, conceives that in this passage John advances a realized eschatology and supposes that judgment, condemnation and passing from death to life are all part of the present 'hour'.

To some scholars the existence of two apparently totally different bases for judgment in one writing is intolerable and has led them to treat the John 5 passage as an apocalyptic development which is not original to the teaching of Jesus.[222] Yet to drive a wedge between the two standards is faulty exegesis, for it is assuming that 'doing good' has no relationship with a man's attitude to Christ. Jesus, on the other hand, declared in John 15:5 'apart from me (the vine) you can do nothing'. When the total teaching of Jesus in John is considered there is no essential contradiction.

It must be recognized, nonetheless, that in John the present aspect of judgment is more prominent that the future aspect. Such a statement as 3:18, 'he who does not believe (*i.e.* in the Son) is condemned already', shows how people's present attitude to Jesus affects the future judgment upon them.[223] In other words anyone who has a definite attitude of rejection towards Jesus in this life must recognize that this will form the basis of future assessment (*cf.* Mt. 10:32f.; Mk. 8:38; Lk. 12:9). Furthermore, the opposite of condemnation in this context is eternal life. Condemnation is thus seen as implying eternal death. The context of this saying makes clear that no judgment, in the sense of condemnation, awaits those who believe in Christ. This does not exclude the thought of believers appearing before the judgment seat, but it means that they already know the verdict. There is a direct connection between present and future.

In one passage, the comment is made (whether by Jesus or by the evangelist is not clear) that judgment is equated with the coming of light into the world with the result that people loved darkness rather than light (Jn. 3:19). This suggests that the incarnation was itself an act of judgment (*krisis*).[224] It is in view of this blanketing of the light on the part of men, that the teaching on judgment in this gospel is so important. It shows that condemnation rests squarely on those who deliberately refuse the light. Jesus himself claims that his judgment is just (Jn. 5:30) and while this is not in the context related to the future judgment, it must have a bearing on the nature of that judgment.

Not only is the incarnation a *krisis* point, but the passion is also.[225] 'Now is the judgment of this world' (Jn. 12:31) is Jesus' assessment as he faces the cross. What takes place later in a future judgment is, therefore, seen enacted in the life and work of Jesus. In this gospel there is a bringing forward of the future into the present, so that no discontinuity exists

---

[222] *Cf.* C. H. Dodd, *The Apostolic Preaching and its Developments*, pp. 65f.; *cf. idem*, *The Interpretation of the Fourth Gospel*, pp. 147f.

[223] Bultmann, *John*, p. 155, reinterprets the saying in Jn. 3:18 of a radical understanding of the appearance of Jesus as an eschatological event. But this removes the future element and regards the saying in existential terms.

[224] *Cf.* Bultmann, *TNT* 2, pp. 38f.

[225] F. Büchsel, article *krima*, *krisis*, *etc.* in *TDNT* 3, p. 941, decides that in John *krisis* is the world judgment of Christ, originally future, but also present already.

between them. The importance of the theme of judgment is also seen in the fact that one of the functions of the Spirit is to convince (or convict) the world of judgment (Jn. 16:8). If it is the Spirit's work to do this, it is also the church's work to draw attention to it. There is no escaping from the theme of judgment.

It is striking that there is very little in John's gospel on the subject of rewards, far less than in the synoptic gospels. In fact the only passage which hints at it is John 4:36 which states that the reaper receives wages, but even this is qualified with the remark that he gathers fruit for eternal life. Indeed, eternal life is regarded in many Johannine passages as so great a prize that any idea of additional rewards seems superfluous. Jesus criticizes those who receive glory from men (Jn. 5:44). The only glory is what comes from God.

Information about judgment is sparse in the Johannine epistles. John is concentrating on the present rather than the future. Abiding in Christ now secures eternal life. But there is one reference to the day of judgment: 'In this is love perfected with us, that we may have confidence for the day of judgment' (1 Jn. 4:17).[226] As a result of this abiding in love, fear is cast out. John says that fear has to do with punishment (1 Jn. 4:18). Although the emphasis is on the present, it has an impingement on the future, and it cannot be said that John knows nothing of a final day of reckoning. When he says that Christians have already passed from death to life (1 Jn. 3:14), he is in agreement with other NT writers who stress the present reality of salvation, but who do not for that reason deny a coming judgment day.

We should also note that John speaks of the world passing away (1 Jn. 2:17)[227] and of the arrival of the 'last hour' (1 Jn. 2:18), both future events expressed in a non-apocalyptic form.[228] Some see this as an evidence of realized eschatology in that the future 'hour' has become present. It may, however, be accounted for by John's acute awareness that the 'hour' permeates the whole of the present era.

Acts

In the earlier part of the book the theme of judgment is implied rather than stated. There is a strong sense of foreboding in the reaction of the hearers on the day of Pentecost (Acts 2:37, 40). The call to repentance in Acts 3:17–19 is made against a background of condemnation, while the case of

[226] I. H. Marshall, *The Epistles of John*, p. 223, explains this statement in the following way: 'This experience of mutual love is fully realized in the fact that we can have confidence on the day of judgment'.

[227] R. Bultmann, *The Johannine Epistles* (Eng. trans. Hermeneia, 1973, from KEK, 1967), p. 34, denies that the word *paragetai* means passing away, and chooses the concept of transitoriness. But the statement implies that as *kosmos* it is due for destruction. Marshall, *op. cit.*, p. 146, correctly links the verb with its meaning in 1 Cor. 7:31.

[228] *Cf.* H. A. Guy, *The New Testament Doctrine of the Last Things* (1948), p. 172.

Ananias and Sapphira (Acts 5:1–11) illustrates the swiftness and justice of God's judgment. In Acts 10:42 Peter affirms that Jesus had been ordained by God to be the judge of the living and the dead, a clear evidence of the conviction that Jesus would perform the same function as God in judgment.

The clearest reference to future condemnation comes in Paul's address at Athens where the call to repentance is directly linked to judgment. God 'commands all men everywhere to repent, because he has fixed a day on which he will judge the world in righteousness by a man whom he has appointed' (Acts 17:30, 31). This is a specific indication of a future day on which all judgment will be executed. There is no suggestion of a continuous process. The emphasis on a fixed day is in line with several statements in Paul's epistles. The judgment theme at Athens evoked little response, but this was probably more the result of the type of audience than of the theme itself. Indeed it may be questioned whether Paul intended to end on such a theme, since he seems to have been prevented from continuing his speech by the dispute over resurrection.[229] One feature of this Acts statement is the support it gives to the significance of Christ's humanity in relation to his position as judge. It is as man that he will execute judgment.

Paul

There is no doubt that for Paul the idea of judgment was an important feature of his teaching about the parousia and the consummation of the age. It would be true to say that judgment is a major function of the parousia. For this reason a clear understanding of his judgment teaching is essential for a comprehensive grasp of his theology. Although we shall find no basic disagreements between Paul's view and those already examined from the gospels and Acts, we shall discover much fuller data. There is still a lack, however, of any systematic presentation and several important questions will remain unanswered. We shall consider the following aspects: the nature of judgment, its scope, and its timing.

THE NATURE OF JUDGMENT

A brief survey must first be made of the various terms which Paul uses for expressing the idea of judgment. It will be possible here to give only the briefest indication of the wide range of such terms, which will enable us to get the feel of Paul's understanding.

(i) The word *wrath* (*orgē*) when applied to God (see pp. 101f. for a discussion of this attribute of God) carries with it the notion of judgment.[230] It is not confined to the judgment day for its expression. Because it is an

---

[229] F. F. Bruce, *The Book of the Acts* (NICNT, 1954), p. 362, sees no reason to suppose that Paul curtailed his speech because of the ridicule. He thinks it was admirably adapted to introduce Christianity to cultured pagans.

[230] For a detailed survey of the theme of the wrath of God in the NT, *cf.* G. Stählin's article on *orgē*, TDNT 5, pp. 422–447.

integral part of the nature of God, it is constantly applicable. Paul sees it as an indispensable aspect of God's righteousness (*cf.* Rom. 1:17–18 where righteousness and wrath are placed side by side). The wrath of God expresses itself against all sin. It comes to particular expression on the day of judgment against those who have deliberately rejected the provisions of the kindness of God (Rom. 2:5). Paul expounds this judgment theme in Romans 2:1–11, but maintains that wrath (*orgē*) and fury (*thymos*) are reserved for those who obey wickedness and do not obey truth.[231]

There is no suggestion in Pauline usage that the wrath of God is ever capricious or the result of passion. It is on the contrary set over against what can be known of God and it is expressed only against a deliberate rejection of that knowledge (*cf.* Rom. 1:17–32). The wrath of God, according to Paul's view, already operates in human history by giving men up to their own passions. So important is this understanding of God's nature, that the idea of judgment was recognized by Paul as an unavoidable expression of what God is. There is on the one hand the inexorable exposure of rebellious sinners to the wrath of God, and on the other hand the promise of salvation from the same wrath for those justified by the blood of Christ (Rom. 5:9). A clear expression of this contrast is found in Romans 9:22–23, where 'vessels of wrath' are set over against 'vessels of mercy'.[232]

(ii) The next group of words are those conveying *judgment* or *condemnation* (*krinein*, and its cognates *krima, katakrinein, krisis*).[233] This series of words is not applied exclusively to God's judgment any more than *orgē* is. But they have special significance in relation to the day of judgment. On that day God will judge the secrets of men by Christ Jesus (Rom. 2:16). Most references to judgment in Paul's epistles imply condemnation and are, with few exceptions, connected with the final judgment. It is God who is judge (Rom. 3:6), and this is the guarantee that the judgment, whether it be commendation or condemnation, will be indisputably just. God shows no partiality. A person's status gives him no exemption (Gal. 5:10). In expounding his Adam theme, Paul claims that the judgment following one man's trespass brought condemnation (Rom. 5:16). The law is said to be the standard of judgment for those under the law (Rom. 2:12). It is in this sense that Paul can speak of the Mosaic era as the 'dispensation of condemnation' (2 Cor. 3:9). It must also be noted that in Paul's mind all are under the same condemnation (Rom. 5:18)[234], where *katakrima* is ex-

---

[231] C. E. B. Cranfield, *Romans*, 1, (*ICC*, 1975), p. 749, sees no distinction between the two words used here, the second simply strengthening the first.

[232] In both of these expressions the genitives are objective, referring respectively to the objects of wrath and of mercy.

[233] G, Vos, *The Pauline Eschatology*, p. 267, notes that the verb *krinein* is basically non-forensic.

[234] F. V. Filson, *St Paul's Conception of Recompense* (1931), p. 52, takes the condemnation in Rom. 5:16, 18, not of final judgment, but of a working of retribution in history.

pressed as the antithesis of righteousness (but see below on the meaning of this word).

(iii) The word group embracing the ideas of *justice* and *justification* (*dikaios, dikaioō*)[235] have considerable bearing on the theme of judgment, because they are a guarantee of absolute justice. In 2 Timothy 4:8, God is seen as the righteous (*dikaios*) judge. Paul further refers to the 'righteous judgment of God' (2 Thes. 1:5). In this latter case the judgment is directly linked with the kingdom of God. In Romans 2:5 the righteous judgment is linked with the day of wrath. It is important to note when considering the judgment of believers that Paul's doctrine of justification is based on the just character of God.

(iv) Another idea is that of *perdition* (*apollyein, apōleia*).[236] Not only is the man of sin called the son of perdition (2 Thess. 2:3), but those who follow him will perish with him (2 Thes. 2:10, they are called the *apollymenoi*). There is no escape from this fate. This destruction is regarded as thoroughly deserved (*cf.* also Rom. 2:12). It is important to note that by the use of these terms Paul is not describing the resultant state as annihilation, as is clear from the occurrence of the same verb in the quotation which affirms that God will destroy the wisdom of the wise (1 Cor. 1:19). At times Paul uses the word in the sense of physical death (1 Cor. 10:9ff.). What then does he mean by 'destruction' as a form of judgment? He must mean to imply that all hope of salvation or restoration is totally excluded.

(v) A similar word, which is used on a few occasions is *olethros, destruction*, found in 1 Corinthians 5:5; 1 Thessalonians 5:3; 2 Thessalonians 1:9; 1 Timothy 6:9. In the first case it relates to the 'flesh' and has a disciplinary purpose (that the man's spirit may be saved in the day of the Lord Jesus). It is not certain what 'the destruction of the flesh' here means. Some relate it to sickness and others to death. It involves a definite restriction on sensual passions and is clearly regarded as a present judgment.[237] In the Thessalonian passages the word is used of unbelievers, and is connected with the day of judgment. Moreover, in 1 Thessalonians 5:3 the destruction is described as 'sudden' (*aiphnidios*) and in 2 Thessalonians 1:9 it is said to be 'eternal' (*aiōnios*). In 1 Timothy 6:9 it is linked with 'ruin' to describe the fate of those who senselessly pursue wealth for its own sake. Since in the context it is said that we cannot take anything out of this world (verse 7), it is evident that the final judgment is in mind.

[235] For a study of *dikaios* and its cognates, *cf.* G. Schrenk, *TDNT* 2, pp. 182–225.

[236] *Cf.* A. Oepke, *TDNT* 1, pp. 394ff., who states that the term is used of eternal destruction, particularly in Paul and John, but also in the synoptics.

[237] J. Schneider, *olethros*, *TDNT* 5, pp. 168f., considers that Paul obviously believed that the curse will be followed by sudden death. *Cf.* also C. K. Barrett, *1 Corinthians*, p. 126, who draws attention to the Jewish belief that a man's death could at times be regarded as an atonement, but he rejects this kind of notion as an explanation of 1 Cor. 5:5 on the grounds that Paul nowhere allows for atonement coming through any other means than through the death of Christ.

From this survey of terms we are in a position to pass on to a consideration of the main features of Paul's teaching on judgment. We may summarize it as follows. (i) Paul asserts both a continuing process of judgment and a final day of judgment. (ii) He speaks of both the judgment seat of Christ and of the judgment seat of God. (iii) He recognizes that non-acceptance of God's provision in Christ merits condemnation. (iv) He assumes as axiomatic that any judgment made by God must be just by reason of his righteous character. (v) He is not afraid to speak of the wrath of God and the consequent severity of his judgment, and does not see in this any clash with either the divine righteousness or the divine love. (vi) He does not restrict his views of judgment to unbelievers, but includes believers.

To understand his whole position, however, it will be necessary to examine it against his total theological exposition. We shall next note the distinctions he draws between unbelievers and believers in relation to judgment. We have already seen when considering the work of Christ (see pp. 492ff.) the relationship between the work and the believer's justification, and the following comments must be considered against that background.

THE UNIVERSAL SCOPE OF JUDGMENT

It is better to examine the destiny of unbelievers before noting the destiny of believers for two reasons. First, the judgment of God on the ungodly is more widely accepted as almost axiomatic. And secondly, the majority of references to judgment in Paul are to believers and the minority to unbelievers.

Paul dwells rather on the certainty of retribution than upon the details of judgment. This retribution may be seen as already at work, but Paul never suggests that it is completed in this life. Indeed, it is abundantly clear that this is not so. It is for this reason that he concentrates his attention on the final judgment. In a few cases he may have regarded death itself as a punishment, but since death is universal, he evidently recognized death and judgment as separate concepts. He regards the judgment day as the focal point of God's judgment on sin and sinners. He says very little on the nature of judgment facing unbelievers, although his teaching has been interpreted to point to annihiliation or to universal salvation or to eternal punishment. What we may deduce in a general sense about the nature of the judgment on unbelievers is that it involves both loss of worthwhile existence (especially in separation from God) and positive punishment, although Paul says little about the latter.

In turning from the judgment of unbelievers to believers, we are at once confronted with a different situation in view of Paul's doctrine of grace. Nevertheless the insistence that believers in Christ have no condemnation alongside the strong warnings about the judgment raises a tension which must be carefully analysed. It has earlier been demonstrated that not only Paul's doctrine, but the whole NT teaching, affirms that justification is not attained through works, but through faith (see pp. 496ff.). At the same time Paul has a definite doctrine of rewards. The idea of merit may be absent from his doctrine of salvation, but it is present in his doctrine of judgment.

The doctrine of justification certainly establishes a believer's standing before God and assures him that he has no need to fear in face of the judgment. The classic statement of this is in Romans 8:1: 'There is therefore now no condemnation (*katakrima*) for those who are in Christ Jesus.' Since it is sin that brings condemnation, Christ's dealings with sin removes the condemnation.[238] But does Paul mean that not only past sins but also future sins are completely covered and that no further accountability will be required? There are many statements which must be considered before a certain answer can be given.

It may at once be observed that at no time did Paul suggest that sin in the lives of believers was anything other than serious. His epistles are full of exhortations which call for the avoidance of all unworthiness. The Christian's target must be blamelessness in the sight of God (1 Thes. 3:13; 5:23; 1 Cor. 1:8). Paul strongly criticizes Christians who fail to live up to Christian standards (as in 1 Cor. 5:9ff.) and even suggests that in some cases physical affliction is visited on people in this life to preserve their entitlement to salvation (*cf.* also 1 Cor. 11:29ff.). Yet does this affect their justification? We have seen reason to suggest that there are no statements in Paul's epistles which lead us to suppose that believers are in definite danger of losing their justification in Christ, for then the final status would rest on their own efforts, an idea alien to Paul's position on grace (see pp. 620ff.).

Yet the apostle clearly states to the Corinthians that 'we must all appear before the judgment seat of Christ' (2 Cor. 5:10) and this focuses attention on a definite day of judgment. Its purpose is that 'each one may receive good or evil, according to what he has done in the body'. It is sometimes supposed that because the statement is made in a Christian epistle, it applies only to Christians. This would necessitate a distinction between the judgment seat of God and the judgment seat of Christ, the former for unbelievers and the latter for believers.[239] But this distinction is difficult to maintain for there seems no logical reason why the expression 'the judgment seat of Christ' should refer to a special tribunal. It occurs only here

---

[238] J. Murray, *Romans* 1, (*NICNT*, 1959), p. 275, connects the freedom from condemnation with release not only from the guilt, but also the power of sin. He supports this by relating the *oun* in Rom. 8:1 to the preceding passage, Rom. 6:1-7:25.

[239] P. E. Hughes, *2 Corinthians* (*NICNT*, 1962), p. 182, regards the judgment seat of Christ not as the universal judgment seat, only as a judgment for the redeemed; but he does not specifically discuss the distinction between the two judgments. However, C. K. Barrett, *2 Corinthians*, p. 160, points out that when Jesus Christ judges his judgment is the judgment of God.

in Paul and nowhere else in the NT. In the similar statement in Romans 14:10, the judgment seat is God's not Christ's, but certainly believers are in mind.

To return to 2 Corinthians 5:10, Paul says good or evil will be received according to works (*ha epraxen*), but it may be wondered in what sense Christians could be said to receive evil.[240] It seems better to suppose that the good and evil apply respectively to Christians and unbelievers. But it leaves room for degrees of rewards. Romans 14:12 is specific that each person will give account of himself to God.

There are many passages in which Paul expounds his idea of rewards for believers.[241] In using an agricultural metaphor he maintains that a man will reap whatever he sows (Gal. 6:7; *cf.* 1 Cor. 3:8). 'Let us not grow weary in well-doing, for in due season we shall reap, if we do not lose heart' (Gal. 6:9). In exchange for a slight affliction, Paul is convinced that believers will receive a much greater eternal weight of glory (2 Cor. 4:17). It is a Christian conviction that an inheritance will be received as a reward (Col. 3:24). Paul speaks of a hope laid up in heaven (Col. 1:5). As he approaches his end, he looks forward to 'the crown of righteousness' (2 Tim. 4:8), which the righteous judge will award on that day.

In the pastoral epistles there is rather more stress on the need for good works, but the idea is not absent from the other epistles.[242] In 2 Corinthians 9:6–8, the apostle urges generosity on the grounds that God may provide in abundance for every good work. The epistles are full of exhortations and Paul clearly expects Christians to maintain high standards of godly living. There is no suggestion that the doctrine of grace lessens moral obligations. Indeed Paul emphatically refutes such a suggestion (Rom. 6:1f.). He assumes that his converts will be preserved guiltless in the day of our Lord Jesus Christ (1 Cor. 1:8). He wants to be proud of them on that day (Phil. 2:16; 1 Cor. 9:15; 2 Cor. 1:14; 7:4; 1 Thes. 2:19).

The most specific passage dealing with rewards is 1 Corinthians 3:12–15, where the apostle discusses the various superstructures which people may build on the one foundation, Jesus Christ. The main point is the building up of the church, to which Paul as a preacher was committed. He wants to bring out the responsibilities inherent in such a calling. He notes that there are wide variations in the different materials which could be used, ranging from gold to stubble. He is thinking, however, of intrinsic value, rather than value for building purposes. The process of testing will destroy the combustible materials, but not the precious metals. Paul's

---

[240] This statement has sometimes been considered as inconsistent with Paul's doctrine of justification. But as R. V. G. Tasker, *2 Corinthians* (*TNTC*, 1958), p. 83, points out the stress on good works here reminds Christians of their moral obligations.

[241] See F. V. Filson's *St Paul's Conception of Recompense*.

[242] Filson, *op. cit.*, pp. 135ff., has a special appendix on the recompense principle in the pastoral epistles.

conclusion from this illustration is that whatever survives will be rewarded, but whatever is destroyed will be sheer loss, with the proviso that the man himself will be saved.

There is no suggestion here that anyone's salvation depends on his service for God. No intimation is given to explain the meaning of the 'fire' which reveals the true nature of the work of building.[243] It cannot, of course, be taken literally, any more than the materials are intended to be taken that way.[244] The passage shows a clear combination of the sole foundation (salvation through Christ alone) and the responsibility of Christians in their life's service. No indication is given in this passage regarding the nature of the reward.

The evidence for Paul's doctrine of rewards is strong and no true understanding of his theology is possible without taking full account of it. We may summarize his position as follows: (i) God will give rewards on the basis of what has been done in this life; (ii) the rewards are partially received here, but mostly reserved in heaven; (iii) the final rewards will be granted on the day of judgment; (iv) the rewards are of a spiritual nature, like 'the crown of righteousness', but their character is not otherwise specified; (v) there is no suggestion that salvation itself comes under the category of a reward.[245]

THE TIMING OF THE JUDGMENT

Comment has already been made above on the theory that the judgment seat of Christ is separate from the judgment seat of God and it was suggested that this is difficult to maintain. Nevertheless, it forms a key idea of those views which place the parousia (and the judgment seat of Christ) at a point in the future prior to the final judgment at the close of the millennium (*cf.* Rev. 20).[246] It must be pointed out, however, that Paul seems to know of only one day of the Lord, and this must be identified as the day of judgment. A study of Paul's epistles alone would not lead anyone to the conclusion that a double judgment day was in his mind. Nor

---

[243] F. W. Grosheide, *1 Corinthians*, p. 87, does not consider that 'fire' is the fire of judgment, but represents narrow escape from destruction. The whole passage, however, connects the idea of rewards with some final assessment.

[244] There is no support in this passage for the idea of purgatory. K. Hanhart, The *Intermediate State*, pp. 185ff., rejects the appeal to this passage and to 1 Cor. 5:5 and Lk. 12:59 in support of purgatory. He notes that the Roman Catholic, J. Gnilka, *1st Kor. 3:10-15 ein Schriftzeugnis für das Fegefeuer?* (1955), concludes that 1 Cor. 3:10ff., cannot be read as referring to purgatory. E.-B. Allo (*Première Épître aux Corinthiens, ad loc.*) thinks that it is only implied in this passage.

[245] Filson, *op. cit.*, p. 102, finds in Gal. 6:8 and Rom. 6:22f. some evidence that Paul thought of eternal life as in some sense a reward. Yet Paul definitely regarded eternal life as a gracious gift of God, as the context in Rom. 6 shows.

[246] *Cf.* J. Walvoord, *The Millennial Kingdom*, pp. 276ff., for a dispensational exposition of the theme of judgment. For a non-dispensational view, *cf.* J. W. Hodges, *Christ's Kingdom and Coming*, pp. 226ff.

can Paul be claimed as a supporter of the view that believers receive their rewards at death, for at times he links the rewards with the second coming.

It may be noted that the apostle is not so much interested in the future for its own sake as in the relation of the future to the present life. There is a salutary effect on believers in the present if they know they will be accountable for their actions in the future, whatever might be the precise time of the judgment. In 1 Corinthians 4:4ff. where Paul declares that the Lord, not men, is the judge of his actions, he warns against judging 'before the time', *i.e.* before the Lord comes.[247] This confirms that judgment belongs essentially to the final judgment day. We may further note from this context one of the essential features of the final judgment, compared with present judgment: the former is open and public, whereas the latter is often hidden. This element of disclosure is naturally associated with the parousia.

Hebrews

There are several allusions to judgment and to the idea of recompense in this epistle. One feature which distinguishes this epistle from Paul's epistles is the absence of any reference to Christ acting as judge. It is the Lord who will judge his people (10:30, a direct quotation from Dt. 32:36; *cf.* also Heb. 12:23). Nevertheless there is a strong sense of divine justice. The writer recognizes that it is a fearful thing to fall into the hands of the living God (10:31). Since he views God as a consuming fire (12:29), his foreboding is understandable.

There is no doubt that judgment will come. As sure as the fact that all people are appointed to die, is the fact of judgment (9:27). Since this refers to the sequence 'death, then judgment', some have supposed that this does not mean final judgment, but judgment pronounced immediately at death.[248] But this would not accord with the other teaching of the epistle. The heroes of the past did not inherit the promises on their deaths (11:39). Moreover in 9:28 the judgment is seen to be closely linked with the second coming of Christ. The theme of future retribution comes out most clearly in the passage 10:27ff. For those who sin deliberately there is 'a fearful prospect of judgment, and a fury of fire which will consume the adversaries' (10:27). The 'fury' must be connected with the wrath of God although this is not mentioned. The writer compares the fate of a man who is guilty of

---

[247] The words *pro kairou* must refer to a specific time, *i.e.* the parousia, *cf.* H. Conzelmann, *1 Corinthians* (Eng. trans. *Hermeneia*, 1975, from *KEK*, 1969), p. 84. C. K. Barrett, *1 Corinthians*, p. 103, relates this to the last judgment.

[248] J. Héring, *Hebrews* (Eng. trans. 1970), p. 84 n. 42, discusses whether this expression implies that judgment immediately follows death, but thinks this is not certain. But *cf.* P. E. Hughes, *Hebrews*, p. 387, who recognizes that although death itself is a judgment there is a further judgment after death, *i.e.* the final judgment.

deliberately violating the law of Moses with that of a person who has spurned the Son of God, and concludes that the punishment of the latter will be much greater (10:29). He is convinced that such punishment will be deserved. There is no question of an arbitrary condemnation by God.

That Christians were expected to have an understanding of the judgment theme is seen from the inclusion of 'eternal judgment' among the elementary principles mentioned in 6:1–2. This seems to be basic to the whole exposition of the high-priest theme. The work of an intermediary is necessary because otherwise all would be under that eternal judgment. The adjective 'eternal' (*aiōnios*) must be given full weight and presumably means that the judgment spoken of has eternal consequences, whether of reward or condemnation. It is the exact parallel of eternal life. It should further be noticed that not all acts of judgment in this epistle are viewed as future. There has already been a destruction of the devil's power (2:14), although there is no suggestion that he has lost his power to molest. He cannot retain the grip over men by fear of death. But the writer says nothing further about any final judgment upon the forces of evil.

The question of rewards must be considered in the same context. Is the 'rest' (*katapausis*) theme in Hebrews 3 and 4 based on the idea of recompense? It is certainly affirmed that it is God who confers the rest, and it is called 'a sabbath rest for the people of God' (4:9). It is clear that entitlement to what is promised depends on people's response 'Today'. But the *katapausis* is available only to faith. It is not defined and therefore some uncertainty must remain over its content. The only indication is the parallel to the sabbath rest of God, which eliminates the idea that rest denotes inactivity. It seems that the rest is intended to inaugurate a continual Lord's day. The passage says nothing, therefore, about recompense for individual merit.

Another aspect which bears on the theme of present judgment is expounded in Hebrews 12, where the reformatory value of chastisement is discussed. In fact the suggestion is that discipline is essential for the development of character. But this passage contributes little to our understanding of future judgment. There are implications in the two warning passages (chapters 6 and 10) that those who adopt a deliberate rejection of God's grace have no further hope. No indications are given which point to a second chance. It is implied that condemnation is absolute.

In the reference to the heavenly Jerusalem in Hebrews 12:22f., the statement assumes an already established community including spirits of just men made perfect. Can we assume that these have already been judged? Nothing is said to this effect, and since the perfection theme in this epistle is expressly linked to the work of Christ, we should assume that salvation and not reward is in mind. Nevertheless, in the same passage there is reference to the kingdom which has already been received (12:28) and which is described as unshakeable.

The rest of the epistles

In *James* judgment is expected and appears to be imminent in that the judge is already standing at the doors (5:9). Since this immediately follows the reference in 5:7f. to the coming of the Lord, the idea of judgment must relate to the future.[249] It is noticeable that the context of this judgment theme is a warning about grumbling against others. It may be paralleled with Matthew's 'idle' words saying (see pp. 849f.).

In *1 Peter* there is a linking of present reality with future hope. Salvation is certain for the new-born, but is nevertheless 'ready to be revealed in the last time' (1:3–5). The genuineness of faith needs testing. Its results will be declared 'at the revelation of Jesus Christ', thus joining the judgment and the parousia (1:7, 13). As in the case of James, the certainty of future judgment in 1 Peter is undeniable. One statement affirms that people will have to give account of themselves, but does not specify the time (4:5). This follows a list of evils which are said to describe what the Gentiles like to do. Judgment will begin with the household of God and then extend to include those who are disobedient (4:17).[250] This does not mean that there are two different judgment days. In fact the expression 'the time has come for judgment to begin' suggests a present rather than a future event. Nevertheless, the readers are exhorted to entrust their souls to a faithful creator in face of present sufferings. It must be remembered that Peter states that the end of all things is at hand (4:7) and that his references to judgment must be seen against this belief in the imminence of the coming and the day.

The obscure passage in 1 Peter 4:6 (see previous section, pp. 842f.) which speaks of judgment following the gospel being preached to the dead is significant in that the standard of judgment is given as being 'according to men in the flesh'. It is suggested that the dead were Christian martyrs who had had the gospel preached to them in their lifetime, were judged (or assessed) from a human point of view then,[251] but now are living according to God in the Spirit. If this is so, it tells us nothing about the final judgment.

Both *2 Peter* and *Jude* make much of the theme of judgment. Jude cites Enoch to the effect that the Lord will execute judgment at his coming (Jude 14–15). He refers to the fallen angels who 'have been kept by him in eternal chains in the nether gloom until the judgment of the great day' (verse 6). For this the destruction of Sodom and Gomorrah is cited as an example of 'punishment of eternal fire' (verse 7). On the other hand such judgment does not face all, for Christians may look forward to the mercy of the Lord

---

[249] It should be noted that in human affairs, James allows that mercy triumphs over judgment (2:13).

[250] E. Best, *1 Peter* (NCB, 1971), p. 165, takes this statement as meaning not a continuous judgment, but the ultimate consummation, as if the final judgment were already beginning. J. N. D. Kelly, *The Epistles of Peter and Jude* (BC, 1969), p. 193, regards the words as pointing to the preordained opening phase in the unfolding of God's plan for the end.

[251] *Cf.* E. G. Selwyn, *1 Peter, ad loc.*

Jesus Christ unto eternal life (verse 21). Certainly some will be saved by being snatched from the 'fire' (verse 23). God is able to present his people 'without blemish before the presence of his glory' (verse 24).

In 2 Peter, those who deny the Master who bought them are said to bring swift destruction on themselves (2 Pet. 2:1). A similar reference to Jude's mention of fallen angels occurs in this epistle (2 Pet. 2:4), as well as the reference to Sodom and Gomorrah (2 Pet. 2:6). Not only is the destruction of ungodly people foretold, but also the destruction of the heavens and earth (2 Pet. 3:7, 10, 12; see next section). Nevertheless, as in Jude, so here, the Christian's hope is in being found 'without spot or blemish' (2 Pet. 3:14). There is no specific reference to rewards.

Revelation

It is at the conclusion of this book that the theme of judgment reaches its climax. It is difficult to deal with it without becoming involved at the same time with chronological issues connected with the millennium, which will be noted in the next section. We shall confine ourselves here to the nature of the final judgment day. There is no denying that the scope of the whole book is a description of the conflict between God and the forces of darkness, and of the final overthrow of the latter. The adverse factors are specifically seen as anti-Christian. All that is true in Christ meets its counterfeit. The hierarchy of evil is portrayed as having its last desperate onslaught before being totally overcome at the consummation of the age. The judgment extends not only to man, but to the devil and his angels. It is a comprehensive idea in which justice is conclusively seen to be done.[252]

We shall note first the strong sense of recompense reflected in the letters to the seven churches (Rev. 2 and 3). Each contains an assessment of the condition of the church and certain reassurances or warnings given on the strength of the assessment. In five of the messages the phrase 'I know your works' occurs. In all of them a special reward is named for the overcomer. But at the same time several serious warnings are given. Those who are faithful are promised a 'crown of life' (Rev. 2:10). Those who hold to false teaching (Nicolaitans) face direct reprisal ('I will . . . war against them with the sword of my mouth' Rev. 2:16). Those practising immorality (called after Jezebel) face tribulation and the visitation of death (Rev. 2:22). The loyal people of the churches will be given what their works deserve (Rev. 2:23). The Philadelphians are urged to hold on so that no-one should seize their crown (Rev. 3:11). The lukewarm are told they will be spewed out of Christ's mouth (Rev. 3:16). There is a mixture of commendation and criticism, but no suggestion of final judgment.

[252] S. G. F. Brandon, *The Judgment of the Dead*, pp. 103f., overstates the case when he affirms that in this book Christ is portrayed primarily as the terrible avenger of the elect, for his function as judge is balanced by his function as the slain Lamb.

The messages to the churches may be summed up in the varied promises. The people of the church at Ephesus will eat the tree of life (2:7); Smyrna will not be hurt by the second death (2:11); Pergamum will have hidden manna, a white stone and a new name (2:17); Thyatira will have power over the nations, and will be given the morning star (2:26–28); Sardis will have the name of God and of the New Jerusalem written on it (3:12); and Laodicea will have the privilege of sitting with Christ on his throne (3:21). There is no clear pattern here. The imagery used points to some future realization. The most surprising is the message to Sardis, which seems to be related to salvation; but even this expresses the final fulfilment of what is already a present reality. The main message is that the future status of Christians is related to their present experience.

In the unfolding drama of the book, the theme of judgment is never far away. The cry of the martyrs from under the altar is a cry for judgment and vengeance (6:9, 10).[253] The delay acts as a prelude to heighten the climax of the coming judgment day. The seven seals, trumpets and bowls all focus attention on judgment, and again appear as preparatory to the final judgment. There are references to God's wrath (*e.g.* 6:16; 11:18; 14:10; 16:19; 19:15) which build up as the judgment day approaches. The description of the judgment on Babylon the harlot (chapter 18) immediately precedes the final crisis. It is, therefore, against this background that we must examine the description in Revelation 20.

The scene of judgment is the great white throne (20:11). It is established after the disappearance of earth and sky. The location is obviously not important. What is important is that all are judged by what was written in the books, *i.e.* by what they had done (20:12). These books are distinct from the book of life, and presumably refer to the doings of each person. It is clear from this passage that the distinction between believers and unbelievers depends on whether their names are written in the book of life. In other words, judgment for unbelievers depends finally on their omission from the book of life, whereas for believers salvation is secured on the grounds of inclusion in that book and rewards are based on the records in the other books.[254] Those who draw a distinction between the judgment

---

[253] G. R. Beasley-Murray, *Revelation*, p. 134, cites 1 Enoch 47 as a parallel to the martyrs' prayer. He considers that this idea was well known in Jewish apocalyptic.

[254] Care must be taken not to regard this description of the last judgment as an act of vindictiveness on the part of God. As J. P. Martin remarks, 'The wrath of God, which is the negative experience of His holy love, nevertheless serves His love (saving purpose),' in 'The Last Judgment', *Dreams, Vision and Oracles* (ed. C. E. Armerding and W. W. Gasque, 1977), p. 201. Martin sees the last judgment as throwing us into the mystery of God's love. A different view of God's wrath in the book of Revelation is advanced by A. T. Hanson, *The Wrath of the Lamb* (1957), pp. 159–178, who denies that wrath has an eschatological significance, but sees it as the process of history in which those who reject God's saving love are involved. He goes as far as to say that in the NT wrath is not an attitude of God, but a condition of men (p 180). G. Caird, *Revelation*, pp. 91f., while partially accepting Hanson's view, points out that he has overlooked the fact that in Revelation the judgment is solely in God's hands.

seat of Christ and the great white throne naturally exclude believers from the final judgment.

It should be noted that in this apocalypse the judge is seen primarily as God, but Christ also exercises the function of judge. This is especially brought out in the account of the coming of the warrior Lord in 19:11ff. The book concludes with the assurance of the imminent coming of Christ who will bring 'his recompense' to repay every one for what he has done' (22:12). There is a final clear distinction between those within the city and those outside (22:14, 15).

NOTE ON THE CONSUMMATION OF THE KINGDOM

When we discussed the teaching of Jesus on the kingdom of God, we noted the dual concept of present and future aspects (see pp. 416ff.). It was observed that Jesus in some ways inaugurated the kingdom among his own disciples, and yet gave many indications that the full establishment of the kingdom would not happen until the future. Our present concern is to point out aspects of future events which will reach their climax at the close of the present age.

Our interpretation on the kingdom theme will be affected by our understanding of the millennium (see next section). But assuming for the moment that there is no difference between the gospel of the kingdom and the gospel of grace, and that the kingdom is a reality in the present age although not precisely identified with the church, we need to note various aspects which belong to the end. We shall concentrate especially on the book of Revelation.

We note first the certainty of tribulation. It is strongly predicted in the apocalyptic sections of the synoptic gospels (Mt. 24; Mk. 13; Lk. 21). Not only is it mentioned in John 16:33, but an assurance is given that Christ has overcome the world, the source of the tribulation. But it is in Revelation 6:12–17; 7:13–14; 12:17; 13:7 that a specific period of tribulation is mentioned. This is described as 'the great tribulation' and although its duration is short, its intensity is great. The main problem which arises is the identity of those who will pass through it. In view of the fact that Jesus predicted that his disciples would face tribulation, it is natural to suppose that that prediction covered the whole period of the future up to the time of the parousia. In this case it included the great tribulation in the book of Revelation, which is the same in kind, but greater in strength.

There is no suggestion that the great tribulation is intended for any different people from the other predictions of persecution. In other words there is no support for the view that Christians will be removed from the earth before the tribulation (the rapture theory), nor the view that the great tribulation will affect only Jews, not Christians. Both these suggestions are based on the view that Revelation 4–19 relates to the great tribulation, which immediately follows the rapture of the saints. Revelation 1–3, according to this view, refers to the pre-rapture state of the church. But there are weaknesses in this theory. There is no evidence anywhere in the NT that the rapture will remove believers from a tribulation which will specifically affect Jews. It cannot be maintained that either Matthew 24 or Revelation 4–19 must be addressed exclusively to Jews, since in both passages it is more natural to suppose that followers of Christ are in mind. There seems to be no justification for supposing that a great tribulation will follow the coming of Christ.

The apocalyptic visions in the book of Revelation with their series of judgments are intended to explain the intensification of the warfare between Satan and the Lamb prior to the latter's coming. We need not for our purpose detail the various woes and plagues. They are all intended to demonstrate the victorious power of God over his enemies. It is the final display of judgment on the people of this world, before all are called to account for their doings on the judgment day. It shows the final triumph of the kingdom of God in this world.

The view that the Jews will have special opportunities to be evangelized through fellow Jews who will preach to them the gospel of the kingdom (not the gospel of grace) is without foundation; for the NT knows of only one gospel, the gospel of the grace of God through Jesus Christ. The age of grace ends, not with the rapture, but with the parousia. It is at the parousia that Jesus Christ will not only be king by right, but will be acknowledged as king.

NOTE ON THE MILLENNIUM

In considering the future destiny of this age, the focal point for many NT interpreters tends to be the millennium, or 1,000-year reign of Christ. Since this is mentioned only in Revelation 20:1–10 and nowhere else in the NT, a caution over its application must at once be raised. It must be borne in mind that its context is a symbolic setting, which means that it cannot be used to provide a key to the interpretation of passages which are not symbolic. The problem arising from the millennium is in fact whether or not it is to be taken literally. There are three main possibilities.[255]

(i) To take it literally and to suppose that Christ will return with his saints after the tribulation and establish his kingdom on earth for 1,000 years. He will reign over a restored nation of Israel, according to this view, which is maintained by the premillennialist school of thought.

[255] For concise summaries of historic premillennialism, dispensational premillennialism, postmillennialism and amillennialism, *cf. The Meaning of the Millennium* (ed. R. G. Clouse, 1977). A. A. Hoekema, in this book (pp. 155–187), gives a concise summary of the amillennial view. For an advocacy of the premillennial view, *cf.* R. H. Gundry, *The Church and the Tribulation*, 1973; and for the postmillennial position, *cf.* I. Murray's *The Puritan Hope* (1971).

(ii) To take it literally, but to maintain that the coming of Christ would be at the conclusion of the millennium, which will be ushered in by the worldwide triumph of the gospel. This school of interpretation is known as postmillennial.

(iii) To take it spiritually and symbolically, and to see in the statement of Revelation 20 an affirmation of the triumph of Christ. This third view, which does not specify a literal period of 1,000 years, but sees it as a symbolic description of the period between the ascension and second coming of Christ, is akin to the second view in that it sees the coming of Christ as the consummation of the age. This is generally known as amillennialism.

Of these three views it should be noted that the first is literal not only with regard to the time span, but also in relation to the nature of the established kingdom, *i.e.* political. Another view ignores the future reference to the kingdom altogether and treats not only this, but also the parousia, as already realized (see the discussion on pp. 797ff.).

In order properly to assess the theological significance of the Revelation 20 passage,[256] it must be recognized that the idea of a limited messianic reign was current in contemporary Judaism (Enoch 91 and 93; Psalms of Solomon 17–18; Apocalypse of Ezra 7:28ff.; 12:34). Jewish messianic hopes were concentrated mainly on national aspirations, although not exclusively so. Especially in the apocalypses of Ezra and Baruch, the prospective joy of the messianic kingdom is expressed in specifically materialistic terms, the earth producing abundant fruits and reapers being exempt from labour (*cf.* Apocalypse of Baruch 29:1–8). But even so the conditions are essentially idealistic, a curious mixture of a new kind of existence which is more than a perfecting of the present. It is also of interest for our purpose to note that the apocalypses of Ezra and Baruch both place the resurrection at the close of the messianic reign. Jewish chiliasm (or millenarianism), however, throws little light on the NT teaching, because the latter is not concerned, as the former is, with a new beginning entirely in the future. It has already begun in Christ.

There are certain features of the Revelation 20 passage which may be summarized as follows: (i) Satan is bound for 1,000 years, during which he is deprived of his power to deceive. It is evident here that the binding cannot be literal since a literal chain could not hold a powerful spiritual being. The binding is followed by a brief release. (ii) What is described as the first resurrection is related to the martyrs who had not worshipped the beast. These are said to reign with Christ for 1,000 years. They are, moreover, described as priests. No data are given about the kind of reign which Christ exercises. (iii) On his brief release, Satan gathers his followers

---

[256] M. Rissi, *The Future of the World* (1972), pp. 29ff., discusses Rev. 20 and its relation to the earlier sections of the book. He draws attention to a striking parallelism between the two parts, which suggests that it may not be correct to treat Rev. 20 as subsequent to the previous sections in time.

and attacks the messianic kingdom, but is completely defeated and ultimately thrown into the lake of fire. It is only after these events that the
vision of the new heavens and new earth is recorded.

Our main question must be whether the passage requires the postulation
of a future millennial kingdom of 1,000 literal years. In some form or other
a reign of Christ is indisputable. Indeed this is supported from other NT
passages (1 Cor. 15:25; 2 Tim. 2:12). But the crux of the matter is whether
this follows or precedes the parousia of Christ. If the book of Revelation
is intended to be understood in chronological order, there would be no
denying that the millennium, whatever its duration, would take place
immediately following the coming. But it is difficult to be certain whether
the book should be interpreted in chronological order. Indeed it is impossible to trace such an order throughout the whole book, and this should
caution us against making the assumption that it occurs here.

When Jesus, on the return of the seventy from their mission work, told
the disciples that he had seen Satan fall like lightning from heaven (Lk.
10:18), and that they were invested with authority over all the power of
the enemy, it looks very much like a parallel with Revelation 20:1–3.
During the present age Satan's power is limited. He may tempt, but he
cannot finally deceive the disciples of Christ. The 'little while' of his release
would then coincide with the final period of great tribulation, when
through his agent antichrist he would make his final opposition to God.
We have already discussed the interpretation of the first resurrection and
suggested a spiritual interpretation of this (see pp. 844f.).[257] It was also
maintained that Revelation 20 does not require us to understand that only
the martyrs would reign with Christ.

That a spiritual interpretation of the millennium is preferable to a literal
interpretation becomes clear when note is taken of the exegetical difficulties
which a literal interpretation faces. Especially is this true of those[258] who
are obliged to postulate two stages for the parousia (a secret coming at the
'rapture', and a public coming after the tribulation), and various resurrections and judgments. The intention is no doubt to clarify, but in point of
fact the result tends to be not only more confusing, but more difficult to
support from other NT statements. Our present task is to resist importing
into these statements what is not implied in their contexts.

For this reason the view that the millennium is the kingdom of heaven,
but not the kingdom of God, must be challenged. We have earlier noted
(pp. 409f.) that 'kingdom of heaven' is found only in Matthew, who also at
times uses the expression 'kingdom of God'. The two expressions cannot
therefore be set against each other; neither is it legitimate to regard the

[257] Cf. G. E. Ladd, *Crucial Questions about the Kingdom of God* (1952), pp. 143ff., for a discussion of the
force of the verb 'came to life' (*ezēsan*) which he thinks nullifies a spiritual resurrection.
[258] Cf. J. W. Hodges, *Christ's Kingdom and Coming*, pp. 185ff.

former as political, relating only to a restored Israel, while the latter alone is treated as being spiritual. This dichotomy is not inherent to the NT use, and there seems no doubt that Jesus in his teaching did not make any such distinction. More serious is the attempt to see the millennium kingdom as political, for there is no NT evidence which suggests that Jesus was aiming to restore Israel in a political sense. Moreover the attempt to divorce the age of grace from the age of the kingdom of heaven, as if the latter has nothing to do with the gospel of the cross, makes that gospel of limited value and detracts from its centrality in the apostolic teaching.

It seems more reasonable to suppose that there is no distinction between the kingdom of God and the kingdom of heaven, and that both are concerned with the age of grace. This means there is one gospel, not two. It means further that although the present reign of Christ is acknowledged only by believers in this age, there will come a time of consummation when his right to rule will be universally recognized. At the manifestation of Christ's power and glory every knee shall bow and acknowledge him as Lord (Phil. 2:9–11). All who give credence to a future coming of Christ in judgment would agree with the final event, whatever their interpretation of the millennium, both in its substance and timing, might be.[259]

How this is to be achieved is not clear. If it be argued that during the present age the gospel would permeate society as leaven permeates a lump of dough (*cf.* Mt. 13:33) until it inaugurated the kingdom at the millennium, this would seem to be contrary to other parables of the kingdom which do not foresee universal acceptance of Christ in this age. This is not to affirm that during this age of grace Christian ideals will have no effect on society in the world; but there is no suggestion in the NT that this world is to experience a golden age, ushered in by the triumph of the gospel through the work of the Holy Spirit.

Is there support for millennialism in Paul's epistles? Some have argued that 1 Corinthians 15:22–25 contains some hint of an interregnum because, after speaking of Christ the first fruits, Paul says 'then (*epeita*) at his coming those who belong to Christ.[260] Then (*eita*) comes the end.' The particular adverbs used in this statement are said to indicate a sequence of events, in which case the coming is seen as distinct from the end.[261] This claim is also supported by an appeal to the words 'each in his own order' (*tagma*). The supposed interval is, moreover, said to be identified with the kingdom of Christ and the end is the point of time at which he delivers the kingdom

---

[259] O. Cullmann, *The Christology of the New Testament* (Eng. trans. ²1963), p. 226, considers that the 1,000 years 'belongs temporally to the final act of Christ's lordship, the act which begins with his return and thus already invades the new aeon'.

[260] *Cf.* Ladd, *op. cit.*, pp. 178ff.

[261] *Cf.* Leivestad, *Christ the Conqueror* (1954), p. 131, for a comment on the *telos* in verse 24. He does not think that Paul's words make room for a millennium.

to God.[262] No-one would dispute that *eita* points to a sequence, but it is by no means necessary to suppose a protracted interval between the coming and the end.[263] The interval could be understood to consist of a very brief period, which would bring the coming and the end into close proximity.

Many commentators favour the view that Paul had the millennium in mind here.[264] 1 Corinthians 15:25 refers to the reign of God as a period during which Christ will subdue his enemies and this has led to the view that the millennium will be occupied with political activity.[265] The words 'each in his own order' do not imply a sequence of three resurrections: Christ's, and a first and second resurrection of believers[266]; for the distinction appears to be between Christ as the first fruits and others who follow later. It must be noted that 1 Corinthians 15:51–58 would not support the idea of an interregnum between the parousia and the end, since the resurrection of the righteous happens at the same time as the establishment of the kingdom. It is further significant that Paul refers in this context to the kingdom of God, not the kingdom of heaven.

Similarly, although it has been argued that some form of millenarian theory is necessary for a right understanding of 1 Thessalonians 4:13–18 and 2 Thessalonians 1:5–12, this is based on a doubtful assessment of the historical background. The Thessalonians do not appear to have been concerned about the fact of resurrection, nor about whether the believers would take part in the parousia, but whether the dead would have any disadvantage compared with the living.

We may conclude that Paul does not specifically support the idea of a coming millennial kingdom on earth. Although there is some slight evidence which might indirectly be pressed into support of it, the evidence does not require such an interpretation. Since the same must be said of the gospels and Acts, we need only enquire whether the rest of the NT has anything to contribute. Our answer must be negative. Even 2 Peter 3:8 with its mention of a thousand years (the only use of the phrase outside the book of Revelation), discourages any idea of a literal millennium. All this isolates the Revelation 20 passage from the rest of the NT and raises a problem for the interpreter. It seems certain that no system which affects the exegesis of other parts of the NT can be constructed entirely on the

---

[262] D. E. H. Whiteley, *The Theology of St Paul*, p. 270, emphatically denies that 1 Cor. 15:22ff. has any reference to a millennial kingdom.

[263] *Cf.* G. Vos, *The Pauline Eschatology*, pp. 237ff., against the view that this passage supports chiliasm.

[264] See Ladd, *op. cit.*, p. 179 n. 59, for a list of such commentators.

[265] G. T. Montague, *The Living Thought of Paul* (1966), p. 127, maintains that 1 Cor. 15:25 shows that the parousia is the consummation, not the beginning, of Christ's reign. This view is supported by many commentators on this passage.

[266] On the question whether or not Paul believed in two resurrections of believers, *cf.* J. Héring, 'Saint Paul a-t-il enseigné deux résurrections?' *RHPR* 12, 1932, pp. 300–320, who thinks it is impossible to find support for this. But for a full discussion, *cf.* W. D. Davies, *Paul and Rabbinic Judaism* (1948), pp. 285–298; E.-B. Allo, *Première Épître aux Corinthiens* (EB ²1956), excursus 18 (pp. 438–454).

foundation of a particular understanding of this enigmatic passage. At most one interpretation can be set against another and the most probable adopted, whether it be a literal or a spiritual understanding of it. But whichever is preferred must be recognized as provisional. This would enter a caution against any structure which treats this millennium as the concluding period of a series of seven such periods spanning the history of man.

Summary

The theme of judgment occurs throughout the NT. It is not confined to one stream of evidence, but it reaches its climax at the scene of the great white throne. There is no denying that man will be answerable for his doings. But the NT teaching about justification must be taken into account in any assessment of this judgment theme. If justification means anything, it must at least mean that the believer in Christ is acquitted from judgment. Nevertheless there is impressive evidence to show that attention must be paid to the basis of judgment generally.

We have noted that although Paul speaks of a judgment seat of Christ, there is nothing to suggest that he thought of this occasion as distinct from the great white throne, although he was mainly concerned with the accountability of believers.

The idea of rewards and recompense is strong in the NT, although it does not serve as the main motive for moral action. Nevertheless many promises are made to those who are overcomers, which suggest that although good works are not the basis for salvation, they are taken into account in the inheritance of the saints. The idea of punishments is inextricably tied up with the theme of judgment.

We shall next consider the state of existence subsequent to the consummation of this age. Because this follows the judgment, it must be considered in two parts: the concept of heaven as the abode of the righteous, and the concept of hell as the abode of the unrighteous.[267]

HEAVEN

It is not fashionable in theological thinking to attach too much importance to a study of the NT teaching on heaven.[268] But it is essential for a complete picture of NT theology. Since the doctrine of the afterlife requires some attention to be given to the final destiny of men, it is fitting to consider what is known about heavenly life in the various parts of the NT. In the OT there are many references to heaven as the abode of God, and this is an important factor in the NT (cf. such passages as Is. 63:15; Ne. 1:4; Dn. 2:37,

---

[267] For a concise discussion on the NT view of heaven, cf. B. Siede, C. Brown, H. Bietenhard, *NIDNTT* 2, pp. 184–196. For a fuller statement see U. Simon, *Heaven in the Christian Tradition* (1958).

[268] N. Pittenger, *'The Last Things' in a Process Perspective* (1970), pp. 61–77, reduces heaven and hell to present experiences, but he does not discuss the biblical evidence.

44). The root idea of habitation is in all the words used of heaven in both the OT and NT. We shall not expect, however, to find a description of a place, so much as the presence of a person. Where localizing expressions are used (like 'above' or 'up' or 'ascend'), these must be recognized to be due to the limitations of human language to express the supra-mundane.

The synoptic gospels

We are at once struck with the remarkable reserve on the subject of heaven in the synoptics. No details are given about the contents of heaven. There are no flights of imagination. And yet the many references to heaven in these gospels underline its importance.

GOD IN HEAVEN

It is the close connection between heaven and God which is most noticeable in the synoptic gospels. In Matthew's gospel alone the expression 'Father in heaven' occurs fourteen times and 'heavenly Father' five times. Mark has no parallels and Luke has one (in the Lord's Prayer). All the occurrences are the words of Jesus, which makes them valuable as an indication not only of how Jesus himself thought of heaven, but also of how he taught his disciples to think. In a prayer to God, Jesus uses the words, 'Father, Lord of heaven and earth' (Mt. 11:25 = Lk. 10:21), which sets heaven as the sphere where God the Father exercises lordship as he does on earth (*cf.* also Mt. 28:18). What is most significant is the combination of heaven with the fatherhood of God. It is not a concept to overawe. It was for Jesus synonymous with his Father's presence. It possessed for him no sense of remoteness. This is especially relevant when it is noted that sometimes Jesus used the expression 'my father in heaven' (Mt. 7:21; 10:32; 33; 12:50; 18:10; 18:19) and sometimes 'your father in heaven (Mt. 5:16, 45, 48; 6:1; 7:11; 18:14; 23:9). The sense of intimacy which he enjoyed was intended to apply equally to his disciples.

This close link between heaven and God is also seen in the Lord's Prayer (Mt. 6:9; Lk. 11:2). It was a reminder that God was other than earthbound, *i.e.* was not restricted by the limitations of material creation.[269] This explains also the voice from heaven (Mt. 3:17 = Mk. 1:11 = Lk. 3:21–22) and the act of Jesus in looking up to heaven when in prayer (Mt. 14:19; Mk. 6:41; 7:34; Lk. 9:16). It also accounts for the description of Jesus' departure as an ascension into heaven (according to some MSS of Lk. 24:51; *cf.* also Mk. 16:19). The idea of location is not important, for it is never enlarged on in the words of Jesus. Heaven is where God is. Jesus points out that those who swear by heaven swear by the throne of God and him

---

[269] *Cf.* E. Lohmeyer, *The Lord's Prayer* (Eng. trans. 1965). pp. 57ff. As against a tendency to think of God in terms of place, the concept of his dwelling in heaven is highly significant.

who sits on it (Mt. 23:22). Heaven implies the presence of God.

Moreover, heaven is linked with the doing of God's will (*cf.* Mt. 12:50; 18:14). In the parable of the prodigal son, a sin against God is described as a sin against heaven (Lk. 15:18) as well as a sin against the father. Similarly in the binding and loosing sayings there is a direct link between what is effected in heaven and on earth (Mt. 16:19; 18:18). Jesus, when confronting his accusers with a question about the baptism of John contrasted 'heaven' with 'men' in the matter of authority, showing again that heaven stood for God (Mt. 21:25 = Mk. 11:30 = Lk. 20:4). We may conclude, therefore, that for Jesus heaven stood for the dwelling place of God.

Some scholars have dismissed the synoptic teaching on heaven on the grounds that it is based on an obsolete cosmology, *i.e.* on a three-tier idea of the universe, with the heavens as the top tier, the earth in the middle and the nether regions as the bottom tier.[270] As a result of this both heaven and hell are designated mythological and the need arises to reinterpret the essential meaning in other terms more acceptable to the modern understanding of the world.

This urge for reinterpretation is understandable, but it has frequently led to a failure to grasp the real meaning. There is, in fact, nothing in the statements of Jesus cited above which requires any stripping of mythological forms, for if heaven is identified with the fullness of the presence of God it does not rest on an acceptance of a three-tier system. If it be argued that the idea of heaven as 'up' points to such a system, it should be recognized, as mentioned above, that in no other way could language explain a removal from the present material earth. It is not satisfactory to restrict the concept of heaven to purely existential terms,[271] for this removes it from the realm of the future. At the same time it is essential to note that Jesus never envisaged a 'future' heaven which bore no relation to present experience.

THE HEAVENLY BEINGS

There is surprisingly little information in the synoptic gospels on this theme. We have already noted the evidence for the presence and activities of angels (see pp. 123ff.) and these are directly connected with heaven (Mt. 18:10; 22:30; 24:36; 28:2; Mk. 12:25; 13:32; Lk. 2:15). From these references we learn of guardian angels for children in heaven, of the absence of marriage among angels, of their ignorance of the time of the coming, and of a descending and ascending movement of angels between heaven and earth. Moreover, the relationship between the angels and Christ forms an important section of the Christology of Hebrews (see below, p. 363). The importance of these heavenly servants of God cannot be denied. It should

[270] So Bultmann, *Jesus Christ and Mythology* (Eng. trans. 1960), pp. 14f.
[271] Pittenger, *op. cit.*, p. 77.

also be noted that Jesus speaks of joy before the angels of God over one sinner who repents (Lk. 15:7), which suggests that the angels share the interests and joy of God over his redemptive activities among men.

With regard to people being in heaven, the only direct reference is to the names of those written in heaven (Lk. 10:20), presumably an allusion to the book of life mentioned in the Apocalypse. It is clear that, since the reference comes in a statement to disciples, a distinction is implied between those whose names are written in heaven and those whose names are not.[272] The gist of the teaching on the kingdom of God (or of heaven) confirms this (*cf.* for instance the distinction between the tares and the wheat).

THE LIFE TO COME

Even less information is given on this subject, but there is a passing allusion to 'treasure' in heaven (Mt. 6:20). This is clearly not material treasure (no moth or rust), but no indication is given about it. It can only represent some kind of spiritual riches. The rich young man was promised heavenly treasure in exchange for giving his earthly possessions to the poor (Mt. 19:21 = Mk. 10:21; *cf.* Lk. 12:33). There are other references to rewards in heaven (Mt. 5:12; 6:1; Lk. 6:23), but again no details. In view of the fact that God's will is done in heaven, this must apply to all who share God's presence. There is no place in heaven for those who oppose that will, *cf.* the casting of Satan out of heaven (Lk. 10:18). Jesus made clear that there would be no marriage in heaven, but made no further comment on human relationships in heaven (Mt. 22:30; Mk. 12:25). The absence of marriage is understandable since procreation will no longer be necessary. But this does not imply the absence of relationships.[273]

A few passages refer to eternal life, a theme more emphasized in John's gospel (*cf.* Mt. 19:16 = Mk. 10:17 = Lk. 18:18; Lk. 10:25; Mk. 10:30). This raises the whole question of the precise meaning of 'eternal' (*aiōnios*) in this context.[274] Eternal life is clearly not life as we now know it made endless, but a different kind of life which no enemy can destroy. What is most significant therefore is the certainty that heavenly life is of a spiritual kind which is indestructible.

The Johannine literature

There is less concentration on the character of the future life of believers in John's gospel than in Matthew's gospel, but nevertheless there are

---

[272] I. H. Marshall, *Luke*, p. 430, discusses the probable reason why Jesus mentions the book of life in this context. He draws attention to the importance of the idea of individual salvation.

[273] On the subject of human relationships in heaven, *cf.* R. Pache, *The Future Life*, pp. 357ff.; U. Simon, *op. cit.*, pp 216ff.

[274] *Cf.* O. Cullmann, *Christ and Time*, pp. 61ff., for a discussion of the relation between time and eternity. He emphatically rejects the idea that primitive Christianity knew anything of a timeless God.

enough indications to show that the theme was in the mind of Jesus according to John's record. There are two main sections where 'heaven' is mentioned. In John 3 the enigmatic saying is found, 'no one has ascended into heaven but he who descended from heaven, the Son of man' (3:13). This is the gist of the 'heavenly things' which Jesus speaks about to Nicodemus. In other words Jesus himself is central to the concept of heaven.[275] The descent idea also occurs several times in John 6 in the description 'bread from heaven' (6:31, 32, 33, 41, 51, 58). Whereas it was applicable in a physical sense to the manna in the wilderness (in which case 'heaven' means 'from above the earth'), yet its meaning is extended to include the thought that God provided it. When Jesus claimed to be the bread from heaven (6:35, 41, 51, 58), he was claiming to provide life of a totally different kind from the natural life sustained by the manna. The spiritual provision guaranteed life for ever (6:58).

This leads to a consideration of the quality of life promised to believers. Several times the idea of 'eternal life' is mentioned (3:15–16; 4:36; 5:39; 6:54; 6:68; 10:28; 12:25; 17:2–3). It is a more central theme in John than the kingdom theme. It is less liable to suffer from materialistic interpretations. It is in fact defined as follows: 'This is eternal life, that they may know thee and Jesus Christ whom thou hast sent' (17:3). Knowing God and knowing Jesus Christ is the main aim of heavenly living.[276] Naturally this process begins in this life, but can reach its goal only in eternal life.[277]

In the beginning of his prayer in John 17:1 Jesus lifted up his eyes to heaven (*i.e.* to God).[278] This fits in with John the Baptist's description of the Spirit descending from heaven (1:32), and with the reference to a voice from heaven in response to a prayer of Jesus to the Father (12:28). The direction indicates the source, *i.e.* God.

It must be admitted that the statements so far have provided little information about heaven itself. One statement in John 14:2 is rather more specific, although all interpreters are by no means agreed on its meaning, 'In my Father's house are many rooms (*monai*); if it were not so, would I have told you that I go to prepare a place for you?' If we understand the words in a spiritual sense,[279] it may be equivalent to saying that ample provision will be made in heaven for the followers of Jesus. We may

---

[275] For a discussion of the significance of the reference to heaven in this context, *cf.* F. J. Moloney, *The Johannine Son of Man*, pp. 51ff.

[276] Eternal life may at first sight seem to be defined in terms of Hellenistic views of salvation. But as B. Lindars, *John*, p. 519, observes, John thinks of knowledge semitically in terms of relationship rather than in terms of intellectual apprehension.

[277] C. H. Dodd, *The Interpretation of the Fourth Gospel*, pp. 144ff., explains 'eternal life' in John in terms of Greek philosophic thought, but he does recognize the importance of the Hebraic antecedents of his thought. He thinks that John's meaning is similar to the Platonic view of the eternal Today.

[278] As L. Morris, *John* (NICNT, 1971), p. 717, points out, the lifting up of eyes to heaven was the accepted posture for prayer. He cites Ps. 123:1 and Mk. 7:34.

[279] Morris, *op. cit.*, p. 638, interprets this statement in the sense of the bliss and permanence of heaven.

perhaps be permitted to deduce that in the mind of Jesus the primary idea of heaven for believers is the idea of an eternal home.[280] In leaving this world, Jesus speaks of going to the Father (16:28). Moreover, although the disciples could not at once follow him in his departure, he promised that they would follow him later (Jn. 13:36).

We may say that there is an essentially spiritual approach in this gospel towards 'heaven'. There is a concentration on the nobler spiritual aspirations which faith in Christ brings and which equip men while on earth for the habitation of heaven. The gospel does not set out to satisfy our curiosities about the blessed state of the spiritual heirs. There is only one statement in 1 John which directly bears on the eternal state and that is 1 John 3:2, in which John assures us that when we see Christ we shall like him. This is regarded as a hope which has a purifying effect for the present. There is a close resemblance between this idea and that of Paul's in Romans 8:29 (predestinated to be conformed to his image).

Acts

In a book with its sights on historical movements it is not surprising that interest in the eternal state of blessedness is minimal. In the few times heaven is mentioned, it almost invariably either denotes the firmament above the earth or else is practically a substitute expression for God. Stephen (7:55), Peter (10:11ff.; 11:5ff.) and Paul (9:3; 22:6) all see heavenly visions and recognize their source as God. Both Peter and Paul heard voices from heaven. But no more details are given about the heavenly scene. The narrative concentrates on the earthly implications. Jesus has gone into heaven (3:21; *cf.* 1:10, 11) and will return out of heaven. Heaven is the dwelling place of God (7:48–49). It is noticeable that Acts is in line with the gospels in the absence of any materialistic conceptions of heaven.

Paul

There is no denying that Paul was constantly looking forward, but in common with other NT writers he says very little about the eternal state of blessedness to which he looks forward. There are, in fact, remarkable similarities between Paul's view and those elsewhere in the NT.

God in heaven. Paul certainly thinks of heaven as the abode of God. He speaks of the wrath of God as being revealed from heaven (Rom. 1:18). He contrasts the second Adam (Christ) from heaven with the first Adam from earth (1 Cor. 15:47). Masters are reminded that they have a master in heaven (Eph. 6:9; Col. 4:1). The believers are to wait for the coming of

---

[280] There is no support in Jn. 14:2 for the view that the *monai* are temporary dwelling places. There is much to be said for the view that the *monai* are spiritual positions in Christ (*cf.* R. H. Gundry, 'In my Father's House are many *Monai* (John 14,2)', *ZNW* 58, 1967, pp. 68ff.

Christ from heaven (1 Thes. 1:10; 4:16; 2 Thes. 1:7).

In one passage Paul speaks of being caught up to the third heaven where he was given revelations of the Lord (2 Cor. 12:1ff.). It is not possible to know exactly what he meant by the 'third heaven', but he proceeds to describe an ecstatic state in which he was aware of divine communications which he was not able to divulge.[281] For this reason the passage tells us nothing about heaven as a final state of blessedness.

From the above brief survey, it will be seen that Paul does not think of heaven as a place, but thinks of it in terms of the presence of God. It should be noted, further, that the activities of the Spirit in the sanctifying processes on earth are preparatory to the heavenly sphere, and that which is now partial will be perfected in heaven.

The heavenly beings. Although Paul concentrates on the status of believers in heaven, he has a few statements about angels, which indicate their activity. He talks about himself and his companions being made a spectacle to the world, to men and to angels (1 Cor. 4:9).[282] Angels are evidently interested in the movements of the servants of God. The enigmatic statement about women's veils in 1 Corinthians 11:10 may point to the same idea. In Galatians 3:19 the law is said to be ordained by angels. Nevertheless their activity is limited. Not even angelic eloquence can match the power of Christian love (1 Cor. 13:1). Paul supports his charge to Timothy 'before the elect angels' (1 Tim. 5:21).

When the apostle says, 'But our commonwealth is in heaven' (Phil. 3:20), he is making a clear distinction between the readers and those who live as the enemies of the cross of Christ; this furnishes us with a clue to the qualifications of those who share the state of eternal blessedness. The idea of 'commonwealth' in the ancient world was associated with privileged Roman citizenship, and Paul is undoubtedly pointing to superior privileges which are enjoyed by the citizens of heaven.[283] Such privileges are not for the unrighteous (1 Cor. 6:9, 10), but for those washed, sanctified, justified (1 Cor. 6:11). In his passage about the resurrection body, Paul maintains that we have 'a house not made with hands, eternal in the heavens' (2 Cor. 5:1). It is this eternal quality for which those still on earth long (2 Cor.

---

[281] C. K. Barrett, *2 Corinthians* (BC, 1973), pp. 309f., cites instances from apocalyptic sources to show that the idea of ecstatic journeys into heaven was familiar (any number up to the tenth). But he inclines to Calvin's view that for Paul the number three may be used as the perfect number to describe what is highest. P. E. Hughes, *2 Corinthians*, pp. 435f., defines the third heaven as Paradise (as in 2 Cor. 12:4), rather than supposing as some have done that there were two stages in the rapture of Paul.

[282] C. K. Barrett, *1 Corinthians*, p. 110, takes the combination of angels and men here in the sense of the world's population, but his reasoning is not obvious. E.-B. Allo, *Première Épître aux Corinthiens* (²1956), p. 75, takes a similar view and thinks of angels and men as two types of spectators.

[283] For a discussion on *politeuma*, cf. P. C. Böttger, 'Die eschatologische Existenz der Christen. Erwägungen zu Philipper 3:20', *ZNW* 60, 1969, pp. 244–263.

5:2). Moreover, Paul uses the analogy of the family to describe the heavenly beings (Eph. 3:15).[284]

The life to come. The apostle sums up the believer's expectancy as 'the hope laid up for you in heaven' (Col. 1:5). It is described, as in the gospels, as eternal life (Rom. 2:7; 5:21; 6:23; 1 Tim. 6:12; 19; Tit. 1:2; 3:7). It is again the qualitative aspect of the believer's life which is in focus. It is real life because it is indestructible. In Romans 6:22 eternal life is said to be the 'end' (*i.e.* goal) of sanctification. It is the free gift of God in Christ Jesus (Rom. 6:23). The prospect of eternal life is used to urge Timothy to fight the good fight of faith (1 Tim. 6:12).

It is not only life which is in prospect, but also glory. The classic passage is 2 Corinthians 3:18, 'And we all, with unveiled face, beholding the glory of the Lord, are being changed into his likeness from one degree of glory to another; for this comes from the Lord who is the Spirit'. It is this progressive glorification of believers linked with the reflective glory of God in them which is most significant.[285] The most glorious work of the Spirit is in this work of transformation. Paul, thinking of his present afflictions, calls them light compared with 'an eternal weight of glory beyond all comparison', which awaits the believers (2 Cor. 4:17). In 2 Timothy 2:10, he speaks of salvation which goes with eternal glory. He is content to leave the Christian's heavenly prospect in these general but nonetheless splendid terms.

In his great hymn of love, the apostle admits that present understanding is fogged, but that future understanding would be unclouded (1 Cor. 13:12). There would be the removal of all hindrances to real appreciation of God. We shall know as we ourselves are known. Since it occurs in the context of a hymn of love, Paul's statement must be meant to focus particularly on a perfect understanding of the nature of love.

Some mention needs to be made of Paul's conception of the heavenly city. Two passages are relevant: Philippians 3:20 and Galatians 4:26. Both suggest a state expressed in political terms, but intended in a heavenly sense.[286] The idea of a community is significant in that it involves fellowship (*cf.* Eph. 2:19). Although fellowship is already experienced, Paul focuses on a heavenly Jerusalem (as *anō* must be understood in Gal. 4:26), in which it will be consummated.

---

[284] For a discussion of the meaning of families in heaven in this view, *cf.* M. Barth, *Ephesians* (AB, 1974), pp. 380ff., who supports the idea of supernatural agencies here. *Cf.* also H. Schlier, *Epheser* ([7]1971), p. 168.

[285] The idea of degrees of glory must not be supposed to refer to progressive steps in heaven, but to the distinction between the believer's present and future glory. *Cf.* U. Simon's discussion in *Heaven in the Christian Tradition*, pp. 243ff. He points out that Paul sees God's glory in the face of Christ, not in a general mystical manner.

[286] *Cf.* J. C. de Young, *Jerusalem in the New Testament* (1960), pp. 117ff.

Hebrews

This epistle is essentially forward looking and contributes significantly to our understanding of the heavenly state. We may note the evidence under four main ideas – the throne, the tabernacle, the rest, and the city – and then note some further points about the quality of the life to come.

The throne. The throne is a central idea in this epistle (1:8; 4:16; 8:1; 12:2; *cf.* 1:3). Since the author is dealing with approach to God, he is conscious of the 'Majesty on high' as his focal point. The heavenly throne is a symbol of the sovereignty of God. Closely akin to the sense of majesty is the sense of awe (12:28). Indeed it is the overwhelming sense of God which makes the high priestly work of Christ relevant. It is from heaven that God warns (12:25). Heaven and God are inextricably linked here as in the other NT books.

The tabernacle. The language of the levitical cultus is used by our author to express concepts which belong to the heavenly sphere. The earthly tent points to a greater and more perfect tent (9:11).[287] The earthly holy of holies becomes a new and better sanctuary (8:2; 9:12), which is described as heaven itself (9:24). Indeed, in one place our high priest is said to be exalted above the heavens (7:26), where the expression is intended to denote the highest possible exaltation. It is highly unlikely that the writer is speaking other than in metaphorical terms in using the language he does, for there is no suggestion that there will be any cultus in heaven. Nevertheless our high priest is permanently at the right hand of God as an assurance of our acceptance.

The rest. An important section of the epistle (chapters 3 and 4) concentrates on the rest which God promises to his people. Since this is likened to God's sabbath rest, its continuance is assured.[288] The author's theme of 'today' cannot be emptied of any future reference. Indeed there is much to be said for the view that Hebrews, like Philo, regards 'today' in terms of an 'eternal always'.[289] It is possible for people to cease from their labours as God did from his (4:9). But rest in this sense cannot be lack of all activity, but rather lack of activity involving change. Labour which never

---

[287] The heavenly tent is greater because the earthly tent is its copy. *Cf.* H. Montiefore, *Hebrews* (BC, 1964), pp. 151ff., on this difficult passage. E. C. Wickham, *Hebrews*, (WC, 1920), p. 68, maintains that the heavenly tabernacle is not the antitype but a figure borrowing its imagery from the type.

[288] P. E. Hughes, *Hebrews*, p. 143, mentions patristic support for the view that three rests are spoken of: the Lord's rest from his work, the Israelites' rest in Palestine, and rest in the kingdom of heaven (*i.e.* the true rest). Hughes wonders whether there is significance in the forty years mentioned in Ps. 95 in view of the period of some forty years between the crucifixion of Jesus and the writing of this epistle.

[289] *Cf.* Philo, *Legum Allegoriarum*, iii.25. U. Simon, *op. cit.*, p. 234, thinks that the author of Hebrews was influenced by Philo.

reaches perfection leads to frustration, but God and heaven are synonymous with perfect poise.

The city. The linking of the idea of a city to the conception of heaven, which is not found in the teaching of Jesus and finds only passing reference in Paul (Gal. 4:24ff.), is a special feature in Hebrews. Abraham the nomad looked forward to an abiding city made by God (11:10). The men of faith desire a better country, *i.e.* a heavenly country (11:16), in which God has prepared a city. The city in mind is identified in 12:22ff. as 'the city of the living God, the heavenly Jerusalem'. It is not surprising that in a Jewish setting Jerusalem should become a symbol of the heavenly state, since Jewish hopes were centred in that city. An idealized earthly city was predicted in Ezekiel 40–48. In apocalyptic literature it became a picture of heaven and was supposed to be pre-existent (Apocalypse of Baruch 4:22ff.; *cf.* 4 Ezra 7:26). The city had become a heavenly Jerusalem (Testament of Daniel 5:12; Enoch 90:28).

It may be wondered why heaven is conceived as a city at all, in view of the fact that cities are human creations. Yet it is highly expressive of a community. Cities depend on cooperation. They cannot exist on isolationism. Their success depends on the sense of community spirit. The city of Jerusalem in its celestial state stands for the perfection of order, for the absence of all polluting agents. The heavenly city swarms with life and festivities among innumerable angels and others whose names are enrolled in heaven (12:22). There is mention also of the 'spirits of just men made perfect'. Those who people the city are of a certain calibre; they have perfections, but they have not made themselves perfect.

There is mention in this context of 'the sprinkled blood' (12:24), and there is no doubt that the atoning sacrifice of Christ appropriated by faith is a *sine qua non* of eligibility. The whole epistle testifies to this. There is no hope for those who re-crucify the Son of God (6:6) and profane the blood (10:29). The heavenly community will be knit together in a common bond to Jesus Christ. It is significant also that the solidity implied in a well-built city is linked with the idea of an unshakeable kingdom in Hebrews 12:28. The epistle ends with an affirmation that the faithful seek a future city (13:14; *cf.* also 10:34).

This latter point leads to a consideration of those realities which are described in Hebrews as 'eternal'. The expression 'eternal life' is missing, but 'eternal salvation' (5:9) includes it and goes beyond it. Similarly, 'eternal redemption' (9:12) shows the abiding nature of Christ's work. It contrasts vividly with the temporary character of the redemption achieved by the old levitical cult. Moreover, the better sacrifice needed to secure it was offered by Christ through the 'eternal Spirit' (9:14). The inheritance thus secured is eternal (9:15), while 'judgment' is also said to be eternal (6:2).

There is an impressive finality about these concepts.

The future heirs will include the OT heroes of faith as well as those who believe in Christ (11:40). Indeed, the great crowd of witnesses surrounding us are probably thought of as already in heaven (12:1). The future glory in store for Christ's people is seen in the statement that Christ's purpose was to bring 'many sons to glory' (2:10). This theme links with Paul's teaching.

The epistles of James and Peter

In the epistle of *James* the concentration of thought on practical living offers no insight into a heavenly state. But the Petrine epistles provide several indications. In *1 Peter* 'an inheritance which is imperishable, undefiled, and unfading, kept in heaven for you' is mentioned in the opening words (1:4). The epistle is aptly known as an epistle of hope. It directs the reader towards the future. No details are given about the inheritance, but its pure and unfading quality is clearly reckoned to be an encouragement for those who are suffering persecution for their faith. The emphasis on enduring quality is further seen in the 'imperishable' seed (*i.e.* the word of God) which has been responsible for the believer's new birth (1:23ff.).

Heaven is the home of the Holy Spirit (1:12)[290] and the location of the risen Christ, who is said to be 'at the right hand of God, with angels, authorities, and powers subject to him' (3:22).[291] This concept is in complete agreement with the other NT literature. The place of the angels in heaven is further developed by comment that they long to look into God's dealings with men (1:12), showing the concern of the heavenly court over man's salvation. There is no reason to suppose that this interest will lessen after the consummation of God's mission on earth. Another aspect in 1 Peter is the theme of glory, which comes out in the reference to 'eternal glory' for those 'in Christ' in 1 Peter 5:10 (*cf.* the doxology in 4:11 which ascribes glory to God and Christ for ever and ever).

The future outlook in *2 Peter* focuses rather on the destiny of the existing heavens and earth, their destruction by fire and their replacement by a new heavens and earth (3:5ff., 10, 12, 13).[292] The recreated heavens and earth

---

[290] Although the expression 'sent from heaven' in 1 Pet. 1:12 has been thought to relate to the giving of the Spirit at Pentecost, this view is unlikely. The expression seems simply to denote divine origin, *cf.* J. N. D. Kelly, *The Epistles of Peter and Jude* (*BC*, 1969), p. 63; E. Best, *1 Peter*, p. 82.

[291] It is generally supposed that the angels, authorities and powers mentioned in 3:22 are malevolent (*cf.* J. N. D. Kelly, *op. cit.*, p. 164). F. W. Beare, *1 Peter* (²1958), pp. 150f., is in agreement, but concedes that there might be a reference here to both good and evil spirits. E. G. Selwyn, *1 Peter*, p. 208, points out that good angels have never been disobedient and therefore the subjection motif would have relevance only to evil spirit-powers.

[292] E. Käsemann, 'An Apologia for Primitive Christian Eschatology', in *Essays on New Testament Themes* (Eng. trans. 1960), pp. 180f., in discussing 3:13 thinks that the passage is a 'little apocalypse' introduced for paraenetic purposes. The whole drama 'serves the single end of giving the pious peace from their adversaries at last'. J. N. D. Kelly, *op. cit.*, p. 368, calls the imagery in this passage 'a Christian development and adaptation of older Jewish hopes and yearnings'. He especially appeals to Is. 65:17 and 66:22.

will be marked by their righteous state. This appears to be a material interpretation of the heavenly state, but it is probable that it was no more intended to be taken literally than Revelation 21:1 (see below). What is clear from Peter's statements is that holiness here is preparatory for righteousness in the future state of existence (3:11). The dissolution of the present, with its preponderance of evil (2 Pet. 2), is to give way to a better state of existence in which only righteousness will hold sway. Again, as in 1 Peter, the theme of glory is present. In 2 Peter 1:17 the voice at the transfiguration is described as the voice borne by the Majestic Glory. Believers are said to be called by God 'to his own glory and excellence' (1:3). Those called by God will have provided for them 'an entrance into the eternal kingdom of our Lord and Saviour Jesus Christ' (1:11).[293]

Revelation

No part of the NT turns the attention of the reader more clearly in a heavenward direction than this book. It supplies several significant insights. It records the merging of this age into its consummation and leads into the description of the eternal state. We may note several distinctive features: visions into heaven itself, descriptions of God and the exalted Lamb, heavenly worship scenes, the marriage of the Lamb and the new Jerusalem.

Visions into heaven. The introduction to the book at once stresses that the revelation is God-given. The first vision, announced by a trumpet-like voice, presents a remarkable picture of the exalted Christ (1:12ff). It is expressed in highly symbolic language, but an impression of majesty is unmistakable. The heavenly figure is seen nonetheless as being in the midst of the candlesticks and as communicating with the seven churches. The vision is followed by others which show that John was given a glimpse into heaven (4:1, 2ff.; 7:1ff.; 8:2; 10:1; 11:15f.; 14:1ff.; 15:1ff.; 19:1ff.; 21:1ff.). Indeed John reports what he saw, including many features about the inhabitants of the heavenly sphere, especially about the activities of angels. The angels engage in the worship of God (5:11), in the revelations of God (*e.g.* 7:1ff.; 10:1ff.), in the blowing of the trumpets of judgment (8:7ff.), in several announcements of doom, in special communications to the seer (*e.g.* 22:6). These angelic activities must be seen as typical of the mingling of worship and service which is ideally offered to God.

What is most characteristic of this book is the presence of the slain Lamb in heaven. The numerous references to Christ under this figure are intended to set him in the centre and indeed to portray him in the same terms as God. The throne is described as the throne of God and of the Lamb (22:1),

---

[293] The expression 'eternal kingdom' occurs only here in the NT. In this context it seems to be equated with heaven, *cf.* J. W. C. Wand, *The General Epistles of St Peter and St Jude* (*WC*, 1934), p. 156.

and the heavenly temple is described in a similar way (21:22). Heavenly worship is directed to him on the throne and to the Lamb (5:13). The exalted state of the Lamb is seen as the dominating theme in heaven, and the Apocalypse gives no indication that it will not continue to be in the ultimate heavenly state.

The vision of heaven which reveals the throne as surrounded with a rainbow and sending out flashes like lightning in a thunderstorm, which might well have overawed with its impression of majesty, nevertheless focuses on the worship of elders and living creatures and others of the heavenly host.

The heavenly beings. Apart from the heavenly creatures just mentioned we need to note special categories of people who are present in heaven. The martyrs are several times referred to as a particular group (6:9; 20:4). Those who had passed through great tribulation are also specified (7:14), as are those 'sealed' as servants of God (*cf.* 7:3ff.; 14:1). The main qualification seems to be that the robes of the saints are washed in the blood of the Lamb (7:14; *cf.* 1:5; 5:9). The robing in white is symbolic of the purity gained through the sacrifice of Christ (*cf.* 7:9, 13f.). Heaven is for the redeemed (14:3). Only those in fact whose names are written in the Lamb's book of life are eligible (20:12, 15; 21:27; *cf.* 3:5; 13:8).

The most significant event related about the future of God's people is the marriage supper of the Lamb (19:6ff.; *cf.* 21:2). In the well-known apocalyptic imagery of the messianic banquet, the completion of the mission of the Lamb is portrayed with certain notable features. The bride, as an image of the church, has been noted under the section on the church (see pp. 786f.). Here the distinctive characteristic is her glorious appearance, for she is dressed in a dazzling wedding garment representing her purity (19:7–8). She has not only made herself ready, but has been granted permission to be clothed with 'the righteous deeds of the saints' (19:8). Does this mean that through her own efforts she has become acceptable? Such a conclusion would run counter to the other testimony of the book and of the rest of the NT. If, however, the main teaching is that the righteous are clothed with the righteousness of Christ, their deeds could be considered righteous only in virtue of his righteousness.[294]

This portrayal of the church in her heavenly state in all her beauty and purity contrasts vividly with that other symbolic woman, Babylon, with her gaudy apparel of purple and scarlet adorned with gold, silver and pearls, who will be destroyed (17:4). The bride imagery sets out the corporate nature of the heavenly community and sees it as an object of love and a supreme example of beauty. Yet the ultimate loveliness of the church

---

[294] As G. R. Beasley-Murray, *Revelation*, p. 274, notes, 'Holiness is the gift of God. It is the holy life of the Redeemer in the redeemed.'

is derived from the Bridegroom himself, which shows the limitations of the analogy.

The new Jerusalem. This age ends with the destruction of the existing heaven and earth and the creation of a new heaven and earth (21:1). This means the establishment of an entirely new order of existence. The centrepiece of it is the new Jerusalem,[295] which is described in terms which cannot be taken literally. The whole vision is clearly symbolic of a perfect state of existence.[296] The new Jerusalem is specifically identified with the bride of the Lamb (21:2, 9, 10). The personal imagery gives way to a city image,[297] which is better able to portray the corporate character of the redeemed community. Nevertheless, as with the bride, so with the city, it is the splendour of its appearance which is particularly noted. It is radiant as a rare jewel (21:11). It is in the form of a cube, which represents its perfection. Even its foundations as well as its gates are bejewelled, while its streets are of gold (21:18–21). Within the city God and the Lamb are worshipped (22:3). Sorrow, death, mourning and pain find no place in it (21:4). It presents a scene of pure joy.

The over-all impression is that redeemed man in communion with God has a glorious future in store for him.[298] The details may be presented in a symbolic way, but the truth is unmistakable. The vision forms a fitting conclusion, not only to the NT canon, but to the whole sweep of NT theology.

HELL

So far we have considered only the eternal state of the blessed. We need next to enquire about the state of the lost, a subject which tends to be neglected or else glossed over.[299] We have already touched on Hades in the section on the afterlife (p. 820), but our concern here is with the final state of those who are not in the book of life.

The synoptic gospels

There are several statements of Jesus which focus attention on hell. Indeed

[295] For a detailed study of the New Jerusalem, *cf.* J. C. de Young, *Jerusalem in the New Testament*, pp. 117–164. *Cf.* also R. A. Harrisville, *The Concept of Newness in the New Testament* (1960), pp. 99ff.; B. Ramm, *Them He Glorified*, pp. 108ff.; M. Rissi, *The Future of the World*, 39ff.

[296] P. S. Minear, *I Saw a New Earth* (1968), p. 273, claims that the difference between the first and the new creation is defined by the community which dwells there (he contrasts Rev. 21:8 with 21:5-7).

[297] A. Farrer, *The Revelation of St John the Divine* (1964), p. 215, points out that the transference from a crown on the lady's brow to a ring of city walls would have been routine for John's contemporaries, since a city's standing emblem was a lady with an embattled crown.

[298] J. C. de Young, *op. cit.*, p. 164, concludes that the holy-city doctrine is seen in two perspectives, one an eternal life of spiritual fellowship with God, and the other the final consummation of the history of redemption.

[299] For a discussion of the moral issues raised by the biblical doctrine of hell, *cf.* J. W. Wenham, *The Goodness of God* (1974), pp. 27–41.

there are more specific sayings in the synoptic gospels than elsewhere in the NT. The expression *Gehenna* occurs several times in Matthew (5:22, 29, 30; 10:28, 18:9, 23:15; 23:33), three times in Mark (9:43, 45, 47), and once in Luke (12:5).[300] *Hades* is also found with the same sense in Matthew 11:23; 16:18 and Luke 10:15; 16:23 as a place of punishment.[301] There is no way of avoiding the conclusion that Jesus firmly accepted that there was a counterpart to heaven for those who were condemned before God.

Those who dislike the whole idea of eternal punishment either regard both heaven and hell as mythological or else dismiss the sayings by assigning them to church tradition. But if Jesus' words are given their face value, hell becomes a terrifying reality. He speaks of 'unquenchable fire' (Mk. 9:43) and expresses the opinion that it would be preferable to inherit life maimed than to have two hands, feet, eyes and be cast into hell. In the same context hell is conceived as a state of continuous punishment (undying worm and unquenched fire; Mk. 9:48). Although the description is undoubtedly symbolical, the meaning conveyed is of an undeniable continuity of judgment. No time limit is set.

In the Matthew contexts the same idea of hell fire occurs, *e.g.* in 5:22 as a liability for those who insultingly underrate others, and in 5:29ff.; 18:8–9, the parallels to the Markan passage just quoted. In the context of the sheep and the goats passage, those cursed are commanded to go 'into the eternal fire prepared for the devil and his angels' (Mt. 25:41). The 'eternal fire' in this context is linked to 'eternal punishment' (25:46).[302] It is God who should be feared because he has power to destroy soul and body in hell (Mt. 10:28 = Lk. 12:5, which has 'power to cast into hell'). In the Matthean parables of the kingdom, a final burning process is seen as the destiny of what is rejected (*cf.* 13:30, 42, 50). In the two latter cases there is mention of wailing and gnashing of teeth (as also in 8:12 and 22:13) to add to the pathos. In addition there is to be an act of binding and a condition of darkness (according to 22:13). Further, in Matthew's account of John the Baptist, the forerunner predicts that the Coming One will burn the chaff with unquenchable fire (Mt. 3:12).

---

[300] On Gehenna, *cf.* J. Jeremias, *TDNT* 2, pp. 657f. He cites a rabbinic reference to show that the followers of Shammai thought of Gehenna as having a purgatorial as well as a penal function. However, the NT evidence supports the latter, but not the former. The passages often cited in support of purgatory (Mk. 9:49; 1 Cor. 3:13-15; 2 Pet. 3:10) can all be otherwise explained.

[301] *Cf. idem*, *TDNT* 1, p. 148, where Jeremias suggests that on three issues the NT evidence is uniform. (i) soul sleep is alien; (ii) Hades lies in the heart of the earth; (iii) the stay in Hades is limited. Jeremias sharply distinguishes Hades from Gehenna since in the former, unlike the latter, the soul is separated from the body. But K. Hanhart, *The Intermediate State in the New Testament*, pp. 32ff., disputes the distinction. *Cf.* also R. H. Charles, *Eschatology, Hebrew, Jewish, Christian* (²1913), pp. 474f., who regards suffering in Gehenna as spiritual not corporeal.

[302] D. Hill, *Matthew*, p. 331, contends that the adjective 'eternal' with reference to both punishment and life means 'that which is characteristic of the Age to come'. He regards the emphasis on temporal lastingness as secondary.

The one reference which occurs only in Luke comes in the story of Dives and Lazarus (Lk. 16:19ff.), which not only contrasts hell with heaven, but gives some indication of conditions in hell (*cf.* pp. 853ff.). It is a state of torment for the rich man, who confesses to being in anguish in the flame of fire. It is, moreover, impossible to bridge the gap between heaven and hell; the gulf between them is fixed (verse 26). In no more vivid way could the finality of the divide be expressed. There is, moreover, an emphatic statement placed on the lips of Abraham to the effect that the anguish is deserved. It must be recognized, of course, that picture language is being used, but the message is unmistakable that hell and torment are inseparable. It is impossible to be certain whether this passage in Luke is describing an intermediate or a final state. This is no indication, however, that the rich man could expect any change in his state. It is noticeable that Luke's other references, which have parallels, do not give any indications of conditions in hell.

In addition to specific mention of hell, all the gospels record sayings which imply a sense of woe or foreboding against those who set themselves against God. Jesus pronounced severe woes on the hypocrites among the scribes and Pharisees (Mt. 23:15), even charging them with making proselytes who became twice as much children of *gehenna* as themselves. A particular woe was uttered over Judas (Mt. 26:24), on whom Jesus comments that it would have been better if he had not been born. In the saying about the narrow door to life, Matthew's account includes the statement that the broad way leads to destruction, although Luke omits all reference to it (Mt. 7:13–14; Lk. 13:24). It seems that Matthew places in general more stress on the punishment aspect than Luke, whose concern is for the more positive side of recompense. Luke does, however, in common with Matthew and Mark record the severe judgment about the millstone (Mt. 18:6, 7; Mk. 9:42; Lk. 17:2), but in his account it is pronounced against those provoking to temptation, whereas in Matthew and Mark it is against those causing 'little ones' to stumble. There is no essential difference between them. In one case Luke records a severe saying (the crushing stone, 20:18), which Matthew, in the most probable texts, omits (*cf.* Mt. 21:44 in TR).

The evidence produced above shows the importance that Jesus placed on punishment. Those who rejected God would certainly not escape from the consequences of doing so. There is no slack approach to the problem of wrongdoing, as was shown in the section on judgment.[303] When we penetrate below the language about hell, the major impression is a sense of separation, a sense expressed in the saying, 'I tell you, I do not know where

---

[303] There is no denying that an acute moral problem is raised by the idea of endless torment of the wicked, but even those who maintain their destruction recognize the need for a period of suffering in which the wicked will receive a punishment for their deeds.

you come from; depart from me, all you workers of iniquity' (Lk. 13:27; *cf.* Mt. 7:23). This is akin to the statement of Jesus, 'Whoever denies me before men, I also will deny before my Father who is in heaven' (Mt. 10:33; *cf.* also Mk. 8:38).

The Johannine literature

There is little in the gospel of John which relates to hell. Indeed, the idea itself does not occur. There is mention of condemnation (3:17) on those who do not believe, but no details are given on the form of judgment. Similarly the wrath of God is said to rest on anyone who does not obey the Son (3:36), but again no information is added as to how that wrath will manifest itself. Although John 5:29 refers to a resurrection of judgment for evil-doers, it is not related to any teaching on hell. It is evident that John is not as interested in this aspect of teaching as the synoptic gospels.

Paul

Of Paul's epistles, 2 Thessalonians has most to say about the final state of the lost, but even in this epistle no details are given. In 2 Thessalonians 1:5–9, those who afflict Christians are promised affliction and this is part of what Paul calls 'the righteous judgment of God'. He further speaks of the appearance of Jesus Christ 'in flaming fire' to inflict vengeance on those who do not know God and who disobey the gospel. The apostle is most specific when he says that they will 'suffer the punishment of eternal destruction' (1:9). This is completely in line with the synoptic references. It is moreover expressed in terms of 'exclusion from the presence of the Lord and from the glory of his might', an indication of the Pauline explanation of eternal punishment. To be excluded from God's presence is the real meaning of hell. Other expressions are used by Paul in describing the fate of the wicked.

In Philippians 3:19 he says of the enemies of the cross that their end is 'destruction' (*apōleia*)[304]. This is the same word as is used in Matthew 7:13 of the end of the broad way. It involves the idea of irreparable loss. Similarly in Romans 9:22 'the vessels of wrath', the very antithesis of the 'vessels of mercy', are said to be made for 'destruction'. This is the opposite of 'glory', but no further indication is given as to its precise meaning.

In two cases Paul uses the strong word 'anathema' (1 Cor. 16:22; Gal. 1:9), which although it originally meant to devote a thing for a holy purpose had come to be understood in an adverse way. It again implies rejection, although it says nothing about the form the rejection will take. It is akin to the 'curse' pronounced on those who rely on the works of the law (Gal. 3:10). The idea of a denial by God is suggested in the formalized statement in 2 Timothy 2:12.

---

[304] *Cf.* A. Oepke, *apōleia, TDNT* 1, pp. 396f.; H. Ridderbos, *Paul*, p. 112.

Paul's approach is to expound fully the theme of Christian salvation, and to give only passing reference to the destiny of the wicked. But there is no doubt that he recognized the certainty and seriousness of the coming judgment, although he did not dwell on the details. He was convinced that God's judgment must be just and therefore that punishment was necessary.

The rest of the New Testament

In *Hebrews* there is only one reference to fires of judgment (Heb. 10:27), which are regarded as a fearful prospect for those who sin deliberately after receiving a knowledge of the truth. The writer is thinking specifically of those who profane the blood of the covenant and outrage the Spirit of grace (verse 29). The 'fury of fire' will consume the adversaries of God (*cf.* Is. 26:11). In the same context in Hebrews comes the statement, 'It is a fearful thing to fall into the hands of the living God (10:31). This is supported by the later saying that our God is a consuming fire (12:29). This is as near as this epistle gets to the concept of fires of judgment. In 10:39 there is mention of the prospect of destruction for those who shrink back.

The destiny of the wicked does not concern the NT letter writers except in *2 Peter* and *Jude*. Jude refers to Sodom and Gomorrah as having undergone 'a punishment of eternal fire', which was seen as a judgment on them for their immorality and unnatural lust (verse 7). Jude also refers to the condemnation designated for those who pervert God's grace and deny Jesus Christ (verse 4). In 2 Peter there is reference to the fallen angels being cast into hell (Gk. *tartarys*) and committed to 'pits of nether gloom to be kept until the judgment' (2 Pet. 2:4). *Tartarys*, which occurs nowhere else in the NT, describes the fallen angels' prison house, where they await the act of consignment to eternal judgment. As far as people are concerned those who are evil are condemned and 'their destruction has not been asleep' (2 Pet. 2:3).

In *Revelation* there is a more graphic representation of hell, particularly in relation to the last judgment. In chapter 14 the blessedness of the redeemed is contrasted with the final judgment on those who worship the beast. They are under the fierce wrath of God (verse 10) which they are made to drink out of the cup of his anger. They are to be 'tormented with fire and brimstone in the presence of the holy angels and in the presence of the Lamb. And the smoke of their torment goes up for ever and ever; and they have no rest, day or night' (verses 10, 11). There is an unquestioned severity about this picture of judgment. It is again echoed in 19:20, where the beast and the false prophet are thrown into 'the lake of fire that burns with brimstone'. The same idea occurs in 20:10 where the devil is consigned to the same lake, and 20:14 where Death and Hades share the same fate. In the latter case the lake of fire is defined as the second death.

The whole book is concerned with the pouring out of wrath and it is not surprising therefore that the lake of fire represents the final overthrow of all opposition. Some concept to mark the judgment of the Lamb over his enemies is essential, but clearly the lake of fire with its interminable flames of torment goes greatly beyond the sense of finality. It involves a definitely punitive element.

SUMMARY

We have noted that the NT writers do not describe heaven as a place, but rather as the presence of God. God and heaven are so closely linked that the latter concept cannot be held without reference to the former. In several books the throne of God is mentioned and this reaches its climax in the book of Revelation where it becomes central in the new Jerusalem. This idea of heaven as a city is particularly seen in the concept of the new Jerusalem, but is also found in Paul's epistles and Hebrews.

In most of the NT books angels play some part, but there is no specific information of their function in heaven. Since their function on earth is always to carry out the commands of God, there is no reason to suppose that their function in heaven is or will be any different.

There is no doubt that the NT view of heaven is closely connected with inheritance and rewards in the form of spiritual treasure. Also connected with the heavenly state of existence is eternal life, a concept in which the adjective emphasizes the qualitative aspect. Another aspect which is frequently emphasized in the NT is the glory which characterizes the future destiny of believers. To dwell in the presence of God is the ultimate bliss for the children of God.

Turning next to the NT teaching about hell, we may summarize this briefly as follows. Although the imagery used sometimes gives the impression of a place, this is less dominant than the idea of a state of condemnation. Judgment on evil-doers is regarded as certain. Moreover, the punishment meted out is just. The major idea is one of separation from God, a complete exclusion from his presence. Another undeniable fact is that judgment is eternal. It is this latter fact which has led some, who consider unending punishment to be unethical, to propound a theory of annihilation. The doctrine of eternal punishment is not an attractive doctrine and the desire to substitute for it the view that, at the judgment, the souls of the wicked will cease to exist, is understandable.

Chapter 9

The New Testament approach to ethics

INTRODUCTORY COMMENTS

No NT theology would be complete without a consideration of the ethical teaching contained in the NT. Our previous studies have shown the way in which the new man in Christ has formed a new humanity. Much has already been said about the fundamental transformation which this has brought about in man's condition, both in relation to God and in relation to his fellow believers. It is not surprising that already some ethical considerations have been brought into the discussion. But our present purpose is to examine the behaviour expected of Christian believers in their present environment. Our enquiry will concentrate on the moral guidance which the NT gives to Christians for their personal lives and will also examine the important issues of social ethics and responsibilities. We shall set out the evidence from the various streams of NT thought for the personal side and then in a more general way for the social side.[1] In doing this we shall pay particular attention to the relationship between theology and ethics.[2]

Because we are approaching ethics via NT theology, it would not be in place to explore the various non-religious ethical systems of the ancient world. Nevertheless in the course of our discussions we shall note the various contrasts between Christian and non-Christian views of ethics. We shall note that Jesus blazed a new trail on the whole subject of ethics and supplied man with new ideals and with the moral dynamic to pursue them.

---

[1] Among standard text books which deal with NT ethics we may note the following: L. H. Marshall, *The Challenge of New Testament Ethics* (1947); W. Lillie, *Studies in New Testament Ethics* (1961); C. A. A. Scott, *New Testament Ethics* (1948); H. Thielicke, *Theological Ethics* 2 vols., (Eng. trans. vol. 1 1966, vol. 2 1969); J. L. Houlden, *Ethics and the New Testament* (1973).

[2] W. N. Pittenger, *The Christian Understanding of Human Nature* (1964), p. 161, in discussing the relation between faith and morality agrees with Kierkegaard that Christian faith comes first and the morality of the Christian tradition second. Pittenger comments that there can be no unethical religion or irreligious morality.

This consideration in and of itself will bring out the practical relevance of our previous theological discussions.

There are certain preliminary factors which need attention in order to place the ethical teaching of Jesus and the apostles in their true perspective. We shall first note that NT ethics is firmly based on the OT ethical teaching. There is no suggestion that Jesus began from scratch. We shall discuss in the final part the way in which he accepted the full authority of the OT and recognized therefore the claims of the law, although he added his own modifications to it (see pp. 957ff.). Since the ten commandments lie at the heart of the OT ethic, it is clear that that ethic is thoroughly theological in character.[3] In his own approach to the commandments, Jesus summed them up in the dual requirement of love to God and love to neighbour (Mt. 22:37–39 = Mk. 12:30 = Lk. 10:27).[4] Set against the ramifications of some rabbinic casuistry this seems an amazingly simple approach, but its genius lies in its combination of simplicity of form with profundity of insight. It at once removes self from the centre of ethics.

A person's relationship to God is the sphere of theology. When he is enabled to love God he has been brought within the orbit of the will of God. This is brought out in the OT by the fact that the commandments and indeed all the injunctions of the law are set within the covenant between God and man. Although the ethical requirements came to be interpreted as legal demands which fostered a purely legalistic approach to ethics (particularly among the Pharisees), the original intention was to reflect what kind of behaviour would be in harmony with the nature of God. Those who entered into a covenant with God would be expected to want to please him.

OT history vividly demonstrates the failure on the part of the Israelites to fulfil their part of the bargain. Jesus alone perfectly fulfilled man's side of the covenantal agreement and this supplies at once the justification for regarding the moral teaching of Jesus as the perfect interpretation of the real intention of the law. The emphatic contrast between 'It was said' and 'But I say' in the Sermon on the Mount must not be regarded as in any sense a debasing of the law, but as brilliantly focusing attention on its inner nature. Examples of how this worked out will be given in the section below on personal ethics; for our present purpose we need to note that the two bases of Jesus' ethics were his acceptance of the authority of the OT, and his recognition of his own personal authority. It is the latter which

---

[3] For a useful study of the ethical implications of the ten commandments, cf. R. S. Wallace, *The Ten Commandments* (1965); H. G. G. Herklots, *The Ten Commandments and Modern Man* (1958).

[4] D. Hill, *Matthew* (NCB, 1972), p. 306, points out that the originality of this summary of the commandments is in the supremacy given to the twin ideas of love to God and to one's neighbour. It is to be noted that in Luke's account it is the lawyer who gives the summary. This suggests that it may have been an already accepted summary of the law.

furnishes the real key to the ethics of Jesus. Indeed NT ethics and Christology are inextricably bound up together.

Another important factor is the relation between ethics and eschatology.[5] In our discussions of the kingdom of God we have noted both future and present aspects (pp. 416ff.). Since we cannot completely divorce the present aspect from the future, we must find an approach to ethics which takes account of both. The present aspect is simpler, unless any credence is given to the *Interimsethik* theory of Schweitzer in which the ethical teaching of Jesus had only a temporary relevance.[6] If the kingdom of God has already come, it must make a difference to the ethical standards of its members.[7]

But it is a crucial question to what extent present values have relevance to the future kingdom. Under the theory of realized eschatology, the ethics of Jesus becomes a vital part of the immediate outworking of the kingdom. In its most extreme form, in which the future coming of Jesus is explained away, the Christian gospel becomes so orientated to the present that ethics becomes its most important feature. The neglect of future hope resulted in the social gospel movement[8] during the early part of the twentieth century. But its failure was due to the fact that neither personal ethics nor social involvement in a way consistent with the teaching of Jesus was possible without the spiritual dynamic which a future hope gives.[9]

On the other hand, attempts to refer the ethics of Jesus entirely to the future also fail to do justice to that teaching, as in the interpretation of some who reserve the relevance of the Sermon on the Mount for the Jews of the millennial kingdom and deny its applicability, except in a decidedly secondary sense, to the Christian church.[10] There is no indication in the

---

[5] *Cf.* A. N. Wilder, *Eschatology and Ethics in the Teaching of Jesus* ([2]1950); *idem*, 'Kerygma, Eschatology and Social Ethics', *The Background of the New Testament and its Eschatology* (ed. W. D. Davies and D. Daube, 1956).

[6] On Schweitzer's *Interimsethik*, *cf.* F. V. Filson, *Jesus Christ the Risen Lord*, pp. 242f., who criticizes the theory on the following grounds: (i) the kingdom was not entirely future; (ii) Jesus did not know the time of the end; (iii) the great bulk of Jesus' teaching did not concern the end, *cf.* R. Otto, *The Kingdom of God and the Son of Man* (Eng. trans. 1938), pp. 59ff. (iv) Jesus saw God's action taking place in his own work. The ethical action grows out of this, *cf.* O. Cullmann, *Christ and Time* (Eng. trans. 1951), pp. 81ff. (v) The eschatological emphasis in the gospels is not lacking in ethical point (*cf.* A. N. Wilder, *Eschatology and Ethics in the Teaching of Jesus*). *Cf.* P. Ramsey, *Basic Christian Ethics* (1950), pp. 29ff. L. H. Marshall *The Challenge of New Testament Ethics*, pp. 191ff., brings out the weakness of the *Interimsethik* idea. He cites approvingly the opinion of E. F. Scott, *The Ethical Teaching of Jesus*, p. 45, that apocalyptic hope did not distort but intensified the moral demands of Jesus.

[7] Those who concentrate on the present aspect of the kingdom see the whole biblical ethic as the ethic of the kingdom. A notable representative of this view was T. W. Manson, *Ethics and the Gospel* (1960).

[8] Among the leading advocates of a social gospel, *cf.* S. Matthews, *Jesus on Social Institutions* (1928); C. J. Cadoux, *The Early Church and the World* (1925).

[9] Many who have put some emphasis on the social gospel have at the same time included some eschatological element. *Cf.* P. Ramsey, *Basic Christian Ethics* (1950).

[10] This is the view advanced in the Scofield Reference Bible (1909). A recent defender of this interpretation is C. C. Ryrie, *Dispensationalism Today* (1965), pp. 65–78. *Cf.* also L. S. Chafer, *Systematic Theology* 5 (1948).

account of the teaching to the effect that it has no present relevance. It would seem, therefore, if both future and present aspects are to be fully taken into account, that the ethics of Jesus must be taken seriously in the present life, and must be seen as perfectly fulfilled only in the future consummation of the kingdom. This will supply for the ethical teaching the necessary dynamic. In view of the end events what kind of persons ought Christians to be (cf. 2 Pet. 3:11)?

Yet another preliminary consideration is the close connection between the NT doctrine of the Spirit and Christian ethics. We have already noted the dynamic supplied by the indwelling Spirit in the believer (pp. 652f.), and it is essential to bear in mind that no attempt to carry out the ethical instruction of Jesus without the aid of the Spirit is a viable proposition. The ethics of Jesus is essentially the ethics of the Spirit.[11] Since the Spirit aims to glorify Jesus, he also aims to make possible to believers the high demands of the teaching of Jesus. By the same token no true account of Christian ethics is intelligible apart from the Christian community, for although the personal side of ethics is essentially a matter of personal responsibility, it is never purely individualistic. The doctrine of the church in the NT has a bearing on the nature of Christian ethics, as will become particularly clear in our study of Acts and of the epistles.

It will be seen from these introductory comments that Christian ethics is no ill-fitting adjunct to NT theology, but an essential part of it. This at once differentiates it from all other ethical systems. Christian ethics is essentially theological ethics.[12] It is meant to be understood in the context of grace. The ethical teaching was not propounded to form the moral basis of secular society, but was designed for those who have already responded to the gospel. NT ethics is essentially for 'committed' people. Its demands will be seen to be far-fetched by those who are not in full sympathy with the mission of Jesus. Those who have tried to divorce his ethical teaching from his redemptive mission and have equated the gospel with the former at the expense of the latter have ended with a totally inadequate view of both. The ethical teaching of Jesus finds its roots in the saving work of Christ.

PERSONAL ETHICS

The synoptic gospels

JESUS' VIEW OF GOODNESS

It is of paramount importance in assessing the ethical teaching of Jesus to consider his idea of the good, for this serves as the norm by which all

[11] H. Thielicke, *Theological Ethics* 1, pp. 648–667, has a section bringing out the significance of the Spirit in the sphere of ethics.

[12] In his second volume, H. Thielicke applies his ethical principles to a wide range of political issues (*Theological Ethics* 2: *Politics*, Eng. trans. 1969).

human acts must be judged.[13] The first observation which must be made is that Jesus declined to assess a person's character by what he did without reference to his inner motives. Such an approach was of particular significance against the contemporary background of rigid observance of legalistic requirements as a means of obtaining merit. Jesus' criticism of the scribes and Pharisees was based on the fact that they paid meticulous attention to external acts but neglected the inner condition. They were like sepulchres which were externally beautiful, but inwardly full of corruption (Mt. 23:27, 28). Jesus' concern was for the weightier matters of the moral law (Mt. 23:23), *i.e.* justice, mercy and faith. Mere observance of the ceremonial law did not find commendation in the teaching of Jesus. He was concerned that people should get their priorities right. Responsible moral action was more important than observance of a legislative code.

For Jesus ethics was fundamentally a matter of a person's character rather than of his activity. What he is, is more important than what he does, for his character will determine his actions. It is no wonder, therefore, that Jesus insisted that the righteousness of the members of his kingdom must exceed that of the scribes and Pharisees (Mt. 5:20).[14] Righteousness for the latter took no account of why a person conformed to the law, only that he did so in an outward manner. Moreover, inherent in the Pharisaic view of righteousness may have been the idea of the accrual of merit, by seeking good deeds in excess of evil deeds.[15] In view of this it is at once clear that, by his insistence on motive as a constituent part of goodness, Jesus could not fail to clash with the religious authorities of his day.

The idea of the inward character of goodness was fundamental to Jesus' ethical teaching.[16] It explains at once why he never legislated over ethical issues and never expected his disciples to do so. When Peter wanted a ruling on the number of times a person should forgive, Jesus suggested that he should not stop before 490 times, a pointed way of declining to legislate at all on a matter of moral attitude (Mt. 18:22; Lk. 17:3, 4).

In emphasizing the importance of motive, Jesus was drawing attention

[13] In his book *New Testament Ethics*, C. A. A. Scott has a chapter on Jesus' concept of goodness, under which some of the more important aspects of his ethical teaching are examined (pp. 48–72.). Scott's conclusion is that the moral ideal, which is to be distinguished from the moral law, is not merely an object of admiration, but is to be regarded as the living force of personality entering our consciousness and directing our wills. L. H. Marshall, *The Challenge of New Testament Ethics*, pp. 63–98, in dealing with Jesus' view of good concentrates mainly on the beatitudes.

[14] P. Bonnard, *Matthieu* (CNT, 1963), p. 62, understands righteousness here, as in Mt. 5:10, in the sense of fidelity to the law as reinterpreted by Christ. He points out also that the statement of Mt. 5:20 does not simply mean that the followers of Jesus were expected quantitively to exceed the righteousness of the Pharisees (as A. Oepke, *TDNT* 4, p. 621 n. 88, maintained), but that their obedience was to be of a new and radical kind.

[15] This theory of accrued merit in Pharisaic thought has recently come under attack. *Cf.* E. P. Sanders, *Paul and Palestinian Judaism* (1977), *passim*, but especially pp. 183ff. He denies support for the idea of the transfer of accrued merit.

[16] On grace and goodness in NT ethics, *cf.* W. Lillie, *Studies in New Testament Ethics*, pp. 34–44.

to the will. No ethic can be imposed on an obstinate will. Jesus expected a full surrender of self to the perfect will of God, which means that the human will becomes exposed to an influence for good which otherwise would not exist. This cannot happen except by individual willingness to surrender. When Jesus demanded that people should take up their cross and follow him, this amounted to self-renunciation and inevitably brought with it profound ethical implications.[17] Obedience then becomes a matter, not of observation of an external code, but of utter devotion to a person. Once the will is committed to the pursuit of conformity to the will of God, it is committed to One whose nature is essentially good and whose decisions must be equally good.

A corollary of Jesus' view of the good is his condemnation of certain undesirable qualities. His ethical teaching has necessarily both a negative and positive side. He was critical of those attitudes and actions which run counter to the character of true goodness. He condemned covetousness, as the law had done before him. The parable of Dives and Lazarus is a commentary on this, since the criticism implied against Dives was not his wealth but his misuse of it (Lk. 16:19–31). His possessions had blinded him to the needs of the man at his gate, and had, in fact, destroyed his social concern.

Another quality which found no place in Jesus' moral standards was hypocrisy. He particularly condemned the scribes and Pharisees for this (Mt. 23). The word 'hypocrisy' did not necessarily denote deliberate 'dissimulation'. Not all the Pharisees were insincere, at least consciously. Nevertheless Jesus recognized that by their actions and attitudes they were, in fact, unconsciously insincere. Purity of motive was so important to Jesus that any lack of it was condemned.

Closely akin to the last is the sin of self-centredness, which may be regarded as a root from which many other evils spring. Greed, immorality, lack of self-control, arrogance, envy, are all due to an inordinate love of self. Jesus called for self-denial in a rigorous way. Those who keep life for themselves lose it (Lk. 17:33). Jesus saw that self-love was the great stumbling block in personal ethics. The call for self-denial was powerfully supported by his own example. His mission centred around a negation of self, which nevertheless proved productive of a standard of ethics previously unknown.[18] Self-centredness is the antithesis of service and is therefore the antithesis of all that Jesus himself came to do and expected his disciples to do.

Jesus condemned sins of the flesh. Not only the act of fornication but

---

[17] On the Christian concept of self-denial, cf. Lillie, op. cit., pp. 151–162; P. Ramsey, *Basic Christian Ethics*, pp. 92–103; D. Bonhoeffer, *The Cost of Discipleship* ([6]1959).

[18] For the obligation of self-assertion in Jewish ethics, cf. E. G. Hirsch, art. Ethics, *Jewish Encyclopedia* 5, p. 249.

the desire to fornicate is regarded as being against the law of God (Mt. 5:28). Moreover, he also condemned anything which causes one to sin, or others to sin, and declared that even if one's own members were responsible they should be cut off (Mk. 9:43–48). Clearly this advice is to be taken symbolically, but the seriousness of such actions cannot be denied. Jesus expected a stringent self-discipline in the interests of the kingdom. Those who have such an approach to their own desires will not regard self-gratification as a worthy end, nor will they exhibit lack of respect for others.

THE BEATITUDES

In a special way the beatitudes, samples of which are preserved in different forms in Matthew 5:3–12 and Luke 6:20–23, have been regarded as epitomizing the ethical teaching of Jesus, although there have been differing opinions about their relevance. There can be no doubt that Jesus intended them to be realized, and yet many of them seem to be impossible as general ethical principles.[19] It must certainly be recognized that they have reference only to those who are willing to accept the discipline of discipleship. In Matthew's setting they are an integral part of the Sermon on the Mount, but even if the context is ignored the spiritual conditions expected in these beatitudes point to a spiritual state which makes no sense apart from the NT concept of the new man in Christ.

Some comment is needed on the word 'blessed' (*makarioi*),[20] for this means more than mere happiness. The word conveys the idea of congratulation, rather than describing a state.[21] The person to whom these beatitudes apply is to be envied. We shall discuss the beatitudes in the order in which Matthew records them, but we shall note the differences where parallel sayings occur in Luke.[22]

(i) In the first beatitude we note a variation between Matthew's account

[19] In his book on *Understanding the Sermon of the Mount* (1961), pp. 80ff., H. K. McArthur stresses that the beatitudes had a future reference and he considered this to be important for an understanding of the sermon as a whole. But E. Schweizer, *Matthew* (Eng. trans. 1976, from *NTD*, 1973), p. 81, points out that as compared with OT and Jewish examples of blessings, the beatitudes of Jesus are totally new in taking a future blessing and declaring it as right now present. Ethiopic Enoch 58:2 is cited as the one parallel. On the ethical content of the beatitudes, *cf.* E. Baker, *The Neglected Factor* (1963); G. Vann, *The Divine Pity, A Study of the Social Implications of the Beatitudes* (1945). The latter book is written from a Roman Catholic point of view.

[20] For a discussion of *makarios* in the NT, *cf.* F. Hauck's article in *TDNT* 4, pp. 367ff.

[21] T. W. Manson, *Ethics and the Gospel*, p. 51 denies that beatitudes are identical with blessings. They are congratulations to people on their present position.

[22] There has been debate over whether it is right to suppose that these beatitudes originally existed as a group in the form that Matthew preserves. *Cf.* G. D. Kilpatrick, *The Origins of the Gospel According to St Matthew* (1946), pp. 15ff. For our present purpose the question of origins may be disregarded. On the differences in wording in the beatitudes between Matthew and Luke, *cf.* J. Jeremias, *The Sermon on the Mount* (Eng. trans. 1961), p. 18, who considers that an Aramaic origin explains many of them.

There is some justification for the view that Luke's beatitudes are addressed to the disciples as 'poor', hence the force of 'you poor'. But Matthew's beatitudes appear to have a different purpose, *i.e.* as entry requirements for the kingdom.

and Luke's. The latter says 'Blessed are you poor', whereas Matthew's has the words 'poor in spirit'. Many prefer Luke's wording on the grounds that it is difficult to attach an intelligible meaning to Matthew's phrase, and they consequently regard the addition as an attempt to soften the harshness of the wording in Luke.[23] In view of the fact that Jesus considered it to be difficult for a rich man to enter the kingdom, he may have been thinking of the spiritual advantages of those who were not encumbered with many of this world's possessions. The difference between Matthew and Luke here suggests that Luke's beatitudes as a whole are making different points compared with Matthew's. His concentrate more on social needs like poverty, misery, hunger and oppression. On the other hand, Matthew's additional words 'in spirit' could be regarded as a true indication of the sense in which Jesus meant the word 'poor' to be understood. If the 'poor' are not those who are materially deprived, but those who recognize their spiritual poverty it makes better sense, but it must be admitted that this is not the most obvious meaning of this first beatitude. It is better to suppose that the 'poor' are those who in the OT sense, although afflicted, trust in God for help (cf. Ps. 69:28–33; 37:14ff.; Is. 61:1). In other words 'poor' has a religious connotation. Since possession of the kingdom of God is the consequence of this 'poverty', it seems to suggest a spiritual element, for the 'kingdom' cannot be understood in any other way. One indisputable fact is that Jesus never gave grounds for supposing that wealth was any passport for claiming a stake in the kingdom. Jesus wanted people to rely on God and not on themselves or their possessions. Whatever interpretation is given to the words, Jesus is clearly setting himself against the trend to assess a person according to his material success. The kingdom of God is not for those who are confident of their own achievements. This first beatitude highlights the fact that Jesus addressed himself only to those who had a sense of need.[24]

(ii) The second beatitude seems to place a high value on suffering (Matthew has 'mourn', while Luke has 'weep').[25] It is paradoxical that such should be regarded as 'blessed'. In the world of Jesus' time this notion would certainly have seemed novel, for people were not in the habit of seeing value in sorrow. But it is not surprising that Jesus should challenge the common view of his own age, in view of the high store that was to be placed on his own suffering. He could promise special comfort to those who learnt the value of affliction. He never promised an unrealistic trouble-free existence, since he knew that in the present imperfect world this would be impossible.

[23] Cf. L. H. Marshall, The Challenge of New Testament Ethics, p. 76.

[24] Cf. D. Hill, Matthew, pp. 110f.

[25] M. Black, An Aramaic Approach to the Gospels and Acts, (³1967), p. 157, regards Matthew's and Luke's Beatitudes, taken together, as forming a parallelismus membrorum.

(iii) A special blessing on meekness would not have met with universal approval in the contemporary world of Jesus.[26] The word used (*praeis*) contains within it more than the normal understanding of meekness. It is not a spineless submissiveness, but an active policy of non self-assertion.[27] The meek person is therefore one who rejects arrogance and domination in favour of a gentle approach. That such should be promised the inheritance of the earth must have appeared to Jesus' contemporaries (as it does to ours) to be a ridiculous ideal. Yet it is true that greater and more enduring conquests have been won by gentle service to others than by political or economic forces. This third beatitude was not intended to be a political manifesto for world conquest, but a directive to those committed to a spiritual ideal. It makes sense only to the new man in Christ.

(iv) The next blessing is for those hungering and thirsting for righteousness. Again, the teaching of Jesus would challenge the current views of Judaism in which a person could earn righteousness by doing good deeds.[28] In this beatitude the blessed person does not earn righteousness, but rather urgently seeks what God alone can give. The sense of lack is particularly acute. Satisfaction comes only to those who are aware of their imperfection. This ties in with the NT teaching on repentance, and the exposition of righteousness and justification in the epistles. This does not mean that Jesus was devaluing good works, but that no-one was to evaluate himself on such grounds. A different emphasis is found in Luke, who includes a blessing on those who hunger now, but links it with a promise of future satisfaction. Whereas physical hunger seems to be the main thought here, the OT contains the idea of hungering for spiritual satisfaction, and this may be the key to the meaning.[29]

(v) Mercy was another quality which was not highly rated in the ancient world.[30] Jewish piety had a deliberately merciless approach to those who did not know the law. To keep the law was of greater moment than sensitivity towards the weakness of those who failed to keep its demands. Mercy, moreover, was totally contrary to the harsh attitude of the ancient pagan world to conquered foes. A Roman triumphal procession found no place for mercy, but customarily exposed the hapless prisoners in chains. The quality of mercy is not weak when it is linked with justice. The kind

[26] Unlike the other beatitudes, this one is based on an OT passage (Ps. 37:11), which is not itself in the form of a beatitude. On the relation of Matthew's words to the OT text, *cf.* R. H. Gundry, *The Use of the Old Testament in St Matthew's Gospel* (1967), pp. 132ff., who maintains their genuineness.

[27] F. Hauck and S. Schulz, art. *praüs, praütēs*, *TDNT* 6, pp. 645f., find support from secular Greek sources for the idea of the word as indicating 'an active attitude and deliberate acceptance, not just a passive submission.'

[28] D. Hill, *Matthew*, p. 112, understands 'righteousness' here in terms of righteousness of life in conformity to God's will.

[29] *Cf.* I. H. Marshall, *Luke* (*NIGTC*, 1978), p. 250.

[30] R. Bultmann, art. *eleos*, *TDNT* 2, p. 478, cites the Stoic view of mercy as a sickness of the soul.

of mercy that Jesus commended is not the kind that excuses wrongdoers at the expense of those they had wronged.

(vi) There is no denying that the rabbis would have approved of the aim of seeing God.[31] But they would not have regarded it as the reward for purity of heart; to them purity was a matter of ceremonial. In this beatitude Jesus once again highlights the inner motives in contrast to external acts. Purity of heart involves purity of mind, and suggests a radical transformation at the centre of a person's thought. A pure person is not so much a person who has achieved sinless perfection as one whose thoughts and desires are dominated by purity rather than defilement.

(vii) In commending peacemakers, Jesus was combating any system which erects barriers between peoples and which therefore fosters strife. The immediate intention was no doubt to oppose narrow Jewish nationalism, and this is borne out by the assurance that the peacemakers will be called 'sons of God', an expression which the rabbis exclusively applied to Israel. The Christian ethic does not see one nationality exalted above another. The gospel is universalistic in scope, and this fact must affect people's relationship to one another. This beatitude is not, however, directed to those who are at peace with others, but to those who actively create conditions of peace. Admittedly the difficulties of creating peace are immense. But Jesus was not simply commending an impossible ideal. The disposition towards peace is a moral and spiritual quality which can be achieved only by spiritual means. Peacemaking makes complete sense only when set against the spiritual potentiality of the new man in Christ. This at least creates within the Christian the disposition, but cannot ensure such a disposition in others. Nevertheless, the more there are who are actively promoting peace, the more possibility there is of peace being achieved. The desire for a just peace[32] reflects a characteristic of God and a person with such a desire is seen as a true 'son of God', in contrast to those who claim sonship on purely nationalistic grounds.

(viii) The last two beatitudes in Matthew deal with the attitude of the 'blessed' person when people revile and persecute him.[33] There is a saying in Luke which parallels Matthew's second saying.[34] Jesus takes it for granted that those who display the qualities of the previous beatitudes will not

---

[31] For the rabbis, the aim to see God was achieved through study of the Scriptures or at the moment of death. Cf. P. Bonnard, *Matthieu*, p. 57.

[32] W. Hendriksen, *Exposition of the Gospel according to Matthew* (1973), p. 279, is right to point out that the peace here is not peace at any price. Hence we must speak of a just or true peace.

[33] According to W. D. Davies, *The Setting of the Sermon on the Mount* (1964), pp. 289ff., the last beatitude relates specifically to the condition of the church faced with the synagogue. But it is expressed in a sufficiently general way to be applicable to all forms of opposition.

[34] For a discussion of the variation in form of this beatitude in Matthew and Luke, cf. D. R. A. Hare, *The Theme of Jewish Persecution of Christians in the Gospel according to St Matthew* (1967), pp. 114ff. He considers that Matthew's use of *diōxōsin* (not in Luke) is secondary. He does not support Lohmeyer's view (*Das Evangelium des Matthäus* ed. E. Lohmeyer- W. Schmauch, *KEK* ²1958), p. 95, that the verb means to

escape persecution. Too many of these qualities run counter to the common ethical standards. Reaction is inevitable. Those who stand for higher standards than current conventions are always seen as critics who are best disposed of. They who represent the kingdom of God among the kingdoms of men face persecution for righteousness' sake (according to Matthew), but their satisfaction is that they already possess the kingdom of God.[35] In no clearer way could the inner nature of the kingdom be demonstrated.

This brief survey of the beatitudes has shown something of the moral qualities expected to be seen in the lives of those committed to Christ. They are not, however, a self-contained unit of teaching. To regard them as such would be to distort their meaning. They give no indication how people may become members of the kingdom. No demand for repentance is given, although this was the first announcement that Jesus made at the inauguration of his public ministry. The beatitudes must not be regarded independently of the whole mission of Jesus. They set out the character which can be achieved only by those who have been transformed by the saving work of Christ. Many who have pronounced them to be impossible, together with the whole Sermon on the Mount, have failed to take account of this fact.

COMMENDABLE VIRTUES

We have already noted certain virtues like humility which were not much valued in the ancient world, but which Jesus rated highly. Apart from the beatitude about the meek, Jesus made clear his own approach to this quality. He described himself as meek and lowly (Mt. 11:29). In his teaching he deplored self-importance and encouraged humility (Lk. 14:7–11).[36] In answer to the question, 'Who is the greatest in the kingdom of heaven?' Jesus set a child before the disciples as an example (Mt. 18:1ff.), and condemned any who caused such little ones to sin. Humility of this kind has a profound effect on behaviour and serves as an important principle in the ethics of Jesus.

The avoidance of stumbling-blocks for others is an extension of the same line of teaching. Jesus paid the temple tax so as not to cause offence (*skandalizomai*) although he did not acknowledge any claim upon him (Mt. 17:24ff.). It must be noted, however, that he did not support the avoidance of offence at any cost, as his criticism of the scribes and Pharisees clearly

---

bring legal charges against someone. The reference to the prophets suggests a much more general and violent opposition.

[35] D. Hill, *Matthew*, p. 114, points out that Matthew uses a word (*agalliasthe*) which does not express physical joy, but is a technical term for joy in persecution.

[36] J. Jeremias, *The Parables of Jesus* (Eng. trans. [2]1963), p. 107, cites a rabbinic parallel to the teaching of Jesus about seeking the lowest places at a banquet, and he reckons that Jesus took over this idea. The main difference is that whereas Jewish teaching was given as a matter of prudence, Jesus was more concerned about men's attitudes in the presence of God. *Cf.* I. H. Marshall, *Luke*, p. 583.

shows (Mt. 15:1ff.). He showed no mercy in face of hypocrisy, and this is proof that there are limits to the exercise of restraint. The temple would not have been cleansed by Jesus if he had not considered the proceedings there to have stretched beyond those limits. The severe criticisms of the religious leaders in Matthew 23 admittedly do not reflect the humility of Jesus, but again their sheer hypocrisy called forth his righteous indignation.

Closely akin to the avoidance of offence is the inculcation of a forgiving spirit. Not only did Jesus hold out promises of forgiveness, but he also expected his followers to forgive as God forgives. This basic principle is starkly stated in the Lord's prayer and in the advice on limitless forgiveness given to Peter (Mt. 18:22 = Lk.17:3–4).[37] It is further supported by the parable of the unmerciful servant (Mt. 18:35). The close correlation between God's forgiveness and man's forgiveness forms an important factor in the ethics of Jesus. Recognition of this will avoid misunderstanding. Man's forgiveness, is not expected any more than God's to be based on an overlooking of evil. Any act of forgiveness is dependent on the willingness of the forgiven party to accept it. A wrong-doer must repent of his wrong before he can expect reconciliation.

A corollary of a forgiving spirit is the renunciation of vindictiveness, another notable feature in the ethics of Jesus. There were, of course, limits on vindictiveness in the Mosaic law, as evidenced by the well-known *lex talionis* (an eye for an eye).[38] Although at first sight this seems revengeful, it offered protection for those who might otherwise have lost two eyes for an eye. The approach of Jesus was revolutionary. The idea of turning the other cheek when one is struck, or going a further mile after a mile of enforced service, seems an impossible ethic (Mt. 5:38–42). Are the aggressive to get away with it without protest from the aggrieved? Jesus' answer is to take the sting out of the grievance. Such action as he recommended is no weak option, for it takes courage and moral resolve deliberately to suppress vindictiveness and inculcate a generous approach. It must, of course, be recognized that Jesus was dealing with personal attitudes and was not here setting out a social ethic. There is no doubt, nevertheless, that the establishing of better relationships between individuals would inevitably have an impact on society as a whole.

The virtues which Jesus saw as essential to living are seen as the direct result of love.[39] Since Jesus summed up the OT law as love for God and for one's neighbour (Mt. 22:34–40 = Mk. 12:30–31 = Lk. 10:25–28), it is evident

---

[37] The need for repeated forgiveness was stressed in Judaism, but not to the unlimited extent insisted on by Jesus. I. H. Marshall, *op. cit.*, p. 643, considers that Luke's version with its reference to repentance is probably primary compared with Matthew's account. But both emphasize unlimited forgiveness.

[38] *Cf.* Ex. 21:24; Dt. 19:21; Lv. 24:20.

[39] On love as a motive in NT ethics, *cf.* W. Lillie, *Studies in New Testament Ethics*, pp. 163–181; *idem, The Law of Christ* (1956), pp. 108–119; C. Spicq, *Agapē in the New Testament* 1 (1963); J. Moffatt, *Love in the New Testament* (1929); A. Nygren, *Agape and Eros* (1953), pp. 61–159; P. Ramsey, *Basic Christian Ethics.*

that love played a dominant part in his approach to religious and social responsibilities. Love for God will lead a person to do his will (*cf.* Mt. 7:21) and to trust in God's care and provision (*cf.* Mt. 7:11). It removes at once the evil of self-sufficiency.

Love for one's neighbour was interpreted by Jesus in the widest possible way to include anyone, even those of a different race (as seen in the parable of the good Samaritan). Such an enlargement of the scope of neighbourly love is another of the revolutionary aspects of Jesus' ethics. It is so revolutionary that it has yet to be achieved except among those who are totally committed to the teaching of Jesus. The modern movement for human rights is based on a principle that Jesus himself laid down, *i.e.* that no kind of person is exempt from respect as an individual. Even so, this modern movement has not gone, and cannot go, as far as Jesus did in insisting on love. It is naturally open to question whether anyone can be commanded to love. In a Hebrew context this would have presented no difficulty, for it would be tantamount to requiring actions to demonstrate that love was present. If our neighbours need care and we show care, we are showing love. But it is important to recognize that love for neighbours is inseparable from love for God. It is the latter which inspires the former.

POWERFUL FACTORS IN THE MORAL LIFE

Even more important than a survey of the specific ethical injunctions of Jesus is a consideration of the controlling factors in the moral life of the disciple. It is difficult to isolate these from the total presentation of the mission of Jesus and its application. Nevertheless certain principles may be discerned which have a special bearing on ethical decisions.

(i) We have already considered love to God and man in our previous section and we need here only mention it again as a dominant imperative. God's love for us draws out our love for him, which in turn produces love for others. This love can become so strong that it can embrace enemies as well as friends (Mt. 5:44). It therefore requires us to do more than simply like people. Jesus expected love to stretch to the seemingly unlovable.[40]

(ii) Some see the golden rule (Mt. 7:12) as a major guide to ethical decisions. Our own actions and attitudes are to be governed by what we expect from others towards ourselves. Jesus gave a positive form to a Jewish rule which was expressed in a negative form, 'Do not do what you do not wish others to do to you.'[41] While it may have some usefulness, this negative form is inadequate to initiate action. It can only prevent.

---

[40] Among the Qumran covenanters love was recommended towards God's elect, but hate towards those whom God had rejected. Nowhere in Jewish sources is a parallel to love towards enemies to be found. *Cf.* D. Hill's discussion on this (*Matthew*, pp. 129f.).

[41] This rule was enunciated by Rabbi Hillel, but in the fourth century BC Isocrates of Athens had stated it in an almost identical negative form. *Cf.* E. Schweizer's comments on these forms, *Matthew*, pp. 174f.

Jesus, however, was concerned with motives which produced positive results. It would be wrong to maintain that he was suggesting a self-centred motive, for his purpose is quite the reverse. Concern for others must not be less than concern for oneself.

(iii) Another factor is the positive rejection of what is contrary to the will of God. Jesus never adopted a legalistic approach to ethics. The standard was nothing less than God's will, and determination of what was right or wrong was dependent on that. It was imperative for the disciples of Jesus to repent of evil as a prerequisite for living a life pleasing to God. Jesus demanded nothing less than the perfection of God, the heavenly Father, as a standard for people (Mt. 5:48). This at once involves a recognition that anything falling short of God's own perfection is unacceptable. In no more vivid way could Jesus have rejected self-love and self-satisfaction as a basis for ethical decision.[42]

(iv) The followers of Jesus have a perfect example in Jesus himself. It is remarkable that the synoptic gospels do not ostensibly state that Jesus is an example for behaviour. In John, Jesus himself makes such a claim (see pp. 908ff.). Yet even in the portrayal of Jesus as a perfect man the synoptic writers, though perhaps unconsciously, provide a powerful moral incentive. If the true humanity of Jesus is established in these gospels (see discussion on pp. 221ff.), it must necessarily follow that he provides a complete pattern for the behaviour of his followers. He becomes the ideal against which ethical decision and action may be judged.

(v) One of the most positive guidelines, which is closely akin to the preceding, is the consciousness in believers that they should act in accordance with their new status as sons of God. Obviously this restricts the relevance of the ethical teaching to those who have entered into a filial relationship with God. They are under obligation to please their heavenly Father. This is the positive side of what is set out in section (iii) above.

(vi) Another principle is regard for truth. Jesus was concerned that, when people spoke, their words would be dependable. He was against the use of oaths to make one's statements seem more impressive (Mt. 5:33–37). It was customary among the Jews to use oaths for this purpose, but Jesus' instruction is clear: a person's word should be truthful without needing to be buttressed with oaths. Respect for truth and especially the reliability of the pledged word is of utmost importance in the ethics of Jesus. The whole field of honesty, in action as well as in word, is essential if people are to have right relations with each other. Deceit was one of the evils which Jesus denounced (cf. Mk. 7:22, where it appears in a list which includes immorality, theft and even murder).

---

[42] On Mt. 5:48, cf. B. Rigaux, 'Révélation des Mystères et Perfection à Qumran et dans le Nouveau Testament', *NTS* 4, 1958, pp. 237–262. (esp. p. 249). D. Hill, *Matthew*, p. 131, does not see in 'perfection' here 'flawless moral character', but whole-hearted devotion to the imitation of God.

(vii) Jesus had an important point to make regarding materialism. In one specific case he told a wealthy young man to sell what he had and give the proceeds to the poor (Mt. 19:21 = Mk. 10:21).[43] But no general rule may be based on this particular case beyond the fact that if wealth is a stumbling-block it is best to dispose of it. Certainly Jesus did not expect his followers to set much store by material possessions. His main teaching about this on a personal level is summed up in the advice, 'Do not lay up for yourselves treasures on earth' (Mt. 6:19f.; *cf.* Lk. 12:33).[44] The key to the meaning is found in the saying, 'Where your treasure is, there will your heart be also' (Mt. 6:21). Jesus is clearly opposed to the idea of making wealth an end in itself. He made it clear that no-one could be ruled by both God and mammon (Mt. 6:24; Lk. 16:13). If he serves mammon (*i.e.* materialism), he cannot serve God. What a person possesses is no indication of his true worth (*cf.* Lk. 12:15). This part of the ethic of Jesus demands a radical reappraisal of the materialistic way of life.

A general rule for priorities is found in the injunction, 'Seek first his kingdom and his righteousness, and all these things shall be yours as well' (Mt. 6:33). This certainly does not mean that spiritual pursuits are a means for economic gain. Jesus was in fact referring to the necessities of life (food and clothing). It implies, therefore, that those devoting themselves to the interests of the kingdom may be sure of these necessities. Jesus himself possessed no property and exemplifies his own injunction. His whole life was a seeking of the kingdom, and nothing more than the necessities were added to him.

John's gospel

Except for certain aspects of the farewell discourses (Chapters 14—16), this gospel is not strong on explicit ethical teaching. This is because its purpose is more definitely theological than that of the synoptic gospels. Since it was aimed to develop faith in the readers (20:30–31), it has more to say about believing than doing. Its goal is essentially spiritual, but this does not eliminate incidental ethical teaching, which is seen to follow naturally from Christian faith. This gospel does not present Jesus as a moral teacher, but as Christ and Son of God. The ethics is subordinate to the Christology. It may further be noted that ethical implications follow from the main themes in the gospel.

The mission of Jesus is summed up as light (1:5; 8:12) and the world is

---

[43] E. Schweizer, *Matthew*, p. 388, rightly denies that Jesus is supporting the idea of a superior class of disciples who were to meet more rigorous demands than others. He concedes, however, that for some a special form of service may be required. P. S. Minear, *Commands of Christ* (1972), p. 105, suggests that Jesus' command may be connected with the sending out of disciples to the mission field (*cf.* Mt. 10:5ff.).

[44] In this case Luke's account of the saying, unlike Matthew's, is dominated by positive imperatives. *Cf.* I. H. Marshall, *Luke*, p. 531.

seen as darkness (3:19; 12:35).[45] The gospel brings about a spiritual transformation which carries over with it a totally new range of ethical values. Darkness is directly linked with evil deeds (3:19). To turn deliberately away from darkness (8:12) is therefore to turn away from evil deeds. The motive for this is the personal dynamic of Jesus ('He who follows me will not walk in darkness'). There is no room for compromise. John presents Jesus as giving men no choice. As light, he expects deeds which can sustain the focus of light upon them. Jesus himself is seen as the standard of good against which all contrary actions and attitudes must be adjudged evil. Jesus contrasts his followers with the *kosmos*, because its deeds are evil (7:7).[46] It is clear, therefore, that Jesus conceived of his mission as precipitating a moral crisis. His followers could no longer live with the same ethic as the contemporary world.

One of the cardinal ethical principles which is supremely exemplified in the life of Jesus in this gospel is obedience to God's will.[47] The same principle has already been noted in the synoptics. In picturesque language Jesus claimed that his food was to do God's will (4:34). He did not seek his own will, but the will of him who sent him (5:30; 6:38ff.). It is not surprising that he expected similar obedience to God's will in his followers (7:17; 9:31). To fulfil God's will involves the surrender of one's own will, which amounts again to the surrender of self. It is important to notice that self-surrender in the teaching and example of Jesus never results in a vacuum. It is not merely a renunciation of self-will, but an adoption of a higher will, *i.e.* God's will.

We turn now specifically to the ethical teaching of the farewell discourses. The keynote of the approach of Jesus to his disciples was love (*agapē*). It was demonstrated in the feet-washing (13:1ff.). Since in this passage the act of service is described as 'an example' (13:15), the love which Jesus demonstrates has a definite content, involving a willingness to perform the most menial task on behalf of others. This concept of a personal example which provides a norm for others to imitate is a decided advance on a legalistic approach to ethics which demands obedience to the letter of a code of laws.[48] This personal aspect is brought out more vividly in John's account of the feet-washing than anywhere in the synoptics. The use of

---

[45] B. Lindars, *John*, p. 161, says that at the incarnation 'the hidden, inner, realities of man's moral state are exposed'. He points out that in Qumran terminology people of moral goodness are under the sway of the Angel of Light, and evil people under the Angel of Darkness.

[46] R. Bultmann, *John* (Eng. trans. 1971), p. 294, takes the mention of 'evil' here, not in the sense of 'immoral', but in the sense of worldly actions, by which he means a world incapable of a true decision. Yet the word *ponēros* cannot be emptied of moral content.

[47] On the example of Christ as a moral imperative, *cf.* W. Lillie, *Studies in New Testament Ethics*, pp. 24ff.

[48] It is not surprising that Bultmann, *John*, p. 476, with his existential viewpoint, denies that Jesus is the *hypodeigma* for an *Imitatio*, and prefers to see this statement as pointing to a new opportunity of existence together. Yet there is no reason to suppose that some definite imitation may not be in mind, especially in view of the imitation theme elsewhere in the NT.

this term 'example' by Jesus is of fundamental importance for a consideration of the nature of the ethics of Jesus.

John has preserved for us a saying which provides a vital motive for right behaviour. It is phrased as a new commandment: that you love one another (13:34). The quality of that love has to conform to the love which Jesus has for his disciples. It was this element of personal example which the Mosaic law lacked, and which justifies the description of a 'new' commandment.[49] Jesus had summed up the law as love to God and to neighbour, but his 'new commandment' adds a powerful new dimension resulting from commitment to himself.[50] Since the farewell discourses are set in the passion narrative, the 'new commandment' in John may be seen as parallel to the inauguration of the 'new covenant' through the institution of the Lord's supper in the synoptics. The dominant feature of the new covenant is its inward character. It was concerned with inward motives rather than adherence to a code of laws. It is for this reason that it would focus on love. No code of law could adjudicate on love.

An even more significant contribution towards motivation in pursuit of ethical standards is found in John's account of the teaching of Jesus on the Holy Spirit (see pp. 527ff.). Since the disciples were promised the indwelling of the Spirit and could therefore rely on his guidance, they were not left to make their own unaided ethical decisions. The Spirit would bring to mind the teaching of Jesus (14:26) which would provide the basis for their behaviour. The Spirit would act as 'another' Counsellor, *i.e.* would repeat the same function that Jesus had performed (14:16). When Jesus promised that the Spirit would guide his disciples into 'all the truth' (16:13), this cannot be restricted to doctrinal truth.[51] The key to the Spirit's guidance is that he glorifies Christ. The believer is promised a helper in all situations to decide what course of action would glorify Christ.

The most specific passage which links the Spirit's activity with moral judgments is 16:8, where it is the Spirit who convinces the world of sin, righteousness and judgment. This special work of the Spirit is seen in the initial conviction of people, which leads them to recognize themselves as sinners in God's sight. The reason given for the sin is lack of faith in Christ. If this is the negative aspect, the positive is that the Spirit will bring to their consciousness standards of righteousness.[52] This will be done by

[49] J. Jeremias, *NTT* 1, p. 213, considers that the breadth of Jesus' commandment to love is without parallel, and justifies the description 'new'.

[50] The new commandment to love one another as a supplement to the requirement to love one's neighbour is not a narrower, but a more comprehensive, view. For comment on this, *cf.* E. C. Hoskyns (ed. F. N. Davey), *The Fourth Gospel* (²1947), p. 451.

[51] R. E. Brown, *John* (*AB*, 1966), p. 715, notes that the Paraclete's guidance here involves more than deeper intellectual understanding. It involves also a way of life.

[52] B. Lindars, *John*, p. 502, regards 'righteousness' here in the sense of judicial vocabulary. He denies that moral perfection is in mind. He suggests that it was probably the best word to express the opposite of *hamartia*.

bringing to mind the pattern of the life of Christ after his departure to the Father. The world will not be left without an effective standard, although the perfect human example is no longer visible. The Spirit's work in judgment would seem to consist of convincing men of the nature of right and wrong and showing them the judgment already pronounced on this world's ruler.

Acts

In view of the nature of this book, with its predominance of historical narrative interspersed with preaching, it is not surprising that there is little specific ethical teaching. Nevertheless Acts makes an important contribution to the whole field of NT ethics in its emphasis on the practical guidance of the Holy Spirit.[53] As already seen in the teaching of Jesus in John's gospel the Spirit was promised as a guide and Acts illustrates the fulfilment of this.

Because of this emphasis on the Spirit after Pentecost, there is a marked difference between the pre- and post-resurrection periods in the approach to Christian ethics. In many ways the teaching of Jesus was impossible. It set the ideal, but it was prospective to the period when the Spirit would supply the dynamic for putting it into practice. Those who have attempted to carry out the injunctions of the Sermon on the Mount without the power of the Spirit have soon discovered the hopelessness of the task. Whereas the book of Acts does not illustrate the specific application of the injunctions of the Sermon on the Mount, it nevertheless shows several ways in which the activity of the Spirit produces surprising ethical results.

The first important principle to note is that the believers in the early church did not rely for moral guidance on the élite group of moral teachers. Every Christian was possessed and led by the Holy Spirit. There was therefore a common basis for approach to ethical issues. The Spirit was known as the Holy Spirit because his nature and also his demands were holy. He was the Spirit of truth who would not lead into decisions involving moral error.

We note first of all that certain virtues are associated with the infilling of the Spirit. There are specific references to the manifestation of wisdom (6:3), faith (6:5; 11:24), grace and power (6:8), directly connected with fullness of the Spirit. In addition, joy, peace and consolation are also the result of the Spirit's work (13:52; 9:31). These virtues were spontaneously manifested in those indwelt by the Spirit. They were not, moreover, confined to those set apart for specific tasks, but were shared by the church

---

[53] For the various ways in which the Spirit effected a transformation in the lives of the early Christians, cf. J. H. E. Hull's *The Holy Spirit in the Acts of the Apostles* (1967), especially pp. 125–168 on the meaning of the gift.

as a whole. Some, however, like Stephen, seem to have shown them in greater measure.

Although among the virtues produced by the Spirit there is no direct reference to love (*agapē*), yet there are incidents included which show the strong bond of affection which existed among the first believers. The spontaneous sharing in 2:44ff. and 4:34ff. was an expression of Christian love. Dorcas gave expression to her love by acts of charity (9:36ff.). There were touching scenes of Christian affection towards Paul when he left the Ephesian elders at Miletus (20:36f.) and similarly at Tyre (21:7ff.). Acts seems to assume the naturalness of Christian love, without the necessity for expounding it as is done in the epistles.

We next note the part played by the Spirit in moral judgment. The case of Ananias and Sapphira (5:1ff.) is notable in this respect, for Peter makes clear that their deceit was against the Holy Spirit, not against the church. The drastic nature of the punishment served to strike fear in the whole community (5:11). The Spirit of God was seen to be the guardian of the moral purity of the church. The clear expression by Peter of the principle underlying private property was under the guidance of the Spirit. He did not condemn possessions, but only the deceit involved in pretending to give all and yet retaining part possession. If the punishment seems harsh, it does at least highlight how important it was for the words of Christians to be dependable.[54] There was to be no place for expediency or double standards in the Christian ethic. The sanction used in this case was more than a punishment to those involved; it was a serious warning which was to have a salutary effect on the developing ethic of the Christian church.

Another issue in which the Spirit played an important part in giving guidance is that of relationships between Jews and Gentiles. The circumcision issue was more than a matter of religious scruples. It was a question whether Christian faith was powerful enough to overcome racial prejudices. The fact that a Jewish Christian such as Peter was prepared to go into the Gentile home of Cornelius was a remarkable advance in human relationships in the contemporary world (Acts 10). It took a special vision and the prompting of the Spirit to achieve it, but it is yet another instance of the development of a new sense of values which would never have been arrived at except through the guidance of the Spirit. Similarly at the Jerusalem Council meeting in Acts 15, James reports that the decision reached was a decision of the Holy Spirit (15:28).

This evidence from Acts is of utmost importance when the ethical teaching of the epistles is considered, for it serves as a link between the ethical teaching of Jesus and those epistles. It supplies the key which is frequently

---

[54] F. F. Bruce, *The Book of the Acts* (*NICNT*, 1954), p. 114, suggests that the judgment on Ananias may have been an act of mercy as well, in the light of 1 Cor. 5:5.

reiterated in the rest of the NT, *i.e.* the moral guidance of the Holy Spirit. Inevitably much of the ethical teaching of the epistles will merge with what has already been said under the section on the new life in Christ. We need to be reminded that a new humanity which emerged 'in Christ' necessarily had to forge new ethical standards which would be consonant with the indwelling Spirit. While Acts shows that new humanity reacting to its old environment without theological debate over the issues involved, it nevertheless presupposes that no approach to moral issues was conceivable except from a theological point of view.

Paul

It has already been seen that Paul's theology gives an important place to the new humanity which has been brought into being in Christ. His exposition of the doctrine of grace has pointed to a transformation of personal ethics, since new creatures in Christ must inescapably evolve a new scale of values in harmony with their new status. In examining Paul's ethical teaching we must avoid treating it in isolation. Indeed, it is an essential part of his whole theological system. Our first consideration must, therefore, be to examine the relation of his ethics both to the ethics of Jesus and to his own theological exposition of the person in Christ.[55] We shall then consider the nature of Paul's position, both in its negative approach (*i.e.* what it does not consist of in relation to other ethical systems), and in its positive approach (*i.e.* what is distinctive about it). Having singled out its characteristic features, we shall examine the motives to which Paul appealed for the enjoining of personal ethics. Our concluding section will attempt to classify Paul's ethical terminology to bring out the particular areas of Christian behaviour which called for special mention.

THE RELATION OF PAUL'S ETHICS TO HIS OTHER TEACHING

It is obviously important to examine the relationship between the ethics of Paul and the ethics of Jesus. We have already noted the seemingly idealistic character of the Sermon on the Mount and the impression of the impossibility created by it. Paul's ethical teaching must have drawn upon the teaching of Jesus, although there is little direct evidence of this, and in any case he received it from others. Nevertheless, he makes many ethical judgments which are developments from the basic premises which Jesus advanced. What is very important to note is that Paul did not forge his ethics *de novo*. In no sense does his ethics stand over against the ethics of Jesus. Indeed, there are no cases where there are contradictions. On the contrary, there are many features which are closely parallel, such as the

[55] For a careful study of the basis of Paul's ethical teaching, *cf.* V. P. Furnish, *Theology and Ethics in Paul* (1968).

constraining power of love (*agapē*), the attitude to the OT law and the necessity for the Spirit's assistance in the making of moral decisions.

In all of these areas, however, Paul theologizes and brings out more clearly the subjects treated. What appears in bud in the ethics of Jesus appears in full flower in Paul.[56] This is to be expected in view of the dawning of the age of the Spirit when the apostle wrote. It was foreshadowed in the teaching of the Master. As we examine the details of Paul's ethical teaching, both his indebtedness to the ethics of Jesus and his own distinctive contribution will become clear.

No approach to Paul's ethics which does not see it rooted in his theology is likely to prove correct, for his theological expositions demand an application which profoundly affects the whole man, not least in his moral decisions. No more than in the teaching of Jesus can the moral advice given become intelligible except in the context of a definite commitment to faith. There is no question, therefore, of taking Paul's ethical injunctions and making them the basis of a general ethical system. Although it would no doubt be valuable for non-Christians to take note of what the apostle says about morals, he never supposes that those not 'in Christ' will have any obligation to do so. He has no doubt, however, that those in 'Christ' will act and think in certain ways which run counter to general conventions. Paul's ethics are definitely for those who are a part of the new humanity in Christ.[57]

The reason why the theological basis is integral to a right understanding of Paul's ethics is that it supplies the dynamic for putting the ethical advice into practice. Those who do not accept the theological basis may admire the moral judgments, but feel totally unable or unwilling to carry them out. Those, however, who have experienced the great Pauline truths of justification, redemption, reconciliation, adoption and sanctification will recognize that at every point doctrine will carry with it ethical implications. A doctrinal position which makes no moral difference can find no support in Paul's epistles. Indeed, it is a characteristic of many of those epistles that an ethical section is added after the doctrinal exposition. The close connection between ethics and doctrine is in no sense accidental for Paul. He could not conceive of a separation between them.

---

[56] There has been much debate over whether or not Paul regarded the example of Jesus to be one of the mainsprings of his ethics. He rarely alludes to the teaching of Jesus, but this does not necessarily mean that he was ignorant of it. As Anderson Scott says, 'Paul may supplement but he never contradicts his Master' (*New Testament Ethics*, p. 75). See further discussion on this on pp. 224f.

[57] J. W. Drane, 'Tradition, Law and Ethics in Pauline Theology', *NovT* 16 (1974), pp. 167–178, writes, 'Morality is not judged by rules and regulations, but according to the kind of existence a man has, whether dominated by *sarx* or *pneuma*' (p. 172). He finds this in Galatians but a rather different picture in 1 Corinthians. In the latter he finds the idea of morality that can be taught. There is certainly a difference in expression, but it may be questioned whether there is the considerable movement towards law-ethics which Drane claims. He admits that the indwelling Christ is still the basis of morality.

PAUL'S PRINCIPLES OF APPROACH

In considering the nature of Paul's ethic we shall first note the negative side and then follow it with the positive.[58]

We first observe the *non-systematic* character of Paul's ethic. He does not set out a moral blueprint either for individuals or society. There is something almost haphazard about the way he arranges the ethical material in his epistles. There is no pattern about it. It is drawn out of his practical concern for the churches to which he writes. He goes into much greater detail than Jesus did, for he had learned from his experience of the churches that the Christians, most of whom had come from a pagan background, needed ethical advice spelt out in such detail. Sometimes his advice touches the obvious, as when he urges the stealer not to steal (Eph. 4:28), which shows the low moral standards of the environment from which many of the early Christians had come.[59] In spite of his profound teaching about the new life and the guidance of the Spirit, Paul was too much of a realist to suppose that his converts would at once reach maturity in their moral judgments. He deals with issues as they arise and this adds considerably to his value as an ethical teacher.

There is nothing remote or artificial about his advice. It was essentially down to earth. Nothing could be farther removed from the ethical systems of philosophers, both ancient and modern. There was no point at which a Christian could say that he had morally attained the ideal. Even Paul himself recognized that he must still press on (Phil. 3:12f.).

The second observation to be made is that Paul's ethics are *non-ascetic*, in spite of giving an occasional appearance of rigour.[60] His approach to marriage is the most striking example of advice to abstain. Yet it must be noted that, although Paul himself abstained from marriage and encouraged others to do the same, he clearly did not consider marriage in any sense to be sinful (*cf.* 1 Cor. 7:28, 39). In advising the single state Paul was governed by what he considered to be the immediate demands of God's service (*cf.* the whole discussion in 1 Cor. 7). He seemed to have been influenced by his belief in the imminence of the parousia (*cf.* 1 Cor. 7:26, 29). There is no suggestions that his advice on marriage could form the basis of a universal ethic on the subject, which would clearly result in the extinction of the race (see further the comment on pp. 950ff.). He takes an eminently sensible view of such matters as material possessions. He does not rigorously deny them, but he counts them of poor value compared with the spiritual riches he has in Christ (Phil. 3). He is not averse to receiving

---

[58] *Cf.* L. H. Marshall, *The Challenge of New Testament Ethics*, 217ff., for a fuller discussion of Paul's approach. The three points mentioned in this section are taken from Marshall.

[59] M. Barth, *Ephesians* (AB, 1974), p. 515, suggests that the word rendered 'thief' may be intended to include those who make money without working. Some in the Christian community may well have been making a living in dubious ways.

[60] *Cf.* L. H. Marshall, *op. cit.*, pp. 220ff., against the view that Paul was ascetic.

contributions of money towards his work (Phil. 4:14ff.).

In one passage Paul rejects the idea of rigorous taboos (do not handle, taste or touch, Col. 2:21). It would seem that some were wanting to make asceticism a test of orthodoxy, but Paul will give no support to this. He will not countenance any ethical standards which would lead to a ritual burden, nor is his ethical approach governed by a list of prohibitions.[61] Christians were intended to be free. Nevertheless he recognized the need for self-discipline, as 1 Corinthians 9:25ff. clearly shows. Such self-discipline was to be exercized within an alien environment and did not consist in escaping from it. Paul gives no warrant for monasticism.

The third point is that Paul's ethics are *non-legalistic*. This is of great importance in assessing his real significance as an ethical teacher. In social ethics laws are the means of setting standards and enforcing them. But a legalistic ethic has serious limitations, for it can deal only with overt acts, not with motives or intentions. Jesus had noted this in relation to the Mosaic law; Paul's approach is similar, although lacking the same authority in re-interpreting the law. He recognizes that the law is 'holy, just and good' (Rom. 7:12)[62], and yet knew from his own experience man's impotence to carry it out. His theology did not depend on his own achievements, but on the grace of God. A legalistic approach to ethics could not, however, find room for grace. The gospel demanded a different moral approach from a written code.[63] The Mosaic law consisted of a series of dos and don'ts which still stand as a pattern, but could do nothing to supply the necessary moral power. It is for this reason that Paul came to see law as an ally of sin, which took advantage of the commandment (Rom. 7:11). We have already discussed Paul's approach to the law (pp. 687ff.), but we need here to note that his rejection of a legalistic approach to salvation necessarily carries with it a non-legalistic approach to ethics.[64]

A person who could not be saved by the law can hardly be expected to live by the law. He needs more than a written code to set out his standard of behaviour. When Paul says that 'the written code kills, but the Spirit gives life' (2 Cor. 3:6), he expresses in a nutshell, both the rejection of a legal ethical code and the assertion of the superiority of the ethic of the Holy Spirit. It is this latter point which furnishes us with the positive principle of Paul's approach.

[61] As F. F. Bruce, *Colossians*, (in *Ephesians & Colossians*, NICNT, 1957, by E. K. Simpson and F. F. Bruce), p. 254, points out, prohibitions of this kind are valuable for children, but not for the age of responsibility.

[62] It is noticeable that in this statement, as C. E. B. Cranfield, *Romans* 1 (*ICC*, 1975), p. 353, points out, it is not only the law as a whole which is declared to be holy, but each individual commandment.

[63] *Cf.* J. F. Bottorff, 'The Relation of Justification and Ethics in the Pauline Epistles', *SJT* 26, 1973, pp. 421ff., who speaks of the need for power to be actualized, and this leads him to emphasize the place of faith. He talks of a believer acting 'in' and 'out' of faith.

[64] L. H. Marshall, *op. cit.*, p. 228, cites Hosten's view that for the Christian 'the Law is abolished, not only as the principle of salvation but also as the principle of conduct'.

We may say that Paul's ethic was essentially *Spirit-directed*. In considering the doctrine of the Spirit we have already commented on the practical effects of the indwelling Spirit (pp. 553ff.). It is necessary here to do no more than reiterate that the Spirit works from within and supplies the dynamic to effect, as well as to provide the guidance to decide, suitable ethical standards. It is the Spirit who produces 'fruit' in the Christian life (Gal. 5:22). Yet it would be wrong to suppose that Paul removes ethics by this means from the sphere of human responsibility. The distinction between legal ethics and Spirit-directed ethics is that the former can produce only rules and regulations and utter condemnation against those who disobey, while the latter brings the mind of the Christian into line with the right standards and attitudes and captures the support of the will. It is the difference in approach between 'thou shalt' and 'I will'. This means neither that the Spirit does everything, nor that the moral guidance is piecemeal. The indwelling Spirit gives such consistent guidance to the Christian that Paul can actually talk of the law of the Spirit (Rom. 8:2); by this he means, not some hard and fast code, but the consistent principles by which the Spirit activates the Christian life.[65]

Paul's teaching on the Spirit elucidates his understanding of the new covenant in which God's law was to be written on people's hearts instead of on tables of stone (Je. 31:31). Although the apostle does not specifically apply this Jeremiah passage to his ethical teaching, his insistence on the inner motives rather than on external directives is fully in line with the superiority of the new over the old covenant.

Moreover, the emphasis on the Spirit makes Paul's moral advice essentially *personal*. The Spirit principle is of paramount importance for a right understanding of the ethical exhortations in the epistles. Although theoretically the apostle knew that the guidance of the Spirit was sufficient of itself to give moral directions, he nevertheless goes into considerable detail on specific issues because he recognized the weakness of human nature, even redeemed human nature, in the Christians to whom he wrote. It is significant that after giving his opinion on the marriage problem which he discusses in 1 Corinthians 7:39–40, Paul says, 'I think that I have the Spirit of God.'[66] His suggestions on moral issues must not be divorced from his conviction that not only he himself but also his readers were led by the Spirit (Rom 8:14). This does not mean that there will be no room for difference of opinion on some moral issues, but it does imply that the Spirit would ensure a basic consistency in behavioural patterns among

---

[65] C. K. Barrett, *Romans* (BC, 1957), p. 155, interprets this law of the Spirit as a way of life, characterized by the gift of the Spirit. The whole process 'is put into effect and operates in Christ'.

[66] C. K. Barrett, *1 Corinthians* (BC, [2]1971), p. 186, suggests that the Corinthians were probably claiming to possess the Spirit, but were unwilling to consider views and practices obtaining elsewhere. F. F. Bruce, *1 and 2 Corinthians*, pp. 77f., takes the expression to imply not spiritual authority, but spiritual wisdom.

those who have submitted themselves to his guidance.

It goes without saying that the Spirit-directed approach to ethics has more point in the realm of personal than of social ethics, but in our consideration of the latter we shall need to bear in mind the social implications of a body of people who are all under the moral guidance of the Holy Spirit.

POWERFUL FACTORS IN PAUL'S ETHICAL TEACHING

What has just been said about the Spirit in Paul's ethics must be extended when our attention is turned to the important subject of motives and other influences. If the indwelling Spirit induces the desire to fulfil the will of God and the believer whole-heartedly responds to it, there will be no need for further impetus. But Paul is not so sanguine about man's whole-heartedness as to suppose that other incentives are not necessary. There are several factors to which he appeals.

The dominant incentive is perhaps love (*agapē*). We have seen how Jesus summed up the law in terms of love (pp. 904f.). Paul is in line with this when he maintains that God's *agapē* 'has been poured into our hearts through the Holy Spirit which has been given to us' (Rom. 5:5). The pattern for our love is nothing less than his love for us.[67] Moreover, Paul also sums up the law in love to one's neighbour (Gal. 5:14; Rom. 13:8). Where love towards others exists, it cannot fail to produce a profound impression on attitudes and relationships. If the Christian has an obligation to love, his moral judgments will need to be in line with that love. Paul's peerless hymn of love (1 Cor. 13) vividly illustrates this point. It is striking what love will prevent a person from doing: many of Paul's statements in 1 Corinthians 13 are set in a negative cast. Altogether the apostle sees love as both a powerful deterrent and a mighty impetus. Since love is a gift of the Spirit, it is but an extension of the Spirit's work. Wherever love transforms human relationships, it is evidence of the Spirit at work.

Another incentive to right moral action is the power of example, the supreme instance of which is the example of Christ.[68] There are surprisingly few references in his epistles to the earthly life of Jesus, but he assumes that the example of Christ's humiliation (Phil. 2:5ff.) is a pattern for Christians. When encouraging the Corinthians to develop liberality, Paul sets out the poverty of Christ as exemplary (2 Cor. 8:9). But he does not

[67] H. Ridderbos, *Paul* (Eng. trans. 1975), p. 297, well brings out the importance of love in Pauline paraenesis by describing the other wide varieties of exhortation as 'forms of love'. He points out that for Paul these virtues are brought under the viewpoint of brotherly communion, in contrast to the use of the same terms in non-Christian Greek ethics, where they are related to character formation. *Cf.* also R. Bultmann, *TNT* 2, p. 225.

[68] For a full discussion of this theme, *cf.* E. J. Tinsley's chapter, 'The Imitation of Christ in Paul', in his *The Imitation of God in Christ* (1960), pp. 134–165.

restrict the power of example to that of Christ. He dares to appeal to his own example, which is in turn patterned on Christ's (1 Cor. 4:15ff.; 11:1; 1 Thes. 1:6). If the invitation to be imitators of Paul seems at first audacious, it must be remembered that the most effective guide to ethics is to look to the manner of life of one who is wholly committed in Christ to the pursuit of the highest end.[69] Since no ethics text books existed in those days, the example of a good-living Christian would stand out among his pagan contemporaries. In a general way Paul uses appeal to Christ's example almost incidentally (cf. Rom. 15:7; Eph. 5:2; 25, 29; Col. 3:13).

We may next note various factors which determine the content of right behaviour for a Christian. We note first the sense of what is fitting. This at once excludes certain evils, such as foul or inane language which are not fitting (Eph. 5:3ff.). In the same passage Paul urges his readers to walk as 'children of light' (Eph. 5:8), which presupposes that they will know the kind of living suitable to the metaphor of light, and also will recognize the difference between this and the 'darkness'. The Christian, in Paul's view, soon develops a sense of what is fitting for his new station 'in Christ'. A similar principle is expressed in 1 Corinthians 6:12; 10:23.[70]

In two passages in 1 Corinthians Paul expounds a principle which, when properly applied, provides a powerful rule for the making of right ethical decisions. He concedes that all things may be lawful, but does not concede that what is permissible is necessarily advisable (1 Cor. 6:12ff.; 10:23ff.). In both passages he applies the principle to essentially practical issues. It is closely linked with his advice to the strong and the weak, and reminds us that the strong must be prepared to waive what is lawful if it would cause a stumblingblock for the weak. A rigid application of the principle of lawfulness would result in a harsh ethic and would ignore the personal problems which arise. Paul's Christian approach will not permit anyone's 'liberty' to ride roughshod over the sensitivity of others.

Another factor in the apostle's approach is his frequent appeals to reason and understanding. He tells his readers that their new life in Christ involves a change of approach to behaviour (Col. 3:1ff.). Certain facets of the old life must be consciously 'put off' and certain specifically Christian virtues must be 'put on'. It is clear that Paul does not expect this to happen automatically. It requires the application of mind to ethical decisions. He expects the spiritual person, who is setting his mind 'on things above', to come to a right understanding of what it means for his life to be hid with

---

[69] It should also be noted, as Tinsley, op. cit., p. 139, points out, that in these passages calling for imitation Paul is dealing with suffering or some form of humiliation. This would guard against abuse or a personality cult. 'What is to be imitated is Paul's self-abnegation.'

[70] The principle expressed here, 'All things are lawful but all things are not expedient', must not be interpreted as an act of compromise. The meaning is that all things do not promote the general well-being, cf. L. H. Marshall, The Challenge of New Testament Ethics, pp. 311f.

Christ in God (Col. 3:3).[71] Closely linked with this is the fact that the renewed mind knows what is the will of God, what is good and acceptable and perfect (Rom. 12:2). Sanctification brings with it new insights into God's will, which are applied in the most practical ways, as the sequence in Romans 12 and 13 shows. The believer is a person who seeks to please God (2 Cor. 5:9; Eph. 5:10). God's will becomes the norm for Christian living, and the Christian mind is expected to seek an understanding of that will.

On one occasion Paul appeals to another consideration which has ethical implications – the expectation of the near return of Christ – as an important factor affecting an ethical decision (1 Cor. 7:26ff.).[72] Paul is advocating the single state as preferable in view of the 'impending distress'. His concern here is not to condemn marriage, but to spare people from having additional worldly troubles. Clearly advice given in conditions of particular stress would not necessarily apply in more normal conditions. It is striking that he does not more often appeal to eschatological motives in view of his strong belief in the parousia. It certainly cannot be said to be a dominant feature of his ethical teaching.

We must not omit the effect of the community principle in Paul's ethics. Since all believers belong to the community, their individual actions affect the community as a whole. Thus what any member of the body does affects the whole community. Paul's frequent use of the body metaphor has ethical implications. In Romans 12:4ff. the body illustration is immediately followed by specific exhortations of an ethical kind, which not only affect oneself but concern others (*e.g.* 'love one another with brotherly affection', Rom. 12:10).

PAUL'S ETHICAL TERMS

In several places in Paul's epistles there are lists either of virtues or of vices. These lists throw a good deal of light on Paul's approach to ethics. They help to redress any impression that for the apostle ethics was merely incidental. The use of ethical lists may moreover be paralleled in non-Christian literature and this shows that Paul is following a contemporary pattern, although undoubtedly putting his own stamp upon it by setting it in a specifically Christian theological framework.[73] Indeed comment has

---

[71] R. P. Martin, *Colossians: The Church's Lord and the Christian's Liberty* (1972), p. 103, points out that Paul's language here must be distinguished from gnostic mysticism which blurred the distinction between the redeemer and the redeemed.

[72] Many scholars have linked ethics with eschatology in Paul's thought. *Cf.* V. P. Furnish, *Theology and Ethics in Paul* (1968); G. Bornkamm, *Paul* (Eng. trans. 1971), pp. 196–227; R. Scroggs, *Paul for a New Day* (1977), pp. 57–82.

[73] For a discussion of the use of house-tables (*i.e.* current lists of ethical duties) in Paul's ethical instructions, *cf.* W. Lillie, 'The Pauline House-Tables', *ExT* 86, 1975, pp. 179ff., who suggests that these tables may represent the more traditional ethical advice and may have been included, at least in Col. 3:18–4:1, to

already been made on some aspects of Christian virtues when the new life in Christ was outlined (see pp. 667ff.), but some further word needs adding to bring these virtues into perspective within personal ethics.

Virtues to be encouraged. The major lists of virtues are found in Galatians 5:22–23 (the fruit of the Spirit), Philippians 4:8 (things to think about), and Colossians 3:12–15 (what to put on). There are wide differences in the contents of these lists, but they all include qualities which may be expected to belong to the new life.

We may summarize these qualities in the following way.[74] The major theological virtues like love, joy and peace are placed at the head of the Galatians 5:22–23 list. The rest are expressions of these three. They sum up a life which is the antithesis of self-centredness, and which shows longsuffering, kindness, meekness and self-control. The two other virtues – goodness and faithfulness – relate in a general way to the Christian character. Altogether these virtues were illustrated *par excellence* in the perfect human life of Jesus, although Paul does not draw attention to this. He contents himself with attributing them all to the work of the Spirit. Since for Paul all Christians are possessed by the Spirit, it follows that all Christians may be expected to display these virtues. A Christian without meekness or self-control is as much an anomaly as a Christian without love. Some of the virtues are regarded with suspicion or even incredulity by many who do not possess the Spirit; they are too unselfish to be popular.

The list in Philippians 4:8 provides an invaluable guide for Christian thought which must then have an effect on action.[75] Indeed the significance of Paul's words is that patterns of thought play an important part in moulding the Christian character. Things true, honourable, just, pure, lovely, gracious, excellent – these are fit subjects for Christian thinking. They at once exclude anything which mars, defiles, creates tensions, or is ugly or second-rate. Paul is here making a profound psychological point, for he recognized that thought always precedes action, and as a person thinks so he is. Someone whose thoughts are pure, for instance, would not act in an impure way.[76]

---

correct a particular situation which had arisen. Other passages which Lillie classes in the same category are: the parallel passage in Eph. 5:21-6:9; Tit. 2:2-10; 3:1-8; 1 Tim. 2:1-15; 6:1; Rom. 13:1-7. Outside Paul's epistles only 1 Pet. 2:18-3:7 is relevant. *Cf.* also W. Schrage, 'Zur Ethik der neutestamentlichen Haustafelen', *NTS* 21, 1974, pp. 1–22; J. E. Crouch, *The Origin and Intention of the Colossian Haustafel* (1972).

[74] J. B. Lightfoot, *St Paul's Epistle to the Galatians* (1876), p. 212, classifies these virtues as follows: (i) Christian habits of mind; (ii) qualities affecting a Christian's relationship to others; (iii) principles which guide a Christian's conduct.

[75] J. N. Sevenster, *Paul and Seneca* (1961), pp. 152ff., finds evidence in Phil. 4:8 that Paul has borrowed from Stoic ethical terminology. He admits however that Paul writes in a different key. Verse 8 must not be isolated from verse 9.

[76] It has been suggested that the instruction in Phil. 4:8 may have been necessary to give guidance on moral standards to a church which was ethically confused, *cf.* R. P. Martin, *Philippians* (NCB, 1976), p. 32.

The Colossians passage contains many similar virtues to the Galatian passage: compassion, kindness, lowliness, meekness, patience, forbearance, a forgiving nature and above all love. Again there is the same absence of self-centredness and the same gentle approach to others. The person who has put on Christ has also put on his moral 'clothing'. The result is a complete transformation of attitudes.

In addition to the terms included in these lists there are many other scattered injunctions. There is, for instance, the penetrating sequence of exhortations in Romans 12 and 13.[77] Such advice as 'Let love be genuine' (Rom. 12:9), or 'Rejoice in your hope' (Rom. 12:12), or 'Live in harmony with one another' (Rom. 12:16), or 'Do not be haughty' (Rom. 12:16), or 'Repay no one evil for evil' (Rom. 12:17), illustrate the same qualities as in the lists of virtue. Again, the hymn of love in 1 Corinthians 13 is a marvellous expression of the quality which is ranked highest in both the Galatians and Colossians lists. The apostle has already prepared for this in the statement of 1 Corinthians 8:1, 'Love builds up.' This essentially practical epistle provides many illustrations of the application to specific problems of the attitudes expressed in the list of the fruit of the Spirit. In Ephesians 4:2, lowliness, meekness, patience and forbearance in love are all enjoined, and we note the similarities with the Colossians list. Again, in 1 Thessalonians 5 the advice given tallies closely with the previous advice: 'Be at peace among yourselves' (1 Thes. 5:13), 'See that none of you repays evil for evil' (1 Thes. 5:15), and 'Rejoice always' (1 Thes. 5:16), are examples of similar applications.

One of the features of the pastoral epistles is the number of ethical lists which are included. Most of these set out vices to be avoided, but some of them contain encouragements to develop virtues. We may first note the ethical qualities required for aspirants to church office, such as being temperate, sensible, dignified, hospitable and gentle[78] (1 Tim. 3:2–3). Deacons are expected to be serious (1 Tim. 3:8), and the women also serious as well as temperate and faithful (1 Tim. 3:11).[79] In the qualifications for bishops in Titus 1:7, 8, the positive qualities are blamelessness, a hospitable nature, love of good, sober-mindedness, justness, holiness, and self-control. All these qualities would have made a person stand out against the moral standards of his environment. It is in this sense that Paul could demand that candidates for office should be thought well of by outsiders (1 Tim.

---

[77] This section of Romans, although in no way giving a complete account of Christian ethics, nevertheless, as C. K. Barrett notes, *Romans*, p. 235, covers a wide field, dealing with moral issues along with comments on church life. It is a reminder again that ethics cannot be isolated in Paul's letters.

[78] Paul uses the word here rendered 'gentle' (*epieikēs*) three times (Phil. 4:5; 1 Tim. 3:3; Tit. 3:2) and the noun (*epieikia*) in 2 Cor. 10:1. See L. H. Marshall, *The Challenge of New Testament Ethics*, pp. 306ff., for a discussion of the meaning of the concept. He renders it 'gracious' or 'graciousness'.

[79] It is generally supposed that 1 Tim. 3:11 relates not to women in general, but to a special group whose task was to minister. *Cf.* J. N. D. Kelly, *The Pastoral Epistles*, (*BC*, 1963), pp. 83f.

3:7). These moral demands cannot, however, be restricted to the office bearers, for it is assumed that such qualities belong to the Christian character.

Another group of recommended qualities occurs in direct advice given to Timothy himself (cf. 1 Tim. 6:11; 2 Tim. 2:22). Here such qualities as righteousness, godliness, faith, love, steadfastness, gentleness, peace, are to be Timothy's aim. Moreover in 2 Timothy 3:10 Paul reminds Timothy of qualities which he has seen in the apostle: faith, patience, love, steadfastness. The consistency which these have with Paul's ethical lists shows that he has a well-defined concept of the character of a Christian person. There is nothing to suggest that he is conscious of expecting from Timothy any virtues which he did not expect from all Christians, including himself.[80]

A third type of list within the Pastorals is the kind which is addressed to Christians generally. 1 Timothy 6:17 contains special advice to wealthy people. Titus 2:2f. gives instruction for older men and women and then to younger men and slaves. The emphasis falls on gravity and sober-mindedness, but also soundness of faith and love. This advice is admittedly more sombre than in Paul's other epistles, but this may be accounted for by the difference of environment. There may have been a tendency to a frivolous approach which needed a corrective. In Titus 3:2 we again meet the demand for gentleness and courtesy, not only towards fellow believers, but towards everyone. It is noteworthy that reference is made in the same context to the goodness and loving kindness of God our Saviour (Tit. 3:4).

From this brief survey of Paul's approach to desirable virtues it is clear that he did not consider these virtues as in any sense optional extras. They are part and parcel of normal Christian standards. They stand out vividly against the background of evils to be avoided, which in themselves reflect clearly the moral environment in the midst of which the patterns of Christian behaviour were forged.

Vices to be avoided. There are even more lists of vices in Paul's letters than lists of virtues, spread over Romans, Corinthians, Galatians,[81] Ephesians, Colossians and the Pastorals. In this case it will probably be best to group the vices under four headings: sexual sins, sins of speech, social sins and selfishness.

(i) Sexual sins. Against the background of widespread sexual immorality, it is not surprising that Paul says so much against sexual sins. There is ample evidence that sexual perversity was not only rife, but was socially

---

[80] It must not be supposed that the appeal to his own example by Paul was a display of egotism. *Cf.* my *The Pastoral Epistles* (*TNTC*, 1957), p. 161, for comment on this point.

[81] R. Scroggs, *Paul for a New Day*, p. 66, suggests that Paul's list of vices may have been taken over from a wandering Cynic or Jewish preacher, but his list of virtues in Gal. 5:22, 23 are too characteristically Pauline.

acceptable.[82] Fornication, adultery and homosexuality were regarded as normal. Sex was a matter of satisfying carnal pleasure irrespective of moral purity or of respect for those who were used for purely selfish ends.[83] It is important to recognize this, if Paul's teaching on sex is to be properly understood. It was a revolutionary step for the current sexual attitudes to be regarded as sins.[84]

We note first that he condemns sexual immorality outright. The kingdom of God has no place for such (1 Cor. 6:9). It is included among the works of the flesh in Galatians 5:19. In Ephesians 5:3 Paul urges that immorality and impurity must not even be named among Christians, for this would be unfitting. No more striking challenge to the sexual standards of the age could be imagined. A similar position is seen in the lists of vices in Colossians 3:5–8. The apostle gives no support for promiscuous sexual relations, nor for adultery. It cannot be argued that his teaching on this theme has no relevance for today, since our permissive society shows many parallels to his contemporary society. The Christian ethic became a bastion for moral purity in sexual relations, and even when the general climate of opinion is against such purity, the Christian who takes his cue from the NT can have no doubt what his standards must be. In two passages Paul mentions homosexual practices (Rom. 1:26; 1 Cor. 6:9). He classifies these as 'dishonourable passions'. These manifestations were rife among both sexes and called for strong disapproval on Paul's part.

It may be said that his doctrine that the body is the temple of the Holy Spirit (1 Cor. 6:19; *cf.* 3:16) introduces a powerful deterrent to sexual sins, for the Christian cannot use his own body or anyone else's body in a manner which dishonours it. The indwelling Spirit makes any sexual acts outside the marriage state totally unacceptable.

(ii) Sins of speech. Because a person often reveals his character by his words, it is not surprising that the evils within are associated with sins of speech. In Romans 1:29f., Paul mentions gossips, slanderers, insolent, haughty, boastful, all of which find expression in words. These vices of the pagan world are unhesitatingly condemned. Christians are forbidden even to eat with anyone who is a reviler (1 Cor. 5:11); revilers have no part in the kingdom (1 Cor. 6:10). Paul fears that he might find 'quarrelling, jealousy, anger, selfishness, slander, gossip, conceit and disorder' when he

---

[82] For a description of the decadence of pagan Roman society, *cf.* R. D. Shaw, *The Pauline Epistles* (⁴1913), pp. 163–183. *Cf.* L. H. Marshall, *op. cit.*, pp. 278f., especially on the excesses of the Roman court. Marshall comments that if court practice was representative of contemporary life, Paul's indictment of Roman life in Rom. 1 was abundantly justified.

[83] C. A. A. Scott, *New Testament Ethics*, p. 118, remarks that it is hard to find in pre-Christian Greek literature a passage in which loose sexual intercourse is regarded as an offence. Sexual indulgence was placed on the same level as eating and drinking.

[84] W. R. Halliday, *The Pagan Background of Early Christianity* (1925), p. 278, states that as regards the sexual morality of the average man, Christians definitely stood on a higher level than their pagan contemporaries.

visits Corinth again (2 Cor. 12:20), and clearly feels that he must condemn these vices and call the people concerned to repentance. Bitterness, wrath, anger, clamour, and slander had all to be put away from the Christian life (Eph. 4:31),[85] and in their place kindness and tenderheartedness towards one another was to be encouraged. All these sins, which are mainly expressed verbally, do not befit Christian profession. Moreover, a special rejection of filthiness, silly talk and levity (Eph. 5:3f.), shows the importance of watching that words do not lead to impurity. Paul found unacceptable the idea of Christians giving vent to filthy language (cf. also Col. 3:8, which also mentions 'foul talk').

What is most noticeable is that so many of these terms express ways in which words can be harmful to other people.[86] Any kind of disparaging or abusive speech which defames the character of another person is unthinkable in the new man in Christ. Nevertheless, Paul is not so blind to realities as to suppose that wrongful speech will not proceed from Christians. Hence he does not hesitate to urge them to put such evils away.

The same concern over the wrong use of the tongue is seen in the pastoral epistles. Word battles, strife, railings and wranglings are found among the false teachers of whom Timothy is being warned (1 Tim. 6:5; cf. Tit. 1:10). Church officers must not be quarrelsome (1 Tim. 3:3), nor double-tongued (1 Tim. 3:8). Titus is to bid older women not to be slanderers (Tit. 2:3) and to show a good example himself by using 'sound speech' which cannot be censured (Tit. 2:8).

(iii) Social sins. Many of the sins of speech mentioned above have social implications in that they affect other people. But we must note certain other evils which have a direct effect on society and which in Paul's view are totally unacceptable for the Christian. Theft is roundly condemned (Eph. 4:28). Indeed materialism as such, mere acquisition for its own sake, finds no support in Paul's teaching; but this does not lead to the conclusion that anyone has the right to seize another's property (see further discussion under social ethics, pp. 943ff.). Closely linked with this is Paul's exposure of the sin of covetousness. In one passage (Col. 3:5, and in the parallel in Eph. 5:5) he declares it to be 'idolatry' by which he presumably means that the urge to acquire becomes so strong that it takes on the status of an object of worship.[87] He mentions greediness in the same list as robbery and idolatry in 1 Corinthians 5:10–11; 6:10. In Romans 1:29 it is linked with evil and malice, and in Ephesians 5:3 with immorality (cf. Col. 3:5).

---

[85] M. Barth, *Ephesians*, p. 521, mentions that in many cultures the raising of the voice is associated with magical incantations and thinks that Paul may have had this in mind here. He also notes, however, other possibilities.

[86] For a discussion of the main terms used, cf. L. H. Marshall, *op. cit.*, pp. 283ff. He notes that because sins of the tongue harm other people they are grave offences against the Christian law of love.

[87] R. P. Martin, *Colossians: the Church's Lord and the Christian's Liberty* (1972), pp. 109f., compares covetousness with the worship of Mammon.

There is no doubt, therefore, that Paul regarded covetousness as wholly incompatible with the Christian position.

All those terms which focus attention on strife, envy, jealousy, factions, divisions, heresies and tumults describe sins which have definite social implications. None of them can exist except in a social setting. They draw attention to the lack of right relationships between people. They have no place in Paul's conception of the Christian life. Indeed his lists of virtues present the very antithesis. Gentleness and loving kindness cannot go hand in hand with factions, nor can they support violent outbursts. All schisms are negations of Christian love. In his hymn of love (1 Cor. 13:4) Paul maintains that love is patient and kind, not jealous or boastful.

Another evil which has social effects is debauchery. This comes out in various passages like 1 Corinthians 5:11; 6:10; Gal. 5:21, and is specifically mentioned in a negative sense in the qualifications of bishops (1 Tim. 3:3; Tit. 1:7). Paul warns against older women being 'slaves to drink' (Tit. 2:3), and exhorts Christians generally not to 'get drunk with wine, for that is debauchery' (Eph. 5:18). Since in this latter case he contrasts it with fullness of the Spirit, it it clear that any form of drunkenness is wholly alien to spiritual life. It is another case of the impairing of the temple of the Spirit, this time through alcohol.

(iv) The sins of selfishness. It goes without saying that Paul's whole theological position is against self-centredness. The man who can affirm, 'I have been crucified with Christ; it is no longer I who live, but Christ who lives in me' (Gal. 2:20), is never likely to make any place for self-seeking in his ethical system. Haughtiness and boastfulness are linked with heartlessness and ruthlessness as characteristics of the pagan Gentile world (Rom. 1:30f.). They form no part of a Christian's moral equipment, for they are the antithesis of the example of Christ. Paul expresses this positively in Philippians 2:3, 'Do nothing from selfishness or conceit, but in humility count others better than yourselves.' In his account of his own experiences in Romans 7, Paul shows that self is the main obstacle in the pursuit of the good and concludes that only Christ can deliver from this obstacle. Indeed, it would not be an exaggeration to claim that the apostle sees the world around him as self-orientated, whereas he sees the Christian as essentially Christ-orientated. This radical shift of centre from self to Christ must inevitably affect ethical standards. The motive of self-advancement at the expense of others is no longer applicable. What is important for the Christian is no more what self wants, but what God wills (Rom. 12:1, 2).

Hebrews

In a manner which differs somewhat from Paul, the writer of this letter intersperses his moral exhortations in the course of his doctrinal exposition.

In no clearer way could he bring out the integral connection between the two. What he says about the high-priest theme was not intended to be an academic exercise. It had an essentially practical purpose. The readers were warned against apostasy. If anyone persisted in a policy of apostasy he would find no repentance (6:4ff.). Or if anyone spurned the Son of God and outraged the Spirit of grace (10:29), he could expect only punishment. Since the epistle is written against a background of such warning, it is not surprising that its ethical requirements are demanding. God himself is described as a consuming fire (12:29), and moral issues therefore cannot be trifled with. There is always the sense of awe when moral challenges are faced (cf. 4:1). This is a sufficient explanation of the apparently greater rigorousness of this epistle than most other parts of the NT (cf. 1 John 5:16 which speaks of 'mortal sin').

Certain qualities receive warm commendation. Among the most notable is the concept of faithfulness which is amply illustrated in chapter 11. It is not 'faith' in the characteristic Pauline sense of the word, but a persistent dependence on the faithfulness of God, a readiness to trust him in face of any difficulties, however insuperable. The people of faith were people whose whole lives were governed by their trust in God. Their religious convictions, in short, governed their moral conduct. Although the heroes of the past are cited as examples for the inspiration of the readers, and indeed the statement is made that they without us could not be made perfect (11:39f.; cf also 6:12), the supreme example of faithfulness is Christ himself (3:6).

Another important quality is patience which is mentioned in Hebrews 6:12, linked with faith. The Greek word (makrothymia) means 'long-suffering'. Another word (hypomonē) is used elsewhere in the epistle in the sense of 'endurance', or 'perseverance' (10:36).[88] The writer seems to set high store on the quality of persistence. The believer is also expected to live a life which is disciplined. It is not so much self-discipline as God-discipline (chapter 12), but there is no question of each person being able to claim freedom to make his own moral choices. This does not mean, however, that people have no responsibility for their own actions, for the so-called 'apostasy' passages would deny this.

Another virtue is obedience. Again Christ is set out as an example of obedience, and is said to have learnt obedience by what he suffered (5:8). Abraham is another who demonstrates the same quality when called to go out to an unknown place which would be his inheritance (11:8). This writer sees obedience as a necessary prerequisite for acquiring salvation (5:9).

---

[88] B. F. Westcott, *Hebrews* (1892), p. 159, distinguishes between *makrothymia* and *hypomonē* by relating the latter to the pressure of distinct trials which have to be borne, and the former to the trial of unsatisfied desire. J. Horst, art. *makrothymia*, *TDNT* 4, p. 386, considers that in this Hebrews passage the word denotes the steadfast endurance of faith which is not vexed by waiting.

Strong warnings are given against disobedience in chapters 3 and 4, where it is almost identified with unbelief. But we need to enquire whether there is any sense in which obedience to a code is expected. The answer must be that, while there is much in this epistle which echoes events and concepts contained in the books of the law, there is no support for an appeal to a legal code in determining moral behaviour. On the contrary an extensive passage in chapter 8 cites the promise from Jeremiah 31:31 about the new covenant and assures the readers that laws are to be written on the hearts, *i.e.* there is to be an internal rather than an external ethic. This is in line with the teaching of Jesus. Obedience is therefore concerned with a personal response to God, a desire to please him (*cf.* 11:5–6; 13:21).

The writer of this epistle expects Christians to produce good works, but it is the result of what Christ has already accomplished (10:24). Moreover, the good works are directly linked with love (*agapē*) in this passage.[89] They are clearly intended to be an expression of love. No indication of their content is given. In the only other reference to *agapē* in this epistle (6:10), it is also linked with work. In this case the love is expressed as 'serving the saints'.

In the concluding exhortations in Hebrews 13, various ethical injunctions are made.[90] There is a commendation of hospitality (13:2), an exhortation to foster brotherly love (13:1), an urge for purity and honour in marriage (13:4), advice about material possession (13:5), a warning about food taboos (13:9), and a commendation for continued good works (13:16). There is clearly no system about this, and in all probability each point mentioned has arisen out of the author's experience with Christians seeking to forge a new way of life. As in Paul's letters, ethical advice arises from a real situation.

Similarly, certain vices are condemned, such as sexual immorality and adultery (13:4), avarice (13:5) and clinging sin (12:1). This latter passage is of some importance for its ethical challenge. The idea of clinging sin is probably taken from the athlete's cloak which he casts off before the race. The metaphor is not precisely applied, but the idea is of putting off anything that hinders. In addition to the clinging sin there is the encumbering weight (*onkos*), which probably refers to the swelling weight of conceit.

We must note that the example of Jesus Christ is reckoned to be powerful, as is seen in 12:2, which urges the readers to look to Jesus, the author and perfecter of our faith. Although Jesus as example is not the most

---

[89] It is significant that the author used a strong word for inciting one another to love (*paroxysmos*). F. F. Bruce, *Hebrews* (NICNT, 1964), p. 253, explains the use of this word here in the sense that love is stimulated by the considerateness and example of other Christians.

[90] F. V. Filson, *Yesterday: A study of Hebrews in the light of chapter 13* (1967), p. 77, rightly warns against assuming that the imperatives in Hebrew 13 point to specific failure on the part of the readers. The author clearly does not set out a social programme, but is concerned to bring out the need for a practical outcome of faith.

927

prominent feature of this epistle, he is nevertheless set out as a perfect high priest (7:26) and becomes for that reason a pattern for his followers. The function of the chapter on faith is intended to set out a 'cloud of witnesses' which are also exemplary.

As a general indication about the power to distinguish good from evil, the writer gives it as his opinion that this power is gained by the mature whose faculties have been trained (5:14).[91] This seems to suggest that only a special group are capable of such discernment. But the writer expects all the readers by now to be mature.

James

Since this is the most practical book in the NT, we might expect to find here a more consistent exposition of ethical principles. But James does not set out a systematic picture. Some of the dominant features which are expounded as motives or standards in other NT books are lacking from this. There is nothing, for instance, to compare with Paul's great hymn of love. On the only three occasions when love is mentioned(1:12; 2:5, 8) it is not expressed in terms of love to Christ. It rather echoes the OT.

It is, in fact, the major feature of the moral teaching of James that it is reminiscent of the moral teaching of the prophets. This is especially so in the realm of social ethics. James is so parallel to Jewish ethics that some have maintained that this letter was originally a Jewish epistle which has been Christianized by the adding of two references to Christ (1:1, 2:1).[92] Others have supposed that the references to Christ are a scribal interpolation into an epistle which was originally sent to unconverted Jews and hence the Christian ethic has been watered down.[93] But there is no need to accept either theory, if it can be assumed that James keeps strictly to his brief to provide practical advice over a wide range of topics. Certainly he does not directly appeal to the example of Christ, but in one passage (3:17) he may well be implying it.

This particular passage gives certain qualities which belong to wisdom, but which are equally applicable to the life of Jesus, although this is not mentioned. The qualities are purity, peaceableness, gentleness, reasonableness, mercy. Where these exist without uncertainty or insincerity James sees the truly wise man (*i.e.* with wisdom from above). There are parallels here with Paul's fruit of the Spirit in Galatians 5:22, although again it is strange that James does not mention the Spirit. These qualities are predominantly non-selfish and non-aggressive. As ethical requirements for personal

---

[91] P. E. Hughes, *Hebrews* (1977), p. 193, does not restrict the references to good and evil to a moral sense, but extends it to doctrine. This is supported by the reference to doctrine in Heb. 6:1. Nevertheless moral teaching would be included in doctrine.

[92] F. Spitta, 'Der Brief des Jacobus', *Zur Geschichte und Literatur des Urchristentums* 2 (1896), pp. 1-239.

[93] *Cf.* L. Dewar, *An Outline of New Testament Ethics* (1949), pp. 260f.

living, they demand a greater thought for others than for oneself. There is perhaps an initial realization of an impossibility to reach such a standard, but in that case the example of Jesus Christ would be invaluable. James gives no support for self-importance, for he talks about the meekness of wisdom (3:13).[94]

The positive virtues are off-set by a criticism of vices such as bitter jealousy and selfish ambition (3:14). This sort of approach comes from earthly wisdom, which James castigates as 'unspiritual and devilish' (3:15). There is clearly a tie up between a true religious disposition, represented by heavenly wisdom, and right living. Although James' words could be understood in a non-religious sense, this is highly improbable, for heavenly wisdom presupposes religious faith. James is in line with the Hebrew wisdom books in taking for granted that the fear of the Lord is the beginning of wisdom. It is therefore evident that James regards his ethical exhortations as something more than prudent advice, although some statements may seem to be of this kind. When he says that disorder and vile practices follow from jealousy and selfish ambition (3:16), he is not introducing a new idea, but making a common observation. Nevertheless observations of this kind form a part of the total impression which James gives that religious faith affects every part of life.

This epistle has special advice about the dangers of speech. A man must be slow to speak and slow to anger (1:19). The two things belong together, for it is the hasty word which breeds anger. Speech and action is to be in accordance with the 'law of liberty' (2:12)[95], which will judge all wrong words and acts. No-one for example, who fails to show mercy can expect mercy (according to 2:13), which echoes Jesus' teaching about the unforgiving debtor (Mt. 18:23ff.). James even goes so far as to say that a person's religion is vain if he does not bridle his tongue (1:26), which shows the high value he places on restraint in speech. This theme is further expanded in 3:1–12, where he calls the tongue 'a restless evil, full of deadly poison' (verse 8). He admits that no one can tame it, but nevertheless says that the same mouth should not bless God and curse people (3:10).[96] The underlying assumption seems to be that devotion to God affects the way people speak.

There are several hints about the perils of riches. It is the rich who oppress (2:6). They are specially condemned in 5:1ff., and are reminded

---

[94] C. L. Mitton, *James* (1966), p. 135, interprets 'the meekness of wisdom' as meekness which is appropriate to wisdom and which true wisdom produces. James uses the same word 'meekness' in 1:21, where it means a readiness to receive the word of God.

[95] It is clear from 2:13 that the 'law of liberty' is closely linked with mercy, which shows the predominance of love. *Cf.* H. Windisch and H. Preisker, *Die Katholischen Briefe* (*LHB*, ³1951), p. 16, who speak of this love as a duty.

[96] M. Dibelius and H. Greeven, *James* (Eng. trans. *Hermeneia*, 1976, from *KEK*, 1964), pp. 201f., regard this saying as taken over by James from Jewish tradition. Whatever the origin of the statement, it fits in well with the strong warnings about misuse of the tongue which are such a notable feature of this epistle.

that they have laid up treasure for the last days (5:3), *i.e.* retribution. From James' strong statements it might be deduced that he regarded material possessions as evil in themselves. But his polemic is not against money as such, but against those who have gained wealth by fraud and even at the expense of others people's lives (5:4–6).

The Petrine epistles and Jude

The most notable feature of the ethical teaching in *1 Peter* is its direct appeal to the example of Christ. For this the classic passage is 2:18ff., where Peter is addressing servants and advising them to be submissive to their masters. Even if they suffer as a consequence, they are to endure patiently as Christ did. He is seen as an example and believers are expected to follow in his steps (2:21).[97] It is remarkable that in order to provide an impetus to moral action, Peter introduces a Christological motive which leads him at once into some profound statements about Christ and his mission. Here is no appeal to the example of Christ as man independent of his soteriological significance. The *imitatio Christi* motive is thoroughly theological as Peter presents it.

In the opening passage of the letter (1:3–9), several virtues are mentioned which set the tone for the whole, such as hope (1:3), faith (1:5, 7), joy (1:6, 8), love (1:8). The emphasis falls on the demonstration of the genuineness of faith (1:7), which is seen in the way in which believers react to trials. The exposition of the epistle is concerned with the ways in which a genuine faith manifests itself in everyday living. Peter recognizes that mental effort is needed in order to aim at a life of holiness (1:13–16). A major manifestation is brotherly love (1:22; 2:17; 3:8; *cf.* 4:8; 5:9).

The most sustained passage which sets out the pattern for Christian living is 3:8–12.[98] Three of the words used, 'likeminded' (*homophrones*), 'sympathy' (*sympatheis*), and 'tender-hearted' (*eusplanchnoi*), are found only here in the NT, although the sentiments expressed occur in other forms. They are essentially communal virtues involving relationships with others, but concentrating on personal initiative. These virtues are linked here with 'love of brethren' and 'humility' which recur in this epistle and elsewhere in the NT. This soft and considerate approach stands in stark contrast to the harsh attitude of the contemporary world. It makes sense only in the context of the total presentation of religious faith seen in this epistle and

---

[97] Both the nouns used in this passage are picturesque. *Hypogrammos* (pattern) comes from an idea taken from the classroom. It described an outline tracing which had to be followed. The word for 'track' or 'step', *ichnos*, referred to footprints and in the plural the line of such footprints. *Cf.* J. N. D. Kelly, *Peter and Jude* (BC, 1969), pp. 119f. The English word 'example' therefore is not really strong enough to represent the true meaning.

[98] For an essay on the ethics of this epistle, *cf.* E. G. Selwyn, *1 Peter* (1946), pp. 101ff. He points out that while much is said about social ethics, there are statements which supply the necessary principles of a personal kind (3:8, 9; 1:13—2:12).

in the NT as a whole. It is essentially self-effacing, as 5:5, 6 shows.

There must also be a definite rejection of sins. Among those specifically mentioned are malice, guile, insincerity, envy, slander (2:1). Christians are not to be conformed to the passions of their former ignorance (1:14), and are abstain from the passions of the flesh which war against the soul (2:11). Some indication of these passions is given in 4:3: licentious living, drunkenness, revels, carousing and lawless idolatory. The Christians addressed had already recognized that these evils must be avoided, for they were being abused because of their attitude. The strong condemnation of sexual sins and drunkenness is significant in view of the widespread nature of these evils. It highlights the unique challenge of the Christian ethic in an environment in which self-control,was disparaged.[99] Add to this Peter's argument about suffering as a Christian, which is set over against suffering on account of murder, stealing, wrongdoing or mischief-making (4:15), all of which are seen to be totally out of keeping for a Christian.

In *2 Peter* and *Jude*, both of which are combating similar situations, the main burden is to contest antinomianism. Many details are given about the nature of the false teaching, most of which focuses on immorality, dissipation and corruption. Both writers are clear that these evils (Peter calls them the 'defilements' of the world', 2 Pet. 2:20) have no place for Christians. To turn back to such a way of life is described in 2 Peter 2:22 as comparable to a cleaned-up sow wallowing again in the mud. The kind of warnings given in 2 Peter and Jude are fully in agreement with other NT teaching, and confirm the lack of moral standards in the world in which the Christian church developed. Jude speaks of those who turn the grace of God into lasciviousness (verse 4), and goes on to describe Sodom and Gomorrah as indulging in immorality and unnatural lust (probably homosexuality, verse 7). He describes those who were acting as irrational animals (verse 10).

But these epistles do more than denounce evils. They seek to encourage good standards. 2 Peter 1:5–8 is a classic passage of this kind, for it sets out a succession of virtues, each of which needs supplementing by the next, in a kind of ladder-effect.[100] It begins with faith and ends with love. In between are virtue, knowledge, self-control, steadfastness, godliness, and brotherly affection. The over-all effect is the impression that the genuine Christian needs to display all these virtues in order to be complete, and that all the preceding virtues are manifestations of the last one, love (*agapē*). Jude contents himself with exhorting his readers, 'Build yourselves up on

---

[99] As F. W. Beare, *1 Peter* ([2]1958), p. 154, points out, in their old life these converted Gentiles were swayed in their conduct by public opinion of a society which was alienated from God. This is the force of the expression 'the will of the Gentiles'.

[100] J. N. D. Kelly, *op. cit.*, p. 305, considers this list has a strong Hellenistic flavour, which he thinks is heightened by the use of *spoudēn pareispherein* (apply effort) and *epichorēgein* (supply in addition).

your most holy faith' and 'Keep yourselves in the love of God' (verses 20–21) — stating the bare structure, whereas 2 Peter enlarges upon it.

The Johannine Epistles

The *first epistle of John* is rich in ethical instruction, but as with other NT writings, it links it closely with doctrine. John is not offering a general ethic, but a specifically Christian ethic. His instruction has relevance only to those who are 'born of God' (3:9), in whom God's nature abides. Indeed, he assumes that those who are in the fellowship will not sin, by which he seems to mean they will not live in a state of sin. He is not suggesting that it is impossible for anyone outside the Christian fellowship to attain to any virtue, but he is implying that the highest moral standards go hand in hand with high spiritual values. It has been suggested that John has overstated his case, because it has been proved that Christian status does not always produce the Christian life,[101] but this is to mispresent his point of view. When he talks about abiding in Christ, he is not simply thinking of Christian status, but of dynamic Christian living. The idea of status without a renewed life is totally alien to John's doctrinal exposition.

In attempting to sum up the ethical approach of this epistle, we note first the dominant factor of love (*agapē*). It may be said to be the most characteristic feature in the writer's theology. Yet nowhere is it assumed that the Christian can work up his own brand of love. It is essentially a derivative of the love of God. God himself is said to be love (4:8, 16).[102] It is he who takes the initiative in loving us, and our love to God is derived from that (4:10, 19). In fact what love we have the Father has given to us (3:1). This sets the tone for the ethical advice. Love will lead to a desire to obey God's will, to observe his commandments (5:3). The perfection of love to God is seen in those who keep his word (2:5). The link between love and commandment prevents the latter from being approached in a legalistic way. Moreover, a major message of this epistle is that love for God must also be translated into love for one another (3:11, 14, 23; 4:7, 20f.). Such love for others has its supreme example in the sacrificial offering of Christ for us, and this kind of love is expected from believers (3:16).

In order to highlight the supreme example of love, John sets it against its antithesis 'hatred'. This author is particularly fond of such antitheses and cannot adopt a compromise.[103] What is not 'love' is 'hate'. This means that 'hate' is essentially the absence of love (*cf* 2:9; 3:15, 4:20). For John there is no possibility of love and hate co-existing and he must, therefore,

---

[101] Cf. L. Dewar, *An Outline of New Testament Ethics*, p. 201.

[102] It must not be supposed that the statement 'God is love' expresses that loving is only one of God's activities, but that all his activities proceed from love. Cf. J. R. W. Stott's comments on this verse, *The Epistles of John* (TNTC, 1964), p. 160.

[103] As F. F. Bruce, *The Epistles of John* (1970), p. 56, remarks, John 'sees life in terms of black and white; intermediate greys have no existence for him'.

be talking about settled states of mind. This is evident when he says that anyone who hates his brother is a murderer (3:15), which reminds us of the teaching of Jesus, which declared the desire to be equivalent to the act (Mt. 5:21, 22). Clearly the inner nature of the ethics of this epistle could not be more vividly brought out. If 'hatred' is a rather strong way of categorizing the absence of love, it shows unmistakably that love is an indispensable factor in Christian ethics.

There is a surprising lack of specific ethical instructions in this epistle. It rather sets out principles than precepts. The believer is expected to know the difference between light and darkness. He is exhorted to walk in the light (1:7), as if the difference between this and walking in darkness is too obvious to need description. Walking in darkness is linked with hate in 2:9, but is otherwise left undefined, except that it is affirmed that in God there is no darkness.

The believer is also expected to know the difference between truth and falsehood (2:21). John assumes that Christians know the truth, although his gives as his purpose that his readers might know they have eternal life (5:13). He several times uses the word 'liar' (*pseustēs*).[104] Those who claim to be without sin make God a liar (1:10); those who claim to know God and do not obey him are liars (2:4); those who deny the truth of the incarnation are liars (2:22); those who hate their brothers are liars (4:20); those who do not believe God make him a liar (5:10). These different uses suggest that 'liar' means more than someone who tells an untruth. In John's view a 'liar' is one who is habitually deviating from God's truth and acting hypocritically. He seems to suggest that even those who make some profession may be as much liars as those who are declared unbelievers. Whatever does not further truth is a lie.

It is noticeable that the example of Christ plays some part in the ethical instruction in this book. The person who abides in Christ is to walk in the way that Christ walked (2:6). Christ is the pattern of righteousness and purity (2:29; 3:3). It is Christ's laying down of his own life which enables people to know the true nature of love (3:16). At the appearing of Christ we shall be like him (3:2). There is no doubt therefore that in this epistle it is assumed that Jesus Christ is the supreme example for Christian living.

In *2 and 3 John* there is little teaching, but there are several references to 'the truth' (2 John 1, 2, 3, 4; 3 John 1, 3, 4, 8, 12). There is also an affirmation of brotherly love (2 John 5), and an exhortation to follow love (2 John 6). Those who use evil words are condemned (3 John 10) and likewise those who deceive, particularly in reference to doctrine (2 John 7ff.). These two brief letters share the same point of view as 1 John.

---

[104] For the meaning and use of this word, *cf.* H. Conzelmann, *TDNT* 9, p. 602; U. Becker and H.-G. Link, *NIDNTT* 2, pp. 473f.

Revelation

It may seem on a cursory reading of this book that its ethical climate is very different from that of the NT generally. We are introduced to cries of vengeance (6:10). The whole future scene centres around judgments. There seems little emphasis on love and kindness. But it would not be true to drive too great a wedge between this book and the rest of the NT. The occasion and purpose of the book clearly affect its presentation. It does not set out the terms for Christian living, but looks forward to the termination of the age. What ethical teaching it gives is therefore incidental and must be recognized as such. In a book which shows the final overthrow of evil, it is inevitable that much emphasis will fall on retribution. Yet the cry for vengeance against the enemies is not a cry for vindictiveness, but for vindication, a wholly different demand.[105]

In the letters to the seven churches, some were commended and others condemned over ethical matters. There is mention of patient endurance (2:2, 3; 2:19; 3:10) and this is undoubtedly an important and necessary quality in a time of persecution (*cf.* 1:9; 13:10; 14:12). Linked with this is the commendation of obedience to the commandments of God (14:12). Since there are special encouragements given to martyrs (6:9ff.; 20:4), it must be supposed that loyalty to the truth is rated particularly highly, especially if as some suppose the first resurrection (20:5) is restricted to martyrs. On the other hand, there is no clear indication that martyrdom for its own sake is valued. It is the faithfulness which led to it which is noted (2:13). Christ himself is introduced as the faithful one (1:5; 3:14), and in his final coming bears the names 'Faithful and True' (19:11). He becomes in this the pattern for his people. A special reward is, moreover, promised to the one who is faithful to death (2:10; *cf.* 17.14).

The churches are called upon to repent where their actions have fallen short of the standard required of them, but special commendations are promised to those who overcome. No details are given to enable the reader to understand precisely what overcoming means, but it is assumed that, since the whole book is set against the background of the opposition of the forces of evil, overcoming consists in pursuit of the good. In fact the whole book, with its final overthrowing of all adverse forces, illustrates this point.

Some of the evils to be avoided are immorality (2:14, 21f.), cowardice, faithlessness, pollution, murder, fornication, sorcery, idolatry and falsehood (21:8), for those guilty of such evils are destined for the second death. They are definitely excluded from the new Jerusalem (22:15). The final triumph inaugurated by the Lamb is the triumph of good over evil. It is noteworthy that in this book cowardice is specifically mentioned, for in an

---

[105] As G. R. Beasley-Murray, *Revelation* (*NCB*, 1974), p. 136, notes, the cry is not for revenge but for vindication of the right and truth of the cause for which they gave their lives.

age when persecution against Christians was widespread, this would be connected with a renunciation of the faith. It would refer to those with no moral backbone. The word rendered 'pollution' (*ebdelygmenoi*) in 21:8 is a general term for pagan abominations.[106]

There are two other passages in this book which have some bearing on the subject of ethics. In 14:4, the 144,000 redeemed from the earth are said to be those who have not defiled themselves with women, for they are chaste (Gk. has *parthenoi*, virgins). Does this suggest a special premium on virginity? First, it must be noted that virginity is here intended to denote the antithesis of adultery, and is probably used in a metaphorical sense. Thus the 'chaste' are those who have a settled disposition of a morally acceptable kind.[107] If, however, virginity is taken in its literal sense, there may be a parallel here with Paul's advice to people not to marry in view of the coming distress (p. 919). What is expedient in a time of acute persecution may not necessarily provide a stable standard for more normal times. There is nothing elsewhere in this book to suggest that celibacy is a virtue. In fact, it is important to note the spiritual use made of the 'bride and bridegroom' imagery in chapters 19ff. In view of the predominantly symbolic nature of the book as a whole, it would place more strain on this passage than it will bear to claim that it must support an ascetic approach to marriage.

The second passage to which reference must be made is the famous taunt song of Revelation 18. Can it be claimed that this song presents such a spirit of vindictiveness that it is out of line with the general NT teaching on the nature of Christian love?[108] It should at once be noted that nowhere in the song is there any rejoicing over the downfall of others. Their torment and tears is recorded as a record of fact. Although the dramatic representation of the desperate plight of the people of Babylon as they watched their trade empires collapse before their eyes is vivid, there is no exultation over it. The whole passage creates the impression of inescapable sadness.

SOCIAL ETHICS

Having seen the approaches of the different parts of the NT to personal ethics, we shall approach the subject of social ethics from the point of view of important themes affecting society rather than attempt to separate the various sources. Our aim will be to seek for guiding principles, for the NT

---

[106] L. Morris, *Revelation* (*TNTC*, 1969), p. 247, suggests that the meaning may be that to accept ideas and practices from heathen religions brings defilement with it.

[107] *Cf.* I. Beckwith, The *Apocalypse of John* (1919, r.p. 1967), pp. 649f. who concludes that the reference here must be to those who have not committed adultery.

[108] R. H. Mounce, *Revelation* (*NICNT*, 1977), p. 321, remarks, 'Squeamishness about his rhetoric results more from a misunderstanding of the literary nature of the prophetic taunt song than from any supposedly sub-Christian ethic being expressed.'

certainly does not provide a blueprint for Christian social action.

The importance of approaching the theme of social responsibility from a theological point of view cannot be over-emphasized. The justification for this is that theology concerns the whole man, which includes his environment. The NT approach is wholly different from those theories which concentrate on the environment in the belief that an improved environment will produce an improved man. In NT thought the transformation of the person is most important, but this leads to a modified approach to society as a whole. We have already discussed the doctrine of God (pp. 75ff.) and the doctrine of man (pp. 150ff.), but we shall need to reiterate the social implications of each doctrine in order to provide a solid theological basis.[109]

The theological basis

Both in the OT and in the NT it is affirmed that man was made in the image of God and this must carry with it certain social implications.[110] The real problem of man's attitude towards his social environment is coloured by the fact that he has fallen from a state of innocence. A true understanding of the nature of man involves the recognition of three stages: man in his original state of creation, man in his fallen state and man in his redeemed state. The first of these no longer exists except in the perfect humanity of Jesus. His perfection shows the true potential of human nature. A perfect social order could clearly exist if all possessed this kind of perfection. Our previous discussion of the doctrine of man has made clear that no such perfection exists (*cf.* Rom. 3:10ff.).[111]

It is man in his fallen state which introduces an environmental tension. In the NT this tension is expressed by a number of antitheses. The world is in darkness (Jn. 1:5; *cf.* 1 Jn. 1:5ff.) It is ignorant of God in the sense of real understanding (Jn. 17:25). Human minds have been blinded by the god of this world (2 Cor. 4:4). Hence a totally alien element has been introduced into the environment in which man is placed. This is in direct contrast to the beneficial elements introduced by the gospel, and gives rise to the tension between light and darkness, truth and error, enlightenment and ignorance, love and hate. The whole of life, both individually and collectively, has been affected. It has even affected the family, the most closely knit of all social groups. This explains the remark of Jesus that human parents are 'evil' (Mt. 7:11) by comparison with the pure motives of God.[112]

---

[109] Sections of this discussion are reproduced in a modified form from my article, 'The New Testament Approach to Social Responsibility', *Vox Evangelica* 9, 1973, pp. 40–59.

[110] For some reflections on the social implications of the 'image', *cf.* J. N. D. Anderson, *Into the World* (1968), pp. 15ff.

[111] J. Murray, *Romans* 1 (*NICNT*, 1959), p. 103, calls the statement in Rom. 3:10 'the precipitate of the Biblical teaching'.

[112] Many commentators regard the *ponēroi* here as merely relative, *i.e.* as compared with God, *cf.* A. H.

The environment in which man finds himself becomes infected by his own nature, biased towards self-centredness (*cf.* Mt. 17:17).[113]

The NT accordingly does not present social teaching without taking account of man's basically sinful nature. It constantly draws attention to social evils (*e.g.* Rom. 1:24f.; Col. 3:5ff.; 1 Pet. 4:3ff.), because these were real problems in the contemporary world. There is no suggestion, therefore, of a purely social solution to these problems, because it was recognized that the root cause is spiritual rather than social.[114]

This leads to the third stage, man in his redeemed state. The NT doctrines of redemption and reconciliation (see pp. 476ff.; 486ff.) are central to the whole Christian message and involve a disarming of man's natural enmity against God and of his self-centredness. The Christian is a new creature (2 Cor. 5:17) and now lives on a new plane (Col. 3:1). The consequence is that redeemed man finds himself with an entirely new set of values and yet remains in his former environment. A tension must at once develop between his former way of looking at social responsibility and his new principles in Christ. The NT concentrates on the latter, because this was the element which was essentially new. The Christian faith demands new attitudes and actions which are of prior importance for those who have just turned away from a pagan background.

This helps to explain the comparative paucity of specific exhortations towards social responsibility. Yet it would be wrong to suppose that this fact absolves Christians from social responsibility. The NT cannot be appealed to as evidence that Christians should not concern themselves with social issues,[115] since the Christian view of redeemed man carries with it some implicit understanding of social responsibility.

The approach of the NT to society tends to be individual, on the principle that redeemed people will have a salutary effect on the environment in which they are placed. The early Christians were not in a position, for instance, to inaugurate a crusade for the abolition of slavery; but the attitude of individuals, both slaves and slave-owners, could do something towards

---

McNeile (1915), *ad loc.* But more must be understood than this. As F. V. Filson, *Matthew* (*BC*, 1960), p. 194, rightly acknowledges, Jesus clearly indicates by this the sinfulness of all men.

[113] When Jesus described his own generation as 'faithless and perverse' in Mt. 17:17, he may be regarding the perversity as consisting in faithlessness (so P. Bonnard, *Matthieu*, p. 260). *Cf.* D. Hill, *Matthew*, p. 270. Filson, *op. cit.*, p. 194, thinks the faithlessness to be a failure to see God's power at work in Jesus.

[114] D. O. Moberg, *Inasmuch: Christian Social Responsibility in the Twentieth Century* (1965), p. 66, points out that although from a theological point of view sin is the source of all social evils, it is not always the sin of the victims which brings about their plight. *Cf.* T. C. Hammond, *Perfect Freedom* (1938), pp. 178ff., on the effects of the doctrine of the fall on ethical theory. A. V. Murray, *The State and the Church in a Free Society* (1958), p. 3. comments that 'all utopias have come to grief on the rock of original sin, and our generation, while it is willing and even eager to admit the failure, is strenuously unwilling to admit the cause of it.'

[115] Against this view, *cf.* Moberg, *op. cit.*, chapter 2.

beginning to undermine the system (see the later section, pp. 941ff.).

Another aspect of human nature which is important in the sphere of society is the sanctity of personality. The NT underlines the value of the individual and lends no support to any social system in which people are treated as less than persons. The basic equality of all classes in the matter of salvation could not fail to have some impact on the Christian approach to social questions. Moreover, the NT has a doctrine of the weak and the strong (Rom. 14), which is diametrically opposed to the idea of the survival of the fittest. Indeed, there is no support for the view that one's own interest must automatically take precedence over the needs of others (*cf.* Gal. 6:2). On all occasions Jesus was concerned about the needs of his contemporaries and is the supreme example of one who shouldered the burdens of others.

It is not only the NT doctrine of man which affects the Christian view of society, but also its view of God. The presentation of a redeemed mankind involves a redeeming God. In discussing the nature of God in the NT, we noted the special emphasis placed on his love, which is an essentially outgoing characteristic. God's love is all-embracing (John 3:16), which testifies to the strong involvement which he has with his creatures. That love is strong enough to persist even in the face of hostility (Rom. 5:8). In NT teaching, moreover, God's love is regarded as the pattern for man (1 Jn. 4:7; Jn. 15:9). Loving is a powerful means of showing concern.[116]

When discussing the work of Christ (pp. 486ff.), we noted the importance of reconciliation, especially in the epistles of Paul. The reconciling work of God in Christ is fundamental to a true approach to social responsibility. A person in society who has been reconciled to God could not logically countenance any method of social reform which would cause alienation between people. Although the NT does not expound on the implications of this, its teaching on the nature of God would seem to exclude the use of violence for the attaining of social ends. The gospel is an agency of reconciliation, not of strife. Some, however, consider that alienation and violence are sometimes justified as the lesser of two evils. But it is difficult to find specific support for this from Paul's epistles.

It must be noted that according to the apostle Paul reconciliation extends beyond the human realm to the material creation. He writes about cosmic groaning for freedom from present bondage (Rom. 8:20ff.), which must reflect to some extent his approach to his environment.[117] This might

---

[116] For a study of the Christian idea of love, *cf.* A. Nygren, *Agape and Eros* (1953); J. Moffatt, *Love in the New Testament* (1929); V. P. Furnish, *The Love Command in the New Testament* (1973).

[117] C. H. Dodd, *Romans* (*MNT*, 1932), p. 134, regards Paul's statement in Rom. 8:22 as 'a truly poetical conception'. F. J. Leenhardt, *Romans* (Eng. trans. 1961, from *CNT*, 1957), pp. 222ff., emphasizes the essential connection between the creature and the creation, while admitting that the mode of expression was determined by Paul's contemporary view of his environment.

Whatever the interpretation of Rom. 8:20ff., it is clear that Paul was convinced that the material creation

provide some indication of Paul's answer to the ecological problem, although he does not give any specific comment on man's responsibility towards his environment. The divine pattern as revealed in NT teaching presupposes that man must be held responsible for polluting his own environment.[118] To disturb the balance of nature for purely selfish ends had not occurred as a problem in NT times, but it can certainly be conjectured that such a procedure would have been recognized in Christian thought as inadmissible. For Paul, the fact that all things will in the end be united with Christ gives a dignity to the creation itself (*cf.* Eph. 1:10).

Another matter of importance in the sphere of social responsibility is to consider the limits within which it is possible for Christians to exert influence. There are inevitably times when the social expectations of the natural man will clash with the standards set by God. It is relevant to enquire whether the NT provides any guidelines for resolving such tensions. The teaching of Jesus makes clear that obedience to God takes precedence over obedience to the state, although ideally they should coincide.[119] Rendering to Caesar what belongs to him and to God what he demands implies the necessity of putting God first. The NT makes clear that a person must follow the dictates of his conscience,[120] in which case there will be times when either explicitly or implicitly he will enter into moral judgment on his social environment. The strong NT warnings against sexual immorality, for instance, are an indictment of the social standards of the time.

Since the NT is concerned primarily with spiritual issues it may give the superficial impression that social concerns are unimportant. But the Christian is first expected to show concern towards those who belong to the Christian community. Paul, for instance, advises that good should be done to all, but especially to those who are of the household of faith (Gal. 6:10).[121] The preference to be given to the Christian community was never intended to exempt Christians from any obligation towards others. There are obvious difficulties in deciding the proportion of responsibility which

---

could not be divorced from the needs and aspirations of man. An older writer, R. Haldane, *Romans* (r.p., 1958), p. 372, maintains that the creation is not what it was before man's sin and therefore shares man's bondage.

For a discussion of the difference between Christian and Jewish ideas about the renovation of nature, *cf.* W. Sanday and A. C. Headlam, *Romans* (*ICC*, ⁵1902), pp. 210ff.

[118] *Cf.* S. E. Wirt, *The Social Conscience of the Evangelical* (1968), pp. 102ff., for a brief statement of a Christian approach to the problem of pollution.

[119] For studies on the Christian approach to the state, *cf.* O. Cullmann, *The State in the New Testament* (Eng. trans. 1957); A. V. Murray, *The State and the Church in a Free Society*; W. Lillie, *Studies in New Testament Ethics*, pp. 82ff.

[120] *Cf.* Lillie, *op. cit.*, pp. 45ff; O. Hallesby, *Conscience* (1939).

[121] Some commentators relate Paul's exhortation in Gal. 6:10 to his appeal fund for the Jerusalem poor *cf.* R. A. Cole, *Galatians* (*TNTC*, 1965), *ad loc.* But it would seem to have a wider application than this. Martin Luther, *Commentary on the Epistle to the Galatians, ad loc.*, applies the term 'household' particularly to ministers and the rest of the faithful.

the Christian must make between the narrower and larger group, but in this the NT offers little specific guidance. It is presumably left to individual consciences.

There are some NT passages which seem to advise Christians to keep themselves unsullied from the world (*e.g.* Jas. 1:27) and this type of teaching has sometimes been seen to support complete non-involvement in social affairs.[122] But, although the Christian must be morally apart from the world, he cannot live apart from it. The teaching of Jesus to his disciples was to the effect that they were to be the salt of the earth (Mt. 5:13), which must mean that they would have a salutary social impact.[123]

Areas of social concern reflected in the New Testament

We shall now consider some of the main areas in which the NT throws light on the possible application of Christian principles to a wider context. Our treatment of these themes must necessarily be in summary form, but references will be given to further reading for fuller exploration.

THE NEW TESTAMENT TEACHING ON WORK

Although there is considerable emphasis in the NT on Christian work, little is said on the subject of the Christian approach to labour in general.[124] Jesus viewed his own mission as 'work' (John 17:4) and most of the NT references to work or good works are from a similar point of view. It has a spiritual basis which cannot apply to a society as a whole where spiritual values are not determinative.

It is to be noted that in NT thinking no distinctions are drawn between various kinds of work or vocation. There is no suggestion of contempt for manual work as among the Greeks. Indeed, both Jesus and Paul were craftsmen, following the established tradition that males should learn a trade, even those destined to become rabbis. The NT does not support any social approach which makes it impossible for someone to have pride in his work, although admittedly it did not have to deal with the complexities of modern industrialized society. When comparing mental work with manual work, the Christian cannot, on the basis of the NT, place the former on a higher rung of the social ladder than the latter. Jesus was not afforded much respect as a teacher by his religious contemporaries because he was

---

[122] *Cf.* J. B. Mayor's comment on *kosmos, James* (³1913, r.p. 1954), pp. 224ff.

[123] J. C. Fenton, *Matthew* (²1977), p. 84, considered that this passage implies that 'the church has a usefulness to God in making the world acceptable to him, by its sacrifice and intercession'. But this is an unwarranted interpretation. It is more probable that salt is here used in its Jewish sense of 'wisdom', in which case Christian thought is seen to have a salutary effect on social thinking (*cf.* D. Hill, *Matthew*, p. 115).

[124] For useful treatments of the theme of work in the NT, *cf.* A. Richardson, *The Christian Doctrine of Work* (1952); Sir Fred Catherwood, *The Christian in Industrial Society* (³1980); W. Lillie, *Studies in New Testament Ethics*, pp. 105ff.; J. N. D. Anderson, *Into the World*, pp. 18ff.

known to be a carpenter (Mk. 6:3), although this was probably more because they considered him to be uneducated (compared with the rabbis) than because of his trade.

The second consideration is that in the NT the emphasis on secular employment is not treated as an end in itself, but as contributing to the service of God.[125] More than once Paul claims to have supported himself by his own labours (Acts 20:34; 1 Thes. 2:9). In this case daily work is no more than a means to an end, but even so the spiritual end in view adds a dimension to the secular which is not present among those who are uncommitted to Christian service. It is to be noticed that the NT does not dismiss the importance of secular vocation. Paul criticized the Thessalonians because of the idleness of some of their members and declares that those who do not work are not entitled to eat (2 Thes. 3:10). This implies, of course, that work was available and that these people were deliberately refusing to work on the ostensible grounds that the parousia was at hand. Paul's advice throws no light on the altogether different situation when prevailing conditions make full employment impossible.[126]

The nearest parallel to the concept of 'worker' in the NT is *doulos* (slave or servant) and to 'employer' is *kyrios* (slave-owner or master). The parallel has serious shortcomings in that the ancient worker had little or no freedom. It was impossible for him to withdraw his labour. Nevertheless, the NT advice to slaves throws some light on the workers' approach to his responsibilities. The main advice on the subject is found in several passages in the form of lists giving instructions on domestic arrangements.[127] These occur in the captivity epistles, the pastoral epistles and 1 Peter. The most striking advice is found in Colossians 3:23 (*cf.* Eph. 6:7), where slaves are exhorted to work heartily 'as serving the Lord and not men'.[128] Again, spiritual principles are seen to dominate a situation in which the slave had no rights and could be exploited by an unscrupulous master. Paul's advice would clearly not be workable in a society in which such a high spiritual approach would be abnormal.

Ideally a Christian should not tolerate a slipshod attitude towards his work responsibility, for in all his activity he is answerable to God. In the pastoral epistles Paul makes the point that where slaves have believing masters, they should serve them all the better (1 Tim. 6:1f.). In writing to Titus, he enjoins true fidelity upon slaves so that they 'may adorn the doctrine of God our Saviour' (Tit. 2:10). Again spiritual motives are seen to be powerful in affecting behaviour within the existing structure of

---

[125] *Cf.* Lillie, *op. cit.*, p. 106.

[126] *Cf.* W. Temple, *Christianity and the Social Order* ([3]1955), pp. 15f.

[127] For a detailed discussion of these ethical codes, *cf.* E. G. Selwyn, *1 Peter*, pp. 419ff. See also footnote 73 on p. 919.

[128] *Cf.* the comments of R. P. Martin, *Colossians: The Church's Lord and the Christian's Liberty*, *ad loc.*

society, and must have been a positive influence in counteracting some of the worst features of that society.

The NT is not wholly concerned with slaves, although a sizeable proportion of the membership of the Christian church was probably in that category. There is advice also for the masters which places considerable social responsibility on them. The clearest example of this is Colossians 4:1, where Paul says, 'Masters, treat your slaves justly and fairly, knowing that you also have a Master in heaven.' Once again, a spiritual reason is given for fair treatment. The implication is that masters, as employers, are accountable to God for their actions and attitudes. In the parallel passage in Ephesians 6:9 the point is made that God is master of both slave and slave-owner alike, which puts both on the same moral footing. Masters have, in fact, less claim on their slaves than God has, a principle which was bound to have revolutionary effects on the existing system.

Christian masters could in fact have a powerful effect on the contemporary society by the force of their example in their treatment of their slaves. Those acting on NT principles would in their day be in the vanguard of progress towards better work relationships. The NT does not condemn masters for owning slaves, but makes sure that they treat the slaves with the utmost respect which the system allowed. A man such as Philemon, had he acted on the advice contained in Paul's letter to him, would have set a noble example in forbearance in a society which reacted with the greatest severity against absconding slaves.[129]

The NT contains no specific teaching on the resolution of the kind of tension which arises from modern trade-union practices, but the total teaching would certainly militate against any restrictive practices which denied to a person liberty of conscience.

A related subject is the NT view of leisure. In the contemporary world there was nothing to compare with the modern problem of leisure.[130] Nevertheless, there is support for a day of rest, in accordance with OT teaching. The exposition of 'rest' in Hebrews 3 and 4 follows directly from the experiences of the Israelites. Although the 'rest' is applied in a spiritual manner, its historical basis is assumed. In any case the clearest directive concerning the whole institution of the sabbath is found in the gospels.[131] The strongest clashes between Jesus and his religious contemporaries were occasioned by disputes over the sabbath. The earliest hint of concerted action against him was on account of his challenge to the *status quo* (Mk. 2:27).[132] The sabbath was intended to be a benefit, not a burden, for Jesus

---

[129] Cf. E. Brunner, *Justice and the Social Order* (Eng. trans. 1949), pp. 97ff.

[130] Cf. A. Richardson, *The Christian Doctrine of Work*, p. 53.

[131] For a balanced comment on the Christian view of the sabbath, cf. J. N. D. Anderson, *Into the World*, pp. 24ff.

[132] C. E. B. Cranfield, *Mark* (*CGTC*, 1959), *ad loc.*, takes this statement as a Markan comment. But V. Taylor, *Mark* (²1966), *ad loc.*, does not reject the view that Jesus could have said it.

942

declared that the Son of man was Lord of the sabbath. This latter feature was to be the controlling factor in the reservation and use of a day of rest. Many problems must have arisen in the Gentile world where the Jewish pattern of the day of rest and worship on the seventh day was not followed, although the NT provides no guidance on such problems.

THE NEW TESTAMENT APPROACH TO THE POOR AND NEEDY

There have been few societies in which there have been no under-privileged people and, therefore, the problem of the attitude of society towards its less fortunate members is always pressing. The NT furnishes certain guidelines for a Christian approach to social welfare.[133]

Jesus himself is presented in the gospels as a poor man, and consequently had a sympathetic understanding of the position of others in similar circumstances. The beatitudes, in Luke's version, contain a special blessing for 'the poor', relating, however, to the poverty of the disciple group.[134] It has already been noted that in Matthew's text this is qualified as 'the poor in spirit', a qualification which gives an understanding which accords better with the general spiritual tenor of Matthew's presentation of the beatitudes. Jesus was not placing a premium on poverty. It must be recognized that the religious use of the word 'poor' has support from the OT and Jewish sources. Jesus did not organize relief for the economic position of the underprivileged. But this is not to say that he had no concern for the poor. His mission was not political, but spiritual.

A person's spiritual condition could not be identified with his social or economic standing. Many of the rich were spiritually more impoverished than many of the poor. Jesus acknowledged the difficulty of rich people coming into the kingdom (Mk. 10:24, 25), but he did not condemn riches as such, only their wrong use and man's wrong attitude towards them (Lk. 12:15). The condemnation of covetousness has an important bearing on a Christian's approach to his own possessions. It also influences the way in which he looks at material prosperity in society as a whole. When Jesus advised the rich young ruler to sell his possessions and give to the poor (Lk. 18:22), he was not giving a general directive to all his followers, but specific advice to one whose great weakness was too great a love for riches.[135] The incident confirms Jesus' concern for the poor. Furthermore, the somewhat similar statements of Luke 12:33 and 14:33 are not cast in

---

[133] R. Batey, in his book, *Jesus and the Poor* (1972), sets out the NT evidence on this subject.

[134] *Cf.* Lk. 6:20 and Mt. 5:3. I. H. Marshall, *Luke: Historian and Theologian* (1970), pp. 122f., regards the 'poor' as indicating those whose wants cannot be supplied by earthly helpers, which would include the idea of Matthew's 'poor in spirit'. E. E. Ellis, *Luke* (*NCB*, 1966), *ad loc.*, regards the 'poor' as the voluntary poor.

[135] Commenting on Lk. 18:22, W. Manson, *The Gospel of Luke* (*MNT*, 1930), favours the view that Jesus may have desired to make the man a member of his band of disciples and for this reason made his request.

the form of specific advice, but of general exhortation.

The question of almsgiving as a social responsibility is also raised in the Sermon on the Mount. The giving of alms is assumed, but Jesus comments on the importance of the manner of it (Mt. 6:2–4). In condemning ostentatious giving, he brought out the importance of motive in the dissemination of social benefits. Secret almsgiving is warmly recommended. In an age when no welfare state existed, this would have been a tremendous boon to the poor. It is an approach which excludes all possibility of a patronizing attitude. The follower of Jesus was not to seek praise from people for the largesse with which he expressed his social concern for the under-privileged.

Similar teaching and similar examples are found in the Acts and epistles. The maintenance of widows was a social problem which the Christians at once faced in respect to their own members (Acts 6). No indication is given whether they extended their care and concern to widows with no connection with the church, but it is probable that resources did not stretch to this extent. In 1 Timothy 5 advice is given about the support of widows. Those able to fend for themselves and those with relatives capable of supporting them are excluded. There appears to have been a register for widows over sixty who had proved themselves by their service to others. It would seem certain, therefore, that the sense of social responsibility was strong towards those within the fellowship who were in real need.

The earliest experiment in Christian communal living (Acts 2:43ff.; 4:32ff.) shows a high degree of social concern among the members, although the motive for the experiment was undoubtedly spiritual rather than social. It was the impulse to share their common faith more closely which induced the idea of common possessions. There was probably no calculation about the economic viability of the scheme, and certainly no economic theory comparable to the basis of modern communism. It is significant that nothing further is heard of the experiment. The epistles contain no hint that it should be emulated. Indeed, the organization of a collection scheme for the Jerusalem church (Rom. 15:25; 1 Cor. 16:1–4; 2 Cor. 8:9) suggests that the experiment may have led to the impoverishment of the Christians there.[136] The apostle Paul was clearly enthusiastic about his relief scheme and was disappointed when the Corinthians were tardy about making an adequate contribution to it. He argues from a theological basis for liberality, but it is noticeable that the recipients are the 'saints'.

When the Christians at Antioch heard Agabus' prophecy of coming famine 'over all the whole world' (Acts 11:28), their thoughts were immediately awakened to the needs of their brethren in Judea. It was again the limited responsibility within the Christian body which found expression

---

[136] Cf. G. S. Duncan, St Paul's Ephesian Ministry (1929), pp. 229ff., in which he discusses in some detail Paul's collection scheme for the saints.

in a contribution being made. In view of the fact that the famine had only been prophesied and was not yet an established fact, the speed with which the relief fund was organized speaks highly for the social concern of the Antioch Christians. Peter commends hospitality but this seems to be concentrated on Christian believers (1 Pet. 4:9). Hebrews 13:2 recommends the practice of showing hospitality to strangers on the grounds that some have unknowingly entertained angels (an obvious allusion to Abraham in Gn. 18:1ff.; 19:1ff.), but the strangers here may be unknown Christians.[137]

THE NEW TESTAMENT VIEW OF JUSTICE

A major part of anyone's approach to social responsibility is his view of justice. What is considered socially desirable is not always directly related to what is morally right. Yet in the NT a standard of justice is assumed and there is a clear differentiation between what is right and what is wrong. There are echoes of the old OT view of social justice as in the condemnation of oppression in James' letter mentioned above. The approach to law in general in the NT is intricately bound up with the Mosaic law, which makes extensive provision for social justice.[138] Jesus upheld the sanctity of the law, declaring that not one part of it should fail (Mt. 5:17–18).[139] Paul describes the law as holy (Rom. 7:12), in spite of his view that it could never effect salvation for anyone (see pp. 687ff. for a discussion on Paul and the law). The importance of the sanctity of the law is that it provides a sound basis for social action. For a stable society law is indispensable, although it is essential for law to be non-repressive if it is to achieve this stability. The NT demand for justice based on the moral character of God would prevent this and would ensure that what is just is good for society.

The trial of Jesus is portrayed in the NT as a miscarriage of justice. Pilate's pathetic attempt to absolve himself from responsibility for justice bears eloquent witness to the impossibility of doing so.[140] Although Christians came at once to recognize a theological significance in the injustice, in that the just died for the unjust (1 Pet. 3:18), nevertheless the fact of the miscarriage of justice remains imprinted on NT thought. Indeed, if the trial were to be considered just, it would be impossible to maintain the sinless-

---

[137] *Cf.* E. C. Wickham, *Hebrews* (*WC*, 1910), *ad loc.*, regards the strangers as Christian strangers in view of the close connection in this passage between love for the brethren and hospitality. For the pressing need for Christians to offer hospitality to their brethren, *cf.* J. Moffatt, *Hebrews*, (*ICC*, 1924), *ad loc.*

[138] An analysis of the use of *nomos* in Paul's letters shows that he frequently, although by no means always, equated the word with the Mosaic law.

[139] *Cf.* G. Barth, in *Tradition and Interpretation in Matthew* (ed. G. Bornkamm, G. Barth and H. J. Held, Eng. trans. 1960), pp. 64ff., for an exposition of the view that Matthew has developed the tradition here. E. P. Blair, *Jesus in the Gospel of Matthew* (1960), pp. 116ff., without discussing origins, concludes that Matthew at any rate understood Jesus' high regard for a true attitude to the law.

[140] For two studies of the trial of Jesus from divergent points of view, *cf.* D. R. Catchpole, *The Trial of Jesus* (1971), and P. Winter, *On the Trial of Jesus* (1961). The latter, a Jewish writer, is highly critical of the gospel accounts.

ness of Jesus. It follows, therefore, that human justice is seen to be particularly fallible, which supports the need for a more objective standard of judgment if social standards are to be maintained, and it is precisely this that the NT provides.

Certainly law is seen as restraint.[141] Civil magistrates have the task of resisting the bad elements in society and encouraging the good (Rom. 13:2–3). This touches on the important function of law and order in society. There is no support for anarchy in the NT. Anarchy is an enemy of social justice and places society as a whole at the mercy of any opportunist who temporarily gains enough control to impose his will on the majority.

Although the Christian church is not a democracy, neither is it an autocracy. Indeed the one instance mentioned in the NT where one man sought to lord it over the community is regarded with strong disfavour (3 John 9–10). The NT idea of the church is a community in which Christ, not man, is the head (Col. 1:18; Eph. 1:22). It is theocratic, not democratic. Its sense of law and order is dominated by God's will (*cf.* 1 Cor. 5:3–5) and in this respect it cannot provide a pattern, except in an ideal sense, for a society which does not acknowledge the government of God. Nevertheless, the fact that even secular magistrates are seen as ministers of God is evidence that the Christian is obliged to come to terms with society as a whole. The Corinthians' practice of taking court cases against fellow Christians to pagan courts is criticized, not on the grounds of the incompetence of pagan magistrates, but because of the incongruity of pagans having to arbitrate between Christian brethren (1 Cor. 6).[142]

The most important aspect of justice in the NT is seen in the exercise of authority. Whether it is in the family or in the state, it is assumed that some must exercise authority while others accept a subordinate position. Children are expected to obey their parents, and slaves their masters (Col. 3:20ff.). Citizens are expected to be subject to the government (Rom. 13:1). In other words the exercise of authority is unquestioned. But it is presupposed that it will be used in a just manner. Fathers must not provoke children, and masters must treat their servants justly and fairly (Col. 3:21; 4:1). Since ultimate authority comes from God, its exercise must be in harmony with his character. This is implicitly understood even when applied to the state. If the government passes legislation which is contrary to an individual's conscience, the NT would not expect obedience to that legislation.[143]

---

[141] For a study of justice and law in biblical thought, *cf.* H.-H. Schrey, H. H. Walz, W. A. Whitehouse, *The Biblical Doctrine of Justice and Law* (1955).

[142] F. F. Bruce, *1 and 2 Corinthians* (*NCB*, 1971), commenting on 1 Cor. 6:1, points out that as every Jewish community had its *bêt-dîn* (for civil justice), the least the Christians could do was to do the same.

[143] As Cullmann, *The State in the New Testament*, p. 59, points out, Paul is here dealing with the state as a matter of principle and is not commenting on the Christian's attitude when the state demands what it has no right to demand.

THE NEW TESTAMENT APPROACH TO POLITICS

It is at once clear that the NT is not a political manifesto. Indeed its kingdom teaching is essentially spiritual. Instead of a pattern for society based on a political programme, the NT concerns itself with a redeemed community whose characteristics appear idealistic to those outside the realm of Christian faith.

Some have seen in the person of Jesus a revolutionary because he so strongly challenged the *status quo* of his own times.[144] Certainly he was critical of the religious leadership, which also exercised considerable political power. Nevertheless Jesus would not allow the crowds to make him king (John 6:15). Although his approach to the establishment was revolutionary in principle, his mission was not accomplished by political means. His example, therefore, gives no indication of what the Christian approach to politics should be. Certain reforms are more within reach of spiritual than of political methods. Man's social conscience needs awakening before some social programmes can be carried out.[145] This happened in later church history, for instance, when slavery was abolished, or factory conditions were improved. The teaching of Jesus can certainly be a handmaid to political action, even if such action found no positive place in his mission.

The use of violence for the effecting of social reforms finds no support in the NT.[146] Jesus discouraged his disciples from the use of the sword (Lk. 22:36–38). Moreover, Christians are urged to live at peace with everyone. Social reform cannot be achieved if this fundamental principle is ignored. Methods which engender strife involve the violation of human rights.[147]

When considering the NT approach to the state we observe that the state is nowhere considered to be necessarily opposed to God. Christian citizens have the obligation to give allegiance to the state (Rom. 13:1f.),[148] and to

---

[144] *Cf.* S. G. F. Brandon, *Jesus and the Zealots* (1967). It is as well to recognize that the idea of Jesus as a member of the Zealot movement found support in the earliest period of NT criticism. A. Richardson, *The Political Christ* (1973), p. 41, points out that the idea originated with Reimarus. O. Cullmann, *Jesus and the Revolutionaries* (Eng. trans. 1970) distinguishes Jesus from the Zealot movement; similarly G. R. Edwards, *Jesus and the Politics of Violence* (1972). M. de Jonge, *VigChr* 23, 1969, pp. 228ff., points out the weaknesses of Brandon's treatment. For the latter's response to his critics, *cf.* 'Jesus and the Zealots: Aftermath', *BJRL* 54, 1971, pp. 47–66.

[145] *Cf.* Brunner, *Justice and the Social Order*, pp. 97ff.

[146] Not all would agree with this statement. *Cf.* the full discussion by J. Ellul, *Violence: Reflections from a Christian Perspective* (1970). For an advocacy of non-violence, *cf.* G. H. C. MacGregor, *The New Testament Basis of Pacifism* (1936); J. Ferguson, *The Politics of Love. The New Testament and Non-Violent Revolution* (n.d.).

[147] *Cf.* C. E. B. Cranfield's discussion, 'The Christian's Political Responsibility according to the New Testament', *SJT* 15, 1962, pp. 176–192. Ellul, *op. cit.*, pp. 133ff., makes the point that violence may sometimes explode facades in a society, but cannot promote a free society. The NT emphasis on freedom arises from its teaching about the value of the individual.

[148] M. Borg, 'A New Context for Romans xiii', *NTS* 19, 1973, pp. 205–218, sets Rom. 13 against the opposition of Roman Judaism to the government. For other discussions of the implications of this passage, *cf.* O. Cullmann, *The State in the New Testament*, pp. 50–70, and his excursus pp. 93–174; J. H. Yoder, *The Politics of Jesus* (1972), pp. 193–214.

pray for its officials (*cf.* 1 Tim. 2:2). This latter action is with a view to leading a 'quiet and peaceable life'. It is acknowledged that governors are ideally appointed to punish wrongdoers and to praise loyal citizens (1 Pet. 2:13). This is the essence of good government. The NT acknowledges, however, that not all government is good, for the Apocalypse portrays the state as an opponent to the people of God and as an ally of the 'beast'.[149] Clearly some discernment is needed to determine the extent to which a Christian's allegiance to the state can be expected.

Social responsibility is to some extent linked with the subject of taxes. Although rejecting any obligation to pay the temple taxes, Jesus nevertheless did not refuse to pay (Mt. 17:24ff.). Paul includes a specific injunction to the Roman Christians to pay taxes on the grounds that the authorities who extract them are 'ministers of God' (Rom. 13:6–7). But the problem arises whether the obligation to pay taxes carries with it any obligation for Christians to interest themselves in the administration of the taxes. There is certainly no indication in the NT that Christians cannot be numbered among the authorities who are 'ministers of God'. Yet because there was in NT times no possibility of Christians seeking administrative office, it is not surprising that the NT gives no guidance on whether Christians should enter local or national politics.

It may be wondered how relevant the advice of Jesus to love enemies (Mt. 5:43f. = Lk. 6:27f.) is in a national context.[150] He was clearly speaking of individual attitudes. Yet since communities consist of individuals, there can be no doubt that if Christian love motivated a large enough group in a community, it would have decided repercussions in reducing political tensions. Nevertheless, Jesus did not specifically deal with the problems of relationships within political groups.

MARRIAGE

The New Testament approach to marriage is an important part of its contribution to social ethics. Its teaching is based on some sayings of Jesus and of Paul. It will be necessary to consider not only the Christian view of marriage, but also the teaching on divorce. It must be recognized that the contemporary Jewish world had various views on the sanctity of marriage. The schools of Shammai and Hillel differed in their approach to divorce, the former being much more rigorous than the latter. It was certainly expected that the Jewish male would marry in order to produce

---

[149] For a full discussion of the state in the Apocalypse, *cf.* O. Cullmann, *op. cit.*, pp. 71–85.

[150] On the historical setting of this saying, *cf.* O. J. F. Seitz, 'Love your Enemies. The Historical Setting of Matthew 5:43f; Luke 6:27f.', *NTS* 16, 1969, pp. 39–54. *Cf.* also V. P. Furnish, *The Love Command in the New Testament*, who sees the double command to love God and to love one's enemy as the starting point for his study. W. A. Meeks, 'The Love Command and its Social Context and Function', *Int* 27, 1973, pp. 95ff., considers that Furnish has not sufficiently taken into account the specific form and social location of the Christian community.

more children to contribute to the continued establishment of the race. It should, however, be noted that in general Jewish opinion assigned to the woman partner in the marriage an inferior position. It is against this background that the teaching of Jesus must be considered.

Although Jesus was himself unmarried there is no evidence that he placed a premium on celibacy for his disciples. Some have attempted to find justification for such an approach from Matthew 19:12, where Jesus appears to commend those who make themselves eunuchs for the sake of the kingdom of heaven. Yet due attention to the context leads to the conclusion that the saying must be seen in the light of Jesus' teaching on marriage and divorce. Some have seen it not as a call to celibacy, but to fidelity in marriage.[151] But the more probable explanation is that Jesus was reckoning on some people voluntarily remaining unmarried for the sake of their Christian work, without in any way suggesting that marriage was not the norm. Another commendation to the disciples concerns those who have left relatives (including a wife, according to Luke 18:29) for the sake of the gospel. But this cannot be treated as a general directive, which would favour the break-up of family life. Jesus is clearly not in support of such a social procedure.[152] In the cause of the gospel there are times when the family stability may have to be temporarily broken, but there can be no doubt that for society as a whole Jesus supported the sanctity of the marriage relationship.

Jesus places a further seal on stable marriage relationships by using the description of the bridegroom for himself (Mt. 25:1–13; Mk. 2:19; *cf.* Mt. 22:1–14). He gave his blessing to a village wedding in Cana (John 2:1–11). In his teaching he makes no distinction between male and female in their standing before God,[153] but he gives no specific teaching on the state of the unmarried. Indeed, Jesus' teaching on marriage almost wholly centres on the problem of divorce.

The passages in the gospels concerned with divorce are Mark 10:11f.; Luke 16:18; Matthew 5:31f.; 19:3–9.[154] From these passages we may deduce certain features about the record of Jesus' teaching on this subject. In both Mark and Luke there is prohibition of divorce, whereas in both the Matthew passages an exceptive clause is introduced (except for unchastity). Many regard the clause in Matthew as a later addition to the more rigorous

[151] This is conceded by A. Kosnik *et al.*, *Human Sexuality* (1977), p. 22, from a Roman Catholic point of view.

[152] For a discussion of the difficulties in such words of Jesus, *cf.* R. A. Harrisville, 'Jesus and the Family', *Int* 23, 1969, pp. 425–438. He finds a duality in Jesus' teaching which he traces to the rejection of all legality.

[153] For a sympathetic appraisal of Jesus' attitude to women, *cf.* A. Feuillet, 'La Dignité et le Rôle de la femme', *NTS* 21, 1975, pp. 157–191. *Cf.* also P. K. Jewett, *Man as Male and Female* (1975), pp. 94ff.

[154] For a careful survey of the NT evidence on divorce, *cf.* D. W. Shaner, *A Christian View of Divorce according to the Teaching of the New Testament* (1969). *Cf.* also J. Murray, *Divorce* (1953).

form of the saying found in the other gospels. A further point is that Mark includes the saying that a woman who divorces her husband and marries another man commits adultery, while all the gospels contain a similar statement about divorced husbands who remarry. In both Mark (10:9) and Matthew (19:6), the creation story (Gn. 1:27) is cited in support of the teaching, but Matthew also includes the comment that Moses allowed a bill of divorcement because of the hardness of the hearts of the people.[155]

There can be no doubt from this evidence that Jesus regarded marriage as a permanent covenant between husband and wife. Nevertheless, if the exceptive clause in Matthew represents a concession on the part of Jesus, it makes provision for the innocent party in a matrimonial breakdown. There is difficulty is supposing that the early Christians attributed the exceptive clause to Jesus in order to promote his sanction for a limited divorce, if there had been no foundation for this in fact.[156] Moreover, Jesus would not be making an additional concession since it was universally acknowledged that adultery broke the marriage. It could be maintained that in Mark and Luke where it does not occur, it is nevertheless assumed.

The apostle Paul gives some consideration to the problem arising from a marriage in which one partner is a Christian and the other partner is not (1 Cor. 7). In principle he upholds the permanency of marriage where the non-Christian partner is willing. Indeed he goes as far as to say that the unbelieving partner may be 'consecrated' by the believer in the case of a mixed marriage (verse 14). On the other hand, if the unbelieving partner wished to separate, Paul agrees that this must be accepted (1 Cor. 7:15). It is clear from this that Paul does not consider that the Christian ethic could have any direct bearing on contemporary conventions regarding marriage. In the Greek world not only was divorce widely practised, but prostitution among married as well as unmarried people was rampant. All that Christians could expect to do was to set an example of stable marriages. Paul recognizes that the attempt by some to live as husband and wife and yet to refrain from sexual intercourse on spiritual grounds was fraught with dangers (cf. 1 Cor. 7:36–38).[157]

A major factor in Paul's teaching about marriage is the strong sense of the impending end of the present age with the result that his advice to the single not to marry must be considered against that background (cf. 1 Cor.

---

[155] It should be noted that Jewish views on divorce were varied. The school of Shammai was strict in its opinions, but the school of Hillel was lax. According to E. Bammel, 'Markus 10:11f und das judische Eherecht', ZNW 61, 1970, pp. 95ff., it was possible in Judaism for divorce to take place on the wife's initiative.

[156] R. N. Soulen, 'Marriage and Divorce', Int 23, 1969, pp. 439–450, finds a development in the NT teaching on divorce in the following order: Jesus, Paul, Mark and Matthew. He considers that Paul and the synoptics interpreted Jesus' teaching with freedom, but he denies that they were guilty of false interpretation.

[157] For a discussion of some of the difficulties in Paul's teaching in 1 Cor. 7, cf. J. K. Elliott, 'Paul's teaching on Marriage in 1 Corinthians: some Problems considered', NTS 19, 1973, pp. 219ff.

7:25ff.). His advice, even to the Corinthians, was not phrased in authoritative terms (see *e.g.* 1 Cor. 7:40). In view of the context it cannot be established as a norm for all circumstances. Although Paul chose the single state and appealed to others to follow it, this must not be construed as evidence that he was a misogynist. That theory is contradicted by the fact that he numbered women among his helpers (Phil. 4:2–3; Rom. 16:3ff.). It is also not without significance that he at times uses feminine imagery in relation to the church (*cf.* the bride imagery in Eph. 5:29–33[158] and the nurse imagery in 1 Thes. 2:7). It must, however, be admitted that there is little evidence in Paul's letters for action towards the emancipation of women.

Nevertheless, inherent in Paul's approach were principles which could not fail to have some impact on society as soon as Christianity grew strong enough to make its influence felt. Too often Paul's teaching has erroneously been cited in support of male superiority. Yet he certainly did not hold that view, as Galatians 3:28 and 1 Corinthians 11:11–12 show. It should be noted of course that he is describing the position 'in Christ', and it is certainly not clear that he would have imagined that his words had relevance in the non-Christian world. For a discussion of Paul's approach to the status of women in general, see pp. 177f.

RACE RELATIONS

Christianity arose in a world in which race relationships constituted a very real social problem, particularly between Jew and Gentile. The deep-seated hostility between the two groups showed no sign of abating. But in the Christian church the barriers were down. Paul affirms that in Christ there is neither Jew nor Greek (Gal. 3:28). In Ephesians 2:11–16 he shows how those who were 'afar off' are made near and that the middle wall of partition was broken down through the death of Christ. This is not to say there were no problems between Christian Jews and Christian Gentiles, but the problems were not racial but religious. It was a remarkable thing that the gospel had enabled the Jews to overcome the prejudices belonging to their religious culture and to accept Gentiles on an equal footing. Paul's discussion of the circumcision issue (in Rom. and Gal.) and the account of the Jerusalem Council (in Acts 15) are an evidence that the battle to remove the barriers was not easily won.

The way in which the Jewish-Gentile controversy was resolved shows the pattern of the NT approach to all race relationships. It is inherent in the doctrine of God that God shows no partiality and could make no distinction between Jew and Gentile over the question of salvation. Moreover, the

---

[158] For a discussion of the implication of Eph. 5:21-33 for the subject of marriage, *cf.* J. P. Sampley, *'And the Two shall become One Flesh'* (1971), pp. 157f. Sampley's conclusion is that the exalted view of the church in this passage leads to an exalted view of marriage.

importance of the individual in NT thought forbids any racial distinctions. A gospel which makes no difference between slaves and freedmen, males and females, could certainly not distinguish between Jew and Gentile, or between one Gentile national and another. In a world of widespread national mistrust and racial rivalries, the NT view of total equality stands out in stark contrast.

The question arises to what extent the revolutionary equality principle within the church has any bearing on relations in society at large. As with the question of slavery, social conventions over race relations could not be changed by direct action. It was only as the striking transformation of relationships within the Christian church permeated society as a whole that any leavening of those conventions could take place. The Christian who had learned to abolish his racial prejudices within the Christian community could not maintain them in the world outside the church. But the NT gives no specific examples of this.

There are many indications of the universality of the gospel in embracing people of all nations (*e.g.* Mt. 28:19; Acts 15:7; Rev. 5:9) and in every case the basis of acceptance is the same. The NT knows of no conditions which apply to one race and not another, and gives absolutely no sanction to any theory of racial superiority.

Chapter 10

Scripture

Introductory comments

Since it is not usual to include in a survey on NT theology a section on Scripture, some justification is needed for its inclusion here. There is no denying the importance of Scripture when surveying the themes that go to make up a NT theology. Two basic assumptions have to be made: (i) the continuity between the OT and the Christian faith, and (ii) the continuing relevance of the NT text. The approach to Scripture adopted within the NT has a direct bearing on the validity and importance of the theological concepts. No further justification is needed. But our field of study must necessarily be limited.

The NT does not expound a full-blown doctrine of Scripture.[1] At most it supplies data on which such a doctrine may be built. We must not expect, therefore, any systematic discussion of such issues, for instance, as the methods of inspiration or the concept of inerrancy. Both lie outside a precise exposition of the NT view of the OT and of the NT testimony to itself. It is salutary to recognize the fragmentary, although powerful, nature of the evidence for the inspiration and authority of Scripture, for this should make more guarded any doctrine based upon it. A careful study of the evidence will lead to a view of the text which has a direct bearing on the authority of the teaching which has been considered in the previous sections.

In the Introduction we noted the problem of the nature of NT theology, whether it is merely descriptive or whether it can be considered normative (see pp. 32ff.). Clearly if the texts from which the concepts have been drawn are authoritative, it must involve more than a descriptive discipline. If it is God-given and revelatory, its relevance must extend beyond the

---

[1] For some general treatments of the NT evidence in relation to the doctrine of Scripture, *cf.* B. B. Warfield, *The Inspiration and Authority of the Bible* (1951), pp. 229ff.; J. N. Geldenhuys, *Supreme Authority* (1953).

borders of its own age. It will need interpreting afresh in each age, to speak coherently to the prevailing intellectual climate; but, precisely for this reason, its basic authority must remain unchanged. The science of hermeneutics will be necessary, but any right interpretation of Scripture will not make any radical change in the authoritative character of the text.

The method to be used in the following discussions on scripture will be to focus attention on authority as the central key for an understanding of the idea of inspiration. It is because of the authority of the text, seen in the approach to it by Jesus, that its testimony to its inspiration must be regarded as valid for his followers. At the same time the text is authoritative by virtue of its inspiration. These are reciprocal truths: the self-evident authority of the text lends weight to the claims it makes for its own inspiration, while at the same time admitting of only one explanation, *i.e.* that in some way it is divinely inspired.

This will explain why in the following study we shall not drive too thick a wedge between authority and inspiration, although recognizing a distinction between them. The real clue to the whole subject is to be found in the personal authority of Jesus himself.[2] His approach to the OT forms the strongest possible grounds for the Christian estimate of it, and his approach to his own teaching provides a solid basis for a right assessment of the NT.

It will be necessary to set the use of the OT by Jesus and the apostles against the current Jewish use in order to bring out both their similarity and distinctiveness. The discovery of the Qumran scrolls has added greatly to our knowledge of contemporary Jewish exegesis and has highlighted the originality of the interpretations of the OT in the teaching of Jesus.

The plan of the following discussion may be set out in three stages: (i) the general use of the OT, (ii) the authority and inspiration of the OT text, and (iii) the basis for an approach to the authority and inspiration of the NT. For a complete survey it would be necessary to discuss the limits of the OT and NT canons, but this lies outside the scope of this book. There are reasonable grounds for supposing that the OT canon known to Jesus and the apostolic church was the same as the Hebrew OT (which excludes the Apocrypha). A discussion of the OT canon belongs to the background and not to the essence of NT theology. A discussion of the NT canon would take us beyond the NT itself into the testimony of the post-apostolic church.[3]

---

[2] Most scholars would agree that Jesus himself must be the key to the problem of authority, but not all would draw the conclusions set out in this section. *Cf.* J. Huxtable, *The Bible Says* (1962), who considers that Jesus' view of authority makes an appeal to insight on the part of his disciples (p. 87). He cites with approval Alan Richardson's remark in his *Christian Apologetics* (1947), p. 222, that God is not authoritarian in the exercise of his authority.

[3] For discussions on the NT canon, *cf.* A. Souter, *The Text and Canon of the New Testament* ([2]1954); A. Wikenhauser, *New Testament Introduction* (Eng. trans. 1958); K. Aland, *The Problem of the New Testament Canon* (1962); C. F. D. Moule, *The Birth of the New Testament* (1962). *Cf.* also J. N. Birdsall,

We have already noted the basic assumption that NT theology assumes a fixed NT canon (pp. 40ff.). Indeed, the study of NT theology itself bears testimony to the remarkable unity of thought within those canonical documents in spite of much diversity of emphasis and expression, and this contributes to the conviction that the books, which were later recognized as belonging exclusively to the NT collection, bear a common authority. This will become clearer in the course of our discussion.

The synoptic gospels

When considering the doctrine of Scripture, it is essential first to examine the approach of Jesus and then to compare with this the approach of the individual evangelists. We shall consider the methods of use and interpretation, the authority and inspiration of the OT as seen in the teaching of Jesus, together with any evidences which point to an approach to the authority of the NT. Then we shall note what relation the attitude of the evengelists has to that of Jesus.

JESUS' GENERAL USE OF THE OLD TESTAMENT

We may begin with the ways in which Jesus incorporated the OT into his teaching. This he did in two main ways, either by direct quotation or by indirect allusion. There can be no doubt that Jesus saw himself as the fulfilment of many OT prophecies.[4] This has already been made clear in the section on Christology, where the titles used were seen to be strongly indebted to an OT background, particularly Son of man, servant of Yahweh and Lord (see pp. 258ff.; 270ff.; 291ff.). It must be noted that even in these cases Jesus gives his own distinctive meaning to the concepts drawn from OT sources. What is significant for our present purpose is the sense of continuity with the OT seen in his use of these concepts. This is particularly true of his own awareness of his messianic office, and must serve as a powerful justification for the Christian conviction that there is a basic unity between the OT and the NT. Although inevitably an NT theology is concerned with the NT teaching, our previous surveys have shown conclusively that the OT background is indispensable for a true understanding of the teaching of the NT. This point is not in dispute in assessing the teaching of Jesus. But important considerations arise from a study of the methods of interpretation used.

The quotations from the OT in the recorded teaching of Jesus are too numerous to be regarded as incidental. They are, moreover, spread throughout all the synoptic gospels, with Matthew's gospel containing the

---

'Canon of the New Testament', *NBD*, pp. 194ff.; D. Guthrie, 'The Canon of the New Testament', *ZPEB* 1, pp. 731–745.

[4] R. T. France, *Jesus and the Old Testament* (1971) provides a detailed examination of Jesus' approach to the OT.

most. Some are introduced with a formula, sometimes specifying the OT writer (Moses, Isaiah, David), but others are found without such a formula. In addition to these precise citations, there are many allusions to OT imagery and to OT characters. We may say that the mind of Jesus was steeped in OT language and thought.

At times his use of Scripture is in accordance with the procedure of his Jewish contemporaries, as when he appears to base his reply to the Sadducees about the reality of the afterlife on the present tense of the verb ('I am the God of Abraham, and the God of Isaac, and the God of Jacob', Mt. 22:32 = Mk. 12:26 = Lk. 20:37, quoting Ex. 3:6). Again, when defending his own less rigid approach to the sabbath in discussion with the Pharisees, Jesus appeals to what David did, as the Lord's anointed, and assumes that what applied to the lesser must also apply to the greater (*i.e.* to himself as Son of man and Lord of the sabbath, Mt. 12:3f. = Mk. 2:25–28 = Lk. 6:3–5). In both these cases there are parallels from rabbinic exegesis.

Sometimes Jesus speaks of the OT as fulfilled in the present as the covenanters of Qumran did.[5] At the commencement of his ministry in the synagogue at Nazareth, Jesus reads from Isaiah 61:1f. and declares that it is fulfilled that very day (Lk. 4:16ff.). This shows that at an early stage of the ministry he was conscious of the idea of fulfilment of passages carried over from the OT. In the passion narrative at the close of the ministry Jesus is seen doing the same thing, as when he cites Zechariah 13:7 in relation to his own passion and the scattering of the disciples (Mt. 26:31 = Mk. 14:27). In the enigmatic saying about the purpose of the parables in Matthew 13:14f., Jesus applies the words of Isaiah 6:9–10 to himself.[6]

There is another method of approach which must be briefly mentioned, although space will not allow more than a passing mention. That is the typological approach. The word 'typology' is used in the sense that persons and events referred to in the OT may be regarded as models (or types) for other persons and events.[7] When OT types are therefore applied to Christ or the disciples, this is done on the basis that there is a consistency about God's dealings with men. There is no doubt that in the OT the exodus was repeatedly seen as such a model. The appeal to type as a method of interpretation, which for a while was out of favour, has reasserted itself in relation to OT people and events. The use of type must be distinguished from the use of prediction, in that type carries within it no necessary reference to the future. It is also sharply distinct from allegory with which it has often been confused. It is not to be thought that appeals to types

---

[5] On the method of interpreting the OT at Qumran, *cf.* F. F. Bruce, *Biblical Exegesis in the Qumran Texts* (1960), pp. 75ff.

[6] *Cf.* Longenecker, *Biblical Exegesis in the Apostolic Period* (1975), pp. 70f., for other examples.

[7] *Cf.* R. T. France, *Jesus and the Old Testament*, pp. 38–80, who gives a detailed discussion of the typological use of the OT. *Cf.* also L. Goppelt, *Typos. Die Typologische Deutung des Alten Testaments im Neuen* (1973).

treat the historical events as anything less than history (as allegory invariably does).

A few examples will suffice to show the importance that Jesus attached to a typological application of OT ideas. He compared himself with Jonah (Mt. 12:39–41 = Lk. 11:29–32), seeing himself as a preacher of repentance. In the same context he compared himself also with Solomon. In the temptation account, Jesus quoted from three sections of Deuteronomy (Dt. 6:13, 16; 8:3); the passage originally related to the people of Israel, whom he sees as typical, and thus he considered himself to be the antitype. There is still debate over how far the use of types is found in the teaching of Jesus. If he used types, the practice would provide firm evidence that Jesus' acceptance of the authority of the OT text rested on more than the obvious predictive passages. For our present purpose we may note the practice because of the evidence it supplies towards an understanding of Jesus' evaluation of the OT. Here, however, we are more concerned to demonstrate the kind of authority which he saw invested in the text, and this will be our next task.

JESUS' VIEW OF THE AUTHORITY AND INSPIRATION OF THE OLD TESTAMENT

The importance attached to what a teacher says is inextricably bound up with what kind of person he is. In the case of Jesus this is supremely important. We have already discussed the person of Christ under Christology, and have seen that the only satisfactory explanation of all the evidence is that Jesus saw himself, and others came to believe him to be, both man and God (see pp. 401ff.). In this case he is unique among men and his teaching must carry with it a unique authority. What Jesus says about the OT must be regarded on the same footing as what he says about his mission. It will be clear from the following evidence that he had the highest possible regard for the OT text and recognized in its words the voice of God.

We first note that Jesus did not question the historicity of the many OT persons or events to which he refers.[8] Such people as Abel, Noah, Abraham, Isaac, Jacob, Lot, from the patriarchal age are treated not as myths, but as actual persons. The same applies to Moses, David, Solomon, Elijah, Elisha and Jonah. The sayings in which these are mentioned would lose some of their authority if the historicity of the persons concerned were in doubt. It has been maintained that Jesus must be regarded as a child of his own time and would therefore reflect the view currently held about the historicity of the OT.[9] In that case it is questioned whether his approach can serve as a pattern for us in view of modern views about the OT. We must

---

[8] For fuller details, *cf.* J. W. Wenham, *Christ and the Bible* (1972), pp. 12f.
[9] *Cf.* for such a view, J. Huxtable, *The Bible Says*, pp. 74f.

consider this objection later, but before we can judge whether Jesus is simply reflecting the views of his times we must first be clear to what extent he showed originality in his view of the OT.

Another important feature is the way Jesus used Scripture in resisting his temptations, for it is clear that he regarded the words of the text as an authoritative answer to the insinuations of the devil. The formula used, 'It is written',[10] invests the words with particular authority, *i.e.* God's authority. They are in no way cited as the words of men, but as words possessing an abiding validity. The text of Scripture also provided for Jesus the words of dereliction from the cross (from Ps. 22:1), which shows how real was the OT text to him in his times of crisis (Mt. 27:46 = Mk. 15:34). In his final commitment of himself to God, he used the words of Psalm 31:5 (Lk. 23:46).

On several occasions Jesus was engaged in controversy with the religious leaders, but in no instance does he detract from the authority of the OT. On the contrary, he criticized the Pharisees for leaving undone the weightier matters of the law (Mt. 23:23), although they were meticulous over the observance of its lesser demands. What the law prescribed, they ought to have done. This sense of obligation to obey the injunctions of the biblical text is further illustrated by Jesus' emphatic announcement that he had come to fulfil the law and the prophets, not to abolish them (Mt. 5:17).[11] He took his stance firmly within the revelation of the OT in such a way as to demonstrate its authority for him. This must be borne in mind when considering the antitheses of Matthew 5:21ff., in which Jesus apparently sets himself against Moses.[12] In no sense is he undermining the authority of Moses, but rather bringing out the deeper meaning of the law. The personal authority of Jesus is seen in the words with which he sets himself over against the Mosaic law, 'But I say to you', as if the supreme authority rests on Jesus' own interpretation of the law (for further comment on this, see pp. 675ff.).

In Matthew 5:19 Jesus condemns any who relax the least of the commandments and commends those who do the commandments and teach others to do the same. He charged the Sadducees with not knowing either the Scriptures or the power of God (Mt. 22:29; *cf.* Mk. 12:24). He clearly meant more than mere acquaintance with, or even respect for, the biblical text, for the Sadducees were not deficient in either. It was real understanding that they lacked, an understanding which could come only through the power of God, not simply through human reason. In the Sermon on the

---

[10] For the uses of the expression *gegraptai*, *cf.* G. Shrenk, art. *graphō*, *TDNT* 1, pp. 747f.

[11] D. Hill, *Matthew* (NCB, 1972), p. 117, who recognizes that the verb *plērōsai* here can have several meanings, prefers the sense 'establish', in which case the meaning is that Jesus establishes the law and prophets by realizing them completely in his teaching and life.

[12] On the antitheses in the Sermon of the Mount, *cf.* R. Banks, *Jesus and the Law in the Synoptic Tradition* (1975), pp. 182ff.

Mount Jesus was concerned with the inner meaning of the commandment. Moreover he considered that the law and prophets could be summed up in two commands: to love God and to love one's neighbour (Mt. 22:37–40; *cf.* Mk. 12:29–31).

In view of the evidence already cited there can be no doubt that Jesus himself accepted the OT as an authoritative text and expected others to regard it in the same way. As a preparation for the future ministry of the disciples, he gave instructions which showed an interpretation of the text in relation to himself (Lk. 24:25–47).[13] What was authoritative for him was also to be authoritative for the Christian church. But before considering the significance of this, we need to enquire what evidence there is that, coupled with his authoritative use of the OT, Jesus also considered its text to be divinely inspired.

In setting out the evidence for Jesus' view of the inspiration of the OT text, we shall be concerned to demonstrate the validity of the words in which God's revelation has come to us. In Mark 12:36 we have the clearest statement when Jesus prefaces a quotation from Psalm 110 with the words, 'David himself, inspired by the Holy Spirit'. This is no mere formula, but a recognition that the text of Psalm 110 was a combination of man's writing and the Spirit of God. Similarly the reference to the 'abomination of desolation' in Matthew's account of the eschatological discourse (Mt. 24:15) is said to be spoken by (Gk. *dia* = 'through') the prophet Daniel. The authors in these cases carried no authority in and of themselves. Their authority was derived from the ultimate source of their messages (*i.e.* God). Hence although at times reference is made to the human authors, it is taken for granted that what they wrote was the revelation of God.

Another passage of great importance for an understanding of Jesus' approach to the words of the OT text is Matthew 5:18 (the jot and tittle saying). There is no escaping from the conclusion that this saying was meant to give the text (*i.e.* of the law) the greatest possible importance. But the qualifying clause (until all is accomplished) sets a limit on its validity and that limit seems to be connected with Christ's fulfilment of the law.[14] It is no wonder that Jesus more than once maintained that the Scripture must be fulfilled (*cf.* Lk. 18:31–33; 21:22; Mt. 26:24; *cf.* also Mk. 14:21; Lk. 22:37; Mt. 26:53–56; and Mk. 14:49). Such complete confidence in the fulfilment of prophecy[15] is intelligible only on the grounds that the

---

[13] Those scholars who regard the Emmaus story as a cult legend naturally put a different complexion on the words of Jesus regarding the OT. *Cf.* H. D. Betz, 'The Origin and Nature of Christian Faith According to the Emmaus Legend (Lk. 24:13-32)', *Int* 23, 1969, pp. 32-46. *Cf.* also A. Ehrhardt, 'The Disciples of Emmaus', *NTS* 10, 1963-4, pp. 182-201, who is not disposed to reject the story simply because it is expressed in an established mythical form.

[14] *Cf.* Wenham, *op. cit.*, p. 47.

[15] On the fulfilment theme in the NT, *cf.* W. G. Kümmel, *Promise and Fulfilment* (Eng. trans. 1957); F. F. Bruce, *This is That* (1968); *idem*, *The Time is Fulfilled* (1978).

prophecy was God-given and therefore thoroughly trustworthy.

This cumulative evidence from the synoptic gospels, which is corroborated by the Johannine evidence, is so strong that it is surprising that it should be called in question. We need to note the grounds on which criticisms have been made. It has been supposed that Jesus, being a child of his age, shared a naïve and totally uncritical approach to the OT in line with his Jewish contemporaries. Some modern criticism has called in question so much of the historicity of the OT that, if its conclusions are correct, the relevance of Jesus' regard for the essential historicity of people and events must be affected. It would then be necessary to maintain either an accommodation theory, in which it is held that Jesus adjusted his view of the OT to the level of his contemporaries, or to suppose that the evidence already cited reflects the convictions of the early church and cannot be considered genuine.

Neither of these views does adequate justice to the nature of Jesus reflected in the gospels. The former leaves unexplained why Jesus did not correct the naïve views of his contemporaries. He could not have taken the view that he must gently begin where his hearers already were in order to lead them on to fuller truth, for on many occasions he did not mince his words when criticizing strongly held opinions. The second explanation supposes that Jesus' genuine views of Scripture left no mark on the early Christians; but it is inconceivable that the strong imprint of authoritative Scripture on the gospel records was due to the imagination of the Christians. A belief in the inspiration and authority of Scripture runs through all the NT books and must have been derived from Jesus himself. It certainly makes better sense to suppose that the Christian church appealed strongly to Scripture because Jesus had done so, than to suppose that the Christians inherited from the Jews high view of Scripture not held by Jesus.

Those who are not disposed to accept the authenticity of much of the teaching of Jesus will naturally put little store on Jesus' approach to the OT. Indeed, the Jewishness is recognized to be an evidence of non-genuineness by many. But it is more credible to suppose that Jesus genuinely accepted the authority of the OT and intended his followers to do the same.[16]

JESUS' CLAIMS FOR THE AUTHORITY OF HIS OWN TEACHING

Of utmost importance for any approach to the authority of the NT is the

---

[16] J. Huxtable, *The Bible Says*, pp. 64ff., criticizes J. I. Packer's position in *'Fundamentalism' and the Word of God* (1958), in which he maintains that Jesus accepted the authority of the OT. Huxtable argues that Jesus was highly selective in his use of the OT and at most all that could be claimed is that Jesus accepted the authority of *part* of it (p. 71). But it is surely reasonable to suppose that when Jesus quotes any part of the OT as authoritative, he regarded the text as a whole in that light. G. S. Hendry, *The Holy Spirit in Christian Theology* (1957), pp. 27ff., thinks that Christians would not have taken over Jewish belief in OT inspiration because of Jewish rejection of Jesus. But the NT evidence does not seem to support this reasoning. To Christians the OT was God speaking.

attitude which Jesus took to his own teaching. We shall list various sayings from the synoptic gospels which show that Jesus not only regarded his own words as true but also as authoritative. The claims are so definite that they rule out any parallels from other teachers. Jesus made astonishing claims for his own teaching which are intelligible only in the light of his nature as both God and man, discussed under the section on Christology. If his claims about himself are taken seriously, it is to be expected that his words will be invested with unique authority.

(i) We begin with the sayings in which Jesus maintains the eternal nature of his own words (Mt. 24:35 = Mk. 13:31 = Lk. 21:33). Since all three evangelists record the words in almost precisely the same form ('Heaven and earth will pass away, but my words will not pass away') they must have regarded the words as of particular significance. In the Greek text of Matthew and Luke the second part is expressed in an emphatic form (*ou mē*),[17] which gives even more point to the eternal validity of the words of Jesus. It is worth noting that the concluding words of the statement are an echo of Isaiah 40:8, which is also about God's word. In this way Jesus places his own teaching on an equal footing with, if not superior to, the law and the prophets (*cf.* Mt. 5:17f.).

(ii) The authoritative 'But I say to you',[18] which occurs several times in the Sermon on the Mount, at once places the sayings of Jesus above the law, in that his teaching reflects the authoritative understanding of the law of Moses. He saw no need to use such a formula as 'Thus says the Lord'. It was enough for him to speak in his own name. His own words carried sufficient authority within themselves. The introductory formula, with its implied contrast with the law of Moses, could have been blasphemous on the lips of anyone whose bearing and words were not in themselves authoritative. As it is, the words imply that what Jesus says must be treated as the words of God.

(iii) An importance is attached to man's attitude to the words of Jesus in the light of the parousia, for the Son of man will be ashamed of those who are ashamed of him and of his words (Mk. 8:38). A similar idea which highlights the importance of the words of Jesus is the comparison of 'teaching' to 'seed' in the parable of the sower (Mt. 13:3–23 = Mk. 4:3–20 = Lk. 8:5–15). The productive seed is what is received and believed. It is expressly identified as the Word of God. One's attitude towards the words of Jesus is regarded as crucial in establishing whether one's life is securely founded or not (*cf.* Mt. 7:24–27 = Lk. 6:46–49). Jesus expected obedience to his words as a basis for right living.

---

[17] In many MSS *ou mē* also appears in Mark, but the *mē* is omitted in B and D and is generally considered to be a later assimilation to Matthew and Luke. *Cf.* V. Taylor, *Mark* (²1966), pp. 521f.

[18] E. Schweizer, *Matthew* (Eng. trans. 1976, from *NTD*, 1973), p. 118, as a result of form-critical examination, admits that this emphatic phrase must go back to Jesus himself.

(iv) Knowledge of God is gained only by those to whom it is revealed by the Son, according to Matthew 11:25ff.[19] and Luke 10:21f. His position is authoritative. This comes out clearly in the concluding commission in Matthew's gospel: 'All authority in heaven and on earth has been given to me. . . . Go therefore and make disciples . . . teaching them to observe all that I have commanded you' (28:18–20). Although this important passage does not specify 'words', the 'all' is so comprehensive that the words must be included. The commandments of Jesus were not codified in tablets of stone as the Mosaic laws, but they were enshrined in the preserved teaching of Jesus. What the disciples possessed was a transferred authority which could be exercised only within the limits of his own teaching. Another remarkable feature of the teaching of Jesus is the number of times that he uses the expression *amēn* to reinforce the authority of his sayings. In John there are many instances of a double *amēn* (see p. 966) which is even more emphatic. The *amēn* certainly draws attention to the extraordinary character of the teaching.[20]

(v) In view of the authority which Jesus claimed for his own teaching it is undeniable that the basis for that authority rests in his person. Not only did others recognize the power of his words, but they saw the effects of his words. By his command people were healed from sickness, raised from the dead, exorcized of possession by evil spirits. Similarly his words demonstrated his authority over the powers of nature, as when he calmed the storm with a command.

(vi) Another factor to note is the complete absence of any awareness that his teaching might be wrong. He does not present his teachings in any sense as tentative. His judgments are expressed in absolute terms and his predictions are certain of fulfilment. The synoptic portrait of Jesus is of a teacher whose very words are charged with infallible authority.

On one occasion Jesus admitted to a limitation of knowledge, over the timing of the parousia (Mk. 13:32), but this in no way lessens his authority. It is clear that he did not consider this a failure of knowledge on his own part, but as an act of filial submission to the will of his Father for the work of redemption (cf. Mt. 11:25–27). This unique and mysterious case can in no way detract from the supreme authority claimed by Jesus throughout his ministry.

THE USE OF THE OLD TESTAMENT BY THE EVANGELISTS

It is important to distinguish between the way in which the evangelists cite the OT and the method used by Jesus, in order to establish the relationship

[19] *Cf.* A. M. Hunter, 'Crux Criticorum - Matt xi. 25-30 - A Reappraisal' *NTS* 8, 1962-2, pp. 241ff.

[20] J. Jeremias, *NTT* 1, p. 36, suggests that the Amen followed by the formula 'I say to you' is analogous to the prophetic 'Thus saith the Lord', although he recognizes that these words of Jesus were created by him to express his authority.

between them. Of the three synoptics there is surprisingly little use of the OT in the comments of Mark and Luke, and considerable use of it by Matthew. The difference is directly related to the purpose of the gospels, since Matthew's alone was designed for a mainly Jewish audience. It is all the more remarkable that Mark and Luke appeal to the OT so little in view of their inclusion of several instances in which Jesus cites the OT text.

We will first comment on Mark. It is only in Mark 1:2f. that he includes a quotation and this is a composite one from Malachi 3:1 and Isaiah 40:3, brought together in a midrashic manner. There is no doubt that Mark treats these texts as fully authoritative. To him what applied to the preparation of the way of the Lord naturally referred to John the Baptist. But having launched his gospel in this way, he makes no other application of OT texts to the ministry of Jesus.

Luke shows little more interest for he has only three citations (Lk. 2:23–24; 3:4–6). In two cases the introductory formula 'It is written' is used, and in the other 'according to what is said'. There is again no doubt that the words of the OT are authoritative. What is 'written' carries considerable weight. But the lack of more extensive citations is probably due to Luke's awareness that his Gentile readers would not appreciate the force of the OT words as readily as Jews would have done.

Matthew has several OT citations which he includes in his narrative, in all but one of which a formula of introduction is used which emphasizes the fulfilment motive. Whether or not these citations were culled, as some suppose,[21] from a testimony book is not certain; but even if they were, it is undeniable that Matthew attaches considerable importance to the formula. What is written in the text may be expected to find fulfilment. Indeed, the form of the expression would suggest that the event itself must happen in order that the text might be fulfilled.

There are similarities between Matthew's use and the principles of interpretation adopted in the Qumran community[22], in that the point of departure in approaching the text is the present events rather than the text itself. By various means, sometimes on the strength of typological correspondence and sometimes on the grounds of a Christian interpretation of messianic foreshadowings, Matthew brings out the significance of the scriptures which he cites. Although his key to interpretation generally comes from the fulfilment event rather than from the original context, he gives no indication that the context of the text of the OT is unimportant. His approach is entirely in line with the method of Jesus in his application of the OT text. The passages which illustrate these features are 1:23, 2:5; 2:15;

---

[21] Among those who have advanced this type of theory, *cf.* F. C. Burkitt, *The Gospel History and its Transmission* (³1911), p. 127; J. R. Harris, *Testimonies*, 2 vols. (1916, 1920); *cf.* J. A. Findlay, 'The First Gospel and the Book of Testimonies', in *Amicitiae Corolla* (ed. H. G. Wood, 1933), pp. 57–71.

[22] For further comments on Qumran exegesis, *cf.* p. 63f.

2:17, 18; 2:23; 3:3; 4:14ff.; 8:17; 12:17–21; 13:35; 21:4–5; 27:9–10. We shall note in our comments on John's use of the OT that there are several similarities between his approach and Matthew's.[23]

John's gospel

As with the synoptic gospels, we shall set out the evidence under the two approaches, that of Jesus and that of the evangelist. We shall discover a close affinity between them.

THE OLD TESTAMENT IN THE TEACHING OF JESUS

Five passages in John record Jesus as quoting from the OT, and in these instances his method of appealing to it is in complete accord with the testimony in the synoptics. The passages are 6:45; 7:38; 10:34; 13:18; 15:25.

In John 6:45 the words 'And they shall all be taught by God' are introduced with the formula 'It is written in the prophets,'[24] and the words are clearly regarded as authoritative. A citation which is difficult to locate in the OT is introduced in 7:38 with the form 'As the scripture has said', another testimony to Jesus' estimate of its prophetic character in terms of his ministry (the pouring out of the Spirit).[25] The quotation from Psalm 82:6 in John 10:34 is introduced with the question, 'Is it not written in your law?' which shows an authoritative appeal to the text of the OT and is followed by the comment 'scripture cannot be broken'. This reflects the contemporary high Jewish regard for the text of Scripture which both Jesus and the evangelist shared.[26] John 13:18 is a definite fulfilment citation, applied to Judas' act of betrayal. There is no doubt that Jesus regarded the words as carrying inviolable authority. It is the same with the citation in John 15:25 'They hated me without a cause' (cf. Ps. 35:19; 69:4), where another fulfilment formula is used.

In addition to these direct quotations, there is a statement in John 17:12 which refers to the fulfilment of Scripture in the case of the 'son of perdition'. Moreover, in the same passage Jesus declares 'Thy word is truth', affirming the validity of the revelation of God (17:17). While the Scripture is not specified here, the 'word' is sufficiently comprehensive to include it. Throughout the teaching of Jesus in this gospel there are many

---

[23] Comparing the Matthean and Johannine *testimonia*, A. Ehrhardt, *NTS* 10, 1963-4, pp. 188ff., considers this shows a change from the old synagogal collections of *testimonia* about the Messiah to a new Christian one. In any case the similar emphasis on *testimonia* in both Matthew and John shows the importance of these fulfilment passages.

[24] The vagueness of the expression 'in the prophets' is not evidence of ignorance of the precise source, but common Jewish practice. Cf. B. Lindars, *John* (NCB, 1972), p. 264.

[25] On this difficult passage, cf. J. Blenkinsopp, 'John vii.37-39: Another note on a notorious crux', *NTS* 6, 1959-60, pp. 95ff.

[26] R. E. Brown, *John* (AB, 1966), pp. 409f., answers the charge that Jesus was adapting his hermeneutical principles to those accepted in his own day. He points out that there is no evidence in the tradition that the early Christians considered Jesus' method of dealing with OT interpretation as unworthy of him.

allusions to OT persons and events (*e.g.* Moses,[27], Abraham, the brazen serpent, the manna), which are all treated as historical although an extended meaning is fastened upon them.

We may observe that there is no essential difference between John and the synoptics in their presentation of Jesus' attitude to the OT. John is clearly nearer to Matthew in recording the manner in which Jesus interprets the text, but all four evangelists show him to be one with his Jewish contemporaries in the high regard he had for its authority. The uniqueness of Jesus' approach was in the way he applied it.

JOHN'S USE OF THE OLD TESTAMENT

On seven occasions John brings in the OT to back up his own comments, all but one of which are in the latter half of the book (2:17; 12:15, 38, 40; 19:24, 36, 37). We must note the significance of these citations for his total presentation.

John sees a correspondence between David's lament in Psalm 69:9 and the cleansing of the temple by Jesus. He notes that the disciples remembered the citation, and considers it to be important to include it in his account of the event.[28] The only conceivable reason is that the backing of Scripture was considered to carry an authoritative significance. Like Matthew, John cites Zechariah 9:9 in his account of the entry of Jesus into Jerusalem (John 12:14, 15). This is a messianic passage and is naturally applied to Jesus. The citation is introduced with the authoritative 'It is written' formula. In 12:38, 40 there is a fuller fulfilment formula in the application of the messianic Isaiah 53:1f. passage to Jesus. John sees the unbelief of Jesus' contemporaries as foreshadowed in the experience of the Isaianic servant. He has no hesitation in identifying Jesus with the servant and sees every reason to cite the Isaiah passage as being in process of fulfilment in Jesus' ministry. In the three citations in John 19, the evangelist uses the events of the passion to explain the real significance of the original texts (the casting of lots for the garments, the avoidance of broken bones and the piercing of the side), which is only discovered when they are applied to Jesus. The citing of these scriptures in the course of the narrative was intended to add weight to the account.[29]

JESUS' CLAIMS FOR THE AUTHORITY OF HIS OWN TEACHING

We have already seen how strongly supported is this feature of the synoptic presentation of Christ. The Johannine Jesus is equally far-reaching in his

---

[27] *Cf.* for example, T. F. Glasson, *Moses in the Fourth Gospel* (1963).

[28] B. Lindars, *John*, p. 140, points out that Ps. 69 was quarried by NT writers more than any other OT passage, which shows the deep impression it made on the early Christians.

[29] R. N. Longenecker, *Biblical Exegesis in the Apostolic Period*, pp. 133ff., finds some significance in the fact that both Matthew and John are nearer to the Qumran *pesher* approach than Mark and Luke, and that they are attributed to direct disciples of Jesus.

claims, if not even more so. We shall first note passages in which Jesus makes statements which underline his authority.

In John 5:30–47 he insists that he is acting and speaking on the authority of the Father. Moreover, the Father bears witness through the words of Scripture (5:39). After the Bread discourse, he describes his words as 'Spirit and life' (6:63), in explaining his saying to the disciples. He disclaims speaking on his own authority, but maintains that his teaching is from God, when he discusses that teaching with the Jews (7:16). In the further debate in chapter 8, Jesus again affirms 'I declare to the world what I have heard from him' (*i.e.* he who sent me, 8:26f.). In referring to coming judgment Jesus even says that the word that he has spoken will judge a person on the last day (12:48). This is because the Father has given Jesus commandment what to say and what to speak (12:49). What he says is only what the Father has bidden him to say (12:50). Before Pilate Jesus declared that he bore witness to the truth (John 18:37), which, although it was cynically received by Pilate, nevertheless bears striking testimony to the validity of what he taught.

In addition to these direct affirmations there are other indications in John that Jesus recognized the authoritative nature of his own teaching. Of special significance is the double *amēn* formula which prefaced several of the sayings of Jesus in this gospel. Its importance for our present purpose lies in the particular emphasis it gives to the following words (*legō soi* or *legō hymin* - I say to you).[30] The strongly authoritative nature of such sayings is borne out by the 'I am' (*egō eimi*) sayings[31] which are a feature of this gospel (see pp. 330f.). The combination of the two (as in John 10:7) conveys a sense of authority which is not paralleled in the sayings of other people.

It is important to note that Jesus did more than affirm the authoritative nature of his own words. John records the highly significant promise of Jesus that the Spirit would recall those words to the minds of the disciples (John 14:26). The promise is that the Spirit would teach them all things and bring to their remembrance 'all that I have said to you'. The importance of this statement for the light it throws on the preservation of the teaching of Jesus cannot be exaggerated. It naturally depends on the value we place on the text and whether or not it is regarded as a genuine promise of Jesus.

The idea that it might have been an early Christian attempt to enhance what the church was officially teaching may be discounted, for this would leave unexplained why the believers invented the connection between the words of Jesus and the Spirit. It is more in accord with the general tenor of John's gospel to suppose that Jesus himself did not neglect to predict the

---

[30] R. E. Brown, *John*, p. 84, contends that for Jesus, *amēn* guarantees the truth of his statements.

[31] For a discussion of the significance of these *egō eimi* sayings, *cf.* J. H. Bernard, *The Gospel according to St John* (*ICC*, 1928), pp. cxvi ff. See pp. 330ff. for details.

means by which his teaching would be preserved. This present statement fits well into the general high esteem for his own teaching which Jesus shows in this gospel. If the Spirit calls that teaching to mind, this must be regarded as an important factor in the transmission of the tradition during the oral period. It would invest the teaching with a special authority, which in turn would explain why the written gospels soon came to be prized on an equal footing with the OT Scriptures (*cf.* also 16:13f.).

We conclude this section with three statements from John 17. Jesus says that he has given to the disciples the words that the Father has given to him (17:8). It is important to note where the authority lies, for this explains the nature of the words in the tradition. The word of God is seen as the agent of man's sanctification (17:17). As Jesus prays for his disciples, he looks ahead and includes those who would come to believe 'through their word' (17:20), which must be interpreted as the 'word' they received from Jesus.

There is seen in embryo in the comments of Jesus recorded by John the basis for the authority of the words and writings of the apostles. They passed on what they received and were conscious that any authority in their own teaching was derived from the one who was the central object of their faith. As we come to consider the apostolic preaching and the writings in the epistles and the Apocalypse, we cannot divorce such consideration from the authoritative tradition which formed the core of their doctrine.

Acts

The early Christians in their proclamation of the gospel relied heavily on OT testimony. In fact, in the preaching of Peter, Stephen, Philip and Paul, and in the statement of James to the assembled church, there are not only OT quotations, but an obvious conviction that what the OT said carried with it the authority of God. Invariably an introductory formula is used which refers sometimes to the human author, as, for instance, Joel (2:16), David (2:25; 34; 4:25), Moses (3:22; 7:37), Isaiah (28:25), and sometimes to the fact that the words stand 'written' (1:20; 7:42; 13:33; 15:15; 23:5).

Two passages are particularly significant in attributing the words of the OT to the Spirit (4:25, which is attributed to the church generally, and 28:25 which is a statement specifically made by Paul). This usage is wholly in line with the current view of inspiration held by the Jews and reflected in the approach of Jesus. In recording these OT citations Luke is more conscious of their importance in his account of the developing mission of the church than he was in recording the ministry of Jesus. In a sense Acts is a commentary on the exposition given by the risen Lord to the disciples on the Emmaus road (Lk. 24:27).[32]

---

[32] On this, *cf.* Longenecker, *op. cit.*, p. 92 n. 40.

In many of the citations, current Jewish methods of exegesis are followed, but in no cases are there evidences that the text is regarded as less than historical. The early Christians clearly had a high regard for the OT and treated it as a voice which must be listened to. Stephen's speech is particularly instructive in this respect, for his weighty appeal to OT history was intended to be authoritative for his hearers. It was not so much his view of the text as his interpretation of it that raised Jewish anger against him (*cf.* Acts 6:11f.). It was inevitable that Christian exegetes would part company with Jewish interpreters when Jesus himself became the key to the understanding of the text. But at no time did they part company over their regard for the authoritative character and divine origin of the text itself. The view reflected in Acts is continued in the epistles.

Paul

Even a most cursory reading of Paul's letters is sufficient to show the extensive use he made of OT citations. His methods of exegesis make a fascinating study, but cannot be debated here since our main concern is to discover what view of Scripture he adopted.[33] Because of his strong Jewish background, it is to be expected that he would share a common Jewish view of the authority and inspiration of Scripture and this is unquestionably reflected in his letters. In addition to examining his view of the OT, we need to enquire what view he had of his own writings, for this has a bearing on the way the Christian church generally came to regard them.

PAUL'S VIEW OF THE OLD TESTAMENT

In attempting a brief summary we shall deal first with Paul's use of the OT, and secondly with his one specific statement about its inspiration in 2 Timothy 3:16.

Paul's use of the Old Testament. There are more OT quotations in Romans than in the other letters, forty-five as compared with fifteen in 1 Corinthians, seven in 2 Corinthians, ten in Galatians, four in Ephesians and two in the Pastorals.[34] It is striking that in the rest of the letters no direct quotations occur. In addition to these eighty-three quotations there are a great number of allusions to OT ideas and OT events and people which are not supported by direct quotations. The sheer weight of evidence shows the powerful influence on Paul's mind of his knowledge of the OT text. This is one of the most important factors to set over against his alleged dependence on Hellenistic thought. Whatever other influences helped to formulate his theology, there is no denying that his greatest indebtedness was to the OT, and no interpreter of Paul can afford to ignore this.

---

[33] *Cf.* E. E. Ellis, *Paul's Use of the Old Testament* (1957), for a discussion of Paul's quotations from Scripture.

[34] The figures quoted are according to Longenecker's reckoning, *op. cit.*, pp. 108f.

In most instances Paul uses introductory formulae which furnish clues to his assessment of the value of the OT text. His most characteristic formula is 'It is written' which is clearly intended to introduce an authoritative text. One or two examples will suffice. He uses it in setting out his key idea at the beginning of his Romans letter in a citation from the OT in Romans 1:17. It recurs in each of the next three chapters (*cf.* Rom. 2:24; 3:10, where it introduces a string of quotations; 4:17), and many other times throughout the argument. It is equally common in the other letters where citations are made.

What is written carries with it for Paul the implication that it makes a claim on every reader. At times he notes the human authors, as Moses (Rom. 10:5, 19), Hosea (Rom. 9:25f.), David (Rom. 11:9), Isaiah (Rom. 9: 29; 10:20; 15:12). At other times, a citation is introduced by the general expression 'he says' (*phēsin*) as in 1 Corinthians 6:16[35], by which he clearly identifies the OT text with the voice of God (*cf.* also 2 Cor. 6:2). Even where the human author is mentioned as in Romans 10:5, this is immediately followed by a citation itself in which the text is almost personified, or else the formula, although mentioning the author, nevertheless distinguishes him from the divine author (as in Rom. 9:25, 'As he says in Hosea').[36] In those cases where the formula does not introduce such a qualification, it is reasonable to suppose that it is implied.

Further confirmation of Paul's regard for the authority of Scripture is found in such an expression as 'then shall come to pass the saying that is written' (1 Cor. 15:54), which is akin to the fulfilment formulae of the gospels. Paul also refers to 'what the promise said' (Rom. 9:9), and introduces one passage with a rhetorical question, 'But what is God's reply (*chrēmatismos*) to him?' (Rom. 11:4). Even more remarkable is the statement in Romans 9:17, 'For the scripture says to Pharoah', in citing a passage from Exodus 9:16 which records the words of God. This identification of the text of Scripture with the voice of God demonstrates Paul's unquestioned belief in the divine origin of the text. Moreover, he expressly says that what was written in former days (*i.e.* in Scripture) was written for our instruction (Rom. 15:4), which highlights its continuing relevance.

We should further note the basic assumption which Paul makes about the continuing of the OT revelation and the Christian gospel. His expositions of Christian doctrinal themes bring out the uniqueness of God's revelation in Christ, but do not depart from a high regard for the OT. This is because for him God's action in Christ is the climax and true fulfilment

---

[35] Since the verb has no expressed subject in Greek in 1 Cor. 6:16, it is permissible to render it as either 'God says' or 'Scripture says', without difference in meaning, C. K. Barrett, *1 Corinthians* (BC, ²1971), p. 149.

[36] It is of course possible to understand the formula here in an impersonal sense, in which case it would be practically equivalent to 'as is said' (so M. Black, *Romans NCB*, 1973, p. 135).

of the content of the OT. Although faith had displaced legal observance as the means of salvation, Paul can still speak of the law as holy (Rom. 7:12). Although some differences in the methods of exegesis might appear when Paul's handling of the OT text is compared with that of Jesus, they stand solidly on the same ground when it comes to their assessment of the authority of the text.

Paul's statement about the inspiration of the Old Testament. Before turning to 2 Timothy 3:16, we note that in Romans 3:2 Paul uses the expression 'oracles of God' in a way that appears to relate to the OT since this was 'entrusted' to the Jewish nation. In the ancient world 'oracles' (*logia*) were divine utterances which carried with them considerable authority.[37] When Paul describes God's revelations in this way, he is no doubt partly thinking of the repeated 'Thus says the Lord' which runs through the prophetic writings. In applying the word, however, he is in all probability thinking further of the whole OT.[38] It is important to recognize that an oracle is not dependent for its authority on the human agent through whose voice the message is conveyed. It is the message itself, not the messenger, which is invested with authority.

The statement in 2 Timothy 3:16 reads as follows: 'All scripture is inspired by God and profitable for teaching, for reproof, for correction and for training in righteousness.' An alternative rendering is 'Every scripture inspired by God is also profitable', which, while possible, is less likely because it does not fit the context so well.[39] Paul is concerned to point out to Timothy the nature of the Scriptures with which he has been acquainted since childhood, and wants him to know they are profitable because they are divinely inspired. The alternative rendering might raise the doubt whether only some parts of Scripture are inspired and therefore profitable, although this is not the most obvious meaning.[40] However conducive this latter translation may be to those schools of thought which adhere to a partial inspiration of Scripture, it is certain that such a notion would never have occurred to Paul and Timothy.

The word *theopneustos* ('inspired by God') has occasioned much discussion and we can do no more than summarize the salient points.[41] The meaning of the word in this context is 'God-breathed', and without doubt implies that what is written in Scripture is of divine origin. It throws no light on the way that this inspiration is brought about. The word itself

[37] *Cf.* J. W. Wenham, *Christ and the Bible*, p. 89.

[38] E. G. Selwyn, *The Oracles in the New Testament* (1911), understands the word *logia* as referring to oracles about Jesus Christ found in the NT.

[39] For a fuller discussion on this, *cf.* my *The Pastoral Epistles* (*TNTC*, 1957), pp. 163f.

[40] J. N. D. Kelly, *The Pastoral Epistles* (*BC*, 1963), p. 203, prefers the first rendering, among other reasons because the alternative would imply that some scriptures were not inspired.

[41] B. B. Warfield, *The Inspiration and Authority of Scripture*, pp. 245–296, has a very full and valuable essay on the interpretation of this word.

does not lend support to a mechanical view of inspiration in which the human writers are supposed to have been completely passive. Such a view does not belong to the manner of thinking in the apostolic age. All that Paul affirms is that the instigator of Scripture is God, not man. The human writers of the OT were the agents through whom writings were produced whose authority goes far beyond the authority of the human writers. Paul does not say that God breathed into the words that men had written to transform them into the words of God. He contents himself with the statement that the finished product was God-breathed. In this way the apostle makes clear that he regards the OT as indeed the Word of God.

The foregoing sketch of Paul's approach to the OT has convincingly shown that he maintained the same approach as Jesus. There is no means of knowing whether he had any knowledge of Jesus' use of the OT, for this depends on whether he knew the gospel traditions. Since in the traditions to which he refers in 1 Corinthians 15:3f. as having been passed on to him there is a double occurrence of the phrase 'in accordance with the Scriptures'.[42] Paul knew at least that the earliest beliefs were supported from the Scriptures. It is most natural to suppose that the early Christian practice, to which Paul was heir, was itself based on the example of Jesus. It is probable that the apostle Paul knew more about the traditions of Jesus' teaching than he reflects in his letters.

PAUL'S VIEW OF HIS OWN WRITINGS

In some respects this subject is more complex than at first appears, for it is inextricably bound up with Paul's view of apostleship. Indeed we must begin with a statement about the apostolic office. In the gospels the apostles are those specifically selected by Jesus to be sharers in his mission activity. None but the twelve were personally appointed by Jesus during his lifetime. But Paul consistently lays claim to the status of apostle. He could not fulfil the conditions laid down in Acts 1:21–22, for he had not accompanied Jesus during his ministry. He goes to considerable trouble, especially in Galatians, to assert that his apostleship was as valid as that of the Jerusalem apostles. It would lie outside our present purpose to conduct an examination into the concept of apostleship (*cf.* the earlier comments on pp. 762ff.), But no discussion of Paul's view of his own writings is possible without some statement about his consciousness of possessing a legitimate claim on the obedience of his readers. He certainly seems to assume this.

We note first of all that in the salutation of most of his letters he calls himself an apostle. The exceptions are Philippians, 1 and 2 Thessalonians and Philemon. Nevertheless in the text of 1 Thessalonians 2:6 Paul claims

---

[42] In his brief but important book entitled *According to the Scriptures* (1952), C. H. Dodd adds a subtitle 'The Sub-structure of New Testament Theology', which brings out the significance attached to this fulfilment theme.

that he and his associates might have made demands on the believers 'as apostles of Christ', although they did not take advantage of this. There is no mistaking the close alignment between the idea of 'apostle' and the idea of 'authority'.[43] Paul himself disclaims any suggestion that his apostleship is either his own idea or that it came about by ecclesiastical appointment. He uses such expressions as 'called to be an apostle' (Rom. 1:1), 'called by the will of God to be an apostle' (1 Cor. 1:1, *cf.* 2 Cor. 1:1; Eph. 1:1; Col. 1:1; 2 Tim. 1:1) 'by command of God' (1 Tim. 1:1), or more specifically 'not from men nor through man, but through Jesus Christ and God the Father' (Gal. 1:1).

Paul expects his readers immediately to accept his claim to an apostolic calling. But the question arises on what grounds he considered his writings to be authoritative. There are two main possibilities. Either his status as apostle is intended to carry with it its own authority, or else his authority is prior to his status and gives the latter its authentic nature. If the former, the idea of apostleship would tend to be equated with legitimacy of office, but if the latter it would consist of a more dynamic concept.[44] In Paul's mind there seems to be some idea that he shared a similar office to the twelve and yet at the same time he derives his authority from his special call to proclaim the gospel. What is most relevant for our present purpose is the consciousness he has of the authority of his own words.

When Paul says, in 1 Corinthians 9:1, 'Am I not an apostle? Have I not seen Jesus our Lord? Are not you my workmanship in the Lord?' he clearly links his claim to apostleship to his special missionary activity among the Corinthians, and supposes as a result a special relationship to them. He calls them 'the seal of my apostleship in the Lord' (1 Cor. 9:2). He immediately sets out certain claims he has upon them as a result. This specific instance may serve as an indication of his general approach to those churches which he has had a hand in founding. Even in those letters to churches which he had not founded, he still claims his apostolic right to address them in an authoritative manner (*cf.* Rom. 1:1; Col. 1:1). This was undoubtedly on the grounds of his calling as 'an apostle to the Gentiles' (Rom. 11:13), *i.e.* an apostle whose special responsibility was to proclaim the gospel to Gentiles.

The crux of the matter as far as the authority of the NT writings is concerned and particularly in relation to Paul's epistles is whether or not the apostolic circle was a particular group which was confined to the twelve and the apostle Paul. Although it would not be unreasonable to suppose

[43] For discussions of the apostolic office in the early church, *cf.* W. Schmithals, *The Office of Apostle in the Early Church* (1969); H. von Campenhausen, *Ecclesiastical Authority and Spiritual Power in the Church of the first Three Centuries* (Eng. trans. 1969); A. A. T. Ehrhardt, *The Apostolic Ministry* (1958); K. H. Rengstorf, art. *apostolos, TDNT* 1. pp. 407ff.

[44] J. H. Schütz, *Paul and the Anatomy of Apostolic Authority* (1975) discusses at length the distinction between apostolic authority and apostolic legitimacy (pp. 121).

that it was, nevertheless the term 'apostle' is not always used, even by Paul, in this exclusive sense. It is possible to draw a distinction between apostles of Christ and apostles of the church. The former would be the exclusive group and the latter special messengers. Although the distinction is somewhat tenuous, it is significant that Paul never calls either the Jerusalem apostles or himself apostles of the church. The basic idea is always of a divine appointment which carried with it a delegated or at least representative authority.

There were occasions when Paul writes in a commanding way as when he says to the Thessalonians that 'we have confidence in the Lord about you, that you are doing and will do the things which we command' (2 Thes. 3:4), He exhorts his readers to work with their hands 'as we charged you' (1 Thes. 4:11). On one occasions Paul draws a distinction between his own command and a command of the Lord's (1 Cor. 7:12), but even so he expects his hearers to heed his words. Indeed, he expresses the view that he has the Spirit of God in respect of the opinions he voices.

But it would be wrong to suppose that he is doing no more than expressing opinions. Even his own advice is in the nature of a command. He expects his readers to take his words seriously. He talks of his 'rule' in all the churches (1 Cor. 7:17). In the same epistle, he says that what he imparts is not taught by human wisdom but by the Spirit (1 Cor. 2:13). He is aware of the authoritative character of what he writes because he is directed by the Spirit. He knows he is specially commissioned to be a master-builder (1 Cor. 3:10). He exhorts his readers to imitate him (1 Cor. 4:16; 11:1). He wants the Corinthians to recognize that what he writes is a command of the Lord (1 Cor. 14:37). He regards his letters as a substitute for his own presence and therefore as carrying the same weight (2 Cor. 10:11; *cf.* 2 Thes. 2:15).[45] Indeed, he condemns those among the Thessalonians who do not obey his word (2 Thes. 3:12–15). In 1 Thessalonians 5:27 he uses strong words ('I adjure you by the Lord') in insisting that his letter should be publicly read in the community. Sufficient evidence has been cited to show that Paul regarded the words he wrote as having a powerful authority over his readers.

Because of Paul's remarkable conversion and his consequent conviction about his divine commission, it might be supposed that his position was unique. We do, however, find some hints of a similar approach to the OT and a similar evaluation of their own writings among other NT writers. The following is a brief survey of this further evidence.

Hebrews
THE OLD TESTAMENT CITATIONS

Dependence on the OT is part of the warp and woof of this epistle. The

---

[45] *Cf.* J. N. Geldenhuys, *Supreme Authority*, p. 84.

initial impression is that the OT text is treated with the utmost respect and this is confirmed by an examination of the introductory formulae used. On several occasions the text is cited as the words of God. This is clear in the recurrent 'He says' (*legei*) in Hebrews 1. In other instances it is assumed that God is the subject of the verb of saying (*cf.* Heb. 4:3–4; 5:5–6, 7:17; 8:5; 10:30; 12:26; 13:5). The writer treats the words of Scripture as the voice of God. In two cases the voice is recognized as the voice of the Spirit (3:7; 10:15). In the first case the words are from a Psalm (95) and in the second from a prophetical book (Je. 31). There can be no dispute that the writer shared with his Jewish and Christian contemporaries belief in the inspiration and authority of the OT texts. He is not particularly interested in the human authors, although on two occasions he mentions Moses in citations from the Pentateuch (9:20; 12:21). His overriding conviction is that what the OT says, God says, even where on occasions he is vague in his introductory formulae (as in 2:6; 4:4).

In spite of the fact that many scholars have maintained a strong indebtedness on the part of the author to Philo of Alexandria in his interpretation of the Old Testament,[46] the approach in Hebrews, unlike Philo, is essentially historical, although also symbolic. It is important to note here the distinction between an allegorical and a symbolical approach. In the latter case, a double meaning is seen, the original historical meaning and an extended meaning. Unlike allegorical interpreters, Hebrews treats the text seriously. Melchizedek, for instance, is a real person although he becomes a symbol for the royal priesthood of Christ. In this, Hebrews is again in line with the other NT writers.

There is a deep conviction that the Christian revelation has a living continuity with the OT revelation, although the new is better than the old. The superiority of Christ as high priest, of his sacrifice, of the heavenly sanctuary, and of the new covenant are never permitted to denigrate the value of the OT. When the writer speaks of the old as obsolete (8:13), he is speaking comparatively of the old as a whole system, not of the OT revelation. The fact that he cites the OT so much, and alludes to it even more, shows conclusively that he does not consider the testimony of its text to be obsolete.

THE AUTHOR'S APPROACH TO HIS OWN WRITING

We at once note a difference between this writer and Paul, in that he does not so readily reveal his thoughts about himself. Nevertheless, there is a certain air of authority about this epistle which in inescapable. The writer is in no sense giving a tentative exposition of his theme. He gives no

---

[46] C. Spicq, *Hébreux* (*EB*, ²1952) was a staunch advocate of this view. But against it, *cf.* R. Williamson, *Philo and the Epistle to the Hebrews* (1970).

suggestion that the Christian interpretation of the OT which he gives might be wrong. In his warning passages he uses authoritative terms to highlight the dangers of falling away from the Christian faith (*cf.* Heb, 2:1–4; 6:1ff.; 10:29). There are many other individual exhortations which are expressed in ways which suggest that the writer expects them to be heeded, although he does not use expressions like Paul's 'I command you'. In his conclusion he writes, 'I appeal to you, brethren, bear with my word of exhortation' (13:22). This is certainly a gentler approach then Paul's, but nonetheless breathes an air of authority, which springs from the conviction of a right understanding of truth and not from the status of a particular office. Indeed, the writer gives no indication of status throughout the epistle.

This highlights more vividly than the Pauline epistles the problem of the real basis of the authority of the text. It suggests that a broader base for the establishment of the authority of the NT texts as a whole is required than can be found in the category of authorship by an apostle. We may perhaps speak of apostolicity in relation to the contents of a book, in the sense that what it contains is apostolic doctrine even if the penman is not an acknowledged apostle. Admittedly apostolic doctrine is easier to recognize than to define. Nevertheless there is a basic affinity between the approach in this epistle and the rest of the NT. This affinity does not merely consist of the absence of any teaching which conflicts with the writings of the acknowledged apostles, but the more positive feature of an authority of its own which is in line with the recognized apostolic authority.

James

Although this epistle is of an essentially practical nature, it is not without direct quotations from the OT which are introduced to add weight to the advice given. James speaks of 'the royal law, according to the scripture' (2:8),[47] cites certain commandments of the law as 'he who said' (2:11), mentions that the text of Genesis 15:6 in relation to Abraham 'was fulfilled' (2:23) and cites Proverbs 3:34 as 'he says' (*legei*, 4:6). He also introduces a general maxim with the words 'the scripture says' (4:5). In addition to these quotations there are many allusions to OT people, events or ideas. James' mind is clearly saturated with the OT and he treats it as authoritative. He expects its dictates to be obeyed.

It is not so easy to determine his approach to his own writing. The question is complicated by differences of opinion over the identity of the author. In any case he was not one of the original apostles, although if he was James, the Lord's brother, as seems most likely, he may have been regarded in the same category as the apostles. He certainly held a position

---

[47] James' word for 'fulfil' in 2:8 is not the usual *plēroō*, but *teleō* (*i.e.* carry out). In 2:23, while *plēroō*, is used, the sense is that Gn. 22:1-19 explicates the statement in Gn. 15:6. This is a rabbinic concept of fulfilment, according to Longenecker, *Biblical Exegesis in the Apostolic Period*, p. 199.

of responsibility in the Jerusalem church according to Acts. But in writing this letter he is content with calling himself 'a servant of God and of the Lord Jesus Christ' (1:1). Whatever authority he assumes, therefore, is strictly theocentric and Christocentric. What he writes, he writes in a representative capacity and his words carry with them the stamp of authority beyond himself.

The Petrine epistles

In both 1 and 2 Peter we are confronted with a situation different from that of James, for in both the writer is introduced as 'Peter an apostle of Jesus Christ'. This is a precise parallel with Paul's practice and cannot be considered accidental. The form is intended to be more than a stereotype. When an apostle speaks, he speaks with some weight. But what general impression do the contents of these epistles give?

We note a positive approach to the authority of the OT again supported by both direct citations and indirect allusions. In *1 Peter* there are several quotations from various parts of the OT. The introductory formulae are much less specific than in Paul's letters and do not throw much light on Peter's view of the text. Nevertheless he speaks of 'the living and abiding word of God' (1:23)[48], and then proceeds to cite the passage from Isaiah 40:6–9 which emphasizes the enduring character of the Word. He mentions the insight that the prophets had been given about the sufferings and glory of the Messiah. Their predictions were due to the Spirit of Christ within them 1:10–11).

In citing Isaiah 28:16, Peter uses the expression, 'it is contained (or stands, *periechei*) in scripture' (2:6), which ummistakably invests it with authority.[49] The familiar 'it is written' formula is used to introduce Leviticus 11:44 as a basis for Peter's own exhortation to the readers to be holy (1:15–16). He can give an authoritative challenge because it is written in Scripture. There is no suggestion that the option of not obeying the Scriptures is considered. Those chosen by God and sanctified by the Spirit for obedience to Jesus Christ (1:1) are expected to respond to the high demands of the scriptural texts. For a similar assumption, compare 1 Peter 5:5. In 4:18 the writer expresses his own challenging question in the words of

---

[48] The use here of *logos* rather than *rhēma*, which occurs in the OT passage cited, is probably to focus attention on the revelatory character of God's communication, particularly in Christ. As E. G. Selwyn, *1 Peter* (1946), p. 152, points out, this significance of God's word is brought out by the adjectives 'living' and 'abiding'. Hence although its primary reference is not to Scripture, the total view of God's word to man would certainly include this.

[49] There is dispute over the significance of *en graphē* in 1 Pet. 2:6. Selwyn suggests 'writing' rather than 'Scripture' and thinks the reference is to a hymn (*op. cit.*, p. 163). But E. Best, *1 Peter* (NCB, 1971), p. 105, is surely correct when he argues that *graphē* here means Scripture. The verb, which is absolute and impersonal, literally means 'includes'.

Proverbs 11:31 LXX, without a specific suggestion that he is even citing Scripture.

As to his own sense of authority, Peter appeals to the elders of the churches addressed, not on the grounds of his apostolic office, but on the grounds of similar responsibilities. He calls himself a fellow elder (5:1). There is nevertheless no tentative nature in the manner in which he addresses these fellow elders. There is no doubt that he considers his words to possess considerable authority.

Although *2 Peter* is much disputed as a genuine Petrine epistle, there are still grounds for considering its claims at its face value. It certainly claims apostolic authorship. Moreover there are personal allusions in 2 Peter 1 which are in harmony with this, particularly the reference to the transfiguration (1:16ff.).[50] The epistle has only one citation from the OT (2:22, from Pr. 26:11), which is introduced with the formula, 'it has happened to them according to the true proverb', showing a fulfilment motive. There are, however, numerous OT allusions, as for instance the use of the words of Psalm 90:4 in 2 Peter 3:8 and the references to Noah, Sodom and Gomorrah, Lot and Balaam.

There are two passages in this epistle which are of some significance for our present study. 2 Peter 1:20, 21 is of particular importance. 'No prophecy of scripture is a matter of one's own interpretation, because no prophecy ever came by the impulse of man, but men moved by the Holy Spirit spoke from God.' This statement, which may refer to the whole of the OT Scriptures, switches attention away from the human authors to the divine acts of inspiration. There is no suggestion, however, that the human authors are without importance. These words cannot support a mechanical view of inspiration. They are concerned with the origin of the prophetic word. The author has no doubt that what the prophets said, God said. The part played by the Spirit is essential, but is defined in no closer terms than 'moving' or 'carrying' men along with him. In other words the Spirit energized or motivated the human writers so that what they wrote was not their views or opinions, but the message of God.

No indication is given of the manner in which this was effected. In common with other OT writings, this epistle reflects the contemporary Jewish conviction that the OT Scriptures were produced under the direction of the Holy Spirit.[51] The implication is that what the Spirit moved men to write carries with it a powerful authority when it is received, as was intended, as the word of God and not simply as the words of men.

Another important statement is 2 Peter 3:15f., which makes reference to

[50] For a discussion on these issues and the problems raised concerning them, see my *New Testament Introduction*, pp. 821f., 828f.

[51] J. N. D. Kelly, *Peter and Jude* (*BC*, 1969), p. 21, shows how widespread the Jewish belief in the inspiration of prophecy was. He refers to Josephus, Philo, Qumran, and rabbinical tradition.

Paul's epistles, and is the only OT passage to refer to any other part in a manner which suggests an evaluation of it. On the one hand there is an acknowledgement of the difficulties of Paul's writings, but on the other there is an obvious recognition of the importance of what Paul has said. Moreover, Paul's epistles appear to be placed on a level with 'the other scriptures'. It is often supposed that such a view of them shows that the epistle must belong to a later date than the apostolic period to allow time for such regard for Paul's letters. But there is no real reason to suppose that a long period must have elapsed before the authoritative nature of Paul's epistles was recognized, especially in view of the apostle's own view of the importance of his writings. Those who were wrongly using the OT could hardly be expected to refrain from doing the same to Paul's writings. The OT was closely linked with the Christian apostolic writings, because the latter constituted an authoritative commentary on the former.

We must accept that 2 Peter 3:16 is a strong witness to the rapid acceptance of Christian literature as authoritative. This is true even if 2 Peter is dated in the sub-apostolic period, but doubly true if its origin is traced back to Peter's own lifetime.[52]

One other statement in 2 Peter might be noted. In 3:2 an exhortation is given to the readers to remember the predictions of the holy prophets and the commandment of the Lord and Saviour 'through your apostles'. The latter phrase suggests some kind of authorized transmission of the teaching of Jesus. The linking of prophetic prediction to the commandments of Jesus shows that the process of building up an authoritative body of Christian teaching to place alongside the OT had already begun.

Jude

Like James, the writer does not claim to be an apostle, but uses the figure of a servant, just as James does. He is important for our purpose mainly because he is the one NT writer who cites from an apocryphal book. His citation from 1 Enoch is introduced by the formula 'Enoch in the seventh generation from Adam prophesied, saying' (verse 14). But did he mean to suggest that Enoch was regarded as Scripture? Since this is the sole instance of a formal citation in the NT from a non-canonical Jewish book, care must be taken to determine whether Jude's verb 'prophesy' (*prophēteuō*) is used to denote a canonical book. It seems most likely that he did not intend the word in this sense, but rather in the sense of 'predicting', since he applies to his own day what purports to come from the antedeluvian world. It would have been different if any of the normal citation-formulae had been used, for then there would have been little doubt that Jude was treating the

---

[52] Kelly, *op. cit.*, pp. 370f., who does not accept the authenticity of 2 Peter finds a major obstacle in the supposed agreement of Peter with Paul in this passage. Even according to this view Paul's writings appear to be placed firmly on the same footing as 'other Scriptures'.

book of Enoch as Scripture. But in the absence of a specific formula, the presumption must be in favour of a more general use of the verb.

In addition to Enoch, Jude probably is making allusion to the Assumption of Moses in reference to the archangel Michael. It must be admitted that Jude has a more respectful view of non-canonical books than most other NT writers. But he is certainly one with them in his regard for the OT text, for although he does not quote it, he makes many allusions to it and certainly treats its people and events as historical.

Jude has a similar statement to 2 Peter 3:2, but restricts himself to 'the predictions of the apostles of our Lord Jesus Christ' (Jude 17). The readers have a duty to remember these predictions, which shows their authoritative character in Jude's mind. All that can be said of Jude's approach to his own writing is that he handles his teaching with the same boldness and certainty as other NT writers.

The Johannine epistles

The writer of *1 John* does not directly introduce himself either by name or by office. But in his opening words he does give some indication of his authority. He had heard, seen and touched 'concerning the word of life' (1:1), which seems to be a clear claim to be an eyewitness. It would certainly be in line with a claim to apostleship, although such a claim is not made. The air of authority throughout the epistle is unmistakable. The author addresses the readers as 'little children' and expects them to take stock of what he writes. There is a firm conviction that what is written is true. It is not open to discussion or doubt. This writer is in harmony with the other writers. He can reiterate 'we know' without suggestion of arrogance or cant.

It should be noted that John does not cite the OT although he does allude to one OT personality (*i.e.* Cain, 3:12), and assumes knowledge of the devil's deceptions 'from the beginning' (3:8). He is more interested in the new commandment than the ancient law (2:8; *cf.* 3:23; 5:2f.), but there is no suggestion that the OT has ceased to be valid.

In *2 and 3 John* the writer introduces himself as 'the elder' without further identity. There are insufficient reasons for maintaining that this pecularity must differentiate this writer from the writer of 1 John.[53] It is more reasonable to suppose that all three epistles ascribed to John belong together. There are, moreover, no convincing reasons why the strong Christian tradition that the writer was the apostle John should be regarded as incorrect. Because 2 and 3 John are brief personal letters, the question of their authority is difficult to settle, but there is the same general air of certainty as in 1 John.

---

[53] See the discussion on this in my *New Testament Introduction*, pp. 886f., 895.

Revelation
In spite of the difficulties of interpretation which surround this book, it is more forthcoming than most of the NT about its own inspiration and authority. It is also a strong witness to the value of the OT for the Christian church.

THE USE OF THE OLD TESTAMENT
This book contains no formal quotation from the OT, but its language is saturated with OT allusions. To whatever other sources the exegete may appeal for parallels to its thought and ideas, the OT must be regarded as the major key to the understanding of its metaphors. It has been calculated that 278 verses out of 404 contain allusions to the OT Scriptures.[54] Since John's mind was so saturated with OT language, it is reasonable to deduce that he accepted its authority. In a book purporting to be a 'revelation' of Jesus Christ, its basic premise seems to be a continuity between the old and the new revelation, although this is nowhere specifically stated.

THE WRITER'S VIEW OF HIS OWN BOOK
Of greater importance are the indications of what John thought about the importance of his book. We begin by noting his description of it as an 'apocalypse'. Whatever superficial correspondence this idea may have with Jewish apocalypses, its distinctive feature is that the apocalypse centres around Jesus Christ. It is essentially a 'given' message and as such demands to be heard. The conclusion of the book matches this impression of authority by its warning against any who tamper with its text (Rev. 22:18f.). The warning is expressed in terms of divine action. Whoever takes away from the 'words' will be taken by God away from the tree of life. Such words are clearly no ordinary words, but convey the impression of special authority.

Moreover, John appears to have been conscious of his own inspiration. He is identified with the 'prophets' in 22:9 (cf. 10:11). He claims to have been 'in the Spirit' when he was commanded to write down what he saw (1:10f.). The command to write was repeated after the overwhelming vision of the risen Lord (1:19). At the conclusion of his writing, he reports the heavenly voice as saying to him, 'These words are trustworthy and true. And the Lord, the God of the spirits of the prophets, has sent his angel to show his servants what must soon take place' (22:6). On occasions John is involved personally in his own visions, as for instance, 5:4; 11:1. Nowhere in the book does he give the impression that he is composing his visions. The impact throughout, with its constant emphasis on angelic

---

[54] Cf. H. B. Swete, *The Apocalypse of St John* (1906), p. cxxxv. This author supplies a valuable table to demonstrate the extent of the indebtedness of the apocalyptist to the OT.

messengers, is one of authoritative revelation of things to come. Even the specific messages to the separate Asiatic churches are expressly stated to be messages from the risen Lord and, as if that were insufficient, the readers are urged to heed what the Spirit says to the churches.

In every way, the book conveys an air of divine authority. The many problems arising from its interpretation must not be allowed to obscure this fact. It was no doubt this feature which led ultimately to the inclusion of the book in the NT canon. Its authoritative conclusion forms a fitting conclusion to the NT as a whole.

Conclusion

From the preceding survey of evidence, it has become clear that, although no formal doctrine of Scripture has been expounded, there are sufficient grounds for maintaining that a common view existed of the importance and authority of the OT Scriptures for Christian thought. We may further say that many of the NT writers give hints of the authoritative nature of their own writings. From this it would be reasonable to claim that the NT supplies the basic materials out of which a more formal doctrine may be worked out.

(i) The approach of Jesus is basic. His approach to the authoritative character of the OT must provide the pattern for the Christian church. Not only so, but his view of the authoritative nature of his own teaching must lead to a high Christian regard for that teaching and to a recognition that it demands obedience.

(ii) The NT writers throughout show the same high view of the OT that Jesus held, and there is no suggestion that it no longer had relevance for the Christian faith. The strong motive for the writers to show that so many events and concepts are fulfilments of OT promises and prophecies under-lines the significance of the OT text. The frequent appeal to Scripture in an authoritative way from earliest times in the Christian era is undeniable. The testimony of Scripture was regarded as the testimony of God, as the citation formulae so frequently emphasize. With regard to their writings, the NT writers vary in their expression of awareness of the authority with which their words were invested. But it would be valid to claim that the awareness seems to be present, especially in the writers' consciousness of being led by the Spirit (notably in the case of Paul and John).

(iii) Our purpose in including this section on Scripture is two-fold. It has first been seen as a necessary part of the totality of early Christian thought. If the phrase 'according to the scriptures' in 1 Corinthians 15:3f. was regarded as so vital that it was necessary to repeat it in a brief early Christian statement of belief, a consideration of the place of Scripture in the NT must be included in our survey. But another reason for its inclusion is the role it has to play in deciding the extent to which NT theology can be considered normative. Clearly since the testimony of the NT is backed by an authoritative and inspired text, its teachings must have more than a descriptive function and must form the basis of the doctrinal position of the on-going Christian church.

Bibliography

Abbott, T. K., *The Epistles to the Ephesians and Colossians, ICC*, Edinburgh, T. & T. Clark, 1899.

Abelson, J., *The Immanence of God*, London, Macmillan, 1912, r.p. New York, Hermon, 1969.

Adamson, J. B., *The Epistle of James, NICNT*, Grand Rapids, Eerdmans, 1976.

Adler, C., *et. al* (eds.), *The Jewish Encyclopedia*, New York, Ktav, 1901.

Aland, K., *The Problem of the New Testament Canon*, London, Mowbray, 1962.

Aland, K. (ed.), *Studia Evangelica* 1, Berlin, Akademie-Verlag, 1959.

Albright, W. F., and Mann, C. S., *Matthew, AB*, New York, Doubleday, 1971.

Alford, H., *The Greek Testament*, (revised by Harrison, E. F.,) Chicago, Moody, 1958.

Allen, W. C., *St Matthew, ICC*, Edinburgh, T. & T. Clark,³1912.

Allo, E.-B., *Première Épître aux Corinthiens, EB*, Paris, Gabalda, ²1956.

Allo, E.-B., *Seconde Épître aux Corinthiens, EB*, Paris, Gabalda, 1956.

Anderson, H., *The Gospel of Mark, NCB*, London, Oliphants, 1976.

Anderson, J. A., *Women's Warfare and Ministry*, London, Christian Herald, 1935.

Anderson, J. N. D., *Into the World*, London, Falcon, 1968.

Argyle, A. W., *God in the New Testament*, London, Hodder, 1965.

Armerding, C. E., and Gasque, W. W. (eds.), *Dreams, Visions and Oracles*, Grand Rapids, Baker Book House, 1977.

Arndt, W. F., *The Gospel According to St Luke*, St Louis, Concordia, 1956.

Atkinson, B. F. C., *Life and Immortality*, Taunton, Phoenix Press, n.d.

Aulén, G., *The Faith of the Christian Church*, Eng. trans. London, SCM, 1954, ²1961.

Aune, D. E., *The Cultic Setting of Realised Eschatology in Early Christianity*, Leiden, Brill, 1972.

BIBLIOGRAPHY

Aune, D. E. (ed.), *Studies in New Testament and Early Christian Literature: Essays in Honour of A. P. Wikgren*, Leiden, Brill, 1972.

Bailey, D. S., *The Man-Woman Relation in Christian Thought*, London, Longmans, 1939.

Baillie, D. M., *God Was in Christ*, London, Faber, [2]1955.

Baker, D. L., *Two Testaments, One Bible*, Leicester, IVP, 1976.

Baker, E., *The Neglected Factor*, London, Epworth, 1963.

Baltensweiler, H., and Reicke, B. (eds.), *Neues Testament und Geschichte: historisches Geschehen und Deutung im Neuen Testament*, Tübingen, Mohr, 1972.

Balz, H., and Schrage, W., *Die 'katholischen' Briefe*, Göttingen, V & R, 1973.

Bammel, E. (ed.), *The Trial of Jesus*, London, SCM, 1970.

Banks, R. J., *Jesus and the Law in the Synoptic Tradition*, Cambridge, CUP, 1975.

Banks, R. J. (ed.), *Reconciliation and Hope*, Exeter, Paternoster, 1974.

Barr, J., *Semantics of Biblical Language*, Oxford, OUP, 1961.

Barrett, C. K., *The Epistle to the Romans, BC,* London, Black, 1957.
The First Epistle to the Corinthians, BC, London, Black, [2]1971.
From First Adam to Last, London, Black, 1962.
The Gospel According to St John, London, SPCK, 1956,[2]1978.
The Holy Spirit and the Gospel Tradition, London, SPCK, 1947.
Jesus and the Gospel Tradition, London, SPCK, 1967.
The Pastoral Epistles, Oxford, Clarendon, 1963.
The Second Epistle to the Corinthians, BC, London, Black, 1973.

Barth, K., *Christ and Adam. Man and Humanity in Romans 5*, Eng. trans. New York, Harper; London, Oliver & Boyd, 1956.
Church Dogmatics, Eng. trans. Edinburgh, T. & T. Clark, 1936–69.
The Epistle to the Romans, Eng. trans. OUP, 1933.
The Faith of the Church, Eng. trans. London, Fontana, 1958.

Barth, M., *The Broken Wall: A Study of the Epistle to the Ephesians*, Valley Forge, Judson Press, 1959.
Ephesians, AB, New York, Doubleday, 1974.
Barth, M., *et al* (eds.), *Foi et Salut selon S. Paul*, Rome, Pontifical Biblical Institute, 1970.
Justification, Eng. trans. Grand Rapids, Eerdmans, 1971.
Was Christ's Death a Sacrifice?, Edinburgh, Oliver & Boyd, 1961.

Bartsch, H.-W. (ed.). *Kerygma and Myth* 1, Eng. trans. London, SPCK, 1953.
Kerygma and Myth 2, Eng. trans. London, SPCK, 1962.

Batey, R., *Jesus and the Poor*, New York, Harper, 1972.

Batey, R. (ed.), *New Testament Issues*, London, SCM, 1970.

Bauer, W., *Das Johannesevangelium, LHB*, Tübingen, Mohr, [2]1925, [3]1933.

Baur, F. C., *Paul*, Eng. trans. London, Williams & Norgate, 1875.

Beare, F. W., *The Earliest Records of Jesus*, New York, Abingdon, 1962.

The Epistle to the Philippians, BC, London, Black,[2]1969.

The First Epistle of Peter, Oxford, Blackwell,[2]1958.

Beasley-Murray, G. R., *Baptism in the New Testament*, London, Macmillan, 1962.

The Book of Revelation, NCB, London, Oliphants, 1974.

A Commentary on Mark Thirteen, London, Macmillan, 1957.

Jesus and the Future, London, Macmillan, 1954.

Beckwith, I. T., *The Apocalypse of John*, Macmillan, 1919, r.p. Grand Rapids, Baker Book House, 1967.

Bell, G. K. A., and Deissmann, A. (eds.), *Mysterium Christi*, London, Longmans, 1930.

Benoit, P., *L'Évangile selon Saint Matthieu*, Paris, Les éditions du Cerf, 1961.

Jesus and the Gospel, Eng. trans. London, Darton, Longman & Todd, 1973.

Bentwich, N., *Philo-Judaeus of Alexandria*, Philadelphia, Jewish Publication Society of America, 1910, r.p. 1948.

Berkouwer, G. C., *Divine Election*, Grand Rapids, Eerdmans, 1960.

The Sacraments, Grand Rapids, Eerdmans, 1969.

Bernard, J. H., *A Critical and Exegetical Commentary on the Gospel according to St John, ICC*, Edinburgh, T. & T. Clark, 1928.

Best, E., *The First and Second Epistles to the Thessalonians, BC*, London, Black, 1972.

One Body in Christ, London, SPCK, 1965.

1 Peter, NCB, London, Oliphants, 1971.

The Temptation and the Passion: The Markan Soteriology, Cambridge, CUP, 1965.

Betz, O., *Der Paraklete*, Leiden, Brill, 1963.

Bieler, L., *THEIOS ANĒR, das Bild des 'göttlichen Menschen' in Spätantike und Frühchristentum*, Vienna, 2 vols, 1935–6, r.p. Darmstadt, Wissenschaftliche Buchgesellschaft, 1967.

Bittlinger, A., *Gifts and Graces*, Eng. trans. London, Hodder, 1967.

Black, M., *An Aramaic Approach to the Gospels and Acts*, Oxford, Clarendon, [3]1967.

Romans, NCB, London, Oliphants, 1973.

The Scrolls and Christian Origins, London, Nelson, 1961.

Blackman, E. C., *Marcion and his Influence*, London, SPCK, 1948.

Blair, E. P., *Jesus in the Gospel of Matthew*, Nashville, Abingdon, 1960.

Blinzler, J., Kuss, O., and Mussner, F. (eds.), *Neutestamentliche Aufsätze: Festschrift für J. Schmid*, Regensburg, Pustet, 1963.

BIBLIOGRAPHY

Bode, E. L., *The First Morning*, Rome, Pontifical Biblical Institute, *Analecta Biblica* 45, 1970.

Boer, H. R., *Pentecost and Missions*, London, Lutterworth, 1961.

Boice, J. M., *Witness and Revelation in the Gospel of John*, Grand Rapids, Zondervan, 1970.

Bonhoeffer, D., *Christology*, Eng. trans. London, Collins, 1966.
The Cost of Discipleship, London, SCM, ⁶1959.

Bonnard, P., *L'épître de S. Paul aux Philippiens, CNT*, Paris, Delachaux & Nestlé, 1950.
L'Évangile selon Saint Matthieu, CNT, Neuchâtel, Delachaux, 1963.

Bonsirven, J., *L'Évangile de Paul*, Paris, Aubier, Éditions Montaigne, 1948.
Théologie du Nouveau Testament, Paris, Aubier, Éditions Montaigne, 1951.

Boobyer, G. H., *St Mark and the Transfiguration Story*, Edinburgh, T. & T. Clark, 1942.

Borchert, O., *The Original Jesus*, Eng. trans. London, Lutterworth, 1933.

Borchsenius, P., *Two Ways to God*, Eng. trans. London, Vallentine: Mitchell, 1968.

Borgen, P., *Bread from Heaven: An Exegetical Study of the Conception of Manna in the Gospel of John and the Writings of Philo*, Leiden, Brill, 1965.

Bornkamm, G., *Early Christian Experience*, Eng. trans. London, SCM, 1969.
Geschichte und Glaube 1, München, Kaiser, 1968.
Jesus of Nazareth, Eng. trans. London, Hodder, 1960.
Paul, Eng. trans. London, Hodder, 1971.

Bornkamm, G., Barth G., and Held, H. J., *Tradition and Interpretation in Matthew*, Eng. trans. London, SCM, 1960.

Borsch, F. H., *The Son of Man in Myth and History*, Eng. trans. London, SCM, 1967.

Boslooper, T., *The Virgin Birth*, London, SCM, 1962.

Bousset, W., *Kyrios Christos* (1913), Eng. trans. Nashville, Abingdon, 1970.

Bouttier, M., *En Christ*, Paris, Presses Universitaires de France, 1962.

Bowker, J., *The Targums and Rabbinic Literature*, Cambridge, CUP, 1969.

Bowman, J. W., *The Intention of Jesus*, London, SCM, 1945.
Prophetic Realism and the Gospel, Philadelphia, Westminster, 1955.

Box, G. H., *The Virgin Birth of Christ*, London, Pitman, 1916.

Braaten, C. E., and Harrisville, R. A., *The Historical Jesus and the Kergymatic Christ*, New York, Abingdon, 1964.

Braaten, C., and Harrisville, R. A. (eds.), *Kerygma and History*, New York, Abingdon, 1962.

Brandenburger, E., *Adam und Christus: Exegetisch-religionsgeschichtliche Un-*

tersuchung zu Römer 5:12–21, Neukirchen, Neukirchener Verlag, 1962.

Brandon, S. G. F., *Jesus and the Zealots*, Manchester, MUP, 1967.

The Judgment of the Dead, London, Weidenfeld and Nicolson, 1967.

Branscomb, B. H., *The Gospel of Mark, MC*, London, Hodder, 1937.

Jesus and the Law of Moses, London, Hodder, 1930.

Braun, F. M., *Jean le Théologien, EB*, Paris, Gabalda, 3 vols, 1959–72.

Bring, R., *Commentary on Galatians*, Eng. trans. Philadelphia, Muhlenburg, 1961.

Brooke, A. E., *The Johannine Epistles, ICC*, Edinburgh, T. & T. Clark, 1912.

Brown, C. (ed.), *The New International Dictionary of New Testament Theology*, Eng. trans. and rvsd., Exeter, Paternoster, 3 vols., 1975–8.

Brown, R. E., *The Birth of the Messiah*, London, Chapman, 1977.

The Gospel According to John, AB, New York, Doubleday, 1966.

Jesus, God and Man, Milwaukee, Bruce, 1967.

New Testament Essays, London, Chapman, 1965.

The Virginal Conception and Bodily Resurrection of Jesus, New Jersey, Paramus, 1973.

Brown, S., *Apostasy and Perseverance in the Theology of Luke*, Rome, Pontifical Biblical Institute, 1969.

Bruce, F. F., *The Acts of the Apostles*, London, Tyndale, 1951, [2]1952.

Biblical Exegesis in the Qumran Texts, Grand Rapids, Eerdmans, 1959.

The Book of the Acts, NICNT, Grand Rapids, Eerdmans, 1954.

1 and 2 Corinthians, NCB, London, Oliphants, 1971.

Ephesians, London, Pickering, 1961.

The Epistle to the Hebrews, NICNT, Grand Rapids, Eerdmans, 1964.

The Epistle of Paul to the Romans, TNTC, London, Tyndale, 1963.

The Epistles of John, London, Pickering, 1970.

Paul and Jesus, Grand Rapids, Baker Book House, 1974.

Second Thoughts on the Dead Sea Scrolls, Exeter, Paternoster, 1956.

This is That, Exeter, Paternoster, 1968.

The Time is Fulfilled, Exeter, Paternoster, 1978.

Bruner, F. D., *A Theology of the Holy Spirit*, London, Hodder, 1970.

Brunner, E., *The Christian Doctrine of the Church, Faith, and the Consummation*, Eng. trans. London, Lutterworth, 1962.

The Christian Doctrine of Creation and Redemption, Eng. trans. London, Lutterworth, 1952.

Justice and the Social Order, Eng. trans. London, Lutterworth, 1949.

The Letter to the Romans, Eng. trans. London, Lutterworth, 1959.

Man in Revolt, Eng. trans. London, Lutterworth, 1939.

Buchanan, C. (ed.), *Evangelical Essays on Church and Sacraments*, London, SPCK, 1972.

Buchanan, G. W., *The Consequences of the Covenant*, Leiden, Brill, 1970.

BIBLIOGRAPHY

Büchsel, F., *Der Geist Gottes im Neuen Testament*, Gütersloh, Bertelsmann, 1926.

Bultmann, R., *Exegetische Probleme des zweiten Korintherbriefes*, Uppsala, Wretmans Boktryckeri A.-B., 1947.

Existence and faith (essays translated by S. M. Ogden), London, Hodder, 1961.

Faith and Understanding, 1933, Eng. trans., London, SCM, 1969, from ⁶1966.

The Gospel of John: A Commentary, Eng. trans. Oxford, Blackwell, 1971.

History and Eschatology, Eng. trans. Edinburgh, Edinburgh University Press, 1957.

The History of the Synoptic Tradition, Eng. trans. Oxford, Blackwell, 1963, ²1968.

Jesus and the Word, Eng. trans. London, Nicholson and Watson, 1935.

Jesus Christ and Mythology, Eng. trans. London, SCM, 1960.

The Johannine Epistles, KEK, 1967, Eng. trans. Philadelphia, 1973.

Primitive Christianity in its Contemporary Setting, Eng. trans. London, Thames & Hudson, 1956.

Theology of the New Testament, Eng. trans. London, SCM, 1956.

and Kundsin, K., *Form Criticism*, Eng. trans. 1934, r.p. New York, Harper, 1962

Buren, P. M. van, *The Secular Meaning of the Gospel*, London, SCM, 1963.

Burger, C., *Jesus als Davidssohn: Eine traditionsgeschichtliche Untersuchung, FRLANT*, Göttingen, V & R. 1970.

Burkitt, F. C., *The Gospel History and its Transmission*, Edinburgh, T. & T. Clark, 1906, ³1911.

Burney, C. F., *The Aramaic Origin of the Fourth Gospel*, Oxford, Clarendon, 1922.

Burrows, M., *The Dead Sea Scrolls*, London, Secker & Warburg, 1956.

Burton, E. D., *Spirit, Soul and Flesh*, Chicago, Chicago University Press, 1918.

Bushnell, H., *The Vicarious Sacrifice*, London, Alexander Strachan, 1866.

Cadbury, H. J., *The Peril of Modernising Jesus*, London, SPCK, 1937.

Cadman, W. H., *The Open Heaven*, Oxford, Blackwell, 1969.

Cadoux, A. T., *The Theology of Jesus*, London, Nicholson and Watson, 1940.

Cadoux, C. J., *The Early Church and the World*, Edindurgh, T. & T. Clark, 1925, r.p. 1955.

Caird, G. B., *A Commentary on the Revelation of St John the Divine, BC*, London, Black, 1966.

The Gospel of St Luke, Harmondsworth, Penguin, 1963; London, Black, 1968.

Principalities and Powers, Oxford, Clarendon, 1956.

Cairns, D., *The Image of God in Man*, London, SCM, 1953.

Campbell, J. V., *Three New Testament Studies*, Leiden, Brill, 1965.

Campenhausen, H. von, *Ecclesiastical Authority and Spiritual Power in the Church of the First Three Centuries*, Eng. trans. London, Black, 1969.

Tradition and Life in the Church, Eng. trans. London, Collins, 1968.

The Virgin Birth in the Theology of the Ancient Church, Eng. trans. London, SCM, 1964.

Candlish, J. S., *The Biblical Doctrine of Sin*, Edinburgh, T. & T. Clark, n.d.

The Christian Doctrine of God, Edinburgh, T. & T. Clark, n.d.

Carey, G., *I Believe in Man*, London, Hodder, 1977.

Catchpole, D. R., *The Trial of Jesus*, Leiden, Brill, 1971.

Catherwood, Sir Fred, *The Christian in Industrial Society*, Leicester, IVP, [3]1980.

Cavallin, H. C. C., *Life after Death*, Lund, Gleerup, 1974.

Cave, S., *The Doctrine of the Work of Christ*, London, University of London Press, 1937.

Cerfaux, L., *The Christian in the Theology of St Paul*, Eng. trans. London, Chapman, 1967.

The Church in the Theology of St Paul, Eng. trans. New York, Herder; London, Nelson, 1959.

Recueil Lucien Cerfaux, Gembloux, Ducelot, 1954.

Chafer, L. S., *Systematic Theology* 5, Dallas, Dallas Seminary Press, 1948.

Charles, R. H., *A Critical and Exegetical Commentary on the Book of Daniel*, Edinburgh, T. & T. Clark, 1929.

A Critical History of the Doctrine of a Future Life, London, Black, [2]1913.

Eschatology, Hebrew, Jewish, Christian, London, Black, [2]1913.

The Revelation of St John, ICC, Edinburgh, T. & T. Clark, 1920.

Charlesworth, J. H. (ed.), *John and Qumran*, London, Chapman, 1972.

Clarke, N., *Interpreting the Resurrection*, London, SCM, 1967.

Clouse, R. G. (ed.), *The Meaning of the Millennium*, Downers Grove, Illinois, IVP, 1977.

Cole, R. A., *The Epistle of Paul to the Galatians, TNTC*, London, Tyndale, 1965.

Collange, J.-F., *L'Épître de Saint Paul aux Philippiens*, Neuchâtel, Delachaux, 1973.

Collingwood, R. G., *The Idea of History*, Oxford, OUP, 1946.

Colpe, C., *Die religionsgeschichtliche Schule*, Göttingen, V. & R, 1961.

Come, A. B., *Human Spirit and Holy Spirit*, Philadelphia, Westminster, 1959.

BIBLIOGRAPHY

Conzelmann, H., *Die Apostelgeschichte, LHB*, Tübingen, Mohr, 1972.

I Corinthians, KEK, 1969, Eng. trans. *Hermeneia*, Philadelphia, Fortress, 1975.

Jesus, Eng. trans. Philadelphia, Fortress, 1978.

An Outline of the Theology of the New Testament, Eng. trans. London, SCM, 1969.

The Theology of St Luke, Eng. trans. London, Faber, 1960.

Corell, A., *Consummatum Est; Eschatology and Church in the Gospel of St John*, London, SPCK, 1958.

Corte, N., *The Origin of Man*, London, Burns & Oates, 1959.

Cranfield, C. E. B., *Commentary on Romans, ICC*, I, Edinburgh, T. & T. Clark, 1975.

1 and 2 Peter and Jude, London, SCM, 1960.

Saint Mark, CGTC, Cambridge, CUP, 1959.

Creed, J. M., *The Gospel according to St Luke*, London, Macmillan, 1930.

Cross, F. L., *1 Peter: A Paschal Liturgy*, London Mowbray, 1954.

(ed.), *The Gospels Reconsidered* (r.p. from *Studia Evangelica* 1, 1957), Oxford, Blackwell, 1960.

(ed.), *Studia Evangelica* 2, Berlin, Akademie-Verlag, 1964.

Studia Evangelica 4, Berlin, Akademie-Verlag, 1968.

Studies in Ephesians, London, Mowbray, 1956.

Crouch, J. E., *The Origin and Intention of the Colossian Haustafel*, Göttingen, V. & R., 1972.

Cullmann, O., and Menoud, P. (eds.), *Aux sources de la tradition chrétienne. Mélanges offerts à M. Goguel*, Paris, Delachaux, 1950.

Cullmann, O., *Baptism in the New Testament*, Eng. trans. London, SCM, 1950.

Christ and Time, Eng. trans. London, SCM, 1951.

The Christology of the New Testament, Eng. trans. London, SCM, [2]1963.

Early Christian Worship, Eng. trans. London, SCM, 1953.

The Early Church, Eng. trans. London, SCM, 1956.

Immortality of the Soul or Resurrection of the Dead? London, Epworth, 1958.

Jesus and the Revolutionaries, Eng. trans. New York, Harper, 1970.

Peter: Disciple, Apostle, Martyr, Eng. trans. London, SCM, 1953, [2]1962.

Salvation in History, Eng. trans. London, SCM, 1967.

The State in the New Testament, Eng. trans. London, SCM, 1957.

Culpepper, R. H., *Interpreting the Atonement*, Grand Rapids, Eerdmans, 1966.

Dahl, M. E., *The Resurrection of the Body*, Eng. trans. London, SCM, 1962.

Dalman, G., *The Words of Jesus*, Eng. trans. Edinburgh, T. & T. Clark, 1902.

Dalton, W. J., *Christ's Proclamation to the Spirits*, Rome, Pontifical Biblical Institute, 1965.

D'Amato, C. (ed.), *Studiorum Paulinorum Congressus Internationalis Catholicus*, Rome, Pontifical Biblical Institute, 1963.

Danby, H., *The Mishnah*, London, Oxford University Press/Cumberlege, 1933.

Daniélou, J., *The Theology of Jewish Christianity*, Eng. trans. London, Darton, Longman & Todd, 1964.

Danker, F. W., *Jesus and the New Age*, St Louis, Clayton, 1974.

Davidson, A. B., *The Epistle to the Hebrews*, ICC, Edinburgh, T. & T. Clark, 1882.

Davies, J. G., *He Ascended into Heaven*, London, Lutterworth, 1958.

Davies, W. D., and Daube, D. (eds.), *The Background of the New Testament and its Eschatology*, Cambridge, CUP, 1964.

Davies, W. D., *Christian Origins and Judaism*, London, Darton, Longman & Todd, 1962.

The Gospel and the Land, Los Angeles, University of California Press, 1974.

Paul and Rabbinic Judaism, London, SPCK, 1948, ²1955.

The Setting of the Sermon on the Mount, Cambridge, CUP, 1964.

Deichgraber, R., *Gotteshymnus und Christushymnus*, Göttingen, V & R, 1967.

Deissmann, A., *Bible Studies*, Eng. trans. Edinburgh, T. & T. Clark, 1901.

Light from the Ancient East, Eng. trans. London, Hodder, 1927.

Die neutestamentliche Formel "In Christo Jesu", Marburg, Siebeck, 1892.

Delling, G., *Studien zum Neuen Testament und zum hellenistischen Judentum*, Göttingen, V & R, 1970.

Worship in the New Testament, Eng. trans. London, Dartmon, Longman & Todd, 1962.

Demarest, B., *A History of Interpretation of Heb. 7:1-10 from the Reformation to the Present*, Tübingen, Mohr, 1976.

Denis, A.-M., *Introduction aux Pseudépigraphes Grecs d'Ancien Testament*, Leiden, Brill, 1970.

Denney, J., *The Christian Doctrine of Reconciliation*, London, Hodder, 1917.

The Death of Christ, London, Hodder, 1911.

Dewar, L., *The Holy Spirit and Modern Thought*, London, Mowbray, 1959.

An Outline of New Testament Ethics, London, University of London Press, 1949.

Dibelius, M., *Der Brief des Paulus an die Philliper*, LHB, Tübingen, Mohr, ³1937.

Die Geisterwelt im Glauben des Paulus, Göttingen, V & R, 1909.

From Tradition to Gospels, Eng. trans. London, Nicholson & Watson, 1934.

Gospel Criticism and Christology, Eng. trans. London, Nicholson & Watson, 1935.

Dibelius, M., *Jungfrauensohn und Krippenkind; Sitzungsberichte der Heidelberger Akademie der Wissenschaften*, Heidelberg, Carl Winters Universitätsbuchhandlung, 1932.

An die Kolosser, Epheser, an Philemon, LHB, Tübingen, Mohr, ³1953.

Studies in the Acts of the Apostles, Eng. trans. London, SCM, 1956.

Dibelius, M., and Conzelmann, H., *The Pastoral Epistles, LHB*, ³1955, Eng. trans. Philadelphia Fortress, 1972.

Dibelius, M., and Greeven, H., *James, KEK* 1964, Eng. trans. Philadelphia, Fortress, 1976.

Dibelius, O., *Die werdende Kirche: Eine Einführung in die Apostelgeshichte*, Hamburg, Im Furche Verlag, ⁵1951.

Dodd, C. H., *According to the Scriptures*, London, Nisbet, 1952.

The Apostolic Preaching and its Developments, London, Hodder, 1936, ²1963.

The Bible and the Greeks, London, Hodder, 1935, ²1954.

The Epistle of Paul to the Romans, MNT, London, Hodder, 1932.

Historical Tradition in the Fourth Gospel, Cambridge, CUP, 1963.

History and the Gospel, London, Nisbet, 1938.

The Interpretation of the Fourth Gospel, Cambridge, CUP, 1953.

The Johannine Epistles, MNT, London, Hodder, 1946.

New Testament Studies, Manchester, MUP, 1953.

The Parables of the Kingdom, London, Nisbet, 1941.

Douglas, J. D., *et al*, (eds.), *The New Bible Dictionary*, London, IVF, 1962.

Driver, G. R., *The Judaean Scrolls*, Oxford, Blackwell, 1965.

Dubarle, A-M., *The Biblical Doctrine of Original Sin*, Eng. trans. New York, Herder, 1964.

Duncan, G. S., *Jesus, Son of Man*, London, Nisbet, 1947.

St Paul's Ephesian Ministry, London, Hodder, 1929.

Dunn, J. D. G., *Baptism in the Holy Spirit*, London, SCM, 1970.

Jesus and the Spirit, London, SCM, 1975.

Unity and Diversity in the New Testament, London, SCM, 1977.

Dupont, J., *Gnosis*, Louvain, Nawalearts; Paris, Gabalda, ²1960

Edwards, D., *The Virgin Birth in History and Faith*, London, Faber, 1943.

Edwards, D. L., *God's Cross in our World*, SCM, 1963.

Edwards, G. R., *Jesus and the Politics of Violence*, New York, Harper, 1972.

Ehrhardt, A. A. T., *The Apostolic Ministry*, Edinburgh, Oliver & Boyd, 1958.

Eichrodt, W., *Man in the Old Testament*, Eng. trans. London, SCM, 1951.

Theology of the Old Testament, 2 vols., Eng. trans. London, SCM, 1961-7.

Elliot, J. H., *The Elect and the Holy*, Leiden, Brill, 1966.

Ellis, E. E., *The Gospel of Luke*, NCB, London, Oliphants, 1966.

Paul and His Recent Interpreters, Grand Rapids, Eerdmans, 1961.

Paul's Use of the Old Testament, London, Oliver & Boyd, 1957.

Prophecy and Hermeneutic in Early Christianity, Tübingen, Mohr, 1978.

Ellis, E. E., and Grässer, E. (eds.), *Jesus und Paulus*, Göttingen, V & R, 1975

Ellul, J., *Violence: reflections from a Christian Perspective*, Eng. trans. London, SCM, 1970.

Eltester, W. (ed.), *Neutestamentliche Studien für Rudolf Bultmann*, Berlin, Töpelmann, ²1957.

Ervin, H. M., *These are not Drunken as ye Suppose*, New Jersey, Plainfield, 1968.

Evans, C. F., *The Resurrection and the New Testament*, London, SCM, 1970.

Evans, P. W., *Sacraments in the New Testament*, London, Tyndale, 1946.

Farmer, W. R. (ed.), *Christian History and Interpretation: Studies Presented to John Knox*, Cambridge, CUP, 1967.

Farrelly, J., *Predestination, Grace and Free Will*, London, Burns & Oates, 1964.

Farrer, A., *The Revelation of St John the Divine*, Oxford, Clarendon, 1964.

Fenton, J. C., *Saint Matthew*, Harmondsworth, Penguin, 1963, London, SCM, 1977.

Ferguson, J., *The Politics of Love. The New Testament and Non-Violent Revolution*, Cambridge, James Clarke, n.d.

Feuillet, A., *Le Christ Sagesse de Dieu d'après les épîtres Pauliniennes*, EB, Paris, Gabalda, 1966.

Filson, F. V., *The Gospel according to St Matthew*, BC, London, Black, 1960.

Jesus Christ, the Risen Lord, New York/Nashville, Abingdon, 1956.

The New Testament against its Environment, London, SCM, 1950.

St Paul's Conception of Recompense, Leipzig, Hinrich, 1931.

Yesterday: A Study of Hebrews in the Light of Chapter 13, London, SCM, 1967.

Findlay, G. G., *Fellowship in the Life Eternal*, London, Hodder, 1909.

Finnegan, J., *Encountering New Testament Manuscripts*, Grand Rapids, Eerdmans, 1974.

Fison, J. E., *The Blessing of the Holy Spirit*, London, Longmans, 1950.

Flemington, W. F., *The New Testament Doctrine of Baptism*, London, SPCK, 1948.

Flender, H., *St Luke, Theologian of Redemptive History*, Eng. trans. London, SPCK, 1967.

Flew, R. N., *The Idea of Perfection in Christian Theology*, Oxford, OUP, 1934.

BIBLIOGRAPHY

Jesus and His Church, London, Epworth, 1938.

Flusser, D., *Jesus*, Eng. trans. New York, Herder, 1969.

Foakes-Jackson, F., and Lake, K., *The Beginnings of Christianity*, 1, London, Macmillan, 1920.

Forestell, J. T., *The Word of the Cross: Salvation as Revelation in the Fourth Gospel*, Rome, Pontifical Biblical Institute, 1974.

Fornberg, T., *An Early Church in a Pluralistic Society: A Study of 2 Peter*, Lund, CWK Gleerup, 1977.

Fortman, E. J., *The Triune God*, London, Hutchinson, 1972.

Foulkes, F., *The Epistle of Paul to the Ephesians*, TNTC, London, Tyndale, 1963.

France, R. T., *Jesus and the Old Testament*, London, Tyndale, 1971.

The Living God, London, Inter-Varsity Press, 1970.

The Man they Crucified, London, Inter-Varsity Press, 1975.

Fraser, J. W., *Jesus and Paul. Paul as Interpreter of Jesus from Harnack to Kümmel*, Abingdon, Marcham Manor, 1972.

Frazer, J. G., *The Golden Bough*, London, Macmillan, [9]1949.

Frye, R. M., *Perspective on Man*, Philadelphia, Westminster, 1961.

Fuchs, E., *Glaube und Erfahrung*, Tübingen, Mohr-Siebeck, 1965.

Studies of the Historical Jesus, Eng. trans. London, SCM, 1964.

Fuller, D. P., *Easter Faith and History*, London, Tyndale, 1968.

Fuller, R. H., *The Formation of the Resurrection Narratives*, London, SPCK, 1972.

The Foundations of New Testament Christology, London, Lutterworth, 1965.

The Mission and Achievement of Jesus, London, SCM, 1954.

Furnish, V. P., *The Love Command in the New Testament*, London, SCM, 1973.

Theology and Ethics in Paul, Nashville, Abingdon, 1968.

Gärtner, B., *The Areopagus Speech and Natural Revelation*, Eng. trans. Lund, Gleerup, 1955.

Gasque, W. W., and Martin, R. P. (eds.), *Apostolic History and the Gospel*, Exeter, Paternoster, 1970.

Gasque, W. W., and LaSor, W. S. (eds.), *Scripture, Tradition and Interpretation*, Grand Rapids, Eerdmans, 1978.

Geldenhuys, J. N., *Supreme Authority*, London, MMS, 1953.

George, A., *Études sur l'Oeuvre de Luc*, Paris, Gabalda, 1978.

George, A. R., *Communion with God in the New Testament*, London, Epworth, 1953.

Gerhardsson, B., *The Testing of God's Son*, Eng. trans. Lund, Gleerup, 1966.

Gibbs, J. C., *Creation and Redemption*, Leiden, Brill, 1971.

994

Gilmour, A. (ed.) *Christian Baptism*, London, Lutterworth, 1959.

Glasson, T. F., *Greek Influence in Jewish Eschatology*, London, SPCK, 1961.

Moses in the Fourth Gospel, London, SCM, 1963.

The Second Advent, London, Epworth, ³1963.

Gnilka, J., *Der Philipperbrief, HTKNT*, Freiburg, Herder, ²1976.

1st Kor. 3:10-15 ein Schriftzeugnis für das Fegefeuer, Düsseldorf, Triltsch, 1955.

Gogarten, F., *Demythologising and History*, London, SCM, 1955.

Goguel, M., *The Primitive Church*, Eng. trans. London, Allen & Unwin, 1964.

Goodenough, E. R., *By Light, Light. The Mystical Gospel of Hellenistic Judaism*, New Haven, Yale University Press, 1935.

An Introduction to Philo Judaeus, Oxford, Blackwell, ²1962.

Goppelt, L., *Apostolic and Post-Apostolic Times*, Eng. trans. London, Black, 1970.

Theologie des Neuen Testaments, Göttingen, V & R, 2 vols. 1975-6.

Typos. Die typologische Deutung des Alten Testaments im Neuen, Darmstadt, Wissenschaftliche Buchgesellschaft, 1973.

Gore, C., *The Body of Christ*, London, Murray, 1901.

Grafe, E., *Die paulinische Lehre vom Gesetz*, Leipzig, Mohr, 1893.

Grant, F. C., *Ancient Judaism and the New Testament*, Edinburgh, Oliver & Boyd, 1960.

The Gospel of the Kingdom, New York, Macmillan, 1940.

Grant, R. M., *An Introduction to New Testament Thought*, New York/Nashville, Abingdon, 1960.

Grässer, E., *Das Problem der Parusieverzögerung in den synoptischen Evangelien und in der Apostelgeschichte*, Berlin, de Gruyter, ³1977.

Der Glaube im Hebräerbrief, Marburg, Elwert-Verlag, 1965.

Gray, G. B., *Sacrifice in the Old Testament*, Oxford, Clarendon, 1925.

Green, E. M. B., *I Believe in the Holy Spirit*, London, Hodder, 1975.

The Second Epistle General of Peter and the General Epistle of Jude, TNTC, London, Tyndale, 1968.

Greeves, F. *The Meaning of Sin*, London, Epworth, 1956.

Grensted, L. W. (ed.), *The Atonement in History and Life*, London, SPCK, 1929.

The Person of Christ, London, Nisbet, 1934.

Grosheide, F.W., *Commentary on the first Epistle to the Corinthians, NICNT*, Grand Rapids, Eerdmans, 1953, ²1954.

Grundman, W., *Das Evangelium nach Lukas, THNT*, Berlin, Evangelische Verlagstalt, ²1961.

Guardini, R., *The Humanity of Jesus*, Eng. trans. London, Burns & Oates, 1964.

Guillebaud, H. E., *Why the Cross?*, London, IVF, 1937.

995

BIBLIOGRAPHY

Gundry, R. H. *The Church and the Tribulation*, Grand Rapids, Zondervan, 1973.

Sōma in Biblical Theology, Cambridge, CUP, 1976.

The Use of the Old Testament in St Matthew's Gospel, Leiden, Brill, 1967.

Guthrie, D., *Galatians, NCB*, London, Oliphants, 1969.

New Testament Introduction, London, Tyndale, ³1970.

The Pastoral Epistles, TNTC, London, Tyndale, 1957.

Guy, H. A., *The New Testament Doctrine of the Last Things*, Oxford, OUP, 1948.

Hackett, H. B., *A Commentary on the Acts of the Apostles*, London, Hamilton, Adams & Co., 1877.

Haenchen, E., *The Acts of the Apostles*, Eng. trans. Oxford, Blackwell, 1971.

Hahn, F., *The Titles of Jesus in Christology*, Eng. trans. London, Lutterworth, 1969.

The Worship of the Early Church, Eng. trans. Philadelphia, Fortress, 1973.

Hahn, W. T., *Das Mitsterben und Mitauferstehen mit Christus bei Paulus*, Gütersloh, Bertelsmann, 1937.

Haldane, R., *Exposition of the Epistle to the Romans*, r.p. London, Banner of Truth, 1958.

Hallesby, O., *Conscience*, London, Hodder, 1939.

Halliday, W. R., *The Pagan Background of Early Christianity*, London, Hodder, 1925.

Hamerton-Kelly, R. G., *Pre-existence, Wisdom, and the Son of Man*, Cambridge, CUP, 1973.

Hamilton, K., *God is Dead: The Anatomy of a Slogan*, Wheaton, Illinois, Tyndale house Publishers, 1966.

Hamilton, N. Q., *The Holy Spirit and Eschatology in Paul*, Edinburgh, Oliver & Boyd, 1957.

Hammerich, L. L., *An Ancient Misunderstanding*, Copenhagen, Munksgaard, 1967.

Hammond, T. C., *Perfect Freedom*, London, IVF, 1938.

Hanhart, K., *The Intermediate State in the New Testament*, Amsterdam University Proefschrift, 1966.

Hanson, A. T., *Studies in the Pastoral Epistles*, London, SPCK, 1968.

Studies in Paul's Technique and Theology, London, SPCK, 1974.

The Wrath of the Lamb, London, SPCK, 1957.

Hanson, P. D., *The Dawn of Apocalyptic*, Philadelphia, Fortress, 1975.

Hanson, R. P. C., *The Acts*, Oxford, Clarendon, 1967.

Hare, D. R. A., *The Theme of Jewish Persecution of Christians in the Gospel according to St Matthew*, Cambridge, CUP, 1967.

Harnack, A. von, *The Constitution and Law of the Church in the First Two*

Centuries, Eng. trans. London, Williams & Norgate, 1910.

The Expansion of Christianity, Eng. trans. London, Williams & Norgate, 1904, ⁵1958.

Marcion: Das Evangelium vom fremden Gott, Leipzig, Hinrichs², 1924; r.p. Darmstadt, Wissenschaftliche Buchgesellschaft, 1960.

What is Christianity?, Eng. trans. London, Williams & Norgate, 1901, ⁵1950, London, Benn.

Harner, P. B., *The 'I am' of the Fourth Gospel*, Philadelphia, Fortress, 1970.

Harper, J., *Women and the Gospel*, London, Christian Brethren Research Fellowship, Occasional Paper 5, 1974.

Harris, H., *The Tübingen School*, Oxford, Clarendon, 1975.

Harris, J. R., *Testimonies*, 2 vols, Cambridge, CUP, 1916-20.

Harrisville, R. A., *The Concept of Newness in the New Testament*, Minneapolis, Augsburg, 1960.

Hartingveld, L. van, *Die Eschatologie des Johannesevangeliums*, Assen, van Gorcum, 1962.

Hay, D. M., *Glory at the Right Hand: Psalm 110 in Early Christianity*, Nashville, Abingdon, 1973.

Heinzelmann, G., *Der Brief an die Philipper*, NTD, Göttingen, V & R, ⁷1955.

Heitmüller, W., *In Namen Jesu: Eine sprach- und religionsgeschichtliche Untersuchung zum Neuen Testament, speziell zur altchristlichen Taufe*, FRLANT, Göttingen, V & R, 1903.

Henderson, I., *Myth in the New Testament*, London, SCM, 1952.

Hendriksen, W., *Commentary on 1 and 2 Timothy and Titus*, London, Banner of Truth, 1959.

Ephesians, London, Banner of Truth, 1972.

Exposition of the Gospel according to Matthew, Edinburgh, Banner of Truth, 1974.

Galatians, London, Banner of Truth, 1969.

The Gospel of John: A commentary, London, Banner of Truth, ²1961.

New Testament Commentary: Exposition of Philippians, London, Banner of Truth, 1962.

More than Conquerors, London, Tyndale, 1962.

Hendry, G. S., *The Holy Spirit in Christian Theology*, London, SCM, 1957.

Hengel, M., *The Son of God*, Eng. trans. London, SCM, 1976.

Victory over Violence, Eng. trans. London, SPCK, 1975.

Was Jesus a Revolutionist?, Eng. trans. Philadelphia, Fortress, 1971.

Henry, C. F. H. (ed.), *Jesus of Nazareth: Saviour and Lord*, London, Tyndale Press, 1966.

Héring, J., *The Epistle to the Hebrews*, Eng. trans. London, Epworth, 1970.

The First Epistle of Saint Paul to the Corinthians, Eng. trans. London, Epworth, 1962.

BIBLIOGRAPHY

Le Royaume de Dieu et sa venue: étude sur l'espérance de Jésus et de S. Paul, Paris, Études d'histoire et de philosophie religieuses, 1937; Neuchâtel, Delachaux, ²1959.

Herklots, H. G. G., *A Fresh Approach to the New Testament*, London, SCM, 1950.

The Ten Commandments and Modern Man, London, Benn, 1958.

Hermann, I., *Kurios und Pneuma*, München, Kösel, 1961.

Hiers, R. H., *The Historical Jesus and the Kingdom of God*, Gainsville, University of Florida Press, 1973.

Higgins, A. J. B., *Jesus and the Son of Man*, London, Lutterworth, 1964.

The Lord's Supper and the New Testament, London, SCM, 1952.

(ed.), *New Testament Essays: Studies in Memory of T. W. Manson*, Manchester, MUP, 1959.

Hill, D., *The Gospel of Matthew*, NCB, London, Oliphants, 1972.

Greek Words and Hebrew Meanings, Cambridge, CUP, 1967.

Hodge, C., *II Corinthians*, r.p. London, Banner of Truth, 1959.

Hodges, J. W., *Christ's Kingdom and Coming*, Grand Rapids, Eerdmans, 1957.

Hodgson, L., *The Doctrine of the Trinity*, London, Nisbet, 1943.

Hoekema, A. A., *Holy Spirit Baptism*, Exeter, Paternoster, 1972.

Holtzmann, H. J., *Lehrbuch der neutestamentlichen Theologie*, Tübingen, Mohr, ²1911.

Holwerda, D. E., *The Holy Spirit and Eschatology in the Gospel of John*, Kampen, Kok, 1959.

Hook, N., *The Eucharist in the New Testament*, London, Epworth, 1964.

Hooke, S. H., *The Resurrection of Christ as History and Experience*, London, Darton, Longman & Todd, 1967.

Hooker, M. D., *Jesus and the Servant*, London, SPCK, 1959.

The Son of Man in Mark, London, SPCK, 1967.

Hopwood, P. G. S., *The Religious Experience of the Primitive Church*, Edinburgh, T. & T. Clark, 1936.

Horton, F. L., *The Melchizedek Tradition*, Cambridge, CUP, 1976.

Hoskyns, E. C., and Davey, F. N., *The Fourth Gospel*, London, Faber, 1940, ²1947.

The Riddle of the New Testament, London, Faber, 1931.

Houlden, J. L., *Ethics and the New Testament*, Baltimore, Penguin, 1973.

Howard, W. F., *Christianity according to St John*, London, Duckworth, 1943.

Hughes, H. M., *The Ethics of Jewish Apocryphal Literature*, London, Kelly, n.d.

What is the Atonement?, London, James Clarke, n.d.

Hughes, P. E., *Commentary on the Second Epistle to the Corinthians*, NICNT, Grand Rapids, Eerdmans, 1962.

The Epistle to the Hebrews, Grand Rapids, Eerdmans, 1977.

Hughes, T. H., *The Atonement*, London, George Allen & Unwin, 1949.

Hughes, H. M., *What is the Atonement?*, London, James Clarke, n.d.

Hull, J. H. E., *The Holy Spirit in the Acts of the Apostles*, London, Lutterworth, 1967.

Hunter, A. M., *Interpreting the Parables*, London, SCM, 1960.

Interpreting Paul's Gospel, London, SCM, 1954.

Introducing New Testament Theology, London, SCM, 1957.

Paul and His Predecessors, London, SCM, ²1961.

The Work and Words of Jesus, London, SCM, 1950.

Hurd, J. C., *The Origin of 1 Corinthians*, London, SPCK, 1965.

Huxtable, J., *The Bible Says*, London SCM, 1962.

Iersel, B. M. F. von, *Der Sohn in den synoptischen Jesusworten*, Leiden, Brill, 1961.

Jacob, E., *Theology of the Old Testament*, Eng. trans. London, Hodder, 1958.

Jauncey, E., *The Doctrine of Grace*, London, SPCK, 1925.

Jeremias, J., *Die Briefe an Timotheus und Titus*, NTD, Göttingen, V & R, 1947.

The Central Message of the New Testament, London, SCM, 1965.

The Eucharistic Words of Jesus, Eng. trans. Oxford, Blackwell, 1955.

Jerusalem in the Time of Jesus, Eng. trans. London, SCM, 1969.

New Testament Theology 1: The Proclamation of Jesus, Eng. trans. London, SCM, 1971.

The Parables of Jesus, Eng. trans. London, SCM, ²1963.

The Prayers of Jesus, Eng. trans. London, SCM, 1967.

Rediscovering the Parables, Eng. trans., London, SCM, 1966.

The Sermon on the Mount, Eng. trans. London, Athlone Press, 1961.

Jervell, J., *Imago Dei*, Göttingen, V & R, 1960.

Luke and the People of God, Minneapolis, Augsburg, 1972.

Jewett, P. K., *Infant Baptism and the Covenant of Grace*, Grand Rapids, Eerdmans, 1978.

Man as Male and Female, Grand Rapids, Eerdmans, 1975.

Jewett, R., *Paul's Anthropological Terms*, Leiden, Brill, 1971.

Johnson, H., *The Humanity of the Saviour*, London, Epworth, 1962.

Johnson, M. D., *The Purpose of the Biblical Genealogies with special reference to the setting of the Genealogies of Jesus*, Cambridge, CUP, 1969.

Johnson, S. E., *The Gospel according to St. Mark*, BC, London, Black, 1960.

Johnston, G., *The Spirit-Paraclete in the Gospel of John*, Cambridge, CUP, 1970.

Jonas, H., *Gnosis und spätantiker Geist* 1, Göttingen, V & R, 1934.

BIBLIOGRAPHY

Jonge, M. de (ed.), *L'Évangile de Jean*, Leuven, Leuven University Press, 1975.

Jülicher, A., *Die Gleichnisreden Jesu*, Tübingen, Mohr, ²1910.

Kähler, E., *Die Frau in den Paulinischen Briefen*, Zurich, Gotthelf, 1960.

Kähler, M., *The So-Called Historical Jesus and the Historic, Biblical Christ* (²1896), Eng. trans. Philadelphia, Fortress, 1964.

Kallas, J., *The Significance of the Synoptic Miracles*, London, SPCK, 1961.

Käsemann, E., *Essays on New Testament Themes*, Eng. trans. London, SCM, 1960.

Leib und die Leib Christi, Tübingen, Mohr, 1933.

New Testament Questions of Today, Eng. trans. London, SCM, 1969.

Perspectives on Paul, Eng. trans. London, SCM, 1971.

The Testament of Jesus, Eng. trans. London, SCM, 1968.

Das wandernde Gottesvolk: Eine Untersuchung zum Hebräerbrief, Göttingen, V & R, 1957.

Keane, A. H., *The Antichrist Legend*, London, Hutchinson, 1896.

Keck, L. E., *A Future for the Historical Jesus*, London, SCM, 1972.

Keck, L. E., and Martyn, J. L. (eds.), *Studies in Luke-Acts*, New York/Nashville, Abingdon, 1966, London, SPCK, 1968.

Kelly, J. N. D., *The Epistles of Peter and of Jude*, BC, London, Black, 1969.

The Pastoral Epistles, BC, London, Black, 1963.

Kemp, E. W., (ed.), *Man, Fallen and Free*, London, Hodder, 1969.

Kendall, E. L., *A Living Sacrifice*, London, SCM, 1960.

Kennedy, H. A. A., *Philo's Contribution to Religion*, London, Hodder, 1919.

St Paul and the Mystery Religions, London, Hodder, 1913.

St Paul's Conceptions of the Last Things, London, Hodder, 1904.

The Theology of the Epistles, London, Duckworth, 1919.

Kertelge, K., *Rechtfertigung bei Paulus*, Münster, Aschendorffsche Verlagsbuchhandlung, 1967.

Kiddle, M., *The Revelation of St John*, MNT, London, Hodder, 1940.

Kilpatrick, G. D., *The Origins of the Gospel according to St Matthew*, Oxford, Clarendon, 1946.

Kirby, J. C., *Ephesians, Baptism and Pentecost*, London, SPCK, 1968.

Kistemaker, S., *The Psalm Citations in the Epistle to the Hebrews*, Amsterdam, van Soest, 1961.

Kittel, G. (ed.), *Theological Dictionary of the New Testament*, Eng. trans. Grand Rapids, Eerdmans, 1964–74.

Kitwood, T. M., *What is Human?* London, IVP, 1970.

Klassen, W., and Snyder, G. F. (eds.), *Current Issues in New Testament Interpretation*, New York, Harper, 1962.

Klausner, J., *The Messianic Idea in Israel*, London, George Allen & Unwin, 1956.

Klos, H., *Die Sakramente im Johannesevangelium*, Stuttgart, Verlag katholisches Bibelwerk, 1970.

Knight, G. A. F., *A Biblical Approach to the Doctrine of the Trinity*, London, Oliver & Boyd, 1953.

Law and Grace, London, SCM, 1962.

Knowling, R. J., *The Epistle of St James*, *WC*, London, Methuen, 1904.

Knox, J., *Chapters in a life of Paul*, New York, Abingdon, 1950.

The Humanity and Divinity of Christ, Cambridge, CUP, 1967.

Jesus, Lord and Christ, New York, Harper, 1958.

Knox, W. L., *St Paul and the Church of the Gentiles*, Cambridge, CUP, 1939, r. p. 1961.

Some Hellenistic Elements in Primitive Christianity, London, British Academy/OUP, 1944.

Koch, K., *The Rediscovery of Apocalyptic*, Eng. trans. London, SCM, 1972.

Koehler, L., *Old Testament Theology*, Eng. trans. London, Lutterworth, 1957.

Kosnik, A., *et al.*, *Human Sexuality*, London, Search Press, 1977.

Kraeling, C. H., *Anthrōpos and Son of Man. A Study in the Religious Syncretism of the Hellenistic Orient*, New York, 1927, r.p. AMS Press, 1966.

John the Baptist, New York, Charles Scribner's Sons, 1951.

Kramer, W., *Christ, Lord and Son of God*, Eng. trans. London, SCM, 1966.

Kümmel, W. G., *Man in the New Testament*, Eng. trans. London, Epworth, 1963.

The New Testament: The History of the Investigation of its Problems, Eng. trans. London, SCM, 1973.

Promise and Fulfilment, Eng. trans. London, SCM, 1957.

Römer 7 und die Bekehrung des Paulus, Leipzig, Hinrichs, 1929.

The Theology of the New Testament, Eng. trans. London, SCM, 1974.

Küng, H., *The Church*, Eng. trans., London, Search Press, 1968.

Why Priests?, Eng. trans. London, Collins, 1972.

Künneth, W., *The Theology of the Resurrection*, Eng. trans. London, SCM, 1965.

Ladd, G. E., *I Believe in the Resurrection of Jesus*, London, Hodder, 1975.

A Commentary on the Revelation of John, Grand Rapids, Eerdmans, 1972.

Crucial Questions about the Kingdom of God, Grand Rapids, Eerdmans, 1952.

The Pattern of New Testament Truth, Grand Rapids, Eerdmans, 1968.

The Presence of the Future, Grand Rapids, Eerdmans, 1974.

A Theology of the New Testament, Grand Rapids, Eerdmans, 1974.

Lake, K. and Cadbury, H. J. (eds.), *The Beginnings of Christianity 5*, London, Macmillan, 1933.

BIBLIOGRAPHY

Lampe, G. W. H. (ed.), *The Doctrine of Justification by Faith*, London, Mowbray, 1954.

God as Spirit, Oxford, OUP, 1977.

The Seal of the Spirit, London, Longmans, 1951.

and Mackinnon, D. M., (eds.), *The Resurrection*, London, Mowbrays, 1966.

Lane, W. L., *The Gospel of Mark*, NICNT, Grand Rapids, Eerdmans, 1974.

Lang, F. G., *2 Korinther 5$^{1-10}$ in der neueren Forschung*, Tübingen, Mohr, 1973.

Langton, E., *Essentials of Demonology*, London, Epworth, 1949.

Good and Evil Spirits, London, SPCK, 1942.

Larrañaga, V., *L'ascension de Notre-Seigneur dans le Nouveau Testament*, Rome, Pontifical Biblical Institute, 1938.

Laurentin, R., *Structure et Théologie de Luc I–II*, EB, Paris, Gabalda, 1964.

Law, R., *The Tests of Life*, Edinburgh, T. & T. Clark, 1909.

Leaney, A. R. C., *The Rule of Qumran and its Meaning*, London, SCM, 1966.

Lee, E. K., *The Religious Thought of St John*, London, SPCK, 1950.

Leenhardt, F. J., *The Epistle to the Romans*, CNT, 1957, Eng. trans. London, Lutterworth, 1961.

Leivestad, R., *Christ the Conqueror*, London, SPCK, 1954.

Lidgett, J. S., *The Fatherhood of God*, Edinburgh, T. & T. Clark, 1902.

Lietzmann, H., *Die Briefe des Apostels Paulus an die Korinther*, LHB, Tübingen, Mohr, ^{4}1933.

Lietzmann H., and Kümmel, W. G., *An die Korinther*, LHB, Tübingen, Mohr, ^{5}1969.

Lightfoot, J. B. *The Epistles to the Colossians and to Philemon*, London, Macmillan, ^{9}1890.

St Paul's Epistle to the Galatians, London, Macmillan, 1876.

St Paul's Epistle to the Philippians, London, Macmillan, ^{4}1878.

Lightfoot, R. H., *The Gospel Message of St Mark*, Oxford, OUP, 1950.

History and Interpretation in the Gospels, London, Hodder, 1935.

St John's Gospel: A Commentary, Oxford, OUP, 1956.

Lillie, W., *The Law of Christ*, London, Hodder, 1956.

Studies in New Testament Ethics, Edinburgh, Oliver & Boyd, 1961.

Lindars, B., *Behind the Fourth Gospel*, London, SPCK, 1971.

The Gospel of John, NCB, London, Oliphants, 1972.

and Smalley, S. S., (eds.), *Christ and Spirit in the New Testament*, Cambridge, CUP, 1973.

Ling, T., *The Significance of Satan*, London, SPCK, 1961.

Lohfink, G., *Die Himmelfahrt Jesu*, München, Kösel, 1971.

Lohmeyer, E., *Die Briefe an die Philipper, Kolosser und Philemon*, KEK, Göttingen, V & R, ^{9}1953.

Das Evangelium des Markus, Göttingen, V & R, [15]1959.

Grundlagen paulinischer Theologie, Tübingen, Mohr, 1929.

Kyrios Jesus. Eine Untersuchung zu Phil. 2.[5-11], *Sitzungberichte der Heidelberger Akademieder Wissenschaften*, Heidelberg, [2]1961.

The Lord's Prayer, Eng. trans. London, Collins, 1965.

Die Offenbarung des Johannes, LHB, Tübingen, Mohr, [3]1933.

and Schmauch, W., *Das Evangelium des Matthäus*, KEK, Göttingen, V & R, [2]1958.

Lohse, E., *Colossians and Philemon*, KEK, 1968, Eng. trans. *Hermeneia*, Philadelphia, Fortress, 1971.

Martyrer und Gottesknecht, FRLANT, Göttingen, V & R., 1955, [2]1963.

The New Testament Environment, Eng. trans. London, SCM, 1974.

Longenecker, R. N., *Biblical Exegesis in the Apostolic Period*, Grand Rapids, Eerdmans, 1975.

The Christology of Early Jewish Christianity, London, SCM, 1970.

Paul, Apostle of Liberty, New York, Harper, 1964.

Longenecker, R. N., and Tenney, M. C. (eds.), *New Dimensions in New Testament Study*, Grand Rapids, Zondervan, 1974.

Lüdemann, H., *Die Anthropologie des Apostels Paulus und ihre Stellung innerhalb seiner Heilslehre. Nach den vier Hauptbriefen*, Kiel, University of Kiel, 1872.

Lundberg, P., *La Typologie Baptismale dans L'Ancienne Église*, Leipzig, Lorentz-Uppsala, Lundequistska, 1942.

Lundström, G., *The Kingdom of God in the Teaching of Jesus*, Eng. trans. London, Oliver & Boyd, 1963.

Lüthi, W., *The Letter to the Romans*, Eng. trans. Edinburgh, Oliver & Boyd, 1961.

Lyonet, S., and Sabourin, L. (eds.), *Sin, Redemption and Sacrifice*, Rome, Pontifical Biblical Institute, 1970.

Macdonald, A. B., *Christian Worship in the Primitive Church*, Edinburgh, T. & T. Clark, 1934.

MacDonald, J., *The Theology of the Samaritans*, London, SCM, 1964.

MacGregor, G. H. C., *The Gospel of John*, MNT, London, Hodder, 1928.

The New Testament Basis of Pacifism, London, Fellowship of Reconciliation, 1936.

Machen, J. G., *The Virgin Birth of Christ*, New York, Harper, 1930.

What is Faith? London, Hodder, 1925.

Mackintosh, H. R., *The Doctrine of the Person of Jesus Christ*, Edinburgh, T. & T. Clark, [3]1914.

Macquarrie, J., *An Existentialist Theology*, London, SCM, 1955.

The Scope of Demythologising, London, SCM, 1960.

BIBLIOGRAPHY

McArthur, H. K. *Understanding the Sermon on the Mount*, London, Epworth, 1961.

McKelvey, R. J., *The New Temple: The Church in the New Testament*, Oxford, OUP, 1969.

McKenzie, J. L., *A Theology of the Old Testament*, London, Chapman, 1974.

McNeile, A. H., *The Gospel according to St Matthew*, London, Macmillan, 1915.

Manson, T. W., *The Church's Ministry*, London, Hodder, 1948.

(ed.), *Companion to the Bible*, Edinburgh, T. & T. Clark, 1939.

Ethics and the Gospel, London, SCM, 1960.

Ministry and Priesthood, London, Epworth, 1958.

On Paul and John, London, SCM, 1963.

The Servant Messiah, Cambridge, CUP, 1953.

The Sayings of Jesus, London, SCM, 1949.

The Teaching of Jesus, Cambridge, CUP, [2]1935, [3]1945.

and Wright, C. J., and Major, H. D. A., *The Mission and Message of Jesus*, London, Macmillan, 1940.

Manson, W., *The Epistle to the Hebrews*, London, Hodder, 1951.

The Gospel of Luke, MNT, London, Hodder, 1930.

Jesus the Messiah, London, Hodder, 1943.

Mansoor, M., *The Thanksgiving Hymns*, Leiden, Brill, 1961.

Marcel, P. C., *The Biblical Doctrine of Infant Baptism*, Eng. trans. London, James Clarke, 1953.

Marmorstein, A., *The Doctrine of Merit in Old Rabbinical Literature*, London, 1920, r.p. New York, Ktav, 1969.

Marsh, H. G., *The Origin and Significance of the New Testament Baptism*, Manchester, MUP, 1941.

Marsh, J., *Saint John*, Harmondsworth, Penguin, 1963, London, SCM, 1968.

Marshall, I. H., *The Epistles of John*, NICNT, Grand Rapids, Eerdmans, 1978.

The Gospel of Luke, NIGTC, Exeter, Paternoster, 1978.

Kept by the Power of God, London, Epworth, 1969.

Luke: Historian and Theologian, Exeter, Paternoster, 1970.

The Origins of New Testament Christology, London, IVP, 1976.

(ed.), *New Testament Interpretation*, Exeter, Paternoster, 1977.

Marshall, L. H., *The Challenge of New Testament Ethics*, London, Macmillan, 1947.

Martin, R. P., *Carmen Christi*, Cambridge, CUP, 1967.

Colossians: The Church's Lord and the Christian's Liberty, Exeter, Paternoster, 1972.

Colossians and Philemon, NCB, London, Oliphants, 1974.

An Early Christian Confession, London, Tyndale, 1960.

The Epistle of Paul to the Philippians, *TNTC*, London, Tyndale, 1959.

Mark: Evangelist and Theologian, Exeter, Paternoster, 1972.

Philippians, NCB, London, Oliphants, 1976.

Worship in the Early Church, London, MMS, 1964.

Martyn, J. L., *History and Theology in the Fourth Gospel*, New York, Harper, 1968.

Marxsen, W., *The Beginnings of Christology. A Study of its Problems*, Philadelphia, Fortress, 1969.

The Lord's Supper as a Christological Problem, Eng. trans. Philadelphia, Fortress, 1970.

Mark the Evangelist, Eng. trans. Nashville, Abingdon, 1969.

The Resurrection of Jesus of Nazareth, Eng. trans. London, SCM, 1970.

Mascall, E. L., *Christ, the Christian and the Church*, London, Longmans, 1946.

Existence and Analogy, London, Longmans, 1949.

Masson, C., *L'Épître de Saint Paul aux Colossiens*, *CNT*, Neuchâtel, Delachaux & Nestlé, 1950.

Matthews, S., *Jesus on Social Institutions*, New York, Macmillan, 1928.

Mayor, J. B. *The Epistle of St James*, London, Macmillan, [2]1897, [3]1913, r.p. Grand Rapids, Zondervan, 1954.

Meeks, W. A., *The Prophet-King*, Leiden, Brill, 1967.

Meinertz, M., *Die Heilige Schrift des Neuen Testaments*, Ergänzungstand 1, *Theologie des Neuen Testaments*, 2 vols, Bonn, Hanstein, 1950.

Metzger, B. M., *Historical and Literary Studies*, Grand Rapids, Eerdmans, 1968.

Meyer, R., *Der Prophet aus Galiläa*, Darmstadt, Wissenschaftliche Buchgesellschaft, [2]1970.

Michael, J. H., *The Epistle to the Philippians*, London, Hodder, 1928.

Miegge, G., *Gospel and Myth in the Thought of Rudolph Bultmann*, Eng. trans. London, SCM, 1960.

Miguens, M., *The Virgin Birth*, Westminster, MD; Christian Classics, 1975.

Milik, J. T., *Ten Years of Discovery in the Wilderness of Judaea*, Eng. trans. London, SCM, 1959.

Milligan, W., *The Ascension and Heavenly Priesthood of our Lord*, London, Macmillan, 1898.

Minear, P. S., *Commands of Christ*, Edinburgh, St Andrew Press, 1972.

Images of the Church in the New Testament, London, Lutterworth, 1961.

I saw a New Earth, Washington, Corpus, 1968.

Mitton, C. L., *Ephesians*, NCB, London, Oliphants, 1976.

The Epistle of James, London, MMS, 1966.

The Epistle to the Ephesians, Oxford, Clarendon, 1951.

BIBLIOGRAPHY

Moburg, D. O., *Inasmuch: Christian Social Responsibility in the Twentieth Century*, Grand Rapids, Eerdmans, 1965.

Moffatt, J., *The Epistle to the Hebrews*, ICC, Edinburgh, T. & T. Clark, 1924.

Grace in the New Testament, London, Hodder, 1931.

An Introduction to the Literature of the New Testament, Edinburgh, T. & T. Clark, ²1912.

Love in the New Testament, London, Hodder, 1929.

The Theology of the Gospels, London, Duckworth, 1948.

Molitor, H., *Die Auferstehung der Christen und Nichtchristen nach dem Apostel Paulus*, Münster in Westphalia, 1933.

Moloney, F. J., *The Johannine Son of Man*, Rome, Las, 1976.

Moltmann, J., *Theology and Joy*, Eng. trans. London, SCM, 1973.

Monod, J., *Chance and Necessity*, Eng. trans. Glasgow, Collins, 1971, Collins/Fontana, 1974.

Montague, G. T., *The Holy Spirit: Growth of a Biblical Tradition*, New York, Hermon, 1976.

The Living Thought of Paul, Milwaukee, Bruce, 1966.

Montefiore, C. G., *Rabbinic Literature and Gospel Teachings*, London, Macmillan, 1930, r.p. New York, Ktav, 1970.

The Synoptic Gospels, London, Macmillan, 1909.

Montefiore, H. W., *The Epistle to the Hebrews*, BC, London, Black, 1964.

(ed.), *Man and Nature*, London, Collins, 1975.

Moore, A. L., *The Parousia in the New Testament*, Leiden, Brill, 1966.

1 and 2 Thessalonians, NCB, London, Oliphants, 1969.

Moore, G. F., *Judaism*, Cambridge (Mass.), Harvard University Press, 1927.

Morgan, R., *The Nature of New Testament Theology*, London, SCM, 1973.

Morris, L., *The Abolition of Religion*, London, IVF, 1964.

Apocalyptic, Grand Rapids, Eerdmans, 1972; London, IVP, 1973.

The Apostolic Preaching of the Cross, London, Tyndale, 1955.

The Biblical Doctrine of Judgment, London, Tyndale, 1960.

The Cross in the New Testament, Grand Rapids, Eerdmans, 1965.

The Epistles of Paul to the Thessalonians, TNTC, London, Tyndale, 1956.

The First Epistle of Paul to the Corinthians, TNTC, London, Tyndale, 1958.

The First and Second Epistles to the Thessalonians, NICNT, Grand Rapids, Eerdmans, 1959.

The Gospel according to John, NICNT, Grand Rapids, Eerdmans, 1971.

The Gospel according to St Luke, TNTC, London, IVP, 1974.

The Lord from Heaven, London, IVP, ²1974.

The Revelation of St John, TNTC, London, Tyndale, 1969.

Spirit of the Living God, London, IVP, 1960.

Studies in the Fourth Gospel, Exeter, Paternoster, 1969.

Morrison, C., *The Powers That Be*, London, SCM, 1960.

Moule, C. F. D., *The Birth of the New Testament*, London, Black, 1962.

The Epistles to the Colossians and Philemon, *CGTC*, Cambridge: CUP, 1957.

The Origin of Christology, Cambridge, CUP, 1977.

The Phenomenon of the New Testament, London, SCM, 1967.

The Sacrifice of Christ, London, Hodder, 1956.

(ed.), *The Significance of the Message of the Resurrection for Faith in Jesus Christ*, Eng. trans. London, SCM, 1968.

Worship in the New Testament, London, Lutterworth, 1961.

Moulton, J. H., *Grammar of New Testament Greek*, Edinburgh, T. & T. Clarke, 1906.

Moulton, J. H., and Milligan, G., *The Vocabulary of the Greek Testament illustrated from the Papyri and other non-literary sources*, London, Hodder, 1930.

Mounce, R. H., *The Book of Revelation*, *NICNT*, Grand Rapids, Eerdmans, 1977.

Mowinkel, S., *He that Cometh*, Eng. trans. New York/Nashville, Abingdon, 1954.

Müller, C., *Gottes Gerechtigkeit und Gottes Volk*, Göttingen, V. & R., 1964.

Müller, J. J., *The Epistles of Paul to the Philippians and to Philemon*, *NICNT*, Grand Rapids, Eerdmans, 1955.

Müller, U., *Prophetie und Predigt im Neuen Testament*, Gütersloh, Gerd Mohn, 1975.

Munck, J., *The Acts of the Apostles*, *AB*, New York, Garden City, 1967.

Murray, A. V., *The State and the Church in a Free Society*, Cambridge, CUP, 1958.

Murray, I., *The Puritan Hope*, London, Banner of Truth, 1971.

Murray, J., *Divorce*, Philadelphia, Presbyterian and Reformed, 1953, r.p. 1976.

The Epistle to the Romans, 2 vols., *NICNT*, Grand Rapids, Eerdmans, 1959–67.

Redemption Accomplished and Applied, Grand Rapids, Eerdmans, 1955; London, Banner of Truth, 1961.

Mussner, F., *The Historical Jesus in the Gospel of St John*, Eng. trans. Freiburg, Herder, 1967.

Der Jacobusbrief, *HTKNT*, Freiburg, Herder, ³1975.

Nauck, W., *Die Tradition und der Charakter des ersten Johannesbriefes*, Tübingen, Mohr, 1957.

Neil, W., *The Acts of the Apostles*, *NCB*, London, Oliphants, 1973.

The Epistles of Paul to the Thessalonians, *MNT*, London, Hodder, 1950.

BIBLIOGRAPHY

Nepper-Christensen, P., *Das Matthäusevangelium. Ein Judenchristliches Evangelium?* Aaraus, Universitetforlaget, 1958.

Neufeld, V. H., *The Earliest Christian Confessions*, Leiden, Brill, 1963.

Neugebauer, F., *In Christus*, Göttingen, V & R, 1961.

Neusner, J., *First-century Judaism in Crisis: Yohanan ben Zakkai and the Renaissance of Torah*, Nashville, Abingdon, 1975.

Nickelsburg, G. W. E., Jnr, *Resurrection, Immortality, and Eternal Life in Intertestamental Judaism*, Harvard Theological Studies 26, Cambridge, Mass., 1972.

Nickle, K. F., *The Collection*, London, SCM, 1966.

Nilsson, M., *Geschichte der griechischen Religion*, (Handbuch der Altertumwissenschaft 5), 2 vols., Munich, Beck, 1940/49, ²1961.

Nineham, D. E., *Saint Mark*, Harmondsworth, Penguin, 1963, London, SCM, 1977.

(ed.), *Studies in the Gospels*, Oxford, Blackwell, 1957.

Nixon, R. E., *The Exodus in the New Testament*, London, Tyndale, 1963.

Noack, B., *Das Gottesreich bei Lukas, Eine Studie zu Luk 17:20–24*, Lund, Gleerup, 1948.

Nock, A. D., and Festugière, A. J. (eds.), *Corpus Hermeticum*, Paris, Société d'Édition la Belle Lettre, 4 vols., 1945–54.

Norden, E., *Agnostos Theos*, Berlin, Teubner, 1913.

Norris, R. (ed.), *Lux in Lumine*, New York, Seabury, 1966.

North, C. R., *The Suffering Servant in Deutero-Isaiah*, Oxford, OUP, 1948.

Noth, M., *The Laws in the Pentateuch and Other Studies*, Eng. trans., Edinburgh, Oliver & Boyd, 1966.

Nygren, A., *Agape and Eros*, London, SPCK, 1953.

Commentary on Romans, Eng. trans., London, SCM, 1952.

Odeburg, H., *The Fourth Gospel*, 1929, r.p. Amsterdam, Gruner, 1974.

Oepke, A., *Der Brief des Paulus an die Galater, THNT*, Berlin, Evangelische Verlagsanstalt, ²1957.

Oesterly, W. O. E., *The Jews and Judaism during the Greek Period*, London, SPCK, 1941.

Oglethorpe, T., *The Death of God Controversy*, London, SCM, 1966.

Oman, J., *Grace and Personality*, Cambridge, CUP, ²1919.

O'Neill, J. C., *Paul's Letter to the Romans*, London, Penguin, 1975.

Orr, J., *The Virgin Birth of Christ*, New York, Charles Scribner's Sons, 1907.

Otto, R., *The Idea of the Holy*, Eng. trans. Oxford, OUP, 1927.

The Kingdom of God and the Son of Man, Eng. trans. London, Lutterworth, 1938.

Pache, R., *The Future Life*, Chicago, Moody, 1962.

Packer, J. I., *'Fundamentalism' and the Word of God*, London, IVF, 1958.

Painter, J., *John, Witness and Theologian*, London, SPCK, 1975.

Panagopoulos, J. (ed.), *Prophetic Vocation in the New Testament and Today*, Leiden, Brill, 1977.

Pancaro, S., *The Law in the Fourth Gospel*, Leiden, Brill, 1975.

Pannenberg, W., *Jesus, God and Man*, Eng. trans. London, SCM, 1968.

Parker, T. H. L. (ed.), *Essays in Christology for Karl Barth*, London, Lutterworth, 1956.

Paulus, H. E. G., *Das Leben Jesus*, Heidelberg, C. F. Winter, 1828.

Pearson, B. A., *The Pneumatikos-Psychikos terminology in 1 Corinthians*, SBL Dissertation Series 12, Missoula, University of Montana, 1973.

Pedersen, J., *Israel: Its Life and Culture*, Oxford, OUP, [2]1959.

Pentecost, J. D., *Things to Come*, Findlay, Ohio, Dunham, 1958, r.p. Grand Rapids, Zondervan, 1964.

Percy, E., *Der Leib Christi*, Lund, Lunds Universitets Årsskrift, 1942.
Untersuchungen über den Ursprung der johanneischen Theologie, Lund, Gleerup, 1939.

Perrin, N., *Jesus and the Language of the Kingdom*, Philadelphia, Fortress, 1976.
The Kingdom of God in the Teaching of Jesus, London, SCM, 1963.
Rediscovering the Teaching of Jesus, London, SCM, 1967.

Pesch, R., *Naherwartungen: Tradition und Redaktion in Markus 13*, Dusseldorf, Patmos, 1968.

Pierce, C. A., *Conscience in the New Testament*, London, SCM, 1955.

Pinnock, C. H. (ed.), *Grace Unlimited*, Minneapolis, Bethany Fellowship, 1975.

Pittenger, W. N. (ed.), *Christ for Us Today*, London, SCM, 1968.
The Christian Understanding of Human Nature, Welwyn, Nisbet, 1964.
'The Last Things' in a Process Perspective, London, Epworth, 1970.

Plummer, A., *The Gospel according to St. John*, Cambridge, CUP, 1899.
St Luke, ICC, Edinburgh, T. & T. Clark, [5]1922.
The Second Epistle of St Paul to the Corinthians, ICC, Edinburgh, T. & T. Clark, 1915.

Pollard, T. E., *Johannine Christology and the Early Church*, Cambridge, CUP, 1970.

Porsche, F., *Pneuma und Wort*, Frankfurt, Knecht, 1974.

Potterie, I. de la, and Lyonnet, S., *The Christian Lives by the Spirit*, Eng. trans. Staten Island, New York, Alba, 1971.

Powell, H. T., *The Fall of Man: its Place in Modern Thought*, London, SPCK, 1934.

Prat, F., *The Theology of St Paul*, Eng. trans., London, Burns, Oates, & Washbourne, [2]1933.

Preisker, H., *Die katholischen Briefe*, Tübingen, Mohr, [3]1951.

Rackham, R. B., *The Acts of the Apostles*, WC, London, Methuen, 1901.

Rad, G. von, Schlier, H., and Wolf, E., *Der alte und neue Mensch: Beiträge zur evangelischen Theologie 8*, Munich, 1942.

Rahner, H., *Greek Myths and Christian Mysteries*, New York, Harper, 1963.

Ramm, B., *Them He Glorified*, Grand Rapids, Eerdmans, 1963.

Ramsey, A. M., *The Glory of God and the Transfiguration of Christ*, London, Longmans, 1949.

The Resurrection of Christ, London, Geoffrey Bles, ²1946.

Ramsey, P., *Basic Christian Ethics*, New York, Charles Scribner's Sons, 1950.

Randall, F., *The Epistle to the Hebrews*, London, Macmillan, 1883.

Rashdall, H., *The Idea of Atonement in Christian Theology*, London, Macmillan, 1919.

Reicke, B., *The Disobedient Spirits and Christian Baptism*, Copenhagen, Munksgaard, 1946.

The Epistles of James, Peter and Jude, AB, New York, Doubleday, 1964.

Reitzenstein, R., *Die hellenistischen Mysterienreligionen nach Ihren Grundgedanken und Wirkungen*, Leipzig, ³1927, r.p. Stuttgart, Teubner, 1956.

Rendall, G. H., *The Epistle of James and Judaic Christianity*, Cambridge, CUP, 1927.

Reumann, J., *Jesus in the Church's Gospel*, Philadelphia, Fortress, 1968, London, SPCK, 1970.

Ricca, P., *Die Eschatologie des vierten Evangeliums*, Zürich, Gotthelf, 1966.

Richards, J. M. (ed.), *Soli Deo Gloria*, Richmond, Va., Knox, 1968.

Richardson, A., *Christian Apologetics*, London, SCM, 1947.

The Christian Doctrine of Work, London, SCM, 1952.

The Political Christ, London, SCM, 1973.

An Introduction to the Theology of the New Testament, London, SCM, 1968.

Ridderbos, H. N., *The Coming of the Kingdom*, Eng. trans, Philadelphia, Presbyterian & Reformed, 1962.

The Epistle of Paul to the Churches of Galatia, NICNT, Grand Rapids, Eerdmans, ²1954.

Paul and Jesus, Philadelphia, Presbyterian and Reformed, 1958.

Paul: An Outline of His Theology, Eng. trans. Grand Rapids, Eerdmans, 1975.

Romans, Kampen, Kok, 1959.

Riesenfeld, H., *The Gospel Tradition*, Eng. trans. Philadelphia, Fortress, 1970.

Jésus Transfiguré, Copenhagen, Munksgaard, 1947.

Rigaux, B., *Dieu l'a ressuscité. Exégèse et théologie biblique*, Gembloux, Ducelot, 1973.

Ringgren, H., *Word and Wisdom*, Lund, Gleerup, 1947.

Rissi, M., *The Future of the World*, London, SCM, 1972.

Time and History, Eng. trans. Richmond, Va., Knox, 1966.

Robertson, A., and Plummer, A., *The First Epistle of St Paul to the Corinthians, ICC*, Edinburgh, T. & T. Clark, 1911.

Robertson, E. H., *Man's Estimate of Man*, London, SCM, 1958.

Robinson, H. Wheeler, *The Christian Doctrine of Man*, Edinburgh, T. & T. Clark, ³1926.

Robinson, J. A. T., *The Body*, London, SCM, 1952.

The Human Face of God, London, SCM, 1973.

In the End, God, London, James Clarke, 1950.

Jesus and His Coming, London, SCM, 1957.

Twelve New Testament Studies, London, SCM, 1962.

Robinson, J. M., *A New Quest of the Historical Jesus*, London, SCM, 1959.

The Problem of History in Mark, London, SCM, ⁴1971.

(ed.), *The Nag Hammadi Library in English*, Leiden, Brill, 1977.

Rohde, E., *Psyche: The Cult of Souls and Belief in Immortality among the Greeks*, r.p. New York, Harper, 1966.

Ropes, J. H., *The Epistle of James*, Edinburgh, T. & T. Clark, 1916.

Rowley, H. H., *From Moses to Qumran*, London, Lutterworth, 1963.

The Relevance of Apocalyptic, London, Lutterworth, 1944, ³1963.

Russell, D. S., *Apocalyptic: Ancient and Modern*, London, SCM, 1978.

The Method and Message of Jewish Apocalyptic, London, SCM, 1964.

Rust, E. C., *Nature and Man in Biblical Thought*, London, Lutterworth, 1953.

Ryrie, C. C., *Dispensationalism Today*, Chicago, Moody, 1965.

Salmon, S. D. F., *The Christian Doctrine of Immortality*, Edinburgh, T. & T. Clark, ³1897.

Sampley, J. P., *'And the Two shall become One Flesh'*, Cambridge, CUP, 1971.

Sand, A., *Der Begriff 'Fleisch' in den paulinischen Hauptbriefen*, Regensburg, Pustet, 1967.

Sanday, W., *The Life of Christ in Recent Research*, Oxford, Clarendon, 1907.

Sanday, W., and Headlam, A. C., *The Epistle to the Romans, ICC*, Edinburgh, T. & T. Clark, 1895, ⁵1902.

Sanders, E. P., *Paul and Palestinian Judaism*, London, SCM, 1977.

Sanders, J. N., and Mastin, B. A., *A Commentary on the Gospel according to St John, BC*, London, Black, 1968.

Sanders, J. T., *The New Testament Christological Hymns*, Cambridge, CUP, 1971.

Sandmel, S., *The Genius of Paul*, New York, Schocken, ²1970.

Sartre, J.-P., *Situations 3*, Paris, Gallimard, 1949.

Scanzoni, L. and Hardesty, N., *All We're Meant to Be*. Texas, Word Books, 1974.

Scheeben, M.-J., *Nature and Grace*, Eng. trans. St. Louis, 1954, from the German *Natur und Gnade*, Freiburg, Herder, 1861, [4]1949.

Schelkle, K. H., *Die Petrusbriefe, Der Judasbrief*, Freiburg, Herder, 1976.

Theologie des Neuen Testaments, Kommentare und Beiträge zum Alten und Neuen Testament, Düsseldorf, Patmos, 4 vols., 1968–76, Eng. trans. *Theology of the New Testament*, Collegeville, Minn., Liturgical Press, 1, 1971, 2, 1976, 3, 1978.

Schep, J. A., *The Nature of the Resurrection Body*, Grand Rapids, Eerdmans, 1964.

Schlatter, A., *Der Glaube im Neuen Testament*, Darmstadt, Wissenschaftliche Buchgesellschaft, 1963, r.p. from Stuttgart edit., [4]1927.

Gottes Gerechtigkeit; ein Kommentar zum Römerbrief, Stuttgart, Calwer Verlag, [4]1965.

Neutestamentliche Theologie, Stuttgart, Calwer Verlag, [2]1922–23.

Paulus der Bote Jesus: Eine Deutung Seiner Briefe an die Korinther, Stuttgart, Calwer Verlag, [2]1956.

Schlier, H., *Der Brief an die Epheser*, Düsseldorf, Patmos, [7]1971.

Principalities and Powers in the New Testament, Eng. trans. New York, Herder, 1961.

The Relevance of the New Testament, Eng. trans. London, Burns & Oates, 1967.

Der Römerbrief, Freiburg, Herder, 1977.

Schmauch, W., *In Christus*, Gütersloh, Bertelsmann, 1935.

Schmidt, K. L. (ed.), *Festgabe für A. Deissmann*, Tübingen, Mohr, 1927.

Schmithals, W., *Gnosticism in Corinth*, 1956, Eng. trans. Nashville, Abingdon, 1971.

The Office of Apostle in the Early Church, Eng. trans. New York, Abingdon, 1969.

Schnackenburg, R., *Baptism in the Thought of St Paul*, Eng. trans. Oxford, Blackwell, 1964.

God's Rule and Kingdom, Eng. trans. New York/London, Nelson, 1963.

Die Johannesbriefe, HTKNT, Freiburg, Herder, 1975.

Das Johannesevangelium 1 HTKNT, Freiburg, Herder, 1965 (Eng. trans. *The Gospel according to St John* 1, London, Burns & Oates, 1968), 2, 1971, 3, 1976.

W. Schneelmelcher (ed.), *Festschrift für Günther Dehn*, Neukirchen, Neukirchener Verlag, 1957.

Schneiwind, J., *Das Evangelium nach Matthäus, NTD*, Göttingen, V & R, [9]1960.

Schoeps, H.-J., *Paul. The Theology of the Apostle in the Light of the History of Jewish Religion*, Eng. trans. London, Lutterworth, 1961.

Schrey, H.-H., Walz, H. H., and Whitehouse, W. A., *The Biblical Doctrine of Justice and Law*, London, SCM, 1955.

Schubert, K., *The Dead Sea Community*, Eng. trans. London, Black, 1959.

Schulz, S., *Q – die Spruchquelle der Evangelisten*, Zurich, Theologischer Verlag, 1972.

Untersuchungen zur Menschensohn – Christologie im Johannesevangelium: Zugleich ein Beitrag zur Methodengeschichte der Auslegung des 4 Evangeliums, Göttingen, V & R, 1957.

Schürmann, H., *Jesu Abschiedsrede: Lk. 22*$^{21-38}$, Münster, Aschendorffsche Verlagsbuchhandlung, 1957.

Schütz, J. H., *Paul and the Anatomy of Apostolic Authority*, Cambridge, CUP, 1975.

Schweitzer, A., *The Mystery of the Kingdom of God* (1901), Eng. trans. London, Black, 1914.

The Mysticism of Paul the Apostle (1930), Eng. trans. London, Black, ^{2}1953.

Paul and his Interpreters, Eng. trans. London, Black, 1912.

The Quest of the Historical Jesus, (1906), Eng. trans. London, Black, ^{3}1954.

Schweizer, E., *Der Brief an die Kolosser, EKK,* Zurich, Benziger Verlag-Neukirchener Verlag, 1976.

The Church as the Body of Christ, Eng. trans. Richmond, Va., Knox, 1964.

Church Order in the New Testament, Eng. trans. London, SCM, 1961.

The Good News according to Mark, NTD, 1967, Eng. trans. London, SPCK, 1971.

The Good News according to Matthew, NTD, 1973, Eng. trans., London SPCK, 1976.

Jesus, Eng. trans. London, SCM, 1971.

Lordship and Discipleship, Eng. trans. London, SCM, 1960.

The Lord's Supper according to the New Testament, Eng. trans. Philadelphia, Fortress, 1967.

Neotestamentica, Zurich, Theologischer Verlag, 1963.

Scobie, C. H. H., *John the Baptist*, London, SCM, 1964.

Scofield, C. I., *Scofield Reference Bible*, Oxford, OUP, 1909.

Scott, C. A. A., *Christianity according to St Paul*, Cambridge, CUP, 1932.

New Testament Ethics, Cambridge, CUP, 1948.

Scott, E. F., *The Epistles of Paul to the Colossians, to Philemon and to the Ephesians, MNT,* London, Hodder, 1930.

The Epistle to the Hebrews, Edinburgh, T. & T. Clark, 1922.

The Epistle to the Philippians, IB, vol. 11, New York, Abingdon, 1955.

The Fourth Gospel, its Purpose and Theology, Edinburgh, T. & T. Clark, ^{2}1908.

Man and Society in the New Testament, New York, Charles Scribner's Sons, 1947.

Scroggs, R., *The Last Adam*, Blackwell, Oxford, 1966.

Paul for a New Day, Philadelphia, Fortress, 1977.

Seesemann, H., *Der Begriff KOINŌNIA im Neuen Testament*, Giessen, Töpelmann, 1933.

Selwyn, E. G., *The First Epistle of Peter*, London, Macmillan, 1946.

The Oracles of the New Testament, London, Hodder, 1911.

Sevenster, J. N., *Paul and Seneca*, Leiden, Brill, 1961.

Sevenster, J. N. and Unnik, W. C. van (eds.), *Studia Paulina in honorem J. de Zwaan*, Haarlem, Bohn, 1953.

Shaner, D. W., *A Christian View of Divorce according to the Teachings of the New Testament*, Leiden, Brill, 1969.

Shaw, R. D., *The Pauline Epistles*, Edinburgh, T. & T. Clark, ⁴1913.

Sidebottom, E. M., *The Christ of the Fourth Gospel*, London, SPCK, 1961.

Simon, D. W., *The Redemption of Man*, London, Melrose, 1906.

Simon, U., *Heaven in the Christian Tradition*, London, Rockliffe, 1958.

Simpson, E. K., *Words Worth Weighing in the Greek New Testament*, London, Tyndale, 1946.

and Bruce, F. F., *The Epistles to the Ephesians and the Colossians, NICNT*, Grand Rapids, Eerdmans, 1957.

Sire, J. W., *The Universe Next Door*, Leicester, IVP, 1977.

Smalley, S. S., *John: Evangelist and Interpreter*, Exeter, Paternoster, 1978.

Smart, J. D., *The Divided Mind of Modern Thought*, Philadelphia, Westminster Press, 1967.

Smedes, L. B., *All Things Made New*, Grand Rapids, Eerdmans, 1970.

Smith, C. Ryder, *The Bible Doctrine of Man*, London, Epworth, 1951.

The Bible Doctrine of Salvation, London, Epworth, 1941.

The Bible Doctrine of Sin, London, Epworth, 1953.

The Bible Doctrine of the Hereafter, London, Epworth, 1958.

Smith, D. M., Jnr, *The Composition and Order of the Fourth Gospel. Bultmann's Literary Theory*, New Haven, Yale University Press, 1965.

Snaith, N. H., *The Distinctive Ideas of the Old Testament*, London, Epworth, 1944.

(ed.), *The Doctrine of the Holy Spirit*, Headingley Lectures, London, Epworth, 1937.

Souter, A., *The Text and Canon of the New Testament*, London, Duckworth, 1913, ²1954.

Spicq, C., *Agapē in the New Testament*, Eng. trans. London, Herder, 1963.

Dieu et l'homme selon le Nouveau Testament, Paris, Les éditions du Cerf, 1961.

L'Épître aux Hébreux, EB, Paris, Gabalda, ²1952.

Les Épîtres Pastorales, EB, Paris, Gabalda, ²1947.

Les Épîtres de Saint Pierre, Paris, Gabalda, 1966.

Spitta, F., *Zur Geschichte und Literatur des Urchristentums*, Göttingen, V & R, 1896.

Stacey, W. D., *The Pauline View of Man*, London, Macmillan, 1956.

Stählin, G., *Die Apostelgeschichte, NTD*, Göttingen, V & R, 1962.

Stanley, D. M., *Christ's Resurrection in Pauline Soteriology*, Rome, Pontifical Biblical Institute, 1961.

Stauffer, E., *Jesus and his Story*, Eng. trans. London, SCM, 1960.

New Testament Theology, Eng. trans. London, SCM, 1955.

Stendahl, K., *The Bible and the Role of Women*, Philadelphia, Fortress, 1966.

(ed.), *Immortality and Resurrection*, New York, Macmillan, 1965.

The Scrolls and the New Testament, London, SCM, 1958.

Stevens, G. B., *The Theology of the New Testament*, Edinburgh, T. & T. Clark, 1899.

Stewart, R. A., *Rabbinic Theology*, Edinburgh, Oliver & Boyd, 1961.

Stibbs, A. M., *The Meaning of the Word 'Blood' in Scripture*, London, Tyndale, 1947.

1 Peter, TNTC, London, Tyndale, 1959.

Stonehouse, N. B., *Paul Before the Areopagus, and other New Testament Studies*, London, Tyndale, 1957.

Stott, J. R. W., *Baptism and Fullness*, London, IVP, [2]1975.

The Epistles of John, TNTC, London, Tyndale, 1964.

Strachan, R. H., *The Fourth Gospel: Its Significance and Environment*, London, SCM, [3]1941.

Strack, H. L., and Billerbeck, P., *Kommentar zum Neuen Testament aus Talmud und Midrasch*, Munich, Beck, [3]1961.

Strathmann, H., *Der Brief an die Hebräer, NTD*, Göttingen, V & R, [6]1953.

Das Evangelium nach Johannes, NTD, Göttingen, V & R, 1954.

Strauss, D., *Das Leben Jesus* (1835), Eng. trans. r.p. *The Life of Jesus Critically Examined*, London, SCM, 1973.

Strawson, W., *Jesus and the Future Life*, London, Epworth, 1959.

Strecker, G. (ed.), *Jesus Christus in Historie und Theologie*, Tübingen, Mohr, 1975.

Das Problem der Theologie des Neuen Testaments, Darmstadt, Wissenschaftliche Buchgesellschaft, 1975.

Stuhlmacher, P., *Gottes Gerechtigkeit bei Paulus*, Göttingen, V & R, 1965.

Suggs, M. J., *Wisdom, Christology and Law in Matthew's Gospel*, Cambridge, Mass., Harvard, 1970.

Suhl, A., *Die Funktion der altetestamentlichen Zitate und Anspielungen im Markusevangelium*, Gütersloh, Gerd Mohn, 1965.

Swete, H. B., *The Apocalypse of St John*, London, Macmillan, [2]1907.

The Ascended Christ, London, Macmillan, 1910.

The Gospel according to St Mark, London, Macmillan, [3]1913.

The Holy Spirit in the New Testament, London, Macmillan, 1931.

Sykes, S. W., and Clayton, J. P., *Christ, Faith and History*, Cambridge, CUP, 1972.

BIBLIOGRAPHY

Tait, A. J., *The Heavenly Session of our Lord*, London, Robert Scott, 1912.

Tanehill, R. C., *Dying and Rising with Christ, A study in Pauline Theology*, Berlin, Töpelmann, 1967.

Tasker, R. V. G., *The Biblical Doctrine of the Wrath of God*, London, Tyndale, 1951.

The General Epistle of James, TNTC, London, Tyndale, 1956.

The Gospel according to Matthew, TNTC, London, Tyndale, 1961.

The Nature and Purpose of the Gospels, London, SCM, 1944.

The Second Epistle of Paul to the Corinthians, TNTC, London, 1958.

Taylor, V., *The Atonement in New Testament Teaching*, London, Epworth, [2]1945, [3]1958.

Behind the Third Gospel, Oxford, Clarendon, 1926.

Forgiveness and Reconciliation, London, Macmillan, 1956.

The Formation of the Gospel Tradition, London, Macmillan, 1957.

The Gospel according to St Mark, London, Macmillan, [2]1966.

The Historical Evidence for the Virgin Birth, Oxford, Clarendon, 1920.

Jesus and His Sacrifice, London, Macmillan, 1937.

The Names of Jesus, London, Macmillan, 1953.

Temple, W., *Christianity and the Social Order*, London, SCM, [3]1955.

Christus Veritas, London, Macmillan, 1925.

Tennant, F. R., *The Concept of Sin*, Cambridge, CUP, 1912.

Tenney, M. C., *The Reality of the Resurrection*, New York, Harper, 1963.

Thielicke, H., *Theological Ethics*, 2 vols., Eng. trans. Philadelphia, Fortress, 1966–9.

Thompson, W. G., *Matthew's Advice to a Divided Community*, Rome, Pontifical Biblical Institute, 1970.

Thomson, J. G. S. S., *The Old Testament View of Revelation*, Grand Rapids, Eerdmans, 1960.

Thornton, L. S., *The Common Life in the Body of Christ*, London, Dacre, [3]1942.

Thüsing, W., *Die Erhöhung und Verherrlichung Jesu in Johannesevangelium*, Münster, Aschendorffsche Verlagsbuchhandlung, [2]1970.

Tillesse, G. M. de, *Le secret messianique dans l'Évangile de Marc*, Paris, du Cerf, 1968.

Tinsley, E. J., *The Imitation of God in Christ*, London, SCM, 1960.

Tödt, H. E., *The Son of Man in the Synoptic Tradition*, Eng. trans. London, London, SCM, 1965.

Trench, R. C., *Synonyms of the New Testament*, London, Macmillan, 1880.

Tulloch, J., *The Christian Doctrine of Sin*, Edinburgh, Blackwood, 1876.

Turner, H. E. W., *Historicity and the Gospel*, London, Mowbray, 1953.

Jesus, Master and Lord, London, Mowbray, 1953.

Turner, N., *Grammatical Insights into the New Testament*, Edinburgh, T. & T. Clark, 1965.

Ullmann, C., *The Sinlessness of Jesus*, Eng. trans. Edinburgh, T. & T. Clark, [7]1901.

Unnik, W. C. van (ed.), *Neotestamentica et Patristica* (Cullmann Freundesgabe) Leiden, Brill, 1962.

Unnik W. C. van *et al.* (eds.), *Studies in John presented to Professor Dr J. N. Sevenster* (Supplements to *NovT*), Leiden, Brill, 1970.

Vann, G., *A Study of the Social Implications of the Beatitudes*, London, Fontana, 1945.

Vawter, B., *This Man Jesus. An Essay toward a New Testament Christology*, New York, Doubleday, 1973.

Vermes, G., *The Dead Sea Scrolls in English*, Harmondsworth, Penguin, [2]1975.

Dead Sea Scrolls: Qumran in Perspective, London, Collins, 1977.

Jesus the Jew, London, Collins, 1973.

Vincent, M. R., *Philippians, and Philemon*, *ICC*, Edinburgh, T. & T. Clark, 1897.

Vögtle, A., *Die Tugend- und Lasterkataloge im Neuen Testament*, Neutestamentliche Abhandlungen 16.4–5, Münster, 1936.

Vos, G., *The Pauline Eschatology*, Grand Rapids, Eerdmans, 1953.

Vriezen, T. C., *An Outline of Old Testament Theology*, Eng. trans. Oxford, Blackwell, [2]1970.

Wagner, G., *Pauline Baptism and the Pagan Mysteries*, Eng. trans. Edinburgh, Oliver & Boyd, 1967.

Wainwright, A. W., *The Trinity in the New Testament*, London, SPCK, 1962.

Wallace, R. S., *The Ten Commandments*, Edinburgh, Oliver & Boyd, 1965.

Walvoord, J., *The Millennial Kingdom*, Findlay, Ohio, Dunham, [2]1963.

Wand, J. W. C., *The Atonement*, London, SPCK, 1963.

The General Epistles of St Peter and St Jude, London, Methuen, 1934.

Wanke, J., *Beobachten zum Eucharistieverständnis des Lukas auf Grund der Lukanischen Mahlberichte*, Leipzig, St Benno, 1973.

Ward, R. A., *Royal Theology*, London, MMS, 1964.

Warfield, B. B., *Christology and Criticism*, New York/London, OUP, 1929.

The Inspiration and Authority of the Bible, London, MMS, 1951.

Weiss, J., *The History of Primitive Christianity* (Eng. trans. 1937), r.p. as *Earliest Christianity: A History of the Period AD 30–150*, Gloucester, Mass., Peter Smith, 1970.

Jesus' Proclamation of the Kingdom of God (1892), Eng. trans. Philadelphia, Fortress, 1971.

Wellhausen, J., *Das Evangelium Marci*, Berlin, Georg Reimer, [2]1909.

BIBLIOGRAPHY

Wenham, J. W., *Christ and the Bible*, London, Tyndale, 1972.

The Goodness of God, London, IVP, 1974.

Werner, M., *The Formation of Christian Dogma*, Eng. trans. London, Black, 1957.

Westcott, B. F., *The Epistle to the Hebrews*, London, Macmillan, 1892.

The Gospel according to St John, London, Macmillan, 1887.

The Epistles of St John, London, Macmillan, ³1892, r.p. Appleford, Marcham Manor, 1966.

Wetter, G. P., *Der Sohn Gottes*, FRLANT, Göttingen, V & R, 1916.

Whiteley, D. E. H., *The Theology of St Paul*, Oxford, Blackwell, 1964.

Wibbing, S., *Die Tugend- und Lasterkatalogue im Neuen Testament und ihre Traditionsgeschichte unter besonderer Berücksichtigung der Qumran-Texte*, Berlin, Töpelmann, 1959.

Wickham, E. C., *The Epistle to the Hebrews*, WC, London, Methuen, 1910.

Wikenhauser, A., *Die Kirche als der mystiche Leib Christi nach dem Apostel Paulus*, Münster, Aschendorffsche Verlagsbuchhandlung, 1937.

New Testament Introduction, Eng. trans. New York, Herder, 1958.

Pauline Mysticism: Christ in the Mystical Teaching of St Paul, Eng. trans. Edinburgh, Nelson, 1960.

Wilckens, V., *Weisheit und Torheit*, Tübingen, Mohr, 1956.

Wilder, A. N., *Eschatology and Ethics in the Teaching of Jesus*, New York, Harper & Bros., ²1950.

Williams, C. S. C., *Alterations to the Text of the Synoptic Gospels and Acts*, Oxford, 1951.

Williams, J. R., *The Era of the Spirit*, New Jersey, Logos, 1971.

Williamson, R., *Philo and the Epistle to the Hebrews*, Leiden, Brill, 1970.

Willoughby, H. R., *Pagan Regeneration*, Chicago, Chicago University Press, 1929.

Wilson, R. M., *Gnosis and the New Testament*, Oxford, Blackwell, 1968.

The Gnostic Problem, London, Mowbray, 1958.

Windisch, H., *The Meaning of the Sermon on the Mount*, Eng. trans. Philadelphia, Westminster, 1937.

The Spirit-Paraclete in the Fourth Gospel, Eng. trans. Philadelphia, Fortress, 1968.

Windisch H., and Preisker, H., *Die katholischen Briefe*, LHB, Tübingen, Mohr, ³1951.

Wingren, G., *Creation and Law*, Edinburgh, Oliver & Boyd, 1961.

Wink, W., *John the Baptist in the Gospel Tradition*, Cambridge, CUP, 1968.

Winter, P., *On the Trial of Jesus*, Berlin, de Gruyter, 1961.

Wirt, S. E., *The Social Conscience of the Evangelical*, London, Scripture Union, 1968.

Wolff, H. W., *Anthropology of the Old Testament*, Eng. trans. London, SCM, 1974.

Wood, H. G. (ed.), *Amicitae Corolla*, London, University of London Press, 1933.

Wrede, W., *Das Messiasgeheimnis in den Evangelien* (1901), Eng. trans. *The Messianic Secret*, London, James Clarke, 1971.

Yamauchi, E. M., *Pre-Christian Gnosticism*, London, Tyndale, 1973.

Yoder, J. H., *The Politics of Jesus*, Grand Rapids, Eerdmans, 1972.

Young, J. C. de, *Jerusalem in the New Testament*, Kampen, Kok, 1960.

Zahn, T., *Das Evangelium des Matthäus*, Leipzig, Deichert, 1903, [4]1922.

Zahrnt, H., *The Historical Jesus*, New York, Harper, 1963.

Ziesler, J. A., *The Meaning of Righteousness in Paul*, Cambridge, CUP, 1972.

Zimmerli, W., and Jeremias, J., *The Servant of God*, Eng. trans. London, SCM, 1957.

Index of references

Index of authors

INDEX OF AUTHORS

Index of Subjects

INDEX OF SUBJECTS

INDEX OF SUBJECTS

INDEX OF SUBJECTS

INDEX OF SUBJECTS

INDEX OF SUBJECTS